W9-CZT-876

A CONCORDANCE
TO THE POEMS OF
RALPH WALDO EMERSON

A CONCORDANCE TO THE POEMS OF RALPH WALDO EMERSON

BY

GEORGE SHELTON HUBBELL, Ph.D.

NEW YORK / RUSSELL & RUSSELL

FIRST PUBLISHED IN 1932
BY H. W. WILSON & COMPANY
REISSUED, 1967, BY RUSSELL & RUSSELL
A DIVISION OF ATHENEUM HOUSE, INC.
L. C. CATALOG CARD NO.: 67–18293

PRINTED IN THE UNITED STATES OF AMERICA

This volume is dedicated to
C. W. H.

INTRODUCTION

The undertaking of a Concordance to Emerson's poetry need not imply any particular theory of Emerson's greatness as a poet. The high estimate which some distinguished critics have held of these poems is not the only excuse for this new attention to them. As Arnold noted in his famous address on Emerson, the man's importance lies not specifically in his philosophy or in his literary art, whether as essayist or poet, but in his service as "the friend and aider of those who would live in the spirit." Because of the spiritual substance of his work, and because of the deftness and point of his phrasing, Emerson's poetry as well as his prose has stuck in many memories, and incidentally got itself widely quoted. Such currency in itself suggests the usefulness of a Concordance. And one might add also that the fragmentary nature of most of this verse, the apparent irrelevancy of many of the titles, and the well-known apparent lack of logical sequence of ideas all unite to make the location of lines from memory very difficult. To such reasons should, of course, be added the recent wholesome and reasonable demand by scholars and critics for more studies of American writers by Americans. It is to be hoped that this piece of unassuming drudgery may help in that program.

Personally, the compiler sought this means of improving some leisure during several years spent far from library resources for more varied studies. The selection of Emerson's poetry, too, was largely a matter of personal taste, strengthened by a rather superstitious sense of gratitude to a writer for treasured insights and inspirations.

The work on this Concordance was started in the fall of 1921. It was finished during the Christmas vacation, 1925. The compiler is personally responsible for every detail of the project up to the printing of the book. Whatever assistance he has received has been rendered under his immediate supervision, and subjected to minute inspection. The text used is that given in Volume IX of the Centenary Edition of Emerson's complete works. Nothing is omitted which that volume furnishes, and no attempt has been made to include further material. The Houghton Mifflin Company, Emerson's publishers, have very kindly furnished without charge ten copies of this basic text. These copies have been extensively mutilated to furnish the actual lines from which this book is printed. A description of the general process by which the lines are arranged on cards according to the requirements of the Concordance may be found in the preface to Lane Cooper's *Concordance to the Poems of William Wordsworth*. Since the printing is done directly from the cards, it is hoped that various inaccuracies incident to copying may be avoided.

Naturally, in so long a task as this, the compiler has availed himself of the services and advice of more friends and helpers than may here be mentioned. To his wife he is indebted for months of labor with the proofs. He is particularly grateful for the wise and generous counsel of Professor C. G. Osgood, of Princeton University, whose experience in compiling the Concordance of Spenser first suggested this undertaking. The following persons have helped in various steps of the work:

Miss J. Jessie Forsyth
Miss Katherine Sheffield
Mr. Clyde Cleveland
Miss Marian Clark
Miss Nellie Clark
Miss Marjorie Malchow
Miss Leonore Walters
Miss Lucille Walters
Miss Alice Stewart
Miss Harriet Stewart

The Alphabetical Order. The alphabetical order of words is mechanically consistent rather than logical. Inflected forms are arranged as if the were different words. This arrangement helps one who looks for a particula form of a word in order to locate a quotation. But in order to collect all the passages in which a word occurs, the user of the Concordance must be sure to look for the separately grouped forms which may be relevant. Thus for the word *go*, there will be *go, goes, going, gone,* and possibly *went.* Between these various forms many other words may intervene. There are no cross references to inflected forms.

Variant spellings of a word are listed separately, with cross references. Example: *skiey, skyey.*

Possessive or contracted forms which have an apostrophe, precede other forms which are identical save for the apostrophe, if the apostrophe occurs within the word. When the apostrophe comes at the end of a word, such a word follows a similar word without the apostrophe. The following sequences are typical: *boy, boy's, boys, boys'; I'll, ill.*

The sequence of quotations under a word is the alphabetical sequence of the catchword titles of the poems from which the quotations are severally taken. If a number of quotations are given from a single poem, they follow the numerical order of lines in that poem. Thus, if one knows in what poem a passage is found, but merely wishes to know the number of the line, he can turn almost immediately to the line he seeks, without having to examine the other quotations.

Line Numbers. It is unfortunate that in most editions of Emerson's poetry the lines are not numbered. The fact will make it rather difficult to locate quotations in some of the longer poems. Since most of the poems are fairly short, however, the difficulty should not ordinarily be great. The various so-called *Fragments on Nature and Life,* and the *Fragments on the Poet and the Poetic Gift* have been numbered by Roman numerals. In the latter there are thirty-five fragments; on Nature there are also thirty-five; on Life there are thirty-seven.

INTRODUCTION

With a few exceptions, each quotation consists of a single line of poetry. From very long lines, irrelevant words were in a few cases omitted; once or twice part of another line was added. As it happens, Emerson's poetry, with its large proportion of end-stopped lines, yields by this system enough context for the purposes of a Concordance.

Partial Lists. Every word that Emerson used in his poetry has been cited in this Concordance at least once. Some words, however, would, if completely represented, add greatly to the bulk and cost of the work without increasing its value. For the following words, therefore, only a partial list of citations is given:

a	did	**if**	over	twixt
about	didst	I'll	own	under
above	do	I'm	quite	until
after	does	in	same	unto
again	done	indeed	shall	up
against	dost	is	she	us
ah	doth	it	since	was
alas	down	its	so	wast
all	each	I've	soon	we
also	either	lest	such	were
am	else	lo	than	what
among	ere	many	that	when
an	ever	may	the	whence
and	for	me	thee	where
any	forth	might	their	whether
are	from	might'st	theirs	which
art	full	more	them	who
as	had	most	then	whom
at	has	much	thence	whose
be	hast	my	there	why
because	hath	myself	these	will
been	have	neither	they	with
before	he	no	thine	within
behind	hence	nor	this	would
being	her	not	those	wouldst
beside	here	now	thou	ye
between	hers	o'er	though	yet
both	herself	of	through	you
but	him	on	thus	your
by	himself	or	thy	yours
can	his	other	thyself	yourself
cannot	hither	ought	till	yourselves
canst	how	our	to	
could	I	ours	toward	
couldst	I'd	out	towards	

The quotations given for illustration of these words are taken not entirely at random. Rime words are always included, since the rime gives the word a certain prominence independent of its inherent meaning. Often words repeated within a line are included, if the repetition gives them emphasis. Words like *as, so,* or *thus* sometimes offer a clue to similes, and in such circumstances are included, affording opportunity for an interesting study of Emerson's figurative language.

Homographs. As in most Concordances, no attempt is made in this work to distinguish between homographs. Such distinctions, if carried out consistently, would complicate the book, involving it in problematic points, and even diminishing somewhat its usefulness as a Concordance. Generally the number of quotations under a word-heading is so small as to cause no serious difficulty, though several parts of speech and several dictionary definitions may be included. In a few exceptional cases (e. g., *art*, noun; and *art*, verb) complicating difficulties were avoided by observing the distinction. Such cases are plainly marked, and should give no trouble to one using the book.

Cross references. When verbal elements are compounded, with or without a hyphen, the second element and any other that may follow are referred to by cross references under those elements in their alphabetical places as independent words. Thus if one were to look under the word *kind,* a cross reference would call attention to *mankind*. But no such cross reference appears under the word *man*. Therefore, to find all the compound words in which a certain word appears as an element, it is necessary to add to the list of cross references, those compounds in the succeeding alphabetical arrangement which introduce that word as their first element.

LIST OF TITLES

(The following is an alphabetical list of catchwords used in this Concordance to designate titles or first lines of poems by Emerson. The full titles which here follow these catchwords are taken as far as possible from the index of titles in the Centenary Edition of Emerson's poems. In the case of poems which have no title, the first line is given, enclosed in quotation marks. After the title or first line of each poem is given the number of the page on which that poem begins in the Centenary Edition. An asterisk before the catchwords indicates that the poem, although included in Emerson's works and hence generally associated with them, is by another writer.)

LIST OF TITLES

A Concordance to the Poems
of Ralph Waldo Emerson

A (Partial list.)
No door-bell heralded a visitor,
              Adirondacs. 65.
A dazzling memory revive;
              Bacchus. 61.
Pray for a beam   Celestial Love. 60.
On a mound an Arab lay,
              Hermione. 1.
A mystic and a cabalist,—
              Initial Love. 61.

Abandon
Abandon all those toys with speed to
obey   Summons. 23.

Abbeys
O'er England's abbeys bends the sky,
              Problem. 37.

Abbots
All ate like abbots, and, if any missed
              Adirondacs. 180.

Abhor
And abhor to feign or seem
              Frag. Life. XXVII. 4.

Abide
If, whilst within thy heart abide
              Angelo. 12.
That each should in his house abide,
              Frag. Life. XXI. 1.
And Genius unspheres all souls that
abide.   Frag. Poet. XXI. 2.
Stars abide—   Hamatreya. 31.
When did he sing? and where abide?
              Harp. 37.
'Here am I, here will I abide
              Sursum Corda. 7.
Since they are transient, and thou dost
abide.   Unbar. 4.
In equal strength through space abide;
              Voluntaries. 116.
Hitherto all things fast abide,
              Woodnotes. II. 256.

Abides
Worship Toil's wisdom that abides.
              Frag. Poet. III. 10.
Fast abides this constant giver,
              Monadnoc. 40.
Stern benefit abides.
              Waldeinsamkeit. 16.

Abode
The strong gods pine for my abode,
              Brahma. 13.
Well-built abode of many a race;
              Monadnoc. 82.
But their heart abode with none.
              Threnody. 157.

Abodes
In the still abodes.
              Celestial Love. 57.
They chant the bliss of their abodes
              Garden. 43.
They hurried down from their deep
abodes   Poet. 147.

Abolishing
The maid, abolishing the past,
              Daemonic Love. 12.

Abound
Till your kinds abound with juice?
              Alphonso. 66.

Abounding
Betrays the more abounding might,
              Monadnoc. 351.

About (Partial list.)
Round about, a hundred miles,
              Monadnoc. 36.
Some went and came about the dead;
              Threnody. 152.

Above (Partial list.)
Above, the eagle flew, the osprey
screamed,   Adirondacs. 146.
The conscious stars accord above,
              Concord Ode. 33.
Around, below, above.   Cupido. 4.
Right above their heads,
              Daemonic Love. 25.
The Powers above: II Eros. 2.
The world above, the world below.
              Frag. Nat. XXVI. 10.
Souls above doubt,   Give. 20.
Above her will, be true;
              Hermione. 70.
Underneath, within, above,—
              Initial Love. 43.
Above the ploughman's highest line,
              Monadnoc. 8.
Above the floral zone,
              Monadnoc. 353.
Above the horizon's hoop,
              Monadnoc. 395.
For there's no rood has not a star
above it;   Musketaquid. 54.
Aught above its rate.   Politics. 8.
Showed them the life of Heaven above
              Robbins Hymn. 19.
Through snows above, mines under-
ground,   Solution. 47.
Above the envy of the crowd,—
              Thought. 3.
Or bow above the tempest bent;
              Threnody. 277.
Still tearless lift its slender form above
the wintry snow?   *Violet. 4.

Abrade
Which, lodged in rock, the rock abrade?
              Wealth. 8.

Abreast
But two cannot go abreast,   Unity. 2.

Abroad
Who bides at home, nor looks abroad,
              Destiny. 49.
Like ample banner flung abroad
              Monadnoc. 34.
Aloft, abroad, the pæan swells;
              Woodnotes II. 100.

Abrogate
And yet, if virtue abrogate the law,
Phi. 3.

Absconds
Absconds and conceals;   Sphinx. 50.

Absolutely
For only it can absolutely deal.
Sursum Corda. 11.

Absorb
The needs of the first sight absorb my
blood,   Day's Ration. 17.

Absorbed
Who, having more absorbed, more
largely yield,   Frag. Nat. V. 11.
This Hermione absorbed Hermione. 12.

Absorbs
Every function he absorbs;
Initial Love. 26.

Abstemious
Ill fits the abstemious Muse a crown to
weave   Phi. 1.

Abundant
Abundant for their bed and board,
Boston. 71.
Just late enough to reap abundant
blame,—   To-Day. 6.

Abuse
I choose a novel theme, a bold abuse
To-Day. 7.

Abysm
In the core of God's abysm,—
Daemonic Love. 127.

Academe
And one in the Academe.
Song of Nature. 68.

Academicians
That not academicians, but some lout,
Adirondacs. 279.

Accelerate
Which none can stay, and none accelerate.'   Poet. 125.

Accent
Or who, with accent bolder,
Channing Ode. 19.
One accent of the Holy Ghost
Problem. 61.

Accents
Sharp accents of my woodland bird;
Miracle. 24.
Seemed, when at last his clarion accents
broke,   Phi. 11.
At the sound of her accents
Sphinx. 59.

Accept
The oar, the guide's. Dare you accept
the tasks   Adirondacs. 102.
Shall the well-born soul accept.
Celestial Love. 70.
Well accept her rule austere;
May-Day. 135.
'Divine Inviters! I accept   Poet. 149.
Brother, accept this fatal hand.
Poet. 264.
Timely wise accept the terms,
Terminus. 17.

Access
Instant and perfect his access
Frag. Life. XVII. 12.

Accessible
See Inaccessible.

Acclimate
So fast will Nature acclimate her sons,
Adirondacs. 54.
Man on earth to acclimate   Art. 21.

Acclivities
Or parties scaled the near acclivities
Adirondacs. 129.

Accompany
Accompany still;   Sphinx. 38.

Accomplice
An oaf, an accomplice,   Sphinx. 55.

Accomplices
Be fine accomplices to fraud?
Chartist. 16.

Accord
The conscious stars accord above,
Concord Ode. 33.

According
With good according to its mind,
May-Day. 284.

Accost
As 't would accost some frivolous
wing,   Titmouse. 92.

Accosts
Some mystic hint accosts the vigilant,
Adirondacs. 203.

Accumulates
Verdict which accumulates
Threnody. 262.

Accursed
Accursed, adored,   Illusions. 2.

Accuse
Or accuse the god of sport?
Initial Love. 80.
Toil's hard hap with scorn accuse.
Monadnoc. 126.

Accuser
Turn on the accuser roundly; say,
Sursum Corda. 6.

Aches
Aches thine unbelieving heart
Poet. 265.

Achieve
And feats achieve before they're named.
Nature. I. 21
'Achieve our peace who can!'
Walden. 24.

Acknowledged
Acknowledged by their hospitable
boughs;   River. 38.

Acorn
From fall to spring, the russet acorn,
Holidays. 1.

Acorn's
The acorn's cup, the raindrop's arc,
Ode to Beauty. 26.

Acorns
Pine-cones and acorns lay on the
ground;   Each. 45.

Acquaintance
And kind acquaintance with the morning stars   Summons. 8.

Acre
I followed in small copy in my acre;
Musketaquid. 53.

Acres
A second crop thine acres yield,
Apology. 19.
What mystic fruit his acres yield
Dirge. 11.

O'er ten thousand, thousand acres,
            Ellen South. 9.
In black acres of the night,
            Frag. Nat. XVIII. 3.
'To find the sitfast acres where you left
    them.'   Hamatreya. 24.
What mystic fruit his acres yield
            Peter. 3.

Acrid
Which feels the acrid juice
            Bacchus. 8.

Across
Shoots across the neutral Dark.
            II Compensation. 14.
Flits across her bosom young,
            Give. 37.
Then flew the sail across the seas
            Wealth. 36.

Act
An act unworthy to be done;
            In Memoriam. 54.
Her every act.   In Memoriam. 96.
To catch the unconscious heart in the
    very act.   Philosopher. 6.
I only follow, when I act aright.
            Self-Reliance. 10.

Action
And lift man's public action to a height
            Adirondacs. 246.
His action won such reverence sweet
            Character. 9.
His lot of action at the urn. Poet. 188.

Action's
For action's field, for victor's car,
            In Memoriam. 29.

Actions
And, I affirm, my actions smack of the
    soil.'   Hamatreya. 10.

Active
Had active hands and smiling lips;
            Saadi. 77.

Acts
Change acts, reacts; back, forward
    hurled,   Poet. 175.

Adam
Though Adam, born when oaks were
    young,   Frag. Nat. VI. 3.
The perfect Adam lives.   Promise, 6.

Adamant
To hew the famous adamant
            House. 15.
Adamant is soft to wit: Monadnoc. 261.
Not of adamant and gold
            Threnody. 272.

Adamantine
With adamantine words.
            Frag. Poet. XIII. 4.
Flies-to the adamantine door   Past. 12.

Adamhood
They discredit Adamhood. Alphonso. 18.

Adam's
And so, perchance, in Adam's race,
            May-Day. 92.

Adapted
Draw from each stratum its adapted
    use   Musketaquid. 39.

Add
Add their nine lives to this cat;
            Alphonso. 71.
You must add the untaught strain
            Destiny. 3.

To bind or unbind, add what lacked,
            Past. 18.

Added
Day by day for her darlings to her
    much she added more;
            Frag. Nat. XII. 1.
Unless to Thought is added Will,
            Frag. Poet. XVIII. 3.
They added ridge to valley, brook to
    pond,   Hamatreya. 17.
And ingots added to the hoard.
            Wealth. 43.

Adder's-tongue
Clover, catchfly, adder's-tongue
            Humble-Bee. 48.

Adding
Adding wings through things to range,
            Insight. 5.
Adding by their mutual gage,
            Merlin. 104.

Address
Plain and cold is their address,
            Celestial Love. 89.

Addresses
Many fashions and addresses,
            Initial Love. 132.

Adds
Ah! the hot owner sees not Death, who
    adds   Hamatreya. 25.
Adds to oak and oxen strength,
            May-Day. 201.
Or how the sacred pine-tree adds
            Problem. 29.
The third adds heat's indulgent spark;
            Woodnotes. II. 291.

Adequately
Can adequately utter none   Harp. 97.

Adhere
Adhere like this foundation strong,
            Monadnoc. 115.

Adhering
From the old adhering sin,
            Woodnotes. II. 64.

Adirondac
The Adirondac lakes. At Martin's Beach
            Adirondacs. 4.
In Adirondac lakes,   Adirondacs. 73.
On Adirondac steeps, I know
            Frag. Nat. IV. 7.

Adjourn
Of thoughts and things at home, but
    still adjourn   Day's Ration. 31.
Constrained by impotence to adjourn
            Poet. 187.

Admired
And then as now from far admired,
            Harp. 117.
Admired, sage doubting whence the
    traveller came,—   River. 4.

Admits
Admits thee to the perfect Mind.
            Saadi. 164.

Admonishment
    See 'Monishment.

Adoped
Adoped them into her race,
            Problem. 42.

Adored
Accursed, adored,   Illusions. 2.

Adoring
From God's adoring lover.   Dull. 14.

Adorn
The past restore, the day adorn,
                            Art. 11.
Each can other best adorn;
                    Love and Thought. 8.
With cloverheads the swamp adorn,
                            Monadnoc. 137.
Adorn her as was none adorned.
                            Rhea. 63.
The gracious boy, who did adorn
                            Threnody. 17.

Adorned
Adorn her as was none adorned.
                            Rhea. 63.
Adorned with them my country's primi-
tive times,   River. 41.

Adorneth
Adorneth, doubleth joy:
                    Frag. Nat. XXIV. 8.

Adorning
Itself with thoughts of thee adorning;
                    Ode to Beauty. 87.
Each the other adorning,   Sphinx. 37.

Adroit
Hereafter,—willing   they,   and   more
    adroit.   Adirondacs. 164.

Adventures
And write my old adventures with the
    pen   Bacchus. 64.

Advice
Ye shall not fail for sound advice.
                        Alphonso. 48.

Advise
Him they beckon, him advise
                    Frag. Poet. XI. 7.

Æneas
Crusoe, Crusader, Pius Æneas, said
    aloud,   Adirondacs. 184.

Æolian
Or like the thrill of Æolian strings
                    Frag. Poet. I. 41.
Æolian harps in the pine   Garden. 33.
Æolian harp,   Harp. 41.

Æon
And the sunny Æon sleeps
                    Celestial Love. 48.
And an æon allows   Frag. Life. VI. 3.
To wait an æon to be born.
                    Threnody. 149.

Æons
Which mocks thy æons to embrace;
                            Nun. 40.
Æons which tardily unfold
                            Nun. 41.
(In dizzy æons dim and mute
                            Wealth. 19.

Aerial
To far eyes, an aerial isle
                    Monadnoc. 42.

Aëry
For aëry intelligence,   Initial Love. 68.

Afar
Framed afar as Fates and Loves.
                    Frag. Poet. XII. 4.
Seen haply from afar,   Monadnoc. 394.
I snuff the breath of my morning afar,
                            Poet. 108.

Affair
Well he knows his own affair,
                    Frag. Nat. I. 12.

The World-soul knows his own affair,
                    Monadnoc. 153.

Affairs
    See Sky-affairs.
He works, plots, fights, in rude affairs,
                            Fate. 7.
He had so sped his wise affairs
                            Guy. 31.
Modulates the king's affairs;
                            Merlin. 78.
And let the world's affairs go by,
                    Threnody. 47.
Crowns all thy mean affairs.
                    Waldeinsamkeit. 48.

Affect
Nor profane affect to hit   Merlin. 66.

Affects
He affects the wood and wild,
                    Initial Love. 96.

Affinities
By sweet affinities to human flesh,
                            Blight. 12.

Affirm
And, I affirm, my actions smack of the
    soil.'   Hamatreya. 10.
And this, at least, I dare affirm,
                            Harp. 73.
And I affirm, the spacious North
                    Titmouse. 58.

Affirmer
Thou grand affirmer of the present tense,
                    Monadnoc. 359.

Afflicted
Afflicted moan, and latest hold
                    May-Day. 19.

Affluence
But the sweet affluence of love and song,
                            Blight. 42.

Affords
Try the might the Muse affords
                    Frag. Poet. X. 1.
All their vocal muse affords;
                    Monadnoc. 176.

Affright
Of grim Disease, that would her peace
    affright.   I Bear. 12.

Afraid
To plant and eat be none afraid.
                            Boston. 12.
To plant and eat be none afraid.
                            Boston. 54.
With no posterity to make the lie afraid,
                            Merlin. 111.
Of that be none afraid.
                    September. 12.

Afric's
From his Afric's torrid plains.
                    Voluntaries. 8.

After (Partial list.)
    See also Hereafter; Thereafter.
After their own genius, clearly,
                    Celestial Love. 122.
After the master's sketch fills and
    o'erfills   Day's Ration. 28.
To each they offer gifts after his will,
                            Days. 5.
I thenceforward and long after
                    Forerunners. 35.
Voices followed after.
                    Frag. Nat. III. 23.
And after Love, the Muse.   Garden. 28.

Justice after as before,—
         Voluntaries. 101.

Afternoon
In the long sunny afternoon Dirge. 13.
[In the long sunny afternoon Peter. 9.
Fine afternoon, old passenger!
         Titmouse. 30.

Again (Partial list.)
Made them to boys again. Happier that
  they   Adirondacs. 61.
Now soar again. What wilt thou, rest-
less bird,   Adirondacs. 208.
And now, again, a hungry company
         Adirondacs. 281.
Within four walls is possible again,—
         Adirondacs. 322.
Time takes fresh start again,
         Adirondacs. 328.
Or tumble all again in heap
         Alphonso. 29.
Give them again to shine; Bacchus. 58.
Or union never more again. Boston. 36.
Help them who cannot help again:
         Boston Hymn. 51.
I keep, and pass, and turn again.
         Brahma. 4.
Unto the same again.'
         Celestial Love. 26.
Again I saw, again I heard,   Each. 48.
Farewell I breathe again *Farewell. 46.
Replunged again into that upper sphere
         Frag. Life. XVI. 8.
Who sought thee once shall seek again.
         Frag. Life. XXII. 4.
Assured to find the token once again
         Frag. Nat. IV. 9.
And all the zone is green again.
         Frag. Nat. XXVIII. 4.
If once again that silent string,
         Harp. 105.
Befalls again what once befell;
         May-Day. 178.
Willows and lilacs brings again,
         May-Day. 183.
Shot up to the height of the sky again,
         May-Day. 322.
Is made whole again.   May-Day. 337.
If Nature give me joy again,
         May-Day. 370.
And take their youth again.
         Merlin's Song. 13.
I know not why I came again
         Miracle. 7.
And when the greater comes again
         Monadnoc. 262.
No dreary repeater now and again,
         Nature. II. 3.
Shall not by the same be loved again;
         Rhea. 38.
That filled their homes again;
         Robbins Hymn. 16.
I looked again,—I thought them hearts
         Rubies. 5.
And mix the bowl again;
         Song of Nature. 74.
Can't trance him again,   Sphinx. 78.
Railing in love to those who rail again,
         Summons. 11.
That winsome voice again might hear;
         Threnody. 51.

Heart's love will meet thee again.
         Threnody. 269.
When here again thy pilgrim comes,
         Titmouse. 81.
Who drink it shall not thirst again;
         Two Rivers. 18.
Once again the pine-tree sung:
         Woodnotes II. 133.
Brings again the Pentecost;
         Woodnotes II. 145.
It cannot be,—I will look again.
         Woodnotes. II. 211.
And straight begins again;
         World-Soul. 92.

Against (Partial list.)
Had not these me against myself de-
fended.   Grace. 8.
Of minds that each can stand against
the world   Oh What. 2.
One over against the mouths of Nile,
         Song of Nature. 67.
Against the being of a line.   Uriel. 20.

Agassiz
Or count the Sioux a match for Agassiz?   Adirondacs. 308.

Agates
Give me agates for my meat;
         Mithridates. 6.

Age
He may, by warrant of his age,
         Alphonso. 79.
Brought the Age of Gold again:
         Character. 8.
Drag a ridiculous age.
         Day's Ration. 19.
No trace of age, no fear to die.
         Frag. Nat. VIII. 8.
Beyond the scope of human age,
         Frag. Poet. XI. 17.
So shall thou pierce the distant age
         Frag. Poet. XIII. 3.
And filled the age his fame;
         Frag. Poet. XXXII. 2.
Age cannot cloud his memory,
         Harp. 5.
That use to undo the limb and sense of
age;   I Bear. 2.
He is not of counted age,
         Initial Love. 140.
And prosperous Age held out his hand,
         In Memoriam. 69.
Soothe pain, and age, and love's dis-
tress,   May-Day. 439.
One to other, health and age.
         Merlin. 105.
Yet they who hear it shed their age,
         Merlin's Song. 12.
Anchored fast for many an age,
         Monadnoc. 283.
Think me not numbed or halt with age,
         Nun. 33.
Here from youth to age I tarry,—
         Poet. 128.
I am not wiser for my age,
         Quat. Climacteric. 1.
Shines the last age, the next with hope
is seen,   Quat. Heri. 1.
Strewing my bed, and, in another age,
         Seashore. 36.
Built in an age, the mad wind's night-
work,   Snow-Storm. 27.

Age—*Continued*

In the next age, are flaming swords.
Solution. 58.

Fitting his age and ken, Threnody. 42.

As love old things for age, and hate
the new.   To-Day. 12.

That works its will on age and hour.
Unity. 11.

Now the iron age is done,
Voluntaries. 44.

In an age of fops and toys,
Voluntaries. 59.

To every age, to every race;
Woodnotes. II. 280.

Unto every race and age
Woodnotes. II. 281.

Aged

Recut the aged prints,   Bacchus. 63.

The halting steps of aged Fate.
May-Day. 155.

Make the aged eye sun-clear,
May-Day. 455.

And out of spent and aged things
Song of Nature. 27.

With aged eyes, short way before,—
Threnody. 180.

With sudden roar the aged pine-tree
falls,—   Woodnotes. I. 73.

Ages

The memory of ages quenched;
Bacchus. 57.

A blessing through the ages thus
Boston. 116.

Counsel which the ages kept
Celestial Love. 69.

United States! the ages plead,—
Concord Ode. 17.

Waits through dark ages for the morn,
Frag. Life. XXIII. 3.

Ever the Rock of Ages melts
Frag. Life. XXIV. 1.

What all the books of ages paint, I
have.   Frag. Nat. V. 1.

Tribes and ages overheard:
Frag. Poet. V. 10.

Will gladly sell ages
Frag. Poet. VIII. 4.

Crowds in a day the sum of ages,
Frag. Poet. IX. 11.

The garnered heat of ages old.
May-Day. 145.

For the next ages, men of mould
Monadnoc. 155.

Ages are thy days,   Monadnoc. 358.

Say, when in lapsed ages
Ode to Beauty. 5.

And Ages went or stayed.   Peter. 24.

Whom the ages must obey: Poet. 80.

Rushing ages moult their wings,
Poet. 132.

·From ancient ages for the bard,
Poet. 151.

Do thou of the Ages ask
Quat. Botanist. 3.

The ages have kept?—   Sphinx. 6.

This child should ills of ages stay,
Threnody. 135.

And ages drop in it like rain.
Two Rivers. 20.

This must the leaves of ages strew
Wealth. 15.

The all-seeing sun for ages hath not
shone;   Woodnotes. I. 65.

Of tendency through endless ages,
Woodnotes. II. 106.

And the ages are effete, World-Soul. 98.

Aggrandize

To aggrandize one funeral.
Threnody. 159.

Agiochook

And in thy valleys, Agiochook!
Channing Ode. 22.

Ago

As when my brothers, long ago,
Dirge. 19.

Not long ago at eventide,   Harp. 107.

This befell how long ago!
Initial Love. 6.

I had the right, few days ago,
Threnody. 32.

Agreeing

With good agreeing with its fate,
May-Day. 286.

Agrees

The hills where health with health
agrees,   Woodnotes. II. 190.

Agrimony

Rue, cinquefoil, gill, vervain and agrimony,   Blight. 5.

Scented fern and agrimony;
Frag. Nat. II. 10.

Scented fern, and agrimony,
Humble-Bee. 47.

Ague

All the fierce enemies, ague, hunger,
cold,   Adirondacs. 317.

Ah (Partial list.)

Ah! late I spoke to silent throngs,
I Compensation. 7.

Ah! the hot owner sees not Death, who
·adds   Hamatreya. 25.

Ah! well I mind the calendar,
May-Day. 372.

Ah, vainly do these eyes recall
Threnody. 58.

Aid

Love calls not to his aid events;
Frag. Life. XVII. 4.

To me their aid preferred,
Hermione. 63.

Cannot withhold his conquering aid.
Nun. 6.

Their doubts, and aid their strife.
Robbins Hymn. 12.

East, west, for aid I looked in vain,
Titmouse. 7.

Ailed

Perchance not he but Nature ailed,
Threnody. 138.

Ails

what ails the warbler? Adirondacs. 206.

'Mid many ails a brittle health,
Poet. 184.

Aim

Of the red deer, to aim at a square mist.
Adirondacs. 120.

Miss the aim whereto I strive.
Angelo. 9.

And aim a telescope at the inviolate
sun.   Letter. 22.

With aim like yours   Poet. 155.

Scorn trifles and embrace a better aim
Rome. 12.

Up! mind thine own aim, and
To J. W. 22.

To the aim which him allures,
Voluntaries. 91.

Aimed
Aimed at him, the blushing blade
Guy. 19.

Aims
Even in the hot pursuit of the best aims
Blight. 58.

And virtue reaching to its aims;
Threnody. 279.

Air
Up with the dawn, they fancied the
light air   Adirondacs. 59.

Insatiate skill in water or in air
Adirondacs. 137.

We trode on air, contemned the distant
town,   Adirondacs. 160.

The clouds are rich and dark, the air
serene,   Adirondacs. 213.

Unbind and give me to the air.
Aeolian Harp. 3.

The air with Cupids full,   April. 6.

Let spouting fountains cool the air,
Art. 7.

In flame, in storm, in clouds of air.
Beauty. 6.

Floating in air or pent in stone,
II Compensation. 26.

The total air was fame;   Cosmos. 10.

Like undulating layer of air,
Daemonic Love. 24.

And, lit by fringent air,
Daemonic Love. 50.

Into the mineral air,
Frag. Life. XXIV. 2.

Transparent air, all-feeding earth,
Frag. Life. XXIX. 3.

Words of the air   Frag. Nat. III. 33.

Which birds of the air
Frag. Nat. III. 34.

How they diffuse themselves into the
air,   Frag. Nat. XVII. 2.

Flashed their small fires in air,
Frag. Nat. XXVII. 9.

Omens and signs that filled the air
Frag. Poet. V. 39.

Wandering voices in the air
Garden. 49.

Pent in a dungeon made of air,—
Harp. 56.

Renewed, I breathe Elysian air,
Harp. 122.

Swimmer through the waves of air;
Humble-Bee. 14.

Hang in the air a bright thermometer
Letter. 21.

And the sweet air with thee was sweet.
Lines. 14.

The air is full of whistlings bland;
May-Day. 7.

Or vagrant booming of the air,
May-Day. 11.

Can this elastic air convey.
May-Day. 14.

The air rings jocund to his call,
May-Day. 70.

In the next field is air more mild,
May-Day. 102.

The bitter-sweet, the haunting air
May-Day. 289.

The air stole into the streets of towns,
May-Day. 342.

Making the splendor of the air,
May-Day. 429.

Purge alpine air by towns defiled,
May-Day. 451.

Scattered on the stormy air,
Merlin. 56.

From air and ocean bring me foods,
Mithridates. 8.

No bird is safe that cuts the air
Monadnoc. 143.

I bathe in the morn's soft and silvered
air,   Musketaquid. 13.

E'en the flowing azure air
Ode to Beauty. 90.

These wonders rose to upper air;
Problem. 40.

Saying, 'Hearken! Earth, Sea, Air!
Rhea. 57.

The wild air bloweth in our lungs,
Romany. 21.

Wedge-like cleave the air the birds,
Saadi. 4.

Seems nowhere to alight: the whited
air   Snow-Storm. 3.

Poets, for the air was fame.
Solution. 42.

The pits of air, the gulf of space,
Song of Nature. 2.

"Sea, earth, air, sound, silence,
Sphinx. 33.

Made of the air that blows outside.'
Titmouse. 78.

Yet on the nimble air benign
Voluntaries. 67.

Aloft, in secret veins of air,
Waldeinsamkeit. 37.

The air is wise, the wind thinks well,
Walden. 37.

From air the creeping centuries drew
Wealth. 13.

Thou canst not wave thy staff in air,
Woodnotes. II. 168.

Of gem, and air, of plants, and worms.
Woodnotes. II. 275.

Air-bells
Air-bells of fortune that shine and
break,   Garden. 55.

Air-borne
And soar to the air-borne flocks
Boston Hymn. 23.

Air-fed
Love is the air-fed fire intense,
Song of Seyd. 15.

Air's
Drink the wild air's salubrity:
Merlin's Song. 32.

Within the air's cerulean round,—
Threnody. 14.

Airs
No city airs or arts pass current here.
Adirondacs. 92.

Incensed and starred with lights and airs
and shapes,   October. 9.

Air-sown
And his air-sown, unheeded words,
Solution. 57.

Air-tight
You captives of your air-tight halls,
Romany. 6.

Airy
Retinues of airy kings,   Art. 15.
Sometimes the airy synod bends,
Daemonic Love. 43.
A score of airy miles will smooth
Frag. Nat. XIV. 1.
And in his airy road benign Lines. 17.
Airy turrets purple-piled, May-Day. 350.
Up! where the airy citadel
Monadnoc. 10.
And airy tongues did taunt the town,
Walden. 23.

Aisled
In the star-lit minster aisled.
May-Day. 50.

Aisles
And on my heart monastic aisles
Problem. 3.
And groined the aisles of Christian
Rome   Problem. 20.
He saw beneath dim aisles, in odorous
beds,   Woodnotes. I. 68.

Alas (Partial list.)
Alas! that neither bonds nor vows
Amulet. 9.
I alas! not well alive,   Angelo. 8.
Alas! that one is born in blight,
Destiny. 18.
Alas! how were they so beguiled,
Poet. 205.
Now Love and Pride, alas! in vain,
Threnody. 80.
'Alas! thine is the bankruptcy,
Woodnotes. II. 217.
Alas! the Sprite that haunts us
World-Soul. 41.

Albeit
Unknown, albeit lying near,
Daemonic Love. 39.
Albeit scorned as none was scorned,
Rhea. 62.

Alchemy
Or hide underground her alchemy.
Woodnotes. II. 167.

Alcohol
The while, one leaden pot of alcohol
Adirondacs. 139.

Alcoran
To recite the Alcoran; Song of Seyd. 22.

Alder
Singing at dawn on the alder bough;
Each. 14.

Ale
Our foaming ale we drank from hunters'
pans,   Adirondacs. 177.
Ale, and a sup of wine. Our steward
gave   Adirondacs. 178.

Alembic
Distilled from heaven's alembic blue,
Walden. 27.

Ali
When Ali prayed and loved
Waterfall. 17.

Alight
Beauty and Force alight.   Poet. 299.

Seems nowhere to alight: the whited air
Snow-Storm. 3.

Alighting
Every night alighting down
May-Day. 26.

Alike
Alike the conqueror silent sleeps;
C. Hymn. 6.
Alike thy memory embalms
In Memoriam. 113.
He roamed, content alike with man and
beast.   Woodnotes. I. 81.
Alike to him the better, the worse,—
Woodnotes. II. 305.

Ali's
Wise Ali's sunbright sayings pass
Saadi. 151.

Alive
I alas! not well alive,   Angelo. 8.
Alive to gentle influence   Culture. 5.
Fleetest couriers alive Forerunners. 23.
Salute the bard who is alive
Frag. Poet. XXVIII. 8.
Stealing grace from all alive; Give. 46.
To keep this fire of faith alive,
Hymn. 6.
Of any woman that is now alive,—
Naples. 20.
The dust is alive,   Poet. 106.
Go, get them where he earned them
when alive;   To J. W. 16.
Lover of all things alive,
Woodnotes. I. 24.

All (Partial list.)
our company all told.   Adirondacs. 6.
Gave an impartial tomb to all the kinds.
Adirondacs. 140.
So Nature shed all beauty lavishly
Adirondacs. 151.
So through all creatures in their form
and ways   Adidondacs. 202.
A melancholy better than all mirth.
Adirondacs. 215.
Superior to all its gaudy skirts.
Adirondacs. 220.
Or tumble all again in heap
Alphonso. 29.
And bestow the shares of all
Alphonso. 69.
Each to all is venerable,   Astraea. 5.
And its depths reflect all forms;
Astraea. 42.
For all I know;—   Bacchus 46
And all their botany is Latin names.
Blight. 22.
Their dauntless ways did all men praise,
Boston. 9.
Whose roads lead everywhere to all;
Boston. 60.
'T is very small,—no load at all,—
Boston. 67.
The rights of all mankind. Boston. 95.
But right is might through all the
world;   Boston. 96.
And the wits of all her wisest,
Boston. 108.
Shield all thy roofs and towers!
Boston. 117.
He serves all who dares be true.
Celestial Love. 132.

It seemed the world was all torches
                    Cosmos. 11.
And the lone seaman all the night
                    Daemonic Love. 54.
Highest Love who shines on all;
                    Daemonic Love. 69.
Sharing all, daring all,
                    Daemonic Love. 81.
and sky that holds them all. Days. 6.
And all the following hours of the day
                    Day's Ration. 18.
And all the costly liquor runs to waste;
                    Day's Ration. 23.
All echoes hearkened for their sound,—
                    Dirge. 35.
One chamber held ye all;   Dirge. 54.
All are needed by each one;   Each. 11.
And all the crowed Past appears
                    Ellen. 3.
When all but Love itself is dead
                    Ellen. 11.
'Thou shalt command us all,—
                    Ellen South. 29.
All too nimble for my treading.
                    Etienne. 4.
Little man, least of all,   Experience. 14.
But all sorts of things and weather
                    Fable. 6.
Talents differ; all is well and wisely put;
                    Fable. 17.
Comes the Genius,—all's forgot,
                    Frag. Life. XVI. 7.
Like the strain of all Frag. Nat. III. 27.
All of worth and beauty set
                    Frag. Nat. XXIII. 3.
Greetings kind to each and all,
                    Frag. Nat. XXIII. 16.
Come and I will show you all
                    Frag. Nat. XXVI. 5.
And all the zone is green again.
                    Frag. Nat. XXVIII. 4.
Leave all for love;   Give. 26.
All the rest he can disguise.
                    Initial Love. 20.
And, if I tell you all my thought,
                    Initial Love. 23.
And holds all stars in his embrace.
                    Initial Love. 117.
Past all balsam or relief;
                    Love and Thought. 10.
All was stiff and stark;   May-Day. 36.
Suddenly betook them all,
                    May-Day. 389.
Made all things in pairs.   Merlin. 80.
Upsurp the seats for which all strive;
                    Merlin's Song. 17.
But wilt thou measure all thy road,
                    Merlin's Song. 22.
The richest of all lords is Use,
                    Merlin's Song. 29.
All my wrath and all my shames,
                    Miracle. 35.
To all the dwellers in the plains
                    Monadnoc. 35.
Is yonder squalid peasant all
                    Monadnoc. 75.
All their vocal muse affords;
                    Monadnoc. 176.
And all town-sprinkled lands that be,
                    Monadnoc. 277.

Sailing through stars with all their his-
    tory.   Monadnoc. 278.
All his county, sea and land,
                    Monadnoc. 320.
Shedding on all its snows and leaves,
                    Monadnoc. 383.
For which we all our lifetime grope,
                    Monadnoc. 388.
To draw all fancies to this spot.
                    Monadnoc Afar. 8.
And all our struggles and our toils
                    Nemesis. 15.
Leads all souls to the Good.   Park. 16.
All to each in kindness bend,
                    Peter. 34.
And throttled all his passion. Is't not
like   Philosopher. 10.
See, all we are rooted here   Poet. 267.
And all thy life is for thy own,
                    Prayer. 3.
Yet not for all his faith can see
                    Problem. 5.
As they lead, so follow all,   Rhea. 31.
And the god, having given all,
                    Rhea. 74.
He hath broke his banks and flooded all
    the vales   River. 9.
Thou heart that lovest all.
                    Robbins Hymn. 28.
And I the lady all the while.
                    Romany. 12.
Be great, be true, and all the Scipios,
                    Rome. 4.
And opens you a welcome in them all.
                    Rome. 10.
Of all mortals the desire,   Saadi. 10.
For all breathing men's behoof,
                    Saadi. 11.
He wants them all,   Saadi. 26.
All the brags of plume and song;
                    Saadi. 150.
Redeemers that can yield thee all:
                    Saadi. 166.
And verses that all verse outlive.
                    Solution. 72.
Shines the peace of all being,
                    Sphinx. 45.
Is master of all I am."   Sphinx. 132.
All woman-born do know, that hoped-
    for days,   Summons. 19.
Abandon all those toys with speed to
    obey   Summons. 23.
All were winnowed through and
    through,   Test. 3.
Covetous death bereaved us all,
                    Threnody. 158.
And all is clear from east to west.
                    Threnody. 208.
The richest flowering of all art:
                    Threnody. 216.
The rash word boded ill to all;
                    Uriel. 30.
But all slid to confusion.   Uriel. 34.
Freedom all winged expands,
                    Voluntaries. 35.
To hazard all in Freedom's fight,—
                    Voluntaries. 62.
All are ghosts beside.   Voluntaries. 122.
Still on the seeds of all he made
                    Waldeinsamkeit. 25.

All (Partial list.) —*Continued*
Though they to all belong!
Waldeinsamkeit. 40.
On all was base in man,   Walden. 22.
And all through which it blows,
Walden. 38.
But all her shows did Nature yield,
Woodnotes. I. 52.
Waneth fast and spendeth all.
Woodnotes. II. 25.
All constellations of the sky
Woodnotes. II. 73.
Gives all to them who all renounce.
Woodnotes. II. 237.
All to yean and all to bury:
Woodnotes. II. 259.
Unto each, and unto all,
Woodnotes. II. 283.
As he giveth to all to drink,
Woodnotes. II. 287.
Hold all the hidden wonders
World-Soul. 39.
It was her stern necessity: all things
Xenophanes. 5.

Allah
'Bard, when thee would Allah teach,
Saadi. 60.
The heaven where unveiled Allah pours
Saadi. 160.

Allayed
Of the same stuff, and so allayed,
Monadnoc. 167.

All-echoing
And what if that all-echoing shell,
Harp. 61.

Alleghanies
And the long Alleghanies here,
Monadnoc. 276.

All-Fair
Build I to the All-Good, All-Fair.
Rhea. 59.

All-feeding
Transparent air, all-feeding earth,
Frag. Life. XXIX. 3.

All-Good
Build I to the All-Good, All-Fair.
Rhea. 49.

All-hail
witness the mute all-hail
Adirondacs. 310.

Alliance
Rich rents and wide alliance shares;
Monadnoc. 59.

Allied
For the prevision is allied   Fate. 13.
For he is sovereignly allied,—
Initial Love. 122.
The centre of the troop allied,
Threnody. 67.
But to each thought and thing allied,
Woodnotes. II. 175.

Allies
"Courage! we are thine allies,
Hermione. 65.

All-knowing
I'm all-knowing, yet unknowing;
Song of Seyd. 19.

All-loving
And, as the great all-loving Day
Threnody. 217.

And be sure the all-loving Nature
World-Soul. 35.

Allowed
A good in Nature not allowed
Frag. Poet. VII. 15.
Not allowed to any liege;
Initial Love. 119.
And if it be to you allowed
May-Day. 363.
Smug routine, and things allowed,
Mithridates. 29.
And Nature have allowed To J. W. 8.
But ours is not allowed.
World-Soul. 80.

Allows
And an æon allows Frag. Life. VI. 3.

All-seeing
The all-seeing sun for ages hath not
shone;   Woodnotes. I. 65.

Allure
Why should the vest on him allure,
Problem. 7.

Allures
Paints, and flavors, and allures,
May-Day. 197.
To the aim which him allures,
Voluntaries. 91.

Alluring
I make some coast alluring, some lone
isle,   Seashore. 48.

All-wise
Not less than was the first; the all-wise
God   Naples. 3.

All-worshipped
As, when the all-worshipped moon attracts the eye,   Musketaquid. 82.

Almanac
I know the trusty almanac
May-Day. 378.

Almighty
Or walks in mask almighty Jove,
May-Day. 215.

Almost
Almost a smile to steal to cheer her
sons,   Adirondacs. 342.
old almost as the shade;
Monadnoc. 204.

Aloes
As the rich aloes flames, I glow,
Song of Seyd. 17.

Aloft
Singing aloft in the tree!   Dirge. 42.
Carry aloft, below, around,
Frag. Nat. III. 35.
Pillar which God aloft had set
Monadnoc. 48.
Aloft, beneath, on left and right
Poet. 99.
Poises Arcturus aloft morning and eve-
ning his spear.   Shah.-Hafiz. 2.
Aloft, in secret veins of air,
Waldeinsamkeit. 37.
Aloft, abroad, the pæan swells;
Woodnotes. II. 100.

Alone
As each would hear the oracle alone.
Adirondacs. 15.
Of keen competing youths, joined or
alone   Adirondacs. 325.
That I walk alone in grove and glen;
Apology. 2.

I sit and mourn alone?
                    I Compensation. 4.
Should mine alone be dumb?
                    I Compensation. 6.
And, by herself, supplants alone
                    Daemonic Love. 15.
Nothing is fair or good alone.
                    Each. 12.
And the hermit never alone,—
                    Etienne. 20.
But if I would walk alone,
                    Frag. Poet. IV. 13.
Pale genius roves alone,
                    Frag. Poet. VI. 1.
I ungrateful, I alone. Frag. Poet. VII. 8.
Through thee alone the sky is arched,
                    Friendship. 11.
Bosomed in yon green hills alone,—
                    Good-Bye. 16.
Now scattered wide thro' earth, and
    each alone,   Good Cheer. 4.
But of the Overgods alone: Harp. 68.
I will follow thee alone,
                    Humble-Bee. 5.
He is headstrong and alone;
                    Initial Love. 95.
Seeks alone his counterpart.
                    Initial Love. 107.
'T is not in the high stars alone,
                    Music. 13.
Alone in Rome.   Rome. 1.
Besides, you need not be alone; the soul
                    Rome. 2.
Virtue alone is sweet society,
                    Rome. 8.
But the poet dwells alone.   Saadi. 8.
Wise Saadi dwells alone.   Saadi. 22.
Good Saadi dwells alone.   Saadi. 33.
In spirt-worlds he trod alone,
                    Solution. 51.
A music heard by thee alone
                    Threnody. 78.
To be alone wilt thou begin
                    Threnody. 187.
Though thou lie alone on the ground.
                    Woodnotes. II. 88.
I see thee in the crowd alone;
                    Woodnotes. II. 221.

Along
The storm-winds urge the heavy weeks
    along,   Adirondacs. 227.
And along the river-side. Berrying. 5.
Along the stormy coast,   Boston. 46.
Along the mountain towers,—
                    Daemonic Love. 110.
He came late along the waste,
                    Initial Love. 11.
Gathering along the centuries
                    Song of Nature. 14.
Like shells along the shore,
                    World-Soul. 66.
Along Thought's causing stream,
                    World-Soul. 70.

Aloof
The great stars did not shine aloof,
                    Poet. 146.
Straitly charged him, 'Sit aloof;'
                    Saadi. 12.
Yet they who listened far aloof
                    Solution. 54.

Aloud
Pius Æneas, said aloud,
                    Adirondacs. 184.
Sings aloud the tune whereto
                    Merlin. 45.
Aloud and cheerfully,   Sphinx. 66.
Alp
Of Alp and Andes, isle and continent,
                    Adirondacs. 263.
As finds its Alp the snowy shower,
                    Frag. Life. XXIII. 6.
Andes, Alp or Himmalee,
                    Frag. Nat. XV. 3.
Etched on Alp and Apennine.
                    Solution. 32.
Alphonse
And, for I'm styled Alphonse the Wise,
                    Alphonso. 47.
Alphonso
I, Alphonso, live and learn,
                    Alphonso. 1.
Alpine
So pure the Alpine element we breathed,
                    Adirondacs. 158.
Like Alpine cataracts frozen as they
    leaped,   Blight. 60.
Whilst his files sweep round yon Alpine
    height;   Each. 8.
She threads dark Alpine forests
                    House. 9.
Purge alpine air by towns defiled,
                    May-Day. 451.
Alps
Under Alps and Andes cold;
                    Frag. Nat. I. 16.
Alps and Caucasus uprear,
                    Monadnoc. 275.
And eat through Alps its home to find.
                    Quat. Love. 4.
Alps'
Link in the Alps' globe-girding chain;
                    Monadnoc. 85.
Already
Wine which is already man,
                    Bacchus. 34.
Forth already on the road,
                    Frag. Life. XXII. 6.
Thou already slumberest deep;
                    Humble-Bee. 60.
Already trembling on their tongue,
                    Hymn. 14.
Already my rocks lie light,
                    Monadnoc. 243.
Already blushes on thy check
                    Nemesis. 1.
Already Heaven with thee its lot has
    cast,   Sursum Corda. 10.
Also (Partial list.)
Also (from the song the wrath
                    Daemonic Love. 62.
Are fugitive also,   Illusions. 18.
Thoughts come also hand in hand;
                    Merlin. 101.
Art thou not also real?
                    Sursum Corda. 4.
Altar
Lead you rightly to my altar,
                    Etienne. 13.
And God hath built his altar here
                    Hymn. 5.
On this altar God hath built Nun. 15.

Alter—*Continued*
On him who by the altar stands,
                    Robbins Hymn. 25.‘
Altar's
To the altar's foot thy fellow seek,—
                    Quat. Pericles. 3.
Alter
Alter or mend eternal Fact.   Past. 21.
The wind may alter twenty ways,
                    Woodnotes. I. 98.
Alterable
        See Unalterable.
Altered
        See Unaltered.
A vixen to his altered eye;   Rhea. 20.
Alternated
Or else alternated;   Merlin. 103.
Alternation
"Eterne alternation   Sphinx. 97.
Altitudes
From all zones and altitudes;—
                    Mithridates. 9.
Altogether
Was not altogether still,
                    Monadnoc. 196.
Alway
Creating fair and good alway,
                    Day by Day. 7.
There alway, alway something sings.
                    Music. 12, 18.
He bridged the gulf from th' alway
    good and wise   Phi. 17.
I am the Muse who sung alway
                    Solution. 1.
Heart-heaving alway;   Sphinx. 102.
Alway it asketh, asketh;   Sphinx. 115.
Always
'Twas always thus, and will be; hand
    and head   Adirondacs. 286.
Meaning always to be young.
                    Initial Love. 141.
Which always find us young
                    Ode to Beauty. 62.
And always keep us so.
                    Ode to Beauty. 63.
Am I not always here, thy summer
    home?   Seashore. 3.
The little needle always knows the
    North,   Self-Reliance. 6.
Am (Partial list.)
I am the doubter and the doubt,
                    Brahma. 11.
If I am I; thou, thou; or thou art I?
                    Flute. 4.
"I am divine, I am not mortal made;
    Frag. Life. XVIII. 3.
I daily dwell in, and am not so blind
                    Frag. Nat. V. 3.
I am a willow of the wilderness,
                    Musketaquid. 70.
There I am full of light;   Peter. 30.
These are the same, but I am not the
    same,   River. 18.
I am the Muse who sung alway
                    Solution. 1.
For I am wont to sing uncalled,
                    Solution. 19.
Is master of all I am."   Sphinx. 132.
I am not poor, but I am proud,
                    Thought. 1.
I am too much bereft.   Threnody. 170.

I am but a thought of hers,   Una. 19.
In forests I am still at home
                    Walden. 47.
Amain
So shall the lights ye pour amain
                    Celestial Love. 23.
Sun and moon must fall amain
                    Frag. Poet. V. 34.
Each star, each god, each grace amain,
                    May-Day. 333.
Is sweetly solemnized. Then flows amain
                    Musketaquid. 21.
They totter now and float amain.
                    Poet. 38.
The brave he loves amain;
                    World-Soul. 90.
Ambassador
The King whose meek ambassador I go.
                    Summons. 24.
Amber
His park where amber mornings break,
                    Chartist. 10.
Except the amber morning wind,
                    Exile. 5.
The moon was making amber of the
    world,   Frag. Nat. XXVII. 3.
Sail swiftly through your amber vault,
                    Poet. 163.
Ambition
Rash ambition, brokenhanded;
                    Alphonso. 24.
Thieving Ambition and paltering Gain!
                    Beauty. 24.
And prizes of ambition, checks its hand,
                    Blight. 59.
By circumspect ambition,
                    Monadnoc. 398.
Ambitious
Not less the ambitious botanist sought
    plants,   Adirondacs. 141.
Thy broad ambitious branches, and thy
    root.   Terminus. 8.
Ambrosia
The nectar and ambrosia, are withheld;
                    Blight. 45.
Ambrosial
Go if thou wilt, ambrosial flower,
                    Frag. Life. XXV. 1.
Amends
In other love should seek amends.
                    From Hafiz. 12.
Americans
Only thy Americans
                    Woodnotes. II. 140.
Amid
        See 'Mid.
Were sought and found, amid the hue
    and cry   Adirondacs. 192.
The lonely Earth amid the balls
                    II Compensation. 9.
Sails, astonished, amid stars.
                    Daemonic Love. 55.
Amid the mountain counties,
                    Letter. 9.
Here amid clouds to stand?
                    Monadnoc. 209.
Amid these coward shapes of joy and
    grief,   Monadnoc. 312.
Amid great Nature's halls
                    Mountain. 7.

Amid the Muses, left thee deaf and
dumb, Terminus. 31.
Amid the gladiators, halt and numb.'
Terminus. 32.

Amidst
Each of these landlords walked amidst
his farm, Hamatreya. 4.
Amidst the deep-eyed dew!
Thine Eyes. 8.

Amiss
Waved the scoop-net, and nothing came
amiss; Adirondacs. 138.
O pilgrim, wandering not amiss!
Monadnoc. 242.

Among (Partial list.)
Among the silver hills of heaven
Bacchus. 16.
Caught among the blackberry vines,
Berrying. 6.
And brier-roses, dwelt among;
Humble-Bee. 49.
Tall and good my kind among;
Monadnoc. 257.
Seek the living among the dead,—
Saadi. 117.
Once, among the Pleiads walking,
Uriel. 7.
'Speak not thy speech my boughs
among: Woodnotes. II. 134.

Ample
Whose ample leaves and tendrils curled
Bacchus. 15.
And the souls of ample fate,
Daemonic Love. 100.
Nor not receive his ample dues.
Guy. 16.
Like ample banner flung abroad
Monadnoc. 34.
To Nature, through her kingdoms ample,
Rhea. 65.
Space is ample, east and west,
Unity. 1.

Amphion
Walls Amphion piled Politics. 13.

Amulet
Give me an amulet Amulet. 5.

Amulets
Needs no amulets nor rings. Guy. 4.
And told his amulets: Hermione. 3.

Amused
And, truth to tell, amused by pain.
II Intellect. 2.

An (Partial list.)
Give me an amulet Amulet. 5.
And an omnipotence in chemistry,
Blight. 25.
And an æon allows Frag. Life. VI. 3.
Or an ungiven maid, Merlin. 109.

Ancestor
Is the ancestor of wars
Daemonic Love. 130.

Ancestors
Ancestors of beauty come
Frag. Life. XXII. 7.
Not ancestors, Merlin. 110.
They were coeval with my ancestors,
River. 40.

Ancestral
In this ancestral place,
In Memoriam. 22.

Anchorage
No anchorage is. Illusions. 4.

Anchored
It is anchored in the ground.
Holidays. 8.
Anchored fast for many an age,
Monadnoc. 283.
And anchored in the tempest ride.
Woodnotes. II. 257.

Ancient
Of the ancient being blow,
Bacchus. 48.
Who climb each night the ancient sky,
Frag. Nat. VIII. 6.
This is not the ancient earth
Frag. Nat. XXVI. 32.
Firm-braced I sought my ancient woods,
May-Day. 39.
As poured the flood of the ancient sea
May-Day. 241.
To greet staid ancient cavaliers
May-Day. 307.
Yet, will you learn our ancient speech,
Monadnoc. 173.
Yet said yon ancient wood, Park. 14.
From ancient ages for the bard,
Poet. 151.
And hark! where overhead the ancient
crows River. 16.
Foolish gossips, ancient drones,
Saadi. 170.
Seethe, Fate! the ancient elements,
Song of Nature. 75.
Waters with tears of ancient sorrow
Threnody. 286.
Safe in their ancient crannies, dark and
deep, To-Day. 3.
I had as lief respect an ancient shoe,
To-Day. 11.
It fell in the ancient periods Uriel. 1.
And I will swim the ancient sea
Woodnotes. II. 45.
The chorus of the ancient Causes!
Woodnotes. II. 119.

And (Partial list.)
And night and day, ocean and continent,
Blight. 34.
And every fair and every good,
Celestial Love. 50.
And write, and reason, and compute,
Initial Love. 28.
And march their feet, Merlin. 47.
Up! mind thine own aim, and
To J. W. 22.

Andes
Of Alp and Andes, isle and continent,
Adirondacs. 263.
Under the Andes to the Cape,
Bacchus. 4.
Under Alps and Andes cold;
Frag. Nat. I. 16.
As in the Andes watched by fleets at
sea, Frag. Nat. IV. 4.
Andes, Alp or Himmalee,
Frag. Nat. XV. 3.
With Andes and with Ararat.
Problem. 44.
The rocky coast, smite Andes into dust,
Seashore. 35.

Anemonies
In cowslips and anemonies.
                    Nature. I. 4.
Anew
Halved and dealt the globe anew,
                    Solution. 64.
I formed the world anew;
                    Song of Nature. 28.
Love wakes anew this throbbing heart,
                    World-Soul. 107.
Angel
    See Archangel.
For the angel Hope aye makes
                    Caritas. 7.
Him an angel whom she leads.
                    Caritas. 8.
An angel as a worm.   Bohemian. 6.
My angel,—his name is Freedom,—
                    Boston Hymn. 13.
As angel blind to trespass done,
                    Frag. Life. XXVIII. 3.
With angel patience labor on,
                    In Memoriam. 76.
Many an angel wander by,   Nun. 24.
No angel from the countless host
                    Threnody. 120.
The glowing angel, the outcast corse.
                    Woodnotes. II. 306.
Our angel, in a stranger's form,
                    World-Soul. 27.
Angelo
In Milton and in Angelo:
                    Frag. Poet. IV. 31.
Angel's
Pure content is angel's lot,   Poet. 251.
Angels
Skirts of angels, starry wings,   Art. 16.
Not angels but divinities attend.
                    Frag. Life. III. 2.
Draws angels nigh to dwell with thee,
                    Freedom. 19.
And bid you let the angels in
                    Hymn. 19.
'Pass in, pass in,' the angels say,
                    Merlin. 34.
Nor sword of angels could reveal
                    Merlin. 76.
Which only angels hear;
                    Merlin's Song. 9.
To whom sweet angels ministered,
                    Poet. 202.
'Sorrow, sorrow!' the angels cried,
                    Poet. 217.
And woke the fear lest angels part.
                    Poet. 256.
But not angels of the deep: Poet. 272.
"Pride ruined the angels,   Sphinx. 89.
That drop from the angels' shoon.
                    Quat. Excelsior. 4.
Shamed the angels' veiling wings;
                    Uriel. 48.
Anger
And dies in anger that it was a dupe;
                    Blight. 55.
Angles
All the angles of the coast   Lines. 3.
Angry
The angry Muse   Channing Ode. 10.
And whether I am angry or content,
                    Day's Ration. 9.

God forbid my angry heart
                    From Hafiz. 11.
Whither the angry farmers came,
                    In Memoriam. 4.
Anguish
And charm the anguish of the worst.
                    Aeolian Harp. 23.
Animals
The animals are sick with love,
                    Merlin. 96.
Animate
To animate new millions, and exhale
                    Pan. 11.
By their animate poles.   Sphinx. 32.
Animated
Thou animated torrid-zone!
                    Humble-Bee. 6.
An animated law, a presence to exalt.'
                    Poet. 164.
Ankles
Painted our necks, hands, ankles, with
    red bands: Adirondacs. 167.
Annals
And I will write our annals new,
                    Titmouse. 99.
Annexed
Annexed a warning, poets say,
                    Saadi. 13.
Announced
    See Self-announced.
Announced by all the trumpets of the
    sky,   Snow-Storm. 1.
Annual
And annual tunes commemorate
                    Mountain. 20.
Painting with morn each annual cell?
                    Problem. 28.
Anointing
'T was coming fast to such anointing,
                    Titmouse. 24.
Another
But, laying hands on another
                    Boston Hymn. 61.
Another round, a higher,
                    Celestial Love. 8.
Have the same mists another side,
                    Chartist. 7.
But Cupid wears another face,
                    Daemonic Love. 89.
And another is born   Destiny. 27.
To-morrow they will wear another face,
                    Experience. 20.
Such another peerless queen
                    Frag. Life. IX. 1.
Pleasures to another stage
                    Frag. Poet. XI. 16.
As if one spake to another,
                    Garden. 30.
And grasping give the orbs another
    whirl.   May-Day. 159.
Strewing my bed, and, in another age,
                    Seashore. 36.
Another heart as large and true.
                    Security. 6.
If Nature hold another heart
                    Security. 9.
To know one element, explore another,
                    Xenophanes. 12.
Another's
If thou pine for another's gift?
                    Destiny. 17.

Yet, greeted in another's eyes,
                    Worship. 17.

Answer
I heard a poet answer   Sphinx. 65.
And each answer is a lie.   Sphinx. 116.

Answered
    See Unanswered.
Answered the pine-tree and the oak,
                    Frag. Nat. III. 11.
Are registered and answered still.
                    Prayer. 8.
The deep Heart answered, 'Weepest
    thou?   Threnody. 176.

Answering
To every tone beat answering tones,
                    Merlin. 83.

Answers
Answers not in word or letter,
                    Astraea. 21.
Leaf answers leaf upon the bough;
                    Merlin. 86.
Lo! the south answers to the north;
                    Monadnoc. 15.

Antelopes
Be swift their feet as antelopes,
                    Boston Hymn. 79.

Ant-hill
Forbore the ant-hill, shunned to tread,
                    Frag. Poet. XXIV. 1.

Anthracite
Is but a straw to anthracite;
                    May-Day. 139.

Anticipate
Impatient to anticipate   May-Day. 154.

Antidote
Vine for vine be antidote,   Bacchus. 53.
My touch thy antidote, my bay thy
    bath?   Seashore. 6.
To find the antidote of fear,
                    Titmouse. 102.

Antipode
To every foot its antipode;   Merlin. 81.

Antipodes
It thrills to the antipodes,
                    Waterfall. 11.

Antique
By this foolish antique patent.
                    Initial Love. 10.

Antiquity
The bald antiquity of China praise.
                    To-Day. 16.

Anxious
Nor when I'm jaded, sick, anxious or
    mean.   Frag. Life. XV. 5.
Deeply soothe his anxious ear.
                    Initial Love. 73.
Thoughtless of its anxious freight,
                    Monadnoc. 333.
And anxious hearts have pondered here
                    Robbins Hymn. 9.

Any (Partial list.)
All ate like abbots, and, if any missed
                    Adirondacs. 180.
Fleeter they than any creature,—
                    Initial Love. 35.
Not allowed to any liege;
                    Initial Love. 119.
Of any woman that is now alive,—
                    Naples. 20.

Apace
His roses bleach apace,
                    Daemonic Love. 91.

Apart
To each apart, lifting her lovely shows
                    Adirondacs. 199.
Shame the times and live apart,—
                    Frag. Poet. IV. 6.
Of a joy apart from thee,   Give. 38.
'Once I dwelt apart,   Hermione. 40.
Gravely it broods apart on joy,
                    II Intellect. 1.
That thou might'st entertain apart
                    Threnody. 215.
This poet, though he live apart,
                    Titmouse. 33.
Leave all thy pedant lore apart;
                    Woodnotes. II. 234.

Ape
Tree and lichen, ape, sea-lion,
                    Mithridates. 12.
To ape thy dare-devil array?
                    Titmouse. 57.

Apennine
Etched on Alp and Apennine.
                    Solution. 32.

Apollo
Apollo is an imbecile.
                    Frag. Poet. XVIII. 4.

Appalled
And sometimes mankind I appalled
                    Solution. 22.
Bound to the stake, no flames appalled,
                    Worship. 9.

Appalling
Peril around, all else appalling,
                    Voluntaries. 93.

Appanage
To be the appanage of pride, Chartist. 8.

Appear
    See Disappear; Reappear.
The vanished gods to me appear;
                    Brahma. 7.
Why the gods will not appear;
                    Frag. Life. XXXIII. 5.
Be what they soothfast appear,
                    May-Day. 360.
The hour of heaven shall come, the man
    appear.   Rome. 27.

Appeared
To me that spectral nook appeared
                    Peter. 25.

Appearest
Nor yet thou appearest.
                    Ellen South. 16.

Appearing
    See Far-appearing.

Appears
And all the crowded Past appears
                    Ellen. 3.
The mill-round of our fate appears
                    Friendship. 15.
Leaves, when the sun appears, astonished
    Art   Snow-Storm. 25.

Appeased
Even the fell Furies are appeased,
                    Celestial Love. 113.

Appeasing
O fair, appeasing presences!
                    Merops. 6.

Appetite
With hunters' appetite and peals of
mirth.   Adirondacs. 182.
A hid unruly appetite   May-Day. 151.
Or by thirst and appetite   Saadi. 89.

Applaud
The good applaud, the lost are eased.
Celestial Love. 114.

Applauded
Others applauded him who spoke the
truth.   Adirondacs. 187.

Applause
To outdo each other and extort applause.
Adirondacs. 326.

Apples
that bears best apples, plant,
Adirondacs. 298.
Took a few herbs and apples, and the
Day   Days. 9.
Hay, corn, roots, hemp, flax, apples,
wool and wood.   Hamatreya. 3.
Are the apples of her eyes;
Nature. I. 8.
Apples of Eden ripe to-morrow.
Threnody. 287.

Apple-tree
Or to his niche in the apple-tree.
May-Day. 391.

Appliances
Means, appliances, delights,
Mithridates. 27.

Apply
Their fragrance, and their chemistry
apply   Blight. 11.

Appointed
See Unappointed; Well-appointed.
The appointed, and the unappointed day;
On Two Days. 2.
I know the appointed hour,   Poet. 114.

Apprehend
Low leaves his quarrel apprehend,
May-Day. 68.

Apprehension
My apprehension? Why seek Italy,
Day's Ration. 29.

Approach
To-day, when friends approach, and
every hour   Day's Ration. 20.

Approaching
Well I hear the approaching feet
Monadnoc. 267.

Approve
And thy behavior approve;
Frag. Life. XXVII. 6.

April
Flowering April cools and dies
Alphonso. 7.
The April winds are magical   April. 1.
April cold with dropping rain
May-Day. 182.
They put their April raiment on;
May-Day. 319.
Morn well might break and April bloom,
Threnody. 16.
Cold April rain and colder snows
Walden. 11.

April's
April's cowslip, summer's clover,
Ellen South. 30.
Their flag to April's breeze unfurled,
C. Hymn. 2.

Sparrows far off, and nearer, April's
bird,   Musketaquid. 15.
As snow-banks thaw in April's beam,
Poet. 35.

Arab
Free as an Arab   Give. 32.
On a mound an Arab lay,
Hermione. 1.

Araby
There are beggars in Iran and Araby,
Frag. Poet. I. 1.

Ararat
With Andes and with Ararat.
Problem. 44.

Arc
The acorn's cup, the raindrop's arc,
Ode to Beauty. 26.

Arcade
Hollow and lake, hillside and pine arcade,   Musketaquid. 23.

Arcades
Beckon thee to their arcades;
Monadnoc. 20.

Arch
Below May's well-appointed arch,
May-Day. 332.
Beneath the crystal arch,   May-Day. 383

Archangel
The archangel Hope
Frag. Life. XXIII. 1.

Archangels
And makes thy thoughts archangels be;
Freedom. 20.

Arched
By the rude bridge that arched the flood,
C. Hymn. 1.
Through thee alone the sky is arched,
Friendship. 11.
But arched o'er him an honoring vault.
Worship. 10.

Arches
Where arches green, the livelong day,
Good-Bye. 19.

Archetypes
In their archetypes endure.
Celestial Love. 53.

Arch-hypocrite
But he is the arch-hypocrite,
Initial Love. 105.

Architect
There is no architect   House. 1.
Be still his arm and architect,
May-Day. 443.
House at once and architect,
Spiritual Laws. 2.

Architecture
I make your sculptured architecture
vain,   Seashore. 11.
The frolic architecture of the snow.
Snow-Storm. 28.

Architrave
Replacing frieze and architrave;—
Monadnoc. 371.

Arcs
In nearer arcs his journeys run,
Peter. 15.

Arctic
One arctic moon had disenchanted.
May-Day. 44.
When you deal with arctic cold,
Titmouse. 2.

Arcturus
Poises Arcturus aloft morning and
evening his spear.   Shah.-Hafiz. 2.
Ardent
Of ardent youth untouched by pain,
Hymn. 11.
Again I meet the ardent beams.
Ode to Beauty. 93.
Are (Partial list.)
Their cords of love so public are,
Celestial Love. 107.
Wise and sure the issues are.
Channing Ode. 77.
And they who truliest love her, heralds
are   Frag. Nat. V. 9.
So deep and large her bounties are,
May-Day. 275.
Makes and moulds them what they are,
Nature. II. 8.
Dark with more clouds than tempests
are,   Threnody. 99.
Her stripes the boreal streamers are.
Voluntaries. 42.
Throes that were, and worlds that are,
Woodnotes. II. 209.
Argument
Nor knowest thou what argument
Each. 9.
Aright
Then, if I read the page aright
Ellen. 5.
I only follow, when I act aright.
Self-Reliance. 10.
Arise
The buried Past arise;   Peter. 18.
When shall that sun arise? Rubies. 12.
Ark
See River-ark.
Arm
Be still his arm and architect,
May-Day. 443.
Can arm impregnably the skin;
Titmouse. 76.
Armed
See Broad-armed; Disarmed; Light-
armed; Unarmed.
armed eyes of experts. Adirondacs. 304.
Our eyes Are armed, but we are
strangers to the stars,
Blight. 29—30.
I armed his hand with skill,
Frag. Poet. XIV. 2.
And his hand was armed with skill;
Power. 2.
When Science armed and guided war,
Solution. 61.
Armies
Or tented armies on a plain.
May-Day. 256.
Armory
The landscape is an armory of powers,
Musketaquid. 34.
Arms
Between two rocky arms, we climb the
bank,   Adirondacs. 31.
And in the left, a gun, his needful arms.
Adirondacs. 79.
Their sinewy arms pull at the oar un-
tired   Adirondacs. 89.
Fold my arms beside the brook;
Apology. 6.

Took Boston in its arms;   Boston. 4.
Had leaped from one fair mother's
arms,   Dirge. 6.
Where far oaks outstretched their arms.
September. 8.
Forging, through swart arms of Offence,
Spiritual Laws. 11.
Has million arms to one of mine:
Titmouse. 6.
Dragged from his mother's arms and
breast,   Voluntaries. 19.
Iron arms, and iron mould,
Woodnotes. II. 41.
Their arms fly open wide.
World-Soul. 96.
Aroma
The aroma of my life is gone
Days Pass. 3.
Which by aroma may compel
Frag. Nat. II. 30.
Aromatic
Breathes aromatic fire;   Threnody. 4.
Around
Where all the sacred mountains drew
around us,   Adirondacs. 9.
Around, below, above.   Cupido. 4.
Around me stood the oaks and firs;
Each. 44.
And paused for them, and looked around,
Dirge. 3.
Around the man who seeks a noble end,
Frag. Life. III. 1.
She walked in flowers around my field
Frag. Life. XIII. 1.
As June herself around the sphere.
Frag. Life. XIII. 2.
Carry aloft, below, around,
Frag. Nat. III. 35.
Around him hover   *Lines. 5.
The cloud was around me,   *Lines. 9.
And wide around, the marriage of the
plants   Musketaquid. 20.
Unseen by such as stood around.
Poet. 16.
From humble tenements around
Robbins Hymn. 13.
Around the radiant fireplace, enclosed
Snow-Storm. 8.
Jealous glancing around,   Sphinx. 54.
Paced by the blessed feet around,
Threnody. 91.
A shudder ran around the sky;
Uriel. 26.
Why wilt thou live when none around
reflects thy pensive ray?   *Violet. 5.
Peril around, all else appalling,
Voluntaries. 93.
Array
And court the flower that cheapens his
array.   Rhodora. 8.
To ape thy dare-devil array?
Titmouse. 57.
Arrive
Never yet could once arrive,
Forerunners. 24.
The gods arrive.   Give. 49.
Say not, the chiefs who first arrive
Merlin's Song. 16.
To the birth they arrive: Poet. 107.
At no goal will arrive;   Sphinx. 84.

Arrive —*Continued*
If once the generous chief arrive
                    Voluntaries. 55.

Arrived
Arrived in time to swell his grain;
                    Guy. 34.
From evils which never arrived!
                    Quat. Borrowing. 4.
From the shore of souls arrived,
                    Song of Seyd. 11.

Arrives
Ere yet arrives the wintry day
                    Monadnoc. 23.
Arrives the snow, and, driving o'er the
fields,   Snow-Storm. 2.
Arrives the wise selecting will,
                    Wealth. 31.

Arriving
        See Late-arriving.
Threading dark ways, arriving late,
                    Worship. 12.

Arrow
I have an arrow that will find its mark,
                    Arrow. 1.
Whose pipe and arrow oft the plough
unburies,   Musketaquid. 29.

Arrows
His arrows he shrouds.   *Lines. 8.

Art (Noun.)
Match God's equator with a zone of art,
                    Adirondacs. 245.
Now speed the gay celerities of art,
                    Adirondacs. 320.
'T is the privilege of Art   Art. 19.
Nor art, nor power, nor toil can find
                    Bohemian. 10.
Where in bright Art each god and sibyl
dwelt   Daemonic Love. 121.
Art its height could never hit;
                    Destiny. 8.
For art, for music over-thrilled,
                    Frag. Poet. XVI. 1.
Not for fame, nor by rules of art,
                    Garden. 19.
(Sweet is art, but sweeter truth,)
                    Harp. 44.
And, through all science and all art,
                    Initial Love. 106.
My stock of art, plant dials in the
grass,   Letter. 20.
Water-line pattern of all art?
                    May-Day. 213.
No jingling serenader's art,   Merlin. 5.
Past clerks' or statesmen's art or pas-
sion.   Monadnoc. 178.
Great is the art,   Merlin. 27.
Asia's rancor, Athens' art,
                    Monadnoc. 300.
Nature, hating art and pains,
                    Nature. I. 5.
And in their vaunted works of Art
                    Nature. II. 22.
Equal trophies of thine art;
                    Ode to Beauty. 89.
Art might obey, but not surpass.
                    Problem. 46.
Through mountains bored by regal art,
                    Saadi. 153.
Leaves, when the sun appears, aston-
ished Art   Snow-Storm. 25.

The richest flowering of all art:
                    Threnody. 216.
Which no false art refines.
                    Waldeinsamkeit. 32.
'T is the chronicle of art.
                    Woodnotes. II. 103.
Strong art and beautiful pretension,
                    Woodnotes. II. 207.

Art (Verb.) (Partial list.)
What art thou? His wicked eye
                    Limits. 11.
Thou art silent and sedate.
                    Monadnoc. 380.
"Thou art the unanswered question;
                    Sphinx. 113.

Arteries
From my great arteries,—nor less, nor
more.'   Day's Ration. 5.

Artery
Vein and artery, though ye kill me!
                    Mithridates. 32.

Artful
Artful thunder, which conveys
                    Merlin. 13.

Arthur
Of Arthur and his peers;   Harp. 26.

Articles
And the articles of arts.   Prudence. 4.

Artificer
Furnished with tile, the fierce artificer
                    Snow-Storm. 12.

Artist
Now must thou be man and artist,—
                    Holidays. 19.
Wealth to the cunning artist who can
work   Seashore. 31.

Artless
Painting artless paradises, May-Day. 249.

Arts
No city airs or arts pass current here.
                    Adirondacs. 92.
Of books and arts and trained experi-
ment,   Adirondacs. 307.
Of better arts and life?
                    Channing Ode. 14.
With the din of city arts;   Merlin. 23.
Sweat and season are their arts,
                    Monadnoc. 133.
To drug their crops or weapon their
arts withal.   Musketaquid. 40.
And the articles of arts.   Prudence. 4.
I too have arts and sorceries;
                    Seashore. 41.
The shop of toil, the hall of arts;
                    Wealth. 35.

As (Partial list.)
Sleep on the fragrant brush, as on
down-beds.   Adirondacs. 58.
With laughter sudden as the crack of
rifle;   Adirondacs. 128.
As water poured through hollows of the
hills   Adirondacs. 149.
As if associates of the sylvan gods.
                    Adirondacs. 156.
As chapels in the city's thoroughfares,
                    Adirondacs. 195.
And as through dreams in watches of
the night,   Adirondacs. 201.
Of such delight and wonder as there
grew,—   Adirondacs. 250.

A burst of joy, as if we told the fact
Adirondacs. 252.
As if we men were talking in a vein
Adirondacs. 256.
As of a luck not quite legitimate,
Adirondacs. 275.
As if one riddle of the Sphinx were
guessed. Adirondacs. 343.
Gaunt as bitterns in the pools,
Alphonso. 16.
O'er your ramparts as ye lean,
Alphonso. 20,
It cheers him as he sails. Bell. 8.
Bold as the engineer who fells the
wood, Blight. 19.
Doth as far transcend Bohemian. 5.
An angel as a worm. Bohemian. 6.
As they sat by the seaside,
Boston Hymn. 3.
As the sculptor uncovers the statue
Boston Hymn. 19.
As planets faithful be. Boston Hymn. 48.
As wind and wandering wave.
Boston Hymn. 56.
As much as he is and doeth,
Boston Hymn. 59.
Be swift their feet as antelopes,
Boston Hymn. 79.
And as behemoth strong.
Boston Hymn. 80.
By races, as snow-flakes,
Boston Hymn. 82.
As the overhanging trees
Celestial Love. 71.
As garment draws the garment's hem,
Celestial Love. 73.
Not glad, as the low-loving herd,
Celestial Love. 117.
As Olympus follows Jove.
Channing Ode. 70.
As, when a shower of meteors
Daemonic Love. 48.
Pouring as wide a flood Dirge. 18.
With sorrow such as mine, Dirge. 46.
If I'm not so large as you, Fable. 12.
Unknown to Cromwell as to me
Fate. 3.
Unknown to him as to his horse,
Fate. 5.
By signs gracious as rainbows.
Forerunners. 34.
As the drop feeds its fated flower,
Frag. Life. XXIII. 5.
As finds its Alp the snowy shower,
Frag. Life. XXIII. 6.
As angel blind to trespass done,
Frag. Life. XXVIII. 3.
As moon from earth, or star from star.
Frag. Nat. VII. 2.
Devour as many as you list,
Frag. Nat. XIX. 5.
And unstained as the sun.
Frag. Nat. XXIII. 18.
Free as an Arab Give. 32.
And as, of old, Polycrates Guy. 7.
As costly wine into his well. Guy. 30.
Know me, as does my dog: we sym-
pathize; Hamatreya. 9.
And strangers, fond as they, their fur-
rows plough. Hamatreya. 12.
Can build as the Muse can; House. 2.

As lions on their prey; Initial Love. 40.
As if it were a living root;
Initial Love. 56.
And waters free as winds shall flow.
May-Day. 110.
As we thaw frozen flesh with snow,
May-Day. 125.
As Southern wrath to Northern right
May-Day. 138.
As in the day of sacrifice, May-Day. 140.
As poured the flood of the ancient sea
May-Day. 241.
Bending forests as bends the sedge,
May-Day. 243.
As if to-morrow should redeem
May-Day. 297.
As if Time brought a new relay
May-Day. 301.
And danced as merrily as young men.
May-Day. 323.
By new delights, as old by old,
May-Day. 366.
To man, as to a lubber friend,
May-Day. 403.
As with diamond dews thereon.
May-Day. 413.
As with hammer or with mace;
Merlin. 11.
Perfect-paired as eagle's wings,
Merlin. 113.
As the two twilights of the day
Merlin. 128.
As you spin a cherry. Mithridates. 24.
Youth, for a moment free as they,
Monadnoc. 21.
On the summit as I stood,
Monadnoc. 193.
Old as the sun, old almost as the shade;
Monadnoc. 204.
As doth this round sky-cleaving boat
Monadnoc. 272.
As in the old poetic fame
Monadnoc. 348.
Ascends as gladly in a single tree
Musketaquid. 56.
As in broad orchards resonant with
bees; Musketaquid. 57.
As is to me when I behold the morn
Naples. 23.
Shines not as on the town, Peter. 14.
As a man unto his friend. Peter. 36.
As on its friends, with kindred eye;
Problem. 38.
For, as the wood-kinds lurk and hide,
Quat. Forester. 3.
As they lead, so follow all, Rhea. 31.
Albeit scorned as none was scorned,
Rhea. 62.
Adorn her as was none adorned.
Rhea. 63.
Hunt knowledge as the lover wooes a
maid, Rome. 14.
Broods over thee, and as God lives in
heaven, Rome. 25.
His tongue can paint as bright, as keen;
Saadi. 122.
Yet beautiful as is the rose in June,
Seashore. 19.
Fresh as the trickling rainbow of July;
Seashore. 20.

As (Partial list.)—*Continued*
Is all his own, retiring, as he were not,
Snow-Storm. 24.
"Erect as a sunbeam,   Sphinx. 17.
As far as the incommunicable;
Threnody. 200.
'I came to thee as to a friend;
Threnody. 209.
And, as the great all-loving Day
Threnody. 217.
As God lives, is permanent;
Threnody. 267.
As resolutely dig or dive. To J. W. 17.
Roving, roving, as it seems, Una. 1.
Lured by 'Union' as the bribe.
Voluntaries. 30.
Justice after as before,—
Voluntaries. 101.
As if by secret sight he knew
Woodnotes. I. 48.
Quit thy friends as the dead in doom,
Woodnotes. II. 223.
We are but such as they.
World-Soul. 56.

Ascendant
Ascendant in the private soul,
Threnody. 252.

Ascending
Ascending thorough just degrees
Frag. Life. XXVIII. 1.
And ever ascending.   Give. 25.

Ascends
And Love ascends his throne,
Cosmos. 22.
Ascends as gladly in a single tree
Musketaquid. 56.

Ashamed
See Unashamed.
They are ashamed.
Frag. Life. XXXIII. 6.

Ashes
We buy ashes for bread; Bacchus. 12.
Ashes and jet all hues outshine.
Titmouse. 55.
If in ashes the fire-seed slept. Uriel. 46.

Asia
Then Asia yeaned her shepherd race,
Solution. 9.

Asia's
Asia's rancor, Athens' art,
Monadnoc. 300.

Aside
Fate grants each to stand aside;
Holidays. 18.
And thrust the weak aside;
World-Soul. 94.

Ask
Ask you, how went the hours?
Adirondacs. 107.
I ask more or not so much:
Aeolian Harp. 7.
And coldly ask their pottage, not their
love.   Blight. 39.
Ask votes of thrushes in the solitudes.
Channing Ode. 74.
None shall ask thee what thou doest,
Destiny. 22.
I ask how far is the Tigris flood,
Exile. 3.
'I ask no bauble miniature,
Hermione. 16.

Means, dear brother, ask them not;
Poet. 249.
Do thou of the Ages ask
Quat. Botanist. 3.
Rhodora! if the sages ask thee why
Rhodora. 9.
I never thought to ask, I never knew:
Rhodora. 14.
Ask not me, as Muftis can,
Song of Seyd. 21.
Ask on, thou clothed eternity;
Sphinx. 119.
High omens ask diviner guess;
Threnody. 228.
The timid it concerns to ask their way,
Woodnotes. I. 86.
'You ask,' he said, 'what guide
Woodnotes. I. 118.

Askance
And water it with wine, nor watch
askance   Adirondacs. 299.

Asked
Content that all we asked was granted?
Fame. 18.
Asked no physician but the wave,
Frag. Poet. V. 20.
He asked, he only asked, to feel.
Poet. 212.

Askest
Askest, 'How long thou shalt stay?'
Visit. 1.
Thou askest in fountains and in fires,
Woodnotes. II. 311.

Asketh
Alway it asketh, asketh;   Sphinx. 115.

Asking
See Light-asking.

Asks
Asks nought his brother cannot give;
Frag. Life. XVII. 2.
Asks nothing, but does all receive.
Frag. Life. XVII. 3.
Asks not of others soft consents,
Frag. Life. XVII. 6.
Asks of the urchin to be tost.
May-Day. 64.
But blest is he, who, playing deep, yet
haply asks not why, Quat. Nature. 3.

Asleep
Pan, half asleep, rolling over
Frag. Nat. I. 7.
Where are these men? Asleep beneath
their grounds: Hamatreya. 11.

Asmodean
The Asmodean feat is mine,
Frag. Poet. XXXIV. 1.

Aspect
Its peace sublime his aspect kept,
In Memoriam. 101.
One aspect to the desert and the lake.
Xenophanes. 4.

Assailed
All day the waves assailed the rock,
Frag. Nat. XXV. 1.

Assign
To assign just place and mates;
Astraea. 20.

Assigned
Knew the strong task to it assigned,
Wealth. 10.

Assimilated
And by the draught assimilated,
Bacchus. 22.

Associates
As if associates of the sylvan gods.
Adirondacs. 156.

Assorted
See Well-assorted.

Assured
Assured to find the token once again
Frag. Nat. IV. 9.
Sole source of light and hope assured,
Hymn. 25.
Looking seaward, well assured
Letters. 4.
Assured that he who made the claim,
Monadnoc. 28.

Aster
Every aster in my hand   Apology. 11.
Where the aster grew
Frag. Nat. III. 4.

Astern
Seeing Nature go astern.   Alphonso. 2.

Asteroid
Supplemental asteroid,
II Compensation. 12.

Astonished
Who stands astonished at the meteor light,   Adirondacs. 123.
Urging astonished Chaos with a thrill
Adirondacs. 264.
The astonished Muse finds thousands at her side   Channing Ode. 97.
Sails, astonished, amid stars.
Daemonic Love. 55.
Leaves, when the sun appears, astonished Art   Snow-Storm. 25.

Astray
Which, from Eden wide astray,
Ode to Beauty. 66.

Astronomy
And human fortunes in astronomy,
Blight. 24.
The true astronomy,
Celestial Love. 67.
Thou, in our astronomy
Monadnoc. 392.
Far-reaching concords of astronomy
Musketaquid. 63.
"Godhead! all this astronomy,
Woodnotes. II. 205.

At (Partial list.)
Or at the foresight of obscurer years?
Adirondacs. 217.
Substances at base divided,
Celestial Love. 44.
At midnight and at morn?   Dirge. 12.
At unawares 't is come and past.
Forerunners. 32.
Sudden, at unawares,   Merlin. 74.
At the burning Lyre,   Monadnoc. 215.
At midnight and at morn?]   Peter. 4.
Pale at overflowing noon   Saadi. 53.
At no goal will arrive;   Sphinx. 84.
At my work I ramble not;   Una. 6.
In at the window-pane;
World-Soul. 30.

Ate
All ate like abbots, and, if any missed
Adirondacs. 180.

Roses he ate, and drank the wind;
Frag. Poet. V. 14.

Atheist
See Theist.
Let theist, atheist, pantheist,   Saadi. 96.

Athens'
Asia's rancor, Athens' art,
Monadnoc. 300.

Athirst
Not mad, athirst, nor garrulous;
Woodnotes II. 68.

Athwart
The sun athwart the cloud thought it no sin   Frag. Nat. IX. 1.
Who athwart space redresses
Merlin. 119.

Atlantic
Or like the Atlantic streams, which run
Bacchus. 29.
And bid the broad Atlantic roll,
Concord Ode. 27.
An Atlantic seat,   Politics. 18.

Atlas
A load your Atlas shoulders cannot lift?
Seashore. 33.

Atmosphere
Give me to the atmosphere,—
Aeolian Harp. 8.
Sailor of the atmosphere;
Humble-Bee. 13.
Be bubbles of the atmosphere.
May-Day. 362.

Atom
Atom from atom yawns as far
Frag. Nat. VII. 1.
The atom displaces all atoms beside,
Frag. Poet. XXI. 1.
Orb and atom forth they prance,
Monadnoc. 249.
And every atom poises for itself,
Musketaquid. 58.
Self-kindled every atom glows
Nature. Mot. 15.
No ray is dimmed, no atom worn,
Song of Nature. 81.
Here was this atom in full breath,
Titmouse. 43.

Atoms
The atom displaces all atoms beside,
Frag. Poet. XXI. 1.
And the atoms march in tune;
Monadnoc. 246.
But borrowed in atoms from iron and stone,   Nature. II. 21.
Thanks the atoms that cohere.
Prudence. 6.
The journeying atoms,   Sphinx. 29.
Are the atoms of his body bright,
World-Soul. 87.

Attain
And some attain his voice to hear,
Harp. 57.
What these with slowest steps attain.
Voluntaries. 54.

Attempered
Attempered to the night and day,
Guy. 2.

Attend
Not angels but divinities attend.
Frag. Life. III. 2.
A little while attend;   Poet. 93.

Attend —*Continued*
So thou attend the enriching Fate
Poet. 124.

Attest
When linked hemispheres attest his deed. Adirondacs. 248.

Attire
Nor knew her beauty's best attire
Each. 31.
The coarseness of my poor attire;
Romany. 2.

Attired
With grace, with genius, well attired,
Harp. 116.

Attracts
As, when the all-worshiped moon attracts the eye, Musketaquid. 82.

Auburn
And dream the dream of Auburn dell.
May-Day. 181.

Audible
These trees and stones are audible to me,
River. 22.

Audience
With Persia for his audience; Saadi. 28.

Aught
Aught unsavory or unclean
Humble-Bee. 40.
Aught above its rate. Politics. 8.
More near than aught thou call'st thy own, Worship. 16.

Augur
He is an augur and a priest,
Initial Love. 109.

Auguries
The birds brought auguries on their wings, Frag. Poet. V. 41.

August
One August evening had a cooler breath;
Adirondacs. 331.

Augustine
Old Chrysostom, best Augustine,
Problem. 65.

Aurora
Aurora of a dearer day. Una. 16.

Aurora's
And lakes, smooth mirrors of Aurora's charms. I Bear. 8.

Ausable
Of the Ausable stream, intent to reach
Adirondacs. 3.

Austere
Well accept her rule austere;
May-Day. 135.
Bitter winds and fasts austere
Monadnoc. 159.

Austerely
And they serve men austerely,
Celestial Love. 121.

Authentic
To him authentic witness bare;
Frag. Poet. V. 40.

Authenticated
See Unauthenticated.
Leave authors' eyes, and fetch your own,
Waldeinsamkeit. 43.

Autumn
From Spring's faint flush to Autumn red.
Garden. 8.
Of a gusty Autumn day,
September. 2.

There's not a blade of autumn grain,
Threnody. 111.
in the clear autumn day. *Violet. 6.
When summer light is fading, and autumn breezes sigh; *Violet. 10.
When Autumn chills the plain.
Walden. 8.

Autumnal
And your autumnal gathering.
Frag. Nat. XXIII. 14.

Autumn-ripe
Autumn-ripe, its juices hold
Monadnoc. 298.

Autumn's
And autumn's sunlit festivals,
Hermione. 73.
Are Autumn's blasts fit music for thee,
*Violet. 2.

Auxiliaries
Nay, we saluted them Auxiliaries,
Adirondacs. 169.

Avail
'T will not now avail to tan
Alphonso. 11.
For what avail the plough or sail,
Boston. 29.
For what avail the plough or sail,
Boston. 80

Avails
But no speed of mine avails
Forerunners. 7.
Ah, what avails it Ode to Beauty. 33.

Avarice
My avarice cooled Hamatreya. 62.
Fear, Craft and Avarice Politics. 9.

Avenger's
Hear the far Avenger's feet: Saadi. 56.

Avenues
Wilt thou seal up the avenues of ill?
Frag. Life. XXXII. 1.
He has avenues to God Voluntaries. 51.

Averted
Of the Genii be averted!
Daemonic Love. 63.
To upstart Wealth's averted eye;
Good-Bye. 9.
Your ne'er averted glance Poet. 242.

Avoid
When each the other shall avoid,
Celestial Love. 97.

Avon
And one by Avon stream,
Song of Nature. 66.

Await
I await a tenderer touch,
Aeolian Harp. 6.
The semigod whom we await?
Culture. 2.
I await the bard and sage,
Monadnoc. 284.

Awaited
I awaited the seer Sphinx. 7.

Awaits
Or say, the foresight that awaits
Fate. 15.

Awake
And gifts awake when givers sleep,
Frag. Life. VII. 2.

Aware
See Unawares.

Away
Then turns to bound away,—is it too
    late?   Adirondacs. 124.
We flee away from cities, but we bring
                    Adirondacs. 302.
The prairie stretched away. Boston. 44.
I wiped away the weeds and foam,
                    Each. 24.
Is the Tigris to float me away. Exile. 20.
Laugh life away; have wine for tears;
                    Fame. 16.
From hearth and home away,
                    *Farewell. 8.
Far away, far away.
    *Farewell. 9. 18. 27. 36. 45. 54.
Breaks up their leaguer, and away.
                    Forerunners. 4.
On and away, their hasting feet
                    Forerunners. 9.
I could walk days, years, away
                    Frag. Nat. XXI. 6.
And fled in pretty frowns away
                    Frag. Poet. I. 38.
Smacks of faint memories far away.
                    May-Day. 78.
Up and away! where haughty woods
                    May-Day. 224.
Visits the valley;—break away the
    clouds,—   Musketaquid. 12.
How lame the other limped away.
                    Nun. 49.
The pious wind took it away, Poet. 17.
Sighed his soul away.   September. 4.
Up and away for life! be fleet!—
                    Titmouse. 11.
Stealing away the memory
                    Voluntaries. 77.
Wild planters, plant away! Walden. 16.
The spans of life away. Walden. 44.
Far away in time, when once,
                    Wealth. 2.

Awe
Saadi held the Muse in awe,
                    Frag. Poet. V. 22.
In strange junctures, felt, with awe,
                    Guy. 11.

Awful
And bid each awful Muse drive the
    damned harpies hence.   I Bear. 14.
Names from awful childhood heard
                    Daemonic Love. 7.
I saw them mask their awful glance.
                    May-Day. 324.
His awful Jove young Phidias brought;
                    Problem. 10.
And shake before those awful Powers,
                    Saadi. 57.
Awful victors, they misguide
                    Voluntaries. 111.

Awkward
And generous, teach his awkward race
                    May-Day. 404.

Awoke
O then I awoke,   *Lines. 25.

Axe
Wield the first axe these echoes ever
    heard.   Adirondacs. 33.
Ring of axe or hum of wheel
                    Frag. Poet. I. 23

Axis
The axis of those eyes sun-clear
                    Celestial love. 21.
Be the axis of the sphere:
                    Celestial Love. 22.
He is the axis of the star;
                    Woodnotes. II. 313.

Axle
Groped for axle of the world.
                    Frag. Nat. XXXIV. 4.

Aye
For the angel Hope aye makes
                    Caritas. 7.
But though aye one in heart,
                    *Farewell. 32.
But sceptred genius, aye inorbed,
                    Hermione. 10.
He shall aye climb   Merlin. 32.
Love is aye the counterforce,—
                    Miracle. 11.
Believed the eloquent was aye the true;
                    Phi. 16.
Ere ye go to quit me for ever and aye.
                    Poet. 262.
The fair moon mounts, and aye the flame
                    Romany. 3.

Aye-rolling
His aye-rolling orb   Sphinx. 83.

Azaleas
Azaleas flush the island floors,
                    May-Day. 261.

Azure
Looks to the azure cope,
                    Frag. Life. XXIII. 2.
E'en the flowing azure air
                    Ode to Beauty. 90.
His hearth the earth,—his hall the azure
    dome;   Woodnotes. I. 93.

Babble
In his flippant chirping babble,
                    Miracle. 34.

Babe
When from the womb the babe was
    loosed,   Quat. Horoscope. 3.
"The babe by its mother   Sphinx. 41.
The babe in willow wagon closed,
                    Threnody. 62.
To guard the babe from fancied foes.
                    Threnody. 69.

Babes
To babes, and to old eyes as well.
                    May-Day. 348.

Baby's
Living in a baby's life.   Holidays. 16.

Bacchic
Nor wanton skip with bacchic dance,
                    May-Day. 129.

Bacchus
Pour, Bacchus! the remembering wine;
                    Bacchus. 51.
Infant Bacchus in the vine,—
                    Garden. 35.

Bachelors
To bachelors and dames.   April. 4.
Most like to bachelors,   Merlin. 108.

Back
    See Coming-back.
Find me, and turn thy back on heaven.
                    Brahma. 16

Back —*Continued*

Back, back to chaos, harlot Day!
    Chartist. 18.
If I cannot carry forests on my back,
    Fable. 18.
Welcome back, you little nations,
    Frag. Nat. XXIII. 7.
Go they ways now, come later back,
    Garden. 59.
'Tis good, when you have crossed the sea
  and back,   Hamatreya. 23.
Would bring back day if it were dark;
    Initial Love. 22.
Back to books and sheltered home,
    May-Day. 54.
Bring hither back the robin's call,
    May-Day. 162.
Bring back the tulip's pride.
    May-Day. 163.
That they may render back
    Merlin. 12.
Change acts, reacts; back, forward
  hurled,
    Poet.175.
The moon comes back,—the Spirit not.
    Poet. 280.
Gives back the bending heavens in dew.
    Song of Nature. 84.
Bring the flown Muses back to men.
    Threnody. 137.

Backed
    See Broad-backed.

Backward

None so backward in the troop,
    Monadnoc. 251.
And wandered backward as in scorn,
    Threnody. 148.

Bad

Bad news from Georgia on the English
  throne;   Boston. 63.
Step by step, lifts bad to good,
    May-Day. 464.
Bad men it will chain and cage—
    Merlin's Song. 7.
That field by spirits bad and good,
    Peter. 5.
The good, the bad with equal zeal,
    Poet. 211.
Bad husbands of their fires,
    Terminus. 24.
Melancholy without bad.
    Woodnotes. I. 15.

Bade

Stars flamed and faded as they bade,
    Dirge. 34.

Badges

All wore thy badges and thy favors
    Lines. 7.

Baffle

Or baffle by a veil, or slight by scorn?
    Adirondacs. 176.

Baffled

Without the baffled North-wind calls.
    May-Day. 57.
Though baffled seers cannot impart
    Nature. Mot. 9.

Baffles

The great Idea baffles wit,
    Bohemian. 7.
Baulks and baffles plotting brains;
    Nature. I. 6.

Bag

And fill the bag to the brim.
    Boston Hymn. 70.

Bagdat

There is no lover in all Bagdat
    Exile. 7.
And all that I see in Bagdat
    Exile. 19.

Baggage

No more baggage than a bird.
    Frag. Poet. XXXIII. 4.

Baked
    See Sun-baked.

Baking
    See Earth-baking.

Balance

Trembling balance duly keep.
    II. Compensation. 4.

Balance-beam

The balance-beam of Fate was bent;
    Uriel. 31.

Balance-loving

Balance-loving Nature   Merlin. 79.

Bald

Time, shake not thy bald head at me.
    Nun. 30.
The bald antiquity of China praise.
    To-Day. 16.

Baldhead

Taháwus, Seaward, MacIntyre, Baldhead,   Adirondacs. 10.

Balk

Never balk the waiting ear.
    Monadnoc. 192.

Ball
    See Eyeball.

Think ye I made this ball
    Boston Hymn. 9.
The fresh ground loves his top and ball,
    May-Day. 69.
Turn swiftlier round, O tardy ball!
    May-Day. 160.
Spin the ball! I reel, I burn,
    Song of Seyd. 1.
Over the lifeless ball,   Wealth. 3.
The shadow sits close to the flying ball;
    Woodnotes. II. 244.

Ballad

Ballad, flag and festival,   Art. 10.

Balls

Nature centres into balls,   Circles. 1.
The lonely Earth amid the balls
    II. Compensation. 9.
Smelting balls and bars,   Merlin. 93.

Balm

And the balm of thoughtful words;
    Frag. Poet. X. 2.
On the first, neither balm nor physician
  can save,   On Two Days. 3.
With spasms of terror for balm of hope.
    Solution. 24.

Balmier

And o'er yon hazy crest is Eden's balmier spring.   May-Day. 103.

Balms

With all his force he gathers balms
    Initial Love. 58.

Balsam

Whose balsam never grew.   Dirge. 40.
Past all balsam or relief;
    Love and Thought. 10.

Baltimore
Penn's town, New York and Baltimore,
Boston. 47.

Band
Chide me not, laborious band,
Apology. 9.
Straight, into double band
Channing Ode. 94.
Next his heart the fireside band
Daemonic Love. 5.
When, foremost of the youthful band,
In Memoriam. 78.
Like the dancers' ordered band,
Merlin. 100.
Ivy for my fillet band;
Mithridates. 14.
Brother, we are no phantom band;
Poet. 263.

Bandaged
With bandaged eyes he never errs,
Cupido. 3.

Bandages
The bandages of purple light; Rhea. 16.

Bands
ankles, with red bands:
Adirondacs. 167.

Banian
Self-planted twice, like the banian.
Miracle. 6.

Banish
'Lowly faithful, banish fear,
Terminus. 37.

Bank
See River-bank.
we climb the bank,   Adirondacs. 31.
On this green bank, by this soft stream,
C. Hymn. 9.

Bankrupt
Would bankrupt nature to repay.
Ode to Beauty. 32.

Bankruptcy
'Alas! thine is the bankruptcy,
Woodnotes. II. 217.

Bank's
Haunting this bank's historic trees?
In Memoriam. 27.

Banks
See Snow-banks.
Through scented banks of lilies white
and gold,   Adirondacs. 19.
The banks slope down to the blue lake-
edge,   Garden. 11.
Long days, and solid banks of flowers;
Humble-Bee. 35.
And these loved banks, whose oak-
boughs bold   In Memoriam. 115.
He hath broke his banks and flooded all
the vales   River. 9.
Thou in thy narrow banks art pent:
Two Rivers. 5.

Banner
For the banner of the free.
Concord Ode. 12.
Like ample banner flung abroad
Monadnoc. 34.

Banner's
The snowflake is her banner's star,
Voluntaries. 41.

Banquets
Houses, banquets, gardens, fountains,
Frag. Poet. IV. 11.

Bantling
Cast the bantling on the rocks,
Quat. Power. 1.
But I, the bantling of a country Muse,
Summons. 22.

Baptize
See Rebaptize.
Environ me and me baptize
Frag. Poet. VII. 5.

Baptized
Baptized with the pure element,
Frag. Nat. XXVI. 27.

Bar
See Unbar.
Merry and manifold without bar,
Nature. II. 7.

Barberry
The wild rose and the barberry thorn
Boston. 37.

Bard
To earn the praise of bard and critic.
Fame. 12.
The bard and mystic held me for their
own,   Frag. Life. XXX. 1.
Darlings of children and of bard,
Frag. Nat. XXIII. 1.
And he the bard, a crystal soul
Frag. Poet. I. 56.
Salute the bard who is alive
Frag. Poet. XXVIII. 8.
Who is the Bard thus magnified?
Harp. 36.
There is no bard in all the choir,
Harp. 75.
The kingly bard   Merlin. 9.
Great be the manners, of the bard.
Merlin. 28.
For bard, for lover and for saint;
Monadnoc. 45.
I await the bard and sage,
Monadnoc. 284.
Nor lives the tragic bard to say
Nun. 47.
From ancient ages for the bard,
Poet. 151.
'Bard, when thee would Allah teach,
Saadi. 60.

Bards
I know the mighty bards,   Dull. 6.
To bards who from its maxims live,
Frag. Poet. IV. 2.
Love of ladies, love of bards,
Frag. Poet. VII. 10.
Bards to say what nations need;
Frag. Poet. XII. 2.
As fits the griefs of bards to be.
Harp. 60.
With the bards and with the crowd.
Initial Love. 87.
When magic wine for bards is brewed;
May-Day. 339.
Beloved of children, bards and Spring,
May-Day. 396.
Bards, Roys, Scanderbegs and Tells;
Monadnoc. 97.
Olympian bards who sung
Ode to Beauty. 60.
Bards to speak what nations need;
Solution. 26.
And bards o'er kings to rule:—
Song of Nature. 70.

Bare
To him authentic witness bare;
                    Frag. Poet. V. 40.
Barefoot
Muffled and dumb like barefoot dervish-
es,   Days. 2.
Barefooted
Barefooted Dervish is not poor,
                    Saadi. 119.
Bareheaded
At morn or noon, the guide rows bare-
headed: Adirondacs. 74.
Barely
Think nature barely serves for one;
                    Alphonso. 36.
Baresark
The Baresark marrow to thy bones,
                    Terminus. 28.
Bark
A mastiff that will bite without a bark.
                    Arrow. 2.
Our eyeless bark sails free
                    Frag. Nat. XV. 1.
Was it a squirrel's pettish bark,
                    May-Day. 21.
The frailest leaf, the mossy bark,
                    Ode to Beauty. 25.
Steers his bark and trims his sail;
                    Quat. Poet. I. 2.
In critic peep or cynic bark,
                    To J. W. 19.
The moss upon the forest bark
                    Woodnotes. I. 133.
Barked
Barked the white spruce to weatherfend
the roof,   Adirondacs. 35.
Barking
Hear wolves barking at the moon;
                    Saadi. 54.
Barley-corn
Is worth one barley-corn at most,
                    From Hafiz. 7.
Barn
Nestle in hedge, or barn, or roof,
                    May-Day. 400.
The poultry-yard, the shed, the barn,—
                    Threnody. 89.
Barren
Teaching barren moors to smile,
                    May-Day. 3.
There's fruit upon my barren soil
                    Monadnoc. 295.
So call not waste that barren cone
                    Monadnoc. 352.
O barren mound, thy plenties fill!
                    Monadnoc. 378.
Barrier
At the barrier of Time,
                    May-Day. 408.
Barriers
'For you,' they said, 'no barriers be,
                    Boston. 55.
Barrows
Give to barrows, trays and pans   Art. 1.
Bars
See Prison-bars.
Have slipped their sacred bars,
                    Daemonic Love. 53.
Smelting balls and bars,   Merlin. 93.
Barter
Being for Seeming bravely barter
                    Fame. 29.

Bartered
Bartered its powdery cap;
                    May-Day. 234.
Basalt
Sit here on the basalt courses
                    Cosmos. 17.
Salt and basalt, wild and tame:
                    Mithridates. 11.
Base
Substances at base divided,
                    Celestial Love. 44.
Nor whether your name is base or brave:
                    Destiny. 40.
Not on its base Monadnoc surer stood,
                    Phi. 13.
And Nile substructs her granite base,—
                    Solution. 10.
On all was base in man,   Walden. 22.
The politics are base;   World-Soul. 17.
Based
Not firmer based than they.
                    Frag. Life. XXXVI. 4.
Bask
He seemed to bask, to dream and play
                    Frag. Poet. V. 4.
Basket-maker's
The sallow knows the basket-maker's
thumb;   Adirondacs. 101.
Baskets
'Onward,' he cries, 'your baskets bring,—
                    May-Day. 101.
Basque
English, German, Basque, Castilian,
                    Woodnotes. II. 151.
Bass
With thy mellow, breezy bass.
                    Humble-Bee. 31.
Bassora's
In old Bassora's schools, I seemed
                    Hermione. 33.
Bastions
Curves his white bastions with projected
roof   Snow-Storm. 13.
Bat
Small bat and wren   Channing Ode. 27.
Bate
Nor bate one jot of heart or hope,
                    In Memoriam. 80.
Bath
My touch thy antidote, my bay thy bath?
                    Seashore. 6.
Bathe
I bathe in the morn's soft and silvered
air,   Musketaquid. 13.
Bathed
See New-bathed.
Lies bathed in joy;   Sphinx. 42.
Bathers
Or, bathers, diving from the rock at
noon;   Adirondacs. 112.
Bathing
Bathing in thy day sublime.   Poet. 133.
Battery
The tremulous battery Earth
                    Waterfall. 9.
Battle
That can give us a glimpse of the battle
                    Cosmos. 15.
Battled
See Embattled.

Battle-field
I mourn upon this battle-field,
                In Memoriam. 1.
Battle-numbers
Borrowed thy battle-numbers bold.
                Titmouse. 98.
Battles
And he who battles on her side,
                Voluntaries. 102.
Battling
Battling for the weak and poor.
                In Memoriam. 43.
Bauble
I ask no bauble miniature,
                Hermione. 16.
Baulks
Baulks and baffles plotting brains;
                Nature. I. 6.
Bay
    See Boston Bay.
Due east a bay makes inward to the
land   Adirondacs. 30.
south to Osprey Bay,   Adirondacs. 109.
the bear is kept at bay, Adirondacs. 315.
The good town on the bay, Boston. 42.
So let each dweller on the Bay
                Boston. 102.
Too fast we leave the bay,
                *Farewell. 6.
I kept the sun and stars at bay,
                Frag. Poet. II. 7.
My touch thy antidote, my bay thy
bath?   Seashore. 6.
Bayonets
Through files of flags that gleamed like
bayonets,   Adirondacs. 17.
Bazaar
Or crowd the market and bazaar;
                Saadi. 110.
Be (Partial list.)
'For you,' they said, 'no barriers be,
                Boston. 55.
Than thine no deeper moat can be,
                Boston. 61.
'Now by these presents be it known
                Boston. 65.
As planets faithful be.
                Boston Hymn. 48.
My will fulfilled shall be,
                Boston Hymn. 85.
O, be my friend, and teach me to be
thine!   Forbearance. 8.
Be it health, or be it sickness;
                Frag. Life. XXVII. 8.
If curses be the wage of love,
                Frag. Life. XXXIII. 1.
The portraiture of things to be.
                Frag. Life. XXXV. 6.
And makes thy thoughts archangels be;
                Freedom. 20.
and let it be   Goethe. 1.
Thine everlasting lovers. Ye shall be
                Good Cheer. 15.
Great be the manners, of the bard.
                Merlin. 28.
Eyes that frame cities where none be,
                Monadnoc. 108.
And all town-sprinkled lands that be,
                Monadnoc. 277.
Would I that cowlèd churchman be.
                Problem. 6.

I would not the good bishop be.
                Problem. 72.
For of this lore be thou sure,—
                Rhea. 27.
These presents be the hostages
                Rhea. 70.
Leaves twinkle, flowers like persons be,
                Saadi. 137.
The yoke of men's opinions. I will be
                Self-Reliance. 2.
The peasant the lord that shall be;
                Woodnotes. II. 19.
All spheres, all stones, his helpers be;
                Woodnotes. II. 78.
A bunch of fragrant lilies be,
                Woodnotes. II. 303.
Finds them who in cellars be;
                World-Soul. 34.
Beach
The Adirondac lakes. At Martin's Beach
                Adirondacs. 4.
Beacon
A beacon set that Freedom's race
                Webster. 3.
Bead
The little cup will hold not a bead more,
                Day's Ration. 22.
Shall string Monadnoc like a bead.
                Monadnoc. 286.
Bead-eyes
Bead-eyes my granite chaos show,
                Monadnoc. 317.
Beads
But rather, like its beads of dew
                Frag. Nat. XXVI. 35.
But beads are of a rosary
                Monadnoc. 233.
Beak
Dove beneath the vulture's beak;—
                Voluntaries. 17.
Beam
    See Balance-beam; Eyebeam; Sun-
    beam.
A private beam into each several heart.
                Adirondacs. 223.
With the beryl beam of the broken
wave;   Beauty. 8.
And beam to the bounds of the universe.
                Beauty. 20.
Came a beam of goodness down
                Caritas. 3.
Pray for a beam   Celestial Love. 60.
Touched with life by every beam.
                Frag. Nat. XXVI. 29.
As snow-banks thaw in April's beam,
                Poet. 35.
Bears nothing on its beam.
                World-Soul. 16.
Beamed
His genius beamed with joy again.
                In Memoriam. 104.
Beaming
Beaming from its counterpart,
                Daemonic Love. 32.
Seest the smile of Reason beaming;—
                Monadnoc. 236.
Beaming from a young man's eyes.
                On Prince. 4.
Beams
She lays her beams in music, House. 17.

Beams —*Continued*
Whose deeps, till beams of noonday
break, May-Day. 18.
Which never strains its rocky beams;
Monadnoc. 273.
Caught with love's cord of twisted
beams, Nun. 35.
Again I meet the ardent beams.
Ode to Beauty. 93.
The stars' own ether beams; Poet. 100.
Beams with a will compassionate
Poet. 243.
With beams December planets dart
Quat. S. H. 1.
With stifling beams on these retreats,
Titmouse. 72.

Beans
Venison and trout, potatoes, beans,
wheat-bread; Adirondacs. 179.

Bear (Verb)
I bear in youth the sad infirmities
I Bear. 1.
Doth it bear hidden in its heart
May-Day. 212.
Ponderous gold and stuffs to bear,
Merlin's Song. 26.
Of him who shall as lightly bear
Monadnoc. 270.

Bear (Noun)
Temper to face wolf, bear, or catamount,
Adirondacs. 85.
'Well done!' he cries; 'the bear is kept
at bay, Adirondacs. 315.
Of wolf and otter, bear and deer;
Monadnoc. 81.
Where feeds the moose, and walks the
surly bear, Woodnotes. I. 66.

Beard
See Graybeard.
Be wise without a beard? Fame. 2.

Bearded
Yet fairest dames and bearded men,
Threnody. 43.
Where bearded mists divide,
Waldeinsamkeit. 34.
The rough and bearded forester
Woodnotes. II. 14.

Bears
Yea, plant the tree that bears best
apples, plant, Adirondacs. 298.
He bears no bow, or quiver, or wand,
Initial Love. 17.
Wave which severs whom it bears
Insight. 3.
Bears nothing on its beam.
World-Soul. 16.

Beast
And strangers to the mystic beast and
bird, Blight. 31.
In the wretched little beast Limits. 6.
They harness beast, bird, insect, to their
work; Musketaquid. 36.
He roamed, content alike with man and
beast. Woodnotes. I. 81.
Are of one pattern made; bird, beast
and flower, Xenophanes. 6.

Beasts
In trees, with beasts, in mines and caves,
Initial Love. 99.

Beat
See Sea-beat.

Our pulses beat not less,
Concord Ode. 6.
My heart shall beat not when
*Farewell. 48.
I feel its finer billows beat
May-Day. 193.
Their pulses beat, Merlin. 46.
To every tone beat answering tones,
Merlin. 83.
On the flinty pathway beat
Monadnoc. 268.
As doth this round sky-cleaving beat
Monadnoc. 272.

Beatified
In me therewith beatified? Poet. 278.

Beatitude
But I, from my beatitude, Rhea. 61.

Beats
In flint and marble beats a heart,
May-Day. 65.
And I like less when Summer beats
Titmouse. 71.
For Nature beats in perfect tune,
Woodnotes. II. 164.

Beauties
Are moles of beauties Time hath slain.
Omar. 4.

Beautiful
Elect, to dreams thus beautiful?'
Berrying. 10.
The beautiful and fortunate,
Daemonic Love. 98.
Made beautiful for God:—
Frag. Nat. III. 7.
Steeped in the light are beautiful.
Frag. Nat. XXVI. 18.
Beauty's not beautiful to me,
Hermione. 9.
No human speech so beautiful Nun. 13.
The prosperous and beautiful Park. 1.
Yet beautiful as is the rose in June,
Seashore. 19.
In beautiful motion Sphinx. 21.
To mark thy beautiful parade,
Threnody. 75.
Of the most beautiful and sweet
Threnody. 107.
Strong art and beautiful pretension,
Woodnotes. II. 207.
Its beautiful disdain. World-Soul. 32.

Beauty
So Nature shed all beauty lavishly
Adirondacs. 151.
Whereon the purple iris dwells in beauty
Adirondacs. 219.
Beauty chased he everywhere,
Beauty. 5.
To die for Beauty, than live for bread.
Beauty. 26.
O North! give him beauty for rags,
Boston Hymn. 73.
Beauty for his sinful weeds, Caritas. 6.
Till dangerous Beauty came, at last,
Daemonic Love. 10.
Till Beauty came to snap all ties;
Daemonic Love. 11.
Beauty of a richer vein,
Daemonic Love. 56.
Friends, foes, joys, fortunes, beauty and
disgust. Day's Ration. 8.
Beauty sits and Music calls; Dearest. 2.

Bed —*Continued*
Well, in this broad bed lie and sleep,—
                                    Titmouse. 17.
I found the water's bed.
                          Woodnotes. I. 121.
Bedeck
The rainbow hours bedeck his glowing
    chair,   Adirondacs. 226.
Beds
  See Myrtle-beds.
Through gold-moth-haunted beds of
    pickerel-flower,   Adirondacs. 18.
in odorous beds,   Woodnotes. I. 68.
Through beds of granite cut my road,
                          Woodnotes. I. 127.
Bee
  See Humble-bee.
Loved of bee,—the tawny hummer.
                              Ellen South. 20.
And the bell of beetle and of bee
                          Woodnotes. II. 227.
As the bee through the garden ranges,
                          Woodnotes. II. 295.
Beech
Oak, cedar, maple, poplar, beech and fir,
                              Adirondacs. 38.
To twilight parks of beech and pine,
                              Monadnoc. 6.
Beechen
Ponderous with beechen forest sloped
    the shore.   Adirondacs. 28.
Bee-infested
Bee-infested quince or plum.
                          Frag. Nat. XXI. 5.
Been (Partial list.)
And, without Jove, the good had never
    been.   Adirondacs. 291.
Beer
East, West, from Beer to Dan,
                                  Fame. 3.
Bees
As in broad orchards resonant with bees;
                          Musketaquid. 57.
Boughs on which the wild bees settle,
                          Woodnotes. I. 20.
Beethoven's
From a log cabin stream Beethoven's
    notes   Adirondacs. 313.
Beetle
And the bell of beetle and of bee
                          Woodnotes. II. 227.
Befall
Who shall tell what did befall,
                                  Wealth. 1.
Befalls
Whatsoever hap befalls Day By Day. 11.
Befalls again what once befell;
                              May-Day. 178.
Befell
This befell how long ago!
                          Initial Love. 6.
Befalls again what once befell;
                              May-Day. 178.
Which in Paradise befell.   Uriel. 6.
Before (Partial list.)
Before ye want a drop of rain,
                              Alphonso. 49.
Or wit be ripe before 't was rotten?
                                  Fame. 6.
Where he goes, goes before him Fate;
                          Frag. Life. XVII. 10.

Tell men what they knew before;
                          Frag. Life. XIX. 1.
He stood before the tumbling main
                          Frag. Poet. I. 50.
That sounded in the soul before,
                                  Hymn. 18.
Heralds high before him run;
                          Initial Love. 74.
This mound shall throb his face before,
                              Monadnoc. 288.
Blue-coated,—flying before from tree to
    tree,   Musketaquid. 16.
And feats achieve before they're named.
                                  Nature. I. 21.
Before me run   Ode To Beauty. 41.
The Book itself before me lies,
                                  Problem. 64.
And shake before those awful Powers,
                                  Saadi. 57.
Yet before the listener's eye Saadi. 133.
And life was larger than before:
                              Solution. 38.
How danced thy form before my path
                              Thine Eyes. 7.
With aged eyes, short way before,—
                              Threnody. 180.
Justice after as before,—
                              Voluntaries. 101.
Before the money-loving herd,
                          Woodnotes. II. 60.
Befriended
But best befriended of the God
                              Voluntaries. 83.
Began
That all things from him began;
                                  Guy. 6.
And how the hills began, Monadnoc. 221.
And I began to catch the sense
                              Titmouse. 66.
Beget
And kiss, and couple, and beget,
                          Initial Love. 31.
Beggar
The beggar begs by God's command,
                          Frag. Life. VII. 1.
Beggar's
Is early frugal, like a beggar's child;
                                  Blight. 57.
Beggars
There are beggars in Iran and Araby,
                          Frag. Poet. I. 1.
Begin
Lend me your ears, and I begin.
                          Aeolian Harp. 11.
To be alone wilt thou begin
                              Threnody. 187.
Beginnings
Who saw the hid beginnings
                                  Cosmos. 1.
I saw the hid beginnings   Cosmos. 5.
Begins
And straight begins again;
                              World-Soul. 92.
Begone
  See Woe-begone.
Begs
The beggar begs by God's command,
                          Frag. Life. VII. 1.
Beguile
Beguile me with the wonted spell.
                              May-Day. 352.

Beguiled
See Unbeguiled.
And of his memory beguiled.
Frag. Poet. I. 34.
Which once my infancy beguiled,
May-Day. 351.
By Sybarites beguiled, Merlin. 49.
Alas! how were they so beguiled,
Poet. 205.
When a god is once beguiled Rhea. 41.

Begun
With the web that's just begun;
Frag. Poet. IX. 5.

Behavior
Nor for the fashion of your behavior;
Destiny. 41.
And loved so well a high behavior,
Forbearance. 5.
And thy behavior approve;
Frag. Life. XXVII. 6.
As if to shame my weak behavior;
Titmouse. 47.

Behaviors
So many high behaviors
Frag. Poet. XXVIII. 7.

Beheld
from the crowd's edge well pleased beheld Frag. Life. XXX. 6.
Whose eyes within his eyes beheld
Threnody. 184.
And are but one. Beheld far off, they part Xenophanes. 9.

Behemoth
And as behemoth strong.
Boston Hymn. 80.

Behest
Bended with joy to his behest
Threnody. 46.
And his behest obey. World-Soul. 88.

Behind (Partial list.)
of duties, leagues behind,
Adirondacs. 62.
Fair rose the planted hills behind
Boston. 41.
I leave it behind with the games of youth:'— Each. 39.
He left each civil scale behind:
Frag. Poet. I. 32.
Slips behind a tomb. Manners. 20.
Tarries yet behind? Merops. 4.
sat watching close behind
Philosopher. 9.
Are hid behind the thrice-piled clouds;
Poet. 178.
With children forward and behind,
Threnody. 64.
The shadows shake on the rock behind,
Woodnotes. II. 94.
Behind thee leave thy merchandise,
Woodnotes. II. 229.
And leave thy peacock wit behind;
Woodnotes. II. 231.
Who never looks behind.
World-Soul. 8.

Behmen
Luther, Fox, Behmen, Swedenborg, grew pale, Adakryn. 3.

Behold
Behold the famous States
Channing Ode. 16.

Behold the miracle!
Frag. Nat. XXVI. 11.
Behold the new majestic birth!
Frag. Nat. XXVI. 16.
Behold the shimmer, Illusions. 24.
Behold the river-bank In Memoriam. 3.
As is to me when I behold the morn
Naples. 23.
By love behold the sun at night.
Poet. 288.
now first behold, Quat. Nature. 1.
And I behold once more River. 1.
Behold, he watches at the door!
Saadi. 157.
Behold his shadow on the floor!
Saadi. 158.
Behold the Sea, Seashore. 17.
As I behold yon evening star,
Thine Eyes. 3.
Behold! were in vain and in vain;—
Woodnotes. II. 210.

Beholding
Beholding the procession of the pines;
Adirondacs. 116.
Beholding his fear;— Sphinx. 58.
Far beholding, without cloud,
Voluntaries. 53.

Beholds
In May beholds the blooming wild,
May-Day. 99.
Which yet beholds not me.
Thine Eyes. 4.

Behoof
For truth's and harmony's behoof;
Channing Ode. 68.
For all breathing men's behoof,
Saadi. 11.

Behooves
What imports, what irks and what behooves, Frag. Poet. XII. 3.

Behoved
One word more thy heart behoved,
Give. 28.

Behoves
Trenchant time behoves to hurry
Woodnotes. II. 258.

Being (Partial list.)
Of the ancient being blow, Bacchus. 48.
Vast the realm of Being is,
Day by Day. 9.
Being for Seeming bravely barter
Fame. 29.
To dissipate their being into it.
Frag. Nat. XVII. 6.
Firm ensign of the fatal Being,
Monadnoc. 361.
And being latent, feel thyself no less?
Musketaquid. 81.
And, being so, the sage unmakes the man. Philosopher. 2.
And sternly calls to being souls
Quat. Fate. 3.
Then Beauty is its own excuse for being: Rhodora. 12.
Shines the peace of all being,
Sphinx. 45.
Against the being of a line. Uriel. 20.

Being's
In Being's deeps past ear and eye;
Ode to Beauty. 95.

Being's—*Continued*
A momentary music. Being's tide
                              Pan. 3.
Beings
On which all beings ride
                    Celestial Love. 34.
Belief
Past utterance, and past belief,
                         Threnody. 203.
Beliefs
What generous beliefs console
                    In Memoriam. 86.
Believed
Charmer who will be believed
                      Frag. Nat. XXXI. 5.
Believed the eloquent was aye the true;
                              Phi. 16.
Believers
I embrace the true believers,
                     Song of Seyd. 29.
Believing
    See Unbelieving.
Wins the believing child with wondrous
    tales;   Enchanter. 5.
Belike
Belike has wider hospitality
                       Frag. Nat. V. 5.
Belike the one they used in parting
                         May-Day. 385.
Bell
    See Church-bell; Death-bell; Door-
    bell; Joy-bell; Lily-bell.
I love thy music, mellow bell,
                              Bell. 1.
The sexton, tolling his bell at noon,
                              Each. 5.
Flower-wreaths gay with bud and bell;
                         May-Day. 315.
I can spare the college bell,
                        Monadnoc. 179.
And hearkens in the berry's bell
                         Nature. I. 13.
And the bell of beetle and of bee
                       Woodnotes. II. 227.
Bellowing
And the bellowing of the savage sea
                              Each. 22.
Bell's
    See Wood-bell's.
Bells
    See Air-bells; Foam-bells; Joy-bells.
And rings the bells of jubilee
                            Cosmos. 27.
But violets and bilberry bells,
                        Humble-Bee. 42.
His feet were shod with golden bells,
                              Poet. 4.
Belly
In the belly of the grape,   Bacchus. 2.
Belong
Ah, not to me those dreams belong!
                       Frag. Poet. XXX. 1.
Thou to the Syrian couldst belong?
                          Hermione. 30.
On thine orchard's edge belong
                            Saadi. 149.
Though they to all belong!
                      Waldeinsamkeit. 40.
Belonged
Belonged to wind and world the toil
                              Guy. 49.

To these their penalty belonged:
                       In Memoriam. 31.
Belongs
Blooms the laurel which belongs
                         Voluntaries. 106.
Beloved
Of man and earth, of world beloved and
    lover,   Blight. 44.
To love and be beloved;   I Eros. 3.
I dare not be beloved and known,
                       Frag. Poet. VII. 7.
Of thy beloved.   Give. 33.
Fruit beloved of maid and boy,
                            Holidays. 2.
Beloved of children, bards and Spring,
                          May-Day. 396.
Though beloved, I miss her not;
                              Una. 10.
Below
And make just laws below the sun,
                         Boston Hymn. 47.
To men below,   Celestial Love. 52.
The waters wild below,
                        Concord Ode. 34.
Around, below, above.   Cupido. 4.
The winding Concord gleamed below,
                              Dirge. 7.
Immortal here below.   Dull. 5.
Carry aloft, below, around,
                        Frag. Nat. III. 35.
The world above, the world below.
                       Frag. Nat. XXVI. 10.
See the world below
                       Frag. Nat. XXVI. 26.
To gauge with glance the roaring gulf
    below,   Grace. 6.
Below May's well-appointed arch,
                         May-Day. 332.
Divine Ideas below,   Ode to Beauty. 61.
Far seen, the river glides below,
                             Peter. 37.
Up from the burning core below,—
                           Problem. 17.
Springs from the life below.
                        Robbins Hymn. 20.
If on the heath, below the moon,
                           Romany. 13.
And a glad delight below,   Security. 2.
The warm rosebuds below.
                         World-Soul. 112.
Belt
Secure as in the zodiac's belt;
                       Daemonic Love. 122.
A belt of mirrors round a taper's flame;
                         Xenophanes. 16.
Belting
From nodding pole and belting zone.
                            Beauty. 12.
Bemoan
And ills to come as evils past bemoan.
                        Woodnotes. I. 89.
Bench
Low on their wooden bench.
                            Boston. 85.
Bend
    See Unbend.
Bend nearer, faint day-moon!
                         Adirondacs. 260.
And bend the exile to his fate, Art. 22.
And each to each shall bend,
                            Boston. 113.

And bend my fancy to your leading,
                         Etienne. 3.
Bend his practice to his prayer
                         Frag. Poet. IV. 4.
Bend happy to the welkin blue.
                         May-Day. 124.
All to each in kindness bend, Peter. 34.

Bended
Bended to fops who bent to him;
                         Poet. 215.
I caught with bended pin my earliest
fish,   River. 12.
Bended with joy to his behest
                         Threnody. 46.

Bending
Daily the bending skies solicit man,
                         Adirondacs. 224.
Bending forests as bends the sedge,
                         May-Day. 243.
Gives back the bending heavens in dew.
                         Song of Nature. 84.
No, but a nest of bending reeds,
                         Threnody. 274.

Bends
Sometimes the airy synod bends,
                         Daemonic Love. 43.
Bending forests as bends the sedge,
                         May-Day. 243.
O'er England's abbeys bends the sky,
                         Problem. 37.

Beneath
The maple eight, beneath its shapely
tower.   Adirondacs. 43.
Or, later yet, beneath a lighted jack,
                         Adirondacs. 117.
Of the wire-cable laid beneath the sea,
                         Adirondacs. 239.
As I spoke, beneath my feet Each. 40.
Beneath the tropic ray,   *Farewell. 51.
And stood beneath the firmanent,
                         Frag. Nat. XXVI. 13.
And when I am stretched beneath the
pines,   Good-Bye. 25.
Where are these men? Asleep beneath
their grounds: Hamatreya. 11.
Lent itself beneath the forest,
                         Holidays. 3.
While the grass beneath the rime
                         May-Day. 119.
Beneath the calm, within the light,
                         May-Day. 150.
Beneath the crystal arch, May-Day. 383.
Open the daunting map beneath,—
                         Monadnoc. 319.
Beneath low hills, in the broad interval
                         Musketaquid. 26.
Ope in such low moist roadside, and be-
neath   Naples. 24.
Aloft, beneath, on left and right
                         Poet. 99.
Beneath the darkling firmament
                         Poet. 227.
Out shone a star beneath the cloud,
                         Poet. 229.
Stuff sharp thorns beneath the head
                         Saadi. 68.
And felt, beneath, the quaking ground;
                         Solution. 56.
I tread the book beneath my feet.
                         Song of Seyd, 24.

Dove beneath the vulture's beak;—
                         Voluntaries. 17.
Beneath the grass that shades the rill,
                         Woodnotes. I. 39.
He saw beneath dim aisles, in odorous
beds,   Woodnotes. I. 68.
Beneath your roofs of slate.
                         World-Soul. 12.

Benediction
With skies of benediction, to Round
Lake,   Adirondacs. 8.

Beneficent
Thy fortune's web to the beneficent
hand   Rome. 22.

Benefit
It is there for benefit;   Astraea. 39.
The benefit of broad mankind.
                         Celestial Love. 120.
Stern benefit abides. Waldeinsamkeit. 16.

Benevolence
Tokens of benevolence.
                         Frag. Poet. VII. 12.

Benighted
Or marked, benighted and forlorn,
                         Harp. 93.

Benign
And in his airy road benign Lines. 17.
Masterpiece of love benign,
                         Threnody. 257.
Yet on the nimble air benign
                         Voluntaries. 67.

Benison
And with a cheerful benison forsake
                         Letter. 5.

Bent
  See Dew-bent.
Nor bent to passion frail.   Harp. 4.
To Heaven's high will his will is bent.
                         In Memoriam. 89.
Short and bent by cold and snow;
                         May-Day. 313.
Loving the wind that bent me. All my
hurts   Musketaquid. 71.
Bended to fops who bent to him;
                         Poet. 215.
And though thy knees were never bent,
                         Prayer. 5.
Or bow above the tempest bent;
                         Threnody. 277.
The balance-beam of Fate was bent;
                         Uriel. 31.
Will thy clear blue eye, upward bent,
still keep its chastened glow,
                         *Violet. 3.

Benzöine
Sassafras, fern, benzöine,
                         Frag. Nat. II. 28.

Bequeath
Failed to bequeath   Terminus. 26.
Bequeathed
Sole estate his sire bequeathed,—
                         Voluntaries. 9.

Bereaved
Bereaved a tyrant of his will,
                         Merlin. 53.
Covetous death bereaved us all,
                         Threnody. 158.

Bereaveth
Their tranquil mien bereaveth him
                         Manners. 15.

Bereft
I am too much bereft.   Threnody. 170.
Thee of thy faith who hath bereft,
    Woodnotes. II. 183.

Berg
  See Iceberg.

Berks
Hants, Franklin, Berks,   Letter. 9.

Berries
No wisdom from our berries went?'
    Berrying. 12.
Garden of berries, perch of birds,
    Monadnoc. 54.
The purple berries in the wood
    Woodnotes. I. 135.

Berry
  See Barberry; Bilberry; Blackberry.
Thine each leaf and berry bore;
    Lines. 6.
The perfumed berry on the spray
    May-Day. 77.
There's a berry blue and gold,—
    Monadnoc. 297.

Berry's
And hearkens in the berry's bell
    Nature. I. 13.

Beryl
With the beryl beam of the broken
wave;   Beauty. 8.

Beseeching
And never poor beseeching glance
    In Memoriam. 46.

Beset
Beset by pensive hosts.   Dirge. 16.
Beset his solitude.   Manners. 8.
Beset by pensive hosts.]   Peter. 12.

Beside (Partial list.)
Fold my arms beside the brook;
    Apology. 6.
O happy town beside the sea,
    Boston. 59.
And peaceful woods beside my cottage
door.   Frag. Nat. IV. 11.
He freelier breathed beside the pine,
    Frag. Poet. V. 15.
The atom displaces all atoms beside,
    Frag. Poet. XXI. 1.
All beside was unknown waste,
    Humble-Bee. 50.
Honor came and sat beside him,
    In Memoriam. 56.
I reached this heath beside the lake,
    Miracle. 16.
Vanish beside these dedicated blocks,
    Monadnoc. 368.
Beside his hut and shading oak,
    Poet. 140.
Beside him sat enduring love, Poet. 195.
And he the chieftain paced beside,
    Threnody. 66.
Half-seen Una sits beside.   Una. 8.
All are ghosts beside.   Voluntaries. 122.
Beside the forest water sate;
    Woodnotes. I. 105.

Besides
Besides, you need not be alone; the soul
    Rome. 2.

Best
Let not him mourn who best entitled
was,   Adirondacs. 296.

Yea, plant the tree that bears best
apples, plant,   Adirondacs. 298.
The best of cities with us, these learned
classifiers,   Adirondacs. 303.
Even in the hot pursuit of the best aims
    Blight. 58.
When he has wrought his best;
    Boston Hymn. 20.
Which at the best is trick,
    Channing Ode. 9.
In coarsest weeds or in the best;
    Destiny. 39.
Nor knew her beauty's best attire
    Each. 31.
But if thou do thy best,
    Frag. Life. XXVII. 1.
And, best with best in sweet consent,
    Frag. Life. XXIX. 5.
Into the very best sole-leather.
    Frag. Poet. XXIII. 2.
That we have drained the best,
    Good Hope. 2.
And best can teach its Delphian chord
    Harp. 103.
Each can other best adorn;
    Love and Thought. 8.
Count your change and cheer the best.
    May-Day. 368.
Best gems of Nature's cabinet,
    May-Day. 394.
Lifting Better up to Best;
    May-Day. 466.
Best of Pan's immortal meat,
    Monadnoc. 304.
Beyond the best conceit of pomp or
power.   October. 11.
O fire of fire! O best of things!
    Poet. 161.
As the best gem upon her zone,
    Problem. 34.
Old Chrysostom, best Augustine,
    Problem. 65.
Minstrels and kings and high-born
dames, and of the best that be.
    Quat. A. H. 4.
The storm is my best galley hand
    Quat. Northman. 3.
Is love of the Best;   Sphinx. 74.
His wistful toil to do his best
    Voluntaries. 21.
But best befriended of the God
    Voluntaries. 83.
Knowledge this man prizes best
    Woodnotes. I. 16.
He is the oldest, and best known,
    Worship. 15.

Bestead
  See Ill-bestead.

Bested
And sore bested with woes.   Riches. 10.

Bestow
And bestow the shares of all
    Alphonso. 69.
So much he shall bestow.
    Boston Hymn. 60.

Bestowed
In well-hung chambers daintily be-
stowed,   Adirondacs. 51.
By lying use bestowed,
    Celestial Love. 65.

And copious language still bestowed
Merops. 11.
With birds and flowers bestowed.
Waterfall. 4.

Bestows
Profuse in love, the king bestows,
Rhea. 56.

Bestriding
I saw fair boys bestriding steeds,
Harp. 111.

Bestrode
Bestrode the tribes that knelt within.
Problem. 50.

Bethink
Bethink, poor heart, what bitter kind of
jest Epitaph. 1.

Bethlehem
When every star is Bethlehem star?
Frag. Poet. XXVIII. 3.

Bethlehem's
Sparta's stoutness, Bethlehem's heart,
Monadnoc. 299.

Betide
What lot soe'er betide,
In Memoriam. 91.

Betimes
So did Guy betimes discover Guy. 9.

Betook
Suddenly betook them all,
May-Day. 389.

Betray
Where twisted hills betray Cosmos. 18.
Or see the fault, or seen betray:
Initial Love. 127.
The scarlet maple-keys betray.
May-Day. 186.
The bias of the will betray.
Quat. Memory. 4.

Betrayed
See Self-betrayed.
And betrayed the fund of joy
May-Day. 344.

Betrays
Like wax, their fashioning skill betrays,
Monadnoc. 148.
Betrays the more abounding might,
Monadnoc. 351.

Better
A melancholy better than all mirth.
Adirondacs. 215.
The latest better than the first,
Aeolian Harp. 21.
Yet is understood the better;
Astraea. 22.
Of better arts and life?
Channing Ode. 14.
Were it not better done, Fame. 13.
If he than his groom be better or
worse. Fate. 6.
We have not better things to say,
Frag. Life. XII. 3.
But surely say them better.
Frag. Life. XII. 4.
I grieve that better souls than mine
Frag. Poet VII. 1.
A better voice peals through my song.
Frag. Poet. XXX. 2.
Of better men than live to-day;
Garden. 62.
Lifting Better up to Best;
May-Day. 466.

Better, the linked purpose of the whole,
Musketaquid. 65.
He builded better than he knew;—
Problem. 23.
Thou are better, and not worse.'—
Rhea. 73.
Scorn trifles and embrace a better aim
Rome. 12.
Draws better deed: Saadi. 44.
Rebuild a continent of better men.
Seashore. 37.
Then by better thought I lead
Solution. 25.
Better it is than gems or gold,
Thought. 5.
And thank thee for a better clew,
Titmouse. 100.
Without better fortune had,
Woodnotes. I. 14.
'Whether is better, the gift or the donor?
Woodnotes II. 5.
Is better than the lord;
Woodnotes II. 15.
Alike to him the better, the worse,—
Woodnotes. II. 305.

Betters
My betters, yet my peers;
*Farewell. 29.

Between (Partial list.)
Between two rocky arms,
Adirondacs. 31.
Though foes and land and seas between
Frag. Life. XVII. 14.
All between that works or grows,
Mithridates. 4.
Under the snow, between the rocks,
Woodnotes. I. 40.
Yon sky between the walls,
World-Soul. 38.

Beurré
See the plum redden, and the beurré
stoop. Quat. Gardener. 4.

Beverage
He emptieth the beverage;
Woodnotes. II. 282.

Beware
Beware from right to swerve.
Boston Hymn. 52.
Beware the fire that Eblis burned."
Frag. Poet. II. 3.
And thou, Cyndyllan's son! beware
Merlin's Song. 25.

Bewilder
None can bewilder;
Daemonic Love. 71.

Beyond
Bound for the just, but not beyond;
Celestial Love. 116.
Beyond the scope of human age,
Frag. Poet. XI. 17.
And look beyond the earth,
Friendship. 14.
Hope beyond hope: Give. 10.
Grains beyond the price of gold.
May-Day. 274.
Islands looming just beyond
May-Day. 424.
Space grants beyond his fated road
Merops. 9.
Realm beyond realm,—extent untold;
Nun. 42.

Beyond —*Continued*
Beyond the best conceit
October. 11.
The Furies wait beyond.
Quat. Pericles. 4.
Seek not beyond thy cottage wall
Saadi. 165.
I taught thy heart beyond the reach
Threnody. 197.

Bias
The bias of the will betray.
Quat. Memory. 4.

Bible
Endured, the Bible says, as long;
Frag. Nat. VI. 4.
The burdens of the Bible old;
Problem. 14.
Of ritual, bible, or of speech;
Threnody. 198.

Bid
Nor bid the unwilling senator
Channing Ode. 73.
Bid Time and Nature gently spare
C. Hymn. 15.
And bid the broad Atlantic roll,
Concord Ode. 27.
Bid my bread feed and my fire warm me
Destiny. 43.
And bid you let the angels in
Hymn. 19.
And bid each awful Muse   I Bear. 14.
Where they were bid, the rivers ran;
Wealth. 39.

Bidding
They do her bidding, nothing loath.
Nature. II. 19.
And at his bidding seemed to come.
Woodnotes. I. 61.

Bide
And Love led Gods therein to bide.
Frag. Poet. XX. 2.
They bide their time, and well can prove,
Monadnoc. 165.
That will not bide the seeing!
Monadnoc. 363.

Bides
Who bides at home, nor looks abroad,
Destiny. 49.

Biding
Biding by his rule and choice,
Voluntaries. 87.

Bids
Than my few needs exhaust, and bids me
read   Frag. Nat. V. 6.
A greater spirit bids thee forth
Monadnoc. 17.
Bids for me her bosom glow.
Security. 4.

Bier
Old cradle, hunting-ground and bier
Monadnoc. 80.

Big
See Big Tupper.
Its timorous ways, big trifles, and we
planned   Adirondacs. 161.
Big with great news, and shouted the re-
port   Adirondacs. 237.
'You are doubtless very big;
Fable. 5.

Biggest
For still, where'er the trees grow biggest,
Quat. Artist. 3.

Big Tupper
Entering Big Tupper, bound for the
foaming Falls   Adirondacs. 232.

Bilberry
But violets and bilberry bells,
Humble-Bee. 42.

Bill
Pay every debt as if God wrote the bill.
Frag. Life. XXXII. 2.

Billets
My billets to his boiler's throat,
Woodnotes. II. 44.

Billows
And billows round her play,
*Farewell. 26.
I feel its finer billows beat
May-Day. 193.

Bind
See Unbind.
There need no vows to bind
Celestial Love. 83.
The distant bind;   Hermione. 68.
What sheaves like those which here we
glean and bind   Monadnoc. 356.
No perfect form could ever bind.
Ode to Beauty. 73.
To bind or unbind, add what lacked,
Past. 18.
My hopes pursue, they cannot bind him.
Threnody. 23.
Which bind the strengths of Nature wild
Wealth. 48.
But if with gold she bind her hair,
Woodnotes. II. 85.

Biped
Or bird or biped knows;   Walden. 40.

Birch
Panax, black birch, sugar maple,
Frag. Nat. II. 15.
Silver birch and black
Frag. Nat. II. 25.

Birches
And finds young pines and budding
birches;   Threnody. 25.

Bird
See Blackbird; Bluebird; Redbird;
Snowbird; Woodbird.
What wilt thou, restless bird,
Adirondacs. 208.
And strangers to the mystic beast and
bird,   Blight. 31.
Like the bird from the woodlands to the
cage;—   Each. 34.
The rolling river, the morning bird;—
Each. 49.
No more baggage than a bird.
Frag. Poet. XXXIII. 4.
The summer bird   Hermione. 4.
'River and rose and crag and bird,
Hermione. 61.
Bird, or deer, or caribou.
Initial Love. 101.
Every bird in carolling,   Lines. 10.
Harp of the wind, or song of bird,
May-Day. 10.
Bird and brier inly warms,
May-Day. 198.

And the colors of joy in the bird,
    May-Day. 235.
Heart of bird the man's heart seeking;
    May-Day. 421.
Bird that from the nadir's floor
    Merlin. 63.
Shall the dumb bird instructed say.
    Miracle. 22.
Sharp accents of my woodland bird;
    Miracle. 24.
When that bird sang, I gave the theme;
    Miracle. 27.
Bird, and reptile, be my game.
    Mithridates. 13.
No bird is safe that cuts the air
    Monadnoc. 143.
It is not only in the bird,   Music. 8.
Sparrows far off, and nearer, April's
  bird,   Musketaquid. 15.
They harness beast, bird, insect, to their
  work;   Musketaquid. 36.
The bird, how far it haply roam
    Nemesis. 3.
Count it flight of bird or dart.
    Poet. 129.
Love-longings of the raptured bird
    Quat. Hafiz. 3.
The bird to him confides.
    Quat. Hafiz. 4.
Light-hearted as a bird, and live with
  God.   Self-Reliance. 3.
The little bird remembereth his note,
    Self-Reliance. 7.
Plant, quadruped, bird,   Sphinx. 34.
As the bird trims her to the gale,
    Terminus. 33.
And every chick of every bird,
    Threnody. 114.
In northern Gaul my dauntless bird,
    Titmouse. 96.
Or bird or biped knows;
    Walden. 40.
In damp fields known to bird and fox.
    Woodnotes. I. 41.
Choosing light, wave, rock and bird,
    Woodnotes II. 59.
To find what bird had piped the strain:—
    Woodnotes. II. 249.
Are of one pattern made; bird, beast and
  flower,   Xenophanes. 6.

Bird-language
The bird-language rightly spell,
    Bacchus. 24.

Bird-like
Firmest cheer, and bird-like pleasure.
    Humble-Bee. 39.
In birdlike heavings unto death,
    Threnody. 101.

Bird's
Of my bird's song: 'Live out of doors
    Titmouse. 67.

Birds
  See Sea-birds.
But birds tell it in the bowers.
    Apology. 16.
I cannot hear your songs, O birds,
    Cosmos. 23.
Hast thou named all the birds without a
  gun?   Forebearance. 1.
Which birds of the air
    Frag. Nat. III. 34.

The birds brought auguries on their
  wings,   Frat. Poet. V. 41.
The wind and the birds which sowed it;
    Garden. 18.
Plants and birds and humble creatures
    May-Day. 134.
The whistle of returning birds,
    May-Day. 184.
On their due days, of the birds,
    May-Day. 380.
O birds, your perfect virtues bring,
    May-Day. 397.
Thy birds, thy songs, thy brooks, thy
  gales,   May-Day. 436.
New tint the plumage of the birds,
    May-Day. 447.
Garden of berries, perch of birds,
    Monadnoc. 54.
Felt in the plants and in the punctual
  birds;   Musketaquid. 64.
Methought like water-haunting birds
    Poet. 19.
O birds of ether without wings!
    Poet. 159.
The birds gave us our wily tongues,
    Romany. 23.
Wedge-like cleave the air the birds,
    Saadi. 4.
To fetch thee birds of paradise:
    Saadi. 148.
With birds and flowers bestowed.
    Waterfall. 4.
To birds and trees who talks?
    Woodnotes. I. 4.

Birth
Child and brother from his birth,
    Daemonic Love. 2.
'They loved thee from their birth;
    Dirge. 50.
Behold the new majestic birth!
    Frag. Nat. XXVI. 16.
And of the kinds that owe her birth.
    Harp. 66.
Take the bounty of thy birth,
    Monadnoc. 25.
To the birth they arrive: Poet. 107.
Is yeaning at the birth. World-Soul. 104.

Bishop
I would not the good bishop be.
    Problem. 72.

Bit
The old Sphinx bit her thick lip,—
    Sphinx. 109.

Bite
A mastiff that will bite without a bark.
    Arrow. 2.

Bitter
  See Bitter-sweet
Bethink, poor heart, what bitter kind of
  jest   Epitaph. 1.
I am bitter, vacant, thwarted,
    Etienne. 7.
Bitter winds and fasts austere
    Monadnoc. 159.
He sends thee from his bitter fount
    Saadi. 62.
With a bitter horoscope,   Solution. 23.

Bittern's
The bittern's boom, a desert make
    Waldeinsamkeit. 31.

Bitterns
Gaunt as bitterns in the pools,
　　　　　　　Alphonso. 16.
Bitter-sweet
The bitter-sweet, the haunting air
　　　　　　　May-Day. 289.
Black
Black by white faces,—
　　　　　　　Channing Ode. 85.
The wings of Time are black and white,
　　　　　　　II. Compensation. 1.
Panax, black birch, sugar maple,
　　　　　　　Frag. Nat. II. 15.
Silver birch and black
　　　　　　　Frag. Nat. II. 25.
In black acres of the night,
　　　　　　　Frag. Nat. XVIII. 3.
Peep the blue violets out of the black
　　loam,　　　　　Naples. 25.
Made the black water with their beauty
　　gay;　　　　　Rhodora. 6.
Why are not diamonds black and gray,
　　　　　　　Titmouse. 56.
The black ducks mounting from the lake,
　　　　　　　Waldeinsamkeit. 29.
Blackberry
Caught among the blackberry vines,
　　　　　　　Berrying. 6.
Blackbird's
Echo the blackbird's roundelay,
　　　　　　　Good-Bye. 20.
Blackbirds
The blackbirds make the maples ring
　　　　　　　May-Day. 166.
Blade
　　See Wheat-blade.
Aimed at him, the blushing blade
　　　　　　　Guy. 19.
There's not a blade of autumn grain,
　　　　　　　Threnody. 111.
Blame
The cargo came! and who could blame
　　　　　　　Boston. 76.
Just late enough to reap abundant
　　blame,—　　　To-Day. 6.
Blamed
　　See Unblamed.
Blameless
Ah! let me blameless gaze upon
　　　　　　　Eva. 7.
Blameless master of the games,
　　　　　　　Merlin. 39.
Bland
The air is full of whistlings bland;
　　　　　　　May-Day. 7.
Blandishment
Thy genius, wiles and blandishment?
　　　　　　　May-Day. 432.
Blasphemy
And past the blasphemy of grief,
　　　　　　　Threnody. 204.
Blast
When the fierce northwestern blast
　　　　　　　Humble-Bee. 58.
Blasts
Which blasts of Northern mountains
　　hymn,　　　　　Nun. 19.
Are Autumn's blasts fit music for thee,
　　fragile one, to hear;　　　*Violet. 2.

Blaze
Blaze near and far,
　　　　　　　Daemonic Love. 51.
The blaze of revellers' feasts outshine.
　　　　　　　Frag. Life. X. 9.
Fires gardens with a joyful blaze
　　　　　　　May-Day. 206.
Sparks of the supersolar blaze.
　　　　　　　Merlin. 15.
An intermittent blaze,　　Poet. 103.
Never in the blaze of light　　Saadi. 51.
Lit by the supersolar blaze.
　　　　　　　Threnody. 202.
Where palms plume, siroccos blaze,
　　　　　　　Voluntaries. 48.
Blazes
Of Gypsy beauty blazes higher.
　　　　　　　Romany. 4.
Lo! the God's love blazes higher,
　　　　　　　Song of Seyd. 25.
Blazing
Ah, brother of the brief but blazing star!
　　　　　　　In Memoriam. 25.
Of rich men blazing hospitable light,
　　　　　　　Naples. 18.
Bleach
Roses bleach, the goats are dry,
　　　　　　　Alphonso. 13.
His roses bleach apace,
　　　　　　　Daemonic Love. 91.
They bleach and dry in the sun.
　　　　　　　Garden. 16.
Sunshine cannot bleach the snow,
　　　　　　　Test. 11.
Bleaching
And bleaching all souls like the sun.
　　　　　　　Frag. Life. XXVIII. 4.
Bleak
And fit the bleak and howling waste
　　　　　　　Monadnoc. 151.
Or on wind-blown sea-marge bleak,
　　　　　　　Solution. 13.
Broadsowing, bleak and void to bless,
　　　　　　　Threnody. 284.
Blear
Thy sight is growing blear;
　　　　　　　Sphinx. 106.
Blend
Blend, ripen race on race,
　　　　　　　Song of Nature. 78.
Blends
Blends the starry fates with thine,
　　　　　　　Freedom. 18.
Flavor gladly blends with flavor;
　　　　　　　Merlin. 85.
Blent
And he who blent both in his line,
　　　　　　　Problem. 66.
Bless
Which children's voices bless.
　　　　　　　Concord Ode. 8.
Fall, stream, from Heaven to bless; re-
　　turn as well;　　Inscription. 1.
To bless that creature day and night:
　　　　　　　Rhea. 48.
Broadsowing, bleak and void to bless,
　　　　　　　Threnody. 284.
Evil will bless, and ice will burn.'
　　　　　　　Uriel. 24.

Blessed
As Hymen yet hath blessed,
Good Hope. 6.
Disappeared in blessed wife;
Holidays. 14.
By his proper bounty blessed,
Monadnoc. 39.
Lone as the blessed Jew.
Quat. Shakespeare. 4.
That blessed gods in servile masks
Saadi. 175.
Paced by the blessed feet around,
Threnody. 91.
And blessed the monument of the man
of flowers, Woodnotes. I. 70.
Blessed Nature so to see.
Woodnotes. II. 218.

Blessing
A blessing through the ages thus
Boston. 116.
And in the church a blessing found
Robbins Hymn. 15.
On him thy blessing fall,
Robbins Hymn. 26.
Blessing all lands with its charity;
Woodnotes. II. 241.

Blessings
The frank blessings of the hill
Monadnoc. 222.
Floods with blessings unawares.
Worship. 20.

Blest
See Unblest.
Of blest and unblest?
Ode to Beauty. 4.
But blest is he, who, playing deep, yet
haply asks not why,
Quat. Nature. 3.
Lit by rays from the Blest. Sphinx. 76.
O Violet, like thee, how blest could I
lie down and die, *Violet. 9.
Thrice the spot is blest; Walden. 2.

Blew
The wizard South blew down the glen,
Frag. Nat. III. 12.
Discoursed of fortune as they blew;
Frag. Poet. V. 38.

Blight
The frost might glitter, it would blight
no crop, Adirondacs. 68.
Alas! that one is born in blight,
Destiny. 18.

Blind
The erring painter made Love blind,—
Daemonic Love. 68.
As angel blind to trespass done,
Frag. Life. XXVIII. 3.
I daily dwell in, and am not so blind
Frag. Nat. V. 3.
Deaf, and dumb, and blind, and cold,
Frag. Poet. VIII. 6.
Him it would straightway blind or craze,
Guy. 22.
The gods are blind and lame,
Monadnoc. 349.
Warning to the blind and deaf,
Rhea. 33.

Blinding
His blinding light Cupido. 5.
Blinding dog-wood in my hand;
Mithridates. 15.

With tempest of the blinding flakes.
Titmouse. 74.

Blindworm
Go, blindworm, go, Channing Ode. 15.

Bliss
They chant the bliss of their abodes
Garden. 43.
It hath pleased Heaven to break the
dream of bliss I Bear. 3.

Blissful
Into blissful orgies sank; Poet. 82.

Block
In its white block; yet it therein shall
find Angelo. 3.
For each eternal block— House. 16.

Blocks
Vanish beside these dedicated blocks,
Monadnoc. 368.

Blood
See Life-blood.
Are no brothers of my blood;—
Alphonso. 17.
Blood of the world, Bacchus. 19.
Let the blood of her hundred thousands
Boston. 106.
And with hand and body and blood,
Celestial Love. 129.
Of blood through veins of kindred
poured. Daemonic Love. 4.
The needs of the first sight absorb my
blood, Day's Ration. 17.
The tie of blood and home was rent;
Frag. Poet. I. 53.
Counsel not with flesh and blood;
Freedom. 22.
A ruddy drop of manly blood
Friendship. 1.
Strong crab with nobler blood did fill;
Guy. 42.
Southwind is my next of blood;
Hermione. 50.
Heaven's oldest blood flows in his side,—
Initial Love. 123.
Their deed of blood
In Memoriam. 7.
Root in the blood of heroes old.
In Memoriam. 116.
To his own blood harsh and strange.
Insight. 6.
For they drew no blood, *Lines. 19.
And wakes the wish in youngest blood
May-Day. 95.
What potent blood hath modest May,
May-Day. 187.
Can make the wild blood start
Merlin. 7.
Kindly to plant and blood and kind,
Monadnoc. 90.
With my north wind chill his blood;
Monadnoc. 341.
I court and play with paler blood,
Romany. 14.
Ah, yes! but by the true heart's blood
They. 3.
As late I found my lukewarm blood
Titmouse. 3.
Curdles the blood to the marble bones,
Titmouse. 14.
Blood is blood which circulates,
Threnody. 243.

Bloody
For haircloth and for bloody whips,
        Saadi. 76.

Bloom
See Pear-bloom.
Maids of as soft a bloom shall marry
        Good Hope. 5.
See youth's glad mates in earliest
bloom,—   Harp. 123.
The year's fresh bloom,
        In Memoriam. 18.
Feels the bloom on the living vine,
        May-Day. 90.
So bloom the unfading petals five,
        Solution. 71.
Morn well might break and April bloom,
        Threnody. 16.
Which bloom and fade like meadow
flowers   Woodnotes. II. 302.

Bloomest
Thou bloomest here a lonely thing
        *Violet. 6.

Blooming
In May beholds the blooming wild,
        May-Day. 99.
A blooming child to children dear,
        Poet. 49.
A blooming hunter of a fairy fine.
        River. 15.

Blooms
When all their blooms the meadows
flaunt   Frag. Nat. VIII. 1.
Blooms in beauty, thinks in wit,
        May-Day. 292.
Thy blooms, thy kinds, May-Day. 437.
Yet wreathed and hid by summer
blooms.   Nun. 28.
Spreading its leafless blooms in a damp
nook,   Rhodora. 3.
Blooms the laurel which belongs
        Voluntaries. 106.

Blossom
Quaintest bud and blossom folds,
        May-Day. 258.
And keep the blossom of the earth,
        Threnody. 124.

Blossoms
Triple blossoms from one root;
        Celestial Love. 43.
She flowered in blossoms red;
        Sphinx. 126.

Blot
Imps, at high midsummer, blot
        Alphonso. 9.
If He should make my web a blot
        Nun. 8.

Blouses
Frocks and blouses, capes, capotes;
        Initial Love. 16.

Blow
See Clover-blow; Elder-blow.
Of the ancient being blow, Bacchus. 48.
In my plot no tulips blow,—
        Garden. 5.
But pipes through which the breath of
Pan doth blow   Pan. 2.
My quiet roses blow.   Walden. 20.
A tempest cannot blow;
        Woodnotes. I. 99.
It may blow north, it still is warm;
        Woodnotes. I. 100.

Blowest
O'er Kernan's meadow blowest,
        Exile. 10.

Bloweth
Creepeth, bloweth everywhere;
        May-Day. 290.
The wild air bloweth in our lungs,
        Romany. 21.

Blowing
We are budding, we are blowing;
        Ellen South. 34.

Blown
See Wind-blown.
Dash our blown hopes as they limp
heavily by.   Summons. 21.
To foreign parts is blown by fame;
        Una. 22.

Blows
Its chords should ring as blows the
breeze,   Merlin. 3.
Merlin's blows are strokes of fate,
        Merlin. 16.
Made of the air that blows outside.'
        Titmouse. 78.
Blows the sweet breath of song,
        Waldeinsamkeit. 38.
And all through which it blows,
        Walden. 38.
Sprung harmless up, refreshed by blows:
        Worship. 2.

Blue
Seeking in that chaste blue
        Adirondacs. 209.
And when you love not, pale and blue.
        Amulet. 8.
Upon the tablets blue, Bacchus. 66.
Or over the town blue ocean flows.
        Boston. 105.
Fills his blue urn with fire;
        Concord Ode. 2.
For He that flung the broad blue fold
        Concord Ode. 9.
The heavy blue chain   Tal. Exile. 1.
From blue mount and headland dim
        Frag. Poet. XI. 5.
When the blue horizon's hoop
        From Hafiz. 13.
The banks slope down to the blue lake-
edge,   Garden. 11.
Blue Walden rolls its cannonade,
        May-Day. 106.
Bend happy to the welkin blue.
        May-Day. 124.
Coat sea and sky with heavenlier blue,
        May-Day. 446.
And lifting man to the blue deep
        Monadnoc. 100.
There's a berry blue and gold,—
        Monadnoc. 297.
Peep the blue violets out of the black
loam,   Naples. 25.
Ye scorn me from your deeps of blue.
        Poet. 240.
My old familiar haunts; here the blue
river,   River. 2.
The same blue wonder that my infant
eye   River. 3.
Will thy clear blue eye, upward bent,
still keep its chastened glow,
        *Violet. 3.

Distilled from heaven's alembic blue,
Walden. 27.

Bluebird
And hears in heaven the bluebird sing,
May-Day. 100.

Bluebird's
And I shall hear my bluebird's note,
May-Day. 180.

Blue-coated
Blue-coated,—flying before from tree to
tree, Musketaquid. 16.

Blue-eyed
Blue-eyed pet of blue-eyed lover.
Ellen South. 32.

Blue-fly
The midge, the blue-fly and the mosquito
Adirondacs. 166.

Bluer
Seeking in that chaste blue a bluer light,
Adirondacs. 209.

Blue-vetch
Blue-vetch and trillium, hawkweed, sassafras, Blight. 6.

Blush
Scarce the first blush has overspread his
cheek, Philosopher. 4.
Has quenched the uneasy blush that
warmed my cheek; Summons. 2.
And a blush tinged the upper sky,
Uriel. 55.
The world would blush in flame;
World-Soul. 50.

Blushes
Already blushes on thy cheek
Nemesis. 1.
'T would bring the blushes of yon maples
September. 15.
"But man crouches and blushes,
Sphinx. 49.

Blusheth
In whose cheek the rose-leaf blusheth,
Woodnotes. II. 39.

Blushing
And blushing Love outwits the sages.
Frag. Poet. IX. 12.
Aimed at him, the blushing blade
Guy. 19.

Board
Abundant for their bed and board,
Boston. 71.
Brought his great forehead to the council
board, Phi. 8.
Sin piles the loaded board.
Woodnotes. II. 17.

Boast
Hide all the stars you boast
From Hafiz. 3.

Boastful
Earth laughs in flowers, to see her boastful boys Hamatreya. 13.

Boasts
That holds and boasts the immeasurable
mind. River. 35.

Boat
We chose our boats; each man a boat
and guide,— Adirondacs. 5.
We made our distance wider, boat from
boat, Adirondacs. 14.
From boat to boat, and to the echoes
round, Adirondacs. 242.

Of our great-hearted Doctor in his boat
Adirondacs. 272.
I give my rafters to his boat,
Woodnotes. II. 43.

Boat's
In the boat's bows, a silent night-hunter
Adirondacs. 118.

Boats
We chose our boats; each man a boat
and guide,— Adirondacs. 5.

Boccace
Nor Boccace in Decameron.
Adirondacs. Motto. 4.

Boded
Boded Merlin wise, Politics. 5.
The rash word boded ill to all; Uriel. 30.

Bodied
See Embodied.

Bodies
Our bodies are weak and worn;
World-Soul. 22.

Boding
And boding Fancy haunted it
Frag. Nat. X. 3.

Body
And with hand and body and blood,
Celestial Love. 129.
His great body in the grass,
Frag. Nat. I. 8.
In one body grooms and brides;
Merlin. 89.
And let thy body lie Mountain. 2.
Thy body food Mountain. 4.
Body with shadow still pursued.
Woodnotes. II. 163.
Are the atoms of his body bright,
World-Soul. 87.

Bog
In quaking bog, on snowy hill,
Woodnotes. I. 38.

Bog River
Of loud Bog River, suddenly confront
Adirondacs. 233.

Boil
Makes flame to freeze and ice to boil;
Spiritual Laws. 10.

Boiled
They boiled the sea, and piled the layers
Song of Nature. 35.

Boiler's
My billets to his boiler's throat,
Woodnotes. II. 44.

Boisterous
Coarse and boisterous, yet mild,
Monadnoc. 131.

Bold
See Overbold.
From bold intrusion of the travelling
crowd,— Adirondacs. 172.
Only the hand secure and bold
Angelo. 4.
Bold as the engineer who fells the wood,
Blight. 19.
'Like us be free and bold!' Boston. 16.
But if, grown bold, the poet dare
Frag. Poet. IV. 3.
Rung loud and bold the song. Harp. 48.
Of thoughtful maids and manhood bold.
Hymn. 12.
By those roving eyeballs bold
Initial Love. 32.

Bold —*Continued*
And these loved banks, whose oak-
boughs bold   In Memoriam. 115.
Recalled thy skill in bold design,
                      Lines. 18.
The sea is the road of the bold,
                      Quat. Alcuin. 1.
Thy softest pleadings seem too bold,
                      Rhea. 21.
Borrowed thy battle-numbers bold.
                      Titmouse. 98.
I choose a novel theme, a bold abuse
                      To-Day. 7.

Bolder
Or who, with accent bolder,
                      Channing Ode. 19.
A bolder foot is still rewarded.
                      Frag. Poet. XXXI. 2.
Stronger and bolder far than I,
                      Harp. 115.
As o'er some bolder height they speed,—
                      Monadnoc. 397.

Bolt
    See Thunderbolt; War-bolt.
Nor plots to ope or bolt a gate,
                      Frag. Life. XVII. 8.
Fell the bolt on the branching oak;
                      In Memoriam. 97.
Turn the key and bolt the door,
                      Past. 6.

Bolted
Bolted down forevermore.   Past. 13.

Bond
Nature is the bond of both:
                      Celestial Love. 86.
Made moon and planets parties to their
bond,   Musketaquid. 8.
Thou inscribest with a bond,
                      Ode to Beauty. 30.

Bondage-days
That the bondage-days are told,
                      May-Day. 109.

Bondmen
These scorned bondmen were my parapet.   Grace. 4.

Bonds
Alas! that neither bonds nor vows
                      Amulet. 9.
I break your bonds and masterships,
                      Boston Hymn. 53.

Bone
In figure, bone and lineament?
                      Threnody. 248.

Bones
His teeth and bones to buy a name,
                      Fame. 10.
The Baresark marrow to thy bones,
                      Terminus. 28.
Curdles the blood to the marble bones,
                      Titmouse. 14.

Bonfires
Saw bonfires of the harlot flies
                      Harp. 91.

Book
Writes a letter in my book. Apology. 8.
Know more than any book.   April. 14.
Brings book, or starbright scroll of
genius,   Day's Ration. 21.
That book is good
                      Frag. Poet. XVIII. 1.
For what need I of book or priest,
                      Frag. Poet. XXVIII. 1.

Write in a book the morning's prime,
                      Garden. 39.
Cannot be carried in book or urn;
                      Garden. 58.
In my coat I bore this book,
                      Goethe. 3.
Knows of Holy Book the spells,
                      Harp. 21.
The Book itself before me lies,
                      Problem. 64.
I tread the book beneath my feet.
                      Song of Seyd. 24.

Book's
Life loiters at the book's first page,—
                      Quat. Climacteric. 3.

Books
Of books and arts and trained experi-
ment,   Adirondacs. 307.
What all the books of ages paint, I
have.   Frag. Nat. V. 1.
Hermit vowed to books and gloom,—
                      Hermione. 34.
There will I bring my books,—my house-
hold gods,   Letter. 16.
Back to books and sheltered home,
                      May-Day. 54.
Shed mocking lustres on shelf of books,
                      May-Day. 356.
Books, Muses, Study,   Summons. 13.
And some in books of solace read;
                      Threnody. 153.
Old mouldy men and books and names
and lands   To-Day. 9.
The fancies found in books;
                      Waldeinsamkeit. 42.

Bookworm
Bookworm, break this sloth urbane;
                      Monadnoc. 16.

Boom
Though with boom and spar
                      Frag. Nat. XV. 2.
The bittern's boom, a desert make
                      Waldeinsamkeit. 31.

Booming
Or vagrant booming of the air,
                      May-Day. 11.

Booms
The cannon booms from town to town,
                      Concord Ode. 5.

Boon
Boon Nature to his poorest shed
                      Monadnoc. 70.
Boon Nature yields each day a brag
which we now first behold,
                      Quat. Nature. 1.

Boots
What boots thy zeal,
                      Channing Ode. 36.
What boots it? What the soldier's
mail,   Destiny. 14.
What boots it here of Thebes or Rome
                      Walden. 45.

Bordering
With salutation to the sea and to the
bordering isles.   Monadnoc. 37.

Borders
To the borders of day.   Sphinx. 104.

Bore
    See Upbore.
In my coat I bore this book,
                      Goethe. 3.

Bore thy colors every flower, Lines. 5.
Thine each leaf and berry bore;
                              Lines. 6.
The follies bore that it invest. Poet. 198.
Wings of what wind the lichen bore,
                              Wealth. 6.

Boreal
Of clouds and the boreal fleece.
                        Boston Hymn. 24.
Like the flitting boreal lights,
                        Frag. Poet. I. 39.
My boreal lights leap upward,
                        Song of Nature. 41.
Her stripes the boreal streamers are.
                        Voluntaries. 42.

Bored
Through mountains bored by regal art,
                        Saadi. 153.

Born
    See High-born; Muse-born; New-
born; Sea-born; Sky-born; Titan-born;
Twin-born; Unborn; Well-born; Wom-
an-born.
Born into Dæmons less divine:
                        Daemonic Love. 90.
When I was born,   Day's Ration. 1.
There's a melody born of melody,
                        Destiny. 5.
Alas! that one is born in blight,
                        Destiny. 18.
And another is born   Destiny. 27.
Defeated day by day, but unto victory
born.   Frag. Life. XXIII. 4.
Though Adam, born when oaks were
young,   Frag. Nat. VI. 3.
There quickened to be born again.
                        Frag. Poet. V. 36.
House you were born in,   Illusions. 7.
Thou born for noblest life,
                        In Memoriam. 28.
He who seemed a soldier born,
                        In Memoriam. 38.
Born for success he seemed,
                        In Memoriam. 60.
Each for other they were born,
                        Love and Thought. 7.
All seeds of beauty to be born?
                        May-Day. 217.
Born and nourished in miracles,
                        Poet. 3.
Ere he was born, the stars of fate
                        Quat. Horoscope. 1.
Earth smiled with flowers, and man was
born.   Solution. 8.
And still the man-child is not born,
                        Song of Nature. 43.
The world whereinto he was born,
                        Threnody. 18.
To wait an æon to be born.
                        Threnody. 149.
Born for the future, to the future lost!
                        Threnody. 175.
Or out of the good of evil born,
                        Uriel. 53.

Borne
    See Air-borne; Upborne; Wind-
borne.

Borrow
Men wait their good and truth to borrow.   Merlin's Song. 21.

Must borrow his winds who there would
come.   Titmouse. 10.

Borrowed
And the second, borrowed money,—
though the smiling lender say
                        Ibn Jemin. 3.
But borrowed in atoms from iron and
stone,   Nature. II. 21.
Borrowed thy battle-numbers bold.
                        Titmouse. 98.

Borrowing
Perversely borrowing from the shop the
tools   Adirondacs. 283.

Bosom
O friend, my bosom said, Friendship. 10.
Flits across her bosom young,
                        Give. 37.
The bosom thought which thou must
speak;   Nemesis. 2.
O friendless Present! than thy bosom
holds.   Quat. Heri. 4.
Bids for me her bosom glow.
                        Security. 4.
Firm to Heaven my bosom clings,
                        Song of Seyd. 31.
When every morn my bosom glowed
                        Threnody. 60.

Bosom-counsel
To make his bosom-counsel good.
                        Celestial Love. 130.

Bosomed
Bosomed in yon green hills alone,—
                        Good-Bye. 16.

Bosom-glow
And a truer bosom-glow
                        Frag. Poet. XI. 10.

Bosom's
If fate unlock his bosom's door,
                        Saadi. 120.

Bosoms
To vacant bosoms brought.
                        Voluntaries. 82.

Bosom-secret
To each his bosom-secret say.
                        Woodnotes. II. 155.

Boston
Took Boston in its arms;   Boston. 4.
If Boston knew the most!   Boston. 48.
'Not so,' said Boston, 'good my lord.
                        Boston. 69.
Fold Boston in his heart,   Boston. 103.
From Boston to Japan.   Waterfall. 12.

Boston Bay
For day by day could Boston Bay
                        Boston. 23.
Boston Bay and Bunker Hill
                        Channing Ode. 41.

Botanist
Not less the ambitious botanist sought
plants,   Adirondacs. 141.

Botany
And all their botany is Latin names.
                        Blight. 22.

Both (Partial list.)
Nature is the bond of both:
                        Celestial Love. 86.
All things return, both sphere and mote,
                        May-Day. 179.
And he who blent both in his line,
                        Problem. 66.
In both I read thy name. Thine Eyes. 12.

Bottom

I find him in the bottom of my heart,
Self-Reliance. 4.

Bottomless

O'er meadows bottomless. So, year by
year, Musketaquid. 46.

Bough

See Hemlock-bough; Maple-bough;
Wood-bough.

Singing at dawn on the alder bough;
Each. 14.

Leaf answers leaf upon the bough;
Merlin. 86.

Hopped on the bough, then, darting low,
Titmouse. 39.

Cut a bough from my parent stem,
Woodnotes. II. 51.

Boughs

See Oak-boughs.

clean without boughs Adirondacs. 83.

And trim the straightest boughs;
Boston Hymn. 34.

When boughs buffet boughs in the wood;
Merlin. 18.

Swing me in the upas boughs,
Mithridates. 18.

By green orchard boughs Politics. 19.

Acknowledged by their hospitable
boughs; River. 38.

I see my trees repair their boughs;
Threnody. 10.

Boughs on which the wild bees settle,
Woodnotes. I. 20.

'Speak not thy speech my boughs among:
Woodnotes. II. 134.

The least breath my boughs which tossed
Woodnotes. II. 144.

Bought

See Dear-bought.

Nothing was ploughed, or reaped, or
bought, or sold; Adirondacs. 67.

Goods and raiment bought and sold;
Celestial Love. 126.

Bound

See Home-bound; Sea-bound; Unbound.

Then turns to bound away,—is it too
late? Adirondacs. 124.

bound for the foaming Falls
Adirondacs. 232.

And a vision without bound:
Celestial Love. 20.

Girds the world with bound and term;
Celestial Love. 37.

Bound for the just, but not beyond;
Celestial Love. 116.

Which older forests bound; Garden. 10.

Since genius too has bound and term,
Harp. 74.

Inextricably bound, Hermione. 75.

Of gulfs of sweetness without bound
Humble-Bee. 36.

The dim horizon's utmost bound;—
May-Day. 425.

When Time thy feet has bound.
Monadnoc. 24.

And, though a pyramid, will bound.
Monadnoc. 255.

Love on his errand bound to go
Quat. Love. 1.

And garden,—they were bound and still.
Threnody. 109.

Hath its unit, bound and metre;
Visit. 5.

Which bound the dusky tribe,
Voluntaries. 28.

Bound in by streams which give and
take Waldeinsamkeit. 7.

Bound to the stake, no flames appalled,
Worship. 9.

Bounded

See Unbounded.

Bounded by dawn and sunset, and the
day Adirondacs. 153.

And sighed for all that bounded their
domain; Hamatreya. 18.

They bounded to the horizon's edge
Poet. 61.

Bounding

I plant his eyes on the sky-hoop bounding; Monadnoc. 324.

Boundless

But the boundless hath no form,
Bohemian. 3.

Boundless is his memory;
Initial Love. 138.

Of the boundless main Tal. Exile. 2.

So long he roved at will the boundless
shade. Woodnotes. I. 85.

Bounds

And beam to the bounds of the universe.
Beauty. 20.

The god of bounds, Terminus. 3.

The bounds of good and ill were rent;
Uriel. 32.

Bounteous

O bounteous seas that never fail!
Boston. 86.

Bounties

So deep and large her bounties are,
May-Day. 275.

Bounty

Take the bounty of thy birth,
Monadnoc. 25.

By his proper bounty blessed,
Monadnoc. 39.

Her manners made of bounty well refined; Quat. A. H. 2.

Bow

See Rainbow.

Bow to the stalwart churls in overalls:
Adirondacs. 94.

Toy with the bow, yet hit the white,
Frag. Poet. V. 2.

Golden curls, and quiver and bow.
Initial Love. 5.

He bears no bow, or quiver, or wand,
Initial Love. 17.

Toy with the bow, yet hit the white.
Merlin's Song. 38.

Nor in the bow that smiles in showers,
Music. 16.

Or bow above the tempest bent;
Threnody. 277.

But it carves the bow of beauty there,
Woodnotes. II. 170.

Bower

Of Eden's bower some dream-like trace
May-Day. 93.

In bower and hall Saadi. 25.

In the bower of dalliance sweet
Saadi. 55.

It opened in its virgin bower,
Woodnotes. I. 43.

Bowers
But birds tell it in the bowers.
Apology. 16.

Flaunting in their bowers;
Frag. Nat. II. 6.

Which breathes his sweet fame through
the northern bowers. Woodnotes. I. 71.

What recks such Traveller if the bowers
Woodnotes. II. 301.

Bowing
The green grass is bowing,
Ellen South. 1.

Bowl
And mix the bowl again;
Song of Nature. 74.

Bows
In the boat's bows, a silent night-hunter
Adirondacs. 118.

Boy
See Plough-boy; Sea-boy.
And the heart of girl and boy,
Harp. 23.

The boy knew on the hills in spring,
Harp. 86.

Fruit beloved of maid and boy,
Holidays. 2.

Boy no more, he wears all coats,
Initial Love. 15.

To the high-school and medalled boy:
May-Day. 345.

From youth to maid, from boy to man,
May-Day. 347.

And Nature squanders on the boy her
pomp, October. 3.

I was a boy; boyhood slid gayly by
Summons. 15.

The hyacinthine boy, for whom
Threnody. 15.

The gracious boy, who did adorn
Threnody. 17.

But the deep-eyed boy is gone.
Threnody. 97.

Boy who made dear his father's home,
Threnody. 167.

The wild-eyed boy, who in the woods
Woodnotes. II. 33.

To the boy with his games undaunted
World-Soul. 7.

Boyhood
I was a boy; boyhood slid gayly by
Summons. 15.

Boy-Rabbi
Boy-Rabbi, Israel's paragon.
Threnody. 223.

Boy's
See School-boy's.
The boy's dream comes to pass,
October. 2.

'Who has drugged my boy's cup?
Sphinx. 61.

Who has mixed my boy's bread?
Sphinx. 62.

Boys
Made them to boys again. Happier that
they Adirondacs. 61.

Five rosy boys with morning light
Dirge. 5.

And boys run out upon their leafy ropes.
Frag. Nat. III. 20.

Earth laughs in flowers, to see her
boastful boys Hamatreya. 13.

Scott, the delight of generous boys,
Harp. 81.

I saw fair boys bestriding steeds,
Harp. 111.

That the maids and boys might name
him. Initial Love. 14.

And games to breathe his stalwart boys:
Monadnoc. 164.

The fault that boys and nations soonest
mend. To-Day. 18.

Who shall nerve heroic boys
Voluntaries. 61.

Braced
See Firm-braced.

Brag
Boon Nature yields each day a brag
which we now first behold,
Quat. Nature. 1.

Braggart
Reputed wrongs and braggart rights,
Mithridates. 28.

Bragged
And bragged his virtues to each other,—
Poet. 204.

Brags
All the brags of plume and song;
Saadi. 150.

Brahmin
And I the hymn the Brahmin sings.
Brahma. 12.

True Brahmin, in the morning meadows
wet, Quat. Gardener. 1.

Brain
weighed the trout's brain,
Adirondacs. 134.

To be a brain, or serve the brain of
man. Adirondacs. 265.

Make sunshine in her brain. Boston. 109.

Puts confusion in my brain.
Channing Ode. 11.

A dull uncertain brain, Dull. 1.

On the nervous brain of man,
Frag. Nat. I. 14.

With joy too tense for sober brain;
Frag. Poet. I. 51.

For all that rattles in thy brain."
Frag. Poet. II. 10.

Like sower's seeds into his brain,
Frag. Poet. V. 35.

Wanting the echo in my brain.
Frag. Poet. XXVI. 2.

Of Cæsar's hand, and Plato's brain,
Informing Spirit. 7.

Not less renew the heart and brain,
May-Day. 453.

He shall not his brain encumber
Merlin. 29.

With my secret in his brain,
Monadnoc. 263.

So the coinage of his brain
Monadnoc. 306.

The order regnant in the yeoman's brain.
Musketaquid. 51.

Hid from men of Northern brain,
Voluntaries. 52.

Brain—*Continued*
If plants or brain, if egg or shell,
Walden. 39.
The reeling brain can ill compute)
Wealth. 20.

Brains
Nor wine nor brains perpetual pump.
Alphonso. 62.
Stuff their nine brains in one hat;
Alphonso. 72.
And the brains of men thenceforth,
Daemonic Love. 45.
Baulks and baffles plotting brains;
Nature. I. 6.

Brake
And the glassy surface in ripples brake
Frag. Poet. I. 37.
Wandering yester morn the brake,
Miracle. 15.
Through brake and fern, the beavers'
camp,   Woodnotes. I. 126.

Brakes
Milkweeds and murky brakes, quaint
pipes and sundew,   Blight. 7.

Branches
Limbs into branches, branches into
twigs,   Frag. Nat. XVII. 4.
Which tore from oaks their branches
broad,   Poet. 29.
Thy broad ambitious branches, and thy
root.   Terminus. 8.
My branches speak Italian,
Woodnotes. II. 150.

Branching
Fell the bolt on the branching oak;
In Memoriam. 97.

Brave
Nor whether your name is base or
brave: Destiny. 40.
Hard to out-do the brave, the true,
Frag. Life. X. 3.
The brave Empedocles, defying fools,
Frag. Life. XVIII. 1.
I scorned the fame of Timour brave;
Frag. Poet. III. 3.
'T is a brave master;   Give. 7.
Be of good cheer, brave spirit; stead-
fastly   Good Cheer. 1.
I was no longer brave;   Hamatreya. 61.
The brave whom Fate denies the goal!
In Memoriam. 87.
The turtle brave in his golden spots;
May-Day. 238.
With the marches of the brave;
Merlin. 25.
But if the brave old mould is broke,
Monadnoc. 118.
Where flowers each stone rosette and
metope brave;   Monadnoc. 372.
To brave the landscape's looks.
Waldeinsamkeit. 44.
The brave he loves amain;
World-Soul. 90.

Braved
The townsmen braved the English king,
Boston. 82.

Bravely
Being for Seeming bravely barter
Fame. 29.
On bravely through the sunshine and
the showers! Frag. Life. XXXVII. 1.

Braw
In braw claithing drest?   Riches. 6.

Brawlers
Heed not what the brawlers say,
Saadi. 102.

Bread
See Wheat-bread.
We buy ashes for bread;   Bacchus. 12.
Water and bread,   Bacchus. 31.
To die for Beauty, than live for bread.
Beauty. 26.
And sailed for bread to every shore.
Boston. 6.
Not to scatter bread and gold,
Celestial Love. 125.
Bread, kingdoms, stars,   Days. 6.
Bid my bread feed and my fire-warm
me   Destiny. 43.
At rich men's tables eaten bread and
pulse?   Forbearance. 3.
With its savory leaf for bread.
Frag. Nat. II. 24.
Like poisoned loaf of elfin bread,
Frag. Nat. III. 3.
Hers to sow the seed of bread,
May-Day. 146.
Bread to eat, and juice to drain;
Monadnoc. 305.
And having thus their bread and growth,
Nature. II. 18.
Serve thou it not for daily bread,—
Poet. 285.
'Eat thou the bread which men refuse;
Saadi. 142.
Who has mixed my boy's bread?
Sphinx. 62.
The innocent mirth which sweetens
daily bread,   Summons. 10.
That thou might'st break thy daily bread
Threnody. 219.
Doubt not, so long as earth has bread,
Titmouse. 83.

Break
I break your bonds and masterships,
Boston Hymn. 53.
His park where amber mornings break
Chartist. 10.
Air-bells of fortune that shine and break,
Garden. 55.
Break not my dream, obtrusive tomb!
Harp. 124.
It hath pleased Heaven to break the
dream of bliss   I Bear. 3.
Hints never loss or cruel break
In Memoriam. 107.
Whose deeps, till beams of noonday
break,   May-Day. 18.
Bookworm, break this sloth urbane;
Monadnoc. 16.
Visits the valley;—break away the
clouds,—   Musketaquid. 12.
Who never break your lawful dance
Poet. 157.
To break enchanted ice,   Rubies. 10.
Morn well might break and April
bloom,   Threnody. 16.
That thou might'st break thy daily bread
Threnody. 219.
They forbore to break the chain
Voluntaries. 27.

Break sharply off their jolly games,
               Voluntaries. 63.

Breaks

Breaks up their leaguer, and away.
               Forerunners. 4.

And breaks the glass of Time.
               Frag. Nat. XXV. 4.

Still breaks that morn, though dim, to
  Memory's eye,   I Bear. 10.

As the wave breaks to foam on shelves,
               Initial Love. 147.

But soft! a sultry morning breaks;
               May-Day. 58.

The forest waves, the morning breaks,
               Saadi. 135.

Breast

See Redbreast.

Slave or master on his breast.
               Astraea. 8.

For a warm breast of maiden to his
  breast,   Epitaph. 3.

In thy breast to make a home.
               Frag. Life. XXII. 8.

But by heaving of the breast:
               Freedom. 10.

So dances his heart in his breast;
               Manners. 14.

Throb thine with Nature's throbbing
  breast,   Nature. Mot. 11.

The keys of this breast,—
               Ode to Beauty. 2.

No mimic; from his breast his counsel
  drew,   Phi. 15.

Of leaves, and feathers from her breast?
               Problem. 26.

From rabbit's coat or grouse's breast;
               Quat. Forester. 2.

Hide thy grief within thy breast,
               Rhea. 11.

Throb thine with Nature's throbbing
  breast,   Threnody. 207.

Single look has drained the breast;
               Visit. 21.

Dragged from his mother's arms and
  breast,   Voluntaries. 19.

Under the tumbling mountain's breast,
               Wealth. 27.

And deck her breast with diamond,
               Woodnotes. II. 86.

Breasts

Smite the white breasts which thee fed,
               Saadi. 67.

Breath

had a cooler breath;   Adirondacs. 331.

I inhaled the violet's breath;   Each. 43.

It trembles to the cosmic breath,—
               Harp. 69.

The poorest that drew breath.
               In Memoriam. 34.

Half-repentant, scant of breath,—
               Monadnoc. 316.

But pipes through which the breath of
  Pan doth blow   Pan. 2.

The gods talk in the breath of the
  woods,   Poet. 73.

I snuff the breath of my morning afar,
               Poet. 108.

No breath therein, no passage out,
               Poet. 190.

A drop can shake, a breath can fan;
               Poet. 222.

Draw the breath of Eternity; Poet. 284.

My breath thy healthful climate in the
  heats,   Seashore. 5.

Creating a sweet climate by my breath,
               Seashore. 23.

Who, when they gave thee breath,
               Terminus. 25.

When thou didst yield thy innocent
  breath   Threnody. 100.

Here was this atom in full breath,
               Titmouse. 43.

That waft the breath of grace divine
               Voluntaries. 69.

Blows the sweet breath of song,
               Waldeinsamkeit. 38.

The least breath my boughs which
  tossed   Woodnotes. II. 144.

Breathe

Farewell I breathe again   *Farewell. 46.

Renewed, I breathe Elysian air,
               Harp. 122.

And games to breathe his stalwart boys:
               Monadnoc. 164.

Breathed

So pure the Alpine element we breathed,
               Adirondacs. 158.

Song breathed from all the forest,
               Cosmos. 9.

He freelier breathed beside the pine,
               Frag. Poet. V. 15.

Was the wailing song he breathed,
               Voluntaries. 11.

Breathed from the everlasting throat.
               Woodnotes. II. 123.

Breathes

Whence a smokeless incense breathes.
               May-Day. 6.

Breathes aromatic fire;   Threnody. 4.

Which breathes his sweet fame through
  the northern bowers.
               Woodnotes. I. 71.

That flows in streams, that breathes in
  wind: Woodnotes. II. 233.

Breathing

For all breathing men's behoof,
               Saadi. 11.

Bred

He comes, but not of that race bred
               Monadnoc. 309.

Breeched

See Yellow-breeched.

Breed

That this proud nursery could breed
               Monadnoc. 76.

Perish like leaves, the highland breed
               Monadnoc. 123.

The sunburnt world a man shall breed
               Song of Nature. 79.

Breeze

Their flag to April's breeze unfurled,
               C. Hymn. 2.

Chained the sunshine and the breeze,
               Guy. 8.

Its chords should ring as blows the
  breeze,   Merlin. 3.

As clouds give rain to the eastern
  breeze,   Poet. 34.

Breeze—*Continued*
Put off thy years, wash in the breeze;
Woodnotes. II. 135.
And lo! he passes like the breeze;
Woodnotes. II. 308.

Breezes
Play glad with the breezes, Sphinx. 27.
When summer light is fading, and
autumn breezes sigh; *Violet. 10.
It seemed as if the breezes brought
him, Woodnotes. I. 46.

Breezy
With thy mellow, breezy bass.
Humble-Bee. 31.

Brewed
When magic wine for bards is brewed;
May-Day. 339.

Bribe
Lured by 'Union' as the bribe.
Voluntaries. 30.

Bribed
Thou hast bribed the dark and lonely
Ode to Beauty. 84.

Bride
On prince or bride no diamond stone
On Prince. 1.

Bridegroom
Ill-bestead for gay bridegroom.
Hermione. 35.

Brides
In one body grooms and brides;
Merlin. 89.

Bridge
By the rude bridge that arched the
flood, C. Hymn. 1.
And Time the ruined bridge has swept
C. Hymn. 7.
Bridge gulfs, drain swamps, build dams
and mills, Monadnoc. 150.

Bridged
He bridged the gulf from th' alway
good and wise Phi. 17.

Bridges
Over yon western bridges I would ride
Letter. 4.

Brief
His brief toilette: at night, or in the
rain, Adirondacs. 76.
If our brief tribe miss thy face,
Ellen South. 23.
Ah, brother of the brief but blazing
star! In Memoriam. 25.

Brier
Bird and brier inly warms,
May-Day. 198.

Brier-roses
And brier-roses, dwelt among;
Humble-Bee. 49.

Brig
Our brig hastes on her way,
*Farewell. 15.

Bright
See Starbright; Sunbright.
By the bright morn the gay flotilla slid
Adirondacs. 16.
His fathers shining in bright fables,
Art. 17.
And treacherously bright to show
Chartist. 11.

When her calm eyes opened bright,
Daemoniac Love. 17.
Mortals deem the planets bright
Daemonic Love. 52.
Where in bright Art each god and sibyl
dwelt Daemonic Love. 121.
Fronted the sun with hope as bright,
Dirge. 7.
Thyself shalt own the page was bright,
Ellen. 7.
From bright, familiar eyes.
*Farewell. 13.
If bright the sun, he tarries,
Frag. Poet. XXXIII. 1.
Which lit my onward way with bright
presage, I Bear. 4.
Hang in the air a bright thermometer
Letter. 21.
To the bright premium,— Saadi. 14.
His tongue can paint as bright, as keen;
Saadi. 122.
Or by knowledge grown too bright
Uriel. 41.
Her morning sun shone bright and calm-
ly purely set; *Violet. 14.
Are the atoms of his body bright,
World-Soul. 87.

Brighter
Brighter than Jami's day. Saadi. 85.
So forth and brighter fares my stream,—
Two Rivers. 17.

Brightest
Had won the brightest laurel of all
time. Adirondacs. 285.

Brim
And fill the bag to the brim.
Boston Hymn. 70.
He came to the green ocean's brim
Frag. Poet. I. 45.

Brimming
The brimming brook invites a leap,
May-Day. 71.

Brims
And brims my little cup; heedless, alas!
Day's Ration. 12.

Brine
A river-ark on the ocean brine,
Good-Bye. 4.

Bring
Full fifty feet, and bring the eaglet down:
Adirondacs. 84.
We flee away from cities, but we bring
Adirondacs. 302.
Bring the moonlight into noon Art. 3.
Bring me wine, but wine which never
grew Bacchus. 1.
New flowerets bring, new prayers uplift,
Celestial Love. 4.
Men their fortunes bring with them.
Celestial Love. 74.
Knows to bring honey
Channing Ode. 86.
Bring diadems and fagots in their hands.
Days. 4.
For I did not bring home the river and
sky;— Each. 17.
To bring their first fruits to the sun.
Frag. Nat. II. 20.
Bring your music and rhythmic flight,
Frag. Nat. XXIII. 9.

And your enchanting manners bring
          Frag. Nat. XXIII. 13.
Bring music to the desolate;
          Frag. Poet. X. 3
Would bring back day if it were dark;
          Initial Love. 22.
There will I bring my books,—my house-
   hold gods,   Letter. 16.
'Onward,' he cries, 'your baskets bring,—
          May-Day. 101.
Bring hither back the robin's call,
          May-Day. 162.
Bring back the tulip's pride.
          May-Day. 163.
To-day shall all her dowry bring,
          May-Day. 264.
O birds, your perfect virtues bring,
          May-Day. 397.
Bring to fair mother fairer child,
          May-Day. 452.
To parting soul bring grandeur near.
          May-Day. 456.
And bring in poetic peace.   Merlin. 58.
You must bring the throbbing heart.
          Miracle. 10.
From air and ocean bring me foods,
          Mithridates. 8.
For wolf and fox, bring lowing herds,
          Monadnoc. 139.
Hither we bring   Monadnoc. 364.
What me the Hours will bring.
          Quat. Botanist. 4.
His words like a storm-wind can bring
          Saadi. 127.
'T would bring the blushes of yon maples
          September. 15.
Bring the flown Muses back to men.
          Threnody. 137.
He shall bring store of seeds and crumbs.
          Titmouse. 82.
I bring round the harvest day.'
          Voluntaries. 34.
See thou bring not to field or stone
          Waldeinsamkeit. 41.
As God and devil; bring them to the
   mind,   Xenophanes. 10.

Brings
Up to my ear the morning brings
          Boston Hymn. 7.
Brings book, or starbright scroll of
   genius,   Day's Ration. 21.
From strength to strength, and for night
   brings day;   Frag. Life. XXXI. 2.
And Time, who keeps God's word, brings
   on the day   Good Cheer. 13.
Every day brings a ship,   Letters. 1.
Every ship brings a word;   Letters. 2.
That the word the vessel brings
          Letters. 5
The next into the farthest brings,
          May-Day. 80.
Willows and lilacs brings again,
          May-Day. 183.
And brings it infantile and fresh.
          Monadnoc. 162.
The next unto the farthest brings;
          Nature. Mot. 2.
The South-wind brings   Threnody. 1.

Where January brings few faces.'
          Titmouse. 32.
Brings again the Pentecost;
          Woodnotes II. 145.
And shares the joy he brings.
          World-Soul. 64.
Brink
Gushed with syrup to the brink.
          May-Day. 341.
Britain's
Slowsure Britain's secular might,
          Monadnoc. 301.
British
Hear what British Merlin sung,
          Merlin's Song. 14.
Briton's
To mark the Briton's friendless grave.
          In Memoriam. 14.
Brittle
'Mid many ails a brittle health,
          Poet. 184.
Broad
The benefit of broad mankind.
          Celestial Love. 120.
Will the sweet sky and ocean broad
          Chartist. 15.
For He that flung the broad blue fold
          Concord Ode. 9.
And bid the broad Atlantic roll,
          Concord Ode. 27.
Broad his shoulders are and strong;
          Destiny. 31.
Broad England harbored not his peer:
          Fate. 10.
Where the fungus broad and red
          Frag. Nat. III. 1.
The meadows broad
          Frag. Nat. XXVII. 6.
The sower scatters broad his seed,
          Frag. Poet. VI. 11.
The sower scatters broad his seed;
          I Intellect. 3.
Broad northward o'er the land,
          May-Day. 248.
That one broad, long midsummer day
          May-Day. 276.
Beneath low hills, in the broad interval
          Musketaquid. 26.
As in broad orchards resonant with bees;
          Musketaquid. 57.
Which tore from oaks their branches
   broad,   Poet. 29.
Yet thou errest far and broad.
          Rhea. 24.
Thy broad ambitious branches, and thy
   root.   Terminus. 8.
Well, in this broad bed lie and sleep,—
          Titmouse. 17.
Her broad van seeks unplanted lands;
          Voluntaries. 37.
Ever fresh the broad creation,
          Woodnotes. II. 262.
And thatch with towns the prairie broad
          World-Soul. 67.
Broad-armed
There broad-armed oaks, the copses'
   maze,   Walden. 5.
Broad-backed
We will climb the broad-backed hills,
          May-Day. 226.

Broader
In schemes of broader scope engage.
Alphonso. 80.
Broad-sowing
Broad-sowing, cheerful, plenteous,
May-Day. 272.
Broadsowing, bleak and void to bless,
Threnody. 284.
Broidered
Yon broidered zodiac girds.
May-Day. 377.
Broke
That broke the gloom of night!
*Farewell. 4.
The rainbow of his hope was broke;
In Memoriam. 98.
But if the brave old mould is broke,
Monadnoc. 118.
Seemed, when at last his clarion accents, broke, Phi. 11.
He hath broke his banks and flooded all the vales River. 9.
Broken
With the beryl beam of the broken wave;
Beauty. 8
In sloven dress and broken rank,
In Memoriam. 5.
That the marble sleep is broken,
May-Day. 33.
I fall, my faith is broken, Poet. 239.
And broken stars I drew,
Song of Nature. 26.
Plight broken, this high face defaced!
Threnody. 151.
O trusted broken prophecy!
Threnody. 173.
Brokenhanded
Rash ambition, brokenhanded;
Alphonso. 24.
Broken-hearted
It is not broken-hearted:
Frag. Nat. XXIV. 6.
Brood
On God's and Satan's brood,
Cupido. 7.
And to all the heavenly brood.
Destiny. 48.
Her callow brood in mantling leaves,—
May-Day. 173.
For the ground-worms' brood
Mountain. 5.
Brooded
I brooded long and held my peace,
Solution. 18.
Brooding
Which the brooding soul surveys,
Uriel. 2.
Broods
What majestic stillness broods
Frag. Nat. XXVI. 19.
Ever on her secret broods. Harp. 14.
Gravely it broods apart on joy,.
II Intellect. 1.
Broods over thee, Rome. 25.
She broods on the world. Sphinx. 4.
He found the tawny thrushes' broods;
Woodnotes. I. 56.
Brook
Fold my arms beside the brook;
Apology. 6.

And court the sunny brook. April. 16.
The brook sings on, but sings in vain
Frag. Poet. XXVI. 1.
They added ridge to valley, brook to pond, Hamatreya. 17.
It throbbed up from the brook.
Hermione. 60.
Even from a brook, and where old woods
Letter. 11.
The brimming brook invites a leap,
May-Day. 71.
To please the desert and the sluggish brook. Rhodora. 4.
From the roadside to the brook
Threnody. 92.
The brook into the stream runs on;
Threnody. 96.
Brooks
Thy birds, thy songs, thy brooks, thy gales, May-Day. 436.
Brother
Where is the wind, my brother,—where?
Aeolian Harp. 9.
To the poor a noble brother,
Boston. 114.
Child and brother from his birth,
Daemonic Love. 2.
Thy heart saith, 'Brother, go thy ways!
Destiny. 21.
Asks nought his brother cannot give;
Frag. Life. XVII. 2.
The brother of the fisher, porter, swain,
Frag. Life. XXX. 5.
Ah, brother of the brief but blazing star!
In Memoriam. 25.
Dear brother, would you know the life,
Letter. 1.
A brother of the world, his song
Poet. 27.
Saluted him each morn as brother,
Poet. 203.
Means, dear brother, ask them not;
Poet. 249.
Brother, we are no phantom band;
Poet. 263.
Brother, accept this fatal hand.
Poet. 264.
Brother, sweeter is the Law Poet. 281.
Brother, no decrepitude Poet. 293.
Thee, dear friend, a brother soothes,
Rhea. 1.
Brothers
Are no brothers of my blood;—
Alphonso. 17.
As when my brothers, long ago,
Dirge. 19.
Farewell, my brothers true,
*Farewell. 28.
I have no brothers and no peers,
Frag. Poet. XXV. 1.
Our brothers have not read it,
World-Soul. 53.
Brought
For the idle flowers I brought:
Apology. 10.
Homeward brought the oxen strong;
Apology. 18.
Brought the Age of Gold again:
Character. 8.
I brought him home, in his nest, at even;
Each. 15.

Have brought us to life's evening hour,
Ellen. 2.
Stronger Custom brought him home.
Frag. Life. XX. 2.
The birds brought auguries on their
wings, Frag. Poet. V. 41.
As if Time brought a new relay
May-Day. 301.
Brought his great forehead to the coun-
cil board, Phi. 8.
His awful Jove young Phidias brought;
Problem. 10.
The self-same Power that brought me
there brought you. Rhodora. 16.
Whence brought his sunny bubbles ere
he washed River. 5.
They brought me rubies from the mine,
Rubies. 1.
And brought Olympian wisdom down
Solution. 67.
Brought the old order into doubt.
Threnody. 145.
To vacant bosoms brought.
Voluntaries. 82.
It seemed as if the breezes brought him,
Woodnotes. I. 46.
And brought me to the lowest land,
Woodnotes. I. 131.
And fanned the dreams it never brought.
Woodnotes. II. 4.

Brow
slips to wipe his brow   Adirondacs. 196.
He wrote on Nature's grandest brow, For
Sale. Webster, 1854. 2.
And torn the ensigns from thy brow,
Woodnotes. II. 184.

Brown
And halfway to the mosses brown;
May-Day. 118.
A brown wren was the Daniel
Miracle. 29.
Its spot of purple, and its streak of
brown, Naples. 8.

Browned
See Unbrowned.

Brows
For living brows; ill fits them to receive:
Phi. 2.

Browse
Browse the mountain sheep in flocks,
Saadi. 6.

Browses
The elephant browses, Sphinx. 19.

Brush
Sleep on the fragrant brush, as on down-
beds. Adirondacs. 58.

Brute
Brute or savage into man;
Freedom. 16.
'Merge me in the brute universe,
Poet. 193.

Brutely
Property will brutely draw
Celestial Love. 77.

Bubble
It rose a bubble from the plain.
Monadnoc. 290.

Bubbles
The bubbles of the latest wave
Each. 20.

Be bubbles of the atmosphere.
May-Day. 362.
Whence brought his sunny bubbles ere
he washed River. 5.

Buck
Is fallen: but hush! it has not scared
the buck Adirondacs. 122.

Bud
See Grass-bud.
Quaintest bud and blossom folds,
May-Day. 258.
Flower-wreaths gay with bud and bell;
May-Day. 315.

Bud-crowned
I saw the bud-crowned Spring go forth,
May-Day. 305.

Budding
We are budding, we are blowing;
Ellen South. 34.
With budding power in college-halls,
In Memoriam. 63.
Nor in the cup of budding flowers,
Music. 14.
And finds young pines and budding
birches; Threnody. 25.
But finds not the budding man;
Threnody. 26.

Buds
Over his head were the maple buds,
Quat. Excelsior. 1.

Buffet
When boughs buffet boughs in the wood;
Merlin. 18.

Buffoons
Rose and vine-leaf deck buffoons;
Heroism. 3.

Build
See Rebuild.
To row, to swim, to shoot, to build a
camp, Adirondacs. 82.
That we should build, hard-by, a spacious
lodge Adirondacs. 162.
We plant and build by foaming seas
Boston. 21.
And build me a wooden house.
Boston Hymn. 36.
To build an equal state,—
Concord Ode. 14.
Delights to build a road:
Daemonic Love. 86.
To be the quarry whence to build
Frag. Life. XXIV. 3.
Can build as the Muse can;   House. 2.
Build this golden portal;   Manners. 2.
and build heroic minds.   May-Day. 440.
Build and unbuild our echoing clay,
Merlin. 127.
build dams and mills,   Monadnoc. 150.
Out of dust to build   Politics. 11.
Build I to the All-Good, All-Fair.
Rhea. 59.
Hermit-thrush comes there to build,
Walden. 3.
To build in matter home for mind.
Wealth. 12.
Whose living towers the years conspired
to build, Woodnotes. I. 78.
And build to them a final tomb;
Woodnotes. II. 224.

Builded
He builded better than he knew;—
                    Problem. 23.
Builder
The hidden-working Builder spy,
                    Monadnoc. 238.
Building
Of the old building Intellect.
                    Monadnoc. 374.
Was ever building like my terraces?
                    Seashore. 7.
The building in the coral sea,
                    Song of Nature. 23.
Building for their sons the State,
                    Voluntaries. 25.
Builds
The last builds town and fleet,
                    Channing Ode. 55.
The Dæmon ever builds a wall,
                    Daemonic Love. 93.
Who builds, yet makes no chips, no din,
                    Monadnoc. 239.
Builds therewith eternal towers;
                    Spiritual Laws. 4.
Built
    See Magic-built; Outbuilt; Well-built.
The steamer built.   Channing Ode. 65.
By Him who built the day,
                    Frag. Life. XXXVI. 2.
And God hath built his altar here
                    Hymn. 5.
'For the world was built in order,'
                    Monadnoc. 245.
Here in pine houses built of new-fallen
trees,   Musketaquid. 30.
On this altar God hath built   Nun. 15.
Our fathers built to God;—
                    Robbins Hymn. 2.
Built in an age, the mad wind's night-
work,   Snow-Storm. 27.
And childhood's castles built or planned;
                    Threnody. 87.
Built he heaven stark and cold;
                    Threnody. 273.
Built of fears and sacred flames,
                    Threnody. 278.
Built of furtherance and pursuing,
                    Threnody. 280.
Then docks were built, and crops were
stored,   Wealth. 42.
Bulkeley
Bulkeley, Hunt, Willard, Hosmer, Meri-
am, Flint,   Hamatreya. 1.
Bullet
Goes like bullet to its mark;
                    Monadnoc. 190.
Of the bullet of the earth
                    Monadnoc. 326.
Bulrush
The fungus and the bulrush spoke,
                    Frag. Nat.. III. 10.
Bun
Bun replied,   Fable. 4.
Bunch
A bunch of fragrant lilies be,
                    Woodnotes. II. 303.
Bundle
Yesterday was a bundle of grass.
                    Woodnotes. II. 277.

Bunker Hill
Boston Bay and Bunker Hill
                    Channing Ode. 41.
Bunting
The hardy bunting does not chide;
                    May-Day. 165.
Burdens
The burdens of the Bible old;
                    Problem. 14.
Buried
Which thus the buried Past can tell,
                    Harp. 62.
The buried Past arise;   Peter. 18.
And trophies buried: To J. W. 15.
Buries
Buries himself in summer waves,
                    Initial Love. 98.
Burly
Burly, dozing humble-bee,
                    Humble-Bee. 1.
Burn
On waves and hedges still they burn.
                    Garden. 60.
For Saadi's nightly stars did burn
                    Saadi. 84.
And cities rise where cities burn,
                    Saadi. 112.
Spin the ball! I reel, I burn,
                    Song of Seyd. 1.
Evil will bless, and ice will burn.'
                    Uriel. 24.
And thou,—go burn thy wormy pages,—
                    Woodnotes. 11. 246.
Burned
As one within whose memory it burned
                    Adirondacs. 278.
Under the cinders burned the fires of
home;   Adirondacs. 333.
Beware the fire that Eblis burned."
                    Frag. Poet. II. 3.
Burned more than others' fire,
                    May-Day. 143.
And burned in noble hearts proverb and
prophecy.   Phi. 22.
If with love thy heart has burned;
                    Rhea. 9.
Prayers of saints that inly burned,—
                    Threnody. 265.
Burning
And pass the burning summer-time
                    Frag. Poet. V. 7.
At the burning Lyre,   Monadnoc. 215.
Up from the burning core below,—
                    Problem. 17.
He roves unhurt the burning ways
                    Voluntaries. 49.
Burnished
Was burnished to a floor of glass,
                    Woodnotes. I. 109.
Burns
Burns up every other tie.
                    Daemonic Love. 115.
What fire burns in that little chest
                    Titmouse. 52.
The rose of beauty burns;
                    Waldeinsamkeit. 26.
Burnt
    See Sunburnt.
Burrs
Running over the club-moss burrs;
                    Each. 42.

Burst
  A burst of joy, as if we told the fact
                            Adirondacs. 252.
Bursting
  When Winter reigned I'd close my eye,
  but wake with bursting Spring,
                            *Violet. 11.
Bursts
  And bursts the hoops at hint of Spring:
                            May-Day. 91.
  The dead log touched bursts into leaf,
                            May-Day. 208.
Bury
  The upheaved land, and bury the folk,
                            Channing Ode. 30.
  All to yean and all to bury:
                            Woodnotes. II. 259.
Bush
  When man in the bush with God may
  meet?   Good-Bye. 30.
Busied
  Too busied with the crowded hour to fear
  to live or die.   Quat. Nature. 4.
Bustle
  'Let the great world bustle on Saadi. 104.
Busy
  Farewell the busy town,   *Farewell. 10.
But. (Partial List.)
  Who but the midge, mosquito and the
  fly,   Adirondacs. 173.
  And none but Toil shall have.
                            Boston Hymn. 28.
  But speechless to the master's mind?
                            Monadnoc. 91.
  But the poet dwells alone.   Saadi. 8.
  But thou, joy-giver and enjoyer,
                            Saadi. 99.
  But the deep-eyed boy is gone.
                            Threnody. 97.
  I am but a thought of hers,   Una. 19.
  We are but such as they. World-Soul. 56.
  They are but sailing foam-bells
                            World-Soul. 69.
  And are but one. Beheld far off, they
  part   Xenophanes. 9.
Butler
  Drug the cup, thou butler sweet,
                            May-Day. 279.
Butterfly
  Have ye seen the butterfly   Riches. 5.
  Over whose flowers I chased the butter-
  fly,   River. 14.
Buy
  We buy ashes for bread;   Bacchus. 12.
  We buy diluted wine;   Bacchus. 13.
  His teeth and bones to buy a name,
                            Fame. 10.
  And buy, and sell, and lose, and win;
                            Initial Love. 47.
  To buy iron and gold;   Politics. 2.
Buys
  Nor kind nor coinage buys   Politics. 7.
By (Partial list.)
  See Hard-by.
  Or baffle by a veil, or slight by scorn?
                            Adirondacs. 176.
  'Now by these presents be it known
                            Boston. 65.
  The sea returning day by day
                            Boston. 100.

The word of the Lord by night
                            Boston Hymn. 1.
As they sat by the seaside,
                            Boston Hymn. 3.
By races, as snow-flakes,
                            Boston Hymn. 82.
By right or wrong,   Celestial Love. 75.
Each other's counsel by his own,
                            Celestial Love. 92.
Not by ribbons or by favors,
                            Celestial Love. 102.
But by heaving of the breast:
                            Freedom. 10.
Year by year the rose-lipped maiden,
                            Holidays. 9.
Or valleys by the sea,   House. 10.
By lapses or by wars,   House. 22.
He has the Muses by the heart,
                            Initial Love. 128.
By the stairway of surprise.' Merlin. 38.
I was a boy; boyhood slid gayly by
                            Summons. 15.
they limp heavily by.   Summons. 21.
And let the world's affairs go by,
                            Threnody. 47.
The kennel by the corded wood;
                            Threnody. 83.
When piped a tiny voice hard by,
                            Titmouse. 25.
Sage and hero, side by side,
                            Voluntaries. 24.
Destiny sat by, and said, Voluntaries. 31.
Biding by his rule and choice,
                            Voluntaries. 87.
Stars taunt us by a mystery
                            World-Soul. 47.
Bye
  See Good-bye.
Byre
  On farmer's byre, on pasture rude,
                            May-Day. 357.
Byron's
  Nor Byron's clarion of disdain,
                            Harp. 80.
Bystander
  The near bystander caught no sound,—
                            Solution. 52.

Cabalist
  A mystic and a cabalist,—
                            Initial Love. 61.
Cabin
  From a log cabin stream Beethoven's
  notes   Adirondacs. 313.
  A cabin hung with curling smoke,
                            Frag. Poet. I. 22.
  For Genius made his cabin wide,
                            Frag. Poet. XX. 1.
Cabinet
  Gems in Nature's cabinet;
                            Frag. Nat. XXIII. 4.
  Best gems of Nature's cabinet,
                            May-Day. 394.
Cable
  See Wire-cable.
  And under, through the cable wove,
                            Concord Ode. 35.
Cadence
  To the cadence of the whirling world
                            House. 19.

Cadent

And, far within those cadent pauses,
Woodnotes. II. 118.

Cæsar

I think old Cæsar must have heard
Titmouse. 95.

Cæsar of his leafy Rome,
Woodnotes. I. 5.

Caesar's

Of Cæsar's hand, and Plato's brain,
Informing Spirit. 7.

Cage

Like the bird from the woodlands to the
cage;— Each. 34.

Bad men it will chain and cage—
Merlin's Song. 7.

Cagèd

The cagèd linnet in the Spring
May-Day. 83.

Calendar

Ah! well I mind the calendar,
May-Day. 372.

Gauge and calendar and dial,
Monadnoc. 52.

Into calendar months and days.
Uriel. 4.

Californian

Found ten years since the Californian
gold? Adirondacs. 280.

Call

See Recall.

Honor enough that we send the call.'
Boston. 68.

Call in the wretch and slave:
Boston Hymn. 26.

Call the people together,
Boston Hymn. 37.

The air rings jocund to his call,
May-Day. 70.

Bring hither back the robin's call,
May-Day. 162.

So call not waste that barren cone
Monadnoc. 352.

And what they call their city way
Nature. II. 9.

Call hither thy mortal enemy, Poet. 219.

Oh, call not Nature dumb; River. 21.

For men mis-hear thy call in Spring,
Titmouse. 91.

But in each pause we heard the call
Walden. 35.

Called

See Uncalled.

Thy summons called our sires, Bell. 10.

And the former called the latter 'Little
Prig;' Fable. 3.

'They called me theirs, Hamatreya. 53.

Not mine,—I never called thee mine,
Threnody. 126.

To the van called not in vain.
Voluntaries. 96.

Callest

See Recallest.

Calling

Him duty through the clarion calling
Voluntaries. 95.

Callow

Her callow brood in mantling leaves,—
May-Day. 173.

Calls

When the South Sea calls. Bacchus. 30.

Which calls the sons of Time. Bell. 4.

Beauty sits and Music calls; Dearest. 2.

Love calls not to his aid events;
Frag. Life. XVII. 4.

Without the baffled North-wind calls.
May-Day. 57.

'Up!—If thou knew'st who calls
Monadnoc. 5.

And sternly calls to being souls
Quat. Fate. 3.

The rain comes when the wind calls;
Woodnotes. II. 238.

Call'st

More near than aught thou call'st thy
own, Worship. 16.

Calm

When her calm eyes opened bright,
Daemonic Love. 17.

But calm delight, *Lines. 14.

Beneath the calm, within the light,
May-Day. 150.

Good men it will calm and cheer,
Merlin's Song. 6.

Calm as the morn the manly patriot sate;
Phi. 10.

Undaunted and calm; Sphinx. 20.

Calmly

Her morning sun shone bright and
calmly purely set; *Violet. 14.

Calmuck

And, Calmuck, in his wagon roam
Poet. 52.

Came

No courier waits, no letter came or
went, Adirondacs. 66.

Waved the scoop-net, and nothing came
amiss; Adirondacs. 138.

So light, so lofty pictures came and went.
Adirondacs. 159.

"Chronic dyspepsia never came from eating Adirondacs. 185.

No tidings since it came. Amulet. 4.

The cargo came! and who could blame
Boston. 76.

To the watching Pilgrims came,
Boston Hymn. 2.

Came a beam of goodness down
Caritas. 3.

Till dangerous Beauty came, at last,
Daemonic Love. 10.

Till Beauty came to snap all ties;
Daemonic Love. 11.

With the flower with which it came.
Days Pass. 4.

It came never out of wit; Destiny. 9.

Came with me to the wood. Dirge. 20.

At last she came to his hermitage,
Each. 33.

That came to every festival.
Frag. Poet. I. 4.

He came a pilgrim to the Mosque
Frag. Poet. I. 5.

And ever the spell of beauty came
Frag. Poet. I. 13.

He came to the green ocean's brim
Frag. Poet. I. 45.

And it lay on my hearth when I came
home. Frag. Poet. IV. 34.

And be sure at last came Love,
Garden. 27.

'T was high time they came; Gifts. 2.

There was no frost but welcome came,
Guy. 47.
When thy meteor glances came,
Hermione. 37.
He came late along the waste,
Initial Love. 11.
Whither the angry farmers came,
In Memoriam. 4.
And Summer came to ripen maids
May-Day. 303.
I know not why I came again
Miracle. 7.
With sounding steps the poet came;
Poet. 2.
The gallant child where'er he came
Poet. 7.
The litanies of nations came,
Problem. 15.
There came a voice without reply,—
Quat. Sacrifice. 2.
Admired, sage doubting whence the
traveller came,—   River. 4.
Came up the pensive train,
Robbins Hymn. 14.
Sudden gusts came full of meaning,
September. 9.
Came to me in his fatal rounds,
Terminus. 5.
Night came, and Nature had not thee;
Threnody. 102.
As if he came unto his own,
Threnody. 143.
Some went and came about the dead;
Threnody. 152.
'I came to thee as to a friend;
Threnody. 209.
I, who dreamed not when 1 came here
Titmouse. 101.
Came Uriel's voice of cherub scorn,
Uriel. 54.

Camel
On trail of camel and caravan,
Frag. Poet. I. 6.
Camel-driver's
Hassan the camel-driver's door,
Frag. Poet. III. 2.
Camest
Whence camest thou, misplaced, mis-
timed,   Woodnotes. II. 179.
Camp
To row, to swim, to shoot, to build a
camp,   Adirondacs. 82.
To thread by night the nearest way to
camp?   Adirondacs. 106.
North from Camp Maple, south to
Osprey Bay,   Adirondacs. 109.
Two Doctors in the camp
Adirondacs. 133.
We struck our camp and left the happy
hills.   Adirondacs. 336.
Their near camp my spirit knows
Forerunners. 33.
Men consort in camp and town,
Saadi. 7.
With war and trade, with camp and
town;   Saadi. 105.
Through brake and fern, the beavers'
camp,   Woodnotes. I. 126.
Camp-fire
Then struck a light and kindled the
camp-fire.   Adirondacs. 36.

Camping
Which o'erhung, like a cloud, our camp-
ing fire.   Adirondacs. 47.
Can (Partial list.)
Which few can put on with impunity.
Adirondacs. 98.
I, a king, for kings can feel.
Alphonso. 44.
Can certify possession;   Amulet. 10.
That can fix a hero's rate;   Astraea. 4.
Food which teach and reason can.
Bacchus. 35.
Nor art, nor power, nor toil can find
Bohemian. 10.
They did what freemen can, Boston. 8.
For you can teach the lightning speech,
Boston. 110.
Can govern the land and sea
Boston Hymn. 46.
They can parley without meeting;
Celestial Love. 93.
They can well communicate
Celestial Love. 95.
The state may follow how it can,
Channing Ode. 69.
Or who can date the morning,
Cosmos. 3.
None can bewilder; Daemonic Love. 71.
Neither can you crack a nut.' Fable. 19.
He lives not who can refuse me;
Frag. Nat. XXVIII. 1.
And, when it lists him, waken can
Freedom. 15.
Is he hapless who can spare Goethe. 7.
Can build as the Muse can;   House. 2.
Each can other best adorn;
Love and Thought. 8.
Can this elastic air convey. May-Day. 14.
Songs can the tempest still,   Merlin. 55.
Who has little, to him who has less, can
spare,   Merlin's Song. 24.
The music that can deepest reach,
Merlin's Song. 35.
His hidden sense interpret can;—
Miracle. 20.
And what obedient Nature can;—
Monadnoc. 88.
'Let him heed who can and will;
Monadnoc. 224.
But well I know, no mountain can,
Monadnoc. 258.
And forget me if he can.'
Monadnoc. 347.
Nor can dispense   Saadi. 27.
Redeemers that can yield thee all:
Saadi. 166.
When frail Nature can no more,
Threnody. 234.
The youth replies, I can. Voluntaries. 74.
'Achieve our peace who can!'
Walden. 24.
Can find with glass in ten times ten.
Walk. 8.
Which well it can supply,
Waterfall. 6.
Canes
Fresh from palms and Cuba's canes.
May-Day. 393
Canister
God fills the scrip and canister,
Woodnotes. II. 16.

Canisters
Weave wood to canisters and mats;
                    Monadnoc. 141.
Cannibals
It is not Iroquois or cannibals,
                    Adirondacs. 292.
Cannon
The cannon booms from town to town,
                    Concord Ode. 5.
Cannon in front and leaden rain
                    Voluntaries. 94.
Cannonade
Or haply 't was the cannonade
                    May-Day. 15.
Blue Walden rolls its cannonade,
                    May-Day. 106.
With the cannonade of wars;
                    Merlin. 24.
Cannot (Partial list.)
Essaying nothing she cannot perform.
                    Adirondacs. 72.
We cannot spare variety.   Alphonso. 58.
It cannot parley with the mean,—
                    Astraea. 43.
Help them who cannot help again:
                    Boston Hymn. 51.
I cannot leave   Channing Ode. 3.
I cannot hear your songs, O birds,
                    Cosmos. 23.
Who cannot circumnavigate the sea
                    Day's Ration. 30.
'You cannot unlock your heart,
                    Dirge. 57.
If I cannot carry forests on my back,
                    Fable. 18.
Ah Fate, cannot a man   Fame. 1.
Which the Omnipotent cannot rebuild.
                    Frag. Life. V. 2.
Who steer the plough, but cannot steer
    their feet   Hamatreya. 15.
If they cannot hold me,   Hamatreya. 58.
What friend to friend cannot convey
                    Miracle. 21.
I cannot spare water or wine,
                    Mithridates. 1.
Cooped in a ship he cannot steer,—
                    Monadnoc. 336.
I cannot shake off the god;   Park. 5.
I cannot publish in my rhyme Peter. 21.
In love, he cannot therefore cease his
    trade;   Philosopher. 3.
I cannot tell rude listeners
                    September. 13.
Sunshine cannot bleach the snow,
                    Test. 11.
And oh! it cannot die,   Thought. 6.
The lost, the lost, he cannot restore;
                    Threnody. 6.
Far and wide she cannot find him;
                    Threnody. 22.
My hopes pursue, they cannot bind him.
                    Threnody. 23.
Speeding Saturn cannot halt;   Visit. 27.
And there I cannot stray.   Walden. 48.
A tempest cannot blow;
                    Woodnotes. I. 99.
It cannot conquer folly,—
                    World-Soul. 13.
We cannot learn the cipher
                    World-Soul. 45.

Canope
When the star Canope shines in May,
                    Merlin's Song. 33.
Canst (Partial list.)
Pluck it now! In vain,—thou canst not;
                    Holidays. 5.
Dost love our manners? Canst thou silent
    lie?   Musketaquid. 77.
Thou canst not catch what they recite
                    Woodnotes. II. 129.
Can't
Can't trance him again,   Sphinx. 78.
Fate let him fall, Fate can't retake him;
                    Threnody. 28.
Cant
For the priest's cant,   Channing Ode. 5.
Cantharids
Give me cantharids to eat;
                    Mithridates. 7.
Canticles
The canticles of love and woe:
                    Problem. 18.
Cap
Bartered its powdery cap; May-Day. 234.
Stately marching in cap and coat
                    Threnody. 76.
Cap-a-pie
Cap-a-pie invulnerable,   Astraea. 6.
Cape
Under the Andes to the Cape,
                    Bacchus. 4.
Capes
Frocks and blouses, capes, capotes;
                    Initial Love. 16.
Capitals
Far capitals and marble courts,
                    Quat. A. H. 3.
Capotes
Frocks and blouses, capes, capotes;
                    Initial Love. 16.
Capped
    See Snow-capped.
Caprice
Grace, Beauty and Caprice   Manners. 1.
Capricious
Mark his capricious ways to draw the
    eye.   Adirondacs. 207.
Captain
Who is the captain he knows not,
                    Monadnoc. 337.
The little captain innocent
                    Threnody. 70.
Captivated
It shook or captivated all who heard,
                    Phi. 20.
Captive
To-day unbind the captive,
                    Boston Hymn. 65.
Where a captive sits in chains,
                    Voluntaries. 6.
Captives
You captives of your air-tight halls,
                    Romany. 6.
Captivity
He to captivity was sold,   Worship. 3.
Captured
Captured the lizard, salamander, shrew,
                    Adirondacs. 135.
Car
For action's field, for victor's car,
                    In Memoriam. 29

Could chain the wheel of Fortune's car,
Poet. 166.

Caravan
On trail of camel and caravan,
Frag. Poet. I. 6.
And speak the lovely caravan.
Threnody. 73.

Carbuncle
Lake Probability,—our carbuncle,
Adirondacs. 132.

Care
Thanks if your genial care
Aeolian Harp. 2.
The lore we care to know. April. 20.
What care though rival cities soar
Boston. 45.
And each shall care for other,
Boston. 112.
Of care and toil, Celestial Love. 64.
Or care a rush for what thou knowest,
Destiny. 23.
I care not how you are dressed,
Destiny. 38.
Thou dost mock at fate and care,
Humble-Bee. 56.
I care not if the pomps you show
May-Day. 359.
What care I, so they stand the same,—
Merops. 1.
Care not to strip the dead To J. W. 11.
Fantastic care derides,
Waldeinsamkeit. 14.
With his chariot and his care;
Woodnotes. II. 27.

Careful
My careful heart was free again,
Friendship. 9.
In cities high the careful crowds
Walden. 17.

Cares
It charms his cares to sleep, Bell. 7.
Or cares that earth to earth engage,
Nun. 34.
So fanciful, so savage, nought cares he
Snow-Storm. 16.
Thy thrift, the sleep of cares;
Waldeinsamkeit. 46.

Caressed
Somewhat not to be caressed,
Ode to Beauty. 71.

Caresses
Piques, reproaches, hurts, caresses.
Initial Love. 133.

Cargo
The cargo came! and who could blame
Botson. 76.

Caribou
Bird, or deer, or caribou.
Initial Love. 101.

Carnival
It was the Carnival of time, Peter. 23.
What time the gods kept carnival,
Song of Nature. 29.
That dizen Nature's carnival,
Threnody. 190.

Carol
And the love in its carol heard,
May-Day. 236.

Carolled
And carolled undeceiving things
Frag. Poet. V. 42.

Carolling
Every bird in carolling, Lines. 10.

Carouse
Vampyre-fanned, when I carouse.
Mithridates. 19.

Carpet
And all unmeet our carpet floors;
May-Day. 221.

Carpets
On carpets green the maskers march
May-Day. 331.

Carried
Cannot be carried in book or urn;
Garden. 57.
The eager fate which carried thee
Threnody. 160.

Carrier-doves
Carrier-doves to nest. Walden. 4.

Carries
Surely he carries a talisman Destiny. 29.
Carries the eagles, and masters the
sword. Destiny. 50.
And when he goes he carries
Frag. Poet. XXXIII. 3.

Carry
See Miscarry.
And carry my purpose forth,
Boston Hymn. 83.
If I cannot carry forests on my back,
Fable. 18.
And carry in my heart, for days,
Forerunners. 37.
Carry aloft, below, around,
Frag. Nat. III. 35.
And carry learning to its height
Monadnoc. 104.
To carry man to new degrees Rhea. 68.

Cart
See Hand-cart.
Makes Romeo of a plough-boy on his
cart; Enchanter. 13.
Toil whistles as he drives his cart.
Saadi. 154.

Carts
Thence, in strong country carts, rode up
the forks Adirondacs. 2.
Their talismans are ploughs and carts;
Monadnoc. 134.

Carve
And carve the coastwise mountain into
caves. Seashore. 13.

Carved
See Stone-incarved.

Carves
He paints, he carves, he chants, he prays,
Initial Love. 116.
But it carves the bow of beauty there,
Woodnotes. II. 170.

Cascades
My leaves and my cascades;
Song of Nature. 52.

Casement
In the casement at my side. Harp. 40.

Cask
The old wine darkling in the cask
May-Day. 89.

Cast

See Downcast; Forecast; Outcast; Recast.

A form which Nature cast in the heroic mould   Phi. 5.

The things whereon he cast his eyes   Poet. 9.

Cast wishful glances at the stars   Poet. 191.

Cast the bantling on the rocks,   Quat. Power. 1.

Already Heaven with thee its lot has cast,   Sursum Corda. 10.

Castile

In my palace of Castile,   Alphonso. 43.

Castilian

English, German, Basque, Castilian,   Woodnotes. II. 151.

Castled

And rankly on the castled steep,—   Voluntaries. 120.

Castles

And childhood's castles built or planned;   Threnody. 87.

Casts

Casts her schemes rarely,   Frag. Life. VI. 2.

Casualty

Casualty and Surprise   Nature. I. 7.

Casuist

Cupid is a casuist,   Initial Love. 60.

Cat

Add their nine lives to this cat;   Alphonso. 71.

Couched like a cat sat watching close behind   Philosopher. 9.

Catamount

Temper to face wolf, bear, or catamount,   Adirondacs. 85.

Cataracts

Like Alpine cataracts frozen as they leaped,   Blight. 60.

Catch

Will you catch crabs? Adirondacs. 100.

Flowers they strew,—I catch the scent;   Forerunners. 11.

Keen ears can catch a syllable,   Garden. 29.

I catch thy meaning, wizard wave;   Peter. 39.

To catch the unconscious heart in the very act.   Philosopher. 6.

And I began to catch the sense   Titmouse. 66.

Thou canst not catch what they recite   Woodnotes. II. 129.

Catches

Those idle catches told the laws   Frag. Poet. V. 11.

Catchfly

Clover, catchfly, adder's-tongue   Humble-Bee. 48.

Caterpillar

Have ye seen the caterpillar   Riches. 1.

Caterpillar-shrouds

Grass-buds and caterpillar-shrouds,   Woodnotes. I. 19.

Cathedrals

Swift cathedrals in the wild;   May-Day. 48.

Catos

The Catos, the wise patriots of Rome,   Rome. 5.

Cattle

Cattle lowed in mellow distance   September. 7.

Caucasus

Alps and Caucasus uprear,   Monadnoc. 275.

Caught

Caught from a late-arriving traveller,   Adirondacs. 236.

Caught among the blackberry vines,   Berrying. 6.

They caught the footsteps of the Same.   Blight. 29.

That suddenly caught the flame.   Cosmos. 12.

That the slave who caught the strain   Freedom. 3.

That he caught Nature in his snares.   Guy. 32.

And saying "You're caught!"   *Lines. 23.

Caught with love's cord of twisted beams,   Nun. 35.

I caught with bended pin   River. 12.

The near bystander caught no sound,—   Solution. 52.

Cause

I cause from every creature   Boston Hymn. 57.

Which publish and which hide the cause.   Celestial Love. 59.

Holding Nature to her cause.   Frag. Poet. V. 12.

Sit with the Cause, or grim or glad.   Frag. Poet. XVII. 2.

Obeying meek the primal Cause,·   Harp. 71.

Worthier cause for passion wild   Threnody. 177.

Causes

And in their causes tells,—   Harp. 12.

The chorus of the ancient Causes!   Woodnotes. II. 119.

Causing

Along Thought's causing stream,   World-Soul. 70.

Cavaliers

To greet staid ancient cavaliers   May-Day. 307.

Cave

No palace but his sea-beat cave.   Frag. Poet. V. 21.

In his windy cave.   Harp. 10.

And prayers of might from martyrs' cave.   Merlin. 26.

No churl, immured in cave or den;   Saadi. 24.

Steeped in each forest cave?   Walden. 28.

Caves

Wake, echoing caves! Adirondacs. 259.

The empire of the ocean caves.   Boston. 18.

In caves and hollow trees he crept   Frag. Poet. I. 43.

In trees, with beasts, in mines and caves,   Initial Love. 99.

Of thought in their mysterious caves   Poet. 276.

And carve the coastwise mountain into
caves. Seashore. 13.
And fear what foe in caves and swamps
can stray, Woodnotes. I. 87.

Cease
In love, he cannot therefore cease his
trade; Philosopher. 3.

Ceased
When he ceased to love me, Gifts. 3.

Cedar
Oak, cedar, maple, poplar, beech and fir,
Adirondacs. 38.
And cedar grove and cliff
Adirondacs. 254.
Or cedar incorruptible, House. 7.

Celebrate
Do these celebrate their loves:
Celestial Love. 100.
Knowing well to celebrate May-Day. 267.
Still celebrate their funerals,
Woodnotes. II. 226.

Celerities
Now speed the gay celerities of art,
Adirondacs. 320.

Celestial
Hear you, then, celestial fellows!
Alphonso. 59.
Read the celestial sign! Monadnoc. 14.
Of a celestial Ceres and the Muse?
Monadnoc. 357.
Stole over the celestial kind, Uriel. 44.

Cell
A cell for prayer, a hall for joy,—
Dirge. 31.
Painting with morn each annual cell?
Problem. 28.
Low and tender in the cell
Voluntaries. 5.
That's writ upon our cell;
World-Soul. 46.

Cellars
Finds them who in cellars be;
World-Soul. 34.

Censer
Yet the censer cannot know.
Song of Seyd. 18.

Cent
But for tribute never a cent.'
Boston. 75.

Centennial
The wood was sovran with centennial
trees,— Adirondacs. 37.
With their centennial wrecks. Letter. 13.

Central
As he holds down central fires
Frag. Nat. I. 15.
What central flowing forces, say,
Frag. Nat. XI. 1.

Centre
But, to his native centre fast,
Culture. 9.
Love works at the centre, Sphinx. 101.
The centre of the troop allied,
Threnody. 67.

Centred
See Self-centred.
From centred and from errant sphere.
Beauty. 14.

Centres
Nature centres into balls, Circles. 1.

Centuries
He left, though goodly centuries old,
Frag. Nat. VI. 7.
Nor sequent centuries could hit
Solution. 39.
Gathering along the centuries
Song of Nature. 14.
From air the creeping centuries drew
Wealth. 13.
My hours are peaceful centuries.
Woodnotes. II. 136.
Thou metest him by centuries,
Woodnotes. II. 307.

Century
Declares the close of its green century.
Woodnotes. I. 75.

Ceremony
Fenced by form and ceremony,
Frag. Poet. I. 28.

Ceres
Of a celestial Ceres and the Muse?
Monadnoc. 357.

Certain
See Uncertain.

Certify
Can certify possession; Amulet. 10.

Cerulean
He could condense cerulean ether
Frag. Poet. XXIII. 1.
Within the air's cerulean round,—
Threnody. 14.

Chafe
Though love repine, and reason chafe,
Quat. Sacrifice. 1.

Chaff
Leave the chaff, and take the wheat.
Humble-Bee. 57.

Chagrin
Nor haughty hope, nor swart chagrin,
Past. 8.

Chain
See Unchain.
And henceforth there shall be no chain,
Concord Ode. 29.
Should throb until he snapped his chain.
Freedom. 4.
A subtle chain of countless rings
May-Day. 79.
Bad men it will chain and cage—
Merlin's Song. 7.
Link in the Alps' globe-girding chain;
Monadnoc. 85.
A subtle chain of countless rings
Nature. Mot. 1.
Could chain the wheel of Fortune's car,
Poet. 166.
The heavy blue chain Tal. Exile. 1.
And his chain when life was done.
Voluntaries. 12.
They forbore to break the chain
Voluntaries. 27.

Chained
Chained the sunshine and the breeze,
Guy. 8.

Chains
Piling mountain chains of phlegm
Frag. Nat. I. 13.
The chains of kind Hermione. 67.
Spilling over mountain chains,
May-Day. 242.

Chains —*Continued*
Where a captive sits in chains,
           Voluntaries. 6.
Mountain chains he can unlock:
           Worship. 6.

Chair
The rainbow hours bedeck his glowing
  chair,   Adirondacs. 226.
Nor to learned jurist's chair;
           Astraea. 14.

Chalice
From all the seas of strength Fate filled
  a chalice,   Day's Ration. 2.
Saying, 'This be thy portion, child; this
  chalice,   Day's Ration. 3.

Chalk
They say, through patience, chalk
           They. 1.
The chalk is crimson grown. They. 4.

Challenging
Challenging Echo by our guns and cries;
        Adirondacs. 113.
I challenge thee to hurry past Nun. 31.
I too therein could challenge part
         Security. 11.

Chamber
One chamber held ye all; Dirge. 54.
In the chamber, on the stairs,
        Frag. Life. VIII. 1.
In her hundred-gated Thebes every
  chamber was a door,
        Frag. Nat. XII. 2.
Weave your chamber weatherproof;
        Frag. Nat. XXIII. 12.
On from hall to chamber ran,
        May-Day. 346.
Here weave your chamber weather-proof,
        May-Day. 401.

Chambered
    See Many-chambered.

Chambers
In well-hung chambers daintily bestowed,
        Adirondacs. 51.
Chambers of the great are jails,
        Heroism. 9.
Through crimson chambers, porphry and
  pearl,   October. 7.
Through smallest chambers takes its way,
        Threnody. 218.
Vice nestles in your chambers,
        World-Soul. 11.

Champion
Thou living champion of the right?
        In Memoriam. 30.

Champlain
We crossed Champlain to Keeseville with
  our friends,   Adirondacs. 1.

Chance
    See Perchance.
Nor when in fair saloons we chance to
  meet;   Frag. Life. XV. 4.
And sweet varieties of chance,
        Monadnoc. 62.
On sons of time and chance, Poet. 244.
If from home chance draw me wide,
        Una. 7.

Chance-dropped
And chance-dropped hints from Nature's
  sphere   Initial Love. 72.

Change
And greet unanimous the joyful
  change.   Adirondacs. 53.
Though it change every minute.
        Ellen South. 4.
To change and to flow, Illusions. 27.
And a change has passed on things.
        May-Day. 34.
Count your change and cheer the best.
        May-Day. 368.
Graced by each change of sum untold,
        Monadnoc. 56.
Change the running sand to corn;
        Monadnoc. 138.
Change acts, reacts; back, forward hurled,
        Poet. 175.
Or the speeding change of water,
        Uriel. 52.
Change I may, but I pass not.
        Woodnotes. II. 255.

Changeable
    See Interchangeable.

Changed
    See Unchanged.
And presently the sky is changed; O
  world!   Adirondacs. 211.
When wrath and terror changed Jove's
  regal port, Frag. Life XXXIV. 1.
Time and tide are strangely changed,
        Initial Love. 7.
But mark what changed my joy to
  fright,—   Miracle. 26.
Have changed not less the guest of gods;
        Poet. 180.

Changes
By million changes skilled to tell
        Monadnoc. **86.**
Not to regret the changes, tho' they cost
        River. 20.
Giving a hint of that which changes not.
        Seashore. 26.
From world to world the godhead
  changes; Woodnotes. II. 296.

Changing
Your letter tells, O changing child!
        Amulet. 3.
In changing moon and tidal wave
        II Compensation. 5.
Or changing colors of the sky,
        Frag. Nat. XXXII. 2.

Channel
Me for the channel of the rivers of God
        Frag. Life. XV. 7.
Or through their channel dry;
        Woodnotes. I. 124.

Channels
Through the channels of that feature,
        Visit. 14.

Chant
They chant the bliss of their abodes
        Garden. 43.
In mightier chant I disappear.
        Monadnoc. 227.
Henceforth I prize thy wiry chant
        Titmouse. 89.

Chanted
Chanted when the sphere was young.
        Woodnotes. II. 99.

Chanting
Trances the heart through chanting
  choirs,   Problem. 53.

Chants
The silent organ loudest chants
Dirge. 59.
He paints, he carves, he chants, he prays,
Initial Love. 116.
Chants his hymn to hills and floods,
Woodnotes II. 34.
Chaos
Urging astonished Choas with a thrill
Adirondacs. 264.
To weltering Chaos and to sleep.
Alphonso. 30.
Shall hear far Chaos talk with me;
Bacchus. 39.
Back, back to chaos, harlot Day!
Chartist. 18.
When Chaos and Order strove,
Cosmos. 2, 6.
From Chaos to the dawning morrow;
May-Day. 460.
Bead-eyes my granite chaos show,
Monadnoc. 317.
Or tapers light the chaos dark?
Nemesis. 12.
The gray old gods whom Chaos knew,
Waldeinsamkeit. 35.
And, out of slime and chaos, Wit
Wealth. 32.
Chapel
In a chapel, which the dew
Frag. Nat. III. 6.
Chapels
As chapels in the city's thoroughfares,
Adirondacs. 195.
Chaplet
Nor chaplet on his head or hand.
Initial Love. 18.
Character
Things writ in vaster character;
Frag. Poet. V. 46.
Song, picture, form, space, thought and
character   Xenophanes. 7.
Characters
I wrote the past in characters
Song of Nature. 21.
Charge
See Surcharge.
For the Muse gave special charge
Poet. 39.
Takes hearts like thine in special charge,
Titmouse. 86.
Charged
Straitly charged him, 'Sit aloof;'
Saadi. 12.
Chariot
The seasons chariot him from this exile,
Adirondacs. 225.
With his chariot and his care;
Woodnotes. II. 27.
Charitable
With charitable Time   To J. W. 7.
Charities
Thy churches and thy charities;
Woodnotes. II. 230.
To him who scorns their charities
World-Soul. 95.
Charity
Dealt out with a God's charity.
Mountain. 13.
Blessing all lands with its charity;
Woodnotes. II. 241.

Charm
And charm the anguish of the worst.
Aeolian Harp. 23.
But whether you charm me,
Destiny. 42.
Far-heard, lows not thine ear to charm;
Each. 4.
Who charm the more their glance for-
bids,   Eva. 10.
This charm is wasted on the earth and
sky,   Rhodora. 10.
Charmed
Charmed from fagot and from steel,
Frag. Poet. V. 30.
Into the charmed snare she shuns;
Nemesis. 6.
And every wave is charmed,'
Terminus. 40.
'Twas one of the charmèd days
Woodnotes. I. 96.
Charmer
Charmer who will be believed
Frag. Nat. XXXI. 5.
Charms
It charms his cares to sleep,   Bell. 7.
And for travelled eyes what charms
Frag. Nat. XXVI. 3.
And lakes, smooth mirrors of Aurora's
charms.   I Bear. 8.
And a few joys, a few peculiar charms,
Naples. 10.
Chart
That were Freedom's whitest chart.
Etienne. 24.
I put no faith in pilot or in chart,
Unbar. 3.
Charters
Of critic charters, an unlaurelled Muse.
To-day. 8.
Chase
This wild plantation will suffice to chase.
Adirondacs. 319.
Let me chase thy waving lines;
Humble-Bee. 8.
The mountain chase, the summer waves,
To J. W. 3.
Chased
Beauty chased he everywhere,
Beauty. 5.
Over whose flowers I chased the butter-
fly,   River. 14.
Chasing
Chasing with words fast-flowing things;
nor try   Frag. Poet. XXIX. 5.
Chaste
Seeking in that chaste blue a bluer light,
Adirondacs. 209.
Grave, chaste, contented, though retired,
Woodnotes II. 69.
Chaste-glowing
Chaste-glowing, underneath their lids,
Eva. 11.
Chastened
Will thy clear blue eye, upward bent, still
keep its chastened glow,   *Violet. 3.
Chattel
'T is the day of the chattel,
Channing Ode. 48.
Chatter
To chatter, frightened, to his clan
Monadnoc. 346.

Chatter —*Continued*
What men chatter know I not.
                Song of Seyd. 34.
Chaucer
Chaucer had no such worthy crew,
                Adirondacs. Motto. 3.
Cheap
And, on cheap summit-levels of the snow,
                Musketaquid. 44.
Cheapens
And court the flower that cheapens his
    array.   Rhodora. 8.
Cheat
Beauty is unripe childhood's cheat;
                Each. 38.
Check
Go, without check or intervals,
                Celestial Love. 24.
Holds in check the frolic light,
                Solution. 44.
Checked
Checked in these souls the turbulent
    heyday   Adirondacs. 189.
Checked by the owners' fierce disdain,
                Voluntaries. 29.
Checkerberry
Sweet willow, checkerberry red,
                Frag. Nat. II. 23.
Checks
And prizes of ambition, checks its hand,
                Blight. 59.
Cheek
Orange cheek or skin of man.
                Alphonso. 12.
Touches a cheek with colors of romance,
                Enchanter. 6.
Upon my cheek to stay;   *Farewell. 24.
Already blushes on thy cheek
                Nemesis. 1.
Scarce the first blush has overspread his
    cheek,   Philosopher. 4.
Has quenched the uneasy blush that
    warmed my cheek;   Summons. 2.
In whose cheek the rose-leaf blusheth,
                Woodnotes II. 39.
Thy cheek too white, thy form too
    slender,   Woodnotes. II. 186.
Cheeked
    See Yellow-cheeked.
Cheek's
Go, keep your cheek's rose from the rain,
                Romany. 17.
Cheeks
His cheeks mantle with mirth;
                World-Soul. 102.
Cheer
Unlocks new sense and loftier cheer.
                Aeolian Harp. 17.
Almost a smile to steal to cheer her sons,
                Adirondacs. 342.
To offer the exile cheer.   Exile. 8.
Be of good cheer, brave spirit; stead-
    fastly   Good Cheer. 1.
Firmest cheer, and bird-like pleasure.
                Humble-Bee. 39.
With social cheer and jubilee;
                May-Day. 167.
With tender light and youthful cheer,
                May-Day. 269.
Count your change and cheer the best.
                May-Day. 368.

Good men it will calm and cheer,
                Merlin's Song. 6.
The Indian cheer, the frosty skies,
                Monadnoc. 106.
In tavern cheer and tavern joke,
                Monadnoc. 120.
I hearken for thy household cheer,
                Threnody. 36.
In a voice of solemn cheer,—
                Woodnotes. II. 147.
The letters do not cheer;
                World-Soul. 18.
Cheered
Till Freedom cheered and joy-bells rung.
                Boston. 99.
That cheered the holy light!
                *Farewell. 2.
With faerie gardens cheered,
                Frag. Nat. X. 2.
Cheerer
Zigzag steerer, desert cheerer,
                Humble-Bee. 7.
The cheerer of men's hearts.   Saadi. 48.
Cheerful
Thus to play its cheerful part,   Art. 20.
And the cheerful round of work.
                Celestial Love. 106.
And with a cheerful benison forsake
                Letter. 5.
While cheerful cries of crag and plain
                May-Day. 239.
Broad-sowing, cheerful, plenteous,
                May-Day. 272.
Pouring many a cheerful river;
                Monadnoc. 41.
Comes that cheerful troubadour,
                Monadnoc. 287.
Peals out a cheerful song.   Music. 6.
Gay and polite, a cheerful cry,
                Titmouse. 26.
And the sky doats on cheerful song.
                Titmouse. 88.
Cheerfully
Aloud and cheerfully,   Sphinx. 66.
Cheerly
Their wonted convenance, cheerly hid
    the loss   Adirondacs. 181.
Forms more cheerly live and go,
                Merlin. 43.
Cheers
It cheers him as he sails.   Bell. 8.
He sings the song, but it cheers not now,
                Each. 16.
Cheers the rough crag and mournful dell,
                Frag. Nat. XXIX. 2.
Chemic
Weatherglass and chemic phial,
                Monadnoc. 53.
How the chemic eddies play,
                Monadnoc. 229.
They turn the frost upon their chemic
    heap,   Musketaquid. 41.
Or from fruit of chemic force,
                Uriel. 50.
Of chemic matter, force and form,
                Woodnotes. II. 110.
Chemist
All substances the cunning chemist Time
                Day's Ration. 6.
Chemist to vamp old worlds with new,
                May-Day. 445.

And, like the chemist 'mid his loaded jars,
Musketaquid. 38.

Chemistry
Their fragrance, and their chemistry
apply   Blight. 11.
And an omnipotence in chemistry,
Blight. 25.

Cherish
That thou might'st cherish for thine own
Threnody. 221

Cherry
As you spin a cherry.   Mithridates. 24.

Cherub
Came Uriel's voice of cherub scorn,
Uriel. 54.

Cherubim
That God has cherubim who go
Dull. 3.

Cherub's
The Seraph's and the Cherub's food.
Saadi. 162.

Cheshire
Dark flower of Cheshire garden,
Monadnoc Afar. 1.

Cheshire's
I turned to Cheshire's haughty hill.
Monadnoc. 32.

Chest
And, chest by chest, let down the same,
Boston. 78.
What fire burns in that little chest
Titmouse. 52.

Chic-a-dee-dee
And, in winter, Chic-a-dee-dee!
Titmouse. 94.

Chic-chic-a-dee-dee
Chic-chic-a-dee-dee! saucy note
Titmouse. 27.

Chick
And every chick of every bird,
Threnody. 114.

Chickadee
In Walden wood the chickadee
Frag. Nat. XIX. 1.

Chid
Whom earlier we had chid with spiteful
names.   Adirondacs. 170.

Chide
Nor Fortune, nor thy coldness, can I
chide,   Angelo. 11.
Chide me not, laborious band,
Apology. 9.
The hardy bunting does not chide;
May-Day. 165.
Trembler, do not whine and chide:
Sursum Corda. 3.

Chidest
Why chidest thou the tardy Spring?
May-Day. 164.

Chiding
I heard or seemed to hear the chiding Sea
Seashore. 1.

Chief
Chief of song where poets feast
Harp. 38.
If once the generous chief arrive
Voluntaries. 55.
To the valiant chief who fights;
Voluntaries. 107.

Chiefest
And, chiefest prize, found I true liberty
Musketaquid. 66.

Chiefly
Wonderer chiefly at himself,
Woodnotes. I. 26.

Chiefs
Say not, the chiefs who first arrive
Merlin's Song. 16.

Chieftain
And he the chieftain paced beside,
Threnody. 66.

Child
See Man-child.
Your letter tells, O changing child!
Amulet. 3.
Is early frugal, like a beggar's child;
Blight. 57.
Each child shall have his school.
Boston. 34.
Fear not, then, thou child infirm,
II. Compensation. 19.
Child and brother from his birth,
Daemonic Love. 2.
Saying, 'This be thy portion, child; this
chalice,   Day's Ration. 3.
Wins the believing child with wondrous
tales;   Enchanter. 5.
Child of the omnific Need,
Frag. Life. XXIII. 7.
Like a flower-hunting child;
Initial Love. 97
Child and parent,   Limits. 8.
And ever when the happy child
May-Day. 98.
Bring to fair mother fairer child,
May-Day. 452.
Strong as giant, slow as child.
Monadnoc. 132.
Of Nature's child the common fate.
Mountain. 21.
The gallant child where'er he came
Poet. 7.
A blooming child to children dear,
Poet. 49.
The child of genius sits forlorn:
Poet. 182.
And they so pure? He, foolish child,
Poet. 206.
To every child they wake,
Promise. 8.
By beauty of a mortal child   Rhea. 42.
Here is the rock where, yet a simple
child,   River. 11.
And he, the wondrous child,
Threnody. 11
O eloquent child!   Threnody. 37.
Could stoop to heal that only child,
Threnody. 122.
This child should ills of ages stay,
Threnody. 135.
O child of paradise,   Threnody. 166.
If I had not taken the child.
Threnody. 178.
The planets' child the planet knows
Waterfall. 13.
To the conscience of a child.
Wealth. 49.
The public child of earth and sky.
Woodnotes. I. 117.

Child—*Continued*
To float my child to victory,
       Woodnotes. II. 46.
But thou, poor child! unbound, un-
rhymed,   Woodnotes. II. 178.
Love shuns the sage, the child it crowns,
       Woodnotes. II. 236.

Childhood
Names from awful childhood heard
       Daemonic Love. 7.
Which once our childhood knew;
       Dirge. 38.
Did in your childhood fall.   Dirge. 56.

Childhood's
And greeted God with childhood's
psalms.   Dirge. 8.
Beauty is unripe childhood's cheat;
       Each. 38.
Ah me! it was my childhood's thought,
       Nun. 7
And childhood's castles built or planned;
       Threnody. 87.

Children
His children fed at heavenly tables.
       Art. 18.
Fond children, ye desire
       Celestial Love. 6.
To die, and leave their children free,
       C. Hymn. 14.
Darlings of children and of bard,
       Frag. Nat. XXIII. 1.
To the children who have faith;
       Harp. 33.
Only to children children sing,
       Harp. 34.
Beloved of children bards and Spring,
       May-Day. 396.
A blooming child to children dear,
       Poet. 49.
Yet here their children pray,
       Robbins Hymn. 22.
With children forward and behind,
       Threnody. 64.

Children's
Which children's voices bless.
       Concord Ode. 8.
Saying, ''Tis mine, my children's and my
name's.   Hamatreya. 5.
To be the children's toy.   Holidays. 4.
The kind Earth takes her children's part,
       May-Day. 66.

Child's
Has turned my child's head?''
       Sphinx. 64.

Chill
Chill and wet, unlighted, mean,
       Chartist. 4.
Like lust in the chill of the grave.
       Hamatreya. 63.
With my north wind chill his blood;
       Monadnoc. 341.

Chilled
Chilled by a ribald jeer.   Voluntaries. 22.
Chilled with a miserly comparison
       Blight. 61.
Chilled wading in the snow-choked wood.
       Titmouse. 4.

Chills
It chills my life, but wittily,
       Frag. Nat. XXIV. 4.
Chills the limbs of Time;   Poet. 294.

When Autumn chills the plain.
       Walden. 8.

Chime
Seas ebbed and flowed in epic chime.
       Beauty. 16.
I love thine iron chime,   Bell. 2.
The joy-bells chime their tidings down,
       Concord Ode. 7.
I heard no church-bell chime,
       Frag. Nat. XXV. 2.
Canst thou copy in verse one chime
       Garden. 37.

Chimes
Primal chimes of sun and shade,
       Woodnotes. II. 160.

Chiming
Chiming with the forest tone,
       Merlin. 17.
Chiming with the gasp and moan
       Merlin. 19.

Chimney-pot
Each chimney-pot and cottage door,
       Poet. 58.

China
The bald antiquity of China praise.
       To-Day. 16.

Chink
Every tree and stem and chink
       May-Day. 340.
Steal in by window, chink, or hole,
       Past. 17.

Chips
For flute or spinet's dancing chips;
       Aeolian Harp. 5.
Who builds, makes no chips, no din,
       Monadnoc. 239.

Chirp
Hark to that petulant chirp! what ails
the warbler?   Adirondacs. 206.

Chirped,
Each snowbird chirped,
       Threnody. 105.

Chirping
In his flippant chirping babble,
       Miracle. 34.

Choice
Biding by his rule and choice,
       Voluntaries. 87.

Choir
And the mighty choir descends,
       Daemonic Love. 44.
Was woven still by the snow-white choir.
       Each. 32.
There is no bard in all the choir,
       Harp. 75.

Choirs
Hafiz and Shakespeare with their shining
choirs.   Adakryn. 5.
Trances the heart through chanting
choirs,   Problem. 53.

Choked
    See Snow-choked.
Till these echoes be choked with snows,
       Boston. 104.
Knee-deep snows choked all the ways,
       May-Day. 37.

Choose
Choose him to be your king;
       Boston Hymn. 14.
They shall choose men to rule
       Boston Hymn. 42.

'Fairest, choose the fairest members
Ellen South. 25.
Slow and warily to choose   House. 5.
I choose a novel theme, a bold abuse
To-Day. 7.

Chooses
To me the heart Fate for me chooses.
Ode To Beauty. 45.

Choosing
Choosing light, wave, rock and bird,
Woodnotes. II. 59.

Choppers
Fishers and choppers and ploughmen
Boston Hymn. 31.

Choral
Hearkens for the choral glee,
May-Day. 84.
I greet with joy the choral trains
May-Day. 392.

Chord
And best can teach its Delphian chord
Harp. 103.
To touch with prophet's hand the chord
Hymn. 15.

Chords
Its chords should ring as blows the
breeze,   Merlin. 3.
Must smite the chords rudely and hard,
Merlin. 10.
On his tense chords all strokes were felt,
Poet. 210.

Chorus
Far distant yet his chorus waits.
Garden. 36.
Into chorus wove.   Merlin. 99.
The chorus of the ancient Causes!
Woodnotes. II. 119.

Chose
We chose our boats; each man a boat
and guide,—   Adirondacs. 5.
Like meteors which chose their way
Poet. 55.

Chosen
Every one to his chosen work;—
Channing Ode. 75.
Graceful women, chosen men,
Manners. 3.

Christian
And groined the aisles of Christian Rome
Problem. 20.

Christ's
Of Lord Christ's heart, and Shakespeare's strain.   Informing Spirit. 8.

Chronic
"Chronic dyspepsia never came from eating   Adirondacs. 185.

Chronicle
'Tis the chronicle of art.
Woodnotes. II. 103.

Chronicles
Whereof old chronicles relate
Frag. Nat. XXVI. 33.

Chrysostom
Old Chrysostom, best Augustine,
Problem. 65.

Church
  See Church-bell.
Nor hymn, nor prayer, nor church.
Bohemian. 12.
In church and state and school.
Boston Hymn. 44.

When the Church is social worth,
Politics. 23.
I like a church; I like a cowl;
Problem. 1.
And in the church a blessing found
Robbins Hymn. 15.
And, though thy rede be church or state,
Visit. 25.

Church-bell
I heard no church-bell chime,
Frag. Nat. XXV. 2.

Churches
Thy churches and thy charities;
Woodnotes. II: 230.

Churchman
Would I that cowlèd churchman be.
Problem. 6.

Churl
Served high and low, the lord and the
churl,   Frag. Poet. I. 20.
No churl, immured in cave or den;
Saadi. 24.
He is no churl nor trifler,
World-Soul. 81.

Churls
Bow to the stalwart churls in overalls:
Adirondacs. 94.
Thou foolish Hafiz! Say, do churls
Friendship. Trans. 1.
And end in churls the mountain folk
Monadnoc. 119.

Chrysolite
The inward sky with chrysolite,
Una. 14.

Cicero
It spoke in Tullius Cicero,
Frag. Poet. IV. 30.

Cinders
Under the cinders burned the fires of
home;   Adirondacs. 333.

Cinquefoil
Rue, cinquefoil, gill, vervain and agrimony,   Blight. 5.

Cinquefoils
Cinquefoils or violets in the grass,
Frag. Poet. XXVIII. 5.

Cipher
We cannot learn cipher
World-Soul. 45.

Circle
In the circle of the earth;
Woodnotes. II. 199.

Circled
That circled freshly in their forest dress
Adirondacs. 60.

Circles
The circles of that sea are laws
Celestial Love. 58.
And round their circles is writ,
Initial Love. 41.

Circling
Whose streams through Nature cricling
go?   Threnody. 239.

Circulates
Blood is blood which circulates,
Threnody. 243.

Circulation
On the wave's circulation,   Illusions. 23.

Circumnavigate
Who cannot circumnavigate the sea
Day's Ration. 30.

Circumspect
By circumspect ambition,
Monadnoc. 398.

Circumstance
Reach his place and circumstance,
Monadnoc. 253.

Circus
Like vaulters in a circus round
Frag. Poet. XIX. 1.

Cit
Which past endurance sting the tender
cit,   Adirondacs. 174.

Citadel
Up! where the airy citadel
Monadnoc. 10.

Cities
We flee away from cities, but we bring
Adirondacs. 302.
The best of cities with us, these learned
classifiers,   Adirondacs. 303.
What care though rival cities soar
Boston. 45.
In cities he was low and mean;
Frag. Poet. V. 16.
And leave the cities void.   Garden. 4.
Eyes that frame cities where none be,
Monadnoc. 108.
Saw rivers run seaward by cities high
Poet. 65.
And cities rise where cities burn,
Saadi. 112.
Cities of mortals woe-begone
Waldeinsamkeit. 13.
In cities high the careful crowds
Walden. 17.
Cities of proud hotels,   World-Soul. 9.
And what it Trade sow cities
World-Soul. 65.

City
No city airs or arts   Adirondacs. 92.
Spy behind the city clock   Art. 14.
A city of the poor;—   Boston. 22.
In city or in solitude,   May-Day. 463.
With the din of city arts;   Merlin. 23.
And what they call their city way
Nature. II. 9.
The leafy dell, the city mart,
Ode To Beauty. 88.
By court and city, dale and down,
Walk. 3.

City's
As chapels in the city's thoroughfares,
Adirondacs. 195.
On the city's paved street   Art. 5.
Whom the city's poisoning spleen
Woodnotes. II. 35.

City-tops
His city-tops a glimmering haze.
Monadnoc. 323.

City Wharf
From South Cove and City Wharf.
Monadnoc. 314.

Civil
He left each civil scale behind:
Frag. Poet. I. 32.
The civil world will much forgive
Frag. Poet. IV. 1.
And earth grow civil, Homer sung.
Solution. 16.

Civilization
Civilization well;   Frag. Nat. XXIV. 2.

Claim
The ill I shun, the good I claim;
Angelo. 7.
Assured that he who made the claim,
Monadnoc. 28.

Clairvoyance
In magic and in clairvoyance,
Initial Love. 65.

Claithing
In braw claithing drest?   Riches. 6.

Clamorous
Where darkling feed the clamorous clans
May-Day. 28.

Clan
At the sophist schools and the learned
clan;   Good-Bye. 28.
To chatter, frightened, to his clan
Monadnoc. 346.

Clans
Where darkling feed the clamorous clans
May-Day. 28.

Clarion
Nor Byron's clarion of disdain,
Harp. 80.
Seemed, when at last his clarion accents
broke,   Phi. 11.
Him duty through the clarion calling
Voluntaries. 95.

Clarionet
Or clarionet of jay? or hark
May-Day. 22.

Classes
While classes or tribes, too weak to
master   Frag. Life. XXXI. 3.

Classifiers
The best of cities with us, these learned
classifiers,   Adirondacs. 303.

Clattering
I lame him, clattering down the rocks;
Monadnoc. 342.

Clay
As a self of purer clay,   Give. 44.
Mortal mixed of middle clay,   Guy. 1.
We must have clay, lime, gravel, granite-
ledge,   Hamatreya. 20.
Build and unbuild our echoing clay,
Merlin. 127.
Something of pity for the puny clay,
River. 34.
Stooping, his finger wrote in clay
Solution. 69.
I rake no coffined clay, nor publish wide
To-Day. 1.
The clay of their departed lover.'
Woodnotes. I. 146.

Clayed
This thin spruce roof, this clayed log-
wall,   Adirondacs. 318.

Clean
See Unclean.
To climb a lofty stem, clean without
boughs   Adirondacs. 83.
Steads not to work on the clean jump,
Alphonso. 61.
The mountains waters washed him clean
Frag. Poet. V. 17.
Clean swept herefrom.   Hamatreya. 52.
Clean shall he be, without, within,
Woodnotes. II. 63.

Cleanness
Without cleanness, without rest.
Riches. 4.

Cleanse
Cleanse the torrent at the fountain,
May-Day. 450

Clear
See Sun-clear.
And, wheresoever their clear eye-beams fell, Blight. 28.
It is clear Frag. Life. XXXIII. 4.
A clear and glorious firmament
Frag. Nat. XXVI. 28.
By searching of a clear and loving eye
Good Cheer. 11.
Clear of the grave. Hamatreya. 16.
Will clear his fame from every cloud
Initial Love. 86.
Till a clear voice spoke,— *Lines. 27.
Free, peremptory, clear. Merlin. 4.
And all is clear from east to west.
Nature. Mot 12.
And prayed the eternal Light to clear
Robbins Hymn. 11.
Her muddy eyes to clear!"
Sphinx. 108.
And all is clear from east to west.
Threnody. 208.
Will thy clear blue eye, upward bent, still keep its chastened glow,
*Violet. 3.
in the clear autumn day. *Violet. 6.
Where his clear spirit leads him, there's his road Woodnotes. I. 94.
Or south, it still is clear;
Woodnotes. I. 101.
To every soul resounding clear
Woodnotes. II. 146.
The voice that speaketh clear.
World-Soul. 20.

Cleared
Not tamed and cleared cumber the ground Letter. 12.

Clearly
Not clearly voiced, Adirondacs. 204.
After their own genius, clearly,
Celestial Love. 122.

Cleave
If earth-fire cleave Channing Ode. 29.
Laurel crowns cleave to deserts,
II. Compensation. 21.
But the meanings cleave to the lake,
Garden. 57.
Wedge-like cleave the air the birds,
Saadi. 4.

Cleaving
See Sky-cleaving.

Clergy
Spare the clergy and libraries,
Monadnoc. 181.

Clerk
Pants up hither the spruce clerk
Monadnoc. 313.

Clerks
And, in the forest, delicate clerks, un-browned, Adirondacs. 57.
And clerks the Janus-gates unbar,
Solution. 62.

Clerks'
Past clerks' or statesmen's art or passion.
Monadnoc. 178.

Clew
And thank thee for a better clew,
Titmouse. 100.

Cliff
And cedar grove and cliff and lake should know Adirondacs. 254.
Are touched with genius. Yonder ragged cliff Musketaquid. 24.
When thou shalt climb the mountain cliff,
Woodnotes. II. 194.

Climate
My breath thy healthful climate in the heats, Seashore. 5.
Creating a sweet climate by my breath,
Seashore. 23.

Climate's
Or mired by climate's gross extremes.
Nun. 36.

Climates
Drugged with spice from climates warm,
Hermione. 52.
In climates of the summer star.
Voluntaries. 50.

Climb
Between two rocky arms, we climb the bank, Adirondacs. 31.
To cilmb a lofty stem, Adirondacs. 83.
Teach him on these as stairs to climb,
Art. 25.
Ye shall climb on the heavenly stair,
Celestial Love. 9.
Up which the incarnate soul must climb,
Dirge. 2.
Climb to their tops, Frag. Nat. III. 19.
Who climb each night the ancient sky,
Frag. Nat. VIII. 6.
How graceful climb those shadows on my hill! Hamatreya. 7.
We will climb the broad-backed hills,
May-Day. 226.
He shall aye climb Merlin. 32.
Only the light-armed climb the hill.
Merlin's Song. 28.
None save dappling shadows climb,
Monadnoc. 202.
Who daily climb my specular head.
Monadnoc. 310.
Ere one man my hill shall climb,
Saadi. 113.
When thou shalt climb the mountain cliff, Woodnotes. II. 194.

Climbed
See Half-climbed.
This morn I climbed the misty hill
Thine Eyes. 5.

Climbing
Climbing the northern zones,
May-Day. 253.
Mark how the climbing Oreads
Monadnoc. 19.

Climbs
He dives the hollow, climbs the steep.
May-Day. 72.

Clime
Where thou art is clime for me.
Humble-Bee. 2.

Cling
Cling with life to the maid; Give. 34.

Clinging
Head downward, clinging to the spray.
Titmouse. 42.

Clinging —*Continued*
Clinging to a colder zone
     Voluntaries. 39.
Clings
Firm to Heaven my bosom clings,
     Song of Seyd. 31.
Clio
The shell of Clio rung.
     Frag. Poet. XXXV. 3.
Clip
The seas their islands clip, II. Eros. 3.
Cloak
Was neither cloak nor crumb my own.
     Frag. Poet. IV. 14.
Loiter not for cloak or food;
     Freedom. 23.
Cloaked
 See Red-cloaked.
Clock
Spy behind the city clock Art. 14.
The sea-beat scorns the minster clock
     Frag. Nat. XXV. 3.
Clods
Fate's grass grows rank in valley clods,
     Voluntaries. 119.
Close
 See Disclose; Enclose.
Close, close to men, Daemonic Love. 23.
Of close low pine-woods Naples. 14.
Works in close conspiracy;
     Ode To Beauty. 83.
watching close behind Philosopher. 9.
When Winter reigned I'd close my eye,
 but wake with bursting Spring,
     *Violet. 11.
Declares the close of its green century.
     Woodnotes. I. 75.
The shadow sits close to the flying ball;
     Woodnotes. II. 244.
Closed
The gate of gifts behind him closed.
     Quat. Horoscope. 4.
The babe in willow wagon closed,
     Threnody. 62.
Cloth
 See Haircloth.
Your rank is all reversed; let men of
 cloth   Adirondacs. 93.
Hid their majesty in cloth
     May-Day. 329.
Clothe
Then clothe these hands with power
     Poet. 245.
To clothe the fiery thought
     Quat. Poet. 2. 1.
The granite slab to clothe and hide,
     Wealth. 16
Clothed
Ask on, thou clothed eternity;
     Sphinx. 119.
Clothing-weeds
Times wore he as his clothing-weeds,
     Poet. 31.
Cloud
 See Thundercloud.
Which o'erhung, like a cloud, our camp-
 ing fire.   Adirondacs. 47.
Worthy the enormous cloud of witnesses,
     Adirondacs. 247.

Each cloud that floated in the sky
     Apology. 7.
The sun athwart the cloud thought it no
 sin   Frag. Nat. IX. 1.
They love me, as I love a cloud
     Frag. Poet. VII.16.
His hired hands were wind and cloud;
     Frag. Poet. XXVII. 2.
Age cannot cloud his memory,
     Harp. 5.
Hills and islands, cloud and tree,
     Hermione. 14.
Will clear his fame from every cloud
     Initial Love. 86.
The silver cloud, In Memoriam. 19.
The saffron cloud that floated warm
     Lines. 15.
The cloud was around me, *Lines. 9.
Flew off in the cloud. *Lines. 24.
To fool me with a shining cloud,
     May-Day. 364.
Minorities, things under cloud!
     Mithridates. 30.
I scowl on him with my cloud,
     Monadnoc. 340.
By cloud or isle, is flying home;
     Nemesis. 4.
And the sailing moon where the cloud
 was rent,   Poet. 68.
Out shone a star beneath the cloud,
     Poet. 229.
Without cloud, in its eyes; Sphinx. 46.
She melted into purple cloud,
     Sphinx. 123.
The moon thy mourner, and the cloud.
     Titmouse. 22.
Withdrew, that hour, into his cloud;
     Uriel. 38.
Far beholding, without cloud,
     Voluntaries. 53.
Of the tree and of the cloud.
     Woodnotes. I. 111.
To hill and cloud his face was known,—
     Woodnotes. I. 114.
Its way up to the cloud and wind;
     Woodnotes. II. 243.
Clouded
A train of gay and clouded days
     Frag. Life. I. 1.
Una lights my clouded dreams;
     Una. 2.
Cloudless
In their cloudless periods; Rhea. 26.
Cloud-rack
From the fixed cone the cloud-rack
 flowed   Monadnoc. 33.
Clouds
 See Thunder-clouds.
And, on the instant, rosier clouds upbore
     Adakryn. 4.
The clouds are rich and dark, the air
 serene,   Adirondacs. 213.
In flame, in storm, in clouds of air.
     Beauty. 6.
Clouds shade the sun, which will not tan
 our hay,   Blight. 51.
Of clouds and the boreal fleece.
     Boston Hymn. 24.
The tenfold clouds that cover Dull. 12.
And largest clouds be flakes of down in
 that enormous sky. Frag. Nat. XX. 2.

The mottled clouds, like scraps of wool,
                    Frag. Nat. XXVI. 17.
Odorous clouds;   *Lines. 6.
'Once more,' the old man cried, 'ye
    clouds,   May-Day. 349.
Under clouds, my lonely head,
                    Monadnoc. 203.
Here amid clouds to stand?
                    Monadnoc. 209.
Visits the valley;—break away the
    clouds,—   Musketaquid. 12.
Sable pageantry of clouds,   Nun. 21.
As clouds give rain to the eastern breeze,
                    Poet. 34.
Are hid behind the thrice-piled clouds;
                    Poet. 178.
A few rods off he deems it gems and
    clouds.   Seashore. 46.
Swandown clouds dappled the farms,
                    September. 6.
Dark with more clouds than the
    tempests are,   Threnody. 99.
Clouds flush their gayest dyes.
                    Waterfall. 16.
Pondering shadows, colors, clouds,
                    Woodnotes. I. 18.
The nearing clouds draw down;
                    World-Soul. 58.

Cloud-shadow
And the cloud-shadow on the lea,
                    Celestial Love. 104.

Cloudy
Like yon slow-sailing cloudy promontory
                    Adirondacs. 218.
The Genius from its cloudy throne.
                    Fate. 12.

Cloven
By the other cloven down.
                    Concord Ode. 24.
My garden is the cloven rock,
                    Woodnotes. II. 9.

Clover
April's cowslip, summer's clover,
                    Ellen South. 30.
Clover, catchfly, adder's-tongue
                    Humble-Bee. 48.

Clover-blow
In columbine and clover-blow,
                    May-Day. 252.

Clover-farm
Or east, it smells like a clover-farm;
                    Woodnotes. I. 102.

Cloverheads
With cloverheads the swamp adorn,
                    Monadnoc. 137.

Clown
Little thinks, in the field, yon red-cloaked
    clown,   Each. 1.

Clowns
Refreshed the wise, reformed the clowns,
                    May-Day. 343.
And idle clowns beside the mere
                    Poet. 21.

Cloy
Nor cloy us with unshaded sun,
                    May-Day. 128.

Club-moss
Running over the club-moss burrs;
                    Each. 42.

Clucking
On clucking hens and prating fools,
                    Woodnotes. II. 202.

Clues
The cobweb clues of Rosamond April. 7.

Clung
Province to province faithful clung,
                    Boston. 97.

Coal
The planting of the coal.
                    Song of Nature. 24.
In the safe herbal of the coal?
                    Wealth. 28.

Coarse
Swainish, coarse and nothing worth:
                    Frag. Poet. XI. 14.
Coarse and boisterous, yet mild,
                    Monadnoc. 131.

Coarseness
The coarseness of my poor attire;
                    Romany 2.

Coarsest
In coarsest weeds or in the best;
                    Destiny. 39.

Coast
And landed on our coast, and pulsating
                    Adirondacs. 240.
Along the stormy coast,   Boston. 46.
Cried him up and down the coast,
                    Initial Love. 2.
All the angles of the coast   Lines. 3.
The rocky coast, smite Andes into dust,
                    Seashore. 35.
I make some coast alluring, some lone
    isle,   Seashore. 48.
That loiters round the crystal coast,
                    Threnody. 121.
Think'st Beauty vanished from the coast
                    Threnody. 181.

Coastwise
And carve the coastwise mountain into
    caves.   Seashore. 13.

Coat
    See Surcoat.
His rank, and quartered his own coat.
                    Astraea. 2.
In my coat I bore this book,
                    Goethe. 3.
Coat sea and sky with heavenlier blue,
                    May-Day. 446.
From rabbit's coat or grouse's breast;
                    Quat. Forester. 2.
Stately marching in cap and coat
                    Threnody. 76.

Coated
    See Blue-coated.

Coats
Boy no more, he wears all coats,
                    Initial Love. 15.
Frog and lizard in holiday coats,
                    May-Day. 237

Coax
Or coax the thunder from its mark?
                    Nemesis. 11.

Cobweb
The cobweb clues of Rosamond April. 7.

Cock
    See Woodcock.

Cockles
Lie like cockles by the main,
May-Day. 255.

Coeval
They were coeval with my ancestors,
River. 140.

Coffined
I rake no coffined clay, nor publish wide
To-Day. 1.

Coffin-lid
Rattles the coffin-lid.   Channing Ode. 35.

Cohere
Thanks the atoms that cohere.
Prudence. 6.

Coil
With the coil of rhythm and number;
Merlin. 30.

Coils
Tighter wind the giant coils.
Nemesis. 16.

Coin
To coin his labor and sweat,
Boston Hymn. 62.
Nevada! coin thy golden crags
Boston Hymn. 75.
Coin the day-dawn into lines
Frag. Poet. XXIX. 1.
Coin the moonlight into verse
Frag. Poet. XXIX. 3.

Coinage
So the coinage of his brain
Monadnoc. 306.
Nor kind nor coinage buys   Politics. 7.

Coincidence
And for strange coincidence.
Inital Love. 69.

Coined
Or ever the wild Time coined itself
Uriel. 3.

Cold
Off soundings, seamen do not suffer cold;
Adirondacs. 56.
All the fierce enemies, ague, hunger, cold,
Adirondacs. 317.
Plain and cold is their address,
Celestial Love. 89.
Under Alps and Andes cold;
Frag. Nat. I. 16.
The cold gray down upon the quinces
lieth   Frag. Nat. XXXIII. 1.
Impassible to heat or cold.
Frag. Poet. I. 49.
Deaf, and dumb, and blind, and cold,
Frag. Poet. VIII. 6.
With passion cold and shy.   Harp. 120.
Even into May the iceberg cold.
May-Day. 20.
Through the cold slab a thousand gates,
May-Day. 122.
Cold is genial and dear.   May-Day. 137.
So Spring guards with surface cold
May-Day. 144.
April cold with dropping rain
May-Day. 182.
Short and bent by cold and snow;
May-Day. 313.
Earth-baking heat, stone-cleaving cold.
Monadnoc. 57.
And for cold mosses, cream and curds:
Monadnoc. 140.

And the cold and purple morning
Ode to Beauty. 86.
His cold eye truth and conduct scanned,
Quat. S. H. 2.
Heat, cold, wet, dry, and peace, and
pain.   Song of Nature. 76.
Cold shuddered the sphere:— Sphinx. 60.
But thought will glow when the sun
grows cold,   Thought. 7.
Built he heaven stark and cold;
Threnody. 273.
When you deal with arctic cold,
Titmouse. 2.
Embalmed by purifying cold;
Titmouse. 19.
The cold sea-wind detain;   Walden. 6.
Cold April rain and colder snows
Walden. 11.
That know not fear, fatigue, or cold.
Woodnotes II. 42.
Of poles and powers, cold, wet, and
warm: Woodnotes II. 111.

Colder
Clinging to a colder zone
Voluntaries. 39.
Cold April rain and colder snows
Walden. 11.

Coldly
And coldly ask their pottage, not their
love.   Blight. 39.
But Saadi coldly thus returned,
Frag. Poet. II. 4.

Coldness
Nor Fortune, nor thy coldness, can I
chide,   Angelo. 11.

College
Was it a college pique of town and gown,
Adirondacs. 277.
I can spare the college bell,
Monadnoc. 179.
How drearily in College hall
Walden. 33.

College-halls
With budding power in college-halls,
In Memoriam. 63.

Collins'
Nor Collins' verse of tender pain,
Harp. 79.

Color
  See Sun-color.
Scent, form and color; to the flowers and
shells   Enchanter. 4.
With a color of romance,
Humble-Bee. 25.
Each color with its counter glowed;
Merlin. 82.
Mysteries of color daily laid
Monadnoc. 60.
Color and sound,   October. 10.
He took the color of his vest
Quat. Forester. 1.

Colored
  See   Leopard-colored;   Rainbow-
colored; Uncolored.
They colored the horizon round;
Dirge. 33.
Over these colored solitudes.
Frag. Nat. XXVI. 20.
And every colored petal of each flower,
Naples. 6.

So shaped, so colored, swift or still,
                          Solution. 30.

Colors
Touches a cheek with colors of romance,
                          Enchanter. 6.
Your colors for our eyes' delight:
                          Frag. Nat. XXIII. 10.
Or changing colors of the sky,
                          Frag. Nat. XXXII. 2.
What parts, what gems, what colors
  shine,—   Frag. Poet. XVIII. 5.
Bore thy colors every flower, Lines. 5.
And the colors of joy in the bird,
                          May-Day. 235.
Showed me the lore of colors and of
  sounds,   Musketaquid. 60.
The fading colors fix,   Poet. 110.
Their colors from the sky;
                          Waldeinsamkeit. 8.
Pondering shadows, colors, clouds,
                          Woodnotes. I. 18.

Colossal
Her colossal portraiture; Hermione. 21.
Is this colossal talisman   Monadnoc. 89.

Columbia
I show Columbia, of the rocks
                          Boston Hymn. 21.

Columbine
Columbine with horn of honey,
                          Frag. Nat. II. 9.
Columbine with horn of honey,
                          Humble-Bee. 46.
In columbine and clover-blow,
                          May-Day. 252.
A wild-rose, or rock-loving columbine,
                          Musketaquid. 74.

Columned
Tented Tartary, columned Nile,—
                          Solution. 11.

Columns
The columns of the firmament
                          Frag. Life. XXXVI. 3.
Gropes for columns strong as he;
                          Frag. Nat. XXXIV. 2.

Comb
  See Honeycomb.

Combine
Lo! how all the tribes combine
                          May-Day. 111.

Combined
Combined a new temperament.
                          Fag. Life. XXIX. 6.
And their members are combined.
                          Merlin. 48.

Come
And how we should come hither with
  our sons,   Adirondacs. 163.
I've come to live with you, sweet friends,
                          Aeolian Harp. 18.
Come, East and West and North,
                          Boston Hymn. 81.
And now their hour is come.
                          I. Compensation. 8.
And they that swiftly come and go
                          Daemonic Love. 41.
Where thy form and favor come,
                          Dearest. 3.
'O come, then, quickly come!
                          Ellen South. 33.
At unawares 't is come and past.
                          Forerunners. 32.

Go and come   Frag. Life. VIII. 3.
Ancestors of beauty come
                          Frag. Life. XXII. 7.
Come search the wood for flowers,—
                          Frag. Nat. II. 1.
Come and I will show you all
                          Frag. Nat. XXVI. 5.
All my force saith, Come and use me:
                          Frag. Nat. XXVIII. 2.
Hated mist if it come near.
                          Frag. Poet. VII. 18.
Go thy ways now, come later back,
                          Garden. 59.
To those who go, and those who come;
                          Good-Bye. 13.
Oft courted will not come;   Harp. 16.
And my kindred come to soothe me.
                          Hermione. 49.
He is come through fragrant wood,
                          Hermione. 51.
Come to us herself to meet."'
                          Hermione. 78.
Wait, I prithee, till I come
                          Humble-Bee. 17.
And hither come the pensive train
                          Hymn. 9.
Come the tumult whence it will,
                          May-Day. 30.
Thoughts come also hand in hand;
                          Merlin. 101.
Things past and things to come.
                          Peter. 28.
The morn is come: the starry crowds
                          Poet. 177.
That curse her when they come.
                          Quat. Fate. 4.
I have come from the spring-woods,
                          Rhea. 5.
Here might the red-bird come his plumes
  to cool,   Rhodora. 7.
The hour of heaven shall come, the man
  appear.   Rome. 27.
Many may come,   Saadi. 17.
Though there come a million, Saadi. 21.
Come ten, or come a million, Saadi. 32.
Say, Pilgrim, why so late and slow to
  come?   Seashore. 2.
Come see the north wind's masonry.
                          Snow-Storm. 10.
His couriers come by squadrons,
                          Song of Nature. 59.
Days that come dancing on fraught with
  delights,   Summons. 20.
Men read the welfare of the times to
  come,   Threnody. 169.
Beckon it when to go and come,
                          Threnody. 253.
Must borrow his winds who there would
  come.   Titmouse. 10.
And, to be valiant, must come down
                          Titmouse. 63.
Hither I come for strength Waterfall. 5.
But he would come in the very hour
                          Woodnotes. I. 42.
And at his bidding seemed to come.
                          Woodnotes. I. 61.
And ills to come as evils past bemoan.
                          Woodnotes. I. 89.
Come to me,'   Woodnotes. II. 6.
Of man to come, of human life,
                          Woodnotes. II. 131.

Come —*Continued*
Come weave with mine a nobler rhyme.
          Woodnotes. II. 139.
'Come learn with me the fatal song
          Woodnotes. II. 156.
Come lift thine eyes to lofty rhymes,
          Woodnotes. II. 158.
Come, lay thee in my soothing shade,
          Woodnotes. II. 219.

Comeliness
Of power and of comeliness. Rhea. 69.

Comely
Shorn from her comely head,
          Hermione. 18.

Comes
Comes the sweet sadness at the retro-
spect,   Adirondacs. 216.
Therefore comes an hour from Jove
          Daemonic Love. 116.
Comes the Genius,—all's forgot,
          Frag. Life. XVI. 7.
The world uncertain comes and goes;
          Friendship. 3.
If who can read them comes at last
          Garden. 63.
And where it comes this courier fleet
          May-Day. 295.
Ever from one who comes to-morrow
          Merlin's Song. 20.
And when the greater comes again
          Monadnoc. 262.
Comes that cheerful troubadour,
          Monadnoc. 287.
He comes, but not of that race bred
          Monadnoc. 309.
The boy's dream comes to pass,
          October. 2.
The moon comes back,—the Spirit not.
          Poet. 280.
He comes not to the gate.
          Song of Nature. 60.
When here again thy pilgrim comes,
          Titmouse. 81.
Hermit-thrush comes there to build,
          Walden. 3.
The rain comes when the wind calls;
          Woodnotes. II. 238.

Comest
And comest thou   Monadnoc. 205.

Comet
I pass with yonder comet free,—
                    Nun. 38.
Pass with the comet into space Nun. 39.

Cometh
And where it cometh, all things are;
          Informing Spirit. 3.
And it cometh everywhere.
          Informing Spirit. 4.
Of him that cometh, and shall come;
          Monadnoc. 269.
When he cometh, I shall shed,
          Monadnoc. 291.

Comfort
To me their comfort plight;—
          Hermione. 64.
And comfort you with their high com-
pany.   Rome. 7.

Comforted
Of them thou shouldst have comforted;
          Saadi. 69.

And henceforth we are comforted,—
          World-Soul. 55.

Comic
Hard fare, hard bed and comic misery,—
          Adirondacs. 165.

Coming
See Coming-back.
As pledged in coming days to forge
          In Memoriam. 64.
I see the coming light,   Poet. 97.
Coming early, coming late,   Poet. 123.
'Twas coming fast to such anointing,
          Titmouse. 24.
And their coming triumph hide
          Voluntaries. 113.
Coming and past eternities?
          Woodnotes. I. 29.
But ever coming in time to crown
          Worship. 13.

Coming-back
Of the punctual coming-back,
          May-Day. 379.

Command
'Thou shalt command us all,—
          Ellen South. 29.
The beggar begs by God's command,
          Frag. Life. VII. 1.
And well the youngest can command
          Monadnoc. 135.
Forget never their command, Rhea. 29.
That shall command a senate to your
side;   Rome. 17.

Commanded
See Self-commanded.

Commandment
'A new commandment,' said the smiling
Muse,   Adakryn. 1.

Commands
The Mighty commands me,   Poet. 119.
Speak through his lips thy pure com-
mands,   Robbins Hymn. 27.

Commemorate
And annual tunes commemorate
          Mountain. 20.

Commissioned
And the commissioned wind to sing
          Mountain. 18.
I am commissioned in my day of joy
          Summons. 3.

Commodore
And Stillman, our guides' guide, and
Commodore,   Adirondacs. 183.

Common
Draw untold juices from the common
earth,   Blight. 9.
So that the common waters fell
          Guy. 29.
Of Nature's child the common fate.
          Mountain. 21.
And reconcile him to the common days.
          Naples. 12.
Than he to common sense and common
good: Phi. 14.

Communicable
See Incommunicable.

Communicate
They can well communicate
          Celestial Love. 95.

Companion
'What am I? companion, say.'
          Astraea. 18.

Condescend
Forgive our harms, and condescend
May-Day. 402.
Condition's
Nor heeds Condition's iron walls,—
Frag. Life. XVII. 9.
Conditions
The flowing conditions of life, give way.
Frag. Life. XXXI. 4.
Conduct
His cold eye truth and conduct scanned,
Quat. S. H. 2.
Cone
From the fixed cone the cloud-rack
flowed Monadnoc. 33.
And soon my cone will spin.
Monadnoc. 244.
So call not waste that barren cone
Monadnoc. 352.
Cones
See Pine-cones.
When the pine tosses its cones
Woodnotes. I. 1.
Confess
For royal man;—they thee confess
Woodnotes. II. 188.
Confessed
What himself confessed records,
Astraea. 27.
Single moment years confessed.
Visit. 22.
Confides
The bird to him confides.
Quat. Hafiz. 4.
Confront
Of loud Bog River, suddenly confront
Adirondacs. 233.
Confusion
Puts confusion in my brain.
Channing Ode. 11.
But all slid to confusion. Uriel. 34.
Conifers
Three conifers, white, pitch and Norway
pine, Adirondacs. 40.
Conjoined
See Fate-conjoined.
Conned
Not to be conned to tediousness
Threnody. 229.
Conquer
Unless he conquer and prevail?
Destiny. 15.
It cannot conquer folly,—
World-Soul. 13.
Conquering
Cannot withhold his conquering aid.
Nun. 6.
Time-and-space-conquering steam,—
World-Soul. 14.
Conqueror
Alike the conqueror silent sleeps;
C. Hymn. 6.
Conquerors
Let kings and conquerors, saints and
soldiers sleep— To-Day. 4.
Conquers
Justice conquers evermore,
Voluntaries. 100.
Conscience
The yoke of conscience masterful,
Park. 3.

As if the conscience of the country
spoke. Phi. 12.
To the conscience of a child.
Wealth. 49.
Conscious
See Unconscious.
The conscious stars accord above,
Concord Ode. 33.
Conscious each of duty done
Frag. Nat. XXIII. 17.
The conscious stone to beauty grew.
Problem. 24.
And conscious Law is King of kings.
Woodnotes. II. 294.
Consent
And, best with best in sweet consent,
Frag. Life. XXIX. 5.
Consents
The rich results of the divine consents
Blight. 43.
Asks not of others soft consents,
Frag. Life. XVII. 6.
Conserver
Fierce conserver, fierce destroyer,—
Saadi. 98.
Consist
Consist with homage to the good
In Memoriam. 36.
Console
What generous beliefs console
In Memoriam. 86.
Consoled
So only new griefs are consoled
May-Day. 365.
Consort
Men consort in camp and town,
Saadi. 7.
Conspiracy
Works in close conspiracy;
Ode to Beauty. 83.
Conspired
Whose living towers the years conspired
to build, Woodnotes. I. 78.
Constant
See Inconstant.
By constant service to that inward law,
Good Cheer. 6.
Fast abides this constant giver,
Monadnoc. 40.
The constant mountain doth dispense;
Monadnoc. 382.
Constellation
The constellation glittered soon,—
Poet. 230.
Constellations
All constellations of the sky
Woodnotes. II. 73.
Constitute
Shall constitute a state.
Boston Hymn. 32.
Constrained
Constrained by impotence to adjourn
Poet. 187.
Consummate
To a consummate holiness,
Frag. Life. XXVIII. 2.
Contemned
We trode on air, contemned the distant
town, Adirondacs. 160.

Contend
That can contend with love. It reigns
forever. Rome. 19.
Content
See Discontent.
And whether I am angry or content,
Day's Ration. 9.
Content that all we asked was granted?
Fame. 18.
If others reach it, is content;
In Memoriam. 88.
Because I was content with these poor
fields, Musketaquid. 1.
My heart's content would find it right.
Nun. 10.
With Gods, with fools, content to live;
Poet. 214.
Pure content is angel's lot, Poet. 251.
I see your forms with deep content,
Poet. 257.
He roamed, content alike with man and
beast. Woodnotes. I. 81.
Contented
Grave, chaste, contented, though retired,
Woodnotes. II. 69.
Continent
Of Alp and Andes, isle and continent,
Adirondacs. 263.
And night and day, ocean and continent,
Blight. 34.
Rebuild a continent of better men.
Seashore. 37.
Continented
See Uncontinented.
Continually
I hear continually his voice therein.
Self-Reliance. 5.
Contoocook
I found by thee, O rushing Contoocook!
Channing Ode. 21.
Contract
Contract thy firmament Terminus. 10.
Contradiction
To sons of contradiction. Saadi. 91.
Contraries
Substance mixed of pure contraries;
Initial Love. 91.
Contrition
And thanks was his contrition;
Saadi. 75.
Contrition's
That knock at meek contrition's door.
Hymn. 20.
Controlled
Who so controlled me; Hamatreya. 54.
Controls
Her planted eye to-day controls,
Quat. Fate. 1.
Convenance
Their wonted convenance, cheerly hid
the loss Adirondacs. 181.
Is the term of convenance, Visit. 24.
Conversation
Hold their sour conversation in the
sky:— River. 17.
Convey
Can this elastic air convey.
May-Day. 14.
What friend to friend cannot convey
Miracle. 21.

Conveyed
But a quiet sense conveyed:
Monadnoc. 197.
Conveyed thy meaning mild.
Threnody. 39.
Conveys
Artful thunder, which conveys
Merlin. 13.
Conviction
And send conviction without phrase,
Monadnoc. 404.
Convoy
I know ye skilful to convoy
May-Day. 353.
To watch the convoy on the road;
Threnody. 61.
Cool
Let spouting fountains cool the air,
Art. 7.
Here might the red-bird come his plumes
to cool, Rhodora. 7.
Cooled
My avarice cooled Hamatreya. 62.
Cooled by the pendent mountain's shade,
May-Day. 17.
Cooler
One August evening had a cooler breath;
Adirondacs. 331.
Cools
Flowering April cools and dies
Alphonso. 7.
Cools sea and land so far and fast,
Humble-Bee. 59.
He cools the present's fiery glow,
Monadnoc. 157.
Coop
On coop or kennel he hangs Parian
wreaths; Snow-Storm. 18.
Cooped
Cooped in a ship he cannot steer,—
Monadnoc. 336.
Cope
Looks to the azure cope,
Frag. Life. XXIII. 2.
Copious
And copious language still bestowed
Merops. 11.
Copper
Copper and iron, lead and gold?
Wealth. 21.
Copse
And modest copse and the forest tall,
Frag. Poet. I. 16.
Crying out of the hazel copse, *Phe-be!*
Titmouse. 93.
Copses'
There broad-armed oaks, the copses'
maze, Walden. 5.
Copy
Canst thou copy in verse one chime
Garden. 37.
I followed in small copy in my acre;
Musketaquid. 53.
Coral
The building in the coral sea,
Song of Nature. 23.
Cord
Tethered by a liquid cord
Daemonic Love. 3.
Caught with love's cord of twisted
beams, Nun. 35.

Corded
The kennel by the corded wood;
Threnody. 83.

Cordial
In severe or cordial mood,   Etienne. 12.
And cure all ill, is cordial speech:
Merlin's Song. 36.
The cordial quality of pear or plum
Musketaquid. 55.
A while to share his cordial game,
Threnody. 48.

Cords
Their cords of love so public are,
Celestial Love. 107.

Core
In the core of God's abysm,—
Daemonic Love. 127.
An eyemark and the country's core,
Monadnoc. 46.
Up from the burning core below,—
Problem. 17.

Coreopis
Coreopsis   Frag. Nat. II. 4.

Corn
See Barley-corn.
Web to weave, and corn to grind;
Channing Ode. 49.
To reap its scanty corn,   Dirge. 10.
But corn of Guy's was there to grind:
Guy. 36.
Hay, corn, roots, hemp, flax, apples,
wool and wood.   Hamatreya. 3.
Change the running sand to corn;
Monadnoc. 138.
To reap its scanty corn,   Peter. 2.

Corners
In the realms and corners of space
Cosmos. 14.
Or in lone corners of a doleful heath,
Frag. Nat. IV. 3.

Corporal
The form is his own corporal form,
Astraea. 29.

Corporate
Of traders, led by corporate sons of
trade,   Adirondacs. 282.

Corrupt
We plot and corrupt each other,
World-Soul. 23.

Corrupted
Corrupted by the present toy
Initial Love. 112.

Corruptible
See Incorruptible.

Corse
The glowing angel, the outcast corse.
Woodnotes. II. 306.

Cosmic
It trembles to the cosmic breath,—
Harp. 69.

Cossack
The Cossack eats Poland,
Channing Ode. 90.

Cossacks
Right Cossacks in their forages;
Initial Love. 34.

Cost
Not to regret the changes, tho' they cost
River. 20.

Costlier
Costlier far than wine or oil.
Monadnoc. 296.

Costly
And all the costly liquor runs to waste;
Day's Ration. 23.
As costly wine into his well.   Guy. 30.
O truth's and nature's costly lie!
Threnody. 172.

Cot
In lowly cot or painful road,
In Memoriam. 57.
Whispered the Muse in Saadi's cot:
Saadi. 86.

Cottage
And peaceful woods beside my cottage
door.   Frag. Nat. IV. 11.
Glittered with silver every cottage pane,
Frag. Nat. XXVII. 8.
Too strait and low our cottage doors,
May-Day. 220.
Each chimney-pot and cottage door,
Poet. 58.
Seek not beyond thy cottage wall
Saadi. 165.

Cotyledons
And match the paired cotyledons.
Merlin. 87.

Couch
Was ever couch magnificent as mine?
Seashore. 8.

Couched
Couched like a cat   Philosopher. 9.

Could. (Partial list.)
Could you slacken and condense?
Alphonso. 64.
For day by day could Boston Bay
Boston. 23.
The cargo came! and who could blame
Boston. 76.
Toil could never compass it;
Destiny. 7.
Its complement; but if I could,
Etienne. 11.
Only could her mirror show.
Frag. Life. IX. 2.
Haply else we could not live,
Frag. Nat. I. 17.
Who could the mystery expound,
Frag. Nat. VI. 2
A twelvemonth he could silence hold,
Frag. Poet. V. 24.
And seldom therein could I look,
Goethe. 4.
Nor sword of angels could reveal
Merlin. 76.
That this proud nursery could breed
Monadnoc. 76.
Ah! could we turn the leaf.
Quat. Climacteric. 4.
Nor sequent centuries could hit
Solution. 39.
These the siroc could not melt,
Test. 7.
For his lips could well pronounce
Threnody. 52.
Was there no star that could be sent,
Threnody. 118.
They could not feed him, and he died,
Threnody. 147.

Strong Hades could not keep his own,
Uriel. 33.
It seemed that Nature could not raise
Woodnotes. I. 36.
Which we could never spell.
World-Soul. 48.

Could'st. (Partial list.)
Out of that delicate lay could'st thou
Dirge. 47.
Thou to the Syrian couldst belong?
Hermione. 30.
Couldst see thy proper eye, Sphinx. 114.

Council
A pause and council: then, where near
the head Adirondacs. 29.
Brought his great forehead to the council board, Phi. 8.

Counsel
See Bosom-counsel.
My counsel is, kill nine in ten,
Alphonso. 68.
Counsel which the ages kept
Celestial Love. 69.
Each other's counsel by his own,
Celestial Love. 92.
Counsel not with flesh and blood;
Freedom. 22.
The counsel of the gods, Harp. 20.
No mimic; from his breast his counsel
drew, Phi. 15.
He would, yet would not, counsel keep,
Poet. 85.
Took counsel from his guiding eyes
Threnody. 56.

Counselled
And murmuring waters counselled me.
Rhea. 8.

Count
Or count the Sioux a match for Agassiz?
Adirondacs. 308.
I count as many as there are
Frag. Poet. XXVIII. 4.
Count your change and cheer the best.
May-Day. 368.
Nor count compartments of the floors,
Merlin. 36.
Count it flight of bird or dart.
Poet. 129.
I do not count the hours I spend
Waldeinsamkeit. 1.

Counted
See Uncounted.
No lineage counted great;
Boston Hymn. 30.
He is not of counted age,
Initial Love. 140.
Counted on the spacious dial
May-Day. 376.
No numbers have counted my tallies,
Song of Nature. 9.

Countenance
Tints the human countenance
Humble-Bee. 24.
Shamed that sculptured countenance.
In Memoriam. 47.
Their sweet and lofty countenance
Manners. 5.
And by his countenance repay
Threnody. 19.

Counter
Each color with its counter glowed;
Merlin. 82.

Counterforce
Love is aye the counterforce,—
Miracle. 11.

Countermanded
Mighty projects countermanded;
Alphonso. 23.

Counterpart
Beaming from its counterpart,
Daemonic Love. 32.
Seeks alone his counterpart.
Initial Love. 107.

Counties
Amid the mountain counties, Hants,
Franklin, Berks, Letter. 9.

Counting
Trade and counting use Merlin. 115.

Countless
Tells of countless sunny hours,
Humble-Bee. 34.
A subtle chain of countless rings
May-Day. 79.
A subtle chain of countless rings
Nature. Mot. 1.
Girds with one flame the countless host,
Problem. 52.
In countless upward-striving waves
Promise. 1.
Of all the zones and countless days.
Song of Nature. 80.
No angel from the countless host
Threnody. 120.
And the countless leaves of the pine are
strings Woodnotes. II. 95.

Country
Thence, in strong country carts,
Adirondacs. 2.
In the country and the town,
Astraea. 10.
In the country or the court.
Forerunners. 22.
As if the conscience of the country
spoke. Phi. 12.
But I, the bantling of a country Muse,
Summons. 22.

Country's
An eyemark and the country's core,
Monadnoc. 46.
Whilst the country's flinty face,
Monadnoc. 147.
Adorned with them my country's primitive times, River. 41.

County
All his county, sea and land,
Monadnoc. 320.

Couple
And kiss, and couple, and beget,
Initial Love. 31.

Couples
In equal couples mated, Merlin. 102.

Courage
Lose courage, and despair.
Daemonic Love. 111.
It requireth courage stout. Give. 19.
"Courage! we are thine allies,
Hermione. 65.
Courage and probity and grace!
May-Day. 405.

Courage —*Continued*
Thanks to each man of courage,
World-Soul. 5.
Courageous
Courageous sing a delicate overture
Musketaquid. 17.
Courages
Undaunted are their courages,
Initial Love. 33.
Courier
No courier waits,   Adirondacs. 66.
To learn of scribe or courier
Frag. Poet. V. 45.
And where it comes this courier fleet
May-Day. 295.
Courier's
The sled and traveller stopped, the
courier's feet   Snow-Storm. 6.
Couriers
Fleetest couriers alive   Forerunners. 23.
His couriers come by squadrons,
Song of Nature. 59.
Course
See Watercourse.
I watch your course,   Poet. 156.
And, shrilling from the solar course,
Uriel. 49.
Courses
Sit here on the basalt courses
Cosmos. 17.
Where stars their perfect courses keep,
Monadnoc. 101.
Suns and stars their courses keep,
Poet. 271.
Right out to sea his courses stand,
Quat. Poet. I. 3.
They laid their courses well,
Song of Nature. 34.
Court
And court the sunny brook.   April. 16.
In the country or the court.
Forerunners. 22.
or held their court   Frag. Nat. XXVII. 9.
At court he sat in the grave Divan.
Frag. Poet. I. 10.
To crowded halls, to court and street;
Good-Bye. 11.
Nor spacious court, nor monarch's hall,
May-Day. 222.
And court the flower that cheapens his
array.   Rhodora. 8.
I court and play with paler blood,
Romany. 14.
To court and mart, to gown and town.
Solution. 68.
To do the honors of his court,
Titmouse. 36.
By court and city, dale and down,
Walk. 3.
Courted
Oft courted will not come;   Harp. 16.
Courtesy
The courtesy ye have shown and kept
Poet. 150.
Courtly
Decked by courtly rites and dress
Frag. Poet. I. 29.
Courts
Far capitals and marble courts,
Quat. A. H. 3.

Cove
See South Cove.
searched every cove,   Adirondacs. 108.
Cover
See Uncover.
The tenfold clouds that cover   Dull. 12.
Under this cover   *Lines. 7.
Nor the June flowers scorn to cover
Woodnotes. I. 145.
Covers
Translucent through the mortal covers,
Daemonic Love. 33.
Covert
Kind leaves of his covert,   Sphinx. 23.
Covet
Then I said, 'I covet truth;   Each. 37.
Covetous
Covetous death bereaved us all,
Threnody. 158.
Cow
Loves nature like a horned cow,
Initial Love. 100.
Coward
Amid these coward shapes of joy and
grief,   Monadnoc. 312.
Hide in false peace your coward head,
Voluntaries. 33.
Not so the wise; no coward watch he
keeps   Woodnotes. I. 90.
Cowardice
The reason of all cowardice
Titmouse. 61.
Cower
And I, who cower mean and small
Frag. Poet. III. 7.
Cowl
I like a church; I like a cowl;
Problem. 1.
Cowlèd
Would I that cowlèd churchman be.
Problem. 6.
I see his cowlèd portrait dear;
Problem. 70.
Cowslip
April's cowslip, summer's clover,
Ellen South. 30.
Mouse-ear, cowslip, wintergreen,
Frag. Nat. II. 29.
Cowslips
In cowslips and anemonies.
Nature. I. 4.
Cowslip-wreaths
Holds a cup with cowslip-wreaths.
May-Day. 5.
Coy
The Muse of men is coy,   Harp. 15.
Daughter of Heaven and Earth, coy
Spring,   May-Day. 1.
Cozen
Can cozen, pique and flatter,   April. 11.
Crab
Crab, mice, snail,   Adirondacs. 136.
Strong crab with nobler blood did fill;
Guy. 42.
Crabs
Will you catch crabs? Truth tries pre-
tension here.   Adirondacs. 100.
Crack
With laughter sudden as the crack of
rifle;   Adirondacs. 128.
Neither can you crack a nut.' Fable. 19.

Cradle
Servant to a wooden cradle,
Holidays. 15.
Old cradle, hunting-ground and bier
Monadnoc. 80.

Craft
By its own craft, to a more rich delight.
Bacchus. 11.
With squires, lords, kings, his craft compares,
Fate. 8.
O, wondrous craft of plant and stone
Monadnoc. 66.
Outran the craft of eloquence. Poet. 200.
Fear, Craft and Avarice Politics. 9.
For still the craft of genius is
Quat. Poet. 2. 3.

Craftsman
The noble craftsman we promote,
Boston. 31.

Crag
Cheers the rough crag and mournful dell,
Frag. Nat. XXIX. 2.
'River and rose and crag and bird,
Hermione. 61.
While cheerful cries of crag and plain
May-Day. 239.
The surge of summer's beauty; dell and
crag, Musketaquid. 22.

Craggy
Of craggy Indian wilderness he hears
Adirondacs. 312.

Crags
Nevada! coin thy golden crags
Boston Hymn. 75.
Man in these crags a fastness find
Monadnoc. 112.
And that these gray crags
Monadnoc. 231.
Not on crags are hung, Monadnoc. 232.

Cramp
And in cramp elf and saurian forms
Song of Nature. 31.

Crannies
Safe in their ancient crannies, dark and
deep, To-Day. 3.

Crash
One crash, the death-hymn of the perfect tree,
Woodnotes. I. 74.

Crave
old empires crave Boston. 92.
To me who only jewels crave?
Song of Seyd. 14.

Craven
No craven cry, no secret tear,—
In Memoriam. 99.

Craving
Or fill my craving ear; Merlin. 2.

Crawls
And crawls through life a paralytic
Fame. 11.
The poor man crawls in web of rags
Riches. 9.

Craze
Him it would straightway blind or craze,
Guy. 22.

Creaking
This poor tooting, creaking cricket,
Frag. Nat. I. 6.
Tooting, creaking, Frag. Nat. I. 9.

Cream
And for cold mosses, cream and curds:
Monadnoc. 140.

Create
Waiting till God create the earth,—
Frag. Nat. XXVI. 16.
All that high God did first create.
May-Day. 442.

Creates
Is the same Genius that creates.
Fate. 16.

Creating
See Sun-creating.
Creating fair and good alway,
Day by Day. 7.
Creating a sweet climate by my breath,
Seashore. 23.

Creation
Low lies the plant to whose creation
went Woodnotes. I. 76.
Ever fresh the broad creation,
Woodnotes. II. 262.

Creator
The freed soul its Creator found?
In Memoriam. 112.
Is the Creator of our human mould
Naples. 2.

Creature
I cause from every creature
Boston Hymn. 57.
Fleeter they than any creature,—
Initial Love. 35.
To bless that creature day and night;
Rhea. 48.
He is the heart of every creature;
Woodnotes. II. 315.

Creatures
So through all creatures in their form
and ways Adirondacs. 202.
All good creatures have their home.
Dearest. 4.
Like creatures of a skiey mould,
Frag. Poet. I. 48.
Plants and birds and humble creatures
May-Day. 134.
My creatures travail and wait;
Song of Nature. 58.

Credit
Plans, credit and the Muse,— Give. 5.

Credits
None credits him till he have shown
Frag. Poet. VI. 3.

Credulous
And, credulous, through the granite
seeming, Monadnoc. 235.
Too credulous lover Ode to Beauty. 3.
With credulous and imaginative man;
Seashore. 44.

Creed
Go put your creed into your deed,
Concord Ode. 19.
Thy life to thy neighbor's creed has lent.
Each. 10.

Creeds
Let war and trade and creeds and song
Song of Nature. 77.

Creep
Silver to silver creep and wind,
Celestial Love. 79.
Where way is none, 't will creep and
wind Quat. Love. 3.

Creep—*Continued*
Though, feigning dwarfs, they crouch
and creep,   Voluntaries. 117.

Creepeth
Creepeth, bloweth everywhere;
May-Day. 290.
He creepeth and peepeth,   Sphinx. 51.

Creeping
Two creeping miles of rushes, pads and
sponge,   Adirondacs. 24.
From air the creeping centuries drew
Wealth. 13.

Creeps
Down the dark stream which seaward
creeps.   C. Hymn. 8.
To spy what danger on his pathway
creeps;   Woodnotes. I. 91.

Crept
intruding duties crept; Adirondacs. 332.
In caves and hollow trees he crept
Frag. Poet. I. 43.

Crest
See Mountain-crest.
And o'er yon hazy crest is Eden's
balmier spring.'   May-Day. 103.

Crew
Chaucer had no such worthy crew,
Adirondacs. Motto. 3.

Cricket
This poor tooting, creaking cricket,
Frag. Nat. I. 6.

Cried
Cried him up and down the coast,
Initial Love. 2.
Cried "Onward!" and the palm-crown
showed,   In Memoriam. 59.
'Once more,' the old man cried, 'ye
clouds,   May-Day. 349.
'Sorrow, sorrow!' the angels cried,
Poet. 217.

Crier
He will read like a crier,
Initial Love. 136.

Cries
Challenging Echo by our guns and cries;
Adirondacs. 113.
With ductile fire. Loud, exulting cries
Adirondacs. 241.
'Well done!' he cries; 'the bear is kept
at bay,   Adirondacs. 315.
Earth, crowded, cries, 'Too many men!'
Alphonso. 67.
Words of pain and cries of fear,
Harp. 58.
'Onward,' he cries, 'your baskets bring,—
May-Day. 101.
While cheerful cries of crag and plain
May-Day. 239.

Crime
The tragic tales of crime and fate;
Frag. Nat. XXVI. 34.
To transmute crime to wisdom, so to
stem   Frag. Poet. XXII. 1.
That Night or Day, that Love or Crime,
Park. 15.
For out of woe and out of crime
Saadi. 70.
Unknowing war, unknowing crime.
Saadi. 100.
What his fault, or what his crime?
Voluntaries. 13.

Crimson
The maple-tops their crimson tint,
May-Day. 60.
Which morn and crimson evening paint
Monadnoc. 44.
Through crimson chambers, porphyry
and pearl,   October. 7.
The chalk is crimson grown.   They. 4.
The crimson morning flames into
World-Soul. 59.

Crimsoning
See Gulf-encrimsoning.

Cripple
A cripple of God, half true, half formed,
Poet. 185.
He kills the cripple and the sick,
World-Soul. 91.

Critic
To earn the praise of bard and critic.
Fame. 12.
But, critic, spare thy vanity,   Saadi. 45.
Of critic charters, an unlaurelled Muse.
To-Day. 8.
In critic peep or cynic bark, To J. W. 19.

Croaked
The raven croaked, owls hooted, the
woodpecker   Adirondacs. 147.

Crocodile
The southern crocodile would grieve.
Channing Ode. 31.

Cromwell
Unknown to Cromwell as to me
Fate. 3.

Cromwell's
Was Cromwell's measure or degree;
Fate. 4.

Crone
Hot midsummer's petted crone,
Humble-Bee. 32.

Crones
Listening to the gray-haired crones,
Saadi. 169.

Crooning
With idle footsteps, crooning rhymes.
Miracle. 2.
Crooning ditties treasured well
Voluntaries. 7.

Crop
it would blight no crop, Adirondacs. 68.
Meagre crop of figs and limes;
Alphonso. 5.
A second crop thine acres yield,
Apology. 19.

Crops
To drug their crops or weapon their arts
withal.   Musketaquid. 40.
Then docks were built, and crops were
stored,   Wealth. 42.

Cross
Cross the orbit of the earth,
Daemonic Love. 49.

Crossed
We crossed Champlain to Keeseville
with our friends,   Adirondacs. 1.
These had crossed them while they slept.
Forerunners. 20.
'Tis good, when you have crossed the
sea and back,   Hamatreya. 23.
When, by false companions crossed,
Love and Thought. 11.

Under east winds crossed with sleet.
                    May-Day. 133.
O richest fortune sourly crossed!
                    Threnody. 174.
Or what ill planet crossed his prime?
                    Voluntaries. 14.
Crosswise
The rope-like pine-roots crosswise grown
                    Woodnotes. I. 106.
Crouch
Though, feigning dwarfs, they crouch
    and creep,   Voluntaries. 117.
Crouched
And crouched no more in stone;
                    Sphinx. 122.
Crouches
"But man crouches and blushes,
                    Sphinx. 49.
To front the fate that crouches near,—
                    Voluntaries. 16.
Crouching
The crouching lion kissed his feet;
                    Worship. 8.
Crow
each fowl must crow;   Threnody. 105.
Crowd
From bold intrusion of the travelling
    crowd,—   Adirondacs. 172.
With the bards and with the crowd.
                    Initial Love. 87.
Dusky sparrows in a crowd,
                    May-Day. 387.
I sing it to the surging crowd,—
                    Merlin's Song. 5.
Or crowd the market and bazaar;
                    Saadi. 110.
Above the envy of the crowd,—
                    Thought. 3.
I see thee in the crowd alone;
                    Woodnotes. II. 221.
Crowded
Earth, crowded, cries, 'Too many men!'
                    Alphonso. 67.
In crowded and in still resorts,
                    Daemonic Love. 46.
And all the crowded Past appears
                    Ellen. 3.
To crowded halls, to court and street;
                    Good-Bye. 11.
Too busied with the crowded hour to
    fear to live or die.   Quat. Nature. 4.
The crowded town, thy feet may well
    delay.   To J. W. 4.
And crowded whole, an infinite paroquet,
                    Xenophanes. 18.
Crowd's
And these from the crowd's edge well
    pleased beheld   Frag. Life. XXX. 6.
Crowds
And crowds a history into a glance;
                    Enchanter. 7.
Crowds each on other, veil on veil,
                    Frag. Nat. XXXI. 4.
Crowds in a day the sum of ages,
                    Frag. Poet. IX. 11.
Long through thy weary crowds I roam;
                    Good-Bye. 3.
The morn is come: the starry crowds
                    Poet. 177.
Crowds every egg out of the nest,
                    Unity. 5.

In cities high the careful crowds
                    Walden. 17.
Crown
    See Palm-crown.
And crowns him with a more than royal
    crown,   October. 4.
a crown to weave   Phi. 1.
But ever coming in time to crown
                    Worship. 13.
Crowned
    See Bud-crowned; Discrowned; Star-
    crowned.
Instead of flowers, crowned with a
    wreath of hills.   Adirondacs. 13.
A woman to thy wife, though she were
    a crowned queen;   Ibn Jemin. 2.
Such sweetness crowned me, *Lines. 11.
Crowning
But over all his crowning grace,
                    Frag. Poet. XI. 1.
Crowns
Laurel crowns cleave to deserts,
                    II. Compensation. 21.
And crowns him with a more than royal
    crown,   October. 4.
Crowns him victor glorified,
                    Voluntaries. 104.
Crowns all thy mean affairs.
                    Waldeinsamkeit. 48.
Love shuns the sage, the child it crowns,
                    Woodnotes. II. 236.
Crows
And hark! where overhead the ancient
    crows   River. 16.
Cruel
O Sun! I curse thy cruel ray:
                    Chartist. 17.
And evermore the cruel god
                    In Memoriam. 58.
Hints never loss or cruel break
                    In Memoriam. 107.
Is cruel to thy cruelty.   Limits. 12.
Cruelty
Is cruel to thy cruelty.   Limits. 12.
Cruise
The port, well worth the cruise, is near,
                    Terminus. 39.
Cruising
three cruising skiffs   Adirondacs. 231.
Crumb
Was neither cloak nor crumb my own.
                    Frag. Poet. IV. 14.
Crumbs
Lit with phosphoric crumbs the forest
    floor.   Adirondacs. 49.
He shall bring store of seeds and
    crumbs.   Titmouse. 82.
Crusader
Crusoe, Crusader, Pius Æneas, said
    aloud,   Adirondacs. 184.
Crusoe
Crusoe, Crusader,   Adirondacs. 184.
Crust
Dissolves the crust, displays the flowers.
                    May-Day. 149.
Cry
Were sought and found, amid the hue
    and cry   Adirondacs. 192.
Lisbon quakes, the people cry.
                    Alphonso. 14.

Cry—*Continued*
Of the wood-bell's peal and cry,
                    Garden. 38.
No craven cry, no secret tear,—
              In Memoriam. 99.
Steering north with raucous cry
              May-Day. 24.
Gay and polite, a cheerful cry,
              Titmouse. 26.

Crying
Crying out of the hazel copse, *Phe-be!*
              Titmouse. 93.

Crypt
Every crypt of every rock.   Bacchus. 44.

Crystal
And split to flakes the crystal ledges.
              Frag. Nat. XXX. 2.
And he the bard, a crystal soul
              Frag. Poet. I. 56.
Beneath the crystal arch,   May-Day. 383.
That loiters round the crystal coast,
              Threnody. 121.

Cuba's
Fresh from palms and Cuba's canes.
              May-Day. 393.

Cuckoo
Yonder masterful cuckoo   Unity. 4.

Cull
Hemlock for my sherbet cull me,
              Mithridates. 16.

Culminating
Culminating in her sphere.
              Hermione. 11.

Culture
Culture and libraries, mysteries of skill,
              Adirondacs. 323.
Of the culture of mankind,
              Channing Ode. 13.

Cumber
Not tamed and cleared cumber the
  ground   Letter. 12.

Cummin
Rue, myrrh and cummin for the Sphinx,
              Sphinx. 107.

Cunning
All substances the cunning chemist Time
              Day's Ration. 6.
Heedless that each cunning word
              Frag. Poet. V. 9.
Never from lips of cunning fell
              Problem. 11.
Foxes are so cunning
              Quat. Orator. 3.
Wealth to the cunning artist who can
  work   Seashore. 31.

Cup
    See Wine-cup.
And brims my little cup; heedless, alas!
              Day's Ration. 12.
The little cup will hold not a bead more,
              Day's Ration. 22.
The cup of life is not so shallow
              Good Hope. 1.
Holds a cup with cowslip-wreaths,
              May-Day. 5.
Drug the cup, thou butler sweet,
              May-Day. 279.
Nor in the cup of budding flowers,
              Music. 14.
The acorn's cup, the raindrop's arc,
              Ode to Beauty. 26.

Who drinks of Cupid's nectar cup
              Rhea. 35.
The cup was never full.
              Song of Nature. 72.
'Who has drugged my boy's cup?
              Sphinx. 61.

Cupid
But Cupid wears another face,
              Daemonic Love. 89.
None will now find Cupid latent
              Initial Love. 9.
Cupid is a casuist,   Initial Love. 60.
For Cupid goes behind all law,
              Initial Love. 120.
Until Cupid laughed loud,   *Lines. 22.

Cupid's
Who drinks of Cupid's nectar cup
              Rhea. 35.

Cupids
The air with Cupids full,   April. 6.
Like Cupids studiously inclined;
              Threnody. 65.

Cups
Said melted the days like cups of pearl,
              Frag. Poet. I. 19.

Curdles
Curdles the blood to the marble bones,
              Titmouse. 14.

Curds
And for cold mosses, cream and curds:
              Monadnoc. 140.

Cure
Haste to cure the old despair,—
              Bacchus. 55.
And cure all ill, is cordial speech:
              Merlin's Song. 36.

Cured
Some of your hurts you have cured,
              Quat. Borrowing. 1.

Cures
He slowly cures decrepit flesh,
              Monadnoc. 161.

Curious
Immensely curious whether you
              Alphonso. 39.
Rendering to a curious eye
              Astraea. 36.

Curled
Whose ample leaves and tendrils curled
              Bacchus. 15.
The ground-pine curled its pretty wreath,
              Each. 41.
When his ringlets grew and curled,
              Frag. Nat. XXXIV. 3.

Curling
A cabin hung with curling smoke,
              Frag. Poet. I. 22.

Curls
Golden curls, and quiver and bow.
              Initial Love. 5.

Current
No city airs or arts pass current here.
              Adirondacs. 92.

Curse
To sun the dark and solve the curse,
              Beauty. 19.
O Sun! I curse thy cruel ray:
              Chartist. 17.
While the solid curse and jeer
              Monadnoc. 191.

That curse her when they come.
Quat. Fate. 4.
Curse, if thou wilt, thy sires,
Terminus. 23.

Curses
If curses be the wage of love,
Frag. Life. XXXIII. 1.

Curtain
A friend to lift the curtain up
Hymn. 21.
Surely now will the curtain rise,
Woodnotes. II. 212.
But the curtain doth *not* rise,
Woodnotes. II. 214.

Curves
Curves his white bastions with projected
roof Snow-Storm. 13.

Custom
Stronger Custom brought him home.
Frag. Life. XX. 2.
Example, custom, fear, occasion slow,—
Grace. 3.

Cut
See Recut.
We cut young trees Adirondacs. 34.
And travelling often in the cut he makes,
Blight. 20.
He shall cut pathways east and west
Boston Hymn. 15.
Go, cut down trees in the forest
Boston Hymn. 33.
Cut down trees in the forest
Boston Hymn. 35.
Swords cannot cut the giving hand
Frag. Life. VII. 3.
Through beds of granite cut my road,
Woodnotes. I. 127.
Cut a bough from my parent stem,
Woodnotes. II. 51.

Cuts
No bird is safe that cuts the air
Monadnoc. 143.

Cyndyllan's
And thou, Cyndyllan's son! beware
Merlin's Song. 25.

Cynic
Youth is (whatever cynic tubs pretend)
To-Day. 17.
In critic peep or cynic bark, To J. W. 19.

Dædalian
Dædalian plan; Sphinx. 12.

Daedalus
Is it Daedalus? is it Love?
May-Day. 214.
For every wave is wealth to Dædalus,
Seashore. 30.

Daemon
Over the flickering Dæmon film,
Celestial Love. 29.
To men, the path to the Dæmon sphere;
Daemonic Love. 40.
The Dæmon ever builds a wall,
Daemonic Love. 93.
The patient Dæmon sits,
World-Soul. 77.

Dæmonic
And ever the Dæmonic Love
Daemonic Love. 129.

Dæmon's
Is the Dæmon's form and face.
Daemonic Love. 34.

Dæmons
The potent plain of Dæmons spreads.
Daemonic Love. 26.
The Dæmons are self-seeking:
Daemonic Love. 65.
Born into Dæmons less divine:
Daemonic Love. 90.

Daffodels
Maple-sap and daffodels,
Humble-Bee. 43.

Dagon's
Samson stark, at Dagon's knee,
Frag. Nat. XXXIV. 1.

Daguerre
Small need have I of Turner or
Daguerre, Frag. Nat. IV. 8.

Daily
Daily the bending skies solicit man,
Adirondacs. 224.
Daily stoops to harbor there.
Astraea. 48.
Daily to a more thin and outward rind,
Blight. 48.
Less than a lily's, thou shalt daily draw
Day's Ration. 4.
You shall not love me for what daily
spends; Frag. Life. XV. 1.
I daily dwell in, and am not so blind
Frag. Nat. V. 3.
Wherefor thanks God his daily praise,
Frag. Poet. XI. 2.
Like daily sunrise there. Friendship. 8.
Daily his own heart he eats;
Heroism. 8.
Stepping daily onward north
May-Day. 306.
He shall daily joy dispense Merlin. 41.
Mysteries of color daily laid
Monadnoc. 60.
Daily over hill and meadow.
Monadnoc. 265.
My daily load of woods and streams,
Monadnoc. 271.
Who daily climb my specular head.
Monadnoc. 310.
Serve thou it not for daily bread,—
Poet. 285.
The innocent mirth which sweetens daily
bread, Summons. 10.
His daily haunts I well discern,—
Threnody. 88.
That thou might'st break thy daily bread
Threnody. 219.
Victors over daily wrongs:
Voluntaries. 110.

Daintily
In well-hung chambers daintily bestowed,
Adirondacs. 51.

Dale
By court and city, dale and down,
Walk. 3.

Dales
Each joy the mountain dales impart;
Woodnotes. I. 35.

Dalliance
In the bower of dalliance sweet
Saadi. 55.

Dame
So hide in thee, thou heavenly dame,
Angelo. 6.

Dame —*Continued*
Who is their Muse and dame.
                    Hermione. 25.
Spoke the universal dame;   Sphinx. 130.
Dames
To bachelors and dames.   April. 4.
Minstrels and kings and high-born
    dames, and of the best that be.
                    Quat. A. H. 4.
And if I take you, dames, to task,
                    Romany. 9.
Yet fairest dames and bearded men,
                    Threnody. 43.
And quit proud homes and youthful
    dames   Voluntaries. 65.
Damnèd
And bid each awful Muse drive the
    damned harpies hence.   I Bear. 14.
Rehearsed to men the damned wails
                    Solution. 49.
Damp
Useful only, triste and damp,
                    Chartist. 5.
Spreading its leafless blooms in a damp
    nook,   Rhodora. 3.
In damp fields known to bird and fox.
                    Woodnotes. I. 41.
They led me through the thicket damp,
                    Woodnotes. I. 125.
Dams
build dams and mills,   Monadnoc. 150.
Dan
East, West, from Beer to Dan,
                    Fame. 3.
Dance
In the snares of Nature's dance;
                    Daemonic Love. 29.
Nor wanton skip with bacchic dance,
                    May-Day. 129.
And the mystic seasons' dance;
                    Monadnoc. 63.
When the music and the dance
                    Monadnoc. 252.
Saw the dance of Nature forward and
    far,   Poet. 70.
Who never break your lawful dance
                    Poet. 157.
Danced
And danced as merrily as young men.
                    May-Day. 323.
How danced thy form before my path
                    Thine Eyes. 7.
Dancers'
Like the dancers' ordered band,
                    Merlin. 100.
Dances
Which dances round the sun—
                    House. 20.
So dances his heart in his breast;
                    Manners. 14.
The panther in our dances flies.
                    Romany. 24.
Dancing
For flute or spinet's dancing chips;
                    Aeolian Harp. 5.
The dancing Pleiads and eternal men.
                    Bacchus. 67.
Or ribbons of a dancing girl
                    Frag. Nat. XXXII. 3.
Days that come dancing on fraught with
    delights,   Summons. 20.

Danger
Unheeded Danger near him strides,
                    Daemonic Love. 87.
Unarmed, faced danger with a heart of
    trust?   Forbearance. 4.
To spy what danger on his pathway
    creeps;   Woodnotes. I. 91.
Dangerous
Till dangerous Beauty came, at last,
                    Daemonic Love. 10.
With the dear, dangerous lords that rule
    our life,   Musketaquid. 7.
Thy dangerous glances
                    Ode to Beauty. 17.
Miles off, three dangerous miles, is home;
                    Titmouse. 9.
Daniel
A brown wren was the Daniel
                    Miracle. 29.
Dante
And Dante searched the triple spheres,
                    Solution. 28.
Dapper
Once more into his dapper town,
                    Monadnoc. 345.
Dappled
Dappled with joy and grief and praise,
                    Frag. Life. I. 2.
Farms the sunny landscape dappled,
                    September. 5.
Swandown clouds dappled the farms,
                    September. 6.
Dappling
None save dappling shadows climb,
                    Monadnoc. 202.
Dare
The oar, the guide's. Dare you accept
    the tasks   Adirondacs. 102.
With the labors he must dare;
                    Alphonso. 74.
Dare praise the freedom-loving moun-
    taineer?   Channing Ode. 20.
Spirit, that made those heroes dare
                    C. Hymn. 13
There's no god dare wrong a worm;
                    II. Compensation. 20.
But if, grown bold, the poet dare
                    Frag. Poet. IV. 3.
I dare not be beloved and known,
                    Frag. Poet. VII. 7.
I dare not peep over this parapet
                    Grace. 5.
And this, at least, I dare affirm,
                    Harp. 73.
How shall I dare to malign him,
                    Initial Love. 79.
That no god dare say him nay,
                    Initial Love. 126.
Queen of things! I dare not die
                    Ode to Beauty. 94.
Me false to mine dare whisper none,—
                    Romany. 15.
O, few to scale those uplands dare,
                    Waldeinsamkeit. 39.
Dared
With malice dared me to proclaim him,
                    Initial Love. 13.
Dare-devil
To ape thy dare-devil array?
                    Titmouse. 57.

Dares
He serves all who dares be true.
Celestial Love. 132.
Daring
Sharing all, daring all,
Daemonic Love. 81.
Dark
The clouds are rich and dark, the air
serene, Adirondacs. 213.
To sun the dark and solve the curse,
Beauty. 19.
For, in daylight or in dark,
Boston Hymn. 86.
Round they roll till dark is light,
Channing Ode. 78.
Down the dark stream C. Hymn. 8.
Shoots across the neutral Dark.
II. Compensation. 14.
Which dazzles me in midnight dark,
Etienne. 16.
And dark, without love, is the day;
Exile. 18.
Waits through dark ages for the morn,
Frag. Life. XXIII. 3.
A watchman in a dark gray tent,
Frag. Nat. XXVI. 14.
And as the light divides the dark
Frag. Poet. XIII. 1.
She threads dark Alpine forests
House. 9.
Would bring back day if it were dark;
Initial Love. 22.
On Life's dark sea, *Lines. 2.
Fled the last plumule of the Dark,
Monadnoc. 312.
Dark flower of Cheshire garden,
Monadnoc Afar. 1.
Or tapers light the chaos dark?
Nemesis. 12.
Thou hast bribed the dark and lonely
Ode to Beauty. 84.
And rived the dark like a new day!
Poet. 56.
And though he speak in midnight dark,—
Saadi. 131.
Dark with more clouds than tempests
are, Threnody. 99.
Safe in their ancient crannies, dark and
deep, To-Day. 3.
'Twill soon be dark; To J. W. 21.
Whose dark sky sheds the snowflake
down, Voluntaries. 40.
Was pole-star when the night was dark;
Woodnotes. I. 134.
The fourth gives light which eats the
dark; Woodnotes. II. 292.
Threading dark ways, arriving late,
Worship. 12.
Darkened
Of the pent and darkened lake,
May-Day. 16.
Darkest
But in the darkest, meanest things
Music. 11.
Darkle
Canst thou shine now, then darkle,
Musketaquid. 80.
Darkling
Where darkling feed the clamorous clans
May-Day. 28.

The old wine darkling in the cask
May-Day. 89.
Beneath the darkling firmament
Poet. 227.
Of woe-worn mortals darkling go,
Walden. 18.
Darkness
That sat in darkness long,—
Boston Hymn. 78.
The darkness haunteth me elsewhere;
Peter. 29.
The reverent darkness hid the lay.
Poet. 18.
No darkness stains its equal gleam,
Two Rivers. 19.
Heeds not the darkness and the dread,
Voluntaries. 86.
Where darkness found him he lay glad
at night; Woodnotes. I. 82.
Darling
'I give my darling son, Thou shalt not
preach';— Adakryn. 2.
Thou darling town of ours!
Boston. 119.
Whispered, 'Darling, never mind!
Experience. 19.
If my darling should depart,
From Hafiz. 9.
Snow-ridges masked each darling spot;
May-Day. 42.
The darling who shall not return.
Threnody. 8.
Of matter, and thy darling lost?
Threnody. 182.
Darlings
Day by day for her darlings to her much
she added more; Frag. Nat. XII. 1.
Darlings of children and of bard,
Frag. Nat. XXIII. 1.
And make the darlings of the earth
Frag. Poet. XI. 13.
Dart
Count it flight of bird or dart.
Poet. 129.
With beams December planets dart
Quat. S. H. 1.
Darting
A flock of finches darting
May-Day. 382.
Driving, darting northward free,
May-Day. 388.
Hopped on the bough, then, darting low,
Titmouse. 39.
Dash
Dash our blown hopes as Summons. 21.
Date
Or who can date the morning,
Cosmos. 3.
And I can date the morning prime
Cosmos. 7.
And granted them an equal date
Problem. 43.
The date fails not on the palm-tree tall;
Woodnotes. II. 245.
Daughter
Daughter of Heaven and Earth, coy
Spring, May-Day. 1.
Muse-born, a daughter of the Muse.
Woodnotes. II. 84.

Daughters

Daughters of Time, the hypocritic Days,
Days. 1.

Daunted

See Undaunted.

Daunting

Open the daunting map beneath,—
Monadnoc. 319.

Dauntless

Their dauntless ways did all men praise,
Boston. 9.

In northern Gaul my dauntless bird,
Titmouse. 96.

Dawn

See Day-dawn.

Up with the dawn, they fancied the light
air Adirondacs. 59.

Bounded by dawn and sunset, and the
day Adirondacs. 153.

Singing at dawn on the alder bough;
Each. 14.

And on his mind at dawn of day
Frag. Poet. V. 47.

Many a day shall dawn and die,
Nun. 23.

By Jove, at dawn of the first day.
Solution. 2.

Whom the dawn and the day-star urgeth,
Woodnotes. II. 38.

Dawned

The morrow dawned with needless glow;
Threnody. 104.

Dawning

From Chaos to the dawning morrow;
May-Day. 460.

Day

See Good-day; Hey-day; Holiday;
Noonday; To-day; Vintage-day.

Where the deer feeds at night, the teal
by day, Adirondacs. 20.

All day we swept the lake,
Adirondacs. 108.

Bounded by dawn and sunset, and the
day Adirondacs. 153.

But, on the second day, we heed them
not, Adirondacs. 168.

And, that no day of life may lack
romance, Adirondacs. 221.

With a vermilion pencil mark the day
Adirondacs. 230.

But day by day, to loving ear
Aeolian Harp. 16.

The past restore, the day adorn,
Art. 11.

Which on the first day drew,
Bacchus. 65.

Of the round day, related to the sun
Blight. 15.

And night and day, ocean and continent,
Blight. 34.

And twice each day the flowing sea
Boston. 3.

For day by day could Boston Bay
Boston. 23.

O day remembered yet! Boston. 87.

The sea returning day by day
Boston. 100.

'Tis the day of the chattel,
Channing Ode. 48.

Day! hast thou two faces, Chartist. 1.

O Day! and is your mightiness
Chartist. 13.

Back, back to chaos, harlot Day!
Chartist. 18.

O tenderly the haughty day
Concord Ode. 1.

Who wrestled here on a day.
Cosmos. 20.

Still keeps that golden day Cosmos. 26.

Day by day returns Day by Day. 1.

But the day of day, Day by Day. 5.

Took a few herbs and apples, and the
Day Days. 9.

And all the following hours of the day
Day's Ration. 18.

Who all the day of life his summer story
tells; Enchanter. 2.

And dark, without love, is the day;
Exile. 18.

Their step is forth, and, ere the day
Forerunners. 3.

Defeated day by day, but unto victory
born. Frag. Life. XXIII. 4.

From strength to strength, and for night
brings day; Frag. Life. XXXI. 2.

By Him who built the day,
Frag. Life. XXXVI. 2.

But I can see the elastic tent of day
Frag. Nat. V. 4.

Make up thy splendor, matchless day?
Frag. Nat. XI. 2.

Day by day for her darlings
Frag. Nat. XII. 1.

Parks and ponds are good by day;
Frag. Nat. XVIII. 1.

All day the waves assailed the rock,
Frag. Nat. XXV. 1.

Makes each day a festival.
Frag. Nat. XXVI. 6.

His diamonds to the day.
Frag. Poet. VI. 4.

And on his mind at dawn of day
Frag. Poet. VI. 47.

Crowds in a day the sum of ages,
Frag. Poet. IX. 11.

When I would spend a lonely day,
Frag. Poet. XXV. 3.

All day his song is heard;
Frag. Poet. XXXIII. 2.

Though her parting dims the day,
Give. 45.

Where arches green, the livelong day,
Good-Bye. 19.

brings on the day Good Cheer. 13.

Attempered to the night and day,
Guy. 2.

To drudge all day for Guy the wise.
Guy. 40.

Knows the law of Night and Day,
Harp. 22.

In the lowland, when day dies;
Harp. 92.

That he will not demand the debt until
the Judgment Day. Ibn Jemin. 4.

Would bring back day if it were dark;
Initial Love. 22.

Plainer than the day, Initial Love. 42.

Every day brings a ship, Letters. 1.

Or a day without night. *Lines. 16.

Voice of a meteor lost in day?
May-Day. 12.

Not idle, since the leaf all day
          May-Day. 115.
As in the day of sacrifice, May-Day. 140.
Giddy with day, to the topmost spire,
          May-Day. 232.
That one broad, long midsummer day
          May-Day. 276.
They were Night and Day, and Day and
  Night,   May-Day. 310.
As the two twilights of the day
          Merlin. 128.
No inch to the god of day; Merops. 10.
Let not unto the stones the Day
          Monadnoc. 12.
Ere yet arrives the wintry day
          Monadnoc. 23.
We are what we are made; each follow-
  ing day   Naples. 1.
The day goes drudging through the
  while,   Nun. 2.
Many a day shall dawn and die,
          Nun. 23.
The appointed, and the unappointed day;
         On Two Days. 2.
That Night or Day, that Love or Crime,
         Park. 15.
The mustering Day of Doom, Peter. 26.
And rived the dark like a new day!
         Poet. 56.
He takes no mark of night or day,
         Poet. 83.
Bathing in thy day sublime. Poet. 133.
The new day lowers, and equal odds
         Poet. 179.
Day and night their turn observe,
         Poet. 273.
But the day of day may swerve.
         Poet. 274.
Shadows of the thoughts of day,
         Quat. Memory. 2.
Boon Nature yields each day a brag
  which we now first behold,
         Quat. Nature. 1.
To bless that creature day and night;
         Rhea. 48.
Brighter than Jami's day. Saadi. 85.
Of a gusty Autumn day, September. 2.
By Jove, at dawn of the first day.
         Solution. 2.
To the borders of day. Sphinx. 104.
I am commissioned in my day of joy
         Summons. 3.
The favor of the loving Day,—
         Threnody. 20.
On that shaded day, Threnody. 98.
Ill day which made this beauty waste,
         Threnody. 150.
And, as the great all-loving Day
         Threnody. 217.
As if it said, 'Good day, good sir!
         Titmouse. 29.
And where he winds is the day of day.
         Two Rivers. 16.
Aurora of a dearer day. Una. 16.
Night and Day were tampered with,
         Unity. 8.
Thou bloomest here a lonely thing in the
  clear autumn day.   *Violet. 6.
Devastator of the day! Visit. 2.
I bring round the harvest day.'
         Voluntaries. 34.

For this the day was made.
         Waldeinsamkeit. 12.
I heed how wears the day;
         Walden. 42.
Or lands of Eastern day? Walden. 46.
But multiplies the image of a day,—
         Xenophanes. 15.

Day-dawn
Coin the day-dawn into lines
         Frag. Poet. XXIX. 1.

Daylight
For, in daylight or in dark,
         Boston Hymn. 86.
Doubling daylight everywhere:
         Caritas. 4.
Watching the daylight fade,
         Hermione. 59.

Day-moon
Bend nearer, faint day-moon! Yon
  thundertops,   Adirondacs. 260.

Day's
Day's toil and its guerdon,
         Illusions. 10.
His day's ride is a furlong space,
         Monadnoc. 322.
Between two sleeps a short day's stealth,
         Poet. 183.
Has disappeared from the Day's eye;
         Threnody. 21.
Returned this day, the South-wind
  searches,   Threnody. 24.
The school-march, each day's festival,
         Threnody. 59.

Days
    See Bondage-days.
For I can mend the happiest days
         Aeolian Harp. 22.
Shorter days and harder times.
         Alphonso. 6.
With the days and firmament, Art. 24.
While thus to love he gave his days
         Beauty. 21.
Daughters of Time, the hypocritic Days,
         Days. 1.
The days pass over me Days Pass. 1.
So to be husbanded for poorer days.
         Day's Ration. 25.
The nearest matters for a thousand
  days?   Day's Ration. 32.
And carry in my heart, for days,
         Forerunners. 37.
A train of gay and clouded days
         Frag. Life. I. 1.
I could walk days, years, away
         Frag. Nat. XXI. 6.
Said melted the days like cups of pearl,
         Frag. Poet. I. 19.
For which I sell days,
         Frag. Poet. VIII. 3.
Friends, kindred, days, Give. 3.
When the south wind, in May days,
         Humble-Bee. 20.
Long days, and solid banks of flowers;
         Humble-Bee. 35.
As pledged in coming days to forge
         In Memoriam. 64.
Nor mourn the unalterable Days
         In Memoriam. 109.
When late I walked, in earlier days,
         May-Day. 35.

Days —_Continued_
I saw the Days deformed and low,
          May-Day. 312.
Exact to days, exact to hours,
          May-Day. 375.
On their due days, of the birds.
          May-Day. 380.
Through tempering nights and flashing
  days,   Monadnoc. 212.
Ages are thy days,   Monadnoc. 358.
The shortness of our days,
          Monadnoc. 406.
And reconcile him to the common days.
          Naples. 12.
On two days it steads not to run from
  thy grave,   On Two Days. 1.
These are but seeds of days, Poet. 101.
Wear out indoors your sickly days,
          Romany. 7.
And in days of evil plight Solution. 20.
In newer days of war and trade,
          Solution. 59
The innumerable days.
         Song of Nature. 4.
Made one of day and one of night
         Song of Nature. 63.
Of all the zones and countless days.
         Song of Nature. 80.
Fears not undermining days,
        Spiritual Laws. 6.
All woman-born do know, that hoped-
  for days,   Summons. 19.
Days that come dancing on fraught with
  delights,   Summons. 20.
I had the right, few days ago,
         Threnody. 32.
Into calendar months and days.
         Uriel. 4.
'Twas one of the charmèd days
        Woodnotes. I. 96.
Day-star
Whom the dawn and the day-star urgeth,
        Woodnotes. II. 38.
Dazzle
But whether it dazzle me with light.
        Destiny. 37.
Dazzle every mortal.   Manners. 4.
Dazzles
Which dazzles me in midnight dark,
        Etienne. 16.
Dazzling
A dazzling memory revive; Bacchus. 61.
Dead
He thought it happier to be dead,
        Beauty. 25.
When all but Love itself is dead
        Ellen. 11.
Nor ringlets dead   Hermione. 17.
The reliquaries of my dead saint, and
  dwell   Letter. 17.
The dead log touched bursts into leaf,
        May-Day. 208.
Seek the living among the dead,—
        Saadi. 117.
But over the dead he has no power,
        Threnody. 5.
Some went and came about the dead;
        Threnody. 152.
Care not to strip the dead To J. W. 11.
Quick or dead, except its own;
        Unity. 6.

And drain his heart till he be dead.
        Voluntaries. 58.
Quit thy friends as the dead in doom,
        Woodnotes. II. 223.
Dead-march
The winds shall sing their dead-march
  old,   Titmouse. 20.
Deaf
Deaf, and dumb, and blind, and cold,
       Frag. Poet. VIII. 6.
Warning to the blind and deaf,
        Rhea. 33.
Amid the Muses, left thee deaf and
  dumb,   Terminus. 31.
This is Jove, who, deaf to prayers,
        Worship. 19.
Deal
For teeth and hair with shopmen deal;
        Romany. 18.
I know what spells are laid. Leave me
  to deal   Seashore. 43.
For only it can absolutely deal.
        Sursum Corda. 11.
When you deal with arctic cold,
        Titmouse. 2.
Dealing
   See Plain-dealing.
Dealing purely and nakedly,—
      Frag. Life. XXVII. 11.
Deals
He has his way, and deals his gifts,—
        World-Soul. 79.
Dealt
Dealt out with a God's charity.
        Mountain. 13.
Thanked Nature for each stroke she
  dealt;   Poet. 209.
Halved and dealt the globe anew,
        Solution. 64.
Dear
Dear memory's stone-incarved traits,
       Daemonic Love. 14.
Dear to the Eumenides, Destiny. 47.
Him by the hand dear Nature took,
       Experience. 17.
To the dear object of his thought,
      Frag. Life. XVII. 13.
'Higher, dear swallows! mind not what I
  say.   Hermione. 26.
Was frolic sunshine, dear to all men,
        Holidays. 11.
More dear to one than mines of gold.
        Holidays. 12.
And sacrifice for love's dear sake,
       In Memoriam. 108.
Dear brother, would you know the life,
        Letter. 1.
Cold is genial and dear. May-Day. 137.
With the dear, dangerous lords that rule
  our life,   Musketaquid. 7.
Dread Power, but dear! if God thou be,
       Ode to Beauty. 98.
A blooming child to children dear,
        Poet. 49.
'Is this dear Nature's manly pride?
        Poet. 218.
And yet, dear stars, I know ye shine
        Poet. 233.
Means, dear brother, ask them not;
        Poet. 249.

I see his cowlèd portrait dear;
                    Problem. 70.
Not less are summer mornings dear
                    Promise. 7.
Tell them, dear, that if eyes were made
  for seeing,   Rhodora. 11.
Of prayer and song that were my dear
  delight,   Summons. 5.
Boy who made dear his father's home,
                    Threnody. 167.

Dear-bought
But will we sacrifice our dear-bought lore
                    Adirondacs. 306.

Dearer
Aurora of a dearer day.   Una. 16.

Dearest
Dearest, where thy shadow falls,
                    Dearest. 1.
And mute thy music's dearest tone,
                    Ellen. 10.
They summon thee, dearest,—
                    Ellen South. 14.
Dearest Nature, strong and kind,
                    Experience. 18.
But when she spread her dearest spells,
                    Frag. Poet. IV. 17.
And the dearest interferes:
                    Frag. Poet. XXV. 2.
Dearest, to thee I did not send
                    Threnody. 210.

Dearly
He never, though he dearly loved his
  race,   Entombed. 3.
But she dearly loves the poor,
                    Nature. I. 9.

Dears
To their kinsfolk and their dears;
                    Astraea. 16.

Death
Both death and pity, my unequal skill
                    Angelo. 13.
Fails of the life, but draws the death
  and ill.   Angelo. 14.
To life or death, to heaven or hell,
                    Bell. 3.
Ah! the hot owner sees not Death, who
  adds   Hamatreya. 25.
Sleep is not, death is not;   Illusions. 5.
I grudge not these their bed of death,
                    In Memoriam. 32.
Life out of death, new out of old,
                    May-Day. 203.
Sweet is death forevermore.   Past. 7.
Life death overtaking;   Sphinx. 15.
In birdlike heavings unto death,
                    Threnody. 101.
Covetous death bereaved us all,
                    Threnody. 158.
My servant Death, with solving rite,
                    Threnody. 236.
Hurling defiance at vast death;
                    Titmouse. 44.
Victor over death and pain.
                    Voluntaries. 105.
Of Death and Fortune, Growth and
  Strife.'   Woodnotes. II. 132.

Death-bell
And soon thy music, sad death-bell,
                    Bell. 13.

Death-hymn
One crash, the death-hymn of the perfect
  tree,   Woodnotes. I. 74.
Deathless
And all but deathless Reason gone.
                    Ellen. 12.

Debility
The general debility;   Alphonso. 21.
Debt
    See Indebted.
For eternal years in debt.
                    Boston Hymn. 64.
Would pay my debt to thee.
                    Farewell. 22.
Pay every debt as if God wrote the bill.
                    Frag. Life. XXXII. 2.
That he will not demand the debt until
  the Judgment Day.   Ibn Jemin. 4.
The debt is paid,   Past. 1.
With glad remembrance of my debt,
                    Titmouse. 79.
Remembering Matter pays her debt:
                    Wealth. 45.

Decameron
Nor Boccace in Decameron.
                    Adirondacs. Motto. 4.
Decay
And slough decay from grazing herds,
                    May-Day. 448.
Endless dirges to decay,   Saadi. 50.
Decayed
Decayed millennial trunks,
                    Adirondacs. 48.
Or taunt us with our hope decayed?
                    May-Day. 427.
Romance forgot, and faith decayed,
                    Solution. 60.

Decays
The school decays, the learning spoils
                    Frag. Life. X. 5.
Grows by decays,   Spiritual Laws. 7.
Deceit
Of such deceit I'll not complain.'
                    May-Day. 371.

Deceive
Though the frail ringlets thee deceive,
                    II. Compensation. 17.
Deceive us, seeming to be many things,
                    Xenophanes. 8.

Deceived
By man who thirts to be deceived.
                    Frag. Nat. XXXI. 6.
'Now, deceived, thou wanderest
                    Hermione. 47.
The much deceived Endymion
                    Manners. 19.
Who thee divorced, deceived and left?
                    Woodnotes. II. 182.

Deceiver
Lest there I find the same deceiver
                    Ode to Beauty. 96.
Deceivers
But I reck not of deceivers.
                    Song of Seyd. 30.
Deceives
Deceives our rash desire;
                    World-Soul. 42.

Deceiving
    See Undeceiving.

December
The low December vault in June be lifted
high,　　　　　Frag. Nat. XX. 1.
With beams December planets dart
　　　　　Quat. S. H. 1.
Decency
That I am laid with decency.
　　　　　Mountain. 17.
Decide
One, with low tones that decide,
　　　　　Uriel. 15.
Decimal
On the remnant decimal.　Alphonso. 70.
Deck
　　See Bedeck.
To deck the morning of the year,
　　　　　Frag. Nat. VIII. 2.
Rose and vine-leaf deck buffoons;
　　　　　Heroism. 3.
And fetch her stars to deck her hair:
　　　　　Rhea. 52.
And deck her breast with diamond,
　　　　　Woodnotes. II. 86.
Decked
Decked by courtly rites and dress
　　　　　Frag. Poet. I. 29.
Decketh
Well used, it decketh joy,
　　　　　Frag. Nat. XXIV. 7.
Declare
Speak what I cannot declare,
　　　　　Garden. 51.
Declared
What himself declared repeats,
　　　　　Astraea. 26.
Declares
Declares the close of its green century.
　　　　　Woodnotes. I. 75.
Decline
He shall no task decline;　Merlin. 50.
Declined
And where the western hills declined
　　　　　Boston. 43.
Decompose
He did their weapons decompose.
　　　　　Guy. 18.
Decrepit
He slowly cures decrepit flesh,
　　　　　Monadnoc. 161.
Decrepitude
Brother, no decrepitude　Poet. 293.
Dedicated
Vanish beside these dedicated blocks,
　　　　　Monadnoc. 368.
Deed
When linkèd hemispheres attest his deed.
　　　　　Adirondacs. 248.
That memory may their deed redeem,
　　　　　C. Hymn. 11.
Hurled into life to do a deed,
　　　　　Frag. Life. XXIII. 8.
Go put your creed into your deed,
　　　　　Concord Ode. 19.
And gives persuasion to a gentle deed.
　　　　　Enchanter. 15.
'The lawyer's deed　　Hamatreya. 37.
Deed thou doest she must do,
　　　　　Hermione. 69.
Their deed of blood　In Memoriam. 7.

Draws better deed:　　　Saadi. 44.
But do the deed thy fellows hate,
　　　　　Saadi. 65.
And the sweet heaven his deed secures.
　　　　　Voluntaries. 92.
Deeds
Not of spent deeds, but of doing.
　　　　　Threnody. 281.
A single will, a million deeds.
　　　　　Woodnotes. II. 265.
Deem
The vines replied, 'And didst thou deem
　　　　　Berrying. 11.
Mortals deem the planets bright
　　　　　Daemonic Love. 52.
Deemest
And deemest thou as those who pore,
　　　　　Threnody. 179.
Deems
Deems not that great Napoleon
　　　　　Each. 6.
A few rods off he deems it gems and
clouds.　　　　　Seashore. 46.
Deep
　　See Knee-deep.
Thy voice upon the deep　　Bell. 5.
The waves that rocked them on the deep
　　　　　Boston. 13.
'Deep, deep are loving eyes,
　　　　　Celestial Love. 15.
Mountain tall and ocean deep
　　　　　II. Compensation. 3.
In the deep heart of man a poet dwells
　　　　　Enchanter. 1.
Deep in the man sits fast his fate
　　　　　Fate. 1.
From deep ideal fontal heavens that
flow.　　　　　Frag. Life. XV. 8.
To the isles of the deep,
　　　　　Frag. Nat. III. 36.
Thou already slumberest deep;
　　　　　Humble-Bee. 60.
Deep in a woodland tract, a sunny farm,
　　　　　Letter. 8.
So deep and large her bounties are,
　　　　　May-Day. 275.
And lifting man to the blue deep
　　　　　Monadnoc. 100.
In the uncontinented deep."
　　　　　Monadnoc. 329.
Sea-valleys and the deep of skies
　　　　　Ode to Beauty. 48.
His learning should be deep and large,
　　　　　Poet. 40.
They hurried down from their deep
abodes　　　　　Poet. 147.
I see your forms with deep content,
　　　　　Poet. 257.
But not angels of the deep:　Poet. 272.
But blest is he, who, playing deep, yet
haply asks not why,　Quat. Nature. 3.
The midway of the eternal deep.
　　　　　Saadi. 146.
Deep underneath deep?　Sphinx. 16.
Deep love lieth under　　Sphinx. 69
In whose deep eyes　　Threnody. 168.
The deep Heart answered, 'Weepest
thou?　　　　　Threnody. 176.

Safe in their ancient crannies, dark and
deep,   To-Day. 3.
Than all it holds more deep, more high.'
Woodnotes. II. 318.

Deeper
Than thine no deeper moat can be,
Boston. 61.
Deeper and older seemed his eye;
Character. 4.
The deeper secret of the hour!
Miracle. 18.
Deeper and older seemed his eye,
Poet. 137.
At home a deeper thought may light
Una. 13.

Deepest
The music that can deepest reach,
Merlin's Song. 35.
The deepest lore of wealth or want:
Poet. 42.

Deep-eyed
The deep-eyed flame, obedient water,
Frag. Life. XXIX. 2.
Amidst the deep-eyed dew!
Thine Eyes. 8.
But the deep-eyed boy is gone.
Threnody. 97.

Deeply
Deeply soothe his anxious ear.
Initial Love. 73.

Deep's
Is the deep's lover;   Ode to Beauty. 38.

Deeps
Folding Nature in its deeps,
Celestial Love. 49.
Whose deeps, till beams of noonday
break,   May-Day. 18.
In Being's deeps past ear and eye;
Ode to Beauty. 95.
Ye scorn me from your deeps of blue.
Poet. 240.
And 't is far in the deeps of history,
World-Soul. 19.

Deer
Where the deer feeds at night, the teal
by day,   Adirondacs. 20.
should drive in deer,   Adirondacs. 110.
Of the red deer, to aim at a square mist.
Adirondacs. 120.
Dissected the slain deer, weighed the
trout's brain,   Adirondacs. 134.
Bird, or deer, or caribou.
Initial Love. 101.
Of wolf and otter, bear and deer;
Monadnoc. 81.

Defaced
Plight broken, this high face defaced!
Threnody. 151.

Defeat
Even at its greatest space is a defeat,
Blight. 54.

Defeated
Defeated day by day, but unto victory
born.   Frag. Life. XXIII. 4.

Defect
Rebuild the ruin, mend defect;
May-Day. 444.

Defence
Him Nature giveth for defence
Woodnotes. II. 75.

Defences
To the defences thou hast round me set;
Grace. 2.

Defend
From all evils to defend her; Rhea. 49.

Defended
Had not these me against myself defended.   Grace. 8.

Defends
For who defends our leafy tabernacle
Adirondacs. 171.

Defiance
Hurling defiance at vast death;
Titmouse. 44.

Defied
And polar frost my frame defied,
Titmouse. 77.
And doubt and reverend use defied,
Uriel. 16.

Defies
Which his ruthless will defies,
Daemonic Love. 117.

Defile
Disgust my reason and defile my hands.
To-Day. 10.

Defiled
See Undefiled.
Purge alpine air by towns defiled,
May-Day. 451.

Define
Define and wrangle how they list,
Saadi. 97.

Deformed
I saw the Days deformed and low,
May-Day. 312.

Defrauded
Whence, O thou orphan and defrauded?
Woodnotes. II. 180.

Defy
And the firm soul does the pale train
defy   I Bear. 11.
All friends to fend, all foes defy,
In Memoriam. 40.
The morrow front, and can defy;
Nun. 4.

De ying
The brave Empedocles, defying fools,
Frag. Life. XVIII. 1.

Degree
Was Cromwell's measure or degree;
Fate. 4.
Falls, in turn, a new degree.   Rhea. 40.
And learn of love a new degree.
Security. 12.

Degrees
Ascending thorough just degrees
Frag. Life. XXVIII. 1.
To carry man to new degrees   Rhea. 68.

Deities
And for the whole. The gentle deities
Musketaquid. 59.
Sylvan deities encamp,   Saadi. 38.
The young deities discussed   Uriel. 11.

Deity
Full of light and of deity;   Each. 47.
Where this deity is shrined,
Freedom. 12.
One deity stirred,—   Sphinx. 36.
And mix with Deity.   Thought. 8.

Dejected
Neither dejected nor elate,   Poet. 168.

Delay
The crowded town, thy feet may well
delay.   To J. W. 4.
Delayed
Delayed, all friends shut out, the house-
mates sit   Snow-Storm. 7.
Delectable
Fortune's delectable mountains;
Frag. Poet. IV. 12.
Delicate
And, in the forest, delicate clerks, un-
browned,   Adirondacs. 57.
Out of that delicate lay could'st thou
Dirge. 47.
The delicate shells lay on the shore;
Each. 19.
Scorch our delicate prime,
Ellen South. 19.
Courageous sing a delicate overture
Musketaquid. 17.
And ever by delicate powers
Song of Nature. 13.
Delight
Of such delight and wonder as there
grew,—   Adirondacs. 250.
By its own craft, to a more rich delight.
Bacchus. 11.
Stops his horse, and lists with delight,
Each. 7.
I do not delight   Frag. Nat. XVIII. 2.
Your colors for our eyes' delight:
Frag. Nat. XXIII. 10.
Mask thy wisdom with delight,
Frag. Poet. V. 1.
Scott, the delight of generous boys,
Harp. 81.
The sweet delight I found in fields and
farms,   I Bear. 6.
But calm delight,   *Lines. 14.
Your manners for the heart's delight,
May-Day. 399.
Mask thy wisdom with delight,
Merlin's Song. 37.
I watched the singer with delight,—
Miracle. 25.
Of untried power and sane delight:
Monadnoc. 105.
On life's fair picture of delight,
Nun. 9.
'T is his study and delight   Rhea. 47.
And a glad delight below,   Security. 2.
Unlock doors of new delight;
Solution. 21.
Of prayer and song that were my dear
delight,   Summons. 5.
Hast thou forgot me in a new delight?
Threnody. 35.
Or for service, or delight,   Visit. 17.
For gods delight in gods,
World-Soul. 93.
Delighted
He rolls them with delighted motion,
Initial Love. 48.
And by her radiant youth delighted,
Rhea. 43.
Delights
Delights to build a road:
Daemonic Love. 86.
By new delights, as old by old,
May-Day. 366.

Means, appliances, delights,
Mithridates. 27.
Days that come dancing on fraught with
delights,   Summons. 20.
Delights the dreadful Destiny
Woodnotes II. 120.
Delivered
See New-delivered.
Dell
Cheers the rough crag and mournful
dell,   Frag. Nat. XXIX. 2.
And dream the dream of Auburn dell.
May-Day. 181.
The surge of summer's beauty; dell and
crag,   Musketaquid. 22.
The leafy dell, the city mart,
Ode to Beauty. 88.
Dells
The summer dells, by genius haunted,
May-Day. 43.
Wales, Scotland, Uri, Hungary's dells:
Monadnoc. 96.
Delphian
And best can teach its Delphian chord
Harp. 103.
Delphic
The thrilling Delphic oracle;
Problem. 12.
Deluge
He planted where the deluge ploughed,
Frag. Poet. XXVII. 1.
Here once the Deluge ploughed,
Garden. 13.
So pours the deluge of the heat
May-Day. 247.
And pour the deluge still;
Song of Nature. 12.
Demand
That he will not demand the debt until
the Judgment Day.   Ibn Jemin. 4.
Den
No churl, immured in cave or den;
Saadi. 24.
Denied
All, all was given, and only health denied.
In Memoriam. 72.
Prometheus proffered, Jove denied;
May-Day. 415.
Denies
But even thy kiss denies   *Farewell. 23.
The brave whom Fate denies the goal!
In Memoriam. 87.
Denounce
Denounce who will, who will deny,
Saadi. 94.
Dens
In dens of passion, and pits of woe,
Beauty. 17.
Deny
I'll not deny you make   Fable. 15.
Denounce who will, who will deny,
Saadi. 94.
Depart
If my darling should depart,
From Hafiz. 9.
The sowers made haste to depart,—
Garden. 17.
Departed
Turned and departed silent. I, too late,
Days. 10.

For when love has once departed
                              Rhea. 13.
The resurrection of departed pride.
                              To-Day. 2.
The clay of their departed lover.'
                              Woodnotes. I. 146.

Departs
Fancy departs: no more invent;
                              Terminus. 9.

Depths
And its depths reflect all forms;
                              Astraea. 42.
Then plunge to depths profound.
                              Garden. 12.
The depths of sin to which I had
  descended,   Grace. 7.

Deranged
Men and manners much deranged:
                              Initial Love. 8.

Derides
Fantastic care derides,
                              Waldeinsamkeit. 14.

Dervish
The Dervish whined to Said,
                              Frag. Poet. II. 1.
Barefooted Dervish is not poor,
                              Saadi. 119.

Dervishes
Muffled and dumb like barefoot dervishes,
                              Days. 2.

Descended
    See Long-descended.
The depths of sin to which I had
  descended,   Grace. 7.

Descends
And the mighty choir descends,
                              Daemonic Love. 44.

Described
That human part may be described and
  taught,   Frag. Life. XVIII. 7.

Desert
What in the desert was impossible
                              Adirondacs. 321.
How much runs over on the desert sands.
                              Days Ration. 14.
How desert without you
                              *Farewell. 30.
Zigzag steerer, desert cheerer,
                              Humble-Bee. 7.
The whited desert knew me not,
                              May-Day. 41.
White hollow shells upon the desert
  shore,   Pan. 9.
To please the desert and the sluggish
  brook.   Rhodora. 4.
Foundling of the desert far,
                              Voluntaries. 47.
The bittern's boom, a desert make
                              Waldeinsamkeit. 31.
One aspect to the desert and the lake.
                              Xenophanes. 4.

Desert's
On the desert's yellow floor,   Saadi. 168.

Deserts
Laurel crowns cleave to deserts,
                              II. Compensation. 21.

Deserving
And in right deserving,
                              Celestial Love. 11.

Design
Ah, but I miss the grand design.
                              Frag. Poet. XVIII. 6.
Worthy her design,   House. 8.
Recalled thy skill in bold design,
                              Lines. 18.
Is sketched and dyed, each with a new
  design,   Naples. 7.
Find to their design   Politics. 17.
And, sculptor-like, his large design
                              Solution. 31.

Designed
But they have heartily designed
                              Celestial Love. 119.

Designs
Which holds the grand designs
                              Ode to Beauty. 53.
Nor plant immense designs   Poet. 247.

Desire
Fond children, ye desire
                              Celestial Love. 6.
And one in our desire.   Concord Ode. 4.
Which drives me mad with sweet desire,
                              Destiny. 13.
Sweet, extravagant desire,
                              Ode to Beauty. 77.
Soul's desire is means enow,
                              Poet. 250.
You must be like them if you desire
  them,   Rome. 11.
Of all mortals the desire,   Saadi. 10.
Life, sunshine and desire,   Threnody. 2.
Deceives our rash desire;
                              World-Soul 42.

Desired
And of all other men desired.
                              Woodnotes II. 70.

Desolate
Bring music to the desolate;
                              Frag. Poet. X. 3.

Despair
Haste to cure the old despair,—
                              Bacchus. 55.
Lose courage, and despair.
                              Daemonic Love. 111.
To master my despair;   Friendship. 18.
Thou hast touched for my despair;
                              Ode to Beauty. 91.
This monument of my despair
                              Rhea. 58.
He forbids to despair;   World-Soul. 101.

Despite
Tyrants despite their guards or walls.
                              In Memoriam. 66.
And the simular despite
                              Monadnoc. 350.

Despoil
And we despoil the unborn.
                              World-Soul. 24.

Destined
High destined youths and holy maids
                              Frag. Poet. VII. 3.

Destiny
Mad Destiny this tender stripling played;
                              Epitaph. 2.
Destiny sat by, and said,
                              Voluntaries. 31.
Delights the dreadful Destiny
                              Woodnotes II. 120.
For Destiny never swerves
                              World-Soul. 73.

Destroy
Ill used, it will destroy,
                    Frag. Nat. XXIV. 9.
Elegantly destroy.
                    Frag. Nat. XXIV. 12.
Whom they will destroy,
                    Voluntaries. 112.

Destroyer
Fierce conserver, fierce destroyer,—
                    Saadi. 98.

Detain
Nor thou detain her vesture's hem,
                    Give. 40.
Than the gray dreams which thee detain.
                    Monadnoc. 18.
The cold sea-wind detain;   Walden. 6.

Detect
His eyes detect the Gods concealed
                    Frag. Poet. XXVII. 3.
I detect far-wandered graces,
                    Ode to Beauty. 65.

Detected
I detected many a god
                    Frag. Life. XXII. 5.

Deteriorate
Things deteriorate in kind;   Alphonso. 3.

Determine
Tell the sun's time, determine the true
   north,   Adirondacs. 104.

Devastate
We devastate them unreligiously,
                    Blight. 38.

Devastator
Devastator of the day!   Visit. 2.

Device
And interpret your device.
                    Initial Love. 63.

Devices
The quaint devices on its mornings gay.
                    Frag. Nat. V. 7.

Devil
As God and devil; bring them to the
   mind,   Xenophanes. 10.

Devils
And stirred the devils everywhere,
                    Uriel. 18.

Devil-Spider
That devil-spider that devours her mate
                    Philosopher. 11.

Devour
His impatient looks devour
                    Daemonic Love. 105.
Devour as many as you list,
                    Frag. Nat. XIX. 5.

Devours
That devil-spider that devours her mate
                    Philosopher. 11.

Dew
   See Sundew.
Draw everlasting dew;   Bacchus. 17.
In a chapel, which the dew
                    Frag. Nat. III. 6.
But rather, like its beads of dew
                    Frag. Nat. XXVI. 35.
The morn and sparkling dew, a snare?
                    May-Day. 430.
Thinly dieted on dew,   Mithridates. 21.
Gives back the bending heavens in dew.
                    Song of Nature. 84.

Amidst the deep-eyed dew!
                    Thine Eyes. 8.
What need I holier dew   Walden. 25.

Dew-bent
And dew-bent violets, fresh and new,
                    Frag. Nat. XXVI. 36.

Dews
With dews of tropic morning wet,
                    May-Day. 395.
As with diamond dews thereon.
                    May-Day. 413.

Diadem
From her summer diadem.   Give. 42.

Diadems
Bring diadems and fagots in their hands.
                    Days. 4.

Dial
Counted on the spacious dial
                    May-Day. 376.
Gauge and calendar and dial,
                    Monadnoc. 52.

Dialogue
With dialogue divine;   Poet. 76.

Dials
My stock of art, plant dials in the grass,
                    Letter. 20.

Diamond
Nor gives the jealous lord one diamond
   drop   Day's Ration. 24.
A rose diamond or a white,   Destiny. 36.
Nor pearl nor diamond   *Farewell. 21.
As with diamond dews thereon.
                    May-Day. 413.
On prince or bride no diamond stone
                    On Prince. 1.
And deck her breast with diamond,
                    Woodnotes. II. 86.

Diamonds
The hedge is gemmed with diamonds,
                    April. 5.
His diamonds to the day.
                    Frag. Poet. VI. 4.
Why are not diamonds black and gray,
                    Titmouse. 56.

Dian's
Sweet and scent for Dian's table,
                    Frag. Nat. II. 16.

Dictionaries
Institutes and dictionaries,
                    Monadnoc. 182.

Did (Partial list.)
   See Undid.
They did what freemen can,   Boston. 8.
Did in your childhood fall.   Dirge. 56
Did as she pleased and went her way.
                    Frag. Nat. XXXV. 2.
So did our sons; Heaven met them as
   they fell.   Inscription. 2
For Saadi's nightly stars did burn
                    Saadi. 84
Which five hundred did survive?
                    Test. 14.
The gracious boy, who did adorn
                    Threnody. 17.
Dearest, to thee I did not send
                    Threnody. 210.
What others did at distance hear,
                    Woodnotes. I. 58.

Didst (Partial list.)
The vines replied, 'And didst thou deem
                    Berrying. 11.

Didst thou, just man, endure.
Tal. Exile. 3.
When thou didst yield thy innocent
breath Threnody. 100.

Die
To die for Beauty, than live for bread.
Beauty. 26.
And die of inanition. If I knew
Blight. 3.
To die, and leave their children free,
C. Hymn. 14.
The seed of gods to die, Fame. 20.
And die to Fame a happy martyr.
Fame. 30.
No trace of age, no fear to die.
Frag. Nat. VIII. 8.
Who seem to die live. Illusions. 6.
Why fear to die Mountain. 1.
It would please me to die, Mountain. 10.
I should like to die in sweets,
Mountain. 14.
Many a day shall dawn and die, Nun. 23.
On earth I dream;—I die to be: Nun. 29.
Queen of things! I dare not die
Ode to Beauty. 94.
Too busied with the crowed hour to live
or die. Quat. Nature. 4.
When for the truth he ought to die.'
Quat. Sacrifice. 4.
To distant men, who must go there, or
die. Seashore. 49.
And oh! it cannot die, Thought. 6.
O Violet, like thee, how blest could I lie
down and die, *Violet. 9.
'T will be time enough to die;
Woodnotes. I. 142.

Died
Died in its last expression. Amulet. 12.
But when at last the patriarch died
Frag. Nat. VI. 5.
His mother died,—the only friend he
had,— Philosopher. 7.
They could not feed him, and he died,
Threnody. 147.
and in the year's rich beauty died.
*Violet. 16.

Dies
Flowering April cools and dies
Alphonso. 7.
And dies in anger that it was a dupe;
Blight. 55.
In the lowland, when day dies;
Harp. 92.
The orphan of the forest dies.
Woodnotes. II. 56.

Diet
Ply us now with a full diet;
Alphonso. 52.

Dieted
Thinly dieted on dew, Mithridates. 21.

Differ
Talents differ; Fable. 17.

Difference
Till all dilerence expire. Song of Seyd. 26.
In difference sweet, Sphinx. 26.

Diffuse
How they diffuse themselves into the air,'
Frag. Nat. XVII. 2.
That never joy or hope shall here diffuse.
In Memoriam. 24.

Thyself thro' Nature to diffuse?
Lines. 2.

Dig
A thousand men shall dig and eat;
Saadi. 106.
As resolutely dig or dive. To J. W. 17.

Digest
There doth digest, and work, and spin,
Initial Love. 46.

Digestible
See Indigestible.

Digger
The digger in the harvest-field,
Boston Hymn. 39.

Diluted
We buy diluted wine; Bacchus. 13.

Dim
To dim New England's shore;
*Farewell. 47.
Ever find me dim regards,
Frag. Poet. VII. 9.
From blue mount and headland dim
Frag. Poet. XI. 5.
Still breaks that morn, though dim, to
Memory's eye, I Bear. 10.
The dim horizon's utmost bound;—
May-Day. 425
Nature's funeral high and dim,— Nun. 20.
(In dizzy æons dim and mute
Wealth. 19.
He saw beneath dim aisles, in odorous
beds, Woodnotes. I. 68.

Dimension
To the titmouse dimension.' Titmouse. 64.

Dimmed
No ray is dimmed, no atom worn,
Song of Nature. 81.

Dimple
Each dimple in the water, April. 9.

Dims
Give the gem which dims the moon
Friendship. Trans. 3.
Though her parting dims the day,
Give. 45.
To light which dims the morning's eye.
Rhea. 4.

Din
With the din of city arts; Merlin. 23.
Who builds, yet makes no chips, no din,
Monadnoc. 239.

Dine
To dine and sleep through forty years;
Fame. 14.
I dine in the sun; when he sinks in the
sea, Titmouse. 69.

Dined
God only knew how Saadi dined;
Frag. Poet. V. 13.

Dip
Which dip their foot in the seas
Boston Hymn. 22.
The moons in ocean dip, II Eros. 4.
And dip it in thy porcelain vase;
Woodnotes. II. 52.
Or dip thy paddle in the lake,
Woodnotes. II. 169.

Dippers
Divers or dippers were his words,
Poet. 20.

Dips
And dips sometimes as low as to her eyes.
Daemonic Love. 38.
And dips sometimes as low as to her eyes.
Frag. Life. XVI. 4.
Dire
Dire and satirical, Woodnotes. II. 201.
Directly
Directly never greeted me,
Frag. Poet. IV. 16.
Dirge
Hearing as now the lofty dirge Nun. 18.
Dirges
Endless dirges to decay, Saadi. 50.
"Say on, sweet Sphinx! thy dirges
Sphinx. 67.
Disappear
In mightier chant I disappear.
Monadnoc. 227.
Disappeared
Disappeared in blessed wife;
Holidays. 14.
Has disappeared from the Day's eye;
Threnody. 21.
Disarmed
Disarmed the thunder's fires. Bell. 12.
Discern
Nor head from foot can I discern,
Song of Seyd. 2.
His daily haunts I well discern,—
Threnody. 88.
Discerning
See Style-discerning.
Disclose
And by the order in the field disclose
Musketaquid. 50.
Disclosing
Disclosing treasure more than true,
May-Day. 416.
Disconcert
Disconcert the searching spy, Astraea. 35.
Disconcerted
It is not disconcerted,
Frag. Nat. XXIV. 5.
Disconcerts
Disconcerts with glad surprise.
Worship. 18.
Discontent
(Perchance I erred), a shade of discontent; Adirondacs. 273.
Discoursed
Discoursed of fortune as they blew;
Frag. Poet. V. 38.
Discourses
O how wise are his discourses!
Initial Love. 104.
Discoursing
What sea and land discoursing say
Harp. 27.
Discover
So did Guy betimes discover Guy. 9.
Discredit
They discredit Adamhood. Alphonso. 18.
Discreet
It seemed his Genius discreet Guy. 25.
Discrete
There are two laws discrete,
Channing Ode. 52.
Discrowned
Discrowned and timid, thoughtless, worn,
Poet. 181.

Discussed
The young deities discused Uriel. 11.
Disdain
Nor Byron's clarion of disdain, Harp. 80.
Checked by the owners' fierce disdain,
Voluntaries. 29.
Its beautiful disdain. World-Soul. 32.
Disdaining
Realms self-upheld, disdaining Fate,
Nun. 44.
Disdains
Now that morning not disdains
Hermione. 19.
I spurn the Past, my mind disdains its
nod, To-Day. 13.
Disease
Of grim Disease, that would her peace
affright. I Bear. 12.
And the wise soul expels disease.
Woodnotes. II. 191.
Disenchanted
One arctic moon had disenchanted.
May-Day. 44.
Disenchants
My twilight realm he disenchants,
Woodnotes. II. 28.
Disfurnished
Displaced, disfurnished here,
Voluntaries. 20.
Disgrace
And I think it no disgrace Fable. 10.
Disguise
All the rest he can disguise.
Initial Love. 20.
Disgust
Friends, foes, joys, fortunes, beauty and
disgust. Day's Ration. 8.
Disgust my reason and defile my hands.
To-Day. 10.
Dishonored
The world dishonored thou hast left.
Threnody. 171.
Disk
Half the sun's disk with a spot;
Alphonso. 10.
Dismal
The dismal Massachusetts ice
May-Day. 142.
Disown
Disown the knave and fool; Boston. 32.
Dispense
His merchants may dispense, Dull. 18.
He shall daily joy dispense Merlin. 41.
The constant mountain doth dispense;
Monadnoc. 382.
Nor can dispense Saadi. 27.
Disperse
The exodus of nations: I disperse
Seashore. 39.
Displace
The green silence dost displace
Humble-Bee. 30.
And nothing jostle or displace,
Woodnotes. II. 2.
Displaced
That so they shall not be displaced
House. 21.
Displaced, disfurnished here,
Voluntaries. 20.

Displaces
The atom displaces all atoms beside,
Frag. Poet. XXI. 1.
Displacing
Levelling, displacing Daemonic Love. 82.
Display
Her lily and rose, her sea and land display.
Monadnoc. 13.
Displays
Dissolves the crust, displays the flowers.
May-Day. 149.
Dissected
Dissected the slain deer, Adirondacs. 134.
Dissipate
To dissipate their being into it.
Frag. Nat. XVII. 6.
Dissipation
The wild dissipation, Illusions. 25.
Dissolves
In one only form dissolves;
Celestial Love. 32.
Dissolves the crust, displays the flowers.
May-Day. 149.
Dissolving
All ill dissolving in the light
Woodnotes. II. 65.
Dissolving all that fixture is,
Woodnotes. II. 113.
Dissuade
Will song dissuade the thirsty spear?
Voluntaries. 18.
Distance
We made our distance wider, boat from
boat, Adirondacs. 14.
Cattle lowed in mellow distance
September. 7.
What others did at distance hear,
Woodnotes. I. 58.
Distant
We trode on air, contemned the distant
town, Adirondacs. 160.
Mixed with mist by distant lochs.
Forerunners. 16.
So shall thou pierce the distant age
Frag. Poet. XIII. 3.
Far distant yet his chorus waits.
Garden. 36.
The distant bind; Hermione. 68.
To distant men, who must go there, or
die. Seashore. 49.
Distilled
Distilled from heaven's alembic blue,
Walden. 27.
Distils
All he distils into sidereal wine
Day's Ration. 11.
Distress
Soothe pain, and age, and love's distress,
May-Day. 439.
Distribute
Of tendency distribute souls.
Celestial Love. 82.
Disturb
Nor my unseasoned step disturb
Frag. Nat. XVIII. 4.
Ditties
Crooning ditties treasured well
Voluntaries. 7.
Divan
At court he sat in the grave Divan.
Frag. Poet. I. 10.

Maple and oak, the old Divan
Miracle. 5.
Dive
Nor mount, nor dive; all good things keep
Saadi. 145.
Man's spirit must dive; Sphinx. 82.
As resolutely dig or dive. To J. W. 17.
Dived
In the sea of sense I dived;
Song of Seyd. 12.
Divers
Divers or dippers were his words,
Poet. 20.
Dives
It dives into noon, Give. 12.
He dives the hollow, climbs the steep.
May-Day. 72.
Divide
I will divide my goods;
Boston Hymn. 25.
The victors divide; Channing Ode. 95.
Where bearded mists divide,
Waldeinsamkeit. 34.
Divided
Substances at base divided,
Celestial Love. 44.
Divides
And as the light divides the dark
Frag. Poet. XIII. 1.
Divine
The rich results of the divine consents
Blight. 43.
Born into Dæmons less divine:
Daemonic Love. 90.
Its heavy tale divine. Dirge. 48.
A sympathy divine. Eva. 6.
Yet can one ray of truth divine
Frag. Life. X. 8.
"I am divine, I am not mortal made;
Frag. Life. XVIII. 3.
Reason's twofold, part human, part divine;
Frag. Life. XVIII. 6.
All things wait for and divine him,—
Initial Love. 78.
Hath such a soul, such divine influence,
Naples. 21.
Divine Ideas below, Ode to Beauty. 61.
With dialogue divine; Poet. 76.
'Divine Inviters! I accept Poet. 149.
Gave his sentiment divine Uriel. 19.
That waft the breath of grace divine
Voluntaries. 69.
By which thy hurt thou may'st divine.
Woodnotes. II. 193.
A divine improvisation,
Woodnotes. II. 263.
Which is human, which divine.
Worship. 23.
Diviner
Or lift to a diviner dream!' Poet. 194.
High omens ask diviner guess;
Threnody. 228.
Divines
Taylor, the Shakespeare of divines.
Problem. 68.
Diving
Or, bathers, diving from the rock at noon;
Adirondacs. 112.
Divinities
Not angels but divinities attend.
Frag. Life. III. 2.

Divorced
Who thee divorced, deceived and left?
Woodnotes. II. 182.

Dizen
That dizen Nature's carnival,
Threnody. 190.

Dizzy
(In dizzy æons dim and mute
Wealth. 19.

Do (Partial list.)
See Outdo; Undo.
Who do the feat, and lift humanity.
Adirondacs. 295.
What it will do when it is man.
Bacchus. 42.
Do these celebrate their loves:
Celestial Love. 100.
Yet do not I implore Channing Ode. 71.
Easy to match what others do,
Frag. Life. X. 1.
Hurled into life to do a deed,
Frag. Life. XXIII. 8.
But if thou do thy best,
Frag. Life. XXVII. 1.
Time hath his work to do and we have
ours. Frag. Life. XXXVII. 2.
I do not delight Frag. Nat. XVIII. 2.
Right thou feelest, rush to do.'
Freedom. 24.
Deed thou doest she must do,
Hermione. 69.
And do well because they please,
Nature. I. 19.
They do her bidding, nothing loath.
Nature. II. 19.
But thou shalt do as do the gods
Rhea. 25.
But do the deed thy fellows hate,
Saadi. 65.
His wistful toil to do his best
Voluntaries. 21.
O what have I to do with time?
Waldeinsamkeit. 11.

Doat
How should not the poet doat Harp. 50.

Doats
And the sky doats on cheerful song.
Titmouse. 88.

Docile
Docile read my measured line:
Frag. Poet. VII. 2.

Docks
Then docks were built, and crops were
stored, Wealth. 42.

Doctor
Of our great-hearted Doctor in his boat
Adirondacs. 272.
The Doctor stretched the hours,
Walden. 34.

Doctors
They are the doctors of the wilderness,
Adirondacs. 95.
Two Doctors in the camp
Adirondacs. 133.

Doer
See Evil-doer.

Doers
See Wrong-doers.

Does (Partial list.)
Asks nothing, but does all receive.
Frag. Life. XVII. 3.

Know me, as does my dog: we sympa-
thize; Hamatreya. 9.
The hardy bunting does not chide;
May-Day. 165.

Doest
None shall ask thee what thou doest,
Destiny. 22.
Deed thou doest she must do,
Hermione. 69.

Doeth
As much as he is and doeth,
Boston Hymn. 59.
And thus the wise Immortal doeth,—
Rhea. 46.

Doffing
Too much of donning and doffing,
Song of Nature. 49.

Doffs
He dons a surcoat which he doffs at
morn: Adirondacs. 77.

Dog
Know me, as does my dog: we sympathize; Hamatreya. 9.

Dogs
Watching when the loud dogs should
drive in deer, Adirondacs. 110.
And the dogs of Fate unties.
Daemonic Love. 118.

Dog-wood
Blinding dog-wood in my hand;
Mithridates. 15.

Doing
Knowing and doing. Ebbs the tide, they
lie Pan. 8.
All my doing, all my leaving,
Song of Seyd. 5.
Not of spent deeds, but of doing.
Threnody. 281.

Doleful
Down with your doleful problems,
April. 15.
Or in lone corners of a doleful heath,
Frag. Nat. IV. 3.
O doleful ghosts, and goblins merry!
Mithridates. 25.

Dolls
On thieves, on drudges and on dolls.
Woodnotes. II. 203.

Domain
And sighed for all that bounded their
domain; Hamatreya. 18.
East, west, north, south, are his domain.
Titmouse. 8.

Dome
The hand that rounded Peter's dome
Problem. 19.
His hearth the earth,—his hall the azure
dome; Woodnotes. I. 93.

Domestic
Farewell, domestic fires *Farewell. 3.

Dominion
Thy sweet dominion o'er my will, Eva. 5.
Joy of thy dominion! Humble-Bee. 12.
But once in your dominion. Poet. 232.
Dominion o'er the palm and vine.
Woodnotes. II. 48.

Donation
With God's unspared donation;
Day by Day. 4.

Done. (Partial list.)
See Undone.
'Well done!' he cries; 'the bear is kept
at bay, Adirondacs. 315.
When the pilgrimage is done, Etienne. 5.
With the errand to be done,—
Etienne. 22.
Were it not better done, Fame. 13.
As angel blind to trespass done,
Frag. Life. XXVIII. 3.
The service done to me as done to them.
Frag. Life. XXX. 7.
Conscious each of duty done
Frag. Nat. XXIII. 17.
What is past, what is done,
Frag. Poet. IX. 4.
The impossible shall yet be done,
Initial Love. 145.
It was well done. In Memoriam. 10.
An act unworthy to be done;
In Memoriam. 54.
Ever have done, ever shall. Rhea. 32.
And his chain when life was done.
Voluntaries. 12.
Now the iron age is done,
Voluntaries. 44.

Donning
Too much of donning and doffing,
Song of Nature. 49.

Donor
'Whether is better, the gift or the donor?
Woodnotes. II. 2.

Dons
He dons a surcoat which he doffs at
morn: Adirondacs. 77.

Don't
For sea and land don't understand,
Concord Ode. 21.

Doom
The tyrants of his doom, Manners. 18.
The mustering Day of Doom, Peter. 26.
Self-announced its hour of doom?
Threnody. 254.
Quit thy friends as the dead in doom,
Woodnotes. II. 223.

Doomed
Whether doomed to long gyration
Uriel. 39.

Dooms
For God hath writ all dooms magnificent, Frag. Life. II. 2.

Door
Paint the prospect from their door.
Frag. Life. XIX. 2.
And peaceful woods beside my cottage
door. Frag. Nat. IV. 11.
every chamber was a door,
Frag. Nat. XII. 2.
A door to something grander,—
Frag. Nat. XII. 3.
Hassan the camel-driver's door,
Frag. Poet. III. 2.
A door into the mountain heart,
Hermione. 44.
That knock at meek contrition's door.
Hymn. 20.
Turn the key and bolt the door, Past. 6.
Flies-to the adamantine door Past. 12.
Each chimney-pot and cottage door,
Poet. 58.

If fate unlock his bosom's door,
Saadi. 120.
Behold, he watches at the door!
Saadi. 157.
While thou sittest at thy door Saadi. 167.
Round every windward stake, or tree, or
door. Snow-Storm. 14.
Unbar the door, since thou the Opener
art, Unbar. 1.

Door-bell
No door-bell heralded a visitor,
Adirondacs. 65.

Doors
See Indoors.
To draw the nations out of doors.
Frag. Nat. XIII. 2.
Too strait and low our cottage doors,
May-Day. 220.
'In to the upper doors, Merlin. 35.
Self-moved, fly-to the doors, Merlin. 75.
Open innumerable doors Saadi. 159.
Those doors are men: the Pariah hind
Saadi. 163.
Then I unbar the doors: my paths lead
out Seashore. 38.
Unlock doors of new delight;
Solution. 21.
Of my bird's song: 'Live out of doors
Titmouse. 67.
Of robins out of doors. Walden. 36.

Dose
Tormenting Pan to double the dose.
Alphonso. 26.

Dost (Partial list.)
What dost thou know? Limits. 5.
Tell me, maiden, dost thou use Lines. 1.
Thou dost succor and remede
Monadnoc. 405.
'You pet! what dost here? and what for?
Titmouse. 49.

Doth (Partial list.)
Of human sense doth overfil. Art. 28.
Reflects his figure that doth pass.
Astraea. 24.
Doth as far transcend Bohemian. 5.
And doth the man unking.
Channing Ode. 57.
He doth elect Daemonic Love. 97.
While the soul it doth surcharge,
Etienne. 18.
Than doth the traveller's shadow on the
rock. Frag. Life. XXVI. 4.
And only sees what he doth give.
Frag. Poet. XXVIII. 9.
There doth digest, and work, and spin,
Initial Love. 46.
As doth this round sky-cleaving boat
Monadnoc. 272.
The constant mountain doth dispense;
Monadnoc. 382.
Yet doth much her love excel
Nature. I. 16.
When the genius of God doth flow;
Woodnotes. I. 97.
But forever doth escape,
Woodnotes. II. 273.

Double
Tormenting Pan to double the dose.
Alphonso. 26.
Straight, into double band
Channing Ode. 94.

Double—*Continued*
Nor speak with double tongue.
                              Concord Ode. 20.
Forging double stars,   Merlin. 94.
Doubleth
Adorneth, doubleth joy:
                              Frag. Nat. XXIV. 8.
Doubling
Doubling daylight everywhere:
                              Caritas. 4.
Doubt
Nor doubt but visitings of graver thought
                              Adirondacs. 188.
I am the doubter and the doubt,
                              Brahma. 11.
Till late he learned, through doubt and
    fear,   Fate. 9.
Souls above doubt,   Give. 20.
You doubt we read the stars on high,
                              Romany. 25.
Was quenched, and all must doubt and
    grope.   Threnody. 133.
Brought the old order into doubt.
                              Threnody. 145.
Doubt not, so long as earth has bread,
                              Titmouse. 83.
And doubt and reverend use defied,
                              Uriel. 16.

Doubter
I am the doubter and the doubt,
                              Brahma. 11.

Doubting
Admired, sage doubting whence the
    traveller came,—   River. 4.
Doubtless
'You are doubtless very big;   Fable. 5.
Doubts
And saddens her with heavenly doubts:
                              Rhea. 54.
Their doubts, and aid their strife.
                              Robbins Hymn. 12.

Dove
    See Carrier-dove.
Dove beneath the vulture's beak;—
                              Voluntaries. 17.

Down (Partial list.)
    See Swandown.
and bring the eaglet down:
                              Adirondacs. 84.
nightly, shedding down Adirondacs. 222.
Down with your doleful problems,
                              April. 15.
I saw men go up and down, Astraea. 9.
And, chest by chest, let down the same,
                              Boston. 78.
Go, cut down trees in the forest
                              Boston Hymn. 33.
Cut down trees in the forest
                              Boston Hymn. 35.
Came a beam of goodness down
                              Caritas. 3.
Are shadows flitting up and down
                              Celestial Love. 56.
Down the dark stream   C. Hymn. 8.
The joy-bells chime their tidings down,
                              Concord Ode. 7.
By the other cloven down.
                              Concord Ode. 24.
I wandered up, I wandered down,
                              Dirge. 15.

Of thee from the hill-top looking down;
                              Each. 2.
And largest clouds be flakes of down in
    that enormous sky. Frag. Nat. XX. 2.
The cold gray down upon the quinces
    lieth   Frag. Nat. XXXIII. 1.
Shine down in the old sea;
                              Hamatreya. 32.
Cried him up and down the coast,
                              Initial Love. 2.
Were tipped with down,   Lines. 18.
Every night alighting down
                              May-Day. 26.
Ere sunset quarrying inches down,
                              May-Day. 117.
I lame him, clattering down the rocks;
                              Monadnoc. 342.
Then, at last, I let him down
                              Monadnoc. 344.
Strikes the loud pretender down.
                              Nature. I. 11.
Bolted down forevermore.   Past. 13.
I wandered up, I wandered down,
                              Peter. 11.
Ridiculously up and down   Poet. 88.
The sun goes down, and with him takes
                              Romany. 1.
Thy foes to hunt, thy enviers to strike
    down,   Shah-Hafiz. 1.
And brought Olympian wisdom down
                              Solution. 67.
Down on earth there, underfoot,
                              Song of Seyd. 33.
Up and down their glances strain.
                              Threnody. 81.
And, to be valiant, must come down
                              Titmouse. 63.
Whose dark sky sheds the snowflake
    down,   Voluntaries. 40.
Or down the oaken glade,
                              Waldeinsamkeit. 10.
Down in yon watery nook,
                              Waldeinsamkeit. 33.
Methought the sky looked scornful down
                              Walden. 21.
By court and city, dale and town,
                              Walk. 3.
Shall fall with purer radiance down;
                              Woodnotes. II. 72.
The nearing clouds draw down;
                              World-Soul. 58.
The truth, and hurl wrong-doers down.
                              Worship. 14.

Down-beds
Sleep on the fragrant brush, as on down-
    beds.   Adirondacs. 58.
Downcast
His lamp, the maiden's downcast eye,
                              Frag. Poet. I. 12.
Downfall
Woe is me for my hope's downfall!
                              Monadnoc. 74.
In our downfall, or our joy:
                              Voluntaries. 114.
Down-lying
This is lordly man's down-lying,
                              Threnody. 163.
Downward
Each street leads downward to the sea.
                              Boston. 57.

Loveth downward, and not up; Rhea. 36.
Head downward, clinging to the spray.
Titmouse. 42.

Dowry
To-day shall all her dowry bring,
May-Day. 264.

Dozing
Burly, dozing humble-bee,
Humble-Bee. 1.

Drag
Drag a ridiculous age. Day's Ration. 19.

Dragged
Dragged from his mother's arms and
breast,   Voluntaries. 19.

Dragon
Yawns the pit of the Dragon,
Sphinx. 75.

Dragon-fly
Crab, mice, snail, dragon-fly, minnow and
moth;   Adirondacs. 136.

Dragons
Wolves shed their fangs, and dragons
scales;   Solution. 6.

Drain
Can drain its wealth of hope and sorrow;
Aeolian Harp. 15.
Drain sweet maple juice in vats.
Monadnoc. 142.
Bridge gulfs, drain swamps,
Monadnoc. 150.
Bread to eat, and juice to drain;
Monadnoc. 305.
And drain his heart till he be dead.
Voluntaries. 58.

Drained
That we have drained the best,
Good Hope. 2.
Single look has drained the breast;
Visit. 21.

Drank
Our foaming ale we drank from hunters'
pans,   Adirondacs. 177.
Roses he ate, and drank the wind;
Frag. Poet. V. 14.
I drank at thy fountain
Ode to Beauty. 13.
One who having nectar drank   Poet. 81.

Draught
And by the draught assimilated,
Bacchus. 22.
Why need I galleries, when a pupil's
draught   Day's Ration. 27.

Draw
Mark his capricious ways to draw the
eye.   Adirondacs. 207.
Draw everlasting dew;   Bacchus. 17.
Draw untold juices from the common
earth,   Blight. 9.
Property will brutely draw
Celestial Love. 77.
Less than a lily's, thou shalt daily draw
Day's Ration. 4.
If a new Muse draw me with splendid
ray,   Day's Ration. 15.
To draw the nations out of doors.
Frag. Nat. XIII. 2.
Draw us to these meadow farms,
Frag. Nat. XXVI. 4.
And right into himself does draw;
Initial Love. 121.

To draw all fancies to this spot.
Monadnoc Afar. 8.
Which, one by one, they know to draw
and use.   Musketaquid. 35.
Draw from each stratum its adapted use
Musketaquid. 39.
And draw me on,   Ode to Beauty. 42.
Draw me to them, self-betrayed?
Ode to Beauty. 51.
One portrait—fact or fancy—we may
draw;   Phi. 4.
Draw the breath of Eternity;   Poet. 283.
Firmly draw, firmly drive,   Sphinx. 31.
The heavens that now draw him
Sphinx. 85.
Exists to draw thy virtue forth.
Titmouse. 59.
If from home chance draw me wide,
Una. 7.
Still, through her motes and masses,
draw   Wealth. 46.
The nearing clouds draw down;
World-Soul. 58.
Draw, if thou canst, the mystic line
Worship. 21.

Drawings
By magical drawings, Ode to Beauty. 11.

Drawn
See Moon-drawn.

Draws
Fails of the life, but draws the death and
ill.   Angelo. 14.
As garment draws the garment's hem,
Celestial Love. 73.
Draws men to their likeness still.
Daemonic Love. 67.
With fire that draws while it repels.
Eva. 12.
Draws angels nigh to dwell with thee,
Freedom. 19.
Draws to the spot the solar ray,
May-Day. 116.
Draws better deed: Saadi. 44.
Draws the heart a lore sublime."'
Saadi. 71.
For Love draws might from terrene force
Waterfall. 7.
Draws the threads of fair and fit.
Wealth. 33.

Dread
What his dread folds would fain con-
ceal?   Harp. 64.
Drooping oft in wreaths of dread,
Heroism. 5.
Dread Power, but dear! if God thou be,
Ode to Beauty. 98.
Heeds not the darkness and the dread,
Voluntaries. 86.

Dreaded
In the dreaded winter time,
Monadnoc. 201.

Dreadful
Every maxim of dreadful Need;
Poet. 44.
Delights the dreadful Destiny
Woodnotes II. 120.

Dream
Never did sculptor's dream unfold
Angelo. 1.
Surface and Dream,   Experience. 7.

Dream—*Continued*

I filled the dream of sad, poetic maids,
Frag. Life. XXX. 2.
He seemed to bask, to dream and play
Frag. Poet. V. 4.
Break not my dream, obtrusive tomb!
Harp. 124.
It hath pleased Heaven to break the
dream of bliss   I Bear. 3.
And dream the dream of Auburn dell.
May-Day. 181.
The vanished rose of evening's dream.
May-Day. 298.
That wood-bird sang my last night's
dream,   Miracle. 28.
On earth I dream;—I die to be:
Nun. 29.
The boy's dream comes to pass,
October. 2.
The solid kingdoms like a dream
Poet. 36.
Or lift to a diviner dream!'   Poet. 194.
Through love and thought, through
power and dream.   Two Rivers. 12.
New slaves fulfilled the poet's dream,
Wealth. 40.
And solid nature to a dream.
Woodnotes.II. 115.
From him that sends the dream.
World-Soul. 72.

Dreamed

And, when I would recall the scenes I
dreamed   Frag. Nat. IV. 6.
I, who dreamed not when I came here
Titmouse. 101.

Dream-like

Of Eden's bower some dream-like trace
May-Day. 93.

Dreams

See Night-dreams.
And as through dreams in watches of the
night,   Adirondacs. 201.
Elect, to dreams thus beautiful?'
Berrying. 10.
What prayers and dreams of youthful
genius feign,   Frag. Nat. V. 2.
The sleeps of trees or dreams of herbs.
Frag. Nat. XVIII. 5.
Reality most like to dreams.
Frag. Nat. XXIII. 6.
Melting matter into dreams,
Frag. Poet. VIII. 7.
Ah, not to me those dreams belong!
Frag. Poet. XXX. 1.
In numbers wild as dreams,   Harp. 30.
Than the gray dreams which thee detain.
Monadnoc. 18.
And, if I languish into dreams,
Ode to Beauty. 92.
Una lights my clouded dreams;
Una. 2.
And fanned the dreams it never brought.
Woodnotes II. 4.

Drear

How drear the part I held in one,
Nun. 48.

Drearily

How drearily in College hall
Walden. 33.

Dreary

I left my dreary page and sallied forth,
Frag. Nat. XXVII. 1.
No dreary repeater now and again,
Nature. II. 3.

Drenched

Reason in Nature's lotus drenched,
Bacchus. 56.

Dress

That circled freshly in their forest dress
Adirondacs. 60.
And dress up Nature in your favor.
Destiny. 44.
Decked by courtly rites and dress
Frag. Poet. I. 29.
In sloven dress and broken rank,
In Memoriam. 5.
their last gay dress put on;   *Violet. 7.

Dressed

All dressed, like Nature, Adirondacs. 71.
I care not how you are dressed,
Destiny. 38.
Saying, 'We have dressed for thee the
ground,   Ellen South. 15.
In his own loom's garment dressed,
Monadnoc. 38.
Form the soul had ever dressed,
Rhea. 18.
Still for journeys she is dressed; Una. 3.
by eldest Nature dressed,
Woodnotes I. 80.

Drest

In braw claithing drest?   Riches. 6.

Drew

Where all the sacred mountains drew
around us,   Adirondacs. 9.
Evening drew on; stars peeped through
maple-boughs,   Adirondacs. 46.
Wise and polite,—and if I drew
Adirondacs. Motto. 1.
Which on the first day drew,
Bacchus. 65.
'Ye drew one mother's milk,   Dirge. 53.
And drew truly every trait.
Hermione. 39.
The poorest that drew breath.
In Memoriam. 34.
Drew his free homage unbeguiled,
In Memoriam. 68.
For they drew no blood,   *Lines. 19.
Hid in milk we drew   May-Day 407.
No mimic; from his breast his counsel
drew,   Phi. 15.
Drew the firm lines of Fate and Life
Solution. 66.
And broken stars I drew,
Song of Nature. 26.
From air the creeping centuries drew
Wealth. 13.

Drift

See Snow-drift.
That pierced my trance its drift to tell,
Miraclce. 30.

Drifted

Struggling through the drifted roads;
May-Day. 40.

Drifting

And drifting sand-heaps feed my stock,
Woodnotes II. 11.

Drink
Then drink in Walden water.
                    Frag. Nat. XIX. 6.
I drink the nectar of the hour:—
                    Frag. Nat. XXVI. 31.
Heaven and earth to eat and drink.
                    Goethe. 6.
Doth eat, and drink, and fish, and shoot,
                    Initial Love. 27.
Drink the wild air's salubrity:
                    Merlin's Song. 32.
And gives them what to drink and eat;
                    Nature. II. 17.
Drink not the Malaga of praise,
                    Saadi. 64.
Who drink it shall not thirst again;
                    Two Rivers. 18.
As he giveth to all to drink,
                    Woodnotes. II. 287.
Drinking
That I, drinking this,   Bacchus. 38.
Drinks
Man drinks the water, drinks the light.
                    Frag. Life. XXIII. 9.
Who drinks of Cupid's nectar cup
                    Rhea. 35.
Drive
Watching when the loud dogs should
    drive in deer,   Adirondacs. 110.
Put in, drive home the sightless wedges
                    Frag. Nat. XXX. 1.
And bid each awful Muse drive the
    damned harpies hence.   I Bear. 14.
Vain beside mine. I drive my wedges
    home,   Seashore. 12.
Firmly draw, firmly drive,   Sphinx. 31.
Right onward drive unharmed;
                    Terminus. 38.
Driven
Long I've been tossed like the driven
    foam;   Good-Bye. 5.
Driver's
    See Camel-driver's
Drives
Which drives me mad with sweet desire,
                    Destiny. 13.
And drives me where I go.
                    Quat. Northman. 4.
Toil whistles as he drives his cart.
                    Saadi. 154.
Driving
Driving the foe and stablishing the
    friend,—   Blight. 13.
Driving, darting northward free,
                    May-Day. 388.
Arrives the snow, and, driving o'er the
    fields,   Snow-Storm. 2.
Drones
Foolish gossips, ancient drones,
                    Saadi. 170.
Drooping
Drooping oft in wreaths of dread,
                    Heroism. 5.
Drop
    See Fountain—drop; Rain-drop.
Before ye want a drop of rain,
                    Alphonso. 49.
They drop their few pale flowers,
                    Daemonic Love. 108.
Nor gives the jealous lord one diamond
    drop   Day's Ration. 24.

As the drop feeds its fated flower,
                    Frag. Life. XXIII. 5.
A ruddy drop of manly blood
                    Friendship. 1.
The ruby of the drop of wine,
                    Ode to Beauty. 28.
A drop can shake, a breath can fan;
                    Poet. 222.
That drop from the angels' shoon.
                    Quat. Excelsior. 4.
Shed in each drop of wine.
                    Quat. Leasts. 4.
And ages drop in it like rain.
                    Two Rivers. 20.
With one drop sheds form and feature;
                    Woodnotes. II. 289.
Dropped
    See Chance—dropped.
Wherein was dropped the mortal spoil.
                    Harp. 127.
Dropping
April cold with dropping rain
                    May-Day. 182.
Drops
And drops from Power's redundant horn
                    May-Day. 216.
I said, they are drops of frozen wine
                    Rubies. 3.
Drove
Which drove them erst to social feats;
                    Alphonso. 34.
Droves
Kine in droves,   Saadi. 2.
Drowsily
Drowsily humming   Frag. Nat. I. 4.
Drowsy
And turned the drowsy world to flame.
                    Frag. Poet. I. 14.
Sweet to me thy drowsy tone
                    Humble-Bee. 33.
The Sphinx is drowsy,   Sphinx. 1.
Drudge
So shall the drudge in dusty frock
                    Art. 13.
To drudge all day for Guy the wise.
                    Guy. 40.
Drudges
On thieves, on drudges and on dolls.
                    Woodnotes. II. 203.
Drudging
The day goes drudging through the while,
                    Nun. 2.
Drug
Drug the cup, thou butler sweet,
                    May-Day. 279.
To drug their crops or weapon their arts
    withal.   Musketaquid. 40.
Drugged
Drugged with spice from climates warm,
                    Hermione. 52.
'Who has drugged my boy's cup?
                    Sphinx. 61.
Drugging
Drugging herbs with Syrian spices,
                    May-Day. 250.
Drugs
She drugs her water and her wheat
                    Nature. II. 15.
Druid
Taught by Plinlimmon's Druid power,
                    Solution. 34.

Drum
He saw the partridge drum in the woods;
    Woodnotes. I. 54.
Drunk
Ruby wine is drunk by knaves,
    Heroism. 1.
Has drunk the life-blood of the great;
    Omar. 2.
Drunken
    See Music—drunken
Drunken with nectar,   Frag. Nat. I. 2.
Dry
Roses bleach, the goats are dry,
    Alphonso. 13.
Say, Seigniors, are the old Niles dry,
    Alphonso. 31.
Wild rose, lily, dry vanilla,—
    Frag. Nat. II. 18.
They bleach and dry in the sun.
    Garden. 16.
To speed his sails, to dry his hay;
    Guy. 38.
And my tears are dry.   *Lines. 28.
Heat, cold, wet, dry, and peace, and pain.
    Song of Nature. 76.
Or through their channel dry;
    Woodnotes. I. 124.
One dry, and one the living tree.
    Woodnotes. II. 21.
Ducks
To northern lakes fly wind-borne ducks,
    Saadi. 5.
The black ducks mounting from the lake,
    Waldeinsamkeit. 29.
Ductile
With ductile fire. Loud, exulting cries
    Adirondacs. 241.
Due
Due east a bay makes   Adirondacs. 30.
Only what to our griping toil is due;
    Blight. 41.
On their due days, of the birds,
    May-Day. 380.
Or in what far to-morrow due;
    May-Day. 417.
Dues
Nor not receive his ample dues.
    Guy. 16.
Nemesis will have her dues,
    Nemesis. 14.
Dug
The ominous hole he dug in the sand,
    Threnody. 86.
Dukedoms
We grant no dukedoms to the few,
    Boston. 25.
Dull
A dull uncertain brain,   Dull. 1.
And the dull idiot might see Merlin. 72.
"Dull Sphinx, Jove keep thy five wits;
    Sphinx. 105.
They dull its edge with their monotony.
    Xenophanes. 11.
Dulness
In dulness now their secret keep;
    Monadnoc. 172.
Duly
Trembling balance duly keep.
    II Compensation. 4.
And duly greet the entering May?
    May-Day. 219.

Marching duly in her train,
    May-Day. 335.
Red evening duly dyes
    Monadnoc Afar. 2.
Dumb
Should mine alone be dumb?
    I Compensation. 6.
Muffled and dumb like barefoot dervishes,
    Days. 2.
When Mirth is dumb and Flattery's fled,
    Ellen. 9.
Lurking dumb,   Frag. Life. VIII. 2.
Deaf, and dumb, and blind, and cold,
    Frag. Poet. VIII. 6.
Entreated, she is dumb;   Harp. 18.
Shall the dumb bird instructed say.
    Miracle. 22.
Oh, call not Nature dumb;   River. 21.
Shall the harp be dumb.   Saadi. 16.
The harp is dumb.   Saadi. 20.
I am dumb in the pealing song,
    Song of Nature. 6.
Amid the Muses, left thee deaf and dumb,
    Terminus. 31.
Dungeon
Pent in a dungeon made of air,—
    Harp. 56.
Dupe
And dies in anger that it was a dupe;
    Blight. 55.
Durance
The durance of a granite ledge.
    Astraea. 37.
Duration
The duration of a glance   Visit. 23.
Dusky
Up! and the dusky race
    Boston Hymn. 77.
Dusky sparrows in a crowd,
    May-Day. 387.
Which bound the dusky tribe,
    Voluntaries. 28.
Dust
    See Star-dust.
Lift up a people from the dust,
    Boston Hymn. 67.
Scatters on every eye dust of his spells,
    Enchanter. 3.
Might grace the dust that is most proud.
    In Memoriam. 20.
O'er thy rich dust the endless smile
    In Memoriam. 105.
Their dust, pervaded by the nerves of
  God,   Pan. 6.
As if the dust were glass and steel.
    Poet. 6.
The dust is alive,   Poet. 106.
Nor less on man's enchanted dust
    Poet. 298.
Out of dust to build   Politics. 11.
What is more than dust,— Politics. 12.
And soon may give my dust their fun-
  eral shade.   River. 42.
Their dust endears the sod.
    Robbins Hymn. 4.
They live with God; their homes are
  dust;   Robbins Hymn. 21.
The rocky coast, smite Andes into dust,
    Seashore. 35.
Hearts are dust, hearts' loves remain;
    Threnody. 268.

So nigh is grandeur to our dust,
Voluntaries. 71.
Dust is their pyramid and mole:
Wealth. 25.

Dusty
So shall the drudge in dusty frock
Art. 13.

Duties
Into each mind intruding duties crept;
Adirondacs. 332.
Toy no longer—it has duties;
Holidays. 7.
Slipped off their park of duties, leagues
behind,　Adirondacs. 62.

Duty
And make of duty fate.
Concord Ode. 16.
Conscious each of duty done
Frag. Nat. XXIII. 17.
Or Duty to grand purpose wrought.
Miracle. 14.
When Duty whispers low, Thou must,
Voluntaries. 73.
Him duty through the clarion calling
Voluntaries. 95.

Dwarfed
Dwarfed to measure of his hand;
Monadnoc. 321.

Dwarfs
Though, feigning dwarfs, they crouch
and creep,　Voluntaries. 117.

Dwell
I daily dwell in, and am not so blind
Frag. Nat. V. 3.
Draws angels nigh to dwell with thee,
Freedom. 19.
The reliquaries of my dead saint, and
dwell　Letter. 17.
Supplanters of the tribe, the farmers
dwell.　Musketaquid. 31.
She will not refuse to dwell
Voluntaries. 45.

Dweller
So let each dweller on the Bay
Boston. 102.
And in low hut the dweller found:
Monadnoc. 73.

Dwellers
We seemed the dwellers of the zodiac,
Adirondacs. 157.
To all the dwellers in the plains
Monadnoc. 35.
And grant to dwellers with the pine
Woodnotes II. 47.

Dwelling-place
Who loved this dwelling-place!
Dirge. 28.

Dwells
Whereon the purple iris dwells in beauty
Adirondacs. 219.
In the deep heart of man a poet dwells
Enchanter. 1.
A love that in the spirit dwells,
Hymn. 2.
But the poet dwells alone.　Saadi. 8.
Wise Saadi dwells alone.　Saadi. 22.
Good Saadi dwells alone.　Saadi. 33.
Be thou ware where Saadi dwells;
Saadi. 34.
Illusion dwells forever with the wave.
Seashore. 42.

Dwelt
Where in bright Art each god and sibyl
dwelt　Daemonic Love. 121.
'Once I dwelt apart,　Hermione. 40.
And brier-roses, dwelt among;
Humble-Bee. 49.

Dwindles
Dwindles here, there magnifies,
Frag. Poet. IX. 7.

Dye
Opal hues and purple dye;
May-Day. 260.

Dyed
Is sketched and dyed, each with a new
design,　Naples. 7.

Dyes
Red evening duly dyes
Monadnoc Afar. 2.
Clouds flush their gayest dyes.
Waterfall. 16.

Dying
For this losing is true dying;
Threnody. 162.
Why lingerest thou, pale violet, to see
the dying year;　*Violet. 1.

Dyspepsia
"Chronic dyspepsia never came from eating　Adirondacs. 185.

Each. (Partial list.)
As each would hear the oracle alone.
Adirondacs. 15.
Rounded by hours where each outdid the
last　Adirondacs. 154.
To each apart, lifting her lovely shows
Adirondacs. 199.
A private beam into each several heart.
Adirondacs. 223.
To outdo each other and extort applause.
Adirondacs. 326.
Into each mind intruding duties crept;
Adirondacs. 332.
Each cloud that floated in the sky
Apology. 7.
Each the herald is who wrote
Astraea. 1.
Each to all is venerable,　Astraea. 5.
Each to each, a looking-glass,
Astraea. 23.
And twice each day the flowing sea
Boston. 3.
Each honest man shall have his vote,
Boston. 33.
Each child shall have his school.
Boston. 34.
So let each dweller on the Bay
Boston. 102.
Throb in each manly vein;　Boston. 107.
And each shall care for other,
Boston. 112.
And each to each shall bend,
Boston. 113.
To please each other well;
Celestial Love. 7.
Each from your proper state,
Celestial Love. 13.
When each the other shall avoid,
Celestial Love. 97.
Shall each by each be most enjoyed.
Celestial Love. 98.

Each (Partial list.)—*Continued*

From each to each, from thee to me,
                    Daemonic Love 79.
Each obstruction, it unites
                    Daemonic Love. 83.
Where in bright Art each god and sibyl
  dwelt   Daemonic Love. 121.
To each they offer gifts after his will,
                    Days. 5.
All are needed by each one;   Each. 11.
For each quality and part
                    Frag. Life. VI. 4.
That each should in his house abide,
                    Frag. Life. XXI. 1.
Greetings kind to each and all,
                    Frag. Nat. XXIII. 16.
Conscious each of duty done
                    Frag. Nat. XXIII. 17.
Makes each day a festival.
                    Frag. Nat. XXVI. 6.
Crowds each on other, veil on veil,
                    Frag. Nat. XXXI. 4.
And made each tide and element
                    Guy. 27.
Each of these landlords walked amidst
  his farm,   Hamatreya. 4.
That each for each doth fast engage;
                    Hermione. 32.
Fate grants each to stand aside;
                    Holidays. 18.
For each eternal block—   House. 16.
Thine each leaf and berry bore;
                    Lines. 6.
Each for other they were born,
                    Love and Thought. 7.
The pilgrims have each other lost.
                    Love and Thought. 12.
Each color with its counter glowed;
                    Merlin. 82.
Each with all propitious Time
                    Merlin. 98.
And mix itself with each event;
                    Monadnoc. 51.
They prove the virtues of each bed of
  rock,   Musketaquid. 37.
Draw from each stratum its adapted use
                    Musketaquid. 39.
We are what we are made; each follow-
  ing day   Naples. 1.
Each spot where tulips prank their state
                    Omar. 1.
All to each in kindness bend,
                    Peter. 34.
Painting with morn each annual cell?
                    Problem. 28.
Shed in each drop of wine.
                    Quat. Leasts. 4.
Thou shalt seem, in each reply,
                    Rhea. 19.
Lighted each transparent word,
                    Saadi. 81.
Each the other adorning,   Sphinx. 37.
And each answer is a lie.   Sphinx. 116.
The school-march, each day's festival,
                    Threnody. 59.
Each village senior paused to scan
                    Threnody. 72.
Each snowbird chirped, each fowl must
  crow;   Threnody. 105.
Each tramper started; but the feet
                    Threnody. 106.

Know, each substance and relation,
                    Visit. 3.
Steeped in each forest cave? Walden. 28.
But in each pause we heard the call
                    Walden. 35.
Each joy the mountain dales impart;
                    Woodnotes. I. 35.
To each his bosom-secret say.
                    Woodnotes II. 155.
Unto each, and unto all,
                    Woodnotes. II. 283.
He is the meaning of each feature;
                    Woodnotes. II. 316.
Thanks to each man of courage,
                    World-Soul. 5.
We plot and corrupt each other,
                    World-Soul. 23.

Eager

Traditioned fame of masters, eager strife
                    Adirondacs. 324.
From the eager opening strings
                    Harp. 47.
To infinite time his eager turn,
                    Poet. 188.
Eager for good, not hating ill,
                    Poet. 208.
The eager fate which carried thee
                    Threnody. 160.

Eagle

Above, the eagle flew, the osprey
  screamed,   Adirondacs. 146.

Eagle's

Perfect-paired as eagle's wings,
                    Merlin. 113.

Eagles

Carries the eagles, and masters the
  sword.   Destiny. 50.

Eaglet

Full fifty feet, and bring the eaglet down:
                    Adirondacs. 84.

Ear

  See Mouse-ear.
But day by day, to loving ear
                    Aeolian Harp. 16.
Up to my ear the morning brings
                    Boston Hymn. 7.
Not unless God made sharp thine ear
                    Dirge. 45.
Far-heard, lows not thine ear to charm;
                    Each. 4.
He sang to my ear,—they sang to my
  eye.   Each. 18.
I gave thee for an hour my ear,
                    Frag. Poet. II. 6.
Than still to entertain his ear
                    Frag. Poet. V. 6.
But the porches of man's ear
                    Garden. 46.
Save to his ear the wind-harp lone.
                    Harp. 98.
Off he keeps his fine ear strained,
                    Initial Love. 66.
Deeply soothe his anxious ear.
                    Initial Love. 73.
Or fill my craving ear;   Merlin. 2.
Never balk the waiting ear.
                    Monadnoc. 192.
For thus the wood-gods murmured in my
  ear: Musketaquid. 76.
music to eye and ear,   October. 10.

In Being's deeps past ear and eye;
                    Ode to Beauty. 95.
His words are music in my ear,
                    Problem. 69.
They must give ear,   Saadi. 29.
Her ear is heavy,   Sphinx. 3.
Still plotting how their hungry ear
                    Threnody. 50.
To the open ear it sings
                    Woodnotes. II. 104.
And shock thy weak ear with a note
                    Woodnotes II. 122.
Hark! in thy ear I will tell the sign
                    Woodnotes. II. 192.

Earlier

Whom earlier we had chid with spite-
    ful names.   Adirondacs. 170.
Stars rose; his faith was earlier up:
                    Character. 2.
When late I walked, in earlier days,
                    May-Day. 35.
Stars rose, his faith was earlier up:
                    Poet. 135.
Product of the earlier found.   Visit. 8.

Earliest

Earliest heats that follow frore
                    Frag. Nat. II. 21.
See youth's glad mates in earliest
    bloom,—   Harp. 123.
Huntsmen find the easiest way.
                    Quat. Artist. 4.
I caught with bended pin my earliest
    fish,   River. 12.

Early

Is early frugal, like a beggar's child;
                    Blight. 57.
That untold early love   *Farewell. 41.
Early or late, the falling rain   Guy. 33.
And mark the rising of the early stars.
                    Letter. 15.
No early morn, no evening late,—
                    Nun. 43.
Coming early, coming late,   Poet. 123.
His early hope, his liberal mien;
                    Threnody. 55.
Grow early old with grief that thou
                    Threnody. 130.

Earn

And teach his nimbleness to earn his
    wage,   Adirondacs. 268.
To earn the praise of bard and critic.
                    Fame. 12.

Earned

Go, get them where he earned them
    when alive;   To J. W. 16.

Earnest

They spoke not, for their earnest sense
                    Poet. 199.

Ears

To ears intelligent; as if gray rock
                    Adirondacs. 253.
Lend me your ears, and I begin.
                    Aeolian Harp. 11.
Keen ears can catch a syllable,
                    Garden. 29.
Sings in my ears, my hands are stones,
                    Titmouse. 13.
To his ears was evident.   Uriel. 10.
O mortal! thy ears are stones;
                    Woodnotes II. 126.

Earshot

Within earshot of thy hum,—
                    Humble-Bee. 18.

Earth

Which fed the veins of earth and sky,
                    Alphonso. 32.
Earth, crowded, cries, 'Too many men!'
                    Alphonso. 67.
Man on earth to acclimate   Art. 21.
Suffer no savor of the earth to scape.
                    Bacchus. 5.
The quaking earth did quake in rhyme,
                    Beauty. 15.
Of man and earth, of world beloved and
    lover,   Blight. 44.
The throbbing sea, the quaking earth,
                    Celestial Love. 109.
The lonely Earth amid the balls
                    II Compensation. 9.
Man was made of social earth,
                    Daemonic Love. 1.
Cross the orbit of the earth,
                    Daemonic Love. 49.
There are no such hearts on earth.
                    Dirge. 52.
Draw untold juices from the common
    earth,   Blight. 9.
Transparent air, all-feeding earth,
                    Frag. Life. XXIX. 3.
And walk on earth as the sun walks in
    the sphere.   Frag. Nat. V. 12.
As moon from earth, or star from star.
                    Frag. Nat. VII. 2.
Waiting till God create the earth,—
                    Frag. Nat. XXVI. 17.
This is not the ancient earth
                    Frag. Nat. XXVI. 32.
And make the darlings of the earth
                    Frag. Poet. XI. 13.
And look beyond the earth,
                    Friendship. 14.
Heaven and earth to eat and drink.
                    Goethe. 6.
Now scattered wide thro' earth, and each
    alone,   Good Cheer. 4.
Earth laughs in flowers, to see her boast-
    ful boys   Hamatreya. 13.
Earth-proud, proud of the earth which is
    not theirs;   Hamatreya. 14.
Hear what the Earth says:—
                    Hamatreya. 27.
Earth endures;   Hamatreya. 30.
It shares the secret of the earth,
                    Harp. 65.
There is no record left on earth,
                    In Memoriam. 48.
Daughter of Heaven and Earth, coy
    Spring,   May-Day. 1.
The kind Earth takes her children's
    part,   May-Day. 66.
What fiery force the earth renews,
                    May-Day. **188.**
Through earth to ripen, through heaven
    endure.   May-Day. 468.
Taste the lordship of the earth.'
                    Monadnoc. 26.
Than all vintage of the earth.
                    Monadnoc. 294.
Of the bullet of the earth
                    Monadnoc. 326.

Earth—*Continued*
On earth I dream;—I die to be:
Nun. 29.
Or cares that earth to earth engage,
Nun. 34.
Earth proudly wears the Partheon,
Problem. 33.
To ransack earth for riches rare,
Rhea. 51.
Saying, 'Hearken! Earth, Sea, Air!
Rhea. 57.
This charm is wasted on the earth and sky,
Rhodora. 10.
In heaven no star, on earth no spark,—
Saadi. 132.
Purger of earth, and medicine of men;
Seashore. 22.
To fire the stagnant earth with thought:
Solution. 4.
Earth smiled with flowers, and man was born.
Solution. 8.
And earth grow civil, Homer sung.
Solution. 16.
But walked the earth unmarked, unknown.
Solution. 52.
Down on earth there, underfoot,
Song of Seyd. 33.
"Sea, earth, air, sound, silence,
Sphinx. 33.
And keep the blossom of the earth,
Threnody. 124.
Voice of earth to earth returned,
Threnody. 264.
Doubt not, so long as earth has bread,
Titmouse. 83.
The tremulous battery Earth
Waterfall. 9.
His hearth the earth,—his hall the azure dome;
Woodnotes. I. 93.
The public child of earth and sky.
Woodnotes. I. 117.
In the circle of the earth;
Woodnotes. II. 199.
Within, without the idle earth,
World-Soul. 61.

Earth-baking
Earth-baking heat, stone-cleaving cold.
Monadnoc. 57.

Earth-fire
If earth-fire cleave   Channing Ode. 29.

Earthly
To make this wisdom earthly wise.
Threnody. 57.

Earth-poles
From the earth-poles to the Line,
Mithridates. 3.

Earth-proud
Earth-proud, proud of the earth which is not theirs;   Hamatreya. 14.

Earth's
Earth's a howling wilderness,
Berrying. 2.
Earth's prime secret, sculpture's seat?
May-Day. 211.
All earth's fleece and food   Politics. 3.
And earth's fit tenant me suprise;—
Woodnotes. II. 213.

Earth-song
When I heard the Earth-song
Hamatreya. 60.

Ease
There, growing slowly old at ease
Alphonso. 77.
To hearts in sloth and ease.
Voluntaries. 70.

Eased
The good applaud, the lost are eased.
Celestial Love. 114.

Easily
Easily to shed the snow,   Nature. I. 2.

East
Due east a bay makes inward to the land
Adirondacs. 30.
He shall cut pathways east and west
Boston Hymn. 15.
Come, East and West and North,
Boston Hymn. 81.
They marched from east to west:
Experience. 13.
East, West, from Beer to Dan, Fame. 3.
Sleeps the vast East in pleased peace,
Frag. Nat. XXVI. 21.
Or sibyl from the mummied East,
Frag. Poet. XXVIII. 2.
He is a Pundit of the East,
Initial Love. 108.
Under east winds crossed with sleet.
May-Day. 133.
From Katskill east to the sea-bound.
Monadnoc. 282.
And all is clear from east to west.
Nature. Mot. 12.
And all is clear from east to west.
Threnody. 208.
East, west, for aid I looked in vain,
Titmouse. 7.
East, west, north, south, are his domain.
Titmouse. 8.
We wander far by east and west. Una. 4.
Space is ample, east and west, Unity. 1.
Or east, it smells like a clover-farm;
Woodnotes. I. 102.

Eastern
On eastern hills I see their smokes,
Forerunners. 15.
Face the eastern star until
Frag. Nat. XXVI. 8.
As clouds give rain to the eastern breeze,
Poet. 34.
Never, son of eastern morning, Saadi. 92.
Or lands of Eastern day?   Walden. 46.

Eastward
Looked eastward from the farms,
Boston. 2.
Eastward it filled all Heathendom
Frag. Poet. IV. 33.
Up and eastward turn thy face;
Poet. 121.

Easy
See Uneasy.
Easy to match what others do,
Frag. Life. X. 1.

Eat
Whether thy sons or strangers eat the fruit: Adirondacs. 300.
Enough that mankind eat and are refreshed.   Adirondacs. 301.
To plant and eat be none afraid.
Boston. 12.
To plant and eat be none afraid.
Boston. 54.

Heaven and earth to eat and drink.
                              Goethe. 6.
Doth eat, and drink, and fish, and shoot,
                        Initial Love. 27.
Give me cantharids to eat; Mithridates. 7.
I will give my son to eat
                          Monadnoc. 303.
Bread to eat, and juice to drain;
                          Monadnoc. 305.
And gives them what to drink and eat;
                            Nature. II. 17.
And eat through Alps its home to find.
                          Quat. Love. 4.
A thousand men shall dig and eat;
                              Saadi. 106.
'Eat thou the bread which men refuse;
                              Saadi. 142.

Eaten
At rich men's tables eaten bread and
    pulse?   Forbearance. 3.
We had eaten fairy fruit, May-Day. 410.

Eater
The eater serves his meat;
                      Channing Ode. 47.

Eating
"Chronic dyspepsia never came from eat-
    ing   Adirondacs. 185.

Eats
The Cossack eats Poland,
                      Channing Ode. 90.
Daily his own heart he eats;
                            Heroism. 8.
The fourth gives light which eats the
    dark;   Woodnotes. II. 292.

Ebb
Five years elapse from flood to ebb.
                              Garden. 24.
Unsure the ebb and flood of thought,
                              Poet. 279.
And, in my mathematic ebb and flow,
                            Seashore. 25.

Ebbed
Seas ebbed and flowed in epic chime.
                              Beauty. 16.

Ebbing
Ebbing later whence it flowed,
                              Garden. 15.
But left a legacy of ebbing veins,
                            Terminus. 29.

Ebbs
Knowing and doing. Ebbs the tide, they
    lie   Pan. 8.

Eblis
Beware the fire that Eblis burned."
                        Frag. Poet. II. 3.

Echo
Challenging Echo by our guns and cries;
                          Adirondacs. 113.
Wanting the echo in my brain.
                      Frag. Poet. XXVI. 2.
Echo the blackbird's roundelay,
                            Good-Bye. 20.
Of sound and echo, man and maid,
                      Woodnotes. II. 161.

Echoed
And, echoed in some frosty wold,
                            Titmouse. 97.

Echoes
Wield the first axe these echoes ever
    heard.   Adirondacs. 33.

From boat to boat, and to the echoes
    round,   Adirondacs. 242.
Till these echoes be choked with snows,
                              Boston. 104.
All echoes hearkened for their sound,—
                              Dirge. 35.
Thy echoes in the wilderness,
                          May-Day. 438.
These echoes are laden with tones
                      Woodnotes. II. 127.

Echoing
    See All-echoing.
Wake, echoing caves!   Adirondacs. 259.
Build and unbuild our echoing clay,
                              Merlin. 127.

Ecliptic
And stars from the ecliptic road.
                              Poet. 30.

Economize
Economize the failing river,
                            Terminus. 14.

Ecstasy
Swims the world in ecstasy,   Saadi. 134.

Eddies
How the chemic eddies play,
                          Monadnoc. 229.

Eden
Which, from Eden wide astray,
                        Ode to Beauty. 66.
Apples of Eden ripe to-morrow.
                            Threnody. 287.

Eden's
Of Eden's bower some dream-like trace
                            May-Day. 93.
And o'er yon hazy crest is Eden's
    balmier spring.'   May-Day. 103.
From Eden's vats that run.   Rubies. 4.

Edge
    See Lake-edge.
To those who gaze from the sea's edge
                            Astraea. 38.
And these from the crowd's edge well
    pleased beheld   Frag. Life. XXX. 6.
To gaze o'er the horizon's edge,
                              Lines. 20.
A world-wide wave with foaming edge
                          May-Day. 245.
They bounded to the horizon's edge
                              Poet. 61.
On thine orchard's edge belong
                              Saadi. 149.
They dull its edge with their monotony.
                          Xenophanes. 11.

Edged
The wide lake, edged with sand and
    grass,   Woodnotes. I. 108.

Edifice
This shining moment is an edifice
                        Frag. Life. V. 1.

Educate
Can rules or tutors educate   Culture. 1.

E'en
E'en the flowing azure air
                        Ode to Beauty. 90.

Effete
And the ages are effete, World-Soul. 98.

Efficacious
Efficacious rhymes;   Merlin. 61.

Egg
Crowds every egg out of the nest,
                              Unity. 5.

Egg—*Continued*
If plants or brain, if egg or shell,
Walden. 39.
Once slept the world an egg of stone,
Woodnotes. II. 266.

Eight
The maple eight, beneath its shapely
tower.   Adirondacs. 43.

Either. (Partial list.)
Rebuild or ruin: either fill
Alphonso. 27.

Elapse
Five years elapse from flood to ebb.
Garden. 24.

Elastic
But I can see the elastic tent of day
Frag. Nat. V. 4.
Can this elastic air convey.
May-Day. 14.

Elate
Neither dejected nor elate,   Poet. 168.

Eld
Taught he not thee—the man of eld,
Threnody. 183.

Elder
His vice some elder virtue's token,
Initial Love. 92.

Elder-blow
Elder-blow, sarsaparilla,
Frag. Nat. II. 17.

Eldest
From the stores of eldest matter,
Frag. Life. XXIX. 1.
Frost and sun and eldest night,
Hermione. 62.
Eldest mason, Frost, had piled
May-Day. 47.
Eldest rite, two married sides
Merlin. 90.
By eldest science wrought and shown!
Monadnoc. 67.
Through these green tents, by eldest Na-
ture dressed,   Woodnotes. I.

Elect
Elect, to dreams thus beautiful?'
Berrying. 10.

Elected
He doth elect   Daemonic Love. 97.
Till his elected hour.   Frag. Poet. V. 8.

Electric
Electric star or pencil plays,
II Compensation. 8.
Electric thrills and ties of law,
Wealth. 47.

Elegantly
Elegantly destroy. Frag. Nat. XXIV. 12.

Elegy
Thine elegy, sweet singer, sainted wife.
Naples. 27.

Element
So pure the Alpine element we breathed,
Adirondacs. 158.
And a prime end of the most subtle ele-
ment   Adirondacs. 258.
And, moulded of one element   Art. 23.
As if they loved the element, and hasted
Frag. Nat. XVII. 5.
Baptized with the pure element,
Frag. Nat. XXVI. 27.
He shared the life of the element,
Frag. Poet. I. 52.

And made each tide and element Guy. 27.
Hymen of element and race,
May-Day. 266.
What god the element obeyed?
Wealth. 5.
Sweet influence from every element;
Woodnotes. I. 77.
To know one element, explore another,
Xenophanes. 12.

Elements
The injured elements say, 'Not in us;'
Blight. 33.
The salt of all the elements, world of the
world.   Good Cheer. 16.
They fight the elements with elements
Musketaquid. 47.
Seethe, Fate! the ancient elements,
Song of Nature. 75.

Elephant
The elephant browses,   Sphinx. 19.

Elf
And in cramp elf and saurian forms
Song of Nature. 31.
Or how meet in human elf
Woodnotes. I. 28.

Elfin
Like poisoned loaf of elfin bread,
Frag. Nat. III. 3.
His elfin length upon the snows,
May-Day. 114.

Ellen
And Ellen, when the graybeard years
Ellen. 1.

Elm
Man's the elm, and Wealth the vine;
II Compensation. 15.

Eloquence
Funeral eloquence   Channing Ode. 34.
The eloquence of truth, the wisdom got
Good Cheer. 10.
Nor wit, nor eloquence,—no, nor even
the song   Naples. 19.
Outran the craft of eloquence. Poet. 200.

Eloquent
Of eloquent lips, of joyful wit:
In Memoriam. 52.
Believed the eloquent was aye the true;
Phi. 16.
It hath a sound more eloquent than
speech.   River. 27.
O eloquent child!   Threnody. 37.

Else (Partial list.)
All else grew foreign in their light.
Daemonic Love. 18.
Haply else we could not live,
Frag. Nat. I. 17.
Feigned to speak to some one else.
Frag. Poet. IV. 18.
Or else alternated;   Merlin. 103.
Peril around, all else appalling,
Voluntaries. 93.

Elsewhere
The darkness haunteth me elsewhere;
Peter. 29.

Elude
And though the substance us elude,
Monadnoc. 390.

Elysian
Renewed, I breathe Elysian air,
Harp. 122.

Emanuel
The Swede Emanuel leads the soul.
Solution. 46.

Embalmed
Embalmed by purifying cold;
Titmouse. 19.

Embalms
Alike thy memory embalms
In Memoriam. 113.

Embattled
Here once the embattled farmers stood
C. Hymn. 3.

Embodied
Well embodied, well ensouled,
Monadnoc. 156.

Embrace
And holds all stars in his embrace.
Initial Love. 117.
Which mocks thy æons to embrace;
Nun. 40.
Scorn trifles and embrace a better aim
Rome. 12.
I embrace the true believers,
Song of Seyd. 29.

Embraces
Scarce freed from her embraces?
Philosopher. 12.

Embryo
An embryo god unborn. Poet. 104.

Emerge
Emerge the winged words in haste.
Poet. 24.

Eminent
In heaven once eminent, the god
Uriel. 37.

Empedocles
The brave Empedocles, defying fools,
Frag. Life. XVIII. 1.

Emperor
Of this young-eyed emperor
Initial Love. 85.
Gave to the mind its emperor,
Solution. 37.

Empire
The empire of the ocean caves.
Boston. 18.

Empires
Kings shook with fear, old empires crave
Boston. 92.

Emptieth
He emptieth the beverage;
Woodnotes. II. 282.

Emptiness
But emptiness on emptiness;
Woodnotes. II. 197.

Empty
I see my empty house, Threnody. 9.

Empyrean
Through from the empyrean walls
Celestial Love. 25.

Emulate
And emulate, vaulted, Illusions. 19.

Enamel
Fresh pearls to their enamel gave,
Each. 21.

Enamoured
More enamoured serve it yet; Poet. 290.

Encamp
Sylvan deities encamp, Saadi. 38.

Enchant
See Disenchant.

Enchanted
His enchanted food; Manners. 6.
Races and planets, its enchanted foam.
Pan. 12.
I know is ground enchanted. Peter. 8.
Nor less on man's enchanted dust
Poet. 298.
To break enchanted ice, Rubies. 10.
By one music enchanted, Sphinx. 35.

Enchanters
Enchanters! Enchantresses! Park. 9.

Enchanting
And your enchanting manners bring
Frag. Nat. XXIII. 13.

Enchantment
The gay enchantment was undone,
Each. 35.
Enchantment fixed me here
Monadnoc. 225.

Enchantresses
Enchanters! Enchantresses! Park. 9.

Enchants
See Disenchants.
Seems, though the soft sheen all enchants, Frag. Nat. XXIX. 1.
The Fairest enchants me, Poet. 118.
And with a million spells enchants
Waldeinsamkeit. 23.
Sure some god his eye enchants:
Woodnotes. I. 11.

Enclosed
Around the radiant fireplace, enclosed
Snow-Storm. 8.

Encloses
Himself encloses and includes,
Daemonic Love. 94.

Encounter
The encounter of the wise,— Visit. 10.

Encumber
He shall not his brain encumber
Merlin. 29.

End
And a prime end of the most subtle element Adirondacs. 258.
The holidays were fruitful, but must end;
Adirondacs. 330.
Wherefore? to what good end?
Channing Ode. 40.
Around the man who seeks a noble end,
Frag. Life. III. 1.
I must end my true report,
Initial Love. 81.
And end in churls the mountain folk
Monadnoc. 119.
Vanish, and end their murmuring,—
Monadnoc. 367.
Fully until the end. Poet. 96.
Oft shall war end, and peace return,
Saadi. 111.
And veils the farm-house at the garden's
end. Snow-Storm. 5.
Unnerves his strength, invites his end.
Woodnotes. II. 50.

Endears
Their dust endears the sod.
Robbins Hymn. 4.

Endeavor
One pulse more of firm endeavor,—
Give. 29.
And, out of endeavor Illusions. 26.

Endless
And marching single in an endless file,
Days. 3.
And endless imbroglio   Illusions. 31.
O'er thy rich dust the endless smile
In Memoriam. 105.
Saw the endless rack of the firmament
Poet. 67.
Endless dirges to decay,   Saadi. 50.
Of tendency through endless ages,
Woodnotes. II. 106.

Ends
fit for her own ends,   Adirondacs. 71.
This home my minstrel-journeyings ends.
Aeolian Harp. 19.
Where I, as others, follow petty ends;
Frag. Life. XV. 3.

Endurance
Which past endurance sting the tender
cit,   Adirondacs. 174.
And to endurance.   Illusions. 37.

Endure
In their archetypes endure.
Celestial Love. 53.
Through earth to ripen, through heaven
endure.   May-Day. 468.
Which I could not on me endure?
Problem. 8.
Didst thou, just man, endure.
Tal. Exile. 3.

Endured
Endured, the Bible says, as long;
Frag. Nat. VI. 4.
But what torments of grief you endured
Quat. Borrowing. 3.

Endures
Each endures;   Hamatreya. 30.

Enduring
Beside him sat enduring love, Poet. 195.

Endymion
The much deceived Endymion
Manners. 19.

Enemies
All the fierce enemies, ague, hunger, cold,
Adirondacs. 317.

Enemy
Call hither thy mortal enemy, Poet. 219.
And he who has one enemy will meet him
everywhere.   Taleb. 2.

Energy
An energy that searches thorough
May-Day. 459.
Throbs with an overmastering energy
Pan. 7.

Engage
In schemes of broader scope engage.
Alphonso. 80.
That Each for each doth fast engage;
Hermione. 32.

Engineer
Bold as the engineer who fells the wood,
Blight. 19.

England
See New England.
Broad England harbored not his peer:
Fate. 10.

England's
O'er England's abbeys bends the sky,
Problem. 37.
England's genius filled all measure
Solution. 35.

English
Bad news from George on the English
throne;   Boston. 63.
The townsmen braved the English king,
Boston. 82.
For that hardy English root
Monadnoc. 183.
English, German, Basque, Castilian,
Woodnotes. II. 151.

Engraved
The rocks uphold thy name engraved,
Lines. 12.

Enjoyed
Shall each by each be most enjoyed.
Celestial Love. 98.
And tell what's there enjoyed, Garden. 2.
And troops of friends enjoyed the tide,—
In Memoriam. 71.

Enjoyer
But thou, joy-giver and enjoyer,
Saadi. 99.

Enlarged
But when it seeks enlarged supplies,
Woodnotes. II. 55.

Enormous
Worthy the enormous cloud of witnesses,
Adirondacs. 247.
Fixed on the enormous galaxy,
Character. 3.
And largest clouds be flakes of down in
that enormous sky.   Frag. Nat. XX. 2.
Fixed on the enormous galaxy,
Poet. 136.
Patient through Heaven's enormous year
Wealth. 11.

Enough
Enough that mankind eat and are re-
freshed.   Adirondacs. 301.
Has lords enough and more;—
Boston. 20.
Honor enough that we send the call.'
Boston. 68.
But wiser than I was, and wise enough
River. 19.
There's not enough for this and that,
Terminus. 12.
'T will be time enough to die;
Woodnotes. I. 142.
Enough for thee the primal mind
Woodnotes. II. 232.

Enow
Soul's desire is means enow,   Poet. 250.

Enriches
Still enriches and transforms,
May-Day. 199.

Enriching
So thou attend the enriching Fate
Poet. 124.

Ensample
I make this maiden an ensample
Rhea. 64.

Ensign
Firm ensign of the fatal Being,
Monadnoc. 361.

Ensigns
And torn the ensigns from thy brow,
Woodnotes. II. 184.

Ensnare
Trade and the streets ensnare us,
World-Soul. 21.

Ensouled
Well embodied, well ensouled,
Monadnoc. 156.
Enter
See Reënter.
Nor murdering hate, can enter in.
Past. 9.
Entering
Entering Big Tupper, Adirondacs. 232.
And duly greet the entering May?
May-Day. 219.
Enterprise
Stings the strong with enterprise,
May-Day. 203.
As the light of enterprise On Prince. 3.
Entertain
Than still to entertain his ear
Frag. Poet. V. 6.
That they may seize and entertain
Initial Love. 51.
Entertain it reverently. Saadi. 36.
That thou might'st entertain apart
Threnody. 215.
Entitled
Let not him mourn who best entitled
was, Adirondacs. 296.
Entombed
And when I am entombed in my place,
Entombed. 1.
Entomologist
O tufted entomologist!
Frag. Nat. XIX. 4.
Entreated
Entreated, she is dumb; Harp. 18.
Enviable
See Unenviable.
Enviers
Thy foes to hunt, thy enviers to strike
down, Shah-Hafiz. 1.
Envies
Yet envies none, none are unenviable.'
Musketaquid. 84.
Environ
Environ me and me baptize
Frag. Poet. VII. 5.
Envy
Above the envy of the crowd,—
Thought. 3.
Ephemerals
And her proud ephemerals, Circles. 2.
Epic
Seas ebbed and flowed in epic chime.
Beauty. 16.
Epicurean
Epicurean of June; Humble-Bee. 16.
Equal
See Unequal.
Equal on Sunday in the pew, Boston. 27.
To the good an equal friend. Boston. 115.
To build an equal state,—
Concord Ode. 14.
In equal couples mated, Merlin. 102.
Equal trophies of thine art;
Ode to Beauty. 89.
The new day lowers, and equal odds
Poet. 179.
The good, the bad with equal zeal,
Poet. 211.
Where equal means are none.' Poet. 248.
And granted them an equal date
Problem. 43.

With equal fire thy heart shalt melt.
Saadi. 124.
Whose voice, an equal messenger,
Threnody. 38.
No darkness stains its equal gleam,
Two Rivers. 19.
In equal strength through space abide;
Voluntaries. 116.
Equalizing
Equalizing small and large, Etienne. 17.
Equals
Equals remote, and seeming opposites.
Daemonic Love. 84.
Equator
Match God's equator with a zone of art,
Adirondacs. 245.
Equipoise
And the equipoise of heaven is thy house's
equipoise. Shah. Enweri. II. 2.
Ere (Partial list.)
Ere freedom out of man.
Concord Ode. 40.
Ere she can find a tree. House. 12.
Ere yet arrives the wintry day
Monadnoc. 23.
Ere he was born, the stars of fate
Quat. Horoscope. 1.
Erebus
Of Styx and Erebus; Bacchus. 9.
The inks of Erebus he found;
Solution. 48.
Erect
Still is the haughty pile erect
Monadnoc. 373.
"Erect as a sunbeam, Sphinx. 17.
Eremite
Seek not, and the little eremite
Woodnotes. II. 250.
Erewhile
With the high port he wore erewhile,
In Memoriam. 77.
Eros
He saw strong Eros struggling through,
Beauty. 18.
The highway, Eros and the Muse.
Love and Thought. 2.
For Eros is older than Saturn or Jove;
Quat. Casella. 2.
Err
If I err not, thus it said:—
Monadnoc. 198.
Nigh persuading gods to err!
Ode to Beauty. 22.
Errand
With the errand to be done,—
Etienne. 22.
Love on his errand bound to go
Quat. Love. 1.
A sterner errand to the silken troop
Summons. 1.
Errands
Her fiery errands go. Concord Ode. 36.
Errant
From centred and from errant sphere.
Beauty. 14.
By errant gain, Monadnoc. 399.
Erred
(Perchance I erred), a shade of discon-
tent; Adirondacs. 273.
Errest
Yet thou errest far and broad. Rhea. 24.

Erring
See Unerring.
Or those we erring own,
Celestial Love. 55.
The erring painter made Love blind,—
Daemonic Love. 68.

Error
By error or intemperance. Poet. 158.

Errors
To wrap the errors of a sage sublime.
To J. W. 9.

Errs
With bandaged eyes he never errs,
Cupido. 3.
And this wise Seer within me never errs.
Self-Reliance. 8.

Erst
Which drove them erst to social feats;
Alphonso. 34.
As erst it wont, would thrill and ring.
Harp. 106.
Step the meek fowls where erst they
ranged; Threnody. 94.

Escape
See Scape.
Greeted their safe escape to me.
Each. 23.
But forever doth escape,
Woodnotes. II. 273.

Escaped
Some tears escaped, but his philosophy
Philosopher. 8.

Escort
Escort us to a little grave.
Frag. Life. I. 4.

Espied
See Unespied.
Seems, by the traveller espied,
Hermione. 43.

Essaying
Essaying nothing she cannot perform.
Adirondacs. 72.

Essence
There the holy essence rolls,
Celestial Love. 46.
He is the essence that inquires.
Woodnotes. II. 312.

Essences
Forest full of esesnces
Frag. Nat. II. 11.

Establish
See Stablish.

Estate
In their innermost estate;
Celestial Love. 96.
Estate, good-fame, Give. 4.
Sole estate his sire bequeathed,—
Voluntaries. 9.

Esteems
These the fables she esteems
Frag. Nat. XXIII. 5.

Estimation
And estimation true, From Hafiz. 5.

Etched
Etched on Alp and Apennine.
Solution. 32.

Eternal
The dancing Pleiads and eternal men.
Bacchus. 67.
The measure of the eternal Mind,
Bohemian. 11.

For eternal years in debt.
Boston Hymn. 64.
Where the starred, eternal worm
Celestial Love. 36.
Nor less the eternal poles
Celestial Love. 81.
That hurry through the eternal halls,
II Compensation. 10.
Over me soared the eternal sky,
Each. 46.
For each eternal block— House. 16.
And those eternal forms, May-Day. 320.
It was as if the eternal gods,
May-Day. 327.
What in the Eternal standeth well,
Monadnoc. 87.
Thou eternal fugitive, Ode to Beauty. 74.
But not the less the eternal wave rolls
on Pan. 10.
Alter or mend eternal Fact. Past. 21.
Feeds those eternal lamps I see.
Poet. 236.
And prayed the eternal Light to clear
Robbins Hymn. 11.
The midway of the eternal deep.
Saadi. 146.
Builds therewith eternal towers;
Spiritual Lows. 4.
Lauding the Eternal Rights,
Voluntaries. 109.
Onward and on, the eternal Pan,
Woodnotes. II. 270.
Stars weave eternal rings;
World-Soul. 62.

Eterne
"Eterne alternation Sphinx. 97.

Eternities
Coming and past eternities?
Woodnotes. I. 29.

Eternity
Roomy Eternity Frag. Life. VI. 1.
Draw the breath of Eternity; Poet. 284.
Ask on, thou clothed eternity;
Sphinx. 119
Or the stars of eternity?
Woodnotes. II. 304.

Ether
He could condense cerulean ether
Frag. Poet. XXIII. 1.
The stars' own ether beams; Poet. 100.
O birds of ether without wings!
Poet. 159.

Ethiops
Feeding on the Ethiops sweet,
Berrying. 7.

Etiquette
And etiquette of gentilesse.
Frag. Poet. I. 30.

Eumenides
Dear to the Eumenides, Destiny. 47.

Europe
Old Europe groans with palaces,
Boston. 19.

Europe's
Pole-star of light in Europe's night,
Boston. 90.

Eve
from morn to eve. Adirondacs. 90.
Freely as task at eve undone
Frag. Poet. XI. 18.
In the hall at summer eve Harp. 45.

Of eve and morn,   In Memoriam. 17.
By morn and eve in light and shade;
                      Monadnoc. 61.
Nor the red rainbow of a summer eve,
                      Naples. 16.
Is not my voice thy music, morn and eve?
                      Seashore. 4.
Obey the voice at eve obeyed at prime:
                      Terminus. 36.

Even
And yet I marked, even in the manly joy
                      Adirondacs. 271.
Thatch his flesh, and even his years
                      Alphonso. 75.
And live on even terms with Time;
                      Art. 26.
Even at its greatest space is a defeat,
                      Blight. 54.
Even in the hot pursuit of the best aims
                      Blight. 58.
Even the fell Furies are appeased,
                      Celestial Love. 113.
Sex to sex, and even to odd;—
                      Channing Ode. 79.
I brought him home, in his nest, at even;
                      Each. 15.
Even to those who thee should love
                      Frag. Life. XXVII. 2.
Even the serene Reason says,
                      In Memoriam. 9.
But even thy kiss denies *Farewell. 23.
Even from a brook, and where old woods
                      Letter. 11.
Even into May the iceberg cold.
                      May-Day. 20.
Who with even matches odd,
                      Merlin. 118.
'T is even so, this treacherous kite,
                      Monadnoc. 331.
Nor wit, nor eloquence,—no, nor even
   the song   Naples. 19.
And give to hold an even state, Poet. 167.

Evening
Evening drew on; stars peeped throuh
   maple-boughs,   Adirondacs. 46.
Or, in the evening twilight's latest red,
                      Adirondacs. 115.
One August evening had a cooler breath;
                      Adirondacs. 331.
Have brought us to life's evening hour,
                      Ellen. 2.
Soft shadows of the evening lay.
                      Frag. Poet. V. 48.
Where the evening star so holy shines,
                      Good-Bye. 26.
Which morn and crimson evening paint
                      Monadnoc. 44.
Red evening duly dyes
                      Monadnoc Afar. 2.
No early morn, no evening late,—
                      Nun. 43.
Poises Arcturus aloft morning and even-
   ing his spear.   Shah.-Hafiz. 2.
As I behold yon evening star,
                      Thine Eyes. 3.
He heard the woodcock's evening hymn;
                      Woodnotes. I. 55.

Evening's
The vanished rose of evening's dream.
                      May-Day. 298.

Event
So in the gladness of the new event
                      Adirondacs. 335.
And mix itself with each event;
                      Monadnoc. 51.
To make no step until the event is
   known,   Woodnotes. I. 88.

Eventide
Not long ago at eventide,   Harp. 107.

Events
Love calls not to his aid events;
                      Frag. Life. XVII. 4.
The livery all events put on,
                      Frag. Poet. IV. 26.

Ever (Partial list.)
   See Forever; Forevermore; How-
   ever; Howsoever.
these echoes ever heard. Adirondacs. 33.
Are ever rivals: but, though this be
   swift,   Adirondacs. 287.
But ever the free race with front sub-
   lime,   Adirondacs. 293.
And ever was. Pay him.
                      Boston Hymn. 72.
It was ever the self-same tale,
                      Daemonic Love. 19.
And ever and forever Love
                      Daemonic Love. 85.
The Dæmon ever builds a wall,
                      Daemonic Love. 93.
And ever the Dæmonic Love
                      Daemonic Love. 129.
Worship him ever.   Ellen South. 12.
Ever the Rock of Ages melts
                      Frag. Life. XXIV. 1.
And, ever subdividing, separate
                      Frag. Nat. XVII. 3.
And ever when the happy child
                      May-Day. 98.
Ever the fiery Pentecost   Problem. 51.
Ever the Poet *from* the land
                      Quat. Poet. I. 1.
Form the soul had ever dressed,
                      Rhea. 18.
Ever have done, ever shall.   Rhea. 32.
And ever in the strife of your own
   thoughts   Rome. 15.
Ever, when twain together play,
                      Saadi. 15.
And ever by delicate powers
                      Song of Nature. 13.
Or ever the wild Time coined itself
                      Uriel. 3.
Ever on thousands shine,   Webster. 2.
For Nature ever faithful is
                      Woodnotes. I. 137.
The ever old, the ever young;
                      Woodnotes II. 117.
Ever fresh the broad creation,
                      Woodnotes. II. 262.

Everlasting
Draw everlasting dew;   Bacchus. 17.
The everlasting sun,   Day by Day. 2.
Would hear the everlasting
                      Frag. Nat. III. 29.
Thine everlasting lovers. Ye shall be
                      Good Cheer. 15.
The stars everlasting,   Illusions. 17.
Breathed from the everlasting throat.
                      Woodnotes II. 123.

Evermore

See Forevermore.

And evermore the cruel god
In Memoriam. 58.

Inspirer, prophet evermore;
Monadnoc. 47.

I with my hammer pounding evermore
Seashore. 34.

Out of an unseen quarry evermore
Snow-Storm. 11.

Justice conquers evermore,
Voluntaries. 100.

Every

All day we swept the lake, searched every
cove,   Adirondacs. 108.

Every aster in my hand   Apology. 11.

Every wayfarer he meets
Astraea. 25.

Every crypt of every rock.   Bacchus. 44.

And sailed for bread to every shore.
Boston. 6.

In every needful faculty,
Boston Hymn. 43.

I cause from every creature
Boston Hymn. 57.

And every fair and every good,
Celestial Love. 50.

Every one to his chosen work;—
Channing Ode. 75.

And every human heart   Cosmos. 25.

Burns up every other tie.
Daemonic Love. 115.

Wherein every siren sung,
Daemonic Love. 124.

To-day, when friends approach, and
every hour   Day's Ration. 20.

They played with it in every mood;
Dirge. 30.

Though it change every minute.
Ellen South. 4.

Every year plays it over
Ellen South. 6.

Scatters on every eve dust of his spells,
Enchanter. 3.

Every shrub and grape leaf
Frag. Nat. III. 24.

For Nature, true and like in every place,
Frag. Nat. IV. 1.

In her hundred-gated Thebes every
chamber was a door,
Frag. Nat. XII. 2.

Touched with life by every beam.
Frag. Nat. XXVI. 29.

I share the good with every flower,
Frag. Nat. XXVI. 30.

Glittered with silver every cottage pane,
Frag. Nat. XXVII. 4.

That came to every festival.
Frag. Poet. I. 4.

Knew every temple and kiosk
Frag. Poet. I. 7.

In every glance of Hassan's eye
Frag. Poet. III. 5.

For every God   Frag. Poet. XV. 1.

When every star is Bethlehem star?
Frag. Poet. XXVIII. 3.

And every god,—none did refuse;
Garden. 26.

Yet every one   Hamatreya. 55.

And drew truly every trait.
Hermione. 39.

And in every twinkling glade,
Hermione. 53.

And quarries every rock,   House. 14.

In music every one,   House. 18.

Every function he absorbs;
Initial Love. 26.

Will clear his fame from every cloud
Initial Love. 86.

With every king on every throne,
Initial Love. 125.

Honor prompted every glance,
In Memoriam. 55.

Which holds to home 'neath every sky,
In Memoriam. 82.

Her every act.   In Memoriam. 96.

Every day brings a ship,   Letters. 1.

Every ship brings a word;   Letters. 2.

Bore thy colors every flower, Lines. 5.

Every moth with painted wing,
Lines. 9.

Every bird in carolling,   Lines. 10.

Every nook of Nature through:
Love and Thought. 6.

Dazzle every mortal.   Manners. 4.

Every night alighting down
May-Day. 26.

See, every patriot oak-leaf throws
May-Day. 113.

Strains every sense to larger scope,
May-Day. 153.

Of shining virgins every May,
May-Day. 302.

Every joy and virtue speed,
May-Day. 334.

Every tree and stem and chink
May-Day. 340.

Every one to his hole in the wall,
May-Day. 390.

To every foot its antipode;   Merlin. 81.

To every tone beat answering tones,
Merlin. 83.

In every mortal meet.   Merlin. 91.

Told every word and syllable
Miracle. 33.

Every thing is kin of mine.
Mithridates. 5.

'Every morn I lift my head,
Monadnoc. 279.

Where every wind that swept my tomb
Mountain. 11.

And every atom poises for itself,
Musketaquid. 58.

Gilds a few points in every several life,
Naples. 4.

And every colored petal of each flower,
Naples. 6.

Self-kindled every atom glows
Nature. Mot. 15.

And every man, in love or pride,
Nemesis. 7.

And every rood in the hemlock wood
Peter. 7.

In every whispering leaf I hear
Peter. 31.

And every flower made obeisance
Peter. 35.

Yet every scroll whereon he wrote
Poet. 13.

Every maxim of dreadful Need;
Poet. 44.

To every child they wake,   Promise. 8.

Every thought is public,   Quat. Hush. 1.
Every nook is wide;   Quat. Hush. 2.
In his every syllable   Saadi. 129.
For every wave is wealth to Dædalus,
                              Seashore. 30.
Round every windward stake, or tree, or
    door.   Snow-Storm. 14.
And every wave is charmed.'
                              Terminus. 40.
And on every mount and meadow
                              Threnody. 3.
Outvalued every pulsing sound
                              Threnody. 13.
When every morn my bosom glowed
                              Threnody. 60.
And every inch of garden ground
                              Threnody. 90.
And every chick of every bird,
                              Threnody. 114.
Crowds every egg out of the nest,
                              Unity. 5.
Every quality and pith   Unity. 9.
And every new compound   Visit. 6.
Sweet influence from every element;
                              Woodnotes. I. 77.
To every soul resounding clear
                              Woodnotes. II. 146.
And rounds with rhyme her every rune,
                              Woodnotes. II. 165.
Is perfect Nature's every part,
                              Woodnotes. II. 176.
To every age, to every race;
                              Woodnotes. II. 280.
Unto every race and age
                              Woodnotes. II. 281.
He is the heart of every creature;
                              Woodnotes. II. 315.

Everywhere
Beauty chased he everywhere,
                              Beauty. 5.
Whose roads lead everywhere to all;
                              Boston. 60.
Doubling daylight everywhere:
                              Caritas. 4.
And it cometh everywhere.
                              Informing Spirit. 4.
Creepeth, bloweth everywhere;
                              May-Day. 290.
Which galls me everywhere.   Park. 4.
And he who has one enemy will meet
    him everywhere.   Taleb. 2.
And stirred the devils everywhere,
                              Uriel. 18.

Evident
The rules to men made evident
                              Frag. Life. XXXVI. 1.
To his ears was evident.   Uriel. 10.

Evil
The evil time's sole patriot,
                              Channing Ode. 2.
The evil and the good.   Cupido. 10.
My few and evil years!   *Farewell. 31.
Nor evil laws or rulers made,
                              May-Day. 105.
And in days of evil plight   Solution. 20.
Evil will bless, and ice will burn.'
                              Uriel. 24.
Or out of the good of evil born,
                              Uriel. 53.
He who, in evil times,   Voluntaries. 84.

Evil-doer
Frowning down the evil-doer,
                              In Memoriam. 42.

Evils
From evils which never arrived!
                              Quat. Borrowing. 4.
From all evils to defend her;   Rhea. 49.
And ills to come as evils past bemoan.
                              Woodnotes. I. 89.

Evil-spoken
And his good is evil-spoken.
                              Initial Love. 93.

Exact
Exact to days, exact to hours,
                              May-Day. 375.

Exalt
An animated law, a presence to exalt.'
                              Poet. 164.

Exalts
When success exalts thy lot,
                              Prayer. 1.

Example
    See Ensample.
Example, custom, fear, occasion slow,—
                              Grace. 3.

Exceeds
The soaring orbit of the muse exceeds
    that journey's length.   Merlin. 65.

Excel
Yet doth much her love excel
                              Nature. I. 16.

Excellent
I know that ye are excellent,   Poet. 258.
Saying, *What is excellent,*
                              Threnody. 266.

Excelling
And a more excelling grace
                              Frag. Poet. XI. 9.

Except
Except the amber morning wind,
                              Exile. 5.
Quick or dead, except its own;   Unity. 6.

Exchange
Exchange in conclave general
                              Frag. Nat. XXIII. 15.

Excuse
Then Beauty is its own excuse for being:
                              Rhodora. 12.
Stoop not then to poor excuse;
                              Sursum Corda. 5.

Executor
And planted world, and full executor
                              Blight. 16.

Exerts
And power to him who power exerts.
                              II Compensation. 22.

Exhalation
An exhalation of the time.
                              Frag. Nat. XXVI. 37.

Exhale
To animate new millions, and exhale
                              Pan. 11.

Exhaust
Than my few needs exhaust, and bids me
    read   Frag. Nat. V. 6.
They feed the spring which they exhaust;
                              Saadi. 42.

Exhausted
    See Unexhausted.

Exile
The seasons chariot him from this exile,
                        Adirondacs. 225.
And bend the exile to his fate,   Art. 22.
To offer the exile cheer.   Exile. 8.
An exile from the wilderness,—
                        Woodnotes. II. 189.

Exile's
And feed once more the exile's eyes;
                        May-Day. 97.

Exists
Exists to draw thy virtue forth.
                        Titmouse. 59.

Exodus
The exodus of nations: I disperse
                        Seashore. 39.

Expands
Freedom all winged expands,
                        Voluntaries. 35.

Expansive
Fairer that expansive reason
                        Threnody. 258.

Expectance
Fans in all hearts expectance sweet,
                        May-Day. 296.

Expels
And the wise soul expels disease.
                        Woodnotes. II. 191.

Experience
The first experience will not fail;
                        Daemonic Love. 20.
Sum their long experience,   Visit. 19.

Experiment
Of books and arts and trained experiment,   Adirondacs. 307.

Experts
armed eyes of experts.
                        Adirondacs. 304.

Expire
Till all difference expire.
                        Song of Seyd. 26.

Explore
Which these explore   Dull. 10.
Explored they teach us to explore.
                        Dull. 22.
His eyes explore the ground,—
                        Manners. 10.
One face explore in foreign faces.
                        Una. 12.
To know one element, explore another,
                        Xenophanes. 12.

Explored
Explored they teach us to explore.
                        Dull. 22.

Expound
Who could the mystery expound,
                        Frag. Nat. VI. 2.
Expound the Vedas of the violet,
                        Quat. Gardener. 2.

Express
To thee the horion shall express
                        Woodnotes. II. 196.

Expressed
    See Unexpressed.
Passion not to be expressed
                        Freedom. 9.

Expression
Died in its last expression.
                        Amulet. 12.

Extend
And our shrinking sky extend.
                        Daemonic Love. 59.

Extense
Men and gods are too extense;
                        Alphonso. 63.

Extent
Realm beyond realm,—extent untold;
                        Nun. 42.

Exterminates
He who exterminates
                        Channing Ode. 83.

Extinguished
Into the winter night's extinguished
    mood?   Musketaquid. 79.

Extort
To outdo each other and extort applause.   Adirondacs. 326.

Extravagant
Sweet, extravagant desire,
                        Ode to Beauty. 77.

Extremes
Modulating all extremes,—   Harp. 31.
Extremes of nature reconciled,—
                        Merlin. 52.
Or mired by climate's gross extremes.
                        Nun. 36.

Exult,
Nay, mourn not one: let him exult,
                        Adirondacs. 297.

Exulting
With ductile fire. Loud, exulting cries
                        Adirondacs. 241.
Surprise the exulting soul.   Hymn. 24.

Exults
In his prowess he exults,
                        Daemonic Love. 103.

Eye
Mark his capricious ways to draw the
    eye.   Adirondacs. 207.
Rendering to a curious eye
                        Astraea. 36.
He smote the lake to feed his eye
                        Beauty. 7.
Deeper and older seemed his eye;
                        Character. 4.
Of man's or maiden's eye: Culture. 8.
And, seeing his eye glare,
                        Daemonic Love. 107.
And his eye is scornful.   Destiny. 32.
He sang to my ear,—they sang to my
    eye.   Each. 18.
Scatters on every eye dust of his spells,
                        Enchanter. 3.
Opens the eye to Virtue's starlike meed
                        Enchanter. 14.
The slow eye of heaven shall show
                        Frag. Nat. XXVI. 9.
That mend her beauty to the eye.
                        Frag. Nat. XXXII. 4.
His lamp, the maiden's downcast eye,
                        Frag. Poet. I. 12.
In every glance of Hassan's eye
                        Frag. Poet. III. 5.
Is the purging of his eye
                        Frag. Poet. XI. 3.
To upstart Wealth's averted eye;
                        Good-Bye. 9.
By searching of a clear and loving eye
                        Good Cheer. 11

His eye the eye 't was seeking found.
Guy. 24.
Still breaks that morn, though dim, to
Memory's eye, I Bear. 10.
Flamed from his martial eye;
In Memoriam. 37.
What art thou? His wicked eye
Limits. 11.
Make the aged eye sun-clear,
May-Day. 455.
Of keenest eye and truest tongue.
Merlin's Song. 15.
Like wise preceptor, lure his eye
Monadnoc. 102.
Can thy style-discerning eye
Monadnoc. 237.
As, when the all-worshipped moon at-
tracts the eye, Musketaquid. 82.
The eye reads omens where it goes,
Nature. Mot. 3.
Color and sound, music to eye and ear,
October. 10.
In Being's deeps past ear and eye;
Ode to Beauty. 95.
He feels it, introverts his learned eye
Philosopher. 5.
With staring eye that seeth none,
Poet. 87.
Deeper and older seemed his eye,
Poet. 137.
As on its friends, with kindred eye;
Problem. 38.
her eye still seemed to see,
Quat. A. H. 3.
Her planted eye to-day controls,
Quat. Fate. 1.
His cold eye truth and conduct scanned,
Quat. S. H. 2.
A vixen to his altered eye; Rhea. 20.
To light which dims the morning's eye.
Rhea. 4.
The same blue wonder that my infant eye
River. 3.
So that what his eye hath seen
Saadi. 121.
Yet before the listener's eye Saadi. 133.
Though her eye seek other forms
Security. 1.
Couldst see thy proper eye,
Sphinx. 114.
Of thine eye I am eyebeam.
Sphinx. 112.
Has disappeared from the Day's eye;
Threnody. 21.
Took the eye with him as he went;
Threnody. 71.
Tutors, but a joyful eye, Threnody. 211.
Revere the Maker; fetch thine eye
Threnody. 270.
As Uriel spoke with piercing eye,
Uriel. 25.
Will thy clear blue eye, upward bent,
still keep its chastened glow,
*Violet. 3.
When Winter reigned I'd close my eye,
but wake with bursting Spring,
*Violet. 11.
Sure some god his eye enchants:
Woodnotes. I. 11.
Shed their virtue through his eye.
Woodnotes II. 74.

And sunk the immortal eye so low?
Woodnotes. II. 185.
And to thine eye the vast skies fall,
Woodnotes. II. 200.

Eyeballs
By those roving eyeballs bold.
Initial Love. 32.
My eyes his eyeballs meet. Park. 8.

Eye-beams
And wheresoever their clear eye-beams
fell, Blight. 28.
Of thine eye I am eyebeam.
Sphinx. 112.

Eyed
See Blue-eyed; Deep-eyed; Far-eyed;
Prophetic-eyed; Sad-eyed; Wild-eyed;
Young-eyed.

Eyelids
Your eyelids to the sphere:
Frag. Life. XXXV. 4.

Eyeless
Our eyeless bark sails free
Frag. Nat. XV. 1.
Plunges eyeless on forever;
Monadnoc. 334.

Eyemark
An eyemark and the country's core,
Monadnoc. 46.

Eyes'
Your colors for our eyes' delight:
Frag. Nat. XXIII. 10.
In the pit of his eye's a spark
Initial Love. 21.

Eyes
See Bead-eyes.
Men knowing what they seek, armed
eyes of experts. Adirondacs. 304.
Eyes of gods! ye must have seen,
Alphonso. 19.
Until he write, where all eyes rest,
Astraea. 7.
Our eyes Are armed, but we are stran-
gers to the stars, Blight. 29-30.
Therefore, to our sick eyes, Blight. 49.
My thunderbolt has eyes to see
Boston Hymn. 87.
'Deep, deep are loving eyes,
Celestial Love. 15.
The axis of those eyes sun-clear
Celestial Love. 21.
With bandaged eyes he never errs,
Cupido. 3.
When her calm eyes opened bright,
Daemonic Love. 17.
And dips sometimes as low as to her
eyes. Daemonic Love. 38.
Whose eyes pierce Daemonic Love. 72.
For fear of human eyes swerved from
his plan. Entombed. 4.
O fair and stately maid, whose eyes
Eva. 1.
From bright, familiar eyes.
*Farewell. 13.
And dips sometimes as low as to her
eyes. Frag. Life. XVI. 4.
And for travelled eyes what charms
Frag. Nat. XXVI. 3.
I shunned his eyes, that faithful man's,
Frag. Poet. III. 11.

Eyes—*Continued*

With light that streams from gracious
eyes.   Frag. Poet. VII. 6.
Nor kind occasion without eyes;
          Frag. Life. XVII. 7.
His eyes detect the Gods concealed.
          Frag. Poet. XXVII. 3.
Leave his weeds and heed his eyes,—
          Initial Love. 19.
And they pounce on other eyes
          Initial Love. 39.
He lives in his eyes;   Initial Love. 45.
With shining gifts that took all eyes,
          In Memoriam. 62.
His eyes explore the ground,—
          Manners. 10.
And feed once more the exile's eyes;
          May-Day. 97.
To babes, and to old eyes as well.
          May-Day. 348.
To far eyes, an aerial isle
          Monadnoc. 42.
Rear purer wits, inventive eyes,—
          Monadnoc. 107.
Eyes that frame cities where none be,
          Monadnoc. 108.
I plant his eyes on the sky-hoop bound-
ing;   Monadnocc. 324.
To fix far-gazing eyes.
          Monadnoc Afar. 4.
Are the apples of her eyes;
          Nature. I. 8.
When first my eyes saw thee,
          Ode to Beauty. 9.
Beaming from a young man's eyes.
          On Prince. 4.
My eyes his eyeballs meet.   Park. 8.
Tossing one sparkle to the eyes:
          Peter. 38.
To that within the vision of small eyes.
          Phi. 18.
Philosophers are lined with eyes within,
          Philosopher. 1.
The things whereon he cast his eyes
          Poet. 9.
He flesh should feel, his eyes should read
          Poet. 43.
But oh, to see his solar eyes   Poet. 54.
Upon him noble eyes did rest,
          Poet. 196.
From the eyes of the false-hearted,
          Rhea. 14.
Tell them, dear, that if eyes were made
for seeing,   Rhodora. 11.
The keen stars twinkle in our eyes,
          Romany. 22.
Wish not to fill the isles with eyes
          Saadi. 147.
Without cloud, in its eyes;   Sphinx. 46.
Which his eyes seek in vain.   Sphinx. 80.
Her muddy eyes to clear!"   Sphinx. 108.
Have you eyes to find the five   Test. 13.
Thine eyes still shined for me, though
far   Thine Eyes. 1.
Took counsel from hic guiding eyes
          Threnody. 56.
Ah, vainly do these eyes recall
          Threnody. 58.
With rolling eyes and face composed;
          Threnody. 63.
In whose deep eyes   Threnody. 168.

With aged eyes, short way before,—
          Threnody. 180.
Whose eyes within his eyes beheld
          Threnody. 184.
Than the meeting of the eyes? Visit. 12.
Leave authors' eyes, and fetch your own,
          Waldeinsamkeit. 43.
Seldom seen by wishful eyes,
          Woodnotes. I. 51.
Take off thine eyes, thy heart forbear,
          Woodnotes. II. 87.
Come lift thine eyes to lofty rhymes,
          Woodnotes II. 158.
Or woman's pleading eyes;
          World-Soul. 28.
Yet, greeted in another's eyes,
          Worship. 17.

Fables

His fathers shining in bright fables,
          Art. 17.
These the fables she esteems
          Frag. Nat. XXIII. 5.
He all the fables knows,   Harp. 11.
Fleeing to fables,   Illusions. 12.

Face

     See Deface; New-face.
Temper to face wolf, bear, or catamount,
          Adirondacs. 85.
Was never form and never face
          Beauty. 1.
And the soldiers face to face?
          Cosmos. 16.
Is the Dæmon's form and face.
          Daemonic Love. 34.
But Cupid wears another face,
          Daemonic Love. 89.
When thou lookest on his face,
          Destiny. 20.
If our brief tribe miss thy face,
          Ellen South. 23.
To-morrow they will wear another face,
          Experience. 20.
Yet I could never see their face.
          Forerunners. 14.
With a face of golden pleasure
          Frag. Nat. XXIV. 11.
Face the eastern star until
          Frag. Nat. XXVI. 8.
I moulded his face to beauty
          Frag. Poet. XIV. 3.
Good-bye to Flattery's fawning face;
          Good-Bye. 7.
But of a kindred face
          In Memoriam. 23.
He looketh seldom in their face,
          Manners. 9.
Whilst the country's flinty face,
          Monadnoc. 147.
This mound shall throb his face before,
          Monadnoc. 288.
I look at my face in the glass,—
          Park. 7.
Up and eastward turn thy face;
          Poet. 121.
His face was the mould of beauty,
          Power. 3.
From many a radiant face,
          Robbins Hymn. 6.

With rolling eyes and face composed;
     Threnody. 63.
With sunny face of sweet repose,
     Threnody. 68.
Plight broken, this high face defaced!
     Threnody. 151.
One face explore in foreign faces.
     Una. 12.
Let Webster's lofty face Webster. 1.
To hill and cloud his face was known,—
     Woodnotes. I. 114.

Faced
Unarmed, faced danger with a heart of
 trust?   Forbearance. 4.

Faces
Black by white faces,—
     Channing Ode. 85.
Day! hast thou two faces, Chartist. 1.
Has thousand faces in a thousand hours.
     Musketaquid. 25.
Statelier forms and fairer faces;
     Rhea. 67.
Where January brings few faces.'
     Titmouse. 32.
One face explore in foreign faces.
     Una. 12.

Facile
A facile, reckless, wandering will,
     Poet. 207.

Fact
For which the world had waited, now
 firm fact, Adirondacs. 238.
A burst of joy, as if we told the fact
     Adirondacs. 252.
Pleads for itself the fact,
     In Memoriam. 94.
Alter or mend eternal Fact. Past. 21.
One portrait—fact or fancy—we may
 draw;   Phi. 4.
Threw to each fact a tuneful name.
     Poet. 8.

Factory
Factory of river and of rain;
     Monadnoc. 84.
Will smile in a factory. World-Soul. 36.

Faculty
In every needful faculty,
     Boston Hymn. 43.

Fade
Watching the daylight fade,
     Hermione. 59.
They fade in the light of Sphinx. 71.
Through times that wear and forms that
 fade,   Waldeinsamkeit. 27.
Which bloom and fade like meadow
 flowers Woodnotes. II. 302.

Faded
Refresh the faded tints, Bacchus. 62.
Stars flamed and faded as they bade,
     Dirge. 34.

Fades
To a beauty that not fades.
     May-Day. 304.
Too slow the rainbow fades,
     Song of Nature. 50.

Fading
 See Unfading.
All these are fading now, *Farewell. 14.
The fading colors fix, Poet. 110.
When summer light is fading, and
 autumn breezes sigh; *Violet. 10.

Faerie
With faerie gardens cheered,
     Frag. Nat. X. 2.

Faery
I understand their faery syllables,
     River. 24.

Fagot
Charmed from fagot and from steel,
     Frag. Poet. V. 30.

Fagots
Bring diadems and fagots in their hands.
     Days. 4.

Fail
Ye shall not fail for sound advice.
     Alphonso. 48.
Or land or life, if freedom fail?
     Boston. 30.
Or land or life, if freedom fail?
     Boston. 81.
O bounteous seas that never fail!
     Boston. 86.
The first experience will not fail;
     Daemonic Love. 20.
Her gay pictures never fail,
     Frag. Nat. XXXI. 3.
Without fail, Hamatreya. 42.
His wisdom will not fail, Harp. 2.
Why only must thy reason fail
     May-Day. 175,
O mariners who never fail! Poet. 162.
Why did all manly gifts in Webster fail?
     Webster, 1854. 1.

Failed
Failed to plant the vantage-ground;
     Merlin's Song. 19.
Failed to bequeath Terminus. 26.
The world and not the infant failed.
     Threnody. 139.

Failing
Failing sometimes of his own,
     Initial Love. 94.
Economize the failing river,
     Terminus. 14.

Fails
Fails of the life, but draws the death and
 ill.   Angelo. 14.
The date fails not on the palm-tree tall;
     Woodnotes. II. 245.

Failure
Into failure, into folly."
     Woodnotes. II. 216.

Fain
What his dread folds would fain conceal?
     Harp. 64.

Fain
When Nature falters, fain would zeal
     May-Day. 157.

Faint
Bend nearer, faint day-moon! Yon
 thundertops, Adirondacs. 260.
From Spring's faint flush to Autumn red.
     Garden. 8.
Smacks of faint memories far away.
     May-Day. 78.
I am neither faint nor weary,
     Poet. 126.

Fainting
And fainting Nature at her need
     May-Day. 336.
Fire fainting will, May-Day. 440

Fair

See All-Fair.
Fair rose the planted hills behind
                 Boston. 41.
Creating fair and good alway,
                 Day by Day. 7.
That you are fair or wise is vain,
                 Destiny. 1.
Had leaped from one fair mother's arms,
                 Dirge. 6.
Nothing is fair or good alone. Each. 12.
O fair and stately maid, whose eyes
                 Eva. 1.
Some had heard their fair report,
                 Forerunners. 21.
Nor when in fair saloons we chance to
  meet;   Frag. Life. XV. 4.
Thought and its mansions fair.
             Frag. Life. XXIV. 4.
Received the fair inscriptions of the
  night;   Frag. Nat. XXVII. 2.
Are through thy friendship fair.
             Friendship. 20.
I saw fair boys bestriding steeds,
                 Harp. 111.
'If it be, as they said, she was not fair,
                 Hermione. 18.
Seeing only what is fair,
                 Humble-Bee. 54.
Bring to fair mother fairer child,
                 May-Day. 452.
Mould the year to fair increase,
                 Merlin. 57.
O fair, appeasing presences!
                 Merops. 6.
Fair fortunes to the mountaineer!
                 Monadnoc. 69.
Who, in large thoughts, like fair pearl-
  seed,   Monadnoc. 285.
From all that's fair, from all that's foul,
                 Music. 5.
The rounded world is fair to see,
               Nature. Mot. 7.
On life's fair picture of delight,
                 Nun. 9.
Fair to old and foul to young;
                 Prudence. 2.
The fair moon mounts, and aye the
  flame   Romany. 3.
Fair the soul's recess and shrine,
              Threnody. 255.
Draws the threads of fair and fit.
               Wealth. 33.
Whence the fair flock of Nature sprang.
           Woodnotes II. 125.

Fairer

And fairer forms are in the quarry
             Good Hope. 7.
Statelier forms and fairer faces;
                 Rhea. 67.
Fairer that expansive reason
             Threnody. 258.
The fairer world complete.
            World-Soul. 100.

Fairest

'Fairest, choose the fairest members
            Ellen South. 25.
Farewell, thou fairest one,
           *Farewell. 37.
The Fairest enchants me,   Poet. 118.

Yet fairest dames and bearded men,
               Threnody. 43.

Fairies

Whose groves the frolic fairies planned;
             Good-Bye. 18.
Swifter-fashioned than the fairies,
            Initial Love. 90.
To some tune by fairies played;—
             Threnody. 77.

Fairly

Were fairly reached at last.
            Adirondacs. 259.
The land is well,—lies fairly to the
  south.   Hamatreya. 22.

Fairy

A gentle wife, but fairy none. Each. 36.
Fit for fairy presences, Frag. Nat. II. 12.
Rang with fairy laughter.
           Frag. Nat. III. 25.
In fairy groves of herds-grass.
          Frag. Nat. XXVII. 10.
We had eaten fairy fruit, May-Day. 410.
A blooming hunter of a fairy fine.
             River. 15.

Faith

Stars rose; his faith was earlier up:
            Character. 2.
Their hands were pure, and pure their
  faith,—   Dirge. 51.
To the children who have faith;
                Harp. 33.
To keep this fire of faith alive,
                Hymn. 6.
And with glad thoughts of faith and
  hope   Hymn. 23.
Stars rose, his faith was earlier up:
               Poet. 135.
I fall, my faith is broken, Poet. 239.
Yet not for all his faith can see
              Problem. 5.
And yet, for all his faith could see,
            Problem. 71.
For faith and peace and mighty love
          Robbins Hymn. 17.
Romance forgot, and faith decayed,
             Solution. 60.
I put no faith in pilot or in chart,
             Unbar. 3.
Thee of thy faith who hath bereft,
          Woodnotes. II. 183.

Faithful

Province to province faithful clung,
            Boston. 97.
As planets faithful be. Boston Hymn. 48.
Love's hearts are faithful, but not fond,
          Celestial Love. 115.
I shunned his eyes, that faithful man's,
          Frag. Poet. III. 11.
Faithful through a thousand years,
           May-Day. 373.
Be thou faithful, but not fond;
          Quat. Pericles. 2.
'Lowly faithful, banish fear,
            Terminus. 37.
For Nature ever faithful is
          Woodnotes. I. 137.

Faithfulness

To such as trust her faithfulness.
          Woodnotes. I. 138.

Fakirs
Sad-eyed Fakirs swiftly say   Saadi. 49.
Thus the sad-eyed Fakirs preach:
                                Saadi. 59.
Fall
    See Befall; Downfall; Waterfall.
'T is fit the forest fall,
                        Channing Ode. 58.
In like sort his love doth fall,
                        Daemonic Love. 96.
Did in your childhood fall.   Dirge. 56.
To the gentian in the fall,
                        Ellen South. 31.
I have heard them fall
                        Frag. Nat. III. 26.
Sun and moon must fall amain
                        Frag. Poet. V. 34.
From fall to spring, the russet acorn,
                        Holidays. 1.
Fall, stream, from Heaven to bless;
                        Inscription. 1.
When forests fall, and man is gone,
                        Monadnoc. 213.
Fall on thee, as fall they will.
                        Monadnoc. 223.
Our towns and races grow and fall,
                        Monadnoc. 386.
His mighty psalm from fall to spring
                        Mountain. 19.
Make him glad thy fall to see! Poet. 220.
I fall, my faith is broken,   Poet. 239.
Fall like sweet strains, or pensive smiles;
                        Problem. 4.
And thy fortunes, as they fall,
                        Quat. Memory. 3.
On him thy blessing fall,
                        Robbins Hymn. 26.
Soften the fall with wary foot;
                        Terminus. 18.
Fate let him fall, Fate can't retake him;
                        Threnody. 28.
Of the snow-tower, when snow should
    fall;   Threnody. 85.
To-morrow, when the masks shall fall
                        Threnody. 189.
Many haps fall in the field
                        Woodnotes. I. 50.
Shall fall with purer radiance down;
                        Woodnotes. II. 72.
And to thine eye the vast skies fall,
                        Woodnotes. II. 200.
Fallen
    See New-fallen; Unfallen.
Is fallen: but hush! it has not scared the
    buck   Adirondacs. 122.
The purple petals, fallen in the pool,
                        Rhodora. 5.
Falling
The falling rain will spoil no holiday.
                        Adirondacs. 69.
Wisp and meteor nightly falling,
                        Frag. Nat. XVI. 1.
Early or late, the falling rain   Guy. 33.
The falling waters led me,
                        Woodnotes. I. 129.
Falls
    See Waterfalls.
Or harebell nodding in the gorge of falls.
                        Adirondacs. 145.
Entering Big Tupper, bound for the
    foaming Falls   Adirondacs. 232.

From his shoulders falls who sees
                        Celestial Love. 66.
Dearest, where thy shadow falls,
                        Dearest. 1.
So sweet and mournful falls the strain.
                        Harp. 102.
Gentler far than falls the snow
                        Poet. 253.
Falls, in turn, a new degree.   Rhea. 40.
Whoever fights, whoever falls,
                        Voluntaries. 99.
With sudden roar the aged pine-tree
    falls,—   Woodnotes. I. 73.
Let the starred shade that nightly falls
                        Woodnotes. II. 225.
Without a pilot it runs and falls,
                        Woodnotes. II. 240.
False
Without a false humility;
                        Celestial Love. 123.
When, by false companions crossed,
                        Love and Thought. 11.
False waters of thirst; Ode to Beauty. 14.
He by false usage pinned about
                        Poet. 189.
Me false to mine dare whisper none,—
                        Romany. 15.
Time is the false reply."   Sphinx. 120.
Hide in false peace your coward head,
                        Voluntaries. 33.
Which no false art refines.
                        Waldeinsamkeit. 32.
False-hearted
From the eyes of the false-hearted,
                        Rhea. 14.
Falsehood
Follow falsehood, follow scorning.
                        Saadi. 93.
Falsely
Sailing falsely in the sphere,
                        Frag. Poet. VII. 17.
Falter
Where the wisest Muses falter,
                        Etienne. 14.
To falter ere thou thy task fulfil,—
                        Merlin's Song. 27.
Faltered
That never faltered from the right.
                        Boston. 91.
Falters
Language falters under it,
                        Bohemian. 8.
When Nature falters, fain would zeal
                        May-Day. 157.
Fame
    See Good-fame.
Traditioned fame of masters, eager
    strife   Adirondacs. 324.
And one to me are shame and fame.
                        Brahma. 8.
The total air was fame;   Cosmos. 10.
For knowledge and for fame   Fame. 8.
Go, sacrifice to Fame;   Fame. 26.
And die to Fame a happy martyr.
                        Fame. 30.
I scorned the fame of Timour brave;
                        Frag. Poet. I. 3.
Fame is profitless as pelf,
                        Frag. Poet. VII. 14.
And filled the age his fame;
                        Frag. Poet. XXXII. 2.

Fame —*Continued*
Not for fame, nor by rules of art,
Garden. 19.
And singers of her fame
Hermione. 24.
Will clear his fame from every cloud
Initial Love. 86.
Nor thought of fame.   In Memoriam. 6.
As in the old poetic fame Monadnoc. 348.
Whose shining sons, too great for fame,
Nun. 45.
Right upward on the road of fame
Poet. 1.
Poets, for the air was fame.
Solution. 42.
Late in the world,—too late perchance
for fame,   To-Day. 5.
To foreign parts is blown by fame;
Una. 22.
What oldest star the fame can save
Wealth. 22.
Which breathes his sweet fame through
the northern bowers. Woodnotes. I. 71.

Famed
See Unfamed.

Familiar
From bright, familiar eyes.
*Farewell. 13.
My old familiar haunts; here the blue
river,   River. 2.

Family
God hath a select family of sons
Good Cheer. 3.

Famine
You have tried famine: no more try it;
Alphonso. 51.
For famine, toil and fray?
Voluntaries. 66.

Famous
Behold the famous States
Channing Ode. 16.
To hew the famous adamant
House. 15.
Tales of many a famous mount,—
Monadnoc. 95.
And, by the famous might that lurks
Spiritual Laws. 8.

Fan
See Vampyre-fan.
And life to fan the flame;   Fame. 28.
Will a woman's fan the ocean smooth?
Nemesis. 9.
A drop can shake, a breath can fan;
Poet. 222.

Fancied
Up with the dawn, they fancied the light
air   Adirondacs. 59.
I fancied he was fled,—   Friendship. 5.

Fancies
Pleasant fancies overtook me.
Berrying. 8.
Solitary fancies go   Merlin. 106.
To draw all fancies to this spot.
Monadnoc. Afar. 8.
The fancies found in books;
Waldeinsamkeit. 42.

Fanciful
So fanciful, so savage, nought cares he
Snow-Storm. 16.

Fancy
And bend my fancy to your leading,
Etienne. 3.
And boding Fancy haunted it
Frag. Nat. X. 3.
I fancy these pure waters and the flags
Hamatreya. 8.
I knew their forms in fancy weeds,
Harp. 112.
By Fancy, ghastly spells undid.
May-Day. 46.
One portrait—fact or fancy—we may
draw;   Phi. 4.
Fancy departs: no more invent;
Terminus. 9.

Fancy-free
Free be she, fancy-free;   Give. 39.

Fancy's
For Fancy's gift   Frag. Poet. IX. 1.
The height of Fancy's far-eyed steep.
Poet. 170.

Fanes
In groves of oak, or fanes of gold,
Problem. 58.

Fangs
Wolves shed their fangs, and dragons
scales;   Solution. 6.

Fanned
And fanned the dreams it never brought.
Woodnotes. II. 4.

Fanning
He felt the flame, the fanning wings,
Frag. Poet. V. 26.
Fanning secret fires which glow
May-Day. 251.

Fans
Fans in all hearts expectance sweet,
May-Day. 296.

Fantastic
Fantastic care derides,
Waldeinsamkeit. 14.
Seems fantastic to the rest:
Woodnotes. I. 17.

Far
Shall hear far Chaos talk with me;
Bacchus. 39.
Doth as far transcend   Bohemian. 5.
Far or forgot to me is near; Brahma. 5.
Higher far into the pure realm,
Celestial Love. 27.
Blaze near and far,   Daemonic Love. 51.
I ask how far is the Tigris flood,
Exile. 3.
Far away, far away.
*Farewell. 9. 18. 27. 36. 45. 54.
Atom from atom yawns as far
Frag. Nat. VII. 1.
Up the far mountain walls
Frag. Nat. XXVI. 22.
Far distant yet his chorus waits.
Garden. 36.
The first far signal-fire of morn.
Harp. 94.
Stronger and bolder far than I,
Harp. 115.
And then as now from far admired,
Harp. 117.
As shepherd's lamp on far hill-side
Hermione. 42.
Wiser far than human seer,
Humble-Bee. 52.

Cools sea and land so far and fast,
    Humble-Bee. 59.
In as far as I took note,
    Initial Love. 83.
The far halloo of human voice;
    May-Day. 76.
Smacks of faint memories far away.
    May-Day. 78.
Or in what far to-morrow due;
    May-Day. 417.
Light's far furnace shines, Merlin. 92.
Thus far to-day your favors reach,
    Merops. 5.
To far eyes, an aerial isle Monadnoc. 42.
When they hear from far the rune;
    Monadnoc. 250.
Costlier far than wine or oil.
    Monadnoc. 296.
Sparrows far off, and nearer, April's
 bird,   Musketaquid. 15.
The bird, how far it haply roam
    Nemesis. 3.
Far seen, the river glides below,
    Peter. 37.
Saw the dance of Nature forward and far,
    Poet. 70.
Gentler far than falls the snow Poet. 253.
Far capitals and marble courts,
    Quat. A. H. 3.
Yet thou errest far and broad. Rhea. 24.
Hear the far Avenger's feet: Saadi. 56.
Saadi, so far thy words shall reach:
    Saadi. 139.
Where far oaks outstretched their arms.
    September. 8.
Far in the North, where polar night
    Solution. 43.
Yet they who listened far aloof
    Solution. 54.
Thine eyes still shined for me, though
 far   Thine Eyes. 1.
Far and wide she cannot find him:
    Threnody. 22.
As far as the incommunicable;
    Threnody. 200.
We wander far by east and west.
    Una. 4.
And I greet from far the ray, Una. 15.
Fleeter far than whirlwinds go,
    Visit. 16.
Haughty thought be far from me;
    Voluntaries. 2.
Foundling of the desert far,
    Voluntaries. 47.
Far beholding, without cloud,
    Voluntaries. 53.
From mountains far and valleys near
    Walden. 13.
Far away in time, when once,
    Wealth. 2.
Where, in far fields, the orchis grew.
    Woodnotes. I. 49.
And, far within those cadent pauses,
    Woodnotes. II. 118.
The wood is wiser far than thou;
    Woodnotes. II. 172.
And 't is far in the deeps of history,
    World-Soul. 19.
And are but one. Beheld far off, they
 part   Xenophanes. 9.

Far-appearing
Oft, my far-appearing peak;
    Monadnoc. 200.
Fare
 See Thoroughfare.
Hard fare, hard bed and comic misery,—
    Adirondacs. 165.
I loved ye with true love, so fare ye
 well!   Summons. 14.
Farer
 See Wayfarer.
Fares
So forth and brighter fares my stream,—
    Two Rivers. 17.
Farewell
Farewell, ye lofty spires *Farewell. 1.
Farewell, domestic fires *Farewell. 3.
Farewell the busy town, *Farewell. 10.
Farewell, my mother fond,
    *Farewell. 19.
Farewell, my brothers true,
    *Farewell. 28.
Farewell, thou fairest one,
    *Farewell. 37.
Farewell to . . . . . ! *Farewell. 44.
Farewell I breathe again *Farewell. 46.
I homeward turn; farewell, my pet!
    Titmouse. 80.
Far-eyed
The height of Fancy's far-eyed steep.
    Poet. 170.
Far-gazing
To fix far-gazing eyes.
    Monadnoc Afar. 4.
Far-heard
Far-heard, lows not thine ear to charm;
    Each. 4.
Farm
 See Clover-farm.
The heifer that lows in the upland farm,
    Each. 3.
Each of these landlords walked amidst
 his farm,   Hamatreya. 4.
Deep in a woodland tract, a sunny farm,
    Letter. 8.
Farmer
One, by humble farmer seen,
    Chartist. 3.
Farmer's
On farmer's byre, on pasture rude,
    May-Day. 357.
Fills up the farmer's lane from wall to
 wall,   Snow-Storm. 20.
Maugre the farmer's sighs; and at the
 gate   Snow-Storm. 21.
Farmers
Here once the embattled farmers stood
    C. Hymn. 3.
Whither the angry farmers came,
    In Memoriam. 4.
Supplanters of the tribe, the farmers
 dwell.   Musketaquid. 31.
Farm-furrowed
Farm-furrowed, town-incrusted sphere,
    Monadnoc. 332.
Farm-gear
Farm-gear and village picket-fence,
    Poet. 59.
Farm-house
And veils the farm-house at the garden's
 end.   Snow-Storm. 5.

Farms
Looked eastward from the farms,
Boston. 2.
Draw us to these meadow farms,
Frag. Nat. XXVI. 4.
The sweet delight I found in fields and
farms, I Bear. 6.
Many farms of mountain men.
Monadnoc. 128.
Farms the sunny landscape dappled,
September. 5.
Swandown clouds dappled the farms,
September. 6.

Far-off
Far-off heats through seas to seek;
Humble-Bee. 4.

Far-reaching
Far-reaching concords of astronomy
Musketaquid. 63.

Farsistan
In Farsistan the violet spreads Exile. 1.

Farther
No farther shoot Terminus. 7.

Farthest
They intertwine the farthest star:
Celestial Love. 108.

Farthest
The next into the farthest brings,
May-Day. 80.
Over the owner's farthest walls!
Monadnoc. 9.
The next unto the farthest brings;
Nature. Mot. 2.

Far-transplanted
In thousands far-transplanted grafts
Promise. 3.

Far-travelled
Far-travelled in the south plantations;
Frag. Nat. XXIII. 8.

Far-wandered
I detect far-wandered graces,
Ode to Beauty. 65.

Fascinate
To fascinate each youthful heart,
Daemonic Love. 31.

Fashion
Nor for the fashion of your behavior;
Destiny. 41.
But they turn them in a fashion
Monadnoc. 177.

Fashioned
See Swifter-fashioned.

Fashioning
Like wax, their fashioning skill betrays,
Monadnoc. 148.

Fashions
Many fashions and addresses,
Initial Love. 132.

Fast
See Sitfast; Soothfast; Steadfast.
So fast will Nature acclimate her sons,
Adirondacs. 54.
But to hold fast his simple sense,
Celestial Love. 127.
Fast to surface and outside, Circles. 3.
But, to his native centre fast,
Culture. 9.
Too fast we leave the bay,
*Farewell. 6.
Deep in the man sits fast his fate
Fate. 1.

Healed as fast the wounds it made.
Guy. 20.
That each for each doth fast engage;
Hermione. 32.
Cools sea and land so far and fast,
Humble-Bee. 59.
Fast abides this constant giver,
Monadnoc. 40.
Anchored fast for many an age,
Monadnoc. 283.
Or for my turn to fly too fast. Nun. 32.
All is now secure and fast; Past. 10.
Life's honeycomb, but not too fast;
Poet. 46.
'T was coming fast to such anointing,
Titmouse. 24.
Waneth fast and spendeth all.
Woodnotes. II. 25.
Hitherto all things fast abide,
Woodnotes. II. 256.

Faster
No faster than his planted trees,
Alphonso. 78.
With the key of the secret he marches
faster, Frag. Life. XXXI. 1.
Faster flowing o'er the plains,—
May-Day. 244.
Never faster, never slower Poet. 116.

Fast-flowing
Chasing with words fast-flowing things;
nor try Frag. Poet. XXIX. 5.

Fasting
You must worship fasting,
Frag. Nat. III. 31.
Inquisitive, and fierce, and fasting,
Initial Love. 37.

Fastness
Man in these crags a fastness find
Monadnoc. 112.

Fasts
Bitter winds and fasts austere
Monadnoc. 159.

Fat
Made not pale, or fat, or lean;
Woodnotes. II. 37.

Fatal
Firm ensign of the fatal Being,
Monadnoc. 361.
Revolves the fatal wheel! Poet. 117.
Brother, accept this fatal hand. Poet. 264.
Came to me in his fatal rounds,
Terminus. 5.
'Come learn with me the fatal song
Woodnotes. II. 156.

Fate
And bend the exile to his fate, Art. 22.
And make of duty fate.
Concord Ode. 16.
And the souls of ample fate,
Daemonic Love. 100.
And the dogs of Fate unties.
Daemonic Love. 118.
From all the seas of strength Fate filled
a chalice, Day's Ration. 2.
Ah Fate, cannot a man Fame. 1.
But Fate will not permit Fame. 19.
Deep in the man sits fast his fate
Fate. 1.
No fate, save by the victim's fault, is low,
Frag. Life. II. 1.

Where he goes, goes before him Fate;
    Frag. Life. XVII. 10.
The tragic tales of crime and fate;
    Frag. Nat. XXVI. 34.
Hang roses on the stony fate.
    Frag. Poet. X. 4.
The mill-round of our fate appears
    Friendship. 15.
Fate and Beauty skilled to weave.
    Harp. 46.
We talked at large of worldly fate,
    Hermione. 38.
Fate grants each to stand aside;
    Holidays. 18.
Thou dost mock at fate and care,
    Humble-Bee. 56.
When Fate by omens takes his part,
    Initial Love. 71.
The brave whom Fate denies the goal!
    In Memoriam. 87.
The halting steps of aged Fate.
    May-Day. 155.
With good agreeing with its fate,
    May-Day. 286.
Merlin's blows are strokes of fate,
    Merlin. 16.
Of Nature's child the common fate.
    Mountain. 21.
Of his fate is never wide.   Nemesis. 8.
Realms self-upheld, disdaining Fate,
    Nun. 44.
As Fate refuses   Ode to Beauty. 44.
To me the heart Fate for me chooses.
    Ode to Beauty. 45.
And be the sport of Fate forever.
    Ode to Beauty. 97.
So thou attend the enriching Fate
    Poet. 124.
With finer fate   Poet. 153.
Or if perchance, ye orbs of Fate,
    Poet. 241.
Ere he was born, the stars of fate
    Quat. Horoscope. 1.
If fate unlock his bosom's door,
    Saadi. 120.
Drew the firm lines of Fate and Life
    Solution. 66.
Seethe, Fate! the ancient elements,
    Song of Nature. 75.
"The fate of the man-child,   Sphinx. 9.
Fate let him fall, Fate can't retake him;
    Threnody. 28.
Nature, Fate, men, him seek in vain.
    Threnody. 29.
The eager fate which carried thee
    Threnody. 160.
'T is not within the force of fate
    Threnody. 193.
Talker! the unreplying Fate?
    Threnody. 250.
Softly,—but this way fate was pointing,
    Titmouse. 23.
The balance-beam of Fate was bent;
    Uriel. 31.
To front the fate that crouches near,—
    Voluntaries. 16.
Of Fate and Will, of Want and Right,
    Woodnotes. II. 130.
And fate and practice and invention,
    Woodnotes. II. 206.

This is he men miscall Fate,
    Worship. 11.
By fate, not option, frugal Nature gave
    Xenophanes. 1.

Fate-conjoined
The fate-conjoined to separate.
    Threnody. 194.

Fated
As the drop feeds its fated flower,
    Frag. Life. XXIII. 5.
Space grants beyond his fated road
    Merops. 9.
Is the fated man of men   Poet. 79.

Fate's
Fate's glowing revolution pause?
    Threnody. 227.
Fate's grass grows rank
    Voluntaries. 119.

Fates
And the world's flowing fates in his own
    mould recast.   Culture. 11.
Framed afar as Fates and Loves.
    Frag. Poet. XII. 4.
Blends the starry fates with thine,
    Freedom. 18.
Ring with the song of the Fates;
    Garden. 34.
These the fates of men forecast,
    Garden. 61.
Long, long concealed by sundering fates,
    Harp. 113.
From lengthening scroll of human fates,
    Threnody. 263.

Father
    See Forefather.
Of mother, father, sister, stand;
    Daemonic Love. 6.

Father's
My father's orchard knowest. Exile. 12.
If thou go as thy father's son,
    Frag. Life. XXVII. 9.
The fragrant flag-roots in my father's
    fields,   River. 6.
Boy who made dear his father's home,
    Threnody. 167.

Fathers
His fathers shining in bright fables,
    Art. 17.
God with the fathers, so with us,
    Boston. 118.
I know what say the fathers wise,—
    Problem. 63.
Our fathers built to God;—
    Robbins Hymn. 2.

Fathom
But without glass we fathom you.
    Romany. 28.

Fatigue
That know not fear, fatigue, or cold.
    Woodnotes. II. 42.

Fatten
Sugar spends to fatten slaves,
    Heroism. 2.

Fault
No fate, save by the victim's fault, is
    low,   Frag. Life. II. 1.
Fault and folly are not mine;
    Frag. Life. XVI. 6.
Or see the fault, or seen betray:
    Initial Love. 127

Fault —*Continued*
And,—fault of novel germs,—
                 Terminus. 21.
The fault that boys and nations soonest
   mend.   To-Day. 18.
Linger,—thou shalt rue the fault:
                 Visit. 28.
What his fault, or what his crime?
             Voluntaries. 13.
Faultless
Fill thy will, O faultless heart! Poet. 127.
Faults
Of her faults I take no note,
            Frag. Life. XVI. 5.
Time and tide their faults may find.
                 Test. 2.
Favor
Where thy form and favor come,
                Dearest. 3.
And dress up Nature in your favor.
              Destiny. 44.
The favor of the loving Day,—
             Threnody. 20.
Favors
Not by ribbons or by favors,
          Celestial Love. 102.
All wore thy badges and thy favors
                Lines. 7.
Thus far to-day your favors reach,
              Merops. 5.
Fawning
Good-bye to Flattery's fawning face;
            Good-Bye. 7.
Fawns
No prayer persuades, no flattery fawns,—
          Celestial Love. 87.
Fawns'
Painting fawns' and leopards' fells,
           May-Day. 204.
Fear
Torments me still the fear that love
              Amulet. 11.
Kings shook with fear, old empires
   crave   Boston. 92.
Fear not, then, thou child infirm,
       II Compensation. 19.
For fear of human eyes swerved from
   his plan.   Entombed. 4.
Nor fear those watchful sentinels,
                 Eva. 9.
Till late he learned, through doubt and
   fear,   Fate. 9.
With forecast or with fear?
          Frag. Nat. VIII. 4.
No trace of age, no fear to die.
          Frag. Nat. VIII. 8.
"Once with manlike love and fear
           Frag. Poet. II. 5.
Without remoter hope or fear
           Frag. Poet. V. 5.
The Muse's hill by Fear is guarded,
         Frag. Poet. XXXI. 1.
Example, custom, fear, occasion slow,—
               Grace. 3.
Words of pain and cries of fear,
              Harp. 58.
And sent his priests in holy fear
              Hymn. 7.
He told no pang, he knew no fear;
          In Memoriam. 100.

Well for those who have no fear,
              Letters. 3.
And to live he is in fear.
          Monadnoc. 343.
Why fear to die   Mountain. 1.
His heart should palpitate with fear.
               Poet. 50.
And woke the fear lest angels part.
              Poet. 256.
With the fear that we must part?
              Poet. 266.
Serve it for pain and fear and need.
              Poet. 286.
Fear, Craft and Avarice   Politics. 9.
Too busied with the crowded hour to
   fear to live or die.   Quat. Nature. 4.
Grow red with joy and white with fear;
              Saadi. 30.
Beholding his fear;—   Sphinx. 58.
'Lowly faithful, banish fear, Terminus. 37.
To find the antidote of fear,
            Titmouse. 102.
Thrive in all weathers without fear,—
             Walden. 15.
And fear what foe in caves and swamps
   can stray,   Woodnotes. I. 87.
Or west, no thunder fear.
         Woodnotes. I. 103.
That know not fear, fatigue, or cold.
         Woodnotes. II. 42.
Without wailing, without fear;
         Woodnotes. II. 80.
Feared
Be loved by few; he feared by none;
              Fame. 15.
Fearing
The maiden fears, and fearing runs
            Nemesis. 5.
Fearless
Fearless Guy had never foes,   Guy. 17.
Fears
The maiden fears, and fearing runs
            Nemesis. 5.
There, while hot heads perplexed with
   fears the state,   Phi. 9.
So I folded me in fears,   Solution. 27.
Fears not undermining days,
         Spiritual Laws. 6.
Feast
Who made this world the feast it was,
              Dirge. 26.
Chief of song where poets feast
              Harp. 38.
Feaster's
Not his the feaster's wine,
          Frag. Poet. VI. 5.
Feasters
Than the wine-fed feasters know.
         Frag. Poet. XI. 11.
By feasters and the frivolous,—
          Monadnoc. 400.
Feasts
Not by jewels, feasts and savors,
          Celestial Love. 101.
The blaze of revellers' feasts outshine.
          Frag. Life. X. 9.
Feat
This feat of wit, this triumph of man-
   kind;   Adirondacs. 255.
Who do the feat, and lift humanity.
          Adirondacs. 295.

As hid all measure of the feat.
                    Character. 10.
Perform the feat as well as they;
                    Frag. Life. X. 2.
No word or feat   Frag. Poet. IX. 10.
The Asmodean feat is mine,
                    Frag. Poet. XXXIV. 1.

Feathered
As fits a feathered lord of land;
                    Titmouse. 37.

Feathers
Of leaves, and feathers from her breast?
                    Problem. 26.

Feats
Which drove them erst to social feats;
                    Alphonso. 34.
And feats achieve before they're named.
                    Nature. I. 21.
Shows feats of his gymnastic play,
                    Titmouse. 41.

Feature
They are his steeds, and not his feature;
                    Initial Love. 36.
Through the channels of that feature,
                    Visit. 14.
With one drop sheds form and feature;
                    Woodnotes. II. 289.
He is the meaning of each feature;
                    Woodnotes. II. 316.

Features
Features that seem at heart my own;
                    Eva. 8.
His purpose woke, his features slept;
                    In Memoriam. 102.
To report thy features only,
                    Ode to Beauty. 85.

Fed
    See Air-fed; Wine-fed.
Which fed the veins of earth and sky,
                    Alphonso. 32.
His children fed at heavenly tables.
                    Art. 18.
Him wood-gods fed with honey wild
                    Frag. Poet. I. 33.
The hero is not fed on sweets,
                    Heroism. 7.
That man and all the kinds be fed;
                    May-Day. 147.
Full fed, but not intoxicated;   Poet. 47.
Smite the white breasts which thee fed,
                    Saadi. 67.
Thou first and foremost shalt be fed;
                    Titmouse. 84.
The foodful waters fed me,
                    Woodnotes. I. 130.

Fee
his world in fee   Rome. 23.

Feeble
She who is old, but nowise feeble,
                    Nature. II. 5.
Talk no more with feeble tongue;
                    Woodnotes. II. 137.

Feebler
To hit the nerve of feebler sight.
                    Uriel. 42.

Feed
To feed this wealth of lakes and rivulets,
                    Adirondacs. 150.
He smote the lake to feed his eye
                    Beauty. 7.

Bid my bread feed and my fire warm me
                    Destiny. 43.
Where darkling feed the clamorous clans
                    May-Day. 28.
And feed once more the exile's eyes;
                    May-Day. 97.
They feed the spring which they exhaust;
                    Saadi. 42.
They could not feed him, and he died,
                    Threnody. 147.
My hedges plant and feed.   Walden. 12.
To feed the North from tropic trees;
                    Wealth. 37.
When sea and land refuse to feed me,
                    Woodnotes. I. 141.
And drifting sand-heaps feed my stock,
                    Woodnotes. II. 11.

Feeding
    See All-feeding.
Feeding on the Ethiops sweet,
                    Berrying. 7.
But, feeding on magnificence,   Poet. 60.
As the sheep go feeding in the waste,
                    Woodnotes. II. 297.

Feeding-grounds
Stealing with paddle to the feeding-
    grounds   Adirondacs. 119.

Feeds
Where the deer feeds at night, the teal
    by day,   Adirondacs. 20.
He that feeds men serveth few;
                    Celestial Love. 131.
As the drop feeds its fated flower,
                    Frag. Life. XXIII. 5.
Feeds those eternal lamps I see.
                    Poet. 236.
Where feeds the moose, and walks the
    surly bear,   Woodnotes. I. 66.

Feel
I, a king, for kings can feel.
                    Alphonso. 44.
Find me a slope where I can feel the sun
                    Letter. 14.
I feel its finer billows beat May-Day. 193.
Are glad to feel the ground.
                    May-Day. 282.
Teach thy feet to feel the ground,
                    Monadnoc. 22.
And being latent, feel thyself no less?
                    Musketaquid. 81.
His flesh should feel, his eyes should
    read   Poet. 43.
He asked, he only asked, to feel.
                    Poet. 212.
I feel as I were welcome to these trees
                    River. 36.

Feelest
Right thou feelest, rush to do.'
                    Freedom. 24.

Feeling
Feeling only the fiery thread
                    Voluntaries. 88.

Feels
Which feels the acrid juice   Bacchus. 8.
But feels and seals this union;
                    Celestial Love. 112.
The joy and pride the pilgrim feels
                    In Memoriam. 83.

Feels —*Continued*
Feels the bloom on the living vine,
                    May-Day. 90.
He feels it, introverts his learned eye
                    Philosopher. 5.

Feet
Our patron pine was fifteen feet in girth,
                    Adirondacs. 42.
Full fifty feet, and bring the eaglet down:
                    Adirondacs. 84.
The feet of millions stride. Boston. 40.
Be swift their feet as antelopes,
                    Boston Hymn. 79.
Hast not thy share? On winged feet,
                    II Compensation. 23.
As I spoke, beneath my feet   Each. 40.
On and away, their hasting feet
                    Forerunners. 9.
To frozen hearts and hasting feet;
                    Good-Bye. 12.
And vulgar feet have never trod
                    Good-Bye. 21.
Who steer the plough, but cannot steer
    their feet   Hamatreya. 15.
Follow not her flying feet;
                    Hermione. 77.
The sod throbbed friendly to my feet,
                    Lines. 13.
The feet that slid so long on sleet
                    May-Day. 281.
And march their feet,   Merlin. 47.
Hands to hands, and feet to feet,
                    Merlin. 88.
Teach thy feet to feel the ground,
                    Monadnoc. 22.
When Time thy feet has bound.
                    Monadnoc. 24.
'Many feet in summer seek,
                    Monadnoc. 199.
Well I hear the approaching feet
                    Monadnoc. 267.
No feet so fleet could ever find,
                    Ode to Beauty. 72.
His feet were shod with golden bells,
                    Poet. 4.
As fleet his feet, his hands as good,
                    Poet. 295.
Power and speed be hands and feet.
                    Quat. Power. 4.
Hear the far Avenger's feet: Saadi. 56.
The sled and traveller stopped, the
    courier's feet   Snow-Storm. 6.
I tread the book beneath my feet.
                    Song of Seyd. 24.
O, whither tend thy feet? Threnody. 31.
Paced by the blessed feet around,
                    Threnody. 91.
Each tramper started; but the feet
                    Threnody. 106.
The frost-king ties my fumbling feet,
                    Titmouse. 12.
The crowded town, thy feet may well
    delay.   To J. W. 4.
In whose feet the lion rusheth,
                    Woodnotes. II. 40.
The crouching lion kissed his feet;
                    Worship. 8.

Feign
What prayers and dreams of youthful
    genius feign,   Frag. Nat. V. 2.

Feigned
Feigned to speak to some one else.
                    Frag. Poet. IV. 18.
Feigning
Though, feigning dwarfs, thy crouch and
    creep,   Voluntaries. 117.
Feigns
Sleeps or feigns slumber,
                    Frag. Nat. I. 3.
Feigns to sleep, sleeping never;
                    Frag. Nat. I. 10.
Fell
    See Befell.
And, wheresoever their clear eye-beams
    fell,   Blight. 28.
Even the fell Furies are appeased,
                    Celestial Love. 113.
And the rash-leaping thunderbolt fell
    short.   Frag. Life. XXXIV. 2.
A wintry storm more fitly fell.
                    Frag. Nat. XXIX. 4.
If I fell within the line,
                    Frag. Poet. IV. 9.
It fell in rain, it grew in grain,
                    Frag. Poet. IV. 27.
When the shadow fell on the lake,
                    Garden. 53.
If on the foeman fell his gaze,   Guy. 21.
So that the common waters fell
                    Guy. 29.
Fell the bolt on the branching oak;
                    In Memoriam. 97.
So did our sons; Heaven met them as
    they fell.   Inscription. 2.
To the souls that never fell,
                    Nature. I. 17.
Fell unregarded to the ground,
                    Poet. 15.
Fell the lesson on his heart   Poet. 255.
Never from lips of cunning fell
                    Problem. 11.
With firmer glory fell.
                    Song of Nature. 20.
But fell the starry influence short,
                    Song of Nature. 71.
It fell in the ancient periods   Uriel. 1.
A sad self-knowledge, withering, fell
                    Uriel. 35.
Felled
This is he, who, felled by foes,
                    Worship. 1.
Felloes
Grasp the felloes of her wheel,
                    May-Day. 158.
Fellow
    See Goodfellow; Playfellow; Yoke-
    fellow.
To the altar's foot thy fellow seek,—
                    Quat. Pericles. 3.
Fellows
Hear you, then, celestial fellows!
                    Alphonso. 59.
When his fellows on the wing
                    May-Day. 85.
But do the deed thy fellows hate,
                    Saadi. 65.
Fellowship
Oh what is Heaven but the fellowship
                    Oh What. 1.

Fells

Bold as the engineer who fells the wood,
Blight. 19.

Painting fawns' and leopards' fells,
May-Day. 204.

Felt

He felt the flame, the fanning wings,
Frag. Poet. V. 26.

In strange junctures, felt, with awe,
Guy. 11.

Felt in the plants and in the punctual
birds; Musketaquid. 64.

On his tense chords all strokes were felt,
Poet. 210.

And what his tender heart hath felt
Saadi. 123.

And felt, beneath, the quaking ground;
Solution. 56.

Fire their fiercer flaming felt, Test. 8.

Fence

See Picket-fence.

No stouter fence, no steeper wall!
Boston. 62.

And hems in life with narrowing fence.
Titmouse. 16.

Fenced

Fenced by form and ceremony,
Frag. Poet. I. 28.

Fend

See Weatherfend.

And fend you with his wing.
Boston Hymn. 16.

All friends to fend, all foes defy,
In Memoriam. 40.

Fended

Into this Oreads' fended Paradise,
Adirondacs. 194.

Fended from the heat, Politics. 20.

Fern

Orchis and gentian, fern and long whip-
scirpus, Adirondacs. 142.

Scented fern and agrimony;
Frag. Nat. II. 10.

Sweet fern, mint and vernal grass,
Frag. Nat. II. 14.

Sassafras, fern, benzöine,
Frag. Nat. II. 28.

Scented fern, and agrimony,
Humble-Bee. 47.

Through brake and fern, the beavers'
camp, Woodnotes. I. 126.

Ferns

From ferns and grapes and from the
folded flowers Frag. Nat. XXVII. 7.

Who saw what ferns and palms were
pressed Wealth. 26.

Ferry

A ferry of the free. Concord Ode. 28.

Fertile

They thank the spring-flood for its fertile slime, Musketaquid. 43.

Festival

Ballad, flag and festival, Art. 10.

Makes each day a festival.
Frag. Nat. XXVI. 6.

That came to every festival.
Frag. Poet. I. 4.

Suffice to hold the festival.
May-Day. 223.

The school-march, each day's festival,
Threnody. 59.

Seemed to the holy festival Uriel. 29.

Festivals

And autumn's sunlit festivals,
Hermione. 73.

Festoons

Thunder-clouds are Jove's festoons,
Heroism. 4.

Fetch

To fetch his word to men. Apology. 4.

To fetch one ingot thence Dull. 16.

And fetch her stars to deck her hair:
Rhea. 52.

To fetch thee birds of paradise:
Saadi. 148.

Revere the Maker; fetch thine eye
Threnody. 270.

Leave authors' eyes, and fetch your own,
Waldeinsamkeit. 43.

Fetched

I fetched my sea-born treasures home;
Each. 25.

Feud

Glows the fued of Want and Have.
II Compensation. 6.

Few

Which few can put on with impunity.
Adirondacs. 98.

We have few moments in the longest life
Adirondacs. 249.

We grant no dukedoms to the few,
Boston. 25.

He that feeds men serveth few;
Celestial Love. 131.

They drop their few pale flowers,
Daemonic Love. 108.

Took a few herbs and apples, and the
Day Days. 9.

Be loved by few; be feared by none;
Fame. 15.

My few and evil years! *Farewell. 31.

Than my few needs exhaust, and bids me
read Frag. Nat. V. 6.

Too long shut in strait and few,
Mithridates. 20.

Gilds a few points Naples. 4.

And a few joys, a few peculiar charms,
Naples. 10.

Are measured but a few;
Quat. Shakespeare. 2.

A few rods off he deems it gems and
clouds. Seashore. 46.

Leave the many and hold the few.
Terminus. 16.

I had the right, few days ago,
Threnody. 32.

Where January brings few faces.'
Titmouse. 32.

O, few to scale those uplands dare,
Waldeinsamkeit. 39.

Fibre

And of the fibre, quick and strong,
Monadnoc. 169.

Field

See Battle-field; Harvest-field.

One harvest from thy field Apology. 17.

A field of havoc and war,
Boston Hymn. 10.

Knows he who tills this lonely field
Dirge. 9.

Field—*Continued*

Little thinks, in the field, yon red-cloaked
clown   Each. 1.
She walked in flowers around my field
                               Frag. Life. XIII. 1.
In the hummock of the field.
                               Frag. Poet. XXVII. 4.
For action's field, for victor's car,
                               In Memoriam. 29.
To fruitful field and sun and moon.
                               Limits. 10.
In the next field is air more mild,
                               May-Day. 102.
'T was the vintage-day of field and wood,
                               May-Day. 338.
And by the order in the field disclose
                               Musketaquid. 50.
The violets yon field which stain
                               Omar. 3.
[Knows he who tills this lonely field
                               Peter. 1.
That field by spirits bad and good,
                               Peter. 5.
See thou bring not to field or stone
                               Waldeinsamkeit. 41.
Many haps fall in the field
                               Woodnotes. I. 50.
A pillow in her greenest field,
                               Woodnotes. I. 144.

Fields

I looked forth on the fields of youth:
                               Harp. 110.
The sweet delight I found in fields and
farms,   I Bear. 6.
Because I was content with these poor
fields,   Musketaquid. 1.
The fields of Thessaly grew green,
                               Peter. 19.
The fragrant flag-roots in my father's
fields,   River. 6.
Much triumphing,—and these the fields
                               River. 13.
Arrives the snow, and, driving o'er the
fields,   Snow-Storm. 2.
In damp fields known to bird and fox.
                               Woodnotes. I. 41.
Where, in far fields, the orchis grew.
                               Woodnotes. I. 49.
Sinew that subdued the fields;
                               Woodnotes. II. 32.

Fiend

"The fiend that man harries
                               Sphinx. 73.

Fierce

All the fierce enemies, ague, hunger, cold,
                               Adirondacs. 317.
Their fierce and limitary will
                               Daemonic Love. 66.
When the fierce northwestern blast
                               Humble-Bee. 58.
Inquisitive, and fierce, and fasting,
                               Initial Love. 37.
Fierce conserver, fierce destroyer,—
                               Saadi. 98.
Furnished with tile, the fierce artificer
                               Snow-Storm. 12.
Than the South more fierce and hot;
                               Test. 6.
Checked by the owners' fierce disdain,
                               Voluntaries. 29.

Fiercely

We must not halt while fiercely speed
                               Walden. 43.

Fiercer

Fire their fiercer flaming felt,
                               Test. 8.

Fiery

Flowed with naphtha fiery sweet;
                               Celestial Love. 16.
Her fiery errands go.   Concord Ode. 36.
And he that paints the oriole's fiery
wings.   Enchanter. 11.
Like fiery honey sucked from roses.
                               Initial Love. 53.
What fiery force the earth renews,
                               May-Day. 188.
Newest knowledge, fiery thought,
                               Miracle. 13.
He cools the present's fiery glow,
                               Monadnoc. 157.
Ever the fiery Pentecost   Problem. 51.
To clothe the fiery thought
                               Quat. Poet 2. 1.
Feeling only the fiery thread
                               Voluntaries. 88.

Fifteen

Our patron pine was fifteen feet in girth,
                               Adirondacs. 42.

Fifth

Into the fifth himself he flings,
                               Woodnotes. II. 293.

Fifty

Full fifty feet, and bring the eaglet down:
                               Adirondacs. 84.

Fight

And fight like a Paladin.
                               Initial Love. 137.
To fight pollution of the mind;
                               Monadnoc. 113.
They fight the elements with elements
                               Musketaquid. 47.
How should I fight? my foreman fine
                               Titmouse. 5.
To hazard all in Freedom's fight,—
                               Voluntaries. 62.

Fights

See rights for which the one hand fights
                               Concord Ode. 23.
He works, plots, fights, in rude affairs,
                               Fate. 7.
Whoever fights, whoever falls,
                               Voluntaries. 99.
To the valiant chief who fights;
                               Voluntaries. 107.

Figs

Meagre crop of figs and limes;
                               Alphonso. 5.

Figure

Reflects his figure that doth pass.
                               Astraea. 24.
In figure, bone and lineament?
                               Threnody. 248.
Some figure of noble guise,—
                               World-Soul. 26.

Figured

But 't is figured in the flowers;
                               Apology. 14.

File

And marching single in an endless file,
                               Days. 3.

Files
Through files of flags that gleamed like
bayonets, Adirondacs. 17.
Whilst his files sweep round you Alpine
height; Each. 8.

Filing
Filing single in stately train.
May-Day. 308.

Fill
See Fulfil; O'erfill; Overfill.
Rebuild or ruin: either fill
Alphonso. 27.
And fill the bag to the brim.
Boston Hymn. 70.
Fill the lake with images,—
Celestial Love. 72.
Strong crab with nobler blood did fill;
Guy. 42.
Fill and saturate each kind
May-Day. 283.
Fill each kind and saturate
May-Day. 285.
Or fill my craving ear; Merlin. 2.
Hither! take me, use me, fill me,
Mithridates. 31.
To fill the hollows, sink the hills,
Monadnoc. 149.
O barren mound, thy plenties fill!
Monadnoc. 378.
And fill the long reach of the old sea-
shore Poet. 75.
Fill thy will, O faultless heart!
Poet. 127.
Wish not to fill the isles with eyes
Saadi. 147.
No tribes my house can fill,
Song of Nature. 10.
Which overflowing Love shall fill,
Threnody. 192.

Filled
See Sun-filled.
And filled their hearts with flame.
Boston Hymn. 4.
From all the seas of strength Fate filled
a chalice, Day's Ration. 2.
I filled the dream of sad,
Frag. Life. XXX. 2.
Filled the straits and filled the wide,
Frag. Nat. III. 13.
Eastward it filled all Heathendom
Frag. Poet. IV. 33.
Omens and signs that filled the air
Frag. Poet. V. 39.
And filled the age his fame;
Frag. Poet. XXXII. 2.
That filled their homes again;
Robbins Hymn. 16.
England's genius filled all measure
Solution. 35.

Fillet
Under her solemn fillet saw the scorn.
Days. 11.
Ivy for my fillet band; Mithridates. 14.

Filling
Filling with thy roseate smell,
Ode to Beauty. 79.

Fills
Fills his blue urn with fire;
Concord Ode. 2.
After the master's sketch fills and o'er-
fills Day's Ration. 28.

And, when the sunlight fills the hours,
May-Day. 148.
Fills the just period, Merlin. 121.
In the love which Nature fills,
Poet. 145.
Fills for his proper sake. Promise. 10.
Fills up the farmer's lane from wall to
wall, Snow-Storm. 20.
God fills the scrip and canister,
Woodnotes II. 16.

Film
Over the flickering Dæmon film,
Celestial Love. 29.

Fin
To Fin and Lap and swart Malay,
Woodnotes. II. 154.

Final
And build to them a final tomb;
Woodnotes. II. 224.

Finches
A flock of finches darting
May-Day. 382.

Find
He shall impose, to find a spring, trap
foxes, Adirondacs. 103.
In its white block; yet it therein shall
find Angelo. 3.
I have an arrow that will find its mark,
Arrow. 1.
Nor art, nor power, nor toil can find
Bohemian. 10.
The secret force to find Boston. 93.
Find me, and turn my back on heaven.
Brahma. 16.
Whom not each other seek, but find.
Celestial Love. 84.
And find a loftier way:
Frag. Life. X. 4.
Assured to find the token once again
Frag. Nat. IV. 9.
Ever find me dim regards,
Frag. Poet. VII. 9.
Yet,—wouldst thou the mountain find
Freedom. 11.
And go find thee in the sphere.
From Hafiz. 16.
To find the sitfast acres where you left
them.' Hamatreya. 24.
She shall find thee, and be found.
Hermione. 76.
Ere she can find a tree. House. 12.
None will now find Cupid latent
Initial Love. 9.
Find me a slope where I can feel the sun
Letter. 14.
I thought to find the patriots
Monadnoc. 92.
Man in these crags a fastness find
Monadnoc. 112.
We in thee the shadow find.
Monadnoc. 391.
My heart's content would find it right.
Nun. 10.
Which always find us young
Ode to Beauty. 62.
No feet so fleet could ever find,
Ode to Beauty. 72.
Lest there I find the same deceiver
Ode to Beauty. 96.
Find to their design Politics. 17.

Find—*Continued*

Hunstmen find the easiest way.
Quat. Artist. 4.

And eat through Alps its home to find.
Quat. Love. 4.

New worlds to find in pinnace frail.
Quat. Poet. I. 4.

To find the narrow way.
Robbins Hymn. 24.

A poet or a friend to find: Saadi. 156.

This matchless strength. Where shall he find, O waves!   Seashore. 32.

She must love me till she find
Security. 5.

I find him in the bottom of my heart,
Self-Reliance. 4.

That wit and joy might find a tongue,
Solution. 15.

Time and tide their faults may find.
Test. 2.

Have you eyes to find the five
Test. 13.

Far and wide she cannot find him;
Threnody. 22.

To find the antidote of fear,
Titmouse. 102.

Can find with glass in ten times ten.
Walk. 8.

The sea tosses and foams to find
Woodnotes. II. 242.

To find what bird had piped the strain:—
Woodnotes. II. 249.

Finder

See Path-finder.

Finds

The astonished Muse finds thousands at her side.   Channing Ode. 97.

As finds its Alp the snowy shower,
Frag. Life. XXIII. 6.

With the flavors she finds meet,
Nature. II. 16.

And finds young pines and budding birches;   Threnody. 25.

But finds not the budding man;
Threnody. 26.

And finds his prison there.
Woodnotes. II. 29.

Finds them who in cellars be;
World-Soul. 34.

Fine

Be fine accomplices to fraud?
Chartist. 16.

They saw not my fine revellers,—
Forerunners. 19.

Oft he keeps his fine ear strained,
Initial Love. 66.

A blooming hunter of a fairy fine.
River. 15.

A genius of so fine a strain,
Threnody. 141.

How should I fight? my foeman fine
Titmouse. 5.

Fine afternoon, old passenger!
Titmouse. 30.

Finer

I feel its finer billows beat
May-Day. 193.

Unploughed, which finer spirits pile,
Monadnoc. 43.

With finer fate   Poet. 153.

Finger

See Finger-tips.

They put their finger on their lip,
II Eros. 1.

Stooping, his finger wrote in clay
Solution. 69.

Fingers

Heat with viewless fingers moulds,
May-Day. 195.

Finger-tips

Keep your lips or finger-tips
Aeolian Harp. 4.

Finish

New-face or finish what is packed,
Past. 20.

Finishes

And finishes the song.   Merlin. 122.

Finite

See Infinite.

Pours finite into infinite.   Threnody. 237.

Fir

poplar, beech and fir,   Adirondacs. 38.

Fire

See Camp-fire; Earth-fire; Wood-fire.

Which o'erhung, like a cloud, our camping fire.   Adirondacs. 47.

With ductile fire. Loud, exulting cries
Adirondacs. 241.

It was from Jove the other stole his fire,
Adirondacs. 290.

The lynx, the rattlesnake, the flood, the fire;   Adirondacs. 316.

Fire, plant and mineral say, 'Not in us;'
Blight. 35.

Fills his blue urn with fire;
Corcord Ode. 2.

Thy beauty, if it lack the fire
Destiny. 12.

Bid my bread feed and my fire warm me
Destiny. 43.

With fire that draws while it repels.
Eva. 12.

Beauty to fire us, saints to save,
Frag. Life. I. 3.

Beware the fire that Eblis burned."
Frag. Poet. II. 3.

To keep this fire of faith alive,
Hymn. 6.

Burned more than others' fire,
May-Day. 143.

Fire fainting will,   May-Day. 440.

With its stars of northern fire,
Monadnoc. 217.

In latent fire his secret thought,
Poet. 14.

O fire of fire! O best of things!
Poet. 161.

But fire to thaw that ruddy snow,
Rubies. 9.

With equal fire thy heart shalt melt.
Saadi. 124.

To fire the stagnant earth with thought:
Solution. 4.

Of rock and fire the scroll,
Song of Nature. 22.

Love is the air-fed fire intense,
Song of Seyd. 15.

Fire their fiercer flaming felt,   Test. 8.

Breathes aromatic fire;   Threnody. 4.

What fire burns in that little chest
Titmouse. 52.

Fired

Which fired the little State to save
Boston. 94.
And fired the shot heard round the world.
C. Hymn. 4.

Fre-fly's

And fire-fly's flight.   Illusions. 21.

Fireplace

Around the radiant fireplace, enclosed
Snow-Storm. 8.

Fires

Under the cinders burned the fires of
home;   Adirondacs. 333.
Disarmed the thunder's fires.   Bell. 12.
Spies oversea the fires of the mountain:
Enchanter. 9.
Farewell, domestic fires   *Farewell. 3.
As he holds down central fires
Frag. Nat. I. 15.
Flashed their small fires in air, or held
their court   Frag. Nat. XXVII. 9.
Fires gardens with a joyful blaze
May-Day. 206.
Fanning secret fires which glow
May-Day. 251.
As when, with inward fires and pain,
Monadnoc. 289.
Bad husbands of their fires,
Terminus. 24.
Thou askest in fountains and in fires,
Woodnotes. II. 311.

Fire-seed

If in ashes the fire-seed slept.   Uriel. 46.

Fireside

Next his heart the fireside band
Daemonic Love 5.
Books, Muses, Study, fireside, friends and
love,   Summons. 13.

Firm

For which the world had waited, now
firm fact,   Adirondacs. 238.
One pulse more of firm endeavor,—
Give. 29.
And the firm soul does the pale train
defy   I Bear. 11.
Firm on his heart relied,
In Memoriam. 90.
Firm ensign of the fatal Being,
Monadnoc. 361.
Drew the firm lines of Fate and Life
Solution. 66.
Firm to Heaven my bosom clings,
Song of Seyd. 31.

Firmament

With the days and firmament,
Art. 24.
The columns of the firmament
Frag. Life. XXXVI. 3.
And stood beneath the firmament,
Frag. Nat. XXVI. 13.
A clear and glorious firmament
Frag. Nat. XXVI. 28.
Saw the endless rack of the firmament
Poet. 67.
Beneath the darkling firmament
Poet. 227.
Contract thy firmament   Terminus. 10.
No watcher in the firmament,
Threnody. 119.
Through flood and sea and firmament;
Two Rivers. 7.

Firm-braced

Firm-braced I sought my ancient woods,
May-Day. 39.

Firmer

Not firmer based than they.
Frag. Life. XXXVI. 4.
With firmer glory fell.
Song of Nature. 20.

Firmest

Firmest cheer, and bird-like pleasure.
Humble-Bee. 39.

Firmly

Firmly draw, firmly drive,   Sphinx. 31.
Speak it firmly, these are gods,
Voluntaries. 121.

Firs

Around me stood the oaks and firs;
Each. 44.
They learned of the oaks and firs.
Nature. II. 12.

First

Wield the first axe   Adirondacs. 33.
At the first mounting of the giant stairs.
Adirondacs. 63.
The latest better than the first,
Aeolian Harp. 21.
Your picture smiles as first it smiled;
Amulet. 1.
Which on the first day drew,
Bacchus. 65.
On its own First of May.   Cosmos. 28.
The first experience will not fail;
Daemonic Love. 20.
The needs of the first sight absorb my
blood,   Day's Ration. 17.
To bring their first fruits to the sun.
Frag. Nat. II. 20.
First vague shadow of surmise
Give. 36.
The first far signal-fire of morn.
Harp. 94.
Then first shalt thou know,
Illusions. 33.
On the first wheels that quit this weary
town   Letter. 3.
All that high God did first create.
May-Day. 442.
Say not, the chiefs who first arrive
Merlin's Song. 16.
Not less than was the first; the all-wise
God   Naples. 3.
When first my eyes saw thee,
Ode to Beauty. 9.
Thou latest and first!
Ode to Beauty. 16.
On the first, neither balm nor physician
can save,   On Two Days. 3.
Scarce the first blush has overspread his
cheek,   Philosopher. 4.
Life loiters at the book's first page,—
Quat. Climacteric. 3.
Boon Nature yields each day a brag
which we now first behold,
Quat. Nature. 1.
By Jove, at dawn of the first day.
Solution. 2.
Thou first and foremost shalt be fed;
Titmouse. 84.
And in the second reappears the first.
Xenophanes. 13.

Fish

Doth eat, and drink, and fish, and shoot,
Initial Love. 27.

No fish, in river or in lake,
Monadnoc. 145.

Or how the fish outbuilt her shell,
Problem. 27.

my earliest fish, River. 12.

Fisher

Yon pale, scrawny fisher fools,
Alphonso. 15.

The brother of the fisher, porter, swain,
Frag. Life. XXX. 5.

Fishers

Fishers and choppers and ploughmen
Boston Hymn. 31.

Fit

See Unfit.

All dressed, like Nature, fit for her own
ends, Adirondacs. 71.

Fit to grace the solar year.
Alphonso. 82.

'T is fit the forest fall,
Channing Ode. 58.

Fit for fairy presences,
Frag. Nat. II. 12.

And fit the bleak and howling waste
Monadnoc. 151.

Are Autumn's blasts fit music for thee,
fragile one, to hear; *Violet. 2.

Draws the threads of fair and fit.
Wealth. 33.

And earth's fit tenant me surprise;—
Woodnotes. II. 213.

Fitly

A wintry storm more fitly fell.
Frag. Nat. XXIX. 4.

Seeks how he may fitly tell Poet. 89.

Fits

Fits not to be overzealous;
Alphonso. 60.

As fits the griefs of bards to be.
Harp. 60.

Ill fits the abstemious Muse Phi. 1.

For living brows; ill fits them to receive:
Phi. 2.

As fits a feathered lord of land;
Titmouse. 37.

Fitting

Fitting his age and ken, Threnody. 42.

Five

Five rosy boys with morning light
Dirge. 5.

Five years elapse from flood to ebb.
Garden. 24.

So bloom the unfading petals five,
Solution. 71.

"Dull Sphinx, Jove keep thy five wits;
Sphinx. 105.

Five lines lasted sound and true;
Test. 4.

Five were smelted in a pot Test. 5.

Have you eyes to find the five Test. 13.

Which five hundred did survive?
Test. 14.

Why Nature loves the number five,
Woodnotes. I. 22.

Five-leaved

Five-leaved, three-leaved and two-leaved,
grew thereby. Adirondacs. 41.

Fix

See Transfix.

That can fix a hero's rate; Astraea. 4.

To fix far-gazing eyes.
Monadnoc Afar. 4.

The fading colors fix, Poet. 110.

Fixed

Fixed on the enormous galaxy,
Character. 3.

From the fixed cone the cloud-rack
flowed Monadnoc. 33.

Enchantment fixed me here
Monadnoc. 225.

Fixed on the enormous galaxy,
Poet. 136.

Fixture

Dissolving all that fixture is,
Woodnotes. II. 113.

Flag

See Waterflag.

Ballad, flag and festival, Art. 10.

Their flag to April's breeze unfurled,
C. Hymn. 2.

Grass with green flag half-mast high,
Frag. Nat. II. 7.

Grass with green flag half-mast high,
Humble-Bee. 44.

Flag-roots

The fragrant flag-roots in my father's
fields, River. 6.

Flags

Through files of flags that gleamed like
bayonets, Adirondacs. 17.

I fancy these pure waters and the flags
Hamatreya. 8.

Flake

See Snowflake.

Flakes

And largest clouds be flakes of down in
that enormous sky. Frag. Nat. XX. 2.

And split to flakes the crystal ledges.
Frag. Nat. XXX. 2.

With tempest of the blinding flakes.
Titmouse. 74.

Flame

In flame, in storm, in clouds of air.
Beauty. 6.

And filled their hearts with flame.
Boston Hymn. 4.

There is smoke in the flame;
Celestial Love. 3.

And purple flame of love. Cosmos. 8.

That suddenly caught the flame.
Cosmos. 12.

When the purple flame shoots up,
Cosmos. 21.

And life to fan the flame; Fame. 28.

The deep-eyed flame, obedient water,
Frag. Life. XXIX. 2.

And turned the drowsy world to flame.
Frag. Poet. I. 14.

He felt the flame, the fanning wings,
Frag. Poet. V. 26.

But lit the sky with flame.
Frag. Poet. XXXII. 4.

Nor freshet, nor midsummer flame.
Guy. 48.

Like the volcano's tongue of flame,
Problem. 16.

Girds with one flame the countless host,
Problem. 52.

The fair moon mounts, and aye the flame
                                Romany. 3.
That knows a purer flame than me,
                                Security. 10.
She spired into a yellow flame;
                                Sphinx. 125.
Makes flame to freeze and ice to boil;
                                Spiritual Laws. 10.
And showed his side of flame;
                                Thines Eyes. 10.
Like wave or flame, into new forms
                                Woodnotes. II. 274.
The world would blush in flame;
                                World-Soul. 50.
A belt of mirrors round a taper's flame;
                                Xenophanes. 16.

Flamed
Stars flamed and faded as they bade,
                                Dirge. 34.
Flamed from his martial eye;
                                In Memoriam. 37.

Flames
As the rich aloes flames, I glow,
                                Song of Seyd. 17.
Built of tears and sacred flames,
                                Threnody. 278.
The crimson morning flames into:
                                World-Soul. 59.
Bound to the stake, no flames appalled,
                                Worship. 9.

Flaming
The purple flaming of love?   Cosmos. 4.
In the next age, are flaming swords.
                                Solution. 58.
Fire their fiercer flaming felt,   Test. 8.

Flannel
Shoes, flannel shirt, and kersey trousers
    make   Adirondacs. 75.
In sooth, red flannel is a saucy test
                                Adirondacs. 97.

Flashed
Flashed their small fires in air,
                                Frag. Nat. XXVII. 9.

Flashing
Through tempering nights and flashing
    days,   Monadnoc. 212.
Or only a flashing sunbeam
                                World-Soul. 29.

Flatter
Can cozen, pique and flatter,   April. 11.
And whine, and flatter, and regret,
                                Initial Love. 30.

Flatteries
Not with flatteries, but truths,   Rhea. 2.

Flattering
For flattering planets seemed to say
                                Threnody. 134.

Flattery
No prayer persuades, no flattery fawns,—
                                Celestial Love. 87.

Flattery's
When Mirth is dumb and Flattery's fled,
                                Ellen. 9.
Good-bye to Flattery's fawning face;
                                Good-Bye. 7.

Flaunt
When all their blooms the meadows
    flaunt   Frag. Nat. VIII. 1.

Flaunting
Flaunting in their bowers;
                                Frag. Nat. II. 6.

Flavors
Paints, and flavors, and allures,
                                May-Day. 197.
Flavor gladly blends with flavor;
                                Merlin. 85.
With the flavors she finds meet,
                                Nature. II. 16.

Flax
Hay, corn, roots, hemp, flax, apples, wool
    and wood.   Hamatreya. 3.

Flecks
like moonlight flecks,   Adirondacs. 48.

Fled
When Mirth is dumb and Flattery's fled,
                                Ellen. 9.
And fled in pretty frowns away
                                Frag. Poet. I. 38.
I fancied he was fled,—   Friendship. 5.
Fled like the flood's foam.
                                Hamatreya. 49.
Fled the last plumule of the Dark,
                                Monadnoc. 312.

Flee
We flee away from cities, but we bring
                                Adirondacs. 302.
From thyself thou canst not flee,—
                                Poet. 269.
Flee from the goods which from thee
    flee;   Saadi. 143.

Fleece
Of clouds and the boreal fleece.
                                Boston Hymn. 24.
All earth's fleece and food   Politics. 3.

Fleeing
Fleeing to fables,   Illusions. 12.
Or like a traveller's fleeing tent,
                                Threnody. 276.

Flees
But when he flees on riches' wings,
                                Riches. 11.

Fleet
When of our little fleet three cruising
    skiffs   Adirondacs. 231.
The last builds town and fleet,
                                Channing Ode. 55.
Shun him, nymphs, on the fleet horses!
                                Initial Love. 102.
And where it comes this courier fleet
                                May-Day. 295.
No feet so fleet could ever find,
                                Ode to Beauty. 72.
As fleet his feet, his hands as good,
                                Poet. 295.
Up and away for life! be fleet!—
                                Titmouse. 11.
Through years, through men, through
    Nature fleet,   Two Rivers. 11.

Fleeter
Fleeter they than any creature,—
                                Initial Love. 35.
Fleeter far than whirlwinds go,
                                Visit. 16.

Fleetest
Fleetest couriers alive   Forerunners. 23.

Fleeting
And in this fleeting lifetime trust
                                Robbins Hymn. 23.

Fleets
As in the Andes watched by fleets at sea,
                                Frag. Nat. IV. 4.

Flesh
Thatch his flesh, and even his years
Alphonso. 75.
By sweet affinities to human flesh,
Blight. 12.
The winds took flesh, the mountains
talked,   Frag. Poet. I. 55.
It put on flesh in friendly form,
Frag. Poet. IV. 28.
Counsel not with flesh and blood;
Freedom. 22.
As we thaw frozen flesh with snow,
May-Day. 125.
He slowly cures decrepit flesh,
Monadnoc. 161.
Hero and maiden, flesh of her flesh;
Nature. II. 14.
His flesh should feel, his eyes should read
Poet. 43.

Flew
Above, the eagle flew, the osprey scream-
ed,   Adirondacs. 146.
Flew off in the cloud.   *Lines. 24.
Piping, as they flew, a march,—
May-Day. 384.
Flew near, with soft wing grazed my
hand,   Titmouse. 38.
Then flew the sail across the seas
Wealth. 36.

Flickering
Over the flickering Dæmon film,
Celestial Love. 29.
And wood-fire flickering on the walls,
May-Day. 55.

Flies
The winged vessel flies,   *Farewell. 25.
To and fro the Genius flies,
Frag. Life. XVI. 1.
harlot flies   Frag. Nat. XXVII. 8.
Saw bonfires of the harlot flies
Harp. 91.
The panther in our dances flies.
Romany. 24.
Now follows, now flies;   Sphinx. 98.
Flies gayly forth and sings in sight.
Woodnotes. II. 251.

Flies-to
Flies-to the adamantine door   Past. 12.

Flight
Bring your music and rhythmic flight,
Frag. Nat. XXIII. 9.
And fire-fly's flight.   Illusions. 21.
Survived the Flight and swam the Flood,
May-Day. 94.
Your song, your forms, your rhythmic
flight,   May-Day. 398.
The soul's pilgrimage and flight;
May-Day. 462.
With hammer soft as snowflake's flight;—
Monadnoc. 240.
And the whole flight, with folded wing,
Monadnoc. 366.

Flight
Count it flight of bird or dart.   Poet. 129.

Fling
To fling his voice into the tree,
Woodnotes. II. 121.

Flings
Into the fifth himself he flings,
Woodnotes. II. 293.

Flingeth
He flingeth white   Cupido. 6.

Flint
Bulkeley, Hunt, Willard, Hosmer, Mer-
iam, Flint,   Hamatreya. 1.
In flint and marble beats a heart,
May-Day. 65.
Of shard and flint makes jewels gay;
Two Rivers. 14.

Flinty
Whilst the country's flinty face,
Monadnoc. 147.
On the flinty pathway beat
Monadnoc. 268.

Flippant
In his flippant chirping babble,
Miracle. 34.

Flit
But sweeter rivers pulsing flit
Two Rivers. 3.

Flits
Flits across her bosom young,
Give. 37.

Flitting
Are shadows flitting up annd down
Celestial Love. 56.
Like the flitting boreal lights,
Frag. Poet. I. 39.

Float
May float at pleasure through all natures;
Bacchus. 23.
Is the Tigris to float me away.
Exile. 20.
Whose timbers, as they silent float,
Monadnoc. 274.
They totter now and float amain.
Poet. 38.
To float my child to victory,
Woodnotes. II. 46.

Floated
Each cloud that floated in the sky
Apology. 7.
The saffron cloud that floated warm
Lines. 15.

Floating
Floating in air or pent in stone,
II Compensation. 26.
Which round the floating isles unite:—
Frag. Nat. XXVI. 25.

Floats
Still floats upon the morning wind,
Problem. 59.

Flock
A flock of finches darting
May-Day. 382.
Shall flock to you and tarry by your side,
Rome. 6.
Whence the fair flock of Nature sprang.
Woodnotes. II. 125.

Flocks
And soar to the air-borne flocks
Boston Hymn. 23.
Where pastoral tribes their flocks infold,
Poet. 64.
Browse the mountain sheep in flocks,
Saadi. 6.

Flood
See Spring-flood.
The lynx, the rattlesnake, the flood, the
fire;   Adirondacs. 316.
By the rude bridge that arched the
flood,   C. Hymn. 1.

Pouring as wide a flood   Dirge. 18.
I ask how far is the Tigris flood,
        Exile. 3.
Five years elapse from flood to ebb.
        Garden. 24.
Mound and flood.   Hamatreya. 47.
Survived the Flight and swam the Flood,
        May-Day. 94.
As poured the flood of the ancient sea
        May-Day. 241.
Of the ice-imprisoned flood;   Merlin. 20.
O'er the floor of plain and flood
        Monadnoc. 194.
Unsure the ebb and flood of thought,
        Poet. 279.
Can swim the flood and wade through
        snow,   Quat. Love. 2.
The flood of truth, the flood of good,
        Saadi. 161.
Through flood and sea and firmament;
        Two Rivers. 7.
The land reflected in the flood,
        Woodnotes. II. 162.

Flooded
He hath broke his banks and flooded all
        the vales   River. 9.

Flood's
Fled like the flood's foam.
        Hamatreya. 49.
Of the old flood's subsiding slime,
        Woodnotes. II. 109.

Floods
Front the liberated floods:
        May-Day. 225.
Chants his hymn to hills and floods,
        Woodnotes. II. 34.
Floods with blessings unawares.
        Worship. 20.

Floor
Lit with phosphoric crumbs the forest
        floor.   Adirondacs. 49.
loftier walls, and vaster floor.
        Frag. Nat. XII. 3.
Bird that from the nadir's floor
        Merlin. 63.
O'er the floor of plain and flood
        Monadnoc. 194.
Behold his shadow on the floor!
        Saadi. 158.
On the desert's yellow floor,
        Saadi. 168.
The planet with a floor of lime?
        Wealth. 24.
He trode the unplanted forest floor,
        whereon   Woodnotes. I. 64.
Was burnished to a floor of glass,
        Woodnotes. I. 109.

Floors
And all unmeet our carpet floors;
        May-Day. 221.
Azaleas flush the island floors,
        May-Day. 261.
Nor count compartments of the floors,
        Merlin. 36.
In the great woods, on prairie floors.
        Titmouse. 68.

Floral
Above the floral zone,   Monadnoc. 353.

Flotilla
By the bright morn the gay flotilla slid
        Adirondacs. 16.

Flow
    See Overflow.
Open and flow.   Bacchus. 50.
His proper good to flow:
        Boston Hymn. 58.
From deep ideal fontal heavens that flow.
        Frag. Life. XV. 8.
Flow, flow the waves hated,
        Illusions. 1.
To change and to flow,   Illusions. 27.
And waters free as winds shall flow.
        May-Day. 110.
The mountains flow, the solids seem,
        Poet. 174.
That from the Godhead flow,
        Robbins Hymn. 18.
And give love's scarlet tides to flow,—
        Rubies. 11.
And, in my mathematic ebb and flow,
        Seashore. 25.
Wilt thou freeze love's tidal flow,
        Threnody. 238.
When the genius of God doth flow;
        Woodnotes. I. 97.

Flowed
Seas ebbed and flowed in epic chime.
        Beauty. 16.
Flowed with naphtha fiery sweet;
        Celestial Love. 16.
Ebbing later whence it flowed,
        Garden. 15.
Planted these, and tempests flowed it.
        Garden. 20.
From the fixed cone the cloud-rack flowed
        Monadnoc. 33.
She flowed into a foaming wave:
        Sphinx. 127.

Flower
    See Wall-flower; Pickerel-flower.
Love not the flower they pluck, and know
        it not,   Blight. 21.
With the flower with which it came.
        Days Pass. 4.
I touch this flower of silken leaf,
        Dirge. 37.
As the drop feeds its fated flower,
        Frag. Life. XXIII. 5.
Go if thou wilt, ambrosial flower,
        Frag. Life. XXV. 1.
He took the flower of all their worth,
        Frag. Life. XXIX. 4.
I share the good with every flower,
        Frag. Nat. XXVI. 30.
Bore thy colors every flower,   Lines. 5.
Many a flower and many a gem,
        May-Day. 316.
Dark flower of Cheshire garden,
        Monadnoc. Afar. 1.
And as each flower upon the fresh hill-
        side,   Naples. 5.
And every colored petal of each flower,
        Naples. 6.
And every flower made obeisance
        Peter. 35.
And court the flower that cheapens his
        array.   Rhodora. 8.
Tricked out in star and flower,
        Song of Nature. 30.
Are of one pattern made; bird, beast and
        flower,   Xenophanes. 6.

Flowered
She flowered in blossoms red;
Sphinx. 126.

Flowerets
New flowerets bring, new prayers uplift,
Celestial Love. 4.

Flower-hunting
Like a flower-hunting child;
Initial Love. 97.

Flowering
See Rainbow-flowering.
Flowering April cools and dies
Alphonso. 7.
The richest flowering of all art:
Threnody. 216.
Flowering grass and scented weeds;
Threnody. 275.

Flowers
Instead of flowers, crowned with a wreath
of hills. Adirondacs. 13.
For the idle flowers I brought;
Apology. 10.
But 't is figured in the flowers;
Apology. 14.
The old men studied magic in the flow-
ers, Blight. 23.
They drop their few pale flowers,
Daemonic Love. 108.
The Flowers—tiny sect of Shakers—
Ellen South. 11.
We poor New England flowers.
Ellen South. 24.
Scent, form and color; to the flowers and
shells Enchanter. 4.
Flowers they strew,—I catch the scent;
Forerunners. 11.
She walked in flowers around my field
Frag. Life. XIII. 1.
Come search the wood for flowers,—
Frag. Nat. II. 1.
From ferns and grapes and from the
folded flowers Frag. Nat. XXVI. 7.
Earth laughs in flowers, to see her boast-
ful boys Hamatreya. 13.
Long days, and solid banks of flowers;
Humble-Bee. 35.
When trellised grapes their flowers un-
mask, May-Day. 87.
Dissolves the crust, displays the flowers.
May-Day. 149.
Of the painted race of flowers,
May-Day. 374.
Speaking by the tongues of flowers,
May-Day. 418.
Thawing snow-drift into flowers.
Monadnoc. 65.
Where flowers each stone rosette and
metope brave; Monadnoc. 372.
Under the flowers of June,
Mountain. 3.
Nor in the cup of budding flowers,
Music. 14.
I stay with the flowers of Spring:
Quat. Botanist. 2.
Over whose flowers I chased the butter-
fly, River. 14.
These idle flowers, that tremble in the
wind, River. 23.
Leaves twinkle, flowers like persons be,
Saadi. 137.
Earth smiled with flowers, and man was
born. Solution. 8.

From race on race the rarest flowers,
Song of Nature. 15.
With birds and flowers bestowed.
Waterfall. 4.
And blessed the monument of the man of
flowers, Woodnotes. I. 70.
Nor the June flowers scorn to cover
Woodnotes. I. 145.
Which bloom and fade like meadow
flowers Woodnotes. II. 302.

Flower-wreaths
Flower-wreaths gay with bud and bell;
May-Day. 315.

Flowing
See Fast-flowing; Overflowing.
And twice each day the flowing sea
Boston. 3.
And the world's flowing fates in his own
mould recast. Culture. 11.
The flowing conditions of life, give way.
Frag. Life. XXXI. 4.
What central flowing forces, say,
Frag. Nat. XI. 1.
Faster flowing o'er the plains,—
May-Day. 244.
The flowing fortunes of a thousand
years;— Merlin. 73.
E'en the flowing azure air
Ode to Beauty. 90.

Flown
Flown to Italy from Greece,
Solution. 17.
Bring the flown Muses back to men.
Threnody. 137.

Flows
Or over the town blue ocean flows.
Boston. 105.
Heaven's oldest blood flows in his side,—
Initial Love. 123.
Flows from the heart of Love, the Lord.
May-Day. 191.
Is sweetly solemnized. Then flows amain
Musketaquid. 21.
Through light, through life, it forward
flows. Two Rivers. 8.
That flows in streams, that breathes in
wind: Woodnotes. II. 233.

Flung
He flung in pebbles well to hear
Beauty. 9.
For He that flung the broad blue fold
Concord Ode. 9.
Nor the palest rose she flung Give. 41.
Like ample banner flung abroad
Monadnoc. 34.

Flush
From Spring's faint flush to Autumn red.
Garden. 8.
the flush of hues; May-Day. 189.
Azaleas flush the island floors,
May-Day. 261.
Clouds flush their gayest dyes.
Waterfall. 16.

Flushed
Flushed in the sky the sweet May-morn,
Solution. 7.

Flute
For flute or spinet's dancing chips;
Aeolian Harp. 5.
Hark what, now loud, now low, the pin-
ing flute complains, Flute. 1.

Flutes
The redwing flutes his *o-ka-lee,*
May-Day. 168.

Fly
See Blue-fly; Dragon-fly; Wood-fly.
Who but the midge, mosquito and the
fly, Adirondacs. 173.
When me they fly, I am the wings;
Brahma. 10.
Hafiz said he was a fly
Frag. Poet. I. 3.
Or for my turn to fly too fast. Nun. 32.
Yet fly me still, Ode to Beauty. 43.
To northern lakes fly wind-borne ducks,
Saadi. 5.
Their arms fly open wide.
World-Soul. 96.

Flying
A makeweight flying to the void,
II Compensation. 11.
Follow not her flying feet;
Hermione. 77.
To rout the flying foe. May-Day. 112.
Blue-coated,—flying before from tree to
tree, Musketaquid. 16.
By cloud or isle, is flying home;
Nemesis. 4.
The shadow sits close to the flying ball;
Woodnotes. II. 244.

Fly's
See Fire-fly's.

Fly-to
Self-moved, fly-to the doors,
Merlin. 75.

Foam
I wiped away the weeds and foam,
Each. 24.
Long I've been tossed like the driven
foam; Good-Bye. 5.
Fled like the flood's foam.
Hamatreya. 49.
As the wave breaks to foam on shelves,
Initial Love. 147.
Races and planets, its enchanted foam.
Pan. 12.

Foam-bells
They are but sailing foam-bells
World-Soul. 69.

Foaming
Our foaming ale we drank from hunters'
pans, Adirondacs. 177.
Entering Big Tupper, bound for the
foaming Falls Adirondacs. 232.
We plant and build by foaming seas
Boston. 21.
A world-wide wave with foaming edge
May-Day. 245.
She flowed into a foaming wave:
Sphinx. 127.
Thanks to the foaming sea,
World-Soul. 2.

Foams
The sea tosses and foams to find
Woodnotes. II. 242.

Foe
Driving the foe and stablishing the
friend,— Blight. 13.
The foe long since in silence slept;
C. Hymn. 5.
Frowned in my foe and growled in storm,
Frag. Poet. IV. 29.

To rout the flying foe. May-Day. 112.
And fear what foe in caves and swamps
can stray, Woodnotes. I. 87.

Foeman
If on the foeman fell his gaze, Guy. 21.

Foes
Friends, foes, joys, fortunes, beauty and
disgust. Day's Ration. 8.
Though foes and land and seas between
Frag. Life. XVII. 14.
Fearless Guy had never foes, Guy. 17.
All friends to fend, all foes defy,
In Memoriam. 40.
Fronting foes of God and man,
In Memoriam. 41.
To help her friends, to plague her foes,
Nature. I. 14.
He laugheth at his foes. Riches. 12.
Thy foes to hunt, thy enviers to strike
down, Shah-Hafiz. 1.
To guard the babe from fancied foes.
Threnody. 69.
This is he, who, felled by foes,
Worship. 1.

Fogs
see beauty in the fogs Naples. 13.

Fold
See Infold; Tenfold; Twofold; Un-
fold.
Fold my arms beside the brook;
Apology. 6.
Fold Boston in his heart, Boston. 103.
For He that flung the broad blue fold
Concord Ode. 9.
Shun passion, fold the hands of thrift,
Frag. Life. XXXV. 1.
Fold us music-drunken in. Merlin. 129.

Folded
From ferns and grapes and from the
folded flowers Frag. Nat. XXVII. 7
And the whole flight, with folded wing,
Monadnoc. 366.
Nine times folded in mystery:
Nature. Mot. 8.
So I folded me in fears, Solution. 27.

Folding
Folding Nature in its deeps,
Celestial Love. 49.

Folds
What his dread folds would fain conceal?
Harp. 64.
Quaintest bud and blossom folds,
May-Day. 258.
Future or Past no richer secret folds,
Quat. Heri. 3.

Foliage
The river, hill, stems, foliage are obscure,
Musketaquid. 83.

Folk
The upheaved land, and bury the folk,
Channing Ode. 30.
And end in churls the mountain folk
Monadnoc. 119.
And to his folk his message sped.
Saadi. 79.

Follansbee
To Follansbee Water and the Lake of
Loons. Adirondacs. 25.
Northward the length of Follansbee we
rowed, Adirondacs. 26.

Follies

The follies bore that it invest. Poet. 198.

Follow

The state may follow how it can,
Channing Ode. 69.

And, like thy shadow, follow thee.
II Compensation. 28.

I serve you not, if you I follow,
Etienne. 1.

Where I, as others, follow petty ends;
Frag. Life. XV. 3.

Earliest heats that follow frore
Frag. Nat. II. 21.

Follow it utterly, Give. 9.

Follow not her flying feet;
Hermione. 77.

I will follow thee alone,
Humble-Bee. 5.

As they lead, so follow all, Rhea 31.

Follow falsehood, follow scorning.
Saadi. 93.

I only follow, when I act aright.
Self-Reliance. 10.

Followed

Long I followed happy guides,
Forerunners. 1.

Voices followed after,
Frag. Nat. III. 23.

Followed with love Harp. 118.

I followed in small copy in my acre;
Musketaquid. 53.

Following

And all the following hours of the day
Day's Ration. 18.

And following his mighty heart
Frag. Poet. IV. 5.

We are what we are made; each following day Naples. 1.

Follows

As Olympus follows Jove.
Channing Ode. 70.

He follows joy, and only joy.
Initial Love. 113.

Now follows, now flies; Sphinx. 98.

Folly

Fault and folly are not mine;
Frag. Life. XVI. 6.

That Genius goes and Folly stays.
In Memoriam. 110.

Into failure, into folly."
Woodnotes. II. 216.

It cannot conquer folly,—
World-Soul. 13.

Fond

Fond children, ye desire
Celestial Love. 6.

Love's hearts are faithful, but not fond,
Celestial Love. 115.

Farewell, my mother fond,
*Farewell. 19.

And strangers, fond as they, their furrows plough. Hamatreya. 12.

Too weak to win, too fond to shun
Manners. 17.

Be thou faithful, but not fond;
Quat. Pericles. 2.

Fontal

From deep ideal fontal heavens that flow.
Frag. Life. XV. 8.

Food

Food indigestible":—then murmered
some, Adirondacs. 186.

Food which needs no transmuting,
Bacchus. 32.

Food which teach and reason can.
Bacchus. 35.

Loiter not for cloak or food;
Freedom. 23.

His enchanted food; Manners. 6.

Thy body food Mountain. 4.

All earth's fleece and food Politics. 3.

The Seraph's and the Cherub's food.
Saadi. 162.

Sea full of food, the nourisher of kinds,
Seashore. 21.

Supplied me necessary food;
Woodnotes. I. 136.

Foodful

The foodful waters fed me,
Woodnotes. I. 130.

Foods

From air and ocean bring me foods,
Mithridates. 8.

Fool

Disown the knave and fool;
Boston. 32.

To fool me with a shining cloud,
May-Day. 364.

We fool and prate; Monadnoc. 379.

No more the fool of space and time,
Woodnotes. II. 138.

Fooled

He is not fooled, but warily knoweth
Rhea. 44.

Foolish

Foolish hands may mix and mar;
Channing Ode. 76.

Thou foolish Hafiz! Say, do churls
Friendship. Trans. 1.

By this foolish antique patent.
Initial Love. 10.

And they so pure? He, foolish child,
Poet. 206.

Foolish gossips, ancient drones,
Saadi. 170.

Fools

Yon pale, scrawny fisher fools,
Alphonso. 15.

The brave Empedocles, defying fools,
Frag. Life. XVIII. 1.

With Gods, with fools, content to live;
Poet. 214.

On clucking hens and prating fools,
Woodnotes. II. 202.

Foot

See Barefoot; Underfoot.

Which dip their foot in the seas
Boston Hymn. 22.

It wets my foot, but prettily
Frag. Nat. XXIV. 3.

A bolder foot is still rewarded.
Frag. Poet. XXXI. 2.

Painting him from head to foot,
Initial Love. 82.

The girl's foot leaves its neater print.
May-Day. 62.

We were quick from head to foot,
May-Day. 411.

To every foot its antipode; Merlin. 81.

To the altar's foot thy fellow seek,—
Quat. Pericles. 3.
Nor head from foot can I discern,
Song of Seyd. 2.
Soften the fall with wary foot;
Terminus. 18.
Set not thy foot on graves;
To J. W. 1. 5. 10.

Footsteps
They caught the footsteps of the Same.
Blight. 29.
With idle footsteps, crooning rhymes.
Miracle. 2.

Fopperies
The fopperies of the town.
World-Soul. 60.

Fops
Bended to fops who bent to him;
Poet. 215.
In an age of fops and toys,
Voluntaries. 59.

For (Partial list.)
See Hoped-for.
Millions for self-government,
Boston. 74.
Weave roses for your mate.
Celestial Love. 14.
Pray for a beam   Celestial Love. 60.
For this fortune wanted root
Daemonic Love. 126.
For bard, for lover and for saint;
Monadnoc. 45.
For the talents not thine own,
Saadi. 90.
For proverbs in the market-place:
Saadi. 152.

Forages
Right Cossacks in their forages;
Initial Love. 34.

Forbear
And selfish preference forbear;
Celestial Love. 10.
Or I might at will forbear;
Frag. Poet. IV. 20.
Take off thine eyes, thy heart forbear,
Woodnotes. II. 87.

Forbearance
Marked forbearance, compliments,
Frag. Poet. VII. 11.

Forbid
God forbid my angry heart
From Hafiz. 11.

Forbidden
To the pair is nought forbidden;
Love and Thought. 4.

Forbids
Who charm the more their glance for-
bids,   Eva. 10.
And to speak my thought if none forbids
May-Day. 326.
He forbids to despair;   World-Soul. 101.

Forbore
Forbore the ant-hill, shunned to tread,
Frag. Poet. XXIV. 1.
They forbore to break the chain
Voluntaries. 27.

Force
See Counterforce; Perforce.
Of vital force the wasted rill,
Alphonso. 28.

Truculent with fraud and force,'
Berrying. 3.
The secret force to find   Boston. 93.
All my force saith, Come and use me:
Frag. Nat. XXVIII. 2.
With all his force he gathers balms
Initial Love. 58.
What fiery force the earth renews,
May-Day. 188.
The miracle of generative force,
Musketaquid. 62.
Beauty and Force alight.   Poet. 299.
They pluck Force thence, and give it to
the wise.   Seashore. 29.
My oldest force is good as new,
Song of Nature. 82.
'T is not within the force of fate
Threnody. 193.
Its onward force too starkly pent
Threnody. 247.
Or from fruit of chemic force,
Uriel. 50.
For Love draws might from terrene
force   Waterfall. 7.
Of chemic matter, force and form,
Woodnotes. II. 110.

Forces
Make his frame and forces square
Alphonso. 73.
The seat of the world-old Forces
Cosmos. 19.
From high to higher forces
Frag. Life. IV. 1.
What central flowing forces, say,
Frag. Nat. XI. 1.

Forecast
With forecast or with fear?
Frag. Nat. VIII. 4.
These the fates of men forecast,
Garden. 61.

Forefathers
The forefathers this land who found
Merlin's Song. 18.

Forego
And my unserviceable limbs forego.
I Bear. 5.
Henceforth, please God, forever I forego
Self-Reliance. 1.

Forehead
Brought his great forehead to the council
board,   Phi. 8.

Foreign
All else grew foreign in their light.
Daemonic Love. 18.
But one I seek in foreign places,
Una. 11.
One face explore in foreign faces.
Una. 12.
To foreign parts is blown by fame;
Una. 22.

Forelooking
Forelooking, when he would prepare
Monadnoc. 154.

Foremost
When, foremost of the youthful band,
In Memoriam. 78.
Thou first and foremost shalt be fed;
Titmouse. 84.

Forerun
So Spring will not her time forerun,
May-Day. 126.

Foreshowed
By God's own light illumined and fore-
showed.   Woodnotes. I. 95.

Foresight
Or at the foresight of obscurer years?
                          Adirondacs. 217.
Or say, the foresight that awaits
                          Fate. 15.

Forest
Ponderous with beechen forest sloped
the shore.   Adirondacs. 28.
And in the twilight of the forest noon
                          Adirondacs. 32.
Lit with phosphoric crumbs the forest
floor.   Adirondacs. 49.
And, in the forest, delicate clerks, un-
browned,   Adirondacs. 57.
That circled freshly in their forest dress
                          Adirondacs. 60.
We were made freemen of the forest
laws,   Adirondacs. 70.
We praise the guide, we praise the forest
life: Adirondacs. 305.
Go, cut down trees in the forest
                          Boston Hymn. 33.
Cut down trees in the forest
                          Boston Hymn. 35.
'T is fit the forest fall,
                          Channing Ode. 58.
Song breathed from all the forest,
                          Cosmos. 9.
Forest full of essences
                          Frag. Nat. II. 11.
And modest copse and the forest tall,
                          Frag. Poet. I. 16.
My garden is a forest ledge   Garden. 9.
Out of the forest way   Hermione. 56.
Lent itself beneath the forest,
                          Holidays. 3.
Might rule the forest to his mind.
                          May-Day. 52.
Chiming with the forest tone,
                          Merlin. 17.
(That one would say, meadow and forest
walked,   Musketaquid. 48.
That rustles down the well-known forest
road—   River. 26.
The rocks and forest know it real.
                          Romany. 20.
The forest waves, the morning breaks,
                          Saadi. 135.
The forest is my loyal friend,
                          Waldeinsamkeit. 3.
Steeped in each forest cave?
                          Walden. 28.
And such I knew, a forest seer,
                          Woodnotes. I. 30.
He trode the unplanted forest floor,
whereon   Woodnotes. I. 64.
Beside the forest water sate;
                          Woodnotes. I. 105.
The moss upon the forest bark
                          Woodnotes. I. 133.
When the forest shall mislead me,
                          Woodnotes. I. 139.
The orphan of the forest dies.
                          Woodnotes. II. 56.
To the green-haired forest free;
                          World-Soul. 4.

Forester
The rough and bearded forester
                          Woodnotes. II. 14.
Into that forester shall pass,
                          Woodnotes. II. 61.

Forests
If I cannot carry forests on my back,
                          Fable. 18.
Which older forests bound;   Garden. 10.
She threads dark Alpine forests
                          House. 9.
Bending forests as bends the sedge,
                          May-Day. 243.
To see strange forests and new snow,
                          Monadnoc. 206.
When forests fall, and man is gone,
                          Monadnoc. 213.
Where forests starve: Monadnoc. 354.
In forests I am still at home
                          Walden. 47.

Foreteller
Foreteller of the vernal ides,
                          Woodnotes. I. 32.

Forethought
But, leaving rule and pale forethought,
                          Merlin. 31.

Forever
Yet shine forever virgin minds,
                          Astraea. 31.
And ever and forever Love
                          Daemonic Love. 85.
One thing is forever good;
                          Destiny. 45.
To-morrow, forever,   Give. 31.
Thyself dost give forever more.
                          Hymn. 28.
Plunges eyeless on forever;
                          Monadnoc. 334.
And be the sport of Fate forever.
                          Ode to Beauty. 97.
Is freed forever from his thrall.
                          Rhea. 75.
That can contend with love. It reigns
forever.   Rome. 19.
Illusion dwells forever with the wave.
                          Seashore. 42.
Henceforth, please God, forever I forego
                          Self-Reliance. 1.
Must time and tide forever run?
                          Song of Nature. 45.
Forever to myself soothfast;
                          Sursum Corda. 8.
And they reply, "Forever mine!"
                          Woodnotes. II. 149.
But forever doth escape,
                          Woodnotes. II. 273.

Forevermore
Forevermore.   Hamatreya. 43.
Sweet is death forevermore.   Past. 7.
Bolted down forevermore.   Past. 13.

For eit
To tread the forfeit Paradise,
                          May-Day. 96.

Forfeited
How have I forfeited the right?
                          Threnody. 34.

Forge
As pledged in coming days to forge
                          In Memoriam. 64.
Time out of mind, this forge of ores;
                          Monadnoc. 78.

Insert a leaf, or forge a name,   Past. 19.
At forge and furnace thousands sweat;
        Saadi. 107.

Forget
So that men might it not forget;
        Monadnoc. 49.
And forget me if he can.'
        Monadnoc. 347.
Nor last posterity forget.   Poet. 12.
If the Law should thee forget,
        Poet. 289.
Though thou forget, the gods, secure,
        Rhea. 28.
Forget never their command,   Rhea. 29.
Would rushing life forget her laws,
        Threnody. 226.
But though light-headed man forget,
        Wealth. 44.

Forgetfulness
O ostrich-like forgetfulness!
        Threnody. 116.

Forgetting
Straightway, a forgetting wind
        Uriel. 43.

Forging
Forging double stars,   Merlin. 94.
Forging, through swart arms of Offence,
        Spiritual Laws. 11.

Forgive
The civil world will much forgive
        Frag. Poet. IV. 1.
Forgive our harms, and condescend
        May-Day. 402.
Who in their pride forgive not ours.
        Saadi. 58.

Forgot
Lone mountain tarn, or isle forgot,
        Astraea. 46.
Far or forgot to me is near;
        Brahma. 5.
Forgot my morning wishes, hastily
        Days. 8.
Comes the Genius,—all's forgot,
        Frag. Life. XVI. 7.
Canst thou, thy pride forgot,
        Musketaquid. **78.**
Romance forgot, and faith decayed,
        Solution. 60.
Hast thou forgot me in a new delight?
        Threnody. 35.

Forgotten
To make the sun forgotten.   Destiny. 28.
Forgotten amid splendid tombs,
        Nun. 27.

Forks
rode up the forks   Adirondacs. 2.

Forlorn
Or marked, benighted and forlorn,
        Harp. 93.
The child of genius sits forlorn:
        Poet. 182.

Form
   See Star-form; Transform.
So through all creatures in their form and
ways   Adirondacs. 202.
A form which marble doth not hold
        Angelo. 2.
The form is his own corporal form,
        Astraea. 29.
Form of forms, and mould to statures,
        Bacchus. 20

Was never form and never face
        Beauty. 1.
But the boundless hath no form,
        Bohemian. 3.
Into vision where all form
        Celestial Love. 31.
In one only form dissolves;
        Celestial Love. 32.
Is the Dæmon's form and face.
        Daemonic Love. 34.
Where thy form and favor come,
        Dearest. 3.
Scent, form and color; to the flowers and
shells   Enchanter. 4.
Fenced by form and ceremony,
        Frag. Poet. I. 28.
It put on flesh in friendly form,
        Frag. Poet. IV. 28.
All things through thee take nobler form,
        Friendship. 13.
In her form and motion.   Hermione. 15.
Unveils thy form.   Hermione. 55.
Studied thy motion, took thy form,
        Lines. 16.
Mounts through all the spires of form.
        May-Day. 82.
In shifting form the formless mind,
        Monadnoc. 389.
Works thy form on human thought;
        Monadnoc Afar. 6.
Mounts through all the spires of form.
        Nature. Mot. 6.
Spirit that lurks each form within
        Nature. Mot. 13.
Thee gliding through the sea of form,
        Ode to Beauty. 68.
No perfect form could ever bind.
        Ode to Beauty. 73.
A form which Nature cast in the heroic
mould   Phi. 5.
Form the soul had ever dressed,
        Rhea. 18.
A swan-like form invests the hidden
thorn;   Snow-Storm. 19.
How danced thy form before my path
        Thine Eyes. 7.
Lovely locks, a form of wonder,
        Threnody. 213.
Laws of form, and metre just,
        Uriel. 12.
Still tearless lift its slender form **above**
the wintry snow?   *Violet. 4.
Of chemic matter, force and form,
        Woodnotes. II. 110.
Thy cheek too white, thy form too
slender,   Woodnotes. II. 186.
With one drop sheds form and feature;
        Woodnotes. II. 289.
From form to form He maketh haste;
        Woodnotes. II. 298.
Our angel, in a stranger's form,
        World-Soul. 27.
Song, picture, form, space, thought and
character   Xenophanes. 7.

Formed
A cripple of God, half true, half formed,
        Poet. 185.
And whether formed for good or ill,
        Prayer. 7.
I formed the world anew;
        Song of Nature. 28.

Former
And the former called the latter 'Little Prig;'   Fable. 3.
Formidable
His formidable innocence;
                          Woodnotes. II. 76.
Formless
In shifting form the formless mind,
                          Monadnoc. 389.
Forms
And its depths reflect all forms;
                          Astraea. 42.
Form of forms, and mould of statures,
                          Bacchus. 20.
In many forms we try   Bohemian. 1.
Need is none of forms of greeting;
                          Celestial Love. 94.
As if on such stern forms and haunts
                          Frag. Nat. XXIX. 3.
And fairer forms are in the quarry
                          Good Hope. 7.
I knew their forms in fancy weeds,
                          Harp. 112.
He need not go to them, their forms
                          Manners. 7.
The wealth of forms,   May-Day. 189.
And those eternal forms, May-Day. 320.
Your song, your forms, your rhythmic flight,   May-Day. 398.
All the forms we looked on shone
                          May-Day. 412.
Forms more cheerly live and go,
                          Merlin. 43.
Shall not be forms of stars, but stars,
                          Monadnoc. 307.
Guest of million painted forms,
                          Ode to Beauty. 23.
Swells hitherward, and myriads of forms
                          Pan. 4.
I see your forms with deep content,
                          Poet. 257.
Statelier forms and fairer faces;
                          Rhea. 67.
Though her eye seek other forms
                          Security. 1.
And in cramp elf and saurian forms
                          Song of Nature. 31.
Through times that wear and forms that fade,   Waldeinsamkeit. 27.
All the forms are fugitive,
                          Woodnotes. II. 260.
into new forms   Woodnotes. II. 274.
Forsake
And with a cheerful benison forsake
                          Letter. 5.
Forsake their comrades gay
                          Voluntaries. 64.
And the ripples in ryhmes the oar forsake.   Woodnotes. II. 171.
Forsook
Old gods forsook the skies.   Peter. 20.
Fort
Sped, when I passed his sylvan fort,
                          Titmouse. 35.
Forth (Partial list.)
   See Henceforth.
And carry my purpose forth,
                          Boston Hymn. 83.
Their step is forth, and, ere the day
                          Forerunners. 3.

Forth already on the road,
                          Frag. Life. XXII. 6.
and salied forth,   Frag. Nat. XXVII. 1.
Friendly hands stretched forth to him,
                          Frag. Poet. XI. 6.
I looked forth on the fields of youth:
                          Harp. 110.
Forth paced it yesterday;
                          Hermione. 57.
I saw the bud-crowned Spring go forth,
                          May-Day. 305.
A greater spirit bids thee forth
                          Monadnoc. 17.
Orb and atom forth they prance,
                          Monadnoc. 249.
Forth speed the strong pulses
                          Sphinx. 103.
Exists to draw thy virtue forth.
                          Titmouse. 59.
So forth and brighter fares my stream,—
                          Two Rivers. 17.
Flies gayly forth and sings in sight.
                          Woodnotes. II. 251.
Forthright
Pilgrims wight with step forthright.
                          May-Day. 311.
Forthright my planets roll,
                          Song of Nature. 42.
Fortunate
The fortunate star that rose on us sank not;   Adirondacs. 337.
The beautiful and fortunate,
                          Daemonic Love. 98.
O, well for the fortunate soul
                          Voluntaries. 75.
Fortune
Since fortune snatched
                          Adirondacs. 276.
Nor Fortune, nor thy coldness, can I chide,   Angelo. 11.
For this fortune wanted root
                          Daemonic Love. 126.
Discoursed of fortune as they blew;
                          Frag. Poet. V. 38.
Air-bells of fortune that shine and break,
                          Garden. 55.
Fortune was his guard and lover;
                          Guy. 10.
A fortune harsh and hard.   Poet. 154.
Seek nothing,—Fortune seeketh thee.
                          Saadi. 144.
O richest fortune sourly crossed!
                          Threnody. 174.
Without better fortune had,
                          Woodnotes. I. 14.
Of Death and Fortune, Growth and Strife.'   Woodnotes. II. 32.
Fortune's
Fortune's delectable mountains;
                          Frag. Poet. IV. 12.
Could chain the wheel of Fortune's car,
                          Poet. 166.
Thy fortune's web to the beneficent hand
                          Rome. 22.
Fortunes
And human fortunes in astronomy,
                          Blight. 24.
Men their fortunes bring with them.
                          Celestial Love. 74.
Friends, foes, joys, fortunes, beauty and disgust.   Day's Ration. 8.

To mould his fortunes, mean or great:
　　　　　　　　　　　Fate. 2.
The flowing fortunes of a thousand
　years;—　　　　　　Merlin. 73.
Fair fortunes to the mountaineer!
　　　　　　　　Monadnoc. 69.
All fortunes made;　　　Past. 5.
And thy fortunes, as they fall,
　　　　　　　Quat. Memory. 3.
Nathless we read your fortunes true;
　　　　　　　　　Romany. 26.

Forty
To dine and sleep through forty years;
　　　　　　　　　　Fame. 14.

Forty-five
Six rods, sixteen, twenty, or forty-five;
　　　　　　　Adirondacs. 126.

Forward
　See Thenceforward.
Saw the dance of Nature forward and
　far,　　　　　　　Poet. 70.
Change acts, reacts; back, forward hurled,
　　　　　　　　　Poet. 175.
Forward stepped the perfect Greek:
　　　　　　　　Solution. 14.
Through light, through life, it forward
　flows.　　　Two Rivers. 8.
With children forward and behind,
　　　　　　　Threnody. 64.
Show me the forward way, since thou art
　guide,　　　　　　Unbar. 2.

Foul
From all that's fair, from all that's foul,
　　　　　　　　　Music. 5.
Fair to old and foul to young;
　　　　　　　Prudence. 2.

Foully
Foully warking in his nest?　Riches. 2.

Found
　See New-found.
Long sought, not found.
　　　　　　Adirondacs. 133.
Were sought and found, amid the hue and
　cry　　　　Adirondacs. 192.
Found ten years since the Californian
　gold?　　　Adirondacs. 280.
Nay, letters found us in our paradise:
　　　　　　Adirondacs. 334.
Found friendship in the French,
　　　　　　　　Boston. 83.
I found by thee, O rushing Contoocook!
　　　　　　　Channing Ode. 21.
Found in polygala root and rind,
　　　　　　Frag. Nat. II. 27.
But never yet the man was found
　　　　　　Frag. Nat. VI. 1.
Vae solis! I found this,
　　　　　　Frag. Poet. IV. 7.
I travelled and found it at Rome;
　　　　　　Frag. Poet. IV. 32.
His eye the eye 't was seeking found.
　　　　　　　　　Guy. 24.
The siroc found it on its way,　Guy. 37.
She shall find thee, and be found.
　　　　　　　　Hermione. 76.
In Indian wildernesses found;
　　　　　　　Humble-Bee. 37.
The sweet delight I found in fields and
　farms,　　　　　I Bear. 6.
The freed soul its Creator found?
　　　　　　In Memoriam. 112.

Whereon their traits are found.
　　　　　　　　Manners. 12.
I found no joy: the icy wind
　　　　　　　　May-Day. 51.
The forefathers this land who found
　　　　　　Merlin's Song. 18.
And in low hut the dweller found:
　　　　　　　Monadnoc. 73.
And found a home in haunts which
　others scorned,　Musketaquid. 3.
And, chiefest prize, found I true liberty
　　　　　　Musketaquid. 66.
The polite found me impolite; the great
　　　　　　Musketaquid. 68.
I found me thy thrall,
　　　　　　Ode to Beauty. 10.
I found the fresh Rhodora in the woods,
　　　　　　　Rhodora. 2.
And in the church a blessing found
　　　　　　Robbins Hymn. 15.
The inks of Erebus he found;
　　　　　　　Solution. 48.
Once found,—for new heavens
　　　　　　　Sphinx. 87.
Lost in God, in Godhead found.'
　　　　　　Threnody. 289.
As late I found my lukewarm blood
　　　　　　Titmouse. 3.
'Line in nature is not found;　Uriel. 21.
Product of the earlier found.　Visit. 8.
The fancies found in books;
　　　　　　Waldeinsamkeit. 42.
He found the tawny thrushes' broods;
　　　　　　Woodnotes. I. 56.
Where darkness found him he lay glad at
　night;　　Woodnotes. I. 82.
I found the water's bed.
　　　　　　Woodnotes. I. 121.
Not one has found the key;
　　　　　　World-Soul. 54.

Foundation
Adhere like this foundation strong,
　　　　　　Monadnoc. 115.

Founder
The founder thou; these are thy race!'
　　　　　　Experience. 21.

Founder's
And promise, on thy Founder's truth,
　　　　　　Monadnoc. 407.

Foundeth
Foundeth a heroic line;
　　　　　　Woodnotes. II. 23.

Foundling
Foundling of the desert far,
　　　　　　Voluntaries. 47.

Fount
He sends thee from his bitter fount
　　　　　　　Saadi. 62.
I sit by the shining Fount of Life
　　　　　　Song of Nature. 11.

Fountain
Gives beauty to the lake and fountain,
　　　　　　Enchanter. 8.
Cleanse the torrent at the fountain,
　　　　　　May-Day. 450.
I drank at thy fountain
　　　　　　Ode to Beauty. 13.
And fountain of the rains.
　　　　　　Quat. Alcuin. 4.

Fountain-drop
Fountain-drop of spicier worth
Monadnoc. 293.
Fountains
Let spouting fountains cool the air,
Art. 7.
Houses, banquets, gardens, fountains,
Frag. Poet. IV. 11.
The fountains of my hidden life
Friendship. 19.
Thou askest in fountains and in fires,
Woodnotes. II. 311.
Four
Within four walls is possible again,—
Adirondacs. 322.
Which the four seasons do not tend
Threnody. 112.
Fourscore
Fourscore or a hundred words
Monadnoc. 175.
Fourth
The fourth gives light which eats the
dark; Woodnotes. II. 292.
Fowl
each fowl must crow; Threnody. 105.
Fowls
Step the meek fowls where erst they
ranged; Threnody. 94.
Fox
Luther, Fox, Behmen, Swedenborg, grew
pale, Adakryn. 3.
For wolf and fox, bring lowing herds,
Monadnoc. 139.
Wintered with the hawk and fox,
Quat. Power. 3.
In damp fields known to bird and fox.
Woodnotes. I. 41.
Foxes
He shall impose, to find a spring, trap
foxes, Adirondacs. 103.
Foxes are so cunning Quat. Orator. 3.
Fox-hole
The fox-hole which the woodchucks rent,
Miracle. 4.
Fragile
Are Autumn's blasts fit music for thee,
fragile one, to hear; *Violet. 2.
Fragrance
Their fragrance, and their chemistry
apply Blight. 11.
Sent a noctural fragrance;
Frag. Nat. XXVII. 8.
Fragrant
Sleep on the fragrant brush, as on down-
beds. Adirondacs. 58.
He is come through fragrant wood,
Hermione. 51.
From the fragrant solitudes;— Rhea. 6.
The fragrant flag-roots in my father's
fields, River. 6.
A bunch of fragrant lilies be,
Woodnotes. II. 303.
Frail
Though the frail ringlets thee deceive,
II Compensation. 17.
Nor bent to passion frail. Harp. 4.
New worlds to find in pinnace frail.
Quat. Poet. I. 4.
When frail Nature can no more,
Threnody. 234.

Frailest
The frailest leaf, the mossy bark,
Ode to Beauty. 25.
Frame
See Wagon-frame.
Make his frame and forces square
Alphonso. 73.
In thee to frame, in me to trust,
Hermione. 29.
He could not frame a word unfit,
In Memoriam. 53.
Eyes that frame cities where none be,
Monadnoc. 108.
And polar frost my frame defied,
Titmouse. 77.
Framed
Framed afar as Fates and Loves.
Frag. Poet. XII. 4.
I framed his tongue to music,
Frag. Poet. XIV. 1.
His tongue was framed to music,
Power. 1.
Frames
And thrill our tuneful frames;
April. 2.
France
Her strength and soul has laughing
France Quat. Leasts. 3.
When France, where poet never grew,
Solution. 63.
Frank
The frank blessings of the hill
Monadnoc. 222.
Her soul is frank as the ocean wind,
Security. 7.
Frankincense
And my heart the frankincense;
Song of Seyd. 16.
Franklin
Amid the mountain counties, Hants,
Franklin, Berks, Letter. 9.
Frankly
Frankly I will be your guest,
May-Day. 367.
And say it frankly without guile,
Romany. 10.
Fraud
Truculent with fraud and force,'
Berrying. 3.
Be fine accomplices to fraud?
Chartist. 16.
Of his wisdom, of his fraud Limits. 4.
Fraudulent
Fraudulent Time in vain concealed,—
Saadi. 174.
Fraught
Days that come dancing on fraught with
delights, Summons. 20.
Fray
For famine, toil and fray?
Voluntaries. 66.
Free
See Fancy-free.
But ever the free race with front sublime,
Adirondacs. 293.
'Like us be free and bold!'
Boston. 16.
Free be his heart and hand henceforth
Boston Hymn. 55.

To die, and leave their children free,
                              C. Hymn. 14.
For the banner of the free.
                              Concord Ode. 12.
A ferry of the free.   Concord Ode. 28.
Our eyeless bark sails free
                              Frag. Nat. XV. 1.
I was free to overhear,
                              Frag. Poet. IV. 19.
The free winds told him what they knew,
                              Frag. Poet. V. 37.
Making free with time and size,
                              Frag. Poet. IX. 6.
My careful heart was free again,
                              Friendship. 9.
Free as an Arab   Give. 32.
Free be she, fancy-free;   Give. 39.
Drew his free homage unbeguiled,
                              In Memoriam. 68.
And waters free as winds shall flow.
                              May-Day. 110.
Driving, darting northward free,
                              May-Day. 388.
Free, peremptory, clear.   Merlin. 4.
When the God's will sallies free,
                              Merlin. 71.
Youth, for a moment free as they,
                              Monadnoc. 21.
Goes loaded with a free perfume
                              Mountain. 12.
I pass with yonder comet free,—
                              Nun. 38.
Himself from God he could not free;
                              Problem. 22.
Who is noble and free?—   Sphinx. 94.
He is free and libertine,
                              Woodnotes. II. 278.
To the green-haired forest free;
                              World-Soul. 4.

Freed
The freed soul its Creator found?
                              In Memoriam. 112.
Scarce freed from her embraces?
                              Philosopher. 12.
Is freed forever from his thrall.
                              Rhea. 75.

Freedom
    See Freedom-loving.
Or land or life, if freedom fail?
                              Boston. 30.
Or land or life, if freedom fail?
                              Boston. 81.
Till Freedom cheered and joy-bells rung.
                              Boston. 99.
My angel,—his name is Freedom,—
                              Boston Hymn. 13.
Freedom praised, but hid;
                              Channing Ode. 33.
Half for freedom strike and stand;—
                              Channing Ode. 96.
Ere freedom out of man.
                              Concord Ode. 40.
In whom the stock of freedom roots;
                              Monadnoc. 93.
And granted me the freedom of their
state,   Musketaquid. 5.
Freedom all winged expands,
                              Voluntaries. 35.
For freedom he will strike and strive,
                              Voluntaries. 57.

Freedom-loving
Dare praise the freedom-loving moun-
taineer?   Channing Ode. 20.
Freedom's
With Freedom's image and name.
                              Boston Hymn. 76.
That were Freedom's whitest chart,
                              Etienne. 24.
Freedom's pæan in my verse,
                              Freedom. 2.
Freedom's secret wilt thou know?—
                              Freedom. 21.
To hazard all in Freedom's fight,—
                              Voluntaries. 62.
A beacon set that Freedom's race
                              Webster. 3.
Freelier
He freelier breathed beside the pine,
                              Frag. Poet. V. 15.
Freely
Freely nestle in our roof,
                              Frag. Nat. XXIII. 11.
Freely as task at eve undone
                              Frag. Poet. XI. 18.
And more to purpose freely pour
                              Walk. 6.
Freemen
We were made freemen of the forest
laws,   Adirondacs. 70.
They did what freemen can,
                              Boston. 8.
Freeze
Who would freeze on frozen lakes?
                              May-Day. 53.
Makes flame to freeze and ice to boil;
                              Spiritual Laws. 10.
Wilt thou freeze love's tidal flow,
                              Threnody. 238.
Freight
The total freight of hope and joy
                              May-Day. 354.
Thoughtless of its anxious freight,
                              Monadnoc. 333.
French
Found friendship in the French,
                              Boston. 83
Frequent
In the frequent interval
                              Frag. Poet. III. 8.
Quit the hut, frequent the palace,
                              Quat. Artist. 1.
Fresh
    See Refresh.
Time takes fresh start again,
                              Adirondacs. 328.
Fresh pearls to their enamel gave,
                              Each. 21.
And dew-bent violets, fresh and new,
                              Frag. Nat. XXVI. 36.
The year's fresh bloom,
                              In Memoriam. 18.
The fresh ground loves his top and ball,
                              May-Day. 69.
Fresh from palms and Cuba's canes.
                              May-Day. 393.
And brings it infantile and fresh.
                              Monadnoc. 162.
And as each flower upon the fresh hill-
side,   Naples. 5.
She spawneth men as mallows fresh,
                              Nature. II. 13.

Fresh—*Continued*
I found the fresh Rhodora in the woods,
Rhodora. 2.
Fresh as the trickling rainbow of July;
Seashore. 20.
And the fresh rose on yonder thorn
Song of Nature. 83.
Ever fresh the broad creation,
Woodnotes. II. 262.

Fresher
By houses lies a fresher green,
May-Day. 299.

Freshet
Nor freshet, nor midsummer flame.
Guy. 48.

Freshly
That circled freshly in their forest dress
Adirondacs. 60.

Friar
He will preach like a friar,
Initial Love. 134.

Friend
See Befriended.
And the friend not hesitates
Astraea. 19.
Driving the foe and stablishing the
friend,— Blight. 13.
And the Universal Friend   Bohemian. 4.
To the good an equal friend.
Boston. 115.
O glowing friend,   Channing Ode. 37.
O, be my friend, and teach me to be
thine!   Forbearance. 8.
O friend, my bosom said,
Friendship. 10.
Thou art not my friend, and I'm not
thine.   Good-bye. 2.
They seek a friend to speak the word
Hymn. 13.
A friend to lift the curtain up
Hymn. 21.
The green lane is the school-boy's
friend,   May-Day. 67.
To man, as to a lubber friend,
May-Day. 403.
What friend to friend cannot convey
Miracle. 21.
As a man unto his friend.   Peter. 36.
His mother died,—the only friend he
had,—   Philosopher. 7.
Impatient friend,—   Poet. 92.
Thee, dear friend, a brother soothes,
Rhea. 1.
Wait then, sad friend, wait in majestic
peace   Rome. 20.
A poet or a friend to find: Saadi. 156.
'I came to thee as to a friend;
Threnody. 209.
The forest is my loyal friend,
Waldeinsamkeit. 3.
Who leaves the pine-tree, leaves his
friend,   Woodnotes. II. 49.

Friendless
To mark the Briton's friendless grave.
In Memoriam. 14.
O friendless Present! than thy bosom
holds.   Quat. Heri. 4.

Friendly
I took the friendly noble by the hand,
Frag. Life. XXX. 3.

It put on flesh in friendly form,
Frag. Poet. IV. 28.
Friendly hands stretch forth to him,
Frag. Poet. XI. 6.
The sod throbbed friendly to my feet,
Lines. 13.

Friends
We crossed Champlain to Keeseville with
our friends,   Adirondacs. 1.
Soft and softlier hold me, friends!
Aeolian Harp. 1.
I've come to live with you, sweet friends,
Aeolian Harp. 18.
Friends year by year more inly known.
Daemonic Love. 16.
Friends, foes, joys, fortunes, beauty and
disgust.   Day's Ration. 8.
To-day, when friends approach, and
every hour   Day's Ration. 20.
Friends to me are frozen wine;
Frag. Life. XIV. 1.
And search the skies for prouder friends,
From Hafiz. 10.
Friends, kindred, days,   Give. 3.
Friends of your spring-time,
Illusions. 8.
All friends to fend, all foes defy,
In Memoriam. 40.
And troops of friends enjoyed the tide,—
In Memoriam. 71.
To help her friends, to plague her foes,
Nature. I. 14.
As on its friends, with kindred eye;
Problem. 38.
Of friends to friends unknown;
Rubies. 6.
Delayed, all friends shut out, the house-
mates sit   Snow-Storm. 7.
Books, Muses, Study, fireside, friends and
love,   Summons. 13.
He who has a thousand friends has not a
friend to spare,   Taleb. 1.
Some to their friends the tidings say;
Threnody. 154.
Quit thy friends as the dead in doom,
Woodnotes. II. 223.

Friendship
Found friendship in the French,
Boston. 83.
Live for friendship, live for love,
Channing Ode. 67.
Are through thy friendship fair.
Friendship. 20.
If Friendship on me smile,   Walden. 30.
And their resistless friendship showed.
Woodnotes. I. 128.

Frieze
Replacing frieze and architrave;—
Monadnoc. 371.

Fright
But mark what changed my joy to
fright,—   Miracle. 26.

Frightened
To chatter, frightened, to his clan
Monadnoc. 346.

Fringent
And, lit by fringent air,
Daemonic Love. 50.

Frivolous
Be feasters and the frivolous,—
Monadnoc. 400.

As 't would accost some frivolous wing,
Titmouse. 92.
Nor vain, sour, nor frivolous;
Woodnotes. II. 67.

Fro
To and fro the Genius hies,—
Daemonic Love. 35.
To and fro perpetually;
Daemonic Love. 80.
To and fro the Genius flies,
Frag. Life. XVI. 1.
Short-lived wandering to and fro,
Merlin. 107.

Frock
So shall the drudge in dusty frock
Art. 13.

Frocks
Frocks and blouses, capes, capotes;
Initial Love. 16.

Frog
Frog and lizard in holiday coats,
May-Day. 237.

Frolic
Sound, ruddy men, frolic and innocent,
Adirondacs. 87.
Whose groves the frolic fairies planned;
Good-bye. 18.
Was frolic sunshine, dear to all men,
Holidays. 11.
The frolic architecture of the snow.
Snow-Storm. 28.
Holds in check the frolic light,
Solution. 44.
So frolic, stout and self-possest?
Titmouse. 53.

From. (Partial list.)
See Herefrom.
We made our distance wider, boat from
boat, Adirondacs. 14.
From a nocturnal root, Bacchus. 7.
Each from your proper state,
Celestial Love. 13.
From each to each, from thee to me,
Daemonic Love. 79.
From high to higher forces
Frag. Life. IV. 1.
From the twins is nothing hidden,
Love and Thought. 3.
From their rifle on their snare;
Monadnoc. 144.
Or coax the thunder from its mark?
Nemesis. 11.
Flee from the goods which from thee
flee; Saadi. 143.
To guard the babe from fancied foes.
Threnody. 69.
From his Afric's torrid plains.
Voluntaries. 8.

Front
But ever the free race with front sublime,
Adirondacs. 293.
Front the liberated floods:
May-Day. 225.
Spoils of a front none need restore,
Monadnoc. 370.
The morrow front, and can defy;
Nun. 4.
Men to all shores that front the hoary
main. Seashore. 40.

To front the fate that couches near,—
Voluntaries. 16.
Cannon in front and leaden rain
Voluntaries. 94.

Fronted
Fronted the sun with hope as bright,
Dirge. 7.

Frontier
Frontier of the wheat-sown plains,
Quat. Alcuin. 2.

Fronting
Fronting foes of God and man,
In Memoriam. 41.

Fronts
Fronts the north-wind in waistcoat gray,
Titmouse. 46.

Frore
Earliest heats that follow frore
Frag. Nat. II. 21.

Frost
The frost might glitter, Adirondacs. 68.
The frost to spare, what scents so well.
Frag. Nat. II. 31.
There was no frost but welcome came,
Guy. 47.
Frost and sun and eldest night,
Hermione. 62.
Eldest mason, Frost, had piled
May-Day. 47.
The pebble loosened from the frost
May-Day. 63.
They turn the frost upon their chemic
heap, Musketaquid. 41.
And polar frost my frame defied,
Titmouse. 77.

Frost-king
The frost-king ties my fumbling feet,
Titmouse. 12.

Frosty
The Indian cheer, the frosty skies,
Monadnoc. 106.
And, echoed in some frosty wold,
Titmouse. 97.

Frown
Nor skies without a frown
Concord Ode. 22.
Kind smile and honest frown
*Farewell. 12.
And they knit no frown. *Lines. 21.

Frowned
Frowned in my foe and growled in storm,
Frag. Poet. IV. 29.
The seraphs frowned from myrtle-beds;
Uriel. 28.

Frowning
Frowning down the evil-doer,
In Memoriam. 42.

Frowns
And fled in pretty frowns away
Frag. Poet. I. 38.

Frozen
Like Alpine cataracts frozen as they
leaped, Blight. 60.
Friends to me are frozen wine;
Frag. Life. XIV. 1.
To froze hearts and hasting feet;
Good-Bye. 12.
Who would freeze on frozen lakes?
May-Day. 53.
As we thaw frozen flesh with snow,
May-Day. 125.

Frozen—*Continued*
And sun this frozen side.   May-Day. 161.
Honey from the frozen land;
                        Monadnoc. 136.
I said, they are drops of frozen wine
                        Rubies. 3.
Or winter's frozen shade?
                        Song of Nature. 56.
Frugal
Is early frugal, like a beggar's child;
                        Blight. 57.
Frugal multiples of that.   Visit. 26.
By fate, not option, frugal Nature gave
                        Xenophanes. 1.
Fruit
Whether thy sons or strangers eat the
   fruit: Adirondacs. 300.
Like stolen fruit;   Channing Ode. 91.
What mystic fruit his acres yield
                        Dirge. 11.
Fruit beloved of maid and boy,
                        Holidays. 2.
We had eaten fairy fruit,   May-Day. 410.
There's fruit upon my barren soil
                        Monadnoc. 295.
What mystic fruit his acres yield
                        Peter. 3.
The parent fruit survives;   Promise. 4.
Known fruit of the unknown;
                        Sphinx. 11.
Mature the unfallen fruit.   Terminus. 22.
Or from fruit of chemic force,
                        Uriel. 50.
Fruitful
The holidays were fruitful, but must end;
                        Adirondacs. 330.
To fruitful field and sun and moon.
                        Limits. 10.
Of fruitful worlds the grain,
                        Waldeinsamkeit. 22.
Fruiting
   See Wisdom-fruiting.
Fruiting-time
Had reached its fruiting-time,
                        Frag. Nat. XXI. 8.
Fruitless
Hide in thy skies, thou fruitless Jove,
                        Frag. Life. XXXIII. 2.
Fruits
To bring their first fruits to the sun.
                        Frag. Nat. II. 20.
Planting strange fruits and sunshine on
   the shore,   Seashore. 47.
Fugitive
Are fugitive also,   Illusions. 18.
Thou eternal fugitive, Ode to Beauty. 74.
All the forms are fugitive,
                        Woodnotes. II. 260.
Fulfil
To falter ere thou thy task fulfil,—
                        Merlin's Song. 27.
Fulfilled
My will fulfilled shall be,
                        Boston Hymn. 85.
New slaves fulfilled the poet's dream,
                        Wealth. 40.
Full (Partial list.)
Full fifty feet,   Adirondacs. 84.
Ply us now with a full diet;
                        Alphonso. 52.
The air with Cupids full,   April. 6.

And planted world, and full executor
                        Blight. 16.
The plain was full of ghosts;
                        Dirge. 14.
Full of light and of deity;   Each. 47.
Forest full of essences
                        Frag. Nat. II. 11.
Yet Nature will not be in full possessed,
                        Frag. Nat. V. 8.
The air is full of whistlings bland;
                        May-Day. 7.
The plain was full of ghosts: Peter. 10.
There I am full of light;   Peter. 30.
Underwoods were full of pleasance,
                        Peter. 33.
Sea full of food, the nourisher of kinds,
                        Seashore. 21.
Sudden gusts came full of meaning,
                        September. 9.
The cup was never full.
                        Song of Nature. 72.
When the scanty shores are full
                        Threnody. 232.
Here was this atom in full breath,
                        Titmouse. 43.
Fully
Fully until the end.   Poet. 96.
Fulness
In its fulness he should taste
                        Poet. 45.
Fumbling
What make you, master, fumbling at the
   oar?   Adirondacs. 99.
The frost-king ties my fumbling feet,
                        Titmouse. 12.
Function
Every function he absorbs;
                        Initial Love. 26.
Functions
Of their imperfect functions. Blight. 17.
Fund
And betrayed the fund of joy
                        May-Day. 344.
But, sober on a fund of joy,
                        Waldeinsamkeit. 19.
Funeral
Funeral eloquence   Channing Ode. 34.
Nature's funeral high and dim,—
                        Nun. 20.
their funeral shade.   River. 42.
To aggrandize one funeral.
                        Threnody. 159.
Funerals
Still celebrate their funerals,
                        Woodnotes. II. 226.
Fungus
Where the fungus broad and red
                        Frag. Nat. III. 1.
The fungus and the bulrush spoke,
                        Frag. Nat. III. 10.
Furies
Even the fell Furies are appeased,
                        Celestial Love. 113.
The Furies laid,   Past. 3.
The Furies wait beyond.
                        Quat. Pericles. 4.
Furl
   See Unfurl.
Furled
Her wings are furled: Sphinx. 2.

Furlong
His day's ride is a furlong space,
Monadnoc. 322.
Furloughed
Of scholars furloughed from their tasks
and let Adirondacs. 193.
Furnace
Light's far furnace shines, Merlin. 92.
At forge and furnace thousands sweat;
Saadi. 107.
What smiths, and in what furnace, rolled
Wealth. 18.
Furnish
See Disfurnish.
Furnished
Furnished several supplies;
Ode to Beauty. 49.
Furnished with tile, the fierce artificer
Snow-Storm. 12.
Furrow
Furrow for the wheat,— Politics. 22.
Furrowed
See Farm-furrowed.
Furrows
And strangers, fond as they, their fur-
rows plough. Hamatreya. 12.
Furtherance
For watch and ward and furtherance,
Daemonic Love. 28.
Built of furtherance and pursuing,
Threnody. 280.
Fuse
Shall into Future fuse the Past,
Culture. 10.
Future
There Past, Present, Future, shoot
Celestial Love. 42.
Shall into Future fuse the Past,
Culture. 10.
Past and future must reveal
Frag. Poet. V. 32.
Should rive the Future, and reveal
Harp. 63.
And tidings of the future tells.
Hymn. 4.
And richly his large future planned,
In Memoriam. 70.
And hints the future which it owes.
Nature. Mot. 16.
Future or Past no richer secret folds,
Quat. Heri. 3.
Born for the future, to the future lost!
Threnody. 175.
Future's
Who the Future's gates unbar,—
Daemonic Love. 101.

Gage
Adding by their mutual gage,
Merlin. 104.
Gain
Thieving Ambition and paltering Gain!
Beauty. 24.
For we invade them impiously for gain;
Blight. 37.
By errant gain, Monadnoc. 399.
Gainsaid
He will never be gainsaid,—
Daemonic Love. 112.

Was not to be gainsaid.
Monadnoc. 30.
Gait
Thy gait too slow, thy habits tender
Woodnotes. II. 187.
Galaxy
Fixed on the enormous galaxy,
Character. 3.
Fixed on the enormous galaxy,
Poet. 136.
Thou seek'st in globe and galaxy,
Woodnotes. II. 309.
Gale
The gale that wrecked you on the sand,
Quat. Northman. 1.
As the bird trims her to the gale,
Terminus. 33.
Gales
Thy birds, thy songs, thy brooks, thy
gales, May-Day. 436.
Gallant
The gallant child where'er he came
Poet. 7.
Galleries
And the galleries and halls,
Daemonic Love. 123.
Why need I galleries, when a pupil's
draught Day's Ration. 27.
I walk in marble galleries, Walden. 31.
Galley
The storm is my best galley hand
Quat. Northman. 3.
Galls
Which galls me everywhere. Park. 4.
Galvanic
Galvanic wire, strong-shouldered steam.
Wealth. 41.
Gambolled
The rivers gambolled onward to the sea,
Adirondacs. 339.
Game
And the inventor of the game
Experience. 10.
Bird, and reptile, be my game.
Mithridates. 13.
Too long the game is played;
Song of Nature. 54.
A while to share his cordial game,
Threnody. 48.
Games
I leave it behind with the games of
youth:'— Each. 39.
To hear, when, 'mid our talk and games,
May-Day. 56.
Blameless master of the games,
Merlin. 39.
And games to breathe his stalwart boys:
Monadnoc. 164.
Break sharply off their jolly games,
Voluntaries. 63.
To the boy with his games undaunted
World-Soul. 7.
Gamesome
She is gamesome and good,
Nature. II. 1.
Gamut
The gamut old of Pan, Monadnoc. 220.
Gang
In unploughed Maine he sought the lum-
berers' gang Woodnotes. I. 62.

Gape
At the new vision gape and jeer.
                              Poet. 22.
I laugh at those who, while they gape
and gaze,   To-Day. 15.
Garden
The garden walks are passional
                              April. 3.
Only two in the garden walked,
                      Daemonic Love. 21.
I, in my pleached garden, watched the
pomp,   Days. 7.
Will hint her secret in a garden patch,
                      Frag. Nat. IV. 2.
Many things the garden shows,
                      Frag. Nat. XXI. 1.
In the garden murmuring,
                      Frag. Nat. XXII. 2.
My garden is a forest ledge
                              Garden. 9.
The zephyr in his garden rolled Guy. 43.
Garden of berries, perch of birds,
                          Monadnoc. 54.
Dark flower of Cheshire garden,
                    Monadnoc Afar. 1.
My garden spade can heal. A woodland
walk,   Musketaquid. 72.
And every inch of garden ground
                          Threnody. 90.
The wintry garden lies unchanged;
                          Threnody. 95.
And garden,—they were bound and still.
                          Threnody. 109.
In my garden three ways meet,
                              Walden. 1.
Self-sown my stately garden grows;
                              Walden. 9.
My garden is the cloven rock,
                      Woodnotes. II. 9.
As the bee through the garden ranges,
                    Woodnotes. II. 295.
Garden-plot
In my house and garden-plot,   Una. 9.
Garden's
And veils the farm-house at the garden's
end.   Snow-Storm. 5.
Gardens
Plant gardens lined with lilacs sweet;
                              Art. 6.
With faerie gardens cheered,
                      Frag. Nat. X. 2.
Houses, banquets, gardens, fountains,
                      Frag. Poet. IV. 11.
All men would to my gardens throng,
                              Garden. 3.
Fires gardens with a joyful blaze
                          May-Day. 206.
My gardens ripened well,
                      Song of Nature. 18.
Garden-side
Waters that wash my garden-side
                              Garden. 21.
Garlanded
Pavilion on pavilion, garlanded,
                              October. 8.
Garment
As garment draws the garment's hem,
                      Celestial Love. 73.
In his own loom's garment dressed,
                          Monadnoc. 38.

Garment's
As garment draws the garment's hem,
                      Celestial Love. 73.
Garnered
The garnered heat of ages old.
                          May-Day. 145.
Garrulous
Not mad, athirst, nor garrulous;
                      Woodnotes. II. 68.
Gas
The gas become solid,   Illusions. 28.
Gasp
Chiming with the gasp and moan
                              Merlin. 19.
Gate
Nor plots to ope or bolt a gate,
                      Frag. Life. XVII. 8.
The gate of gifts behind him closed.
                      Quat. Horoscope. 4.
Maugre the farmer's sighs; and at the
gate   Snow-Storm. 21.
He comes not to the gate.
                      Song of Nature. 60.
Gated
    See Hundred-gated.
Gates
    See Janus-gates.
Who the Future's gates unbar,—
                      Daemonic Love. 101.
Through the cold slab a thousand gates,
                          May-Day. 122.
Gather
Which I gather in a song.
                          Apology. 20.
Might gather omens from that radiant
sign.   Webster. 4.
Gathered
Gathered with hope to please,
                      Daemonic Love. 109.
His gathered sticks to stanch the wall
                          Threnody. 84.
Gathering
And your autumnal gathering.
                      Frag. Nat. XXIII. 14.
Gathering along the centuries
                      Song of Nature. 14.
Gathers
With all his force he gathers balms
                      Initial Love. 58.
Gaudy
Superior to all its gaudy skirts.
                          Adirondacs. 220.
Gauge
Gauge of more and less through space,
                      II. Compensation. 7.
To gauge with glance the roaring gulf
below,   Grace. 6.
Gauge and calendar and dial,
                          Monadnoc. 52.
Gaul
In northern Gaul my dauntless bird,
                          Titmouse. 96.
Gaunt
Whither gaunt Labor slips to wipe his
brow   Adirondacs. 196.
Gaunt as bitterns in the pools,
                          Alphonso. 16.
Gave
Gave an impartial tomb to all the kinds.
                          Adirondacs. 140.

Ale, and a sup of wine. Our steward
gave   Adirondacs. 178.
The ring you gave is still the same;
                        Amulet. 2.
The moment's music which they gave.
                        Beauty. 10.
While thus to love he gave his days
                        Beauty. 21.
Fresh pearls to their enamel gave,
                        Each. 21.
I gave my heart to thee. *Farewell. 40.
I gave thee for an hour my ear,
                        Frag. Poet. II. 6.
Which more of pride than pity gave
                        In Memoriam. 13.
Gave the law which others took,
                        In Memoriam. 45.
When that bird sang, I gave the theme;
                        Miracle. 27.
Nay, God is witness, gave the names.
                        Miracle. 36.
In the glad home plain-dealing Nature
gave.   Musketaquid. 67.
Who gave thee, O Beauty,
                        Ode to Beauty. 1.
For the Muse gave special charge
                        Poet. 39.
And Nature gladly gave them place,
                        Problem. 41.
The birds gave us our wily tongues,
                        Romany. 23.
God, who gave to him the lyre,
                        Saadi. 9.
Gave to the mind its emperor,
                        Solution. 37.
Who, when they gave thee breath,
                        Terminus. 25.
I gave thee sight—where is it now?
                        Threnody. 196.
Gave his sentiment divine   Uriel. 19.
By fate, not option, frugal Nature gave
                        Xenophanes. 1.

Gay
By the bright morn the gay flotilla slid
                        Adirondacs. 16.
Now speed the gay celerities of art,
                        Adirondacs. 320.
Why but because, when these are gay,
                        I. Compensation. 3.
The gay enchantment was undone,
                        Each. 35.
Together sad or gay,   *Farewell. 33.
A train of gay and clouded days
                        Frag. Life. I. 1.
The quaint devices on its mornings gay.
                        Frag. Nat. V. 7.
Her gay pictures never fail,
                        Frag. Nat. XXXI. 3.
The tragic and the gay,   Harp. 24.
Gay for youth, gay for youth,   Harp. 43.
Ill-bestead for gay bridegroom.
                        Hermione. 35.
Flower-wreaths gay with bud and bell;
                        May-Day. 315.
Shepherds are thankful and nations gay.
                        Merlin's Song. 34.
Made the black water with their beauty
gay;   Rhodora. 6.
Gay and polite, a cheerful cry,
                        Titmouse. 26.

Of shard and flint makes jewels gay;
                        Two Rivers. 14.
their last gay dress put on;   *Violet. 7.
Forsake their comrades gay
                        Voluntaries. 64.

Gayest
Gayest pictures rose to win me,
                        Monadnoc. 3.
Clouds flush their gayest dyes.
                        Waterfall. 16.

Gayly
I was a boy; boyhood slid gayly by
                        Summons. 15.
Flies gayly forth and sings in sight.
                        Woodnotes. II. 251.

Gaze
To those who gaze from the sea's edge
                        Astraea. 38.
Ah! let me blameless gaze upon
                        Eva. 7.
If on the foeman fell his gaze,   Guy. 21.
To gaze o'er the horizon's edge,
                        Lines. 20.
Where I gaze, and still shall gaze,
                        Monadnoc. 211.
To gaze upon the Pyramids;
                        Problem. 36.
I laugh at those who, while they gape
and gaze,   To-Day. 15.

Gazed
Who gazed upon the sun and moon
                        Threnody. 142.

Gazing
    See Far-gazing.
The gazing urchin walks   October. 6.

Gear
    See Farm-gear.

Gem
Rough Monadnoc to a gem.
                        Frag. Nat. XIV. 2.
Give the gem which dims the moon
                        Friendship Trans. 3.
Many a flower and many a gem,
                        May-Day. 316.
As the best gem upon her zone,
                        Problem. 34.
Living gem of Solomon;
                        Song of Seyd. 10.
A little while each russet gem
                        Woodnotes. II. 53.
Of gem, and air, of plants, and worms.
                        Woodnotes. II. 275.

Gemmed
The hedge is gemmed with diamonds,
                        April. 5.

Gems
And gems from the sea-washed strand,
                        Exile. 14.
Gems in Nature's cabinet;
                        Frag. Nat. XXIII. 4.
What parts, what gems, what colors
shine,—   Frag. Poet. XVIII. 5.
Best gems of Nature's cabinet,
                        May-Day. 394.
A few rods off he deems it gems and
clouds.   Seashore. 46.
Better it is than gems or gold,
                        Thought. 5.

General
The general debility;   Alphonso. 21.
Exchange in conclave general
     Frag. Nat. XXIII. 15.
'Tis because a general hope
     Threnody. 132.

Generates
Life is life which generates,
     Threnody. 244.

Generation
In the sea of generation,   Uriel. 40.

Generative
The miracle of generative force,
     Musketaquid. 62.

Generous
Or was it for mankind a generous shame,
     Adirondacs. 274.
Or strong, or rich, or generous;
     Destiny. 2.
Scott, the delight of generous boys,
     Harp. 81.
What generous beliefs console
     In Memoriam. 86.
And, generous, teach his awkward race
     May-Day. 404.
Was mingled from the generous whole;
     Ode to Beauty. 47.
If once the generous chief arrive
     Voluntaries. 55.

Generously
The hour of heaven. Generously trust
     Rome. 21.

Genesis
A new genesis were here.   Circles. 6.
Sweet the genesis of things,
     Woodnotes. II. 105.

Genial
Thanks if your genial care
     Aeolian Harp. 2.
Cold is genial and dear.
     May-Day. 137.

Genii
Of the Genii be averted!
     Daemonic Love. 63.

Genius
On for a thousand years of genius more.'
     Adirondacs. 329.
Of genius the sterility;   Alphonso. 22.
After their own genius, clearly,
     Celestial Love. 122.
To and fro the Genius hies,—
     Daemonic Love. 35.
Brings book, or starbright scroll of
genius,   Day's Ration. 21.
When they with torch of genius pierce
     Dull. 11.
The Genius from its cloudy throne.
     Fate. 12.
Is the same Genius that creates.
     Fate. 16.
To and fro the Genius flies,
     Frag. Life. XVI. 1.
Comes the Genius,—all's forgot,
     Frag. Life. XVI. 7.
Him strong Genius urged to roam,
     Frag. Life. XX. 1.
What prayers and dreams of youthful
genius feign,   Frag. Nat. V. 2.
Pale genius roves alone,
     Frag. Poet. VI. 1.

For Genius made his cabin wide,
     Frag. Poet. XX. 1.
And Genius unspheres all souls that
abide.   Frag. Poet. XXI. 2.
It seemed his Genius discreet   Guy. 25.
Since genius too has bound and term,
     Harp. 74.
With grace, with genius, well attired,
     Harp. 116.
But sceptred genius, aye inorbed,
     Hermione. 10.
His genius beamed with joy again.
     In Memoriam. 104.
That Genius goes and Folly stays.
     In Memoriam. 110.
The summer dells, by genius haunted,
     May-Day. 43.
Thy genius, wiles and blandishment?
     May-Day. 432.
Are touched with genius. Yonder ragged
cliff   Musketaquid. 24.
The child of genius sits forlorn:
     Poet. 182.
Which, for the Genius that there strove,
     Poet. 197.
For still the craft of genius is
     Quat. Poet. 2. 3.
England's genius filled all measure
     Solution. 35.
A genius of so fine a strain,
     Threnody. 141.
Nor see the genius of the whole
     Threnody. 251.
When the genius of God doth flow;
     Woodnotes. I. 97.
Of Genius sire and son.   World-Soul. 84.

Gentian
Orchis and gentian, fern and long whip-
scirpus,   Adirondacs. 142.
To the gentian in the fall,
     Ellen South. 31.

Gentilesse
And etiquette of gentilesse.
     Frag. Poet. I. 30.

Gentle
For gentle harp to gentle hearts
     Aeolian Harp. 12.
Alive to gentle influence   Culture. 5.
A gentle wife, but fairy none.   Each. 36.
And gives persuasion to a gentle deed.
     Enchanter. 15.
Under gentle types, my Spring
     May-Day. 457.
'Gentle pilgrim, if thou know
     Monadnoc. 219.
And for the whole. The gentle deities
     Musketaquid. 59.
'O gentle Saadi, listen not,   Saadi. 87.
Gentle Saadi, mind thy rhyme;
     Saadi. 101.
So gentle, wise and grave, Threnody. 45.
So the gentle poet's name   Una. 21.

Gentlemen!
Look to yourselves, ye polished gentlemen!   Adirondacs. 91.

Gentler
Gentler far than falls the snow
     Poet. 253.

Gentlest
Grafts gentlest scion
     Channing Ode. 88.

Gentlest guardians marked serene
Threnody. 54.

Gently
Bid Time and Nature gently spare
C. Hymn. 15.

Genuine
Self-centred; when he launched the genuine word
Phi. 19.

George
Bad news from George on the English throne;
Boston. 63.

German
English, German, Basque, Castilian,
Woodnotes. II. 151.

German's
And the German's inward sight.
Monadnoc. 302.

Germs
And,—fault of novel germs,—
Terminus. 21.

Get
Go, get them where he earned them when alive:
To J. W. 16.

Getting
'Tis the poor man getting siller,
Riches. 3.

Ghastly
By Fancy, ghastly spells undid.
May-Day. 46.

Ghost
Were tenanted by thy sweet ghost,
Lines. 4.
One accent of the Holy Ghost
Problem. 61.

Ghosts
The plain was full of ghosts; Dirge. 14.
The piny hosts were sheeted ghosts
May-Day. 49.
O doleful ghosts, and goblins merry!
Mithridates. 25.
The plain was full of ghosts: Peter. 10.
All are ghosts beside. Voluntaries. 122.

Giant
At the first mounting of the giant stairs.
Adirondacs. 63.
Mind wakes a new-born giant from her sleep.
Adirondacs. 327.
Strong as giant, slow as child.
Monadnoc. 132.
Tighter wind the giant coils.
Nemesis. 16.

Giant's
Karnak and Pyramid and Giant's Stairs
Seashore. 15.

Giaours
What are Moslems? what are Giaours?
Song of Seyd. 27.

Gibbous
The sportive sun, the gibbous moon,
Song of Nature. 3.

Giddy
Giddy with day, to the topmost spire,
May-Day. 232.
Giddy with motion Nature reels,
Poet. 172.
Whose giddy top the morning loved to gild.
Woodnotes. I. 79.

Gift
'I will have a purer gift;
Celestial Love. 2.

If thou pine for another's gift?
Destiny. 17.
For Fancy's gift Frag. Poet. IX. 1.
Gift too precious to be prayed,
Freedom. 8.
'Whether is better, the gift or the donor?
Woodnotes. II. 5.

Gifted
But gifted yet to know Dull. 2.

Gifts
To each they offer gifts after his will,
Days. 5.
But what is gold for, but for gifts?
Exile. 17.
And gifts awake when givers sleep,
Frag. Life. VII. 2.
Gifts of one who loved me,— Gifts. 1.
That seeth as God seeth. These are their gifts,
Good Cheer. 12.
With shining gifts that took all eyes,
In Memoriam. 62.
The gate of gifts behind him closed.
Quat. Horoscope. 4.
Rich are the sea-gods:—who gives gifts but they?
Seashore. 27.
And know my higher gifts unbind
Threnody. 230.
Why did all manly gifts in Webster fail?
Webster, 1854. 1.
He has his way, and deals his gifts,—
World-Soul. 79.

Gild
Whose giddy top the morning loved to gild.
Woodnotes. I. 79.

Gilds
Gilds a few points Naples. 4.

Gill
Rue, cinquefoil, gill, vervain and agrimony,
Blight. 5.

Girding
See Globe-girding.

Girds
Girds the world with bound and term;
Celestial Love. 37.
Yon broidered zodiac girds.
May-Day. 377.
Girds with one flame the countless host,
Problem. 52.
The zone that girds the incarnate mind.
Threnody. 231.

Girl
Or ribbons of a dancing girl
Frag. Nat. XXXII. 3.
And the heart of girl and boy,
Harp. 23.

Girl's
The girl's foot leaves its neater print.
May-Day. 62.

Girls
Pale Northern girls! you scorn our race;
Romany. 5.

Girt
Girt in by mountain walls
Mountain. 8.

Girth
was fifteen feet in girth, Adirondacs. 42.

Give
'I give my darling son, Thou shalt not preach';—
Adakryn. 2.
Unbind and give me to the air.
Aeolian Harp. 3.

Give —*Continued*
Give me to the atmosphere,—
         Aeolian Harp. 8.
Give me an amulet   Amulet. 5.
Give to barrows, trays and pans   Art. 1.
Give me of the true,—   Bacchus. 14.
Give them again to shine;   Bacchus. 58.
Give me truths;   Blight. 1.
O North! give him beauty for rags,
         Boston Hymn. 73.
They give and take no pledge or oath,—
         Celestial Love. 85.
That can give us a glimpse of the battle
         Cosmos. 15.
Asks nought his brother cannot give;
         Frag. Life. XVII. 2.
The flowing conditions of life, give way.
         Frag. Life. XXXI. 4.
And only sees what he doth give.
         Frag. Poet. XXVIII. 9.
Give the gem which dims the moon
         Friendship Trans. 3.
Give all to love;   Give. 1.
Thyself dost give forever more.
         Hymn. 28.
And grasping give the orbs another
   whirl.   May-Day. 159.
If Nature give me joy again,
         May-Day. 370.
How long the power to give them name
         Merops. 3.
Give me agates for my meat;
         Mithridates. 6.
Give me cantharids to eat;
         Mithridates. 7.
I will give my son to eat
         Monadnoc. 303.
Wilt not give the lips to taste
         Ode to Beauty. 80.
Unmake me quite, or give thyself to me!
         Ode to Beauty. 99.
As clouds give rain to the eastern breeze,
         Poet. 34.
And give to hold an even state,
         Poet. 167.
And soon may give my dust their funeral
   shade.   River. 42.
And give love's scarlet tides to flow,—
         Rubies. 11.
They must give ear,   Saadi. 29.
And give or take the stroke of war,
         Saadi. 109.
They pluck Force thence, and give it to
   the wise.   Seashore. 29.
Bound in by streams which give and take
         Waldeinsamkeit. 7.
I give my rafters to his boat,
         Woodnotes. II. 43.

Given
   See Ungiven.
And if to me it is not given   Dull. 15.
All, all was given, and only health denied.
         In Memoriam. 72.
And the god, having given all,
         Rhea. 74.

Giver
   See Joy-giver.
Mediator, royal giver;
         Daemonic Love. 75.
Fast abides this constant giver,
         Monadnoc. 40.

Not the less revere the Giver,
         Terminus. 15.
'I am the giver of honor.
         Woodnotes. II. 8.

Givers
And gifts awake when givers sleep,
         Frag. Life. VII. 2.

Gives
The joyful traveller gives, when on the
   verge   Adirondacs. 311.
Nor gives the jealous lord one diamond
   drop   Day's Ration. 24.
Gives beauty to the lake and fountain,
         Enchanter. 8.
And gives persuasion to a gentle deed.
         Enchanter. 15.
Who gives to seas and sunset skies
         Freedom. 13.
Gives the reed and lily length,
         May-Day. 200.
And gives them what to drink and eat;
         Nature. II. 17.
Rich are the sea-gods:—who gives gifts
   but they?   Seashore. 27.
Gives back the bending heavens in dew.
         Song of Nature. 84.
Gives all to them who all renounce.
         Woodnotes. II. 237.
The fourth gives light which eats the
   dark;   Woodnotes. II. 292.

Giveth
Him Nature giveth for defence
         Woodnotes. II. 75.
As he giveth to all to drink,
         Woodnotes. II. 287.

Giving
Swords cannot cut the giving hand
         Frag. Life. VII. 3.
Giving a hint of that which changes not.
         Seashore. 26.

Glaciers
Over the winter glaciers
         World-Soul. 109.

Glad
Greet the glad miracle. Thought's new-
   found path   Adirondacs. 243.
Not glad, as the low-loving herd,
         Celestial Love. 117.
They made the woodlands glad or mad.
         Dirge. 36.
Glad when the solid mountain swims
         Frag. Poet. V. 28.
Sit with the Cause, or grim or glad.
         Frag. Poet. XVII. 2.
See youth's glad mates in earliest
   bloom,—   Harp. 123.
And with glad thoughts of faith and hope
         Hymn. 23.
Are glad to feel the ground.
         May-Day. 282.
In the glad home plain-dealing Nature
   gave.   Musketaquid. 67.
Make him glad thy fall to see!
         Poet. 220.
And a glad delight below,   Security. 2.
Play glad with the breezes, ' Sphinx. 27.
And the glad hey-day of my household
   hours,   Summons. 9.
With glad remembrance of my debt,
         Titmouse. 79.

The woods at heart are glad.
                    Waldeinsamkeit. 20.
Disconcerts with glad surprise.
                    Worship. 18.

Glade
Or down the oaken glade,
                    Waldeinsamkeit. 10.
In the wood he travels glad,
                    Woodnotes. I. 13.
Where darkness found him he lay glad
    at night;   Woodnotes. I. 82.
And in every twinkling glade,
                    Hermione. 53.

Gladiators
Amid the gladiators, halt and numb.'
                    Terminus. 32.

Gladly
Flavor gladly blends with flavor;
                    Merlin. 85.
Will gladly sell ages
                    Frag. Poet. VIII. 4.
Teach him gladly to postpone
                    Frag. Poet. XI. 15.
Ascends as gladly in a single tree
                    Musketaquid. 56.
And Nature gladly gave them place,
                    Problem. 41.
Theme no poet gladly sung,
                    Prudence. 1.
Gladly round that golden lamp
                    Saadi. 37.

Gladness
So in the gladness of the new event
                    Adirondacs. 335.

Glance
And crowds a history into a glance;
                    Enchanter. 7.
Who charm the more their glance for-
    bids,   Eva. 10.
In every glance of Hassan's eye
                    Frag. Poet. III. 5.
I shunned the toiling Hassan's glance."
                    Frag. Poet. III. 12.
To gauge with glance the roaring gulf
    below,   Grace. 6.
The glance that to their glance opposes,
                    Initial Love. 52.
The wise and simple have one glance
                    In Memoriam. 11.
And never poor beseeching glance
                    In Memoriam. 46.
Honor prompted every glance,
                    In Memoriam. 55.
I saw them mask their awful glance
                    May-Day. 324.
Your ne'er averted glance   Poet. 242.
The duration of a glance   Visit. 23.
Can read thy line, can meet thy glance,
                    Woodnotes. II. 141.

Glances
Where their glances meet:
                    Celestial Love. 18.
When thy meteor glances came,
                    Hermione. 37.
Thy dangerous glances
                    Ode to Beauty. 17.
Cast wishful glances at the stars
                    Poet. 191.
Up and down their glances strain.
                    Threnody. 81.

Glancing
Jealous glancing around,   Sphinx. 54.

Glare
And, seeing his eye glare,
                    Daemonic Love. 107.

Glass
    See Looking-glass.
Shiver the palaces of glass;
                    Daemonic Love. 119.
And breaks the glass of Time.
                    Frag. Nat. XXV. 4.
I look at my face in the glass,—
                    Park. 7.
As if the dust were glass and steel.
                    Poet. 6.
But without glass we fathom you.
                    Romany. 28.
Can find with glass in ten times ten.
                    Walk. 8.
Was burnished to a floor of glass,
                    Woodnotes. I. 109.

Glassy
And the glassy surface in ripples brake
                    Frag. Poet. I. 37.

Gleam
A gleam which plays and hovers
                    Daemonic Love. 36.
In silver lakes that unexhausted gleam
                    Frag. Nat. IV. 10.
A gleam of sun, a summer rain,
                    Frag. Nat. XXVIII. 3.
Or gleam which use can paint on steel,
                    Frag. Poet. I. 24.
No darkness stains its equal gleam,
                    Two Rivers. 19.

Gleamed
Through files of flags that gleamed like
    bayonets,   Adirondacs. 17.
The winding Concord gleamed below,
                    Dirge. 17.

Gleaming
Hid in gleaming piles of stone;
                    Art. 4.
But hovered gleaming and was gone.
                    Beauty. 4.
By lake and stream and gleaming hall
                    Frag. Poet. I. 15.

Gleams
We will mark the leaps and gleams
                    May-Day. 228.
I see the scattered gleams,   Poet. 98.
The sunset gleams his smile.
                    Song of Nature. 40.

Glean
What sheaves like those which here we
    glean and bind   Monadnoc. 356.

Glebe
The glebe tilled,   Channing Ode. 63.

Glee
Hearkens for the choral glee,
                    May-Day. 84.

Glen
That I walk alone in grove and glen;
                    Apology. 2.
The wizard South blew down the glen,
                    Frag. Nat. III. 12.

Glide
Pleased with these grand companions,
    we glide on,   Adirondacs. 12.
Glide its hours uncounted,—   Sphinx. 43.

Glides
I shall pass, as glides my shadow
          Monadnoc. 264.
Far seen, the river glides below,
          Peter. 37.

Gliding
Thee gliding through the sea of form,
          Ode to Beauty. 68.

Glimmer
Grace and glimmer of romance;
          Art. 2.

Glimmering
His city-tops a glimmering haze.
          Monadnoc. 323.

Glimpse
That can give us a glimpse of the battle
          Cosmos. 15.

Glitter
The frost might glitter, it would blight
no crop,   Adirondacs. 68.

Glittered
Glittered with silver
          Frag. Nat. XXVII. 4.
The constellation glittered soon,—
          Poet. 230.

Glittering
Glittering twins and trines.   Merlin. 95.
And hemmed me in their glittering troop.
          Poet. 148.

Globe
And round the globe your voices reach.
          Boston. 111.
Halved and dealt the globe anew,
          Solution. 64.
Thou seek'st in globe and galaxy,
          Woodnotes. II. 309.

Globe-girding
Link in the Alps' globe-girding chain;
          Monadnoc. 85.

Globes
I tire of globes and races,
          Song of Nature. 53.

Gloom
That broke the gloom of night!
          *Farewell. 4.
yet ominous with gloom.
          Frag. Nat. XXVII. 5.
Hermit vowed to books and gloom,—
          Hermione. 34.
'Through all time, in light, in gloom
          Monadnoc. 266.
And guessed within the thicket's gloom,
          Woodnotes. I. 59.

Glories
'Mid all the hints and glories of the
home.   Adirondacs. 190.
June's glories and September's
          Ellen South. 27.

Glorified
Crowns him victor glorified,
          Voluntaries. 104.

Glorious
A clear and glorious firmament
          Frag. Nat. XXVI. 28.
But he, the man-child glorious,—
          Song of Nature. 37.
It whispers of the glorious gods,
          World-Soul. 43.

Glory
Which in turn thy glory warms!
          Ode to Beauty. 24.
I hide in the solar glory,
          Song of Nature. 5.
With firmer glory fell.
          Song of Nature. 20.

Gloves
Not with scarfs or perfumed gloves
          Celestial Love. 99.

Glow
     See Bosom-glow.
His planted isle where roses glow?
          Chartist. 12.
On windy hills, whose tops with morning
glow,   I Bear. 7.
Mix polar night with tropic glow,
          May-Day. 127.
Fanning secret fires which glow
          May-Day. 251.
Or if yon realms in sunset glow
          May-Day. 361.
He cools the present's fiery glow,
          Monadnoc. 157.
Bids for me her bosom glow.
          Security. 4.
As the rich aloes flames, I glow,
          Song of Seyd. 17.
But thought will glow when the sun
grows cold,   Thought. 7.
The morrow dawned with needless glow;
          Threnody. 104.
Will thy clear blue eye, upward bent,
still keep its chastened glow,
          *Violet. 3.
In summer's scorching glow.
          Woodnotes. II. 12.
I see the summer glow,
          World-Soul. 110.

Glowed
Glowed unexhausted kindliness,
          Friendship. 7.
I said to heaven that glowed above,
          From Hafiz. 1.
To search where now thy beauty glowed,
          Lines. 21.
Each color with its counter glowed;
          Merlin. 82.
'You have no lapse; so have ye glowed
          Poet. 231.
When every morn my bosom glowed
          Threnody. 60.

Glowing
     See Chaste-glowing.
The rainbow hours bedeck his glowing
chair,   Adirondacs. 226.
O glowing friend,   Channing Ode. 37.
In vain: the stars are glowing wheels,
          Poet. 171.
Yet whirl the glowing wheels once more,
          Song of Nature. 73.
Fate's glowing revolution pause?
          Threnody. 227.
Or trundle on the glowing rail, Una. 18.
The glowing angel, the outcast corse.
          Woodnotes. II. 306.

Glows
Glows the feud of Want and Have.
          II. Compensation. 6.
And whatever glows or seems
          Frag. Poet. VIII. 9.
Not only where the rainbow glows,
          Music. 9.

Self-kindled every atom glows
Nature. Mot. 15.
This vault which glows immense with
light   Woodnotes. II. 299.

Gnawed
Since the world was, he has gnawed;
Limits. 3.

Go
See Forego.
Seeing Nature go astern.   Alphonso. 2.
I go to the god of the wood   Apology. 3.
I saw men go up and down,   Astraea. 9.
Go, cut down trees in the forest
Boston Hymn. 33.
Go, without check or intervals,
Celestial Love. 24.
Lands and goods go to the strong.
Celestial Love. 76.
Go, blindworm, go,   Channing Ode. 15.
Go put your creed into your deed,
Concord Ode. 19.
Her fiery errands go.   Concord Ode. 36.
And they that swiftly come and go
Daemonic Love. 41.
Thy heart saith, 'Brother, go thy ways!
Destiny. 21.
'Go, lonely man,' it saith;   Dirge. 49.
That God has cherubim who go   Dull. 3.
Go then, sad youth, and shine;
Fame. 25.
Go, sacrifice to Fame;   Fame. 26.
Go and come   Frag. Life. VIII. 3.
Go if thou wilt, ambrosial flower,
Frag. Life. XXV. 1.
Go match thee with thy seeming peers;
Frag. Life. XXV. 2.
If thou go in thine own likeness,
Frag. Life. XXVII. 7.
If thou go as thy father's son,
Frag. Life. XXVII. 9.
Go, speed the stars of Thought
Frag. Poet. VI. 9.
And go find thee in the sphere.
From Hafiz. 16.
Go thy ways now, come later back,
Garden. 59.
When half-gods go,   Give. 48.
To those who go, and those who come;
Good-Bye. 13.
And misty lowland, where to go for peat.
Hamatreya. 21.
Go, speed the stars of Thought
I. Intellect. 1.
Hand in hand the comrades go
Love and Thought. 5.
He need not go to them, their forms
Manners. 7.
I saw the bud-crowned Spring go forth,
May-Day. 305.
Forms more cheerly live and go,
Merlin. 43.
Solitary fancies go   Merlin. 106.
Let me go where'er I will,   Music. 1.
He cannot go, he cannot stay,
Poet. 84.
I will not go under a wooden roof:
Poet. 143.
Ere ye go to quit me for ever and aye.
Poet. 262.
Go thou to thy learned task,
Quat. Botanist. 1.

Love on his errand bound to go
Quat. Love. 1.
And drives me where I go.
Quat. Northman. 4.
Go, keep your cheek's rose from the
rain,   Romany. 17.
Wormwood,—saying, "Go thy ways;
Saadi. 63.
To distant men, who must go there, or
die.   Seashore. 49.
The King whose meek ambassador I go.
Summons. 24.
Go thou, sweet Heaven, or at thy
pleasure stay!'   Sursum Corda. 9.
And let the world's affairs go by,
Threnody. 47.
Must to the wastes of Nature go,—
Threnody. 131.
Whose streams through Nature circling
go?   Threnody. 239.
Beckon it when to go and come,
Threnody. 253.
House and tenant go to ground,
Threnody. 288.
Go, get them where he earned them
when alive;   To J. W. 16.
But two cannot go abreast,   Unity. 2.
Fleeter far than whirlwinds go,   Visit. 16.
Go where he will, the wise man is at
home,   Woodnotes. I. 92.
And thou,—go burn thy wormy pages,—
Woodnotes. II. 246.
As the sheep go feeding in the waste,
Woodnotes. II. 297.

Goal
That hides from man the mortal goal,
Hymn. 22.
The brave whom Fate denies the goal!
In Memoriam. 87.
In trance upborne past mortal goal
Solution. 45.
At no goal will arrive;   Sphinx. 84.

Goals
On to their shining goals:—
Frag. Poet. VI. 10.
On to their shining goals;—
I. Intellect. 2.

Goats
Roses bleach, the goats are dry,
Alphonso. 13.

Goblin
Musketaquit, a goblin strong,
Two Rivers. 13.

Goblins
Goodfellow, Puck and goblins,   April. 13.
O doleful ghosts, and goblins merry!
Mithridates. 25.

God
See Overgod; Sea-god; Semigod;
Wood-god.
I go to the god of the wood
Apology. 3.
To house of God and heavenly joys
Bell. 9.
God with the fathers, so with us,
Boston. 118.
God said, I am tired of kings,
Boston Hymn. 5.
But God said,   Celestial Love. 1.
The God who made New Hampshire
Channing Ode. 24.

God —*Continued*

There's no god dare wrong a worm;
II. Compensation. 20.
Him, radiant, sharpest-sighted god,
Daemonic Love. 70.
Where in bright Art each god and sibyl
dwelt Daemonic Love. 121.
And greeted God with childhood's
psalms. Dirge. 8.
Not unless God made sharp thine ear
Dirge. 45.
That God has cherubim who go Dull. 3.
For God hath writ all dooms magnificent,
Frag. Life. II. 2.
Me for the channel of the rivers of God
Frag. Life. XV. 7.
Whom he uniteth, God installs;
Frag. Life. XVII. 12.
I detected many a god
Frag. Life. XXII. 5.
Pay every debt as if God wrote the bill.
Frag. Life. XXXII. 2.
Made beautiful for God:—
Frag. Nat. III. 7.
But the Stars of God remain.
Frag. Nat. XVI. 2.
Waiting till God create the earth,—
Frag. Nat. XXVI. 15.
By want and pain God screeneth him
Frag. Poet. V. 7.
God only knew how Saadi dined;
Frag. Poet. V. 13.
Wherefor thanks God his daily praise,
Frag. Poet. XI. 2.
For every God Frag. Poet. XV. 1.
God forbid my angry heart
From Hafiz. 11.
And every god,—none did refuse;
Garden. 26.
But it is a god, Give. 15.
A spot that is sacred to thought and God.
Good-Bye. 22.
When man in the bush with God may
meet? Good-Bye. 30.
God hath a select family of sons
Good Cheer. 3.
That seeth as God seeth. These are their
gifts, Good Cheer. 12.
How much, preventing God, how much
I owe Grace. 1.
And God hath built his altar here
Hymn. 5.
Which God in human hearts hath strung.
Hymn. 16.
Please God, I'll wrap me in mine innocence,
I Bear. 13.
Or accuse the god of sport?
Initial Love. 80.
That no god dare say him nay,
Initial Love. 126.
Fronting foes of God and man,
In Memoriam. 41.
And evermore the cruel god
In Memoriam. 58.
Please God, that I would lead?
Letter. 2.
Then would I seek where God might
guide my steps, Letter. 7.
The shafts of the god *Lines. 17.
No inch to the god of day; Merops. 10.

Nay, God is witness, gave the names.
Miracle. 36.
What god is this imperial Heat,
May-Day. 210.
Each star, each god, each grace amain,
May-Day. 333.
All that high God did first create.
May-Day. 442.
Pillar which God aloft had set
Monadnoc. 48.
And like wise God she judges well.
Nature. I. 15.
Though I am weak, yet God, when
prayed, Nun. 5.
On this altar God hath built Nun. 15.
Dread Power, but dear! if God thou be,
Ode to Beauty. 98.
Their dust, pervaded by the nerves of
God, Pan. 6.
I cannot shake off the god; Park. 5.
An embryo god unborn. Poet. 104.
A cripple of God, half true, half
formed, Poet. 185.
He whom God had thus preferred,—
Poet. 201.
God for thy virtue lays a plot:
Prayer. 2.
Himself from God he could not free;
Problem. 22.
And the god, having given all, Rhea. 74.
When a god is once beguiled Rhea. 41.
Our fathers built to God;—
Robbins Hymn. 2.
They live with God; their homes are
dust; Robbins Hymn. 21.
Broods over thee, and as God lives in
heaven, Rome. 25.
God, who gave to him the lyre,
Saadi. 9.
Henceforth, please God, forever I forego
Self-Reliance. 1.
Light-hearted as a bird, and live with
God. Self-Reliance. 3.
The god of bounds, Terminus. 3.
The mystic gulf from God to man?
Threnody. 186.
As God lives, is permanent;
Threnody. 267.
Lost in God, in Godhead found.'
Threnody. 289.
Nor kneels in homage to so mean a God.
To-Day. 14.
God speed the mark! To J. W. 23.
In heaven once eminent, the god
Uriel. 37.
He has avenues to God Voluntaries. 51.
So near is God to man, Voluntaries. 72.
But best befriended of the God
Voluntaries. 83.
God, though he were ten times slain,
Voluntaries. 103.
Like God it unseth me.
Waldeinsamkeit. 4.
What god the element obeyed?
Wealth. 5.
Sure some god his eye enchants:
Woodnotes. I. 11.
When the genius of God doth flow;
Woodnotes. I. 97.
God fills the scrip and canister,
Woodnotes. II. 16.

God hid the whole world in thy heart.
Woodnotes. II. 235.

From the heart of God proceeds,
Woodnotes. II. 264.

And God said, "Throb!" and there was motion Woodnotes. II. 268.

As God and devil; bring them to the mind, Xenophanes. 10.

Godhead

Yet, in the name of Godhead, I
Nun. 3.

That from the Godhead flow,
Robbins Hymn. 18.

Lost in God, in Godhead found.'
Threnody. 289.

"Godhead! all this astronomy,
Woodnotes. II. 205.

From world to world the godhead changes; Woodnotes. II. 296.

God's

Match God's equator with a zone of art,
Adirondacs. 245.

To utter God's infinity, Bohemian. 2.

On God's and Satan's brood, Cupido. 7.

In the core of God's abysm,—
Daemonic Love. 127.

With God's unspared donation;
Day by Day. 4.

From God's adoring lover. Dull. 14.

The beggar begs by God's command,
Frag. Life. VII. 1.

And Time, who keeps God's word, brings on the day Good Cheer. 13.

When the God's will sallies free,
Merlin. 71.

For God's vicegerency and stead?
Monadnoc. 77.

Dealt out with a God's charity.
Mountain. 13.

Lo! the God's love blazes higher,
Song of Seyd. 25.

By God's own light illumined and fore-showed. Woodnotes. I. 95.

Gods

See Half-gods; War-gods; Wind-gods; Wood-gods.

As if associates of the sylvan gods.
Adirondacs. 156.

Eyes of gods! ye must have seen,
Alphonso. 19.

And vex the gods with question pert,
Alphonso. 38.

Men and gods are too extense;
Alphonso. 63.

The vanished gods to me appear;
Brahma. 7.

The strong gods pine for my abode,
Brahma. 13.

The race of gods, Celestial Love. 54.

Men and gods have not outlearned it;
I. Eros. 4.

The seed of gods to die, Fame. 20.

The gods upon their spheres.
Frag. Life. IV. 4.

Why the gods will not appear;
Frag. Life. XXXIII. 5.

And Love led Gods therein to bide.
Frag. Poet. XX. 2.

His eyes detect the Gods concealed
Frag. Poet. XXVII. 3.

Wonderful verse of the gods,
Garden. 41.

Ever the words of the gods resound;
Garden. 45.

The gods arrive. Give. 49.

The counsel of the gods, Harp. 20.

There will I bring my books,—my household gods, Letter. 16.

Of the gods, whereof she is one,—
May-Day. 131.

It was as if the eternal gods,
May-Day. 327.

The gods are blind and lame,
Monadnoc. 349.

Nigh persuading gods to err!
Ode to Beauty. 22.

Not the gods can shake the Past;
Past. 11.

Old gods forsook the skies. Peter. 20.

The gods talk in the breath of the woods, Poet. 73.

'I have supped to-night with gods,
Poet. 142.

Have changed not less the guest of gods;
Poet. 180.

With Gods, with fools, content to live;
Poet. 214.

And the gods from side to side.
Quat. Hush. 4.

But thou shalt do as do the gods
Rhea. 25.

Though thou forget, the gods, secure,
Rhea. 28.

He who loves, of gods or men,
Rhea. 37.

Wisdom of the gods is he,—
Saadi. 35.

That the high gods love tragedy;
Saadi. 73.

That blessed gods in servile masks
Saadi. 175.

What time the gods kept carnival,
Song of Nature. 29.

Seyd overheard the young gods talking; Uriel. 8.

And the gods shook, they knew not why.
Uriel. 56.

Speak it firmly, these are gods,
Voluntaries. 121.

The gray old gods whom Chaos knew,
Waldeinsamkeit. 35.

It whispers of the glorious gods,
World-Soul. 43.

For gods delight in gods,
World-Soul. 93.

Goes

Goes home loaded with a thought.
Apology. 12.

He goes in pawn to his victim
Boston Hymn. 63.

Goes light the nimble zephyr;
Ellen South. 10.

Where he goes, goes before him Fate;
Frag. Life. XVII. 10.

And when he goes he carries
Frag. Poet. XXXIII. 3.

The world uncertain comes and goes;
Friendship. 3.

He spreads his welcome where he goes,
Initial Love. 76.

Goes—*Continued*

For Cupid goes behind all law,
                    Initial Love. 120.
That Genius goes and Folly stays.
                    In Memoriam. 110.
The youth sees omens where he goes,
                    May-Day. 73.
Goes like bullet to its mark;
                    Monadnoc. 190.
Goes loaded with a free perfume
                    Mountain. 12.
The eye reads omens where it goes,
                    Nature. Mot. 3.
The day goes drudging through the
    while,   Nun. 2.
The sun goes down, and with him takes
                    Romany. 1.
I think no virtue goes with size;
                    Titmouse. 60.
The stream I love unbounded goes
                    Two Rivers. 6.
He goes to the river-side,—
                    Woodnotes. I. 7.
He goes to my savage haunts,
                    Woodnotes. II. 26.

Goethe

Goethe, raised o'er joy and strife,
                    Solution. 65.

Going

But now, proud world! I'm going home.
                    Good-Bye. 6.
Good-bye, proud world! I'm going home:
                    Good-Bye. 1. 14.
I am going to my own hearth-stone,
                    Good-Bye. 15.
Stand not, pause not, in my going.
                    Song of Seyd. 20.

Gold

Through scented banks of lilies white
    and gold,   Adirondacs. 19.
Found ten years since the California
    gold?   Adirondacs. 280.
Not to scatter bread and gold,
                    Celestial Love. 125.
Brought the Age of Gold again:
                    Character. 8.
Of the unfading gold of Heaven
                    Dull. 17.
But what is gold *for*, but for gifts?
                    Exile. 17.
Nor land, nor gold, nor power,
                    Frag. Poet. VI. 6.
He gold or jewel could not lose,
                    Guy. 15.
From plum-trees vegetable gold;
                    Guy. 44.
More dear to one than mines of gold.
                    Holidays. 12.
Grains beyond the price of gold.
                    May-Day. 274.
Ponderous gold and stuffs to bear,
                    Merlin's Song. 26.
There's a berry blue and gold,—
                    Monadnoc. 297.
through tents of gold,   October. 6.
Your gold makes you seem wise;
                    Park. 10.
Gold and iron are good   Politics. 1.
To buy iron and gold;   Politics. 2.
In groves of oak, or fanes of gold,
                    Problem. 58.

Better it is than gems or gold,
                    Thought. 5.
Not of adamant and gold
                    Threnody. 272.
Copper and iron, lead and gold?
                    Wealth. 21.
But if with gold she bind her hair,
                    Woodnotes. II. 85.

Golden

Nevada! coin thy golden crags
                    Boston Hymn. 75.
Still keeps that golden day   Cosmos. 26.
With a face of golden pleasure
                    Frag. Nat. XXIV. 11.
Golden curls, and quiver and bow.
                    Initial Love. 5.
Build this golden portal;   Manners. 2.
The turtle brave in his golden spots;
                    May-Day. 238.
His feet were shod with golden bells,
                    Poet. 4.
The younger *Golden Lips* or mines,
                    Problem. 67.
Gladly round that golden lamp
                    Saadi. 37.
Who can turn the golden rhyme.
                    Saadi. 114.
Ere wheat can wave its golden pride.
                    Wealth. 17.

Goldenrod

With the social goldenrod,
                    Frag. Nat. III. 5.

Gold-moth-haunted

Through gold-moth-haunted beds of
    pickerel-flower,   Adirondacs. 18.

Gone

But hovered gleaming and was gone.
                    Beauty. 4.
When, like our sires, our sons are gone.
                    C. Hymn. 12.
The aroma of my life is gone
                    Days Pass. 3.
But they are gone,—the holy ones
                    Dirge. 21.
The key is gone with them;   Dirge. 58.
And all but deathless Reason gone.
                    Ellen. 12.
Wished to stay, and is gone,
                    Hamatreya. 56.
When forests fall, and man is gone,
                    Monadnoc. 213.
But the deep-eyed boy is gone.
                    Threnody. 97.
There will be nought to shelter thee
    when their sweet leaves are gone.
                    *Violet. 8.

Good

    See All-good.

And, without Jove, the good had never
    been.   Adirondacs. 291.
The ill I shun, the good I claim;
                    Angelo. 7.
And good men thought thy sacred voice
                    Bell. 11.
The good town on the bay,
                    Boston. 42.
The mountains said, 'Good-day!
                    Boston. 50.
'Not so,' said Boston, 'good my lord,
                    Boston. 69.

Through good and ill the war-bolt hurled,   Boston. 98.
To the good an equal friend.   Boston. 115.
His proper good to flow: Boston Hymn. 58.
But thou, meek lover of the good!   Brahma. 15.
Where good and ill,   Celestial Love. 39.
And every fair and every good,   Celestial Love. 50.
The good applaud, the lost are eased.   Celestial Love. 114.
To make his bosom-counsel good.   Celestial Love. 130.
Wherefore? to what good end?   Channing Ode. 40.
The evil and the good.   Cupido. 10.
Creating fair and good alway,   Day by Day. 7.
All good creatures have their home.   Dearest. 4.
One thing is forever good;   Destiny. 45.
My good, my noble, in their prime,   Dirge. 25.
Nothing is fair or good alone.   Each. 12.
Too kind, too good to me;   Farewell. 20.
Parks and ponds are good by day;   Frag. Nat. XVIII. 1.
I share the good with every flower,   Frag. Nat. XXVI. 30.
A good in Nature not allowed   Frag. Poet. VII. 15.
That book is good   Frag. Poet. XVIII. 1.
Be of good cheer, brave spirit; steadfastly   Good Cheer. 1.
'Tis good, when you have crossed the sea and back,   Hamatreya. 23.
And his good is evil-spoken.   Initial Love. 93.
Consist with homage to the good   In Memoriam. 36.
With good according to its mind,   May-Day. 284.
With good agreeing with its fate,   May-Day. 286.
Step by step, lifts bad to good,   May-Day. 464.
Good men it will calm and cheer,   Merlin's Song. 6.
Men wait their good and truth to borrow.   Merlin's Song. 21.
Tall and good my kind among;   Monadnoc. 257.
And imagest the stable good   Monadnoc. 387.
She is gamesome and good,   Nature. II. 1.
All that's good and great with thee   Ode to Beauty. 82.
Leads all souls to the Good.   Park. 16.
That field by spirits bad and good,   Peter. 5.
Than he to common sense and common good: Phi. 14.
He bridged the gulf from th' alway good and wise   Phi. 17.
Eager for good, not hating ill,   Poet. 208.

The good, the bad with equal zeal,   Poet. 211.
As fleet his feet, his hands as good,   Poet. 295.
Gold and iron are good   Politics. 1.
And whether formed for good or ill,   Prayer. 7.
I would not the good bishop be.   Problem. 72.
All grace, all good his great heart knows,   Rhea. 55.
Not for a private good,   Rhea. 60.
One sallow horseman knows me good.   Romany. 16.
Good Saadi dwells alone.   Saadi. 33.
Nor mount, nor dive; all good things keep   Saadi. 145.
The flood of truth, the flood of good,   Saadi. 161.
My oldest force is good as new,   Song of Nature. 82.
As if it said, 'Good day, good sir!   Titmouse. 29.
'Tis good will makes intelligence,   Titmouse. 65.
The bounds of good and ill were rent;   Uriel. 32.
Or out of the good of evil born,   Uriel. 53.
And the unimagined good of men   World-Soul. 103.

Good-bye
Good-bye to Flattery's fawning face;   Good-Bye. 7.
Good-bye, proud world! I'm going home: Good-Bye. 1. 14.

Good-fame
Estate, good-fame,   Give. 4.

Goodfellow
Goodfellow, Puck and goblins,   April. 13.

Goodly
He left, though goodly centuries old,   Frag. Nat. VI. 7.

Goodness
Came a beam of goodness down   Caritas. 3.

Goods
I will divide my goods;   Boston Hymn. 25.
Lands and goods go to the strong.   Celestial Love. 76.
Goods and raiment bought and sold;   Celestial Love. 126.
What all the goods thy pride which lift,   Destiny. 16.
That of goods I could not miss   Frag. Poet. IV. 8.
Flee from the goods which from thee flee;   Saadi. 143.

Good-will
Right good-will my sinews strung,   Forerunners. 6.

Gordian
The Gordian noose was still untied.   Frag. Nat. VI. 6.

Gorge
Or harebell nodding in the gorge of falls.   Adirondacs. 145.

Gossamer
Sidewise meek in gossamer lids;
                    May-Day. 325.
Gossips
Thy gossips spread each whisper,
                    Quat. Hush. 3.
Foolish gossips, ancient drones,
                    Saadi. 170.
Got
The eloquence of truth, the wisdom got
                    Good Cheer. 10.
Gotten
That wisdom might in youth be gotten,
                    Fame. 5.
'Tis the poor man gotten rich,
                    Riches. 7.
Govern
Can govern the land and sea
                    Boston Hymn. 46.
Government
    See Self-government.
Governors
We pay your governors here
                    Boston. 70.
Gown
Was it a college pique of town and
    gown,   Adirondacs. 277.
To court and mart, to gown and town.
                    Solution. 68.
Grace
Fit to grace the solar year.
                    Alphonso. 82.
Grace and glimmer of romance;
                    Art. 2.
So sweet to Seyd as only grace
                    Beauty. 2.
And the lustre and the grace
                    Daemonic Love. 30.
And princes offer me grace   Exile. 15.
But over all his crowning grace,
                    Frag. Poet. XI. 1.
And a more excelling grace
                    Frag. Poet. XI. 9.
Stealing grace from all alive;
                    Give. 46.
With grace, with genius, well attired,
                    Harp. 116.
Might grace the dust that is most proud.
                    In Memoriam. 20.
Of the grace that on him shone,
                    In Memoriam. 51.
With grace to win, with heart to hold,
                    In Memoriam. 61.
Grace, Beauty and Caprice   Manners. 1.
The love of kind, the joy, the grace,
                    May-Day. 265.
Each star, each god, each grace amain,
                    May-Day. 333.
Courage and probity and grace!
                    May-Day. 405.
Hint summits of heroic grace;
                    Monadnoc. 111.
Than all the grace Love ever saw;
                    Poet. 282.
All grace, all good his great heart knows,
                    Rhea. 55.
That waft the breath of grace divine
                    Voluntaries. 69.
Will swell and rise with wonted grace;
                    Woodnotes. II. 54.

From these companions, power and
    grace.   Woodnotes. II. 62.
Graced
Graced by each change of sum untold,
                    Monadnoc. 56.
Graceful
The lover watched his graceful maid,
                    Each. 29.
How graceful climb those shadows on
    my hill!   Hamatreya. 7.
Graceful women, chosen men,
                    Manners. 3.
Graces
Graces of a subtler strain,
                    Daemonic Love. 57.
I detect far-wandered graces,
                    Ode to Beauty. 65.
Gracing
Gracing the rich man's wood and lake,
                    Chartist. 9.
Gracious
By signs gracious as rainbows.
                    Forerunners. 34.
With light that streams from gracious
    eyes.   Frag. Poet. VII. 6.
Half so gracious ever shone,
                    On Prince. 2.
The gracious boy, who did adorn
                    Threnody. 17.
Graded
The steep be graded,
                    Channing Ode. 59.
Grafts
Grafts gentlest scion
                    Channing Ode. 88.
In thousand far-transplanted grafts
                    Promise. 3.
Grain
It fell in rain, it grew in grain,
                    Frag. Poet. IV. 27.
Arrived in time to swell his grain;
                    Guy. 34.
They set the wind to winnow pulse and
    grain,   Musketaquid. 42.
My swarthy tint is in the grain,
                    Romany. 19.
There's not a blade of autumn grain,
                    Threnody. 111.
Of fruitful worlds the grain,
                    Waldeinsamkeit. 22.
Grains
Grains beyond the price of gold.
                    May-Day. 274.
Grand
Pleased with these grand companions,
    we glide on,   Adirondacs. 12.
Ah, but I miss the grand design.
                    Frag. Poet. XVIII. 6.
Or teach thou, Spring! the grand recoil
                    Harp. 125.
The grand return   In Memoriam. 16.
Or Duty to grand purpose wrought.
                    Miracle. 14.
Thou grand affirmer of the present tense,
                    Monadnoc. 359.
Which holds the grand designs
                    Ode to Beauty. 53.
Grander
A door to something grander,—
                    Frag. Nat. XII. 3.

And, pregnant with his grander thought,
Threnody. 144.

Grandest
He wrote on Nature's grandest brow, *For Sale.* Webster, 1854. 2.

Grandeur
To Grandeur with his wise grimace;
Good-Bye. 8.
To parting soul bring grandeur near.
May-Day. 456.
Grandeur of the perfect sphere
Prudence. 5.
So nigh is grandeur to our dust,
Voluntaries. 71.

Granite
The durance of a granite ledge.
Astraea. 37.
And, credulous, through the granite seeming, Monadnoc. 235.
Bead-eyes my granite chaos show,
Monadnoc. 317.
And Nile substructs her granite base,—
Solution. 10.
Of granite, marl and shell.
Song of Nature. 36.
The granite slab to clothe and hide,
Wealth. 16.
Through beds of granite cut my road,
Woodnotes. I. 127.

Granite-ledge
We must have clay, lime, gravel, granite-ledge, Hamatreya. 20.

Grant
We grant no dukedoms to the few,
Boston. 25.
And grant to dwellers with the pine
Woodnotes. II. 47.

Granted
The prairie granted,
Channing Ode. 64.
Content that all we asked was granted?
Fame. 18.
And granted me the freedom of their state, Musketaquid. 5.
Hath granted his throne?
Ode to Beauty. 36.
And granted them an equal date
Problem. 43.

Grants
Fate grants each to stand aside;
Holidays. 18.
Space grants beyond his fated road
Merops. 9.

Grape
In the belly of the grape, Bacchus. 2.
And the grape requite the lote!
Bacchus. 54.
Every shrub and grape leaf
Frag. Nat. III. 24.

Grapes
See River-grapes.
Let its grapes the morn salute
Bacchus. 6.
From ferns and grapes and from the folded flowers Frag. Nat. XXVII. 7.
When trellised grapes their flowers unmask, May-Day. 87.

Grapevine
Grapevine and succory, Frag. Nat. II. 3.

Grasp
Grasp the felloes of her wheel,
May-Day. 158.

Grasping
And grasping give the orbs another whirl.
May-Day. 159.

Grass
See Herds—grass.
And the poor grass shall plot and plan
Bacchus. 41.
The green grass is bowing,
Ellen South. 1.
His great body in the grass,
Frag. Nat. I. 8.
Grass with green flag half-mast high,
Frag. Nat. II. 7.
Sweet fern, mint and vernal grass,
Frag. Nat. II. 14.
Cinquefoils or violets in the grass,
Frag. Poet. XXVIII. 5.
Grass with green flag half-mast high,
Humble-Bee. 44.
plant dials in the grass, Letter. 20.
The green grass is a looking-glass
Manners. 11.
While the grass beneath the rime
May-Day. 119.
These temples grew as grows the grass;
Problem. 45.
The stream, the trees, the grass, the sighing wind, River. 28.
Flowering grass and scented weeds;
Threnody. 275.
Fate's grass grows rank in valley clods,
Voluntaries. 119.
Beneath the grass that shades the rill,
Woodnotes. I. 39.
The wide lake, edged with sand and grass, Woodnotes. I. 108.
The lord is hay, the peasant grass,
Woodnotes. II. 20.
Yesterday was a bundle of grass.
Woodnotes. II. 277.

Grass-buds
Grass-buds and caterpillar-shrouds,
Woodnotes. I. 19.

Grasses
And what the whispering grasses smother. Garden. 32.

Grassy
Winding through grassy shallows in and out, Adirondacs. 23.

Grateful
See Ungrateful.
In heaven are kept their grateful vows,
Robbins Hymn. 3.
I travelled grateful by their side,
Woodnotes. I. 123.

Grave
Escort us to a little **grave**.
Frag. Life. I. 4.
At court he sat in the **grave** Divan.
Frag. Poet. I. 10.
Instant to my grave I stoop,
From Hafiz. 15.
Clear of the grave. Hamatreya. 16.
Like lust in the chill of the grave.
Hamatreya. 63.
To mark the Briton's friendless grave.
In Memoriam. 14.

Grave—*Continued*

And thy grave smiled on by the visiting
moon.   Mountain. 6.
On two days it steads not to run from
thy grave,   On Two Days. 1.
And grave parental love.   River. 30.
So gentle, wise and grave,
                               Threnody. 45.
Grave, chaste, contented, though retired,
                               Woodnotes. II. 69.

Gravel

We must have clay, lime, gravel, granite-
ledge,   Hamatreya. 20.

Gravely

Gravely it broods apart on joy,
                               II Intellect. 1.

Graver

Nor doubt but visitings of graver
thought   Adirondacs. 188.
Higher or graver;   Merlin. 84.

Graves

Set not thy foot on graves;
                               To J. W. 1. 5. 10.

Gravitate

From thy worth and weight the stars
gravitate,   Shah, Enweri. II. 1.

Gray

To ears intelligent; as if gray rock
                               Adirondacs. 253.
A watchman in a dark gray tent,
                               Frag. Nat. XXVI. 14.
The cold gray down upon the quinces
lieth   Frag. Nat. XXXIII. 1.
As Jelaleddin old and gray;
                               Frag. Poet. V. 3.
Than the gray dreams which thee detain.
                               Monadnoc. 18.
And that these gray crags
                               Monadnoc. 231.
"See there the grim gray rounding
                               Monadnoc. 325.
Fronts the north-wind in waistcoat gray,
                               Titmouse. 46.
Why are not diamonds black and gray,
                               Titmouse. 56.
The gray old gods whom Chaos knew,
                               Waldeinsamkeit. 35.

Graybeard

And Ellen, when the graybeard years
                               Ellen. 1.

Gray-haired

Listening to the gray-haired crones,
                               Saadi. 169.

Grazed

Flew near, with soft wing grazed my
hand,   Titmouse. 38.

Grazing

And slough decay from grazing herds,
                               May-Day. 448.
Not lazy grazing on all they saw,
                               Poet. 57.

Great

Big with great news, and shouted the
report   Adirondacs. 237.
The great Idea baffles wit,
                               Bohemian. 7.
Where tyrants great and tyrants small
                               Boston Hymn. 11.
No lineage counted great;
                               Boston Hymn. 30.

From my great arteries,—nor less, nor
more.'   Day's Ration. 5.
Deems not that great Napoleon
                               Each. 6.
To mould his fortunes, means or great:
                               Fate. 2.
His great body in the grass,
                               Frag. Nat. I. 8.
I read great years of victory,
                               Frag. Poet. III. 6.
Chambers of the great are jails,
                               Heroism. 9.
There is no great and no small
                               Informing Spirit. 1.
Great is the art,   Merlin. 27.
Great be the manners, of the bard.
                               Merlin. 28.
Amid great Nature's halls Mountain. 7.
The polie found me impolite; the great
                               Musketaquid. 68.
Whose shining sons, too great for fame,
                               Nun. 45.
All that's good and great with thee
                               Ode to Beauty. 82.
Has drunk the life-blood of the great;
                               Omar. 2.
Brought his great forehead to the council
board,   Phi. 8.
The great stars did not shine aloof,
                               Poet. 146.
And by great sparks Promethean
warmed,   Poet. 186.
Proved Napoleon great,   Politics. 6.
Plotted to make him rich and great:
                               Quat. Horoscope. 2.
All grace, all good his great heart knows,
                               Rhea. 55.
Be great, be true, and all the Scipios,
                               Rome. 4.
'Let the great world bustle on
                               Saadi. 104.
"Out spoke the great mother,
                               Sphinx. 57.
And, as the great all-loving Day
                               Threnody. 217.
In the great woods, on prairie floors.
                               Titmouse. 68.
Great men in the Senate sate,
                               Voluntaries. 23.
There the great Planter plants
                               Waldeinsamkeit. 21.
Three moons his great heart him a her-
mit made,   Woodnotes. I. 84.
The musing peasant, lowly great,
                               Woodnotes. I. 104.
He is great who can live by me:
                               Woodnotes II. 13.
Houses of rich and great,
                               World-Soul. 10.

Greater

A greater spirit bids thee forth
                               Monadnoc. 17.
And when the greater comes again
                               Monadnoc. 262.
For greater need   Saadi. 43.

Greatest

Even at its greatest space is a defeat,
                               Blight. 54.

Great-hearted

Of our great-hearted Doctor in his boat
                               Adirondacs. 272.

Greece
I tread on the pride of Greece and Rome;
Good-Bye. 24.
Flown to Italy from Greece,
Solution. 17.

Greek
Well and wisely said the Greek,
Quat. Pericles. 1.
Forward stepped the perfect Greek:
Solution. 14.

Green
See Wintergreen.
On this green bank, by this soft stream,
C. Hymn. 9.
The green grass is bowing,
Ellen South. 1.
In yon green palmy isle, *Farewell. 50.
Grass with green flag half-mast high,
Frag. Nat. II. 7.
In our green Musketaquid,
Frag. Nat. XXVI. 2.
And all the zone is green again.
Frag. Nat. XXVIII. 4.
He came to the green ocean's brim
Frag. Poet. I. 45.
Bosomed in yon green hills alone,—
Good-Bye. 16.
Where arches green, the livelong day,
Good-Bye. 19.
The green silence dost displace
Humble-Bee. 30.
Grass with green flag half-mast high,
Humble-Bee. 44.
The green grass is a looking-glass
Manners. 11.
The ground-pines wash their rusty green,
May-Day. 59.
The green lane is the school-boy's friend,
May-Day. 67.
Till green lances peering through
May-Day. 123.
Which for a spike of tender green
May-Day. 233.
By houses lies a fresher green,
May-Day. 299.
On carpets green the maskers march
May-Day. 331.
The fields of Thessaly grew green,
Peter. 19.
By green orchard boughs
Politics. 19.
The tall green trees, that shelter thee,
*Violet. 7.
Declares the close of its green century.
Woodnotes. I. 75.
Through these green tents, by eldest
Nature dressed, Woodnotes. I. 80.
Painted with shadows green and proud
Woodnotes. I. 110.

Greenest
A pillow in her greenest field,
Woodnotes. I. 144.

Green-haired
To the green-haired forest free;
World-Soul. 4.

Greenwood
What pranks the greenwood played;
Peter. 22.

Greet
And greet unanimous the joyful change.
Adirondacs. 53.
Greet the glad miracle. Adirondacs. 243.
We greet you well, you Saxon men,
Boston. 51.
To greet you stern head-stone,
In Memoriam. 12.
And duly greet the entering May?
May-Day. 219.
To greet staid ancient cavaliers
May-Day. 307.
I greet with joy the choral trains
May-Day. 392.
I greet my office well, Poet. 115.
And I greet from far the ray, Una. 15.

Greeted
And greeted God with childhood's
psalms. Dirge. 8.
Greeted their safe escape to me.
Each. 23.
Directly never greeted me,
Frag. Poet. IV. 16.
I greeted loud my little savior,
Titmouse. 48.
Yet, greeted in another's eyes,
Worship. 17.

Greeting
Need is none of forms of greeting;
Celestial Love. 94.

Greetings
Greetings kind to each and all,
Frag. Nat. XXIII. 16.

Grew
Luther, Fox, Behmen, Swedenborg, grew
pale, Adakryn. 3.
Five-leaved, three-leaved and two-leaved,
grew thereby. Adirondacs. 41.
Of such delight and wonder as there
grew,— Adirondacs. 250.
Bring me wine, but wine which never
grew Bacchus. 1.
Or grew on vine whose tap-roots, reach-
ing through Bacchus. 3.
All else grew foreign in their light.
Daemonic Love. 18.
Whose balsam never grew. Dirge. 40.
Where the aster grew Frag. Nat. III. 4.
When his ringlets grew and curled,
Frag. Nat. XXXIV 3.
It fell in rain, it grew in grain,
Frag. Poet. IV. 27.
Harvests grew upon his tongue,
Frag. Poet. V. 31.
The fields of Thessaly grew green,
Peter. 19.
The conscious stone to beauty grew.
Problem. 24.
Such and so grew these holy piles,
Problem. 31.
These temples grew as grows the grass;
Problem. 45.
When France, where poet never grew,
Solution. 63.
Where, in far fields, the orchis grew.
Woodnotes. I. 49.

Grief
Its soft leaves wound me with a grief
Dirge. 39.
Dappled with joy and grief and praise,
Frag. Life. I. 2.

Grief —*Continued*

Nor grief untune his voice,   Harp. 6.

They know one only mortal grief
          Love and Thought. 9.

Amid these coward shapes of joy and
grief,   Monadnoc. 362.

One joy it joys, one grief it grieves.
          Monadnoc. 384.

But what torments of grief you endured
          Quat. Borrowing. 3.

Nor skilful by my grief;
          Quat. Climacteric. 2.

Hide thy grief within thy breast,
          Rhea. 11.

Grow early old with grief that thou
          Threnody. 130.

And past the blasphemy of grief,
          Threnody. 204.

They lose their grief who hear his song,
          Two Rivers. 15.

Griefs

As fits the griefs of bards to be.
          Harp. 60.

So only new griefs are consoled
          May-Day. 365.

Washing out harms and griefs from
memory,   Seashore. 24.

Grieve

Though loath to grieve
          Channing Ode. 1.

The southern crocodile would grieve.
          Channing Ode. 31.

I grieve that better souls than mine
          Frag. Poet. VI. 1.

Grieves

He nor repents nor grieves,
          In Memoriam. 93.

One joy it joys, one grief it grieves.
          Monadnoc. 384.

When happy stoic Nature grieves,
          Nun. 12.

Grim

Portly and grim,—   Experience. 5.

Sit with the Cause, or grim or glad.
          Frag. Poet. XVII. 2.

Of grim Disease, that would her peace
affright.   I Bear. 12.

"See there the grim gray rounding
          Monadnoc. 325.

Grimace

To Grandeur with his wise grimace;
          Good-Bye. 8.

Grind

Web to weave, and corn to grind;
          Channing Ode. 49.

But corn of Guy's was there to grind:
          Guy. 36.

Griping

Only what to our griping toil is due;
          Blight. 41.

Grisly

Hunted by Sorrow's grisly train
          In Memoriam. 74.

Groans

Old Europe groans with palaces,
          Boston. 19.

Groined

And groined the aisles of Christian Rome
          Problem. 20.

Groom

See Bridegroom.

If he than his groom be better or worse.
          Fate. 6.

Grooms

In one body grooms and brides;
          Merlin. 89.

Grope

For which we all our lifetime grope,
          Monadnoc. 388.

They grope the sea for pearls, but more
than pearls: Seashore. 28.

Was quenched, and all must doubt and
grope.   Threnody. 133.

Groped

Groped for axle of the world.
          Frag. Nat. XXXIV. 4.

Gropes

Gropes for columns strong as he;
          Frag. Nat. XXXIV. 2.

Gross

Or mired by climate's gross extremes.
          Nun. 36.

Grot

For there's no sequestered grot,
          Astraea. 45.

Grottoes

His quarantines and grottoes, where
          Monadnoc. 160.

Ground

See Hunting-ground; Underground;
Vantage-ground.

Pine-cones and acorns lay on the
ground;   Each. 45.

Saying, 'We have dressed for thee the
ground,   Ellen South. 15.

Who leap from horse to horse, but never
touch the ground.   Frag. Poet. XIX. 2.

An inch of ground the lightning strook
          Frag. Poet. XXXII. 3.

The sympathetic swallow swept the
ground.   Hermione. 7.

It is anchored in the ground.
          Holidays. 8.

What matters how, or from what ground,
          In Memoriam. 111.

Not tamed and cleared cumber the
ground   Letter. 12.

His eyes explore the ground,—
          Manners. 10.

The fresh ground loves his top and ball,
          May-Day. 69.

Are glad to feel the ground.
          May-Day. 282.

Teach thy feet to feel the ground,
          Monadnoc. 22.

Which keeps the ground and never soars,
          Monadnoc. 187.

I know is ground enchanted.   Peter. 8.

Fell unregarded to the ground,
          Poet. 15.

And felt, beneath, the quaking ground;
          Solution. 56.

He poisons the ground.   Sphinx. 56.

And every inch of garden ground
          Threnody. 90.

House and tenant go to ground,
          Threnody. 288.

Leading over heroic ground,
          Voluntaries. 89.

Though thou lie alone on the ground.
                    Woodnotes. II. 88.

Ground-pine
The ground-pine curled its pretty wreath,
                    Each. 41.

Ground-pines
The ground-pines wash their rusty green,
                    May-Day. 59.

Grounds
    See Feeding-grounds; Pleasure-
grounds.
Where are these men? Asleep beneath
    their grounds: Hamatreya. 11.
The morning mist within your grounds
                    Park. 11.
For in those lonely grounds the sun
                    Peter. 13.

Ground-worms'
For the ground-worms' brood
                    Mountain. 5.

Grouse's
The heavy grouse's sudden whir,
                    Harp. 89.
From rabbit's coat or grouse's breast;
                    Quat. Forester. 2.

Grove
    See Orange-grove; Palm-grove;
Pine-grove.
And cedar grove and cliff and lake should
    know   Adirondacs. 254.
That I walk alone in grove and glen;
                    Apology. 2.
He heard, when in the grove, at intervals,
                    Woodnotes. I. 72.

Groves
In fairy groves of herds-grass.
                    Frag. Nat. XXVII. 10.
Whose groves the frolic fairies planned;
                    Good-Bye. 18.
In groves of oak, or fanes of gold,
                    Problem. 58.
Trees in groves,   Saadi. 1.

Grow
And willing grow old
                    Frag. Poet. VIII. 5.
And rank the savage maples grow
                    Garden. 7.
Our towns and races grow and fall,
                    Monadnoc. 386.
For still, where'er the trees grow big-
    gest,   Quat. Artist. 3.
Grow red with joy and white with fear;
                    Saadi. 30.
And earth grow civil, Homer sung.
                    Solution. 16.
Grow early old with grief that thou
                    Threnody. 130.

Growing
There, growing slowly old at ease
                    Aphonso. 77.
Thy sight is growing blear;
                    Sphinx. 106.

Growled
Frowned in my foe and growled in
    storm,   Frag. Poet. IV. 29.

Grown
    See Overgrown.
Now, to a savage selfness grown,
                    Alphonso. 35.

Till the poor is wealthy grown,
                    Etienne. 19.
But if, grown bold, the poet dare
                    Frag. Poet. IV. 3.
The chalk is crimson grown. They. 4.
Or by knowledge grown too bright
                    Uriel. 41.
The rope-like pine-roots crosswise grown
                    Woodnotes. I. 106.

Grows
And the vine that grows thereby?
                    Exile. 4.
Power that by obedience grows,
                    Insight. 1.
Slow grows the palm,   May-Day. 156.
All between that works or grows,
                    Mithridates. 4.
These temples grew as grows the grass;
                    Problem. 45.
Grows by decays,   Spiritual Laws. 7.
But thought will glow when the sun
    grows cold,   Thought. 7.
Fate's grass grows rank in valley clods,
                    Voluntaries. 119.
Self-sown my stately garden grows;
                    Walden. 9.

Growth
    See Overgrowth.
And having thus their bread and growth,
                    Nature. II. 18.
Of Death and Fortune, Growth and
    Strife.'   Woodnotes. II. 32.

Grudge
I grudge not these their bed of death,
                    In Memoriam. 32.

Guard
Fortune was his guard and lover;
                    Guy. 10.
Weapons to guard the State, or scourge
                    In Memoriam. 65.
To guard the babe from fancied foes.
                    Threnody. 69.

Guarded
The Muse's hill by Fear is guarded,
                    Frag. Poet. XXXI. 1.

Guardians
Among the legs of his guardians tall,
                    Experience. 15.
Gentlest guardians marked serene
                    Threnody. 54.

Guards
Tyrants despite their guards or walls.
                    In Memoriam. 66.
So Spring guards with surface cold
                    May-Day. 144.

Guercino
Of Salvator, of Guercino,
                    Ode to Beauty. 54.

Guerdon
Its guerdon in the sky,   Fame. 22.
Day's toil and its guerdon, Illusions. 10.

Guess
High omens ask diviner guess;
                    Threnody. 228.

Guessed
As if one riddle of the Sphinx were
    guessed.   Adirondacs. 343.
Some to see, some to be guessed,
                    Experience. 12.
And guessed within the thicket's gloom,
                    Woodnotes. I. 59.

Guest

Frankly I will be your guest,
                    May-Day. 367.
Guest of million painted forms,
                    Ode to Beauty. 23.
Have changed not less the guest of gods;
                    Poet. 180.
And thoughtest thou such guest
                    Threnody. 224.

Guide

See Misguide.
We chose our boats; each man a boat
    and guide,—   Adirondacs. 5.
At morn or noon, the guide rows bare-
    headed: Adirondacs. 74.
And Stillman, our guides' guide, and
    Commodore,   Adirondacs. 183.
We praise the guide, we praise the forest
    life: Adirondacs. 305.
Guide lovers to the pool.   April. 8.
Thee to guide and to redeem.
                    Celestial Love. 62.
Where'er he went, the magic guide
                    Frag. Poet. I. 17.
Then would I seek where God might
    guide my steps,   Letter. 7.
Show me the forward way, since thou
    art guide,   Unbar. 2.
'You ask,' he said, 'what guide
                    Woodnotes. I. 118.
The watercourses were my guide;
                    Woodnotes. I. 122.

Guided

Spelling with guided tongue man's mes-
    sages   Adirondacs. 269.
When Science armed and guided war,
                    Solution. 61.
By wondrous tongue, and guided pen,
                    Threnody. 136.

Guide's

The oar, the guide's. Dare you accept
    the tasks   Adirondacs. 102.

Guides

Ten men, ten guides,   Adirondacs. 6.
By turns we praised the stature of our
    guides,   Adirondacs. 80.
In winter, lumberers; in summer, guides;
                    Adirondacs. 88.
Long I followed happy guides,
                    Forerunners. 1.

Guides'

our guides' guide,   Adirondacs. 183.

Guiding

Took counsel from his guiding eyes
                    Threnody. 56.

Guile

And say it frankly without guile,
                    Romany. 10.

Guilt

So guilt not traverses his tender will.
                    Frag. Life. II. 3.
I lay my vanity and guilt;   Nun. 16.

Guise

In their own guise,   Experience. 3.
Some figure of noble guise,—
                    World-Soul. 26.

Gulf

To gauge with glance the roaring gulf
    below,   Grace. 6.

He bridged the gulf from th' alway good
    and wise   Phi. 17.
The pits of air, the gulf of space,
                    Song of Nature. 2.
The mystic gulf from God to man?
                    Threnody. 186.

Gulf-encrimsoning

Seethes the gulf-encrimsoning shells,
                    May-Day. 205.

Gulfs

Of gulfs of sweetness without bound
                    Humble-Bee. 36.
Bridge gulfs, drain swamps, build dams
    and mills,   Monadnoc. 150.

Gun

And in the left, a gun, his needful arms.
                    Adirondacs. 79.
Hast thou named all the birds without a
    gun?   Forbearance. 1.
Nor gun nor scythe to see.
                    Woodnotes. I. 10.

Guns

Challenging Echo by our guns and cries;
                    Adirondacs. 113.

Gushed

Gushed with syrup to the brink.
                    May-Day. 341.

Gusts

Sudden gusts came full of meaning,
                    September. 9.

Gusty

Of a gusty Autumn day,
                    September. 2.

Guy

Guy possessed the talisman   Guy. 5.
So did Guy betimes discover   Guy. 9.
Fearless Guy had never foes,   Guy. 17.
To drudge all day for Guy the wise.
                    Guy. 40.
And venture, and to Guy the oil.
                    Guy. 50.

Guy's

But corn of Guy's was there to grind:
                    Guy. 36.

Gymnastic

Shows feats of his gymnastic play,
                    Titmouse. 41.

Gypsies

Then you are Gypsies in a mask,
                    Romany. 11.

Gypsy

Of Gypsy beauty blazes higher.
                    Romany. 4.

Gyration

Whether doomed to long gyration
                    Uriel. 39.

Habits

Thy gait too slow, thy habits tender
                    Woodnotes. II. 187.

Had (Partial list.)

Had won the brightest laurel of all time.
                    Adirondacs. 285.
the good had never been.
                    Adirondacs. 291.
One August evening had a cooler breath;
                    Adirondacs. 331.
Chaucer had no such worthy crew,
                    Adirondacs. Motto. 3.
Had a quarrel,   Fable. 2.

Had reached its fruiting-time,
Frag. Nat. XXI. 8.
For I had too much to think,
Goethe. 5.
I muse what sercet purpose had he
Monadnoc Afar. 7.
His mother died,—the only friend he
had,— Philosopher. 7.
Had active hands and smiling lips;
Saadi. 77.
I had the right, few days ago,
Threnody. 32.
Night came, and Nature had not thee;
Threnody. 102.
If I had not taken the child.
Threnody. 178.
I had as lief respect an ancient shoe,
To-Day. 11.
I had a sister once who seemed just like
a violet; *Violet. 13.
Without better fortune had,
Woodnotes. I. 14.

Hades
Strong Hades could not keep his own,
Uriel. 33.

Hafiz
Hafiz and Shakspeare with their shining
choirs. Adakryn. 5.
Hafiz said he was a fly
Frag. Poet. I. 3.
Thou foolish Hafiz! Say, do churls
Friendship. Trans. 1.
From Hafiz never hides;
Quat. Hafiz. 2.

Hail
See All-hail.

Hails
The home-bound sea-boy hails, Bell. 6.

Hair
And fetch her stars to deck her hair:
Rhea. 52.
For teeth and hair with shopmen deal:
Romany. 18.
But if with gold she bind her hair,
Woodnotes. II. 85.

Haircloth
For haircloth and for bloody whips,
Saadi. 76.

Haired
See Gray-haired; Green-haired.

Half
Half the sun's disk with a spot;
Alphonso. 10.
Half for freedom strike and stand;—
Channing Ode. 96.
And not half so spry. Fable. 14.
Pan, half asleep, rolling over
Frag. Nat. I. 7.
Half so gracious ever shone,
On Prince. 2.
A cripple of God, half true, half formed,
Poet. 185.
Half piled or prostrate; and my newest
slab Seashore. 16.
Half the tell-tale South-wind said,—
September. 14.
O wise man! hear'st thou half it tells?
Woodnotes. II. 101.

Half-climbed
On the half-climed zodiac?
Threnody. 241.

Half-gods
When half-gods go, Give. 48.

Half-mast
Grass with green flag half-mast high,
Frag. Nat. II. 7.
Grass with green flag half-mast high,
Humble-Bee. 44.

Half-repentant
Half-repentant, scant of breath,—
Monadnoc. 316.

Half-seen
Half-seen Una sits beside. Una. 8.

Halfway
And halfway to the mosses brown;
May-Day. 118.

Hall
Let statue, picture, park and hall,
Art. 9.
A cell for prayer, a hall for joy,—
Dirge. 31.
By lake and stream and gleaming hall
Frag. Poet. I. 15.
In the hall at summer eve Harp. 45.
Nor spacious court, nor monarch's hall,
May-Day. 222.
On from hall to chamber ran,
May-Day. 346.
In bower and hall Saadi. 25.
Would in thy hall take up his rest?
Threnody. 225.
How drearily in College hall
Walden. 33.
The shop of toil, the hall of arts;
Wealth. 35.
His hearth the earth,—his hall the azure
dome; Woodnotes. I. 93.
Who liveth in the palace hall
Woodnotes. II. 24.

Halloo
The far halloo of human voice;
May-Day. 76.

Hallow
Hallow these my orchard shades;
Frag. Poet. VII. 4.

Hallows
Peace that hallows rudest ways.
Forerunners. 38.

Halls
See College-halls.
That hurry through the eternal halls,
II Compensation. 10.
And the galleries and halls,
Daemonic Love. 123.
To crowded halls, to court and street;
Good-Bye. 11.
Amid great Nature's halls
Mountain. 7.
Nor Rome, nor joyful Paris, nor the
halls Naples. 17.
From the lighted halls Poet. 226.
You captives of your air-tight halls,
Romany. 6.

Halt
Think me not numbed or halt with age,
Nun. 33.
Amid the gladiators, halt and numb.'
Terminus. 32.

Halt —*Continued*
Speeding Saturn cannot halt;
                        Visit. 27.
We must not halt while fiercely speed
                        Walden. 43.

Halteth
Halteth never in one shape,
                        Woodnotes. II. 272.

Halting
The halting steps of aged Fate.
                        May-Day. 155.
Without halting, without rest,
                        May-Day. 465.

Halts
Which neither halts nor shakes.
                        Boston Hymn. 84.

Halved
Halved and dealt the globe anew,
                        Solution. 64.

Hamlets
In hamlets, palaces and parks,
                        Initial Love. 3.
Many hamlets sought I then,
                        Monadnoc. 127.

Hammer
As with hammer or with mace;
                        Merlin. 11.
With hammer soft as snowflake's
flight;—   Monadnoc. 240.
I with my hammer pounding evermore
                        Seashore. 34.

Hammered
Loud hammered, and the heron rose in
the swamp.   Adirondacs. 148.

Hampshire
   See New Hampshire.

Hand
A paddle in the right hand, or an oar,
                        Adirondacs. 78.
'T was always thus, and will be; hand
and head   Adirondacs. 286.
On the piano, played with master's hand.
                        Adirondacs. 314.
Only the hand secure and bold
                        Angelo. 4.
Every aster in my hand   Apology. 11.
And prizes of ambition, checks its hand,
                        Blight. 59.
Free be his heart and hand henceforth
                        Boston Hymn. 55.
And with hand and body and blood,
                        Celestial Love. 129.
See rights for which the one hand fights
                        Concord Ode. 23.
Him by the hand dear Nature took,
                        Experience. 17.
Swords cannot cut the giving hand
                        Frag. Life. VII. 3.
I took the friendly noble by the hand,
                        Frag. Life. XXX. 3.
I armed his hand with skill,
                        Frag. Poet. XIV. 2.
The virtue of his lucky hand.   Guy. 14.
To touch with prophet's hand the chord
                        Hymn. 15.
Of Cæsar's hand, and Plato's brain,
                        Informing Spirit. 7.
Nor chaplet on his head or hand.
                        Initial Love. 18.

Imbibing virtue by his hand
                        Initial Love. 55.
And prosperous Age held out his hand,
                        In Memoriam. 69.
Work of his hand   In Memoriam. 92.
Hand in hand the comrades go
                        Love and Thought. 5.
Thoughts come also hand in hand;
                        Merlin. 101.
Blinding dog-wood in my hand;
                        Mithridates. 15.
Dwarfed to measure of his hand;
                        Monadnoc. 321.
My hand upon the silent string,
                        Poet. 95.
Brother, accept this fatal hand.
                        Poet. 264.
And his hand was armed with skill;
                        Power. 2.
The hand that rounded Peter's dome
                        Problem. 19.
The passive Master lent his hand
                        Problem. 47.
The storm is my best galley hand
                        Quat. Northman. 3.
October in his liberal hand.
                        Quat. S. H. 4.
Thy fortune's web to the beneficent hand
                        Rome. 22.
And thrice outstretched my hand,
                        Song of Nature. 62.
Flew near, with soft wing grazed my
hand,   Titmouse. 38.

Hand-cart
I was the trustee of the hand-cart man,
                        Frag. Life. XXX. 4.

Handed
   See Brokenhanded; Million-handed;
Myriad-handed.

Hands
Painted our necks, hands, ankles, with
red bands: Adirondacs. 167.
But, laying hands on another
                        Boston Hymn. 61.
Foolish hands may mix and mar;
                        Channing Ode. 76.
Bring diadems and fagots in their hands.
                        Days. 4.
Their hands were pure, and pure their
faith,—   Dirge. 51.
Shun passion, fold the hands of thrift,
                        Frag. Life. XXXV. 1.
Friendly hands stretch forth to him,
                        Frag. Poet. XI. 6.
His hired hands were wind and cloud;
                        Frag. Poet. XXVII. 2.
The pulse of hands will make him mute;
                        Initial Love. 57.
Hands to hands, and feet to feet,
                        Merlin. 88.
And hands that stablish what these see;
                        Monadnoc. 109.
But their long hands it thence will take;
                        Monadnoc. 146.
Then clothe these hands with power
                        Poet. 245.
As fleet his feet, his hands as good,
                        Poet. 295.
He who has no hands
                        Quat. Orator. 1.

Power and speed be hands and feet.
Quat. Power. 4.

Had active hands and smiling lips;
Saadi. 77.

Sings in my ears, my hands are stones,
Titmouse. 13.

Disgust my reason and defile my hands.
To-Day. 10.

Hang
Hang roses on the stony fate.
Frag. Poet. X. 4.

Hang in the air a bright thermometer
Letter. 21.

The slight Linnæa hang its twin-born
heads,   Woodnotes. I. 69.

Would hang his head for shame.
World-Soul. 52.

Hanging
See Overhanging.

Hangs
On coop or kennel he hangs Parian
wreaths;   Snow-Storm. 18.

Hants
Amid the mountain counties, Hants,
Franklin, Berks,   Letter. 9.

Hap
Whatsoever hap befalls
Day by Day. 11.

Toil's hard hap with scorn accuse.
Monadnoc. 126.

Hapless
Is he hapless who can spare
Goethe. 7.

Hapless sire to hapless son,—
Voluntaries. 10.

Haply
Haply else we could not live,
Frag. Nat. I. 17.

Or haply 't was the cannonade
May-Day. 15.

Seen haply from afar,   Monadnoc. 394.
The bird, how far it haply roam
Nemesis. 3.

That haply man upraised might keep
Poet. 169.

But blest is he, who, playing deep, yet
haply asks not why,
Quat. Nature. 3.

Happier
Made them to boys again. Happier that
they   Adirondacs. 61.

He thought it happier to be dead,
Beauty. 25.

Yet happier he whose inward sight,
Voluntaries. 79.

Happiest
For I can mend the happiest days
Aeolian Harp. 22.

Happiness
To swains that live in happiness
Nature. I. 18.

Happy
See Unhappy.
We struck our camp and left the happy
hills.   Adirondacs. 336.

O happy town beside the sea,
Boston. 59.

O happy port that spied the sail
Boston. 88.

And die to Fame a happy martyr.
Fame. 30.

Long I followed happy guides,
Forerunners. 1.

But for the love of happy souls
House. 23.

And ever when the happy child
May-Day. 98.

Bend happy to the welkin blue.
May-Day. 124.

Wreaths for May! for happy Spring
May-Day. 263.

'Happy,' I said, 'whose home is here!
Monadnoc. 68.

Such resurrection of the happy past,
Naples. 22.

When happy stoic Nature grieves,
Nun. 12.

Ah, happy if a sun or star   Poet. 165.
Happy to meet you in these places,
Titmouse. 31.

He shall be happy in his love,
Woodnotes. II. 81.

He shall be happy whilst he wooes,
Woodnotes. II. 83.

Haps
Many haps fall in the field
Woodnotes. I. 50.

Harbinger
The rainbow shines his harbinger,
Song of Nature. 39.

Wise harbinger of spheres and tides,
Woodnotes. I. 33.

Harbingers
And harbingers of a majestic race,
Frag. Nat. V. 10.

Harbor
Daily stoops to harbor there.
Astraea. 48.

Harbored
Broad England harbored not his peer:
Fate. 10.

Hard
Hard fare, hard bed and comic misery,—
Adirondacs. 165.

Hard to out-do the brave, the true,
Frag. Life. X. 3.

Princely women hard to please,
Frag. Poet. I. 27.

Must smite the chords rudely and hard,
Merlin. 10.

Toil's hard hap with scorn accuse.
Monadnoc. 126.

A fortune harsh and hard.   Poet. 154.
When piped a tiny voice hard by,
Titmouse. 25.

Hard-by
That we should build, hard-by, a spacious
lodge   Adirondacs. 162.

Harder
Shorter days and harder times.
Alphonso. 6.

Hardy
Titan-born, to hardy natures
May-Day. 136.

The hardy bunting does not chide;
May-Day. 165.

For that hardy English root
Monadnoc. 183.

Harebell
Or harebell nodding in the gorge of falls.
Adirondacs. 145.

Harebells
Loved harebells nodding on a rock,
Frag. Poet. I. 21.

Hark
Hark to that muffled roar! a tree in the woods
Adirondacs. 121.
Hark to that petulant chirp!
Adirondacs. 206.
Hark to the winning sound!
Ellen South. 13.
Hark what, now loud, now low, the pining flute complains,
Flute. 1.
Hark in the wall to the rat:
Limits. 2.
Or clarionet of jay? or hark
May-Day. 22.
Hushed myriads hark in vain,
Merlin's Song. 11.
And hark! where overhead the ancient crows
River. 16.
Hark! in thy ear I will tell the sign
Woodnotes. II. 192.

Harlequin
And jump like Harlequin;
Initial Love. 135.

Harlot
Back, back to chaos, harlot Day!
Chartist. 18.
Sent a nocturnal fragrance; harlot flies
Frag. Nat. XXVII. 8.
Saw bonfires of the harlot flies
Harp. 91.

Harmed
See Unharmed.

Harmless
Sprung harmless up, refreshed by blows
Worship. 2.

Harmonies
What pictures and what harmonies are thine!
Adirondacs. 212.

Harmony's
For truth's and harmony's behoof;
Channing Ode. 68.

Harms
Forgive our harms, and condescend
May-Day. 402.
Washing out harms and griefs from memory,
Seashore. 24.

Harness
They harness beast, bird, insect, to their work;
Musketaquid. 36.

Harp
See Wind-harp.
For gentle harp to gentle hearts
Aeolian Harp. 12.
Æolian harp,
Harp. 41.
Of Merlin locked the harp within,—
Harp. 54.
Harp of the wind, or song of bird,
May-Day. 10.
Thy trivial harp will never please
Merlin. 1.
Shall the harp be dumb.
Saadi. 16.
The harp is dumb.
Saadi. 20.

Harpies
drive the damned harpies
I Bear. 14.

Harp-like
Listen for their harp-like laughter,
Forerunners. 36.

Harps
Æolian harps in the pine
Garden. 33.

Harries
"The fiend that man harries
Sphinx. 73.

Harry
Might harry the weak and poor?
Boston Hymn. 12.

Harrying
Harrying Mexico
Channing Ode. 17.

Harsh
To his own blood harsh and strange.
Insight. 6.
A fortune harsh and hard.
Poet. 154.

Harvest
One harvest from thy field
Apology. 17.
The heaped-up harvest of the moon
From Hafiz. 6.
With their own harvest honored were.
Guy. 46.
I bring round the harvest day.'
Voluntaries. 34.

Harvest-field
The digger in the harvest-field,
Boston Hymn. 39.

Harvests
Harvests grew upon his tongue,
Frag. Poet. V. 31.
Which all her harvests were not worth?
Threnody. 125.
The harvests sown to-day
Walden. 14.

Has (Partial list.)
Is fallen: but hush! it has not scared the buck
Adirondacs. 122.
Has lords enough and more;—
Boston. 20.
My thunderbolt has eyes to see
Boston Hymn. 87.
That God has cherubim who go
Dull. 3.
Is to live well with who has none.
Frag. Life. XI. 2.
Belike has wider hospitality
Frag. Nat. V. 5.
Toy no longer—it has duties;
Holidays. 7.
He has a total world of wit;
Initial Love. 103.
He has the Muses by the heart,
Initial Love. 128.
Has hints of the propitious time,
May-Day. 120.
But she has the temperance
May-Day. 130.
Who has little, to him who has less, can spare,
Merlin's Song. 24.
Is to live well with who has none.
Merlin's Song. 40.
Has royal pleasure-grounds outspread.'
Monadnoc. 71.
Has thousand faces in a thousand hours.
Musketaquid. 25.
He who has no hands
Quat. Orator. 1.
That until now has put his world in fee
Rome. 23.

But he has no companion;   Saadi. 31.
And the world has only two.
                              Security. 8.
But over the dead he has no power,
                              Threnody. 5.
Has disappeared from the Day's eye;
                              Threnody. 21.
He has avenues to God   Voluntaries. 51.
He has his way, and deals his gifts,—
                              World-Soul. 79.

Hassan
Hassan the camel-driver's door,
                              Frag. Poet. III. 2.
Timour, to Hassan, was a slave.
                              Frag. Poet. III. 4.

Hassan's
In every glance of Hassan's eye
                              Frag. Poet. III. 5.
I shunned the toiling Hassan's glance."
                              Frag. Poet. III. 12.

Hast (Partial list.)
Hast thou named all the birds without
  a gun?   Forbearance. 1.
To the defences thou hast round me set;
                              Grace. 2.
Of the nectar which thou hast.
                              Ode to Beauty. 81.
Hast thou forgot me in a new delight?
                              Threnody. 35.
The world dishonored thou hast left.
                              Threnody. 171.

Haste
Suns haste to set, that so remoter lights
                              Adirondacs. 228.
Haste to cure the old despair,—
                              Bacchus. 55.
The sowers made haste to depart,—
                              Garden. 17.
Shod like a traveller for haste;
                              Initial Love. 12.
Emerge the winged words in haste.
                              Poet. 24.
And Morning opes with haste her lids
                              Problem. 35.
From form to form He maketh haste;
                              Woodnotes. II. 298.

Hasted
As if they loved the element, and hasted
                              Frag. Nat. XVII. 5.
Hither hasted, in old time, Jove,
                              Garden. 25.

Hasten
'O hasten;' 't is our time,
                              Ellen South. 17.

Hastes
Our brig hastes on her way,
                              *Farewell. 15.

Hastily
Forgot my morning wishes, hastily
                              Days. 8.

Hasting
On and away, their hasting feet
                              Forerunners. 9.
To frozen hearts and hasting feet;
                              Good-Bye. 12.
Restless, predatory, hasting;
                              Initial Love. 38.

Hat
Stuff their nine brains in one hat;
                              Alphonso. 72.

Hate
Virtue, to love, to hate them, vice;
                              Daemonic Love. 9.
Pronounced the word that mortals hate
  to hear—   Frag. Life. XVIII. 2.
Nor murdering hate, can enter in.
                              Past. 9.
Though it hate thee, suffer long;
                              Poet. 291.
But do the deed thy fellows hate,
                              Saadi. 65.
As love old things for age, and hate the
  new.   To-Day. 12.

Hated
Hated mist if it come near.
                              Frag. Poet. VII. 18.
Flow, flow the waves hated,
                              Illusions. 1.
He should be loved; he should be hated;
                              Poet. 48.

Hath (Partial list.)
But the boundless hath no form,
                              Bohemian. 3.
God hath a select family of sons
                              Good Cheer. 3.
What potent blood hath modest May,
                              May-Day. 187.
The world hath overmuch of pain,—
                              May-Day. 369.
Hath such a soul, such divine influence,
                              Naples. 21.
So that what his eye hath seen
                              Saadi. 121.
And what his tender heart hath felt
                              Saadi. 123.
Hath its unit, bound and metre;
                              Visit. 5.
Not hook nor line hath he;
                              Woodnotes. I. 8.
The all-seeing sun for ages hath not
  shone;   Woodnotes. I. 65.
Thee of thy faith who hath bereft,
                              Woodnotes. II. 183.

Hating
Nature, hating art and pains,
                              Nature. I. 5.
Eager for good, not hating ill,
                              Poet. 208.

Hatred's
Hatred's swift repulsions play.
                              Visit. 30.

Hats
They shook the snow from hats and
  shoon,   May-Day. 318.

Haughtily
And haughtily return us stare tor stare.
                              Blight. 36.

Haughty
O tenderly the haughty day
                              Concord Ode. 1.
Up and away! where haughty woods
                              May-Day. 224.
I turned to Cheshire's haughty hill.
                              Monadnoc. 32.
Still is the haughty pile erect
                              Monadnoc. 373.
Nor haughty hope, nor swart chagrin,
                              Past. 8.
Haughty thought be far from me;
                              Voluntaries. 2.

Haunted
See Gold-moth-haunted.
And boding Fancy haunted it
Frag. Nat. X. 3.
The summer dells, by genius haunted,
May-Day. 43.
By Hell and Heaven is haunted,
Peter. 6.
Than Walden's haunted wave,
Walden. 26.

Haunteth
The darkness haunteth me elsewhere;
Peter. 29.

Haunting
See Pool-haunting; Water-haunting.
Haunting this bank's historic trees?
In Memoriam. 27.
The bitter-sweet, the haunting air
May-Day. 289.

Haunts
As if on such stern forms and haunts
Frag. Nat. XXIX. 3.
And found a home in haunts which
others scorned, Musketaquid. 3.
My old familiar haunts; here the blue,
river, River. 2.
His daily haunts I well discern,—
Threnody. 88.
He goes to my savage haunts,
Woodnotes. II. 26.
Alas! the Sprite that haunts us
World-Soul. 41.

Have (Partial list.)
We have few moments in the longest
life Adirondacs. 249.
We must have society, Alphonso. 57.
So shall ye have a man of the sphere
Alphonso. 81.
I have an arrow that will find its mark,
Arrow. 1.
Each honest man shall have his vote,
Boston. 33.
Each child shall have his school.
Boston. 34.
And none but Toil shall have.
Boston Hymn. 28.
I will have never a noble,
Boston Hymn. 29.
'I will have a purer gift;
Celestial Love. 2.
Power have they for tenderness;
Celestial Love. 90.
But they have heartily designed
Celestial Love. 119.
When other men have none?
I Compensation. 2.
Glows the feud of Want and Have.
II Compensation. 6.
Laugh life away; have wine for tears;
Fame. 16.
We have not better things to say,
Frag. Life. XII. 3.
Time hath his work to do and we have
ours. Frag. Life. XXXVII. 2.
Small need have I of Turner or
Daguerre, Frag. Nat. IV. 8.
What all the books of ages paint, I
have. Frag. Nat. V. 1.
I have no brothers and no peers,
Frag. Poet. XXV. 1.

And ride, and run, and have, and hold,
Initial Love. 29.
Well for those who have no fear,
Letters. 3.
So each man's life shall have its proper
lights, Naples. 9.
Nemesis will have her dues,
Nemesis. 14.
Have ye seen the caterpillar Riches. 1.
Have ye seen the butterfly Riches. 5.
Here holy thoughts a light have shed
Robbins Hymn. 5.
Shall have society of its own rank.
Rome. 3.
Of them thou shouldst have comforted;
Saadi. 69.
Oh, south winds have long memories,
September. 11.
Have I a lover Sphinx. 93.
Have you eyes to find the five
Test. 13.
How have I forfeited the right?
Threnody. 34.

Having
Who, having more absorbed, more large-
ly yield, Frag. Nat. V. 11.
And having thus their bread and growth,
Nature. II. 18.
One who having nectar drank
Poet. 81.
And the god, having given all,
Rhea. 74.

Havoc
A field of havoc and war,
Boston Hymn. 10.

Hawk
Wintered with the hawk and fox,
Quat. Power. 3.
And the shy hawk did wait for him;
Woodnotes. I. 57.

Hawkweed
Blue-vetch and trillium, hawkweed, sassafras, Blight. 6.

Hay
Clouds shade the sun, which will not tan
our hay, Blight. 51.
To speed his sails, to dry his hay;
Guy. 38.
Hay, corn, roots, hemp, flax, apples, wool
and wood. Hamatreya. 3.
The lord is hay, the peasant grass,
Woodnotes. II. 20.

Hazard
To hazard all in Freedom's fight,—
Voluntaries. 62.

Hazarded
Have not hazarded their state;
Astraea. 34.

Haze
With a net of shining haze
Humble-Bee. 21.
His city-tops a glimmering haze.
Monadnoc. 323.

Hazel
Crying out of the hazel copse, Phe-be!
Titmouse. 93.

Hazy
Out of the hazy land? May-Day. 9.
And o'er yon hazy crest is Eden's balmier
spring.' May-Day. 103.

He (Partial list.)
He dons a surcoat which he doffs at
morn: Adirondacs. 77.
'You are thriving well,' said he;
Boston. 64.
He to his wants can well suffice:
Frag. Life. XVII. 5.
Gropes for columns strong as he;
Frag. Nat. XXXIV. 2.
He asked, he only asked, to feel.
Poet. 212.
Wisdom of the gods is he,—
Saadi. 35.
Not hook nor line hath he;
Woodnotes. I. 8.

Head
See Baldhead; Forehead; Godhead;
Overhead.
A pause and council: then, where near
the head Adirondacs. 29.
'T was always thus, and will be; hand
and head Adirondacs. 286.
Over the maiden's head,
Daemonic Love. 37.
She laid a slab of marble on his head.
Epitaph. 4.
Over the maiden's head
Frag. Life. XVI. 3.
Lifts its head, Frag. Nat. III. 2.
In mercy, on one little head.
Frag. Poet. XXIV. 2.
Shorn from her comely head,
Hermione. 18.
Lightning-knotted round his head;
Heroism. 6.
Nor chaplet on his head or hand.
Initial Love. 18.
Painting him from head to foot,
Initial Love. 82.
We were quick from head to foot,
May-Day. 411.
Under clouds, my lonely head,
Monadnoc. 203.
'Every morn I lift my head
Monadnoc. 279.
From this wellspring in my head,
Monadnoc. 292.
Who daily climb my specular head.
Monadnoc. 310.
Thy sombre head with rosy hues
Monadnoc Afar. 3.
Time, shake not thy bald head at me.
Nun. 30.
Over his head were the maple buds,
Quat. Excelsior. 1.
Stuff sharp thorns beneath the head
Saadi. 68.
Nor head from foot can I discern,
Song of Seyd. 2.
Has turned my child's head?'"
Sphinx. 64.
She stood Monadnoc's head.
Sphinx. 128.
With prophet, savior and head;
Threnody. 220.
Head downward, clinging to the spray.
Titmouse. 42.
Hide in false peace your coward head,
Voluntaries. 33.

Would hang his head for shame.
World-Soul. 52.
Headed
See Bareheaded; Light-headed.
Headland
From blue mount and headland dim
Frag. Poet. XI. 5.
Poet on a sunny headland
September. 3
Heads
See Cloverheads.
Right above their heads,
Daemonic Love. 25.
There, while hot heads perplexed with
fears the state, Phi. 9.
The stern old war-gods shook their
heads, Uriel. 27.
The slight Linnæa hang its twin-born
heads, Woodnotes. I. 69.
Head-stone
To greet yon stern head-stone,
In Memoriam. 12.
Headstrong
He is headstrong and alone;
Initial Love. 95.
Head-winds
And head-winds right for royal sails.
Heroism. 10.
Heal
My garden spade can heal. A woodland
talk, Musketaquid. 72.
Could stoop to heal that only child,
Threnody. 122.
And heal the hurts which sin has made.
Woodnotes. II. 220.
Healed
Healed as fast the wounds it made.
Guy. 20.
Health
Put youth, joy, health upon the shrine,
Fame. 27.
Be it health, or be it sickness;
Frag. Life. XXVII. 8.
All, all was given, and only health denied.
In Memoriam. 72.
One to other, health and age.
Merlin. 105.
And ruddy Health the loftiest Muse.
Merlin's Song. 30.
'Mid many ails a brittle health,
Poet. 184.
The hills where health with health
agrees, Woodnotes. II. 190.
Healthful
My breath thy healthful climate in the
heats, Seashore. 5.
Healthy
New-bathed, new-trimmed, on healthy
wing, Poet. 25.
Heap
See Sand-heap.
Or tumble all again in heap
Alphonso. 29.
They turn the frost upon their chemic
heap, Musketaquid. 41.
Will heap in me their highest tide,
Poet. 277.
Heaped-up
The heaped-up harvest of the moon
From Hafiz. 6.

Hear

See Mis-hear; Overhear.

As each would hear the oracle alone.
Adirondacs. 15.

Let them hear well!   Adirondacs. 261.

Hear the sentiment of Spain.
Alphonso. 50.

Hear you, then, celestial fellows!
Alphonso. 59.

Shall hear far Chaos talk with me;
Bacchus. 39.

He flung in pebbles well to hear
Beauty. 9.

He heard a voice none else could hear
Beauty. 13.

I cannot hear your songs, O birds,
Cosmos. 23.

Pronounced the word that mortals hate
to hear—   Frag. Life. XVIII. 2.

Would hear the everlasting
Frag. Nat. III. 29.

Are unsealed, that he may hear.
Garden. 48.

Yet hear me, yet,   Give. 27.

Hear what the Earth says:—
Hamatreya. 27.

And some attain his voice to hear,
Harp. 57.

Therein I hear the Parcæ reel
Harp. 99.

Is the word they wish to hear.
Letters. 6.

To hear, when, 'mid our talk and games,
May-Day. 56.

And I shall hear my bluebird's note,
May-Day. 180.

Hear the uproar of their joy;
May-Day. 227.

Which only angels hear;
Merlin's Song. 9.

Yet they who hear it shed their age,
Merlin's Song. 12.

Hear what British Merlin sung,
Merlin's Song. 14.

When they hear from far the rune;
Monadnoc. 250.

Well I hear the approaching feet
Monadnoc. 267.

I hear a sky-born music still:
Music. 2.

I hear the lofty pæans
Ode to Beauty. 56.

In every whispering leaf I hear
Peter. 31.

I hear the rustle of wings,   Poet. 360.

Hear wolves barking at the moon;
Saadi. 54.

Hear the far Avenger's feet:
Saadi. 56.

I heard or seemed to hear the chiding
Sea   Seashore. 1.

I hear continually his voice therein.
Self-Reliance. 5.

That winsome voice again might hear;
Threnody. 51.

Now hear thee say in Roman key,
Titmouse. 103.

Hear what wine and roses say;
To J. W. 2.

I hear the spending of the stream
Two Rivers. 10.

They lose their grief who hear his song,
Two Rivers. 15.

Are Autumn's blasts fit music for thee,
fragile one, to hear;   *Violet. 2.

I see the wreath, I hear the songs
Voluntaries. 108.

What others did at distance hear,
Woodnotes. I. 58.

Which only the pure can hear;
Woodnotes. II. 128.

Heard

See Far-heard; Overheard.

these echoes ever heard.
Adirondacs. 33.

He heard a voice none else could hear
Beauty. 13.

'May be true what I had heard,—
Berrying. 1.

And fired the shot heard round the world.
C. Hymn. 4.

Names from awful childhood heard
Daemonic Love. 7.

Again I saw, again I heard,   Each. 48.

Say, was it never heard   Fame. 4.

Some had heard their fair report,
Forerunners. 21.

I have heard them fall.
Frag. Nat. III. 26.

I heard no church-bell chime,
Frag. Nat. XXV. 2.

He heard their medicinal song,
Frag. Poet. V. 19.

All day his song is heard;
Frag. Poet. XXXIII. 2.

When I heard the Earth-song
Hamatreya. 60.

When pacing through the oaks he heard
Harp. 87.

His sorrow heard,   Hermione. 5.

What was that I heard   May-Day. 8.

And the love in its carol heard,
May-Day. 236.

Passing yonder oak, I heard
Miracle. 23.

I heard, and I obeyed,—
Monadnoc. 27.

Nor in the song of woman heard,
Music. 10.

Never heard thy weary name;   Nun. 46.

Who heard the starry music
Ode to Beauty. 58.

It shook or captivated all who heard,
Phi. 20.

I heard or seemed to hear the chiding
Sea   Seashore. 1.

Heard rendings of the skyey roof,
Solution. 55.

I heard a poet answer   Sphinx. 65.

Who heard the sweet request,
Threnody. 44.

A music heard by thee alone
Threnody. 78.

I think old Cæsar must have heard
Titmouse. 95.

But in each pause we heard the call
Walden. 35.

He heard the woodcock's evening hymn;
Woodnotes. I. 55.

He heard, when in the grove, at intervals,
Woodnotes. I. 72.

Hearer
Keep me nearer, me thy hearer,
                    Humble-Bee. 9.
Hearest
Hearest thou, O traveller,   Dirge. 43.
Heareth
As it heareth, so it saith;   Harp. 70.
Hearing
Hearing as now the lofty dirge
                    Nun. 18.
Hearken
Hearken to yon pine-warbler   Dirge. 41.
Saying, 'Hearken! Earth, Sea, Air!
                    Rhea. 57.
I hearken for thy household cheer,
                    Threnody. 36.
Hearken! Hearken!   Woodnotes. II. 97.
'Hearken once more!
                    Woodnotes. II. 252.
Hearkened
All echoes hearkened for their sound,—
                    Dirge. 35.
Hearkens
Hearkens for the choral glee,
                    May-Day. 84.
And hearkens in the berry's bell
                    Nature. I. 13.
Hears
    See Overhears.
Of craggy Indian wilderness he hears
                    Adirondacs. 312.
And hears in heaven the bluebird sing,
                    May-Day. 100.
Hear'st
O wise man! hear'st thou half it tells?
                    Woodnotes. II. 101.
O wise man! hear'st thou the least part?
                    Woodnotes. II. 102.
Heart
    See Sweetheart.
into each several heart.   Adirondacs. 223.
If, whilst within thy heart abide
                    Angelo. 12.
Fold Boston in his heart,   Boston. 103.
Free be his heart and hand henceforth
                    Boston Hymn. 55.
And every human heart   Cosmos. 25.
Next his heart the fireside band
                    Daemonic Love. 5.
To fascinate each youthful heart,
                    Daemonic Love. 31.
Thy heart saith, 'Brother, go thy ways!
                    Destiny. 21.
'You cannot unlock your heart,
                    Dirge. 57.
In the deep heart of man a poet dwells
                    Enchanter. 1.
The little Shakspeare in the maiden's
    heart   Enchanter. 12.
Bethink, poor heart, what bitter kind of
    jest   Epitaph. 1.
And your heart is unsupported.
                    Etienne. 8.
Features that seem at heart my own;
                    Eva. 8.
But though aye one in heart,
                    *Farewell. 32.
I gave my heart to thee.   *Farewell. 40.
My heart shall beat not when
                    *Farewell. 48.

Unarmed, faced danger with a heart of
    trust?   Forbearance. 4.
Keen my sense, my heart was young,
                    Forerunners. 5.
And carry in my heart, for days,
                    Forerunners. 37.
And many-chambered heart.
                    Frag. Life. VI. 6.
And following his mighty heart
                    Frag. Poet. IV. 5.
All their heart when Saadi sung;
                    Frag. Poet. V. 33.
They turn his heart from lovely maids,
                    Frag. Poet. XI. 12.
And his heart the throne of Will.
                    Frag. Poet. XIV. 4.
Or, if in thy heart he shine,
                    Freedom. 17.
My careful heart was free again,
                    Friendship. 9.
God forbid my angry heart
                    From Hafiz. 11.
Obey thy heart;   Give. 2.
One word more thy heart behoved,
                    Give. 28.
And the heart of girl and boy,
                    Harp. 23.
A door into the mountain heart,
                    Hermione. 44.
Daily his own heart he eats;
                    Heroism. 8.
Of Lord Christ's heart, and Shakespeare's
    strain.   Informing Spirit. 8.
But it touches his quick heart
                    Initial Love. 70.
He has the Muses by the heart,
                    Initial Love. 128.
Save in tables of the heart,
                    In Memoriam. 49.
With grace to win, with heart to hold,
                    In Memoriam. 61.
Nor bate one jot of heart or hope,
                    In Memoriam. 80.
Firm on his heart relied,
                    In Memoriam. 90.
Is life and heart,   Limits. 7.
So dances his heart in his breast;
                    Manners. 14.
In flint and marble beats a heart,
                    May-Day. 65.
Flows from the heart of Love, the Lord.
                    May-Day. 191.
Doth it bear hidden in its heart
                    May-Day. 212.
Heart of bird the man's heart seeking;
                    May-Day. 421.
Not less renew the heart and brain,
                    May-Day. 453.
In the heart of the music peals a strain
                    Merlin's Song. 8.
You must bring the throbbing heart.
                    Miracle. 10.
Sparta's stoutness, Bethlehem's heart,
                    Monadnoc. 299.
The secret of its laboring heart,
                    Nature. Mot. 10.
To me the heart Fate for me chooses.
                    Ode to Beauty. 45.
To catch the unconscious heart in the
    very act.   Philosoper. 6.

Heart —*Continued*
His heart should palpitate with fear.
                                    Poet. 50.
Fill thy will, O faultless heart!
                                    Poet. 127.
My heart at the heart of things
                                    Poet. 130.
Fell the lesson on his heart
                                    Poet. 255.
Aches thine unbelieving heart   Poet. 265.
And his heart the throne of will.
                                    Power. 4.
And on my heart monastic aisles
                                    Problem. 3.
Out from the heart of nature rolled
                                    Problem. 13.
Trances the heart through chanting
   choirs,   Problem. 53.
High was her heart, and yet was well in-
   clined,   Quat. A. H. 1.
July was in his sunny heart,
                              Quat. S. H. 3.
If with love thy heart has burned;
                                    Rhea. 9.
All grace, all good his great heart knows,
                                    Rhea. 55.
Thou heart that lovest all.
                           Robbins Hymn. 28.
Draws the heart a lore sublime."'
                                    Saadi. 71.
Sunshine in his heart transferred
                                    Saadi. 80.
And what his tender heart hath felt
                                    Saadi. 123.
With equal fire thy heart shalt melt.
                                    Saadi. 124.
Another heart as large and true.
                                    Security. 6.
If Nature hold another heart
                                    Security. 9.
I find him in the bottom of my heart,
                                Self-Reliance. 4.
Of heart and soul, of strength and
   pleasure,   Solution. 36.
Nor my heart from love of mine,
                              Song of Seyd. 3.
And my heart the frankincense;
                             Song of Seyd. 16.
But their heart abode with none.
                                    Threnody. 157.
The deep Heart answered, 'Weepest
   thou?   Threnody. 176.
I taught thy heart beyond the reach
                                    Threnody. 197.
The mysteries of Nature's heart;
                                    Threnody. 205.
Wilt thou not ope thy heart to know
                                    Threnody. 260.
Out of sound heart and merry throat,
                                    Titmouse. 28.
Moved by his hospitable heart,
                                    Titmouse. 34.
Heart too soft and will too weak
                                    Voluntaries. 15.
And drain his heart till he be dead.
                                    Voluntaries. 58.
The woods at heart are glad.
                              Waldeinsamkeit. 20.
A lover true, who knew by heart
                                    Woodnotes. I. 34.

Three moons his great heart him a her-
   mit made,   Woodnotes. I. 84.
He was the heart of all the scene;
                              Woodnotes. I. 112.
Take off thine eyes, thy heart forbear,
                              Woodnotes. II. 87.
Rooted in the mighty Heart.
                              Woodnotes. II. 177.
God hid the whole world in thy heart.
                              Woodnotes. II. 235.
From the heart of God proceeds,
                              Woodnotes. II. 264.
He is the heart of every creature;
                              Woodnotes. II. 315.
Love wakes anew this throbbing heart,
                                    World-Soul. 107.

Hearted
   See Broken-hearted; False-hearted;
   Great-hearted; Light-hearted.

Hearth
From hearth and home away,
                                    *Farewell. 8.
And it lay on my hearth when I came
   home.   Frag. Poet. IV. 34.
In hearts which round the hearth at
   home   In Memoriam. 84.
Rude poets of the tavern hearth,
                                    Monadnoc. 185.
When the state-house is the hearth,
                                    Politics. 24.
His hearth the earth,—his hall the azure
   dome;   Woodnotes. I. 93.

Heart-heaving
Heart-heaving alway;   Sphinx. 102.

Hearth-stone
I am going to my own hearth-stone,
                                    Good-Bye. 15.

Heartily
But they have heartily designed
                              Celestial Love. 119.
Heartily know,   Give. 47.
The sun himself shines heartily,
                                    World-Soul. 63.

Heart-o'erlading
The heart-o'erlading miracle.
                                    Poet. 90.

Heart's
Your manners for the heart's delight,
                                    May-Day. 399.
My heart's content would find it right.
                                    Nun. 10.
Ah, yes! but by the true heart's blood
                                    They. 3.
Heart's love will meet thee again.
                                    Threnody. 269.

Hearts
For gentle harp to gentle hearts
                              Aeolian Harp. 12.
And filled their hearts with flame.
                              Boston Hymn. 4.
Love's hearts are faithful, but not fond,
                              Celestial Love. 115.
There are no such hearts on earth.
                                    Dirge. 52.
To frozen hearts and hasting feet;
                                    Good-Bye. 12.
Which God in human hearts hath strung.
                                    Hymn. 16.
In hearts which round the hearth at
   home   In Memoriam. 84.

Fans in all hearts expectance sweet,
May-Day. 296.
With the pulse of manly hearts;
Merlin. 21.
And burned in noble hearts proverb and prophecy. Phi. 22.
And anxious hearts have pondered here
Robbins Hymn. 9.
It keeps the key to all heroic hearts,
Rome. 9.
I looked again,—I thought them hearts
Rubies. 5.
The cheerer of men's hearts.
Saadi. 48.
Hearts are dust, hearts' loves remain;
Threnody. 268.
Takes hearts like thine in special charge,
Titmouse. 86.
Hearts to hearts their meaning show,
Visit. 18.

Hearts'
Hearts are dust, hearts' loves remain;
Threnody. 268.

Heart-strings
Tugs at the heart-strings, numbs the sense, Titmouse. 15.

Heart-warming
And thou, heart-warming nightingale!
Exile. 11.

Heat
Impassible to heat or cold.
Frag. Poet. I. 49.
The lambent heat lightning
Illusions. 20.
Masks her treasury of heat
May-Day. 132.
The garnered heat of ages old.
May-Day. 145.
Hither rolls the storm of heat;
May-Day. 192.
Heat with viewless fingers moulds,
May-Day. 195.
What god is this imperial Heat,
May-Day. 210.
So pours the deluge of the heat
May-Day. 247.
Earth-baking heat, stone-cleaving cold.
Monadnoc. 57.
Fended from the heat, Politics. 20.
Heat, cold, wet, dry, and peace, and pain. Song of Nature. 76.
Inconstant heat and nerveless reins,—
Terminus. 30.

Heated
Where now on heated pavements worn
Boston. 39.

Heath
Or in lone corners of a doleful heath,
Frag. Nat. IV. 3.
I reached this heath beside the lake,
Miracle. 16.
If on the heath, below the moon,
Romany. 13.

Heathendom
Eastward it filled all Heathendom
Frag. Poet. IV. 33.

Heat's
The third adds heat's indulgent spark;
Woodnotes. II. 291.

Heats
That mortals miss the loyal heats,
Alphonso. 33.
Earliest heats that follow frore
Frag. Nat. II. 21.
Far-off heats through seas to seek;
Humble-Bee. 4.
And infusing subtle heats,
Humble-Bee. 26.
My breath thy healthful climate in the heats, Seashore. 5.

Heaved
See Upheaved.
And, when he heaved a sigh profound,
Hermione. 6.

Heaven
Among the silver hills of heaven
Bacchus. 16.
To life or death, to heaven or hell,
Bell. 3.
Find me, and turn thy back to heaven.
Brahma. 16.
One morn is in the mighty heaven,
Concord Ode. 3.
And I uplift myself into its heaven,
Day's Ration. 16.
Of the unfading gold of Heaven
Dull. 17.
I thought the sparrow's note from heaven, Each. 13.
The slow eye of heaven shall show
Frag. Nat. XXVI. 9.
Inundating the heaven
Frag. Nat. XXVI. 23.
I cannot sell my heaven again
Frag. Poet. II. 9.
I said to heaven that glowed above,
From Hafiz. 1.
Heaven and earth to eat and drink.
Goethe. 6.
It hath pleased Heaven to break the dream of bliss I Bear. 3.
Fall, stream, from Heaven to bless; return as well; Inscription. 1.
So did our sons; Heaven met them as they fell. Inscription. 2.
Daughter of Heaven and Earth, coy Suring, May-Day. 1.
And hears in heaven the bluebird sing,
May-Day. 100.
And the tints of heaven reply.
May-Day. 262.
Through earth to ripen, through heaven endure. May-Day. 468.
The heaven high over
Ode to Beauty. 37.
Oh what is Heaven but the fellowship
Oh What. 1.
By Hell and Heaven is haunted,
Peter. 6.
Right to the heaven they steer and sing.
Poet. 26.
To Heaven thy hourly prayers are sent,
Prayer. 6.
In heaven are kept their grateful vows,
Robbins Hymn. 3.
Showed them the life of Heaven above
Robbins Hymn. 19.
The hour of heaven. Generously trust
Rome. 21.

Heaven—*Continued*

and as God lives in heaven, Rome. 25.
The hour of heaven shall come, the man
  appear. Rome. 27.
In heaven no star, on earth no spark,—
  Saadi. 132.
The heaven where unveiled Allah pours
  Saadi. 160.
And the equipoise of heaven is thy
  house's equipoise.
  Shah, Enweri. II. 2.
Hides hills and woods, the river, and the
  heaven, Snow-Storm. 4.
Firm to Heaven my bosom clings,
  Song of Seyd. 31.
The living Heaven thy prayers respect,
  Spiritual Laws. 1.
Go thou, sweet Heaven, or at thy
  pleasure stay!' Sursum Corda. 9.
Already Heaven with thee its lot has
  cast, Sursum Corda. 10.
Built he heaven stark and cold;
  Threnody. 273.
In heaven once eminent, the god
  Uriel. 37.
And the sweet heaven his deed secures.
  Voluntaries. 92.
Upward the ninth heaven thrilled and
  moved Waterfall. 19.

Heavenlier

Of heavenlier prosperities
  Frag. Poet. XI. 8.
Coat sea and sky with heavenlier blue,
  May-Day. 446.

Heavenly

So hide in thee, thou heavenly dame,
  Angelo. 6.
His children fed at heavenly tables.
  Art. 18.
To house of God and heavenly joys
  Bell. 9.
Ye shall climb on the heavenly stair,
  Celestial Love. 9.
Leave no track on the heavenly snow.
  Daemonic Love. 42.
And to all the heavenly brood.
  Destiny. 48.
Things of the heavenly mind,—
  Merops. 2.
O heavenly ships without a sail!
  Poet. 160.
And saddens her with heavenly doubts:
  Rhea. 54.

Heaven's

And meditate a moment on Heaven's
  rest. Adirondacs. 197.
Know Heaven's truth from lies that
  shine— Dull. 21.
I will wait Heaven's perfect hour
  Frag. Life. XXV. 3.
Heaven's oldest blood flows in his side,—
  Initial Love. 123.
To Heaven's high will his will is bent.
  In Memoriam. 89.
Heaven's numerous hierarchy span
  Threnody. 185.
Distilled from heaven's alembic blue,
  Walden. 27.
Patient through Heaven's enormous year
  Wealth. 11.

Heavens

From deep ideal fontal heavens that
  flow. Frag. Life. XV. 8.
Gives back the bending heavens in dew.
  Song of Nature. 84.
The heavens that now draw him
  Sphinx. 85.
Once found,—for new heavens
  Sphinx. 87.

Heavily

Dash our blown hopes as they limp heavily by. Summons. 21.

Heaving

See Heart-heaving.
But by heaving of the breast:
  Freedom. 10.

Heavings

In birdlike heavings unto death,
  Threnody. 101.

Heavy

The storm-winds urge the heavy weeks
  along, Adirondacs. 227.
Its heavy tale divine. Dirge. 48.
The heavy grouse's sudden whir,
  Harp. 89.
Her ear is heavy, Sphinx. 3.
The heavy blue chain Tal. Exile. 1.

Hedge

The hedge is gemmed with diamonds,
  April. 5.
Nestle in hedge, or barn, or roof,
  May-Day. 400.

Hedges

On waves and hedges still they burn.
  Garden. 60.
My hedges plant and feed.
  Walden. 12.

Heed

But, on the second day, we heed them
  not, Adirondacs. 168.
They heed not moon or solar tide,—
  Garden. 22.
Leave his weeds and heed his eyes,—
  Initial Love. 19.
'Let him heed who can and will;
  Monadnoc. 224.
Heed not what the brawlers say,
  Saadi. 102.
Heed thou only Saadi's lay.
  Saadi. 103.
Heed thou only Saadi's lay. Saadi. 116.
And oft at home 'mid tasks I heed,
  Walden. 41.
I heed how wears the day;
  Walden. 42.
'Heed the old oracles,
  Woodnotes. II. 89.

Heeded

See Unheeded.

Heedless

And brims my little cup; heedless, alas!
  Day's Ration. 12.
Heedless that each cunning word
  Frag. Poet. V. 9.
Ah! heedless how the weak are strong,
  Hermione. 27.
The heedless world hath never lost.
  Problem. 62.
Heedless of inferior things;
  Song of Seyd. 32.

Heeds
Nor heeds Condition's iron walls,—
          Frag. Life. XVII. 9.
The Titan heeds his sky-affairs,
          Monadnoc. 58.
Heeds no longer lapse of time,
          Poet. 131.
Heeds not the darkness and the dread,
          Voluntaries. 86.
Heifer
The heifer that lows in the upland farm,
          Each. 3.
Height
And lift man's pubic action to a height
          Adirondacs. 246.
Art its height could never hit;
          Destiny. 8.
Whilst his files sweep round yon Alpine
height;   Each. 8.
Shot up to the height of the sky again,
          May-Day. 322.
And carry learning to its height
          Monadnoc. 104.
As o'er some bolder height they speed,—
          Monadnoc. 397.
The height of Fancy's far-eyed steep.
          Poet. 170.
To the height of mighty Nature,
          Saadi. 172.
Heir
But Nature's heir,—if I repine,
          Threnody. 127.
Heirs
To them, and to their heirs
          Hamatreya. 40.
Held
One held a printed journal waving high
          Adirondacs. 235.
One chamber held ye all;   Dirge. 54.
The bard and mystic held me for their
 own,
          Frag. Life. XXX. 1.
or held their court
          Frag. Nat. XXVII. 9.
Saadi held the Muse in awe,
          Frag. Poet. V. 22.
And prosperous Age held out his hand,
          In Memoriam. 69.
How drear the part I held in one,
          Nun. 48.
And held them to the sun;   Rubies. 2.
I brooded long and held my peace,
          Solution. 18.
Hell
To life or death, to heaven or hell,
          Bell. 3.
By Hell and Heaven is haunted,
          Peter. 6.
Hellebore
Nervèd leaf of hellebore,
          Frag. Nat. II. 22.
Helm
Nor yields to men the helm;
          World-Soul. 74.
Helmet
He should have the helmet worn,
          In Memoriam. 39.
Helmsman
Our helmsman he.   *Lines. 4.

Help
Help them who cannot help again:
          Boston Hymn. 51.
To help her friends, to plague her foes,
          Nature. I. 14.
Helped
It helped my rowers to row;
          Quat. Northman. 2.
Helpers
All spheres, all stones, his helpers be;
          Woodnotes. II. 78.
Helps
Helps who for their own need are strong,
          Titmouse. 87.
Hem
As garment draws the garment's hem,
          Celestial Love. 73.
Nor thou detain her vesture's hem,
          Give. 40.
When worlds of lovers hem thee in?
          Threnody. 188.
Hemispheres
When linkèd hemispheres attest his deed.
          Adirondacs. 248.
Hemlock
Hemlock for my sherbet cull me,
          Mithridates. 16.
And every rood in the hemlock wood
          Peter. 7.
Hemlock-boughs
Lie here on hemlock-boughs, like Sacs
and Sioux,   Adirondacs. 52.
Hemlocks
In the hemlocks tall, untamable,
          Garden. 31.
Hemmed
And hemmed me in their glittering troop.
          Poet. 148.
Hemp
Hay, corn, roots, hemp, flax, apples,
wool and wood.   Hamatreya. 3.
Hems
And hems in life with narrowing fence.
          Titmouse. 16.
Hence (Partial list.)
Virtue palters; Right is hence;
          Channing Ode. 32.
drive the damned harpies hence.
          I Bear. 14.
Henceforth
Shall supplement henceforth all trodden
ways,   Adirondacs. 244.
Free be his heart and hand henceforth
          Boston Hymn. 55.
And henceforth there shall be no chain,
          Concord Ode. 29.
Henceforth, please God, forever I forego
          Self-Reliance. 1.
Henceforth I wear no stripe but thine;
          Titmouse. 54.
Henceforth I prize thy wiry chant
          Titmouse. 89.
And henceforth we are comforted,—
          World-Soul. 55.
Hens
On clucking hens and prating fools,
          Woodnotes. II. 202.
Her (Partial list.)
All dressed, like Nature, fit for her own
ends,   Adirondacs. 71.

Her (Partial list.)—*Continued*
Casts her schemes rarely,
Frag. Life. VI. 2.
Her gay pictures never fail,
Frag. Nat. XXXI. 3.
Well accept her rule austere;
May-Day. 135.
She drugs her water and her wheat
Nature. II. 15.
From all evils to defend her;
Rhea. 49.

Herald
Each the herald is who wrote
Astraea. 1.

Heralded
No door-bell heralded a visitor,
Adirondacs. 65.

Heralds
And they who truliest love her, heralds
are Frag. Nat. V. 9.
They her heralds be, Hermione. 22.
Heralds high before him run;
Initial Love. 74.

Herbal
In the safe herbal of the coal?
Wealth. 28.

Herbs
Only the herbs and simples of the wood,
Blight. 4.
Took a few herbs and apples, and the
Day Days. 9.
The sleeps of trees or dreams of herbs.
Frag. Nat. XVIII. 5.
Drugging herbs with Syrian spices,
May-Day. 250.

Herd
See Neatherd.
Not glad, as the low-loving herd,
Celestial Love. 117.
Before the money-loving herd,
Woodnotes. II. 60.

Herds
And trumpet-lowing of the herds.
May-Day. 185.
And slough decay from grazing herds,
May-Day. 448.
Pasture of pool-haunting herds,
Monadnoc. 55.
For wolf and fox, bring lowing herds,
Monadnoc. 139.
In ocean sport the scaly herds,
Saadi. 3.

Herds-grass
In fairy groves of herds-grass.
Frag. Nat. XXVII. 10.

Here (Partial list.)
Lie here on hemlock-boughs, like Sacs
and Sioux, Adirondacs. 52.
pass current here. Adirondacs. 92.
Truth tries pretension here.
Adirondacs. 101.
We pay your governors here
Boston. 70.
And here in a pine state-house
Boston Hymn. 41.
Here once the embattled farmers stood
C. Hymn. 3.
A new genesis were here. Circles. 6.
Sit here on the basalt courses
Cosmos. 17.

Who wrestled here on a day.
Cosmos. 20.
He scatters wide and wild its lustres here.
Frag. Life. XVI. 9.
'Here is the land, Hamatreya. 44.
And God hath built his altar here
Hymn. 5.
'Happy,' I said, 'whose home is here!
Monadnoc. 68.
Thrives here, unvalued, underfoot.
Monadnoc. 184.
Here amid clouds to stand?
Monadnoc. 209.
Enchantment fixed me here
Monadnoc. 225.
And the long Alleghanies here,
Monadnoc. 276.
What sheaves like those which here we
glean and bind Monadnoc. 356.
Here in pine houses Musketaquid. 30.
Here might the red-bird come his plumes
to cool, Rhodora. 7.
And anxious hearts have pondered here
Robbins Hymn. 9.
Yet here their children pray,
Robbins Hymn. 22.
'Here am I, here will I abide
Sursum Corda. 7.
One tarried here, there hurried one;
Threnody. 156.
Displaced, disfurnished here,
Voluntaries. 20.
What boots it here of Thebes or Rome
Walden. 45.

Hereafter
Hereafter,—willing they, and more adroit.
Adirondacs. 164.

Herefrom
Clean swept herefrom. Hamatreya. 52.

Heritors
But the heritors?— Hamatreya. 48.

Hermione
This Hermione absorbed
Hermione. 12.

Hermit
State of hermit, state of lover;
Alphonso. 56.
And the hermit never alone,—
Etienne. 20.
Hermit vowed to books and gloom,—
Hermione. 34
him a hermit made, Woodnotes. I. 84

Hermitage
At last she came to his hermitage,
Each. 33.

Hermit-thrush
Hermit-thrush comes there to build,
Walden. 3.

Hero
The hero is not fed on sweets,
Heroism. 7.
Hero and maiden, flesh of her flesh;
Nature. II. 14.
Sage and hero, side by side,
Voluntaries. 24.
If but one hero knew it,
World-Soul. 49.

Heroes
Our heroes' tried their rifles at a mark,
Adirondacs. 125.

Spirit, that made those heroes dare
C. Hymn. 13.
The heroes on their horses,
Frag. Life. IV. 3.
Root in the blood of heroes old.
In Memoriam. 116.
When heroes piled the pyre,
May-Day. 141.
O what are heroes, prophets, men,
Pan. 1.

Heroic
and build heroic minds. May-Day. 440.
Hint summits of heroic grace;
Monadnoc. 111.
A form which Nature cast in the heroic
mould Phi. 5.
It keeps the key to all heroic hearts,
Rome. 9.
Who shall. nerve heroic boys
Voluntaries. 61.
Leading over heroic ground,
Voluntaries. 89.
Foundeth a heroic line;
Woodnotes. II. 23.

Heron
Loud hammered, and the heron rose in
the swamp. Adirondacs. 148.

Hero's
That can fix a hero's rate; Astraea. 4.

Hers (Partial list.)
Hers to sow the seed of bread,
May-Day. 146.
Is not their way, but hers,
Nature. II. 10.
I am but a thought of hers, Una. 19.

Herself (Partial list.)
And, by herself, supplants alone
Daemonic Love. 15.
As June herself around the sphere.
Frag. Life. XIII. 2.
Come to us herself to meet."'
Hermione. 78.

Hesitates
And the friend not hesitates
Astraea. 19.

Hew
To hew the famous adamant House. 15.

Heyday
Checked in these souls the turbulent hey-
day Adirondacs. 189.
And the glad hey-day of my household
hours, Summons. 9.

Hid
Their wonted convenance, cheerly hid
the loss Adirondacs. 181.
And that the Jove,—yet, howsoever hid,
Adirondacs. 289.
Hid in gleaming piles of stone; Art. 4.
Which I hid of old time in the West,
Boston Hymn. 18.
Freedom praised, but hid;
Channing Ode. 33.
As hid all measure of the feat.
Character. 10.
Who saw the hid beginnings
Cosmos. 1.
I saw the hid beginnings Cosmos. 5.
Would you know what joy is hid
Frag. Nat. XXVI. 1.

All the sweet secrets therein hid
May-Day. 45.
A hid unruly appetite May-Day. 151.
Hid their majesty in cloth
May-Day. 329.
Hid in milk we drew May-Day. 407.
Whispering hints of treasure hid
May-Day. 422.
Hid in song's sweet influence.
Merlin. 42.
Yet wreathed and hid by summer
blooms. Nun. 28.
The reverent darkness hid the lay.
Poet. 18.
Are hid behind the thrice-piled clouds;
Poet. 178.
Or, hid in vines, peeping through many
a loop, Quat. Gardener. 3.
Hid from men of Northern brain,
Voluntaries. 52.
God hid the whole world in thy heart.
Woodnotes. II. 235.

Hidden
The fountains of my hidden life
Friendship. 19.
From the twins is nothing hidden,
Love and Thought. 3.
Doth it bear hidden in its heart
May-Day. 212.
Poets praise that hidden wine
May-Day. 406.
His hidden sense interpret can;—
Miracle. 20.
A swan-like form invests the hidden
thorn; Snow-Storm. 19.
He is hidden and unknown. Una. 24.
Hold all the hidden wonders
World-Soul. 39.
He shoots his thought, by hidden nerves,
World-Soul. 75.

Hidden-working
The hidden-working Builder spy,
Monadnoc. 238.

Hide
So hide in thee, thou heavenly dame,
Angelo. 6.
Which publish and which hide the cause.
Celestial Love. 59.
Nor let us hide, whate'er our pleasure,
Fame. 23.
Hide in thy skies, thou fruitless Jove,
Frag. Life. XXXIII. 2.
O hide yon sun-filled zone,
From Hafiz. 2.
Hide all the stars you boast;
From Hafiz. 3.
Secure the osier yet will hide
May-Day. 172.
Hide in thy skies, O sovereign lamp!
Monadnoc. 122.
To hide or to shun Ode to Beauty. 34.
Nor Time's snows hide the names he set,
Poet. 11.
Love it, though it hide its light;
Poet. 287.
For, as the wood-kinds lurk and hide,
Quat. Forester. 3.
Hide thy grief within thy breast,
Rhea. 11.
The stars may hide in the upper sky,
Romany. 27.

Hide—*Continued*
I hide in the solar glory,
          Song of Nature. 5.
Seek not the spirit, if it hide
          Sursum Corda. 1.
Hide in false peace your coward head,
          Voluntaries. 33.
And their coming triumph hide
          Voluntaries. 113.
The sires of Nature, hide.
          Waldeinsamkeit. 36.
The granite slab to clothe and hide,
          Wealth. 16.
Or hide underground her alchemy.
          Woodnotes. II. 167.

Hides
That hides from man the mortal goal,
          Hymn. 22.
From Hafiz never hides;
          Quat. Hafiz. 2.
Hides hills and woods, the river, and the
heaven,   Snow-Storm. 4.
He hides in pure transparency;
          Woodnotes. II. 310.

Hierarchy
Heaven's numerous hierarchy span
          Threnody. 185.

Hies
To and fro the Genius hies,—
          Daemonic Love. 35.

High
   See Most High.
One held a printed journal waving high
          Adirondacs. 235.
Imps, at high midsummer, blot
          Alphonso. 9.
Is none so high, so mean is none,
          Celestial Love. 111.
For He that worketh high and wise,
          Concord Ode. 37.
He pays too high a price   Fame. 7.
And loved so well a high behavior,
          Forbearance. 5.
From high to higher forces
          Frag. Life. IV. 1.
Grass with green flag half-mast high,
          Frag. Nat. II. 7.
And all we see are pictures high;
          Frag. Nat. III. 16.
Many a high hillside,
          Frag. Nat. III. 17.
The low December vault in June be
lifted high,   Frag. Nat. XX. 1.
Served high and low, the lord and the
churl,   Frag. Poet. I. 20.
And thus the high Muse treated me,
          Frag. Poet. IV. 15.
High destined youths and holy maids.
          Frag. Poet. VII. 3.
So many high behaviors
          Frag. Poet. XXVIII. 7.
'T was high time they came;   Gifts. 2.
High and more high   Give. 11.
To supple Office, low and high;
          Good-Bye. 10.
For what are they all, in their high con-
ceit,   Good-Bye. 29.
Grass with green flag half-mast high,
          Humble-Bee. 44.

Heralds high before him run;
          Initial Love. 74.
With the high port he wore erewhile,
          In Memoriam. 77.
To Heaven's high will his will is bent.
          In Memoriam. 89.
All that high God did first create.
          May-Day. 442.
High over the river intervals,
          Monadnoc. 7.
'T is not in the high stars alone,
          Music. 13.
Nature's funeral high and dim,—
          Nun. 20.
The heaven high over
          Ode to Beauty. 37.
Saw rivers run seaward by cities high
          Poet. 65.
High was her heart, and yet was well in-
clined,   Quat. A. H. 1.
You doubt we read the stars on high,
          Romany. 25.
And comfort you with their high com-
pany.   Rome. 7.
That the high gods love tragedy;
          Saadi. 73.
Plight broken, this high face defaced!
          Threnody. 151.
High omens ask diviner guess;
          Threnody. 228.
In cities high the careful crowds
          Walden. 17.
Than all it holds more deep, more high.'
          Woodnotes. II. 318.

High-born
Minstrels and kings and high-born
dames, and of the best that be.
          Quat. A. H. 4.

Higher
Another round, a higher,
          Celestial Love. 8.
Higher far into the pure realm,
          Celestial Love. 27.
From high to higher forces
          Frag. Life. IV. 1.
Spirits of a higher strain
          Frag. Life. XXII. 3.
Higher, dear swallows! mind not what
I say.   Hermione. 26.
Higher or graver;   Merlin. 84.
Of Gypsy beauty blazes higher.
          Romany. 4.
Lo! the God's love blazes higher,
          Song of Seyd. 25.
And know my higher gifts unbind
          Threnody. 230.

Highest
And, in its highest noon and wantonness,
          Blight. 56.
Highest Love who shines on all;
          Daemonic Love. 69.
Above the ploughman's highest line,
          Monadnoc. 8.
Will heap in me their highest tide,
          Poet. 277.

Highland
Perish like leaves, the highland breed
          Monadnoc. 123.
Nestle warm the highland people,
          Monadnoc. 130.

Highlanders
Mountain speech to Highlanders,
Woodnotes. II. 152.

Highness
(Your Highness knows our homely
word) Boston. 73.

High-school
To the high-school and medalled boy:
May-Day. 345.

Highway
The highway, Eros and the Muse.
Love and Thought. 2.

Highways
Highways for me through the rock.
Hermione. 46.

Hill
See Ant-hill; Bunker Hill.
Shadowlike, o'er hill and hollow;
Etienne. 2.
Stand upon this pasture hill,
Frag. Nat. XXVI. 7.
The Muse's hill by Fear is guarded,
Frag. Poet. XXXI. 1.
How graceful climb those shadows on my
hill! Hamatreya. 7.
Only the light-armed climb the hill.
Merlin's Song. 28.
I turned to Cheshire's haughty hill.
Monadnoc. 32.
Seemed to me, the towering hill
Monadnoc. 195.
The frank blessings of the hill
Monadnoc. 222.
Daily over hill and meadow.
Monadnoc. 265.
The river, hill, stems, foliage are ob-
scure, Musketaquid. 83.
Ere one man my hill shall climb,
Saadi. 113.
The vapor the hill. Sphinx. 40.
This morn I climbed the misty hill
Thine Eyes. 5.
Of human youth had left the hill
Threnody. 108.
In quaking bog, on snowy hill,
Woodnotes. I. 38.
To hill and cloud his face was known,—
Woodnotes. I. 114.

Hill's
A hill's leaves for winding-sheets,
Mountain. 15.

Hills
Instead of flowers, crowned with a
wreath of hills. Adirondacs. 13.
As water poured through hollows of the
hills Adirondacs. 149.
We struck our camp and left the happy
hills. Adirondacs. 336.
Among the silver hills of heaven
Bacchus. 16.
But these young scholars, who invade our
hills, Blight. 18.
Fair rose the planted hills behind
Boston. 41.
And where the western hills declined
Boston. 43.
Will rive the hills and swim the sea,
II Compensation. 27.
Where twisted hills betray Cosmos. 18.

On eastern hills I see their smokes,
Forerunners. 15.
Northward he went to the snowy hills,
Frag. Poet. I. 9.
Bosomed in yon green hills alone,—
Good-Bye. 16.
The boy knew on the hills in spring,
Harp. 86.
Hills and islands, cloud and tree,
Hermione. 14.
On windy hills, whose tops with morn-
ing glow, I Bear. 7.
We will climb the broad-backed hills,
May-Day. 226.
'Our music's in the hills;'—
Monadnoc. 2.
To fill the hollows, sink the hills,
Monadnoc. 149.
And how the hills began,
Monadnoc. 221.
Beneath low hills, in the broad interval
Musketaquid. 26.
As I walked among the hills Poet. 144.
And pile the hills to scale the sky;
Saadi. 95.
Hides hills and woods, the river, and the
heaven, Snow-Storm. 4.
And, looking over the hills, I mourn
Threnody. 7.
Of skirting hills to lie,
Waldeinsamkeit. 6.
Chants his hymn to hills and floods,
Woodnotes. II. 34.
The hills where health with health agrees,
Woodnotes. II. 190.

Hillside
Many a high hillside,
Frag. Nat. III. 17.
As shepherd's lamp on far hill-side
Hermione. 42.
Hollow and lake, hillside and pine arcade,
Musketaquid. 23.
And as each flower upon the fresh hill-
side, Naples. 5.

Hill-top
Of thee from the hill-top looking down;
Each. 2.

Hilltops
The rocky nook with hilltops three
Boston. 1.

Him (Partial list.)
And ever was. Pay him.
Boston Hymn. 72.
Him strong Genius urged to roam,
Frag. Life. XX. 1.
Him to beckon, him to warn;
Frag. Poet. V. 43.
With malice dared me to proclaim him,
Initial Love. 13.
I travail in pain for him,
Song of Nature. 57.
The heavens that now draw him
Sphinx. 85.
Far and wide she cannot find him;
Threnody. 22.
My hopes pursue, they cannot bind him.
Threnody. 23.
Nature, who lost, cannot remake him;
Threnody. 27.
Fate let him fall, Fate can't retake him;
Threnody. 28.

Him (Partial list.)—*Continued*
To the aim which him allures,
　　　　　Voluntaries. 91.
Him duty through the clarion calling
　　　　　Voluntaries. 95.
It seemed as if the breezes brought him,
　　　　　Woodnotes. I. 46.
It seemed as if the sparrows taught him;
　　　　　Woodnotes. I. 47.
And the shy hawk did wait for him;
　　　　　Woodnotes. I. 57.
Him Nature giveth for defence
　　　　　Woodnotes. II. 75.

Himmaleh
Or the sky-piercing horns of Himmaleh;
　　　　　Frag. Nat. IV. 5.

Himmalee
Andes, Alp or Himmalee,
　　　　　Frag. Nat. XV. 3.

Himself (Partial list.)
What himself declared repeats,
　　　　　Astraea. 26.
What himself confessed records,
　　　　　Astraea. 27.
Himself encloses and includes,
　　　　　Daemonic Love. 94.
Himself and his love intervene.
　　　　　Frag. Life. XVII. 15.
Thus to himself the poet spoke,
　　　　　Poet. 141.
Himself from God he could not free;
　　　　　Problem. 22.
Wonderer chiefly at himself,
　　　　　Woodnotes. I. 26.
Into the fifth himself he flings,
　　　　　Woodnotes. II. 293.

Hind
Those doors are men: the Pariah hind
　　　　　Saadi. 163.

Hint
Some mystic hint accosts the vigilant,
　　　　　Adirondacs. 203.
Will hint her secret in a garden patch,
　　　　　Frag. Nat. IV. 2.
And with this hint be wise,—
　　　　　Hermione. 66.
And bursts the hoops at hint of Spring:
　　　　　May-Day. 91.
Hint summits of heroic grace;
　　　　　Monadnoc. 111.
Giving a hint of that which changes not.
　　　　　Seashore. 26.

Hints
'Mid all the hints and glories of the
　home. 　　　Adirondacs. 190.
And chance-dropped hints from Nature's
　sphere 　　　Initial Love. 72.
Hints never loss or cruel break
　　　　　In Memoriam. 107.
Has hints of the propitious time,
　　　　　May-Day. 120.
Whispering hints of treasure hid
　　　　　May-Day. 422.
And hints the future which it owes.
　　　　　Nature. Mot. 16.

Hired
His hired hands were wind and cloud;
　　　　　Frag. Poet. XXVII. 2.

Hireling
Hireling and him that hires;
　　　　　Boston Hymn. 40.

Hires
Hireling and him that hires;
　　　　　Boston Hymn. 40.

His (Partial list.)
And teach his nimbleness to earn his
　wage, 　　　Adirondacs. 268.
His hot tyranny 　Daemonic Love. 114.
In the waste one nook is his;
　　　　　Day by Day. 10.
Of his wisdom, of his fraud
　　　　　Limits. 4.
His city-tops a glimmering haze.
　　　　　Monadnoc. 323.
And thanks was his contrition;
　　　　　Saadi. 75.
What his fault, or what his crime?
　　　　　Voluntaries. 13.

Historic
Haunting this bank's historic trees?
　　　　　In Memoriam. 27.

History
Was never secret history 　Apology. 15.
A very tender history 　　Dirge. 55.
And crowds a history into a glance;
　　　　　Enchanter. 7.
Sailing through stars with all their his-
　tory. 　　　Monadnoc. 278.
I've learned the sum of that sad history
　　　　　Summons. 18.
And 't is far in the deeps of history,
　　　　　World-Soul. 19.

Hit
Art its height could never hit;
　　　　　Destiny. 8.
Toy with the bow, yet hit the white,
　　　　　Frag. Poet. V. 2.
Nor profane affect to hit 　Merlin. 66.
Toy with the bow, yet hit the white.
　　　　　Merlin's Song. 38.
Nor sequent centuries could hit
　　　　　Solution. 39.
To hit the nerve of feebler sight.
　　　　　Uriel. 42.
The sage, till he hit the secret,
　　　　　World-Soul. 51.

Hither (Partial list.)
　See Hitherward.
And how we should come hither with
　our sons, 　　Adirondacs. 163.
Hither hasted, in old time, Jove,
　　　　　Garden. 25.
And hither come the pensive train
　　　　　Hymn. 9.
Bring hither back the robin's call,
　　　　　May-Day. 162.
Hither rolls the storm of heat;
　　　　　May-Day. 192.
Hither! take me, use me, fill me,
　　　　　Mithridates. 31.
Pants up hither the spruce clerk
　　　　　Monadnoc. 313.
Hither we bring 　　Monadnoc. 364.
Call hither thy mortal enemy,
　　　　　Poet. 219.
Hither I come for strength
　　　　　Waterfall. 5.

Hitherto
Hitherto all things fast abide,
　　　　　Woodnotes. II. 256.

Hitherward
Swells hitherward, and myriads of forms
Pan. 4.

Hoard
And ingots added to the hoard.
Wealth. 43.

Hoary
Men to all shores that front the hoary
main. Seashore. 40.

Hold
See Uphold; Withhold.
Soft and softlier hold me, friends!
Aeolian Harp. 1.
A form which marble doth not hold
Angelo. 2.
We hold like rights, and shall;—
Boston. 26.
But to hold fast his simple sense,
Celestial Love. 127.
Of all he sheds how little it will hold,
Day's Ration. 13.
The little cup will hold not a bead more,
Day's Ration. 22.
I hold it of little matter Destiny. 34.
A twelvemonth he could silence hold,
Frag. Poet. V. 24.
Hold of the Maker, not the Made;
Frag. Poet. XVII. 1.
If they cannot hold me,
Hamatreya. 58.
But I hold them?' Hamatreya. 59.
And ride, and run, and have, and hold,
Initial Love. 29.
With grace to win, with heart to hold,
In Memoriam. 61.
Afflicted moan, and latest hold
May-Day. 19.
Suffice to hold the festival.
May-Day. 223.
Autumn-ripe, its juices hold
Monadnoc. 298.
And give to hold an even state,
Poet. 167.
Hold their sour conversation in the
sky:— River. 17.
If Nature hold another heart
Security. 9.
Leave the many and hold the few.
Terminus. 16.
Hold all the hidden wonders
World-Soul. 39.
But him no prison-bars would hold:
Worship. 4.

Holder
See Negro-Holder.

Holding
Holding Nature to her cause.
Frag. Poet. V. 12.
Holding us at vantage still,
Monadnoc. 376.

Holds
and sky that holds them all. Day. 6.
As he holds down central fires
Frag. Nat. I. 15.
Yet holds he them with tautest rein,
Initial Love. 50.
And holds all stars in his embrace.
Initial Love. 117.
Which holds to home 'neath every sky,
In Memoriam. 82.

Holds a cup with cowslip-wreaths,
May-Day. 5.
Which holds the grand designs
Ode to Beauty. 53.
O friendless Present! than thy bosom
holds. Quat. Heri. 4.
That holds and boasts the immeasurable
mind. River. 35.
Holds in check the frolic light,
Solution. 44.
Than all it holds more deep, more high.'
Woodnotes. II. 318.

Hole
See Fox-hole.
Every one to his hole in the wall,
May-Day. 390.
Steal in by window, chink, or hole,
Past. 17.
The ominous hole he dug in the sand,
Threnody. 86.
I too have a hole in a hollow tree;
Titmouse. 70.

Holiday
The falling rain will spoil no holiday.
Adirondacs. 69.
Why should I keep holiday
I Compensation. 1.
Where shall we keep the holiday,
May-Day. 218.
Frog and lizard in holiday coats,
May-Day. 237.

Holidays
The holidays were fruitful, but must end;
Adirondacs. 330.

Holier
What need I holier dew Walden. 25.

Holiness
To a consummate holiness,
Frag. Life. XXVIII. 2.

Hollow
Shadowlike, o'er hill and hollow;
Etienne. 2.
In caves and hollow trees he crept
Frag. Poet. I. 43.
He dives the hollow, climbs the steep.
May-Day. 72.
Hollow and lake, hillside and pine arc-
ade, Musketaquid. 23.
White hollow shells upon the desert
shore, Pan. 9.
I too have a hole in a hollow tree;
Titmouse. 70.

Hollows
As water poured through hollows of the
hills Adirondacs. 149.
To fill the hollows, sink the hills,
Monadnoc. 149.

Holy
There the holy essence rolls,
Celestial Love. 46.
But they are gone,—the holy ones
Dirge. 21.
That cheered the holy light!
*Farewell. 2.
High destined youths and holy maids
Frag. Poet. VII. 3.
Where the evening star so holy shines,
Good-Bye. 26.
Knows of Holy Book the spells,
Harp. 21.

Holy—*Continued*
And sent his priests in holy fear
                    Hymn. 7.
Such and so grew these holy piles,
                    Problem. 31.
One accent of the Holy Ghost
                    Problem. 61.
Here holy thoughts a light have shed
                    Robbins Hymn. 5.
And lift thee to his holy mount,
                    Saadi. 61.
Thought's holy light.   Thought. 4.
Seemed to the holy festival   Uriel. 29.
To the maids of holy mind,
                    World-Soul. 6.

Homage
Consist with homage to the good
                    In Memoriam. 36.
Drew his free homage unbeguiled,
                    In Memoriam. 68.
Nor kneels in homage to so mean a God.
                    To-Day. 14.

Home
'Mid all the hints and glories of the
    home.   Adirondacs. 190.
To spiritual lessons pointed home,
                    Adirondacs. 200.
Beckon the wanderer to his vaster home.
                    Adirondacs. 229.
Under the cinders burned the fires of
    home;   Adirondacs. 333.
This home my minstrel-journeyings ends.
                    Aeolian Harp. 19.
Goes home loaded with a thought.
                    Apology. 12.
His way home to the mark.
                    Boston Hymn. 88.
Be just at home; then write your scroll
                    Concord Ode. 25.
Of thoughts and things at home, but still
    adjourn   Day's Ration. 31.
All good creatures have their home.
                    Dearest. 4.
Who bides at home, nor looks abroad,
                    Destiny. 49.
I brought him home, in his nest, at even;
                    Each. 15.
For I did not bring home the river and
    sky;—   Each. 17.
I fetched my sea-born treasures home;
                    Each. 25.
From hearth and home away,
                    *Farewell. 8.
Stronger Custom brought him home.
                    Frag. Life. XX. 2.
In thy breast to make a home.
                    Frag. Life. XXII. 8.
Put in, drive home the sightless wedges
                    Frag. Nat. XXX. 1.
The tie of blood and home was rent:
                    Frag. Poet. I. 53.
And it lay on my hearth when I came
    home.   Frag. Poet. IV. 34.
Good-bye, proud world! I'm going home:
                    Good-Bye. 1. 14.
But now, proud world! I'm going home.
                    Good-Bye. 6.
O, when I am safe in my sylvan home,
                    Good-Bye. 23.
Which holds to home 'neath every sky,
                    In Memoriam. 82.

In hearts which round the hearth at
    home   In Memoriam. 84.
Back to books and sheltered home,
                    May-Day. 54.
'Happy,' I said, 'whose home is here!
                    Monadnoc. 68.
And found a home in haunts which
    others scorned,   Musketaquid. 3.
In the glad home plain-dealing Nature
    gave.   Musketaquid. 67.
By cloud or isle, is flying home;
                    Nemesis. 4.
And well he loved to quit his home
                    Poet. 51.
The republican at home.   Politics. 26.
Is in the morrow most at home,
                    Quat. Fate. 2.
And eat through Alps its home to find.
                    Quat. Love. 4.
Am I not always here, thy summer
    home?   Seashore. 3.
Vain beside mine. I drive my wedges
    home,   Seashore. 12.
Boy who made dear his father's home,
                    Threnody. 167.
Miles off, three dangerous miles, is home;
                    Titmouse. 9.
If from home chance draw me wide,
                    Una. 7.
At home a deeper thought may light
                    Una. 13.
And oft at home 'mid tasks I heed,
                    Walden. 41.
In forests I am still at home
                    Walden. 47.
To build in matter home for mind.
                    Wealth. 12.
There the poet is at home.
                    Woodnotes. I. 6.
Go where he will, the wise man is at
    home,   Woodnotes. I. 92.

Home-bound
The home-bound sea-boy hails,
                    Bell. 6.

Homely
(Your Highness knows our homely
    word)   Boston. 73.
Into rude and homely nooks,
                    May-Day. 355.
In the homstead, homely thought,
                    Una. 5.

Homer
And earth grow civil, Homer sung.
                    Solution. 16.

Homer's
Not Homer's self, the poet sire,
                    Harp. 76.

Homes
For homes of virtue, sense and taste.
                    Monadnoc. 152.
In lowly homes have lost their way.
                    Ode to Beauty. 67.
That filled their homes again;
                    Robbins Hymn. 16.
They live with God; their homes are
    dust;   Robbins Hymn. 21.
And quit proud homes and youthful
    dames   Voluntaries. 65.

Homestead
In the homestead, homely thought,
                    Una. 5.

Homeward
Homeward brought the oxen strong;
                          Apology. 18.
I homeward turn; farewell, my pet!
                          Titmouse. 80.
Honest
The world was made for honest trade,—
                          Boston. 11.
The honest waves refused to slaves
                          Boston. 17.
Their honest labor overpay.
                          Boston. 24.
Each honest man shall have his vote,
                          Boston. 33.
A union then of honest men,
                          Boston. 35.
The world was made for honest trade,—
                          Boston. 53.
Kind smile and honest frown
                          *Farewell. 12.
Honey
Knows to bring honey
                          Channing Ode. 86.
Columbine with horn of honey,
                          Frag. Nat. II. 9.
Him wood-gods fed with honey wild
                          Frag. Poet. I. 33.
Columbine with horn of honey,
                          Humble-Bee. 46.
Like fiery honey sucked from roses.
                          Initial Love. 53.
Honey from the frozen land;
                          Monadnoc. 136.
Sheen will tarnish, honey cloy,
                          Waldeinsamkeit. 17.
Honeycomb
Life's honeycomb, but not too fast;
                          Poet. 46.
Honied
My honied thought
                          Channing Ode. 4.
Honor
    See Dishonor.
Honor enough that we send the call.'
                          Boston. 68.
And honor joined the patriot ring
                          Boston. 84.
And honor, O South! for his shame;
                          Boston Hymn. 74.
Of honor o'er the sea,
                          Concord Ode. 26.
Honor prompted every glance,
                          In Memoriam. 55.
Honor came and sat beside him,
                          In Memoriam. 56.
'I am the giver of honor.
                          Woodnotes. II. 8.
Honored
With their own harvest honored were.
                          Guy. 46.
Honoring
And well could honoring Persia learn
                          Saadi. 82.
But arched o'er him an honoring vault.
                          Worship. 10.
Honors
To do the honors of his court,
                          Titmouse. 36.
Hook
Not hook nor line hath he;
                          Woodnotes. I. 8.

Hoop
    See Sky-hoop.
When the blue horizon's hoop
                          From Hafiz. 13.
Above the horizon's hoop,
                          Monadnoc. 395.
Hoops
And bursts the hoops at hint of Spring:
                          May-Day. 91.
Hooted
The raven croaked, owls hooted, the
    woodpecker   Adirondacs. 147.
Hope
Can drain its wealth of hope and sor-
    row;   Aeolian Harp. 15.
For the angel Hope aye makes
                          Caritas. 7.
The sun set, but set not his hope:
                          Character. 1.
Gathered with hope to please,
                          Daemonic Love. 109.
Fronted the sun with hope as bright,
                          Dirge. 7.
Where Hope, the soothsayer, reads our
    lot,   Ellen. 6.
The archangel Hope
                          Frag. Life. XXIII. 1.
Without remoter hope or fear
                          Frag. Poet. V. 5.
Hope beyond hope: Give. 10.
And with glad thoughts of faith and
    hope   Hymn. 23.
Sole source of light and hope assured,
                          Hymn. 25.
That never joy or hope shall here diffuse.
                          In Memoriam. 24.
Nor bate one jot of heart or hope,
                          In Memoriam. 80.
The rainbow of his hope was broke;
                          In Memoriam. 98.
Of swifter life, a surer hope,
                          May-Day. 152.
The total freight of hope and joy
                          May-Day. 354.
Or taunt us with our hope decayed?
                          May-Day. 427.
Terror and Hope and wild Remorse,
                          Miracle. 12.
Nor me can Hope or Passion urge
                          Nun. 17.
Nor haughty hope, nor swart chagrin,
                          Past. 8.
The sun set, but set not his hope:—
                          Poet. 134.
Shines the last age, the next with hope
    is seen,   Quat. Heri. 1.
With spasms of terror for balm of hope.
                          Solution. 24.
His early hope, his liberal mien;
                          Threnody. 55.
'T is because a general hope
                          Threnody. 132.
Hoped-for
All woman-born do know, that hoped-for
    days,   Summons. 19.
Hope's
Woe is me for my hope's downfall!
                          Monadnoc. 74.

Hopes
Dash our blown hopes as they limp
heavily by. Summons. 21.
My hopes pursue, they cannot bind him.
Threnody. 23.
She laid her hopes at rest,
*Violet. 16.

Hopped
Hopped on the bough, then, darting low,
Titmouse. 39.

Horizon
Up the horizon walls, Bacchus. 28.
They colored the horizon round;
Dirge. 33.
Silvers the horizon wall,
Humble-Bee. 22.
But leave us the horizon walls.
Romany. 8.
To thee the horizon shall express
Woodnotes. II. 196.

Horizon's
When the blue horizon's hoop
From Hafiz. 13.
To gaze o'er the horizon's edge,
Lines. 20.
The dim horizon's utmost bound;—
May-Day. 425.
Above the horizon's hoop,
Monadnoc. 395.
They bounded to the horizon's edge
Poet. 61.

Horn
From her redundant horn.
Adirondacs. 152.
Columbine with horn of honey,
Frag. Nat. II. 9.
Soothing with thy summer horn
Frag. Nat. XXII. 3.
Columbine with horn of honey,
Humble-Bee. 46.
And drops from Power's redundant horn
May-Day. 216.

Hornèd
Loves nature like a hornèd cow,
Initial Love. 100.

Horns
Or the sky-piercing horns of Himmaleh;
Frag. Nat. IV. 5.

Horoscope
With a bitter horoscope,
Solution. 23.

Horse
The horseman serves the horse,
Channing Ode. 44.
Stops his horse, and lists with delight,
Each. 7.
Unknown to him as to his horse,
Fate. 5.
Who leap from horse to horse, but never
touch the ground.
Frag. Poet. XIX. 2.

Horsed
Horsed on the Proteus, Illusions. 35.

Horseman
The horseman serves the horse,
Channing Ode. 44.
One sallow horseman knows me good.
Romany. 16.

Horses
The heroes on their horses,
Frag. Life. IV. 3.

Shun him, nymphs, on the fleet horses!
Initial Love. 102.

Hosmer
Bulkeley, Hunt, Willard, Hosmer,
Meriam, Flint, Hamatreya. 1.

Hospitable
Of rich men blazing hospitable light,
Naples. 18.
Acknowledged by their hospitable
boughs; River. 38.
Moved by his hospitable heart,
Titmouse. 34.

Hospitality
Belike has wider hospitality
Frag. Nat. V. 5.

Host
Girds with one flame the countless host,
Problem. 52.
No angel from the countless host
Threnody. 120.

Hostages
These presents be the hostages
Rhea. 70.

Hosts
Beset by pensive hosts. Dirge. 16.
The piny hosts were sheeted ghosts
May-Day. 49.
Beset by pensive hosts.] Peter. 12.

Hot
Even in the hot pursuit of the best aims
Blight. 58.
His hot tyranny Daemonic Love. 114.
Ah! the hot owner sees not Death, who
adds Hamatreya. 25.
Hot midsummer's petted crone,
Humble-Bee. 32.
There, while hot heads perplexed with
fears the state, Phi. 9.
Than the South more fierce and hot;
Test. 6.

Hotels
Cities of proud hotels, World-Soul. 9.

Hour
And now their hour is come.
I Compensation. 8.
Therefore comes an hour from Jove
Daemonic Love. 116.
To-day, when friends approach, and every
hour Day's Ration. 20.
Have brought us to life's evening hour,
Ellen. 2.
I will wait Heaven's perfect hour
Frag. Life. XXV. 3.
I drink the nectar of the hour:—
Frag. Nat. XXVI. 31.
I gave thee for an hour my ear,
Frag. Poet. II. 6.
Till his elected hour. Frag. Poet. V. 8.
The deeper secret of the hour!
Miracle. 18.
I know the appointed hour, Poet. 114.
Too busied with the crowded hour to
fear to live or die.
Quat. Nature. 4.
The hour of heaven. Generously trust
Rome. 21.
The hour of heaven shall come, the man
appear. Rome. 27.
Then the Spirit strikes the hour:
Threnody. 235.

Self-announced its hour of doom?
Threnody. 254.
That works its will on age and hour.
Unity. 11.
Withdrew, that hour, into his cloud;
Uriel. 38.
But he would come in the very hour
Woodnotes. I. 42.

Hourly
To Heaven thy hourly prayers are sent,
Prayer. 6.

Hours
Ask you, how went the hours?
Adirondacs. 107.
Rounded by hours where each outdid the
last Adirondacs. 154.
The rainbow hours bedeck his glowing
chair, Adirondacs. 226.
And all the following hours of the day
Day's Ration. 18.
And all the hours of the year
Guy. 45.
Tells of countless sunny hours,
Humble-Bee. 34.
And, when the sunlight fills the hours,
May-Day. 148.
Exact to days, exact to hours,
May-Day. 375.
There are open hours Merlin. 70.
And thief-like step of liberal hours
Monadnoc. 64.
Has thousand faces in a thousand hours.
Musketaquid. 25.
For him round-in the melancholy hours
Naples. 11.
What me the Hours will bring.
Quat. Botanist. 4.
And when his hours are numbered, and
the world Snow-Storm. 23.
Glide its hours uncounted,—
Sphinx. 43.
Quarrying man's rejected hours,
Spiritual Laws. 3.
And the glad hey-day of my household
hours, Summons. 9.
I do not count the hours I spend
Waldeinsamkeit. 1.
The Doctor stretched the hours,
Walden. 34.
My hours are peaceful centuries.
Woodnotes. II. 136.

House
See Farm-house; State-house.
To house of God and heavenly joys
Bell. 9.
And build me a wooden house.
Boston Hymn. 36.
House in the oak:—
Channing Ode. 28.
At the house where these sojourned.
Forerunners. 26.
That each should in his house abide,
Frag. Life. XXI. 1.
Thou shalt make thy house
Frag. Life. XXII. 1.
House you were born in, Illusions. 7.
Murmur in the house of life,
Merlin. 124.
We love the venerable house
Robbins Hymn. 1.

No tribes my house can fill,
Song of Nature. 10.
House at once and architect,
Spiritual Laws. 2.
I see my empty house, Threnody. 9.
House and tenant go to ground,
Threnody. 288.
In my house and garden-plot, Una. 9.

Household
There will I bring my books,—my house-
hold gods, Letter. 16.
Plied for thee thy household tasks.'
Saadi. 176.
And the glad hey-day of my household
hours, Summons. 9.
I hearken for thy household cheer,
Threnody. 36.

Houseless
In the houseless wood,
Frag. Nat. III. 22.

Housemates
Delayed, all friends shut out, the house-
mates sit Snow-Storm. 7.

House's
And the equipoise of heaven is thy
house's equipoise. Shah. Enweri. II. 2.

Houses
Houses, banquets, gardens, fountains,
Frag. Poet. IV. 11.
By houses lies a fresher green,
May-Day. 299.
Here in pine houses built of new-fallen
trees, Musketaquid. 30.
Not in their houses stand the stars,
Shah. Enweri. I. 1.
Houses of rich and great,
World-Soul. 10.

Hover
Around him hover *Lines. 5.

Hovered
But hovered gleaming and was gone.
Beauty. 4.

Hovering
Hovering over all that live,
Ode to Beauty. 75.

Hovers
A gleam which plays and hovers
Daemonic Love. 36.
A light which plays and hovers
Frag. Life. XVI. 2.

How (Partial list.)
Ask you, how went the hours?
Adirondacs. 107.
And how we should come hither with
our sons, Adirondacs. 163.
The state may follow how it can,
Channing Ode. 69.
Of all he sheds how little it will hold,
Day's Ration. 13.
Or how thy supper is sodden;'
Destiny. 26.
And, how oft soe'er they've turned it,
I Eros. 5.
How much, preventing God, how much
I owe Grace. 1.
How am I theirs, Hamatreya. 57.
This befell how long ago!
Initial Love. 6.
How long the power to give them name
Merops. 3.

How (Partial list.)—*Continued*
Knew my quarrel, how and why,
     Miracle. 31.
Mark how the climbing Oreads
     Monadnoc. 19.
And think how Nature in these towers
     Monadnoc. 98.
And how the hills began,
     Monadnoc. 221.
How the chemic eddies play,
     Monadnoc. 229.
Or how the sacred pine-tree adds
     Problem. 29.
Define and wrangle how they list,
     Saadi. 97.
Let them manage how they may,
     Saadi. 115.
How have I forfeited the right?
     Threnody. 34.
Askest, 'How long thou shalt stay?'
     Visit. 1.
How drearily in College hall
     Walden. 33.
I heed how wears the day;
     Walden. 42.
Or how meet in human elf
     Woodnotes. I. 28.

However
However long thou walkest solitary,
     Rome. 26.

Howling
Earth's a howling wilderness,
     Berrying. 2.
And fit the bleak and howling waste
     Monadnoc. 151.

Howsoever
And that the Jove,—yet, howsoever hid,
     Adirondacs. 289.

Hoyden
Whither went the lovely hoyden?
     Holidays. 13.

Hue
Were sought and found, amid the hue
and cry   Adirondacs. 192.
With song and hue and star and state,
     May-Day. 268.

Hues
the flush of hues; May-Day. 189.
Opal hues and purple dye;
     May-Day. 260.
Thy sombre head with rosy hues
     Monadnoc Afar. 3.
Ashes and jet all hues outshine.
     Titmouse. 55.

Hum
Ring of axe or hum of wheel
     Frag. Poet. I. 23.
Within earshot of thy hum,—
     Humble-Bee. 18.

Human
Of human sense doth overfill.
     Art. 28.
By sweet affinities to human flesh,
     Blight. 12.
And human fortunes in astronomy,
     Blight. 24.
And every human heart Cosmos. 25.
Stands to each human soul its own,
     Daemonic Love. 27.

For fear of human eyes swerved from his
plan.   Entombed. 4.
I am superior to my human weeds."
     Frag. Life. XVIII. 4.
Reason's twofold, part human, part
divine;   Frag. Life. XVIII. 6.
That human part may be described and
taught,   Frag. Life. XVIII. 7.
Beyond the scope of human age,
     Frag. Poet. XI. 17.
Tints the human countenance
     Humble-Bee. 24.
Wiser far than human seer,
     Humble-Bee. 52.
Which God in human hearts hath strung.
     Hymn. 16.
The far halloo of human voice;
     May-Day. 76.
Into all our human plight,
     May-Day. 461.
Complement of human kind,
     Monadnoc. 375.
Works thy form on human thought;
     Monadnoc Afar. 6.
Is the Creator of our human mould
     Naples. 2.
No human speech so beautiful
     Nun. 13.
I see all human wits
     Quat. Shakespeare. 1.
Of human youth had left the hill
     Threnody. 108.
From lengthening scroll of human fates,
     Threnody. 263.
Or how meet in human elf
     Woodnotes. I. 28.
Of man to come, of human life,
     Woodnotes. II. 131.
Which is human, which divine.
     Worship. 23.

Humanity
Who do the feat, and lift humanity.
     Adirondacs. 295.

Humble
None shall rule but the humble,
     Boston Hymn. 27.
One, by humble farmer seen,
     Chartist. 3.
Oft the humble and the poor;
     Daemonic Love. 106.
Plants and birds and humble creatures
     May-Day. 134.
And prayers of humble virtue made
     Robbins Hymn. 7.
From humble tenements around
     Robbins Hymn. 13.

Humble-bee
Burly, dozing humble-bee,
     Humble-Bee. 1.

Humblest
Oft, in streets or humblest places,
     Ode to Beauty. 64.

Humility
Without a false humility;
     Celestial Love. 123.

Hummer
Loved of bee,—the tawny hummer.
     Ellen South. 20.

Humming
Drowsily humming Frag. Nat. I. 4.

The threads of man at their humming
wheel,   Harp. 100.

Hummock
In the hummock of the field.
                    Frag. Poet. XXVII. 4.

Humors
To a thousand humors shift it,
                    Mithridates. 23.

Hundred
Let the blood of her hundred thousands
                    Boston. 106.
I have trod this path a hundred times
                    Miracle. 1.
Round about, a hundred miles,
                    Monadnoc. 36.
Fourscore or a hundred words
                    Monadnoc. 175.
Which five hundred did survive?
                    Test. 14.
Where from a hundred lakes young rivers
sprang;   Woodnotes. I. 63.

Hundred-gated
In her hundred-gated Thebes
                    Frag. Nat. XII. 2.

Hung
    See Low-hung; O'erhung; Well-hung.
Hung out their summer pride,
                    Boston. 38.
A cabin hung with curling smoke,
                    Frag. Poet. I. 22.
Not on crags are hung,
                    Monadnoc. 232.
I hung my verses in the wind,   Test. 1.
Hung idle stars and suns?
                    Wealth. 4.

Hungary's
Wales, Scotland, Uri, Hungary's dells:
                    Monadnoc. 96.

Hunger
All the fierce enemies, ague, hunger, cold,
                    Adirondacs. 317.

Hungrier
Said was hungrier than all;
                    Frag. Poet. I. 2.

Hungry
And now, again, a hungry company
                    Adirondacs. 281.
Still plotting how their hungry ear
                    Threnody. 50.

Hunt
To hunt upon their shining trails.
                    Forerunners. 8.
Bulkeley, Hunt, Willard, Hosmer,
    Meriam, Flint,   Hamatreya. 1.
Hunt knowledge   Rome. 14.
Thy foes to hunt, thy enviers to strike
down,   Shah-Hafiz. 1.

Hunted
Hunted by Sorrow's grisly train
                    In Memoriam. 74.

Hunter
    See Night-hunter.
A blooming hunter of a fairy fine.
                    River. 15.

Hunters'
Our foaming ale we drank from hunters'
pans,   Adirondacs. 177.
With hunters' appetite and peals of mirth.
                    Adirondacs. 182.

Hunting
    See Flower-hunting

Hunting-ground
Old cradle, hunting-ground and bier
                    Monadnoc. 80.

Huntsmen
Huntsmen find the easiest way.
                    Quat. Artist. 4.

Hurl
The truth, and hurl wrong-doers down.
                    Worship. 14.

Hurled
Through good and ill the war-bolt hurled,
                    Boston. 98.
Hurled into life to do a deed,
                    Frag. Life. XXIII. 8.
Change acts, reacts; back, forward
hurled,   Poet. 175.

Hurling
Hurling defiance at vast death;
                    Titmouse. 44.

Hurried
They hurried down from their deep
abodes   Poet. 147.
One tarried here, there hurried one;
                    Threnody. 156.

Hurry
But they hurry to their peers,
                    Astraea. 15.
That hurry through the eternal halls,
                    II Compensation. 10.
I challenge thee to hurry past
                    Nun. 31.
Trenchant time behoves to hurry
                    Woodnotes. II. 258.

Hurt
    See Unhurt.
With science poorly mask their hurt;
                    Alphonso. 37.
Indebted or insulted, loved or hurt,
                    Day's Ration. 10.
By which thy hurt thou may'st divine.
                    Woodnotes. II. 193.

Hurts
Piques, reproaches, hurts, caresses.
                    Initial Love. 133.
To stand the hurts of time, until
                    Monadnoc. 226.
Loving the wind that bent me. All my
hurts   Musketaquid. 71.
Some of your hurts you have cured,
                    Quat. Borrowing. 1.
And heal the hurts which sin has made.
                    Woodnotes. II. 220.

Husbanded
So to be husbanded for poorer days.
                    Day's Ration. 25.

Husbands
Bad husbands of their fires,
                    Terminus. 24.

Hush
Is fallen: but hush! it has not scared the
buck
                    Adirondacs. 122.

Hushed
Hushed myriads hark in vain,
                    Merlin's Song. 11.

Hut
And in low hut the dweller found:
                    Monadnoc. 73.
Beside his hut and shading oak,
                    Poet. 140.

Hut—*Continued*
Quit the hut, frequent the palace,
Quat. Artist. 1.
A little hut suffices like a town.
Seashore. 10.

Huts
And huts and tents; nor loved he less
Frag. Poet. I. 25.

Hyacinthine
The hyacinthine boy, for whom
Threnody. 15.

Hydnum
Hypnum and hydnum, mushroom, sponge
and moss, Adirondacs. 144.

Hymen
As Hymen yet hath blessed,
Good Hope. 6.
Hymen of element and race,
May-Day. 266.

Hymn
See Death-hymn.
Nor hymn, nor prayer, nor church.
Bohemian. 12.
And I the hymn the Brahmin sings.
Brahma. 12.
Obeys the hymn, obeys the ode.
Frag. Poet. XV. 2.
Which blasts of Northern mountains
hymn, Nun. 19.
He heard the woodcock's evening hymn;
Woodnotes. I. 55.
Chants his hymn to hills and floods,
Woodnotes. II. 34.

Hymns
In music and uplifting hymns.
Frag. Poet. V. 29.

Hypnum
Hypnum and hydnum, mushroom, sponge
and moss, Adirondacs. 144.

Hypocrite
See Arch-hypocrite.

Hypocritic
Daughters of Time, the hypocritic Days,
Days. 1.

Hyson
One scent to hyson and to wall-flower,
Xenophanes. 2.

I (Partial list.)
I, Alphonso, live and learn,
Alphonso. 1.
I, a king, for kings can feel.
Alphonso. 44.
Tax not my sloth that I Apology. 5.
'What am I? companion, say.'
Astraea. 18.
That I intoxicated, Bacchus. 21.
That I, drinking this, Bacchus. 38.
Quickened so, will I unlock
Bacchus. 43.
I thank the joyful juice Bacchus. 45.
For all I know;— Bacchus. 46.
For I am weary of the surfaces,
Blight. 2.
O, that were much, and I could be a
part Blight. 14.
Lo! I uncover the land
Boston Hymn. 17.
I show Columbia, of the rocks
Boston Hymn. 21.

And I unchain the slave:
Boston Hymn. 54.
When me they fly, I am the wings;
Brahma. 10.
I am the doubter and the doubt,
Brahma. 11.
And I the hymn the Brahmin sings.
Brahma. 12.
If I refuse Channing Ode. 7.
Yet do not I implore Channing Ode. 71.
When I was born,
Day's Ration. 1.
And whether I am angry or content,
Day's Ration. 9.
I wandered up, I wandered down,
Dirge. 15.
I serve you not, if you I follow,
Etienne. 1.
You are not so small as I, Fable. 13.
If I cannot carry forests on my back,
Fable. 18.
I tuneful voices overhear;
Forerunners. 30.
When I, as others, follow petty ends;
Frag. Life. XV. 3.
I do not delight Frag. Nat. XVIII. 2.
And pleased I stray
Frag. Nat. XXI. 2.
Come and I will show you all
Frag. Nat. XXVI. 5.
The depths of sin to which I had de-
scended, Grace. 7.
I sing it to the surging crowd,—
Merlin's Songs. 5.
What care I, so they stand the same,—
Merops. 1.
I heard, and I obeyed,—
Monadnoc. 27.
If I err not, thus it said:—
Monadnoc. 198.
I will give my son to eat
Monadnoc. 303.
I am a willow of the wilderness,
Musketaquid. 70.
There in a moment I have seen
Peter. 17.
And if I take you, dames, to task,
Romany. 9.
And I the lady all the while.
Romany. 12.
And sometimes mankind I appalled
Solution. 22.
So I folded me in fears, Solution. 27.
But I, the bantling of a country Muse,
Summons. 22.
I hung my verses in the wind, Test. 1.
The youth replies, I can.
Voluntaries. 74.
What need I holier dew Walden. 25.
I talk with kings the while.]
Walden. 32.
And there I cannot stray. Walden. 48.

Ice
The dismal Massachusetts ice
May-Day. 142.
To break enchanted ice, Rubies. 10.
Makes flame to freeze and ice to boil;
Spiritual Laws. 10.
Evil will bless, and ice will burn.'
Uriel. 24.

Iceberg
Even into May the iceberg cold.
May-Day. 20.
As melts the iceberg in the seas,
Poet. 33.

Ice-imprisoned
Of the ice-imprisoned flood; Merlin. 20.

Icy
I found no joy: the icy wind
May-Day. 51.

I'd (Partial list.)
When Winter reigned I'd close my eye,
*Violet. 11.

Idea
The great Idea baffles wit,
Bohemian. 7.
From deep ideal fontal heavens that flow.
Frag. Life. XV. 8.

Ideas
Divine Ideas below, Ode to Beauty. 61.

Ides
Forteller of the vernal ides,
Woodnotes. I. 32.

Idiot
And the dull idiot might see
Merlin. 72.

Idle
For the idle flowers I brought;
Apology. 10.
Yet mark me well, that idle word
Frag. Poet. IV. 21.
Those idle catches told the laws
Frag. Poet. V. 11.
Not idle, since the leaf all day
May-Day. 115.
With idle footsteps, crooning rhymes.
Miracle. 2.
And idle clowns beside the mere
Poet. 21.
These idle flowers, that tremble in the
wind, River. 23.
Hung idle stars and suns? Wealth. 4.
Within, without the idle earth,
World-Soul. 61.

Idleness
For a proud idleness like this
Waldeinsamkeit. 47.

Idolatry
His sweetheart's idolatry Rhea. 39.

If (Partial list.)
As if associates of the sylvan gods.
Adirondacs. 156.
To ears intelligent; as if gray rock
Adirondacs. 253.
Wise and polite,—and if I drew
Adirondacs. Motto. 1.
And die of inanition. If I knew
Blight. 3.
If Indians seized the tea, Boston. 77.
As if in him the welkin walked,
Frag. Poet. I. 54.
Or, if in thy heart he shine,
Freedom. 17.
If on the foeman fell his gaze, Guy. 21.
And, if I tell you all my thought,
Initial Love. 23.
If thou trowest Monadnoc. 228.
But Nature's heir,—if I repine,
Threnody. 127.

If I had not taken the child.
Threnody. 178.
But if upon the seas I sail, Una. 17.
If in ashes the fire-seed slept. Uriel. 46.
If but one hero knew it,
World-Soul. 49.

Ignoble
The snow is no ignoble shroud,
Titmouse. 21.

Ignorance
But, in my simple ignorance, suppose
Rhodora. 15.

I'll (Partial list.)
Masters, I'll be plain with you;
Alphonso. 42.
I'll not deny you make Fable. 15.

Ill
The ill I shun, the good I claim;
Angelo. 7.
Fails of the life, but draws the death and
ill. Angelo. 14.
Through good and ill the war-bolt
hurled, Boston. 98.
They reckon ill who leave me out;
Brahma. 9.
Where good and ill, Celestial Love. 39.
Wilt thou seal up the avenues of ill?
Frag. Life. XXXII. 1.
Ill used, it will destroy,
Frag. Nat. XXIV. 9.
And cure all ill, is cordial speech:
Merlin's Song. 36.
Ill fits the abstemious Muse Phi. 1.
For living brows; ill fits them to receive:
Phi. 2.
Eager for good, not hating ill,
Poet. 208.
And whether formed for good or ill,
Prayer. 7.
Ill day which made this beauty waste,
Threnody. 150.
The rash word boded ill to all;
Uriel. 30.
The bounds of good and ill were rent;
Uriel. 32.
Or what ill planet crossed his prime?
Voluntaries. 14.
The reeling brain can ill compute)
Wealth. 20.
All ill dissolving in the light
Woodnotes. II. 65.

Ill-bestead
Ill-bestead for gay bridegroom.
Hermione. 35.

Ills
This child should ills of ages stay,
Threnody. 135.
And ills to come as evils past bemoan.
Woodnotes. I. 89.

Illumined
By God's own light illumined and fore-
showed. Woodnotes. I. 95.

Illusion
Illusion works impenetrable,
Frag. Nat. XXXI. 1.
Illusion dwells forever with the wave.
Seashore. 42.

Illusions
Illusions like the tints of pearl,
Frag. Nat. XXXII. 1.

I'm (Partial list.)
Masters, I'm in pain with you;
          Alphonso. 41.
And, for I'm styled Alphonse the Wise,
          Alphonso. 47.
If I'm not so large as you,   Fable. 12.
Nor when I'm jaded, sick, anxious or
   mean.   Frag. Life. XV. 5.

Image
With Freedom's image and name.
          Boston Hymn. 76.
Twice I have moulded an image,
          Song of Nature. 61.
But multiplies the image of a day,—
          Xenophanes. 15.

Images
Fill the lake with images,—
          Celestial Love. 72.

Imagest
And imagest the stable good
          Monadnoc. 387.

Imaginative
With credulous and imaginative man;
          Seashore. 44.

Imagined
  See Unimagined.

Imbecile
Apollo is an imbecile.
          Frag. Poet. XVIII. 4.

Imbibing
Imbibing virtue by his hand
          Initial Love. 55.

Imbroglio
And endless imbroglio   Illusions. 31.

Immeasurable
That holds and boasts the immeasurable
   mind.   River. 35.

Immense
Plans immense his term prolong;
          Initial Love. 139.
Nor plant immense designs   Poet. 247.
This vault which glows immense with
   light   Woodnotes. II. 299.

Immensely
Immensely curious whether you
          Alphonso. 39.

Immortal
Singing an immortal strain,   Dull. 4.
Immortal here below.   Dull. 5.
Rafters of immortal pine,   House. 6.
Of Syrian peace, immortal leisure,
          Humble-Bee. 38.
Best of Pan's immortal meat,
          Monadnoc. 304.
And thus the wise Immortal doeth,—
          Rhea. 46.
Immortal youth returns.
          Waldeinsamkeit. 28.
And sunk the immortal eye so low?
          Woodnotes. II. 185.

Immured
No churl, immured in cave or den;
          Saadi. 24.

Impart
To read the sense the woods impart
          Miracle. 9.
Though baffled seers cannot impart
          Nature. Mot. 9.

And though no Muse can these impart,
          Threnody. 206.
Each joy the mountain dales impart;
          Woodnotes. I. 35.

Impartial
Gave an impartial tomb to all the kinds.
          Adirondacs. 140.

Imparts
The secret of the world imparts;
          Aeolian Harp. 13.

Impassible
Impassible to heat or cold.
          Frag. Poet. I. 49.

Impatient
His impatient looks devour
          Daemonic Love. 105.
Impatient to anticipate   May-Day. 154.
Impatient friend,—   Poet. 92.
And the impatient years that trod on it
          Summons. 16.

Impenetrable
Illusion works impenetrable,
          Frag. Nat. XXXI. 1.

Imperfect
Of their imperfect functions.
          Blight. 17.

Imperial
What god is this imperial Heat,
          May-Day. 210.

Impertinent
Shall his own sorrow seem impertinent,
          Frag. Life. XXVI. 2.

Impiously
For we invade them impiously for gain;
          Blight. 37.

Implore
Yet do not I implore
          Channing Ode. 71.

Impolite
The polite found me impolite; the great
          Musketaquid. 68.

Import
Of one import, of varied tone;
          Garden. 42.
And import intelligence.   Visit. 20.

Imports
What imports, what irks and what behooves,   Frag. Poet. XII. 3.

Impose
He shall impose, to find a spring, trap
   foxes,   Adirondacs. 103.

Impossible
What in the desert was impossible
          Adirondacs. 321.
The impossible shall yet be done,
          Initial Love. 145.

Impotence
Constrained by impotence to adjourn
          Poet. 187.

Impregnably
Can arm impregnably the skin;
          Titmouse. 76.

Impress
Prints his small impress on the snow,
          Titmouse. 40.

Impressional
Tremulous, impressional,   Culture. 4.

Imprisoned
  See Ice-imprisoned.

To man imprisoned in his own.
Garden. 44.
Man in man is imprisonèd; Saadi. 118.

Improved
Not to be improved. I Eros. 6.

Improvisation
A divine improvisation,
Woodnotes. II. 263.

Imps
Imps, at high midsummer, blot
Alphonso. 9.

Impulse
Obey the nobler impulse; that is Rome:
Rome. 16.

Impunity
Which few can put on with impunity.
Adirondacs. 98.

Impure
Pure by impure is not seen.
Astraea. 44.
Known in part, or known impure,
Celestial Love. 51.
He has not tasted wine impure,
Harp. 3.

In (Partial list.)
See Round-in; Wherein.
In winter, lumberers; in summer, guides;
Adirondacs. 88.
Insatiate skill in water or in air
Adirondacs. 137.
Nor Boccace in Decameron.
Adirondacs. Motto. 4.
Died in its last expression. Amulet. 12.
In their summits are united;
Celestial Love. 45.
In the still abodes. Celestial Love. 57.
Solitude in solitudes:
Daemonic Love. 95.
The morning wind is in it;
Ellen South. 2.
To use my land to put his rainbow in.
Frag. Nat. IX. 2.
In Walden wood the chickadee
Frag. Nat. XIX. 1.
Disappeared in blessed wife;
Holidays. 14.
Living in a baby's life. Holidays. 16.
And bid you let the angels in
Hymn. 19.
House you were born in,
Illusions. 7.
'Pass in, pass in,' the angels say,
Merlin. 34.
Fold us music-drunken in. Merlin. 129.
Nor murdering hate, can enter in.
Past. 9.
When worlds of lovers hem thee in?
Threnody. 188.
In at the window-pane; World-Soul. 30.
And in the second reappears the first.
Xenophanes. 13.

Inaccessible
Slide with the sledge to inaccessible
woods Musketaquid. 45.

Inalienable
Of one inalienable right,
Thought. 2.

Inanition
And die of inanition. If I knew
Blight. 3.

Inborn
All inborn power that could
In Memoriam. 35.

Incarnate
Up which the incarnate soul must climb,
Dirge. 2.
The zone that girds the incarnate mind.
Threnody. 231.

Incarved
See Stone-incarved.

Incense
Whence a smokeless incense breathes.
May-Day. 6.

Incensed
Incensed and starred October. 9.

Incessant
Who layeth the world's incessant plan,
Woodnotes. II. 271.

Inch
An inch of ground the lightning strook
Frag. Poet. XXXII. 3.
No inch to the god of day; Merops. 10.
And every inch of garden ground
Threnody. 90.

Inches
Ere sunset quarrying inches down,
May-Day. 117.

Inclined
Publishes when 't is inclined.
Merlin. 69.
High was her heart, and yet was well
inclined, Quat. A. H. 1.
Like Cupids studiously inclined;
Threnody. 65.

Includes
Himself encloses and includes,
Daemonic Love. 94.

Incommunicable'
As far as the incommunicable;
Threnody. 200.

Inconstant
Inconstant heat and nerveless reins,—
Terminus. 30.

Incontinent
Each street and spire and roof, incontinent. Letter. 6.

Incorruptible
Or cedar incorruptible, House. 7.
By its own meek and incorruptible will?
Oh What. 3.

Increase
the streams increase
Frag. Nat. XXVI. 22.
Mould the year to fair increase,
Merlin. 57.
And tides of life and increase lend;
Threnody. 113.

Incrusted
See Town-incrusted.

Indebted
Indebted or insulted, loved or hurt,
Day's Ration. 10.

Indian
Of craggy Indian wilderness he hears
Adirondacs. 312.
In Indian wildernesses found;
Humble-Bee. 37.

Indian—*Continued*
Makes travellers long for Indian skies,
May-Day. 294.
The Indian cheer, the frosty skies,
Monadnoc. 106.
Through which at will our Indian rivulet
Musketaquid. 26.

Indians
If Indians seized the tea,
Boston. 77.

Indigence
Our sumptuous indigence,
Monadnoc. 377.

Indigestible
Food   indigestible":—then   murmured
some,   Adirondacs. 186.

Indignant
That would indignant rend
Channing Ode. 38.

Indoors
Wear out indoors your sickly days,
Romany. 7.

Indulgent
The third adds heat's indulgent spark;
Woodnotes. II. 291.

Industry
By mind's industry sharpening the love
of life—   Summons. 12.

Inevitable
The inevitable morning   World-Soul. 33.

Inexorable
Inexorable to thy zeal:
Sursum Corda. 2.

Inextricably
Inextricably bound,   Hermione. 75.

Infancy
Which once my infancy beguiled,
May-Day. 351.

Infant
Infant Bacchus in the vine,—
Garden. 35.
The same blue wonder that my infant eye
River. 3.
The world and not the infant failed.
Threnody. 139.

Infantile
And brings it infantile and fresh.
Monadnoc. 162.

Infection
And where the infection slid,
Bacchus. 60.

Inferior
Heedless of inferior things;
Song of Seyd. 32.

Infested
See Bee-infested.

Infinite
Permitted on her infinite repose
Adirondacs. 341.
Whom the Infinite One
Ode to Beauty. 35.
To infinite time his eager turn,
Poet. 188.
Pours finite into infinite.
Threnody. 237.
And crowded whole, an infinite paroquet,
Xenophanes. 18.

Infinity
To utter God's infinity,   Bohemian. 2.

Infirm
Fear not, then, thou child infirm,
II Compensation. 19.
Infirm, melancholy,   Sphinx. 53.

Infirmities
I bear in youth the sad infirmities
I Bear. 1.

Influence
I said, 'What influence me preferred,
Berrying. 9.
Alive to gentle influence   Culture. 5.
Hid in song's sweet influence.
Merlin. 42.
Hath such a soul, such divine influence,
Naples. 21.
But fell the starry influence short,
Song of Nature. 71.
Sweet influence from every element;
Woodnotes. I. 77.

Infold
Transforming what it doth infold,
May-Day. 202.
Where pastoral tribes their flocks infold,
Poet. 64.
Which Music's wings infold,
Voluntaries. 76.

Infolds
Like a sea which me infolds;
May-Day. 194.

Informed
Informed by thee,   Ode to Beauty. 40.

Infusing
And infusing subtle heats,
Humble-Bee. 26.

Ingot
To fetch one ingot thence   Dull. 16.

Ingots
And ingots added to the hoard.
Wealth. 43.

Inhabiteth
And inhabiteth the wood,
Woodnotes. II. 58.

Inhaled
I inhaled the violet's breath;   Each. 43.

Inherent
Of the rich inherent worth,
In Memoriam. 50.

Injured
The injured elements say, 'Not in us;'
Blight. 33.

Inks
The inks of Erebus he found;
Solution. 48.

Inly
Friends year by year more inly known.
Daemonic Love. 16.
Bird and brier inly warms,
May-Day. 198.
Prayers of saints that inly burned,—
Threnody. 265.

Inmost
Revealer of the inmost powers
May-Day. 414.

Inn
Is the inn where he lodges for a night.
Woodnotes. II. 300.

Innermost
In   their   innermost   estate;
Celestial Love. 96.

Innocence
And speak the speech of innocence,
    Celestial Love. 128.
Please God, I'll wrap me in mine innocence,   I Bear. 13.
The silver seat of Innocence.
    Spiritual Laws. 12.
Innocence that matched the sky,
    Threnody. 212.
His formidable innocence;
    Woodnotes. II. 76.

Innocent
Sound, ruddy men, frolic and innocent,
    Adirondacs. 87.
The innocent mirth which sweetens daily
 bread,   Summons. 10.
The little captain innocent
    Threnody. 70.
When thou didst yield thy innocent
 breath   Threnody. 100.

Innumerable
Through the innumerable years.
    Frag. Life. XXV. 4.
Weaving webs innumerable,
    Frag. Nat. XXXI. 2.
The innumerable tenements of beauty,
    Musketaquid. 61.
Open innumerable doors Saadi. 159.
The innumerable days.
    Song of Nature. 4.

Inorbed
But sceptred genius, aye inorbed,
    Hermione. 10.

Inquires
He is the essence that inquires.
    Woodnotes. II. 312.

Inquisitive
Inquisitive, and fierce, and fasting,
    Initial Love. 37.

Insanity
The insanity of towns to stem
    Monadnoc. 116.

Insatiate
Insatiate skill in water or in air
    Adirondacs. 137.

Inscribest
Thou inscribest with a bond,
    Ode to Beauty. 30.

Inscriptions
Received the fair inscriptions of the
 night; Frag. Nat. XXVII. 2.

Inscrutable
And Nature, the inscrutable and mute,
    Adirondacs. 340.
Shy, untamed, inscrutable,
    Initial Love. 89.

Insect
Intent on insect slaughter:
    Frag. Nat. XIX. 3.
Solar insect on the wing
    Frag. Nat. XXII. 1.
Insect lover of the sun,
    Humble-Bee. 11.
Hath my insect never seen;
    Humble-Bee. 41.
Our insect miseries to thy rocks;
    Monadnoc. 365.
They harness beast, bird, insect, to their
 work; Musketaquid. 36.

Insert
Insert a leaf, or forge a name,
    Past. 19.

Inspire
Quick and skilful to inspire
    Ode to Beauty. 76.

Inspirer
Inspirer, prophet evermore;
    Monadnoc. 47.

Inspires
And through the priest the mind inspires.
    Problem. 54.

Installs
Whom he uniteth, God installs;
    Frag. Life. XVII. 12.

Instant
And, on the instant, rosier clouds upbore
    Adakryn. 4.
Instant and perfect his access
    Frag. Life. XVII. 12.
His instant thought a poet spoke,
    Frag. Poet. XXXII. 1.
Instant to my grave I stoop,
    From Hafiz. 15.

Instead
Instead of flowers, crowned with a wreath
 of hills.   Adirondacs. 13.
Snow-loving pines and oaks instead;
    Garden. 7.

Institutes
Institutes and dictionaries,
    Monadnoc. 182.

Instructed
And these instructed by their wisest too,
    Adirondacs. 294.
Shall the dumb bird instructed say.
    Miracle. 22.

Instruction
Then for mankind's instruction shown;
    Prayer. 4.

Instrument
Or tone of silver instrument
    Forerunners. 12.

Insufficient
In the insufficient skies. Alphonso. 8.

Insulted
Indebted or insulted, loved or hurt,
    Day's Ration. 10.

Insults
And the multitude insults.
    Daemonic Love. 104.

Intellect
And the sons of intellect,
    Daemonic Love. 99.
Of the old building Intellect.
    Monadnoc. 374.

Intelligence
That keeps intelligence with you,—
    Amulet. 6.
For aëry intelligence, Initial Love. 68.
'T is good will makes intelligence,
    Titmouse. 65.
And import intelligence. Visit. 20.

Intelligent
To ears intelligent; as if gray rock
    Adirondacs. 253.

Intemperance
By error or intemperance. Poet. 158.

Intense
Love is the air-fed fire intense,
Song of Seyd. 15.
Intent
Of the Ausable stream, intent to reach
Adirondacs. 3.
And where they went on trade intent
Boston. 7.
Intent on insect slaughter:
Frag. Nat. XIX. 3.
Untold intent; Give. 14.
Intent, I searched the region round,
Monadnoc. 72.
Interchangeable
Interchangeable with things, Guy. 3.
Interchangeably
And interchangeably at one
Initial Love. 124.
Interferes
And the dearest interferes:
Frag. Poet. XXV. 2.
Interior
For out of Thought's interior sphere
Problem. 39.
Intermittent
An intermittent blaze, Poet. 103.
Interpret
For so I must interpret still Eva. 4.
And interpret your device.
Initial Love. 63.
His hidden sense interpret can;—
Miracle. 20.
Interrogate
Wilt thou, uncalled, interrogate,
Threnody. 249.
Intertwine
They intertwine the farthest star:
Celestial Love. 108.
Interval
In the frequent interval
Frag. Poet. III. 8.
Beneath low hills, in the broad interval
Musketaquid. 26.
Intervals
Go, without check or intervals,
Celestial Love. 24.
High over the river intervals,
Monadnoc. 7.
He heard, when in the grove, at intervals,
Woodnotes. I. 72.
In scanty intervals. World-Soul. 40.
Intervene
Himself and his love intervene.
Frag. Life. XVII. 15.
Intimacy
And his wish is intimacy,
Initial Love. 142.
Intimater intimacy, Initial Love. 143.
Intimate
Thou intimate stranger,
Ode to Beauty. 15.
Intimater
Intimater intimacy, Initial Love. 143.
Into
See Whereinto.
Into this Oreads' fended Paradise,
Adirondacs. 194.
A private beam into each several heart.
Adirondacs. 223.

Into each mind Adirondacs. 332.
Bring the moonlight into noon Art. 3.
Into the laughing sea? Boston. 79.
Higher far into the pure realm,
Celestial Love. 27.
Into vision where all form
Celestial Love. 31.
Melt into one. Celestial Love. 41.
Straight, into double band
Channing Ode. 94.
Nature centres into balls, Circles. 1.
Go put your creed into your deed,
Concord Ode. 19.
Shall into Future fuse the Past,
Culture. 10.
Melts down into that liquor of my life,—
Day's Ration. 7.
All he distils into sidereal wine
Day's Ration. 11.
And I uplift myself into its heaven,
Day's Ration. 16.
And crowds a history into a glance;
Enchanter. 7.
Replunged again into that upper sphere
Frag. Life. XVI. 8.
Hurled into life to do a deed,
Frag. Life. XXIII. 8.
Into the mineral air,
Frag. Life. XXIV. 2.
Limbs into branches, branches into twigs,
Frag. Nat. XVII. 4.
Like sower's seeds into his brain,
Frag. Poet. V. 35.
Melting matter into dreams,
Frag. Poet. VIII. 7.
Into substance, into Law.
Frag. Poet. VIII. 10.
Into the very best sole-leather.
Frag. Poet. XXIII. 2.
Coin the day-dawn into lines
Frag. Poet. XXIX. 1.
Coin the moonlight into verse
Frag. Poet. XXIX. 3.
Brute or savage into man;
Freedom. 16.
It dives into noon, Give. 12.
As costly wine into his well. Guy. 30.
A door into the mountain heart,
Hermione. 44.
And right into himself does draw;
Initial Love. 121.
Then runs into a wave again,
Initial Love. 148.
Even into May the iceberg cold.
May-Day. 20.
The next into the farthest brings,
May-Day. 80.
The dead log touched bursts into leaf,
May-Day. 208.
The air stole into the streets of towns,
May-Day. 342.
Into rude and homely nooks,
May-Day. 355.
Into all our human plight,
May-Day. 461.
Into chorus wove. Merlin. 99.
Thawing snow-drift into flowers.
Monadnoc. 65.
Once more into his dapper town,
Monadnoc. 345.

Into the winter night's extinguished mood?   Musketaquid. 79.
Pours her power into the people,
          Nature. II. 6.
Into the charmed snare she shuns;
          Nemesis. 6.
Into nature again.   Ode to Beauty. 20.
Into blissful orgies sank;   Poet. 82.
Adopted them into her race,
          Problem. 42.
And carve the coastwise mountain into caves.   Seashore. 13.
The rocky coast, smite Andes into dust,
          Seashore. 35.
She spired into a yellow flame;
          Sphinx. 125.
She flowed into a foaming wave:
          Sphinx. 127.
The brook into the stream runs on;
          Threnody. 96.
Brought the old order into doubt.
          Threnody. 145.
Pours finite into infinite.
          Threnody. 237.
Into calendar months and days.
          Uriel. 4.
Withdrew, that hour, into his cloud;
          Uriel. 38.
Nature poureth into nature   Visit. 13.
The crimson morning flames into
          World-Soul. 59.
To fling his voice into the tree,
          Woodnotes. II. 121.
Into failure, into folly."
          Woodnotes. II. 216.
Like wave or flame, into new forms
          Woodnotes. II. 274.
Into the fifth himself he flings,
          Woodnotes. II. 293.

Intoxicated
That I intoxicated,   Bacchus. 21.
Full fed, but not intoxicated;
          Poet. 47.

Introverts
He feels it, introverts his learned eye
          Philosopher. 5.

Intruding
Into each mind intruding duties crept;
          Adirondacs. 332.

Intrusion
From bold intrusion of the travelling crowd,—   Adirondacs. 172.

Inundating
Inundating the heaven
          Frag. Nat. XXVI. 23.

Inundation
I see the inundation sweet,
          Two Rivers. 9.

Invade
For we invade them impiously for gain;
          Blight. 37.
But these young scholars, who invade our hills,   Blight. 18.

Invent
Fancy departs: no more invent;
          Terminus. 9.

Invented
He invented oaths to swear;
          Initial Love. 115.

Invention
And fate and practice and invention,
          Woodnotes. II. 206.

Inventive
Rear purer wits, inventive eyes,—
          Monadnoc. 107.

Inventor
And the inventor of the game
          Experience. 10.

Invest
The follies bore that it invest.
          Poet. 198.

Invests
A swan-like form invests the hidden thorn;   Snow-Storm. 19.

Inviolate
And aim a telescope at the inviolate sun.
          Letter. 22.

Invite
And invite the sunbeam,
          Frag. Life. XXVII. 3.

Inviters
'Divine Inviters! I accept   Poet. 149.

Invites
The brimming brook invites a leap,
          May-Day. 71.
Unnerves his strength, invites his end.
          Woodnotes. II. 50.

Inviting
Inviting to new knowledge, one with old.
          Adirondacs. 205.

Invulnerable
Cap-a-pie invulnerable,   Astraea. 6.

Inward
Due east a bay makes inward to the land
          Adirondacs. 30.
By constant service to that inward law,
          Good Cheer. 6.
From tone of joy to inward wail,
          Harp. 8.
As when, with inward fires and pain,
          Monadnoc. 289.
And the German's inward sight.
          Monadnoc. 302.
The inward sky with chrysolite,
          Una. 14.
Yet happier he whose inward sight,
          Voluntaries. 79.
Warned by an inward voice,
          Voluntaries. 85.

Iran
There are beggars in Iran and Araby,
          Frag. Poet. I. 1.

Iris
Whereon the purple iris dwells in beauty
          Adirondacs. 219.

Irks
What imports, what irks and what behooves,   Frag. Poet. XII. 3.

Iron
I love thine iron chime,   Bell. 2.
Nor heeds Condition's iron walls,—
          Frag. Life. XVII. 9.
But borrowed in atoms from iron and stone,   Nature. II. 21.
Gold and iron are good   Politics. 1.
To buy iron and gold;   Politics. 2.
'T is written on the iron leaf,   Rhea. 34.
Now the iron age is done,
          Voluntaries. 44.

Iron —*Continued*
Copper and iron, lead and gold?
                              Wealth. 21.
Iron arms, and iron mould,
                    Woodnotes. II. 41.

Ironed
With railways ironed o'er?—
                    World-Soul. 68.

Iroquois
It is not Iroquois or cannibals,
                    Adirondacs. 292.

Is (Partial list.)
     See There's; 'T is.
Wine that is shed   Bacchus. 26.
Wine which Music is,—   Bacchus. 36.
As much as he is and doeth,
                    Boston Hymn. 59.
Vast the realm of Being is,
                    Day by Day. 9.
To share the sunshine that so spicy is.
                    Frag. Nat. XXXIII. 3.
There is no architect   House. 1.
Great is the art,   Merlin. 27.
Man in man is imprisonèd;   Saadi. 118.
Saying, What is excellent,
                    Threnody. 266.
Say, what other metre is it   Visit. 11.
So near is God to man,
                    Voluntaries. 72.
Who can tell him what he is?
                    Woodnotes. I. 27.
For Nature ever faithful is
                    Woodnotes. I. 137.
Dissolving all that fixture is,
                    Woodnotes. II. 113.

Island
Azaleas flush the island floors,
                    May-Day. 261.

Islanders
Ocean tongues to islanders,
                    Woodnotes. II. 153.

Islands
The seas their islands clip,
                    II Eros. 3.
Hills and islands, cloud and tree,
                    Hermione. 14.
Islands looming just beyond
                    May-Day. 424.

Isle
Of Alp and Andes, isle and continent,
                    Adirondacs. 263.
Lone mountain tarn, or isle forgot,
                    Astraea. 46.
His planted isle where roses glow?
                    Chartist. 12.
In yon green palmy isle,
                    *Farewell. 50.
Of Nature in thy Spanish isle
                    In Memoriam. 106.
That orange-grove, that isle of palms,
                    In Memoriam. 114.
To far eyes, an aerial isle
                    Monadnoc. 42.
By cloud or isle, is flying home;
                    Nemesis. 4.
I make some coast alluring, some lone
     isle,   Seashore. 48.
And, under vines, on rocky isle,
                    Solution. 12.

Isles
To the isles of the deep,
                    Frag. Nat. III. 36.
Which round the floating isles unite:—
                    Frag. Nat. XXVI. 25.
With salutation to the sea and to the
     bordering isles.   Monadnoc. 37.
Wish not to fill the isles with eyes
                    Saadi. 147.

Ispahan
Out from Mecca to Ispahan;
                    Frag. Poet. I. 8.

Israel's
Boy-Rabbi, Israel's paragon.
                    Threnody. 223.

Issues
Wise and sure the issues are.
                    Channing Ode. 77.

It (Partial list.)
     See 'T is; 'T was; 'T will.
It is not Iroquois or cannibals,
                    Adirondacs. 292.
no more try it;   Alphonso. 51.
No tidings since it came.   Amulet. 4.
Language falters under it,
                    Bohemian. 8.
The morning wind is in it;
                    Ellen South. 2.
Men and gods have not outlearned it;
                    I Eros. 4.
Loved the wood-rose, and left it on its
     stalk?   Forbearance. 2.
For joy and beauty planted it,
                    Frag. Nat. X. 1.
And boding Fancy haunted it
                    Frag. Nat. X. 3.
To dissipate their being into it.
                    Frag. Nat. XVII. 6.
Speak it not, or speak it low;
                    Freedom. 6.
It is anchored in the ground.
                    Holidays. 8.
Though I comprehend it not,
                    Initial Love. 24.
It preys on all, all prey on it,
                    May-Day. 291.
So that men might it not forget;
                    Monadnoc. 49.
For there's no rood has not a star above
     it;   Musketaquid. 54.
Entertain it reverently.   Saadi. 36.
And the impatient years that trod on it
                    Summons. 16.
For only it can absolutely deal.
                    Sursum Corda. 11.
Roving, roving, as it seems,   Una. 1.
Say, what other metre is it   Visit. 11.

Italian
My branches speak Italian,
                    Woodnotes. II. 150.

Italy
My apprehension? Why seek Italy,
                    Day's Ration. 29.
Flown to Italy from Greece,
                    Solution. 17.

Its (Partial list.)
Folding Nature in its deeps,
                    Celestial Love. 49.
Its heavy tale divine.   Dirge. 48.
Thought and its mansions fair.
                    Frag. Life. XXIV. 4.

Gave to the mind its emperor,
Solution. 37.
"The babe by its mother   Sphinx. 41.

Itself
When all but Love itself is dead
Ellen. 11.
Lent itself beneath the forest,
Holidays. 3.
Pleads for itself the fact,
In Memoriam. 94.
And mix itself with each event;
Monadnoc. 51.
And every atom poises for itself,
Musketaquid. 58.
The Book itself before me lies,
Problem. 64.
Or ever the wild Time coined itself
Uriel. 3.

I've (Partial list.)
Long I've been tossed like the driven
foam;   Good-Bye. 5.

Ivy
Ivy for my fillet band;
Mithridates. 14.

Jack
Or, later yet, beneath a lighted jack,
Adirondacs. 117.

Jackals
The jackals of the negro-holder.
Channing Ode. 23.

Jaded
Nor when I'm jaded, sick, anxious or
mean.   Frag. Life. XV. 5.

Jails
Chambers of the great are jails,
Heroism. 9.

Jake
While Jake retorts and Reuben roars;
Monadnoc. 188.

Jami's
Brighter than Jami's day.   Saadi. 85.

January
Where January brings few faces.'
Titmouse. 32.

Janus-gates
And clerks the Janus-gates unbar,
Solution. 62.

Japan
From Boston to Japan.
Waterfall. 12.

Japhet
The vice of Japhet by the thought of
Shem.   Frag. Poet. XXII. 2.

Jars
And, like the chemist 'mid his loaded jars,
Musketaquid. 38.

Jay
Or clarionet of jay? or hark
May-Day. 22.

Jealous
Nor gives the jealous lord one diamond
drop   Day's Ration. 24.
Jealous glancing around,   Sphinx. 54.

Jeer
While the solid curse and jeer
Monadnoc. 191.
At the new vision gape and jeer.
Poet. 22.

Chilled by a ribald jeer.
Voluntaries. 22.

Jelaleddin
As Jelaleddin old and gray;
Frag. Poet. V. 3.

Jest
Bethink, poor heart, what bitter kind of
jest   Epitaph. 1.

Jet
Ashes and jet all hues outshine.
Titmouse. 55.

Jew
Lone as the blessed Jew.
Quat. Shakespeare. 4.

Jewel
Whether your jewel be of pure water,
Destiny. 35.
He gold or jewel could not lose,
Guy. 15.

Jewels
Not by jewels, feasts and savors,
Celestial Love. 101.
To me who only jewels crave?
Song of Seyd. 14
Of shard and flint makes jewels gay;
Two Rivers. 14.

Jingling
No jingling serenader's art,
Merlin. 5.

Jocund
The air rings jocund to his call,
May-Day. 70.

Joined
      See Fate-conjoined.
Of keen competing youths, joined or
alone   Adirondacs. 325.
And honor joined the patriot ring
Boston. 84.

Joke
In tavern cheer and tavern joke,
Monadnoc. 120.

Jolly
Break sharply off their jolly games,
Voluntaries. 63.

Jostle
And nothing jostle or displace,
Woodnotes. II. 2.

Jot
Nor bate one jot of heart or hope,
In Memoriam. 80.

Journal
One held a printed journal waving high
Adirondacs. 235.

Journeying
But Justice, journeying in the sphere,
Astraea. 47.
The journeying atoms,   Sphinx. 29.

Journeyings
      See Minstrel—journeyings.

Journey's
The soaring orbit of the muse exceeds
that journey's length.   Merlin. 65.

Journeys
In nearer arcs his journeys run,
Peter. 15.
Still for journeys she is dressed;
Una. 3.

Jove
And that the Jove,—yet, howsoever hid,
Adirondacs. 289.

Jove—*Continued*

It was from Jove the other stole his
fire,   Adirondacs. 290.
And, without Jove, the good had never
been.   Adirondacs. 291.
As Olympus follows Jove.
    Channing Ode. 70.
Therefore comes an hour from Jove
    Daemonic Love. 116.
Well may Jove and Juno scorn.
    Destiny. 11.
Hide in thy skies, thou fruitless Jove,
    Frag. Life. XXXIII. 2.
Hither hasted, in old time, Jove,
    Garden. 25.
Or walks in mask almighty Jove,
    May-Day. 215.
Prometheus proffered, Jove denied;
    May-Day. 415.
If need were, their line from Jove;
    Monadnoc. 167.
Nor pictures pale, but Jove and Mars.
    Monadnoc. 308.
His awful Jove young Phidias brought;
    Problem. 10.
For Eros is older than Saturn or Jove;
    Quat. Casella. 2.
By Jove, at dawn of the first day.
    Solution. 2.
"Dull Sphinx, Jove keep thy five wits;
    Sphinx. 105.
This is Jove, who, deaf to prayers,
    Worship. 19.

Jove's

When wrath and terror changed Jove's
regal port,   Frag. Life. XXXIV. 1.
Thunder-clouds are Jove's festoons,
    Heroism. 4.

Joy

    See Enjoyed; Enjoyer.
A burst of joy, as if we told the fact
    Adirondacs. 252.
And yet I marked, even in the manly
joy   Adirondacs. 271.
And joy and moan,   Celestial Love. 40.
A cell for prayer, a hall for joy,—
    Dirge. 31.
Put youth, joy, health upon the shrine,
    Fame. 27.
Dappled with joy and grief and praise,
    Frag. Life. I. 2.
For joy and beauty planted it,
    Frag. Nat. X. 1.
Well used, it decketh joy,
    Frag. Nat. XXIV. 7.
Adorneth, doubleth joy:
    Frag. Nat. XXIV. 8.
Would you know what joy is hid
    Frag. Nat. XXVI. 1.
With joy too tense for sober brain;
    Frag. Poet. I. 51.
But leaped with joy when on the wind
    Frag. Poet. XXXV. 2.
Of a joy apart from thee,   Give. 38.
From tone of joy to inward wail,
    Harp. 8.
O joy, for what recoveries rare!
    Harp. 121.
Joy of thy dominion!
    Humble-Bee. 12.

He follows joy, and only joy.
    Initial Love. 113.
That never joy or hope shall here diffuse.
    In Memoriam. 24.
The joy and pride the pilgrim feels
    In Memoriam. 83.
His genius beamed with joy again.
    In Memoriam. 104.
Gravely it broods apart on joy,
    II Intellect. 1.
I found no joy: the icy wind
    May-Day. 51.
What joy in rosy waves outpoured
    May-Day. 190.
Hear the uproar of their joy;
    May-Day. 227.
And the colors of joy in the bird,
    May-Day. 235.
The love of kind, the joy, the grace,
    May-Day. 265.
Every joy and virtue speed,
    May-Day. 334.
And betrayed the fund of joy
    May-Day. 344.
The total freight of hope and joy
    May-Day. 354.
If Nature give me joy again,
    May-Day. 370.
I greet with joy the choral trains
    May-Day. 392.
He shall daily joy dispense
    Merlin. 41.
Whether it waken joy or rage
    Merlin's Song. 10.
But mark what changed my joy to
fright,—   Miracle. 26.
Amid these coward shapes of joy and
grief,   Monadnoc. 362.
One joy it joys, one grief it grieves.
    Monadnoc. 384.
Grow red with joy and white with fear;
    Saadi. 30.
That wit and joy might find a tongue,
    Solution. 15.
Goethe, raised o'er joy and strife,
    Solution. 65.
Lies bathed in joy;   Sphinx. 42.
Lurks the joy that is sweetest
    Sphinx. 91.
I am commissioned in my day of joy
    Summons. 3.
Bended with joy to his behest
    Threnody. 46.
In our downfall, or our joy:
    Voluntaries. 114.
But, sober on a fund of joy,
    Waldeinsamkeit. 19.
And to his joy replies;
    Waterfall. 14.
Each joy the mountain dales impart;
    Woodnotes. I. 35.
And shares the joy he brings.
    World-Soul. 64.

Joy-bells

Till Freedom cheered and joy-bells rung.
    Boston. 99.
The joy-bells chime their tidings down,
    Concord Ode. 7.

Joyful

And greet unanimous the joyful change.
    Adirondacs. 53.

The joyful traveller gives, when on the verge   Adirondacs. 311.
I thank the joyful juice   Bacchus. 45.
Of joyful and transparent mien.
Daemonic Love. 77.
Of eloquent lips, of joyful wit:
In Memoriam. 52.
Fires gardens with a joyful blaze
May-Day. 206.
Nor Rome, nor joyful Paris, nor the halls
Naples. 17.
Tutors, but a joyful eye,
Threnody. 211.
Like to like shall joyful prove;
Woodnotes. II. 82.

Joy-giver
But thou, joy-giver and enjoyer,
Saadi. 99.

Joys
To house of God and heavenly joys
Bell. 9.
Friends, foes, joys, fortunes, beauty and disgust.   Day's Ration. 8.
One joy it joys, one grief it grieves.
Monadnoc. 384.
And a few joys, a few peculiar charms,
Naples. 10.
What though the pains and joys
Threnody. 40.

Joy-tides
Joy-tides swell their mimic ocean.
Initial Love. 49.

Jubilant
In sleep their jubilant troop is near,—
Forerunners. 29.
Why tinge thy lustres jubilant
Frag. Nat. VIII. 3.
At the tread of the jubilant soul.
Waterfall. 20.

Jubilee
And rings the bells of jubilee
Cosmos. 27.
With social cheer and jubilee;
May-Day. 167.

Judæan
One in a Judæan manger,
Song of Nature. 65.

Judge
Judge with what sweet surprises Nature spoke   Adirondacs. 198.
'Judgment and a judge we seek.'
Astraea. 12.
Not Sense but Reason is the Judge of truth;   Frag. Life. XVIII. 5.

Judges
And like wise God she judges well.
Nature. I. 15.

Judgment
'Judgment and a judge we seek.'
Astraea. 12.
That he will not demand the debt until the Judgment Day.   Ibn Jemin. 4.

Juice
Till your kinds abound with juice?
Alphonso. 66.
Which feels the acrid juice
Bacchus. 8.
I thank the joyful juice   Bacchus. 45.
And the prussic juice to lull me;
Mithridates. 17.

Drain sweet maple juice in vats.
Monadnoc. 142.
Bread to eat, and juice to drain;
Monadnoc. 305.

Juices
Draw untold juices from the common earth,   Blight. 9.
Autumn-ripe, its juices hold
Monadnoc. 298.

July
July was in his sunny heart,
Quat. S. H. 3.
Fresh as the trickling rainbow of July;
Seashore. 20.

July's
Than July's meridian light.   Test. 10.

Jump
Steads not to work on the clean jump,
Alphonso. 61.
And jump like Harlequin;
Initial Love. 135.

Junctures
In strange junctures, felt, with awe,
Guy. 11.

June
As June herself around the sphere.
Frag. Life. XIII. 2.
The low December vault in June be lifted high,   Frag. Nat. XX. 1.
Epicurean of June;   Humble-Bee. 16.
Under the flowers of June,
Mountain. 3.
Yet beautiful as is the rose in June,
Seashore. 19.
Nor the June flowers scorn to cover
Woodnotes. I. 145.

June's
June's glories and September's
Ellen South. 27.

Juno
Well may Jove and Juno scorn.
Destiny. 11.

Jurist's
Nor to learned jurist's chair;
Astraea. 14.

Just
To assign just place and mates;
Astraea. 20.
And make just laws below the sun,
Boston Hymn. 47.
Bound for the just, but not beyond;
Celestial Love. 116.
Be just at home; then write your scroll
Concord Ode. 25.
Ascending thorough just degrees
Frag. Life. XXVIII. 1.
With the web that's just begun;
Frag. Poet. IX. 5.
Say, was it just,   Hermione. 28.
Islands looming just beyond
May-Day. 424.
Fills the just period,   Merlin. 121.
In just proportion,   Poet. 246.
Didst thou, just man, endure.
Tal. Exile. 3.
This scrap of valor just for play
Titmouse. 45.
Laws of form, and metre just,
Uriel. 12.
I had a sister once who seemed just like a violet;   *Violet. 13.

Just—*Continued*
Just late enough to reap abundant blame,—   To-Day. 6.

Justice
But Justice, journeying in the syhere, Astraea. 47.
Justice is the rhyme of things; Merlin. 114.
Justice conquers evermore, Voluntaries. 100.
Justice after as before,— Voluntaries. 101.

Karnak
Karnak and Pyramid and Giant's Stairs Seashore. 15.

Katskill
From Katskill east to the sea-bound. Monadnoc. 282.

Keen
Of keen competing youths, joined or alone   Adirondacs. 325.
Keen my sense, my heart was young, Forerunners. 5.
Keen ears can catch a syllable, Garden. 29.
The keen stars twinkle in our eyes, Romany. 22.
His tongue can paint as bright, as keen; Saadi. 122.

Keenest
Of keenest eye and truest tongue. Merlin's Song. 15.

Keep
Keep your lips or finger-tips Aeolian Harp. 4.
I keep, and pass, and turn again. Brahma. 4.
Why should I keep holiday I Compensation. 1.
Trembling balance duly keep. II Compensation. 4.
Nor stab the love that orphans keep. Frag. Life. VII. 4.
Keep thee to-day,   Give. 30.
Keep me nearer, me thy hearer, Humble-Bee. 9.
To keep this fire of faith alive, Hymn. 6.
Keep pulse for pulse with those who roam.   In Memoriam. 85.
Where shall we keep the holiday, May-Day. 218.
Or keep truth undecayed. Merlin. 112.
Where stars their perfect courses keep, Monadnoc. 101.
In dulness now their secret keep; Monadnoc. 172.
And always keep us so. Ode to Beauty. 63.
He would, yet would not, counsel keep, Poet. 85.
That haply man upraised might keep Poet. 169.
Suns and stars their courses keep, Poet. 271.
Go, keep your cheek's rose from the rain,   Romany. 17.

Nor mount, nor dive; all good things keep   Saadi. 145.
"Dull Sphinx, Jove keep thy five wits; Sphinx. 105.
And keep the blossom of the earth, Threnody. 124.
The punctual stars will vigil keep,— Titmouse. 18.
Strong Hades could not keep his own, Uriel. 33.
Will thy clear blue eye, upward bent, still keep its chastened glow, *Violet. 3.

Keeps
That keeps intelligence with you,— Amulet. 6.
Still keeps that golden day Cosmos. 26.
And Time, who keeps God's word, brings on the day   Good Cheer. 13.
Oft he keeps his fine ear strained, Initial Love. 66.
Which keeps the ground and never soars, Monadnoc. 187.
It keeps the key to all heroic hearts, Rome. 9.
Not so the wise; no coward watch he keeps   Woodnotes. I. 90.

Keeseville
We crossed Champlain to Keeseville with our friends,   Adirondacs. 1.

Ken
Fitting his age and ken, Threnody. 42.

Kennel
On coop or kennel he hangs Parian wreaths;   Snow-Storm. 18.
The kennel by the corded wood; Threnody. 83.

Kept
'Well done!' he cries; 'the bear is kept at bay,   Adirondacs. 315.
Counsel which the ages kept Celestial Love. 69.
Who the road had surely kept; Forerunners. 18.
Kept its place by the poet's side. Frag. Poet. I. 18.
I kept the sun and stars at bay, Frag. Poet. II. 7.
Its peace sublime his aspect kept, In Memoriam. 101.
The courtesy ye have shown and kept Poet. 150.
Though thou kept the straightest road, Rhea. 23.
In heaven are kept their grateful vows, Robbins Hymn. 3.
What time the gods kept carnival, Song of Nature. 29.
The ages have kept?—   Sphinx. 6.
And their lips the secret kept, Uriel. 45.

Kernan's
O'er Kernan's meadow blowest, Exile. 10.

Kersey
Shoes, flannel shirt, and kersey trousers make   Adirondacs. 75.

Key
The key is gone with them;
                    Dirge. 58.
With the key of the secret he marches
  faster,   Frag. Life. XXXI. 1.
Turn the key and bolt the door.
                    Past. 6.
It keeps the key to all heroic hearts,
                    Rome. 9.
Now hear thee say in Roman key,
                    Titmouse. 103.
Not one has found the key;
                    World-Soul. 54.

Keys
  See Maple-keys.
The keys of this breast,—
                    Ode to Beauty. 2.

Kill
My counsel is, kill nine in ten,
                    Alphonso. 68.
Vein and artery, though ye kill me!
                    Mithridates. 32.

Kills
He kills the cripple and the sick,
                    World-Soul. 91.

Kin
Every thing is kin of mine.
                    Mithridates. 5.
Beckons to spirit of its kin;
                    Nature. Mot. 14.

Kind
  See Mankind; Unkind.
Things deteriorate in kind;
                    Alphonso. 3.
And kind to kind.   Celestial Love. 80.
The men are ripe of Saxon kind
                    Concord Ode. 13.
Bethink, poor heart, what bitter kind of
  jest   Epitaph. 1.
Dearest Nature, strong and kind,
                    Experience. 18.
Kind smile and honest frown
                    *Farewell. 12.
Too kind, too good to me;
                    *Farewell. 20.
Nor kind occasion without eyes;
                    Frag. Life. XVII. 7.
Greetings kind to each and all,
                    Frag. Nat. XXIII. 16.
The chains of kind   Hermione. 67.
The kind Earth takes her children's part,
                    May-Day. 66.
The love of kind, the joy, the grace,
                    May-Day. 265.
Fill and saturate each kind
                    May-Day. 283.
Fill each kind and saturate
                    May-Day. 285.
Kindly to plant and blood and kind,
                    Monadnoc. 90.
Tall and good my kind among;
                    Monadnoc. 257.
Complement of human kind,
                    Monadnoc. 375.
Nor kind nor coinage buys   Politics. 7.
Kind leaves of his covert,   Sphinx. 23.
And kind acquaintance with the morning
  stars   Summons. 8.
Stole over the celestial kind,   Uriel. 44.

Kindled
  See Self-kindled.
Then struck a light and kindled the
  camp-fire.   Adirondacs. 36.
Were kindled in the upper skies
                    Eva. 2.

Kindliness
Glowed unexhausted kindliness,
                    Friendship. 7.
Kindly to plant and blood and kind,
                    Monadnoc. 90.

Kindness
All to each in kindness bend,   Peter. 34.

Kindred
Of blood through veins of kindred
  poured.   Daemonic Love. 4.
Friends, kindred, days,   Give. 3.
Who are thy spiritual kindred, and each
  one   Good Cheer. 5.
And my kindred come to soothe me.
                    Hermione. 49.
But of a kindred face
                    In Memoriam. 23.
As on its friends, with kindred eye;
                    Problem. 38.

Kinds
  See Wood-kinds.
Gave an impartial tomb to all the kinds.
                    Adirondacs. 140.
Till your kinds abound with juice?
                    Alphonso. 66.
Perfect kinds by vice unmarred,
                    Frag. Nat. XXIII. 2.
And of the kinds that owe her birth.
                    Harp. 66.
That man and all the kinds be fed;
                    May-Day. 147.
Thy blooms, thy kinds,   May-Day. 437.
To myriad kinds and times one sense
                    Monadnoc. 381.
Sea full of food, the nourisher of kinds,
                    Seashore. 21.

Kine
Kine in droves,   Saadi. 2.

King
  See Frost king; Unking.
I, a king, for kings can feel.
                    Alphonso. 44.
There is no king nor sovereign state
                    Astraea. 3.
Choose him to be your king;
                    Boston Hymn. 14.
The townsmen braved the English king,
                    Boston. 82.
King Oberon's minstrelsy.
                    Frag. Nat. III. 28.
With every king on every throne,
                    Initial Love. 125.
Masks the might of Nature's king,
                    May-Day. 458.
King of sport that never shames,
                    Merlin. 40.
To mask a king in weeds.
                    Quat. Poet. 2. 4.
Profuse in love, the king bestows,
                    Rhea. 56.
The King whose meek ambassador I go.
                    Summons. 24.
And conscious Laws is King of kings.
                    Woodnotes. II. 294.

Kingdom
And the kingdom,   Hamatreya. 51.

Kingdoms
Bread, kingdoms, stars, and sky that
holds them all.   Days. 6.
The solid kingdoms like a dream
      Poet. 36.
To Nature, through her kingdoms ample,
      Rhea. 65.

Kingfisher
The rattle of the kingfisher;   Harp. 90.

Kingly
The kingly bard   Merlin. 9.

King's
Modulates the king's affairs;
      Merlin. 78.

Kings
I, a king, for kings can feel.
      Alphonso. 44.
Retinues of airy kings,   Art. 15.
Kings unborn shall walk with me;
      Bacchus. 40.
Kings shook with fear,   Boston. 92.
God said, I am tired of kings,
      Boston Hymn. 5.
With squires, lords, kings, his craft com-
pares,   Fate. 8.
Minstrels and kings and high-born dames,
and of the best that be. Quat. A. H. 4.
I moulded kings and saviors,
      Song of Nature. 69.
And bards o'er kings to rule;—
      Song of Nature. 70.
Let kings and conquerors, saints and
soldiers sleep—   To-Day. 4.
I talk with kings the while.]
      Walden. 32.
And conscious Law is King of kings.
      Woodnotes. II. 294.

Kinsfolk
To their kinsfolk and their dears;
      Astraea. 16.

Kiosk
Knew every temple and kiosk
      Frag. Poet. I. 7.

Kiss
But even thy kiss denies   *Farewell. 23.
And kiss, and couple, and beget,
      Initial Love. 31.

Kissed
The crouching lion kissed his feet;
      Worship. 8.

Kite
'T is even so, this treacherous kite,
      Monadnoc. 331.

Knave
Disown the knave and fool;   Boston. 32.

Knaves
Ruby wine is drunk by knaves,
      Heroism. 1.

Knee
Samson stark, at Dagon's knee,
      Frag. Nat. XXXIV. 1.

Knee-deep
Knee-deep snows choked all the ways,
      May-Day. 37.

Kneels
Nor kneels in homage to so mean a God.
      To-Day. 14.

Knees
And though thy knees were never bent,
      Prayer. 5.

Knell
Knell their melodious memory.
      Woodnotes. II. 228.

Knelt
Bestrode the tribes that knelt within.
      Problem. 50.

Knew
And die of inanition. If I knew
      Blight. 3.
If Boston knew the most!   Boston. 48.
Knew they what that signified,
      Circles. 5.
Which once our childhood knew;
      Dirge. 38.
Nor knew her beauty's best attire
      Each. 31.
Tell men what they knew before;
      Frag. Life. XIX. 1.
Knew every temple and kiosk
      Frag. Poet. I. 7.
God only knew how Saadi dined;
      Frag. Poet. V. 13.
The free winds told him what they knew,
      Frag. Poet. V. 37.
The boy knew on the hills in spring,
      Harp. 86.
I knew their forms in fancy weeds,
      Harp. 112.
They knew not of,   Harp. 119.
He told no pang, he knew no fear;
      In Memoriam. 100.
I knew not why   *Lines. 10.
I knew of them not   *Lines. 20.
The whited desert knew me not,
      May-Day. 41.
Knew my quarrel, how and why,
      Miracle. 31.
Well the Planter knew how strongly
      Monadnoc Afar. 5.
Thee knew I of old?   Ode to Beauty. 6.
He builded better than he knew;—
      Problem. 23.
I never thought to ask, I never knew:
      Rhodora. 14.
And the gods shook, they knew not why.
      Uriel. 56.
The gray old gods whom Chaos knew,
      Waldeinsamkeit. 35.
Knew the strong task to it assigned,
      Wealth. 10.
And such I knew, a forest seer,
      Woodnotes. I. 30.
A lover true, who knew by heart
      Woodnotes. I. 34.
As if by secret sight he knew
      Woodnotes. I. 48.
They knew by secret sympathy
      Woodnotes. I. 116.
If but one hero knew it,
      World-Soul. 49.

Knew'st
'Up!—If thou knew'st who calls
      Monadnoc. 5.

Knife
With rifle and with knife!
      Channing Ode. 18.

Knit
And they knit no frown.   *Lines. 21.
The Muse can knit   Frag. Poet. IX. 3.

Knits
Which knits the world in music strong,
   Woodnotes. II. 157.

Knock
That knock at meek contrition's door.
   Hymn. 20.

Knotted
   See Lighting-knotted.

Know
and lake should know   Adirondacs. 254.
know more than any book.   April. 14.
The lore we care to know.   April. 20.
For all I know;—   Bacchus. 46.
Love not the flower they pluck, and know
   it not,   Blight. 21.
They laughed to know the world so wide;
   Boston. 49.
They know not well the subtle ways
   Brahma. 3.
But gifted yet to know   Dull. 2.
I know the mighty bards,   Dull. 6.
And now I know   Dull. 8.
Yet well I know the royal mine,
   Dull. 19.
And know the sparkle of its ore,
   Dull. 20.
Know Heaven's truth   Dull. 21.
I know that thou, O morning wind!
   Exile. 9.
You shall not know me in the noisy
   street,   Frag. Life. XV. 2.
But love me then and only, when you
   know   Frag. Life. XV. 6.
And know the only strong?
   Frag. Nat. III. 30.
On Adirondac steeps, I know
   Frag. Nat. IV. 7.
Would you know what joy is hid
   Frag. Nat. XXVI. 1.
Than the wine-fed feasters know.
   Frag. Poet. XI. 11.
Freedom's secret wilt thou know?—
   Freedom. 21.
Know the worth of Oman's pearls?
   Friendship. Trans. 2.
Heartily know,   Give. 47.
Serve that low whisper thou hast served;
   for know,   Good Cheer. 2.
Know me, as does my dog: we sympa-
   thize;   Hamatreya. 9.
Know the stars yonder,   Illusions. 16.
Then first shalt thou know,   Illusions. 33.
Dear brother, would you know the life,
   Letter. 1.
What dost thou know?   Limits. 5.
They know one only mortal grief
   Love and Thought. 9.
The robins know the melting snow;
   May-Day. 169.
I know ye skilful to convoy
   May-Day. 353.
I know the trusty almanac
   May-Day. 378.
I know each nest and web-worm's tent,
   Miracle. 3.
I know not why I came again
   Miracle. 7.

'Gentle pilgrim, if thou know
   Monadnoc. 219.
But well I know, no mountain can,
   Monadnoc. 258.
Which, one by one, they know to draw
   and use.   Musketaquid. 35.
Winters know   Nature. I. 1.
I know is ground enchanted.   Peter. 8.
I know the appointed hour,   Poet. 114.
And yet, dear stars, I know ye shine
   Poet. 233.
I know that ye are excellent,
   Poet. 258.
I know what say the fathers wise,—
   Problem. 63.
They know me as their son, for side by
   side,   River. 39.
The rocks and forest know it real.
   Romany. 20.
I know what spells are laid. Leave me to
   deal   Seashore. 43.
And know only that I love.
   Song of Seyd. 8.
Yet the censer cannot know.
   Song of Seyd. 18.
What men chatter know I not.
   Song of Seyd. 34.
All woman-born do know, that hoped-for
   days,   Summons. 19.
Nor time unmake what poets know.
   Test. 12.
Thy steps to watch, thy place to know:
   Threnody. 33.
And know my higher gifts unbind
   Threnody. 230.
Wilt thou not ope thy heart to know
   Threnody. 260.
Know, each substance and relation,
   Visit. 3.
That know not fear, fatigue, or cold.
   Woodnotes. II. 42.
If thou wouldst know the mystic song
   Woodnotes. II. 98.
The wood and wave each other know
   Woodnotes. II. 173.
To know one element, explore another,
   Xenophanes. 12.

Knowest
Or care a rush for what thou knowest,
   Destiny. 23.
Nor knowest thou what argument
   Each. 9.
My father's orchard knowest.   Exile. 12.
Knowest thou this?   Monadnoc. 241.

Knoweth
He is not fooled, but warily knoweth
   Rhea. 44.

Knowing
   See Unknowing.
Men knowing what they seek,
   Adirondacs. 304.
'T is a tune worth thy knowing,
   Ellen South. 3.
Sings a tune that's worth the knowing.'
   Ellen South. 36.
Knowing well to celebrate
   May-Day. 267.
Knowing and doing. Ebbs the tide, they
   lie   Pan. 8.
Knowing this,—and knows no more,—
   Voluntaries. 98.

Knowledge
    See Self-knowledge.
Inviting to new knowledge, one with old.
                Adirondacs. 205.
For knowledge and for fame   Fame. 8.
Knowledge which its source not knows,
                Insight. 2.
Planting seeds of knowledge pure,
                May-Day. 467.
Newest knowledge, fiery thought,
                Miracle. 13.
Test of the poet is knowledge of love,
                Quat. Casella. 1.
And yet have knowledge of our moral
  race,   River. 32.
Hunt knowledge as the lover wooes a
  maid,   Rome. 14.
Or by knowledge grown too bright
                Uriel. 41.
Knowledge this man prizes best
                Woodnotes. I. 16.

Known
    See Unknown; Well-known.
'Welcome, though late, unknowing, yet
  known to me.'   Adirondacs. 45.
'Now by these presents be it known
                Boston. 65.
Known in part, or known impure,
                Celestial Love. 51.
And, so thoroughly is known
                Celestial Love. 91.
Friends year by year more inly known.
                Daemonic Love. 16.
I dare not be beloved and known,
                Frag. Poet. VII. 7.
Well known, but loving not a name,
                Monadnoc. 29.
Known fruit of the unknown;
                Sphinx. 11.
In damp fields known to bird and fox.
                Woodnotes. I. 41.
To make no step until the event is known,
                Woodnotes. I. 88.
To hill and cloud his face was known,—
                Woodnotes. I. 114.
He is the oldest, and best known,
                Worship. 15.

Knows
The sallow knows the basket-maker's
  thumb;   Adirondacs. 101.
(Your Highness knows our homely
  word)   Boston. 73.
Knows to bring honey
                Channing Ode. 86.
Knows he who tills this lonely field
                Dirge. 9.
Their near camp my spirit knows
                Forerunners. 33.
Well he knows his own affair,
                Frag. Nat. I. 12.
Knows its own path   Give. 16.
He all the fables knows,   Harp. 11.
Knows Nature's rarest moods,
                Harp. 13.
But my minstrel knows and tells
                Harp. 19.
Knows of Holy Book the spells,
                Harp. 21.
Knows the law of Night and Day,
                Harp. 22.

Knowledge which its source not knows,
                Insight. 2.
Who knows this or that?   Limits. 1.
The World-soul knows his own affair,
                Monadnoc. 153.
But knows the sun-creating sound,
                Monadnoc. 254.
Who is the captain he knows not,
                Monadnoc. 337.
[Knows he who tills this lonely field
                Peter. 1.
All grace, all good his great heart knows,
                Rhea. 55.
One sallow horseman knows me good.
                Romany. 16.
That knows a purer flame than me,
                Security. 10.
The little needle always knows the
  North,   Self-Reliance. 6.
Or bird or biped knows;
                Walden. 40.
And wary Nature knows her own
                Walk. 2.
The planets' child the planet knows
                Waterfall. 13.
What he knows nobody wants.
                Woodnotes. I. 12.
The river knows the way to the sea;
                Woodnotes. II. 239.

Know'st
Know'st thou what wove yon woodbird's
  nest   Problem. 25.

Labor
Whither gaunt Labor slips to wipe his
  brow   Adirondacs. 196.
Their honest labor overpay. Boston. 24.
To coin his labor and sweat,
                Boston Hymn. 62.
With angel patience labor on,
                In Memoriam. 76.

Laborer's
Serving for a laborer's lamp?
                Chartist. 6.

Laboring
The secret of its laboring heart,
                Nature. Mot. 10.

Laborious
Chide me not, laborious band,
                Apology. 9.

Labors
With the labors he must dare;
                Alphonso. 74.

Labrador
In these woods, thy small Labrador,
                Titmouse. 50.

Lack
And, that no day of life may lack
  romance,   Adirondacs. 221.
Thy beauty, if it lack the fire
                Destiny. 12.

Lacked
To bind or unbind, add what lacked,
                Past. 18.

Laden
These echoes are laden with tones
                Woodnotes. II. 127.

Ladies
Love of ladies, love of bards,
                Frag. Poet. VII. 10.

Lading
  See O'erlading.
Lads
Said the winds that sung the lads to sleep, Boston. 15.
Lady
And I the lady all the while. Romany. 12.
Lafayette
Which wafted Lafayette! Boston. 89.
Laid
Of the wire-cable laid beneath the sea, Adirondacs. 239.
She laid a slab of marble on his head. Epitaph. 4.
Laid the terraces, one by one; Garden. 14.
Mysteries of color daily laid Monadnoc. 60.
Which who can tell what mason laid? Monadnoc. 369.
That I am laid with decency. Mountain. 17.
Mourning summer laid in shrouds. Nun. 22.
The Furies laid, Past. 3.
Whilst love and terror laid the tiles. Problem. 32.
I know what spells are laid. Leave me to deal Seashore. 43.
They laid their courses well, Song of Nature. 34.
A spell is laid on sod and stone, Unity. 7.
She laid her hopes at rest, *Violet. 16.
Lair
And wit to trap or take him in his lair. Adirondacs. 86.
Lake
With skies of benediction, to Round Lake, Adirondacs. 8.
To Follansbee Water and the Lake of Loons. Adirondacs. 25.
All day we swept the lake, searched every cove, Adirondacs. 108.
Competing seekers of a rumored lake, Adirondacs. 130.
Lake Probability,—our carbuncle, Adirondacs. 132.
And cedar grove and cliff and lake should know Adirondacs. 254.
Wild Tupper Lake; witness the mute all-hail Adirondacs. 310.
He smote the lake to feed his eye Beauty. 7.
Fill the lake with images,— Celestial Love. 72.
Gracing the rich man's wood and lake, Chartist. 9.
Gives beauty to the lake and fountain, Enchanter. 8.
By lake and stream and gleaming hall Frag. Poet. I. 15.
When the wing of the south-wind whipt the lake Frag. Poet. I. 36.
When the shadow fell on the lake, Garden. 53.
But the meanings cleave to the lake, Garden. 57.

Of the pent and darkened lake, May-Day. 16.
I reached this heath beside the lake, Miracle. 16.
Published it to lake and sky, Miracle. 32.
No fish, in river or in lake, Monadnoc. 145.
Hollow and lake, hillside and pine arcade, Musketaquid. 23.
The black ducks mounting from the lake, Waldeinsamkeit. 29.
The wide lake, edged with sand and grass, Woodnotes. I. 108.
Or dip thy paddle in the lake, Woodnotes. II. 169.
One aspect to the desert and the lake. Xenophanes. 4.
Lake-edge
The banks slope down to the blue lake-edge, Garden. 11.
Lake-margin's
Rosy polygonum, lake-margin's pride, Adirondacs. 143.
Lakes
The Adirondac lakes. At Martin's Beach Adirondacs. 4.
In Adirondac lakes, Adirondacs. 73.
To feed this wealth of lakes and rivulets, Adirondacs. 150.
In silver lakes that unexhausted gleam Frag. Nat. IV. 10.
And lakes, smooth mirrors of Aurora's charms. I Bear. 8.
By lonely lakes to men unknown. May-Day. 29.
Who would freeze on frozen lakes? May-Day. 53.
To northern lakes fly wind-borne ducks, Saadi. 5.
The pastures sleep, ripple the lakes, Saadi. 136.
Where from a hundred lakes young rivers sprang; Woodnotes. I. 63.
Lambent
The lambent heat lightning Illusions. 20.
Lame
I lame him, clattering down the rocks; Monadnoc. 342.
How lame the other limped away. Nun. 49.
Lamp
Serving for a laborer's lamp? Chartist. 6.
His lamp, the maiden's downcast eye, Frag. Poet. I. 12.
As shepherd's lamp on far hill-side Hermione. 42.
Hide in thy skies, O sovereign lamp! Monadnoc. 122.
The gods are blind and lame, Monadnoc. 349.
Gladly round that golden lamp Saadi. 37.
Lamps
Feeds those eternal lamps I see. Poet. 236.
Lances
Till green lances peering through May-Day. 123.

Land

    See Headland; Highland; Lowland;
Northland; Upland; Woodland.

inward to the land   Adirondacs. 30.

The prodigal sunshine rested on the land,
         Adirondacs. 338.

Or land or life, if freedom fail?
         Boston. 30.

Or land or life, if freedom fail?
         Boston. 81.

Lo! I uncover the land
         Boston Hymn. 17.

Can govern the land and sea
         Boston Hymn. 46.

Taunted the lofty land
         Channing Ode. 25.

The upheaved land, and bury the folk,
         Channing Ode. 30.

O'er-mantling land and sea,
         Concord Ode. 10.

For sea and land don't understand,
         Concord Ode. 21.

To stay in the Syrian land; ·   Exile. 16.

Though foes and land and seas between
         Frag, Life. XVII. 14.

To use my land to put his rainbows in.
         Frag. Nat. IX. 2.

Nor land, nor gold, nor power,
         Frag. Poet. VI. 6.

A secret nook in a pleasant land,
         Good-Bye. 17.

Possessed the land which rendered to
their toil   Hamatreya. 2.

The land is well,—lies fairly to the south.
         Hamatreya. 22.

Him to his land, a lump of mould the
more.   Hamatreya. 26.

'Here is the land,   Hamatreya. 44.

What sea and land discoursing say
         Harp. 27.

The lustre of the land and ocean,
         Hermione. 13.

Cools sea and land so far and fast,
         Humble-Bee. 59.

Out of the hazy land?   May-Day. 9.

Broad northward o'er the land,
         May-Day. 248.

The forefathers this land who found
         Merlin's Song. 18.

Her lily and rose, her sea and land display.   Monadnoc. 13.

Honey from the frozen land;
         Monadnoc. 136.

And tread uplifted land?
         Monadnoc. 207.

All his county, sea and land,
         Monadnoc. 320.

Ever the Poet from the land
         Quat. Poet. I. 1.

But make the statute of this land.
         Rhea. 30.

But what is land, or what is wave,
         Song of Seyd. 13.

I lonely roved the land or sea:
         Thine Eyes. 2.

As fits a feathered lord of land;
         Titmouse. 37.

And brought me to the lowest land,
         Woodnotes. I. 131.

When sea and land refuse to feed me,
         Woodnotes. I. 141.

The land reflected in the flood,
         Woodnotes. II. 162.

Whether she work in land or sea,
         Woodnotes. II. 166.

Is thy land peeled, thy realm marauded?
         Woodnotes. II. 181.

The seeds of land and sea
         World-Soul. 86.

Landed

And landed on our coast, and pulsating
         Adirondacs. 240.

Landlords

Each of these landlords walked amidst
his farm,   Hamatreya. 4.

Lands

    See Uplands.

Lands and goods go to the strong.
         Celestial Love. 76.

In strange lands unblest;
         Hermione. 48.

In many lands, with painful steps,
         House. 11.

In lands remote, in toil and pain,
         In Memoriam. 75.

And all town-sprinkled lands that be,
         Monadnoc. 277.

books and names and lands
         To-Day. 9.

Her broad van seeks unplanted lands;
         Voluntaries. 37.

Or lands of Eastern day?   Walden. 46.

Blessing all lands with its charity;
         Woodnotes. II. 241.

Landscape

Of landscape and of sky,   Culture. 6.

And we've the landscape overrun,
         Etienne. 6.

The landscape is an armory of powers,
         Musketaquid. 34.

Farms the sunny landscape dappled,
         September. 5.

But in the serious landscape lone
         Waldeinsamkeit. 15.

Yon ridge of purple landscape,
         World-Soul. 37.

Landscape's

O'erlooks the surging landscape's swell!
         Monadnoc. 11.

To brave the landscape's looks.
         Waldeinsamkeit. 44.

Landscapes

In new landscapes of romance,
         May-Day. 27.

To read new landscapes and old skies;
         Poet. 53.

Landward

Or landward to the west.'   Boston. 58.

Landward they reached the mountains
old   Poet. 63.

Lane

The green lane is the school-boy's friend,
         May-Day. 67.

Fills up the farmer's lane from wall to
wall,   Snow-Storm. 20.

Language

    See Bird-language.

Language falters under it,   Bohemian. 8.

The other portion language cannot speak.
Frag. Life. XVIII. 8.
And copious language still bestowed
Merops. 11.

Languages
And speaks all languages the rose,
May-Day. 74.
And speaks all languages the rose;
Nature. Mot. 4.

Languish
And, if I languish into dreams,
Ode to Beauty. 92.

Languishing
With sudden passion languishing,
May-Day. 2.

Lap
In her lap to pour all splendor;
Rhea. 50.
To Fin and Lap and swart Malay,
Woodnotes. II. 124.

Lapse
The soothing lapse of morn to mirk,
Celestial Love. 105.
Heeds no longer lapse of time,
Poet. 131.
'You have no lapse; so have ye glowed
Poet. 231.
This was the lapse of Uriel,   Uriel. 5.

Lapsed
Say, when in lapsed ages
Ode to Beauty. 5.

Lapses
By lapses or by wars,   House. 22.

Larch
Last year from yon oak or larch;
May-Day. 386.

Large
Of sympathy so large, that ours was
theirs,   Adirondacs. 257.
Equalizing small and large, Etienne. 17.
If I'm not so large as you,   Fable. 12.
We talked at large of worldly fate,
Hermione. 38.
And richly his large future planned,
In Memoriam. 70.
So deep and large her bounties are,
May-Day. 275.
Who, in large thoughts, like fair pearl-
seed,   Monadnoc. 285.
What these strong masters wrote at large
in miles,   Musketaquid. 52.
His learning should be deep and large,
Poet. 40.
Another heart as large and true.
Security. 6.
And, sculptor-like, his large design
Solution. 31.
The Providence that is most large
Titmouse. 85.

Largely
Who, having more absorbed, more largely yield,   Frag. Nat. V. 11.

Larger
Strains every sense to larger scope,
May-Day. 153.
And life was larger than before:
Solution. 38.
O loss of larger in the less!
Threnody. 117.

Largest
And largest clouds be flakes of down
Frag. Nat. XX. 2.
Took the largest part of me:
Threnody. 161.

Lark's
To the lark's trill unfolds the rose,
Waterfall. 15.

Lars
Lemurs and Lars.   Frag. Life. VIII. 4.

Last
Rounded by hours where each outdid the
last   Adirondacs. 154.
Were fairly reached at last. Wake, echo-
ing caves!   Adirondacs. 259.
Died in its last expression.   Amulet. 12.
The last builds town and fleet,
Channing Ode. 55.
Her last noble is ruined,
Channing Ode. 92.
Her last poet mute: Channing Ode. 93.
Till dangerous Beauty came, at last,
Daemonic Love. 10.
At last she came to his hermitage,
Each. 33.
Obeying time, the last to own   Fate. 11.
But when at last the patriarch died
Frag. Nat. VI. 5.
And be sure at last came Love,
Garden. 27.
If who can read them comes at last
Garden. 63.
Last year from yon oak or larch;
May-Day. 386.
That wood-bird sang my last night's
dream,   Miracle. 28.
Fled the last plumule of the Dark,
Monadnoc. 312.
Then, at last, I let him down
Monadnoc. 344.
Seemed, when at last his clarion accents
broke,   Phi. 11.
Nor last posterity forget.   Poet. 12.
Shines the last age, the next with hope
is seen,   Quat. Heri. 1.
Magic-built to last a season;
Threnody. 256.
their last gay dress put on;   *Violet. 7.

Lasted
Five lines lasted sound and true;
Test. 4.

Lasting
See Everlasting.

Late
'Welcome, though late, unknowing, yet
known to me.'   Adirondacs. 45.
Though late returning to her pristine
ways.   Adirondacs. 55.
Then turns to bound away,—is it too
late?   Adirondacs. 124.
Ah! late I spoke to silent throngs,
I Compensation. 7.
Turned and departed silent. I, too late,
Days. 10.
Till late he learned, through doubt and
fear,   Fate. 9.
Early or late, the falling rain   Guy. 33.
He came late along the waste,
Initial Love. 11.
When late I walked, in earlier days,
May-Day. 35.

Late—*Continued*

No early morn, no evening late,—
Nun. 43.

Coming early, coming late,   Poet. 123.

Never was poet, of late or of yore,
Quat. Casella. 3.

Say, Pilgrim, why so late and slow to
come?   Seashore. 2.

As late I found my lukewarm blood
Titmouse. 3.

Late in the world,—too late perchance for
fame,   To-Day. 5.

Just late enough to reap abundant
blame,—   To-Day. 6.

Threading dark ways, arriving late,
Worship. 12.

Late-arriving

Caught from a late-arriving traveller,
Adirondacs. 236.

Latent

None will now find Cupid latent
Initial Love. 9.

And being latent, feel thyself no less?
Musketaquid. 81.

In latent fire his secret thought,
Poet. 14.

Later

Or, later yet, beneath a lighted jack,
Adirondacs. 117.

Ebbing later whence it flowed,
Garden. 15.

Go thy ways now, come later back.
Garden. 59.

Latest

Or, in the evening twilight's latest red,
Adirondacs. 115.

The latest better than the first,
Aeolian Harp. 21.

The bubbles of the latest wave
Each. 20.

Afflicted moan, and latest hold
May-Day. 19.

Thou latest and first!
Ode to Beauty. 16.

Latin

And all their botany is Latin names.
Blight. 22.

Latter

And the former called the latter 'Little
Prig;'   Fable. 3.

Lauding

Lauding the Eternal Rights,
Voluntaries. 109.

Laugh

Laugh life away;   Fame. 16.

I laugh at the lore and the pride of man,
Good-Bye. 27.

Maidens laugh and weep; Composure
Poet. 223.

I laugh at those who, while they gape
and gaze,   To-Day. 15.

Laughed

They laughed to know the world so
wide;   Boston. 49.

Until Cupid laughed loud,   *Lines. 22.

Laugheth

He laugheth at his foes.   Riches. 12.

Laughing

Into the laughing sea?   Boston. 79.

Her strength and soul has laughing
France   Quat. Leasts. 3.

Laughs

Love laughs, and on a lion rides.
Daemonic Love. 88.

Earth laughs in flowers, to see her boastful boys   Hamatreya. 13.

Laughter

Or listening to the laughter of the loon;
Adirondacs. 114.

With laughter sudden as the crack of
rifle;   Adirondacs. 128.

Listen for their harp-like laughter,
Forerunners. 36.

Rang with fairy laughter.
Frag. Nat. III. 25.

Laughter rich as woodland thunder,
Threnody. 214.

Launched

Self-centred; when he launched the
genuine word   Phi. 19.

Laurel

Had won the brightest laurel of all
time.   Adirondacs. 285.

Laurel crowns cleave to deserts,
II Compensation. 21.

By the ten-tongued laurel speaking,
May-Day. 419.

Blooms the laurel which belongs
Voluntaries. 106.

Laurelled

See Unlaurelled.

Lavish

Lavish, lavish promiser,
Ode to Beauty. 21.

Lavishly

So Nature shed all beauty lavishly
Adirondacs. 151.

Law

Law for man, and law for thing;
Channing Ode. 54.

Let man serve law for man;
Channing Ode. 66.

She was his mistress and his law;
Frag. Poet. V. 23.

Into substance, into Law.
Frag. Poet. VIII. 10.

By constant service to that inward law,
Good Cheer. 6.

His own symmetry with law;   Guy. 12.

Knows the law of Night and Day,
Harp. 22.

Is law and the world,—   Illusions. 32.

For Cupid goes behind all law,
Initial Love. 120.

Gave the law which others took,
In Memoriam. 45.

And yet, if virtue abrogate the law,
Phi. 3.

An animated law, a presence to exalt.'
Poet. 164.

Brother, sweeter is the Law   Poet. 281.

If the Law should thee forget,   Poet. 289.

Electric thrills and ties of law,
Wealth. 47.

And conscious Law is King of kings.
Woodnotes. II. 294.

Lawful

Play not in Nature's lawful web,
Garden. 22.

Who never break your lawful dance
                              Poet. 157.

Lawrence
  See Saint Lawrence.

Laws
  We were made freemen of the forest
    laws,   Adirondacs. 70.
  And make just laws below the sun,
                              Boston Hymn. 47.
  The circles of that sea are laws
                              Celestial Love. 58.
  There are two laws discrete,
                              Channing Ode. 52.
  Those idle catches told the laws
                              Frag. Poet. V. 11.
  The lawyer, and the laws,
                              Hamatreya. 50.
  It is the tongue of mundane laws.
                              Harp. 72.
  Nor evil laws or rulers made,
                              May-Day. 105.
  Would rushing life forgot her laws,
                              Threnody. 226.
  Laws of form, and metre just,   Uriel. 12.

Lawyer
  The lawyer, and the laws,
                              Hamatreya. 50.

Lawyer's
  'The lawyer's deed   Hamatreya. 37.

Lay
  Lift the sash, lay me within,
                              Aeolian Harp. 10.
  Out of that delicate lay could'st thou
                              Dirge. 47.
  The delicate shells lay on the shore;
                              Each. 19.
  Pine-cones and acorns lay on the ground;
                              Each. 45.
  And it lay on my hearth when I came
    home.   Frag. Poet. IV. 34.
  Soft shadows of the evening lay.
                              Frag. Poet. V. 48.
  On a mound an Arab lay,
                              Hermione. 1.
  I lay my vanity and guilt;   Nun. 16.
  The reverent darkness hid the lay.
                              Poet. 18.
  Heed thou only Saadi's lay.   Saadi. 103.
  Heed thou only Saadi's lay.   Saadi. 116.
  Where darkness found him he lay glad
    at night;   Woodnotes. I. 82.
  Tuned to the lay the wood-god sings.
                              Woodnotes. II. 96.
  Come, lay thee in my soothing shade,
                              Woodnotes. II. 219.

Layer
  Like undulating layer of air,
                              Daemonic Love. 24.

Layers
  They boiled the sea, and piled the layers
                              Song of Nature. 35.

Layeth
  Who layeth the world's incessant plan,
                              Woodnotes. II. 271.

Laying
  But, laying hands on another
                              Boston Hymn. 61.

Laymen
  And we the low-prized laymen.
                              Adirondacs. 96.

Lays
  Many and subtle are my lays,
                              Aeolian Harp. 20.
  She lays her beams in music,
                              House. 17.
  God for thy virtue lays a plot:
                              Prayer. 2.

Lazy
  Not lazy grazing on all they saw,
                              Poet. 57.

Lea
  And the cloud-shadow on the lea,
                              Celestial Love. 104.

Lead (Verb, guide.)
  See Mislead.
  Whose roads lead everywhere to all;
                              Boston. 60.
  Lead you rightly to my altar,
                              Etienne. 13.
  By thoughts I lead
                              Frag. Poet. XII. 1.
  Please God, that I would lead?
                              Letter. 2.
  To lead the tardy concert of the year.
                              Musketaquid. 18.
  As they lead, so follow all,   Rhea. 31.
  Then I unbar the doors: my paths lead
    out   Seashore. 38.
  Then by better thought I lead
                              Solution. 25.
  To lead him willing to be led,
                              Voluntaries. 56.

Lead (Noun, metal.)
  His sheet of lead,   To J. W. 14.
  Copper and iron, lead and gold?
                              Wealth. 21.

Leaden
  The while, one leaden pot of alcohol
                              Adirondacs. 139.
  Cannon in front and leaden rain
                              Voluntaries. 94.

Leader's
  His from youth the leader's look
                              In Memoriam. 44.

Leading
  And bend my fancy to your leading,
                              Etienne. 3.
  Leading over heroic ground,
                              Voluntaries. 89.

Leads
  Each street leads downward to the sea,
                              Boston. 57.
  Him an angel whom she leads.
                              Caritas. 8.
  Where yon wedged line the Nestor leads,
                              May-Day. 23.
  Leads all souls to the Good.   Park. 16.
  The Swede Emanuel leads the soul.
                              Solution. 46.
  Where his clear spirit leads him, there's
    his road   Woodnotes. I. 94.

Leaf
  See Oak-leaf; Rose-leaf; Tobacco-
    leaf; Vine-leaf.
  Each leaf that shades the rock
                              April. 10.
  I touch this flower of silken leaf,
                              Dirge. 37.
  Nervèd leaf of hellebore,
                              Frag. Nat. II. 22.

Leaf—*Continued*
With its savory leaf for bread.
Frag. Nat. II. 24.
Each maple leaf turned up its silver side.
Frag. Nat. III. 14.
Every shrub and grape leaf
Frag. Nat. III. 24.
Thine each leaf and berry bore;
Lines. 6.
Not idle, since the leaf all day
May-Day. 115.
The dead log touched bursts into leaf,
May-Day. 208.
Leaf answers leaf upon the bough;
Merlin. 86.
The frailest leaf, the mossy bark,
Ode to Beauty. 25.
Insert a leaf, or forge a name,
Past. 19.
In every whispering leaf I hear
Peter. 31.
Ah! could we turn the leaf.
Quat. Climacteric. 4.
'T is written on the iron leaf,   Rhea. 34.

Leafless
See yonder leafless trees against the sky,
Frag. Nat. XVII. 1.
Spreading its leafless blooms in a damp
nook,   Rhodora. 3.

Leafy
For who defends our leafy tabernacle
Adirondacs. 171.
And boys run out upon their leafy ropes.
Frag. Nat. III. 20.
But for a leafy sign   May-Day. 107.
The leafy dell, the city mart,
Ode to Beauty. 88.
Cæsar of his leafy Rome,
Woodnotes. I. 5.

Leaguer
Breaks up their leaguer, and away.
Forerunners. 4.

Leagues
Slipped off their pack of duties, leagues
behind,   Adirondacs. 62.

Lean
O'er your ramparts as ye lean,
Alphonso. 20.
Made not pale, or fat, or lean;
Woodnotes. II. 37.

Leap
And take the mortal leap undaunted,
Fame. 17.
Who leap from horse to horse, but never
touch the ground.
Frag. Poet. XIX. 2.
The brimming brook invites a leap,
May-Day. 71.
My boreal lights leap upward,
Song of Nature. 41.

Leaped
Like Alpine cataracts frozen as they
leaped,   Blight. 60.
Had leaped from one fair mother's arms,
Dirge. 6.
But leaped with joy when on the wind
Frag. Poet. XXXV. 2.

Leaping
See Rash-leaping.
Is leaping o'er the sea,   *Farewell. 17.

Leaps
We will mark the leaps and gleams
May-Day. 228.

Learn
See Outlearn.
But which we learn to scatter with a
smudge,   Adirondacs. 175.
He must to school and learn his verb
and noun   Adirondacs. 267.
I, Alphonso, live and learn,
Alphonso. 1.
To learn of scribe or courier
Frag. Poet. V. 45.
Unless to learn it ten times ten.
Miracle. 8.
Yet, will you learn our ancient speech,
Monadnoc. 173.
And well could honoring Persia learn
Saadi. 82.
Lie on the warm rock-ledges, and there
learn   Seashore. 9.
And learn of love a new degree.
Security. 12.
'Come learn with me the fatal song
Woodnotes. II. 156.
We cannot learn the cipher
World-Soul. 45.

Learned
The best of cities with us, these learned
classifiers,   Adirondacs. 303.
Nor to learned jurist's chair;
Astraea. 14.
It leaves the learned in the lurch;
Bohemian. 9.
Who learned with me the lore of time,
Dirge. 27.
Till late he learned, through doubt and
fear,   Fate. 9.
Slighted Minerva's learnèd tongue,
Frag. Poet. XXXV. 1.
At the sophist schools and the learned
clan;   Good-Bye. 28.
Of Merlin wise I learned a song,—
Merlin's Song. 1.
And the learned lecture, well;
Monadnoc. 180.
They learned of the oaks and firs.
Nature. II. 12.
He feels it, introverts his learned eye
Philosopher. 5.
Go thou to thy learned task,
Quat. Botanist. 1.
I've learned the sum of that sad history
Summons. 18.
In one wood walk, than learned men
Walk. 7.

Learning
The school decays, the learning spoils
Frag. Life. X. 5.
And carry learning to its height
Monadnoc. 104.
His learning should be deep and large,
Poet. 40.

Least
Little man, least of all,
Experience. 14.
And this, at least, I dare affirm,
Harp. 73.
And, least of all, the loyal tie
In Memoriam. 81.

O wise man! hear'st thou the least part?
Woodnotes. II. 102.
The least breath my boughs which tossed
Woodnotes. II. 144.

Leather
See Sole-leather.

Leave
They reckon ill who leave me out;
Brahma. 9.
I cannot leave   Channing Ode. 3.
To die, and leave their children free,
C. Hymn. 14.
Leave no track on the heavenly snow.
Daemonic Love. 42.
I leave it behind with the games of
youth:'—   Each. 39.
Too fast we leave the bay,
*Farewell. 6.
I leave untold to-day,   *Farewell. 42.
And leave the cities void.   Garden. 4.
Leave all for love;   Give. 26.
Leave the chaff, and take the wheat.
Humble-Bee. 57.
Leave his weeds and heed his eyes,—
Initial Love. 19.
But leave us the horizon walls.
Romany. 8.
I know what spells are laid. Leave me
to deal   Seashore. 43.
To leave my woods and streams and the
sweet sloth   Summons. 4.
To leave the rudeness of my woodland
life,   Summons. 6.
Leave the many and hold the few.
Terminus. 16.
Leave authors' eyes, and fetch your own,
Waldeinsamkeit. 43.
Behind thee leave thy merchandise,
Woodnotes. II. 229.
And leave thy peacock wit behind;
Woodnotes. II. 231.
Leave all thy pedant lore apart;
Woodnotes. II. 234.

Leaved
See Five-leaved; Three-leaved; Two-leaved.

Leaves (verb).
It leaves the learned in the lurch;
Bohemian. 9.
Leaves on the wind melodious trace;
Forerunners. 13.
As unrepenting Nature leaves
In Memoriam. 95.
The girl's foot leaves its neater print.
May-Day. 62.
Leaves, when the sun appears, astonish-
ed Art   Snow-Storm. 25.
Who leaves the pine-tree, leaves his
friend,   Woodnotes. II. 49.
And leaves us in the mire.
World-Soul. 44.

Leaves (noun).
'Welcome!' the wood-god murmured
through the leaves,—
Adirondacs. 44.
Lemons run to leaves and rind;
Alphonso. 4.
Whose ample leaves and tendrils curled
Bacchus. 15.

Its soft leaves wound me with a grief
Dirge. 39.
Its leaves to the rival sky;   Exile. 2.
Low leaves his quarrel apprehend,
May-Day. 68.
Her callow brood in mantling leaves,—
May-Day. 173.
Perish like leaves, the highland breed
Monadnoc. 123.
Shedding on all its snows and leaves,
Monadnoc. 383.
A hill's leaves for winding-sheets,
Mountain. 15.
But O, these waves and leaves,—
Nun. 11.
Of leaves, and feathers from her breast?
Problem. 26.
To her old leaves new myriads?
Problem. 30.
Leaves twinkle, flowers like persons be,
Saadi. 137.
My leaves and my cascades;
Song of Nature. 52.
Kind leaves of his covert,   Sphinx. 23.
There will be nought to shelter thee
when their sweet leaves are gone.
*Violet. 8.
This must the leaves of ages strew
Wealth. 15.
And the countless leaves of the pine
are strings   Woodnotes. II. 95.

Leavest
And leavest thou thy lowland race,
Monadnoc. 208.

Leaving
Leaving on space no shade, no scars,
Frag. Nat. VIII. 7.
But, leaving rule and pale forethought,
Merlin. 31.
All my doing, all my leaving,
Song of Seyd. 5.

Lecture
And the learned lecture, well;
Monadnoc. 180.

Led
Of traders, led by corporate sons of
trade,   Adirondacs. 282.
And Love led Gods therein to bide.
Frag. Poet. XX. 2.
To works as noble led thee on.
Threnody. 79.
To lead him willing to be led,
Voluntaries. 56.
Me through trackless thickets led,
Woodnotes. I. 119.
They led me through the thicket damp,
Woodnotes. I. 125.
The falling waters led me,
Woodnotes. I. 129.

Ledge
See Granite-ledge; Rock-ledge.
The durance of a granite ledge.
Astraea. 37.
My garden is a forest ledge
Garden. 9.

Ledges
And split to flakes the crystal ledges.
Frag. Nat. XXX. 2.
She ransacks mines and ledges
House. 13.

Lees
And lees make all the rest.
Good Hope. 4.

Left
And in the left, a gun, his needful arms.
Adirondacs. 79.
We struck our camp and left the happy
hills. Adirondacs. 336.
Had left their beauty on the shore
Each. 27.
Loved the wood-rose, and left it on its
stalk? Forbearance. 2.
He left, though goodly centuries old,
Frag. Nat. VI. 7.
I left my dreary page
Frag. Nat. XXVII. 1.
He left each civil scale behind:
Frag. Poet. I. 32.
To find the sitfast acres where you left
them.' Hamatreya. 24.
There is no record left on earth,
In Memoriam. 48.
Aloft, beneath, on left and right
Poet. 99.
But left a legacy of ebbing veins,
Terminus. 29.
Amid the Muses, left thee deaf and
dumb, Terminus. 31.
Of human youth had left the hill
Threnody. 108.
The world dishonored thou hast left.
Threnody. 171.
Who thee divorced, deceived and left?
Woodnotes. II. 182.

Legacy
But left a legacy of ebbing veins,
Terminus. 29.

Legitimate
As of a luck not quite legitimate,
Adirondacs. 275.

Legs
Among the legs of his guardians tall,
Experience. 15.

Leisure
Of Syrian peace, immortal leisure,
Humble-Bee. 38.

Lemons
Lemons run to leaves and rind;
Alphonso. 4.

Lemurs
Lemurs and Lars. Frag. Life. VIII. 4.

Lend
Lend me your ears, and I begin.
Aeolian Harp. 11.
Unto men these moonmen lend,
Daemonic Love. 58.

Lender
And the second, borrowed money,—
though the smiling lender say
Ibn Jemin. 3.

Lend
And tides of life and increase lend;
Threnody. 113.

Length
Northward the length of Follansbee we
rowed, Adirondacs. 26.
And life, shorn of its venerable length,
Blight. 53.
Of the toy's purchase with the length
of life. Blight. 62.

His elfin length upon the snows,
May-Day. 114.
Gives the reed and lily length,
May-Day. 200.
The soaring orbit of the muse exceeds
that journey's length. Merlin. 65.

Lengthening
From lengthening scroll of human fates,
Threnody. 263.

Lent
Thy life to thy neighbor's creed has lent.
Each. 10.
Lent itself beneath the forest,
Holidays. 3.
The passive Master lent his hand
Problem. 47.

Leopard-colored
Leopard-colored rills. Monadnoc. 4.

Leopards'
Painting fawns' and leopards' fells,
May-Day. 204.

Less
Not less the ambitious botanist sought
plants, Adirondacs. 141.
Nor less the eternal poles
Celestial Love. 81.
Gauge of more and less through space,
II Compensation. 7.
Our pulses beat not less,
Concord Ode. 6.
Born into Dæmons less divine:
Daemonic Love. 90.
Less than a lily's, thou shalt daily draw
Day's Ration. 4.
From my great arteries,—nor less, nor
more.' Day's Ration. 5.
And huts and tents; nor loved he less
Frag. Poet. I. 25.
Little and less he says to them,
Manners. 13.
Not less renew the heart and brain,
May-Day. 453.
Who has little, to him who has less, can
spare, Merlin's Song. 24.
And being latent, feel thyself no less?
Musketaquid. 81.
Not less than was the first; the all-wise
God Naples. 3.
But not the less the eternal wave rolls
on Pan. 10.
Have changed not less the guest of gods;
Poet. 180.
Nor less on man's enchanted dust
Poet. 298.
Not less are summer mornings dear
Promise. 7.
Not the less revere the Giver,
Terminus. 15.
O loss of larger in the less!
Threnody. 117.
And I like less when Summer beats
Titmouse. 71.

Lesson
Fell the lesson on his heart Poet. 255.

Lessons
To spiritual lessons pointed home,
Adirondacs. 200.
Taught me new lessons in the lore of
life. Summons. 17.

Lest (Partial list.)
Lest there I find the same deceiver
    Ode to Beauty. 96.

Let
 See Outlet.
Your rank is all reversed; let men of
cloth   Adirondacs. 93.
Of scholars furloughed from their tasks
and let   Adirondacs. 193.
Let them hear well! Adirondacs. 261.
Let not him mourn who best entitled was,
    Adirondacs. 296.
Nay, mourn not one: let him exult,
    Adirondacs. 297.
Let spouting fountains cool the air,
     Art. 7.
Let statue, picture, park and hall,
     Art. 9.
Let its grapes the morn salute
    Bacchus. 6.
Let wine repair what this undid;
    Bacchus. 59.
And, chest by chest, let down the same,
    Boston. 78.
So let each dweller on the Bay
    Boston. 102.
Let the blood of her hundred thousands
    Boston. 106.
Let man serve law for man;
    Channing Ode. 66.
Ah! let me blameless gaze upon
     Eva. 7.
Nor let us hide, whate'er our pleasure,
    Fame. 23.
Let it have scope: Give. 8.
Six thankful weeks,—and let it be
    Goethe. 1.
Let them sail for Porto Rique,
    Humble-Bee. 3.
Let me chase thy waving lines;
    Humble-Bee. 8.
And bid you let the angels in
    Hymn. 19.
Let not unto the stones the Day
    Monadnoc. 12.
Soft! let not the offended muse
    Monadnoc. 125.
'Let him heed who can and will;
    Monadnoc. 224.
Then, at last, I let him down
    Monadnoc. 344.
And let thy body lie Mountain. 2.
Let me go where'er I will, Music. 1.
Let theist, atheist, pantheist, Saadi. 96.
'Let the great world bustle on
    Saadi. 104.
Let them manage how they may,
    Saadi. 115.
Let war and trade and creeds and song
    Song of Nature. 77.
Fate let him fall, Fate can't retake him;
    Threnody. 28.
And let the world's affairs go by,
    Threnody. 47.
Let Webster's lofty face Webster. 1.
Let the starred shade that nightly falls
    Woodnotes. II. 225.

Lethe
The Lethe of Nature Sphinx. 77.

Letter
No courier waits, no letter came or went,
    Adirondacs. 66.
Your letter tells, O changing child!
    Amulet. 3.
Writes a letter in my book.
    Apology. 8.
Answers not in word or letter,
    Astraea. 21.
Not so the pen, for in a letter
    Frag. Life. XII. 2.

Letters
Nay, letters found us in our paradise:
    Adirondacs. 334.
The letters do not cheer;
    World-Soul. 18.

Levelling
Levelling, displacing
    Daemonic Love. 82.

Levels
 See Summit-levels.

Liatris
And liatris, Frag. Nat. II. 5.

Liberal
And thief-like step of liberal hours
    Monadnoc. 64.
October in his liberal hand.
    Quat. S. H. 4.
His early hope, his liberal mien;
    Threnody. 55.
As sunbeams stream through liberal
space   Woodnotes. II. 1.

Liberated
Front the liberated floods:
    May-Day. 225.

Libertine
He is free and libertine,
    Woodnotes. II. 278.

Liberty
Sweet songs of liberty.
    Concord Ode. 32.
And, chiefest prize, found I true liberty
    Musketaquid. 66.
Of them who rescued liberty of old;
    Phi. 6.

Libraries
Culture and libraries, mysteries of skill,
    Adirondacs. 323.
Spare the clergy and libraries,
    Monadnoc. 181.

Lichen
Tree and lichen, ape, sea-lion,
    Mithridates. 12.
Wings of what wind the lichen bore,
    Wealth. 6.

Lid
 See Coffin-lid.
Under morn's unlifted lid,
    May-Day. 423.

Lids
Chaste-glowing, underneath their lids,
    Eva. 11.
Sidewise meek in gossamer lids;
    May-Day. 325.
And Morning opes with haste her lids
    Problem. 35.

Lie
Ten scholars, wonted to lie warm and
soft   Adirondacs. 50.

Lie—*Continued*

Lie here on hemlock-boughs,
     Adirondacs. 52.

If thou wear no mask or lie,
     Frag. Life. XXVII. 10.

Lie like cockles by the main,
     May-Day. 255.

With no posterity to make the lie afraid,
     Merlin. 111.

Already my rocks lie light,
     Monadnoc. 243.

And let thy body lie   Mountain. 2.

Dost love our manners? Canst thou silent lie?   Musketaquid. 77.

Lie on the warm rock-ledges, and there learn   Seashore. 9.

And each answer is a lie. Sphinx. 116.

O truth's and nature's costly lie!
     Threnody. 172.

Well, in this broad bed lie and sleep,—
     Titmouse. 17.

O Violet, like thee, how blest could I lie down and die,   *Violet. 9.

Of skirting hills to lie,
     Waldeinsamkeit. 6.

When the night and morning lie,
     Woodnotes. I. 140.

Though thou lie alone on the ground.
     Woodnotes. II. 88.

Lief

I had as lief respect an ancient shoe,
     To-Day. 11.

Liege

Not allowed to any liege;
     Initial Love. 119.

Lies

Know Heaven's truth from lies that shine—   Dull. 21.

The land is well,—lies fairly to the south.
     Hamatreya. 22.

By houses lies a fresher green,
     May-Day. 299.

More proudly rolls, more softly lies.
     Park. 12.

The Book itself before me lies,
     Problem. 64.

Lies bathèd in joy;   Sphinx. 42.

In soft miniature lies. Sphinx. 48.

Under pleasure, pain lies. Sphinx. 100.

The wintry garden lies unchanged;
     Threnody. 95.

Low lies the plant to whose creation went   Woodnotes. I. 76.

Liest

Or remember where thou liest,
     Destiny. 25.

Lieth

The cold gray down upon the quinces lieth   Frag. Nat. XXXIII. 1.

Deep love lieth under Sphinx. 69.

Life

And, that no day of life may lack romance,   Adirondacs. 221.

We have few moments in the longest life   Adirondacs. 249.

We praise the guide, we praise the forest life: Adirondacs. 305.

Fails of the life, but draws the death and ill.   Angelo. 14.

Whilst upper life the slender rill
     Art. 27.

To life or death, to heaven or hell,
     Bell. 3.

And life, shorn of its venerable length,
     Blight. 53.

Of the toy's purchase with the length of life.   Blight. 62.

Or land or life, if freedom fail?
     Boston. 30.

Or land or life, if freedom fail?
     Boston. 81.

Of better arts and life?
     Channing Ode. 14.

The aroma of my life is gone
     Days Pass. 3.

Melts down into that liquor of my life,—
     Day's Ration. 7.

Thy life to thy neighbor's creed has lent.
     Each. 10.

Who all the day of life his summer story tells;   Enchanter. 2.

The lords of life, the lords of life,—
     Experience. 1.

And crawls through life a paralytic
     Fame. 11.

Laugh life away; have wine for tears;
     Fame. 16.

And life to fan the flame; Fame. 28.

Hurled into life to do a deed,
     Frag. Life. XXIII. 8.

The flowing conditions of life, give way.
     Frag. Life. XXXI. 4.

Life would be too wild an ode.
     Frag. Nat. I. 18.

It chills my life, but wittily,
     Frag. Nat. XXIV. 4.

Touched with life by every beam.
     Frag. Nat. XXVI. 29.

He shared the life of the element,
     Frag. Poet. I. 52.

The fountains of my hidden life
     Friendship. 19.

Cling with life to the maid; Give. 34.

The cup of life is not so shallow
     Good Hope. 1.

The threads of life and power and pain,
     Harp. 101.

Of life resurgent from the soil
     Harp. 126.

Living in a baby's life. Holidays. 16.

Thou born for noblest life,
     In Memoriam. 28.

Dear brother, would you know the life,
     Letter. 1.

Is life and heart,   Limits. 7.

Of swifter life, a surer hope,
     May-Day. 152.

Life out of death, new out of old,
     May-Day. 203.

When our life was new.
     May-Day. 409.

Murmur in the house of life,
     Merlin. 124.

With the dear, dangerous lords that rule our life,   Musketaquid. 7.

in every several life, Naples. 4.

So each man's life shall have its proper lights,   Naples. 9.

The River of my Life replies.
Peter. 40.
Light-loving, light-asking life in me
Poet. 235.
And all thy life is for thy own,
Prayer. 3.
And each with novel life his sphere
Promise. 9.
Life loiters at the book's first page,—
Quat. Climacteric. 3.
The mystery of life,
Robbins Hymn. 10.
Showed them the life of Heaven above
Robbins Hymn. 19.
Springs from the life below.
Robbins Hymn. 20.
Tides that should warm each neighbor-
ing life Rubies. 7.
And life pulsates in rock or tree.
Saadi. 138.
And life was larger than before:
Solution. 38.
Drew the firm lines of Fate and Life
Solution. 66.
I sit by the shining Fount of Life
Song of Nature. 11.
Life death overtaking; Sphinx. 15.
To leave the rudeness of my woodland
life, Summons. 6.
By mind's industry sharpening the love
of life— Summons. 12.
Taught me new lessons in the lore of
life. Summons. 17.
Life, sunshine and desire,
Threnody. 2.
And tides of life and increase lend;
Threnody. 113.
Would rushing life forget her laws,
Threnody. 226.
Life is life which generates,
Threnody. 244.
And many-seeming life is one,—
Threnody. 245.
Up and away for life! be fleet!—
Titmouse. 11.
And hems in life with narrowing fence.
Titmouse. 16.
Life is too short to waste To J. W. 18.
Through light, through life, it forward
flows. Two Rivers. 8.
And his chain when life was done.
Voluntaries. 12.
The spans of life away. Walden. 44.
Of man to come, of human life,
Woodnotes. II. 131.

Life-blood
Has drunk the life-blood of the great;
Omar. 2.

Lifeless
Over the lifeless ball, Wealth. 3.

Life-pulse
Sets the life-pulse strong but slow:
Monadnoc. 158.

Life's
Have brought us to life's evening hour,
Ellen. 2.
Seldom in this low life's round
Garden. 47.
On Life's dark sea, *Lines. 2.

It should be their life's ornament,
Monadnoc. 50.
On life's fair picture of delight, Nun. 9.
Life's honeycomb, but not too fast;
Poet. 46.

Lifetime
For which we all our lifetime grope,
Monadnoc. 388.
And in this fleeting lifetime trust
Robbins Hymn. 23.

Lift
See Uplift.
And lift man's public action to a height
Adirondacs. 246.
Who do the feat, and lift humanity.
Adirondacs. 295.
Lift the sash, lay me within,
Aeolian Harp. 10.
Shall lift its notes once more, Bell. 14.
Lift up a people from the dust,
Boston Hymn. 67.
What all the goods thy pride which
lift, Destiny. 16.
Can mountains lift;
Frag. Poet. IX. 2.
A friend to lift the curtain up
Hymn. 21.
See thou lift the lightest load.
Merlin's Song. 23.
'Every morn I lift my head,
Monadnoc. 279.
Or lift to a diviner dream!' Poet. 194.
And lift thee to his holy mount,
Saadi. 61.
A load your Atlas shoulders cannot lift?
Seashore. 33.
Still tearless lift its slender form above
the wintry snow? *Violet. 4.
Come lift thine eyes to lofty rhymes,
Woodnotes. II. 158.

Lifted
See Unlifted; Uplifted.

Lifting
See Uplifting.
To each apart, lifting her lovely shows
Adirondacs. 199.
Lifting Better up to Best;
May-Day. 466.
And lifting man to the blue deep
Monadnoc. 100.

Lifts
Lifts its head, Frag. Nat. III. 2.
Step by step, lifts bad to good,
May-Day. 464.

Light
See Daylight; Moonlight; Sunlight.
Then struck a light and kindled the
camp-fire. Adirondacs. 36.
Up with the dawn, they fancied the
light air Adirondacs. 59.
Who stands astonished at the meteor
light, Adirondacs. 123.
So light, so lofty pictures came and
went. Adirondacs. 159.
Seeking in that chaste blue a bluer light,
Adirondacs. 209.
It is there for purging light;
Astraea. 40.
Pole-star of light in Europe's night,
Boston. 90.

Light—*Continued*
Round they roll till dark is light,
        Channing Ode. 78.
His blinding light   Cupido. 5.
All else grew foreign in their light.
        Daemonic Love. 18.
But whether it dazzle me with light.
        Destiny. 37.
Five rosy boys with morning light
        Dirge. 5.
Full of light and of deity;   Each. 47.
Goes light the nimble zephyr;
        Ellen South. 10.
The world's light underneath a measure.
        Fame. 24.
That cheered the holy light!
        *Farewell. 2.
A light which plays and hovers
        Frag. Life. XVI. 2.
Man drinks the water, drinks the light.
        Frag. Life. XXIII. 9.
Steeped in the light are beautiful.
        Frag. Nat. XXVI. 18.
With spouting streams and waves of light
        Frag. Nat. XXVI. 24.
The light wherewith all planets shone,
        Frag. Poet. IV. 25.
With light that streams from gracious
  eyes.   Frag. Poet. VII. 6.
And as the light divides the dark
        Frag. Poet. XIII. 1.
Voyager of light and noon;
        Humble-Bee. 15.
Sole source of light and hope assured,
        Hymn. 25.
Beneath the calm, within the light,
        May-Day. 150.
With tender light and youthful cheer,
        May-Day. 269.
By morn and eve in light and shade;
        Monadnoc. 61.
Already my rocks lie light,
        Monadnoc. 243.
'Through all time, in light, in gloom
        Monadnoc. 266.
Of rich men blazing hospitable light,
        Naples. 18.
Or tapers light the chaos dark?
        Nemesis. 12.
And passing, light my sunken turf
        Nun. 25.
As the light of enterprise
        On Prince. 3.
There I am full of light;   Peter. 30.
I see the coming light,   Poet. 97.
And I to whom your light has spoken,
        Poet. 237.
Love it, though it hide its light;
        Poet. 287.
To light which dims the morning's eye.
        Rhea. 4.
The bandages of purple light;
        Rhea. 16.
Here holy thoughts a light have shed
        Robbins Hymn. 5.
And prayed the eternal Light to clear
        Robbins Hymn. 11.
Never in the blaze of light   Saadi. 51.
Holds in check the frolic light,
        Solution. 44.

And light from meliorating stars
        Song of Nature. 19.
They fade in the light of   Sphinx. 71.
Than July's meridian light.   Test. 10.
Thought's holy light.   Thought. 4.
Light is light which radiates,
        Threnody. 242.
Through light, through life, it forward
  flows.   Two Rivers. 8.
At home a deeper thought may light
        Una. 13.
When summer light is fading, and
  autumn breezes sigh;   *Violet. 10.
There the red morning touched him with
  its light.   Woodnotes. I. 83.
By God's own light illumined and fore-
  showed.   Woodnotes. I. 95.
Choosing light, wave, rock and bird,
        Woodnotes. II. 59.
All ill dissolving in the light
        Woodnotes. II. 65.
On him the light of star and moon
        Woodnotes. II. 71.
And pulse, and sound, and light was
  none;   Woodnotes. II. 267.
The fourth gives light which eats the
  dark;   Woodnotes. II. 292.
This vault which glows immense with
  light   Woodnotes. II. 299.
Thanks to the morning light,
        World-Soul. 1.

Light-armed
Only the light-armed climb the hill.
        Merlin's Song. 28.

Light-asking
Light-loving, light-asking life in me
        Poet. 235.

Lighted
Or, later yet, beneath a lighted jack,
        Adirondacs. 117.
At the same torch that lighted mine;
        Eva. 3.
Lighted each transparent word,
        Saadi. 81.
From the lighted halls   Poet. 226.
Lightest
See thou lift the lightest load.
        Merlin's Song. 23.

Light-headed
But though light-headed man forget,
        Wealth. 44.

Light-hearted
Light-hearted as a bird, and live with
  God.   Self-Reliance. 3.

Light-loving
Light-loving, light-asking life in me
        Poet. 235.

Lightly
Name not lightly to be said,
        Freedom. 7.
Of him who shall as lightly bear
        Monadnoc. 270.

Lightning
The lightning has run masterless too
  long;   Adirondacs. 266.
For you can teach the lightning speech,
        Boston. 110.
An inch of ground the lightning strook
        Frag. Poet. XXXII. 3.
The lambent heat lightning Illusions. 20.

Like (preposition, etc.)—*Continued*
Like thee the youth or maid:
    May-Day. 435.
Self-planted twice, like the banian.
    Miracle. 6.
Like wise preceptor, lure his eye
    Monadnoc. 102.
Adhere like this foundation strong,
    Monadnoc. 115.
Perish like leaves, the highland breed
    Monadnoc. 123.
Like wax, their fashioning skill betrays,
    Monadnoc. 148.
Goes like bullet to its mark;
    Monadnoc. 190.
Who, in large thoughts, like fair pearl-seed,
    Monadnoc. 285.
Shall string Monadnoc like a bead.
    Monadnoc. 286.
And, like the chemist 'mid his loaded jars,
    Musketaquid. 38.
Transmuted in these men to rule their like),
    Musketaquid. 49.
Canst thou, thy pride forgot, like Nature pass
    Musketaquid. 78.
And like wise God she judges well.
    Nature. I. 15.
Like the lightning through the storm,
    Ode to Beauty. 69.
Couched like a cat sat   Philosopher. 9.
And throttled all his passion. Is't not like
    Philosopher. 10.
Methought like water-haunting birds
    Poet. 19.
Sounded like a tempest strong
    Poet. 28.
The solid kingdoms like a dream
    Poet. 36.
Like meteors which chose their way
    Poet. 55.
And rived the dark like a new day!
    Poet. 56.
But, like a walker in his sleep   Poet. 86.
With aim like yours   Poet. 155.
For their like are sold.   Politics. 4.
Fall like sweet strains, or pensive smiles;
    Problem. 4.
Like the volcano's tongue of flame,
    Problem. 16.
You must be like them if you desire them,
    Rome. 11.
His words like a storm-wind can bring
    Saadi. 127.
Leaves twinkle, flowers like persons be,
    Saadi. 137.
Was ever building like my terraces?
    Seashore. 7.
A little hut suffices like a town.
    Seashore. 10.
Like Cupids studiously inclined;
    Threnody. 65.
Or like a traveller's fleeing tent,
    Threnody. 276.
And ages drop in it like rain.
    Two Rivers. 20.
Takes hearts like thine in special charge,
    Titmouse. 86.
O Violet, like thee, how blest could I lie
  down and die,   *Violet. 9.

I had a sister once who seem just like a violet;
    *Violet. 13.
Like God it useth me.
    Waldeinsamkeit. 4.
For a proud idleness like this
    Waldeinsamkeit. 47.
And like a lover volunteers,   Walk. 4.
Or east, it smells like a clover-farm;
    Woodnotes. I. 102.
Like to like shall joyful prove;
    Woodnotes. II. 82.
Like wave or flame,
    Woodnotes. II. 274.
Which bloom and fade like meadow flowers
    Woodnotes. II. 302.
And lo! he passes like the breeze;
    Woodnotes. II. 308.
Like shells along the shore,
    World-Soul. 66.

Likeness
Draws men to their likeness still.
    Daemonic Love. 67.
If thou go in thine own likeness,
    Frag. Life. XXVII. 7.
It seemed the likeness of their own;
    Woodnotes. I. 115.

Lilacs
Plant gardens lined with lilacs sweet;
    Art. 6.
Willows and lilacs brings again,
    May-Day. 183.

Lilies
Through scented banks of lilies white and gold,
    Adirondacs. 19.
A bunch of fragrant lilies be,
    Woodnotes. II. 303.

Lily
Wild rose, lily, dry vanilla,—
    Frag. Nat. II. 18.
Gives the reed and lily length,
    May-Day. 200.
Her lily and rose, her sea and land display.
    Monadnoc. 13.

Lily-bell
Starry space and lily-bell
    Ode to Beauty. 78.

Lily's
Less than a lily's, thou shalt daily draw
    Day's Ration. 4.

Limb
That use to undo the limb and sense of age;
    I Bear. 2.

Limbs
Limbs into branches, branches into twigs,
    Frag. Nat. XVII. 4.
And my unserviceable limbs forego.
    I Bear. 5.
Chills the limbs of Time;   Poet. 294.

Lime
We must have clay, lime, gravel, granite-ledge,
    Hamatreya. 20.
The planet with a floor of lime?
    Wealth. 24.

Limes
Meagre crop of figs and limes;
    Alphonso. 5.

Limitary
Their fierce and limitary will
    Daemonic Love. 66.

Limp
Dash our blown hopes as they limp heav-
ily by.   Summons. 21.
Limped
How lame the other limped away.
Nun. 49.
Linden
Linden and spruce. In strict society
Adirondacs. 39.
Line
See Water-line.
If I fell within the line,
Frag. Poet. IV. 9.
Docile read my measured line:
Frag. Poet. VII. 2.
Where yon wedged line the Nestor leads,
May-Day. 23.
Merlin's mighty line   Merlin. 51.
From the earth-poles to the Line,
Mithridates. 3.
Above the ploughman's highest line,
Monadnoc. 8.
If need were, their line from Jove;
Monadnoc. 167.
The swinging spider's silver line
Ode to Beauty. 27.
And he who blent both in his line,
Problem. 66.
Against the being of a line.   Uriel. 20.
'Line in nature is not found;   Uriel. 21.
Not hook nor line hath he;
Woodnotes. I. 8.
Foundeth a heroic line;
Woodnotes. II. 23.
Can read thy line, can meet thy glance,
Woodnotes. II. 141.
Draw, if thou canst, the mystic line
Worship. 21.
Lineage
No lineage counted great;
Boston Hymn. 30.
'I am of a lineage   Hermione. 31.
Lineament
In figure, bone and lineament?
Threnody. 248.
Lined
Plant gardens lined with lilacs sweet;
Art. 6.
Philosophers are lined with eyes within,
Philosopher. 1.
Lines
Coin the day-dawn into lines
Frag. Poet. XXIX. 1.
Let me chase thy waving lines;
Humble-Bee. 8.
And Piranesi's lines.
Ode to Beauty. 55.
Drew the firm lines of Fate and Life
Solution. 66.
Five lines lasted sound and true;
Test. 4.
Linger
Linger,—thou shalt rue the fault:
Visit. 28.
Lingerest
Why lingerest thou, pale violet, to see the
dying year;   *Violet. 1.
Link
Link in the Alps' globe-girding chain;
Monadnoc. 85.

Linkèd
When linked hemispheres attest his deed.
Adirondacs. 248.
Better, the linked purpose of the whole,
Musketaquid. 65.
Linnæa
The slight Linnæa hang its twin-born
heads,   Woodnotes. I. 69.
Linnet
The cagèd linnet in the Spring
May-Day. 83
Lion
See Sea-lion.
Out of the lion;   Channing Ode. 87.
Love laughs, and on a lion rides.
Daemonic Love. 88.
And made the lion mild.   Merlin. 54.
In whose feet the lion rusheth,
Woodnotes. II. 40.
The crouching lion kissed his feet;
Worship. 8.
Lion's
from wit the lion's part?
Adirondacs. 276.
Lions
As lions on their prey;
Initial Love. 40.
Thrown to lions for their meat,
Worship. 7.
Lip
They put their finger on their lip,
II Eros. 1.
The old Sphinx bit her thick lip,—
Sphinx. 109.
Lipped
See Rose-lipped.
Lips
Keep your lips or finger-tips
Aeolian Harp. 4.
My lips in whisper move   *Farewell. 43.
O touch thy servant's lips with power,
Hymn. 26.
Of eloquent lips, of joyful wit:
In Memoriam. 52.
Ye taught my lips a single speech,
Merops. 7.
Wilt not give the lips to taste
Ode to Beauty. 80.
Never from lips of cunning fell
Problem. 11.
The younger Golden Lips or mines,
Problem. 67.
Speak through his lips thy pure com-
mands,   Robbins Hymn. 27.
Had active hands and smiling lips;
Saadi. 77.
For his lips could well pronounce
Threnody. 52.
And their lips the secret kept, Uriel. 45.
Liquid
Tethered by a liquid cord
Daemonic Love. 3.
Liquor
Melts down into that liquor of my life,—
Day's Ration. 7.
And all the costly liquor runs to waste;
Day's Ration. 23.
Lisbon
Lisbon quakes, the people cry.
Alphonso. 14.

List

Devour as many as yau list,
　　　　　Frag. Nat. XIX. 5.
Define and wrangle how they list,
　　　　　Saadi. 97.

Listen

Or listen when thou repliest,
　　　　　Destiny. 24.
I listen when they sing,　　Dull. 7.
Listen for their harp-like laughter,
　　　　　Forerunners. 36.
You must listen long.
　　　　　Frag. Nat.III. 32.
Listen what the poplar-tree　　Rhea. 7.
'O gentle Saadi, listen not,　　Saadi. 87.
O, listen to the undersong,
　　　　　Woodnotes. II. 116.

Listened

Yet they who listened far aloof
　　　　　Solution. 54.

Listener's

Yet before the listener's eye　　Saadi. 133.

Listeners

I cannot tell rude listeners
　　　　　September. 13.

Listening

Or listening to the laughter of the loon;
　　　　　Adirondacs. 114.
It seemed, so listening, at my side
　　　　　Harp. 108.
Listening to the gray-haired crones,
　　　　　Saadi. 169.

Listens

For Nature listens in the rose
　　　　　Nature. I. 12.

Lists

Stops his horse, and lists with delight,
　　　　　Each. 7.
And, when it lists him, waken can
　　　　　Freedom. 15.
The prizes in all lists he won;
　　　　　In Memoriam. 79.

Lit

　　See Star-lit; Sunlit.
Lit with phosphoric crumbs the forest
floor.　　　　　Adirondacs. 49.
And, lit by fringent air,
　　　　　Daemonic Love. 50.
But lit the sky with flame.
　　　　　Frag. Poet. XXXII. 4.
Which lit my onward way with bright
presage,　　　　　I Bear. 4.
Lit by rays from the Blest.　　Sphinx. 76.
Lit by the supersolar blaze.
　　　　　Threnody. 202.

Litanies

The litanies of nations came,
　　　　　Problem. 15.

Lithe

Of our lithe society;　　Ellen South. 26.

Little

When of our little fleet three cruising
skiffs　　　　　Adirondacs. 231.
Which fired the little State to save
　　　　　Boston. 94.
With little men;—　　Channing Ode. 26.
And brims my little cup; heedless, alas!
　　　　　Day's Ration. 12.
Of all he sheds how little it will hold,
　　　　　Day's Ration. 13.

The little cup will hold not a bead more,
　　　　　Day's Ration. 22.
I hold it of little matter　　Destiny. 34.
Little thinks, in the field, yon red-cloaked
clown　　　　　Each. 1.
The little Shakespeare in the maiden's
heart　　　　　Enchanter. 12.
Little man, least of all,　　Experience. 14.
And the former called the latter 'Little
Prig;'　　　　　Fable. 3.
Escort us to a little grave.
　　　　　Frag. Life. I. 4.
Wait a little, you shall see
　　　　　Frag. Life. XXXV. 5.
Welcome back, you little nations,
　　　　　Frag. Nat. XXIII. 7.
In mercy, on one little head.
　　　　　Frag. Poet. XXIV. 2.
Me a little pinches here,　From Hafiz. 14.
In the wretched little beast　　Limits. 6.
Little and less he says to them,
　　　　　Manners. 13.
Who has little, to him who has less, can
spare,　　　　　Merlin's Song. 24.
A little while attend;　　　Poet. 93.
A little hut suffices like a town.
　　　　　Seashore. 10.
The little needle always knows the
North,　　　　　Self-Reliance. 6.
The little bird remembereth his note,
　　　　　Self-Reliance. 7.
A little while　　　　Terminus. 19.
The little captain innocent
　　　　　Threnody. 70.
I greeted loud my little savior,
　　　　　Titmouse. 48.
What fire burns in that little chest
　　　　　Titmouse. 52.
A little while each russet gem
　　　　　Woodnotes. II. 53.
Seek not, and the little eremite
　　　　　Woodnotes. II. 250.

Live

　　See Alive; Outlive.
I've come to live with you, sweet friends,
　　　　　Aeolian Harp. 18.
I, Alphonso, live and learn,
　　　　　Alphonso. 1.
And live on even terms with Time;
　　　　　Art. 26.
To die for Beauty, than live for bread.
　　　　　Beauty. 26.
Live for friendship, live for love,
　　　　　Channing Ode. 67.
Is to live well with who has none.
　　　　　Frag. Life. XI. 2.
Haply else we could not live,
　　　　　Frag. Nat. I. 17.
To bards who from its maxims live,
　　　　　Frag. Poet. IV. 2.
Shame the times and live apart,—
　　　　　Frag. Poet. IV. 6.
Of better men than live to-day;
　　　　　Garden. 62.
Who seem to die live.　　Illusions. 6.
Forms more cheerly live and go,
　　　　　Merlin. 43.
Live in the sunshine, swim the sea,
　　　　　Merlin's Song. 31.

Is to live well with who has none.
Merlin's Song. 40.
And to live he is in fear.
Monadnoc. 343.
To swains that live in happiness
Nature. I. 18.
Hovering over all that live,
Ode to Beauty. 75.
Live, robed with beauty, painted by the
sun; Pan. 2.
With Gods, with fools, content to live;
Poet. 214.
Too busied with the crowded hour to fear
to live or die. Quat. Nature. 4.
They live with God; their homes are
dust; Robbins Hymn. 21.
Light-hearted as a bird, and live with
God. Self-Reliance. 3.
This poet, though he live apart,
Titmouse. 33.
Of my bird's song: 'Live out of doors
Titmouse. 67.
Why wilt thou live when none around
reflects thy pensive ray? *Violet. 5.
And live with living nature, a pure re-
joicing thing. *Violet. 12.
He is great who can live by me:
Woodnotes. II. 13.

Lived
See Short-lived.
And I lived but to sigh, *Lines. 26.
The men who lived with him became
Solution. 41.

Livelong
Where arches green, the livelong day,
Good-Bye. 19.

Livery
The livery all events put on,
Frag. Poet. IV. 26.

Lives
Add their nine lives to this cat;
Alphonso. 71.
He lives not who can refuse me;
Frag. Nat. XXVIII. 1.
He lives in his eyes; Initial Love. 45.
Nor lives the tragic bard to say
Nun. 47.
The perfect Adam lives. Promise. 6.
and as God lives in heaven, Rome. 25
As God lives, is permanent;
Threnody. 267.
There lives no man of Nature's worth
Woodnotes. II. 198.

Liveth
Who liveth by the ragged pine
Woodnotes. II. 22.
Who liveth in the palace hall
Woodnotes. II. 24.

Living
Through with living swords,
Frag. Poet. XIII. 2.
Living in a baby's life. Holidays. 16.
As if it were a living root;
Initial Love. 56.
Thou living champion of the right?
In Memoriam. 30.
Feels the bloom on the living vine,
May-Day. 90.
For living brows; ill fits them to receive:
Phi. 2.

Seek the living among the dead,—
Saadi. 117.
Living gem of Solomon;
Song of Seyd. 10.
The living Heaven thy prayers respect,
Spiritual Laws. 1.
And live with living nature, a pure re-
joicing thing. *Violet. 12.
Whose living towers the years conspired
to build, Woodnotes. I. 78.
One dry, and one the living tree.
Woodnotes. II. 21.

Lizard
Captured the lizard, salamander, shrew,
Adirondacs. 135.
Frog and lizard in holiday coats,
May-Day. 237.

Lo (Partial list.)
Lo! I uncover the land
Boston Hymn. 17.
Lo, now! if these poor men
Boston Hymn. 45.
Lo! the south answers to the north;
Monadnoc. 15.
Lo! here is Rome and Nineveh and
Thebes, Seashore. 14.
And lo! he passes like the breeze;
Woodnotes. II. 308.

Load
'T is very small,—no load at all,—
Boston. 67.
O, what a load Celestial Love. 63.
See thou lift the lightest load.
Merlin's Song. 23.
My daily load of woods and streams,
Monadnoc. 271.
A load your Atlas shoulders cannot lift?
Seashore. 33.

Loaded
Goes home loaded with a thought.
Apology. 12.
Goes loaded with a free perfume
Mountain. 12.
And, like the chemist 'mid his loaded
jars, Musketaquid. 38.
Sin piles the loaded board.
Woodnotes. II. 17.

Loaf
Like poisoned loaf of elfin bread,
Frag. Nat. III. 3.

Loam
Peep the blue violets out of the black
loam, Naples. 25.

Loath
Though loath to grieve
Channing Ode. 1.
They do her bidding, nothing loath.
Nature. II. 19.

Lochs
Mixed with mist by distant lochs.
Forerunners. 16.

Lock
See Unlock.

Locked
Of Merlin locked the harp within.—
Harp. 54.
Are locked in sparkling stone.
Rubies. 8.

Locks
Lovely locks, a form of wonder,
Threnody. 213.

Lodge
That we should build, hard-by, a spacious
   lodge   Adirondacs. 162.
Lodged
Which, lodged in rock, the rock abrade?
                         Wealth. 8.
Lodges
Is the inn where he lodges for a night.
                    Woodnotes. II. 300.
Loftier
Unlocks new sense and loftier cheer.
                     Aeolian Harp. 17.
And find a loftier way:
                     Frag. Life. X. 4.
A door to something grander,—loftier
   walls, and vaster floor.
                     Frag. Nat. XII. 3.
Loftiest
And ruddy Health the loftiest Muse.
                     Merlin's Song. 30.
Lofty
To climb a lofty stem, clean without
   boughs   Adirondacs. 83.
So light, so lofty pictures came and went.
                     Adirondacs. 159.
Oft pealed for him a lofty tone
                         Beauty. 11.
Taunted the lofty land
                     Channing Ode. 25.
Farewell, ye lofty spires   *Farewell. 1.
Their sweet and lofty countenance
                         Manners. 5.
Hearing as now the lofty dirge   Nun. 18.
I hear the lofty pæans
                     Ode to Beauty. 56.
Let Webster's lofty face   Webster. 1.
Come lift thine eyes to lofty rhymes,
                    Woodnotes. II. 158.
Log
From a log cabin stream Beethoven's
   notes   Adirondacs. 313.
The dead log touched bursts into leaf,
                     May-Day. 208.
Log-wall
This thin spruce roof, this clayed log-
   wall,   Adirondacs. 318.
Loiter
Loiter not for cloak or food;
                         Freedom. 23.
And loiter willing by yon loitering
   stream.   Musketaquid. 14.
Loitering
by yon loitering stream.
                     Musketaquid. 14.
Loiters
Life loiters at the book's first page,—
                     Quat. Climacteric. 3.
That loiters round the crystal coast,
                     Threnody. 121.
Lone
Lone mountain tarn, or isle forgot,
                         Astraea. 46.
And the lone seaman all the night
                     Daemonic Love. 54.
Or in lone corners of a doleful heath,
                     Frag. Nat. IV. 3.
Save to his ear the wind-harp lone.
                         Harp. 98.
Lone as the blessed Jew.
                     Quat. Shakespeare. 4.

I make some coast alluring, some lone
   isle,   Seashore. 48.
But in the serious landscape lone
                     Waldeinsamkeit. 15.
Lonely
The lonely Earth amid the balls
                     II Compensation. 9.
Knows he who tills this lonely field
                         Dirge. 9.
'Go, lonely man,' it saith;   Dirge. 49.
When I would spend a lonely day,
                     Frag. Poet. XXV. 3.
By lonely lakes to men unknown.
                         May-Day. 29.
Under clouds, my lonely head,
                     Monadnoc. 203.
Thou hast bribed the dark and lonely
                     Ode to Beauty. 84.
[Knows he who tills this lonely field
                         Peter. 1.
For in those lonly grounds the sun
                         Peter. 13.
Alone in Rome. Why, Rome is lonely
   too;—   Rome. 1.
I lonely roved the land or sea:
                     Thine Eyes. 2.
Thou bloomest here a lonely thing
                        *Violet. 6.
Long
   See Livelong.
Long sought, not found.
                     Adirondacs. 133.
Orchis and gentian, fern and long whip-
   scirpus,   Adirondacs. 142.
The lightning has run masterless too
   long;   Adirondacs. 266.
That sat in darkness long,—
                     Boston Hymn. 78.
The foe long since in silence slept;
                         C. Hymn. 5.
In the long sunny afternoon   Dirge. 13.
As when my brothers, long ago,
                         Dirge. 19.
Long and various the report,—
                         I Eros. 2.
Long I followed happy guides,
                     Forerunners. 1.
I thenceforward and long after
                     Forerunners. 35.
You must listen long.   Frat. Nat. III. 32.
Endured, the Bible says, as long;
                     Frag. Nat. VI. 4.
Nor think it long.   Frag. Nat. XXI. 9.
Long through thy weary crowds I roam;
                         Good-Bye. 3.
Long I've been tossed like the driven
   foam;   Good-Bye. 5.
Not long ago at eventide,   Harp. 107.
Long, long concealed by sundering
   fates,   Harp. 113.
Long days, and solid banks of flowers;
                     Humble-Bee. 35.
Two things thou shalt not long for, if
   thou love a mind serene;—
                     Ibn Jemin. 1.
This befell how long ago!
                     Initial Love. 6.
That one broad, long midsummer day
                     May-Day. 276.

The feet that slid so long on sleet
                    May-Day. 281.
Makes travellers long for Indian skies,
                    May-Day. 294.
How long the power to give them name
                    Merops. 3.
Too long shut in strait and few,
                    Mithridates. 20.
But their long hands it thence will take;
                    Monadnoc. 146.
And the long Alleghanies here,
                    Monadnoc. 276.
Long morrow to this mortal youth.
                    Monadnoc. 408.
[In the long sunny afternoon   Peter. 9.
And fill the long reach of the old sea-
    shore   Poet. 75.
Though it hate thee, suffer long;
                    Poet. 291.
After long months of weary wandering,
                    River. 37.
However long thou walkest solitary,
                    Rome. 26.
Oh, south winds have long memories,
                    September. 11.
Star-crowned, sole-sitting, long I wrought
                    Solution. 3.
I brooded long and held my peace,
                    Solution. 18.
Too long the game is played;
                    Song of Nature. 54.
Doubt not, so long as earth has bread,
                    Titmouse. 83.
And the treason, too long pent,   Uriel. 9.
Whether doomed to long gyration
                    Uriel. 39.
Askest, 'How long thou shalt stay?'
                    Visit. 1.
Sum their long experience,   Visit. 19.
Long she loved the Northman well;
                    Voluntaries. 43.
So long he roved at will the boundless
    shade.   Woodnotes. I. 85.

Long-descended
And tell its long-descended race.
                    Woodnotes. I. 45.

Longer
I was no longer brave;   Hamatreya. 61.
Toy no longer—it has duties;
                    Holidays. 7.
Heeds no longer lapse of time,
                    Poet. 131.

Longest
We have few moments in the longest
    life   Adirondacs. 249.

Longings
    See Love-longings.

Look
Look to yourselves, ye polished gentle-
    men!   Adirondacs. 91.
The stunted trees look sick,   Blight. 50.
Walked about with puzzled look.
                    Experience. 16.
And look beyond the earth,
                    Friendship. 14.
And seldom therein could I look,
                    Goethe. 4.
His from youth the leader's look
                    In Memoriam. 44.
I look at my face in the glass,—
                    Park. 7.

Look, here he is, unaltered, save that now
                    River. 8.
From the window I look out
                    Threnody. 74.
Whereinto he loved to look.
                    Threnody. 93.
With a look that solved the sphere,
                    Uriel. 17.
Single look has drained the breast;
                    Visit. 21.
It cannot be,—I will look again.
                    Woodnotes. II. 211.

Looked
Looked eastward from the farms,
                    Boston. 2.
And paused for them, and looked around,
                    Dirge. 3.
I looked forth on the fields of youth:
                    Harp. 110.
All the forms we looked on shone
                    May-Day. 412.
I looked again,—I though them hearts
                    Rubies. 5.
East, west, for aid I looked in vain,
                    Titmouse. 7.
Methought the sky looked scornful down
                    Walden. 21.
On him the sun looked more serene;
                    Woodnotes. I. 113.

Lookest
When thou lookest on his face,
                    Destiny. 20.

Looketh
He looketh seldom in their face,
                    Manners. 9.

Looking
    See Forelooking.
Of thee from the hill-top looking down;
                    Each. 2.
Looking seaward, well assured
                    Letters. 4.
And, looking over the hills, I mourn
                    Threnody. 7.

Looking-glass
Each to each a looking-glass,
                    Astraea. 23.
The green grass is a looking-glass
                    Manners. 11.

Looks
His impatient looks devour
                    Daemonic Love. 105.
Who bides at home, nor looks abroad,
                    Destiny. 49.
Looks to the azure cope,
                    Frag. Life. XXIII. 2.
He looks on that, and he turns pale.
                    Monadnoc. 330.
To brave the landscape's looks.
                    Waldeinsamkeit. 44.
Who never looks behind.
                    World-Soul. 8.

Looming
Islands looming just beyond
                    May-Day. 424.

Loom's
In his own loom's garment dressed,
                    Monadnoc. 38.

Loon
Or listening to the laughter of the loon;
                    Adirondacs 114

Loons
To Follansbee Water and the Lake of
Loons.　　　　　　Adirondacs. 25.
Loop
Or, hid in vines, peeping through many
a loop,　　　　Quat. Gardener. 3.
Loosed
When from the womb the babe was
loosed,　　　Quat. Horoscope. 3.
Loosened
The pebble loosened from the frost
　　　　　　　　　May-Day. 63.
Lord
　　See Landlord.
'Not so,' said Boston, 'good my lord,
　　　　　　　　　Boston. 69.
The word of the Lord by night
　　　　　　　　Boston Hymn. 1.
Nor gives the jealous lord one diamond
drop　　　　　Day's Ration. 24.
Served high and low, the lord and the
churl,　　　　Frag. Poet. I. 20.
Of Lord Christ's heart, and Shakspeare's
strain.　　Informing Spirit. 8.
Flows from the heart of love, the Lord.
　　　　　　　　　May-Day. 191.
Silent rushes the swift Lord
　　　　　　　　　Threnody. 282.
As fits a feathered lord of land;
　　　　　　　　　Titmouse. 37.
Is better than the lord;
　　　　　　　Woodnotes. II. 15.
The lord is the peasant that was,
　　　　　　　Woodnotes. II. 18.
The peasant the lord that shall be;
　　　　　　　Woodnotes. II. 19.
The lord is hay, the peasant grass,
　　　　　　　Woodnotes. II. 20.
Lordly
This is lordly man's down-lying,
　　　　　　　　　Threnody. 163.
Lords
Lords of this realm,　Adirondacs. 152.
Has lords enough and more;—
　　　　　　　　　Boston. 20.
The lords of life, the lords of life,—
　　　　　　　　Experience. 1.
With squires, lords, kings, his craft com-
pares,　　　　　　Fate. 8.
Stately lords in palaces,
　　　　　　　Frag. Poet. I. 26.
The richest of all lords is Use,
　　　　　　　Merlin's Song. 29.
With the dear, dangerous lords that rule
our life,　　　Musketaquid. 7.
Lordship
Taste the lordship of the earth.'
　　　　　　　　　Monadnoc. 26.
Lore
　　See Love-lore.
But will we sacrifice our dear-bought
lore　　　　　Adirondacs. 306.
The lore we care to know.　April. 20.
Who learned with me the lore of time,
　　　　　　　　　Dirge. 27.
I laugh at the lore and the pride of man,
　　　　　　　　Good-Bye. 27.
He renders all his lore　　Harp. 29.
Showed me the lore of colors and of
sounds,　　　Musketaquid. 60.

The deepest lore of wealth or want:
　　　　　　　　　Poet. 42.
For of this lore be thou sure,—
　　　　　　　　　Rhea. 27.
Draws the heart a lore sublime."'
　　　　　　　　　Saadi. 71.
Taught me new lessons in the lore of
life.　　　　　Summons. 17.
Leave all thy pedant lore apart;
　　　　　　　Woodnotes. II. 234.
I will tell thee the mundane lore.
　　　　　　　Woodnotes. II. 253.
Lose
Lose courage, and despair.
　　　　　　　Daemonic Love. 111.
The tongue is prone to lose the way,
　　　　　　　Frag. Life. XII. 1.
He gold or jewel could not lose,
　　　　　　　　　Guy. 15.
And buy, and sell, and lose, and win;
　　　　　　　　Initial Love. 47.
Lose the shudder of midnight;
　　　　　　　　　Saadi. 52.
They lose their grief who hear his song,
　　　　　　　Two Rivers. 15.
Losing
For this losing is true dying;
　　　　　　　　　Threnody. 162.
Loss
Their wonted convenance, cheerly hid
the loss　　　Adirondacs. 181.
Retrieve the loss of me and mine!
　　　　　　　　　Bacchus. 52.
Hints never loss or cruel break
　　　　　　　In Memoriam. 107.
O loss of larger in the less!
　　　　　　　　　Threnody. 117.
Lost
The good applaud, the lost are eased.
　　　　　　　Celestial Love. 114.
Too soon those spires are lost,
　　　　　　　　*Farewell. 5.
Venus, when her son was lost,
　　　　　　　　Initial Love. 1.
The pilgrims have each other lost.
　　　　　　　Love and Thought. 12.
Voice of a meteor lost in day?
　　　　　　　　May-Day. 12.
In lowly homes have lost their way.
　　　　　　　Ode to Beauty. 67.
The heedless world hath never lost.
　　　　　　　　Problem. 62.
Lost in whirling spheres I rove,
　　　　　　　Song of Seyd. 7.
The lost, the lost, he cannot restore;
　　　　　　　　Threnody. 6.
Nature, who lost, cannot remake him;
　　　　　　　　Threnody. 27.
Born for the future, to the future lost!
　　　　　　　　Threnody. 175.
Of matter, and thy darling lost?
　　　　　　　　Threnody. 182.
Lost in God, in Godhead found.'
　　　　　　　　Threnody. 289.
Lot
Where Hope, the soothsayer, reads our
lot,　　　　　　　Ellen. 6.
What lot soe'er betide,
　　　　　　　In Memoriam. 91.
His lot of action at the urn.　Poet. 188.

Pure content is angel's lot,   Poet. 251.
When success exalts thy lot,
                                Prayer. 1.
Already Heaven with thee its lot has
    cast,   Sursum Corda. 10.
Lote
And the grape requite the lote!
                                Bacchus. 54.
Lotus
Reason in Nature's lotus drenched,
                                Bacchus. 56.
With lotus wine obliterates
                        Daemonic Love. 13.
Loud
Watching when the loud dogs should
    drive in deer,   Adirondacs. 110.
Loud hammered, and the heron rose in
    the swamp.   Adirondacs. 148.
Of loud Bog River, suddenly confront
                        Adirondacs. 233.
With ductile fire. Loud, exulting cries
                        Adirondacs. 241.
Hark what, now loud, now low, the pin-
    ing flute complains,   Flute. 1.
Rung loud and bold the song.
                                Harp. 48.
Until Cupid laughed loud,   *Lines. 22.
Sing it low or sing it loud,
                        Merlin's Song. 2.
Strikes the loud pretender down.
                                Nature. I. 11.
I greeted loud my little savior,
                                Titmouse. 48.
Louder
Louder than with speech they pray,—
                                Astraea. 17.
Loudest
The silent organ loudest chants
                                Dirge. 59.
Lout
That not academicians, but some lout,
                        Adirondacs. 279.
Love
Red when you love, and rosier red,
                                Amulet. 7.
And when you love not, pale and blue.
                                Amulet. 8.
Torments me still the fear that love
                                Amulet. 11.
Not love, nor beauty's pride,
                                Angelo. 10.
While thus to love he gave his days
                                Beauty. 21.
I love thy music, mellow bell,
                                Bell. 1.
I love thine iron chime,   Bell. 2.
Love not the flower they pluck, and know
    it not,   Blight. 21.
And coldly ask their pottage, not their
    love.   Blight. 39.
But the sweet affluence of love and song,
                                Blight. 42.
And love without a name.
                        Celestial Love. 5.
Thou must mount for love;
                        Celestial Love. 30.
Their cords of love so public are,
                        Celestial Love. 107.
Live for friendship, live for love,
                        Channing Ode. 67.

The purple flaming of love?
                                Cosmos. 4.
And purple flame of love.   Cosmos. 8.
And Love ascends his throne,
                                Cosmos. 22.
Is pervious to Love;   Cupido. 2.
Virtue, to love, to hate them, vice;
                        Daemonic Love. 9.
The erring painter made Love blind,—
                        Daemonic Love. 68.
Highest Love who shines on all;
                        Daemonic Love. 69.
And ever and forever Love
                        Daemonic Love. 85.
Love laughs, and on a lion rides.
                        Daemonic Love. 88.
In like sort his love doth fall.
                        Daemonic Love. 96.
And ever the Dæmonic Love
                        Daemonic Love. 129.
When all but Love itself is dead
                                Ellen. 11.
Show our love and piety.
                                Ellen South. 28.
To love and be beloved;   I Eros. 3.
They love, but name not love.
                                II Eros. 5.
And dark, without love, is the day;
                                Exile. 18.
That untold early love   *Farewell. 41.
Nor stab the love that orphans keep.
                        Frag. Life. VII. 4.
You shall not love me for what daily
    spends;   Frag. Life. XV. 1.
But love me then and only, when you
    know   Frag. Life. XV. 6.
Love   Frag. Life. XVII. 1.
Love calls not to his aid events;
                        Frag. Life. XVII. 4.
Himself and his love intervene.
                        Frag. Life. XVII. 15.
Even to those who thee should love
                        Frag. Life. XXVII. 5.
If curses be the wage of love,
                        Frag. Life. XXXIII. 1.
And they who truest love her, heralds
    are   Frag. Nat. V. 9.
"Once with manlike love and fear
                        Frag. Poet. II. 5.
And love, for words thy tongue could
    say.   Frag. Poet. II. 8.
Love of ladies, love of bards,
                        Frag. Poet. VII. 10.
What then, can I love myself?
                        Frag. Poet. VII. 13.
They love me, as I love a cloud
                        Frag. Poet. VII. 16.
And blushing Love outwits the sages.
                        Frag. Poet. IX. 12.
And Love led Gods therein to bide.
                        Frag. Poet. XX. 2.
For, in the world of love
                        From Hafiz. 4.
In other love should seek amends.
                        From Hafiz. 12.
And be sure at last came Love,
                                Garden. 27.
And after Love, the Muse.
                                Garden. 28.
When he ceased to love me,   Gifts. 3.

Love—*Continued*

Give all to love;   Give. 1.
Leave all for love;   Give. 26.
Followed with love   Harp. 118.
But for the love of happy souls
                                      House. 23.
A love that in the spirit dwells,
                                      Hymn. 2.
if thou love a mind serene;—
                                      Ibn Jemin. 1.
Love—love—love—love.
                                      Initial Love. 44.
Love scatters oil   *Lines. 1.
Flows from the heart of Love, the Lord.
                                      May-Day. 191.
Is it Daedalus? is it Love?
                                      May-Day. 214.
And the love in its carol heard,
                                      May-Day. 236.
The love of kind, the joy, the grace,
                                      May-Day. 265.
The animals are sick with love,
                                      Merlin. 96.
Love is aye the counterforce,—
                                      Miracle. 11.
Whose throbs are love, whose thrills are
  song.   Monadnoc. 170.
The partial wood-gods overpaid my love,
                                      Musketaquid. 4.
Dost love our manners? Canst thou silent
  lie?   Musketaquid. 77.
Yet doth much her love excel
                                      Nature. I. 16.
And every man, in love or pride,
                                      Nemesis. 7.
That Night or Day, that Love or Crime,
  of life—   Park. 15.
In love, he cannot therefore cease his
  trade;   Philosopher. 3.
In the love which Nature fills,
                                      Poet. 145.
Beside him sat enduring love,
                                      Poet. 195.
Than all the grace Love ever saw;
                                      Poet. 282.
Love it, though it hide its light;
                                      Poet. 287.
By love behold the sun at night.
                                      Poet. 288.
I love a prophet of the soul;
                                      Problem. 2.
The canticles of love and woe:
                                      Problem. 18.
Whilst love and terror laid the tiles.
                                      Problem. 32.
Scorn not thou the love of parts,
                                      Prudence. 3.
Test of the poet is knowledge of love,
                                      Quat. Casella. 1.
Love on his errand bound to go
                                      Quat. Love. 1.
Though love repine, and reason chafe,
                                      Quat. Sacrifice. 1.
If with love thy heart has burned;
                                      Rhea. 9.
If thy love is unreturned;   Rhea. 10.
For when love has once departed
                                      Rhea. 13.
His love shall never be requited.
                                      Rhea. 45.

Profuse in love, the king bestows,
                                      Rhea. 56.
And grave parental love.   River. 30.
We love the venerable house
                                      Robbins Hymn. 1.
For faith and peace and mighty love
                                      Robbins Hymn. 17.
That can contend with love. It reigns
  forever.   Rome. 19.
To thee. He watches for thee still. His
  love   Rome. 24.
That the high gods love tragedy;
                                      Saadi. 73.
Yet the love the world that warms
                                      Security. 3.
She must love me till she find
                                      Security. 5.
And learn of love a new degree.
                                      Security. 12.
Nor my heart from love of mine,
                                      Song of Seyd. 3.
And know only that I love.
                                      Song of Seyd. 8.
Love is the air-fed fire intense,
                                      Song of Seyd. 15.
Well I love the meaning sweet,—
                                      Song of Seyd. 23.
Lo! the God's love blazes higher,
                                      Song of Seyd. 25.
Deep love lieth under   Sphinx. 69.
Is love of the Best;   Sphinx. 74.
Than to love me.   Sphinx. 96.
Love works at the centre,   Sphinx. 101.
Railing in love to those who rail again,
                                      Summons. 11.
By mind's industry sharpening the love
  of life—   Summons. 12.
fireside, friends and love,   Summons. 13.
I loved ye with true love, so fare ye
  well!   Summons. 14.
Now Love and Pride, alas! in vain,
                                      Threnody. 80.
Which overflowing Love shall fill,
                                      Threnody. 192.
Masterpiece of love benign,
                                      Threnody. 257.
Heart's love will meet thee again.
                                      Threnody. 269.
As love old things for age,
                                      To-Day. 12.
The stream I love unbounded goes
                                      Two Rivers. 6.
Through love and thought, through
  power and dream.   Two Rivers. 12.
If Love his moment overstay,
                                      Visit. 29.
For Love draws might from terrene force
                                      Waterfall. 7.
He shall be happy in his love,
                                      Woodnotes. II. 81.
Love shuns the sage, the child it crowns,
                                      Woodnotes. II. 236.
Love wakes anew this throbbing heart,
                                      World-Soul. 107.

Loved
    See Beloved.
Loved by stars and purest winds,
                                      Astraea. 32.
Indebted or insulted, loved or hurt,
                                      Day's Ration. 10.

Who loved this dwelling-place!
                    Dirge. 28.
'They loved thee from their birth;
                    Dirge. 50.
Well that we loved, woe had we not,
                    Ellen. 8.
Loved of bee,—the tawny hummer.
                    Ellen South. 20.
He never, though he dearly loved his
    race,   Entombed. 3.
Be loved by few; be feared by none;
                    Fame. 15.
Loved the wood-rose, and left it on its
    stalk?   Forbearance. 2.
And loved so well a high behavior,
                    Forbearance. 5.
As if they loved the element, and hasted
                    Frag. Nat. XVII. 5.
Loved harebells nodding on a rock,
                    Frag. Poet. I. 21.
And huts and tents; nor loved he less
                    Frag. Poet. I. 25.
He loved to watch and wake
                    Frag. Poet. I. 35.
Gifts of one who loved me,—
                    Gifts. 1.
Though thou loved her as thyself,
                    Give. 43.
Who but loved the wind-harp's note?
                    Harp. 49.
And these loved banks, whose oak-
    boughs bold   In Memoriam. 115.
He should be loved; he should be hated;
                    Poet. 48.
And well he loved to quit his home
                    Poet. 51.
Shall not by the same be loved again;
                    Rhea. 38.
Yet Saadi loved the race of men,—
                    Saadi. 23.
I loved ye with true love, so fare ye
    well!   Summons. 14.
Whereinto he loved to look.
                    Threnody. 93.
Not what I made, but what I loved,
                    Threnody. 129.
Long she loved the Northman well;
                    Voluntaries. 43.
When Ali prayed and loved
                    Waterfall. 17.
Whose giddy top the morning loved to
    gild.   Woodnotes. I. 79.

Loveliest
Though thou wert the loveliest
                    Rhea. 17.
Loveliest of travellers.   Una. 20.

Love-longings
Love-longings of the raptured bird
                    Quat. Hafiz. 3.

Love-lore
Who was not tremulous with love-lore.
                    Quat. Casella. 4.

Lovely
To each apart, lifting her lovely shows
                    Adirondacs. 199.
Who trod with me this lovely vale;
                    Dirge. 22.
They turn his heart from lovely maids,
                    Frag. Poet. XI. 12.

Whither went the lovely hoyden?
                    Holidays. 13.
And speak the lovely caravan.
                    Threnody. 73.
Lovely locks, a form of wonder,
                    Threnody. 213.

Lover
State of hermit, state of lover;
                    Alphonso. 56.
Of man and earth, of world beloved and
    lover,   Blight. 44.
But thou, meek lover of the good!
                    Brahma. 15.
From God's adoring lover.   Dull. 14.
The lover watched his graceful maid,
                    Each. 29.
And to the pausing lover.
                    Ellen South. 8.
Blue-eyed pet of blue-eyed lover.
                    Ellen South. 32.
There is no lover in all Bagdat
                    Exile. 7.
The lover rooted stays.   Friendship. 4.
Fortune was his guard and lover;
                    Guy. 10.
Insect lover of the sun,
                    Humble-Bee. 11.
For bard, for lover and for saint;
                    Monadnoc. 45.
Too credulous lover   Ode to Beauty. 3.
Is the deep's lover;   Ode to Beauty. 38.
Hunt knowledge as the lover wooes a
    maid,   Rome. 14.
Have I a lover   Sphinx. 93.
And like a lover volunteers,   Walk. 4.
Lover of all things alive,
                    Woodnotes. I. 24.
A lover true, who knew by heart
                    Woodnotes. I. 34.
The clay of their departed lover.'
                    Woodnotes. I. 146.

Lover's
That were a man's and lover's part,
                    Etienne. 23.

Lovers
Guide lovers to the pool.   April. 8.
Thine everlasting lovers. Ye shall be
                    Good Cheer. 15.
So lovers melt their sundered selves,
                    Initial Love. 149.
When worlds of lovers hem thee in?
                    Threnody. 188.

Love's
Love's hearts are faithful, but not fond,
                    Celestial Love. 115.
For this is Love's nobility,—
                    Celestial Love. 124.

Loves
Do these celebrate their loves:
                    Celestial Love. 100.
Loves nature like a hornèd cow,
                    Initial Love. 100.
Framed afar as Fates and Loves.
                    Frag. Poet. XII. 4.
And sacrifice for love's dear sake,
                    In Memoriam. 108.
The fresh ground loves his top and
    ball,   May-Day. 69.
Soothe pain, and age, and love's dis-
    tress,   May-Day. 439.

Loves—*Continued*
But she dearly loves the poor,
Nature. I. 9.
Caught with love's cord of twisted beams, Nun. 35.
Only by needs and loves of mine;
Poet. 234.
He who loves, of gods or men,
Rhea. 37.
And give love's scarlet tides to flow,—
Rubies. 11.
All are Love's, and all are ours,
Song of Seyd. 28.
Wilt thou freeze love's tidal flow,
Threnody. 238.
Hearts are dust, hearts' loves remain;
Threnody. 268.
She loves a poor and virtuous race.
Voluntaries. 38.
Why Nature loves the number five,
Woodnotes. I. 22.
The brave he loves amain;
World-Soul. 90.

Lovesick
Lovesick with rhyme; Merlin. 97.

Lovest
Thou heart that lovest all.
Robbins Hymn. 28.

Loveth
Loveth downward, and not up;
Rhea. 36.

Love-without-weakness
Love-without-weakness,—Of Genius sire and son. World-Soul. 83.

Loving
See All-loving; Balance-loving; Freedom-loving; Light-loving; Low-loving; Money-loving; Rock-loving; Snow-loving.
But day by day, to loving ear
Aeolian Harp. 16.
'Deep, deep are loving eyes,
Celestial Love. 15.
By searching of a clear and loving eye
Good Cheer. 11.
Well known, but loving not a name,
Monadnoc. 29.
Loving the wind that bent me. All my hurts Musketaquid. 71.
The favor of the loving Day,—
Threnody. 20.

Low
Under low mountains, whose unbroken ridge Adirondacs. 27.
Low on their wooden bench.
Boston. 85.
And dips sometimes as low as to her eyes. Daemonic Love. 38.
Are silent, low and pale. Dirge. 24.
Hark what, now loud, now low, the pining flute complains, Flute. 1.
No fate, save by the victim's fault, is low, Frag. Life. II. 1.
And dips sometimes as low as to her eyes. Frag. Life. XVI. 4.
The low December vault in June be lifted high, Frag. Nat. XX. 1.
Served high and low, the lord and the churl, Frag. Poet. I. 20.

In cities he was low and mean;
Frag. Poet. V. 16.
Speak it not, or speak it low;
Freedom. 6.
Seldom in this low life's round
Garden. 47.
To supple Office, low and high;
Good-Bye. 10.
Serve that low whisper thou hast served; for know, Good Cheer. 2.
Low leaves his quarrel apprehend,
May-Day. 68.
Too strait and low our cottage doors,
May-Day. 220.
I saw the Days deformed and low,
May-Day. 312.
Sing it low or sing it loud,
Merlin's Song. 2.
And in low hut the dweller found:
Monadnoc. 73.
Low, open meads, slender and sluggish streams, Musketaquid. 2.
Beneath low hills, in the broad interval
Musketaquid. 26.
Of close low pine-woods in a river town;
Naples. 14.
Ope in such low moist roadside, and beneath Naples. 24.
In the woodwalks still and low
Poet. 254.
Hopped on the bough, then, darting low,
Titmouse. 39.
One, with low tones that decide,
Uriel. 15.
Low and mournful be the strain,
Voluntaries. 1.
Low and tender in the cell
Voluntaries. 5.
When Duty whispers low, Thou must,
Voluntaries. 73.
The matted thicket low and wide,
Wealth. 14.
Low lies the plant to whose creation went Woodnotes. I. 76.
And sunk the immortal eye so low?
Woodnotes. II. 185.

Lowed
Cattle lowed in mellow distance
September. 7.

Lowers
The new day lowers, and equal odds
Poet. 179.

Lowest
And brought me to the lowest land,
Woodnotes. I. 131.

Low-hung
And the seas wash the low-hung sky;
Poet. 66.

Lowing
See Trumpet-lowing.
For wolf and fox, bring lowing herds,
Monadnoc. 139.

Lowland
And misty lowland, where to go for peat. Hamatreya. 21.
In the lowland, when day dies;
Harp. 92.
And leavest thou thy lowland race,
Monadnoc. 208.

Low-loving
Not glad, as the low-loving herd,
                    Celestial Love. 117.

Lowly
In lowly cot or painful road,
                    In Memoriam. 57.
In lowly homes have lost their way.
                    Ode to Beauty. 67.
'Lowly faitful, banish fear,
                    Terminus. 37.
The musing peasant, lowly great,
                    Woodnotes. I. 104.

Low-prized
And we the low-prized laymen.
                    Adirondacs. 96.

Lows
The heifer that lows in the upland farm,
                    Each. 3.
Far-heard, lows not thine ear to charm;
                    Each. 4.

Loyal
That mortals miss the loyal heats,
                    Alphonso. 33.
In loyal worship, scorning praise,
                    Beauty. 22.
And, least of all, the loyal tie
                    In Memoriam. 81.
The forest is my loyal friend,
                    Waldeinsamkeit. 3.

Lubber
To man, as to a lubber friend,
                    May-Day. 403.

Luck
As of a luck not quite legitimate,
                    Adirondacs. 275.

Lucky
The virtue of his lucky hand.   Guy. 14.

Lukewarm
As late I found my lukewarm blood
                    Titmouse. 3.

Lull
And the prussic juice to lull me;
                    Mithridates. 17.
As their murmurs mine to lull.   Nun. 14.

Lumberers
In winter, lumberers; in summer, guides;
                    Adirondacs. 88.

Lumberers'
In unploughed Maine he sought the
    lumberers' gang   Woodnotes. I. 62.

Lump
Him to his land, a lump of mould the
    more.   Hamatreya. 26.

Lungs
The wild air bloweth in our lungs,
                    Romany. 21.

Lurch
It leaves the learned in the lurch;
                    Bohemian. 9.

Lure
Like wise preceptor, lure his eye
                    Monadnoc. 102.

Lured
Lured by 'Union' as the bribe.
                    Voluntaries. 30.

Lures
How spread their lures for him in vain
                    Beauty. 23.

Lurk
For, as the wood-kinds lurk and hide,
                    Quat. Forester. 3.

Lurketh
Lurketh Nature veritable;   Saadi. 130.

Lurking
Lurking dumb,   Frag. Life. VIII. 2.
Can your lurking thought surprise,
                    Initial Love. 62.

Lurks
Spirit that lurks each form within
                    Nature. Mot. 13.
Lurks the joy that is sweetest
                    Sphinx. 91.
And, by the famous might that lurks
                    Spiritual Laws. 8.

Lust
Like lust in the chill of the grave.
                    Hamatreya. 63.

Lustre
And the lustre and the grace
                    Daemonic Love. 30.
The lustre of the land and ocean,
                    Hermione. 13.

Lustres
He scatters wide and wild its lustres
    here.   Frag. Life. XVI. 9.
Why tinge thy lustres jubilant
                    Frag. Nat. VIII. 3.
Shed mocking lustres on shelf of books,
                    May-Day. 356.
I see the pale lustres condense to a star:
                    Poet. 109.

Lute
Thy praying lute will seem to scold;
                    Rhea. 22.

Luther
Luther, Fox, Behmen, Swedenborg, grew
    pale,   Adakryn. 3.

Lying
    See Down-lying.
By lying use bestowed,
                    Celestial Love. 65.
Unknown, albeit lying near,
                    Daemonic Love. 39.

Lynx
The lynx, the rattlesnake, the flood, the
    fire;   Adirondacs. 316.

Lyre
At the burning Lyre,   Monadnoc. 215.
God, who gave to him the lyre,
                    Saadi. 9.

Mace
As with hammer or with mace;
                    Merlin. 11.

MacIntyre
Taháwus, Seaward, MacIntyre, Baldhead,
                    Adirondacs. 10.

Mad
Which drives me mad with sweet de-
    sire,   Destiny. 13.
They made the woodlands glad or mad.
                    Dirge. 36.
Mad Destiny this tender stripling played;
                    Epitaph. 2.
Built in an age, the mad wind's night-
    work,   Snow-Storm. 28.

Mad—*Continued*
Not mad, athirst, nor garrulous;
Woodnotes. II. 68.

Made
We made our distance wider, boat from
boat,   Adirondacs. 14.
Made them to boys again. Happier that
they   Adirondacs. 61.
We were made freemen of the forest
laws,   Adirondacs. 70.
The world was made for honest trade,—
Boston. 11.
The world was made for honest trade,—
Boston. 53.
Think ye I made this ball
Boston Hymn. 9.
The God who made New Hampshire
Channing Ode. 24.
Spirit, that made those heroes dare
C. Hymn. 13.
Man was made of social earth,
Daemonic Love. 1.
The erring painter made Love blind,—
Daemonic Love. 68.
Who made this world the feast it was,
Dirge. 26.
They made the woodlands glad or mad.
Dirge. 36.
Not unless God made sharp thine ear
Dirge. 45.
"I am divine, I am not mortal made;
Frag. Life. XVIII. 3.
The rules to men made evident
Frag. Life. XXXVI. 1.
Made beautiful for God:—
Frag. Nat. III. 7.
Hold of the Maker, not the Made;
Frag. Poet. XVII. 1.
For Genius made his cabin wide,
Frag. Poet. XX. 1.
The sowers made haste to depart,—
Garden. 17.
Healed as fast the wounds it made.
Guy. 20.
And made each tide and element
Guy. 27.
Pent in a dungeon made of air,—
Harp. 56.
Or made what other purlieus proud.
Lines. 22.
Nor evil laws or rulers made,
May-Day. 105.
Is made whole again.   May-Day. 337.
And made the lion mild.   Merlin. 54.
Made all things in pairs.   Merlin. 80.
Assured that he who made the claim,
Monadnoc. 28.
As that whereof the sun is made,
Monadnoc. 168.
Made moon and planets parties to their
bond,   Musketaquid. 8.
We are what we are made; each follow-
ing day   Naples. 1.
And what they say they made to-day,
Nature. II. 11.
And the sands whereof I'm made
Ode to Beauty. 50.
All fortunes made;   Past. 5.
And every flower made obeisance
Peter. 35.

Her manners made of bounty well re-
fined;   Quat. A. H. 2.
Made the black water with their beauty
gay;   Rhodora. 6.
Tell them, dear, that if eyes were made
for seeing,   Rhodora. 11.
And prayers of humble virtue made
Robbins Hymn. 7.
Made one of day and one of night
Song of Nature. 63.
Not what I made, but what I loved,
Threnody. 129.
Ill day which made this beauty waste,
Threnody. 150.
Boy who made dear his father's home,
Threnody. 167.
Made of the air that blows outside.'
Titmouse. 78.
For this the day was made.
Waldeinsamkeit. 12.
Still on the seeds of all he made
Waldeinsamkeit. 25.
him a hermit made,   Woodnotes. I. 84.
Made not pale, or fat, or lean;
Woodnotes. II. 36.
And heal the hurts which sin has made.
Woodnotes. II. 220.
Are of one pattern made; bird, beast
and flower,   Xenophanes. 6.

Madness
Who, with sadness and madness,
Sphinx. 63.

Magic
The old men studied magic in the flowers,
Blight. 23.
Where'er he went, the magic guide
Frag. Poet. I. 17.
In magic and in clairvoyance,
Initial Love. 65.
When magic wine for bards is brewed;
May-Day. 339.

Magical
The April winds are magical
April. 1.
By magical drawings,
Ode to Beauty. 11.

Magic-built
Magic-built to last a season;
Threnody. 256.

Magnificence
Yet unto me not morn's magnificence,
Naples. 15.
But, feeding on magnificence,
Poet. 60.

Magnificent
For God hath writ all dooms magnificent,
Frag. Life. II. 2.
Was ever couch magnificent as mine?
Seashore. 8.

Magnified
Who is the Bard thus magnified?
Harp. 36

Magnifies
Dwindles here, there magnifies,
Frag. Poet. IX. 7

Maid
The maid, abolishing the past,
Daemonic Love. 12
The lover watched his graceful maid.
Each. 29

O fair and stately maid, whose eyes
                                Eva. 1.
In man or maid, that thou from speech
    refrained,   Forbearance. 6.
Cling with life to the maid;   Give. 34.
Fruit beloved of maid and boy,
                            Holidays. 2.
Old man and young maid,
                            Illusions. 9.
From youth to maid, from boy to man,
                        May-Day. 347.
Like thee the youth or maid:
                        May-Day. 435.
Or an ungiven maid,   Merlin. 109.
as the lover wooes a maid,   Rome. 14.
To a man and to a maid.   September. 16.
Of sound and echo, man and maid,
                        Woodnotes. II. 161.

Maiden
For a warm breast of maiden to his
    breast,   Epitaph. 3.
Year by year the rose-lipped maiden,
                            Holidays. 9.
Tell me, maiden, dost thou use? Lines. 1.
Willow and violet, maiden and man.
                        May-Day. 288.
Hero and maiden, flesh of her flesh;
                            Nature. II. 14.
The maiden fears, and fearing runs
                            Nemesis. 5.
I make this maiden an ensample
                            Rhea. 64.

Maiden's
Of man's or maiden's eye: Culture. 8.
Over the maiden's head,
                    Daemonic Love. 37.
The little Shakspeare in the maiden's
    heart   Enchanter. 12.
Over the maiden's head
                    Frag. Life. XVI. 3.
His lamp, the maiden's downcast eye,
                    Frag. Poet. I. 12.

Maidens
Maidens laugh and weep; Composure
                            Poet. 223.

Maids
poetic maids,   Frag. Life. XXX. 2.
High destined youths and holy maids
                    Frag. Poet. VII. 3.
They turn his heart from lovely maids,
                    Frag. Poet. XI. 12.
Maids of as soft a bloom shall marry
                    Good Hope. 5.
Of thoughtful maids and manhood bold.
                            Hymn. 12.
That the maids and boys might name
    him.   Initial Love. 14.
On men and maids a ruddier mien,
                        May-Day. 300.
And Summer came to ripen maids
                        May-Day. 303.
And simple maids and noble youth
                            Saadi. 39.
To the maids of holy mind,
                        World-Soul. 6.

Mail
What boots it? What the soldier's mail,
                            Destiny. 14.

Main
The wires shall murmur through the main
                        Concord Ode. 31.
Of all wit's uses the main one
                    Frag. Life. XI. 1.
He stood before the tumbling main
                    Frag. Poet. I. 50.
Reply to the thunder of river and main.
                        May-Day. 240.
Lie like cockles by the main,
                        May-Day. 255.
Of all wit's uses, the main one
                    Merlin's Song. 39.
Men to all shores that front the hoary
    main.   Seashore. 40.
Of the boundless main   Tal. Exile. 2.

Maine
In unploughed Maine he sought the lum-
    berers' gang   Woodnotes. I. 62.

Majestic
And harbingers of a majestic race,
                    Frag. Nat. V. 10.
Behold the new majestic birth!
                    Frag. Nat. XXVI. 16.
What majestic stillness broods
                    Frag. Nat. XXVI. 19.
And somewhat of majestic sympathy,
                            River. 33.
Wait then, sad friend, wait in majestic
    peace   Rome. 20.

Majesty
Hid their majesty in cloth
                        May-Day. 329.

Make
    See Unmake.
We cut young trees to make our poles
    and thwarts,   Adirondacs. 34.
and kersey trousers make
                        Adirondacs. 75.
What make you, master, fumbling at the
    oar?   Adirondacs. 99.
Make his frame and forces square
                            Alphonso. 73.
And make to-morrow a new morn.
                            Art. 12.
Make sunshine in her brain.
                            Boston. 109.
And make just laws below the sun,
                        Boston Hymn. 47.
To make his bosom-counsel good.
                        Celestial Love. 130.
And make of duty fate.
                        Concord Ode. 16.
To make the sun forgotten.
                            Destiny. 28.
To make up a year   Fable. 8.
I'll not deny you make   Fable. 15.
Make the morning proud and sweet;
                        Forerunners. 10.
Thou shalt make thy house
                    Frag. Life. XXII. 1.
In thy breast to make a home.
                    Frag. Life. XXII. 8.
Make up thy splendor, matchless day?
                    Frag. Nat. XI. 2.
And make the darlings of the earth
                    Frag. Poet. XI. 13.
And lees make all the rest.
                        Good Hope. 4.

Make—*Continued*
The pulse of hands will make him mute;
     Initial Love. 57.
The blackbirds make the maples ring
     May-Day. 166.
Make the aged eye sun-clear,
     May-Day. 455.
Can make the wild blood start
     Merlin. 7.
With no posterity to make the lie afraid,
     Merlin. 111.
If He should make my web a blot
     Nun. 8.
Make women of men;
     Ode to Beauty. 18.
Make him glad thy fall to see!
     Poet. 220.
Plotted to make him rich and great:
     Quat. Horoscope. 2.
But make the statute of this land.
     Rhea. 30.
I make this maiden an ensample
     Rhea. 64.
I make your sculptured architecture vain,
     Seashore. 11.
I make some coast alluring, some lone
isle,   Seashore.47.
Make thy option which of two;
     Terminus. 13.
To make this wisdom earthly wise.
     Threnody. 57.
Wilt thou transfix and make it none?
     Threnody. 246.
In plains that room for shadows make
     Waldeinsamkeit. 5.
The bittern's boom, a desert make
     Waldeinsamkeit. 31.
To make no step until the event is known,
     Woodnotes. I. 88.

Maker
 See Basket-maker.
Hold of the Maker, not the Made;
     Frag. Poet. XVII. 1.
Revere the Maker; fetch thine eye
     Threnody. 270.
Maker and original.
     Woodnotes. II. 284.

Maker's
Worked on the Maker's own receipt,
     Guy. 26.

Makes
 See Unmakes.
Due east a bay makes inward to the land
     Adirondacs. 30.
And travelling often in the cut he makes,
     Blight. 20.
For the angel Hope aye makes
     Caritas. 7.
Makes Romeo of a plough-boy on his
cart;   Enchanter. 13.
Makes each day a festival.
     Frag. Nat. XXVI. 6.
And makes thy thoughts archangels be;
     Freedom. 20.
Thy sleep makes ridiculous.
     Humble-Bee. 63.
Makes travellers long for Indian skies,
     May-Day. 294.
Who builds, yet makes no chips, no din,
     Monadnoc. 239.

Makes and moulds them what they are,
     Nature. II. 8.
On my neck he makes his seat;
     Park. 6.
Your gold makes you seem wise;
     Park. 10.
'T is good will makes intelligence,
     Titmouse. 65.
Than noontide twilights which snow
makes   Titmouse. 73.
Of shard and flint makes jewels gay;
     Two Rivers. 14.
Spring still makes spring in the mind
     World-Soul. 105.

Makest
And makest sane.   Monadnoc. 402.

Maketh
To the Soul that maketh all:
     Informing Spirit. 2.
From form to form He maketh haste;
     Woodnotes. II. 298.

Makeweight
A makeweight flying to the void,
     II Compensation. 11.

Making
Making one place two places?
     Chartist. 2.
The moon was making amber of the
world,   Frag. Nat. XXVII. 3.
Making free with time and size,
     Frag. Poet. IX. 6.
Making the splendor of the air,
     May-Day. 429.

Malaga
Drink not the Malaga of praise,
     Saadi. 64.

Malay
To Fin and Lap and swart Malay,
     Woodnotes. II. 154.

Malice
Peace now each for malice takes,
     Caritas. 5.
With malice dared me to proclaim him,
     Initial Love. 13.

Malign
How shall I dare to malign him,
     Initial Love. 79.

Mall
On Monday in the mall, Boston. 28.

Mallows
She spawneth men as mallows fresh,
     Nature. II. 13.

Man
 See Craftsman; Foeman; Freeman;
Horseman; Layman; Northman;
Ploughman; Seaman; Shopman; States-
man; Townsman; Watchman; Wood-
man.
We chose our boats; each man a boat
and guide,—   Adirondacs. 5.
Daily the bending skies solicit man,
     Adirondacs. 224.
To be a brain, or serve the brain of man.
     Adirondacs. 265.
Orange cheek or skin of man.
     Alphonso. 12.
Puny man and scentless rose
     Alphonso. 25.
So shall ye have a man of the sphere
     Alphonso. 81.

Man on earth to acclimate   Art. 21.
Wine which is already man,
                    Bacchus. 34.
What it will do when it is man.
                    Bacchus. 42.
Of man and earth, of world beloved and
    lover,   Blight. 44.
The merchant was a man.   Boston. 10.
Each honest man shall have his vote,
                    Boston. 33.
Law for man, and law for thing;
                Channing Ode. 54.
And doth the man unking.
                Channing Ode. 57.
Let man serve law for man;
                Channing Ode. 66.
Ere freedom out of man.
                Concord Ode. 40.
Man was made of social earth,
                Daemonic Love. 1.
'Go, lonely man,' it saith;   Dirge. 49.
In the deep heart of man a poet dwells
                    Enchanter. 1.
Be it remembered of a single man,
                    Entombed. 2.
Little man, least of all,   Experience. 14.
Ah Fate, cannot a man   Fame. 1.
Deep in the man sits fast his fate
                        Fate. 1.
In man or maid, that thou from speech
    refrained,   Forbearance. 6.
Around the man who seeks a noble end,
                Frag. Life. III. 1.
Man drinks the water, drinks the light.
                Frag. Life. XXIII. 9.
I was the trustee of the hand-cart man,
                Frag. Life. XXX. 4.
On the nervous brain of man,
                Frag. Nat. I. 14.
But never yet the man was found
                Frag. Nat. VI. 1.
By man who thirsts to be deceived.
                Frag. Nat. XXXI. 6.
Brute or savage into man;
                    Freedom. 16.
To man imprisoned in his own.
                    Garden. 44.
I laugh at the lore and the pride of man,
                    Good-Bye. 27.
When man in the bush with God may
    meet?   Good-Bye. 30.
The threads of man at their humming
    wheel,   Harp. 100.
Now must thou be man and artist,—
                    Holidays. 19.
That hides from man the mortal goal,
                    Hymn. 22.
Old man and young maid,   Illusions. 9.
Fronting foes of God and man,
                In Memoriam. 41.
And, striving to be man, the worm
                    May-Day. 81.
That man and all the kinds be fed;
                    May-Day. 147.
Willow and violet, maiden and man.
                    May-Day. 288.
From youth to maid, from boy to man,
                    May-Day. 347.
'Once more,' the old man cried, 'ye
    clouds,   May-Day. 349.

To man, as to a lubber friend,
                    May-Day. 403.
Nature, the supplement of man,
                    Miracle. 19.
And lifting man to the blue deep
                    Monadnoc. 100.
Man in these crags a fastness find
                    Monadnoc. 112.
When forests fall, and man is gone,
                    Monadnoc. 213.
Zion or Meru, measure with man.
                    Monadnoc. 259.
And, striving to be man, the worm
                    Nature. Mot. 5.
And every man, in love or pride,
                    Nemesis. 7.
As a man unto his friend.   Peter. 36.
And, being so, the sage unmakes the man.
                    Philosopher. 2.
And through man and woman and sea
    and star   Poet. 69.
Is the fated man of men   Poet. 79.
That haply man upraised might keep
                    Poet. 169.
Sun, moon, man, undulate and stream,
                    Poet. 173.
Is the pudency of man.'   Poet. 224.
To carry man to new degrees
                    Rhea. 68.
'T is the poor man getting siller,
                    Riches. 3.
'T is the poor man gotten rich,
                    Riches. 7.
The poor man crawls in web of rags
                    Riches. 9.
The hour of heaven shall come, the man
    appear.   Rome. 27.
Are welcome to the man of truth.
                    Saadi. 40.
Ere one man my hill shall climb,
                    Saadi. 113.
Man in man is imprisonèd;   Saadi. 118.
With credulous and imaginative man;
                    Seashore. 44.
To a man and to a maid.   September. 16.
Earth smiled with flowers, and man was
    born.   Solution. 8.
The sunburnt world a man shall breed
                Song of Nature. 79.
The meaning of man;   Sphinx. 10.
"But man crouches and blushes,
                    Sphinx. 49.
"The fiend that man harries
                    Sphinx. 73.
Didst thou, just man, endure.
                    Tal. Exile. 3.
I man the rudder, reef the sail,
                    Terminus. 35.
But finds not the budding man;
                    Threnody. 26.
Taught he not thee—the man of eld,
                    Threnody. 183.
The mystic gulf from God to man?
                    Threnody. 186.
So near is God to man,   Voluntaries. 72.
On all was base in man,   Walden. 22.
Responds to the touch of man;
                    Waterfall. 10.
But though light-headed man forget,
                    Wealth. 44.

Man—*Continued*
Knowledge this man prizes best
                    Woodnotes. I. 16.
And blessed the monument of the man of
flowers,   Woodnotes. I. 70.
He roamed, content alike with man and
beast.   Woodnotes. I. 81.
Go where he will, the wise man is at
home,   Woodnotes. I. 92.
O wise man! hear'st thou half it tells?
                    Woodnotes. II. 101.
O wise man! hear'st thou the least part?
                    Woodnotes. II. 102.
Of man to come, of human life,
                    Woodnotes. II. 131.
Of sound and echo, man and maid,
                    Woodnotes. II. 161.
For royal man;—they thee confess
                    Woodnotes. II. 188.
There lives no man of Nature's worth
                    Woodnotes. II. 198.
Thanks to each man of courage,
                    World-Soul. 5.

Manage
Let them manage how they may,
                    Saadi. 115.

Man-child
But he, the man-child glorious,—
                    Song of Nature. 37.
"The fate of the man-child,   Sphinx. 9.

Manger
One in a Judæan manger,
                    Song of Nature. 65.

Manhood
The manhood that should yours resist,—
                    Etienne. 10.
Of thoughtful maids and manhood bold.
                    Hymn. 12.

Manifold
He has not one mode, but manifold,
                    Initial Love. 131.
Merry and manifold without bar,
                    Nature. II. 7

Mankind
This feat of wit, this triumph of man-
kind;   Adirondacs. 255.
Or was it for mankind a generous shame,
                    Adirondacs. 274.
Enough that mankind eat and are re-
freshed.   Adirondacs. 301.
The rights of all mankind.   Boston. 95.
The benefit of broad mankind.
                    Celestial Love. 120.
Of the culture of mankind,
                    Channing Ode. 13.
And ride mankind.   Channing Ode. 51.
All mankind praise;   In Memoriam. 8.
Nor scour the seas, nor sift mankind,
                    Saadi. 155.
And sometimes mankind I appalled
                    Solution. 22.

Mankind's
Then for mankind's instruction shown;
                    Prayer. 4.

Manlike
"Once with manlike love and fear
                    Frag. Poet. II. 5.

Manly
And yet I marked, even in the manly joy
                    Adirondacs. 271.

Throb in each manly vein;   Boston. 107.
A ruddy drop of manly blood
                    Friendship. 1.
With the pulse of manly hearts;
                    Merlin. 21.
Calm as the morn the manly patriot sate;
                    Phi. 10.
'Is this dear Nature's manly pride?
                    Poet. 218.
Why did all manly gifts in Webster fail?
                    Webster, 1854. 1.

Manner
'T is his manner,   Frag. Nat. I. 11.

Manners
And your enchanting manners bring
                    Frag. Nat. XXIII. 13.
Men and manners much deranged:
                    Initial Love. 8.
The wood-boughs with thy manners
waved,   Lines. 11.
Your manners for the heart's delight,
                    May-Day. 399.
Great be the manners, of the bard.
                    Merlin. 28.
Dost love our manners? Canst thou silent
lie?   Musketaquid. 77.
Her manners made of bounty well re-
fined;   Quat. A. H. 2.
Up to his style, and manners of the sky.
                    Threnody. 271.

Man's
And lift man's public action to a height
                    Adirondacs. 246.
Spelling with guided tongue man's mes-
sages   Adirondacs. 269.
Gracing the rich man's wood and lake,
                    Chartist. 9.
Man's the elm, and Wealth the vine;
                    II Compensation. 15.
Of man's or maiden's eye: Culture. 8.
So is man's narrow path
                    Daemonic Love. 60.
There were a man's and lover's part,
                    Etienne. 23.
I shunned his eyes, that faithful man's,
                    Frag. Poet. III. 11.
But the porches of man's ear
                    Garden. 46.
Heart of bird the man's heart seeking;
                    May-Day. 421.
So each man's life   Naples. 9.
Beaming from a young man's eyes.
                    On Prince. 4.
Nor less on man's enchanted dust
                    Poet. 298.
'T is man's perdition to be safe,
                    Quat. Sacrifice. 3.
Man's spirit must dive;   Sphinx. 82.
Quarrying man's rejected hours,
                    Spiritual Laws. 3.
This is lordly man's down-lying,
                    Threnody. 163.

Mansions
Thought and its mansions fair.
                    Frag. Life. XXIV. 4.

Mantle
His cheeks mantle with mirth;
                    World-Soul. 102.

Mantling
See O'er-mantling.

Her callow brood in mantling leaves,—
　　　　　　　　May-Day. 173.
Manure
And my manure the snow;
　　　　　　　　Woodnotes. II. 10.
Many (Partial list.)
Many and subtle are my lays,
　　　　　　　　Aeolian Harp. 20.
Earth, crowded, cries, 'Too many men!'
　　　　　　　　Alphonso. 67.
In many forms we try　　Bohemian. 1.
I met many travellers　Forerunners. 17.
I detected many a god
　　　　　　　　Frag. Life. XXII. 5.
Many a high hillside,　Frag. Nat. III. 17.
Devour as many as you list,
　　　　　　　　Frag. Nat. XIX. 5.
Many things the garden shows,
　　　　　　　　Frag. Nat. XXI. 1.
I count as many as there are
　　　　　　　　Frag. Poet. XXVIII. 4.
So many saints and saviors,
　　　　　　　　Frag. Poet. XXVIII. 6.
So many high behaviors
　　　　　　　　Frag. Poet. XXVIII.7.
In many lands, with painful steps,
　　　　　　　　House. 11.
He has ushers many a one;
　　　　　　　　Initial Love. 75.
His many signs cannot be told;
　　　　　　　　Initial Love. 130.
Many fashions and addresses,
　　　　　　　　Initial Love. 132.
Many a flower and many a gem,
　　　　　　　　May-Day. 316.
Pouring many a cheerful river;
　　　　　　　　Monadnoc. 41.
Well-built abode of many a race;
　　　　　　　　Monadnoc. 82.
Tales of many a famous mount,—
　　　　　　　　Monadnoc. 95.
Many hamlets sought I then,
　　　　　　　　Monadnoc. 127.
Many farms of mountain men.
　　　　　　　　Monadnoc. 128.
Many feet in summer seek,
　　　　　　　　Monadnoc. 199.
In many a thousand years?
　　　　　　　　Monadnoc. 218.
Anchored fast for many an age,
　　　　　　　　Monadnoc. 283.
Not many men　　　　Naples. 13.
Many a day shall dawn and die,
　　　　　　　　Nun. 23.
Many an angel wander by,　Nun. 24.
Or, hid in vines, peeping through many a
　loop,　　　Quat. Gardener. 3.
Me many a sigh.　　　River. 21.
From many a radiant face,
　　　　　　　　Robbins Hymn. 6.
Many may come,　　　Saadi. 17.
And many a thousand summers
　　　　　　　　Song of Nature. 17.
Leave the many and hold the few.
　　　　　　　　Terminus. 16.
Many haps fall in the field
　　　　　　　　Woodnotes. I. 50.
Deceive us, seeming to be many things,
　　　　　　　　Xenophanes. 8.

Many-chambered
And many-chambered heart.
　　　　　　　　Frag. Life. VI. 6.
Many-seeming
And many-seeming life is one,—
　　　　　　　　Threnody. 245.
Map
Open the daunting map beneath,—
　　　　　　　　Monadnoc. 319.
Maple
Oak, cedar, maple, poplar, beech and fir,
　　　　　　　　Adirondacs. 38.
The maple eight, beneath its shapely
　tower.　　　　Adirondacs. 43.
North from Camp Maple, south to Os-
　prey Bay,　　　Adirondacs. 109.
Panax, black birch, sugar maple,
　　　　　　　　Frag. Nat. II. 15.
Each maple leaf turned up its silver side.
　　　　　　　　Frag. Nat. III. 14.
The maple street　Frag. Nat. III. 21.
Runs round the pine and maple tree
　　　　　　　　Frag. Nat. XIX. 2.
Maple and oak, the old Divan
　　　　　　　　Miracle. 5.
Drain sweet maple juice in vats.
　　　　　　　　Monadnoc. 142.
Over his head were the maple buds,
　　　　　　　　Quat. Excelsior. 1.
Maple-boughs
Evening drew on; stars peeped through
　maple-boughs,　Adirondacs. 46.
Maple-keys
The scarlet maple-keys betray
　　　　　　　　May-Day. 186.
Maples
And rank the savage maples grow
　　　　　　　　Garden. 7.
The blackbirds make the maples ring
　　　　　　　　May-Day. 166.
'T would bring the blushes of yon
　maples　　　　September. 15.
Maple-sap
Maple-sap and daffodels,
　　　　　　　　Humble-Bee. 43.
Maple-tops
The maple-tops their crimson tint,
　　　　　　　　May-Day. 60.
Mar
Foolish hands may mix and mar;
　　　　　　　　Channing Ode. 76.
Marauded
Is thy land peeled, thy realm marauded?
　　　　　　　　Woodnotes. II. 181.
Marble
With the marble which he rears.
　　　　　　　　Alphonso. 76.
A form which marble doth not hold
　　　　　　　　Angelo. 2.
She laid a slab of marble on his head.
　　　　　　　　Epitaph. 4.
That the marble sleep is broken,
　　　　　　　　May-Day. 33.
In flint and marble beats a heart,
　　　　　　　　May-Day. 65.
Far capitals and marble courts,
　　　　　　　　Quat. A. H. 3.
Curdles the blood to the marble bones,
　　　　　　　　Titmouse. 14.
I walk in marble galleries,　Walden. 31.

Marbles
Through treacherous marbles.
Illusions. 15.
March
See School-march.
Music to the march of time.
Frag. Nat. I. 5.
On carpets green the maskers march
May-Day. 331.
Piping, as they flew, a march,—
May-Day. 384.
And march their feet,   Merlin. 47.
And the atoms march in tune;
Monadnoc. 246.
Marched
They marched from east to west:
Experience. 13.
Marches
With the key of the secret he marches
faster,   Frag. Life. XXXI. 1.
With the marches of the brave;
Merlin. 25.
Marching
And marching single in an endless file,
Days. 3.
Marching duly in her train,
May-Day. 335.
Stately marching in cap and coat
Threnody. 76.
Marge
See Sea-marge.
Margin
See Lake-margin.
Mariners
O mariners who never fail!
Poet. 162.
Mark
See Eyemark.
Our heroes tried their rifles at a mark,
Adirondacs. 125.
Mark his capricious ways to draw the
eye.   Adirondacs. 207.
With a vermilion pencil mark the day
Adirondacs. 230.
I have an arrow that will find its mark,
Arrow. 1.
His way home to the mark.
Boston Hymn. 88.
Yet mark me well, that idle word
Frag. Poet. IV. 21.
To mark the Briton's friendless grave.
In Memoriam. 14.
And mark the rising of the early stars.
Letter. 15.
We will mark the leaps and gleams
May-Day. 228.
But mark what changed my joy to
fright,—   Miracle. 26.
Mark how the climbing Oreads
Monadnoc. 19.
Goes like bullet to its mark;
Monadnoc. 190.
Or coax the thunder from its mark?
Nemesis. 11.
He takes no mark of night or day,
Poet. 83.
To mark thy beautiful parade,
Threnody. 75.
God speed the mark!   To J. W. 23.

Marked
See Unmarked.
And yet I marked, even in the manly joy
Adirondacs. 271.
Marked forbearance, compliments,
Frag. Poet. VII. 11.
Or marked, benighted and forlorn,
Harp. 93.
I marked them yestermorn,
May-Day. 381.
Gentlest guardians marked serene
Threnody. 54.
Market
In palaces and market squares Harp. 17.
Or crowd the market and bazaar;
Saadi. 110.
Market-place
For proverbs in the market-place:
Saadi. 152.
Marks
And told the truant by his marks,—
Initial Love. 4.
Marl
Of granite, marl and shell.
Song of Nature. 36.
Marred
See Unmarred.
Marriage
To seal the marriage of these minds with
thine,   Good Cheer. 14.
And wide around, the marriage of the
plants   Musketaquid. 20.
Married
Eldest rite, two married sides
Merlin. 90.
Marries
Who marries Right to Might,
Channing Ode. 81.
Marrow
The Baresark marrow to thy bones,
Terminus. 28.
Marry
Maids of as soft a bloom shall marry
Good Hope. 5.
Mars
Nor pictures pale, but Jove and Mars,
Monadnoc. 308.
Mart
Restores the world-wide mart;
Boston. 101.
The leafy dell, the city mart,
Ode to Beauty. 88.
To court and mart, to gown and town.
Solution. 68.
Martial
Flamed from his martial eye;
In Memoriam. 37.
Martin's
The Adirondac lakes. At Martin's Beach
Adirondacs. 4.
Marts
Then temples rose, and towns, and marts,
Wealth. 34.
Martyr
And die to Fame a happy martyr.
Fame. 30.
Martyrdom
All without is martyrdom.
Humble-Bee. 19.

Martyrs'
And prayers of might from martyrs' cave.
Merlin. 26.

Marvel
Which all its marvel shall rehearse,
Frag. Poet. XXIX. 4.
And, by marvel of her own,
Nature. I. 10.
Nature's sweet marvel undefiled,
Threnody. 123.

Mary's
The riches of sweet Mary's Son,
Threnody. 222.

Mask
See Unmask.
With science poorly mask their hurt;
Alphonso. 37.
If thou wear no mask or lie,
Frag. Life. XXVII. 10.
Mask thy wisdom with delight,
Frag. Poet. V. 1.
There is no mask but he will wear;
Initial Love. 114.
Or walks in mask almighty Jove,
May-Day. 215.
I saw them mask their awful glance
May-Day. 324.
Mask thy wisdom with delight,
Merlin's Song. 37.
To mask a king in weeds.
Quat. Poet. 2. 4.
Then you are Gypsies in a mask,
Romany. 11.
And merry is only a mask of sad,
Waldeinsamkeit. 18.

Masked
Snow-ridges masked each darling spot;
May-Day. 42.

Maskers
On carpets green the maskers march
May-Day. 331.

Masks
Masks her treasury of heat
May-Day. 132.
Masks the might of Nature's king,
May-Day. 458.
That blessed gods in servile masks
Saadi. 175.
To-morrow, when the masks shall fall
Threnody. 189.

Mason
Eldest mason, Frost, had piled
May-Day. 47.
Which who can tell what mason laid?
Monadnoc. 369.

Masonry
Come see the north wind's masonry.
Snow-Storm. 10.

Mass
O'er all that mass and minster vaunt;
Titmouse. 90.
And the vast mass became vast ocean.
Woodnotes. II. 269.

Massachusetts
The dismal Massachusetts ice
May-Day. 142.

Masses
Still, through her motes and masses,
draw   Wealth. 46.

Mast
See Half-mast.
And up the tall mast runs the wood-
pecker.   Woodnotes. I. 67.

Master
What make you, master, fumbling at the
oar?   Adirondacs. 99.
Slave or master on his breast.
Astraea. 8.
While classes or tribes, too weak to
master   Frag. Life. XXXI. 3.
To master my despair;   Friendship. 18.
'T is a brave master;   Give. 7.
Blameless master of the games,
Merlin. 39.
The passive Master lent his hand
Problem. 47.
Is master of all I am."   Sphinx. 132.

Masterful
The yoke of conscience masterful,
Park. 3.
Yonder masterful cuckoo   Unity. 4.

Mastering
See Overmastering.

Masterless
The lightning has run masterless too
long;   Adirondacs. 266.

Masterpiece
Masterpiece of love benign,
Threnody. 257.

Master's
On the piano, played with master's hand.
Adirondacs. 314.
After the master's sketch fills and o'er-
fills   Day's Ration. 28.
The master's requiem.'   Dirge. 60.
But speechless to the master's mind?
Monadnoc. 91.

Masters
Traditioned fame of masters, eager strife
Adirondacs. 324.
Masters, I'm in pain with you;
Alphonso. 41.
Masters, I'll be plain with you;
Alphonso. 42.
The masters quite omitted   April. 19.
Carries the eagles, and masters the
sword.   Destiny. 50.
These the masters who can teach.
Monadnoc. 174.
What these strong masters wrote at
large in miles,   Musketaquid. 52.
Of the masters of the shell,
Ode to Beauty. 57.

Masterships
I break your bonds and masterships,
Boston Hymn. 53.

Master-stroke
The master-stroke is still her part.
Nature. II. 23.

Mastiff
A mastiff that will bite without a bark.
Arrow. 2.

Match
Match God's equator with a zone of art,
Adirondacs. 245.
Or count the Sioux a match for Agassiz?
Adirondacs. 308.
Easy to match what others do,
Frag. Life. X. 1.

Match —*Continued*
Go match thee with thy seeming peers;
        Frag. Life. XXV. 2.
Succory to match the sky,
        Frag. Nat. II. 8.
Or match with words that tender sky?
        Garden. 40.
Succory to match the sky,
        Humble-Bee. 45.
And match the paired cotyledons.
        Merlin. 87.

Matched
And matched his sufferance sublime
        Character. 5.
And matched his sufferance sublime
        Poet. 138.
Innocence that matched the sky,
        Threnody. 212.

Matches
Who with even matches odd,
        Merlin. 118.

Matchless
Make up thy splendor, matchless day?
        Frag. Nat. XI. 2.
Trusting well the matchless power
        Initial Love. 84.
This matchless strength. Where shall he
find, O waves!   Seashore. 32.

Mate
    See Housemate.
Weave roses for your mate.
        Celestial Love. 14.
But when the mate of the snow and wind,
        Frag. Poet. I. 31.
That devil-spider that devours her mate
        Philosopher. 11.

Mated
In equal couples mated,   Merlin. 102.

Material
Replenishing material urns
        Day by Day. 3.

Materials
Materials for her plan;   House. 4.

Mates
Two of our mates returning with swift
oars.   Adirondacs. 234.
To assign just place and mates;
        Astraea. 20.
Mates of my youth,—yet not my mates,
        Harp. 114.
See youth's glad mates in earliest
bloom,—   Harp. 123.
I said, 'We are mates in misery.'
        Threnody. 103.

Mathematic
And, in my mathematic ebb and flow,
        Seashore. 25.

Mats
Weave wood to canisters and mats;
        Monadnoc. 141.

Matted
The matted thicket low and wide,
        Wealth. 14.

Matter
There my thoughts the matter roll,
        Alphonso. 45.
I hold it of little matter   Destiny. 34.
From the stores of eldest matter,
        Frag. Life. XXIX. 1.

Melting matter into dreams,
        Frag. Poet. VIII. 7.
Of matter, and thy darling lost?
        Threnody. 182.
Procession of a soul in matter,
        Uriel. 51.
To build in matter home for mind.
        Wealth. 12.
Remembering Matter pays her debt:
        Wealth. 45.
Of chemic matter, force and form,
        Woodnotes. II. 110.

Matters
The nearest matters for a thousand days?
        Day's Ration. 32.
What matters how, or from what ground,
        In Memoriam. 111.

Mature
Mature the unfallen fruit.
        Terminus. 22.

Matures
Swells, and mellows, and matures,
        May-Day. 196.

Maugre
Maugre the farmer's sighs; and at the
gate   Snow-Storm. 21.

Maxim
Every maxim of dreadful Need;
        Poet. 44.

Maxims
To bards who from its maxims live,
        Frag. Poet. IV. 2.

May (Partial list.)
And, that no day of life may lack ro-
mance,   Adirondacs. 221.
He may, by warrant of his age,
        Alphonso. 79.
May float at pleasure through all natures;
        Bacchus. 23.
May be true what I had heard,—
        Berrying. 1.
The state may follow how it can,
        Channing Ode. 69.
Foolish hands may mix and mar;
        Channing Ode. 76.
That memory may their deed redeem,
        C. Hymn. 11.
On its own First of May.   Cosmos. 28.
Which by aroma may compel
        Frag. Nat. II. 30.
When the south wind, in May days,
        Humble-Bee. 20.
That they may seize and entertain
        Initial Love. 51.
Even into May the iceberg cold.
        May-Day. 20.
In May beholds the blooming wild,
        May-Day. 99.
What potent blood hath modest May,
        May-Day. 187.
And duly greet the entering May?
        May-Day. 219.
Wreaths for May! for happy Spring
        May-Day. 263.
Of shining virgins every May,
        May-Day. 302.
That they may render back
        Merlin. 12.
When the star Canope shines in May.
        Merlin's Song. 33.

Onward and nearer rides the sun of May;
　　　　　　Musketaquid. 19.
Or, it may be, a picture; to these men,
　　　　　　Musketaquid. 33.
In May, when sea-winds pierced our soli-
　　tudes,　　　　Rhodora. 1.
The stars may hide in the upper sky,
　　　　　　Romany. 27.
Many may come,　　　　Saadi. 17.
Let them manage how they may,
　　　　　　Saadi. 115.
Time and tide their faults may find.
　　　　　　Test. 2.
At home a deeper thought may light
　　　　　　Una. 13.

May-morn
Flushed in the sky the sweet May-morn,
　　　　　　Solution. 7.

May's
Below May's well-appointed arch,
　　　　　　May-Day. 332.

May'st
By which thy hurt thou may'st divine.
　　　　　　Woodnotes. II. 193.

Maze
There broad-armed oaks, the copses'
　　maze,　　　　Walden. 5.

Me (Partial list.)
So like the soul of me, what if 't were
　　me?　　　Adirondacs. 214.
Give me an amulet　　　Amulet. 5.
Think me not unkind and rude
　　　　　　Apology. 1.
Kings unborn shall walk with me;
　　　　　　Bacchus. 40.
Give me truths;　　　　Blight. 1.
The days pass over me　　Days Pass. 1.
What he singeth to me?　　Dirge. 44.
Greeted their safe escape to me.
　　　　　　Each. 23.
Too kind, too good to me;
　　　　　　*Farewell. 20.
Unplighted yet to me,　　*Farewell. 38.
Unknown to Cromwell as to me
　　　　　　Fate. 3.
Me for the channel of the rivers of God
　　　　　　Frag. Life. XV. 7.
He lives not who can refuse me;
　　　　　　Frag. Nat. XXVIII. 1.
All my force saith, Come and use me:
　　　　　　Frag. Nat. XXVIII. 2.
Beauty's not beautiful to me,
　　　　　　Hermione. 9.
In thee to frame, in me to trust,
　　　　　　Hermione. 29.
Thousand minstrels woke within me,
　　　　　　Monadnoc. 1.
Gayest pictures rose to win me,
　　　　　　Monadnoc. 3.
Nearing me,　　　Monadnoc. 216.
Enchantment fixed me here
　　　　　　Monadnoc. 225.
Pathetic silent poets that sing to me
　　　　　　Naples. 26.
Time, shake not thy bald head at me.
　　　　　　Nun. 30.
And murmuring waters counselled me.
　　　　　　Rhea. 8.
These trees and stones are audible to me,
　　　　　　River. 22.

They brought me rubies from the mine,
　　　　　　Rubies. 1.
And yet it seemeth not to me
　　　　　　Saadi. 72.
Bids for me her bosom glow.
　　　　　　Security. 4.
That knows a purer flame than me,
　　　　　　Security. 10.
I never taught it what it teaches me;
　　　　　　Self-Reliance. 9.
So I folded me in fears,　　Solution. 27.
Are pleasant songs to me.　　Sphinx. 68.
Than to love me.　　　Sphinx. 96.
Which yet beholds not me.
　　　　　　Thine Eyes. 4.
Took the largest part of me:
　　　　　　Threnody. 161.
Haughty thought be far from me;
　　　　　　Voluntaries. 2.
Me through trackless thickets led,
　　　　　　Woodnotes. I. 119.
The falling waters led me,
　　　　　　Woodnotes. I. 129.
The foodful waters fed me,
　　　　　　Woodnotes. I. 130.
When the forest shall mislead me,
　　　　　　Woodnotes. I. 139.
When sea and land refuse to feed me,
　　　　　　Woodnotes. I. 141.
Come to me,　　　Woodnotes. II. 6.
He is great who can live by me:
　　　　　　Woodnotes. II. 13.

Meadow
O'er Kernan's meadow blowest,
　　　　　　Exile. 10.
Draw us to these meadow farms,
　　　　　　Frag. Nat. XXVI. 4.
What the spangled meadow saith
　　　　　　Harp. 32.
Daily over hill and meadow.
　　　　　　Monadnoc. 265.
(That one would say, meadow and forest
　　walked,　　　Musketaquid. 48.
And on every mount and meadow
　　　　　　Threnody. 3.
A patch of meadow upland
　　　　　　Waterfall. 1.
Which bloom and fade like meadow flow-
　　ers　　　Woodnotes. II. 302.

Meadows
When all their blooms the meadows
　　flaunt　　　Frag. Nat. VIII. 1.
The meadows broad
　　　　　　Frag. Nat. XXVII. 6.
O'er meadows bottomless. So, year by
　　year,　　　Musketaquid. 46.
True Brahmin, in the morning meadows
　　wet,　　　Quat. Gardener. 1.
He stands in the meadows wide,—
　　　　　　Woodnotes. I. 9.

Meads
Low, open meads, slender and sluggish
　　streams,　　　Musketaquid. 2.

Meagre
Meagre crop of figs and limes;
　　　　　　Alphonso. 5

Mean
It cannot parley with the mean,—
　　　　　　Astraea. 43.

Mean —*Continued*
Is none so high, so mean is none,
Celestial Love. 111.
Chill and wet, unlighted, mean,
Chartist. 4.
To mould his fortunes, mean or great:
Fate. 2.
Nor when I'm jaded, sick, anxious or
mean. Frag. Life. XV. 5.
And I, who cower mean and small
Frag. Poet. III. 7.
In cities he was low and mean;
Frag. Poet. V. 16.
It was never for the mean; Give. 18.
Nor kneels in homage to so mean a God.
To-Day. 14.
Crowns all thy mean affairs.
Waldeinsamkeit. 48.

Meanest
But in the darkest, meanest things
Music. 11.

Meaning
Meaning always to be young.
Initial Love. 141.
I catch thy meaning, wizard wave;
Peter. 39.
Sudden gusts came full of meaning,
September. 9.
Well I love the meaning sweet,—
Song of Seyd. 23.
The meaning of man; Sphinx. 10.
Their meaning sublime. Sphinx. 72.
And the meaning was more white
Test. 9.
Conveyed thy meaning mild.
Threnody. 39.
Hearts to hearts their meaning show,
Visit. 18.
He is the meaning of each feature;
Woodnotes. II. 316.

Meanings
Their noble meanings are their pawns.
Celestial Love. 88.
But the meanings cleave to the lake,
Garden. 57.
"Who telleth one of my meanings
Sphinx. 131.

Means
Means, appliances, delights,
Mithridates. 27.
Where equal means are none.'
Poet. 248.
Means, dear brother, ask them not;
Poet. 249.
Soul's desire is means enow,
Poet. 250.
But when the quarried means were piled,
Wealth. 29.

Measurable
See Immeasurable.

Measure
The measure of the eternal Mind,
Bohemian. 11.
As hid all measure of the feat.
Character. 10.
The world's light underneath a measure.
Fame. 24.
Was Cromwell's measure or degree;
Fate. 4.

In perfect time and measure
Frag. Nat. XXIV. 10
Or-Shakspeare, whom no mind can meas-
ure, Harp. 78.
In perfect time and measure they
Merlin. 126.
But wilt thou measure all thy road,
Merlin's Song. 22.
Zion or Meru, measure with man.
Monadnoc. 259.
Dwarfed to measure of his hand;
Monadnoc. 321.
England's genius filled all measure
Solution. 35.

Measured
See Unmeasured.
Docile read my measured line:
Frag. Poet. VII. 2.
Are measured but a few;
Quat. Shakespeare. 2.

Meat
The eater serves his meat;
Channing Ode. 47.
Give me agates for my meat;
Mithridates. 6.
Best of Pan's immortal meat,
Monadnoc. 304.
Thrown to lions for their meat,
Worship. 7.

Mecca
Out from Mecca to Ispahan;
Frag. Poet. I. 8.

Medalled
To the high-school and medalled boy:
May-Day. 345.

Meddling
Or compass that, by meddling wit,
Merlin. 67.

Mediator
Mediator, royal giver;
Daemonic Love. 75.

Medicinal
He heard their medicinal song,
Frag. Poet. V. 19.

Medicine
Purger of earth, and medicine of men;
Seashore. 22.

Meditate
And meditate a moment on Heaven's
rest. Adirondacs. 197.
Ye meditate what to say Poet. 261.

Meed
to Virtue's starlike meed
Enchanter. 14.

Meek
But thou, meek lover of the good!
Brahma. 15.
Meek Nature's secret still untold.
Frag. Nat. VI. 8.
Obeying meek the primal Cause,
Harp. 71.
That knock at meek contrition's door.
Hymn. 20.
The sparrow meek, prophetic-eyed,
May-Day. 170.
Sidewise meek in gossamer lids;
May-Day. 325.
By its own meek and incorruptible will?
Oh What. 3.

Meet

The King whose meek ambassador I go.
Summons. 24.
Step the meek fowls where erst they
ranged; Threnody. 94.

Meet

See Unmeet.
Where their glances meet:
Celestial Love. 18.
Lo! it rushes thee to meet;
II Compensation. 24.
Nor when in fair saloons we chance to
meet; Frag. Life. XV. 4.
When man in the bush with God may
meet?
Good-Bye. 30.
Come to us herself to meet."'
Hermione. 78.
In every mortal meet. Merlin. 91.
With the flavors she finds meet,
Nature. II. 16.
Again I meet the ardent beams.
Ode to Beauty. 93.
My eyes his eyeballs meet. Park. 8.
With the Virtues meet, Politics. 16.
Old playfellows meet; Sphinx. 28.
And he who has one enemy will meet
him everywhere. Taleb. 2.
Heart's love will meet thee again.
Threnody. 269.
Happy to meet you in these places,
Titmouse. 31.
In my garden three ways meet,
Walden. 1.
Or how meet in human elf
Woodnotes. I. 28.
He shall meet the speeding year,
Woodnotes. II. 79.
Can read thy line, can meet thy glance,
Woodnotes. II. 141.

Meeting

They can parley without meeting;
Celestial Love. 93.
Than the meeting of the eyes? Visit. 12.

Meets

Every wayfarer he meets Astraea. 25.
Wonderer at all he meets,
Woodnotes. I. 25.

Melancholy

A melancholy better than all mirth.
Adirondacs. 215.
For him round-in the melancholy hours
Naples. 11.
Infirm, melancholy, Sphinx. 53.
Melancholy without bad.
Woodnotes. I. 15.

Meliorating

And light from meliorating stars
Song of Nature. 19.

Mellow

I love thy music, mellow bell, Bell. 1.
With thy mellow, breezy bass.
Humble-Bee. 31.
Nor in the redbreast's mellow tone,
Music. 15.
Cattle lowed in mellow distance
September. 7.

Mellows

Swells, and mellows, and matures,
May-Day. 196.

Melodious

Leaves on the wind melodious trace;
Forerunners. 13.
Knell their melodious memory.
Woodnotes. II. 228.

Melody

There's a melody born of melody,
Destiny. 5.
But pillowed all on melody, Harp. 59.

Melt

Melt into one. Celestial Love. 41.
And his soul will melt in prayer,
Initial Love. 110.
So lovers melt their sundered selves,
Initial Love. 149.
With equal fire thy heart shalt melt.
Saadi. 124.
These the siroc could not melt, Test. 7.

Melted

Said melted the days like cups of pearl,
Frag. Poet. I. 19.
Yet melted would be twain.
Initial Love. 150.
She melted into purple cloud,
Sphinx. 123.

Melting

Melting matter into dreams,
Frag. Poet. VIII. 7.
The robins know the melting snow;
May-Day. 169.
New-born, we are melting
Ode to Beauty. 19.

Melts

Melts down into that liquor of my life,—
Day's Ration. 7.
Which melts the world into a sea.
Destiny. 6.
Ever the Rock of Ages melts
Frag. Life. XXIV. 1.
As melts the iceberg in the seas,
Poet. 33.
Melts things that be to things that seem,
Woodnotes. II. 114.

Member

Once a member, all was mine,
Frag. Poet. IV. 10.

Members

'Fairest, choose the fairest members
Ellen South. 25.
And their members are combined.
Merlin. 48.

Memories

Smacks of faint memories far away.
May-Day. 78.
Oh, south winds have long memories,
September. 11.

Memory

As one within whose memory it burned
Adirondacs. 278.
The memory of ages quenched;
Bacchus. 57.
A dazzling memory revive;
Bacchus. 61.
That memory may their deed redeem,
C. Hymn. 11.
And of his memory beguiled.
Frag. Poet. I. 34.
The riches of a spotless memory,
Good Cheer. 9.
Age cannot cloud his memory,
Harp. 5.

Memory —*Continued*
With its primeval memory,   Harp. 52.
Boundless is his memory;
          Initial Love. 138.
Alike thy memory embalms
          In Memoriam. 113.
In the sweet odor of her memory.
          Letter. 18.
Washing out harms and griefs from memory,   Seashore. 24.
Stealing away the memory
          Voluntaries. 77.
Knell their melodious memory.
          Woodnotes. II. 228.

Memory's
Dear memory's stone-incarved traits,
          Daemonic Love. 14.
Still breaks that morn, though dim, to Memory's eye,   I Bear. 10.
Night-dreams trace on Memory's wall
          Quat. Memory. 1.

Men
    See Bondmen; Huntsmen; Moon-men; Shopmen.
Ten men, ten guides,   Adirondacs. 6.
Sound, ruddy men, frolic and innocent,
          Adirondacs. 87.
Your rank is all reversed; let men of cloth   Adirondacs. 93.
As if we men were talking in a vein
          Adirondacs. 256.
Men knowing what they seek,
          Adirondacs. 304.
Men and gods are too extense;
          Alphonso. 63.
Earth, crowded, cries, 'Too many men!'
          Alphonso. 67.
To fetch his word to men.
          Apology. 4.
I saw men go up and down,
          Astraea. 9.
The dancing Pleiads and eternal men.
          Bacchus. 67.
And good men thought thy sacred voice
          Bell. 11.
The old men studied magic in the flowers,
          Blight. 23.
Preferring things to names, for these were men,   Blight. 26.
The men of yore were stout and poor,
          Boston. 5.
Their dauntless ways did all men praise,
          Boston. 9.
A union then of honest men,
          Boston. 35.
you Saxon men,   Boston. 51.
The young men and the sires,
          Boston Hymn. 38.
They shall choose men to rule
          Boston Hymn. 42.
Lo, now! if these poor men
          Boston Hymn. 45.
And ye shall succor men;
          Boston Hymn. 49.
To men below,   Celestial Love. 52.
Men their fortunes bring with them.
          Celestial Love. 74.
And they serve men austerely,
          Celestial Love. 121.

He that feeds men serveth few;
          Celestial Love. 131.
With little men;—
          Channing Ode. 26.
When other men have none?
          I Compensation. 2.
The men are ripe of Saxon kind
          Concord Ode. 13.
Close, close to men,
          Daemonic Love. 23.
To men, the path to the Dæmon sphere;
          Daemonic Love. 40.
And the brains of men thenceforth,
          Daemonic Love. 45.
Unto men these moonmen lend,
          Daemonic Love. 58.
Draws men to their likeness still.
          Daemonic Love. 67.
Men and gods have not outlearned it;
          I Eros. 4.
Tell men what they knew before;
          Frag. Life. XIX. 1.
The rules to men made evident
          Frag. Life. XXXVI. 1.
With men and women weird.
          Frag. Nat. X. 4.
All men would to my gardens throng;
          Garden. 3.
These the fates of men forecast,
          Garden. 61.
Of better men than live to-day;
          Garden. 62.
Where are these men? Asleep beneath their grounds: Hamatreya. 11.
But where are old men? Hamatreya. 34.
The Muse of men is coy,   Harp. 15.
Was frolic sunshine, dear to all men,
          Holidays. 11.
There is in all the sons of men
          Hymn. 1.
Men and manners much deranged:
          Initial Love. 8.
Graceful women, chosen men,
          Manners. 3.
By lonely lakes to men unknown.
          May-Day. 29.
On men and maids a ruddier mien,
          May-Day. 300.
And danced as merrily as young men.
          May-Day. 323.
Good men it will calm and cheer,
          Merlin's Song. 6.
Bad men it will chain and cage—
          Merlin's Song. 7.
Men wait their good and truth to borrow.
          Merlin's Song. 21.
So that men might it not forget;
          Monadnoc. 49.
Many farms of mountain men.
          Monadnoc. 128.
For the next ages, men of mould
          Monadnoc. 155.
Or, it may be, a picture; to these men,
          Musketaquid. 33.
Transmuted in these men to rule their like),   Musketaquid. 49.
Not many men see beauty in the fogs
          Naples. 13.
Of rich men blazing hospitable light,
          Naples. 18.

She will be all things to all men.
Nature. II. 4.
She spawneth men as mallows fresh,
Nature. II. 13.
Make women of men;
Ode to Beauty. 18.
O what are heroes, prophets, men,
Pan. 1.
Is the fated man of men   Poet. 79.
He who loves, of gods or men,
Rhea. 37.
Men consort in camp and town,
Saadi. 7.
Yet Saadi loved the race of men,—
Saadi. 23.
A thousand men shall dig and eat;
Saadi. 106.
'Eat thou the bread which men refuse;
Saadi. 142.
Those doors are men: the Pariah hind
Saadi. 163.
Purger of earth, and medicine of men
Seashore. 22.
Rebuild a continent of better men.
Seashore. 37.
Men to all shores that front the hoary
main.   Seashore. 40.
To distant men, who must go there, or
die.   Seashore. 49.
The men who lived with him became
Solution. 41.
Rehearsed to men the damnèd wails
Solution. 49.
What men chatter know I not.
Song of Seyd. 34.
Nature, Fate, men, him seek in vain.
Threnody. 29.
Yet fairest dames and bearded men,
Threnody. 43.
Bring the flown Muses back to men.
Threnody. 137.
Men read the welfare of the times to
come,   Threnody. 169.
Is, that men are overgrown,
Titmouse. 62.
For men mis-hear thy call in Spring,
Titmouse. 91.
Old mouldy men and books and names
and lands   To-Day. 9.
Through years, through men, through
Nature fleet,   Two Rivers. 11.
Great men in the Senate sate,
Voluntaries. 23.
Hid from men of Northern brain,
Voluntaries. 52.
In one wood walk, than learned men
Walk. 7.
And of all other men desired.
Woodnotes. II. 70.
Nor yields to men the helm;
World-Soul. 74.
And the unimagined good of men
World-Soul. 103.
This is he men miscall Fate,
Worship. 11.

Mend
For I can mend the happiest days
Aeolian Harp. 22.
That mend her beauty to the eye.
Frag. Nat. XXXII. 4.

Rebuild the ruin, mend defect;
May-Day. 444.
Alter or mend eternal Fact.   Past. 21.
Or mend his wicker-frame, Threnody. 49.
The fault that boys and nations soonest
mend.   To-Day. 18.
Men's
At rich men's tables eaten bread and
pulse?   Forbearance. 3.
For all breathing men's behoof, Saadi. 11.
The cheerer of men's hearts.   Saadi. 48.
The yoke of men's opinions. I will be
Self-Reliance. 2.
Merchandise
Behind thee leave thy merchandise,
Woodnotes. II. 229.
Merchant
The merchant was a man.   Boston. 10.
The merchant serves the purse,
Channing Ode. 46.
The merchant hath stuffs of price,
Exile. 13.
Merchants
His merchants may dispense,   Dull. 18.
Mercy
In mercy, on one little head.
Frag. Poet. XXIV. 2.
Mere
And idle clowns beside the mere
Poet. 21.
Merge
'Merge me in the brute universe,
Poet. 193.
Meriam
Bulkeley, Hunt, Willard, Hosmer, Meri-
am, Flint,   Hamatreya. 1.
Meridian
Than July's meridian light.   Test. 10.
Merlin
Of Merlin locked the harp within,—
Harp. 54.
Merlin paying the pain of sin,   Harp. 55.
Of Merlin wise I learned a song,—
Merlin's Song. 1.
Hear what British Merlin sung,
Merlin's Song. 14.
Boded Merlin wise,   Politics. 5.
Merlin's
Merlin's blows are strokes of fate,
Merlin. 16.
Merlin's mighty line   Merlin. 51
Merrily
And danced as merrily as young men.
May-Day. 323.
Merry
The merry Spring threw wreaths on
them,   May-Day. 314.
O doleful ghosts, and goblins merry!
Mithridates. 25.
Merry and manifold without bar,
Nature. II. 7.
Uprose the merry Sphinx,   Sphinx. 121.
Out of sound heart and merry throat,
Titmouse. 28.
And merry is only a mask of sad,
Waldeinsamkeit. 18.
Meru
Zion or Meru, measure with man
Monadnoc. 259.

Message
And to his folk his message sped.
Saadi. 79.
Messages
Spelling with guided tongue man's mes-
sages Adirondacs. 269.
Speed nimbler messages, Voluntaries. 68.
Messenger
Whose voice, an equal messenger,
Threnody. 38.
Met
I met many travellers Forerunners. 17.
So did our sons; Heaven met them as
they fell. Inscription. 2.
Metamorphosis
The rushing metamorphosis
Woodnotes. II. 112.
Meteor
Who stands astonished at the meteor
light, Adirondacs. 123.
Like a meteor pass. Daemonic Love. 125.
Wisp and meteor nightly falling,
Frag. Nat. XVI. 1.
When thy meteor glances came,
Hermione. 37.
Voice of a meteor lost in day?
May-Day. 12.
Meteors
As, when a shower of meteors
Daemonic Love. 48.
Like meteors which chose their way
Poet. 55.
Meter
See Metre.
A meter of prosperity,— Goethe. 2.
Metest
Thou metest him by centuries,
Woodnotes. II. 307.
Methods
O all you virtues, methods, mights,
Mithridates. 26.
Methought
Methought like water-haunting birds
Poet. 19.
Methought the sky looked scornful down
Walden. 21.
Metope
Where flowers each stone rosette and
metope brave; Monadnoc. 372.
Metre
See Meter.
Laws of form, and metre just, Uriel. 12.
Hath its unit, bound and metre;
Visit. 5.
Say, what other metre is it Visit. 11.
Mexico
Harrying Mexico Channing Ode. 17.
Mice
Crab, mice, snail, dragon-fly, minnow and
moth; Adirondacs. 136.
'Mid
See Amid.
'Mid all the hints and glories of the home.
Adirondacs. 190.
As 'mid the virgin train she strayed,
Each. 30.
To hear, when, 'mid our talk and games,
May-Day. 56.
And, like the chemist 'mid his loaded jars,
Musketaquid. 38.

'Mid many ails a brittle health,
Poet. 184.
And oft at home 'mid tasks I heed,
Walden. 41.
Middle
I reached the middle of the mount
Dirge. 1.
Mortal mixed of middle clay, Guy. 1.
Midge
The midge, the blue-fly and the mosquito
Adirondacs. 166.
Who but the midge, mosquito and the fly,
Adirondacs. 173.
Midnight
At midnight and at morn? Dirge. 12.
Which dazzles me in midnight dark,
Etienne. 16.
At midnight and at morn?] Peter. 4.
Lose the shudder of midnight;
Saadi. 52.
And though he speak in midnight dark,—
Saadi. 131.
Sweet twilight walks and midnight soli-
tude Summons. 7.
Midst
And in the midst of spoils and slaves, we
thieves Blight. 46.
Midsummer
Imps, at high midsummer, blot
Alphonso. 9.
Nor freshet, nor midsummer flame.
Guy. 48.
That one broad, long midsummer day
May-Day. 276.
And my midsummer snow:
Monadnoc. 318.
Midsummer's
Hot midsummer's petted crone,
Humble-Bee. 32.
Midway
The midway of the eternal deep.
Saadi. 146.
Mien
Of joyful and transparent mien.
Daemonic Love. 77.
Their tranquil mien bereaveth him
Manners. 15.
On men and maids a ruddier mien,
May-Day. 300.
His early hope, his liberal mien;
Threnody. 55.
Might (Partial list.)
The frost might glitter, it would blight
no crop, Adirondacs. 68.
But right is might through all the world;
Boston. 96.
Might harry the weak and poor?
Boston Hymn. 12.
Who marries Right to Might,
Channing Ode. 81.
Try the might the Muse affords
Frag. Poet. X. 1.
Once I wished I might rehearse
Freedom. 1.
That the maids and boys might name
him. Initial Love. 14.
Masks the might of Nature's king,
May-Day. 458.
And prayers of might from martyrs'
cave. Merlin. 26.

And the dull idiot might see Merlin. 72.
So that men might it not forget;
                Monadnoc. 49.
Slowsure Britain's secular might,
                Monadnoc. 301.
Betrays the more abounding might,
                Monadnoc. 351.
Art might obey, but not surpass.
                Problem. 46.
Here might the red-bird come his plumes
    to cool,   Rhodora. 7.
For there is no might in the universe
                Rome. 18.
That wit and joy might find a tongue,
                Solution. 15.
And, by the famous might that lurks
            Spiritual Laws. 8.
Morn well might break and April bloom,
                Threnody. 16.
That winsome voice again might hear;
                Threnody. 51.
For Love draws might from terrene force
                Waterfall. 7.

Mightier
It is mightier than the strong,
            Merlin's Song. 3.
In mightier chant I disappear.
            Monadnoc. 227.

Mightiness
O Day! and is your mightiness
            Chartist. 13.

Mights
O all you virtues, methods, mights,
            Mithridates. 26.

Might'st. (Partial list.)
That thou might'st entertain apart
            Threnody. 215.
That thou might'st break thy daily bread
            Threnody. 219.
That thou might'st cherish for thine own
            Threnody. 221.

Mighty
Mighty projects countermanded;
            Alphonso. 23.
One morn is in the mighty heaven,
            Concord Ode. 3.
And the mighty choir descends,
            Daemonic Love. 44.
I know the mighty bards,   Dull. 6.
And following his mighty heart
            Frag. Poet. IV. 5.
Merlin's mighty line   Merlin. 51.
His mighty psalm from fall to spring
            Mountain. 19.
The Mighty commands me,   Poet. 119.
For faith and peace and mighty love
            Robbins Hymn. 17.
To the height of mighty Nature,
            Saadi. 172.
Rooted in the mighty Heart.
            Woodnotes. II. 177.

Migrate
Migrate from the Southern Sea;
            May-Day. 86.

Mild
In the next field is air more mild,
            May-Day. 102.
And made the lion mild.   Merlin. 54.
Coarse and boisterous, yet mild,
            Monadnoc. 131.

Conveyed thy meaning mild.
            Threnody. 39.

Mildew
Still are rulers, or Mildew?
            Alphonso. 40.

Mile
Painting pictures mile on mile,
            May-Day. 4.
Reached by a mile of road,
            Waterfall. 2.

Miles
Two creeping miles of rushes, pads and
    sponge,   Adirondacs. 24.
A score of airy miles will smooth
            Frag. Nat. XIV. 1.
Round about, a hundred miles,
            Monadnoc. 36.
What these strong masters wrote at large
    in miles,   Musketaquid. 52.
Miles off, three dangerous miles, is home;
            Titmouse. 9.

Milk
'Ye drew one mother's milk,   Dirge. 53.
Hid in milk we drew   May-Day. 407.

Milkweeds
Milkweeds and murky brakes, quaint
    pipes and sundew,   Blight. 7.

Millennial
Decayed millennial trunks, like moonlight
    flecks,   Adirondacs. 48.

Million
By million changes skilled to tell
            Monadnoc. 86.
Shot million rays of thought and tender-
    ness.   Musketaquid. 10.
Guest of million painted forms,
            Ode to Beauty. 23.
Though there come a million, Saadi. 21.
Come ten, or come a million,   Saadi. 32.
Has million arms to one of mine:
            Titmouse. 6.
And with a million spells enchants
            Waldeinsamkeit. 23.
A single will, a million deeds.
            Woodnotes. II. 265.

Million-handed
The million-handed sculptor moulds
            May-Day. 257.
The million-handed painter pours
            May-Day. 259.

Millions
The feet of millions stride.   Boston. 40.
Millions for self-government,
            Boston. 74.
To animate new millions, and exhale
            Pan. 11.
So, in the new-born millions, Promise. 5.

Mill-round
The mill-round of our fate appears
            Friendship. 15.

Mills
Bridge gulfs, drain swamps, build dams
    and mills,   Monadnoc. 150.

Milton
In Milton and in Angelo:
            Frag. Poet. IV. 31.

Milton's
Wise Milton's odes of pensive pleasure,
            Harp. 77.

Mimic

Joy-tides swell their mimic ocean.
Initial Love. 49.
No mimic; from his breast his counsel
drew, Phi. 15.
To mimic in slow structures, stone by
stone, Snow-Storm. 26.

Mind

Mind wakes a new-born giant from her
sleep. Adirondacs. 327.
Into each mind intruding duties crept;
Adirondacs. 332.
Which still obeys the mind. Angelo. 5.
The measure of the eternal Mind,
Bohemian. 11.
To take the statute from the mind
Concord Ode. 15.
The orb within the mind,
Day by Day. 6.
Whispered, 'Darling, never mind!
Experience. 19.
And on his mind at dawn of day
Frag. Poet. V. 47.
Or Shakespeare, whom no mind can
measure, Harp. 78.
'Higher, dear swallows! mind not what
I say. Hermione. 26.
Two things thou shalt not long for, if
thou love a mind serene;—
Ibn Jemin. 1.
Might rule the forest to his mind.
May-Day. 52.
With good according to its mind,
May-Day. 284.
Ah! well I mind the calendar,
May-Day. 372.
What time the subtle mind Merlin. 44.
Which only the propitious mind
Merlin. 68.
Things of the heavenly mind,—
Merops. 2.
Time out of mind, this forge of ores;
Monadnoc. 78.
But speechless to the master's mind?
Monadnoc. 91.
To fight pollution of the mind;
Monadnoc. 113.
In shifting form the formless mind,
Monadnoc. 389.
And through the priest the mind inspires.
Problem. 54.
Still whispers to the willing mind.
Problem. 60.
That holds and boasts the immeasurable
mind. River. 35.
Gentle Saadi, mind thy rhyme;
Saadi. 101.
Admits thee to the perfect Mind.
Saadi. 164.
Gave to the mind its emperor,
Solution. 37.
The zone that girds the incarnate mind.
Threnody. 231.
I spurn the Past, my mind disdains its
nod, To-Day. 13.
Up! mind thine own aim, and
To J. W. 22.
To build in matter home for mind.
Wealth. 12.

Enough for thee the primal mind
Woodnotes. II. 232.
And his mind is the sky.
Woodnotes. II. 317.
To the maids of holy mind,
World-Soul. 6.
Spring still makes spring in the mind.
World-Soul. 105.
As God and devil; bring them to the
mind, Xenophanes. 10.

Mindful

Winds mindful still of sannup and of
squaw, Musketaquid. 28.

Mind's

By mind's industry sharpening the love
of life— Summons. 12.
Wrote in thy mind's transparent table,
Threnody. 199.

Minds

Yet shine forever virgin minds,
Astraea. 31.
To seal the marriage of these minds with
thine, Good Cheer. 14.
and build heroic minds.
May-Day. 440.
Of minds that each can stand against the
world Oh What. 2.

Mine

See Undermine.
Retrieve the loss of me and mine!
Bacchus. 52.
And strangers to the plant and to the
mine. Blight. 32.
Should mine alone be dumb?
I. Compensation. 6.
With sorrow such as mine, Dirge. 46.
Yet well I know the royal mine,
Dull. 19.
At the same torch that lighted mine;
Eva. 3.
But no speed of mine avails
Forerunners. 7.
Fault and folly are not mine;
Frag. Life. XVI. 6.
Once a member, all was mine,
Frag. Poet. IV. 10.
I grieve that better souls than mine
Frag. Poet. VII. 1.
The Asmodean feat is mine,
Frag. Poet. XXXIV. 1.
Saying, "T is mine, my children's and my
name's. Hamatreya. 5.
'Mine and yours; Hamatreya. 28.
Mine, not yours. Hamatreya. 29.
Please God, I'll wrap me in mine inno-
cence, I Bear. 13.
Every thing is kin of mine.
Mithridates. 5.
As their murmurs mine to lull. Nun. 14.
Only by needs and loves of mine;
Poet. 234.
Me false to mine dare whisper none,—
Romany. 15.
They brought me rubies from the mine,
Rubies. 1.
Was ever couch magnificent as mine?
Seashore. 8.
Vain beside mine. I drive my wedges
home, Seashore. 12.

Mine are the night and morning,
Song of Nature. 1.
Nor my heart from love of mine,
Song of Seyd. 3.
Not mine,—I never called thee mine,
Threnody. 126.
Has million arms to one of mine:
Titmouse. 6.
Come weave with mine a nobler rhyme.
Woodnotes. II. 139.
And they reply, "Forever mine!"
Woodnotes. II. 149.

Mineral
Fire, plant and mineral say, 'Not in us;'
Blight. 35.
Into the mineral air,
Frag. Life. XXIV. 2.

Minerva's
Slighted Minerva's learnèd tongue,
Frag. Poet. XXXV. 1.

Mines
More dear to one than mines of gold.
Holidays. 12.
She ransacks mines and ledges
House. 13.
In trees, with beasts, in mines and caves,
Initial Love. 99.
The younger Golden Lips or mines,
Problem. 67.
Through snows above, mines underground,
Solution. 47.

Mingled
Was mingled from the generous whole;
Ode to Beauty. 47.

Miniature
'I ask no bauble miniature,
Hermione. 16.
In soft miniature lies. Sphinx. 48.

Minions
Minions of the Morning Star.
Daemonic Love. 102.

Ministered
To whom sweet angels ministered,
Poet. 202.

Minnow
Crab, mice, snail, dragon-fly, minnow and
moth; Adirondacs. 136.

Minorities
Minorities, things under cloud!
Mithridates. 30.

Minster
The sea-beat scorns the minster clock.
Frag. Nat. XXV. 3.
In the star-lit minster aisled.
May-Day. 50.
O'er all that mass and minster vaunt;
Titmouse. 90.

Minstrel
But my minstrel knows and tells
Harp. 19.
A minstrel of the natural year,
Woodnotes. I. 31.

Minstrel-journeyings
This home my minstrel-journeyings ends.
Aeolian Harp. 19.

Minstrels
Reporting what old minstrels told
The Harp. 53.

Thousand minstrels woke within me,
Monadnoc. 1.
Minstrels and kings and high-born dames,
and of the best that be. Quat. A. H. 4.

Minstrelsy
King Oberon's minstrelsy.
Frag. Nat. III. 28.

Mint
Sweet fern, mint and vernal grass,
Frag. Nat. II. 14.

Minute
Though it change every minute.
Ellen South. 4.

Miracle
Greet the glad miracle. Thought's new-
found path Adirondacs. 243.
Behold the miracle! Frag. Nat. XXVI. 11.
The miracle of generative force,
Musketaquid. 62.
The heart-o'erlading miracle. Poet. 90.

Miracles
In miracles of pomp, we must be proud,
Adirondacs. 155.
Born and nourished in miracles,
Poet. 3.
And the play of his miracles.
Woodnotes. II. 286.

Mire
And leaves us in the mire. World-Soul. 44.

Mired
Or mired by climate's gross extremes.
Nun. 36.

Mirk
The soothing lapse of morn to mirk,
Celestial Love. 105.

Mirror
Is there never a retroscope mirror
Cosmos. 13.
Only could her mirror show.
Frag. Life. IX. 2.

Mirrors
And lakes, smooth mirrors of Aurora's
charms. I Bear. 8.
A belt of mirrors round a taper's flame;
Xenophanes. 16.

Mirth
With hunters' appetite and peals of mirth.
Adirondacs. 182.
A melancholy better than all mirth.
Adirondacs. 215.
Yield sympathy and signs of mirth;
Celestial Love. 110.
And why, when mirth unseals all tongues,
I. Compensation. 5.
When Mirth is dumb and Flattery's fled,
Ellen. 9.
Squandering your unquoted mirth,
Monadnoc. 186.
The innocent mirth which sweetens daily
bread, Summons. 10.
His cheeks mantle with mirth;
World-Soul. 102.

Miscall
This is he men miscall Fate,
Worship. 11.

Miscarried
And Nature has miscarried wholly
Woodnotes. II. 215.

Miseries
Our insect miseries to thy rocks;
Monadnoc. 365.

Miserly
Chilled with a miserly comparison
Blight. 61.

Misery
Hard fare, hard bed and comic misery,—
Adirondacs. 165.
I said, 'We are mates in misery.'
Threnody. 103.

Misguide
Awful victors, they misguide
Voluntaries. 111.

Mis-hear
For men mis-hear thy call in Spring,
Titmouse. 91

Mislead
When the forest shall mislead me,
Woodnotes. I. 139.

Misplaced
Whence camest thou, misplaced, mistimed,
Woodnotes. II. 179.

Miss
That mortals miss the loyal heats,
Alphonso. 33.
Miss the aim whereto I strive. Angelo. 9.
If our brief tribe miss thy face,
Ellen South. 23.
That of goods I could not miss
Frag. Poet. IV. 8.
Ah, but I miss the grand design.
Frag. Poet. XVIII. 6.
My wreath shall nothing miss.
Song of Nature. 16.
Though beloved, I miss her not;
Una. 10.

Missed
All ate like abbots, and, if any missed
Adirondacs. 180.
Vainly valiant, you have missed
Etienne. 9.

Mist
Of the red deer, to aim at a square mist.
Adirondacs. 120.
Mixed with mist by distant lochs.
Forerunners. 16.
Hated mist if it come near.
Frag. Poet. VII. 18.
The morning mist within your grounds
Park. 11.

Mistimed
Whence camest thou, misplaced, mistimed,
Woodnotes. II. 179.

Mistress
She was his mistress and his law;
Frag. Poet. V. 23.

Mistrust
The world rolls round,—mistrust it not,—
May-Day. 177.

Mists
Have the same mists another side,
Chartist. 7.
Seethed in mists of Penmanmaur,
Solution. 33.
Where bearded mists divide,
Waldeinsamkeit. 34.

Misty
And misty lowland, where to go for peat.
Hamatreya. 21.

Mountains and the misty plains
Hermione. 20.
This morn I climbed the misty hill
Thine Eyes. 5.

Mix
And mix my requiem with the wind
Bell. 15.
Foolish hands may mix and mar;
Channing Ode. 76.
Mix polar night with tropic glow,
May-Day. 127.
And mix itself with each event;
Monadnoc. 51.
And mix the bowl again;
Song of Nature. 74.
And mix with Diety. Thought. 8.

Mixed
Mixed with mist by distant lochs.
Forerunners. 16.
Mortal mixed of middle clay, Guy. 1.
Substance mixed of pure contraries;
Initial Love. 91.
Who has mixed my boy's bread?
Sphinx. 62.

Mixes
He mixes music with her thoughts,
Rhea. 53.

Mixture
That no mixture could withstand
Guy. 13.

Moan
Afflicted moan, and latest hold
May-Day. 19.
Chiming with the gasp and moan
Merlin. 19.
And joy and moan, Celestial Love. 40.

Moanings
Moanings of the tropic sea;
Voluntaries. 4.

Moat
Than thine no deeper moat can be,
Boston. 61.

Mock
Thou dost mock at fate and care,
Humble-Bee. 56.

Mocking
Shed mocking lustres on shelf of books,
May-Day. 356.
A quest of river-grapes, a mocking thrush,
Musketaquid. 73.

Mockingly
For number or proportion. Mockingly,
Snow-Storm. 17.

Mocks
The wood-fly mocks with tiny voice
May-Day. 75.
Which mocks thy æons to embrace;
Nun. 40.

Mode
He has not one mode, but manifold,
Initial Love. 131.

Model
Whereby to model newer races,
Rhea. 66.

Modest
And modest copse and the forest tall,
Frag. Poet. I. 16.
What potent blood hath modest May,
May-Day. 187.

Modulate
To modulate   Poet. 152.
Modulates
Modulates the king's affairs;   Merlin. 78.
Modulating
Modulating all extremes,—   Harp. 31.
Moist
Ope in such low moist roadside, and be-
neath   Naples. 24.
Moist perhaps by ocean surf,   Nun. 26.
Mole
Dust is their pyramid and mole:
Wealth. 25.
Moles
Are moles of beauties Time hath slain.
From Omar. 4.
Moment
And meditate a moment on Heaven's rest.
Adirondacs. 197.
This shining moment is an edifice
Frag. Life. V. 1.
Youth, for a moment free as they,
Monadnoc. 21.
A moment, by the railway troop,
Monadnoc. 396.
There in a moment I have seen
Peter. 17.
Single moment years confessed. Visit. 22.
If Love his moment overstay,   Visit. 29.
Momentary
In thy momentary play,
Ode to Beauty. 31.
A momentary music. Being's tide
Pan. 3.
Moment's
The moment's music which they gave.
Beauty. 10.
Moments
We have few moments in the longest life
Adirondacs. 249.
Monadnoc
Rough Monadnoc to a gem.
Frag. Nat. XIV. 2.
'Monadnoc is a mountain strong,
Monadnoc. 256.
Shall string Monadnoc like a bead.
Monadnoc. 286.
Not on its base Monadnoc surer stood,
Phi. 13.
Monadnoc's
She stood Monadnoc's head. Sphinx. 128.
Monarch's
Of a true monarch's soul. Beauty and
strength,   Good Cheer. 8.
Nor spacious court, nor monarch's hall,
May-Day. 222.
Monarchs
Not to monarchs they repair,
Astraea. 13.
Monastic
And on my heart monastic aisles
Problem. 3.
Monday
On Monday in the mall,   Boston. 28.
Money
And the second, borrowed money,—
though the smiling lender say
Ibn Jemin. 3.
Money-loving
Before the money-loving herd,
Woodnotes. II. 60.

'Monishment
All of them utter sounds of 'monishment
River. 29.
Monotony
They dull its edge with their monotony.
Xenophanes. 11.
Month
See Twelvemonth.
Months
After long months of weary wandering,
River. 37.
Into calendar months and days.
Uriel. 4.
Monument
This monument of my despair   Rhea. 58.
And blessed the monument of the man of
flowers,   Woodnotes. I. 70.
Mood
They played with it in every mood;
Dirge. 30.
In severe or cordial mood,   Etienne. 12.
Teach me your mood, O patient stars!
Frag. Nat. VIII. 5.
Which puts me in a working mood.
Frag. Poet. XVIII. 2.
Into the winter night's extinguished
mood?   Musketaquid. 79.
But of mutable mood,—   Nature. II. 2.
Moods
Knows Nature's rarest moods, Harp. 13.
Moon
See Day-moon.
In changing moon and tidal wave
II. Compensation. 5.
As moon from earth, or star from star.
Frag. Nat. VII. 2.
Strikes never moon or star.
Frag. Nat. XV. 4.
The moon was making amber of the
world,   Frag. Nat. XXVII. 3.
Sun and moon must fall amain
Frag. Poet. V. 34.
Sun and moon are in my way.
Frag. Poet. XXV. 4.
Give the gem which dims the moon
Friendship Trans. 3.
The heaped-up harvest of the moon
From Hafiz. 6.
They heed not moon or solar tide,—
Garden. 23.
To fruitful field and sun and moon.
Limits. 10
One arctic moon had disenchanted.
May-Day. 44.
The sun obeys them and the moon.
Monadnoc. 248.
And thy grave smiled on by the visiting
moon.   Mountain. 6.
Made moon and planets parties to their
bond,   Musketaquid. 8.
As, when the all-worshipped moon at-
tracts the eye,   Musketaquid. 82.
And nearer stoops the moon.   Peter. 16.
He sowed the sun and moon for seeds.
Poet. 32.
And the sailing moon where the cloud
was rent,   Poet. 68.
Sun, moon, man, undulate and stream,
Poet. 173.
The moon comes back,—the Spirit not.
Poet. 280.

Moon —*Continued*
And over the tree was the moon,
        Quat. Excelsior. 2.
And over the moon were starry studs
        Quat. Excelsior. 3.
The fair moon mounts, and aye the flame
        Romany. 3.
If on the heath, below the moon,
        Romany. 13.
Hear wolves barking at the moon;
        Saadi. 54.
The sportive sun, the gibbous moon,
        Song of Nature. 3.
She silvered in the moon;   Sphinx. 124.
Who gazed upon the sun and moon
        Threnody. 142.
The moon thy mourner, and the cloud.
        Titmouse. 22.
On him the light of star and moon
        Woodnotes. II. 71.

Moon-drawn
The moon-drawn tide-wave strives;
        Promise. 2.

Moonlight
Decayed millennial trunks, like moonlight
  flecks,   Adirondacs. 48.
Bring the moonlight into noon   Art. 3.
Coin the moonlight into verse
        Frag. Poet. XXIX. 3.

Moonmen
Unto men these moonmen lend,
        Daemonic Love. 58.

Moons
The moons in ocean dip,   II. Eros. 4.
Three moons his great heart him a hermit
  made,   Woodnotes. I. 84.

Moored
How Nature to the soul is moored,
        Harp. 104.
Cannot be moored.   Illusions. 13.

Moors
She paints with white and red the moors
        Frag. Nat. XIII. 1.
Teaching barren moors to smile,
        May-Day. 3.

Moose
Where feeds the moose, and walks the
  surly bear,   Woodnotes. I. 66.

Moral
And by the moral of his place
        Monadnoc. 110.
And yet have knowledge of our moral
  race,   River. 32.

More (Partial list.)
  See Evermore; Forevermore.
Hereafter,—willing they, and more adroit.
        Adirondacs. 164.
On for a thousand years of genius more.'
        Adirondacs. 329.
You have tried famine: no more try it;
        Alphonso. 51.
By its own craft, to a more rich delight.
        Bacchus. 11.
Shall lift its notes once more, Bell. 14.
Has lords enough and more;—
        Boston. 20.
Or union never more again. Boston. 36.
I suffer them no more; Boston Hymn. 6.
Their reach shall yet be more profound,
        Celestial Love. 19.

Gauge of more and less through space,
        II. Compensation. 7.
From my great arteries,—nor less, nor
  more.'   Day's Ration. 5.
The little cup will hold not a bead more,
        Day's Ration. 22.
I pant for thee no more.   *Farewell. 49.
Nobility more nobly to repay?
        Forbearance. 7.
A thing that takes no more root in the
  world   Frag. Life. XXVI. 3.
Who, having more absorbed, more large-
  ly yield,   Frag. Nat. V. 11.
to her much she added more;
        Frag. Nat. XII. 1.
A wintry storm more fitly fell.
        Frag. Nat. XXIX. 4.
High and more high   Give. 11.
More than they were,   Give. 24.
Him to his land, a lump of mould the
  more.   Hamatreya. 26.
More dear to one than mines of gold.
        Holidays. 12.
Thyself dost give forever more.
        Hymn. 28.
Boy no more, he wears all coats,
        Initial Love. 15.
And feed once more the exile's eyes;
        May-Day. 97.
Burned more than others' fire,
        May-Day. 143.
Forms more cheerly live and go,
        Merlin. 43.
One word, no more, to say. Merops. 12.
Once more into his dapper town,
        Monadnoc. 345.
Betrays the more abounding might,
        Monadnoc. 351.
And crowns him with a more than royal
  crown,   October. 4.
More proudly rolls, more softly lies.
        Park. 12.
More sense than sages write. Peter. 32.
From thyself no more can we. Poet. 270.
More enamoured serve it yet; Poet. 290.
And I behold once more   River. 1.
It hath a sound more eloquent than
  speech.   River. 27.
Yet whirl the glowing wheels once more,
        Song of Nature. 73.
And crouched no more in stone;
        Sphinx. 122.
And said: 'No more!   Terminus. 6.
Fancy departs: no more invent;
        Terminus. 9.
Than the South more fierce and hot;
        Test. 6.
And the meaning was more white
        Test. 9.
When frail Nature can no more,
        Threnody. 234.
Knowing this,—and knows no more,—
        Voluntaries. 98.
And to her son will treasures more
        Walk. 5.
And more to purpose freely pour
        Walk. 6.
On him the sun looked more serene;
        Woodnotes. I. 113.

Talk no more with feeble tongue;
                    Woodnotes. II. 137.
No more the fool of space and time,
                    Woodnotes. II. 138.
'Hearken once more! Woodnotes. II. 252.
Than all it holds more deep, more high.'
                    Woodnotes. II. 318.
More near than aught thou call'st thy own,
                    Worship. 16.

Morn
        See May-morn; Yestermorn.
Next morn, we swept with oars the Sara-
nac,   Adirondacs. 7.
By the bright morn the gay flotilla slid
                    Adirondacs. 16.
At morn or noon, the guide rows bare-
headed: Adirondacs. 74.
He dons a surcoat which he doffs at morn:
                    Adirondacs. 77.
from morn to eve.   Adirondacs. 90.
And make to-morrow a new morn.
                    Art. 12.

Let its grapes the morn salute
                    Bacchus. 6.
The soothing lapse of morn to mirk,
                    Celestial Love. 105.
One morn is in the mighty heaven,
                    Concord Ode. 3.
At midnight and at morn?   Dirge. 12.
Waits through dark ages for the morn,
                    Frag. Life. XXIII. 3.
The first far signal-fire of morn.
                    Harp. 94.
Still breaks that morn, though dim, to
    Memory's eye,   I Bear. 10.
Of eve and morn,   In Memoriam. 17.
The morn and sparkling dew, a snare?
                    May-Day. 430.
Wandering yester morn the brake,
                    Miracle. 15.
Which morn and crimson evening paint
                    Monadnoc. 44.
By morn and eve in light and shade;
                    Monadnoc. 61.
'Every morn I lift my head,
                    Monadnoc. 279.
As is to me when I behold the morn
                    Naples. 23.
No early morn, no evening late, –
                    Nun. 43.
At midnight and at morn?]   Peter. 14.
Calm as the morn the manly patriot sate;
                    Phi. 10.
Not yet a steadfast morn,   Poet. 102.
The morn is come: the starry crowds
                    Poet. 177.
Saluted him each morn as brother,
                    Poet. 203.
Painting with morn each annual cell?
                    Problem. 28.
Is not my voice thy music, morn and
eve?   Seashore. 4.
This morn I climbed the misty hill
                    Thine Eyes. 5.
Morn well might break and April bloom,
                    Threnody. 16.
When every morn my bosom glowed
                    Threnody. 60.

Morning
Up to my ear the morning brings
                    Boston Hymn. 7.

Pied with morning and with night.
                    II. Compensation. 2.
Or who can date the morning,
                    Cosmos. 3.
And I can date the morning prime
                    Cosmos. 7.
Minions of the Morning Star.
                    Daemonic Love. 102.
Forgot my morning wishes, hastily
                    Days. 8.
Five rosy boys with morning light
                    Dirge. 5.
The rolling river, the morning bird;—
                    Each. 49.
The morning wind is in it;
                    Ellen South. 2.
Except the amber morning wind,
                    Exile. 5.
I know that thou, O morning wind!
                    Exile. 9.
Make the morning proud and sweet;
                    Forerunners. 10.
To deck the morning of the year,
                    Frag. Nat. VIII. 2.
Now that morning not disdains
                    Hermione. 19.
On windy hills, whose tops with morning
glow,   I Bear. 7.
But soft! a sultry morning breaks;
                    May-Day. 58.
With dews of tropic morning wet,
                    May-Day. 395.
Oft as morning wreathes my scarf,
                    Monadnoc. 311.
And the cold and purple morning
                    Ode to Beauty. 86.
The morning mist within your grounds
                    Park. 11.
I snuff the breath of my morning afar,
                    Poet. 108.
As mountains for the morning wait,
                    Poet. 122.
And Morning opes with haste her lids
                    Problem. 35.
Still floats upon the morning wind,
                    Problem. 59.
True Brahmin, in the morning meadows
wet,   Quat. Gardener. 1.
Never, son of eastern morning,
                    Saadi. 92.
The forest waves, the morning breaks,
                    Saadi. 135.
Poises Arcturus aloft morning and eve-
ning his spear.   Shah-Hafiz. 2.
Mine are the night and morning,
                    Song of Nature. 1.
Night veileth the morning,
                    Sphinx. 39.
And kind acquaintance with the morning
stars   Summons. 8.
Her morning sun shone bright and calm-
ly purely set;   *Violet. 14.
Whose giddy top the morning loved to
gild.   Woodnotes. I. 79.
There the red morning touched him with
its light.   Woodnotes. I. 83.
When the night and morning lie,
                    Woodnotes. I. 140.

Morning —*Continued*
Thanks to the morning light,
World-Soul. 1.
The inevitable morning   World-Soul. 33.
The crimson morning flames into
World-Soul. 59.

Morning's
Write in a book the morning's prime,
Garden. 39.
Of tulips, in the morning's rays.
May-Day. 207.
To light which dims the morning's eye.
Rhea. 4.

Mornings
His park where amber mornings break,
Chartist. 10.
The quaint devices on its mornings gay.
Frag. Nat. V. 7.
Not less are summer mornings dear
Promise. 7.

Morn's
Under morn's unlifted lid,
May-Day. 423.
I bathe in the morn's soft and silvered
air,   Musketaquid. 13.
Yet unto me not morn's magnificence,
Naples. 15.

Morrow
From Chaos to the dawning morrow;
May-Day. 460.
Long morrow to this mortal youth.
Monadnoc. 408.
The morrow front, and can defy;
Nun. 4.
Is in the morrow most at home,
Quat. Fate. 2.
The morrow dawned with needless glow;
Threnody. 104.

Mortal
See Immortal.
Translucent through the mortal covers,
Daemonic Love. 33.
And take the mortal leap undaunted,
Fame. 17.
"I am divine, I am not mortal made;
Frag. Life. XVIII. 3.
Mortal mixed of middle clay,   Guy. 1.
Wherein was dropped the mortal spoil.
Harp. 127.
That hides from man the mortal goal,
Hymn. 22.
They know one only mortal grief
Love and Thought. 9.
Dazzle every mortal.   Manners. 4.
In every mortal meet.   Merlin. 91.
Long morrow to this mortal youth.
Monadnoc. 408.
Call hither thy mortal enemy,   Poet. 219.
By beauty of a mortal child   Rhea. 42.
In trance upborne past mortal goal
Solution. 45.
Walled with mortal terror round,
Voluntaries. 90.
O mortal! thy ears are stones;
Woodnotes. II. 126.

Mortals
That mortals miss the loyal heats,
Alphonso. 33.
Mortals deem the planets bright
Daemonic Love. 52.

Pronounced the word that mortals hate
to hear—   Frag. Life. XVIII. 2.
Of all mortals the desire,   Saadi. 10.
Cities of mortals woe-begone
Waldeinsamkeit. 13.
Of woe-worn mortals darkling go,
Walden. 18.
Or Music pours on mortals
World-Soul. 31.

Mortify
Would mortify me, but in vain; for still
Musketaquid. 69.

Moslems
What are Moslems? what are Giaours?
Song of Seyd. 27.

Mosque
He came a pilgrim to the Mosque
Frag. Poet. I. 5.

Mosquito
The midge, the blue-fly and the mosquito
Adirondacs. 166.
Who but the midge, mosquito and the fly,
Adirondacs. 173.

Moss
See Club-moss; Rock-moss.
Hypnum and hydnum, mushroom, sponge
and moss,   Adirondacs. 144.
The moss upon the forest bark
Woodnotes. I. 133.

Mosses
And halfway to the mosses brown;
May-Day. 118.
And for cold mosses, cream and curds:
Monadnoc. 140.

Mossy
The frailest leaf, the mossy bark,
Ode to Beauty. 25.

Most (Partial list.)
See Inmost; Innermost; Topmost;
Utmost.
And a prime end of the most subtle ele-
ment   Adirondacs. 258.
If Boston knew the most!
Boston. 48.
Shall each by each be most enjoyed.
Celestial Love. 98.
Reality most like to dreams.
Frag. Nat. XXIII. 6.
Is worth one barley-corn at most,
From Hafiz. 7.
Most like to bachelors,   Merlin. 108.
What's most theirs is not their own,
Nature. II. 20.
Is in the morrow most at home,
Quat. Fate. 2.
Most welcome they who need him most,
Saadi. 41.
Of the most beautiful and sweet
Threnody. 107.
The Providence that is most large
Titmouse. 85.

Most High
And thou shalt say to the Most High,
Woodnotes. II. 204.

Mote
All things return, both sphere and mote,
May-Day. 179.

Motes
Still, through her motes and masses,
draw   Wealth. 46.

Moth
 See Gold-moth.
dragon-fly, minnow and moth;
     Adirondacs. 136.
Every moth with painted wing,
     Lines. 9.
Woven of tulips and painted moth.
     May-Day. 330.

Mother
Of mother, father, sister, stand;
     Daemonic Love. 6.
Farewell, my mother fond,
     *Farewell. 19.
Bring to fair mother fairer child,
     May-Day. 452.
His mother died,—the only friend he
 had,—   Philosopher. 7.
"The babe by its mother Sphinx. 41.
"Out spoke the great mother,
     Sphinx. 57.

Mother's
Had leaped from one fair mother's arms,
     Dirge. 6.
'Ye drew one mother's milk,
     Dirge. 53.
Dragged from his mother's arms and
 breast,   Voluntaries. 19.
Then will yet my mother yield
     Woodnotes. I. 143.

Motion
In her form and motion. Hermione. 15.
He rolls them with delighted motion,
     Initial Love. 48.
Studied thy motion, took thy form
     Lines. 16.
Giddy with motion Nature reels,
     Poet. 172.
In beautiful motion Sphinx. 21.
And God said, "Throb!" and there was
 motion   Woodnotes. II. 268.

Motive
Resist in vain his motive strain,
     Poet. 37.

Mottled
The mottled clouds, like scraps of wool,
     Frag. Nat. XXVI. 17.

Mould
Form of forms, and mould of statures,
     Bacchus. 20.
And the world's flowing fates in his own
 mould recast.   Culture. 11.
To mould his fortunes, mean or great:
     Fate. 2.
Like creatures of a skiey mould,
     Frag. Poet. I. 48.
Him to his land, a lump of mould the
 more.   Hamatreya. 26.
Quickening underneath the mould
     May-Day. 273.
Mould the year to fair increase,
     Merlin. 57.
But if the brave old mould is broke,
     Monadnoc. 118.
For the next ages, men of mould
     Monadnoc. 155.
Is the Creator of our human mould
     Naples. 2.
A form which Nature cast in the heroic
 mould   Phi. 5.
His face was the mould of beauty.
     Power. 3.

Iron arms, and iron mould,
     Woodnotes. II. 41.

Moulded
And, moulded of one element Art. 23.
I moulded his face to beauty
     Frag. Poet. XIV. 3.
Twice I have moulded an image,
     Song of Nature. 61.
I moulded kings and saviors,
     Song of Nature. 69.

Moulding
Moulding Nature at his will,
     Solution. 29.

Moulds
Heat with viewless fingers moulds,
     May-Day. 195.
The million-handed sculptor moulds
     May-Day. 257.
Makes and moulds them what they are,
     Nature. II. 8.

Mouldy
Old mouldy men and books and names
 and lands   To-Day. 9.

Moult
Rushing ages moult their wings,
     Poet. 132.

Mound
Mound and flood. Hamatreya. 47.
On a mound an Arab lay, Hermione. 1.
Its root has pierced yon shady mound;
     Holidays. 6.
This mound shall throb his face before,
     Monadnoc. 288.
O barren mound, thy plenties fill!
     Monadnoc. 378.

Mount
Thou must mount for love;
     Celestial Love. 30.
I reached the middle of the mount
     Dirge. 1.
From blue mount and headland dim
     Frag. Poet. XI. 5.
Mount on the pipes of the trees,
     May-Day. 231.
But mount to paradise Merlin. 37.
Tales of many a famous mount,—
     Monadnoc. 95.
And lift thee to his holy mount,
     Saadi. 61.
Nor mount, nor dive; all good things
 keep   Saadi. 145.
And on every mount and meadow
     Threnody. 3.

Mountain
 See Mountain-crest.
Lone mountain tarn, or isle forgot,
     Astraea. 46.
The mountain tunnelled,
     Channing Ode. 60.
Mountain tall and ocean deep
     II Compensation. 3.
Along the mountain towers,—
     Daemonic Love. 110.
Spies oversea the fires of the mountain;
     Enchanter. 9.
The mountain and the squirrel
     Fable. 1.
Piling mountain chains of phlegm
     Frag. Nat. I. 13.
Up the far mountain walls the streams
 increase Frag. Nat. XXVI. 22.

Mountain —*Continued*
The mountain waters washed him clean
Frag. Poet. V. 17.
Glad when the solid mountain swims
Frag. Poet. V. 28.
Yet,—wouldst thou the mountain find
Freedom. 11.
A door into the mountain heart,
Hermione. 44.
Amid the mountain counties, Hants,
Franklin, Berks, Letter. 9.
Spilling over mountain chains,
May-Day. 242.
Sweep ruins from the scarped mountain,
May-Day. 449.
Quarry of spars in mountain pores;
Monadnoc. 79.
And end in churls the mountain folk
Monadnoc. 119.
Sink, O mountain, in the swamp!
Monadnoc. 121.
Many farms of mountain men.
Monadnoc. 128.
'Monadnoc is a mountain strong,
Monadnoc. 256.
But well I know, no mountain can,
Monadnoc. 258.
The constant mountain doth dispense;
Monadnoc. 382.
Girt in by mountain walls
Mountain. 8.
Yet spake yon purple mountain,
Park. 13.
Browse the mountain sheep in flocks,
Saadi. 6.
And carve the coastwise mountain into
caves. Seashore. 13.
The mountain chase, the summer waves,
To J. W. 3.
Each joy the mountain dales impart;
Woodnotes. I. 35.
Mountain speech to Highlanders,
Woodnotes. II. 152.
When thou shalt climb the mountain cliff,
Woodnotes. II. 194.
Mountain chains he can unlock:
Worship. 6.

Mountain-crest
Or on the mountain-crest sublime,
Waldeinsamkeit. 9.

Mountaineer
Dare praise the freedom-loving mountain-
eer? Channing Ode. 20.
Fair fortunes to the mountaineer!
Monadnoc. 69.

Mountain's
Cooled by the pendent mountain's shade,
May-Day. 17.
Under the tumbling mountain's breast,
Wealth. 27.

Mountains
Where all the sacred mountains drew
around us, Adirondacs. 9.
Under low mountains, whose unbroken
ridge Adirondacs. 27.
The mountains said, 'Good-day!
Boston. 50.
The winds took flesh, the mountains
talked, Frag. Poet. I. 55.

Fortune's delectable mountains;
Frag. Poet. IV. 12.
Can mountains lift;
Frag. Poet. VIII. 2.
Mountains and the misty plains
Hermione. 20.
Which blasts of Northern mountains
hymn, Nun. 19.
Ran from his mouth to mountains and the
sea, Phi. 21.
Landward they reached the mountains
old Poet. 63.
As mountains for the morning wait,
Poet. 122.
The mountains flow, the solids seem,
Poet. 174.
Through mountains bored by regal art,
Saadi. 153.
From mountains far and valleys near
Walden. 13.

Mounting
At the first mounting of the giant stairs.
Adirondacs. 63.
The black ducks mounting from the lake,
Waldeinsamkeit. 29.
The mounting sap, the shells, the sea,
Woodnotes. II. 77.

Mounts
Mounts through all the spires of form.
May-Day. 82.
Mounts through all the spires of form.
Nature. Mot. 6.
The fair moon mounts, and aye the flame
Romany. 3.

Mourn
Let not him mourn who best entitled was,
Adirondacs. 296.
Nay, mourn not one: let him exult,
Adirondacs. 297.
I sit and mourn alone?
I Compensation. 4.
I mourn upon this battle-field,
In Memoriam. 1.
Nor mourn the unalterable Days
In Memoriam. 109.
And, looking over the hills, I mourn
Threnody. 7.

Mourner
The moon thy mourner, and the cloud.
Titmouse. 22.

Mournful
Cheers the rough crag and mournful dell,
Frag. Nat. XXIX. 2.
So sweet and mournful falls the strain.
Harp. 102.
Low and mournful be the strain.
Voluntaries. 1.

Mourning
Mourning summer laid in shrouds.
Nun. 22.

Mouse-ear
Mouse-ear, cowslip, wintergreen,
Frag. Nat. II. 29.

Mouth
Ran from his mouth to mountains and
the sea, Phi. 21.

Mouths
One over against the mouths of Nile,
Song of Nature. 67.

Move
My lips in whisper move   *Farewell. 43.
Moved
  See Self-moved.
And seeing rashly torn and moved
                        Threnody. 128.
Moved by his hospitable heart,
                        Titmouse. 34.
Upward the ninth heaven thrilled and
moved   Waterfall. 19.
Much (Partial list.)
  See Overmuch.
't is theirs as much as ours.
                        Adirondacs. 261.
I ask more or not so much:
                        Aeolian Harp. 7.
O, that were much, and I could be a part
                        Blight. 14.
As much as he is and doeth,
                        Boston Hymn. 59.
So much he shall bestow.
                        Boston Hymn. 60.
How much runs over on the desert sands.
                        Day's Ration. 14.
Day by day for her darlings to her much
she added more;   Frag. Nat. XII. 1.
For I had too much to think, Goethe. 5.
How much, preventing God, how much I
owe   Grace. 1.
I who have seen much,   Hamatreya. 35.
Men and manners much deranged:
                        Initial Love. 8.
The much deceived Endymion
                        Manners. 19.
Yet doth much her love excel
                        Nature. I. 16.
Much triumphing,—and these the fields
                        River. 13.
All too much to him they said,
                        September. 10.
They swathed their too much power.
                        Song of Nature. 32.
Too much of donning and doffing,
                        Song of Nature. 49.
I am too much bereft.   Threnody. 170.
Mud
But in the mud and scum of things
                        Music. 17.
Muddy
Her muddy eyes to clear!"   Sphinx. 108.
Muffled
Hark to that muffled roar! a tree in the
woods   Adirondacs. 121.
Muffled and dumb like barefoot dervishes,
                        Days. 2.
Muftis
Ask not me, as Muftis can,
                        Song of Seyd. 21.
Multiples
Frugal multiples of that.   Visit. 26.
Multiplies
But multiplies the image of a day,—
                        Xenophanes. 15.
Multitude
And the multitude insults.
                        Daemonic Love. 104.
Multitudinous
Of the multitudinous   Frag. Life. VI. 5.
Mummied
Or sibyl from the mummied East,
                        Frag. Poet. XXVIII. 2.

Mundane
It is the tongue of mundane laws.
                        Harp. 72.
I will tell thee the mundane lore.
                        Woodnotes. II. 253.
Murdering
Nor murdering hate, can enter in.
                        Past. 9.
Murky
Milkweeds and murky brakes, quaint
pipes and sundew,   Blight. 7.
Murmur
The wires shall murmur through the main
                        Concord Ode. 31.
I murmur never while   *Farewell. 52.
Murmur in the house of life, Merlin. 124.
Murmured
'Welcome!' the wood-god murmured
through the leaves,—   Adirondacs. 44.
Food indigestible":—then murmured
some,   Adirondacs. 186.
For thus the wood-gods murmured in my
ear: Musketaquid. 76.
Murmuring
In the garden murmuring,
                        Frag. Nat. XXII. 2.
And the murmuring rivers of sap
                        May-Day. 230.
Vanish, and end their murmuring,—
                        Monadnoc. 367.
And murmuring waters counselled me.
                        Rhea. 8.
Murmurs
And murmurs in the wold   Garden. 50.
As their murmurs mine to lull.   Nun. 14.
Muse
'A new commandment,' said the smiling
Muse   Adakryn. 1.
And other Titans without muse or name.
                        Adirondacs. II.
The angry Muse   Channing Ode. 10.
The astonished Muse finds thousands at
her side.   Channing Ode. 97.
The Muse the truth uncolored speaking)
                        Daemonic Love. 64.
If a new Muse draw me with splendid ray,
                        Day's Ration. 15.
And thus the high Muse treated me,
                        Frag. Poet. IV. 15.
Saadi held the Muse in awe,
                        Frag. Poet. V. 22.
The Muse can knit   Frag. Poet. IX. 3.
Try the might the Muse affords
                        Frag. Poet. X. 1.
And after Love, the Muse.   Garden. 28.
Plans, credit and the Muse,—   Give. 5.
The Muse of men is coy,   Harp. 15.
Who is their Muse and dame.
                        Hermione. 25.
Can build as the Muse can;   House. 2.
And bid each awful Muse drive the
damned harpies hence.   I Bear. 14.
Yet not of these I muse
                        In Memoriam. 21.
The highway, Eros and the Muse.
                        Love and Thought. 2.
The soaring orbit of the muse exceeds
that journey's length.   Merlin. 65.
The self-same tuneful muse;
                        Merlin. 116.

Muse —*Continued*
And ruddy Health the loftiest Muse.
                              Merlin's Song. 30.
Soft! let not the offended muse
                              Monadnoc. 125.
All their vocal muse affords;
                              Monadnoc. 176.
Of a celestial Ceres and the Muse?
                              Monadnoc. 357.
I muse what secret purpose had he
                              Monadnoc Afar. 7.
In spite of Virtue and the Muse,
                              Nemesis. 13.
Ill fits the abstemious Muse a crown to
    weave   Phi. 1.
For the Muse gave special charge
                              Poet. 39
Whispered the Muse in Saadi's cot:
                              Saadi. 86.
And thus to Saadi said the Muse:
                              Saadi. 141.
I am the Muse who sung alway
                              Solution. 1.
But I, the bantling of a country Muse,
                              Summons. 22.
And though no Muse can these impart,
                              Threnody. 206.
Of critic charters, an unlaurelled Muse.
                              To-Day. 8.
Muse-born, a daughter of the Muse.
                              Woodnotes. II. 84.

Muse-born
Muse-born, a daughter of the Muse.
                              Woodnotes. II. 84.

Muse's
The Muse's hill by Fear is guarded,
                              Frag. Poet. XXXI. 1.

Muses
Where the wisest Muses falter,
                              Etienne. 14.
He has the Muses by the heart,
                              Initial Love. 128.
When the Muses nine   Politics. 15.
For, whom the Muses smile upon,
                              Saadi. 125.
Books, Muses, Study, fireside, friends and
    love,   Summons. 13.
Amid the Muses, left thee deaf and dumb,
                              Terminus. 31.
Bring the flown Muses back to men.
                              Threnody. 137.

Mushroom
Hypnum and hydnum, mushroom, sponge
    and moss,   Adirondacs. 144.

Music
Wine which Music is,—   Bacchus. 36.
Music and wine are one,—   Bacchus. 37.
The moment's music which they gave.
                              Beauty. 10.
I love thy music, mellow bell,   Bell. 1.
And soon thy music, sad death-bell,
                              Bell. 13.
Beauty sits and Music calls;
                              Dearest. 2.
But a music music-born   Destiny. 10.
Music to the march of time.
                              Frag. Nat. I. 5.
Bring your music and rhythmic flight,
                              Frag. Nat. XXIII. 9.

His music was the south-wind's sigh,
                              Frag. Poet. I. 11.
In music and uplifting hymns.
                              Frag. Poet. V. 29.
Bring music to the desolate:
                              Frag. Poet. X. 3
I framed his tongue to music,
                              Frag. Poet. XIV. 1.
For art, for music over-thrilled,
                              Frag. Poet. XVI. 1.
To music, and to music's thought,
                              Hermione. 74.
She lays her beams in music,
                              House. 17
In music every one,   House. 18.
In the heart of the music peals a strain
                              Merlin's Song. 8.
The music that can deepest reach,
                              Merlin's Song. 35.
On prayer and music strung;
                              Monadnoc. 234
When the music and the dance
                              Monadnoc. 252
I hear a sky-born music still:
                              Music. 2.
Color and sound, music to eye and ear,
                              October. 10.
Who heard the starry music
                              Ode to Beauty. 58.
A momentary music. Being's tide
                              Pan. 3
His tongue was framed to music,
                              Power. 1.
His words are music in my ear,
                              Problem. 69.
He mixes music with her thoughts,
                              Rhea. 53.
Is not my voice thy music, morn and eve?
                              Seashore. 4.
On which the seraph music sails.
                              Solution. 50.
By one music enchanted,   Sphinx. 35.
A music heard by thee alone
                              Threnody. 78.
Repeats the music of the rain;
                              Two Rivers. 2.
Are Autumn's blast fit music for thee,
    fragile one, to hear;   *Violet. 2.
In music he repeats the pang
                              Woodnotes. II. 124.
Which knits the world in music strong,
                              Woodnotes II. 157.
Or Music pours on mortals
                              World-Soul. 31.

Musical
He must be musical,   Culture. 3.
Saw musical order and pairing rhymes.
                              Poet. 72.

Music-born
But a music music-born   Destiny. 10.

Music-drunken
Fold us music-drunken in.   Merlin. 129.

Musician
One musician is sure,   Harp. 1.

Music's
And mute thy music's dearest tone,
                              Ellen. 10.
To music, and to music's thought,
                              Hermione. 74.
'Our music's in the hills;'—
                              Monadnoc. 2.

Which Music's wings infold,
Voluntaries. 76.

Musing
The musing peasant, lowly great,
Woodnotes. I. 104.

Musketaquid
In our green Musketaquid,
Frag. Nat. XXVI. 2.
Thy summer voice, Musketaquit,
Two Rivers. 1.
Musketaquit, a goblin strong,
Two Rivers. 13.

Must
In miracles of pomp, we must be proud,
Adirondacs. 155.
He must to school and learn his verb and
noun   Adirondacs. 267.
The holidays were fruitful, but must end;
Adirondacs. 330.
Eyes of gods! ye must have seen,
Alphonso. 19.
We must have society,   Alphonso. 57.
With the labors he must dare;
Alphonso. 74.
Thou must mount for love;
Celestial Love. 30.
He must me musical,   Culture. 3.
Up which the incarnate soul must climb,
Dirge. 2.
For so I must intepret still   Eva. 4.
Must be taken in together,   Fable. 7.
You must worship fasting,
Frag. Nat. III. 31.
You must listen long. Frag. Nat. III. 32.
Past and future must reveal
Frag. Poet. V. 32.
Sun and moon must fall amain
Frag. Poet. V. 34.
We must have clay, lime, gravel, granite-
ledge,   Hamatreya. 20.
Deed thou doest she must do,
Hermione. 69.
Now must thou be man and artist,—
Holidays. 19.
I must end my true report,
Initial Love. 81.
Why only must thy reason fail
May-Day. 175.
Must smite the chords rudely and hard,
Merlin. 10.
You must bring the throbbing heart.
Miracle. 10.
Risk or ruin he must share.
Monadnoc. 339.
The bosom thought which thou must
speak;   Nemesis. 2.
Whom the ages must obey: Poet. 80.
Not yet I sing: but I must wait,
Poet. 94.
With the fear that we must part?
Poet. 266.
Phœbus stablish must.   Politics. 14.
You must be like them if you desire
them,   Rome. 11.
They must give ear,   Saadi. 29.
To distant men, who must go there, or
die.   Seashore. 49.
She must love me till she find
Security. 5.
Must time and tide forever run?
Song of Nature. 45.

Man's spirit must dive;   Sphinx. 82.
Each snowbird chirped, each fowl must
crow;   Threnody. 105.
Must to the wastes of Nature go,—
Threnody. 131.
Was quenched, and all must doubt and
grope.   Threnody. 133.
When Duty whispers low, *Thou must,*
Voluntaries. 73.
We must not halt while fiercely speed
Walden. 43.
This must the leaves of ages strew
Wealth. 15.

Mustering
The mustering Day of Doom,
Peter. 26.

Mutable
He is wilful, mutable,
Initial Love. 88.
But of mutable mood,—   Nature. II. 2.

Mutation
The waves of mutation;   Illusions. 3.

Mute
Wild Tupper Lake; witness the mute all-
hail   Adirondacs. 310.
And Nature, the inscrutable and mute,
Adirondacs. 340.
Her last poet mute:
Channing Ode. 93.
And mute thy music's dearest tone,
Ellen. 10.
The pulse of hands will make him mute;
Initial Love. 57.
Mute orator! well skilled to plead,
Monadnoc. 403.
(In dizzy æons dim and mute
Wealth. 19.

Mutual
Adding by their mutual gage,
Merlin. 104.

My. (Partial list.)
My angel,—his name is Freedom,—
Boston Hymn. 13.
All too nimble for my treading.
Etienne. 4.
All my wrath and all my shames,
Miracle. 35.
Disgust my reason and defile my hands.
To-Day. 10.

Myriad
To myriad kinds and times one sense
Monadnoc. 381.

Myriad-handed
Speeding, the myriad-handed, his wild
work   Snow-Storm. 15.

Myriads
Hushed myriads hark in vain,
Merlin's Song. 11.
Swells hitherward, and myriads of forms
Pan. 4.
To her old leaves new myriads?
Problem. 30.

Myrrh
Rue, myrrh and cummin for the Sphinx,
Sphinx. 107.
His myrrh, and wine, and rings,
To J. W. 13.

Myrtle-beds
The seraphs frowned from myrtle-beds;
Uriel. 28.

Myself. (Partial list.)
And I uplift myself into its heaven,
               Day's Ration. 16.
I yielded myself to the perfect whole.
               Each. 51.
What then, can I love myself?
               Frag. Poet. VII. 13.
Had not these me against myself defended.
               Grace. 8.
To myself I oft recount
               Monadnoc. 94.
I trim myself to the storm of time,
               Terminus. 34.

Mysteries
Culture and libraries, mysteries of skill,
               Adirondacs. 323.
Mysteries of color daily laid
               Monadnoc. 60.
The mysteries of Nature's heart;
               Threnody. 205.
[If Thought unlock her mysteries,
               Walden. 29.

Mysterious
Of thought in their mysterious caves
               Poet. 276.

Mystery
There was never mystery   Apology. 13.
Saying, Sweetheart! the old mystery remains,—
               Flute. 3.
Who could the mystery expound
               Frag. Nat. VI. 2.
Nine times folded in mystery:
               Nature. Mot. 8.
The mystery of life,   Robbins Hymn. 10.
Stars taunt us by a mystery
               World-Soul. 47

Mystic
Some mystic hint accosts the vigilant,
And strangers to the mystic beast and
  bird,   Blight. 31.
By mystic wiles   Cupido. 9.
What mystic fruit his acres yield
               Dirge. 11.
The bard and mystic held me for their
  own,   Frag. Life. XXX. 1.
On its mystic tongue,   Harp. 51.
Speaks not of self that mystic tone,
               Harp. 67.
A mystic and a cabalist,—
               Initial Love. 61.
In its mystic springs.   Merlin. 8.
And the mystic seasons' dance;
               Monadnoc. 63.
What mystic fruit his acres yield
               Peter. 3.
The mystic gulf from God to man?
               Threnody. 186.
If thou wouldst know the mystic song
               Woodnotes. II. 98.
Draw, if thou canst, the mystic line
               Worship. 21.

Nadir's
Bird that from the nadir's floor
               Merlin. 63.

Nail
Nail the wild star to its track
               Threnody. 240.

Nakedly
Dealing purely and nakedly,—
               Frag. Life. XXVII. 11.

Name
And other Titans without muse or name.
               Adirondacs. 11.
My angel,—his name is Freedom,—
               Boston Hymn. 13.
With Freedom's image and name.
               Boston Hymn. 76.
And love without a name.
               Celestial Love. 5.
Nor whether your name is base or brave:
               Destiny. 40.
They love, but name not love.
               II Eros. 5.
Omnipresent without name;—
               Experience. 11.
His teeth and bones to buy a name,
               Fame. 10.
Name not lightly to be said,
               Freedom. 7.
That the maids and boys might name
  him.   Initial Love. 14.
The rocks uphold thy name engraved,
               Lines. 12.
How long the power to give them name
               Merops. 3.
Well known, but loving not a name,
               Monadnoc. 29.
Yet, in the name of Godhead, I
               Nun. 3.
Never heard thy weary name;   Nun. 46.
Threw to each fact a tuneful name.
               Poet. 8.
Insert a leaf, or forge a name,
               Past. 19.
Said, "Who taught thee me to name?
               Sphinx. 110.
In both I read thy name.
               Thine Eyes. 12.
So the gentle poet's name   Una. 21.

Named
Whose unauthenticated waves we named
               Adirondacs. 131.
Hast thou named all the birds without a
  gun?   Forbearance. 1.
Not to be named:
               Frag. Life. XXXIII. 3.
And feats achieve before they're named.
               Nature. I. 21.

Name's
Saying, "T is mine, my children's and my
  name's.   Hamatreya. 5.

Names
Whom earlier we had chid with spiteful
  names.   Adirondacs. 170.
And all their botany is Latin names.
               Blight. 22.
Preferring things to names, for these
  were men,   Blight. 26.
Names from awful childhood heard
               Daemonic Love. 7.
Nay, God is witness, gave the names.
               Miracle. 36.
Nor Time's snows hide the names he
  set,   Poet. 11.
Old mouldy men and books and names
  and lands   To-Day. 9.

Naphtha
Flowed with naphtha fiery sweet;
Celestial Love. 16.

Napoleon
Deems not that great Napoleon.
Each. 6.
Proved Napoleon great,   Politics. 6.

Narrow
So is man's narrow path
Daemonic Love. 60.
In his vision's narrow walls
Day by Day. 12.
To find the narrow way.
Robbins Hymn. 24.
Thou in thy narrow banks are pent:
Two Rivers. 5.
Nor perches in a narrow place;
Voluntaries. 36.

Narrowing
And hems in life with narrowing fence.
Titmouse. 16.

Nathless
Nathless we read your fortunes true;
Romany. 26.

Nation's
The temple of a nation's vows.
Frag. Life. XXII. 2.

Nations
To draw the nations out of doors.
Frag. Nat. XIII. 2.
Welcome back, you little nations,
Frag. Nat. XXIII. 7.
Bards to say what nations need;
Frag. Poet. XII. 2.
Shepherds are thankful and nations gay.
Merlin's Song. 34.
Could not the nations rebaptize,
Poet. 10.
The litanies of nations came,
Problem. 15.
The exodus of nations: I disperse
Seashore. 39.
Bards to speak what nations need;
Solution. 26.
The fault that boys and nations soonest
mend.   To-day. 18.

Native
That sweeps my native shore.   Bell. 16.
But, to his native centre fast, Culture. 9.
Seek him in his native town, Una. 23.

Natural
And nothing thrives to reach its natural
term;   Blight. 52.
A minstrel of the natural year,
Woodnotes. I. 31.

Nature
So fast will Nature acclimate her sons,
Adirondacs. 54.
All dressed, like Nature, fit for her own
ends,   Adirondacs. 71.
So Nature shed all beauty lavishly
Adirondacs. 151.
Judge with what sweet surprises Nature
spoke   Adirondacs. 198.
And Nature, the inscrutable and mute,
Adirondacs. 340.
Seeing Nature go astern.   Alphonso. 2.
Think nature barely serves for one;
Alphonso. 36.
Folding Nature in its deeps,
Celestial Love. 49.

Nature is the bond of both:
Celestial Love. 86.
Nature centres into balls,   Circles. 1.
Bid Time and Nature gently spare
C. Hymn. 15.
And all that Nature made thy own,
Compensation. II. 25.
And dress up Nature in your favor.
Destiny. 44.
They treated Nature as they would.
Dirge. 32.
Him by the hand dear Nature took,
Experience. 17.
Dearest Nature, strong and kind,
Experience. 18.
O what would Nature say?
Frag. Nat. III. 8.
For Nature, true and like in every place,
Frag. Nat. IV. 1.
Yet Nature will not be in full possessed,
Frag. Nat. V. 8.
But Nature whistled with all her winds,
Frag. Nat. XXXV. 1.
Holding Nature to her cause.
Frag. Poet. V. 12.
A good in Nature not allowed
Frag. Poet. VII. 15.
That he caught Nature in his snares.
Guy. 32.
These syllables that Nature spoke,
Harp. 95.
How Nature to the soul is moored,
Harp. 104.
Loves nature like a hornèd cow,
Initial Love. 100.
As unrepenting Nature leaves
In Memoriam. 95.
Of Nature in thy Spanish isle
In Memoriam. 106.
Thyself thro' Nature to diffuse?
Lines. 2.
Every nook of Nature through:
Love and Thought. 6.
When Nature falters, fain would zeal
May-Day. 157.
And fainting Nature at her need
May-Day. 336.
If Nature give me joy again,
May-Day. 370.
Extremes of nature reconciled,—
Merlin. 52.
Balance-loving Nature   Merlin. 79.
Nature, the supplement of man,
Miracle. 19.
Boon Nature to his poorest shed
Monadnoc. 70.
And what obedient Nature can;—
Monadnoc. 88.
And think how Nature in these towers
Monadnoc. 98.
In the glad home plain-dealing Nature
gave.   Musketaquid. 67.
Canst thou, thy pride forgot, like Nature
pass   Musketaquid. 78.
Nature, hating art and pains,
Nature. I. 5.
For Nature listens in the rose
Nature. I. 12.
When happy stoic Nature grieves.
Nun. 12.

Nature—*Continued*

And Nature squanders on the boy her pomp,   October. 3.
Into nature again.   Ode to Beauty. 20.
Would bankrupt nature to repay.
                          Ode to Beauty. 32.
A form which Nature cast in the heroic mould   Phi. 5.
Saw the dance of Nature forward and far,   Poet. 70.
In the love which Nature fills,
                               Poet. 145.
Giddy with motion Nature reels,
                               Poet. 172.
Thanked Nature for each stroke she dealt;   Poet. 209.
Out from the heart of nature rolled
                               Problem. 13.
And Nature gladly gave them place,
                               Problem. 41.
Boon Nature yields each day a brag which we now first behold,
                          Quat. Nature. 1.
To Nature, through her kingdoms ample,
                               Rhea. 65.
Oh, call not Nature dumb;   River. 21.
Lurketh Nature veritable;   Saadi. 130.
To the height of mighty Nature,
                               Saadi. 172.
If Nature hold another heart
                             Security. 9.
Moulding Nature at his will,
                             Solution. 29.
The Lethe of Nature   Sphinx. 77.
So take thy quest through nature,
                             Sphinx. 117.
Nature, who lost, cannot remake him;
                             Threnody. 27.
Nature, Fate, men, him seek in vain.
                             Threnody. 29.
Night came, and Nature had not thee;
                             Threnody. 102.
Must to the wastes of Nature go,—
                             Threnody. 131.
Perchance not he but Nature ailed,
                             Threnody. 138.
When frail Nature can no more,
                             Threnody. 234.
Whose streams through Nature circling go?   Threnody. 239.
And Nature have allowed   To J. W. 8.
Through years, through men, through Nature fleet,   Two Rivers. 11.
'Line in nature is not found;   Uriel. 21.
And live with living nature, a pure re-joicing thing.   *Violet. 12.
Nature poureth into nature   Visit. 13.
The sires of Nature, hide.
                          Waldeinsamkeit. 36.
And wary Nature knows her own
                                Walk. 2.
Which bind the strengths of Nature wild
                              Wealth. 48.
Why Nature loves the number five,
                          Woodnotes. I. 22.
It seemed that Nature could not raise
                          Woodnotes. I. 36.
But all her shows did Nature yield,
                          Woodnotes. I. 52.
Through these green tents, by eldest Nature dressed,   Woodnotes. I. 80.

For Nature ever faithful is
                          Woodnotes. I. 137.
Him Nature giveth for defence
                          Woodnotes. II. 75.
And solid nature to a dream.
                          Woodnotes. II. 115.
Whence the fair flock of Nature sprang.
                          Woodnotes. II. 125.
For Nature beats in perfect tune,
                          Woodnotes. II. 164.
And Nature has miscarried wholly
                          Woodnotes. II. 215.
Blessed Nature so to see.
                          Woodnotes. II. 218.
With the next a special nature;
                          Woodnotes. II. 290.
And be sure the all-loving Nature
                           World-Soul. 35.
By fate, not option, frugal Nature gave
                           Xenophanes. 1.
And universal Nature, through her vast
                           Xenophanes. 17.

Nature's

Reason in Nature's lotus drenched,
                              Bacchus. 56.
In the snares of Nature's dance;
                          Daemonic Love. 29.
Meek Nature's secret still untold.
                          Frag. Nat. VI. 8.
Gems in Nature's cabinet;
                          Frag. Nat. XXIII. 4.
Play not in Nature's lawful web,
                              Garden. 22.
Knows Nature's rarest moods, Harp. 13.
And chance-dropped hints from Nature's sphere   Initial Love. 72.
Best gems of Nature's cabinet,
                             May-Day. 394.
Masks the might of Nature's king,
                             May-Day. 458.
Amid great Nature's halls   Mountain. 7.
Of Nature's child the common fate.
                             Mountain. 21.
Throb thine with Nature's throbbing breast,   Nature. Mot. 11.
Nature's funeral high and dim,—
                                Nun. 20.
'Is this dear Nature's manly pride?
                               Poet. 218.
On Nature's wheels there is no rust;
                               Poet. 297.
But Nature's heir,—if I repine,
                             Threnody. 127.
Nature's sweet marvel undefiled,
                             Threnody. 123.
O truth's and nature's costly lie!
                             Threnody. 172.
That dizen Nature's carnival,
                             Threnody. 190.
The mysteries of Nature's heart;
                             Threnody. 205.
Throb thine with Nature's throbbing breast,   Threnody. 207.
Thorough nature's operation,   Visit. 4.
He wrote on Nature's grandest brow, For Sale.   Webster, 1854. 2.
Is perfect Nature's every part,
                          Woodnotes. II. 176.
There lives no man of Nature's worth
                          Woodnotes. II. 198.

Natures
May float at pleasure through all natures;
                         Bacchus. 23.
Titan-born, to hardy natures
                         May-Day. 136.
From all natures, sharp and slimy,
                         Mithridates. 10.
It through thousand natures ply;
                         Sphinx. 118.

Navigate
    See Circumnavigate.

Nay
Nay, we saluted them Auxiliaries,
                         Adirondacs. 169.
Nay, mourn not one: let him exult,
                         Adirondacs. 297.
Nay, letters found us in our paradise:
                         Adirondacs. 334.
That no god dare say him nay,
                         Initial Love. 126.
Nay, God is witness, gave the names.
                         Miracle. 36.

Near
A pause and council: then, where near the
    head   Adirondacs. 29.
Or parties scaled the near acclivities
                         Adirondacs. 129.
Far or forgot to me is near; Brahma. 5.
Unknown, albeit lying near,
                         Daemonic Love. 39.
Blaze near and far,   Daemonic Love. 51.
Unheeded Danger near him strides,
                         Daemonic Love. 87.
In sleep their jubilant troop is near,—
                         Forerunners. 29.
Their near camp my spirit knows
                         Forerunners. 33.
Sit still and Truth is near:
                         Frag. Life. XXXV. 2.
And near the wolf and panther slept.
                         Frag. Poet. I. 44.
Hated mist if it come near.
                         Frag. Poet. VII. 18.
To parting soul bring grandeur near.
                         May-Day. 456.
The near bystander caught no sound,—
                         Solution. 52.
The port, well worth the cruise, is near,
                         Terminus. 39.
Flew near, with soft wing grazed my
    hand,   Titmouse. 38.
To front the fate that crouches near,—
                         Voluntaries. 16.
So near is God to man,   Voluntaries. 72.
From mountains far and valleys near
                         Walden. 13.
More near than aught thou call'st thy
    own,   Worship. 16.

Nearer
Bend nearer, faint day-moon! Yon
    thundertops,   Adirondacs. 260.
Keep me nearer, me thy hearer,
                         Humble-Bee. 9.
Sparrows far off, and nearer, April's bird,
                         Musketaquid. 15.
Onward and nearer rides the sun of May;
                         Musketaquid. 19.
In nearer arcs his journeys run,
                         Peter. 15.
And nearer stoops the moon.   Peter. 16.

Nearest
To thread by night the nearest way to
    camp?   Adirondacs. 106.
The nearest matters for a thousand days?
                         Day's Ration. 32.

Nearing
Nearing me,   Monadnoc. 216.
The nearing clouds draw down;
                         World-Soul. 58.

Neat
The neatherd serves the neat,
                         Channing Ode. 45.

Neater
The girl's foot leaves its neater print.
                         May-Day. 62.

'Neath
    See Underneath.
Which holds to home 'neath every sky,
                         In Memoriam. 82.

Neatherd
The neatherd serves the neat,
                         Channing Ode. 45.

Necessary
Supplied me necessary food;
                         Woodnotes. I. 136.

Necessity
It was her stern necessity: all things
                         Xenophanes. 5.

Neck
With this tablet on their neck,
                         Astraea. 11.
On my neck he makes his seat;
                         Park. 6.

Necks
Painted our necks, hands, ankles, with
    red bands: Adirondacs. 167.

Nectar
The nectar and ambrosia, are withheld;
                         Blight. 45.
His nectar smacks of wine.
                         Daemonic Love. 92.
Drunken with nectar,   Frag. Nat. I. 2.
I drink the nectar of the hour:—
                         Frag. Nat. XXVI. 31.
And send the nectar round;
                         May-Day. 280.
Of the nectar which thou hast.
                         Ode to Beauty. 81.
One who having nectar drank   Poet. 81.
Who drinks of Cupid's nectar cup
                         Rhea. 35.

Need
There need no vows to bind
                         Celestial Love. 83.
Need is none of forms of greeting;
                         Celestial Love. 94.
Why need I volumes, if one word suffice?
                         Day's Ration. 26.
Why need I galleries, when a pupil's
    draught   Day's Ration. 27.
Child of the omnific Need,
                         Frag. Life. XXIII. 7.
Small need have I of Turner or Daguerre,
                         Frag. Nat. IV. 8.
Bards to say what nations need;
                         Frag. Poet. XII. 2.
For what need I of book or priest.
                         Frag. Poet. XXVIII. 1.
He need not go to them, their forms
                         Manners. 7.

Need—*Continued*

And fainting Nature at her need
     May-Day. 336.
If need were, their line from Jove;
     Monadnoc. 166.
Spoils of a front none need restore,
     Monadnoc. 370.
Every maxim of dreadful Need;
     Poet. 44.
Serve it for pain and fear and need.
     Poet. 286.
Besides, you need not be alone; the soul
     Rome. 2.
Most welcome they who need him most,
     Saadi. 41.
For greater need Saadi. 43.
Bards to speak what nations need;
     Solution. 26.
Helps who for their own need are strong,
     Titmouse. 87.
What need I holier dew Walden. 25.

Needed

All are needed by each one; Each. 11.

Needful

And in the left, a gun, his needful arms.
     Adirondacs. 79.
In every needful faculty,
     Boston Hymn. 43.
The needful sinew stark as once,
     Terminus. 27.

Needle

The little needle always knows the
 North, Self-Reliance. 6.

Needless

The morrow dawned with needless glow;
     Threnody. 104.

Needs

Food which needs no transmuting,
     Bacchus. 32.
The needs of the first sight absorb my
 blood, Day's Ration. 17.
Than my few needs exhaust, and bids me
 read Frag. Nat. V. 6.
Needs no amulets nor rings. Guy. 4.
Only by needs and loves of mine;
     Poet. 234.

Ne'er

Your ne'er averted glance Poet. 242.

Negro-holder

The jackals of the negro-holder.
     Channing Ode. 23.

Neighboring

Tides that should warm each neighboring
 life Rubies. 7.

Neighbor's

Thy life to thy neighbor's creed has lent.
     Each. 10.

Neither (Partial list.)

Alas! that neither bonds nor vows
     Amulet. 9.
Which neither halts nor shakes.
     Boston Hymn. 84.
Neither can you crack a nut.' Fable. 19.
On the first, neither balm nor physician
 can save, On Two Days. 3.

Nemesis

And Nemesis, Merlin. 117.
Nemesis will have her dues,
     Nemesis. 14.

Nerve

To hit the nerve of feebler sight.
     Uriel. 42.
Who shall nerve heroic boys
     Voluntaries. 61.

Nervèd

Nervèd leaf of hellebore,
     Frag. Nat. II. 22.

Nerveless

Inconstant heat and nerveless reins,—
     Terminus. 30.

Nerves

 See Unnerves.
Their dust, pervaded by the nerves of
 God, Pan. 6.
He shoots his thought, by hidden nerves,
     World-Soul. 75.

Nervous

On the nervous brain of man,
     Frag. Nat. I. 14.

Nest

I brought him home, in his nest, at even;
     Each. 15.
Her nest beside the snow-drift weaves,
     May-Day. 171.
I know each nest and web-worm's tent,
     Miracle. 3.
Know'st thou what wove yon woodbird's
 nest Problem. 25.
Foully warking in his nest? Riches. 2.
No, but a nest of bending reeds,
     Threnody. 274.
Crowds every egg out of the nest,
     Unity. 5.
Carrier-doves to nest. Walden. 4.

Nestle

Freely nestle in our roof,
     Frag. Nat. XXIII. 11.
Nestle in hedge, or barn, or roof,
     May-Day. 400.
Nestle warm the highland people,
     Monadnoc. 130.

Nestles

Vice nestles in your chambers,
     World-Soul. 11

Nestor

Where yon wedged line the Nestor leads,
     May-Day. 23.

Net

 See Scoop-net.
With a net of shining haze
     Humble-Bee. 21.

Network

Composed the network of his throne;
     Woodnotes. I. 107.

Neutral

Shoots across the neutral Dark.
     II Compensation. 14.

Nevada

Nevada! coin thy golden crags
     Boston Hymn. 75.

Never

"Chronic dyspepsia never came from
 eating Adirondacs. 185.
And, without Jove, the good had never
 been. Adirondacs. 291.
Never did sculptor's dream unfold
     Angelo. 1.
There was never mystery Apology. 13.
Was never secret history Apology. 15.

Bring me wine, but wine which never
grew   Bacchus. 1.
Was never form and never face
                            Beauty. 1.
Or union never more again.
                            Boston. 36.
But for tribute never a cent.'
                            Boston. 75.
O bounteous seas that never fail!
                            Boston. 86.
That never faltered from the right.
                            Boston. 91.
I will have never a noble,
                        Boston Hymn. 29.
Is there never a retroscope mirror
                            Cosmos. 13.
With bandaged eyes he never errs,
                            Cupido. 3.
He will never be gainsaid,—
                        Daemonic Love. 112.
Toil could never compass it;
                            Destiny. 7.
Art its height could never hit;
                            Destiny. 8.
It came never out of wit;   Destiny. 9.
Whose balsam never grew.   Dirge. 40.
He never, though he dearly loved his race,
                            Entombed. 3.
And the hermit never alone,—
                            Etienne. 20.
Whispered, 'Darling, never mind!
                        Experience. 19.
Say, was it never heard   Fame. 4.
I murmur never while   *Farewell. 52.
I could never reach their sides;
                        Forerunners. 2.
Yet I could never see their face.
                        Forerunners. 14.
Never yet could once arrive,
                        Forerunners. 24.
Feigns to sleep, sleeping never;
                        Frag. Nat. I. 10.
But never yet the man was found
                        Frag. Nat. VI. 1.
Strikes never moon or star.
                        Frag. Nat. XV. 4.
Directly never greeted me,
                        Frag. Poet. IV. 16.
It was never for the mean;   Give. 18.
And vulgar feet have never trod
                            Good-Bye. 21.
Fearless Guy had never foes,   Guy. 17.
Such have I never seen.
                        Hamatreya. 36.
Hath my insect never seen;
                        Humble-Bee. 41.
That never joy or hope shall here diffuse.
                        In Memoriam. 24.
And never poor beseeching glance
                        In Memoriam. 46.
Hints never loss or cruel break
                        In Memoriam. 107.
Thy trivial harp will never please
                            Merlin. 1.
King of sport that never shames,
                            Merlin. 40.
Which keeps the ground and never soars,
                        Monadnoc. 187.
Never balk the waiting ear.
                        Monadnoc. 192.

Which never strains its rocky beams;
                        Monadnoc. 273.
To the souls that never fell,
                        Nature. I. 17.
Of his fate is never wide.   Nemesis. 8.
The yesterday doth never smile,
                            Nun. 1.
Never heard thy weary name;   Nun. 46.
Never faster, never slower   Poet. 116.
Who never break your lawful dance
                            Poet. 157.
And though thy knees were never bent,
                            Prayer. 5.
Never from lips of cunning fell
                            Problem. 11.
The heedless world hath never lost.
                            Problem. 62.
From evils which never arrived!
                        Quat. Borrowing. 4.
Never was poet, of late or of yore,
                        Quat. Casella. 3.
From Hafiz never hides;
                        Quat. Hafiz. 2.
Forget never their command,   Rhea. 29.
His love shall never be requited.
                            Rhea. 45.
I never thought to ask, I never knew:
                        Rhodora. 14.
Never in the blaze of light   Saadi. 51.
Never, son of eastern morning,
                            Saadi. 92.
And this wise Seer within me never
errs.   Self-Reliance. 8.
I never taught it what it teaches me;
                        Self-Reliance. 9.
When France, where poet never grew,
                        Solution. 63.
Will never my winds go sleep in the
west?   Song of Nature. 46.
Will never my wheels which whirl the
sun   Song of Nature. 47.
The cup was never full.
                    Song of Nature. 72.
Not mine,—I never called thee mine,
                        Threnody. 126.
They reach no term, they never sleep,
                        Voluntaries. 115.
And fanned the dreams it never brought.
                        Woodnotes. 11. 4.
Halteth never in one shape,
                        Woodnotes. II. 272.
Who never looks behind.   World-Soul. 8.
Which we could never spell.
                        World-Soul. 48.
For Destiny never swerves
                        World-Soul. 73.
And we are never old;   World-Soul. 108.

New
    See Renew.
'A new commandment,' said the smiling
Muse,   Adakryn. 1.
but waking a new sense Adirondacs. 204.
Inviting to new knowledge, one with old.
                        Adirondacs. 205.
So in the gladness of the new event
                        Adirondacs. 335.
Unlocks new sense and loftier cheer.
                        Aeolian Harp. 17.
And make to-morrow a new morn.
                            Art. 12.

New—*Continued*

New flowerets bring, new prayers uplift,
                    Celestial Love. 4.
A new genesis were here.   Circles. 6.
If a new Muse draw me with splendid
    ray,   Day's Ration. 15.
Combined a new temperament.
                    Frag. Life. XXIX. 6.
Behold the new majestic birth!
                    Frag. Nat. XXVI. 16.
And dew-bent violets, fresh and new,
                    Frag. Nat. XXVI. 36.
In new landscapes of romance,
                    May-Day. 27.
Life out of death, new out of old,
                    May-Day. 203.
As if Time brought a new relay
                    May-Day. 301.
So only new griefs are consoled
                    May-Day. 365.
By new delights, as old by old,
                    May-Day. 366.
When our life was new.   May-Day. 409.
Chemist to vamp old worlds with new,
                    May-Day. 445.
New tint the plumage of the birds,
                    May-Day. 447.
To see strange forests and new snow,
                    Monadnoc. 206.
Is sketched and dyed, each with a new
    design,   Naples. 7.
To animate new millions, and exhale
                    Pan. 11.
At the new vision gape and jeer.
                    Poet. 22.
To read new landscapes and old skies;
                    Poet. 53.
And rived the dark like a new day!
                    Poet. 56.
The new day lowers, and equal odds
                    Poet. 179.
To her old leaves new myriads?
                    Problem. 30.
And trains us on to slight the new, as
    if it were the old: Quat. Nature. 2.
New worlds to find in pinnace frail.
                    Quat. Poet. I. 4.
Falls, in turn, a new degree.   Rhea. 40.
To carry man to new degrees   Rhea. 68.
And learn of love a new degree.
                    Security. 12.
Unlock doors of new delight;
                    Solution. 21.
My oldest force is good as new,
                    Song of Nature. 82.
Once found,—for new heavens
                    Sphinx. 87.
Taught me new lessons in the lore of
    life.   Summons. 17.
Hast thou forgot me in a new delight?
                    Threnody. 35.
And I will write our annals new,
                    Titmouse. 100.
and hate the new.   To-Day. 12.
And every new compound   Visit. 6.
Of sorrows new and old!
                    Voluntaries. 78.
New slaves fulfilled the poet's dream,
                    Wealth. 40.
into new forms   Woodnotes. II. 274.

New-bathed

New-bathed, new-trimmed, on healthy
    wing,   Poet. 25.

New-born

Mind wakes a new-born giant from her
    sleep.   Adirondacs. 327.
And the new-born tendrils twine,
                    May-Day. 88.
The spousals of the new-born year.
                    May-Day. 270.
New-born, we are melting
                    Ode to Beauty. 19.
So, in the new-born millions,
                    Promise. 5.

New-delivered

Of the new-delivered streams,
                    May-Day. 229.

New England

We poor New England flowers.
                    Ellen South. 24.
See New England underspread,
                    Monadnoc. 280.

New England's

To dim New England's shore;
                    *Farewell. 47.

Newer

Whereby to model newer races,
                    Rhea. 66.
In newer days of war and trade,
                    Solution. 59.

Newest

Outlive the newest stars.   House. 24.
Newest knowledge, fiery thought,
                    Miracle. 13.
Half piled or prostrate; and my newest
    slab   Seashore. 16.

New-face

New-face or finish what is packed,
                    Past. 20.

New-fallen

built of new-fallen trees,
                    Musketaquid. 30.

New-found

Greet the glad miracle. Thought's new-
    found path   Adirondacs. 243.

New Hampshire

The God who made New Hampshire
                    Channing Ode. 24.
To the uplands of New Hampshire,
                    World-Soul. 3.

New-trimmed

New-bathed, new-trimmed, on healthy
    wing,   Poet. 25.

New York

Penn's town, New York and Baltimore,
                    Boston. 47.

News

Big with great news, and shouted the
    report   Adirondacs. 237.
Bad news from George on the English
    throne;   Boston. 63.

Next

Next morn, we swept with oars the
    Saranac,   Adirondacs. 7.
Next his heart the fireside band
                    Daemonic Love. 5.
Southwind is my next of blood;
                    Hermione. 50.
The next into the farthest brings,
                    May-Day. 80.

In the next field is air more mild,
May-Day. 102.
For the next ages, men of mould
Monadnoc. 155.
The next unto the farthest brings;
Nature. Mot. 2.
Shines the last age, the next with hope
is seen, Quat. Heri. 1.
In the next age, are flaming swords.
Solution. 58.
With the next a special nature;
Woodnotes. II. 290.

Niche
Or to his niche in the apple-tree.
May-Day. 391.

Nigh
Draws angels nigh to dwell with thee,
Freedom. 19.
Nigh persuading gods to err!
Ode to Beauty. 22.
So nigh is grandeur to our dust,
Voluntaries. 71.

Night
See Midnight.
Where the deer feeds at night, the teal
by day, Adirondacs. 20.
His brief toilette: at night, or in the
rain, Adirondacs. 76.
To thread by night the nearest way to
camp? Adirondacs. 106.
And as through dreams in watches of the
night, Adirondacs. 201.
And turns the woe of Night,
Bacchus. 10.
And night and day, ocean and continent,
Blight. 34.
Pole-star of light in Europe's night,
Boston. 90.
The word of the Lord by night
Boston Hymn. 1.
Pied with morning and with night.
II Compensation. 2.
And the lone seaman all the night
Daemonic Love. 54.
That broke the gloom of night!
*Farewell. 4.
From strength to strength, and for night
brings day; Frag. Life. XXXI. 2.
Who climb each night the ancient sky,
Frag. Nat. VIII. 6.
In black acres of the night,
Frag. Nat. XVIII. 3.
Received the fair inscriptions of the
night; Frag. Nat. XXVII. 2.
Attempered to the night and day,
Guy. 2.
Knows the law of Night and Day,
Harp. 22.
Frost and sun and eldest night,
Hermione. 62.
Yet I think on them in the silent night,
I Bear. 9.
Or a day without night. *Lines. 16.
Every night alighting down
May-Day. 26.
Mix polar night with tropic glow,
May-Day. 127.
They were Night and Day, and Day and
Night, May-Day. 310.

That Night or Day, that Love or Crime,
Park. 15.
He takes no mark of night or day,
Poet. 83.
Again by night the poet went
Poet. 225.
Day and night their turn observe,
Poet. 273.
By love behold the sun at night.
Poet. 288.
To bless that creature day and night;
Rhea. 48.
Far in the North, where polar night
Solution. 43.
Mine are the night and morning,
Song of Nature. 1.
Made one of day and one of night
Song of Nature. 63.
Night veileth the morning,
Sphinx. 39.
Night came, and Nature had not thee;
Threnody. 102.
Night and Day were tampered with,
Unity. 8.
Where darkness found him he lay glad
at night; Woodnotes. I. 82.
Was pole-star when the night was dark;
Woodnotes. I. 134.
When the night and morning lie,
Woodnotes. I. 140.
Is the inn where he lodges for a night.
Woodnotes. II. 300.

Night-dreams
Night-dreams trace on Memory's wall
Quat. Memory. 1.

Night-hunter
In the boat's bows, a silent night-hunter
Adirondacs. 118.

Nightingale
And thou, heart-warming nightingale!
Exile. 11.

Nightly
The spiritual stars rise nightly, shedding
down Adirondacs. 222.
Wisp and meteor nightly falling,
Frag. Nat. XVI. 1.
For Saadi's nightly stars did burn
Saadi. 84.
Let the starred shade that nightly falls
Woodnotes. II. 225.

Night's
That wood-bird sang my last night's
dream, Miracle. 28.
Into the winter night's extinguished
mood? Musketaquid. 79.

Nights
Rippling roses in northern nights,
Frag. Poet. I. 40.
Through tempering nights and flashing
days, Monadnoc. 212.

Night-work
Built in an age, the mad wind's night-
work, Snow-Storm. 27.

Nile
And Nile substructs her granite base,—
Solution. 10.
Tented Tartary, columned Nile,—
Solution. 11.
One over against the mouths of Nile,
Song of Nature. 67.

Niles
Say, Seigniors, are the old Niles dry,
           Alphonso. 31.

Nimble
Goes light the nimble zephyr;
           Ellen South. 10.
All too nimble for my treading.
           Etienne. 4.
Yet on the nimble air benign
           Voluntaries. 67.

Nimbleness
And teach his nimbleness to earn his
    wage,   Adirondacs. 268.

Nimbler
Speed nimbler messages,
           Voluntaries. 68.

Nine
My counsel is, kill nine in ten,
           Alphonso. 68.
Add their nine lives to this cat;
           Alphonso. 71.
Stuff their nine brains in one hat;
           Alphonso. 72.
Nine times folded in mystery:
           Nature. Mot. 8.
When the Muses nine   Politics. 15.

Nineveh
Lo! here is Rome and Nineveh and
    Thebes,   Seashore. 14.

Ninth
Upward the ninth heaven thrilled and
    moved   Waterfall. 19.

No (Partial list.)
O no, not we! Witness the shout that
    shook   Adirondacs. 309.
No tidings since it came.   Amulet. 4.
No stouter fence, no steeper wall!
           Boston. 62.
I suffer them no more;
           Boston Hymn. 6.
There are no such hearts on earth.
           Dirge. 52.
There is no architect   House. 1.
No sire survive, no son succeed!
           Monadnoc. 124.
In heaven no star, on earth no spark,—
           Saadi. 132.
And crouched no more in stone;
           Sphinx. 122.
No, but a nest of bending reeds,
           Threnody. 274.

Nobility
For this is Love's nobility,—
           Celestial Love. 124.
Nobility more nobly to repay?
           Forbearance. 7.

Noble
The noble craftsman we promote,
           Boston. 31.
To the poor a noble brother,
           Boston. 114.
I will have never a noble,
           Boston Hymn. 29.
Their noble meanings are their pawns.
           Celestial Love. 88.
Her last noble is ruined,
           Channing Ode. 92.
My good, my noble, in their prime,
           Dirge. 25.

Around the man who seeks a noble end,
           Frag. Life. III. 1.
I took the friendly noble by the hand,
           Frag. Life. XXX. 3.
And burned in noble hearts proverb and
    prophecy.   Phi. 22.
Upon him noble eyes did rest,
           Poet. 196.
And simple maids and noble youth
           Saadi. 39.
Who is noble and free?—   Sphinx. 94.
To works as noble led thee on.
           Threnody. 79.
Some figure of noble guise,—
           World-Soul. 26.

Nobleness
'T is nobleness to serve;
           Boston Hymn. 50.
Me too thy nobleness has taught
           Friendship. 17.

Nobler
All things through thee take nobler
    form,   Friendship. 13.
Strong crab with nobler blood did fill;
           Guy. 42.
Obey the nobler impulse; that is Rome:
           Rome. 16.
I would he were nobler   Sphinx. 95.
Come weave with mine a nobler rhyme.
           Woodnotes. II. 139.

Noblest
To the noblest, or to none.
           Friendship. Trans. 4.
Thou born for noblest life,
           In Memoriam. 28.

Nobly
Nobility more nobly to repay?
           Forbearance. 7.

Nobody
What he knows nobody wants.
           Woodnotes. I. 12.

Nocturnal
From a nocturnal root,   Bacchus. 7.
Sent a nocturnal fragrance; harlot flies
           Frag. Nat. XXVII. 8.

Nod
I spurn the Past, my mind disdains its
    nod,   To-Day. 13.

Nodding
Or harebell nodding in the gorge of falls.
           Adirondacs. 145.
From nodding pole and belting zone.
           Beauty. 12.
Loved harebells nodding on a rock,
           Frag. Poet. I. 21.

Noisome
But the poor, unsightly, noisome things
           Each. 26.

Noisy
You shall not know me in the noisy
    street,   Frag. Life. XV. 2.
But when the noisy scorn was past,
           Poet. 23.

None
He heard a voice none else could hear
           Beauty. 13.
To plant and eat be none afraid.
           Boston. 12.
To plant and eat be none afraid.
           Boston. 54.

None shall rule but the humble,
Boston Hymn. 27.
And none but Toil shall have.
Boston Hymn. 28.
Need is none of forms of greeting;
Celestial Love. 94.
Is none so high, so mean is none,
Celestial Love. 111.
When other men have none?
I Compensation. 2.
None from its stock that vine can reave.
II Compensation. 18.
None can bewilder;
Daemonic Love. 71.
None shall ask thee what thou doest,
Destiny. 22.
A gentle wife, but fairy none.
Each. 36.
Be loved by few; be feared by none;
Fame. 15.
Is to live well with who has none.
Frag. Life. XI. 2.
None credits him till he have shown
Frag. Poet. VI. 3.
To the noblest, or to none.
Friendship. Trans. 4.
And every god,—none did refuse;
Garden. 26.
Can adequately utter none   Harp. 97.
None will now find Cupid latent
Initial Love. 9.
And to speak my thought if none forbids
May-Day. 326.
Is to live well with who has none.
Merlin's Song. 40.
Eyes that frame cities where none be,
Monadnoc. 108.
None save dappling shadows climb,
Monadnoc. 202.
None so backward in the troop,
Monadnoc. 251.
Spoils of a front none need restore,
Monadnoc. 370.
Yet envies none, none are unenviable.'
Musketaquid. 84.
None can reënter there,—   Past. 14.
With staring eye that seeth none,
Poet. 87.
Which none can stay, and none accelerate.'
Poet. 125.
Where equal means are none.'
Poet. 248.
Where way is none, 't will creep and
wind   Quat. Love. 3.
Albeit scorned as none was scorned,
Rhea. 62.
Adorn her as was none adorned.
Rhea. 63.
Me false to mine dare whisper none,—
Romany. 15.
Of that be none afraid.   September. 12.
But their heart abode with none.
Threnody. 157.
Wilt thou transfix and make it none?
Threnody. 246.
Why wilt thou live when none around
reflects thy pensive ray?   *Violet. 5.
And pulse, and sound, and light was
none;   Woodnotes. II. 267.

And his viceroy is none,—
World-Soul. 82.

Nook
The rocky nook with hilltops three
Boston. 1.
In the waste one nook is his;
Day by Day. 10.
A secret nook in a pleasant land,
Good-Bye. 17.
And twilight nook,   Hermione. 54.
Every nook of Nature through:
Love and Thought. 6.
To me that spectral nook appeared
Peter. 25.
Every nook is wide;   Quat. Hush. 2.
Spreading its leafless blooms in a damp
nook,   Rhodora. 3.
Down in yon watery nook,
Waldeinsamkeit. 33.

Nooks
Into rude and homely nooks,
May-Day. 355.

Noon
See Afternoon.
And in the twilight of the forest noon
Adirondacs. 32.
At morn or noon, the guide rows bare-
headed: Adirondacs. 74.
Or, bathers, diving from the rock at
noon;   Adirondacs. 112.
Bring the moonlight into noon   Art. 3.
And, in its highest noon and wantonness,
Blight. 56.
The sexton, tolling his bell at noon,
Each. 5.
It dives into noon,   Give. 12.
Voyager of light and noon;
Humble-Bee. 15.
Pale at overflowing noon   Saadi. 53.

Noonday
Whose deeps, till beams of noonday
break,   May-Day. 18.

Noontide
Than noontide twilights which snow
makes   Titmouse. 73.

Noose
The Gordian noose was still untied.
Frag. Nat. VI. 6.

Nor (Partial list.)
Nor Boccace in Decameron.
Adirondacs. Motto. 4.
Nor wine nor brains perpetual pump.
Alphonso. 62.
Nor hymn, nor prayer, nor church.
Bohemian. 12.
From my great arteries,—nor less, nor
more.'   Day's Ration. 5.
Nor not receive his ample dues.
Dues. 16.
He nor repents nor grieves,
In Memoriam. 93.
Nor mount, nor dive; all good things
keep   Saadi. 145.
Nor scour the seas, nor sift mankind,
Saadi. 155.
Nor perches in a narrow place;
Voluntaries. 36.

North
determine the true north,
Adirondacs. 104.

North —*Continued*

North from Camp Maple,
                    Adirondacs. 109.
O North! give him beauty for rags,
                    Boston Hymn. 73.
Come, East and West and North,
                    Boston Hymn. 81.
Steering north with raucous cry
                    May-Day. 24.
Stepping daily onward north
                    May-Day. 306.
Lo! the south answers to the north;
                    Monadnoc. 15.
With my north wind chill his blood;
                    Monadnoc. 341.
The little needle always knows the North,
                    Self-Reliance. 6.
Come see the north wind's masonry.
                    Snow-Storm. 10.
Far in the North, where polar night
                    Solution. 43.
East, west, north, south, are his domain.
                    Titmouse. 8.
And I affirm, the spacious North
                    Titmouse. 58.
To feed the North from tropic trees;
                    Wealth. 37.
It may blow north, it still is warm;
                    Woodnotes. I. 100.

Northern

Rippling roses in northern nights,
                    Frag. Poet. I. 40.
As Southern wrath to Northern right
                    May-Day. 138.
Climbing the northern zones,
                    May-Day. 253.
With its stars of northern fire,
                    Monadnoc. 217.
Which blasts of Northern mountains
hymn,   Nun. 19.
Pale Northern girls! you scorn our
race;   Romany. 5.
To northern lakes fly wind-borne ducks,
                    Saadi. 5.
In northern Gaul my dauntless bird,
                    Titmouse. 96.
Hid from men of Northern brain,
                    Voluntaries. 52.
Which breathes his sweet fame through
the northern bowers.
                    Woodnotes. I. 71.

Northland

The northland from the south?
                    Channing Ode. 39.

Northman

Long she loved the Northman well;
                    Voluntaries. 43.

Northward

Northward the length of Follansbee we
rowed,   Adirondacs. 26.
Northward he went to the snowy hills,
                    Frag. Poet. I. 9.
Broad northward o'er the land,
                    May-Day. 248.
Driving, darting northward free,
                    May-Day. 388.

Northwestern

When the fierce northwestern blast
                    Humble-Bee. 58.

North-wind

Without the baffled North-wind calls.
                    May-Day. 57.
Fronts the north-wind in waistcoat gray,
                    Titmouse. 46.

Norway

Three conifers, white, pitch and Norway
pine,   Adirondacs. 40.

Not (Partial list.)

See Cannot.
But, on the second day, we heed them
not,   Adirondacs. 168.
The fortunate star that rose on us sank
not;   Adirondacs. 337.
Love not the flower they pluck, and
know it not,   Blight. 21.
Not reconciled,—   Channing Ode. 53.
Well that we loved, woe had we not,
                    Ellen. 8.
But the Spirit said, 'Not so;
                    Freedom. 5.
Mine, not yours.   Hamatreya. 29.
Pluck it now! In vain,—thou canst not;
                    Holidays. 5.
Though I comprehend it not,
                    Initial Love. 24.
The whited desert knew me not,
                    May-Day. 41.
The world rolls round,—mistrust it not,—
                    May-Day. 177.
Not ancestors,   Merlin. 110.
Who is the captain he knows not,
                    Monadnoc. 337.
Port or pilot trows not,—
                    Monadnoc. 338.
'O gentle Saadi, listen not,   Saadi. 87.
What men chatter know I not.
                    Song of Seyd. 34.
At my work I ramble not;   Una. 6.
Though beloved, I miss her not;
                    Una. 10.
But the curtain doth not rise,
                    Woodnotes. II. 214.
Change I may, but I pass not.
                    Woodnotes. II. 255.

Note

I thought the sparrow's note from
heaven,   Each. 13.
Of her faults I take no note,
                    Frag. Life. XVI. 5.
Who but loved the wind-harp's note?
                    Harp. 49.
In as far as I took note,
                    Initial Love. 83.
And I shall hear my bluebird's note,
                    May-Day. 180.
The little bird remembereth his note,
                    Self-Reliance. 7.
Chic-chic-a-dee-dee! saucy note
                    Titmouse. 27.
And shock thy weak ear with a note
                    Woodnotes. II. 122.
Repeats one note.   Xenophanes. 19.

Notes

From a log cabin stream Beethoven's
notes   Adirondacs. 313.
Shall lift its notes once more,   Bell. 14.

Nothing

Nothing was ploughed,
                    Adirondacs. 67.

Essaying nothing she cannot perform.
Adirondacs. 72.

Waved the scoop-net, and nothing came amiss; Adirondacs. 138.

And nothing thrives to reach its natural term; Blight. 52.

Nothing is fair or good alone.
Each. 12.

Asks nothing, but does all receive.
Frag. Life. XVII. 3.

Swainish, coarse and nothing worth:
Frag. Poet. XI. 14.

Nothing refuse. Give. 6.

From the twins is nothing hidden,
Love and Thought. 3.

They do her bidding, nothing loath.
Nature. II. 19.

Seek nothing,—Fortune seeketh thee.
Saadi. 144.

My wreath shall nothing miss.
Song of Nature. 16.

And nothing jostle or displace,
Woodnotes. II. 2.

Bears nothing on its beam.
World-Soul. 16.

Nothings
And phantoms and nothings
Illusions. 29.

Nought
Asks nought his brother cannot give;
Frag. Life. XVII. 2.

To the pair is nought forbidden;
Love and Thought. 4.

So fanciful, so savage, nought cares he
Snow-Storm. 16.

There will be nought to shelter thee when their sweet leaves are gone.
*Violet. 8.

Noun
He must to school and learn his verb and noun Adirondacs. 267.

Nourished
Born and nourished in miracles,
Poet. 3.

Nourisher
Sea full of food, the nourisher of kinds,
Seashore. 21.

Novel
And each with novel life his sphere
Promise. 9.

And,—fault of novel germs,—
Terminus. 21.

I choose a novel theme, a bold abuse
To-Day. 7.

Now (Partial list.)
Now soar again. Adirondacs. 208.

He sings the song, but it cheers not now,
Each. 16.

Now I live with all; Hermione. 41.

Pluck it now! In vain,—thou canst not;
Holidays. 5.

Look, here he is, unaltered, save that now River. 8.

Now follows, now flies; Sphinx. 98.

I gave thee sight—where is it now?
Threnody. 196.

Nowhere
Seems nowhere to alight: the whited air
Snow-Storm. 3.

Nowise
She who is old, but nowise feeble,
Nature. II. 5.

Numb
Amid the gladiators, halt and numb.'
Terminus. 32.

Numbed
Think me not numbed or halt with age,
Nun. 33.

Number
See Battle-number.
With the coil of rhythm and number;
Merlin. 30.

For number or proportion. Mockingly,
Snow-Storm. 17.

Why Nature loves the number five,
Woodnotes. I. 22.

Numbered
And when his hours are numbered, and the world Snow-Storm. 23.

Numbers
In numbers wild as dreams, Harp. 30.

And recount the numbers well;
Ode to Beauty. 59.

No numbers have counted my tallies,
Song of Nature. 9.

Older am I than thy numbers wot,
Woodnotes. II. 254.

Numbs
Tugs at the heart-strings, numbs the sense, Titmouse. 15.

Numerable
See Innumerable.

Numerous
Heaven's numerous hierarchy span
Threnody. 185.

Nurseries
In his rich nurseries, timely skill
Guy. 41.

Nursery
That this proud nursery could breed
Monadnoc. 76.

Nut
Neither can you crack a nut.'
Fable. 19.

Nymphs
Shun him, nymphs, on the fleet horses!
Initial Love. 102.

O

And presently the sky is changed; O world! Adirondacs. 211.

O no, not we! Witness the shout that shook Adirondacs. 309.

Your letter tells, O changing child!
Amulet. 3.

O, that were much, and I could be a part Blight. 14.

O happy town beside the sea,
Boston. 59.

O bounteous seas that never fail!
Boston. 86.

O day remembered yet! Boston. 87.

O happy port that spied the sail
Boston. 88.

O North! give him beauty for rags,
Boston Hymn. 73.

And honor, O South! for his shame;
Boston Hymn. 74.

O—*Continued*

O, what a load   Celestial Love. 63.

I found by thee, O rushing Contoocook!
    Channing Ode. 21.

O glowing friend,   Channing Ode. 37.

O Day! and is your mightiness
    Chartist. 13.

O Sun! I curse thy cruel ray:
    Chartist. 17.

O tenderly the haughty day
    Concord Ode. 1.

I cannot hear your songs, O birds,
    Cosmos. 23.

Hearest thou, O traveller,   Dirge. 43.

'O hasten;' 't is our time,
    Ellen South. 17.

'O pride of thy race!   Ellen South. 21.

'O come, then, quickly come!
    Ellen South. 33.

O fair and stately maid, whose eyes
    Eva. 1.

I know that thou, O morning wind!
    Exile. 9.

O what would Nature say?
    Frag. Nat. III. 8.

Teach me your mood, O patient stars!
    Frag. Nat. VIII. 5.

O tufted entomologist!
    Frag. Nat. XIX. 4.

O hide you sun-filled zone,
    From Hafiz. 2.

O touch thy servant's lips with power,
    Hymn. 26.

O how wise are his discourses!
    Initial Love. 104.

O then I awoke,   *Lines. 25.

Turn swiftlier round, O tardy ball!
    May-Day. 160.

O birds, your perfect virtues bring,
    May-Day. 397.

For thou, O Spring, canst renovate
    May-Day. 441.

O fair, appeasing presences!
    Merops. 6.

O, wondrous craft of plant and stone
    Monadnoc. 66.

Sink, O mountain, in the swamp!
    Monadnoc. 121.

Hide in thy skies, O soverign lamp!
    Monadnoc. 122.

O pilgrim, wandering not amiss!
    Monadnoc. 242.

O barren mound, thy plenties fill!
    Monadnoc. 378.

Who gave thee, O Beauty,
    Ode to Beauty. 1.

O what are heroes, prophets, men,
    Pan. 1.

Fill thy will, O faultless heart!
    Poet. 127.

O birds of ether without wings!
    Poet. 159.

O heavenly ships without a sail!
    Poet. 160.

O fire of fire! O best of things!
    Poet. 161.

O mariners who never fail!   Poet. 162.

O friendless Present! than thy bosom
holds.   Quat. Heri. 4.

See to thyself, O Universe!   Rhea. 72.

'O gentle Saadi, listen not,   Saadi. 87.

O, whither tend thy feet?
    Threnody. 31.

O eloquent child!   Threnody. 37.

O ostrich-like forgetfulness!
    Threnody. 116.

O loss of larger in the less!
    Threnody. 117.

O child of paradise,   Threnody. 166.

O truth's and nature's costly lie!
    Threnody. 172.

O trusted broken prophecy!
    Threnody. 173.

O richest fortune sourly crossed!
    Threnody. 174.

O Violet, like thee, how blest could I
lie down and die,   *Violet. 9.

O, well for the fortunate soul
    Voluntaries. 75.

O wise man!   Woodnotes. II. 102.

O, listen to the undersong,
    Woodnotes. II. 116.

O mortal! thy ears are stones;
    Woodnotes. II. 126.

Whence, O thou orphan and defrauded?
    Woodnotes. II. 180.

Oaf

An oaf, an accomplice,   Sphinx. 55.

Oak

Oak, cedar, maple,   Adirondacs. 38.

House in the oak:—
    Channing Ode. 28.

Answered the pine-tree and the oak,
    Frag. Nat. III. 11.

Fell the bolt on the branching oak;
    In Memoriam. 97.

Adds to oak and oxen strength,
    May-Day. 201.

Last year from yon oak or larch;
    May-Day. 386.

Maple and oak, the old Divan
    Miracle. 5.

Passing yonder oak, I heard
    Miracle. 23.

Beside his hut and shading oak,
    Poet. 140.

In groves of oak, or fanes of gold,
    Problem. 58.

Oak-boughs

And these loved banks, whose oak-
boughs bold   In Memoriam. 115.

Oaken

Or down the oaken glade,
    Waldeinsamkeit. 10.

Oak-leaf

See, every patriot oak-leaf throws
    May-Day. 113.

Oaks

Around me stood the oaks and firs;
    Each. 44.

Snow-loving pines and oaks instead;
    Garden. 6.

While oaks of pride   Frag. Nat. III. 18.

Though Adam, born when oaks were
young,   Frag. Nat. VI. 3.

When pacing through the oaks he heard
    Harp. 87.

They learned of the oaks and firs.
    Nature. II. 12.

Which tore from oaks their branches broad,   Poet. 29.
Where far oaks outstretched their arms.   September. 8.
There broad-armed oaks, the copses' maze,   Walden. 5.

Oar
A paddle in the right hand, or an oar,   Adirondacs. 78.
Their sinewy arms pull at the oar untired   Adirondacs. 89.
What make you, master, fumbling at the oar?   Adirondacs. 99.
The oar, the guide's. Dare you accept the tasks   Adirondacs. 102.
And the ripples in rhymes the oar forsake.   Woodnotes. II. 171.

Oars
Next morn, we swept with oars the Saranac,   Adirondacs. 7.
Two of our mates returning with swift oars.   Adirondacs. 234.

Oath
They give and take no pledge or oath,—   Celestial Love. 85.

Oaths
He invented oaths to swear;   Initial Love. 115.

Obedience
Power that by obedience grows,   Insight. 1.

Obedient
The deep-eyed flame, obedient water,   Frag. Life. XXIX. 2.
And what obedient Nature can;—   Monadnoc. 88.

Obeisance
And every flower made obeisance   Peter. 35.

Oberon's
King Oberon's minstrelsy.   Frag. Nat. III. 28.

Obey
Obey thy heart;   Give. 2.
Whom the ages must obey: Poet. 80.
Art might obey, but not surpass.   Problem. 46.
Obey the nobler impulse; that is Rome: Rome. 16.
Abandon all those toys with speed to obey   Summons. 23.
Obey the voice at eve obeyed at prime: Terminus. 36.
And his behest obey.   World-Soul. 88.

Obeyed
I heard, and I obeyed,—   Monadnoc. 27.
Obey the voice at eve obeyed at prime: Terminus. 36.
What god the element obeyed?   Wealth. 5.

Obeying
Obeying time, the last to own   Fate. 11.
Obeying meek the primal Cause,   Harp. 71.

Obeys
Which still obeys the mind.   Angelo. 5.
Obeys the hymn, obeys the ode.   Frag. Poet. XV. 2.
The sun obeys them and the moon.   Monadnoc. 248.

Object
To the dear object of his thought,   Frag. Life. XVII. 13.

Obliterates
With lotus wine obliterates   Daemonic Love. 13.

Oblivion
Oblivion here thy wisdom is,   Waldeinsamkeit. 45.

Obscure
The river, hill, stems, foliage are obscure,   Musketaquid. 83.

Obscurer
Or at the foresight of obscurer years?   Adirondacs. 217.

Observance
Tower of observance searching space;   Monadnoc. 83.

Observe
Day and night their turn observe,   Poet. 273.

Obstruction
Each obstruction, it unites   Daemonic Love. 83.

Obtrusive
Break not my dream, obtrusive tomb!   Harp. 124.

Occasion
Nor kind occasion without eyes;   Frag. Life. XVII. 7.
Example, custom, fear, occasion slow,—   Grace. 3.

Occult
He is versed in occult science,   Initial Love. 64.

Occupy
To occupy my place.   Fable. 11.

Ocean
And night and day, ocean and continent,   Blight. 34.
The empire of the ocean caves.   Boston. 18.
Or over the town blue ocean flows.   Boston. 105.
Will the sweet sky and ocean broad   Chartist. 15.
Mountain tall and ocean deep   Compensation. II. 3.
The moons in ocean dip,   Eros. II. 4.
Too soon by ocean tost   *Farewell. 7.
Rude ocean doth us part;   *Farewell. 34.
A river-ark on the ocean brine,   Good-Bye. 4.
The lustre of the land and ocean,   Hermione. 13.
Joy-tides swell their mimic ocean.   Initial Love. 49.
From air and ocean bring me foods,   Mithridates. 8.
Will a woman's fan the ocean smooth?   Nemesis. 9.
Moist perhaps by ocean surf,   Nun. 26.
And wishful saw the Ocean stream:—   Poet. 192.
In ocean sport the scaly herds,   Saadi. 3.
Her soul is frank as the ocean wind,   Security. 7.
Unerring to the ocean sand.   Woodnotes. I. 132.
Ocean tongues to islanders,   Woodnotes. II. 153.

Ocean *—Continued*
And the vast mass became vast ocean.
Woodnotes. II. 269.

Ocean's
He came to the green ocean's brim
Frag. Poet. I. 45.

October
October woods wherein   October. 1
October in his liberal hand.
Quat. S. H. 4.

Odd
Sex to sex, and even to odd;—
Channing Ode. 79.
Who with even matches odd, Merlin. 118.

Odds
The new day lowers, and equal odds
Poet. 179.

Ode
Life would be too wild an ode.
Frag. Nat. I. 18.
Obeys the hymn, obeys the ode.
Frag. Poet. XV. 2.

Odes
Wise Milton's odes of pensive pleasure,
Harp. 77.

Odious
To vex with odious subtlety   Saadi. 47.

Odor
In the sweet odor of her memory.
Letter. 18.

Odorous
Odorous clouds;   *Lines. 6.
He saw beneath dim aisles, in odorous
beds,   Woodnotes. I. 68.

O'er (Partial list.)
O'er your ramparts as ye lean,
Alphonso. 20.
Which, o'er passion throned sedate,
Astraea. 33.
Of honor o'er the sea, Concord Ode. 26.
Shadowlike, o'er hill and hollow;
Etienne. 2.
Is leaping o'er the sea,   *Farewell. 17.
To gaze o'er the horizon's edge,
Lines. 20.
And o'er yon hazy crest is Eden's balm-
ier spring.'   May-Day. 103.
O'er the floor of plain and flood
Monadnoc. 194.
As o'er some bolder height they speed,—
Monadnoc. 397.
O'er meadows bottomless. So, year by
year,   Musketaquid. 46.
O'er England's abbeys bends the sky,
Problem. 37.
To the vast soul that o'er him planned:
Problem. 48.
Arrives the snow, and, driving o'er the
fields,   Snow-storm. 2.
And bards o'er kings to rule;—
Song of Nature. 70.
With railways ironed o'er?—
World-Soul. 68.

O'erfills
After the master's sketch fills and o'erfills   Day's Ration. 28.

O'erhung
Which o'erhung, like a cloud, our camping fire.   Adirondacs. 47.

O'erlading
See Heart-o'erlading.

O'erlooks
O'erlooks the surging landscape's swell!
Monadnoc. 11.

O'er-mantling
O'er-mantling land and sea,
Concord Ode. 10.

Of (Partial list.)
See Whereof.
Give me of the true,—   Bacchus. 14.
Wine of wine,   Bacchus. 18.
Form of forms, and mould of statures,
Bacchus. 20.
Of care and toil,   Celestial Love. 64.
Of all wit's uses, the main one
Merlin's Song. 39.
Showed me the lore of colors and of
sounds,   Musketaquid. 60.
Of all mortals the desire,   Saadi. 10.
For out of woe and out of crime
Saadi. 70.
Of ritual, bible, or of speech;
Threnody. 198.

Off
See Far-off.
Off soundings, seamen do not suffer cold;
Adirondacs. 56.
Slipped off their pack of duties, leagues
behind,   Adirondacs. 62.
Flew off in the cloud.   *Lines. 24.
Sparrows far off, and nearer, April's bird,
Musketaquid. 15.
I cannot shake off the god;   Park. 5.
To-day slinks poorly off unmarked be-
tween: Quat. Heri. 2.
And one by one has torn off quite
Rhea. 15.
A few rods off he deems it gems and
clouds.   Seashore. 46.
Break sharply off their jolly games,
Voluntaries. 63.
Put off thy years, wash in the breeze;
Woodnotes. II. 135.
And are but one. Beheld far off, they
part   Xenophanes. 9.

Offence
Forging, through swart arms of Offence,
Spiritual Laws. 11

Offended
Soft! let not the offended muse
Monadnoc. 125.

Offer
To each they offer gifts after his will,
Days. 5.
To offer the exile cheer.   Exile. 8.
And princes offer me grace   Exile. 15.

Offered
Nor offered words till they were things,
Frag. Poet. V. 27.

Office
To supple Office, low and high;
Good-Bye. 10.
I greet my office well,   Poet. 115.

Offspring
With the offspring of the Sun;
Voluntaries. 46.

Oft
And solve and oft resolve the whole.
Alphonso. 46.

Oft pealed for him a lofty tone
                    Beauty. 11.
Oft the humble and the poor;
                    Daemonic Love. 106.
And, how oft soe'er they've turned it,
                    I Eros. 5.
Oft courted will not come;   Harp. 16.
Drooping oft in wreaths of dread,
                    Heroism. 5.
Oft he keeps his fine ear strained,
                    Initial Love. 66.
To myself I oft recount   Monadnoc. 94.
Oft, my far-appearing peak;
                    Monadnoc. 200.
Oft as morning wreathes my scarf,
                    Monadnoc. 311.
oft the plough unburies,
                    Musketaquid. 29.
Oft, in streets or humblest places,
                    Ode to Beauty. 64.
Oft shall war end, and peace return,
                    Saadi. 111.
And oft at home 'mid tasks I heed,
                    Walden. 41.
Oft didst thou thread the woods in vain
                    Woodnotes. II. 248.

Often
And travelling often in the cut he makes,
                    Blight. 20.

Oh
And oh, the wonder of the power,
                    Miracle. 17.
Oh what is Heaven but the fellowship
                    Oh What. 1.
But oh, to see his solar eyes   Poet. 54.
Me many a sigh. Oh, call not Nature
dumb;   River. 21.
Oh, south winds have long memories,
                    September. 11.
And oh! it cannot die,   Thought. 6.

Oil
And venture, and to Guy the oil.
                    Guy. 50.
Love scatters oil   *Lines. 1.
Costlier far than wine or oil.
                    Monadnoc. 296.

O-ka-lee
The redwing flutes his *o-ka-lee,*
                    May-Day. 168.

Old
   See World-old.
Inviting to new knowledge, one with old.
                    Adirondacs. 205.
Twirl the old wheels!   Adirondacs. 328.
Say, Seigniors, are the old Niles dry,
                    Alphonso. 31.
There, growing slowly old at ease
                    Alphonso. 77.
Haste to cure the old despair,—
                    Bacchus. 55.
And write my old adventures with the
pen   Bacchus. 64.
The old men studied magic in the flowers,
                    Blight. 23.
Old Europe groans with palaces,
                    Boston. 19.
Kings shook with fear, old empires crave
                    Boston. 92.
Which I hid of old time in the West,
                    Boston Hymn. 18.

Saying, Sweetheart! the old mystery re-
mains,—   Flute. 3.
He left, though goodly centuries old,
                    Frag. Nat. VI. 7.
Whereof old chronicles relate
                    Frag. Nat. XXVI. 33.
As Jelaleddin old and gray;
                    Frag. Poet. V. 3.
And willing grow old
                    Frag. Poet. VIII. 5.
Hither hasted, in old time, Jove,
                    Garden. 25.
And as, of old, Polycrates   Guy. 7.
Shine down in the old sea;
                    Hamatreya. 32.
Old are the shores;   Hamatreya. 33.
But where are old men?
                    Hamatreya. 34.
With its old valley,   Hamatreya. 46.
Reporting what old minstrels told
                    Harp. 53.
In old Bassora's schools, I seemed
                    Hermione. 33.
Playfellow of young and old,
                    Holidays. 10.
Of rich and poor, of young and old,
                    Hymn. 10.
Old man and young maid,   Illusions. 9.
Root in the blood of heroes old.
                    In Memoriam. 116.
Even from a brook, and where old woods
                    Letter. 11.
The old wine darkling in the cask
                    May-Day. 89.
The garnered heat of ages old.
                    May-Day. 145.
Life out of death, new out of old,
                    May-Day. 203.
To babes, and to old eyes as well.
                    May-Day. 348.
'Once more,' the old man cried, 'ye clouds,
                    May-Day. 349.
By new delights, as old by old,
                    May-Day. 366.
Chemist to vamp old worlds with new,
                    May-Day. 445.
Maple and oak, the old Divan
                    Miracle. 5.
Old cradle, hunting-ground and bier
                    Monadnoc. 80.
But if the brave old mould is broke,
                    Monadnoc. 118.
Old as the sun, old almost as the shade;
                    Monadnoc. 204.
The gamut old of Pan,   Monadnoc. 220.
As in the old poetic fame
                    Monadnoc. 348.
Of the old building Intellect.
                    Monadnoc. 374.
It sounds from all things old,   Music. 3.
She who is old, but nowise feeble,
                    Nature. II. 5.
Thee knew I of old?   Ode to Beauty. 6.
Old gods forsook the skies.   Peter. 20.
Of them who rescued liberty of old;
                    Phi. 6.
To read new landscapes and old skies;
                    Poet. 53.
Landward they reached the mountains old
                    Poet. 63.

Old—*Continued*
And fill the long reach of the old seashore
                              Poet. 75.
To the seashore, to the old seawalls,
                              Poet. 228.
The burdens of the Bible old;
                              Problem. 14.
To her old leaves new myriads?
                              Problem. 30.
Old Chrysostom, best Augustine,
                              Problem. 65.
Fair to old and foul to young;
                              Prudence. 2.
And trains us on to slight the new, as if
  it were the old: Quat. Nature. 2.
My old familiar haunts; here the blue
  river,   River. 2.
Old playfellows meet;   Sphinx. 28.
He spurneth the old.   Sphinx. 88.
The old Sphinx bit her thick lip,—
                              Sphinx. 109.
It is time to be old,   Terminus. 1.
Grow early old with grief that thou
                              Threnody. 130.
Brought the old order into doubt.
                              Threnody. 145.
The winds shall sing their dead-march old,
                              Titmouse. 20.
Fine afternoon, old passenger!
                              Titmouse. 30.
I think old Cæsar must have heard
                              Titmouse. 95.
Old mouldy men and   To-Day. 9.
As love old things for age, and hate the
  new.   To-Day. 12.
The stern old war-gods shook their
  heads,   Uriel. 27.
Of sorrows new and old!
                              Voluntaries. 78.
The gray old gods whom Chaos knew,
                              Waldeinsamkeit. 35.
When the old world is sterile
                              World-Soul. 97.
And we are never old;   World-Soul. 108.
From the old adhering sin,
                              Woodnotes. II. 64.
'Heed the old oracles,
                              Woodnotes. II. 89.
Of the old flood's subsiding slime,
                              Woodnotes. II. 109.
The ever old, the ever young,
                              Woodnotes. II. 117.

Older
Deeper and older seemed his eye;
                              Character. 4.
Which older forests bound;
                              Garden. 10.
Deeper and older seemed his eye,
                              Poet. 137.
For Eros is older than Saturn or Jove;
                              Quat. Casella. 2.
Older than all thy race.   Seashore. 17.
Older am I than thy numbers wot,
                              Woodnotes. II. 254.

Oldest
Heaven's oldest blood flows in his side,—
                              Initial Love. 123.
My oldest force is good as new,
                              Song of Nature. 82.

What oldest star the fame can save
                              Wealth. 22.
He is the oldest, and best known,
                              Worship. 15.

Olympian
Olympian bards who sung
                              Ode to Beauty. 60.
And brought Olympian wisdom down
                              Solution. 67.

Olympus
As Olympus follows Jove.
                              Channing Ode. 70.

Oman's
Know the worth of Oman's pearls?
                              Friendship. Trans. 2.

Omen
Whose omen 't is, and sign.
                              Threnody. 259.

Omens
Omens and signs that filled the air
                              Frag. Poet. V. 39.
And omens above thought.   Garden. 56.
When Fate by omens takes his part,
                              Initial Love. 71.
The youth sees omens where he goes,
                              May-Day. 73.
The eye reads omens where it goes,
                              Nature. Mot. 3.
High omens ask diviner guess;
                              Threnody. 228.
Might gather omens from that radiant
  sign.   Webster. 4.

Ominous
The trees were rich, yet ominous with
  gloom.   Frag. Nat. XXVII. 5.
The ominous hole he dug in the sand,
                              Threnody. 86.

Omitted
The masters quite omitted   April. 19.

Omnific
Child of the omnific Need,
                              Frag. Life. XXIII. 7.

Omnipotence
And an omnipotence in chemistry,
                              Blight. 25.

Omnipotent
Which the Omnipotent cannot rebuild.
                              Frag. Life. V. 2.

Omnipresent
Omnipresent without name;—
                              Experience. 11.

On (Partial list.)
    See Thereon; Upon; Whereon.
Pleased with these grand companions, we
  glide on,   Adirondacs. 12.
They put their April raiment on;
                              May-Day. 319.
And draw me on,   Ode to Beauty. 42.
But not the less the eternal wave rolls on
                              Pan. 10.
To works as noble led thee on.
                              Threnody. 79.
The brook into the stream runs on;
                              Threnody. 96.

Once
Shall lift its notes once more, Bell. 14.
Here once the embattled farmers stood
                              C. Hymn. 3.
Shines not as once it shined.
                              Day by Day. 8.

Which once our childhood knew;
                              Dirge. 38.
Never yet could once arrive.
                              Forerunners. 24.
Who sought thee once shall seek again.
                              Frag. Life. XXII. 4.
Assured to find the token once again
                              Frag. Nat. IV. 9.
'Once with manlike love and fear
                              Frag. Poet. II. 5.
Once a member, all was mine,
                              Frag. Poet. IV. 10.
Once I wished I might rehearse
                              Freedom. 1.
Here once the Deluge ploughed,
                              Garden. 13.
That all the wine at once we swallow
                              Good Hope. 3.
If once again that silent string,
                              Harp. 105.
'Once I dwelt apart,   Hermione. 40.
And feed once more the exile's eyes;
                              May-Day. 97.
Befalls again what once befell;
                              May-Day. 178.
'Once more,' the old man cried, 'ye
  clouds,   May-Day. 349.
Which once my infancy beguiled,
                              May-Day. 351.
Once more into his dapper town,
                              Monadnoc. 345.
But once in your dominion.   Poet. 232.
For when love has once departed
                              Rhea. 13.
When a god is once beguiled   Rhea. 41.
And I behold once more   River. 1.
Yet whirl the glowing wheels once more,
                              Song of Nature. 73.
Once found,—for new heavens
                              Sphinx. 87.
House at once and architect,
                              Spiritual Laws. 2.
His beauty once their beauty tried;
                              Threnody. 146.
The needful sinew stark as once,
                              Terminus. 27.
Once, among the Pleiads walking,
                              Uriel. 7.
In heaven once eminent, the god
                              Uriel. 37.
I had a sister once who seemed just like
  a violet,   *Violet. 13.
If once the generous chief arrive
                              Voluntaries. 55.
Far away in time, when once, Wealth. 2.
Once again the pine-tree sung:—
                              Woodnotes. II. 133.
Hearken once more! Woodnotes. II. 252.
Once slept the world an egg of stone,
                              Woodnotes. II. 266.

One
The while, one leaden pot of alcohol
                              Adirondacs. 139.
Inviting to new knowledge, one with old.
                              Adirondacs. 205.
One held a printed journal waving high
                              Adirondacs. 235.
As one within whose memory it burned
                              Adirondacs. 278.
Nay, mourn not one: let him exult,
                              Adirondacs. 297.

One August evening   Adirondacs. 331.
As if one riddle of the Sphinx were
  guessed.   Adirondacs. 343.
Think nature barely serves for one;
                              Alphonso. 36.
For one sun supply us twenty.
                              Alphonso. 54.
Stuff their nine brains in one hat;
                              Alphonso. 72.
One harvest from thy field   Apology. 17.
And, moulded of one element   Art. 23.
Music and wine are one,—   Bacchus. 37.
And one to me are shame and fame.
                              Brahma. 8.
In one only form dissolves;
                              Celestial Love. 32.
Melt into one.   Celestial Love. 41.
Triple blossoms from one root;
                              Celestial Love. 43.
One through separated souls;
                              Celestial Love. 47.
Every one to his chosen work;—
                              Channing Ode. 75.
Making one place two places?
                              Chartist. 2.
One, by humble farmer seen,
                              Chartist. 3.
One morn is in the mighty heaven,
                              Concord Ode. 3.
And one in our desire.   Concord Ode. 4.
One third part of the sky unrolled
                              Concord Ode. 11.
See rights for which the one hand fights
                              Concord Ode. 23.
In the waste one nook is his;
                              Day by Day. 10.
Nor gives the jealous lord one diamond
  drop   Day's Ration. 24.
Why need I volumes, if one word suffice?
                              Day's Ration. 26.
Alas! that one is born in blight,
                              Destiny. 18.
One thing is forever good;   Destiny. 45.
That one thing is Success,—   Destiny. 46.
Had leaped from one fair mother's arms,
                              Dirge. 6.
'Ye drew one mother's milk,   Dirge. 53.
One chamber held ye all;   Dirge. 54.
To fetch one ingot thence   Dull. 16.
All are needed by each one;   Each. 11.
The traveller and the road seem one
                              Etienne. 21.
Not one salutes me here;   Exile. 6.
But though aye one in heart,
                              *Farewell. 32.
Farewell, thou fairest one,
                              *Farewell. 37.
Yet can one ray of truth divine
                              Frag. Life. X. 8.
Of all wit's uses the main one
                              Frag. Life. XI. 1.
Feigned to speak to some one else.
                              Frag. Poet. IV. 18.
In mercy, on one little head.
                              Frag. Poet. XXIV. 2.
Laid the terraces, one by one;
                              Garden. 14.
As if one spake to another,   Garden. 30.
Canst thou copy in verse one chime
                              Garden. 37.

One —*Continued*

Of one import, of varied tone;
Garden. 42.

Gifts of one who loved me,— Gifts. 1.

One word more thy heart behoved,
Give. 28.

One pulse more of firm endeavor,—
Give. 29.

Who are thy spiritual kindred, and each
one Good Cheer. 5.

Yet every one Hamatreya. 55.

One musician is sure, Harp. 1.

Not one of all can put in verse,
Harp. 83.

More dear to one than mines of gold.
Holidays. 12.

In music every one, House. 18.

The wise and simple have one glance
In Memoriam. 11.

Nor bate one jot of heart or hope,
In Memoriam. 80.

He has ushers many a one:
Initial Love. 75.

And interchangeably at one
Initial Love. 124.

He has not one mode, but manifold,
Initial Love. 131.

And, being two, shall still be one.
Initial Love. 146.

They know one only mortal grief
Love and Thought. 9.

One arctic moon had disenchanted.
May-Day. 44.

Of the gods, whereof she is one,—
May-Day. 131.

That one broad, long midsummer day
May-Day. 276.

Belike the one they used in parting
May-Day. 385.

Every one to his hole in the wall,
May-Day. 390.

In one body grooms and brides;
Merlin. 89.

One to other, health and age.
Merlin. 105.

Ever from one who comes to-morrow
Merlin's Song. 20.

Of all wit's uses, the main one
Merlin's Song. 39.

One word, no more, to say. Merops. 12.

To myriad kinds and times one sense
Monadnoc. 381.

One joy it joys, one grief it grieves.
Monadnoc. 384.

Which, one by one, they know to draw
and use. Musketaquid. 35.

(That one would say, meadow and forest
walked, Musketaquid. 48.

How drear the part I held in one,
Nun. 48.

Whom the Infinite One
Ode to Beauty. 35.

Tossing one sparkle to the eyes:
Peter. 38.

One portrait—fact or fancy—we may
draw; Phi. 4.

One who having nectar drank
Poet. 81.

I, pining to be one of you, Poet. 238.

By one thought to one same sphere;
Poet. 268.

Girds with one flame the countless host,
Problem. 52.

One accent of the Holy Ghost
Problem. 61.

And one by one has torn off quite
Rhea. 15.

One sallow horseman knows me good.
Romany. 16.

But one shall sing; Saadi. 18.

Ere one man my hill shall climb,
Saadi. 113.

Made one of day and one of night
Song of Nature. 63.

And one of the salt sea-sand.
Song of Nature. 64.

One in a Judæan manger,
Song of Nature. 65.

And one by Avon stream,
Song of Nature. 66.

One over against the mouths of Nile,
Song of Nature. 67.

And one in the Academe.
Song of Nature. 68.

By one music enchanted, Sphinx. 35.

One deity stirred,— Sphinx. 36.

"Who telleth one of my meanings
Sphinx. 131.

And he who has one enemy will meet him
everywhere. Taleb. 2.

Of one inalienable right, Thought. 2.

One tarried here, there hurried one;
Threnody. 156.

To aggrandize one funeral.
Threnody. 159.

And many-seeming life is one,—
Threnody. 245.

Has million arms to one of mine:
Titmouse. 6.

But one I seek in foreign places,
Una. 11.

One face explore in foreign faces.
Una. 12.

One, with low tones that decide,
Uriel. 15.

Are Autumn's blasts fit music for thee,
fragile one, to hear; *Violet. 2.

In one wood walk, than learned men
Walk. 7.

One crash, the death-hymn of the perfect
tree, Woodnotes. I. 74.

'T was one of the charmed days
Woodnotes. I. 96.

One dry, and one the living tree.
Woodnotes. II. 21.

Halteth never in one shape,
Woodnotes. II. 272.

With one drop sheds form and feature;
Woodnotes. II. 289.

If but one hero knew it, World-Soul. 49.

Not one has found the key;
World-Soul. 54.

One scent to hyson and to wall-flower,
Xenophanes. 2.

One sound to pine-groves and to waterfalls, Xenophanes. 3.

One aspect to the desert and the lake.
Xenophanes. 4.

Are of one pattern made; bird, beast and
flower, Xenophanes. 6.

And are but one. Beheld far off, they
  part   Xenophanes. 9.
To know one element, explore another,
                  Xenophanes. 12.
Repeats one note.   Xenophanes. 19.

Ones
But they are gone,—the holy ones
                  Dirge. 21.

Only
Only the hand secure and bold
                  Angelo. 4.
So sweet to Seyd as only grace
                  Beauty. 2.
Only the herbs and simples of the wood,
                  Blight. 4.
Only what to our griping toil is due;
                  Blight. 41.
So only are ye unbound;
                  Boston Hymn. 66.
In one only form dissolves;
                  Celestial Love. 32.
Useful only, triste and damp,
                  Chartist. 5.
Only two in the garden walked,
                  Daemonic Love. 21.
Only could her mirror show.
                  Frag. Life. IX. 2.
But love me then and only, when you
  know   Frag. Life. XV. 6.
And know the only strong?
                  Frag. Nat. III. 30.
God only knew how Saadi dined;
                  Frag. Poet. V. 13.
And only. sees what he doth give.
                  Frag. Poet. XXVIII. 9.
Only to children children sing, Harp. 34.
Only to youth will spring be spring.
                  Harp. 35.
Seeing only what is fair,
                  Humble-Bee. 54.
Sipping only what is sweet,
                  Humble-Bee. 55.
He follows joy, and only joy.
                  Initial Love. 113.
All, all was given, and only health denied.
                  In Memoriam. 72.
They know one only mortal grief
                  Love and Thought. 9.
Why only must thy reason fail
                  May-Day. 175.
So only new griefs are consoled
                  May-Day. 365.
Which only the propitious mind
                  Merlin. 68.
Which only angels hear;
                  Merlin's Song. 9.
Only the light-armed climb the hill.
                  Merlin's Song. 28.
It is not only in the rose,   Music. 7.
It is not only in the bird,   Music. 8.
Not only where the rainbow glows,
                  Music. 9.
To report thy features only,
                  Ode to Beauty. 85.
His mother died,—the only friend he
  had,—   Philosopher. 7.
He asked, he only asked, to feel.
                  Poet. 212.
Only by needs and loves of mine;
                  Poet. 234.
Heed thou only Saadi's lay. Saadi. 103.

Heed thou only Saadi's lay. Saadi. 116.
And the world has only two.
                  Security. 8.
I only follow, when I act aright.
                  Self-Reliance. 10.
And know only that I love.
                  Song of Seyd. 8.
To me who only jewels crave?
                  Song of Seyd. 14.
For only it can absolutely deal.
                  Sursum Corda. 11.
Could stoop to heal that only child,
                  Threnody. 122.
Feeling only the fiery thread
                  Voluntaries. 88.
And merry is only a mask of sad,
                  Waldeinsamkeit. 18.
Only what the pine-tree yields;
                  Woodnotes. II. 31.
Which only the pure can hear;
                  Woodnotes. II. 128.
Only thy Americans
                  Woodnotes. II. 140.
Or only a flashing sunbeam
                  World-Soul. 29.

Onward
The rivers gambolled onward to the sea,
                  Adirondacs. 339.
Which lit my onward way with bright
  presage,   I Bear. 4.
Cried "Onward!" and the palm-crown
  showed,   In Memoriam. 59.
'Onward,' he cries, 'your baskets bring,—
                  May-Day. 101.
Stepping daily onward north
                  May-Day. 306.
Onward and nearer rides the sun of May;
                  Musketaquid. 19.
Right onward drive unharmed;
                  Terminus. 38.
Its onward force too starkly pent
                  Threnody. 247.
Onward and on, the eternal Pan,
                  Woodnotes. II. 270.

Ooze
In the wide thaw and ooze of wrong,
                  Monadnoc. 114.

Opaker
An opaker star,   Monadnoc. 393.

Opal
Opal hues and purple dye;
                  May-Day. 260.

Opaline
The opaline, the plentiful and strong,
                  Seashore. 18.

Ope
When thrushes ope their throat, 't is he
  that sings,   Enchanter. 10.
Nor plots to ope or bolt a gate,
                  Frag. Life. XVII. 8.
Ope in such low moist roadside, and be-
  neath   Naples. 24.
Wilt thou not ope thy heart to know
                  Threnody. 260.

Open
Open and flow.   Bacchus. 50.
There are open hours   Merlin. 70.
Open the daunting map beneath,—
                  Monadnoc. 319.

Open —*Continued*
Low, open meads, slender and sluggish
streams, Musketaquid. 2.
Open innumerable doors Saadi. 159.
The open secret of to-day.
Solution. 70.
To the open ear it sings
Woodnotes. II. 104.
Their arms fly open wide.
World-Soul. 96.

Opened
When her calm eyes opened bright,
Daemonic Love. 17.
It opened in its virgin bower,
Woodnotes. I. 43.

Opener
Unbar the door, since thou the Opener
art, Unbar. 1.

Opening
From the eager opening strings
Harp. 47.

Opens
Opens the eye Enchanter. 14.
And opens you a welcome in them all.
Rome. 10.

Operation
Thorough nature's operation, Visit. 4.

Opes
And Morning opes with haste her lids
Problem. 35.

Opinions
The yoke of men's opinions. I will be
Self-Reliance. 2.

Opposes
The glance that to their glance opposes,
Initial Love. 52.

Opposites
Equals remote, and seeming opposites.
Daemonic Love. 84.

Option
Make thy option which of two;
Terminus. 13.
By fate, not option, frugal Nature gave
Xenophanes. 1.

Opulent
Is it that my opulent soul
Ode to Beauty. 46.

Or. (Partial list.)
Nothing was ploughed, or reaped, or
bought, or sold; Adirondacs. 67.
Or if the slain think he is slain,
Brahma. 2.
Impassible to heat or cold.
Frag. Poet. I. 49.
Or else alternated; Merlin. 103.
Or for service, or delight, Visit. 17.

Oracle
As each would hear the oracle alone.
Adirondacs. 15.
The thrilling Delphic oracle;
Problem. 12.

Oracles
'Heed the old oracles,
Woodnotes. II. 89.

Orange
Orange cheek or skin of man.
Alphonso. 12.

Orange-grove
That orange-grove, that isle of palms,
In Memoriam. 114.

Orator
There is no orator prevails
May-Day. 433.
Mute orator! well skilled to plead,
Monadnoc. 403.

Orators
With the voice of orators; Merlin. 22.

Orb
The orb within the mind, Day by Day. 6.
Orb and atom forth they prance,
Monadnoc. 249.
His aye-rolling orb Sphinx. 83.
Orb, quintessence, and sunbeams,
Uriel. 13.

Orbed
See Enorbed.

Orbit
Cross the orbit of the earth,
Daemonic Love. 49.
The soaring orbit of the muse exceeds
that journey's length. Merlin. 65.
Orbit and sum of Shakespeare's wit.
Solution. 40.

Orbs
In those unfathomable orbs
Initial Love. 25.
And grasping give the orbs another
whirl. May-Day. 159.
Or if perchance, ye orbs of Fate,
Poet. 241.

Orchard
The orchard planted, Channing Ode. 62.
My father's orchard knowest. Exile. 12.
Hallow these my orchard shades;
Frag. Poet. VII. 4.
By green orchard boughs Politics. 19.

Orchard's
On thine orchard's edge belong
Saadi. 149.

Orchards
As in broad orchards resonant with bees;
Musketaquid. 57.

Orchis
Orchis and gentian, fern and long whip-
scirpus, Adirondacs. 142.
Where, in far fields, the orchis grew.
Woodnotes. I. 49.

Order
When Chaos and Order strove,
Cosmos. 2, 6.
'For the world was built in order,
Monadnoc. 245.
And by the order in the field disclose
Musketaquid. 50.
The order regnant in the yeoman's brain.
Musketaquid. 51.
Saw musical order and pairing rhymes.
Poet. 72.
Brought the old order into doubt.
Threnody. 145.

Ordered
Like the dancers' ordered band,
Merlin. 100.

Ore
And know the sparkle of its ore,
Dull. 20.

Oreads
Mark how the climbing Oreads
Monadnoc. 19.

Oreads'
Into this Oreads' fended Paradise,
Adirondacs. 194.

Ores
Time out of mind, this forge of ores;
Monadnoc. 78.

Organ
The silent organ loudest chants
Dirge. 59.

Orgies
Into blissful orgies sank;   Poet. 82.

Original
Maker and original.   Woodnotes. II. 284.

Oriole
Singing by the oriole songs,
May-Day. 420.

Oriole's
And he that paints the oriole's fiery
wings.   Enchanter. 11.

Ornament
It should be their life's ornament,
Monadnoc. 50.
Of his sad ornament,   To J. W. 12.

Orphan
The orphan of the forest dies.
Woodnotes. II. 56.
Whence, O thou orphan and defrauded?
Woodnotes. II. 180.

Orphans
Nor stab the love that orphans keep.
Frag. Life. VII. 4.

Osier
Secure the osier yet will hide
May-Day. 172.
Yon waterflag, yon sighing osier,
Poet. 221.

Osprey
North from Camp Maple, south to Osprey Bay,   Adirondacs. 109.
Above, the eagle flew, the osprey
screamed,   Adirondacs. 146.

Ostrich-like
O ostrich-like forgetfulness!
Threnody. 116.

Other (Partial list.)
And other Titans without muse or name.
Adirondacs. 11.
The other slow,—this the Prometheus,
Adirondacs. 288.
It was from Jove the other stole his fire,
Adirondacs. 290.
To outdo each other and extort applause.
Adirondacs. 326.
And each shall care for other,
Boston. 112.
To please each other well;
Celestial Love. 7.
Whom not each other seek, but find.
Celestial Love. 84.
When each the other shall avoid,
Celestial Love. 97.
Of self in other still preferred,
Celestial Love. 118.
When other men have none?
I Compensation. 2.
By the other cloven down.
Concord Ode. 24.
Burns up every other tie.
Daemonic Love. 115.

The other portion language cannot
speak.   Frag. Life. XVIII. 8.
Crowds each on other, veil on veil,
Frag. Nat. XXXI. 4.
Or made what other purlieus proud.
Lines. 22.
Each for other they were born,
Love and Thought. 7.
Each can other best adorn;
Love and Thought. 8.
The pilgrims have each other lost.
Love and Thought. 12.
One to other, health and age.
Merlin. 105.
Though her eye seek other forms
Security. 1.
Each the other adorning,   Sphinx. 37.
Say, what other metre is it   Visit. 11.
And of all other men desired.
Woodnotes. II. 70.
The wood and wave each other know
Woodnotes. II. 173.
We plot and corrupt each other,
World-Soul. 23.

Other's
Each other's counsel by his own,
Celestial Love. 92.

Others
Others applauded him who spoke the
truth.   Adirondacs. 187.
Easy to match what others do,
Frag. Life. X. 1.
Where I, as others, follow petty ends;
Frag. Life. XV. 3.
Asks not of others soft consents,
Frag. Life. XVII. 6.
Gave the law which others took,
In Memoriam. 45.
If others reach it, is content;
In Memoriam. 88.
And found a home in haunts which others
scorned,   Musketaquid. 3.
Where others did at distance hear,
Woodnotes. I. 58.

Others'
Burned more than others' fire,
May-Day. 143.

Otter
Of wolf and otter, bear and deer;
Monadnoc. 81.

Our (Partial list.)
Our heroes tried their rifles at a mark,
Adirondacs. 125.
But these young scholars, who invade
our hills,   Blight. 18.
When, like our sires, our sons are gone.
C. Hymn. 12.
And one in our desire.
Concord Ode. 4.
Our pulses beat not less, Concord Ode. 6.
In our green Musketaquid,
Frag. Nat. XXVI. 2.
Our sumptuous indigence,
Monadnoc. 377.
Thou, in our astronomy Monadnoc. 392.
Is the Creator of our human mould
Naples. 2.
And all our struggles and our toils
Nemesis. 15.

Our. (Partial list.)—*Continued*
So nigh is grandeur to our dust,
    Voluntaries. 71.
In our downfall, or our joy:
    Voluntaries. 114.
Ours. (Partial list.)
't is theirs as much as ours.
    Adirondacs. 261.
Of sympathy so large, that ours was
theirs,   Adirondacs. 257.
Thou darling town of ours!   Boston. 119.
Sad, in sooth, it were to ours,
    Ellen South. 22.
Time hath his work to do and we have
ours.   Frag. Life. XXXVII. 2.
Who in their pride forgive not ours.
    Saadi. 58.
Out. (Partial list.)
    See Light-outspeeding; Without.
Winding through grassy shallows in and
out,   Adirondacs. 23.
And pirates of the universe, shut out
    Blight. 47.
They reckon ill who leave me out;
    Brahma. 9.
Out of that sphere,   Celestial Love. 61.
Will take the sun out of the skies
    Concord Ode. 39.
Ere freedom out of man.
    Concord Ode. 40.
Out of that delicate lay could'st thou
    Dirge. 47.
To draw the nations out of doors.
    Frag. Nat. XIII. 2.
Out from the heart of nature rolled
    Problem. 13.
For out of woe and out of crime
    Saadi. 70.
Out of sleeping a waking,   Sphinx. 13.
"Out spoke the great mother,
    Sphinx. 57.
From the window I look out
    Threnody. 74.
Or out of the good of evil born,
    Uriel. 53.
Or how the fish outbuilt her shell,
    Problem. 26.
Outcast
The glowing angel, the outcast corse.
    Woodnotes. II. 306.
Outdid
Rounded by hours where each outdid the
last   Adirondacs. 154.
Out-do
To outdo each other and extort applause.
    Adirondacs. 326.
Hard to out-do the brave, the true,
    Frag. Life. X. 3.
Outlearned
Men and gods have not outlearned it;
    Eros. I. 4.
Outlets
And the outlets of the sky.   Give 17.
Outlive
Outlive the newest stars.   House. 24.
And verses that all verse outlive.
    Solution. 72.
Outpoured
What joy in rosy waves outpoured
    May-Day. 190.

Outrage
The outrage of the poor.
    Boston Hymn. 8.
Outran
Outran the craft of eloquence.
    Poet. 200.
Outsee
Shalt outsee seers, and outwit sages.
    Woodnotes. II. 247.
Outshine
The blaze of revellers' feasts outshine.
    Frag. Life. X. 9.
Ashes and jet all hues outshine.
    Titmouse. 55.
Outside
Fast to surface and outside,   Circles. 3.
Made of the air that blows outside.'
    Titmouse. 78.
Outsleep
Woe and want thou canst outsleep;
    Humble-Bee. 61.
Outspeeding
    See Sight-outspeeding
Outspread
Has royal pleasure-grounds outspread.'
    Monadnoc. 71.
Outstretched
Where far oaks outstretched their arms.
    September. 8.
And thrice outstretched my hand,
    Song of Nature. 62.
Outstride
The strong they slay, the swift outstride:
    Voluntaries. 118.
Outvalued
Outvalued every pulsing sound
    Threnody. 13.
Outward
Daily to a more thin and outward rind,
    Blight. 48.
Outweighs
The surging sea outweighs,
    Friendship. 2.
Outwit
Shalt outsee seers, and outwit sages.
    Woodnotes. II. 247.
Outwits
And blushing Love outwits the sages.
    Frag. Poet. IX. 12.
Over (Partial list.)
    See O'er.
I have thought it thoroughly over,—
    Alphonso. 55.
Over the flickering Dæmon film,
    Celestial Love. 29.
Pan, half asleep, rolling over
    Frag. Nat. I. 7.
I dare not peep over this parapet
    Grace. 5.
Over tribes and over times,
    Monadnoc. 214.
The heaven high over
    Ode to Beauty. 37.
One over against the mouths of Nile,
    Song of Nature. 67.
But over the dead he has no power,
    Threnody. 5.
Victor over death and pain.
    Voluntaries. 105.
Victors over daily wrongs:
    Voluntaries. 110.

Over the winter glaciers
     World-Soul. 109.

Overalls
Bow to the stalwart churls in overalls:
     Adirondacs. 94.

Overbold
You shall not be overbold
     Titmouse. 1.

Overfill
Of human sense doth overfill. Art. 28.

Overflowing
Pale at overflowing noon Saadi. 53.
Which overflowing Love shall fill,
     Threnody. 192.

Over-god
The over-god Channing Ode. 80.

Overgods
But of the Overgods alone: Harp. 68.

Overgrown
Is, that men are overgrown,
     Titmouse. 62.

Overgrowths
Your rank overgrowths reduce
     Alphonso. 65.

Overhanging
As the overhanging trees
     Celestial Love. 71.

Overhead
And hark! where overhead the ancient
 crows   River. 16.

Overhear
I tuneful voices overhear;
     Forerunners. 30.
I was free to overhear,
     Frag. Poet. IV. 19.

Overheard
Thus at random overheard
     Frag. Poet. IV. 22.
Tribes and ages overheard:
     Frag. Poet. V. 10.
Seyd overheard the young gods talking;
     Uriel. 8.

Overhears
And the poet who overhears Poet. 77.

Overmastering
Throbs with an overmastering energy
     Pan. 7.

Overmuch
The world hath overmuch of pain,—
     May-Day. 369.

Overpaid
The partial wood-gods overpaid my love,
     Musketaquid. 4.

Overpay
Their honest labor overpay.
     Boston. 24.
Shall to the planet overpay
     May-Day. 277.

Overrun
And we've the landscape overrun,
     Etienne. 6.

Oversea
Spies oversea the fires of the mountain;
     Enchanter. 9.

Overspread
Scarce the first blush has overspread his
 cheek,   Philosopher. 4.

Overstay
If Love his moment overstay,
     Visit. 29

Overstays
Here sultry Summer overstays
     Walden. 7.

Overtaken
Though they are not overtaken;
     Forerunners. 28.

Overtaking
Life death overtaking; Sphinx. 15.

Over-thrilled
For art, for music over-thrilled,
     Frag. Poet. XVI. 1

Overtook
Pleasant fancies overtook me.
     Berrying. 8.

Overtops
A tapering turret overtops the work.
     Snow-Storm. 22.

Overture
Courageous sing a delicate overture
     Musketaquid. 17.

Overzealous
Fits not to be overzealous;
     Alphonso. 60.

Owe
How much, preventing God, how much I
 owe   Grace. 1
And of the kinds that owe her birth.
     Harp. 66

Owes
And hints the future which it owes.
     Mature. Mot. 16.

Owls
The raven croaked, owls hooted, the
 woodpecker Adirondacs. 147.

Own. (Partial list.)
 See Disown.
fit for her own ends, Adirondacs. 71.
Their several portraits, you would own
     Adirondacs. Motto. 2.
His rank, and quartered his own coat.
     Astraea. 2.
The form is his own corporal form,
     Astraea. 29.
Or those we erring own,
     Celestial Love. 55.
Each other's counsel by his own,
     Celestial Love. 92.
After their own genius, clearly,
     Celestial Love. 122.
And all that Nature made thy own,
     Compensation. II. 25.
For the witchery of my own.
     Cosmos. 24.
On its own First of May. Cosmos. 28.
Stands to each human soul its own,
     Daemonic Love. 27.
Thyself shalt own the page was bright,
     Ellen. 7.
Features that seem at heart my own;
     Eva. 8.
Uncertain of thine own *Farewell. 39.
Obeying time, the last to own Fate. 11.
Shall his own sorrow seem impertinent,
     Frag. Life. XXVI. 2.
The bard and mystic held me for their
 own,   Frag. Life. XXX. 1.
Well he knows his own affair,
     Frag. Nat. I. 12.
To man imprisoned in his own.
     Garden. 44.

Own. (Partial list.)—*Continued*
I am going to my own hearth-stone,
Good-Bye. 15.
His own symmetry with law;   Guy. 12.
Worked on the Maker's own receipt,
Guy. 26.
With their own harvest honored were.
Guy. 46.
Failing sometimes of his own,
Initial Love. 94.
To his own blood harsh and strange.
Insight. 6.
In his own loom's garment dressed,
Monadnoc. 38.
The World-soul knows his own affair,
Monadnoc. 153.
And, by marvel of her own,
Nature. I. 10.
What's most theirs is not their own,
Nature. II. 20.
By its own meek and incorruptible will?
Oh What. 3.
And all thy life is for thy own,
Prayer. 3.
Then Beauty is its own excuse for being:
Rhodora. 12.
And ever in the strife of your own
thoughts   Rome. 15.
For the talents not thine own,   Saadi. 90.
Is all his own, retiring, as he were not,
Snow-Storm. 24.
As if he came unto his own,
Threnody. 143.
The pure shall see by their own will,
Threnody. 191.
That thou might'st cherish for thine own
Threnody. 221.
Helps who for their own need are strong,
Titmouse. 87.
Up! mind thine own aim, and
To J. W. 22.
Strong Hades could not keep his own,
Uriel. 33.
Leave authors' eyes, and fetch your own,
Waldeinsamkeit. 43.
And wary Nature knows her own
Walk. 2.
By God's own light illumined and fore-
showed.   Woodnotes. I. 95.
It seemed the likeness of their own;
Woodnotes. I. 115.
More near than aught thou call'st thy
own,   Worship. 16.

Owner
Pay ransom to the owner
Boston Hymn. 69.
Who is the owner? The slave is owner,
Boston Hymn. 71.
Ah! the hot owner sees not Death, who
adds   Hamatreya. 25.
I am owner of the sphere,
Informing Spirit. 5.

Owner's
Over the owner's farthest walls!
Monadnoc. 9.
Checked by the owners' fierce disdain,
Voluntaries. 29.

Oxen
Homeward brought the oxen strong;
Apology. 18.

Adds to oak and oxen strength,
May-Day. 201.

Pace
    See Apace.
Paced
Forth paced it yesterday; Hermione. 57.
And he the chieftain paced beside,
Threnody. 66.
Paced by the blessed feet around,
Threnody. 91.
Pacing
When pacing through the oaks he heard
Harp. 87.
Pack
Slipped off their pack of duties, leagues
behind,   Adirondacs. 62.
Packed,
New-face or finish what is packed,
Past. 20.
Paddle
A paddle in the right hand, or an oar,
Adirondacs. 78.
Stealing with paddle to the feeding-
grounds   Adirondacs. 119.
Or dip thy paddle in the lake,
Woodnotes. II. 169.
Pads
Two creeping miles of rushes, pads and
sponge,   Adirondacs. 24.
Pæan
Freedom's pæan in my verse,
Freedom. 2.
Pæan! Veni, vidi, vici.   Titmouse. 104.
Aloft, abroad, the pæan swells;
Woodnotes. II. 100.
Pæans
I hear the lofty pæans
Ode to Beauty. 56.
Page
Then if I read the page aright
Ellen. 5.
Thyself shalt own the page was bright,
Ellen. 7.
I left my dreary page and sallied forth,
Frag. Nat. XXVII. 1.
Life loiters at the book's first page,—
Quat. Climacteric. 3.
Pageantry
Sable pageantry of clouds,   Nun. 21.
Pages
And thou,—go burn thy wormy pages,—
Woodnotes. II. 246.
Paid
    See Overpaid.
The debt is paid,   Past. 1.
Pain
Masters, I'm in pain with you;
Alphonso. 41.
By want and pain God screeneth him
Frag. Poet. V. 7.
Merlin paying the pain of sin,
Harp. 55.
Words of pain and cries of fear,
Harp. 58.
Nor Collins' verse of tender pain,
Harp. 79.
The threads of life and power and pain,
Harp. 101.

Or ardent youth untouched by pain,
                    Hymn. 11.
In lands remote, in toil and pain,
              In Memoriam. 75.
And yet between the spasms of pain
            In Memoriam. 103.
And, truth to tell, amused by pain.
              Intellect. II. 2.
No pain was within,   *Lines. 13.
The world hath overmuch of pain,—
              May-Day. 369.
Soothe pain, and age, and love's distress,
              May-Day. 439.
As when, with inward fires and pain,
              Monadnoc. 289.
Serve it for pain and fear and need.
              Poet. 286.
I travail in pain for him,
           Song of Nature. 57.
Heat, cold, wet, dry, and peace, and pain.
           Song of Nature. 76.
And under pain, pleasure,—   Sphinx. 99.
Under pleasure, pain lies.   Sphinx. 100.
Tones of penitence and pain,
             Voluntaries. 3.
Victor over death and pain.
           Voluntaries. 105.
The souls that walk in pain.
        Waldeinsamkeit. 24.

Pained
And Reason on her tiptoe pained
            Initial Love. 67.

Painful
In many lands, with painful steps,
             House. 11.
In lowly cot or painful road,
          In Memoriam. 57.

Pains
Nature, hating art and pains,
           Nature. I. 5.
What though the pains and joys
          Threnody. 40.

Paint
Paint the prospect from their door.
        Frag. Life. XIX. 2.
What all the books of ages paint, I have.
         Frag. Nat. V. 1.
Or gleam which use can paint on steel,
        Frag. Poet. I. 24.
Which morn and crimson evening paint
         Monadnoc. 44.
His tongue can paint as bright, as keen;
           Saadi. 122.

Painted
Painted our necks, hands,
         Adirondacs. 167.
Every moth with painted wing,
           Lines. 9.
Woven of tulips and painted moth.
         May-Day. 330.
Of the painted race of flowers,
         May-Day. 374.
Guest of million painted forms,
        Ode to Beauty. 23.
Live, robed with beauty, painted by the
sun;   Pan. 5.
In rings and painted vest.   Riches. 8.
The painted sled stands where it stood;
          Threnody. 82.
Painted with shadows green and proud
        Woodnotes. I. 110.

Painter
The erring painter made Love blind,—
        Daemonic Love. 68.
The million-handed painter pours
         May-Day. 259.

Painting
Painting him from head to foot,
        Initial Love. 82.
Painting pictures mile on mile,
         May-Day. 4.
Painting fawns' and leopards' fells,
         May-Day. 204.
Painting artless paradises,
         May-Day. 249.
Painting with morn each annual cell?
        Problem. 28.

Paints
And he that paints the oriole's fiery
  wings.   Enchanter. 11.
She paints with white and red the moors
        Frag. Nat. XIII. 1.
He paints, he carves, he chants, he prays,
        Initial Love. 116.
Paints, and flavors, and allures,
        May-Day. 197.

Pair
To the pair is nought forbidden;
        Love and Thought. 4.

Paired
  See Perfect-paired.
And match the paired cotyledons.
           Merlin. 87.

Pairing
Saw musical order and pairing rhymes.
          Poet. 72.

Pairs
Made all things in pairs.   Merlin. 80.

Palace
In my palace of Castile,   Alphonso. 43.
No palace but his sea-beat cave.
        Frag. Poet. V. 21.
Quit the hut, frequent the palace,
        Quat. Artist. 1.
Who liveth in the palace hall
        Woodnotes. II. 24.

Palaces
Old Europe groans with palaces,
         Boston. 19.
Shiver the palaces of glass;
        Daemonic Love. 119.
Stately lords in palaces,
        Frag. Poet. I. 26.
In palaces and market squares Harp. 17.
In hamlets palaces and parks,
        Initial Love. 3.

Paladin
And fight like a Paladin.
        Initial Love. 137.

Pale
Luther, Fox, Behmen, Swedenborg, grew
  pale,   Adakryn. 3.
Yon pale, scrawny fisher fools,
        Alphonso. 15.
And when you love not, pale and blue.
        Amulet. 8.
Turn pale and starve.   Blight. 49.
They drop their few pale flowers,
        Daemonic Love. 108.
Are silent, low and pale.   Dirge. 24.
Pale genius roves alone,
        Frag. Poet. VI. 1.

Pale —*Continued*
And the firm soul does the pale train
defy I Bear. 11.
But, leaving rule and pale forethought,
Merlin. 31.
Nor pictures pale, but Jove and Mars.
Monadnoc. 308.
He looks on that, and he turns pale.
Monadnoc. 330.
I see the pale lustres condense to a star:
Poet. 109.
Pale Northern girls! you scorn our race;
Romany. 5.
Pale at overflowing noon Saadi. 53.
Why lingerest thou, pale violet, to see
the dying year; *Violet. 1.
Made not pale, or fat, or lean;
Woodnotes. II. 36.

Paler
I court and play with paler blood,
Romany. 14.

Palest
Nor the palest rose she flung Give. 41.

Pallid
Where a thousand pallid towns
May-Day. 254.

Palm
Slow grows the palm, May-Day. 156.
For, though he scoop my water in his
palm, Seashore. 45.
Upspringeth the palm; Sphinx. 18.
Dominion o'er the palm and vine.
Woodnotes. II. 48.

Palm-crown
Cried "Onward!" and the palm-crown
showed, In Memoriam. 59.

Palm-grove
In the palm-grove with a rhyme;
Frag. Poet. V. 8.

Palmistry
He palmistry can understand,
Initial Love. 54.

Palms
Into those wise, thrilling palms.
Initial Love. 59.
That orange-grove, that isle of palms,
In Memoriam. 114.
Fresh from palms and Cuba's canes.
May-Day. 393.
Where palms plume, siroccos blaze,
Voluntaries. 48.
Who saw what ferns and palms were
pressed Wealth. 26.

Palm-tree
The date fails not on the palm-tree tall;
Woodnotes. II. 245.

Palmy
In yon green palmy isle, *Farewell. 50.

Palpitate
His heart should palpitate with fear.
Poet. 50.

Palsy
And pause were palsy to the world.—
Poet. 176.

Paltering
Thieving Ambition and paltering Gain!
Beauty. 24.

Palters
Virtue palters; Right is hence;
Channing Ode. 32.

He palters and steals; Sphinx. 52.

Pan
Tormenting Pan to double the dose.
Alphonso. 26.
The patient Pan, Frag. Nat. I. 1.
Pan, half asleep, rolling over
Frag. Nat. I. 7.
The gamut old of Pan, Monadnoc. 220.
But pipes through which the breath of
Pan doth blow Pan. 2.
Onward and on, the eternal Pan,
Woodnotes. II. 270.

Panax
Panax, black birch, sugar maple,
Frag. Nat. II. 15.

Pane
See Window-pane.
every cottage pane,
Frag. Nat. XXVII. 4.

Pang
He told no pang, he knew no fear;
In Memoriam. 100.
'Pang for pang your seed shall pay,
Voluntaries. 32.
In music he repeats the pang
Woodnotes. II. 124.

Panorama
The specious panorama of a year
Xenophanes. 14.

Panoramas
Panoramas which I saw
Frag. Poet. VIII. 8.

Pan's
Or Wordsworth, Pan's recording voice,—
Harp. 82.
Best of Pan's immortal meat,
Monadnoc. 304.

Pans
Our foaming ale we drank from hunters'
pans, Adirondacs. 177.
Give to barrows, trays and pans Art. 1.

Pant
I pant for thee no more. *Farewell. 49.

Panteth
That panteth after things unseen,
Hymn. 3.

Pantheist
See Theist.
Let theist, atheist, pantheist, Saadi. 96.

Panther
And near the wolf and panther slept.
Frag. Poet. I. 44.
The panther in our dances flies.
Romany. 24.

Pants
Pants up hither the spruce clerk
Monadnoc. 313.

Parade
Not for a regiment's parade,
May-Day. 104.
To mark thy beautiful parade,
Threnody. 75.

Paradise
Into this Oreads' fended Paradise,
Adirondacs. 194.
Nay, letters found us in our paradise:
Adirondacs. 334.
And the point is paradise,
Celestial Love. 17.
To tread the forfeit Paradise,
May-Day. 96.

But mount to paradise   Merlin. 37.
To fetch thee birds of paradise:
        Saadi. 148.
O child of paradise,   Threnody. 166.
Which in Paradise befell.   Uriel. 6.

Paradises
Painting artless paradises,
        May-Day. 249.

Paragon
Boy-Rabbi, Israel's paragon.
        Threnody. 223.

Paralytic
And crawls through life a paralytic
        Fame. 11.

Parapet
These scorned bondmen were my para-
    pet.   Grace. 4.
I dare not peep over this parapet
        Grace. 5.

Parasite
And he, poor parasite,   Monadnoc. 335.

Parcæ
Therein I hear the Parcæ reel
        Harp. 99.
And the stern Parcæ on his part.
        Initial Love. 129.
Or prayers the stony Parcæ soothe,
        Nemesis. 10.

Parent
And the parent of remorse.
        Daemonic Love. 131.
Child and parent,   Limits. 8.
The parent fruit survives;   Promise. 4.
Cut a bough from my parent stem,
        Woodnotes. II. 51.

Parental
And grave parental love.   River. 30.

Pariah
Those doors are men: the Pariah hind
        Saadi. 163.

Parian
On coop or kennel he hangs Parian
    wreaths;   Snow-Storm. 18.

Paris
Nor Rome, nor joyful Paris, nor the halls
        Naples. 17.

Parish
Rallying round a parish steeple
        Monadnoc. 129.

Park
Let statue, picture, park and hall,
        Art. 9.
His park where amber mornings break,
        Chartist. 10.
'This suits me for a pasture; that's my
    park;   Hamatreya. 19.

Parks
Parks and ponds are good by day;
        Frag. Nat. XVIII. 1.
In hamlets, palaces and parks,
        Initial Love. 3.
To twilight parks of beech and pine,
        Monadnoc. 6.

Parley
Can parley and provoke.   April. 12.
It cannot parley with the mean,—
        Astraea. 43.
They can parley without meeting;
        Celestial Love. 93.

Parlor
Yet there in the parlor sits
        World-Soul. 25.

Paroquet
And crowded whole, an infinite paroquet,
        Xenophanes. 18.

Part
    See Depart; Impart.
from wit the lion's part?
        Adirondacs. 276.
Thus to play its cheerful part,   Art. 20.
O, that were much, and I could be a
    part   Blight. 14.
Known in part, or known impure,
        Celestial Love. 51.
One third part of the sky unrolled
        Concord Ode. 11.
That were a man's and lover's part,
        Etienne. 23.
Rude ocean doth us part;
        *Farewell. 34.
For each quality and part
        Frag. Life. VI. 4.
Reason's twofold, part human, part di-
    vine;   Frag. Life. XVIII. 6.
That human part may be described and
    taught,   Frag. Life. XVIII. 7.
When Fate by omens takes his part,
        Initial Love. 71.
And the stern Parcæ on his part.
        Initial Love. 129.
The kind Earth takes her children's
    part,   May-Day. 66.
The master-stroke is still her part.
        Nature. II. 23.
How drear the part I held in one,
        Nun. 48.
And woke the fear lest angels part.
        Poet. 256.
With the fear that we must part?
        Poet. 266.
I too therein could challenge part
        Security. 11.
Took the largest part of me:
        Threnody. 161.
hear'st thou the least part?
        Woodnotes. II. 102.
Is perfect Nature's every part,
        Woodnotes. II. 176.
And are but one. Beheld far off, they
    part   Xenophanes. 9.

Parthenon
Earth proudly wears the Parthenon,
        Problem. 33.

Partial
    See Impartial.
The partial wrong,   Merlin. 120.
The partial wood-gods overpaid my love,
        Musketaquid. 4.

Parties
Or parties scaled the near acclivities
        Adirondacs. 129.
Made moon and planets parties to their
    bond,   Musketaquid. 8.

Parting
Though her parting dims the day,
        Give. 45.
Belike the one they used in parting
        May-Day. 385.

Parting —*Continued*
To parting soul bring grandeur near.
May-Day. 456.

Partridge
He saw the partridge drum in the woods;
Woodnotes. I. 54.

Parts
What parts, what gems, what colors shine,— Frag. Poet. XVIII. 5.
Scorn not thou the love of parts,
Prudence. 3.
Nor show thy pompous parts,
Saadi. 46.
To foreign parts is blown by fame;
Una. 22.

Party
He, when the rising storm of party roared, Phi. 7.

Pass
Père Raquette stream, to a small tortuous pass Adirondacs. 22.
No city airs or arts pass current here.
Adirondacs. 92.
Reflects his figure that doth pass.
Astraea. 24.
I keep, and pass, and turn again.
Brahma. 4.
Like a meteor pass.
Daemonic Love. 125.
The days pass over me
Days Pass. 1.
I saw them pass Experience. 2.
And pass the burning summer-time
Frag. Poet. V. 7.
'Pass in, pass in,' the angels say,
Merlin. 34.
I shall pass, as glides my shadow
Monadnoc. 264.
like Nature pass Musketaquid. 78.
I pass with yonder comet free,—
Nun. 38.
Pass with the comet into space
Nun. 39.
The boy's dream comes to pass,
October. 2.
Wise Ali's sunbright sayings pass
Saadi. 151.
Into that forester shall pass,
Woodnotes. II. 61.
Change I may, but I pass not.
Woodnotes. II. 255.

Passage
No breath therein, no passage out,
Poet. 190.

Passed
All was picture as he passed.
Humble-Bee. 51.
And a change has passed on things.
May-Day. 34.
Sped, when I passed his sylvan fort,
Titmouse. 35.

Passenger
Fine afternoon, old passenger!
Titmouse. 30.

Passes
And lo! he passes like the breeze;
Woodnotes. II. 308.

Passing
'T is a sparkle passing
Daemonic Love. 78.

Passing yonder oak, I heard
Miracle. 23.
And passing, light my sunken turf
Nun. 25.

Passion
Which, o'er passion throned sedate,
Astraea. 33.
In dens of passion, and pits of woe,
Beauty. 17.
Shun passion, fold the hands of thrift,
Frag. Life. XXXV. 1.
Passion not to be expressed
Freedom. 9.
Nor bent to passion frail. Harp. 4.
With passion cold and shy. Harp. 120.
With sudden passion languishing,
May-Day. 2.
Past clerks' or statesmen's art or passion.
Monadnoc. 178.
Nor me can Hope or Passion urge
Nun. 17.
And throttled all his passion. Is't not like
Philosopher. 10.
Worthier cause for passion wild
Threnody. 177.

Passional
The garden walks are passional
April. 3.

Passions
Her passions the shy violet
Quat. Hafiz. 1.

Passive
The passive Master lent his hand
Problem. 47.

Past
Which past endurance sting the tender cit, Adirondacs. 174.
The past restore, the day adorn,
Art. 11.
There Past, Present, Future, shoot
Celestial Love. 42.
Present and Past in under-song,—
Concord Ode. 18.
Shall into Future fuse the Past,
Culture. 10.
The maid, abolishing the past,
Daemonic Love. 12.
And all the crowded Past appears
Ellen. 3.
At unawares 't is come and past.
Forerunners. 32.
Past and future must reveal
Frag. Poet. V. 32.
What is past, what is done,
Frag. Poet. IX. 4.
Which thus the buried Past can tell,
Harp. 62.
Past all balsam or relief;
Love and Thought. 10.
Past clerks' or statesmen's art or passion.
Monadnoc. 178.
Such resurrection of the happy past,
Naples. 22.
I challenge thee to hurry past Nun. 31.
In Being's deeps past ear and eye;
Ode to Beauty. 95.
Not the gods can shake the Past;
Past. 11.
The buried Past arise; Peter. 18.
Things past and things to come.
Peter. 28.

But when the noisy scorn was past,
                              Poet. 23.
Future or Past no richer secret folds,
                              Quat. Heri. 3.
In trance upborne past mortal goal
                              Solution. 45.
I wrote the past in characters
                              Song of Nature. 21.
Past utterance, and past belief,
                              Threnody. 203.
And past the blasphemy of grief,
                              Threnody. 204.
I spurn the Past, my mind disdains its
  nod,   To-Day. 13.
Coming and past eternities?
                              Woodnotes. I. 29.
And ills to come as evils past bemoan.
                              Woodnotes. I. 89.

Pastoral
Where pastoral tribes their flocks infold,
                              Poet. 64.

Pasture
Stand upon this pasture hill,
                              Frag. Nat. XXVI. 7.
'This suits me for a pasture; that's my
  park;   Hamatreya. 19.
On farmer's byre, on pasture rude,
                              May-Day. 357.
Pasture of pool-haunting herds,
                              Monadnoc. 55.

Pastures
Said I, strolling through the pastures,
                              Berrying. 4.
The pastures sleep, ripple the lakes,
                              Saadi. 136.
And roamed the pastures through;
                              Thine Eyes. 6.

Patch
Will hint her secret in a garden patch,
                              Frag. Nat. IV. 2.
A patch of meadow upland
                              Waterfall. 1

Patent
By this foolish antique patent.
                              Initial Love. 10.

Path
    See Sun-path.
Thought's new-found path
                              Adirondacs. 243.
To men, the path to the Dæmon sphere;
                              Daemonic Love. 40.
So is man's narrow path
                              Daemonic Love. 60.
Knows its own path   Give. 16.
On the soft path each track is seen,
                              May-Day. 61.
I have trod this path a hundred times
                              Miracle. 1.
How danced thy form before my path
                              Thine Eyes. 7.

Pathetic
Pathetic silent poets that sing to me
                              Naples. 26.

Path-finder
Path-finder, road-builder,
                              Daemonic Love. 74.

Paths
Then I unbar the doors: my paths lead
  out   Seashore. 38.

Pathway
The stony pathway to the wood.
                              May-Day. 358.
On the flinty pathway beat
                              Monadnoc. 268.
To spy what danger on his pathway
  creeps;   Woodnotes. I. 91.

Pathways
He shall cut pathways east and west
                              Boston Hymn. 15.

Patience
With angel patience labor on,
                              In Memoriam. 76.
They say, through patience, chalk
                              They. 1.

Patient
    See Impatient.
The patient Pan,   Frag. Nat. I. 1.
Teach me your mood, O patient stars!
                              Frag. Nat. VIII. 5.
Patient through Heaven's enormous year
                              Wealth. 11.
The patient Dæmon sits,
                              World-Soul. 77.

Patriarch
But when at last the patriarch died
                              Frag. Nat. VI. 5.

Patriot
And honor joined the patriot ring
                              Boston. 84.
The evil time's sole patriot,
                              Channing Ode. 2.
See, every patriot oak-leaf throws
                              May-Day. 113.
Calm as the morn the manly patriot sate;
                              Phi. 10.

Patriots
I thought to find the patriots
                              Monadnoc. 92.
The Catos, the wise patriots of Rome,
                              Rome. 5.

Patron
Our patron pine was fifteen feet in girth,
                              Adirondacs. 42.

Pattern
Are of one pattern made; bird, beast and
  flower,   Xenophanes. 6.

Patterns
Water-line patterns of all art?
                              May-Day. 213.

Pause
A pause and council: then, where near
  the head   Adirondacs. 29.
And pause were palsy to the world.—
                              Poet. 176.
Stand not, pause not, in my going.
                              Song of Seyd. 20.
Fate's glowing revolution pause?
                              Threnody. 227.
But in each pause we heard the call
                              Walden. 35.

Paused
And paused for them, and looked around,
                              Dirge. 3.
Each village senior paused to scan
                              Threnody. 72.

Pauses
Nor pauses in his plan,
                              Concord Ode. 38.
And, far within those cadent pauses,
                              Woodnotes II. 118.

Pausing
And to the pausing lover.
                 Ellen South. 8.
Pave
Of races perishing to pave   Wealth. 23.
Paved
On the city's paved street   Art. 5.
Pavements
Where now on heated pavements worn
                 Boston. 39.
Pavilion
Pavilion on pavilion, garlanded,
                 October. 8.
Pawn
He goes in pawn to his victim
             Boston Hymn. 63.
Which I pawn for my release.   Rhea. 71.
Pawns
Their noble meanings are their pawns.
             Celestial Love. 88.
Pay
   See Overpay; Repay.
You shall pay us a tax on tea;
                 Boston. 66.
We pay your governors here
                 Boston. 70.
Pay ransom to the owner
             Boston Hymn. 69.
And ever was. Pay him.
             Boston Hymn. 72.
Would pay my debt to thee.
               *Farewell. 22.
Pay every debt as if God wrote the bill.
           Frag. Life. XXXII. 2.
'Pang for pang your seed shall pay,
            Voluntaries. 32.
Paying
Merlin paying the pain of sin, Harp. 55.
Pays
He pays too high a price   Fame. 7.
Remembering Matter pays her debt:
                 Wealth. 45.
Pea
Wild tea and wild pea, Frag. Nat. II. 2.
Peace
Peace now each for malice takes,
                 Caritas. 5.
The period of peace. Celestial Love. 68.
Peace that hallows rudest ways.
             Forerunners. 38.
in pleasèd peace,   Frag. Nat. XXVI. 21.
Of Syrian peace, immortal leisure,
             Humble-Bee. 38.
Of grim Disease, that would her peace
  affright.   I Bear. 12.
Its peace sublime his aspect kept,
          In Memoriam. 101.
And bring in poetic peace.   Merlin. 58.
For faith and peace and mighty love
           Robbins Hymn. 17.
Wait then, sad friend, wait in majestic
  peace   Rome. 20.
Oft shall war end, and peace return,
                 Saadi. 111.
I brooded long and held my peace,
               Solution. 18.
Heat, cold, wet, dry, and peace, and pain.
          Song of Nature. 76.
Shines the peace of all being,
               Sphinx. 45.

Hide in false peace your coward head,
             Voluntaries. 33.
'Achieve our peace who can!'
                 Walden. 24.
Peaceful
And peaceful woods beside my cottage
  door.   Frag. Nat. IV. 11.
And compromise thy peaceful state;
                 Saadi. 66.
My hours are peaceful centuries.
          Woodnotes II. 136.
Peacock
And leave thy peacock wit behind;
          Woodnotes. II. 231.
Peak
Oft, my far-appearing peak;
             Monadnoc. 200.
Peal
Of the wood-bell's peal and cry,
               Garden. 38.
Or where he stepped the soil did peal
                Poet. 5.
Pealed
Oft pealed for him a lofty tone
               Beauty. 11.
Pealing
I am dumb in the pealing song,
          Song of Nature. 6.
Peals
With hunters' appetite and peals of mirth.
          Adirondacs. 182.
A better voice peals through my song.
         Frag. Poet. XXX. 2.
In the heart of the music peals a strain
         Merlin's Song. 8.
Peals out a cheerful song.   Music. 6.
Pear
The cordial quality of pear or plum
          Musketaquid. 55.
Pear-bloom
Watching the white pear-bloom,
         Frag. Nat. XXI. 4.
Pearl
Nor pearl nor diamond   *Farewell. 21.
Illusions like the tints of pearl,
        Frag. Nat. XXXII. 1.
Said melted the days like cups of pearl,
        Frag. Poet. I. 19.
too slow the pearl: May-Day. 156.
Through crimson chambers, porphyry
  and pearl,   October. 7.
Pearls
Fresh pearls to their enamel gave,
               Each. 21.
Know the worth of Oman's pearls?
        Friendship. Trans. 2.
They grope the sea for pearls, but more
  than pearls: Seashore. 28.
Pearl-seed
Who, in large thoughts, like fair pearl-
  seed.   Monadnoc. 285.
Peasant
Is yonder squalid peasant all
             Monadnoc. 75.
The musing peasant, lowly great,
          Woodnotes. I. 104.
The lord is the peasant that was,
         Woodnotes. II. 18.
The peasant the lord that shall be;
         Woodnotes II. 19.

The lord is hay, the peasant grass,
                    Woodnotes II. 20.
Peat
And misty lowland, where to go for peat.
                    Hamatreya. 21.
Pebble
The pebble loosened from the frost
                    May-Day. 63.
The shining pebble of the pond,
                    Ode to Beauty. 29.
Pebbles
He flung in pebbles well to hear
                    Beauty. 9.
Pecker
See Woodpecker
Peculiar
And a few joys, a few peculiar charms,
                    Naples. 10.
Pedant
Leave all thy pedant lore apart;
                    Woodnotes. II. 234.
Pedantry
To plant thy shrivelled pedantry
                    Frag. Poet. XXIX. 6.
Pedestals
A spasm throbbing through the pedestals
                    Adirondacs. 262.
Peeled
Is thy land peeled, thy realm maraudéd?
                    Woodnotes. II. 181.
Peep
I dare not peep over this parapet
                    Grace. 5.
Peep the blue violets out of the black
loam,   Naples. 25.
In critic peep or cynic bark, To J. W. 19.
Peeped
Evening drew on; stars peeped through
maple-boughs,   Adirondacs. 46.
Peepeth
He creepeth and peepeth,   Sphinx. 51.
Peeping
Or, hid in vines, peeping through many
a loop,   Quat. Gardener. 3.
Peer
Broad England harbored not his peer:
                    Fate. 10.
Peering
Till green lances peering through
                    May-Day. 123.
Peerless
Such another peerless queen
                    Frag. Life. IX. 1.
Peers
But they hurry to their peers,
                    Astraea. 15.
My betters, yet my peers;
                    *Farewell. 29.
Go match thee with my seeming peers;
                    Frag. Life. XXV. 2.
I have no brothers and no peers,
                    Frag. Poet. XXV. 1.
Of Arthur and his peers;   Harp. 26.
A queen rejoices in her peers;
                    Walk. 1.
Pelf
Fame is profitless as pelf,
                    Frag. Poet. VII. 14.

Pen
And write my old adventures with the
pen   Bacchus. 64.
Not so the pen, for in a letter
                    Frag. Life. XII. 2.
By wondrous tongue, and guided pen,
                    Threnody. 136.
Penal
And his thought the penal worm.
                    Astraea. 30.
Penalty
To these their penalty belonged:
                    In Memoriam. 31.
Pencil
With a vermilion pencil mark the day
                    Adirondacs. 230.
Electric star or pencil plays,
                    II Compensation. 8.
Pendent
Cooled by the pendent mountain's shade,
                    May-Day. 17.
Penitence
Tones of penitence and pain,
                    Voluntaries. 3.
Penmanmaur
Seethed in mists of Penmanmaur,
                    Solution. 33.
Penn's
Penn's town, New York and Baltimore,
                    Boston. 47.
Pensive
Beset by pensive hosts.   Dirge. 16.
Wise Milton's odes of pensive pleasure,
                    Harp. 77.
And hither come the pensive train
                    Hymn. 9.
Beset by pensive hosts.]   Peter. 12.
Fall like sweet strains, or pensive smiles;
                    Problem. 4.
Came up the pensive train,
                    Robbins Hymn. 14.
Why wilt thou live when none around re-
flects thy pensive ray?   *Violet. 5.
Pent
Floating in air or pent in stone,
                    II Compensation. 26.
Pent in a dungeon made of air,—
                    Harp. 56.
Of the pent and darkened lake,
                    May-Day. 16.
Its onward force too starkly pent
                    Threnody. 247.
Thou in thy narrow banks art pent:
                    Two Rivers. 5.
And the treason, too long pent,
                    Uriel. 9.
Pentecost
Ever the fiery Pentecost   Problem. 51.
Brings again the Pentecost;
                    Woodnotes. II. 145.
People
Lisbon quakes, the people cry.
                    Alphonso. 14.
Call the people together,
                    Boston Hymn. 37.
Life up a people from the dust,
                    Boston Hymn. 67.
To see the people of the sky:
                    Frag. Poet. XI. 4.

People—*Continued*
Nestle warm the highland people,
                Monadnoc. 130.
Pours her power into the people,
                Nature. II. 6.
Reck not what the people say;
                Quat. Artist. 2.

Peoples
  See Unpeoples.
Who peoples, unpeoples,—
                Channing Ode. 82.

Peppermint
Peppermint and sassafras,
                Frag. Nat. II. 13.

Perceiving
Reaches not to my perceiving;
                Song of Seyd. 6.

Perch
Garden of berries, perch of birds,
                Monadnoc. 54.

Perchance
(Perchance I erred), a shade of discontent;   Adirondacs. 273.
And so, perchance, in Adam's race,
                May-Day. 92.
Traveller, to thee, perchance, a tedious road,   Musketaquid. 32.
Or if perchance, ye orbs of Fate,
                Poet. 241.
Perchance not he but Nature ailed,
                Threnody. 138.
Late in the world,—too late perchance
for fame,   To-Day. 5.

Perches
Nor perches in a narrow place;
                Voluntaries. 36.

Perdition
"T is man's perdition to be safe,
                Quat. Sacrifice. 3.

Père Raquette
Père Raquette stream, to a small tortuous pass   Adirondacs. 22.

Peremptory
Free, peremptory, clear.   Merlin. 4.

Perfect
  See Imperfect.
I yielded myself to the perfect whole.
                Each. 51.
Instant and perfect his access
                Frag. Life. XVII. 12.
I will wait Heaven's perfect hour
                Frag. Life. XXV. 3.
Perfect kinds by vice unmarred,
                Frag. Nat. XXIII. 2.
In perfect time and measure
                Frag. Nat. XXIV. 10.
O birds, your perfect virtues bring,
                May-Day. 397.
In perfect time and measure they
                Merlin. 126.
Where stars their perfect courses keep,
                Monadnoc. 101.
No perfect form could ever bind.
                Ode to Beauty. 73.
Then the perfect State is come,
                Politics. 25.
The perfect Adam lives.   Promise. 6.
Grandeur of the perfect sphere
                Prudence. 5.

Admits thee to the perfect Mind.
                Saadi. 164.
Forward stepped the perfect Greek:
                Solution. 14.
Whose soul sees the perfect,
                Sphinx. 79.
One crash, the death-hymn of the perfect tree,   Woodnotes. I. 74.
For Nature beats in perfect tune,
                Woodnotes. II. 164.
Is perfect Nature's every part,
                Woodnotes. II. 176.

Perfection
And soft perfection of its plan—
                May-Day. 287.

Perfect-paired
Perfect-paired as eagle's wings,
                Merlin. 113.

Perforates
And upward pries and perforates
                May-Day. 121.

Perforce
Perforce must use his tongue;
                Quat. Orator. 2.

Perform
Essaying nothing she cannot perform.
                Adirondacs. 72.
Perform the feat as well as they;
                Frag. Life. X. 2.

Perfume
And the wind that we perfume
                Ellen South. 35.
Goes loaded with a free perfume
                Mountain. 12.
The perfume of the place.
                Robbins Hymn. 8.

Perfumed
Not with scarfs or perfumed gloves
                Celestial Love. 99.
The perfumed berry on the spray
                May-Day. 77.

Perhaps
Moist perhaps by ocean surf,   Nun. 26.

Peril
Peril around, all else appalling,
                Voluntaries. 93.

Perilous
With Thought's• perilous, whirling pool;
                Threnody. 233.

Period
The period of peace.
                Celestial Love. 68.
Fills the just period,   Merlin. 121.

Periods
Tired of their starry periods,
                May-Day. 328.
In their cloudless periods;   Rhea. 26.
It fell in the ancient periods   Uriel. 1.

Perish
Perish like leaves, the highland breed
                Monadnoc. 123.

Perished
But not for those who perished here.
                In Memoriam. 2.

Perishing
Of races perishing to pave
                Wealth. 23.

Permanence
And type of permanence!
                Monadnoc. 360.

Permanent
As God lives, is permanent;
Threnody. 267.

Permit
But Fate will not permit   Fame. 19.

Permitted
Permitted on her infinite repose
Adirondacs. 341.

Perpetual
Nor wine nor brains perpetual pump.
Alphonso. 62.
Victim of perpetual slight: Destiny. 19.

Perpetually
To and fro perpetually;
Daemonic Love. 80.

Perplexed
There, while hot heads perplexed with
fears the state,   Phi. 9.

Persia
With Persia for his audience;
Saadi. 28.
And well could honoring Persia learn
Saadi. 82.

Persons
Leaves twinkle, flowers like persons be,
Saadi. 137.

Persuade
Or who like thee persuade,
May-Day. 428.
To beckon or persuade   May-Day. 434.

Persuades
No prayer persuades, no flattery fawns,—
Celestial Love. 87.

Persuading
Nigh persuading gods to err!
Ode to Beauty. 22.

Persuasion
And gives persuasion to a gentle deed.
Enchanter. 15.
And touch with soft persuasion,
Saadi. 126.

Persuasions
Words that were persuasions.
Threnody. 53.

Pert
And vex the gods with question pert,
Alphonso. 38.

Pervaded
Their dust, pervaded by the nerves of
God,   Pan. 6.

Perversely
Perversely borrowing from the shop the
tools   Adirondacs. 283.
Stream could not so perversely wind
Guy. 35.

Pervious
Is pervious to Love;   Cupido. 2.

Pet
Blue-eyed pet of blue-eyed lover.
Ellen South. 32.
'You pet! what dost here? and what for?
Titmouse. 49.
I homeward turn; farewell, my pet!
Titmouse. 80.

Petal
And every colored petal of each flower,
Naples. 6.
Tints that spot the violet's petal,
Woodnotes. I. 21.

Petals
The purple petals, fallen in the pool,
Rhodora. 5.
So bloom the unfading petals five,
Solution. 71.

Peter's
The hand that rounded Peter's dome
Problem. 19.

Petted
Hot midsummer's petted crone,
Humble-Bee. 32.

Pettish
Was it a squirrel's pettish bark,
May-Day. 21.

Petty
Where I, as others, follow petty ends;
Frag. Life. XV. 3.

Petulant
Hark to that petulant chirp!
Adirondacs. 206.

Pew
Equal on Sunday in the pew,
Boston. 27.

Phantom
Brother, we are no phantom band;
Poet. 263.

Phantoms
And phantoms and nothings
Illusions. 29.

Phe-be
Crying out of the hazel copse, Phe-be!
Titmouse. 93.

Phial
Weatherglass and chemic phial,
Monadnoc. 53.

Phidias
Than Phidias released.
Good Hope. 8.
His awful Jove young Phidias brought;
Problem. 10.

Philosopher
Yellow-breeched philosopher!
Humble-Bee. 53.
Was shown to this philosopher,
Woodnotes. I. 60.

Philosophers
Of science, not from the philosophers,
Adirondacs. 284.
Philosophers are lined with eyes within,
Philosopher. 1.

Philosophy
Some tears escaped, but his philosophy
Philosopher. 8.

Phlegm
Piling mountain chains of phlegm
Frag. Nat. I. 13.

Phœbus
Phœbus stablish must.   Politics. 14.

Phosphoric
Lit with phosphoric crumbs the forest
floor.   Adirondacs. 49.

Phrase
And send conviction without phrase,
Monadnoc. 404.

Physician
Asked no physician but the wave,
Frag. Poet. V. 20.
On the first, neither balm nor physician
can save,   On Two Days. 3.

Piano
On the piano, played with master's hand.
Adirondacs. 314.
Nor tinkle of piano strings,   Merlin. 6.

Pickerel-flower
Through gold-moth-haunted beds of
pickerel-flower,   Adirondacs. 18.

Picket-fence
Farm-gear and village picket-fence,
Poet. 59.

Picture
Your picture smiles as first it smiled;
Amulet. 1.
Let statue, picture, park and hall,
Art. 9.
All was picture as he passed.
Humble-Bee. 51.
Or, it may be, a picture; to these men,
Musketaquid. 33.
On life's fair picture of delight,
Nun. 9.
Song, picture, form, space, thought and
character   Xenophanes. 7.

Pictures
So light, so lofty pictures came and
went.   Adirondacs. 159.
What pictures and what harmonies are
thine!   Adirondacs. 212.
And all we see are pictures high;
Frag. Nat. III. 16.
Her gay pictures never fail,
Frag. Nat. XXXI. 3.
Painting pictures mile on mile,
May-Day. 4.
Gayest pictures rose to win me,
Monadnoc. 3.
Nor pictures pale, but Jove and Mars.
Monadnoc. 308.
These pictures of time;   Sphinx. 70.

Piece
See Masterpiece.

Pied
Pied with morning and with night.
II Compensation. 2.

Pierce
Whose eyes pierce
Daemonic Love. 72.
When they with torch of genius pierce
Dull. 11.
So shall thou pierce the distant age
Frag. Poet. XIII. 3.

Pierced
Its root has pierced yon shady mound;
Holidays. 6.
That pierced my trance its drift to tell,
Miracle. 30.
In May, when sea-winds pierced our soli-
tudes,   Rhodora. 1.

Piercing
See Sky-piercing.
As Uriel spoke with piercing eye,
Uriel. 25.
Of his triumphant piercing sight:
Woodnotes. II. 66.

Piety
Show our love and piety.
Ellen South. 28.

Pigeon
The pigeon in the pines,
Waldeinsamkeit. 30.

Pile
Unploughed, which finer spirits pile,
Monadnoc. 43.
Still is the haughty pile erect
Monadnoc. 373.
And pile the hills to scale the sky;
Saadi. 95.

Piled
See Purple-piled; Thrice-piled; Wild-
piled.
Eldest mason, Frost, had piled
May-Day. 47.
When heroes piled the pyre,
May-Day. 141.
Walls Amphion piled   Politics. 13.
Half piled or prostrate; and my newest
slab   Seashore. 16.
They boiled the sea, and piled the layers
Song of Nature. 35.
But when the quarried means were
piled,   Wealth. 29.

Piles
Hid in gleaming piles of stone;
Art. 4.
Such and so grew these holy piles,
Problem. 31.
Sin piles the loaded board.
Woodnotes. II. 17.

Pilgrim
He came a pilgrim to the Mosque
Frag. Poet. I. 5.
The joy and pride the pilgrim feels
In Memoriam. 83.
'Gentle pilgrim, if thou know
Monadnoc. 219.
O pilgrim, wandering not amiss!
Monadnoc. 242.
Say, Pilgrim, why so late and slow to
come?   Seashore. 2.
When here again thy pilgrim comes,
Titmouse. 81.
To please and win this pilgrim wise.
Woodnotes. I. 53.

Pilgrimage
See Star-pilgrimage.
When the pilgrimage is done,
Etienne. 5.
The soul's pilgrimage and flight;
May-Day. 462.

Pilgrims
To the watching Pilgrims came,
Boston Hymn. 2.
The pilgrims have each other lost.
Love and Thought. 12.
Pilgrims wight with step forthright.
May-Day. 311.

Piling
Piling mountain chains of phlegm
Frag. Nat. I. 13.

Pillar
Pillar which God aloft had set
Monadnoc. 48.

Pillow
A pillow in her greenest field,
Woodnotes. I. 144.

Pillowed
But pillowed all on melody,   Harp. 59.

Pilot
Port or pilot trows not,—
Monadnoc. 338.

I put no faith in pilot or in chart,
Unbar. 3.
Without a pilot it runs and falls,
Woodnotes. II. 240.

Pin
I caught with bended pin my earliest
fish, River. 12.

Pinch
At this pinch, wee San Salvador!
Titmouse. 51.

Pinched
Swains by winter pinched and worn.
Frag. Nat. XXII. 4.

Pinches
Me a little pinches here,
From Hafiz. 14.

Pine
See Ground-pine.
pitch and Norway pine,
Adirondacs. 40.
Our patron pine was fifteen feet in girth,
Adirondacs. 42.
And here in a pine state-house
Boston Hymn. 41.
The strong gods pine for my abode,
Brahma. 13.
And pine in vain the sacred Seven;
Brahma. 14.
If thou pine for another's gift?
Destiny. 17.
Runs round the pine and maple tree
Frag. Nat. XIX. 2.
He freelier breathed beside the pine,
Frag. Poet. V. 15.
Æolian harps in the pine Garden. 33.
Rafters of immortal pine, House. 6.
To twilight parks of beech and pine,
Monadnoc. 6.
Hollow and lake, hillside and pine arcade,
Musketaquid. 23.
Here in pine houses Musketaquid. 30.
They talk in the shaken pine, Poet. 74.
So sings in the wind a sprig of the pine;
Quat. Leasts. 2.
When the pine tosses its cones
Woodnotes. I. 1.
Who liveth by the ragged pine
Woodnotes. II. 22.
And grant to dwellers with the pine
Woodnotes. II. 47.
And the countless leaves of the pine are
strings Woodnotes. II. 95.
I, that to-day am a pine,
Woodnotes. II. 276.

Pine-cones
Pine-cones and acorns lay on the ground;
Each. 45.

Pine-groves
One sound to pine-groves and to waterfalls, Xenophanes. 3.

Pine-roots
The rope-like pine-roots crosswise grown
Woodnotes. I. 106.

Pines
See Ground-pines.
Beholding the procession of the pines;
Adirondacs. 116.
Snow-loving pines and oaks instead;
Garden. 6.

And when I am stretched beneath the
pines, Good-Bye. 25.
And finds young pines and budding
birches; Threnody. 25.
The pigeon in the pines,
Waldeinsamkeit. 30.

Pine-tree
Answered the pine-tree and the oak,
Frag. Nat. III. 11.
Or how the sacred pine-tree adds
Problem. 29.
As sings the pine-tree in the wind,
Quat. Leasts. 1.
With sudden roar the aged pine-tree
fall,— Woodnotes. I. 73.
So waved the pine-tree through my
thought Woodnotes. II. 3.
Quoth the pine-tree, Woodnotes. II. 7.
Only what the pine-tree yields;
Woodnotes. II. 31.
Who leaves the pine-tree, leaves his
friend, Woodnotes. II. 49.
Once again the pine-tree sung:—
Woodnotes. II. 133.

Pine-warbler
Hearken to yon pine-warbler Dirge. 41.

Pine-woods
Of close low pine-woods in a river town;
Naples. 14.

Pining
Hark what, now loud, now low, the pin-
ing flute complains, Flute. 1.
I, pining to be one of you, Poet. 238.

Pinnace
New worlds to find in pinnace frail.
Quat. Poet. I. 4.

Pinnacles
But o'er the pinnacles of thine!
Shah. Enweri. I. 2.
Song wakes in my pinnacles
Woodnotes. II. 91.

Pinned
He by false usage pinned about
Poet. 189.

Piny
The piny hosts were sheeted ghosts
May-Day. 49.

Pioneer
And well the primal pioneer
Wealth. 9.

Pious
The pious wind took it away,
Poet. 17.

Piously
See Impiously.

Pipe
Rhyme the pipe, and Time the warder,
Monadnoc. 247.
Whose pipe and arrow Musketaquid. 29.

Piped
When piped a tiny voice hard by,
Titmouse. 25.
To find what bird had piped the strain:—
Woodnotes. II. 249.

Pipes
Milkweeds and murky brakes, quaint
pipes and sundew, Blight. 7.
Mount in the pipes of the trees.
May-Day. 231.
But pipes through which the breath of
Pan doth blow Pan. 2.

Piping

Piping, as they flew, a march,—
                 May-Day. 384.

Pique

Was it college pique of town and gown,
                 Adirondacs. 277.
Can cozen, pique and flatter,   April. 11.

Piques

Piques, reproaches, hurts, caresses.
                 Initial Love. 133.

Piranesi's

And   Piranesi's   lines.
                 Ode to Beauty. 55.

Pirate

On pirate and Turk.   Channing Ode. 89.

Pirates

And pirates of the universe, shut out
                 Blight. 47.

Pit

Shot through the weltering pit of the salt
   sea.   Adirondacs. 270.
In the pit of his eye's a spark
                 Initial Love. 21.
The pit wherein the streams are rolled
                 Quat. Alcuin. 3.
Yawns the pit of the Dragon,
                 Sphinx. 75.

Pitch

Three conifers, white, pitch and Norway
   pine,   Adirondacs. 40.
Tempering the pitch of all   Harp. 9.
I rest on the pitch of the torrent,
                 Song of Nature. 7.

Pith

Every quality and pith   Unity. 9.

Pitiless

Pitiless, will not be stayed;
                 Daemonic Love. 113.

Pits

In dens of passion, and pits of woe,
                 Beauty. 17.
The pits of air, the gulf of space,
                 Song of Nature. 2.

Pity

Both death and pity, my unequal skill
                 Angelo. 13.
Which more of pride than pity gave
                 In Memoriam. 13.
Something of pity for the puny clay,
                 River. 34.

Pius

Crusoe, Crusader, Pius Æneas, said aloud,
                 Adirondacs. 184.

Placard

No placard on these rocks warned to the
   polls,   Adirondacs. 64.

Place

    See Displace; Dwelling-place; Market-
place; Misplace.
To assign just place and mates;
                 Astraea. 20.
Making one place two places?
                 Chartist. 2.
And when I am entombèd in my place,
                 Entombed. 1.
To occupy my place.   Fable. 11.
For Nature, true and like in every place,
                 Frag. Nat. IV. 1.
Kept its place by the poet's side.
                 Frag. Poet. I. 18.

In this ancestral place,
                 In Memoriam. 22.
And by the moral of his place
                 Monadnoc. 110.
Reach his place and circumstance,
                 Monadnoc. 253.
Saying, 'Stand in thy place;   Poet. 120.
And Nature gladly gave them place,
                 Problem. 41.
The perfume of the place.
                 Robbins Hymn. 8.
Thy steps to watch, thy place to know:
                 Threnody. 33.
Nor perches in a narrow place;
                 Voluntaries. 36.
A plant in any secret place,
                 Woodnotes. I. 37.
As if a sunbeam showed the place,
                 Woodnotes. I. 44.

Places

Making one place two places?
                 Chartist. 2.
Oft, in streets or humblest places,
                 Ode to Beauty. 64.
Happy to meet you in these places,
                 Titmouse. 31.
But one I seek in foreign places,
                 Una. 11.

Placing

    See Replacing.

Plague

To help her friends, to plague her foes,
                 Nature. I. 14.
The plague is stayed.   Past. 4.

Plain

Masters, I'll be plain with you;
                 Alphonso. 42.
Plain and cold is their address,
                 Celestial Love. 89.
The potent plain of Dæmons spreads.
                 Daemonic Love. 26.
The plain was full of ghosts;   Dirge. 14.
To speak the plain reproof of sin
                 Hymn. 17.
While cheerful cries of crag and plain
                 May-Day. 239.
Or tented armies on a plain.
                 May-Day. 256.
O'er the floor of plain and flood
                 Monadnoc. 194.
It rose a bubble from the plain.
                 Monadnoc. 290.
The plain was full of ghosts:
                 Peter. 10.
Through thee, as thou through Concord
   Plain.   Two Rivers. 4.
When Autumn chills the plain.
                 Walden. 8.

Plain-dealing

In the glad home plain-dealing Nature
   gave.   Musketaquid. 67.

Plainer

Plainer than the day,   Initial Love. 42.

Plains

Mountains and the misty plains
                 Hermione. 20.
Faster flowing o'er the plains,—
                 May-Day. 244.
To all the dwellers in the plains
                 Monadnoc. 35.

Frontier of the wheat-sown plains,
Quat. Alcuin. 2.
From his Afric's torrid plains.
Voluntaries. 8.
In plains that room for shadows make
Waldeinsamkeit. 5.

Plan
And the poor grass shall plot and plan
Bacchus. 41.
Nor pauses in his plan,
Concord Ode. 38.
For fear of human eyes swerved from
his plan.   Entombed. 4.
Materials for her plan;   House. 4.
And soft perfection of its plan—
May-Day. 287.
Dædalian plan;   Sphinx. 12.
Still plan and smile,   Terminus. 20.
Who layeth the world's incessant plan,
Woodnotes. II. 271.

Planet
Shall to the planet overpay
May-Day. 277.
Or what ill planet crossed his prime?
Voluntaries. 14.
The planets' child the planet knows
Waterfall. 13.
The planet with a floor of lime?
Wealth. 24.

Planets
As planets faithful be.
Boston Hymn. 48.
Mortals deem the planets bright
Daemonic Love. 52.
The light wherewith all planets shone,
Frag. Poet. IV. 25.
Made moon and planets parties to their
bond,   Musketaquid. 8.
Races and planets, its enchanted foam.
Pan. 12.
With beams December planets dart
Quat. S. H. 1.
Forthright my planets roll,
Song of Nature. 42.
For flattering planets seemed to say
Threnody. 134.

Planets'
The planets' child the planet knows
Waterfall. 13.

Planned
Its timorous ways, big trifles, and we
planned   Adirondacs. 161.
Whose groves the frolic fairies planned;
Good-Bye. 18.
And richly his large future planned,
In Memoriam. 70.
And childhood's castles built or planned;
Threnody. 87.
To the vast soul that o'er him planned;
Problem. 48.

Plans
Plans, credit and the Muse,—   Give. 5.
Plans immense his term prolong;
Initial Love. 139.

Plant
  See Transplant.
Yea, plant the tree that bears best apples,
plant,   Adirondacs. 298.
Plant gardens lined with lilacs sweet;
Art. 6.

And strangers to the plant and to the
mine.   Blight. 32.
Fire, plant and mineral say, 'Not in us;'
Blight. 35.
To plant and eat be none afraid.
Boston. 12.
We plant and build by foaming seas
Boston. 21.
To plant and eat be none afraid.
Boston. 54.
To plant thy shrivelled pedantry
Frag. Poet. XXIX. 6.
My stock of art, plant dials in the grass,
Letter. 20.
Failed to plant the vantage-ground;
Merlin's Song. 19.
O, wondrous craft of plant and stone
Monadnoc. 66.
Kindly to plant and blood and kind,
Monadnoc. 90.
I plant his eyes on the sky-hoop bound-
ing;   Monadnoc. 324.
Nor plant immense designs
Poet. 247.
Plant, quadruped, bird,   Sphinx. 34.
My hedges plant and feed.   Walden. 12.
Wild planters, plant away! Walden. 16.
A plant in any secret place,
Woodnotes. I. 37.
Low lies the plant to whose creation went
Woodnotes. I. 76.

Plantation
This wild plantation will suffice to chase.
Adirondacs. 319.

Plantations
Far-travelled in the south plantations;
Frag. Nat. XXIII. 8.

Planted
  See Self-planted; Unplanted.
No faster than his planted trees,
Alphonso. 78.
And planted world, and full executor
Blight. 16.
Fair rose the planted hills behind
Boston. 41.
The orchard planted,
Channing Ode. 62.
His planted isle where roses glow?
Chartist. 12.
For joy and beauty planted it,
Frag. Nat. X. 1.
He planted where the deluge ploughed,
Frag. Poet. XXVII. 1.
Planted these, and tempests flowed it.
Garden. 20.
Her planted eye to-day controls,
Quat. Fate. 1.

Planter
Well the Planter knew how strongly
Monadnoc Afar. 5.
There the great Planter plants
Waldeinsamkeit. 21.

Planters
Wild planters, plant away!   Walden. 16.

Planting
Planting seeds of knowledge pure,
May-Day. 467.
Planting strange fruits and sunshine on
the shore,   Seashore. 47.
The planting of the coal.
Song of Nature. 24.

Plants
Not less the ambitious botanist sought
plants, Adirondacs. 141.
Spices in the plants that run
Frag. Nat. II. 19.
Plants and birds and humble creatures
May-Day. 134.
And wide around, the marriage of the
plants, Adirondacs. 141.
Felt in the plants and in the punctual
birds; Musketaquid. 64.
Plants with worlds the wilderness;
Threnody. 285.
There the great Planter plants
Waldeinsamkeit. 21.
If plants or brain, if egg or shell,
Walden. 39.
Of gem, and air, of plants, and worms.
Woodnotes. II. 275.

Plato's
Of Cæsar's hand, and Plato's brain,
Informing Spirit. 7.

Play
Thus to play its cheerful part, Art. 20.
And billows round her play,
*Farewell. 26.
He seemed to bask, to dream and play
Frag. Poet. V. 4.
Play not in Nature's lawful web,
Garden. 22.
How the chemic eddies play,
Monadnoc. 229.
In thy momentary play,
Ode to Beauty. 31.
I court and play with paler blood,
Romany. 14.
Ever, when twain together play,
Saadi. 15.
Play glad with the breezes,
Sphinx. 27.
Shows feats of his gymnastic play,
Titmouse. 41.
This scrap of valor just for play
Titmouse. 45.
Hatred's swift repulsions play. Visit. 30.
And the play of his miracles.
Woodnotes. II. 286.

Played
On the piano, played with master's hand.
Adirondacs. 314.
They played with it in every mood;
Dirge. 30.
Mad Destiny this tender stripling played;
Epitaph. 2.
What pranks the greenwood played;
Peter. 22.
Too long the game is played;
Song of Nature. 54.
To some tune by fairies played;—
Threnody. 77.

Playest
Still thou playest;—short vacation
Holidays. 17.

Playfellow
Playfellow of young and old,
Holidays. 10.

Playfellows
Old playfellows meet; Sphinx. 28.

Playing
But blest is he, who, playing deep, yet
haply asks not why, Quat. Nature. 3.

Plays
Electric star or pencil plays,
Compensation. II. 8.
A gleam which plays and hovers
Daemonic Love. 36.
Every year plays it over Ellen South. 6.
A light which plays and hovers
Frag. Life. XVI. 2.

Pleached
I, in my pleached garden, watched the
pomp, Days. 7.

Plead
United States! the ages plead,—
Concord Ode. 17.
Mute orator! well skilled to plead,
Monadnoc. 403.

Pleading
Or woman's pleading eyes;
World-Soul. 28.

Pleadings
Thy softest pleadings seem too bold,
Rhea. 21.

Pleads
Pleads for itself the fact,
In Memoriam. 94.

Pleasance
Underwoods were full of pleasance,
Peter. 33.

Pleasant
Pleasant fancies overtook me.
Berrying. 8.
A secret nook in a pleasant land,
Good-Bye. 17.
Are pleasant songs to me.
Sphinx. 68.

Please
To please each other well;
Celestial Love. 7.
Gathered with hope to please,
Daemonic Love. 109.
Princely women hard to please,
Frag. Poet. I. 27.
Please God, I'll wrap me in mine in-
nocence, I Bear. 13.
Please God, that I would lead?
Letter. 2.
Thy trivial harp will never please
Merlin. 1.
It would please me to die,
Mountain. 10.
And do well because they please,
Nature. I. 19.
To please the desert and the sluggish
brook. Rhodora. 4.
Henceforth, please God, forever I forego
Self-Reliance. 1.
To please and win this pilgrim wise.
Woodnotes. I. 53.

Pleased
Pleased with these grand companions, we
glide on, Adirondacs. 12.
And these from the crowd's edge well
pleased Frag. Life. XXX. 6.
And pleased I stray
Frag. Nat. XXI. 2.
Sleeps the vast East in pleasèd peace,
Frag. Nat. XXVI. 21.
Did as she pleased and went her way.
Frag. Nat. XXXV. 2.
It hath pleased Heaven to break the
dream of bliss I Bear. 3.

Pleasure
May float at pleasure through all natures;
                                Bacchus. 23.
Nor let us hide, whate'er our pleasure,
                                Fame. 23.
With a face of golden pleasure
                                Frag. Nat. XXIV. 11.
Wise Milton's odes of pensive pleasure,
                                Harp. 77.
Firmest cheer, and bird-like pleasure.
                                Humble-Bee. 39.
Of heart and soul, of strength and
    pleasure,   Solution. 36.
And under pain, pleasure,—
                                Sphinx. 99.
Under pleasure, pain lies.   Sphinx. 100.
Go thou, sweet Heaven, or at thy
    pleasure stay!'   Sursum Corda. 9.
Pleasure-grounds
Has royal pleasure-grounds outspread.'
                                Monadnoc. 71.
Pleasures
Pleasures to another stage
                                Frag. Poet. XI. 16.
Pledge
They give and take no pledge or oath,—
                                Celestial Love. 85.
Pledged
As pledged in coming days to forge
                                In Memoriam. 64.
Pleiads
The dancing Pleiads and eternal men.
                                Bacchus. 67.
Once, among the Pleiads walking,
                                Uriel. 7.
Pleiads'
The Pleiads' sheaf but two.
                                From Hafiz. 8.
Plenteous
Broad-sowing, cheerful, plenteous,
                                May-Day. 272.
Plenties
O barren mound, thy plenties fill!
                                Monadnoc. 378.
Plentiful
The opaline, the plentiful and strong,
                                Seashore. 18.
Plenty
Teach your pupils now with plenty,
                                Alphonso. 53.
In his plenty things so rare?
                                Goethe. 8.
Plied
Plied for thee thy household tasks.'
                                Saadi. 176.
Plies
The thrush plies his wings;   Sphinx. 22.
Plight
To me their comfort plight;—
                                Hermione. 64.
Into all our human plight,
                                May-Day. 461.
And in days of evil plight
                                Solution. 20.
Plight broken, this high face defaced!
                                Threnody. 151.
Plighted
    See Unplighted.
Plinlimmon's
Taught by Plinlimmon's Druid power,
                                Solution. 34.

Plot
    See Garden-plot.
And the poor grass shall plot and plan
                                Bacchus. 41.
In my plot no tulips blow,—
                                Garden. 5.
God for thy virtue lays a plot:
                                Prayer. 2.
We plot and corrupt each other,
                                World-Soul. 23.
Plots
He works, plots, fights, in rude affairs,
                                Fate. 7.
Nor plots to ope or bolt a gate,
                                Frag. Life. XVII. 8.
Plotted
Plotted to make him rich and great:
                                Quat. Horoscope. 2.
Plotting
Baulks and baffles plotting brains;
                                Nature. I. 6.
Still plotting how their hungry ear
                                Threnody. 50.
Plough
For what avail the plough or sail,
                                Boston. 29.
For what avail the plough or sail,
                                Boston. 80.
And strangers, fond as they, their fur-
    rows plough.   Hamatreya. 12.
Who steer the plough, but cannot steer
    their feet   Hamatreya. 15.
Whose pipe and arrow oft the plough un-
    buries,   Musketaquid. 29.
Plough-boy
Makes Romeo of a plough-boy on his
    cart;   Enchanter. 13.
Ploughed
    See Unploughed.
Nothing was ploughed, or reaped, or
    bought, or sold;   Adirondacs. 67.
He planted where the deluge ploughed,
                                Frag. Poet. XXVII. 1.
Here once the Deluge ploughed,
                                Garden. 13.
Ploughman's
Above the ploughman's highest line,
                                Monadnoc. 8.
Ploughmen
Fishers and choppers and ploughmen
                                Boston Hymn. 31.
Ploughs
Their talismans are ploughs and carts;
                                Monadnoc. 134.
Where the statesman ploughs
                                Politics. 21.
Plow
    See Plough.
Pluck
Love not the flower they pluck, and know
    it not,   Blight. 21.
Pluck it now! In vain,—thou canst not;
                                Holidays. 5.
They pluck Force thence, and give it to
    the wise.   Seashore. 29.
Plum
Bee-infested quince or plum.
                                Frag. Nat. XXI. 5.
The cordial quality of pear or plum
                                Musketaquid. 55.

Plum —*Continued*
See the plum redden, and the beurré
stoop. Quat. Gardener. 4.
Plumage
New tint the plumage of the birds,
May-Day. 447.
Plume
All the brags of plume and song;
Saadi. 150.
Where palms plume, siroccos blaze,
Voluntaries. 48.
Plumes
Here might the red-bird come his plumes
to cool, Rhodora. 7.
Plum-trees
From plum-trees vegetable gold;
Guy. 44.
Plumule
Fled the last plumule of the Dark,
Monadnoc. 312.
Plunge
Then plunge to depths profound.
Garden. 12.
Plunged
See Replunged.
Plunges
Plunges eyeless on forever;
Monadnoc. 334.
Ply
Ply us now with a full diet;
Alphonso. 52.
It through thousand natures ply;
Sphinx. 118.
Poet
Her last poet mute: Channing Ode. 93.
In the deep heart of man a poet dwells
Enchanter. 1.
But if, grown bold, the poet dare
Frag. Poet. IV. 3.
Well might then the poet scorn
Frag. Poet. V. 44.
His instant thought a poet spoke,
Frag. Poet. XXXII. 1.
How should not the poet doat
Harp. 50.
Not Homer's self, the poet sire,
Harp. 76.
The rhyme of the poet Merlin. 77.
With sounding steps the poet came;
Poet. 2.
And the poet who overhears Poet. 77.
Thus to himself the poet spoke,
Poet. 141.
Again by night the poet went Poet. 225.
Theme no poet gladly sung,
Prudence. 1.
Test of the poet is knowledge of love,
Quat. Casella. 1.
Never was poet, of late or of yore,
Quat. Casella. 3.
Ever the Poet from the land
Quat. Poet. I. 1.
But the poet dwells alone. Saadi. 8.
A poet or a friend to find: Saadi. 156.
Poet on a sunny headland September. 3.
When France, where poet never grew,
Solution. 63.
I heard a poet answer Sphinx. 65.
This poet, though he live apart,
Titmouse. 33.

There the poet is at home.
Woodnotes. I. 6.
Poetic
I filled the dream of sad, poetic maids,
Frag. Life. XXX. 2.
And bring in poetic peace. Merlin. 58.
As in the old poetic fame
Monadnoc. 348.
Poet's
Kept its place by the poet's side.
Frag. Poet. I. 18.
So the gentle poet's name Una. 21.
New slaves fulfilled the poet's dream,
Wealth. 40.
Poets
Chief of song where poets feast
Harp. 38.
Poets praise that hidden wine
May-Day. 406.
Rude poets of the tavern hearth,
Monadnoc. 185.
Pathetic silent poets that sing to me
Naples. 26.
Annexed a warning, poets say,
Saadi. 13.
Poets, for the air was fame.
Solution. 42.
Nor time unmake what poets know.
Test. 12.
Point
And the point is paradise,
Celestial Love. 17.
Pointed
To spiritual lessons pointed home,
Adirondacs. 200.
Pointing
Softly,—but this way fate was pointing,
Titmouse. 23.
Points
Gilds a few points in every several life,
Naples. 4.
Poises
And every atom poises for itself,
Musketaquid. 58.
Poises Arcturus aloft morning and eve-
ning his spear. Shah-Hafiz. 2.
Poisoned
Like poisoned loaf of elfin bread,
Frag. Nat. III. 3.
Poisoning
Whom the city's poisoning spleen
Woodnotes. II. 35.
Poisons
He poisons the ground. Sphinx. 56.
Poland
The Cossack eats Poland,
Channing Ode. 90.
Polar
Mix polar night with tropic glow,
May-Day. 127.
Far in the North, where polar night
Solution. 43.
And polar frost my frame defied,
Titmouse. 77.
Pole
From nodding pole and belting zone.
Beauty. 12.
Pole to pole, and what they say;
Monadnoc. 230.

Poles
See Earth-poles.
We cut young trees to make our poles
and thwarts, Adirondacs. 34.
Nor less the eternal poles
Celestial Love. 81.
By their animate poles. Sphinx. 32.
Of poles and powers, cold, wet, and
warm: Woodnotes. II. 111.
Pole-star
Pole-star of light in Europe's night,
Boston. 90.
Was pole-star when the night was dark;
Woodnotes. I. 134.
Polished
Look to yourselves, ye polished gentle-
men! Adirondacs. 91.
Polite
See Impolite.
Wise and polite,—and if I drew
Adirondacs. Motto. 1.
The polite found me impolite; the great
Musketaquid. 68.
Gay and polite, a cheerful cry,
Titmouse. 26.
Politic
No thief so politic, Past. 15.
Politics
The politics are base; World-Soul. 17.
Politique
My study for their politique,
Channing Ode. 8.
Polls
No placard on these rocks warned to the
polls, Adirondacs. 64.
Pollution
To fight pollution of the mind;
Monadnoc. 113.
Polycrates
And as, of old, Polycrates Guy. 7.
Polygala
Found in polygala root and rind,
Frag. Nat. II. 27.
Polygonum
Rosy polygonum, lake-margin's pride,
Adirondacs. 143.
Pomp
In miracles of pomp, we must be proud,
Adirondacs. 155.
I, in my pleached garden, watched the
pomp, Days. 7.
And Nature squanders on the boy her
pomp, October. 3.
Beyond the best conceit of pomp or
power. October. 11.
What without him is summer's pomp,
Song of Nature. 55.
This radiant pomp of sun and star,
Woodnotes. II. 208.
Pompous
Nor show thy pompous parts,
Saadi. 46.
Pomps
I care not if the pomps you show
May-Day. 359.
Pond
They added ridge to valley, brook to
pond, Hamatreya. 17.
The shining pebble of the pond,
Ode to Beauty. 29.

Ponder
Ponder my spells; Woodnotes. II. 90.
Pondered
And anxious hearts have pondered here
Robbins Hymn. 9.
Pondering
Pondering shadows, colors, clouds,
Woodnotes. I. 18.
Ponderous
Ponderous with beechen forest sloped the
shore. Adirondacs. 28.
Ponderous gold and stuffs to bear,
Merlin's Song. 26.
Ponds
Parks and ponds are good by day;
Frag. Nat. XVIII. 1.
Pool
Guide lovers to the pool. April. 8.
The purple petals, fallen in the pool,
Rhodora. 5.
With Thought's perilous, whirling pool;
Threnody. 233.
Pool-haunting
Pasture of pool-haunting herds,
Monadnoc. 55.
Pools
Gaunt as bitterns in the pools,
Alphonso. 16.
Poor
And the poor grass shall plot and plan
Bacchus. 41.
The men of yore were stout and poor,
Boston. 5.
A city of the poor;— Boston. 22.
To the poor a noble brother,
Boston. 114.
The outrage of the poor.
Boston Hymn. 8.
Might harry the weak and poor?
Boston Hymn. 12.
Lo, now! if these poor men
Boston Hymn. 45.
Oft the humble and the poor;
Daemonic Love. 106.
But the poor, unsightly, noisome things
Each. 26.
We poor New England flowers.
Ellen South. 24.
Bethink, poor heart, what bitter kind of
jest Epitaph. 1.
Till the poor is wealthy grown,
Etienne. 19.
This poor tooting, creaking cricket,
Frag. Nat. I. 6.
And the poor spinners weave their webs
thereon Frag. Nat. XXXIII. 2.
Of rich and poor, of young and old,
Hymn. 10.
Battling for the weak and poor.
In Memoriam. 43.
And never poor beseeching glance
In Memoriam. 46.
And he, poor parasite, Monadnoc. 335.
Because I was content with these poor
fields, Musketaquid. 1.
But she dearly loves the poor,
Nature. I. 9.
'T is the poor man getting siller,
Riches. 3.

Poor —*Continued*
'T is the poor man gotten rich,
                              Riches. 7.
The poor man crawls in web of rags
                              Riches. 9.
The coarseness of my poor attire;
                              Romany. 2.
Barefooted Dervish is not poor,
                              Saadi. 119.
Stoop not then to poor excuse;
                              Sursum Corda. 5.
I am not poor, but I am proud,
                              Thought. 1.
She loves a poor and virtuous race.
                              Voluntaries. 38.
But thou, poor child! unbound, unrhymed,
                              Woodnotes. II. 178.

Poorer
So to be husbanded for poorer days.
                              Day's Ration. 25.

Poorest
The poorest that drew breath.
                              In Memoriam. 34.
Boon Nature to his poorest shed
                              Monadnoc. 70.

Poorly
With science poorly mask their hurt;
                              Alphonso. 37.
To-day slinks poorly off unmarked between:
                              Quat. Heri. 2.

Poplar
Oak, cedar, maple, poplar, beech and fir,
                              Adirondacs. 38.

Poplar-tree
Listen what the poplar-tree   Rhea. 7.

Poppy
Tobacco-leaf, or poppy, or rose;
                              Mithridates. 2.

Porcelain
And dip it in thy porcelain vase;
                              Woodnotes. II. 52.

Porches
But the porches of man's ear
                              Garden. 46.

Pore
And deemest thou as those who pore,
                              Threnody. 179.

Pores
Quarry of spars in mountain pores;
                              Monadnoc. 79.

Porphyry
Through crimson chambers, porphyry and pearl,
                              October. 7.

Port
O happy port that spied the sail
                              Boston. 88.
When wrath and terror changed Jove's regal port,   Frag. Life. XXXIV. 1.
With the high port he wore erewhile,
                              In Memoriam. 77.
Port or pilot trows not,—
                              Monadnoc. 338.
The port, well worth the cruise, is near,
                              Terminus. 39.

Portal
Build this golden portal;   Manners. 2.

Porter
The brother of the fisher, porter, swain,
                              Frag. Life. XXX. 5.

Portfolio
I turn the proud portfolio
                              Ode to Beauty. 52.

Portion
Saying, 'This be thy portion, child; this chalice,   Day's Ration. 3.
The other portion language cannot speak.   Frag. Life. XVIII. 8.

Portly
Portly and grim,—   Experience. 5.

Porto Rique
Let them sail for Porto Rique,
                              Humble-Bee. 3.

Portrait
One portrait—fact or fancy—we may draw;   Phi. 4.
I see his cowlèd portrait dear;
                              Problem. 70.

Portraits
Their several portraits, you would own
                              Adirondacs. Motto. 2.

Portraiture
The portraiture of things to be.
                              Frag. Life. XXXV. 6.
Her colossal portraiture;
                              Hermione. 21.

Possessed
Yet Nature will not be in full possessed,
                              Frag. Nat. V. 8.
Guy possessed the talisman   Guy. 5.
Possessed the land which rendered to their toil   Hamatreya. 2.
Somewhat not to be possessed,
                              Ode to Beauty. 70.

Possession
Can certify possession;   Amulet. 10.

Possible
  See Impossible.
Within four walls is possible again,—
                              Adirondacs. 322.

Posterity
With no posterity to make the lie afraid,
                              Merlin. 111.
Nor last posterity forget.   Poet. 12.

Postpone
Teach him gladly to postpone
                              Frag. Poet. XI. 15.

Pot
  See Chimney-pot.
The while, one leaden pot of alcohol
                              Adirondacs. 139.
Five were smelted in a pot   Test. 5.

Potatoes
Venison and trout, potatoes, beans, wheat-bread;   Adirondacs. 179.

Potencies
And potencies of sky.   Waterfall. 8.

Potent
The potent plain of Dæmons spreads.
                              Daemonic Love. 26.
What potent blood hath modest May,
                              May-Day. 187.

Pottage
And coldly ask their pottage, not their love.   Blight. 39.

Poultry-yard
The poultry-yard, the shed, the barn,—
                              Threnody. 89.

Pounce
And they pounce on other eyes
                              Initial Love. 39.

Pounding
I with my hammer pounding evermore
                    Seashore. 34.
Pounds
Six thousand pounds a year.   Boston. 72.
Pour
    See Outpour.
Pour, Bacchus! the remembering wine;
                    Bacchus. 51.
So shall the lights ye pour amain
                    Celestial Love. 23.
In her lap to pour all splendor;
                    Rhea. 50.
And pour the deluge still;
                    Song of Nature. 12.
And more to purpose freely pour
                    Walk. 6.
Poured
As water poured through hollows of the
    hills   Adirondacs. 149.
Of blood through veins of kindred
    poured.   Daemonic Love. 4.
As poured the flood of the ancient sea
                    May-Day. 241.
Poureth
Nature poureth into nature   Visit. 13.
Pouring
Pouring as wide a flood   Dirge. 18.
Pouring many a cheerful river;
                    Monadnoc. 41.
Pouring of his power the wine
                    Woodnotes. II. 279.
Pours
So pours the deluge of the heat
                    May-Day. 247.
The million-handed painter pours
                    May-Day. 259.
Pours her power into the people,
                    Nature. II. 6.
The heaven where unveiled Allah pours
                    Saadi. 160.
Pours finite into infinite.   Threnody. 237.
Or Music pours on mortals
                    World-Soul. 31.
Powdery
Bartered its powdery cap;
                    May-Day. 234.
Power
Nor art, nor power, nor toil can find
                    Bohemian. 10.
Power have they for tenderness;
                    Celestial Love. 90.
And power to him who power exerts.
                    Compensation. II. 22.
The scale of power uprears,
                    Frag. Life. IV. 2.
Nor land, nor gold, nor power,
                    Frag. Poet. VI. 6.
The threads of life and power and pain,
                    Harp. 101.
O touch thy servant's lips with power,
                    Hymn. 26.
Thou ridest to power,   Illusions. 36.
Trusting well the matchless power
                    Initial Love. 84.
All inborn power that could
                    In Memoriam. 35.
With budding power in college-halls,
                    In Memoriam. 63.

Power that by obedience grows,
                    Insight. 1.
How long the power to give them name
                    Merops. 3.
And oh, the wonder of the power,
                    Miracle. 17.
Of untried power and sane delight:
                    Monadnoc. 105.
Pours her power into the people,
                    Nature. II. 6.
of pomp or power.   October. 11.
Dread Power, but dear! if God thou be,
                    Ode to Beauty. 98.
Then clothe these hands with power
                    Poet. 245.
And the same power that reared the
    shrine   Problem. 49.
Power and speed be hands and feet.
                    Quat. Power. 4.
Of power and of comeliness.   Rhea. 69.
The self-same Power that brought me
    there brought you.   Rhodora. 16.
Taught by Plinlimmon's Druid power,
                    Solution. 34.
They swathed their too much power.
                    Song of Nature. 32.
But over the dead he has no power,
                    Threnody. 5.
Through love and thought, through
    power and dream.   Two Rivers. 12.
Surcharged and sultry with a power
                    Unity. 10.
Wafting the puny seeds of power,
                    Wealth. 7.
From these companions, power and
    grace.   Woodnotes. II. 62.
Pouring of his power the wine
                    Woodnotes. II. 279.
Power's
And drops from Power's redundant horn
                    May-Day. 216.
Powers
The Powers above: II Eros. 2.
Revealer of the inmost powers
                    May-Day. 414.
Uplifted shall condense her powers,
                    Monadnoc. 99.
The landscape is an armory of powers,
                    Musketaquid. 34.
And shake before those awful Powers.
                    Saadi. 57.
And ever by delicate powers
                    Song of Nature. 13.
Of poles and powers, cold, wet, and
    warm: Woodnotes. II. 111.
Practice
Bend his practice to his prayer
                    Frag. Poet. IV. 4.
And fate and practice and invention,
                    Woodnotes. II. 206.
Prairie
The prairie stretched away.
                    Boston. 44.
The prairie granted,   Channing Ode. 64.
In the great woods, on prairie floors.
                    Titmouse. 68.
And thatch with towns the prairie broad
                    World-Soul. 67.

Praise

We praise the guide, we praise the forest
life: Adirondacs. 305.
In loyal worship, scorning praise,
Beauty. 22.
Their dauntless ways did all men praise,
Boston. 9.
Dare praise the freedom-loving moun-
taineer? Channing Ode. 20.
To earn the praise of bard and critic.
Fame. 12.
Dappled with joy and grief and praise,
Frag. Life. I. 2.
For thought, and not praise;
Frag. Poet. VIII. 1.
Wherefor thanks God his daily praise,
Frag. Poet. XI. 2.
All mankind praise;
In Memoriam. 8.
Poets praise that hidden wine
May-Day. 406.
Than wine or sleep or praise;
Rome. 13.
Drink not the Malaga of praise,
Saadi. 64.
Tempted by thy praise of wit,
Saadi. 88.
The bald antiquity of China praise.
To-Day. 16.

Praised

By turns we praised the stature of our
guides, Adirondacs. 80.
Freedom praised, but hid;
Channing Ode. 33.

Prance

Orb and atom forth they prance,
Monadnoc. 249.

Prank

Each spot where tulips prank their state
Omar. 1.

Pranks

What pranks the greewood played;
Peter. 22.

Prate

We fool and prate; Monadnoc. 379.

Prates

But who is he that prates
Channing Ode. 12.

Prating

On clucking hens and prating fools,
Woodnotes. II. 202.

Pray

Louder than with speech they pray,—
Astraea. 17.
Pray for a beam Celestial Love. 60.
For thee and thine I pray;
*Farewell. 53.
Yet here their children pray,
Robbins Hymn. 22.
Some went to write, some went to pray;
Threnody. 155.

Prayed

"Thou didst not tarry while I prayed.
Frag. Poet. II. 2.
Gift too precious to be prayed,
Freedom. 8.
Though I am weak, yet God, when pray-
ed, Nun. 5.
And prayed the eternal Light to clear
Robbins Hymn. 11.

When Ali prayed and loved
Waterfall. 17.

Prayer

Nor hymn, nor prayer, nor church.
Bohemian. 12.
No prayer persuades, no flattery fawns,—
Celestial Love. 87.
A cell for prayer, a hall for joy,—
Dirge. 31.
Bend his practice to his prayer
Frag. Poet. IV. 4.
And his soul will melt in prayer,
Initial Love. 110.
On prayer and music strung;
Monadnoc. 234.
Of prayer and song that were my dear
delight, Summons. 5.

Prayers

New flowerets bring, new prayers uplift,
Celestial Love. 4.
What prayers and dreams of youthful
genius feign, Frag. Nat. V. 2.
And prayers of might from martyrs' cave.
Merlin. 26.
Or prayers the stony Parcæ soothe,
Nemesis. 10.
To Heaven thy hourly prayers are sent,
Prayer. 6.
And prayers of humble virtue made
Robbins Hymn. 7.
The living Heaven thy prayers respect,
Spiritual Laws. 1.
Prayers of saints that inly burned,—
Threnody. 265.
This is Jove, who, deaf to prayers,
Worship. 19.

Praying

Thy praying lute will seem to scold;
Rhea. 22.

Prays

He paints, he carves, he chants, he prays,
Initial Love. 116.

Preach

'I give my darling son, Thou shalt not
preach';— Adakryn. 2.
He will preach like a friar,
Initial Love. 134.
Thus the sad-eyed Fakirs preach:
Saadi. 59.

Preceptor

Like wise preceptor, lure his eye
Monadnoc. 102.

Precious

Gift too precious to be prayed,
Freedom. 8.

Predatory

Restless, predatory, hasting;
Initial Love. 38.

Preference

And selfish preference forbear;
Celestial Love. 10.

Preferred

I said, 'What influence me preferred,
Berrying. 9.
Of self in other still preferred,
Celestial Love. 118.
To me their aid preferred.
Hermione. 63.
He whom God had thus preferred,—
Poet. 201.

And weed and rock-moss is preferred.
                        Threnody. 115.
Preferring
Preferring things to names, for these
  were men,   Blight. 26.
Pregnant
And, pregnant with his grander thought,
                        Threnody. 144.
Premium
To the bright premium,—
                        Saadi. 14.
Prepare
Forelooking, when he would prepare
                        Monadnoc. 154.
Presage
Which lit my onward way with bright
  presage,   I Bear. 4.
Presence
Or to this presence could rehearse
                        Harp. 84.
An animated law, a presence to exalt.'
                        Poet. 164.
Presences
Fit for fairy presences,
                        Frag. Nat. II. 12.
O fair, appeasing presences!
                        Merops. 6.
Present
        See Omnipresent.
There Past, Present, Future, shoot
                        Celestial Love. 42.
Present and Past in under-song,—
                        Concord Ode. 18.
Corrupted by the present toy
                        Initial Love. 112.
Thou grand affirmer of the present tense,
                        Monadnoc. 359.
O friendless Present! than thy bosom
  holds.   Quat. Heri. 4.
Presently
And presently the sky is changed; O
  world!   Adirondacs. 211.
Present's
He cools the present's fiery glow,
                        Monadnoc. 157.
Presents
'Now by these presents be it known
                        Boston. 65.
These presents be the hostages
                        Rhea. 70.
Pressed
Who saw what ferns and palms were
  pressed   Wealth. 26.
Presses
Still, still the secret presses;
                        World-Soul. 57.
Pretend
Youth is (whatever cynic tubs pretend)
                        To-Day. 17.
Pretender
Strikes the loud pretender down.
                        Nature. I. 11.
Pretension
Will you catch crabs? Truth tries pre-
  tension here.   Adirondacs. 100.
Strong art and beautiful pretension,
                        Woodnotes. II. 207.
Prettily
It wets my foot, but prettily
                        Frag. Nat. XXIV. 3.

Pretty
The ground-pine curled its pretty wreath,
                        Each. 41.
A very pretty squirrel track;   Fable. 16.
And fled in pretty frowns away
                        Frag. Poet. I. 38.
Prevail
Unless he conquer and prevail?
                        Destiny. 15.
Prevailed
And in their secret senate have prevailed
                        Musketaquid. 6.
Prevails
There is no orator prevails
                        May-Day. 433.
On spawning slime my song prevails,
                        Solution. 5.
Preventing
How much, preventing God, how much
  I owe   Grace. 1.
Prevision
For the prevision is allied   Fate. 13.
Prey
As lions on their prey;
                        Initial Love. 40.
It preys on all, all prey on it,
                        May-Day. 291.
Preys
It preys on all,   May-Day. 291.
Price
The merchant hath stuffs of price,
                        Exile. 13.
He pays too high a price   Fame. 7.
Grains beyond the price of gold.
                        May-Day. 274.
Pride
Rosy polygonum, lake-margin's pride,
                        Adirondacs. 143.
Not love, nor beauty's pride,
                        Angelo. 10.
Hung out their summer pride,
                        Boston. 38.
To be the appanage of pride,
                        Chartist. 8.
What all the goods thy pride which lift,
                        Destiny. 16.
'O pride of thy race!
                        Ellen South. 21.
While oaks of pride
                        Frag. Nat. III. 18.
I tread on the pride of Greece and Rome;
                        Good-Bye. 24.
I laugh at the lore and the pride of man,
                        Good-Bye. 27.
Which more of pride than pity gave
                        In Memoriam. 13.
The joy and pride the pilgrim feels
                        In Memoriam. 83.
Bring back the tulip's pride.
                        May-Day. 163.
Canst thou, thy pride forgot, like Na-
  ture pass   Musketaquid. 78.
And every man, in love or pride,
                        Nemesis. 7.
'Is this dear Nature's manly pride?
                        Poet. 218.
Who in their pride forgive not ours.
                        Saadi. 58.
"Pride ruined the angels,   Sphinx. 89.

Pride—*Continued*
Now Love and Pride, alas! in vain,
                    Threnody. 80.
The resurrection of departed pride.
                    To-Day. 2.
When the violets were in their shrouds,
and Summer in its pride,   *Violet. 15.
Which they shall rule with pride.
                    Voluntaries. 26.
Ere wheat can wave its golden pride.
                    Wealth. 17.

Pries
And upward pries and perforates
                    May-Day. 121.

Priest
For what need I of book or priest,
                    Frag. Poet. XXVIII. 1.
He is an augur and a priest,
                    Initial Love. 109.
And through the priest the mind in-
spires.   Problem. 54.

Priest's
For the priest's cant,
                    Channing Ode. 5.

Priests
And sent his priests in holy fear
                    Hymn. 7.

Prig
And the former called the latter 'Little
Prig;'   Fable. 3.

Primal
Obeying meek the primal Cause,
                    Harp. 71.
And well the primal pioneer
                    Wealth. 9.
Primal chimes of sun and shade,
                    Woodnotes. II. 160.
Enough for thee the primal mind
                    Woodnotes. II. 232.

Prime
And a prime end of the most subtle
element   Adirondacs. 258.
And I can date the morning prime
                    Cosmos. 7.
My good, my noble, in their prime,
                    Dirge. 25.
Scorch our delicate prime,
                    Ellen South. 19.
Write in a book the morning's prime,
                    Garden. 39.
Earth's prime secret, sculpture's seat?
                    May-Day. 211.
Obey the voice at eve obeyed at prime:
                    Terminus. 36.
Or what ill planet crossed his prime?
                    Voluntaries. 14.

Primeval
With its primeval memory,   Harp. 52.

Primitive
Adorned with them my country's primitive times,   River. 41.

Primordial
Primordial wholes,   Sphinx. 30.

Prince
On prince or bride no diamond stone
                    On Prince. 1.

Princely
Princely women hard to please,
                    Frag. Poet. I. 27.

Princes
And princes offer me grace   Exile. 15.

Print
The girl's foot leaves its neater print.
                    May-Day. 62.

Printed
One held a printed journal waving high
                    Adirondacs. 235.

Prints
Recut the aged prints,   Bacchus. 63.
Prints his small impress on the snow,
                    Titmouse. 40.

Prison
    See Imprison.
And finds his prison there.
                    Woodnotes. II. 29.

Prison-bars
But him no prison-bars would hold:
                    Worship. 4.

Prisoned
    See Imprisoned.

Pristine
Though late returning to her pristine
ways.   Adirondacs. 55.

Prithee
Wait, I prithee, till I come
                    Humble-Bee. 17.

Privacies
For who can tell what sudden privacies
                    Adirondacs. 191.

Privacy
And a stricter privacy;
                    Initial Love. 144.
In a tumultuous privacy of storm.
                    Snow-Storm. 9.

Private
A private beam   Adirondacs. 223.
Not for a private good,   Rhea. 60.
Taught thee each private sign to raise
                    Threnody. 201.
Ascendant in the private soul,
                    Threnody. 252.

Privilege
'T is the privilege of Art   Art. 19.
He takes a sovran privilege
                    Initial Love. 118.
Or seemed to use his privilege
                    Lines. 19.
And searched with the sun's privilege.
                    Poet. 62.

Prize
And, chiefest prize, found I true liberty
                    Musketaquid. 66.
Henceforth I prize thy wiry chant
                    Titmouse. 89.

Prized
    See See Low-prized.

Prizes
And prizes of ambition, checks its hand,
                    Blight. 59.
The prizes in all lists he won;
                    In Memoriam. 79.
Knowledge this man prizes best
                    Woodnotes. I. 16.
'What prizes the town and the tower?
                    Woodnotes. II. 30.

Probability
Lake Probability,—our carbuncle,
                    Adirondacs. 132.

Probity
Courage and probity and grace!
May-Day. 405.

Problems
Down with your doleful problems,
April. 15.

Proceeds
From the heart of God proceeds,
Woodnotes. II. 264.

Procession
Beholding the procession of the pines;
Adirondacs. 116.
Procession of a soul in matter,
Uriel. 51.

Proclaim
With malice dared me to proclaim him,
Initial Love. 13.

Prodigal
The prodigal sunshine rested on the land,
Adirondacs. 338.

Produced
In vain produced, all rays return;
Uriel. 23.

Product
Is some product and repeater,—
Visit. 7.
Product of the earlier found.   Visit. 8.

Profane
Nor profane affect to hit   Merlin. 66.

Proffered
Prometheus proffered, Jove denied;
May-Day. 415.

Profile
Scan the profile of the sphere;
Circles. 4.

Profitless
Fame is profitless as pelf,
Frag. Poet. VII. 14.

Profound
Their reach shall yet be more profound,
Celestial Love. 19.
Then plunge to depths profound.
Garden. 12.
And, when he heaved a sigh profound,
Hermione. 6.

Profounder
"To vision profounder,   Sphinx. 81.

Profuse
Profuse in love, the king bestows,
Rhea. 56.

Projected
Curves his white bastions with projected
roof   Snow-Storm. 13.

Projects
Mighty projects countermanded;
Alphonso. 23.

Prolong
Plans immense his term prolong;
Initial Love. 139.

Promethean
And by great sparks Promethean warmed,   Poet. 186.

Prometheus
The other slow,—this the Prometheus,
Adirondacs. 288.
Prometheus proffered, Jove denied;
May-Day. 415.

Promise
On his young promise Beauty smiled,
In Memoriam. 67.

And promise, on thy Founder's truth,
Monadnoc. 407.

Promiser
Lavish, lavish promiser,
Ode to Beauty. 21.

Promontory
Like yon slow-sailing cloudy promontory   Adirondacs. 218.

Promote
The noble craftsman we promote,
Boston. 31.

Prompted
Honor prompted every glance,
In Memoriam. 55.

Prone
The tongue is prone to lose the way,
Frag. Life. XII. 1.

Pronounce
For his lips could well pronounce
Threnody. 52.

Pronounced
Pronounced the word that mortals hate
to hear—   Frag. Life. XVIII. 2.

Proof
See Weather-proof.

Proper
His proper good to flow:
Boston Hymn. 58.
Each from your proper state,
Celestial Love. 13.
In which its proper splendor shines;
Frag. Poet. 2.
By his proper bounty blessed,
Monadnoc. 39.
So each man's life shall have its proper
lights,   Naples. 9.
Fills for his proper sake.   Promise. 10.
Couldst see thy proper eye,
Sphinx. 114.

Property
Property will brutely draw
Celestial Love. 77.

Prophecy
And burned in noble hearts proverb and
prophecy.   Phi. 22.
O trusted broken prophecy!
Threnody. 173.

Prophet
Inspirer, prophet evermore;
Monadnoc. 47.
I love a prophet of the soul;
Problem. 2.
The word unto the prophet spoken
Problem. 55.
With prophet, savior and head;
Threnody. 220.

Prophetic
Soundeth the prophetic wind,
Woodnotes. II. 93.

Prophetic-eyed
The sparrow meek, prophetic-eyed,
May-Day. 170.

Prophet's
To touch with prophet's hand the chord
Hymn. 15.

Prophets
O what are heroes, prophets, men,
Pan. 1.

Propitious
Has hints of the propitious time,
May-Day. 120.

Propitious—*Continued*
Which only the propitious mind
           Merlin. 68.
Each with all propitious Time
           Merlin. 98.

Proportion
In just proportion,   Poet. 246.
For number or proportion. Mockingly,
           Snow-Storm. 17.

Proportions
Is weaving the sublime proportions
           Good Cheer. 7.

Proprietor
Still to the proprietor;
           Celestial Love. 78.

Prospect
Paint the prospect from ttheir door.
           Frag. Life. XIX. 2.

Prosperities
Of heavenlier prosperities
           Frag. Poet. XI. 8.

Prosperity
A meter of prosperity,—   Goethe. 2.

Prosperous
And prosperous Age held out his hand,
           In Memoriam. 69.
The prosperous and beautiful
           Park. 1.

Prostrate
Half piled or prostrate; and my newest
slab   Seashore. 16.

Proteus
Horsed on the Proteus,   Illusions. 35.

Proud
    See Earth-proud.
In miracles of pomp, we must be proud,
           Adirondacs. 155.
And her proud ephemerals,   Circles. 2.
Make the morning proud and sweet;
           Forerunners. 10.
Good-bye, proud world! I'm going home:
           Good-Bye. 1. 14.
But now, proud world! I'm going home.
           Good-Bye. 6.
Earth-proud, proud of the earth which
is not theirs;   Hamatreya. 14.
Might grace the dust that is most proud.
           In Memoriam. 20.
Or made what other purlieus proud.
           Lines. 22.
And punishes the proud.
           Merlin's Song. 4.
That this proud nursery could breed
           Monadnoc. 76.
I turn the proud portfolio
           Ode to Beauty. 52.
I am not poor, but I am proud,
           Thought. 1.
And quit proud homes and youthful
dames   Voluntaries. 65.
For a proud idleness like this
           Waldeinsamkeit. 47.
Painted with shadows green and proud
           Woodnotes. I. 110.
Cities of proud hotels,
           World-Soul. 9.

Prouder
And search the skies for prouder friends,
           From Hafiz. 10.

Proudly
More proudly rolls, more softly lies.
           Park. 12.
Earth proudly wears the Parthenon,
           Problem. 33.

Prove
They bide their time, and well can
prove,   Monadnoc. 165.
They prove the virtues of each bed of
rock,   Musketaquid. 37.
Like to like shall joyful prove;
           Woodnotes. II. 82.

Proved
Proved Napoleon great,   Politics. 6.

Proverb
And proverb of a thousand years,
           Frag. Poet. IV. 24.
For proverbs in the market-place:
           Saadi. 152.
And burned in noble hearts proverb and
prophecy.   Phi. 22.

Providence
The Providence that is most large
           Titmouse. 85.

Province
Province to province faithful clung,
           Boston. 97.

Provinces
Through tracts and provinces of sky,
           May-Day. 25.

Provoke
Can parley and provoke.   April. 12.

Prow
Her unremembering prow
           *Farewell. 16.

Prowess
In his prowess he exults,
           Daemonic Love. 103.

Prussic
And the prussic juice to lull me;
           Mithridates. 17.

Psalm
His mighty psalm from fall to spring
           Mountain. 19.

Psalms
And greeted God with childhood's psalms.
           Dirge. 8.

Public
And lift man's public action to a height
           Adirondacs. 246.
Their cords of love so public are,
           Celestial Love. 107.
Every thought is public,
           Quat. Hush. 1.
The public child of earth and sky.
           Woodnotes. I. 117.

Publish
Which publish and which hide the cause.
           Celestial Love. 59.
I cannot publish in my rhyme
           Peter. 21.
I rake no coffined clay, nor publish wide
           To-Day. 1.

Published
Published it to lake and sky,
           Miracle. 32.

Publishes
Publishes when 't is inclined.
           Merlin. 69.

Puck
Goodfellow, Puck and goblins,
                    April. 13.
Pudency
Is the prudency of man.'   Poet. 224.
Pull
Their sinewy arms pull at the oar un-
tired   Adirondacs. 89.
Pulsates
And life pulsates in rock or tree.
                    Saadi. 138.
Pulsating
And landed on our coast, and pulsating
                    Adirondacs. 240.
Pulse
    See Life-pulse.
eaten bread and pulse?
                    Forbearance. 3.
One pulse more of firm endeavor,—
                    Give. 29.
The pulse of hands will make him mute;
                    Initial Love. 57.
Keep pulse for pulse with those who
roam.   In Memoriam. 85.
With the pulse of manly hearts;
                    Merlin. 21.
They set the wind to winnow pulse and
grain,   Musketaquid. 42.
And pulse, and sound, and light was
none;   Woodnotes. II. 267.
Pulses
Our pulses beat not less,
                    Concord Ode. 6.
Their pulses beat,   Merlin. 46.
Forth speed the strong pulses
                    Sphinx. 103.
Pulsing
Outvalued every pulsing sound
                    Threnody. 13.
But sweeter rivers pulsing flit
                    Two Rivers. 3.
Pump
Nor wine nor brains perpetual pump.
                    Alphonso. 62.
Punctual
Of the punctual coming-back,
                    May-Day. 379.
Felt in the plants and in the punctual
birds;   Musketaquid. 64.
The punctual stars will vigil keep,—
                    Titmouse. 18.
Pundit
He is a Pundit of the East,
                    Initial Love. 108.
Punishes
And punishes the proud.
                    Merlin's Song. 4.
Puny
Puny man and scentless rose
                    Alphonso. 25.
Something of pity for the puny clay,
                    River. 34.
Wafting the puny seeds of power,
                    Wealth. 7.
Pupil's
Why need I galleries, when a pupil's
draught   Day's Ration. 27.
Pupils
Teach your pupils now with plenty,
                    Alphonso. 53.

Purchase
Of the toy's purchase with the length of
life.   Blight. 62.
Pure
    See Impure.
So pure the Alpine element we breathed,
                    Adirondacs. 158.
Thirsting in that pure for a purer sky?
                    Adirondacs. 210.
Pure by impure is not seen.
                    Astraea. 44.
Higher far into the pure realm,
                    Celestial Love. 27.
Whether your jewel be of pure water,
                    Destiny. 35.
Their hands were pure, and pure their
faith,—   Dirge. 51.
Baptized with the pure element,
                    Frag. Nat. XXVI. 27.
I fancy these pure waters and the flags
                    Hamatreya. 8.
Substance mixed of pure contraries;
                    Initial Love. 91.
Planting seeds of knowledge pure,
                    May-Day. 467.
It is pure use;—   Monadnoc. 355.
And they so pure? He, foolish child,
                    Poet. 206.
Pure content is angel's lot,   Poet. 251.
Speak through his lips thy pure com-
mands,   Robbins Hymn. 27.
The pure shall see by their own will,
                    Threnody. 191.
And live with living nature, a pure re-
joicing thing.   *Violet. 12.
Which only the pure can hear;
                    Woodnotes. II. 128.
He hides in pure transparency;
                    Woodnotes. II. 310.
Purely
Dealing purely and nakedly,—
                    Frag. Life. XXVII. 11.
Her morning sun shone bright and calmly
purely set;   *Violet. 14.
Purer
for a purer sky?   Adirondacs. 210.
'I will have a purer gift;
                    Celestial Love. 2.
As a self of purer clay,   Give. 44.
Rear purer wits, inventive eyes,—
                    Monadnoc. 107.
That knows a purer flame than me,
                    Security. 10.
Shall fall with purer radiance down;
                    Woodnotes. II. 72.
Purest
Loved by stars and purest winds,
                    Astraea. 32.
Purge
Purge alpine air by towns defiled,
                    May-Day. 451.
Purger
Purger of earth, and medicine of men;
                    Seashore. 22.
Purgeth
Whom the rain and the wind purgeth,
                    Woodnotes. II. 37.
Purging
It is there for purging light;
                    Astraea. 40.

Purging—*Continued*
Is the purging of his eye
                    Frag. Poet. XI. 3.
Purify
Which tarnish not, but purify   Rhea. 3.
Purifying
There for purifying storms;
                    Astraea. 41.
Embalmed by purifying cold;
                    Titmouse. 19.
Purlieus
Or made what other purlieus proud.
                    Lines. 22.
Purple
Whereon the purple iris dwells in beauty
                    Adirondacs. 219.
The purple flaming of love?   Cosmos. 4.
And purple flame of love.   Cosmos. 8.
When the purple flame shoots up,
                    Cosmos. 21.
Opal hues and purple dye;
                    May-Day. 260.
Its spot of purple, and its streak of
brown,   Naples. 8.
And the cold and purple morning
                    Ode to Beauty. 86.
Yet spake yon purple mountain,
                    Park. 13.
The bandages of purple light;   Rhea. 16.
The purple petals, fallen in the pool,
                    Rhodora. 5.
And thousands sail the purple sea,
                    Saadi. 108.
She melted into purple cloud,
                    Sphinx. 123.
The purple berries in the wood
                    Woodnotes. I. 135.
Yon ridge of purple landscape,
                    World-Soul. 37.
Purple-piled
Airy turrets purple-piled,   May-Day. 350.
Purpose
And carry my purpose forth,
                    Boston Hymn. 83.
His purpose woke, his features slept;
                    In Memoriam. 102.
Or Duty to grand purpose wrought.
                    Miracle. 14.
I muse what secret purpose had he
                    Monadnoc Afar. 7.
Better, the linked purpose of the whole,
                    Musketaquid. 65.
And more to purpose freely pour
                    Walk. 6.
Purse
The merchant serves the purse,
                    Channing Ode. 46.
Pursue
My hopes pursue, they cannot bind him.
                    Threnody. 23.
Pursued
Body with shadow still pursued.
                    Woodnotes. II. 163.
Pursuing
Built of furtherance and pursuing,
                    Threnody. 280.
Pursuit
Even in the hot pursuit of the best aims
                    Blight. 58.

Put
Which few can put on with impunity.
                    Adirondacs. 98.
Go put your creed into your deed,
                    Concord Ode. 19.
They put their finger on their lip,
                    II Eros. 1.
Talents differ; all is well and wisely put;
                    Fable. 17.
Put youth, joy, health   Fame. 27.
To use my land to put his rainbows in.
                    Frag. Nat. IX. 2.
Put in, drive home the sightless wedges
                    Frag. Nat. XXX. 1.
It put on flesh in friendly form,
                    Frag. Poet. IV. 28.
If I could put my woods in song
                    Garden. 1.
Not one of all can put in verse,
                    Harp. 83.
They put their April raiment on;
                    May-Day. 319.
Put the Spirit in the wrong;   Poet. 292.
That until now has put   Rome. 23.
I put on faith in pilot or in chart,
                    Unbar. 3.
their last gay dress put on;
                    *Violet. 7.
Put off thy years, wash in the breeze;
                    Woodnotes. II. 135.
Puts
Puts confusion in my brain.
                    Channing Ode. 11.
Which puts me in a working mood.
                    Frag. Poet. XVIII. 2.
Puzzled
Walked about with puzzled look.
                    Experience. 16.
Pyramid
And, though a pyramid, will bound.
                    Monadnoc. 255.
Karnak and Pyramid and Giant's Stairs
                    Seashore. 15.
Dust is their pyramid and mole:
                    Wealth. 25.
Pyramids
To gaze upon the Pyramids;
                    Problem. 36.
Pyre
When heroes piled the pyre,
                    May-Day. 141.

Quadruped
Plant, quadruped, bird,   Sphinx. 34.
Quaint
Milkweeds and murky brakes, quaint
pipes and sun-dew,   Blight. 7.
The quaint devices on its mornings gay.
                    Frag. Nat. V. 7.
Quaintest
Quaintest bud and blossom folds,
                    May-Day. 258.
Quake
The quaking earth did quake in rhyme,
                    Beauty. 15.
Quakes
Lisbon quakes, the people cry.
                    Alphonso. 14.

Quaking
The quaking earth did quake in rhyme,
                         Beauty. 15.
The throbbing sea, the quaking earth,
                         Celestial Love. 109.
And felt, beneath, the quaking ground;
                         Solution. 56.
In quaking bog, on snowy hill,
                         Woodnotes. I. 38.

Quality
For each quality and part
                         Frag. Life. VI. 4.
Steeped in her quality,   Hermione. 23.
The cordial quality of pear or plum
                         Musketaquid. 55.
Every quality and pith   Unity. 9.

Quarantines
His quarantines and grottoes, where
                         Monadnoc. 160.

Quarrel
Had a quarrel,   Fable. 2.
Low leaves his quarrel apprehend,
                         May-Day. 68.
Knew my quarrel, how and why,
                         Miracle. 31.
Quarrel or reprimand: To J. W. 20.

Quarried
But when the quarried means were piled,
                         Wealth. 29.

Quarries
And quarries every rock,   House. 14.

Quarry
To be the quarry whence to build
                         Frag. Life. XXIV. 3.
And fairer forms are in the quarry
                         Good Hope. 7.
So didst thou quarry and unlock
                         Hermione. 45.
Quarry of spars in mountain pores;
                         Monadnoc. 79.
Out of an unseen quarry evermore
                         Snow-Storm. 11.

Quarrying
Ere sunset quarrying inches down,
                         May-Day. 117.
Quarrying man's rejected hours,
                         Spiritual Laws. 3.

Quartered
His rank, and quartered his own coat.
                         Astraea. 2.

Queen
Such another peerless queen
                         Frag. Life. IX. 1.
A woman to thy wife, though she were a
   crowned queen;   Ibn Jemin. 2.
Queen of things! I dare not die
                         Ode to Beauty. 94.
A queen rejoices in her peers,   Walk. 1.

Quenched
The memory of ages quenched;
                         Bacchus. 57.
Has quenched the uneasy blush that
   warmed my cheek;   Summons. 2.
Was quenched, and all must doubt and
   grope.   Threnody. 133.

Queries
Sharp queries of the sentry-bird,
                         Harp. 88.

Quest
A quest of river-grapes, a mocking
   thrush,   Musketaquid. 73.

So take thy quest through nature,
                         Sphinx. 117.

Question
And vex the gods with question pert,
                         Alphonso. 38.
"Thou art the unanswered question;
                         Sphinx. 113.

Quick
But it touches his quick heart
                         Initial Love. 70.
We were quick from head to foot,
                         May-Day. 411.
And of the fibre, quick and strong,
                         Monadnoc. 169.
Quick and skilful to inspire
                         Ode to Beauty. 76.
Quick or dead, except its own;
                         Unity. 6.

Quickened
Quickened so, will I unlock
                         Bacchus. 43.
There quickened to be born again.
                         Frag. Poet. V. 36.

Quickening
Quickening underneath the mould
                         May-Day. 273.

Quickly
'O come, then, quickly come!
                         Ellen South. 33.

Quick-witted
The south-winds are quick-witted,
                         April. 17.

Quiet
But a quiet sense conveyed:
                         Monadnoc. 197.
My quiet roses blow.   Walden. 20.

Quince
Bee-infested quince or plum.
                         Frag. Nat. XXI. 5.

Quinces
The cold gray down upon the quinces
   lieth   Frag. Nat. XXXIII. 1.

Quintessence
Orb, quintessence, and sunbeams,
                         Uriel. 13.

Quit
On the first wheels that quit this weary
   town   Letter. 3.
And well he loved to quit his home
                         Poet. 51.
Ere ye go to quit me for ever and aye.
                         Poet. 262.
Quit the hut, frequent the palace,
                         Quat. Artist. 1.
And quit proud homes and youthful
   dames   Voluntaries. 65.
Quit thy friends as the dead in doom,
                         Woodnotes. II. 223.

Quite. (Partial list.)
As of a luck not quite legitimate,
                         Adirondacs. 275.
The masters quite omitted   April. 19.
Unmake me quite, or give thyself to me!
                         Ode to Beauty. 99.
And one by one has torn off quite
                         Rhea. 15.

Quiver
Golden curls, and quiver and bow.
                         Initial Love. 5.
He bears no bow, or quiver, or wand,
                         Initial Love. 17.

Quoted
See Unquoted.

Quoth
Quoth the pine-tree,
Woodnotes. II. 7.

Rabbi
See Boy-Rabbi.

Rabbit's
From rabbit's coat or grouse's breast;
Quat. Forester. 2.

Race
But ever the free race with front sublime,
Adirondacs. 293.
Up! and the dusky race
Boston Hymn. 77.
The race of gods,
Celestial Love. 54.
'O pride of thy race!   Ellen South. 21.
He never, though he dearly loved his race,
Entombed. 3.
The founder thou; these are thy race!"
Experience. 21.
And harbingers of a majestic race,
Frag. Nat. V. 10.
And so, perchance, in Adam's race,
May-Day. 92.
Hymen of element and race,
May-Day. 266.
Of the painted race of flowers,
May-Day. 374.
And, generous, teach his awkward race
May-Day. 404.
Well-built abode of many a race;
Monadnoc. 82.
And leavest thou thy lowland race,
Monadnoc. 208.
He comes, but not of that race bred
Monadnoc. 309.
Adopted them into her race,
Problem. 42
They are not of our race, they seem to say,
River. 31.
And yet have knowledge of our moral race,
River. 32.
Pale Northern girls! you scorn our race;
Romany. 5.
Yet Saadi loved the race of men,—
Saadi. 23.
Older than all thy race.   Seashore. 17.
Then Asia yeaned her shepherd race,
Solution. 9.
From race on race the rarest flowers,
Song of Nature. 15.
Blend, ripen race on race,
Song of Nature. 78.
She loves a poor and virtuous race.
Voluntaries. 38.
A beacon set that Freedom's race
Webster. 3.
And tell its long-descended race.
Woodnotes. I. 45.
To every age, to every race;
Woodnotes. II. 280.
Unto every race and age
Woodnotes. II. 281.

Races
By races, as snow-flakes,
Boston Hymn. 82.
Races by stronger races,
Channing Ode. 84.
Our towns and races grow and fall,
Monadnoc. 386.
Races and planets, its enchanted foam.
Pan. 12.
Through worlds and races and terms and times
Poet. 71.
Whereby to model newer races,
Rhea. 66.
I tire of globes and races,
Song of Nature. 53.
Of races perishing to pave   Wealth. 23.

Rack
See Cloud-rack.
Saw the endless rack of the firmament
Poet. 67.

Radiance
Shall fall with purer radiance down;
Woodnotes. II. 72.

Radiant
Him, radiant, sharpest-sighted god,
Daemonic Love. 70.
And by her radiant youth delighted,
Rhea. 43.
From many a radiant face,
Robbins Hymn. 6.
Around the radiant fireplace, enclosed
Snow-Storm. 8.
Might gather omens from that radiant sign.   Webster. 4.
This radiant pomp of sun and star,
Woodnotes. II. 208.

Radiates
Light is light which radiates,
Threnody. 242.

Rafters
Rafters of immortal pine,   House. 6.
I give my rafters to his boat,
Woodnotes. II. 43.

Rage
See Outrage.
Whether it waken joy or rage
Merlin's Song. 10.

Ragged
Are touched with genius. Yonder ragged cliff   Musketaquid. 24.
Who liveth by the ragged pine
Woodnotes. II. 22.

Rags
O North! give him beauty for rags,
Boston Hymn. 73.
Who can, like thee, our rags upbraid,
May-Day. 426.
The poor man crawls in web of rags
Riches. 9.

Rail
Railing in love to those who rail again,
Summons. 11.
Or trundle on the glowing rail,
Una. 18.

Railing
Railing in love to those who rail again
Summons. 11.

Railway
On the railway, in the square,
Caritas. 2.
A moment, by the railway troop,
Monadnoc. 396.

Railways
With railways ironed o'er?—
World-Soul. 68.
Raiment
Goods and raiment bought and sold;
Celestial Love. 126.
They put their April raiment on;
May-Day. 319.
Rain
The falling rain will spoil no holiday.
Adirondacs. 69.
His brief toilette: at night, or in the rain,
Adirondacs. 76.
Before ye want a drop of rain,
Alphonso. 49.
He spoke, and words more soft than rain
Character. 7.
A gleam of sun, a summer rain,
Frag. Nat. XXVIII. 3.
It fell in rain, it grew in grain,
Frag. Poet. IV. 27.
Early or late, the falling rain   Guy. 33.
April cold with dropping rain
May-Day. 182.
Factory of river and of rain;
Monadnoc. 84.
As clouds give rain to the eastern breeze,
Poet. 34.
Go, keep your cheek's rose from the rain,
Romany. 17.
Repeats the music of the rain;
Two Rivers. 2.
And ages drop in it like rain.
Two Rivers. 20.
Cannon in front and leaden rain
Voluntaries. 94.
Cold April rain and colder snows
Walden. 11.
Whom the rain and the wind purgeth,
Woodnotes. II. 37.
The rain comes when the wind calls;
Woodnotes. II. 238.
Rainbow
The rainbow hours bedeck his glowing
chair,   Adirondacs. 226.
The rainbow of his hope was broke;
In Memoriam. 98.
Not only where the rainbow glows,
Music. 9.
Nor the red rainbow of a summer eve,
Naples. 16.
Fresh as the trickling rainbow of July;
Seashore. 20.
The rainbow shines his harbinger,
Song of Nature. 39.
Too slow the rainbow fades,
Song of Nature. 50.
Rainbow-colored
Shrivel the rainbow-colored walls,
Daemonic Love. 120.
Rainbow-flowering
Rainbow-flowering, wisdom-fruiting,
Bacchus. 33.
Rainbows
By signs gracious as rainbows.
Forerunners. 34.
To use my land to put his rainbows in.
Frag. Nat. IX. 2.
What rainbows teach, and sunsets show?
Threnody. 261.

Rain-drop
Swells a rain-drop to a tun;
Frag. Poet. IX. 8.
Raindrop's
The acorn's cup, the raindrop's arc,
Ode to Beauty. 26.
Rains
And fountain of the rains.
Quat. Alcuin. 4.
Raise
See Upraise.
The shaft we raise to them and thee.
C. Hymn. 16.
Taught thee each private sign to raise
Threnody. 201.
It seemed that Nature could not raise
Woodnotes. I. 36.
Raised
Goethe, raised o'er joy and strife,
Solution. 65.
Rake
I rake no coffined clay, nor publish wide
To-Day. 1.
Rallying
Rallying round a parish steeple
Monadnoc. 129.
Ramble
At my work I ramble not;
Una. 6.
Ramparts
O'er your ramparts as ye lean,
Alphonso. 20.
Ran
See Outran.
Nor ran to speak till she him told;
Frag. Poet. V. 25.
Ran sure,   Hamatreya. 38.
On from hall to chamber ran,
May-Day. 346.
Ran from his mouth to mountains and the
sea,   Phi. 21.
A shudder ran around the sky; Uriel. 26.
Where they were bid, the rivers ran;
Wealth. 39.
Rancor
Asia's rancor, Athens' art,
Monadnoc. 300.
Random
Thus at random overheard
Frag. Poet. IV. 22.
Some random word they say   Poet. 78.
Rang
Rang with fairy laughter.
Frag. Nat. III. 25.
Range
Adding wings through things to range,
Insight. 5.
Ranged
Step the meek fowls where erst they
ranged;   Threnody. 94.
Ranges
As the bee through the garden ranges,
Woodnotes. II. 295.
Ranging
Ranging down the ruled scale
Harp. 7.
Rank
Your rank is all reversed; let men of
cloth   Adirondacs. 93.
Your rank overgrowths reduce
Alphonso. 65.

Rank—*Continued*
His rank, and quartered his own coat.
Astraea. 2.
And rank the savage maples grow
Garden. 7.
In sloven dress and broken rank,
In Memoriam. 5.
Shall have society of its own rank.
Rome. 3.
Fate's grass grows rank in valley clods,
Voluntaries. 119.

Rankly
And rankly on the castled steep,—
Voluntaries. 120.

Ransack
To ransack earth for riches rare,
Rhea. 51.

Ransacks
She ransacks mines and ledges
House. 13.

Ransom
Pay ransom to the owner
Boston Hymn. 69.

Rant
Or statesman's rant.
Channing Ode. 6.

Raptured
Love-longings of the raptured bird
Quat. Hafiz. 3.

Raquette
See Père Raquette.

Rare
And rare and virtuous roots, which in
these woods Blight. 8.
In his plenty things so rare?
Goethe. 8.
O joy, for what recoveries rare!
Harp. 121.
To ransack earth for riches rare,
Rhea. 51.

Rarely
Casts her schemes rarely,
Frag. Life. VI. 3.

Rarest
Knows Nature's rarest moods,
Harp. 13.
From race on race the rarest flowers,
Song of Nature. 15.

Rash
See Rash-leaping.
Rash ambition, brokenhanded;
Alphonso. 24.
The rash word boded ill to all;
Uriel. 30.
Deceives our rash desire;
World-Soul. 42.

Rash-leaping
And the rash-leaping thunderbolt fell
short. Frag. Life. XXXIV. 2.

Rashly
And seeing rashly torn and moved
Threnody. 128.

Rat
Hark in the wall to the rat: Limits. 2.

Rate
That can fix a hero's rate;
Astraea. 4.
Aught above its rate. Politics. 8.

Rather
But rather, like its beads of dew
Frag. Nat. XXVI. 35.

Rattle
The rattle of the kingfisher; Harp. 90.

Rattles
Rattles the coffin-lid. Channing Ode. 35.
For all that rattles in thy brain."
Frag. Poet. II. 10.

Rattlesnake
The lynx, the rattlesnake, the flood, the
fire; Adirondacs. 316.

Raucous
Steering north with raucous cry
May-Day. 24.

Ravage
The ravage of a year of war.
May-Day. 278.

Raven
The raven croaked, owls hooted, the
woodpecker Adirondacs. 147.

Ravine
Where down the rock ravine a river
roars, Letter. 10.

Ravishing
The sights and voices ravishing
Harp. 85.

Ray
O Sun! I curse thy cruel ray:
Chartist. 17.
If a new Muse draw me with splendid
ray, Day's Ration. 15.
Beneath the tropic ray, *Farewell. 51.
Yet can one ray of truth divine
Frag. Life. X. 8.
All things shine in his smoky ray,
Frag. Nat. III. 15.
Draws to the spot the solar ray,
May-Day. 116.
No ray is dimmed, no atom worn,
Song of Nature. 81.
And I greet from far the ray, Una. 15.
Why wilt thou live when none around re-
flects thy pensive ray? *Violet. 5.
Riding on the ray of sight, Visit. 15.

Rays
Of tulips, in the morning's rays.
May-Day. 207.
Shot million rays of thought and tender-
ness. Musketaquid. 10.
Lit by rays from the Blest. Sphinx. 76.
In vain produced, all rays return;
Uriel. 23.

Reach
Of the Ausable stream, intent to reach
Adirondacs. 3.
And nothing thrives to reach its natural
term; Blight. 52.
And round the globe your voices reach.
Boston. 111.
Their reach shall yet be more profound,
Celestial Love. 19.
I could never reach their sides;
Forerunners. 2.
If others reach it, is content;
In Memoriam. 88.
The music that can deepest reach,
Merlin's Song. 35.
Thus far to-day your favors reach,
Merops. 5.
Reach his place and circumstance,
Monadnoc. 253.
And fill the long reach of the old seashore
Poet. 75.

Saadi, so far thy words shall reach:
Saadi. 139.
I taught thy heart beyond the reach
Threnody. 197.
They reach no term, they never sleep,
Voluntaries. 115.

Reached
Were fairly reached at last.
Adirondacs. 259.
I reached the middle of the mount
Dirge. 1.
Had reached its fruiting-time,
Frag. Nat. XXI. 8.
I reached this heath beside the lake,
Miracle. 16.
Landward they reached the mountains old
Poet. 63.
Reached by a mile of road, Waterfall. 2.

Reaches
Reaches not to my perceiving;
Song of Seyd. 6.

Reaching
See Far-reaching.
Or grew on vine whose tap-roots, reaching through
Bacchus. 3.
And virtue reaching to its aims;
Threnody. 279.

Reaction
In reaction and recoil, Spiritual Laws. 9.

Reacts
Change acts, reacts; back, forward hurled,
Poet. 175.

Read
Then, if I read the page aright
Ellen. 5.
Than my few needs exhaust, and bids me read
Frag. Nat. V. 6.
I read great years of victory,
Frag. Poet. III. 6.
Docile read my measured line:
Frag. Poet. VII. 2.
If who can read them comes at last
Garden. 63.
He will read like a crier,
Initial Love. 136.
To read the sense the woods impart
Miracle. 9.
Read the celestial sign! Monadnoc. 14.
His flesh should feel, his eyes should read
Poet. 43.
To read new landscapes and old skies;
Poet. 53.
You doubt we read the stars on high,
Romany. 25.
Nathless we read your fortunes true;
Romany. 26.
And yet his runes he rightly read,
Saadi. 78.
In both I read thy name. Thine Eyes. 12.
And some in books of solace read;
Threnody. 153.
Men read the welfare of the times to come,
Threnody. 169.
Can read thy line, can meet thy glance,
Woodnotes. II. 141.
Our brothers have not read it,
World-Soul. 53.

Reads
Where Hope, the soothsayer, reads our lot,
Ellen. 6.

The eye reads omens where it goes,
Nature. Mot. 3.

Real
The rocks and forest know it real.
Romany. 20.
Art thou not also real?
Sursum Corda. 4.

Reality
Reality most like to dreams.
Frag. Nat. XXIII. 6.

Realm
Lords of this realm, Adirondacs. 152.
Higher far into the pure realm,
Celestial Love. 27.
Vast the realm of Being is,
Day by Day. 9.
Realm beyond realm,—extent untold;
Nun. 42.
My twilight realm he disenchants,
Woodnotes. II. 28.
Is thy land peeled, thy realm marauded?
Woodnotes. II. 181.
Throughout the solid realm.
World-Soul. 76.

Realms
In the realms and corners of space
Cosmos. 14.
Or if yon realms in sunset glow
May-Day. 361.
Realms self-upheld, disdaining Fate,
Nun. 44.

Reap
To reap its scanty corn, Dirge. 10.
To reap its scanty corn, Peter. 2.
Just late enough to reap abundant blame,—
To-Day. 6.

Reaped
Nothing was ploughed, or reaped, or bought, or sold; Adirondacs. 67.

Reappears
And in the second reappears the first.
Xenophanes. 13.

Rear
See Uprear.
Rear purer wits, inventive eyes,—
Monadnoc. 107.
Cannot rear a State. Politics. 10.

Reared
And the same power that reared the shrine
Problems. 49.

Rears
With the marble which he rears.
Alphonso. 76.

Reason
Food which teach and reason can.
Bacchus. 35.
Reason in Nature's lotus drenched,
Bacchus. 56.
And all but deathless Reason gone.
Ellen. 12.
Not Sense but Reason is the Judge of truth; Frag. Life. XVIII. 5.
And write, and reason, and compute,
Initial Love. 28.
And Reason on her tiptoe pained
Initial Love. 67.
Even the serene Reason says,
In Memoriam. 9.
Why only must thy reason fail
May-Day. 175.

Reason —*Continued*
Seest the smile of Reason beaming;—
　　　　　　　　Monadnoc. 236.
Though love repine, and reason chafe,
　　　　　　　　Quat. Sacrifice. 1.
Fairer that expansive reason
　　　　　　　　Threnody. 258.
The reason of all cowardice
　　　　　　　　Titmouse. 61.
Disgust my reason and defile my hands.
　　　　　　　　To-Day. 10.

Reason's
Reason's twofold, part human, part
　divine; 　　　Frag. Life. XVIII. 6.

Reave
None from its stock that vine can reave.
　　　　　　　　II Compensation. 18.

Rebaptize
Could not the nations rebaptize,
　　　　　　　　Poet. 10.

Rebuild
Rebuild or ruin: either fill
　　　　　　　　Alphonso. 27.
Which the Omnipotent cannot rebuild.
　　　　　　　　Frag. Life. V. 2.
Rebuild the ruin, mend defect;
　　　　　　　　May-Day. 444.
Rebuild a continent of better men.
　　　　　　　　Seashore. 37.

Recall
And, when I would recall the scenes I
　dreamed 　　　Frag. Nat. IV. 6.
Ah, vainly do these eyes recall
　　　　　　　　Threnody. 58.

Recalled
Recalled thy skill in bold design,
　　　　　　　　Lines. 18.

Recallest
Recallest us, 　　　Monadnoc. 401.

Recast
And the world's flowing fates in his own
　mould recast. 　　　Culture. 11.

Receipt
Worked on the Maker's own receipt,
　　　　　　　　Guy. 26.

Receive
Asks nothing, but does all receive.
　　　　　　　　Frag. Life. XVII. 3.
Nor not receive his ample dues. Guy. 16.
For living brows; ill fits them to receive:
　　　　　　　　Phi. 2.

Received
Received the fair inscriptions of the
　night; 　　　Frag. Nat. XXVII. 2.

Recess
Fair the soul's recess and shrine,
　　　　　　　　Threnody. 255.

Recite
To recite the Alcoran; Song of Seyd. 22.
Thou canst not catch what they recite
　　　　　　　　Woodnotes. II. 129.

Reck
Reck not what the people say;
　　　　　　　　Quat. Artist. 2.
But I reck not of deceivers.
　　　　　　　　Song of Seyd. 30.

Reckless
A facile, reckless, wandering will,
　　　　　　　　Poet. 207.

Reckon
They reckon ill who leave me out;
　　　　　　　　Brahma. 9.

Recks
What recks such Traveller if the bowers
　　　　　　　　Woodnotes. II. 301.

Reclining
This his slow but sure reclining,
　　　　　　　　Threnody. 164.

Recoil
Or teach thou, Spring! the grand recoil
　　　　　　　　Harp. 125.
In reaction and recoil,
　　　　　　　　Spiritual Laws. 9.

Reconcile
And reconcile him to the common days.
　　　　　　　　Naples. 12.

Reconciled
Not reconciled,— 　Channing Ode. 53.
Extremes of nature reconciled,—
　　　　　　　　Merlin. 52.

Reconciles
And reconciles 　　　Cupido. 8.

Record
There is no record left on earth,
　　　　　　　　In Memoriam. 48.

Recording
Or Wordsworth, Pan's recording voice,—
　　　　　　　　Harp. 82.

Records
What himself confessed records,
　　　　　　　　Astraea. 27.

Recount
To myself I oft recount Monadnoc. 94.
And recount the numbers well;
　　　　　　　　Ode to Beauty. 59.

Recoveries
O joy, for what recoveries rare!
　　　　　　　　Harp. 121.

Recut
Recut the aged prints, 　Bacchus. 63.

Red
In sooth, red flannel is a saucy test
　　　　　　　　Adirondacs. 97.
Or, in the evening twilight's latest red,
　　　　　　　　Adirondacs. 115.
Of the red deer, to aim at a square mist.
　　　　　　　　Adirondacs. 120.
Painted our necks, hands, ankles, with red
　bands: 　　　Adirondacs. 167.
Red when you love, and rosier red,
　　　　　　　　Amulet. 7.
If the red slayer think he slays,
　　　　　　　　Brahma. 1.
Ere yet the red Summer
　　　　　　　　Ellen South. 18.
Sweet willow, checkerberry red,
　　　　　　　　Frag. Nat. II. 23.
Where the fungus broad and red
　　　　　　　　Frag. Nat. III. 1.
She paints with white and red the moors
　　　　　　　　Frag. Nat. XIII. 1.
Through thee the rose is red;
　　　　　　　　Friendship. 12.
From Spring's faint flush to Autumn red.
　　　　　　　　Garden. 8.
Red evening duly dyes
　　　　　　　　Monadnoc Afar. 2.
Nor the red rainbow of a summer eve,
　　　　　　　　Naples. 16.

Grow red with joy and white with fear;
                    Saadi. 30.

She flowered in blossoms red;
                    Sphinx. 126.

There the red morning touched him with
  its light.   Woodnotes. I. 83.

Red-bird
  Here might the red-bird come his plumes
    to cool,   Rhodora. 7.

  When the redbird spread his sable wing,
                  Thine Eyes. 9.

Redbreast's
  Nor in the redbreast's mellow tone.
                  Music. 15.

Red-cloaked
  Little thinks, in the field, yon red-cloaked
    clown   Each. 1.

Redden
  See the plum redden, and the beurré
    stoop.   Quat. Gardener. 4

Rede
  And, though thy rede be church or state,
                  Visit. 25.

Redeem
  Thee to guide and to redeem.
          Celestial Love. 62.

  That memory may their deed redeem,
              C. Hymn. 11.

  As if to-morrow should redeem
           May-Day. 297.

Redeemed
  I was by thy touch redeemed;
           Hermione. 36.

Redeemers
  Redeemers that can yield thee all:
              Saadi. 166.

Redresses
  Who athwart space redresses
            Merlin. 119.

Reduce
  Your rank overgrowths reduce
          Alphonso. 65.

Redundant
  From her redundant horn.
         Adirondacs. 152.

  And drops from Power's redundant horn
         May-Day. 216.

  With his redundant waves.   River. 10.

Redwing
  The redwing flutes his o-ka-lee,
          May-Day. 168.

Reed
  Gives the reed and lily length,
          May-Day. 200.

Reeds
  No, but a nest of bending reeds,
         Threnody. 274.

Reef
  I man the rudder, reef the sail,
         Terminus. 35.

Reel
  Therein I hear the Parcæ reel
         Harp. 99.

  Spin the ball! I reel, I burn,
        Song of Seyd. 1.

Reeling
  The reeling brain can ill compute)
         Wealth. 20.

Reels
  Giddy with motion Nature reels,
         Poet. 172.

Reënter
  None can reënter there,—   Past. 14.

Refined
  Her manners made of bounty well refined;   Quat. A.H. 2.

Refines
  Which no false art refines.
        Waldeinsamkeit. 32.

Reflect
  And its depths reflect all forms;
         Astraea. 42.

Reflected
  The land reflected in the flood,
        Woodnotes. II. 162.

Reflects
  Reflects his figure that doth pass.
         Astraea. 24.

  Why wilt thou live when none around reflects thy pensive ray?
          *Violet. 5.

Reformed
  Refreshed the wise, reformed the clowns,
        May-Day. 343.

Refrained
  In man or maid, that thou from speech
  refrained,   Forbearance. 6.

Refresh
  Refresh the faded tints,   Bacchus. 62.

Refreshed
  Enough that mankind eat and are refreshed.   Adirondacs. 301.

  They were refreshed by the smell,
        May-Day. 317.

  Refreshed the wise, reformed the clowns,
        May-Day. 343.

  Sprung harmless up, refreshed by blows:
        Worship. 2.

Refuse
  If I refuse   Channing Ode. 7

  He lives not who can refuse me;
        Frag. Nat. XXVIII. 1.

  And every god,—none did refuse;
        Garden. 26.

  Nothing refuse.   Give. 6.

  'Eat thou the bread which men refuse;
        Saadi. 142.

  She will not refuse to dwell
        Voluntaries. 45.

  When sea and land refuse to feed me,
        Woodnotes. I. 141.

Refused
  The honest waves refused to slaves
        Boston. 17.

Refuses
  As Fate refuses   Ode to Beauty. 44.

Regal
  changed Jove's regal port,
        Frag. Life. XXXIV. 1.

  Through mountains bored by regal art,
        Saadi. 153.

Regarded
  See Unregarded.

Regards
  Ever find me dim regards,
        Frag. Poet. VII. 9.

Regiment's
  Not for a regiment's parade,
        May-Day. 104.

Region
  In a region where the wheel
        Celestial Love. 33.

Region—*Continued*
Intent, I searched the region round,
                 Monadnoc. 72.

Registered
Are registered and answered still.
                 Prayer. 8.

Regnant
The order regnant in the yeoman's brain.
                 Musketaquid. 51.

Regret
And whine, and flatter, and regret,
                 Initial Love. 30.
Not to regret the changes, tho' they cost
                 River. 20.

Regrets
And sung his sweet regrets
                 Hermione. 2.

Rehearse
Which all its marvel shall rehearse,
                 Frag. Poet. XXIX. 4.
Once I wished I might rehearse
                 Freedom. 1.
Or to this presence could rehearse
                 Harp. 84.
But the runes that I rehearse
                 Woodnotes. II. 142.

Rehearsed
Rehearsed to men the damnèd wails
                 Solution. 49.

Reigned
When Winter reigned I'd close my eye,
but wake with bursting Spring,
                 *Violet. 11.

Reigns
That can contend with love. It reigns
forever.   Rome. 19.

Rein
Yet holds he them with tautest rein,
                 Initial Love. 50.

Reins
Inconstant heat and nerveless reins,—
                 Terminus. 30.

Rejected
Quarrying man's rejected hours,
                 Spiritual Laws. 3.

Rejoices
A Queen rejoices in her peers,
                 Walk. 1.

Rejoicing
And live with living nature, a pure re-
joicing thing.   *Violet. 12.

Relate
Whereof old chronicles relate
                 Frag. Nat. XXVI. 33.

Related
     See Unrelated.
Of the round day, related to the sun
                 Blight. 15.

Relation
Not without relation   Limits. 9.
Know, each substance and relation,
                 Visit. 3.

Relay
As if Time brought a new relay
                 May-Day. 301.

Release
Which I pawn for my release.
                 Rhea. 71.

Released
Than Phidias released.   Good Hope. 8.

Relied
Firm on his heart relied,
                 In Memoriam. 90.

Relief
Past all balsam or relief;
                 Love and Thought. 10.

Religion
Throbs of a wild religion stirred;—
                 Daemonic Love. 8.

Religiously
     See Unreligiously.

Reliquaries
The reliquaries of my dead saint, and
dwell   Letter. 17.

Remain
But the Stars of God remain.
                 Frag. Nat. XVI. 2.
Hearts are dust, hearts' loves remain;
                 Threnody. 268.

Remains
Saying, Sweetheart! the old mystery remains,—   Flute. 3.

Remake
Nature, who lost, cannot remake him;
                 Threnody. 27.

Remede
Thou dost succor and remede
                 Monadnoc. 405.

Remember
Or remember where thou liest,
                 Destiny. 25.

Remembered
O day remembered yet!   Boston. 87.
Be it remembered of a single man,
                 Entombed. 2.

Remembereth
The little bird remembereth his note,
                 Self-Reliance. 7.

Remembering
     See Unremembering.
Winds of remembering   Bacchus. 47.
Pour, Bacchus! the remembering wine;
                 Bacchus. 51.
Remembering Matter pays her debt:
                 Wealth. 45.

Remembrance
With glad remembrance of my debt,
                 Titmouse. 79.

Remission
Without remission, without rest,
                 Frag. Life. XXVII. 2.

Remnant
On the remnant decimal.   Alphonso. 70.

Remorse
And the parent of remorse.
                 Daemonic Love. 131.
Terror and Hope and wild Remorse,
                 Miracle. 12.
In stings of remorse.   Sphinx. 92.

Remote
Equals remote, and seeming opposites.
                 Daemonic Love. 84.
In lands remote, in toil and pain,
                 In Memoriam. 75.

Remoter
Suns haste to set, that so remoter lights
                 Adirondacs. 228.
Without remoter hope or fear
                 Frag. Poet. V. 5.

Rend
That would indignant rend
                        Channing Ode. 38.

Render
That they may render back   Merlin. 12.

Rendered
Possessed the land which rendered to
their toil   Hamatreya. 2.

Rendering
Rendering to a curious eye   Astraea. 36.

Renders
He renders all his lore   Harp. 29.

Rendings
Heard rendings of the skyey roof,
                        Solution. 55.

Renew
Not less renew the heart and brain,
                        May-Day. 453.

Renewed
Renewed, I breathe Elysian air,
                        Harp. 122.

Renews
What fiery force the earth renews,
                        May-Day. 188.

Renounce
Gives all to them who all renounce.
                        Woodnotes. II. 237.

Renovate
For thou, O Spring, canst renovate
                        May-Day. 441.

Rent
The tie of blood and home was rent:
                        Frag. Poet. I. 53.
Stewards of stipend and of rent;
                        Guy. 28.
The fox-hole which the woodchucks rent,
                        Miracle. 4.
And the sailing moon where the cloud
was rent,   Poet. 68.
The bounds of good and ill were rent;
                        Uriel. 32.

Rents
Rich rents and wide alliance shares;
                        Monadnoc. 59.

Repair
Not to monarchs they repair,
                        Astraea. 13.
Let wine repair what this undid;
                        Bacchus. 59.
I see my trees repair their boughs;
                        Threnody. 10.

Repay
Nobility more nobly to repay?
                        Forbearance. 7.
Would bankrupt nature to repay.
                        Ode to Beauty. 32.
And by his countenance repay
                        Threnody. 19.

Repeat
So to repeat   Frag. Poet. IX. 9.

Repeater
No dreary repeater now and again,
                        Nature. II. 3.
Is some product and repeater,—
                        Visit. 7.

Repeats
What himself declared repeats,
                        Astraea. 26.
Repeats the music of the rain;
                        Two Rivers. 2.

And why the star-form she repeats:
                        Woodnotes. I. 23.
In music he repeats the pang
                        Woodnotes. II. 124.
Repeats one note.   Xenophanes. 19.

Repels
With fire that draws while it repels.
                        Eva. 12.

Repentant
See Half-repentant.

Repenting
See Unrepenting.

Repents
He nor repents nor grieves,
                        In Memoriam. 93.

Repine
Though love repine, and reason chafe,
                        Quat. Sacrifice. 1.
But Nature's heir,—if I repine,
                        Threnody. 127.

Replacing
Replacing frieze and architrave:—
                        Monadnoc. 371.

Replenishing
Replenishing material urns
                        Day by Day. 3.

Replied
The vines replied, 'And didst thou deem
                        Berrying. 11.
Bun replied,   Fable. 4.

Replies
The River of my Life replies.   Peter. 40.
The youth replies, I can.
                        Voluntaries. 74.
And to his joy replies;   Waterfall. 14.

Repliest
Or listen when thou repliest,
                        Destiny. 24.

Replunged
Replunged again into that upper sphere
                        Frag. Life. XVI. 8.

Reply
Reply to the thunder of river and main.
                        May-Day. 240.
And the tints of heaven reply.
                        May-Day. 262.
There came a voice without reply,—
                        Quat. Sacrifice. 2.
Thou shalt seem, in each reply,
                        Rhea. 19.
Time is the false reply."   Sphinx. 120.
And they reply, "Forever mine!"
                        Woodnotes. II. 149.

Replying
See Unreplying.

Report
Big with great news, and shouted the
report   Adirondacs. 237.
Long and various the report,—
                        I Eros. 2.
Some had heard their fair report,
                        Forerunners. 21.
I must end my true report,
                        Initial Love. 81.
To report thy features only,
                        Ode to Beauty. 85.

Reporting
Reporting what old minstrels told
                        Harp. 53.

Repose
Permitted on her infinite repose
Adirondacs. 341.
With sunny face of sweet repose,
Threnody. 68.

Reprimand
Quarrel or reprimand: To J. W. 20.

Reproaches
Piques, reproaches, hurts, caresses.
Initial Love. 133.

Reproof
To speak the plain reproof of sin
Hymn. 17.

Reptile
Bird, and reptile, be my game.
Mithridates. 13.

Republican
The republican at home. Politics. 26.

Repulsions
Hatred's swift repulsions play.
Visit. 30.

Reputed
Reputed wrongs and braggart rights,
Mithridates. 28.

Request
Who heard the sweet request,
Threnody. 44.

Requiem
And mix my requiem with the wind
Bell. 15.
The master's requiem.' Dirge. 60.

Requireth
It requireth courage stout. Give. 19.

Requite
And the grape requite the lote!
Bacchus. 54.

Requited
His love shall never be requited.
Rhea. 45.

Rescue
Trump of their rescue, sound!
Boston Hymn. 68.

Rescued
Of them who rescued liberty of old;
Phi. 6.

Resent
Or who resent May-Day. 431.

Resides
When wisdom not with me resides,
Frag. Poet. III. 9.

Resigning
Star by star his world resigning.
Threnody. 165.

Resist
The manhood that should yours resist,—
Etienne. 10.
Resist in vain his motive strain,
Poet. 37.

Resistless
And their resistless friendship showed.
Woodnotes. I. 128.

Resolutely
As resolutely dig or dive. To J. W. 17.

Resolve
And solve and oft resolve the whole.
Alphonso. 46.

Resonant
As in broad orchards resonant with bees;
Musketaquid. 57.

Resort
And, in her strict resort Hermione. 71.

Resorts
In crowded and in still resorts,
Daemonic Love. 46.

Resound
Ever the words of the gods resound;
Garden. 45.

Resounding
To every soul resounding clear
Woodnotes. II. 146.

Respect
The living Heaven thy prayers respect,
Spiritual Laws. 1.
I had as lief respect an ancient shoe,
To-Day. 11.

Responds
Responds to the touch of man;
Waterfall. 10.

Rest
And meditate a moment on Heaven's
rest. Adirondacs. 197.
Until he write, where all eyes rest,
Astraea. 7.
For you no sluggard rest; Boston. 56.
Without remission, without rest,
Frag. Life. XXVII. 2.
And lees make all the rest.
Good Hope. 4.
All the rest he can disguise.
Initial Love. 20.
Of wit, of words, of rest. Manners. 16.
Without halting, without rest,
May-Day. 465.
Upon him noble eyes did rest, Poet. 196.
Without cleanness, without rest.
Riches. 4.
I rest on the pitch of the torrent,
Song of Nature. 7.
And satellites have rest?
Song of Nature. 48.
Would in thy hall take up his rest?
Threnody. 225.
She laid her hopes at rest, *Violet. 16.
Seems fantastic to the rest:
Woodnotes. I. 17.

Rested
The prodigal sunshine rested on the land,
Adirondacs. 338.

Restless
What wilt thou, restless bird,
Adirondacs. 208.
Restless, predatory, hasting;
Initial Love. 38.

Restore
The past restore, the day adorn,
Art. 11.
Spoils of a front none need restore,
Monadnoc. 370.
The lost, the lost, he cannot restore;
Threnody. 6.

Restored
Through ruined systems still restored,
Threnody. 283.

Restores
Restores the world-wide mart;
Boston. 101.
Their shame them restores; Sphinx. 90.

Results
The rich results of the divine consents
Blight. 43.

Resurgent
Of life resurgent from the soil
                            Harp. 126.
Resurrection
Such resurrection of the happy past,
                            Naples. 22.
The resurrection of departed pride.
                            To-Day. 2.
Retake
Fate let him fall, Fate can't retake him;
                            Threnody. 28.
Retinues
Retinues of airy kings,   Art. 15.
Retired
Grave, chaste, contented, though retired,
                            Woodnotes. II. 69.
Retiring
Is all his own, retiring, as he were not,
                            Snow-Storm. 24.
Retort
Sometimes their wits at sally and retort,
                            Adirondacs. 127.
Retorts
While Jake retorts and Reuben roars;
                            Monadnoc. 188.
Retreats
With stifling beams on these retreats,
                            Titmouse. 72.
Retrieve
Retrieve the loss of me and mine!
                            Bacchus. 52.
Retroscope
Is there never a retroscope mirror
                            Cosmos. 12.
Retrospect
Comes the sweet sadness at the retro-
    spect,   Adirondacs. 216.
Return
And haughtily return us stare for stare.
                            Blight. 36.
They shall return   Give. 23.
When thou dost return   Illusions. 22.
Return to be things,   Illusions. 30.
The grand return   In Memoriam. 16.
Fall, stream, from Heaven to bless; re-
    turn as well;   Inscription. 1.
All things return, both sphere and mote,
                            May-Day. 179.
Oft shall war end, and peace return,
                            Saadi. 111.
The darling who shall not return.
                            Threnody. 8.
In vain produced, all rays return;
                            Uriel. 23.
Returned
    See Unreturned.
As they went or they returned,
                            Forerunners. 25.
But Saadi coldly thus returned,
                            Frag. Poet. II. 4
Returned this day, the South-wind search-
    es,   Threnody. 24.
Voice of earth to earth returned,
                            Threnody. 264.
Returning
Though late returning to her pristine
    ways.   Adirondacs. 55.
Two of our mates returning with swift
    oars.   Adirondacs. 234.

The sea returning day by day
                            Boston. 100.
The whistle of returning birds,
                            May-Day. 184.
Wait his returning strength.
                            Merlin. 62.
Returns
Day by day returns   Day by Day. 1.
Immortal youth returns.
                            Waldeinsamkeit. 28.
Reuben
While Jake retorts and Reuben roars;
                            Monadnoc. 188.
Reveal
Past and future must reveal
                            Frag. Poet. V. 32.
Should rive the Future, and reveal
                            Harp. 63.
Nor sword of angels could reveal
                            Merlin. 76.
Revealed
And the secret stands revealed
                            Saadi. 173.
Revealer
Revealer of the inmost powers
                            May-Day. 414.
Revellers
They saw not my fine revellers,—
                            Forerunners. 19.
Revellers'
The blaze of revellers' feasts outshine.
                            Frag. Life. X. 9.
Revere
Not the less revere the Giver,
                            Terminus. 15.
Revere the Maker; fetch thine eye
                            Threnody. 270.
Reverence
His action won such reverence sweet
                            Character. 9.
Reverend
And doubt and reverend use defied,
                            Uriel. 16.
Reverent
The reverent darkness hid the lay.
                            Poet. 18.
Reverently
Entertain it reverently.   Saadi. 36.
Reversed
Your rank is all reversed; let men of
    cloth   Adirondacs. 93.
Revive
A dazzling memory revive;
                            Bacchus. 61.
Revolution
Fate's glowing revolution pause?
                            Threnody. 227.
Revolves
Visibly revolves;   Celestial Love. 35.
Revolves the fatal wheel!   Poet. 117.
Reward
It will reward,—   Give. 22.
Rewarded
A bolder foot is still rewarded.
                            Frag. Poet. XXXI. 2.
Rhodora
I found the fresh Rhodora in the woods,
                            Rhodora. 2.
Rhodora! if the sages ask thee why
                            Rhodora. 9.

Rhyme

The quaking earth did quake in rhyme,
Beauty. 15.
In the palm-grove with a rhyme;
Frag. Poet. V. 8.
For his rhyme.   Merlin. 33.
The rhyme of the poet   Merlin. 77.
Lovesick with rhyme;   Merlin. 97.
Justice is the rhyme of things;
Merlin. 114.
Rhyme the pipe, and Time the warder,
Monadnoc. 247.
I cannot publish in my rhyme
Peter. 21.
Gentle Saadi, mind thy rhyme;
Saadi. 101.
Who can turn the golden rhyme.
Saadi. 114.
Come weave with mine a nobler rhyme.
Woodnotes. II. 139.
And rounds with rhyme her every rune,
Woodnotes. II. 165.

Rhymed

See Unrhymed.

Rhymes

Efficacious rhymes;   Merlin. 61.
Subtle rhymes, with ruin rife,
Merlin. 123.
With idle footsteps, crooning rhymes.
Miracle. 2.
Saw musical order and pairing rhymes.
Poet. 72.
Come lift thine eyes to lofty rhymes,
Woodnotes. II. 158.
And the ripples in rhymes the oar for-
sake.   Woodnotes. II. 171.

Rhythm

With the coil of rhythm and number;
Merlin. 30.

Rhythmic

Bring your music and rhythmic flight,
Frag. Nat. XXIII. 9.
Your song, your forms, your rhythmic
flight,   May-Day. 398.

Ribald

Chilled by a ribald jeer. Voluntaries. 22.

Ribbons

Not by ribbons or by favors,
Celestial Love. 102.
Or ribbons of a dancing girl
Frag. Nat. XXXII. 3.

Rich

See Enrich.

The clouds are rich and dark, the air
serene,   Adirondacs. 213.
By its own craft, to a more rich delight,
Bacchus. 11.
The rich results of the divine consents
Blight. 43.
Gracing the rich man's wood and lake,
Chartist. 9.
Or strong, or rich, or generous;
Destiny. 2.
At rich men's tables   Forbearance. 3.
The trees were rich, yet ominous with
gloom.   Frag. Nat. XXVII. 5.
In his rich nurseries, timely skill
Guy. 41.
Of rich and poor, of young and old,
Hymn. 10.

Of the rich inherent worth,
In Memoriam. 50.
O'er thy rich dust the endless smile
In Memoriam. 105.
Rich rents and wide alliance shares;
Monadnoc. 59.
Of rich men blazing hospitable light,
Naples. 18.
Plotted to make him rich and great:
Quat. Horoscope. 2.
'T is the poor man gotten rich,
Riches. 7.
Rich are the sea-gods:—who gives gifts
but they?   Seashore. 27.
As the rich aloes flames, I glow,
Song of Seyd. 17.
Laughter rich as woodland thunder,
Threnody. 214.
and in the year's rich beauty died.
*Violet. 16.
Houses of rich and great,
World-Soul. 10.

Richer

Beauty of a richer vein,
Daemonic Love. 56.
Future or Past no richer secret folds,
Quat. Heri. 3.

Riches

The riches of the universe   Dull. 13.
The riches of a spotless memory,
Good Cheer. 9.
To ransack earth for riches rare,
Rhea. 51.
The riches of sweet Mary's Son,
Threnody. 222.

Riches'

But when he flees on riches' wings,
Riches. 11.

Richest

The richest of all lords is Use,
Merlin's Song. 29.
O richest fortune sourly crossed!
Threnody. 174.
The richest flowering of all art:
Threnody. 216.

Richly

And richly his large future planned,
In Memoriam. 70.

Riddle

As if one riddle of the Sphinx were
guessed.   Adirondacs. 343.

Ride

On which all beings ride
Celestial Love. 34.
And ride mankind.   Channing Ode. 51.
And ride, and run, and have, and hold,
Initial Love. 29.
Over yon western bridges I would ride
Letter. 4.
His day's ride is a furlong space,
Monadnoc. 322.
And anchored in the tempest ride.
Woodnotes. II. 257.

Rides

Love laughs, and on a lion rides.
Daemonic Love. 88.
Onward and nearer rides the sun of May;
Musketaquid. 19.

Ridest

Thou ridest to power,   Illusions. 36.

Ridge
Under low mountains, whose unbroken
ridge   Adirondacs. 27.
They added ridge to valley, brook to
pond,   Hamatreya. 17.
Yon ridge of purple landscape,
World-Soul. 37.

Ridges
     See Snow-ridges.

Ridiculous
Drag a ridiculous age. Day's Ration. 19.
Thy sleep makes ridiculous.
Humble-Bee. 63.

Ridiculously
Ridiculously up and down   Poet. 88.

Riding
Riding on the ray of sight,   Visit. 15.

Rife
Subtle rhymes, with ruin rife,
Merlin. 123

Rifle
With laughter sudden as the crack of
rifle;   Adirondacs. 128.
With rifle and with knife!
Channing Ode. 18.
From their rifle or their snare;
Monadnoc. 144.

Rifles
Our heroes tried their rifles at a mark,
Adirondacs. 125.

Right
     See Aright; Forthright.
A paddle in the right hand, or an oar,
Adirondacs. 78.
That never faltered from the right.
Boston. 91.
But right is might through all the world;
Boston. 96.
Beware from right to swerve.
Boston Hymn. 52.
And in right deserving,
Celestial Love. 11.
By right or wrong,   Celestial Love. 75.
Virtue palters; Right is hence;
Channing Ode. 32.
Who marries Right to Might,
Channing Ode. 81.
Right above their heads,
Daemonic Love. 25.
Right good-will my sinews strung,
Forerunners. 6.
Right thou feelest, rush to do.'
Freedom. 24.
And head-winds right for royal sails.
Heroism. 10.
Right Cossacks in their forages;
Initial Love. 34.
And right into himself does draw;
Initial Love. 121.
Thou living champion of the right?
In Memoriam. 30.
As Southern wrath to Northern right
May-Day. 138.
My heart's content would find it right.
Nun. 10.
Right upward on the road of fame
Poet. 1.
Right to the heaven they steer and sing.
Poet. 26.
Aloft, beneath, on left and right
Poet. 99.

Right out to sea his courses stand,
Quat. Poet. I. 3.
Right onward drive unharmed;
Terminus. 38.
Of one inalienable right,
Thought. 2.
I had the right, few days ago,
Threnody. 32.
How have I forfeited the right?
Threnody. 34.
Wanting wisdom, void of right,
Voluntaries. 60.
Of Fate and Will, of Want and Right,
Woodnotes. II. 130.

Rightly
The bird-language rightly spell,
Bacchus. 24.
Rightly seeing, rightly seen,
Daemonic Love. 76.
Lead you rightly to my altar,
Etienne. 13.
And yet his runes he rightly read,
Saadi. 78.
Severing rightly his from thine,
Worship. 22.

Rights
We hold like rights, and shall;—
Boston. 26.
The rights of all mankind.
Boston. 95.
See rights for which the one hand fights
Concord Ode. 23.
Reputed wrongs and braggart rights,
Mithridates. 28.
Lauding the Eternal Rights,
Voluntaries. 109.

Rill
Of vital force the wasted rill,
Alphonso. 28.
Whilst upper life the slender rill
Art. 27.
Beneath the grass that shades the rill,
Woodnotes. I. 39.

Rills
Leopard-colored rills.   Monadnoc. 4.

Rime
     See Rhyme.
While the grass beneath the rime
May-Day. 119.

Rims
That rims the running silver sheet,—
May-Day. 246.

Rind
Lemons run to leaves and rind;
Alphonso. 4.
Daily to a more thin and outward rind,
Blight. 48.
Found in polygala root and rind,
Frag. Nat. II. 27.

Ring
The ring you gave is still the same;
Amulet. 2.
And honor joined the pariot ring
Boston. 84.
Ring of axe or hum of wheel
Frag. Poet. I. 23.
Ring with the song of the Fates;
Garden. 34.
As erst it wont, would thrill and ring.
Harp. 106.

Ring—*Continued*
The blackbirds make the maples ring
May-Day. 166.
Its chords should ring as blows the breeze,   Merlin. 3.
The world is the ring of his spells,
Woodnotes. II. 285.

Ringlets
Though the frail ringlets thee deceive,
II Compensation. 17.
When his ringlets grew and curled,
Frag. Nat. XXXIV. 3.
Nor ringlets dead   Hermione. 17.

Rings
And rings the bells of jubilee
Cosmos. 27.
In which the sudden wind-god rings.
Frag. Poet. I. 42.
Needs no amulets nor rings.   Guy. 4.
The air rings jocund to his call,
May-Day. 70.
A subtle chain of countless rings
May-Day. 79.
A subtle chain of countless rings
Nature Mot. 1.
In rings and painted vest.   Riches. 8.
And thefts from satellites and rings
Song of Nature. 25.
His myrrh, and wine, and rings,
To J. W. 13.
Stars weave eternal rings;
World-Soul. 62.

Ripe
See Autumn-ripe; Unripe.
The men are ripe of Saxon kind
Concord Ode. 13.
Or wit be ripe before 't was rotten?
Fame. 6.
It was not ripe yet to sustain
Threnody. 140.
Apples of Eden ripe to-morrow.
Threnody. 287.

Ripen
And Summer came to ripen maids
May-Day. 303.
Through earth to ripen, through heaven endure.   May-Day. 468.
Blend, ripen race on race,
Song of Nature. 78.

Ripened
My gardens ripened well,
Song of Nature. 18.
When the rosebud ripened to the rose,
Thine Eyes. 11.

Ripening
Till the slow ripening, secular tree
Frag. Nat. XXI. 7.

Ripple
The pastures sleep, ripple the lakes,
Saadi. 136.

Ripples
And the glassy surface in ripples brake
Frag. Poet. I. 37.
The whirlwind in ripples wrote
Garden. 54.
And the ripples in rhymes the oar forsake.   Woodnotes. II. 171.

Rippling
Rippling roses in northern nights,
Frag. Poet. I. 40.

Rise
The spiritual stars rise nightly, shedding down   Adirondacs. 222.
And the world's sun seemed to rise
Guy. 39.
And cities rise where cities burn,
Saadi. 112.
Suns rise and set in Saadi's speech.'
Saadi. 140.
Saadi, see! they rise in stature
Saadi. 171.
Will swell and rise with wonted grace;
Woodnotes. II. 54.
Surely now will the curtain rise,
Woodnotes. II. 212.
But the curtain doth not rise,
Woodnotes. II. 214.

Rising
And mark the rising of the early stars.
Letter. 15.
He, when the rising storm of party roared,   Phi. 7.

Risk
Risk or ruin he must share.
Monadnoc. 339.

Rite
Eldest rite, two married sides
Merlin. 90.
My servant Death, with solving rite,
Threnody. 236.

Rites
Decked by courtly rites and dress
Frag. Poet. I. 29.

Ritual
Of ritual, bible, or of speech;
Threnody. 198.

Rival
Their rival strength and suppleness, their skill   Adirondacs. 81.
What care though rival cities soar
Boston. 45.
Its leaves to the rival sky;   Exile. 2.
Why thou wert there, O rival of the rose!   Rhodora. 13.

Rivals
Are ever rivals: but, though this be swift,
Adirondacs. 287.

Rive
Will rive the hills and swim the sea,
II Compensation. 27.
Should rive the Future, and reveal
Harp. 63.

Rived
And rived the dark like a new day!
Poet. 56.

River
Of loud Bog River, suddenly confront
Adirondacs. 233.
For I did not bring home the river and sky;—   Each. 17.
The rolling river, the morning bird;—
Each. 49.
'River and rose and crag and bird,
Hermione. 61.
Where down the rock ravine a river roars,   Letter. 10.
Reply to the thunder of river and main.
May-Day. 240.
High over the river intervals,
Monadnoc. 7.

Pouring many a cheerful river;
                    Monadnoc. 41.
Factory of river and of rain;
                    Monadnoc. 84.
No fish, in river or in lake,
                    Monadnoc. 145.
The river, hill, stems, foliage are obscure,
                    Musketaquid. 83.
Of close low pine-woods in a river town;
                    Naples. 14.
Far seen, the river glides below,
                    Peter. 37.
The River of my Life replies.
                    Peter. 40.
My old familiar haunts; here the blue
    river,   River. 2.
Hides hills and woods, the river, and the
    heaven,   Snow-Storm. 4.
Economize the failing river,
                    Terminus. 14.
The river knows the way to the sea;
                    Woodnotes. II. 239.

River-ark
A river-ark on the ocean brine,
                    Good-Bye. 4.

River-bank
Behold the river-bank
                    In Memoriam. 3.

River-grapes
A quest of river-grapes, a mocking
    thrush,   Musketaquid. 73.

Rivers
The rivers gambolled onward to the sea,
                    Adirondacs. 339.
Me for the channel of the rivers of God
                    Frag. Life. XV. 7.
And the murmuring rivers of sap
                    May-Day. 230.
Saw rivers run seaward by cities high
                    Poet. 65.
But sweeter rivers pulsing flit
                    Two Rivers. 3.
Where they were bid, the rivers ran;
                    Wealth. 39.
Where from a hundred lakes young rivers
    sprang;   Woodnotes. I. 63.

River-side
And along the river-side.   Berrying. 5.
He goes to the river-side,—
                    Woodnotes. I. 7.

Rivulet
Through which at will our Indian rivulet
                    Musketaquid. 27.

Rivulets
To feed this wealth of lakes and rivulets,
                    Adirondacs. 150.

Road
Delights to build a road:
                    Daemonic Love. 86.
The traveller and the road seem one
                    Etienne. 21.
Who the road had surely kept;
                    Forerunners. 18.
Forth already on the road,
                    Frag. Life. XXII. 6.
In lowly cot or painful road,
                    In Memoriam. 57.
And in his airy road benign   Lines. 17.
But wilt thou measure all thy road,
                    Merlin's Song. 22.

Space grants beyond his fated road
                    Merops. 9.
Traveller, to thee, perchance, a tedious
    road,   Musketaquid. 32.
Right upward on the road of fame
                    Poet. 1.
And stars from the ecliptic road.
                    Poet. 30.
The sea is the road of the bold,
                    Quat. Alcuin. 1.
Though thou kept the straightest road,
                    Rhea. 23.
That rustles down the well-known forest
    road—   River. 26.
To watch the convoy on the road;
                    Threnody. 61.
Reached by a mile of road,
                    Waterfall. 2.
Where his clear spirit leads him, there's
    his road   Woodnotes. I. 94.
Through beds of granite cut my road,
                    Woodnotes. I. 127.

Road-builder
Path-finder, road-builder,
                    Daemonic Love. 74.

Roads
Whose roads lead everywhere to all;
                    Boston. 60.
Struggling through the drifted roads;
                    May-Day. 40.

Roadside
Ope in such low moist roadside, and be-
    neath   Naples. 24.
From the roadside to the brook
                    Threnody. 92.

Roam
Him strong Genius urged to roam,
                    Frag. Life. XX. 1.
Long through thy weary crowds I roam;
                    Good-Bye. 3.
Keep pulse for pulse with those who
    roam.   In Memoriam. 85.
The bird, how far it haply roam
                    Nemesis. 3.
And, Calmuck, in his wagon roam
                    Poet. 52.

Roamed
And roamed the pastures through;
                    Thine Eyes. 6.
He roamed, content alike with man and
    beast.   Woodnotes. I. 81.

Roar
    See Uproar.
Hark to that muffled roar! a tree in the
    woods   Adirondacs. 121.
With sudden roar the aged pine-tree
    falls,—   Woodnotes. I. 73.

Roared
He, when the rising storm of party
    roared,   Phi. 7.

Roaring
To gauge with glance the roaring gulf
    below,   Grace. 6.

Roars
Where down the rock ravine a river
    roars,   Letter. 10.
While Jake retorts and Reuben roars;
                    Monadnoc. 188.

Robe
I weary of my robe of snow,
                    Song of Nature. 51.

Robed
Live, robed with beauty, painted by the
    sun;   Pan. 5.
Robin
To the robin on the wing,
                    Ellen South. 7.
Robin's
Bring hither back the robin's call,
                    May-Day. 162.
Robins
The robins know the melting snow;
                    May-Day. 169.
Of robins out of doors.   Walden. 36.
Rock
Or, bathers, diving from the rock at
    noon;   Adirondacs. 112.
To ears intelligent; as if gray rock
                    Adirondacs. 253.
Each leaf that shades the rock
                    April. 10.
Every crypt of every rock.
                    Bacchus. 44.
Ever the Rock of Ages melts
                    Frag. Life. XXIV. 1.
Than doth the traveller's shadow on the
    rock.   Frag. Life. XXVI. 4.
All day the waves assailed the rock,
                    Frag. Nat. XXV. 1.
Loved harebells nodding on a rock,
                    Frag. Poet. I. 21.
Highways for me through the rock.
                    Hermione. 46.
And quarries every rock,   House. 14.
Where down the rock ravine a river
    roars,   Letter. 10.
They prove the virtues of each bed of
    rock,   Musketaquid. 37.
Here is the rock where, yet a simple
    child,   River. 11.
And life pulsates in rock or tree.
                    Saadi. 138.
Of rock and fire the scroll,
                    Song of Nature. 22.
Which, lodged in rock, the rock abrade?
                    Wealth. 8.
My garden is the cloven rock,
                    Woodnotes. II. 9.
Choosing light, wave, rock and bird,
                    Woodnotes. II. 59.
The shadows shake on the rock behind,
                    Woodnotes. II. 94.
Though they sealed him in a rock,
                    Worship. 5.
Rocked
The waves that rocked them on the deep
                    Boston. 13.
Rock-ledges
Lie on the warm rock-ledges, and there
    learn   Seashore. 9.
Rock-like
And through my rock-like, solitary wont
                    Musketaquid. 9.
Rock-loving
A wild-rose, or rock-loving columbine,
                    Musketaquid. 74.
Rock-moss
And weed and rock-moss is preferred.
                    Threnody. 115.
Rocks
No placard on these rocks warned to the
    polls,   Adirondacs. 64.

I show Columbia, of the rocks
                    Boston Hymn. 21.
The rocks uphold thy name engraved,
                    Lines. 12.
Already my rocks lie light,
                    Monadnoc. 243.
I lame him, clattering down the rocks;
                    Monadnoc. 342.
Our insect miseries to thy rocks;
                    Monadnoc. 365.
Cast the bantling on the rocks,
                    Quat. Power. 1.
The rocks and forest know it real.
                    Romany. 20.
Under the snow, between the rocks,
                    Woodnotes. I. 40.
Rocky
Between two rocky arms, we climb the
    bank,   Adirondacs. 31
The rocky nook with hilltops three
                    Boston. 1.
Which never strains its rocky beams;
                    Monadnoc. 273.
The rocky coast, smite Andes into dust,
                    Seashore. 35.
And, under vines, on rocky isle,
                    Solution. 12.
Rode
rode up the forks   Adirondacs. 2.
Rods
Six rods, sixteen, twenty, or forty-five;
                    Adirondacs. 126.
A few rods off he deems it gems and
    clouds.   Seashore. 46.
Roll
    See Unroll.
There my thoughts the matter roll,
                    Alphonso. 45.
Round they roll till dark is light,
                    Channing Ode. 78.
And bid the broad Atlantic roll,
                    Concord Ode. 27.
Forthright my planets roll,
                    Song of Nature. 42.
Where Syrian waters roll,
                    Waterfall. 18.
Rolled
The zephyr in his garden rolled
                    Guy. 43.
Out from the heart of nature rolled
                    Problem. 13.
The pit wherein the streams are rolled
                    Quat. Alcuin. 3.
What smiths, and in what furnace, rolled
                    Wealth. 18.
Rolling
    See Aye-rolling.
The rolling river, the morning bird;—
                    Each. 49.
Pan, half asleep, rolling over
                    Frag. Nat. I. 7.
With rolling eyes and face composed;
                    Threnody. 63.
Rolls
There the holy essence rolls,
                    Celestial Love. 46.
He rolls them with delighted motion,
                    Initial Love. 48.
Blue Walden rolls its cannonade,
                    May-Day. 106.
The world rolls round,—   May-Day. 177

Hither rolls the storm of heat;
May-Day. 192.

But not the less the eternal wave rolls on
Pan. 10.

More proudly rolls, more softly lies.
Park. 12.

Roman
Now hear thee say in Roman key,
Titmouse. 103.

Romance
And, that no day of life may lack romance,
Adirondacs. 221.

Grace and glimmer of romance; Art. 2.

Touches a cheek with colors of romance,
Enchanter. 6.

With a color of romance,
Humble-Bee. 25.

In new landscapes of romance,
May-Day. 27.

Romance forgot, and faith decayed,
Solution. 60.

Rome
I travelled and found it at Rome;
Frag. Poet. IV. 32.

I tread on the pride of Greece and
Rome;
Good-Bye. 24.

Nor Rome, nor joyful Paris, nor the
halls
Naples. 17.

And groined the aisles of Christian Rome
Problem. 20.

Alone in Rome. Why, Rome is lonely
too;—
Rome. 1.

The Catos, the wise patriots of Rome,
Rome. 5.

Obey the nobler impulse; that is Rome:
Rome. 16.

Lo! here is Rome and Nineveh and
Thebes,
Seashore. 14.

What boots it here of Thebes or Rome
Walden. 45.

Cæsar of his leafy Rome,
Woodnotes. I. 5.

Romeo
Makes Romeo of a plough-boy on his
cart;
Enchanter. 13.

Rood
For there's no rood has not a star above
it;
Musketaquid. 54.

And every rood in the hemlock wood
Peter. 7.

Roof
Barked the white spruce to weatherfend
the roof,
Adirondacs. 35.

This thin spruce roof, this clayed log-
wall,
Adirondacs. 318.

Freely nestle in our roof,
Frag. Nat. XXIII. 11.

Each street and spire and roof, incontinent.
Letter. 6.

Nestle in hedge, or barn, or roof,
May-Day. 400.

I will not go under a wooden roof:
Poet. 143.

Curves his white bastions with projected
roof
Snow-Storm. 13.

Heard rendings of the skyey roof,
Solution. 55.

Roofs
Shield all thy roofs and towers!
Boston. 117.

Beneath your roofs of slate.
World-Soul. 12.

Room
In plains that room for shadows make
Waldeinsamkeit. 5.

Roomy
Roomy Eternity Frag. Life. VI. 1.

Root
See Flag-root; Pine-root.

From a nocturnal root, Bacchus. 7.

Triple blossoms from one root;
Celestial Love. 43.

For this fortune wanted root
Daemonic Love. 126.

A thing that takes no more root in the
world Frag. Life. XXVI. 3.

Found in polygala root and rind,
Frag. Nat. II. 27.

Its root has pierced yon shady mound;
Holidays. 6.

As if it were a living root;
Initial Love. 56.

Root in the blood of heroes old.
In Memoriam. 116.

For that hardy English root
Monadnoc. 183.

Thy broad ambitious branches, and thy
root.
Terminus. 8.

Rooted
The lover rooted stays. Friendship. 4.

See, all we are rooted here Poet. 267.

Rooted in the mighty Heart.
Woodnotes. II. 177.

Roots
See Tap-roots.

And rare and virtuous roots, which in
these woods
Blight. 8.

Hay, corn, roots, hemp, flax, apples, wool
and wood. Hamatreya. 3.

In whom the stock of freedom roots;
Monadnoc. 93.

Rope-like
The rope-like pine-roots crosswise grown
Woodnotes. I. 106.

Ropes
And boys run out upon their leafy ropes.
Frag. Nat. III. 20.

Rosamond
The cobweb clues of Rosamond
April. 7.

Rosary
But beads are of a rosary
Monadnoc. 233.

Rose. (Noun and adjective).
See Briar-rose; Wild-rose; Wood-
rose.

Puny man and scentless rose
Alphonso. 25.

The wild rose and the barberry thorn
Boston. 37.

That sheds beauty on the rose.
Destiny. 4.

A rose diamond or a white,
Destiny. 36.

Wild rose, lily, dry vanilla,—
Frag. Nat. II. 18.

Through thee the rose is red;
Friendship. 12.

Nor the palest rose she flung Give. 41.

'River and rose and crag and bird,
Hermione. 61.

Rose. (Noun and adjective)—*Continued*

Rose and vine-leaf deck buffoons;
  Heroism. 3.
And touches all things with his rose.
  Initial Love. 77.
And speaks all languages the rose,
  May-Day. 74.
The vanished rose of evening's dream.
  May-Day. 298.
Tobacco-leaf, or poppy, or rose;
  Mithridates. 2.
Her lily and rose, her sea and land dis-
play.
  Monadnoc. 13.
It is not only in the rose, Music. 7.
For Nature listens in the rose
  Nature. I. 12.
And speaks all languages the rose;
  Nature. Mot. 4.
Why thou wert there, O rival of the rose!
  Rhodora. 13.
Go, keep your cheek's rose from the rain,
  Romany. 17.
Yet beautiful as is the rose in June,
  Seashore. 19.
And the fresh rose on yonder thorn
  Song of Nature. 83.
When the rosebud ripened to the rose,
  Thine Eyes. 11.
The rose of beauty burns;
  Waldeinsamkeit. 26.
To the lark's trill unfolds the rose,
  Waterfall. 15.

Rose. (Verb).

See Uprose.

Loud hammered, and the heron rose in
the swamp. Adirondacs. 148.
The fortunate star that rose on us sank
not; Adirondacs. 337.
Fair rose the planted hills behind
  Boston. 41.
Stars rose; his faith was earlier up:
  Character. 2.
A window rose, and, to say sooth,
  Harp. 109.
Gayest pictures rose to win me,
  Monadnoc. 3.
It rose a bubble from the plain.
  Monadnoc. 290.
Stars rose, his faith was earlier up:
  Poet. 135.
These wonders rose to upper air;
  Problem. 40.
Then temples rose, and towns, and marts,
  Wealth. 34.

Roseate

Filling with thy roseate smell,
  Ode to Beauty. 79.

Rosebud

When the rosebud ripened to the rose,
  Thine Eyes. 11.

Rosebuds

The warm rosebuds below.
  World-Soul. 112.

Rose-leaf

In whose cheek the rose-leaf blusheth,
  Woodnotes. II. 39.

Rose-lipped

Year by year the rose-lipped maiden,
  Holidays. 9.

Roses

Roses bleach, the goats are dry,
  Alphonso. 13.
And that which roses say so well.
  Bacchus. 25.
Weave roses for your mate.
  Celestial Love. 14.
His planted isle where roses glow?
  Chartist. 12.
His roses bleach apace,
  Daemonic Love. 91.
Rippling roses in northern nights,
  Frag. Poet. I. 40.
Roses he ate, and drank the wind;
  Frag. Poet. V. 14.
Hang roses on the stony fate.
  Frag. Poet. X. 4.
Like fiery honey sucked from roses.
  Initial Love. 53.
Hear what wine and roses say;
  To J. W. 2.
My quiet roses blow. Walden. 20.
With roses and a shroud.
  World-Soul. 78.

Rosette

Where flowers each stone rosette and
metope brave; Monadnoc. 372.

Rosier

And, on the instant, rosier clouds upbore
  Adakryn. 4.
Red when you love, and rosier red,
  Amulet. 7.

Rosy

Rosy polygonum, lake-margin's pride,
  Adirondacs. 143.
Five rosy boys with morning light
  Dirge. 5.
What joy in rosy waves outpoured
  May-Day. 190.
Thy sombre head with rosy hues
  Monadnoc Afar. 3.

Rotten

Or wit be ripe before 't was rotten?
  Fame. 6.

Rough

Or whipping its rough surface for a
trout; Adirondacs. 111.
Rough Monadnoc to a gem.
  Frag. Nat. XIV. 2.
Cheers the rough crag
  Frag. Nat. XXIX. 2.
Through thick-stemmed woodlands rough
and wide. Woodnotes. I. 120.
The rough and bearded forester
  Woodnotes. II. 14.

Round

See Will-round.

From boat to boat, and to the echoes
round, Adirondacs. 242.
Of the round day, related to the sun
  Blight. 15.
And round the globe your voices reach.
  Boston. 111.
Another round, a higher,
  Celestial Love. 8.
And the cheerful round of work.
  Celestial Love. 106.
Round they roll till dark is light,
  Channing Ode. 78.
And fired the shot heard round the world.
  C. Hymn. 4.

They colored the horizon round;
Dirge. 33.
Whilst his files sweep round yon Alpine
height; Each. 8.
And billows round her play,
*Farewell. 26.
Runs round the pine and maple tree
Frag. Nat. XIX. 2.
Which round the floating isles unite:—
Frag. Nat. XXVI. 25.
Like vaulters in a circus round
Frag. Poet. XIX. 1.
Seldom in this low life's round
Garden. 47.
To the defences thou hast round me set;
Grace. 2.
In the street, if he turned round,
Guy. 23.
And what is writ on Table Round
Harp. 25.
Lightning-knotted round his head;
Heroism. 6.
Which dances round the sun—
House. 20.
And round their circles is writ,
Initial Love. 41.
In hearts which round the hearth at home
In Memoriam. 84.
Turn swiftlier round, O tardy ball!
May-Day. 160.
The world rolls round,— May-Day. 177.
And send the nectar round;
May-Day. 280.
Round about, a hundred miles,
Monadnoc. 36.
Intent, I searched the region round,
Monadnoc. 72.
Rallying round a parish steeple
Monadnoc. 129.
As doth this round sky-cleaving boat
Monadnoc. 272.
And round me swarmed in shadowy troop
Peter. 27.
Gladly round that golden lamp
Saadi. 37.
Round every windward stake, or tree, or
door. Snow-Storm. 14.
Within the air's cerulean round,—
Threnody. 14.
That loiters round the crystal coast,
Threnody. 121.
Unit and universe are round; Uriel. 22.
I bring round the harvest day.'
Voluntaries. 34.
Walled with mortal terror round,
Voluntaries. 90.
A belt of mirrors round a taper's flame;
Xenophanes. 16.

Rounded
Rounded by hours where each outdid the
last Adirondacs. 154.
The rounded world is fair to see,
Nature. Mot. 7.
The hand that rounded Peter's dome
Problem. 19.
Of rounded worlds, of space and time,
Woodnotes. II. 108.

Roundelay
Echo the blackbird's roundelay,
Good-Bye. 20.

Round-in
For him round-in the melancholy hours
Naples. 11.
Rounding
"See there the grim gray rounding
Monadnoc. 325.
Round Lake
With skies of benediction, to Round
Lake, Adirondacs. 8.
Roundly
Turn on the accuser roundly; say,
Sursum Corda. 6.
Rounds
Came to me in his fatal rounds,
Terminus. 5.
And rounds with rhyme her every rune,
Woodnotes. II. 165.
Rout
To rout the flying foe. May-Day. 112.
Routine
Smug routine, and things allowed,
Mithridates. 29.
Rove
Lost in whirling spheres I rove,
Song of Seyd. 7.
Roved
I lonely roved the land or sea:
Thine Eyes. 2.
So long he roved at will the boundless
shade. Woodnotes. I. 85.
Rover
Rover of the underwoods,
Humble-Bee. 29.
Roves
Pale genius roves alone,
Frag. Poet. VI. 1.
He roves unhurt the burning ways
Voluntaries. 49.
Roving
By those roving eyeballs bold.
Initial Love. 32.
Roving, roving, as it seems, Una. 1.
Row
To row, to swim, to shoot, to build a
camp, Adirondacs. 82.
It helped my rowers to row;
Quat. Northman. 2.
Rowed
Northward the length of Follansbee we
rowed, Adirondacs. 26.
Rowers
It helped my rowers to row;
Quat. Northman. 2.
Rows
At morn or noon, the guide rows bare-
headed: Adirondacs. 74.
Royal
Mediator, royal giver;
Daemonic Love. 75.
Yet well I know the royal mine,
Dull. 19.
And head-winds right for royal sails.
Heroism. 10.
Has royal pleasure-grounds outspread.'
Monadnoc. 71.
And crowns him with a more than royal
crown, October. 4.
No Satan with a royal trick Past. 16.
For royal man;—they thee confess
Woodnotes. II. 188.

Roys
Bards, Roys, Scanderbegs and Tells;
　　　　　　　Monadnoc. 97.
Rubies
They brought me rubies from the mine,
　　　　　　　Rubies. 1.
Ruby
Ruby wine is drunk by knaves,
　　　　　　　Heroism. 1.
The ruby of the drop of wine,
　　　　　　　Ode to Beauty. 28.
Becomes a ruby stone;　　They. 2.
Rudder
I man the rudder, reef the sail,
　　　　　　　Terminus. 35.
Ruddier
On men and maids a ruddier mien,
　　　　　　　May-Day. 300.
Ruddy
Sound, ruddy men, frolic and innocent,
　　　　　　　Adirondacs. 87.
A ruddy drop of manly blood
　　　　　　　Friendship. 1.
And ruddy Health the loftiest Muse.
　　　　　　　Merlin's Song. 30.
But fire to thaw that ruddy snow,
　　　　　　　Rubies. 9.
Rude
Think me not unkind and rude
　　　　　　　Apology. 1.
By the rude bridge that arched the flood,
　　　　　　　C. Hymn. 1.
Rude ocean doth up part;　*Farewell. 34.
He works, plots, fights, in rude affairs,
　　　　　　　Fate. 7.
Into rude and homely nooks,
　　　　　　　May-Day. 355.
On farmer's byre, on pasture rude,
　　　　　　　May-Day. 357.
Rude poets of the tavern hearth,
　　　　　　　Monadnoc. 185.
I cannot tell rude listeners
　　　　　　　September. 13.
Rudely
Must smite the chords rudely and hard,
　　　　　　　Merlin. 10.
Rudeness
To leave the rudeness of my woodland
life,　　　　　Summons. 6.
Rudest
Peace that hallows rudest ways.
　　　　　　　Forerunners. 38.
Rue
Rue, cinquefoil, gill, vervain and agri-
mony,　　　　Blight. 5.
Rue, myrrh and cummin for the Sphinx,
　　　　　　　Sphinx. 107.
Linger,—thou shalt rue the fault:
　　　　　　　Visit. 28.
Rugged
I take him up my rugged sides,
　　　　　　　Monadnoc. 315.
Ruin
Rebuild or ruin: either fill
　　　　　　　Alphonso. 27.
Rebuild the ruin, mend defect;
　　　　　　　May-Day. 444.
Subtle rhymes, with ruin rife,
　　　　　　　Merlin. 123.
Risk or ruin he must share.
　　　　　　　Monadnoc. 339.

Ruined
Her last noble is ruined,
　　　　　　　Channing Ode. 92.
And Time the ruined bridge has swept
　　　　　　　C. Hymn. 7.
"Pride ruined the angels,　Sphinx. 89.
Through ruined systems still restored,
　　　　　　　Threnody. 283.
Ruins
Sweep ruins from the scarped mountain,
　　　　　　　May-Day. 449.
Rule
None shall rule but the humble,
　　　　　　　Boston Hymn. 27.
They shall choose men to rule
　　　　　　　Boston Hymn. 42.
Might rule the forest to his mind.
　　　　　　　May-Day. 52.
Well accept her rule austere;
　　　　　　　May-Day. 135.
But, leaving rule and pale forethought,
　　　　　　　Merlin. 31.
With the dear, dangerous lords that rule
our life,　　Musketaquid. 7.
Transmuted in these men to rule their
like),　　　Musketaquid. 49.
And bard o'er kings to rule;—
　　　　　　　Song of Nature. 70.
Which they shall rule with pride.
　　　　　　　Voluntaries. 26.
Biding by his rule and choice,
　　　　　　　Voluntaries. 87.
Ruled
Ranging down the ruled scale
　　　　　　　Harp. 7.
Rulers
Still are rulers, or Mildew?
　　　　　　　Alphonso. 40.
Nor evil laws or rulers made,
　　　　　　　May-Day. 105.
Rules
Can rules or tutors educate　Culture. 1.
The rules to men made evident
　　　　　　　Frag. Life. XXXVI. 1.
Not for fame, nor by rules of art,
　　　　　　　Garden. 19.
Ruly
　　See Unruly.
Rumored
Competing seekers of a rumored lake,
　　　　　　　Adirondacs. 130.
Run
　　See Forerun; Overrun
The lightning has run masterless too
long;　　　Adirondacs. 266.
Lemons run to leaves and rind;
　　　　　　　Alphonso. 4.
Or like the Atlantic streams, which run
　　　　　　　Bacchus. 29.
Spices in the plants that run
　　　　　　　Frag. Nat. II. 19.
And boys run out upon their leafy ropes.
　　　　　　　Frag. Nat. III. 20.
And ride, and run, and have, and hold,
　　　　　　　Initial Love. 29.
Heralds high before him run;
　　　　　　　Initial Love. 74.
Before me run　　Ode to Beauty. 41.
On two days it steads not to run from
thy grave,　　On Two Days. 1

In nearer arcs his journeys run,
Peter. 15.
Saw rivers run seaward by cities high
Poet. 65.
From Eden's vats that run. Rubies. 4.
Must time and tide forever run?
Song of Nature. 45.

Rune
When they hear from far the rune;
Monadnoc. 250.
And rounds with rhyme her every rune,
Woodnotes. II. 165.

Runes
And yet his runes he rightly read,
Saadi. 78.
But the runes that I rehearse
Woodnotes. II. 142.

Rung
Till Freedom cheered and joy-bells rung.
Boston. 99.
The shell of Clio rung.
Frag. Poet. XXXV. 3.
Rung loud and bold the song. Harp. 48.

Running
Running over the club-moss burrs;
Each. 42.
That rims the running silver sheet,—
May-Day. 246.
Change the running sand to corn;
Monadnoc. 138.

Runs
But it runs wild, Channing Ode. 56.
How much runs over on the desert
sands.   Day's Ration. 14.
And all the costly liquor runs to waste;
Day's Ration. 23.
Runs round the pine and maple tree
Frag. Nat. XIX. 2.
Then runs into a wave again,
Initial Love. 148.
The maiden fears, and fearing runs
Nemesis. 5.
The brook into the stream runs on;
Threnody. 96.
And up the tall mast runs the wood-
pecker.   Woodnotes. I. 67.
Without a pilot it runs and falls,
Woodnotes. II. 240.

Rush
Or care a rush for what thou knowest,
Destiny. 23.
Right thou feelest, rush to do.'
Freedom. 24.
Voice of sport, or rush of wings,
May-Day. 31.
I tire of shams, I rush to be: Nun. 37.

Rushes
Two creeping miles of rushes, pads and
sponge,   Adirondacs. 24.
Lo! it rushes thee to meet;
II. Compensation. 24.
Silent rushes the swift Lord
Threnody. 282.

Rusheth
In whose feet the lion rusheth,
Woodnotes. II. 40.

Rushing
I found by thee, O rushing Contoocook!
Channing Ode. 21.
Rushing ages moult their wings,
Poet. 132.

Would rushing life forget her laws,
Threnody. 226.
The rushing metamorphosis
Woodnotes. II. 112.

Russet
From fall to spring, the russet acorn,
Holidays. 1.
A little while each russet gem
Woodnotes. II. 53.

Rust
On Nature's wheels there is no rust;
Poet. 297.

Rustle
I hear the rustle of wings, Poet. 260.

Rustles
That rustles down the well-known forest
road—   River. 26.

Rusty
The ground-pines wash their rusty green,
May-Day. 59.

Ruthless
Which his ruthless will defies,
Daemonic Love. 117.

Saadi
See Said; Seyd.
But Saadi coldly thus returned,
Frag. Poet. II. 4.
Said Saadi, "When I stood before
Frag. Poet. III. 1.
God only knew how Saadi dined;
Frag. Poet. V. 13.
Saadi held the Muse in awe,
Frag. Poet. V. 22.
All their heart when Saadi sung;
Frag. Poet. V. 33.
Wise Saadi dwells alone. Saadi. 22.
Yet Saadi loved the race of men,—
Saadi. 23.
Good Saadi dwells alone. Saadi. 33.
Be thou ware where Saadi dwells;
Saadi. 34.
For Saadi sat in the sun, Saadi. 74.
What Saadi wished to say; Saadi. 83.
'O gentle Saadi, listen not, Saadi. 87.
Gentle Saadi, mind thy rhyme;
Saadi. 101.
Saadi, so far thy words shall reach:
Saadi. 139.
And thus to Saadi said the Muse:
Saadi. 141.
Saadi, see! they rise in stature
Saadi. 171.

Saadi's
For Saadi's nightly stars did burn
Saadi. 84.
Whispered the Muse in Saadi's cot:
Saadi. 86.
Heed thou only Saadi's lay. Saadi. 103.
Heed thou only Saadi's lay. Saadi. 116.
Suns rise and set in Saadi's speech!'
Saadi. 140.

Sable
Sable pageantry of clouds, Nun. 21.
When the redbird spread his sable wing,
Thine Eyes. 9.

Sacred
Where all the sacred mountains drew
around us,   Adirondacs. 9.

Sacred—*Continued*
And good men thought thy sacred voice
                     Bell. 11.
And pine in vain the sacred Seven;
                   Brahma. 14.
Have slipped their sacred bars,
             Daemonic Love. 53.
A spot that is sacred to thought and
  God.   Good-Bye. 22.
Or how the sacred pine-tree adds
                 Problem. 29.
Built of tears and sacred flames,
               Threnody. 278.

Sacrifice
But will we sacrifice our dear-bought lore
            Adirondacs. 306.
Go, sacrifice to Fame;   Fame. 26.
And sacrifice for love's dear sake,
          In Memoriam. 108.
As in the day of sacrifice, May-Day. 140.

Sacs
like Sacs and Sioux,   Adirondacs. 52.

Sad
The schools are sad and slow,
                   April. 18.
And soon thy music, sad death-bell,
                    Bell. 13.
Sad, in sooth, it were to ours,
            Ellen South. 22.
Go then, sad youth, and shine;
                  Fame. 25.
Together sad or gay,   *Farewell. 33.
I filled the dream of sad, poetic maids,
          Frag. Life. XXX. 2.
Thou saw'st but now the twilight sad
         Frag. Nat. XXVI. 12.
I bear in youth the sad infirmities
                I Bear. 1.
Wrought in a sad sincerity;
               Problem. 21.
And all their sad significance. The wind,
                 River. 25.
Wait then, sad friend, wait in majestic
  peace   Rome. 20.
I've learned the sum of that sad history
              Summons. 18.
Of his sad ornament,   To J. W. 12.
A sad self-knowledge, withering, fell
                  Uriel. 35.
And merry is only a mask of sad,
          Waldeinsamkeit. 18.

Saddens
And saddens her with heavenly doubts:
                  Rhea. 54.

Saddle
Things are in the saddle,
           Channing Ode. 50.

Sad-eyed
Sad-eyed Fakirs swiftly say   Saadi. 49.
Thus the sad-eyed Fakirs preach:
                  Saadi. 59.

Sadness
Comes the sweet sadness at the retro-
  spect,   Adirondacs. 216.
Who, with sadness and madness,
                Sphinx. 63.

Safe
Greeted their safe escape to me.
                 Each. 23.

O, when I am safe in my sylvan home,
             Good-Bye. 23.
No bird is safe that cuts the air
             Monadnoc. 143.
''Tis man's perdition to be safe,
         Quat. Sacrifice. 3.
Safe in their ancient crannies, dark and
  deep,   To-Day. 3.
In the safe herbal of the coal?
                Wealth. 28.

Saffron
The saffron cloud that floated warm
                 Lines. 15.

Sage
I await the bard and sage,
            Monodnac. 284.
And, being so, the sage unmakes the
  man.   Philosopher. 2.
Admired, sage doubting whence the
  traveller came,—   River. 4.
To wrap the errors of a sage sublime.
               To J. W. 9.
Sage and hero, side by side,
           Voluntaries. 24.
Love shuns the sage, the child it crowns,
         Woodnotes. II. 236.
The sage, till he hit the secret,
           World-Soul. 51.

Sages
And blushing Love outwits the sages.
         Frag. Poet. IX. 12.
More sense than sages write.   Peter. 32.
Rhodora! if the sages ask thee why
             Rhodora. 9.
Shalt outsee seers, and outwit sages.
         Woodnotes. II. 247.

Said
    See Saadi; Seyd
Said was hungrier than all;
          Frag. Poet. I. 2.
Said melted the days like cups of pearl,
         Frag. Poet. I. 19.
The Dervish whined to Said,
         Frag. Poet. II. 1.

Said. (verb).
    See Gainsaid; Saith, Say, Sayeth.
'A new commandment,' said the smiling
  Muse,   Adakryn. 1.
Crusoe, Crusader, Pius Æneas, said
  aloud,   Adirondacs. 184.
Said I, strolling through the pastures,
            Berrying. 4.
I said, 'What influence me preferred,
            Berrying. 9.
Said the winds that sung the lads to
  sleep,   Boston. 15.
The mountains said, 'Good-day!
           Boston. 50.
'For you,' they said, 'no barriers be,
           Boston. 55.
'You are thriving well,' said he;
           Boston. 64.
'Not so,' said Boston, 'good my lord.
           Boston. 69.
God said, I am tired of kings,
         Boston Hymn. 5.
But God said,   Celestial Love. 1.
Then I said, 'I covet truth;   Each. 37.
Hafiz said he was a fly
          Frag. Poet. I. 3.

Said Saadi, "When I stood before
          Frag. Poet. III. 1.
But the Spirit said, 'Not so;
          Freedom. 5.
Name not lightly to be said,
          Freedom. 7.
O friend, my bosom said,
          Friendship. 10.
I said to heaven that glowed above,
          From Hafiz. 1.
'If it be, as they said, she was not fair,
          Hermione. 8.
'Happy,' I said, 'whose home is here!
          Monadnoc. 68.
If I err not, thus it said:—
          Monadnoc. 198.
Yet said yon ancient wood,
          Park. 14.
The verdict said,   Past. 2.
Well and wisely said the Greek,
          Quat. Pericles. 1.
I said, they are drops of frozen wine
          Rubies. 3.
And thus to Saadi said the Muse:
          Saadi. 141.
All too much to him they said,
          September. 10.
Half the tell-tale South-wind said,—
          September. 14.
Said, "Who taught thee me to name?
          Sphinx. 110.
And said: 'No more!   Terminus. 6.
I said, 'We are mates in misery.'
          Threnody. 103.
As if it said, 'Good day, good sir!
          Titmouse. 29.
Destiny sat by, and said,
          Voluntaries. 31.
'You ask,' he said, 'what guide
          Woodnotes. I. 118.
And God said, "Throb!" and there was
  motion   Woodnotes. II. 268.

Sail
For what avail the plough or sail,
          Boston. 29.
For what avail the plough or sail,
          Boston. 80.
O happy port that spied the sail
          Boston. 88.
Let them sail for Porto Rique,
          Humble-Bee. 3.
Whereon ye sail,   Monadnoc. 327.
O heavenly ships without a sail!
          Poet. 160.
Sail swiftly through your amber vault,
          Poet. 163.
Steers his bark and trims his sail;
          Quat. Poet. I. 2.
And thousands sail the purple sea,
          Saadi. 108.
To take in sail:—   Terminus. 2.
I man the rudder, reef the sail,
          Terminus. 35.
But if upon the seas I sail,   Una. 17.
Then flew the sail across the seas
          Wealth. 36.

Sailed
And sailed for bread to every shore.
          Boston. 6.

Sailing
  See Slow-sailing..
Sailing falsely in the sphere,
          Frag. Poet. VII. 17.
Sailing through stars with all their history.   Monadnoc. 278.
And the sailing moon where the cloud was rent,   Poet. 68.
They are but sailing foam-bells
          World-Soul. 69.

Sailor
Sailor of the atmosphere;
          Humble-Bee. 13.

Sails
It cheers him as he sails.   Bell. 8.
Sails, astonished, amid stars.
          Daemonic Love. 55.
Our eyeless bark sails free
          Frag. Nat. XV. 1.
To speed his sails, to dry his hay;
          Guy. 38.
And head-winds right for royal sails.
          Heroism. 10.
On which the seraph music sails.
          Solution. 50.

Saint
The reliquaries of my dead saint, and dwell   Letter. 17.
For bard, for lover and for saint;
          Monadnoc. 45.

Sainted
Thine elegy, sweet singer, sainted wife.
          Naples. 27.

Saint Lawrence
South from Saint Lawrence to the Sound,   Monadnoc. 281.

Saints
Beauty to fire us, saints to save,
          Frag. Life. I. 3.
So many saints and saviors,
          Frag. Poet. XXVIII. 6.
Prayers of saints that inly burned,—
          Threnody. 265.
Let kings and conquerors, saints and soldiers sleep—   To-Day. 4.

Saith
Thy heart saith, 'Brother, go thy ways!
          Destiny. 21.
'Go, lonely man,' it saith;   Dirge. 49.
All my force saith, Come and use me:
          Frag. Nat. XXVIII. 2.
What the spangled meadow saith
          Harp. 32.
As it heareth, so it saith;   Harp. 70.

Sake
And sacrifice for love's dear sake,
          In Memoriam. 108.
Fills for his proper sake.   Promise. 10.

Salamander
Captured the lizard, salamander, shrew,
          Adirondacs. 135.

Sale
He wrote on Nature's grandest brow, *For Sale.*   Webster, 1854. 2.

Sallied
I left my dreary page and sallied forth,
          Frag. Nat. XXVII. 1.

Sallies
When the God's will sallies free,
          Merlin. 71.

Sallow
The sallow knows the basket-maker's thumb; Adirondacs. 101.
One sallow horseman knows me good. Romany. 16.

Sally
Sometimes their wits at sally and retort, Adirondacs. 127.

Saloons
Nor when in fair saloons we chance to meet; Frag. Life. XV. 4.

Salt
Shot through the weltering pit of the salt sea. Adirondacs. 270.
The salt of all the elements, world of the world. Good Cheer. 16.
Salt and basalt, wild and tame: Mithridates. 11.
And one of the salt sea-sand. Song of Nature. 64.

Salubrity
Drink the wild air's salubrity: Merlin's Song. 32.

Salutation
With salutation to the sea and to the bordering isles. Monadnoc. 37.

Salute
Let its grapes the morn salute Bacchus. 6.
Salute the bard who is alive Frag. Poet. XXVIII. 8.

Saluted
Nay, we saluted them Auxiliaries, Adirondacs: 169.
Saluted him each morn as brother, Poet. 203.

Salutes
Not one salutes me here; Exile. 6.

Salvador
At this pinch, wee San Salvador! Titmouse. 51.

Salvator
Of Salvator, of Guercino, Ode to Beauty. 54.

Salve
Salve my worst wounds. Musketaquid. 75.

Same (Partial list.)
See Self-same.
The ring you gave is still the same; Amulet. 2.
They caught the footsteps of the Same. Blight. 29.
And, chest by chest, let down the same, Boston. 78.
Shadow and sunlight are the same; Brahma. 6.
Unto the same again.' Celestial Love. 26.
Have the same mists another side, Chartist. 7.
And I am still the same; Days Pass. 2.
At the same torch that lighted mine; Eva. 3.
Is the same Genius that creates. Fate. 16.
What care I, so they stand the same,— Merops. 1.
Of the same stuff, and so allayed, Monadnoc. 167.

Lest there I find the same deceiver Ode to Beauty. 96.
By one thought to one same sphere; Poet. 268.
And the same power that reared the shrine Problem. 49.
Shall not by the same be loved again; Rhea. 38.
The same blue wonder that my infant eye River. 3.
These are the same, but I am not the same, River. 18.

Samson
Samson stark, at Dagon's knee, Frag. Nat. XXXIV. 1.

Sand
See Sea-sand.
The sand shaded, Channing Ode. 61.
With the sun and the sand and the wild uproar. Each. 28.
Change the running sand to corn; Monadnoc. 138.
The gale that wrecked you on the sand, Quat. Northman. 1.
The ominous hole he dug in the sand, Threnody. 86.
The wide lake, edged with sand and grass, Woodnotes. I. 108.
Unerring to the ocean sand. Woodnotes. I. 132.

Sand-heap
To spin my sand-heap into twine. Frag. Poet. XXXIV. 2.

Sand-heaps
And drifting sand-heaps feed my stock, Woodnotes. II. 11.

Sands
How much runs over on the desert sands. Day's Ration. 14.
And the sands whereof I'm made Ode to Beauty. 50.

Sane
Of untried power and sane delight: Monadnoc. 105.
And makest sane. Monadnoc. 402.

Sang
He sang to my ear,—they sang to my eye. Each. 18.
When that bird sang, I gave the theme; Miracle. 27.
That wood-bird sang my last night's dream, Miracle. 28.

Sank
The fortunate star that rose on us sank not; Adirondacs. 337.
Into blissful orgies sank; Poet. 82.

Sannup
Winds mindful still of sannup and of squaw, Musketaquid. 28.

Sap
See Maple-sap.
And the murmuring rivers of sap May-Day. 230.
The mounting sap, the shells, the sea, Woodnotes. II. 77.

Saranac
Next morn, we swept with oars the Saranac, Adirondacs. 7.
On through the Upper Saranac, and up Adirondacs. 21.

Sark
   See Baresark.
Sarsaparilla
   Elder-blow, sarsaparilla,
                 Frag. Nat. II. 17.
Sash
   Lift the sash, lay me within,
                 Aeolian Harp. 10.
Sassafras
   Blue-vetch and trillium, hawkweed, sassa-
     fras,   Blight. 6.
   Peppermint and sassafras,
                 Frag. Nat. II. 13.
   Sassafras, fern, benzöine,
                 Frag. Nat. II. 28.
Sat
   See Sate.
   As they sat by the seaside,
                 Boston Hymn. 3.
   That sat in darkness long,—
                 Boston Hymn. 78.
   At court he sat in the grave Divan.
                 Frag. Poet. I. 10.
   And when I sat by the watercourse,
                 Hermione. 58.
   Honor came and sat beside him,
                 In Memoriam. 56.
   Couched like a cat sat watching close be-
   hind   Philosopher. 9.
   Beside him sat enduring love,   Poet. 195.
   For Saadi sat in the sun,   Saadi. 74.
   Destiny sat by, and said,
                 Voluntaries. 31.
Satan
   No Satan with a royal trick   Past. 16.
Satan's
   On God's and Satan's brood,   Cupido. 7.
Sate
   See Sat.
   Calm as the morn the manly patriot sate;
                 Phi. 10.
   Great men in the Senate sate,
                 Voluntaries. 23.
   Beside the forest water sate;
                 Woodnotes. I. 105.
Satellites
   And thefts from satellites and rings
                 Song of Nature. 25.
   And satellites have rest?
                 Song of Nature. 48.
Satiate
   See Insatiate.
Satirical
   Dire and satirical,   Woodnotes. II. 201.
Saturate
   Fill and saturate each kind
                 May-Day. 283.
   Fill each kind and saturate
                 May-Day. 285.
Saturn
   For Eros is older than Saturn or Jove;
                 Quat. Casella. 2.
   Speeding Saturn cannot halt;   Visit. 27.
Saucy
   In sooth, red flannel is a saucy test
                 Adirondacs. 97.
   Chic-chic-a-dee-dee! saucy note
                 Titmouse. 27.
Saurian
   And in cramp elf and saurian forms
                 Song of Nature. 31.

Savage
   Now, to a savage selfness grown,
                 Alphonso. 35.
   And the bellowing of the savage sea
                 Each. 22.
   Brute or savage into man; Freedom. 16.
   And rank the savage maples grow
                 Garden. 7.
   So fanciful, so savage, nought cares he
                 Snow-Storm. 16.
   He goes to my savage haunts,
                 Woodnotes. II. 26.
Save
   Which fired the little State to save
                 Boston. 94.
   Save underneath the sea
                 Concord Ode. 30.
   Beauty to fire us, saints to save,
                 Frag. Life. I. 3.
   No fate, save by the victim's fault, is low,
                 Frag. Life. II. 1.
   Save to his ear the wind-harp lone.
                 Harp. 98.
   Save in tablets of the heart,
                 In Memoriam. 49.
   None save dappling shadows climb,
                 Monadnoc. 202.
   On the first, neither balm nor physician
   can save,   On Two Days. 3.
   Look, here he is, unaltered, save that
   now   River. 8.
   What oldest star the fame can save
                 Wealth. 22.
Savior
   With prophet, savior and head;
                 Threnody. 220.
   I greeted loud my little savior,
                 Titmouse. 48.
Saviors
   So many saints and saviors,
                 Frag. Poet. XXVIII. 6.
   I moulded kings and saviors,
                 Song of Nature. 69.
Savor
   Suffer no savor of the earth to scape.
                 Bacchus. 5.
Savors
   Not by jewels, feasts and savors,
                 Celestial Love. 101.
   In their scent or in their savors,
                 Lines. 8.
Savory
   See Unsavory.
   With its savory leaf for bread.
                 Frag. Nat. II. 24.
Saw
   I saw men go up and down,
                 Astraea. 9.
   He saw strong Eros struggling through,
                 Beauty. 18.
   Who saw the hid beginnings
                 Cosmos. 1.
   I saw the hid beginnings   Cosmos. 5.
   Under her solemn fillet saw the scorn.
                 Days. 11.
   Again I saw, again I heard,   Each. 48.
   I saw them pass   Experience. 2.
   They saw not my fine revellers,—
                 Forerunners. 19.
   And saw the wheeling sea-birds skim,
                 Frag. Poet. I. 46.

Saw—*Continued*

Panoramas which I saw
  Frag. Poet. VIII. 8.
Saw bonfires of the harlot flies
  Harp. 91.
I saw fair boys bestriding steeds,
  Harp. 111.
I saw the bud-crowned Spring go forth,
  May-Day. 305.
I saw the Days deformed and low,
  May-Day. 312
I saw them mask their awful glance
  May-Day. 324.
When first my eyes saw thee,
  Ode to Beauty. 9.
Not lazy grazing on all they saw,
  Poet. 57.
Saw rivers run seaward by cities high
  Poet. 65.
Saw the endless rack of the firmament
  Poet. 67.
Saw the dance of Nature forward and far,
  Poet. 70.
Saw musical order and pairing rhymes.
  Poet. 72.
And wishful saw the Ocean stream:—
  Poet. 192.
Than all the grace Love ever saw;
  Poet. 282.
Who saw what ferns and palms were
  pressed   Wealth. 26.
He saw the partridge drum in the woods;
  Woodnotes. I. 54.
He saw beneath dim aisles,
  Woodnotes. I. 68.

Saw'st

Thou saw'st but now the twilight sad
  Frag. Nat. XXVI. 12.

Saxon

We greet you well, you Saxon men,
  Boston. 51.
The men are ripe of Saxon kind
  Concord Ode. 13.

Say

  See Said, Saith, Sayeth, Saying, Says.
Say, Seigniors, are the old Niles dry,
  Alphonso. 31.
'What am I? companion, say.'
  Astraea. 18.
And that which roses say so well.
  Bacchus. 25.
The injured elements say, 'Not in us;'
  Blight. 33.
Fire, plant and mineral say, 'Not in us;'
  Blight. 35.
Say, was it never heard   Fame. 4.
Or say, the foresight that awaits
  Fate. 15.
We have not better things to say,
  Frag. Life. XII. 3.
But surely say them better.
  Frag. Life. XII. 4.
O what would Nature say?
  Frag. Nat. III. 8.
What central flowing forces, say,
  Frag. Nat. XI. 1.
And love, for words thy tongue could
  say.   Frag. Poet. II. 8.
Bards to say what nations need;
  Frag. Poet. XII. 2.

Thou foolish Hafiz! Say, do churls
  Friendship Trans. 1.
What sea and land discoursing say
  Harp. 27.
A window rose, and, to say sooth,
  Harp. 109.
'Higher, dear swallows! mind not what I
  say.   Hermione. 26.
Say, was it just,   Hermione. 28.
And the second, borrowed money,—
  though the smiling lender say
  Ibn Jemin. 3.
That no god dare say him nay,
  Initial Love. 126.
'Pass in, pass in,' the angels say,
  Merlin. 34.
Say not, the chiefs who first arrive
  Merlin's Song. 16.
One word, no more, to say.   Merops. 12.
Shall the dumb bird instructed say.
  Miracle. 22.
Pole to pole, and what they say;
  Monadnoc. 230.
(That one would say, meadow and forest
  walked,   Musketaquid. 48.
And what they say they made to-day,
  Nature. II. 11.
Nor lives the tragic bard to say
  Nun. 47.
Say, when in lapsed ages
  Ode to Beauty. 5.
Some random word they say   Poet. 78.
Ye meditate what to say   Poet. 261.
I know what say the fathers wise,—
  Problem. 63.
Reck not what the people say;
  Quat. Artist. 2.
They are not of our race, they seem to
  say,   River. 31.
And say it frankly without guile,
  Romany. 10.
Annexed **a** warning, poets say,
  Saadi. 13.
Sad-eyed Fakirs swiftly say   Saadi. 49.
What Saadi wished to say;   Saadi. 83.
Heed not what the brawlers say,
  Saadi. 102.
Say, Pilgrim, why so late ͵and slow to
  come?   Seashore. 2.
"Say on, sweet Sphinx! thy dirges
  Sphinx. 67.
Turn on the accuser roundly; say,
  Sursum Corda. 6.
They say, through patience, chalk
  They. 1.
For flattering planets seemed to say
  Threnody. 134.
Some to their friends the tidings say;
  Threnody. 154.
Now hear thee say in Roman key,
  Titmouse. 103.
Hear what wine and roses say;
  To J. W. 2.
Say, what other meter is it   Visit. 11.
To each his bosom-secret say.
  Woodnotes. II. 155.
And thou shalt say to the Most High,
  Woodnotes. II. 204.

Sayer

  See Soothsayer.

Saying

Saying, 'This be thy portion, child; this
chalice,   Day's Ration. 3.
Saying, 'We have dressed for thee the
ground,   Ellen South. 15.
Saying, Sweetheart! the old mystery re-
mains,—   Flute. 3.
Saying, "T is mine, my children's and my
name's.   Hamatreya. 5.
And saying "You're caught!"
                              *Lines. 23.
Saying 'Stand in thy place;   Poet. 120.
Saying, 'Hearken! Earth, Sea, Air!'
                              Rhea. 57.
Wormwood,—saying, "Go thy ways;
                              Saadi. 63.
Saying, *What is excellent,*
                          Threnody. 266.

Sayings

Wise Ali's sunbright sayings pass
                              Saadi. 151.

Says

Endured, the Bible says, as long;
                          Frag. Nat. VI. 4.
Hear what the Earth says:—
                          Hamatreya. 27.
Even the serene Reason says,
                          In Memoriam. 9.
Little and less he says to them,
                              Manners. 13.

Scale

The scale of power uprears,
                          Frag. Life. IV. 2.
He left each civil scale behind:
                          Frag. Poet. I. 32.
Ranging down the ruled scale
                              Harp. 7.
And pile the hills to scale the sky;
                              Saadi. 95.
O, few to scale those uplands dare,
                          Waldeinsamkeit. 39.

Scaled

Or parties scaled the near acclivities
                          Adirondacs. 129.

Scales

Wolves shed their fangs, and dragons
scales;   Solution. 6.

Scaly

In ocean sport the scaly herds,
                              Saadi. 3.

Scan

Scan the profile of the sphere;
                              Circles. 4.
Each village senior paused to scan
                          Threnody. 72.

Scanderbegs

Bards, Roys, Scanderbegs and Tells;
                          Monadnoc. 97.

Scanned

His cold eye truth and conduct scanned,
                          Quat. S. H. 2.

Scant

Half-repentant, scant of breath,—
                          Monadnoc. 316.
And his training should not scant
                              Poet. 41.

Scanty

To reap its scanty corn,   Dirge. 10.
To reap its scanty corn,   Peter. 2.
When the scanty shores are full
                          Threnody. 232.

In scanty intervals.   World-Soul. 40.

Scape

See Escape.
Suffer no savor of the earth to scape.
                              Bacchus. 5.

Scarce

Scarce the first blush has overspread his
cheek,   Philosopher. 4.
Scarce freed from her embraces?
                          Philosopher. 12.

Scared

Is fallen: but hush! it has not scared
the buck   Adirondacs. 122.

Scarf

Oft as morning wreathes my scarf,
                          Monadnoc. 311.

Scarfs

Not with scarfs or perfumed gloves
                          Celestial Love. 99.

Scarlet

The scarlet maple-keys betray
                          May-Day. 186.
And give love's scarlet tides to flow,—
                              Rubies. II.

Scarped

Sweep ruins from the scarped mountain,
                          May-Day. 449.

Scars

Leaving on space no shade, no scars,
                          Frag. Nat. VIII. 7.

Scatter

But which we learn to scatter with a
smudge,   Adirondacs. 175.
Not to scatter bread and gold,
                          Celestial Love. 125.
Scatter the sloth, wash out the stain,
                          May-Day. 454.

Scattered

Now scattered wide thro' earth, and each
alone,   Good Cheer. 4.
Scattered on the stormy air,   Merlin. 56.
I see the scattered gleams,   Poet. 98.

Scatters

Scatters on every eye dust of his spells,
                          Enchanter. 3.
He scatters wide and wild its lustres
here.   Frag. Life. XVI. 9.
The sower scatters broad his seed,
                          Frag. Poet. VI. 11.
The sower scatters broad his seed;
                          I. Intellect. 3.
Love scatters oil   *Lines. 1.

Scene

A tiny scene of sun and shower,
                              Ellen. 4.
He was the heart of all the scene;
                          Woodnotes. I. 112.

Scenes

And, when I would recall the scenes I
dreamed   Frag. Nat. IV. 6.

Scent

Scent, form and color; to the flowers and
shells   Enchanter. 4.
Flowers they strew,—I catch the scent;
                          Forerunners. 11.
Sweet and scent for Dian's table,
                          Frag. Nat. II. 16.
In their scent or in their savors,
                              Lines. 8.
One scent to hyson and to wall-flower,
                          Xenophanes. 2.

Scented
Through scented banks of lilies white
and gold, Adirondacs. 19.
Scented fern and agrimony;
Frag. Nat. II. 10.
Scented fern, and agrimony,
Humble-Bee. 47.
Flowering grass and scented weeds;
Threnody. 275.

Scentless
Puny man and scentless rose
Alphonso. 25.

Scents
The frost to spare, what scents so well.
Frag. Nat. II. 31.

Sceptred
But sceptred genius, aye inorbed,
Hermione. 10.

Schemes
In schemes of broader scope engage.
Alphonso. 80.
Casts her schemes rarely,
Frag. Life. VI. 2.

Schism
Was a weed of self and schism;
Daemonic Love. 128.

Scholars
Ten scholars, wonted to lie warm and
soft Adirondacs. 50.
Of scholars furloughed from their tasks
and let Adirondacs. 193.
But these young scholars, who invade our
hills, Blight. 18.

School
See High-school.
He must to school and learn his verb and
noun Adirondacs. 267.
Each child shall have his school.
Boston. 34.
In church and state and school.
Boston Hymn. 44.
The school decays, the learning spoils
Frag. Life. X. 5.

School-boy's
The green lane is the school-boy's friend,
May-Day. 67.

School-march
The school-march, each day's festival,
Threnody. 59.

Schools
The schools are sad and slow,
April. 18.
At the sophist schools and the learned
clan; Good-Bye. 28.
In old Bassora's schools, I seemed
Hermione. 33.

Science
Of science, not from the philosophers,
Adirondacs. 284.
With science poorly mask their hurt;
Alphonso. 37.
He is versed in occult science,
Initial Love. 64.
And, through all science and all art,
Initial Love. 106.
And thou, by science all undone,
May-Day. 174.
By eldest science wrought and shown!
Monadnoc. 67.
To sound the science of the sky,
Monadnoc. 103.

When Science armed and guided war,
Solution. 61.

Scion
Grafts gentlest scion
Channing Ode. 88.

Scipios
Be great, be true, and all the Scipios,
Rome. 4.

Scirpus
See Whip-scirpus

Scoff
Scoff of yeoman strong and stark,
Monadnoc. 189.

Scold
Thy praying lute will seem to scold;
Rhea. 22.

Scoop
For, though he scoop my water in his
palm, Seashore. 45.

Scoop-net
Waved the scoop-net, and nothing came
amiss; Adirondacs. 138.

Scope
In schemes of broader scope engage.
Alphonso. 80.
Beyond the scope of human age,
Frag. Poet. XI. 17.
Let it have scope: Give. 8.
Strains every sense to larger scope,
May-Day. 153.

Scorch
Scorch our delicate prime,
Ellen South. 19.

Scorching
In summer's scorching glow.
Woodnotes. II. 12.

Score
See Fourscore.
A score of airy miles will smooth
Frag. Nat. XIV. 1.

Scorn
Or baffle by a veil, or slight by scorn?
Adirondacs. 176.
Under her solemn fillet saw the scorn.
Days. 11.
Well may Jove and Juno scorn.
Destiny. 11.
Well might then the poet scorn
Frag. Poet. V. 44.
Toil's hard hap with scorn accuse.
Monadnoc. 126.
But when the noisy scorn was past,
Poet. 23.
Ye scorn me from your deeps of blue.
Poet. 240.
Scorn not thou the love of parts,
Prudence. 3.
Pale Northern girls! you scorn our race;
Romany. 5.
Scorn trifles and embrace a better aim
Rome. 12.
And wandered backward as in scorn,
Threnody. 148.
Came Uriel's voice of cherub scorn,
Uriel. 54.
Nor the June flowers scorn to cover
Woodnotes. I. 145.

Scorned
I scorned the fame of Timour brave;
Frag. Poet. III. 3.

These scorned bondmen were my para-
pet. Grace. 4.
And found a home in haunts which others
scorned, Muketaquid. 3.
Albeit scorned as none was scorned,
Rhea. 62.

Scornful
And his eye is scornful, Destiny. 32.
Methought the sky looked scornful down
Walden. 21.

Scorning
In loyal worship, scorning praise,
Beauty. 22.
Follow falsehood, follow scorning.
Saadi. 93.

Scorns
The sea-beat scorns the minster clock
Frag. Nat. XXV. 3.
To him who scorns their charities
World-Soul. 95.

Scotland
Wales, Scotland, Uri, Hungary's dells:
Monadnoc. 96.

Scott
Scott, the delight of generous boys,
Harp. 81.

Scour
Nor scour the seas, nor sift mankind,
Saadi. 155.

Scourge
Weapons to guard the State, or scourge
In Memoriam. 65.

Scout
No scout can track his way,
Frag. Poet. VI. 2.

Scowl
I scowl on him with my cloud,
Monadnoc. 340.

Scrap
This scrap of valor just for play
Titmouse. 45.

Scraps
The mottled clouds, like scraps of wool,
Frag. Nat. XXVI. 17.

Scrawny
Yon pale, scrawny fisher fools,
Alphonso. 15.

Screamed
Above, the eagle flew, the osprey
screamed, Adirondacs. 146.

Screeneth
By want and pain God screeneth him
Frag. Poet. V. 7.

Scribe
To learn of scribe or courier
Frag. Poet. V. 45.

Scrip
God fills the scrip and canister,
Woodnotes. II. 16.

Scroll
Be just at home; then write your scroll
Concord Ode. 25.
Bring book, or starbright scroll of genius,
Day's Ration. 21.
Yet every scroll whereon he wrote
Poet. 13.
Of rock and fire the scroll,
Song of Nature. 22.
From lengthening scroll of human fates,
Threnody. 263.

Sculptor
As the sculptor uncovers the statue
Boston Hymn. 19.
The million-handed sculptor moulds
May-Day. 257.

Sculptor-like
And, sculptor-like, his large design
Solution. 31.

Sculptor's
Never did sculptor's dream unfold
Angelo. 1.

Sculpture
He will spell in the sculpture, 'Stay.'
Garden. 64.

Sculptured
Shamed that sculptured countenance.
In Memoriam. 47.
I make your sculptured architecture vain,
Seashore. 11.

Sculpture's
Earth's prime secret, sculpture's seat?
May-Day. 211.

Scum
But in the mud and scum of things
Music. 17.

Scythe
Nor gun nor scythe to see.
Woodnotes. I. 10.

Sea
See Oversea.
Of the wire-cable laid beneath the sea,
Adirondacs. 239.
Shot through the weltering pit of the
salt sea. Adirondacs. 270.
The rivers gambolled onward to the sea,
Adirondacs. 339.
When the South Sea calls.
Bacchus. 30.
And twice each day the flowing sea
Boston. 3.
Each street leads downward to the sea,
Boston. 57.
O happy town beside the sea,
Boston. 59.
Into the laughing sea? Boston. 79.
The sea returning day by day
Boston. 100.
Can govern the land and sea
Boston Hymn. 46.
The circles of that sea are laws
Celestial Love. 58.
But by the sun-spark on the sea,
Celestial Love. 103.
The throbbing sea, the quaking earth,
Celestial Love. 109.
Will rive the hills and swim the sea,
II. Compensation. 27.
O'er-mantling land and sea,
Concord Ode. 10.
For sea and land don't understand,
Concord Ode. 21.
Of honor o'er the sea, Concord Ode. 26.
Save underneath the sea
Concord Ode. 30.
Who cannot circumnavigate the sea
Day's Ration. 30.
Which melts the world into a sea.
Destiny. 6.
And the bellowing of the savage sea
Each. 22.

Sea —*Continued*
Is leaping o'er the sea,   *Farewell. 17.
As in the Andes watched by fleets at sea,
                    Frag. Nat. IV. 4.
The   surging   sea   outweighs,
                    Friendship. 2.
'T is good, when you have crossed the
    sea and back,   Hamatreya. 23.
Shine down in the old sea;
                    Hamatreya. 32.
What sea and land discoursing say
                    Harp. 27.
Or valleys by the sea,   House. 10.
Cools sea and land so far and fast,
                    Humble-Bee. 59.
On Life's dark sea,   *Lines. 2.
Migrate from the Southern Sea;
                    May-Day. 86.
Like a sea which me infolds;
                    May-Day. 194.
As poured the flood of the ancient sea
                    May-Day. 241.
Coat sea and sky with heavenlier blue,
                    May-Day. 446.
Live in the sunshine, swim the sea,
                    Merlin's Song. 31.
Her lily and rose, her sea and land dis-
    play.   Monadnoc. 13.
With salutation to the sea and to the
    bordering isles.   Monadnoc. 37.
All his county, sea and land,
                    Monadnoc. 320.
The sun and sea,   Ode to Beauty. 39.
Thee gliding through the sea of form,
                    Ode to Beauty. 68.
Ran from his mouth to mountains and
    the sea,   Phi. 21.
And through man and woman and sea
    and star   Poet. 69.
The sea is the road of the bold,
                    Quat. Alcuin. 1.
Right out to sea his courses stand,
                    Quat. Poet. I. 3.
Saying, 'Hearken! Earth, Sea, Air!
                    Rhea. 57.
And thousands sail the purple sea,
                    Saadi. 108.
I heard or seemed to hear the chiding
    Sea   Seashore. 1.
Behold the Sea,   Seashore. 17.
Sea full of food, the nourisher of kinds,
                    Seashore. 21.
They grope the sea for pearls, but more
    than pearls: Seashore. 28.
The building in the coral sea,
                    Song of Nature. 23.
They boiled the sea, and piled the layers
                    Song of Nature. 35.
In the sea of sense I dived;
                    Song of Seyd. 12.
"Sea, earth, air, sound, silence,
                    Sphinx. 33.
I lonely roved the land or sea:
                    Thine Eyes. 2.
I dine in the sun; when he sinks in the
    sea,   Titmouse. 69.
Through flood and sea and firmament;
                    Two Rivers. 7.
In the sea of generation,   Uriel. 40.
Moanings of the tropic sea;
                    Voluntaries. 4.

In wandering by the sea;
                    Waldeinsamkeit. 2.
When sea and land refuse to feed me,
                    Woodnotes. I. 141.
And I will swim the ancient sea
                    Woodnotes. II. 45.
The mounting sap, the shells, the sea,
                    Woodnotes. II. 77.
Whether she work in land or sea,
                    Woodnotes. II. 166.
The river knows the way to the sea;
                    Woodnotes. II. 239.
The sea tosses and foams to find
                    Woodnotes. II. 242.
Thanks to the foaming sea,
                    World-Soul. 2.
The seeds of land and sea
                    World-Soul. 86.
Sea-beat
The sea-beat scorns the minster clock
                    Frag. Nat. XXV. 3.
No palace but his sea-beat cave.
                    Frag. Poet. V. 21.
Sea-birds
And saw the wheeling sea-birds skim,
                    Frag. Poet. I. 46.
Sea-born
I fetched my sea-born treasures home;
                    Each. 25.
Sea-bound
From Katskill east to the sea-bound.
                    Monadnoc. 282.
Sea-boy
The home-bound sea-boy hails,
                    Bell. 6.
Sea-gods
Rich are the sea-gods:—who gives gifts
    but they?   Seashore. 27.
Seal
    See Unseal.
Wilt thou seal up the avenues of ill?
                    Frag. Life. XXXII. 1.
To seal the marriage of these minds with
    thine,   Good Cheer. 14.
Sealed
Though they sealed him in a rock,
                    Worship. 5.
Sea-lion
Tree and lichen, ape, sea-lion,
                    Mithridates. 12.
Seals
    See Unseals.
But feels and seals this union;
                    Celestial Love. 112.
Seaman
And the lone seaman all the night
                    Daemonic Love. 54.
Sea-marge
Or on wind-blown sea-marge bleak,
                    Solution. 13.
Seamen
Off soundings, seamen do not suffer cold;
                    Adirondacs. 56.
Search
Come search the wood for flowers,—
                    Frag. Nat. II. 1.
And search the skies for prouder friends,
                    From Hafiz. 10.
To search where now thy beauty glowed,
                    Lines. 21.

Searched

All day we swept the lake, searched every cove,   Adirondacs. 108.

Intent, I searched the region round,
          Monadnoc. 72.

And searched with the sun's privilege.
          Poet. 62.

And Dante searched the triple spheres,
          Solution. 28.

Searches

An energy that searches thorough
          May-Day. 459.

Returned this day, the South-wind searches,   Threnody. 24.

Searching

Disconcert the searching spy,
          Astraea. 35.

By searching of a clear and loving eye
          Good Cheer. 11.

Tower of observance searching space;
          Monadnoc. 83.

And the searching sun to see
          Mountain. 16.

Sea's

To those who gaze from the sea's edge
          Astraea. 38.

Seas

Seas ebbed and flowed in epic chime.
          Beauty. 16.

We plant and build by foaming seas
          Boston. 21.

O bounteous seas that never fail!
          Boston. 86.

Which dip their foot in the seas
          Boston Hymn. 22.

From all the seas of strength Fate filled a chalice,   Day's Ration. 2.

The seas their islands clip,   II Eros. 3.

Though foes and land and seas between
          Frag. Life. XVII. 14.

Who gives to seas and sunset skies
          Freedom. 13.

Far-off heats through seas to seek;
          Humble-Bee. 4.

As melts the iceberg in the seas,
          Poet. 33.

And the seas wash the low-hung sky;
          Poet. 66.

Nor scour the seas, nor sift mankind,
          Saadi. 155.

Who sets to seas a shore,
          Terminus. 4.

But if upon the seas I sail,   Una. 17.

Then flew the sail across the seas
          Wealth. 36.

Sea-sand

And one of the salt sea-sand.
          Song of Nature. 64.

Seashore

And fill the long reach of the old sea-shore   Poet. 75.

To the seashore, to the old seawalls,
          Poet. 228.

Seaside

As they sat by the seaside,
          Boston Hymn. 3.

Season

Sweat and season are their arts,
          Monadnoc. 133.

Magic-built to last a season;
          Threnody. 256.

Seasoned

See Unseasoned.

Seasons

The seasons chariot him from this exile,
          Adirondacs. 225.

Which the four seasons do not tend
          Threnody. 112.

Seasons'

And the mystic seasons' dance;
          Monadnoc. 63.

Seat

The seat of the world-old Forces
          Cosmos. 19.

Earth's prime secret, sculpture's seat?
          May-Day. 211.

On my neck he makes his seat;
          Park. 6.

An Atlantic seat,   Politics. 18.

The silver seat of Innocence.
          Spiritual Laws. 12.

Seats

Usurp the seats for which all strive;
          Merlin's Song. 17.

Sea-valleys

Sea-valleys and the deep of skies
          Ode to Beauty. 48.

Seawalls

To the seashore, to the old seawalls,
          Poet. 228.

Seaward

Taháwus, Seaward, MacIntyre, Baldhead,
          Adirondacs. 10.

Down the dark stream which seaward creeps.   C. Hymn. 8.

Looking seaward, well assured
          Letters. 4.

Saw rivers run seaward by cities high
          Poet. 65.

Sea-washed

And gems from the sea-washed strand,
          Exile. 14.

Sea-waves

And by the sea-waves he was strong;
          Frag. Poet. V. 18.

Sea-wind

The cold sea-wind detain;
          Walden. 6.

Sea-winds

In May, when sea-winds pierced our solitudes,   Rhodora. 1.

Second

But, on the second day, we heed them not,   Adirondacs. 168.

A second crop thine acres yield,
          Apology. 19.

And the second, borrowed money,— though the smiling lender say
          Ibn Jemin. 3.

Nor thee, on the second, the Universe slay.   On Two Days. 4.

And in the second reappears the first.
          Xenophanes. 13.

Secret

See Bosom-secret.

The secret of the world imparts;
          Aeolian Harp. 13.

Was never secret history   Apology. 15.

To them their secret told;   Boston. 14.

The secret force to find   Boston. 93.

The secret store   Dull. 9.

Secret—*Continued*

With the key of the secret he marches
faster,   Frag. Life. XXXI. 1.
Will hint her secret in a garden patch,
                    Frag. Nat. IV. 2.
Meek Nature's secret still untold.
                    Frag. Nat. VI. 8.
Freedom's secret wilt thou know?—
                    Freedom. 21.
A secret nook in a pleasant land,
                    Good-Bye. 17.
Ever on her secret broods.   Harp. 14.
It shares the secret of the earth,
                    Harp. 65.
No craven cry, no secret tear,—
                    In Memoriam. 99.
Earth's prime secret, sculpture's seat?
                    May-Day. 211.
Fanning secret fires which glow
                    May-Day. 251.
The deeper secret of the hour!
                    Miracle. 18.
In dulness now their secret keep;
                    Monadnoc. 172.
With my secret in his brain,
                    Monadnoc. 263.
I muse what secret purpose had he
                    Monadnoc Afar. 7.
And in their secret senate have prevailed
                    Musketaquid. 6.
The secret of its laboring heart,
                    Nature. 10.
In latent fire his secret thought,
                    Poet. 14.
Future or Past no richer secret folds,
                    Quat. Heri. 3.
And the secret stands revealed
                    Saadi. 173.
The open secret of to-day.
                    Solution. 70.
"Who'll tell me my secret, Sphinx. 5.
And their lips the secret kept,
                    Uriel. 45.
Aloft, in secret veins of air,
                    Waldeinsamkeit. 37.
A plant in any secret place,
                    Woodnotes. I. 37.
As if by secret sight he knew
                    Woodnotes. I. 48.
They knew by secret sympathy
                    Woodnotes. I. 116.
The sage, till he hit the secret,
                    World-Soul. 51.
Still, still the secret presses;
                    World-Soul. 57.

Secrets

All the sweet secrets therein hid
                    May-Day. 45.
Secrets of the solar track,   Merlin. 14.

Sect

The Flowers—tiny sect of Shakers—
                    Ellen South. 11.

Secular

Till the slow ripening, secular tree
                    Frag. Nat. XXI. 7.
Slowsure Britain's secular might,
                    Monadnoc. 301.

Secure

Only the hand secure and bold
                    Angelo. 4.

Secure as in the zodiac's belt;
                    Daemonic Love. 122.
Secure the osier yet will hide
                    May-Day. 172.
All is now secure and fast;   Past. 10.
Though thou forget, the gods, secure,
                    Rhea. 28.

Secures

And the sweet heaven his deed secures.
                    Voluntaries. 92.

Sedate

Which, o'er passion throned sedate,
                    Astraea. 33.
Thou art silent and sedate.
                    Monadnoc. 380.

Sedge

Bending forests as bends the sedge,
                    May-Day. 243.

Sediment

He will from wrecks and sediment
                    World-Soul. 99.

See

        See Outsee.
My thunderbolt has eyes to see
                    Boston Hymn. 87.
See rights for which the one hand fights
                    Concord Ode. 23.
Some to see, some to be guessed,
                    Experience. 12.
Yet I could never see their face.
                    Forerunners. 14.
On eastern hills I see their smokes,
                    Forerunners. 15.
Wait a little, you shall see
                    Frag. Life. XXXV. 5.
And all we see are pictures high;
                    Frag. Nat. III. 16.
But I can see the elastic tent of day
                    Frag. Nat. V. 4.
See yonder leafless trees against the
sky,   Frag. Nat. XVII. 1.
See the world below
                    Frag. Nat. XXVI. 26.
To see the people of the sky:
                    Frag. Poet. XI. 4.
Earth laughs in flowers, to see her boast-
ful boys   Hamatreya. 13.
See youth's glad mates in earliest
bloom,—   Harp. 123.
See the stars through them,
                    Illusions. 14.
Or see the fault, or seen betray:
                    Initial Love. 127.
I see him with superior smile
                    In Memoriam. 73.
See, every patriot oak-leaf throws
                    May-Day. 113.
To see the southing of the sun?
                    May-Day. 176.
And the dull idiot might see
                    Merlin. 72.
See thou lift the lightest load.
                    Merlin's Song. 23.
And hands that stablish what these see:
                    Monadnoc. 109.
To see strange forests and new snow,
                    Monadnoc. 206.
See New England underspread,
                    Monadnoc. 280.
"See there the grim gray rounding
                    Monadnoc. 325.

And the searching sun to see
                    Mountain. 16.
Not many men see beauty in the fogs
                    Naples. 13.
The rounded world is fair to see,
                    Nature. Mot. 7.
But oh, to see his solar eyes   Poet. 54.
I see the coming light,   Poet. 97.
I see the scattered gleams,   Poet. 98.
I see the pale lustres condense to a star:
                    Poet. 109.
Make him glad thy fall to see!
                    Poet. 220.
Feeds those eternal lamps I see.
                    Poet. 236.
I see your forms with deep content,
                    Poet. 257.
See, all we are rooted here   Poet. 267.
Yet not for all his faith can see
                    Problem. 5.
I see his cowlèd portrait dear;
                    Problem. 70.
And yet, for all his faith could see,
                    Problem. 71.
her eye still seemed to see,
                    Quat. A. H. 3.
See the plum redden, and the beurré
stoop.   Quat. Gardener. 4.
I see all human wits
                    Quat. Shakespeare. 1.
See to thyself, O Universe!   Rhea. 72.
Saadi, see! they rise in stature
                    Saadi. 171.
Come see the north wind's masonry.
                    Snow-Storm. 10.
Couldst see thy proper eye,
                    Sphinx. 114.
I see my empty house,   Threnody. 9.
I see my trees repair their boughs;
                    Threnody. 10.
The pure shall see by their own will,
                    Threnody. 191.
Nor see the genius of the whole
                    Threnody. 251.
I see the inundation sweet,
                    Two Rivers. 9.
Why lingerest thou, pale violet, to see
the dying year;   *Violet. 1.
I see the wreath, I hear the songs
                    Voluntaries. 108.
See thou bring not to field or stone
                    Waldeinsamkeit. 41.
Nor gun nor scythe to see.
                    Woodnotes. I. 10.
Or see the wide shore from thy skiff,
                    Woodnotes. II. 195.
Blessed Nature so to see.
                    Woodnotes. II. 218.
I see thee in the crowd alone;
                    Woodnottes. II. 221.
I see the summer glow,
                    World-Soul. 110.

Seed
        See Fire-seed; Pearl-seed.
The seed of gods to die,   Fame. 20.
The sower scatters broad his seed,
                    Frag. Poet. VI. 11.
The sower scatters broad his seed;
                    I Intellect. 3.
Hers to sow the seed of bread,
                    May-Day. 146.

'Pang for pang your seed shall pay,
                    Voluntaries. 32.
The winds and wind-blown seed,
                    Walden. 10.
Seeds
Like sower's seeds into his brain,
                    Frag. Poet. V. 35.
All seeds of beauty to be born?
                    May-Day. 217.
Planting seeds of knowledge pure,
                    May-Day. 467.
He sowed the sun and moon for seeds
                    Poet. 32.
These are but seeds of days,   Poet. 101.
He shall bring store of seeds and
crumbs.   Titmouse. 82.
Still on the seeds of all he made
                    Waldeinsamkeit. 25.
Wafting the puny seeds of power,
                    Wealth. 7.
The seeds of land and sea
                    World-Soul. 86.
Seeing
        See All-seeing.
Seeing Nature go astern.   Alphonso. 2.
Rightly seeing, rightly seen,
                    Daemonic Love. 76.
And, seeing his eye glare,
                    Daemonic Love. 107.
Seeing only what is fair,
                    Humble-Bee. 54.
That will not bide the seeing!
                    Monadnoc. 363.
Tell them, dear, that if eyes were made
for seeing,   Rhodora. 11.
And seeing rashly torn and moved
                    Threnody. 128.
Seek
Men knowing what they seek, armed
eyes of experts.   Adirondacs. 304.
'Judgment and a judge we seek.'
                    Astraea. 12.
Whom not each other seek, but find.
                    Celestial Love. 84.
My apprehension? Why seek Italy,
                    Day's Ration. 29.
Who sought thee once shall seek again.
                    Frag. Life. XXII. 4.
In other love should seek amends.
                    From Hafiz. 12.
Far-off heats through seas to seek;
                    Humble-Bee. 4.
They seek a friend to speak the word
                    Hymn. 13.
Then would I seek where God might
guide my steps,   Letter. 7.
He shall not seek to weave,   Merlin. 59.
'Many feet in summer seek,
                    Monadnoc. 199.
To the altar's foot thy fellow seek,—
                    Quat. Pericles. 3.
Seek the living among the dead,—
                    Saadi. 117.
Seek nothing,—Fortune seeketh thee.
                    Saadi. 144.
Seek not beyond thy cottage wall
                    Saadi. 165.
Though her eye seek other forms
                    Security. 1.
Which his eyes seek in vain.
                    Sphinx. 80.

Seek —*Continued*
Seek not the spirit, if it hide
                    Sursum Corda. 1.
Nature, Fate, men, him seek in vain.
                    Threnody. 29.
Nor seek to unwind the shroud
                    To J. W. 6.
But one I seek in foreign places,
                    Una. 11.
Seek him in his native town,   Una. 23.
Seek not, and the little eremite
                    Woodnotes. II. 250.

Seeker
I am seeker of the stone,
                    Song of Seyd. 9.

Seekers
Competing seekers of a rumored lake,
                    Adirondacs. 130.

Seeketh
Fortune seeketh thee.   Saadi. 144.

Seeking
        See Self-seeking.
Seeking in that chaste blue a bluer light,
                    Adirondacs. 209.
His eye the eye 't was seeking found.
                    Guy. 24.
Heart of bird the man's heart seeking;
                    May-Day. 421.

Seeks
Around the man who seeks a noble end,
                    Frag. Life. III. 1.
Seeks alone his counterpart.
                    Initial Love. 107.
Seeks how he may fitly tell   Poet. 89.
Her broad van seeks unplanted lands;
                    Voluntaries. 37.
But when it seeks enlarged supplies,
                    Woodnotes. II. 55.

Seek'st
Thou seek'st in globe and galaxy,
                    Woodnotes. II. 309.

Seem
The traveller and the road seem one
                    Etienne. 21.
Features that seem at heart my own;
                    Eva. 8.
Shall his own sorrow seem impertinent,
                    Frag. Life. XXVI. 2.
And abhor to feign or seem
                    Frag. Life. XXVII. 4.
Who seem to die live.   Illusions. 6.
To me seem not to wear   Park. 2.
Your gold makes you seem wise;
                    Park. 10.
The mountains flow, the solids seem,
                    Poet. 174.
Thou shalt seem, in each reply,
                    Rhea. 19.
Thy softest pleadings seem too bold,
                    Rhea. 21.
Thy praying lute will seem to scold;
                    Rhea. 22.
They are not of our race, they seem to
say,   River. 31.
Melts things that be to things that seem,
                    Woodnotes. II. 114.

Seemed
We seemed the dwellers of the zodiac,
                    Adirondacs. 157.
Deeper and older seemed his eye;
                    Character. 4.

It seemed the world was all torches
                    Cosmos. 11.
He seemed to bask, to dream and play
                    Frag. Poet. V. 4.
It seemed his Genius discreet   Guy. 25.
And the world's sun seemed to rise
                    Guy. 39.
It seemed, so listening, at my side
                    Harp. 108.
In old Bassora's schools, I seemed
                    Hermione. 33.
He who seemed a soldier born,
                    In Memoriam. 38.
Born for success he seemed,
                    In Memoriam. 60.
Or seemed to use his privilege
                    Lines. 19.
Seemed to me, the towering hill
                    Monadnoc. 195.
Seemed, when at last his clarion accents
broke,   Phi. 11.
Deeper and older seemed his eye,
                    Poet. 137.
her eye still seemed to see,
                    Quat. A. H. 3.
I heard or seemed to hear the chiding
Sea   Seashore. 1.
For flattering planets seemed to say
                    Threnody. 134.
Seemed to the holy festival   Uriel. 29.
I had a sister once who seemed just like
a violet;   *Violet. 13.
It seemed that Nature could not raise
                    Woodnotes. I. 36.
It seemed as if the breezes brought him,
                    Woodnotes. I. 46.
It seemed as if the sparrows taught him;
                    Woodnotes. I. 47.
And at his bidding seemed to come.
                    Woodnotes. I. 61.
It seemed the likeness of their own;
                    Woodnotes. I. 115.

Seemeth
And yet it seemeth not to me
                    Saadi. 72.

Seeming
        See Many-seeming.
Equals remote, and seeming opposites.
                    Daemonic Love. 84.
Being for Seeming bravely barter
                    Fame. 29.
Go match thee with thy seeming peers;
                    Frag. Life. XXV. 2.
And, credulous, through the granite
seeming,   Monadnoc. 235.
Deceive us, seeming to be many things,
                    Xenophanes. 8.

Seeming-solid
And seeming-solid walls of use
                    Bacchus. 49.

Seems
Seems, though the soft sheen all en-
chants,   Frag. Nat. XXV. 1.
And whatever glows or seems
                    Frag. Poet. VIII. 9.
Seems, by the traveller espied,
                    Hermione. 43.
Seems nowhere to alight: the whited air
                    Snow-Storm. 3.
Roving, roving, as it seems,   Una. 1.

What subsisteth, and what seems.
Uriel. 14.
Seems fantastic to the rest:
Woodnotes. I. 17.

Seen
See Half-seen; Unseen.
Eyes of gods! ye must have seen,
Alphonso. 19.
Pure by impure is not seen.
Astraea. 44.
One, by humble farmer seen,
Chartist. 3.
Rightly seeing, rightly see,
Daemonic Love. 76.
I who have seen much,
Hamatreya. 35.
Such have I never seen.
Hamatreya. 36.
Hath my insect never seen;
Humble-Bee. 41.
Or see the fault, or seen betray:
Initial Love. 127.
On the soft path each track is seen,
May-Day. 61.
Seen haply from afar, Monadnoc. 394.
There in a moment I have seen
Peter. 17.
Far seen, the river glides below,
Peter. 37.
The vanishing are seen, Poet. 111.
Shines the last age, the next with hope
is seen, Quat. Heri. 1.
Have ye seen the caterpillar Riches. 1.
Have ye seen the butterfly Riches. 5.
So that what his eye hath seen
Saadi. 121.
Seldom seen by wishful eyes,
Woodnotes. I. 51.

Seer
Wiser far than human seer,
Humble-Bee. 52.
And this wise Seer within me never errs.
Self-Reliance. 8.
I awaited the seer Sphinx. 7.
And such I knew, a forest seer,
Woodnotes. I. 30.

Seers
Though baffled seers cannot impart
Nature. Mot. 9.
The word by seers or sibyls told,
Problem. 57.
Shalt outsee seers, and outwit sages.
Woodnotes. II. 247.

Sees
From his shoulders falls who sees
Celestial Love. 66.
And only sees what he doth give.
Frag. Poet. XXVIII. 9.
Ah! the hot owner sees not Death, who
adds Hamatreya. 25.
The youth sees omens where he goes,
May-Day. 73.
Whose soul sees the perfect,
Sphinx. 79.

Seest
Is the wind-harp which thou seest
Harp. 39.
Seest the smile of Reason beaming;—
Monadnoc. 236.
Thou seest, O watchman tall,
Monadnoc. 385.

Seeth
That seeth as God seeth. These are their
gifts, Good Cheer. 12.
With staring eye that seeth none,
Poet. 87.

Seethe
Seethe, Fate! the ancient elements,
Song of Nature. 75.

Seethed
Seethed in mists of Penmanmaur,
Solution. 33.

Seethes
Seethes the gulf-encrimsoning shells,
May-Day. 205.

Seigniors
Say, Seigniors, are the old Niles dry,
Alphonso. 31.

Seize
That they may seize and entertain
Initial Love. 31.

Seized
If Indians seized the tea, Boston. 77.

Seldom
Seldom in this low life's round
Garden. 47.
And seldom therein could I look,
Goethe. 4.
He looketh seldom in their face,
Manners. 9.
Seldom seen by wishful eyes,
Woodnotes. I. 51.

Select
God hath a select family of sons
Good Cheer. 3.
She is skilful to select House. 3.

Selecting
Arrives the wise selecting will,
Wealth. 31.

Self
See Itself; Yourself.
Of self in other still preferred,
Celestial Love. 118.
Was a weed of self and schism;
Daemonic Love. 128.
As a self of purer clay, Give. 44.
Speaks not of self that mystic tone,
Harp. 67.
Not Homer's self, the poet sire,
Harp. 76.

Self-announced
Self-announced its hour of doom?
Threnody. 254.

Self-betrayed
Draw me to them, self-betrayed?
Ode to Beauty. 51.

Self-centred
Self-centred; when he launched the genuine word Phi. 19.

Self-commanded
Sole and self-commanded works,
Spiritual Laws. 5.

Self-government
Millions for self-government,
Boston. 74.

Selfish
And selfish preference forbear;
Celestial Love. 10.

Self-kindled
Self-kindled every atom glows
Nature. Mot. 15.

Self-knowledge
A sad self-knowledge, withering, fell
                        Uriel. 35.
Self-moved
Self-moved, fly-to the doors,
                        Merlin. 75.
Selfness
Now, to a savage selfness grown,
                        Alphonso. 35.
Self-planted
Self-planted twice, like the banian.
                        Miracle. 6.
Self-pleasing
Timid, self-pleasing, sensitive,
                        Poet. 213.
Self-possest
So frolic, stout and self-possest?
                        Titmouse. 53.
Self-same
It was ever the self-same tale,
                      Daemonic Love. 19.
With the selfsame spice
                      Frag. Nat. II. 26.
The self-same tuneful muse;
                      Merlin. 116.
The self-same Power that brought me
  there brought you.   Rhodora. 16.
Self-seeking
The Dæmons are self-seeking:
                      Daemonic Love. 65.
Self-similar
Or stumbling on through vast self-similar
  woods   Adirondacs. 105.
Self-sown
Self-sown my stately garden grows;
                      Walden. 9.
Self-upheld
Realms self-upheld, disdaining Fate,
                      Nun. 44.
Sell
I cannot sell my heaven again
                    Frag. Poet. II. 9.
For which I sell days,
                  Frag. Poet. VIII. 3.
Will gladly sell ages
                  Frag. Poet. VIII. 4.
And buy, and sell, and lose, and win;
                  Initial Love. 47.
Sells
Who sells his sinews to be wise,
                      Fame. 9.
Selves
So lovers melt their sundered selves,
                  Initial Love. 149.
Semigod
The semigod whom we await?
                      Culture. 2.
Senate
And in their secret senate have prevailed
                  Musketaquid. 6.
That shall command a senate to your
  side;   Rome. 17.
Great men in the Senate sate,
                  Voluntaries. 23.
Senator
Nor bid the unwilling senator
                  Channing Ode. 73.
Send
Honor enough that we send the call.'
                  Boston. 68.

And send the nectar round;
                  May-Day. 280.
And send conviction without phrase,
                  Monadnoc. 404.
Dearest, to thee I did not send
                  Threnody. 210.
Sends
He sends thee from his bitter fount
                  Saadi. 62.
From him that sends the dream.
                  World-Soul. 72.
Senior
Each village senior paused to scan
                  Threnody. 72.
Sense
but waking a new sense
                  Adirondacs. 204.
Unlocks new sense and loftier cheer.
                  Aeolian Harp. 17.
Of human sense doth overfill.   Art. 28.

But to hold fast his simple sense,
                  Celestial Love. 127.
The sense of the world is short,—
                  I. Eros. 1.
Not suffer sense to win from wit
                  Fame. 21.
Keen my sense, my heart was young,
                  Forerunners. 5.
Not Sense but Reason is the Judge of
  truth;   Frag. Life. XVIII. 5.
That use to undo the limb and sense of
  age;   I Bear. 2.
Strains every sense to larger scope,
                  May-Day. 153.
To read the sense the woods impart
                  Miracle. 9.
His hidden sense interpret can;—
                  Miracle. 20.
For homes of virtue, sense and taste.
                  Monadnoc. 152.
But a quiet sense conveyed:
                  Monadnoc. 197.
To myriad kinds and times one sense
                  Monadnoc. 381.
More sense than sages write.
                  Peter. 32.
Than he to common sense and common
  good: Phi. 14.
They spoke not, for their earnest sense
                  Poet. 199.
In the sea of sense I dived;
                  Song of Seyd. 12.
Tugs at the heart-strings, numbs the
  sense,   Titmouse. 15.
And I began to catch the sense
                  Titmouse. 66.
Shuts his sense on toys of time,
                  Voluntaries. 81.
Senses
Beauty through my senses stole;
                  Each. 50.
Sensitive
Timid, self-pleasing, sensitive,
                  Poet. 213.
Sent
Sent a nocturnal fragrance; harlot flies
              Frag. Nat. XXVII. 8.
And sent his priests in holy fear
                  Hymn. 7.

To Heaven thy hourly prayers are sent,
Prayer. 6.
Was there no star that could be sent,
Threnody. 118.

Sentences
Sentences him in his words;
Astraea. 28.

Sentiment
Hear the sentiment of Spain.
Alphonso. 50.
Gave his sentiment divine   Uriel. 19.

Sentinels
Nor fear those watchful sentinels,
Eva. 9.

Sentry-bird
Sharp queries of the sentry-bird,
Harp. 88.

Separate
We separate to-day,   * Farewell. 35.
And, ever subdividing, separate
Frag. Nat. XVII. 3.
The fate-conjoined to separate.
Threnody. 194.

Separated
One through separated souls;
Celestial Love. 47.

September's
June's glories and September's
Ellen South. 27.

Sequent
Nor sequent centuries could hit
Solution. 39.

Sequestered
For there's no sequestered grot,
Astraea. 45.

Seraph
And with snake and seraph talked.
Daemonic Love. 22.
On which the seraph music sails.
Solution. 50.

Seraph's
The Seraph's and the Cherub's food.
Saadi. 162.

Seraphs
The seraphs frowned from myrtle-beds;
Uriel. 28.

Serenader's
No jingling serenader's art,   Merlin. 5.

Serene
The clouds are rich and dark, the air
serene,   Adirondacs. 213.
Two things thou shalt not long for, if
thou love a mind serene;—
Ibn Jemin. 1.
Even the serene Reason says,
In Memoriam. 9.
Gentlest guardians marked serene
Threnody. 54.
On him the sun looked more serene;
Woodnotes. I. 113.

Serious
But in the serious landscape lone
Waldeinsamkeit. 15.

Servant
Servant to a wooden cradle,
Holidays. 15.
My servant Death, with solving rite,
Threnody. 236.
He serveth the servant, World-Soul. 89.

Servant's
O touch thy servant's lips with power,
Hymn. 26.

Serve
To be a brain, or serve the brain of man.
Adirondacs. 265.
'Tis nobleness to serve;
Boston Hymn. 50.
And they serve men austerely,
Celestial Love. 121.
Would serve things still;—
Channing Ode. 42.
Let man serve law for man;
Channing Ode. 66.
I serve you not, if you I follow,
Etienne. 1.
Serve that low whisper thou hast served;
for know,   Good Cheer. 2.
Serve thou it not for daily bread,—
Poet. 285.
Serve it for pain and fear and need.
Poet. 286.
More enamoured serve it yet;
Poet. 290.

Served
Served high and low, the lord and the
churl,   Frag. Poet. I. 20.
Serve that low whisper thou hast served;
for know,   Good Cheer. 2.

Serves
Think nature barely serves for one;
Alphonso. 36.
He serves all who dares be true,
Celestial Love. 132.
The horseman serves the horse,
Channing Ode. 44.
The neatherd serves the neat,
Channing Ode. 45.
The merchant serves the purse,
Channing Ode. 46.
The eater serves his meat;
Channing Ode. 47.

Serveth
He that feeds men serveth few;
Celestial Love. 131.
He serveth the servant,   World-Soul. 89.

Service
The service done to me as done to them.
Frag. Life. XXX. 7.
By constant service to that inward law,
Good Cheer. 6.
Or what was the service
Ode to Beauty. 7.
Or for service, or delight,   Visit. 17.

Serviceable
See Unserviceable.

Servile
That blessed gods in servile masks
Saadi. 175.

Serving
Serving for a laborer's lamp?
Chartist. 6.

Set
See Sunset.
Suns haste to set, that so remoter lights
Adirondacs. 228.
The sun set, but set not his hope:
Character. 1.
We set to-day a votive stone;
C. Hymn. 10.

Set—*Continued*

All of worth and beauty set
　　　　　Frag. Nat. XXIII. 3.
To the defences thou hast round me set;
　　　　　Grace. 2.
Pillar which God aloft had set
　　　　　Monadnoc. 48.
They set the wind to winnow pulse and
grain,　　　　Musketaquid. 42.
Nor Time's snows hide the names he set,
　　　　　Poet. 11.
The sun set, but set not his hope:—
　　　　　Poet. 134.
Suns rise and set in Saadi's speech!'
　　　　　Saadi. 140.
Set not thy foot on graves;
　　　　　To J. W. 1. 5. 10.
Her morning sun shone bright and calm-
ly purely set;　　　　*Violet. 14.
A beacon set that Freedom's race
　　　　　Webster. 3.

Sets

Sets the life-pulse strong but slow:
　　　　　Monadnoc. 158.
Who sets to seas a shore,
　　　　　Terminus. 4.

Settle

Boughs on which the wild bees settle,
　　　　　Woodnotes. I. 20.

Seven

And pine in vain the sacred Seven;
　　　　　Brahma. 14.
Of the seven stars and the solar year,
　　　　　Informing Spirit. 6.

Several

A private beam into each several heart.
　　　　　Adirondacs. 223.
Their several portraits, you would own
　　　　　Adirondacs. Motto. 2.
in every several life,　　Naples. 4.
Furnished several supplies;
　　　　　Ode to Beauty. 49.

Severe

In severe or cordial mood,　Etienne. 12.

Severing

Severing rightly his from thine,
　　　　　Worship. 22.

Severs

Wave which severs whom it bears
　　　　　Insight. 3.

Sex

Sex to sex, and even to odd;—
　　　　　Channing Ode. 79.

Sexton

The sexton, tolling his bell at noon,
　　　　　Each. 5.

Seyd

See Saadi, Said.
So sweet to Seyd as only grace
　　　　　Beauty. 2.
Seyd overheard the young gods talking;
　　　　　Uriel. 8.

Shade

Clouds shade the sun, which will not tan
our hay,　　　　Blight. 51.
Leaving on space no shade, no scars,
　　　　　Frag. Nat. VIII. 7.
Cooled by the pendent mountain's shade,
　　　　　May-Day. 17.
By morn and eve in light and shade;
　　　　　Monadnoc. 61.

Old as the sun, old almost as the shade;
　　　　　Monadnoc. 204.
And soon may give my dust their funeral
shade.　　　　River. 42.
Or winter's frozen shade?
　　　　　Song of Nature. 56.
So long he roved at will the boundless
shade.　　　　Woodnotes. I. 85.
Primal chimes of sun and shade,
　　　　　Woodnotes. II. 160.
Come, lay thee in my soothing shade,
　　　　　Woodnotes. II. 219.
Let the starred shade that nightly falls
　　　　　Woodnotes. II. 225.

Shaded

See Unshaded.
The sand shaded,　　Channing Ode. 61.
On that shaded day,　　Threnody. 98.

Shades

Each leaf that shades the rock
　　　　　April. 10.
Hallow these my orchard shades;
　　　　　Frag. Poet. VII. 4.
Beneath the grass that shades the rill,
　　　　　Woodnotes. I. 39.

Shading

Beside his hut and shading oak,
　　　　　Poet. 140.

Shadow

See Cloud-shadow.
Shadow and sunlight are the same;
　　　　　Brahma. 6.
And, like thy shadow, follow thee.
　　　　　II Compensation. 28.
Dearest, where thy shadow falls,
　　　　　Dearest. 1.
Than doth the traveller's shadow on the
rock.　　　　Frag. Life. XXVI. 4.
When the shadow fell on the lake,
　　　　　Garden. 53.
First vague shadow of surmise
　　　　　Give. 36.
I shall pass, as glides my shadow
　　　　　Monadnoc. 264.
We in thee the shadow find.
　　　　　Monadnoc. 391.
Behold his shadow on the floor!
　　　　　Saadi. 158.
Body with shadow still pursued.
　　　　　Woodnotes. II. 163.
The shadow sits close to the flying ball;
　　　　　Woodnotes. II. 244.

Shadowlike

Shadowlike, o'er hill and hollow;
　　　　　Etienne. 2.

Shadows

Are shadows flitting up and down
　　　　　Celestial Love. 56.
Soft shadows of the evening lay.
　　　　　Frag. Poet. V. 48.
How graceful climb those shadows on my
hill!　　　　Hamatreya. 7.
None save dappling shadows climb,
　　　　　Monadnoc. 202.
Shadows of the thoughts of day,
　　　　　Quat. Memory. 2.
In plains that room for shadows make
　　　　　Waldeinsamkeit. 5.
Pondering shadows, colors, clouds,
　　　　　Woodnotes. I. 18.

Shadows
Painted with shadows green and proud
            Woodnotes. I. 110.
The shadows shake on the rock behind,
            Woodnotes. II. 94.

Shadowy
And round me swarmed in shadowy
  troop   Peter. 27.

Shady
Its root has pierced yon shady mound;
            Holidays. 6.

Shaft
The shaft we raise to them and thee.
            C. Hymn. 16.

Shafts
The shafts of the god   *Lines. 17.

Shaggy
Shaggy with wood,   Hamatreya. 45.

Shake
Time, shake not thy bald head at me.
            Nun. 30.
I cannot shake off the god;   Park. 5.
Not the gods can shake the Past;
            Past. 11.
A drop can shake, a breath can fan;
            Poet. 222.
And shake before those awful Powers,
            Saadi. 57.
The shadows shake on the rock behind,
            Woodnotes. II. 94.

Shaken
They talk in the shaken pine,   Poet. 74.

Shakers
The Flowers—tiny sect of Shakers—
            Ellen South. 11.

Shakes
Which neither halts nor shakes.
            Boston Hymn. 84
The wine-cup shakes, the wine is spilled.
            Frag. Poet. XVI. 2.

Shakspeare
Hafiz and Shakespeare with their shining
  choirs.   Adakryn. 5.
The little Shakspeare in the maiden's
  heart   Enchanter. 12.
Or Shakspeare, whom no mind can
  measure,   Harp. 78.
Taylor, the Shakspeare of divines.
            Problem. 68.
Unmeasured still my Shakspeare sits,
            Quat. Shakespeare. 3.

Shakspeare's
Of Lord Christ's heart, and Shakspeare's
  strain.   Informing Spirit. 8.
Orbit and sum of Shakspeare's wit.
            Solution. 40.

Shall. (Partial list.)
We hold like rights, and shall;—
            Boston. 26.
Of him that cometh, and shall come;
            Monadnoc. 269.
When he cometh, I shall shed,
            Monadnoc. 291.
Ever have done, ever shall.   Rhea. 32.
Shall the harp be dumb.   Saadi. 16.

Shallow
The cup of life is not so shallow
            Good Hope. 1.
Not from a vain or shallow thought
            Problem. 9.

Shallows
Winding through grassy shallows in and
  out,   Adirondacs. 23.

Shalt
'I give my darling son, Thou shalt not
  preach';—   Adakryn. 2.
Less than a lily's, thou shalt daily draw
            Day's Ration. 4.
Thyself shalt own the page was bright,
            Ellen. 7.
'Thou shalt command us all,—
            Ellen South. 29.
Thou shalt make thy house
            Frag. Life. XXII. 1.
Two things thou shalt not long for, if
  thou love a mind serene;—
            Ibn Jemin. 1.
Then first shalt thou know,
            Illusions. 33.
Thou shalt seem, in each reply,
            Rhea. 19.
But thou shalt do as do the gods
            Rhea. 25.
With equal fire thy heart shalt melt.
            Saadi. 124.
Askest, 'How long thou shalt stay?'
            Visit. 1.
Linger,—thou shalt rue the fault:
            Visit. 28.
When thou shalt climb the mountain
  cliff,   Woodnotes. II. 194.
Shalt outsee seers, and outwit sages.
            Woodnotes. II. 247.

Shame
Or was it for mankind a generous shame,
            Adirondacs. 274.
And honor, O South! for his shame;
            Boston Hymn. 74.
And one to me are shame and fame.
            Brahma. 8.
Shame the times and live apart,—
            Frag. Poet. IV. 6.
Time they stopped for shame. Gifts. 4.
Their shame them restores; Sphinx. 90.
As if to shame my weak behavior;
            Titmouse. 47.
Would hang his head for shame.
            World-Soul. 52.

Shamed
    See Ashamed.
Shamed that sculptured countenance.
            In Memoriam. 47.
Shamed the angels' veiling wings;
            Uriel. 48.

Shames
King of sport that never shames,
            Merlin. 40.
All my wrath and all my shames,
            Miracle. 35.

Shams
I tire of shams, I rush to be: Nun. 37.

Shape
Halteth never in one shape,
            Woodnotes. II. 272.
And take their shape and sun-color
            World-Soul. 71.

Shaped
So shaped, so colored, swift or still,
            Solution. 30

Shapely
The maple eight, beneath its shapely
tower.   Adirondacs. 43.

Shapes
Amid these coward shapes of joy and
grief,   Monadnoc. 362.
with lights and airs and shapes,
                          October. 9.

Shard
Of shard and flint makes jewels gay;
                          Two Rivers. 14.

Share
Hast not thy share? On winged feet,
                  II. Compensation. 23.
I share the good with every flower,
                  Frag. Nat. XXVI. 30.
To share the sunshine that so spicy is.
                  Frag. Nat. XXXIII. 3.
Risk or ruin he must share.
                          Monadnoc. 339.
A while to share his cordial game,
                          Threnody. 48.

Shared
He shared the life of the element,
                  Frag. Poet. I. 52.

Shares
And bestow the shares of all
                          Alphonso. 69.
It shares the secret of the earth,
                          Harp. 65.
Rich rents and wide alliance shares;
                          Monadnoc. 59.
And shares the joy he brings.
                          World-Soul. 64.

Sharing
Sharing all, daring all,
                  Daemonic Love. 81.

Sharp
Not unless God made sharp thine ear
                          Dirge. 45.
Sharp queries of the sentry-bird,
                          Harp. 88.
Sharp accents of my woodland bird;
                          Miracle. 24.
From all natures, sharp and slimy,
                          Mithridates. 10.
Stuff sharp thorns beneath the head
                          Saadi. 68.

Sharpening
By mind's industry sharpening the love
of life—   Summons. 12.

Sharpest
And the sharpest you still have survived,
                  Quat. Borrowing. 2.

Sharpest-sighted
Him, radiant, sharpest-sighted god,
                  Daemonic Love. 70.

Sharply
Break sharply off their jolly games,
                          Voluntaries. 63.

She. (Partial list.)
Essaying nothing she cannot perform.
                          Adirondacs. 72.
She was his mistress and his law;
                  Frag. Poet. V. 23.
'If it be, as they said, she was not fair,
                          Hermione. 8.
But she dearly loves the poor,
                          Nature. I. 9.
Far and wide she cannot find him;
                          Threnody. 22.

Still for journeys she is dressed;
                          Una. 3.

Sheaf
The Pleiads' sheaf but two.
                          From Hafiz. 8.
The wheat-blade whispers of the sheaf.
                          May-Day. 209.

Sheaves
What sheaves like those which here we
glean and bind   Monadnoc. 356.

Shed
So Nature shed all beauty lavishly
                          Adirondacs. 151.
Wine that is shed   Bacchus. 26.
Shed mocking lustres on shelf of books,
                          May-Day. 356.
Yet they who hear it shed their age,
                          Merlin's Song. 12.
Boon Nature to his poorest shed
                          Monadnoc. 70.
When he cometh, I shall shed,
                          Monadnoc. 291.
Easily to shed the snow,   Nature. I. 2.
Shed in each drop of wine.
                          Quat. Leasts. 4.
Here holy thoughts a light have shed
                          Robbins Hymn. 5.
Wolves shed their fangs, and dragons
scales;   Solution. 6.
The poultry-yard, the shed, the barn,—
                          Threnody. 89.
Shed their virtue through his eye.
                          Woodnotes. II. 74.

Shedding
The spiritual stars rise nightly, shedding
down   Adirondacs. 222.
Shedding on all its snows and leaves,
                          Monadnoc. 383.

Sheds
That sheds beauty on the rose.
                          Destiny. 4.
Of all he sheds how little it will hold,
                          Day's Ration. 13.
Whose dark sky sheds the snowflake
down,   Voluntaries. 40.
With one drop sheds form and feature;
                          Woodnotes. II. 289.

Sheen
Seems, though the soft sheen all en-
chants,   Frag. Nat. XXIX. 1.
Sheen will tarnish, honey cloy,
                          Waldeinsamkeit. 17.

Sheep
Browse the mountain sheep in flocks,
                          Saadi. 6.
As the sheep go feeding in the waste,
                          Woodnotes. II. 297.

Sheet
See Winding-sheet.
That rims the running silver sheet,—
                          May-Day. 246.
His sheet of lead,   To J. W. 14.

Sheeted
The piny hosts were sheeted ghosts
                          May-Day. 49.

Shelf
Shed mocking lustres on shelf of books,
                          May-Day. 356.

Shell
The shell of Clio rung.
                  Frag. Poet. XXXV. 3.

And what if that all-echoing shell,
Harp. 61.

Of the masters of the shell,
Ode to Beauty. 57.

Or how the fish outbuilt her shell,
Problem. 27.

Of granite, marl and shell.
Song of Nature. 36.

If plants or brain, if egg or shell,
Walden. 39.

Shells
The delicate shells lay on the shore;
Each. 19.

Scent, form and color; to the flowers and shells
Enchanter. 4.

Seethes the gulf-encrimsoning shells,
May-Day. 205.

White hollow shells upon the desert shore,
Pan. 9.

The mounting sap, the shells, the sea,
Woodnotes. II. 77.

Like shells along the shore,
World-Soul. 66.

Shelter
The tall green trees, that shelter thee,
*Violet. 7.

There will be nought to shelter thee when their sweet leaves are gone.
*Violet. 8.

Sheltered
Back to books and sheltered home,
May-Day. 54.

Shelves
As the wave breaks to foam on shelves,
Initial Love. 147.

Shem
The vice of Japhet by the thought of Shem.
Frag. Poet. XXII. 2.

Shepherd
Then Asia yeaned her shepherd race,
Solution. 9.

Shepherd's
As shepherd's lamp on far hill-side
Hermione. 42.

Shepherds
Shepherds are thankful and nations gay.
Merlin's Song. 34.

Sherbet
Hemlock for my sherbet cull me,
Mithridates. 16.

She-wolf's
Suckle him with the she-wolf's teat,
Quat. Power. 2.

Shield
Shield all thy roofs and towers!
Boston. 117.

Shift
To a thousand humors shift it,
Mithridates. 23.

Shifting
In shifting form the formless mind,
Monadnoc. 389.

Shimmer
Behold the shimmer,
Illusions. 24.

Shine
See Outshine; Sunshine.
Yet shine forever virgin minds,
Astraea. 31.

Give them again to shine;   Bacchus. 58.

from lies that shine—   Dull. 21.

Go then, sad youth, and shine;
Fame. 25.

I wait the sun on them should shine.
Frag. Life. XIV. 2.

All things shine in his smoky ray,
Frag. Nat. III. 15.

What parts, what gems, what colors shine,—   Frag. Poet. XVIII. 5.

Or, if in thy heart he shine,
Freedom. 17.

Air-bells of fortune that shine and break,
Garden. 55.

Shine down in the old sea;
Hamatreya. 32.

Canst thou shine now, then darkle,
Musketaquid. 80.

The great stars did not shine aloof,
Poet. 146.

And yet, dear stars, I know ye shine
Poet. 233.

Ever on thousands shine,   Webster. 2.

Shined
Shines not as once it shined.
Day by Day. 8.

Thine eyes still shined for me, though far
Thine Eyes. 1.

Shines
Highest Love who shines on all;
Daemonic Love. 69.

Shines not as once it shined.
Day by Day. 8.

In which its proper splendor shines;
Frag. Poet. XXIX. 2.

Where the evening star so holy shines,
Good-Bye. 26.

Light's far furnace shines,   Merlin. 92.

When the star Canope shines in May,
Merlin's Song. 33.

Shines not as on the town,   Peter. 14.

Shines the last age, the next with hope is seen,   Quat. Heri. 1.

The rainbow shines his harbinger,
Song of Nature. 39.

Shines the peace of all being,
Sphinx. 45.

The sun himself shines heartily,
World-Soul. 63.

Shining
Hafiz and Shakspeare with their shining choirs.   Adakryn. 5.

His fathers shining in bright fables,
Art. 17.

To hunt upon their shining trails.
Forerunners. 8.

The shining moment is an edifice
Frag. Life. V. 1.

On to their shining goals:—
Frag. Poet. V. 10.

With a net of shining haze
Humble-Bee. 21.

With shining gifts that took all eyes,
In Memoriam. 62.

On to their shining goals;—
I Intellect. 2.

Of shining virgins every May,
May-Day. 302.

To fool me with a shining cloud,
May-Day. 364.

Whose shining sons, too great for fame,
Nun. 45.

Shining —*Continued*
The shining pebble of the pond,
Ode to Beauty. 29.
I sit by the shining Fount of Life
Song of Nature. 11.

Ship
Every day brings a ship, Letters. 1.
Every ship brings a word; Letters. 2.
Cooped in a ship he cannot steer,—
Monadnoc. 336.

Ships
O heavenly ships without a sail!
Poet. 160.

Shirt
Shoes, flannel shirt, and kersey trousers
make Adirondacs. 75.

Shiver
Shiver the palaces of glass;
Daemonic Love. 119.

Shock
And shock thy weak ear with a note
Woodnotes. II. 122.

Shod
Shod like a traveller for haste;
Initial Love. 12.
His feet were shod with golden bells,
Poet. 4.

Shoe
I had as lief respect an ancient shoe,
To-Day. 11.

Shoes
See Shoon.
Shoes, flannel shirt, and kersey trousers
make Adirondacs. 75.

Shone
The light wherewith all planets shone,
Frag. Poet. IV. 25.
Of the grace that on him shone,
In Memoriam. 51.
All the forms we looked on shone
May-Day. 412.
Half so gracious ever shone,
On Prince. 2.
Out shone a star beneath the cloud,
Poet. 229.
Her morning sun shone bright and
calmly purely set; * Violet. 14.
The all-seeing sun for ages hath not
shone; Woodnotes. I. 65.

Shook
O no, not we! Witness the shout that
shook Adirondacs. 309.
Kings shook with fear, old empires crave
Boston. 92.
They shook the snow from hats and
shoon, May-Day. 318.
It shook or captivated all who heard,
Phi. 20.
The stern old war-gods shook their
heads,· Uriel. 27.
And the gods shook, they knew not why.
Uriel. 56.

Shoon
See Shoes
They shook the snow from hats and
shoon, May-Day. 318.
That drop from the angels' shoon.
Quat. Excelsior. 4.

Shoot
To row, to swim, to shoot, to build a
camp, Adirondacs. 82.

There Past, Present, Future, shoot
Celestial Love. 42.
Doth eat, and drink, and fish, and shoot,
Initial Love. 27.
No farther shoot Terminus. 7.

Shoots
Shoots across the neutral Dark.
II. Compensation. 14.
When the purple flame shoots up,
Cosmos. 21.
He shoots his thought, by hidden nerves,
World-Soul. 75.

Shop
Perversely borrowing from the shop the
tools Adirondacs. 283.
The shop of toil, the hall of arts;
Wealth. 35.

Shopman
The wrinkled shopman to my sounding
woods, Channing Ode. 72.

Shopmen
For teeth and hair with shopmen deal;
Romany. 18.

Shore
See Seashore.
Ponderous with beechen forest sloped the
shore. Adirondacs. 28.
That sweeps my native shore. Bell. 16.
And sailed for bread to every shore.
Boston. 6.
The delicate shells lay on the shore;
Each. 19.
Had left their beauty on the shore
Each. 27.
To dim New England's shore;
* Farewell. 47.
White hollow shells upon the desert
shore, Pan. 9.
Planting strange fruits and sunshine on
the shore, Seashore. 47.
From the shore of souls arrived,
Song of Seyd. 11.
Who sets to seas a shore, Terminus. 4.
Or see the wide shore from the skiff,
Woodnotes. II. 195.
Like shells along the shore,
World-Soul. 66.

Shores
Old are the shores; Hamatreya. 33.
Men to all shores that front the hoary
main. Seashore. 40.
When the scanty shores are full
Threnody. 232.

Shorn
And life, shorn of its venerable length,
Blight. 53.
Shorn from her comely head,
Hermione. 18.

Short
the summer short, Blight. 50.
The sense of the world is short,—
I. Eros. 1.
And the rash-leaping thunderbolt fell
short. Frag. Life. XXXIV. 2.
Still thou playest;—short vacation
Holidays. 17.
Short and bent by cold and snow;
May-Day. 313.
Between two sleeps a short day's stealth,
Poet. 183.

But fell the starry influence short,
Song of Nature. 71.
With aged eyes, short way before,—
Threnody. 180.
Life is too short to waste   To J. W. 18.

Shorter
Shorter days and harder times.
Alphonso. 6.

Short-lived
Short-lived wandering to and fro,
Merlin. 107.

Shortness
The shortness of our days,
Monadnoc. 406.

Shot
Shot through the weltering pit of the salt
sea.   Adirondacs. 270.
And fired the shot heard round the
world.   C. Hymn. 4.
While Time shot by.   * Lines. 12.
Shot up to the height of the sky again,
May-Day. 322.
Shot million rays of thought and tender-
ness.   Musketaquid. 10.

Should
Watching when the loud dogs should
drive in deer,   Adirondacs. 110.
That we should build, hard-by, a spa-
cious lodge   Adirondacs. 162.
And how we should come hither with
our sons,   Adirondacs. 163.
And cedar grove and cliff and lake should
know   Adirondacs. 254.
Why should I keep holiday
I. Compensation. 1.
Should mine alone be dumb?
I. Compensation. 6.
The manhood that should yours resist,—
Etienne. 10.
I wait the sun on them should shine.
Frag. Life. XIV. 2.
That each should in his house abide,
Frag. Life. XXI. 1.
Even to those who thee should love
Frag. Life. XXVII. 5.
Should throb until he snapped his chain.
Freedom. 4.
If my darling should depart,
From Hafiz. 9.
In other love should seek amends.
From Hafiz. 12.
How should not the poet doat
Harp. 50.
As if to-morrow should redeem
May-Day. 297.
Its chords should ring as blows the
breeze,   Merlin. 3.
It should be their life's ornament,
Monadnoc. 50.
I should like to die in sweets,
Mountain. 14.
And his training should not scant
Poet. 4.
His learning should be deep and large,
Poet. 40.
His flesh should feel, his eyes should
read   Poet. 43.
In its fulness he should taste   Poet. 45.
He should be loved; he should be hated;
Poet. 48.

His heart should palpitate with fear.
Poet. 50.
If the Law should thee forget, Poet. 289.
Why should the vest on him allure,
Problem. 7.
Tides that should warm each neighbor-
ing life   Rubies. 7.
Of the snow-tower, when snow should
fall;   Threnody. 85.
This child should ills of ages stay,
Threnody. 136.

Shouldered
See Strong-shouldered.

Shoulders
From his shoulders falls who sees
Celestial Love. 66.
Broad his shoulders are and strong;
Destiny. 31.
On the shoulders of the sky.
Frag. Poet. XXIX. 7.
A load your Atlas shoulders cannot lift?
Seashore. 33.

Shouldst
Of them thou shouldst have comforted;
Saadi. 69.

Shout
O no, not we! Witness the shout that
shook   Adirondacs. 309.

Shouted
Big with great news, and shouted the
report   Adirondacs. 237.

Shove
Therefore they shove us from them,
yield to us   Blight. 40.

Show
See Foreshow.
I show Columbia, of the rocks
Boston Hymn. 21.
And treacherously bright to show
Chartist. 11.
Show our love and piety.
Ellen South. 28.
Only could her mirror show.
Frag. Life. IX. 2.
Come and I will show you all
Frag. Nat. XXVI. 5.
The slow eye of heaven shall show
Frag. Nat. XXVI. 9.
I care not if the pomps you show
May-Day. 350.
Bead-eyes my granite chaos show,
Monadnoc. 317.
Nor show thy pompous parts,
Saadi. 46.
What rainbows teach, and sunsets show?
Threnody. 261.
Show me the forward way, since thou
art guide,   Unbar. 2.
Hearts to hearts their meaning show,
Visit. 18.

Showed
Cried "Onward!" and the palm-crown
showed,   In Memoriam. 59.
Showed me the lore of colors and of
sounds,   Musketaquid. 60.
Showed them the life of Heaven above
Robbins Hymn. 19.
And showed his side of flame;
Thine Eyes. 10.
As if a sunbeam showed the place,
Woodnotes. I. 44.

Showed—*Continued*
And their resistless friendship showed.
Woodnotes. I. 128.
Shower
As, when a shower of meteors
Daemonic Love. 48.
A tiny scene of sun and shower,
Ellen. 4.
As finds its Alp the snowy shower,
Frag. Life. XXIII. 6.
Showers
On bravely through the sunshine and the showers!   Frag. Life. XXXVII. 1.
Nor in the bow that smiles in showers,
Music. 16.
For me, in showers, in sweeping showers, the Spring   Musketaquid. 11.
Shown
None credits him till he have shown
Frag. Poet. VI. 3.
By eldest science wrought and shown!
Monadnoc. 67.
The courtesy ye have shown and kept
Poet. 150.
Then for mankind's instruction shown;
Prayer. 4.
Was shown to this philosopher,
Woodnotes. I. 60.
Shows
To each apart, lifting her lovely shows
Adirondacs. 199.
Many things the garden shows,
Frag. Nat. XXI. 1.
Shows feats of his gymnastic play,
Titmouse. 41.
But all her shows did Nature yield,
Woodnotes. I. 52.
Shrew
Captured the lizard, salamander, shrew,
Adirondacs. 135.
Shrilling
And, shrilling from the solar course,
Uriel. 49.
Shrine
upon the shrine,   Fame. 27.
And the same power that reared the shrine   Problem. 49.
Fair the soul's recess and shrine,
Threnody. 255.
Shrined
Where this deity is shrined,
Freedom. 12.
Shrinking
And our shrinking sky extend.
Daemonic Love. 59.
Shrivel
Shrivel the rainbow-colored walls,
Daemonic Love. 120.
Shrivelled
To plant thy shrivelled pedantry
Frag. Poet. XXIX. 6.
Shroud
See Caterpillar-shroud.
The snow is no ignoble shroud,
Titmouse. 21.
Nor seek to unwind the shroud
To J. W. 6.
With roses and a shroud;
World-Soul. 78.
Shrouds
His arrows he shrouds.   *Lines. 8.

Mourning summer laid in shrouds.
Nun. 22.
When the violets were in their shrouds, and Summer in its pride,   *Violet. 15.
Shrub
Every shrub and grape leaf
Frag. Nat. III. 24.
Shrubs
Singing over shrubs and vines.
Humble-Bee. 10.
Shudder
Lose the shudder of midnight;
Saadi. 52.
A shudder ran around the sky;
Uriel. 26.
Shuddered
Cold shuddered the sphere:—
Sphinx. 60.
Shun
The ill I shun, the good I claim;
Angelo. 7.
Shun passion,   Frag. Life. XXXV. 1.
Shun him, nymphs, on the fleet horses!
Initial Love. 102.
Too weak to win, too fond to shun
Manners. 17.
To hide or to shun   Ode to Beauty. 34.
Shunned
I shunned the toiling Hassan's glance."
Frag. Poet. I. 12.
I shunned his eyes, that faithful man's,
Frag. Poet. III. 11.
Forbore the ant-hill, shunned to tread,
Frag. Poet. XXIV. 1.
Shuns
Into the charmed snare she shuns;
Nemesis. 6.
Love shuns the sage, the child it crowns,
Woodnotes. II. 236.
Shut
And pirates of the universe, shut out
Blight. 47.
Too long shut in strait and few,
Mithridates. 20.
Delayed, all friends shut out, the house-mates sit   Snow-Storm. 7.
Shuts
Shuts his sense on toys of time,
Voluntaries. 81.
Shy
With passion cold and shy.   Harp. 120.
Shy, untamed, inscrutable,
Initial Love. 89.
Her passions the shy violet
Quat. Hafiz. 1.
And the shy hawk did wait for him;
Woodnotes. I. 57.
Sibyl
Where in bright Art each god and sibyl dwelt   Daemonic Love. 121.
Or sibyl from the mummied East,
Frag. Poet. XXVIII. 2.
Sibyls
The word by seers or sibyls told,
Problem. 57.
Sick
See Lovesick.
Therefore, to our sick eyes,
Blight. 49.

The stunted trees look sick,   Blight. 50.
Nor when I'm jaded, sick, anxious or
  mean.   Frag. Life. XV. 5.
The animals are sick with love,
      Merlin. 96.
He kills the cripple and the sick,
      World-Soul. 91.

Sickly
Wear out indoors your sickly days,
      Romany. 7.

Sickness
Be it health, or be it sickness;
      Frag. Life. XXVII. 8.

Side
    See Fireside; Garden-side; Hillside;
River-Side; Roadside; Seaside.
The astonished Muse finds thousands at
  her side.   Channing Ode. 97.
Have the same mists another side,
      Chartist. 7.
Each maple leaf turned up its silver side.
      Frag. Nat. III. 14.
Kept its place by the poet's side.
      Frag. Poet. I. 18.
In the casement at my side.   Harp. 40.
It seemed, so listening, at my side
      Harp. 108.
Heaven's oldest blood flows in his side,—
      Initial Love. 123.
And sun this frozen side.   May-Day. 161.
And the gods from side to side.
      Quat. Hush. 4.
They know me as their son, for side by
  side,   River. 39.
Shall flock to you and tarry by your side,
      Rome. 6.
That shall command a senate to your
  side;   Rome. 17.
And showed his side of flame;
      Thine Eyes. 10.
Sage and hero, side by side,
      Voluntaries. 24.
And he who battles on her side,
      Voluntaries. 102.
I travelled grateful by their side,
      Woodnotes. I. 123.

Sidereal
All he distils into sidereal wine
      Day's Ration. 11.

In sidereal years.   Harp. 28.

Sides
I could never reach their sides;
      Forerunners. 2.
Eldest rite, two married sides
      Merlin. 90.
I take him up my rugged sides,
      Monadnoc. 315.

Sidewise
Sidewise meek in gossamer lids;
      May-Day. 325.

Sift
I will use the world, and sift it.
      Mithridates. 22.
Nor scour the seas, nor sift mankind,
      Saadi. 155.

Sigh
Without tongue, yellow-cheeked, full of
  winds that wail and sigh;   Flute. 2.
His music was the south-wind's sigh,
      Frag. Poet. I. 11.

And, when he heaved a sigh profound,
      Hermione. 6.
And I lived but to sigh,   * Lines. 26.
Me many a sigh.   River. 21.
When summer light is fading, and autumn
  breezes sigh;   * Violet. 10.

Sighed
And sighed for all that bounded their
  domain;   Hamatreya. 18.
Sighed his soul away.   September. 4.

Sighing
Yon waterflag, yon sighing osier,
      Poet. 221.
The stream, the trees, the grass, the
  sighing wind,   River. 28.

Sighs
Maugre the farmer's sighs; and at the
  gate   Snow-Storm. 21.

Sight
    See Foresight.
The needs of the first sight absorb my
  blood,   Day's Ration. 17.
And the German's inward sight.
      Monadnoc. 302.
Thy sight is growing blear;   Sphinx. 106.
I gave thee sight—where is it now?
      Threnody. 196.
To hit the nerve of feebler sight.
      Uriel. 42.
Riding on the ray of sight,   Visit. 15.
Yet happier he whose inward sight,
      Voluntaries. 79.
As if by secret sight he knew
      Woodnotes. I. 48.
Of his triumphant piercing sight:
      Woodnotes. II. 66.
Flies gayly forth and sings in sight.
      Woodnotes. II. 251.

Sighted
    See Sharpest-sighted.

Sightless
Put in, drive home the sightless wedges
      Frag. Nat. XXX. 1.

Sightly
    See Unsightly.

Sights
The sights and voices ravishing
      Harp. 85.

Sign
But for a leafy sign   May-Day. 107.
Read the celestial sign!   Monadnoc. 14.
Taught thee each private sign to raise
      Threnody. 201.
Whose omen 'tis, and sign.
      Threnody. 259.
Might gather omens from that radiant
  sign.   Webster. 4.
Hark! in thy ear I will tell the sign
      Woodnotes. II. 192.

Signal-fire
The first far signal-fire of morn.
      Harp. 94.

Significance
And all their sad significance. The wind,
      River. 25.

Signified
Knew they what that signified,
      Circles. 5.
Unto the thing so signified;   Fate. 14.

Signs
Yield sympathy and signs of mirth;
Celestial Love. 110.
By signs gracious as rainbows.
Forerunners. 34.
Omens and signs that filled the air
Frag. Poet. V. 39.
His many signs cannot be told;
Initial Love. 130.
Silence
The foe long since in silence slept;
C. Hymn. 5.
A twelvemonth he could silence hold,
Frag. Poet. V. 24.
The green silence dost displace
Humble-Bee. 30.
Your silence he sings. Sphinx. 24.
"Sea, earth, air, sound, silence,
Sphinx. 33.
Silences
And a thousand silences. Merops. 8.
Silent
In the boat's bows, a silent night-hunter
Adirondacs. 118.
Alike the conqueror silent sleeps;
C. Hymn. 6.
Ah! late I spoke to silent throngs,
I. Compensation. 7.
Turned and departed silent. I, too late,
Days. 10.
Are silent, low and pale. Dirge. 24.
The silent organ loudest chants
Dirge. 59.
If once again that silent string,
Harp. 105.
Yet I think on them in the silent night,
I Bear. 9.
Whose timbers, as they silent float,
Monadnoc. 274.
Thou art silent and sedate.
Monadnoc. 380.
Dost love our manners? Canst thou
silent lie? Musketaquid. 77.
Pathetic silent poets that sing to me
Naples. 26.
My hand upon the silent string,
Poet. 95.
Silent rushes the swift Lord
Threnody. 282.
Silken
I touch this flower of silken leaf,
Dirge. 37.
A sterner errand to the silken troop
Summons. 1.
Siller
'Tis the poor man getting siller,
Riches. 3.
Silver
Among the silver hills of heaven
Bacchus. 16.
Silver to silver creep and wind,
Celestial Love. 79.
Or tone of silver instrument
Forerunners. 12.
Silver birch and black Frag. Nat. II. 25.
Each maple leaf turned up its silver side.
Frag. Nat. III. 14.
In silver lakes that unexhausted gleam
Frag. Nat. IV. 10.
Glittered with silver every cottage pane,
Frag. Nat. XXVII. 4.

The silver cloud, In Memoriam. 19.
That rims the running silver sheet,—
May-Day. 246.
The swinging spider's silver line,
Ode to Beauty. 27.
The silver seat of Innocence.
Spiritual Laws. 12.
Whose silver warble wild Threnody. 12.
Silvered
I bathe in the morn's soft and silvered
air, Musketaquid. 13.
She silvered in the moon; Sphinx. 124.
Silvers
Silvers the horizon wall,
Humble-Bee. 22.
Similar
See Self-similar.
Simple
But to hold fast his simple sense,
Celestial Love. 127.
The wise and simple have one glance
In Memoriam. 11.
In simple words succeeds,
Quat. Poet. 2. 2.
But, in my simple ignorance, suppose
Rhodora. 15.
Here is the rock where, yet a simple
child, River. 11.
And simple maids and noble youth
Saadi. 39.
Simpleness
With simpleness for stratagem.
Monadnoc. 117.
Simples
Only the herbs and simples of the wood,
Blight. 4.
Simular
And the simular despite Monadnoc. 350.
Sin
thought it no sin Frag. Nat. IX. 1.
The depths of sin to which I had de-
scended, Grace. 7.
Merlin paying the pain of sin,
Harp. 55.
To speak the plain reproof of sin
Hymn. 17.
Like a world without sin, * Lines. 15.
Sin piles the loaded board.
Woodnotes. II. 17.
From the old adhering sin,
Woodnotes. II. 64.
And heal the hurts which sin has made.
Woodnotes. II. 220.
Since. (Partial list.)
Since fortune snatched
Adirondacs. 276.
No tidings since it came. Amulet. 4.
The foe long since in silence slept;
C. Hymn. 5.
Since genius too has bound and term,
Harp. 74.
Since the world was, he has gnawed;
Limits. 3.
Not idle, since the leaf all day
May-Day. 115.
Sincerity
Wrought in a sad sincerity;
Problem. 21.
Sinew
The needful sinew stark as once,
Terminus. 27.

Sinew that subdued the fields;
                    Woodnotes. II. 32.

Sinews
Who sells his sinews to be wise,
                    Fame. 9.
Right good-will my sinews strung,
                    Forerunners. 6.

Sinewy
Their sinewy arms pull at the oar un-
    tired   Adirondacs. 89.

Sinful
Beauty for his sinful weeds,
                    Caritas. 6.

Sing
I listen when they sing,   Dull. 7.
Only to children children sing,
                    Harp. 34.
When did he sing? and where abide?
                    Harp. 37.
And hears in heaven the bluebird sing,
                    May-Day. 100.
Sing it low or sing it loud,
                    Merlin's Song. 2.
I sing it to the surging crowd,—
                    Merlin's Song. 5.
And the commissioned wind to sing
                    Mountain. 18.
Courageous sing a delicate overture
                    Musketaquid. 17.
Pathetic silent poets that sing to me
                    Naples. 26.
Right to the heaven they steer and sing.
                    Poet. 26.
Not yet I sing: but I must wait,
                    Poet. 94.
But one shall sing;   Saadi. 18.
For I am wont to sing uncalled,
                    Solution. 19.
The winds shall sing their dead-march
    old,   Titmouse. 20.

Singer
I watched the singer with delight.—
                    Miracle. 25.
Thine elegy, sweet singer, sainted wife.
                    Naples. 27.

Singers
And singers of her fame   Hermione. 24.

Singeth
What he singeth to me?   Dirge. 44.

Singing
Singing in the sun-baked square;
                    Art. 8.
Singing aloft in the tree!   Dirge. 42.
Singing an immortal strain,   Dull. 4.
Singing at dawn on the alder bough;
                    Each. 14.
Singing over shrubs and vines.
                    Humble-Bee. 10.
Singing by the oriole songs,
                    May-Day. 420.

Single
And marching single in an endless file,
                    Days. 3.
Be it remembered of a single man,
                    Entombed. 2.
Filing single in stately train.
                    May-Day. 308.
Ye taught my lips a single speech,
                    Merops. 7.
Ascends as gladly in a single tree
                    Musketaquid. 56.

Single look has drained the breast;
                    Visit. 21.
Single moment years confessed.
                    Visit. 22.
A single will, a million deeds.
                    Woodnotes. II. 265.

Sings
And I the hymn the Brahmin sings.
                    Brahma. 12.
He sings the song, but it cheers not now,
                    Each. 16.
Sings a tune that's worth the knowing.'
                    Ellen South. 36.
When thrushes ope their throat, 't is he
    that sings,   Enchanter. 10.
The brook sings on, but sings in vain
                    Frag. Poet. XXVI. 1.
Sings aloud the tune whereto
                    Merlin. 45.
There alway, alway something sings.
                    Music. 12, 18.
As sings the pine-tree in the wind,
                    Quat. Leasts. 1.
So sings in the wind a sprig of the pine;
                    Quat. Leasts. 2.
Your silence he sings.   Sphinx. 24.
Sings in my ears, my hands are stones,
                    Titmouse. 13.
Tuned to the lay the wood-god sings.
                    Woodnotes. II. 96.
To the open ear it sings
                    Woodnotes. II. 104.
Flies gayly forth and sings in sight.
                    Woodnotes. II. 251.

Sink
Sink, O mountain, in the swamp!
                    Monadnoc. 121.
To fill the hollows, sink the hills,
                    Monadnoc. 149.

Sinks
I dine in the sun; when he sinks in the
    sea,   Titmouse. 69.

Sioux
Lie here on hemlock-boughs, like Sacs
    and Sioux,   Adirondacs. 52.
Or count the Sioux a match for Agassiz?
                    Adirondacs. 308.

Sipping
Sipping only what is sweet,
                    Humble-Bee. 55.

Sir
As if it said, 'Good day, good sir!
                    Titmouse. 29.

Sire
Not Homer's self, the poet sire.
                    Harp. 76.
No sire survive, no son succeed!
                    Monadnoc. 124.
Sole estate his sire bequeathed,—
                    Voluntaries. 9.
Hapless sire to hapless son,——
                    Voluntaries. 10.
Of Genius sire and son.   World-Soul. 84.

Siren
Wherein every siren sung,
                    Daemonic Love. 124.

Sires
Thy summons called our sires,
                    Bell. 10.

Sires —*Continued*
The young men and the sires,
                    Boston Hymn. 38.
When, like our sires, our sons are gone.
                    C. Hymn. 12.
Curse, if thou wilt, thy sires,
                    Terminus. 23.
The sires of Nature, hide.
                    Waldeinsamkeit. 36.

Siroc
The siroc found it on its way,   Guy. 37.
These the siroc could not melt,   Test. 7.

Siroccos
Where palms plume, siroccos blaze,
                    Voluntaries. 48.

Sister
Of mother, father, sister, stand;
                    Daemonic Love. 6.
I had a sister once who seemed just like
  a violet;   *Violet. 13.

Sisters
Sung by the Sisters as they spin;
                    Merlin. 125.

Sit
I sit and mourn alone?
                    I Compensation. 4.
Sit here on the basalt courses
                    Cosmos. 17.
Sit still and Truth is near:
                    Frag. Life. XXXV. 2.
Sit with the Cause, or grim or glad.
                    Frag. Poet. XVII. 2.
Straitly charged him, 'Sit aloof;'
                    Saadi. 12.
Delayed, all friends shut out, the house-
  mates sit   Snow-Storm. 7.
I sit by the shining Fount of Life
                    Song of Nature. 11.

Sitfast
To find the sitfast acres where you left
  them.'   Hamatreya. 24.

Sits
Beauty sits and Music calls;   Dearest. 2.
Deep in the man sits fast his fate
                    Fate. 1.
The child of genius sits forlorn:
                    Poet. 182.
Unmeasured still my Shakspeare sits,
                    Quat. Shakespeare. 3.
Half-seen Una sits beside.   Una. 8.
Where a captive sits in chains,
                    Voluntaries. 6.
The shadow sits close to the flying ball;
                    Woodnotes. II. 244.
Yet there in the parlor sits
                    World-Soul. 25.
The patient Dæmon sits,
                    World-Soul. 77.

Sittest
While thou sittest at thy door
                    Saadi. 167.

Sitting
  See Sole-sitting.

Six
Six rods, sixteen, twenty, or forty-five;
                    Adirondacs. 126.
Six thousand pounds a year.
                    Boston. 72.
Six thankful weeks,—   Goethe. 1.

Sixteen
Six rods, sixteen, twenty, or forty-five;
                    Adirondacs. 126.

Sixty
When sixty years are told;
                    World-Soul. 106.

Size
Making free with time and size,
                    Frag. Poet. IX. 6.
I think no virtue goes with size;
                    Titmouse. 60.

Sketch
After the master's sketch fills and o'erfills   Day's Ration. 28.

Sketched
Is sketched and dyed, each with a new
  design,   Naples. 7.

Skies
With skies of benediction, to Round
  Lake,   Adirondacs. 8.
Daily the bending skies solicit man,
                    Adirondacs. 224.
In the insufficient skies.   Alphonso. 8.
Nor skies without a frown
                    Concord Ode. 22.
Will take the sun out of the skies
                    Concord Ode. 39.
Were kindled in the upper skies   Eva. 2.
Hide in thy skies, thou fruitless Jove,
                    Frag. Life. XXXIII. 2.
Who gives to seas and sunset skies
                    Freedom. 13.
And search the skies for prouder friends,
                    From Hafiz. 10.
Makes travellers long for Indian skies,
                    May-Day. 294.
The Indian cheer, the frosty skies,
                    Monadnoc. 106.
Hide in thy skies, O sovereign lamp!
                    Monadnoc. 122.
Sea-valleys and the deep of skies
                    Ode to Beauty. 48.
Old gods forsook the skies.
                    Peter. 20.
To read new landscapes and old skies;
                    Poet. 53.
And to thine eye the vast skies fall,
                    Woodnotes. II. 200.

Skiey
  See Skyey.
Like creatures of a skiey mould,
                    Frag. Poet. I. 48.

Skiff
Or see the wide shore from thy skiff,
                    Woodnotes. II. 195.

Skiffs
When of our little fleet three cruising
  skiffs   Adirondacs. 231.

Skilful
She is skilful to select   House. 3.
I know ye skilful to convoy
                    May-Day. 353.
Quick and skilful to inspire
                    Ode to Beauty. 76.
Nor skilful by my grief;
                    Quat. Climacteric. 2.

Skill
Their rival strength and suppleness,
  their skill   Adirondacs. 81

Insatiate skill in water or in air
            Adirondacs. 137.
Culture and libraries, mysteries of skill,
            Adirondacs. 323.
Both death and pity, my unequal skill
            Angelo. 13.
I armed his hand with skill,
            Frag. Poet. XIV. 2.
In his rich nurseries, timely skill
            Guy. 41.
Recalled thy skill in bold design,
            Lines. 18.
Like wax, their fashioning skill betrays,
            Monadnoc. 148.
And his hand was armed with skill;
            Power. 2.

Skilled
Fate and Beauty skilled to weave.
            Harp. 46.
By million changes skilled to tell
            Monadnoc. 86.
Mute orator! well skilled to plead,
            Monadnoc. 403.

Skim
And saw the wheeling sea-birds skim,
            Frag. Poet. I. 46.

Skin
Orange cheek or skin of man.
            Alphonso. 12.
Can arm impregnably the skin;
            Titmouse. 76.

Skip
Nor wanton skip with bacchic dance,
            May-Day. 129.

Skirted
By strength and terror skirted;
            Daemonic Love. 61.

Skirting
Of skirting hills to lie,
            Waldeinsamkeit. 6.

Skirts
Superior to all its gaudy skirts.
            Adirondacs. 220.
Skirts of angels, starry wings,   Art. 16.

Sky
Thirsting in that pure for a purer sky?
            Adirondacs. 210.
And presently the sky is changed; O
  world!   Adirondacs. 211.
Which fed the veins of earth and sky,
            Alphonso. 32.
Each cloud that floated in the sky
            Apology. 7.
Will the sweet sky and ocean broad
            Chartist. 15.
One third part of the sky unrolled
            Concord Ode. 11.
Of landscape and of sky,   Culture. 6.
And our shrinking sky extend.
            Daemonic Love. 59.
Bread, kingdoms, stars, and sky that
  holds them all.   Days. 6.
For I did not bring home the river and
  sky;—   Each. 17.
Over me soared the eternal sky,
            Each. 46.
Its leaves to the rival sky;   Exile. 2.
Its guerdon in the sky,   Fame. 22.
Succory to match the sky,
            Frag. Nat. II. 8.

Who climb each night the ancient sky,
            Frag. Nat. VIII. 6.
See yonder leafless trees against the sky,
            Frag. Nat. XVII. 1.
in that enormous sky. Frag. Nat. XX. 2.
Or changing colors of the sky,
            Frag. Nat. XXXII. 2
To see the people of the sky:
            Frag. Poet. XI. 4.
On the shoulders of the sky.
            Frag. Poet. XXIX. 7.
But lit the sky with flame.
            Frag. Poet. XXXII. 4.
Through thee alone the sky is arched,
            Friendship. 11.
Or match with words that tender sky?
            Garden. 40.
And the outlets of the sky.   Give. 17.
Succory to match the sky,
            Humble-Bee. 45.
Which holds to home 'neath every sky,
            In Memoriam. 82.
Through tracts and provinces of sky,
            May-Day. 25.
In the sky no spark;   May-Day. 38.
Shot up to the height of the sky again,
            May-Day. 322.
Coat sea and sky with heavenlier blue,
            May-Day. 446.
Published it to lake and sky,
            Miracle. 32.
To sound the science of the sky,
            Monadnoc. 103.
And the seas wash the low-hung sky;
            Poet. 66.
O'er England's abbeys bends the sky,
            Problem. 37.
This charm is wasted on the earth and
  sky,   Rhodora. 10.
Hold their sour conversation in the
  sky:—   River. 17.
The stars may hide in the upper sky,
            Romany. 27.
And pile the hills to scale the sky;
            Saadi. 95.
Announced by all the trumpets of the
  sky,   Snow-Storm. 1.
Flushed in the sky the sweet May-morn,
            Solution. 7.
Innocence that matched the sky,
            Threnody. 212.
Up to his style, and manners of the sky.
            Threnody. 271.
And the sky doats on cheerful song.
            Titmouse. 88.
The inward sky with chrysolite,   Una. 14.
A shudder ran around the sky;
            Uriel. 26.
And a blush tinged the upper sky,
            Uriel. 55.
Whose dark sky sheds the snowflake
  down,   Voluntaries. 40.
Their colors from the sky;
            Waldeinsamkeit. 8.
Methought the sky looked scornful down
            Walden. 21.
And potencies of sky.   Waterfall. 8.
The public child of earth and sky.
            Woodnotes. I. 117.
All constellations of the sky
            Woodnotes. II. 73.

Sky—*Continued*
And his mind is the sky.
     Woodnotes. II. 317.
Yon sky between the walls,
     World-Soul. 38.
Sky-affairs
The Titan heeds his sky-affairs,
     Monadnoc. 58.
Sky-born
I hear a sky-born music still:
     Music. 2.
Sky-cleaving
As doth this round sky-cleaving beat
     Monadnoc. 272.
Skyey
 See Skiey.
Heard rendings of the skyey roof,
     Solution. 55.
Sky-hoop
I plant his eyes on the sky-hoop bound-
ing;   Monadnoc. 324.
Sky-piercing
Or the sky-piercing horns of Himmaleh;
     Frag. Nat. IV. 5.
Slab
She laid a slab of marble on his head.
     Epitaph. 4.
Through the cold slab a thousand gates,
     May-Day. 122.
Half piled or prostrate; and my newest
slab   Seashore. 16.
The granite slab to clothe and hide,
     Wealth. 16.
Slacken
Could you slacken and condense?
     Alphonso. 64.
Sometimes their strong speed they
slacken, Forerunners. 27.
Slain
Dissected the slain deer, weighed the
trout's brain, Adirondacs. 134.
Or if the slain think he is slain,
     Brahma. 2.
Are moles of beauties Time hath slain.
     Omar. 4.
God, though he were ten times slain,
     Voluntaries. 103.
Slate
Beneath your roofs of slate.
     World-Soul. 12.
Slaughter
Intent on insect slaughter:
     Frag. Nat. XIX. 3.
Slave
Slave or master on his breast.
     Astraea. 8.
Call in the wretch and slave:
     Boston Hymn. 26.
And I unchain the slave:
     Boston Hymn. 54.
Who is the owner? The slave is owner,
     Boston Hymn. 71.
Timour, to Hassan, was a slave.
     Frag. Poet. III. 4.
That the slave who caught the strain
     Freedom. 3.
Slaves
And in the midst of spoils and slaves, we
thieves   Blight. 46.
The honest waves refused to slaves
     Boston. 17.

Sugar spends to fatten slaves,
     Heroism. 2.
New slaves fulfilled the poet's dream,
     Wealth. 40.
Slay
Nor thee, on the second, the Universe
slay.   On Two Days. 4.
The strong they slay, the swift outstride:
     Voluntaries. 118.
Slayer
If the red slayer think he slays,
     Brahma. 1.
Slays
If the red slayer think he slays,
     Brahma. 1.
Sled
The sled and traveller stopped, the cour-
ier's feet Snow-Storm. 6.
The painted sled stands where it stood;
     Threnody. 82.
Sledge
Slide with the sledge to inaccessible
woods Musketaquid. 45.
Sleep
 See Asleep; Outsleep.
Sleep on the fragrant brush, as on down-
beds.   Adirondacs. 58.
Mind wakes a new-born giant from her
sleep.   Adirondacs. 327.
To weltering Chaos and to sleep.
     Alphonso. 30.
It charms his cares to sleep,
     Bell. 7.
Said the winds that sung the lads to
sleep,   Boston. 15.
To dine and sleep through forty years;
     Fame. 14.
In sleep their jubilant troop is near,—
     Forerunners. 29.
And gifts awake when givers sleep,
     Frag. Life. VII. 2.
Feigns to sleep, Frag. Nat. I. 10.
Thy sleep makes ridiculous.
     Humble-Bee. 63.
Sleep is not, death is not; Illusions. 5.
That the marble sleep is broken,
     May-Day. 33.
Now in sordid weeds they sleep,
     Monadnoc. 171.
But, like a walker in his sleep Poet. 86.
Than wine or sleep or praise; Rome. 13.
The pastures sleep, ripple the lakes,
     Saadi. 136.
Will never my winds go sleep in the
west? Song of Nature. 46.
Out of waking a sleep; Sphinx. 14.
Well, in this broad bed lie and sleep.
     Titmouse. 17.
Let kings and conquerors, saints and
soldiers sleep— To-Day. 4.
They reach no term, they never sleep,
     Voluntaries. 115.
Thy thrift, the sleep of cares;
     Waldeinsamkeit. 46.
Sleeping
Feigns to sleep, sleeping never;
     Frag. Nat. I. 10.
Out of sleeping a waking, Sphinx. 13.
Sleeps
And the sunny Æon sleeps
     Celestial Love. 48.

Alike the conqueror silent sleeps;
              C. Hymn. 6.
Sleeps or feigns slumber,
              Frag. Nat. I. 3.
The sleeps of trees or dreams of herbs.
              Frag. Nat. XVIII. 5.
Sleeps the vast East
              Frag. Nat. XXVI. 21.
Between two sleeps a short day's stealth,
              Poet. 183.

Sleet
Under east winds crossed with sleet.
              May-Day. 133.
The feet that slid so long on sleet
              May-Day. 281.

Slender
Whilst upper life the slender rill Art. 27.
Low, open meads, slender and sluggish
  streams,   Musketaquid. 2.
Still tearless lift its slender form above
  the wintry snow?   *Violet. 4.
Thy cheek too white, thy form too slen-
  der,   Woodnotes. II. 186.

Slept
The foe long since in silence slept;
              C. Hymn. 5.
These had crossed them while they slept.
              Forerunners. 20.
And near the wolf and panther slept.
              Frag. Poet. I. 44.
His purpose woke, his features slept;
              In Memoriam. 102.
While they slumbered and slept:—
              Sphinx. 8.
If in ashes the fire-seed slept. Uriel. 46.
Once slept the world an egg of stone,
              Woodnotes. II. 266.

Slid
By the bright morn the gay flotilla slid
              Adirondacs. 16.
And where the infection slid,
              Bacchus. 60.
The feet that slid so long on sleet
              May-Day. 281.
I was a boy; boyhood slid gayly by
              Summons. 15.
But all slid to confusion.   Uriel. 34.

Slide
Slide with the sledge to inaccessible
  woods   Musketaquid. 45.

Slight
Or baffle by a veil, or slight by scorn?
              Adirondacs. 176.
Victim of perpetual slight: Destiny. 19.
And trains us on to slight the new, as
  if it were the old: Quat. Nature. 2.
The slight Linnæa hang its twin-born
  heads,   Woodnotes. I. 69.

Slighted
Slighted Minerva's learnèd tongue,
              Frag. Poet. XXXV. 1.

Slime
They thank the spring-flood for its fer-
  tile slime,   Musketaquid. 43.
On spawning slime my song prevails,
              Solution. 5.
And, out of slime and chaos, Wit
              Wealth. 32.
Of the old flood's subsiding slime,
              Woodnotes. II. 109.

Slimy
From all natures, sharp and slimy,
              Mithridates. 10.

Slinks
To-day slinks poorly off unmarked between: Quat. Heri. 2.

Slip
      See Cowslip.

Slipped
Slipped off their pack   Adirondacs. 62.
Have slipped their sacred bars,
              Daemonic Love. 53.

Slips
Whither gaunt Labor slips to wipe his
  brow   Adirondacs. 196.
Siips behind a tomb.   Manners. 20.

Slope
The banks slope down to the blue lake-
  edge,   Garden. 11.
Find me a slope where I can feel the sun
              Letter. 14.

Sloped
Ponderous with beechen forest sloped the
  shore.   Adirondacs. 28.

Sloth
Tax not my sloth that I   Apology. 5.
Scatter the sloth, wash out the stain,
              May-Day. 454.
Bookworm, break this sloth urbane;
              Monadnoc. 16.
To leave my woods and streams and the
  sweet sloth   Summons. 4.
To hearts in sloth and ease.
              Voluntaries. 70.

Slough
And slough decay from grazing herds,
              May-Day. 448.

Sloven
In sloven dress and broken rank,
              In Memoriam. 5.

Slow
The other slow,—this the Prometheus,
              Adirondacs. 288.
The schools are sad and slow,   April. 18.
Till the slow ripening, secular tree
              Frag. Nat. XXI. 7.
The slow eye of heaven shall show
              Frag. Nat. XXVI. 9.
Example, custom, fear, occasion slow,—
              Grace. 3.
Slow and warily to choose   House. 5.
Slow grows the palm, too slow the pearl:
              May-Day. 156.
Strong as giant, slow as child.
              Monadnoc. 132.
Sets the life-pulse strong but slow:
              Monadnoc. 158.
Say, Pilgrim, why so late and slow to
  come   Seashore. 2.
To mimic in slow structures, stone by
  stone,   Snow-Storm. 26.
Too slow, the rainbow fades,
              Song of Nature. 50.
This his slow but sure reclining,
              Threnody. 164.
Thy gait too slow, thy habits tender
              Woodnotes. II. 187.

Slower
Never faster, never slower   Poet. 116.

Slowest
What these with slowest steps attain.
Voluntaries. 54.
Slowly
There, growing slowly old at ease
Alphonso. 77.
Slowly
He slowly cures decrepit flesh,
Monadnoc. 161.
Slow-sailing
Like yon slow-sailing cloudy promontory
Adirondacs. 218.
Slowsure
Slowsure Britain's secular might,
Monadnoc. 301.
Sluggard
For you no sluggard rest;   Boston. 56.
Sluggish
Low, open meads, slender and sluggish
streams,   Musketaquid. 2.
To please the desert and the sluggish
brook.   Rhodora. 4.
Slumber
Which did not slumber like a stone,
Beauty. 3.
Sleeps or feigns slumber,
Frag. Nat. I. 3.
In slumber I am strong.
Song of Nature. 8.
Slumbered
While they slumbered and slept:—
Sphinx. 8.
Slumberest
Thou already slumberest deep;
Humble-Bee. 60.
Smack
And, I affirm, my actions smack of the
soil.'   Hamatreya. 10.
Smacks
His nectar smacks of wine.
Daemonic Love. 92.
Smacks of faint memories far away.
May-Day. 78.
Small
Père Raquette stream, to a small tortu-
ous pass   Adirondacs. 22.
'Tis very small,—no load at all,—
Boston. 67.
Where tyrants great and tyrants small
Boston Hymn. 11.
Small bat and wren
Channing Ode. 27.
Equalizing small and large,
Etienne. 17.
You are not so small as I,
Fable. 13.
Small need have I of Turner or Daguerre,
Frag. Nat. IV. 8.
Flashed their small fires in air, or held
their court   Frag. Nat. XXVII. 9.
And I, who cower mean and small
Frag. Poet. III. 7.
There is no great and no small
Informing Spirit. 1.
I followed in small copy in my acre;
Musketaquid. 53.
To that within the vision of small eyes.
Phi. 18.
Prints his small impress on the snow,
Titmouse. 40.

In these woods, thy small Labrador,
Titmouse. 50.
Smallest
Through smallest chambers takes its
way,   Threnody. 218.
Smell
They were refreshed by the smell,
May-Day. 317.
Filling with thy roseate smell,
Ode to Beauty. 79.
Smells
Or east, it smells like a clover-farm;
Woodnotes. I. 102.
Smelted
Five were smelted in a pot   Test. 5.
Smelting
Smelting balls and bars,   Merlin. 93.
Smile
Almost a smile to steal to cheer her sons,
Adirondacs. 342.
Kind smile and honest frown
* Farewell. 12.
I see him with superior smile
In Memoriam. 73.
O'er thy rich dust the endless smile
In Memoriam. 105.
Teaching barren moors to smile,
May-Day. 3.
Seest the smile of Reason beaming;—
Monadnoc. 236.
The yesterday doth never smile,
Nun. 1.
For, whom the Muses smile upon,
Saadi. 125.
The sunset gleams his smile.
Song of Nature. 40.
Still plan and smile,   Terminus. 20.
If Friendship on me smile,   Walden. 30.
Will smile in a factory.   World-Soul. 36.
Smiled
Your picture smiles as first it smiled;
Amulet. 1.
On his young promise Beauty smiled,
In Memoriam. 67.
And thy grave smiled on by the visiting
moon.   Mountain. 6.
Earth smiled with flowers, and man was
born.   Solution. 8.
Smiles
Your picture smiles   Amulet. 1.
Nor in the bow that smiles in showers,
Music. 16.
Fall like sweet strains, or pensive smiles;
Problem. 4.
Smiling
'A new commandment,' said the smiling
Muse,   Adakryn. 1.
And the second, borrowed money,—
though the smiling lender say
Ibn Jemin. 3.
Had active hands and smiling lips;
Saadi. 77.
Smite
Must smite the chords rudely and hard.
Merlin. 10.
Smite the white breasts which thee fed.
Saadi. 67.
The rocky coast, smite Andes into dust,
Seashore. 35.

Smiths
What smiths, and in what furnace, rolled
Wealth. 18.

Smoke
There is smoke in the flame;
Celestial Love. 3.
A cabin hung with curling smoke,
Frag. Poet. I. 22.

Smokeless
Whence a smokeless incense breathes.
May-Day. 6.

Smokes
On eastern hills I see their smokes,
Forerunners. 15.

Smoky
All things shine in his smoky ray,
Frag. Nat. III. 15.

Smooth
A score of airy miles will smooth
Frag. Nat. XIV. 1.
And lakes, smooth mirrors of Aurora's
charms. I Bear. 8.
Will a woman's fan the ocean smooth?
Nemesis. 9.

Smote
He smote the lake to feed his eye
Beauty. 7.

Smother
And what the whispering grasses
smother. Garden. 32.

Smudge
But which we learn to scatter with a
smudge, Adirondacs. 175.

Smug
A sycophant to smug success?
Chartist. 14.
Smug routine, and things allowed,
Mithridates. 29.

Snail
Crab, mice, snail, dragon-fly, minnow and
moth; Adirondacs. 136.

Snake
See Rattlesnake.
Things are of the snake.
Channing Ode. 43.
And with snake and seraph talked.
Daemonic Love. 22.

Snap
Till Beauty came to snap all ties;
Daemonic Love. 11.

Snapped
Should throb until he snapped his chain.
Freedom. 4.

Snare
But word and wisdom is a snare;
Initial Love. 111.
The morn and sparkling dew, a snare?
May-Day. 430.
From their rifle or their snare;
Monadnoc. 144.
Into the charmed snare she shuns;
Nemesis. 6.

Snares
In the snares of Nature's dance;
Daemonic Love. 29.
That he caught Nature in his snares.
Guy. 32.

Snatch
How snatch the stripling from their
toils?— Frag. Life. X. 7.

Snatched
Since fortune snatched from wit the
lion's part? Adirondacs. 276.

Snow
Leave no track on the heavenly snow.
Daemonic Love. 42.
But when the mate of the snow and wind,
Frag. Poet. I. 31.
As we thaw frozen flesh with snow,
May-Day. 125.
The robins know the melting snow;
May-Day. 169.
Short and bent by cold and snow;
May-Day. 314.
They shook the snow from hats and
shoon, May-Day. 318.
To see strange forests and new snow,
Monadnoc. 206.
And my midsummer snow:
Monadnoc. 318.
And, on cheap summit-levels of the snow,
Musketaquid. 44.
Easily to shed the snow, Nature. I. 2.
Gentler far than falls the snow
Poet. 253.
Can swim the flood and wade through
snow, Quat. Love. 2.
But fire to thaw that ruddy snow,
Rubies. 9.
Arrives the snow, and, driving o'er the
fields, Snow-Storm. 2.
The frolic architecture of the snow.
Snow-Storm. 28.
I weary of my robe of snow,
Song of Nature. 51.
Sunshine cannot bleach the snow,
Test. 11.
Of the snow-tower, when snow should
fall; Threnody. 85.
The snow is no ignoble shroud,
Titmouse. 21.
Prints his small impress on the snow,
Titmouse. 40.
Than noontide twilights which snow
makes Titmouse. 73.
Still tearless lift its slender form above
the wintry snow? *Violet. 4.
Under the snow, between the rocks,
Woodnotes. I. 40.
And my manure the snow;
Woodnotes. II. 10.

Snow-banks
As snow-banks thaw in April's beam,
Poet. 35.

Snowbird
Each snowbird chirped, Threnody. 105.

Snow-capped
To the snow-capped steep,
Frag. Nat. III. 37.

Snow-choked
Chilled wading in the snow-choked wood.
Titmouse. 4.

Snow-drift
Her nest beside the snow-drift weaves,
May-Day. 171.
Thawing snow-drift into flowers.
Monadnoc. 65.
And through the wild-piled snow-drift
World-Soul. 111.

Snowflake
Whose dark sky sheds the snowflake down,   Voluntaries. 40.
The snowflake is her banner's star,   Voluntaries. 41.

Snowflake's
With hammer soft as snowflake's flight;—   Monadnoc. 240.

Snowflakes
By races, as snow-flakes,   Boston Hymn. 82.

Snow-loving
Snow-loving pines and oaks instead;   Garden. 6.

Snow-ridges
Snow-ridges masked each darling spot;   May-Day. 42.

Snows
Till these echoes be choked with snows,   Boston. 104.
Knee-deep snows choked all the ways,   May-Day. 37.
His elfin length upon the snows,   May-Day. 114.
Shedding on all its snows and leaves,   Monadnoc. 383.
Nor Time's snows hide the names he set,   Poet. 11.
Through snows above, mines underground,   Solution. 47.
Cold April rain and colder snows   Walden. 11.

Snow-tower
Of the snow-tower, when snow should fall;   Threnody. 85.

Snow-white
Was woven still by the snow-white choir.   Each. 32.

Snowy
As finds its Alp the snowy shower,   Frag. Life. XXIII. 6.
Northward he went to the snowy hills,   Frag. Poet. I. 9.
In quaking bog, on snowy hill,   Woodnotes. I. 38.

Snuff
I snuff the breath of my morning afar,   Poet. 108.

So (Partial list.)
See Howsoever.
So like the soul of me, what if 't were me?   Adirondacs. 214.
So much he shall bestow.   Boston Hymn. 60.
Is none so high, so mean is none,   Celestial Love. 111.
So to be husbanded for poorer days.   Day's Ration. 25.
Unto the thing so signified;   Fate. 14.
But the Spirit said, 'Not so;   Freedom. 5.
Stream could not so perversely wind   Guy. 35.
Who so controlled me;   Hamatreya. 54.
So the coinage of his brain   Monadnoc. 306.
And always keep us so.   Ode to Beauty. 63.
And, being so, the sage unmakes the man.   Philosopher. 2.

Such and so grew these holy piles,   Problem. 31.
Foxes are so cunning   Quat. Orator. 3.
As they lead, so follow all,   Rhea. 31.
So take thy quest through nature,   Sphinx. 117.
A genius of so fine a strain,   Threnody. 141.
So the gentle poet's name   Una. 21.
So nigh is grandeur to our dust,   Voluntaries. 71.

Soar
Now soar again.   Adirondacs. 208.
What care though rival cities soar   Boston. 45.
And soar to the air-borne flocks   Boston Hymn. 23.
To the zenith's top can soar,—   Merlin. 64.

Soared
Over me soared the eternal sky,   Each. 46.

Soaring
The soaring orbit of the muse exceeds that journey's length.   Merlin. 65.

Soars
Which keeps the ground and never soars,   Monadnoc. 187.

Sober
With joy too tense for sober brain;   Frag. Poet. I. 51.
But, sober on a fund of joy,   Waldeinsamkeit. 19.

Social
Which drove them erst to social feats;   Alphonso. 34.
Man was made of social earth,   Daemonic Love. 1.
With the social goldenrod,   Frag. Nat. III. 5.
With social cheer and jubilee;   May-Day. 167.
When the Church is social worth,   Politics. 23.

Society
Linden and spruce. In strict society   Adirondacs. 39.
We must have society,   Alphonso. 57.
Of our lithe society;   Ellen South. 26.
Shall have society of its own rank.   Rome. 3.
Virtue alone is sweet society,   Rome. 8.

Sod
Turns the sod to violets,   Humble-Bee. 27.
The sod throbbed friendly to my feet,   Lines. 13.
Their dust endears the sod.   Robbins Hymn. 4.
A spell is laid on sod and stone,   Unity. 7.

Sodden
Or how thy supper is sodden;'   Destiny. 26.

Soe'er
And, how oft soe'er they've turned it,   I Eros. 5.
What lot soe'er betide,   In Memoriam. 91.

Soft
to lie warm and soft   Adirondacs. 50.
Soft and softlier hold me, friends!
    Aeolian Harp. 1.
He spoke, and words more soft than rain
    Character. 7.
On this green bank, by this soft stream,
    C. Hymn. 9.
Its soft leaves wound me with a grief
    Dirge. 39.
Asks not of others soft consents,
    Frag. Life. XVII. 6.
Seems, though the soft sheen all en-
chants,   Frag. Nat. XXIX. 1.
Soft shadows of the evening lay.
    Frag. Poet. V. 48.
Maids of as soft a bloom shall marry
    Good Hope. 5.
But soft! a sultry morning breaks;
    May-Day. 58.
On the soft path each track is seen,
    May-Day. 61.
And soft perfection of its plan—
    May-Day. 287.
Soft! let not the offended muse
    Monadnoc. 125.
With hammer soft as snowflake's flight;—
    Monadnoc. 240.
Adamant is soft to wit: Monadnoc. 261.
I bathe in the morn's soft and silvered
air,   Musketaquid. 13.
And touch with soft persuasion,
    Saadi. 126.
In soft miniature lies.   Sphinx. 48.
Flew near, with soft wing grazed my
hand,   Titmouse. 38.
Heart too soft and will too weak
    Voluntaries. 15.

Soften
Soften the fall with wary foot;
    Terminus. 18.

Softest
Thy softest pleadings seem too bold,
    Rhea. 21.

Softlier
Soft and softlier hold me, friends!
    Aeolian Harp. 1.

Softly
More proudly rolls, more softly lies.
    Park. 12.
Softly,—but this way fate was pointing,
    Titmouse. 23.

Softness
And with softness touching all,
    Humble-Bee. 23.

Soil
And, I affirm, my actions smack of the
soil.'   Hamatreya. 10.
Of life resurgent from the soil
    Harp. 126.
There's fruit upon my barren soil
    Monadnoc. 295.
Or where he stepped the soil did peal
    Poet. 5.

Sojourned
At the house where these sojourned.
    Forerunners. 26.

Solace
And some in books of solace read;
    Threnody. 153.

Solar
    See Supersolar.
Fit to grace the solar year.
    Alphonso. 82.
Solar insect on the wing
    Frag. Nat. XXII. 1.
They heed not moon or solar tide,—
    Garden. 23.
Of the seven stars and the solar year,
    Informing Spirit. 6.
Draws to the spot the solar ray,
    May-Day. 116.
Secrets of the solar track,   Merlin. 14.
But oh, to see his solar eyes   Poet. 54.
I hide in the solar glory,
    Song of Nature. 5.
And, shrilling from the solar course,
    Uriel. 49.

Sold
or reaped, or bought, or sold;
    Adirondacs. 67.
Goods and raiment bought and sold;
    Celestial Love. 126.
For which I was sold?
    Ode to Beauty. 8.
For their like are sold.   Politics. 4.
He to captivity was sold,   Worship. 3.

Soldier
He who seemed a soldier born,
    In Memoriam. 38.
Stainless soldier on the walls,
    Voluntaries. 97.

Soldier's
What boots it? What the soldier's mail,
    Destiny. 14.

Soldiers
And the soldiers face to face?
    Cosmos. 16.
Let kings and conquerors, saints and
    soldiers sleep—   To-Day. 4.

Sole
The evil time's sole patriot,
    Channing Ode. 2.
Sold source of light and hope assured,
    Hymn. 25.
Sole and self-commanded works,
    Spiritual Laws. 5.
Sole estate his sire bequeathed,—
    Voluntaries. 9.

Sole-leather
Into the very best sole-leather.
    Frag. Poet. XXIII. 2.

Solemn
Under her solemn fillet saw the scorn.
    Days. 11.
In a voice of solemn cheer,—
    Woodnotes. II. 147.

Solemnized
Is sweetly solemnized. Then flows amain
    Musketaquid. 21.

Sole-sitting
Star-crowned, sole-sitting, long I wrought
    Solution. 3.

Solicit
Daily the bending skies solicit man,
    Adirondacs. 224.

Solid
    See Seeming-solid.
The solid, solid universe   Cupido. 1.
Glad when the solid mountain swims
    Frag. Poet. V. 28.

Solid—*Continued*

Long days, and solid banks of flowers;
Humble-Bee. 35.

The gas become solid,   Illusions. 28

While the solid curse and jeer
Monadnoc. 191.

The solid kingdoms like a dream
Poet. 36.

And solid nature to a dream.
Woodnotes. II. 115.

Throughout the solid realm.
World-Soul. 76.

Solids

The mountains flow, the solids seem,
Poet. 174.

Solis

Væ solis! I found this,
Frag. Poet. IV. 7.

Solitary

Solitary fancies go   Merlin. 106.

And through my rock-like, solitary wont
Musketaquid. 9.

However long thou walkest solitary,
Rome. 26.

Solitude

Nor yet unsuited to that solitude:
Adirondacs. 251.

Solitude in solitudes:
Daemonic Love. 95.

Then in the uncouth solitude unlock
Letter. 19.

Beset his solitude.   Manners. 8.

In city or in solitude,   May-Day. 463.

Sweet twilight walks and midnight
solitude   Summons. 7.

Whoso walks in solitude
Woodnotes. II. 57.

Solitudes

Ask votes of thrushes in the solitudes.
Channing Ode. 74

Solitude in solitudes:
Daemonic Love. 95.

Over these colored solitudes.
Frag. Nat. XXVI. 20.

Thou, in sunny solitudes,
Humble-Bee. 28.

From the fragrant solitudes;—
Rhea. 6.

In May, when sea-winds pierced our
solitudes,   Rhodora. 1.

But in these sunny solitudes
Walden. 19.

Solomon

Living gem of Solomon;
Song of Seyd. 10.

Solve

And solve and oft resolve the whole.
Alphonso. 46.

To sun the dark and solve the curse,
Beauty. 19.

Solved

With a look that solved the sphere,
Uriel. 17.

Solving

My servant Death, with solving rite,
Threnody. 236.

Sombre

Thy sombre head with rosy hues
Monadnoc Afar. 3.

Some

Food   indigestible":—then   murmured
some,   Adirondacs. 186.

Some mystic hint accosts the vigilant,
Adirondacs. 203.

That not academicians, but some lout,
Adirondacs. 278.

Some to see, some to be guessed,
Experience. 12.

Some had heard their fair report,
Forerunners. 21.

Feigned to speak to some one else.
Frag. Poet. IV. 18.

And some attain his voice to hear,
Harp. 57.

His vice some elder virtue's token,
Initial Love. 92.

Of Eden's bower some dream-like trace
May-Day. 93.

As o'er some bolder height they speed,—
Monadnoc. 397.

Some tears escaped, but his philosophy
Philosopher. 8.

Some random word they say
Poet. 78.

Some of your hurts you have cured,
Quat. Borrowing. 1

I make some coast alluring, some lone
isle,   Seashore. 48.

To some tune by fairies played;—
Threnody. 77.

Some went and came about the dead;
Threnody. 152.

And some in books of solace read;
Threnody. 153.

Some to their friends the tidings say;
Threnody. 154.

Some went to write, some went to pray;
Threnody. 155.

And, echoed in some frosty wold,
Titmouse. 97.

Is some product and repeater,—
Visit. 7.

Sure some god his eye enchants:
Woodnotes. I. 11.

Some figure of noble guise,—
World-Soul. 26.

Something

A door to something grander,—
Frag. Nat. XII. 3.

There alway, alway something sings.
Music. 12, 18.

Something of pity for the puny clay,
River. 34.

Sometimes

Sometimes their wits at sally and retort,
Adirondacs. 127.

And dips sometimes as low as to her
eyes.   Daemonic Love. 38.

Sometimes the airy synod bends,
Daemonic Love. 43.

Sometimes their strong speed they slack-
en,   Forerunners. 27.

And dips sometimes as low as to her
eyes.   Frag. Life. XVI. 4.

Yes, sometimes to the sorrow-stricken
Frag. Life. XXVI. 1.

Failing sometimes of his own,
Initial Love. 94.

And sometimes mankind I appalled
Solution. 22.

Somewhat

Somewhat not to be possessed,
Ode to Beauty. 70.
Somewhat not to be caressed,
Ode to Beauty. 71.
And somewhat of majestic sympathy,
River. 33.

Son

'I give my darling son, Thou shalt not
preach';— Adakryn. 2.
If thou go as thy father's son,
Frag. Life. XXVII. 9.
Venus, when her son was lost,
Initial Love. 1.
And thou, Cyndyllan's son! beware
Merlin's Song. 25.
No sire survive, no son succeed!
Monadnoc. 124.
I will give my son to eat Monadnoc. 303.
They know me as their son, for side by
side, River. 39.
Never, son of eastern morning,
Saadi. 92.
The riches of sweet Mary's Son,
Threnody. 222.
Hapless sire to hapless son,—
Voluntaries. 10.
And to her son will treasures more
Walk. 5.
Of Genius sire and son.
World-Soul. 84.

Song

See Earth-song; Under-song.
Which I gather in a song. Apology. 20.
But the sweet affluence of love and song,
Blight. 42.
Song breathed from all the forest,
Cosmos. 9.
Also (from the song the wrath
Daemonic Love. 62.
He sings the song, but it cheers not now,
Each. 16.
He heard their medicinal song,
Frag. Poet. V. 19.
A better voice peals through my song.
Frag. Poet. XXX. 2.
All day his song is heard;
Frag. Poet. XXXIII. 2.
If I could put my woods in song
Garden. 1.
Ring with the song of the Fates;
Garden. 34.
Chief of song where poets feast
Harp. 38.
Rung loud and bold the song.
Harp. 48.
Harp of the wind, or song of bird,
May-Day. 10.
With song and hue and star and state,
May-Day. 268.
Your song, your forms, your rhythmic
flight, May-Day. 398.
And finishes the song. Merlin. 122.
Of Merlin wise I learned a song,—
Merlin's Song. 1.
Whose throbs are love, whose thrills are
song. Monadnoc. 170.
Peals out a cheerful song. Music. 6.
Nor in the song of woman heard,
Music. 10.

Nor wit, nor eloquence,—no, nor even the
song Naples. 19.
A Brother of the world, his song
Poet. 27.
All the brags of plume and song;
Saadi. 150.
On spawning slime my song prevails,
Solution. 5.
I am dumb in the pealing song,
Song of Nature. 6.
Let war and trade and creeds and song
Song of Nature. 77.
Of prayer and song that were my dear
delight, Summons. 5.
Of my bird's song: 'Live out of doors
Titmouse. 67.
And the sky doats on cheerful song.
Titmouse. 88.
They lose their grief who hear his song,
Two Rivers. 15.
Was the wailing song he breathed,
Voluntaries. 11.
Will song dissuade the thirsty spear?
Voluntaries. 18.
Blows the sweet breath of song,
Waldeinsamkeit. 38.
To the song of its waterfall tones,
Woodnotes. I. 2.
Song wakes in my pinnacles
Woodnotes. II. 91.
If thou wouldst know the mystic song
Woodnotes. II. 98.
'Come learn with me the fatal song
Woodnotes. II. 156.
Song, picture, form, space, thought and
character Xenophanes. 7.

Song's

Hid in song's sweet influence.
Merlin. 42.

Songs

Sweet songs of liberty. Concord Ode. 32.
I cannot hear your songs, O birds,
Cosmos. 23.
Singing by the oriole songs,
May-Day. 420.
Thy birds, thy songs, thy brooks, thy
gales, May-Day. 436.
Songs can the tempest still, Merlin. 55.
Are pleasant songs to me. Sphinx. 68.
I see the wreath, I hear the songs
Voluntaries. 108.

Sons

So fast will Nature acclimate her sons,
Adirondacs. 54.
And how we should come hither with our
sons, Adirondacs. 163.
Of traders, led by corporate sons of
trade, Adirondacs. 282.
Whether thy sons or strangers eat the
fruit: Adirondacs. 300.
Almost a smile to steal to cheer her sons,
Adirondacs. 342.
Which calls the sons of Time. Bell. 4.
When, like our sires, our sons are gone.
C. Hymn. 12.
And the sons of intellect,
Daemonic Love. 99.
Because of the sons of wine;
Frag. Life. X. 6.
God hath a select family of sons
Good Cheer. 3.

Sons —*Continued*
There is in all the sons of men
Hymn. 1.
So did our sons; Heaven met them as
they fell. Inscription. 2.
Whose shining sons, too great for fame,
Nun. 45.
On sons of time and chance, Poet. 244.
To sons of contradiction. Saadi. 91.
Building for their sons the State,
Voluntaries. 25.

Soon (Partial list.)
And soon thy music, sad death-bell,
Bell. 13.
Too soon those spires are lost,
*Farewell. 5.
Too soon by ocean tost *Farewell. 7.
And soon my cone will spin.
Monadnoc. 244.
The constellation glittered soon,—
Poet. 230.
And soon may give my dust River. 42.
'T will soon be dark; To J. W. 21.

Soonest
The fault that boys and nations soonest
mend. To-Day. 18.

Sooth
In sooth, red flannel is a saucy test
Adirondacs. 97.
Sad, in sooth, it were to ours,
Ellen South. 22.
A window rose, and, to say sooth,
Harp. 109.

Soothe
And my kindred come to soothe me.
Hermione. 49.
Deeply soothe his anxious ear.
Initial Love. 73.
Soothe pain, and age, and love's distress,
May-Day. 439.
Or prayers the stony Parcæ soothe,
Nemesis. 10.

Soothed
Soothed by the voice of waters,
Waterfall. 3.

Soothes
Thee, dear friend, a brother soothes,
Rhea. 1.

Soothfast
Be what they soothfast appear,
May-Day. 360.
Forever to myself soothfast;
Sursum Corda. 8.

Soothing
The soothing lapse of morn to mirk,
Celestial Love. 105.
Soothing with thy summer horn
Frag. Nat. XXII. 3.
Come, lay thee in my soothing shade,
Woodnotes. II. 219.

Soothsayer
Where Hope, the soothsayer, reads our
lot, Ellen. 6.

Sophist
At the sophist schools and the learned
clan; Good-Bye. 28.

Sorceries
I too have arts and sorceries;
Seashore. 41.

Sordid
Now in sordid weeds they sleep,
Monadnoc. 171.
And sore bested with woes. Riches. 10.

Sorrow
Can drain its wealth of hope and sorrow;
Aeolian Harp. 15.
With sorrow such as mine, Dirge. 46.
Shall his own sorrow seem impertinent,
Frag. Life. XXVI. 2.
His sorrow heard, Hermione. 5.
'Sorrow, sorrow!' the angels cried,
Poet. 217.
Waters with tears of ancient sorrow
Threnody. 286.

Sorrow's
Hunted by Sorrow's grisly train
In Memoriam. 74.

Sorrows
Of sorrows new and old!
Voluntaries. 78.

Sorrow-stricken
Yes, sometimes to the sorrow-stricken
Frag. Life. XXVI. 1.

Sort
In like sort his love doth fall.
Daemonic Love. 96.

Sorts
But all sorts of things and weather
Fable. 6.

Sought
Long sought, not found.
Adirondacs. 133.
Not less the ambitious botanist sought
plants, Adirondacs. 141.
Were sought and found, amid the hue and
cry Adirondacs. 192.
Who sought thee once shall seek again.
Frag. Life. XXII. 4.
Firm-braced I sought my ancient woods,
May-Day. 39.
Many hamlets sought I then,
Monadnoc. 127.
In unploughed Maine he sought the lum-
berers' gang Woodnotes. I. 62.

Soul
See World-soul.
So like the soul of me, what if 't were me?
Adirondacs. 214.
Shall the well-born soul accept.
Celestial Love. 70.
Stands to each human soul its own,
Daemonic Love. 27.
Up which the incarnate soul must climb,
Dirge. 2.
While the soul it doth surcharge,
Etienne. 18.
And he the bard, a crystal soul
Frag. Poet. I. 56.
Of a true monarch's soul. Beauty and
strength, Good Cheer. 8.
How Nature to the soul is moored,
Harp. 104.
That sounded in the soul before,
Hymn. 18.
Surprise the exulting soul. Hymn. 24.
And the firm soul does the pale train
defy I Bear. 11.
To the Soul that maketh all:
Informing Spirit. 2.

And his soul will melt in prayer,
Initial Love. 110.
The freed soul its Creator found?
In Memoriam. 112.
To parting soul bring grandeur near.
May-Day. 456.
Hath such a soul, such divine influence,
Naples. 21.
Is it that my opulent soul
Ode to Beauty. 46.
I love a prophet of the soul;
Problem. 2.
To the vast soul that o'er him planned;
Problem. 48.
Her strength and soul has laughing
France Quat. Leasts. 3.
Form the soul had ever dressed,
Rhea. 18.
Besides, you need not be alone; the soul
Rome. 2.
Her soul is frank as the ocean wind,
Security. 7.
Sighed his soul away. September. 4.
Of heart and soul, of strength and
pleasure, Solution. 36.
The Swede Emanuel leads the soul.
Solution. 46.
Whose soul sees the perfect, Sphinx. 79.
Ascendant in the private soul,
Threnody. 252.
For well the soul, if stout within,
Titmouse. 75.
Which the brooding soul surveys,
Uriel. 2.
Procession of a soul in matter, Uriel. 51.
O, well for the fortunate soul
Voluntaries. 75.
At the tread of the jubilant soul.
Waterfall. 20.
To every soul resounding clear
Woodnotes. II. 146.
And the wise soul expels disease.
Woodnotes. II. 191.

Souled
See Ensouled.

Soul's
The soul's pilgrimage and flight;
May-Day. 462.
Soul's desire is means enow, Poet. 250.
Fair the soul's recess and shrine,
Threnody. 255.

Souls
Checked in these souls the turbulent hey-
day Adirondacs. 189.
One through separated souls;
Celestial Love. 47.
Of tendency distribute souls.
Celestial Love. 82.
And the souls of ample fate,
Daemonic Love. 100.
And bleaching all souls like the sun.
Frag. Life. XXVIII. 4.
I grieve that better souls than mine
Frag. Poet. VII. 1.
The wheat thou strew'st be souls.
Frag. Poet. VI. 12.
And Genius unspheres all souls that abide.
Frag. Poet. XXI. 2.
Souls above doubt, Give. 20.

But for the love of happy souls
House. 23.
The wheat thou strew'st be souls.
I Intellect. 4.
To the souls that never fell,
Nature. I. 17.
Leads all souls to the Good.
Park. 16.
And sternly calls to being souls
Quat. Fate. 3.
From the shore of souls arrived,
Song of Seyd. 11.
The souls that walk in pain.
Waldeinsamkeit. 24.

Sound
Sound, ruddy men, frolic and innocent,
Adirondacs. 87.
Ye shall not fail for sound advice.
Alphonso. 48.
Trump of their rescue, sound!
Boston Hymn. 68.
All echoes hearkened for their sound,—
Dirge. 35.
Hark to the winning sound!
Ellen South. 13.
It is a sound, it is a token May-Day. 32.
To sound the science of the sky,
Monadnoc. 103.
But knows the sun-creating sound,
Monadnoc. 254.
South from Saint Lawrence to the Sound,
Monadnoc. 281.
Color and sound, music to eye and ear,
October. 10.
It hath a sound more eloquent than
speech. River. 27.
The near bystander caught no sound,—
Solution. 53.
"Sea, earth, air, sound, silence,
Sphinx. 33.
At the sound of her accents Sphinx. 59.
Five lines lasted sound and true;
Test. 4.
Outvalued every pulsing sound
Threnody. 13.
Out of sound heart and merry throat,
Titmouse. 28.
Of sound and echo, man and maid,
Woodnotes. II. 161.
And pulse, and sound, and light was none;
Woodnotes. II. 267.
One sound to pine-groves and to water-
falls, Xenophanes. 3.

Sounded
That sounded in the soul before,
Hymn. 18.
Sounded like a tempest strong
Poet. 28.

Soundeth
Soundeth the prophetic wind,
Woodnotes. II. 93.

Sounding
The wrinkled shopman to my sounding
woods, Channing Ode. 72.
With sounding steps the poet came;
Poet. 2.

Soundings
Off soundings, seamen do not suffer cold;
Adirondacs. 56

Sounds
How sweet the west wind sounds in my
own trees!   Hamatreya. 6.
It sounds from all things old,   Music. 3.
It sounds from all things young,
Music. 4.
Showed me the lore of colors and of
sounds,   Musketaquid. 60.
All of them utter sounds of 'monishment
River. 29.

Sour
Hold their sour conversation in the sky:—
River. 17.
Not vain, sour, nor frivolous;
Woodnotes. II. 67.

Source
Sole source of light and hope assured,
Hymn. 25.
Knowledge which its source not knows,
Insight. 2.

Sourly
O richest fortune sourly crossed!
Threnody. 174.

South
North from Camp Maple, south to Osprey
Bay,   Adirondacs. 109.
When the South Sea calls.   Bacchus. 30.
And honor, O South! for his shame;
Boston Hymn. 74.
The northland from the south?
Channing Ode. 39.
The wizard South blew down the glen,
Frag. Nat. III. 12.
Far-travelled in the south plantations;
Frag. Nat. XXIII. 8.
The land is well,—lies fairly to the south.
Hamatreya. 22.
When the south wind, in May days,
Humble-Bee. 20.
Lo! the south answers to the north;
Monadnoc. 15.
South from Saint Lawrence to the Sound,
Monadnoc. 281.
Oh, south winds have long memories,
September. 11.
Than the South more fierce and hot;
Test. 6.
East, west, north, south, are his domain.
Titmouse. 8.
Or south, it still is clear;
Woodnotes. I. 101.

South Cove
From South Cove and City Wharf.
Monadnoc. 314.

Southern
The southern crocodile would grieve.
Channing Ode. 31.
Migrate from the Southern Sea;
May-Day. 86.
As Southern wrath to Northern right
May-Day. 138.

Southing
To see the southing of the sun?
May-Day. 176.

South Sea
When the South Sea calls.   Bacchus. 30.

South-wind
When the wing of the south-wind whipt
the lake   Frag. Poet. I. 36.
Southwind is my next of blood;
Hermione. 50.

Half the tell-tale South-wind said,—
September. 14.
The South-wind brings   Threnody. 1.
Returned this day, the South-wind
searches,   Threnody. 24.

South-wind's
His music was the south-wind's sigh,
Frag. Poet. I. 11.

South-winds
The south-winds are quick-witted,
April. 17.

Sovereign
There is no king nor sovereign state
Astraea. 3.
Hide in thy skies, O sovereign lamp!
Monadnoc. 122.

Sovereignly
For he is sovereignly allied,—
Initial Love. 122.

Sovran
The wood was sovran with centennial
trees,—   Adirondacs. 37.
He takes a sovran privilege
Initial Love. 118.

Sow
Hers to sow the seed of bread,
May-Day. 146.
And what if Trade sow cities
World-Soul. 65.

Sowed
The wind and the birds which sowed it;
Garden. 18.
He sowed the sun and moon for seeds.
Poet. 32.

Sower
The sower scatters broad his seed,
Frag. Poet. VI. 11.
The sower scatters broad his seed;
I Intellect. 3.

Sower's
Like sower's seeds into his brain,
Frag. Poet. V. 35.

Sowers
The sowers made haste to depart,—
Garden. 17.

Sowing
See Broad-sowing.

Sown
See Air-sown; Self-sown; Wheat-
sown.
The harvests sown to-day   Walden. 14.

Space
Even at its greatest space is a defeat,
Blight. 54.
Gauge of more and less through space,
II Compensation. 7.
In the realms and corners of space
Cosmos. 14.
With me who walked through space and
time   Dirge. 4.
Leaving on space no shade, no scars,
Frag. Nat. VIII. 7.
Who athwart space redresses
Merlin. 119.
Space grants beyond his fated road
Merops. 9.
Tower of observance searching space;
Monadnoc. 83.
His day's ride is a furlong space,
Monadnoc. 322.

Pass with the comet into space
Nun. 39.
Starry space and lily-bell
Ode to Beauty. 78.
The pits of air, the gulf of space,
Song of Nature. 2.
Space is ample, east and west,
Unity. 1.
In equal strength through space abide;
Voluntaries. 116.
As sunbeams stream through liberal
space Woodnotes. II. 1.
Of rounded worlds, of space and time,
Woodnotes. II. 108.
No more the fool of space and time,
Woodnotes. II. 138.
Time-and-space-conquering steam,—
World-Soul. 14.
Song, picture, form, space, thought and
character Xenophanes. 7.

Spacious
That we should build, hard-by, a spacious
lodge Adirondacs. 162.
Nor spacious court, nor monarch's hall,
May-Day. 222.
Counted on the spacious dial
May-Day. 376.
And I affirm, the spacious North
Titmouse. 58.

Spade
My garden spade can heal. A woodland
walk, Musketaquid. 72.

Spain
Hear the sentiment of Spain.
Alphonso. 50.

Spake
As if one spake to another, Garden. 30.
Yet spake yon purple mountain,
Park. 13.

Span
Heaven's numerous hierarchy span
Threnody. 185.
The storm-wind wove, the torrent span,
Wealth. 38.

Spangled
What the spangled meadow saith
Harp. 32.

Spanish
Of Nature in thy Spanish isle
In Memoriam. 106.

Spans
The spans of life away. Walden. 44.

Spar
Though with boom and spar
Frag. Nat. XV. 2.
He is the sparkle of the spar;
Woodnotes. II. 314.

Spare
We cannot spare variety. Alphonso. 58.
Bid Time and Nature gently spare
C. Hymn. 15.
The frost to spare, what scents so well.
Frag. Nat. II. 31.
Is he hapless who can spare Goethe. 7.
Who has little, to him who has less, can
spare, Merlin's Song. 24.
I cannot spare water or wine,
Mithridates. 1.
I can spare the college bell,
Monadnoc. 179.

Spare the clergy and libraries,
Monadnoc. 181.
But, critic, spare thy vanity, Saadi. 45.
He who has a thousand friends has not a
friend to spare, Taleb. 1.

Spared
See Unspared.
She spared no speech to-day:
Frag. Nat. III. 9.

Spark
See Sun-spark.
Or compensatory spark,
Compensation. 13.
And worship that world-warming spark
Etienne. 15.
In the pit of his eye's a spark
Initial Love. 21.
In the sky no spark; May-Day. 38.
In heaven no star, on earth no spark,—
Saadi. 132.
The third adds heat's indulgent spark;
Woodnotes. II. 291.

Sparkle
'T is a sparkle passing
Daemonic Love. 78.
And know the sparkle of its ore,
Dull. 20.
Tossing one sparkle to the eyes:
Peter. 38.
How all things sparkle, Poet. 105.
He is the sparkle of the spar;
Woodnotes. II. 314.

Sparkling
The morn and sparkling dew, a snare?
May-Day. 430.
Are locked in sparkling stone. Rubies. 8.

Sparks
Sparks of the supersolar blaze.
Merlin. 15.
And by great sparks Promethean warmed,
Poet. 186.

Sparrow
The sparrow meek, phophetic-eyed,
May-Day. 170.
There's not a sparrow or a wren,
Threnody. 110.

Sparrow's
I thought the sparrow's note from heaven,
Each. 13.

Sparrows
Dusky sparrows in a crowd,
May-Day. 387.
Sparrows far off, and nearer, April's bird,
Musketaquid. 15.
It seemed as if the sparrows taught him;
Woodnotes. I. 47.

Spars
Quarry of spars in mountain pores;
Monadnoc. 79.

Sparta's
Sparta's stoutness, Bethlehem's heart,
Monadnoc. 299.

Spasm
A spasm throbbing through the pedestals
Adirondacs. 262.

Spasms
And yet between the spasms of pain
In Memoriam. 103.
With spasms of terror for balm of hope.
Solution. 24.

Spawneth
She spawneth men as mallows fresh,
                    Nature. II. 13.
Spawning
On spawning slime my song prevails,
                    Solution. 5.
Speak
And speak the speech of innocence,
                    Celestial Love. 128.
Nor speak with double tongue.
                    Concord Ode. 20.
The other portion language cannot speak.
                    Frag. Life. XVIII. 8.
Feigned to speak to some one else.
                    Frag. Poet. IV. 18.
Nor ran to speak till she him told;
                    Frag. Poet. V. 25.
Speak it not, or speak it low;
                    Freedom. 6.
Speak what I cannot declare,
                    Garden. 51.
To speak the truth—for truth to strive.
                    Hymn. 8.
They seek a friend to speak the word
                    Hymn. 13.
To speak the plain reproof of sin
                    Hymn. 17.
So shall he speak to us the word
                    Hymn. 27.
And to speak my thought if none forbids
                    May-Day. 326.
The bosom thought which thou must
speak;   Nemesis. 2.
Speak through his lips thy pure com-
mands,   Robbins Hymn. 27.
And though he speak in midnight dark,—
                    Saadi. 131.
Bards to speak what nations need;
                    Solution. 26.
And speak the lovely caravan.
                    Threnody. 73.
Speak it firmly, these are gods,
                    Voluntaries. 121.
'Speak not thy speech my boughs among:
                    Woodnotes. II. 134.
My branches speak Italian,
                    Woodnotes II. 150.
Speaketh
The voice that speaketh clear.
                    World-Soul. 20.
Speaking
    See Truth-speaking.
The Muse the truth uncolored speaking)
                    Daemonic Love. 64.
Speaking by the tongues of flowers,
                    May-Day. 418.
By the ten-tongued laurel speaking,
                    May-Day. 419.
Speaks
Speaks not of self that mystic tone,
                    Harp. 67.
And speaks all languages the rose,
                    May-Day. 74.
And speaks all languages the rose;
                    Nature. Mot. 4.
Spear
Poises Arcturus aloft morning and even-
ing his spear.   Shah.-Hafiz. 2.
Will song dissuade the thirsty spear?
                    Voluntaries. 18.
Special
For the Muse gave special charge
                    Poet. 39.

Takes hearts like thine in special charge,
                    Titmouse. 86.
With the next a special nature;
                    Woodnotes. II. 290.
Specious
The specious panorama of a year
                    Xenophanes. 14.
Spectral
Succession swift and spectral Wrong,
                    Experience. 8.
To me that spectral nook appeared
                    Peter. 25.
Specular
Who daily climb my specular head.
                    Monadnoc. 310.
Sped
He had so sped his wise affairs   Guy. 31.
And to his folk his message sped.
                    Saadi. 79.
Sped, when I passed his sylvan fort,
                    Titmouse. 35.
Speech
Louder than with speech they pray,—
                    Astraea. 17.
For you can teach the lightning speech,
                    Boston. 110.
And speak the speech of innocence,
                    Celestial Love. 128.
In man or maid, that thou from speech
refrained,   Forbearance. 6.
She spared no speech to-day:
                    Frag. Nat. III. 9.
And cure all ill, is cordial speech:
                    Merlin's Song. 36.
Ye taught my lips a single speech,
                    Merops. 7.
Yet, will you learn our ancient speech,
                    Monadnoc. 173.
No human speech so beautiful   Nun. 13.
It hath a sound more eloquent than
speech.   River. 27.
Suns rise and set in Saadi's speech!'
                    Saadi. 140.
Of ritual, bible, or of speech;
                    Threnody. 198.
'Speak not thy speech my boughs among:
                    Woodnotes II. 134.
Mountain speech to Highlanders,
                    Woodnotes II. 152.
Speechless
But speechless to the master's mind?
                    Monadnoc. 91.
Speed
Now speed the gay celerities of art,
                    Adirondacs. 320.
But no speed of mine avails
                    Forerunners. 7.
Sometimes their strong speed they
slacken,   Forerunners. 27.
Go, speed the stars of Thought
                    Frag. Poet. V. 9.
To speed his sails, to dry his hay;
                    Guy. 38.
Go, speed the stars of Thought
                    I Intellect. 1.
Every joy and virtue speed,
                    May-Day. 334.
As o'er some bolder height they speed,—
                    Monadnoc. 397.
Power and speed be hands and feet.
                    Quat. Power. 4.
Forth speed the strong pulses
                    Sphinx. 103.
Abandon all those toys with speed to
obey   Summons. 23.

God speed the mark!   To J.W. 23.
Speed nimbler messages,
                    Voluntaries. 68.
We must not halt while fiercely speed
                    Walden. 43.

Speeding
Speeding, the myriad-handed, his wild
    work   Snow-Storm. 15.
Or the speeding change of water,
                    Uriel. 52.
Speeding Saturn cannot halt;   Visit. 27.
He shall meet the speeding year,
                    Woodnotes. II. 79.

Speeds
Who speeds to the woodland walks?
                    Woodnotes. I. 3.

Spell
The bird-language rightly spell,
                    Bacchus. 24.
Untold, unknown, and I could surely
    spell   Blight. 10.
And ever the spell of beauty came
                    Frag. Poet. I. 13.
He will spell in the sculpture, 'Stay.'
                    Garden. 64.
Beguile me with the wonted spell.
                    May-Day. 352.
A spell is laid on sod and stone,
                    Unity. 7.
Which we could never spell.
                    World-Soul. 48.

Spelling
Spelling with guided tongue man's mes-
    sages   Adirondacs. 269.

Spells
Scatters on every eye dust of his spells,
                    Enchanter. 3.
But when she spread her dearest spells,
                    Frag. Poet. IV. 17.
Knows of Holy Book the spells,
                    Harp. 21.
By Fancy, ghastly spells undid.
                    May-Day. 46.
I know what spells are laid. Leave me to
    deal   Seashore. 43.
And with a million spells enchants
                    Waldeinsamkeit. 23.
Ponder my spells;   Woodnotes. II. 90.
The world is the ring of his spells,
                    Woodnotes. II. 285.

Spend
When I would spend a lonely day,
                    Frag. Poet. XXV. 3.
I do not count the hours I spend
                    Waldeinsamkeit. 1.

Spendeth
Waneth fast and spendeth all.
                    Woodnotes. II. 25.

Spending
I hear the spending of the stream
                    Two Rivers. 10.

Spends
You shall not love me for what daily
    spends;   Frag. Life. XV. 1.
Sugar spends to fatten slaves,
                    Heroism. 2.

Spent
    See Unspent.
And out of spent and aged things
                    Song of Nature. 27.

Not of spent deeds, but of doing.
                    Threnody. 281.

Sphere
    See Hemisphere.
So shall ye have a man of the sphere
                    Alphonso. 81.
But Justice, journeying in the sphere,
                    Astraea. 47.
From centred and from errant sphere.
                    Beauty. 14.
Be the axis of the sphere:
                    Celestial Love. 22.
Out of that sphere,   Celestial Love. 61.
Scan the profile of the sphere;
                    Circles. 4.
To men, the path to the Dæmon sphere;
                    Daemonic Love. 40.
And a sphere.   Fable. 9.
As June herself around the sphere.
                    Frag. Life. XIII. 2.
Replunged again into that upper sphere
                    Frag. Life. XVI. 8.
Your eyelids to the sphere:
                    Frag. Life. XXXV. 4.
And walk on earth as the sun walks in the
    sphere.   Frag. Nat. V. 12.
Sailing falsely in the sphere,
                    Frag. Poet. VII. 17.
And go find thee in the sphere.
                    From Hafiz. 16.
Culminating in her sphere.
                    Hermione. 11.
I am owner of the sphere,
                    Informing Spirit. 5.
And chance-dropped hints from Nature's
    sphere   Initial Love. 72.
Such tidings of the starry sphere
                    May-Day. 13.
All things return, both sphere and mote,
                    May-Day. 179.
Farm-furrowed, town-incrusted sphere,
                    Monadnoc. 332.
By one thought to one same sphere;
                    Poet. 268.
For out of Thought's interior sphere
                    Problem. 39.
And each with novel life his sphere
                    Promise. 9.
Grandeur of the perfect sphere
                    Prudence. 5.
Cold shuddered the sphere:—
                    Sphinx. 60.
With a look that solved the sphere,
                    Uriel. 17.
Chanted when the sphere was young.
                    Woodnotes II. 99.

Sphered
Sphered and concentric with the whole.
                    Frag. Poet. I. 57.

Spheres
    See Unspheres.
The gods upon their spheres.
                    Frag. Life. IV. 4.
Was the symphony of spheres,
                    Frag. Poet. IV. 23.
And Dante searched the triple spheres,
                    Solution. 28.
Lost in whirling spheres I rove,
                    Song of Seyd. 7.
Wise harbinger of spheres and tides,
                    Woodnotes. I. 33.

Spheres—*Continued*
All spheres, all stones, his helpers be;
Woodnotes II. 78.

Sphinx
As if one riddle of the Sphinx were
guessed. Adirondacs. 343.
The Sphinx is drowsy, Sphinx. 1.
"Say on, sweet Sphinx! thy dirges
Sphinx. 67.
"Dull Sphinx, Jove keep thy five wits;
Sphinx. 105.
Rue, myrrh and cummin for the Sphinx,
Sphinx. 107.
The old Sphinx bit her thick lip,—
Sphinx. 109.
Uprose the merry Sphinx, Sphinx. 121.

Spice
With the selfsame spice
Frag. Nat. II. 26.
Drugged with spice from climates warm,
Hermione. 52.

Spices
Spices in the plants that run
Frag. Nat. II. 19.
Drugging herbs with Syrian spices,
May-Day. 250.

Spicier
Fountain-drop of spicier worth
Monadnoc. 293.

Spicy
To share the sunshine that so spicy is.
Frag. Nat. XXXIII. 3.

Spider
See Devil-spider.

Spider's
The swinging spider's silver line,
Ode to Beauty. 27.

Spied
O happy port that spied the sail
Boston. 88.

Spies
Spies oversea the fires of the mountain;
Enchanter. 9.

Spike
Which for a spike of tender green
May-Day. 233.

Spilled
The wine-cup shakes, the wine is spilled.
Frag. Poet. XVI. 2.

Spilling
Spilling over mountain chains,
May-Day. 242.

Spin
To spin my sand-heap into twine.
Frag. Poet. XXXIV. 2.
There doth digest, and work, and spin,
Initial Love. 46.
Sung by the Sisters as they spin;
Merlin. 125.
As you spin a cherry. Mithridates. 24.
And soon my cone will spin.
Monadnoc. 244.
Spin the ball! I reel, I burn,
Song of Seyd. 1.

Spinet's
For flute or spinet's dancing chips;
Aeolian Harp. 5.

Spinners
And the poor spinners weave their webs
thereon Frag. Nat. XXXIII. 2.

Spire
Each street and spire and roof, incon-
tinent. Letter. 6.
Giddy with day, to the topmost spire,
May-Day. 232.

Spired
She spired into a yellow flame;
Sphinx. 125.

Spires
Farewell, ye lofty spires *Farewell. 1.
Too soon those spires are lost,
*Farewell. 5.
Mounts through all the spires of form.
May-Day. 82.
Mounts through all the spires of form.
Nature. Mot. 6.

Spirit
Spirit, that made those heroes dare
C. Hymn. 13.
Their near camp my spirit knows
Forerunners. 33.
But the Spirit said, 'Not so;
Freedom. 5.
Be of good cheer, brave spirit; steadfastly
Good Cheer. 1.
A love that in the spirit dwells,
Hymn. 2.
A greater spirit bids thee forth
Monadnoc. 17.
Spirit that lurks each form within
Nature. Mot. 13.
Beckons to spirit of its kin;
Nature. Mot. 14.
The moon comes back,—the Spirit not.
Poet. 280.
Put the Spirit in the wrong; Poet. 292.
Man's spirit must dive; Sphinx. 82.
I am thy spirit, yoke-fellow;
Sphinx. 111.
Seek not the spirit, if it hide
Sursum Corda. 1.
Then the Spirit strikes the hour:
Threnody. 235.
Where his clear spirit leads him, there's
his road Woodnotes. I. 94.

Spirits
Spirits of a higher strain
Frag. Life. XXII. 3.
Unploughed, which finer spirits pile,
Monadnoc. 43.
That field by spirits bad and good,
Peter. 5.

Spirit-touch
And tender to the spirit-touch Culture. 7.

Spiritual
To spiritual lessons pointed home,
Adirondacs. 200.
The spiritual stars rise Adirondacs. 222.
Who are thy spiritual kindred, and each
one Good Cheer. 5.

Spirit-worlds
In spirit-worlds he trod alone,
Solution. 51.

Spite
In spite of Virtue and the Muse,
Nemesis. 13.

Spiteful
Whom earlier we had chid with spiteful
names. Adirondacs. 170.

Spleen
Whom the city's poisoning spleen
Woodnotes II. 35.

Splendid
If a new Muse draw me with splendid
ray, Day's Ration. 15.
Forgotten amid splendid tombs,
Nun. 27.

Splendor
Make up thy splendor, matchless day?
Frag. Nat. XI. 2.
In which its proper splendor shines;
Frag. Poet. XXIX. 2.
Making the splendor of the air,
May-Day. 429.
And unimagined splendor waits his steps.
October. 5.
In her lap to pour all splendor;
Rhea. 50.

Split
And split to flakes the crystal ledges.
Frag. Nat. XXX. 2.

Spoil
The falling rain will spoil no holiday.
Adirondacs. 69.
Wherein was dropped the mortal spoil.
Harp. 127.

Spoils
And in the midst of spoils and slaves, we thieves Blight. 46.
The school decays, the learning spoils
Frag. Life. X. 5.
Spoils of a front none need restore,
Monadnoc. 370.

Spoke
Others applauded him who spoke the truth. Adirondacs. 187.
Judge with what sweet surprises Nature spoke Adirondacs. 198.
He spoke, and words more soft than rain
Character. 7.
Ah! late I spoke to silent throngs,
I Compensation. 7.
As I spoke, beneath my feet Each. 40.
The fungus and the bulrush spoke,
Frag. Nat. III. 10.
It spoke in Tullius Cicero,
Frag. Poet. IV. 30.
His instant thought a poet spoke,
Frag. Poet. XXXII. 1.
These syllables that Nature spoke,
Harp. 95.
Till a clear voice spoke,— *Lines. 27.
As if the conscience of the country spoke.
Phi. 12.
Thus to himself the poet spoke,
Poet. 141.
They spoke not, for their earnest sense
Poet. 199.
"Out spoke the great mother,
Sphinx. 57.
Spoke the universal dame; Sphinx. 130.
Whereof it spoke were toys
Threnody. 41.
As Uriel spoke with piercing eye,
Uriel. 25.

Spoken
See Evil—spoken
And I to whom your light has spoken,
Poet. 237.
The word unto the phophet spoken
Problem. 55.

Sponge
of rushes, pads and sponge,
Adirondacs. 24.
Hypnum and hydnum, mushroom, sponge
and moss, Adirondacs. 144.

Sport
Or accuse the god of sport?
Initial Love. 80.
Voice of sport, or rush of wings,
May-Day. 31.

King of sport that never shames,
Merlin. 40.
And be the sport of Fate forever.
Ode to Beauty. 97.
In ocean sport the scaly herds,
Saadi. 3.

Sportive
The sportive sun, the gibbous moon,
Song of Nature. 3.

Spot
Half the sun's disk with a spot;
Alphonso. 10.
A spot that is sacred to thought and God. Good-Bye. 22.
Snow-ridges masked each darling spot;
May-Day. 42.
Draws to the spot the solar ray,
May-Day. 116.
To draw all fancies to this spot.
Monadnoc Afar. 8.
Its spot of purple, and its streak of
brown, Naples. 8.
Each spot where tulips prank their state
Omar. 1.
Thrice the spot is blest; Walden. 2.
Tints that spot the violet's petal,
Woodnotes. I. 21.

Spotless
The riches of a spotless memory,
Good Cheer. 9.

Spots
The turtle brave in his golden spots;
May-Day. 238.

Spousals
The spousals of the new-born year.
May-Day. 270

Spouting
Let spouting fountains cool the air,
Art. 7.
With spouting streams and waves of light
Frag. Nat. XXVI. 24.

Sprang
Where from a hundred lakes young
rivers sprang; Woodnotes. I. 63.
Whence the fair flock of Nature sprang.
Woodnotes. II. 125.

Spray
The perfumed berry on the spray
May-Day. 77.
Head downward, clinging to the spray.
Titmouse. 42.

Spread
See Outspread; Overspread; Under-spread.
How spread their lures for him in vain
Beauty. 23.
But when she spread her dearest spells,
Frag. Poet. IV. 17.
Thy gossips spread each whisper,
Quat. Hush. 3.
When the redbird spread his sable wing,
Thine Eyes. 9.

Spreading
Spreading its leafless blooms in a damp
nook, Rhodora. 3.

Spreads
The potent plain of Dæmons spreads.
Daemonic Love. 26.
In Farsistan the violet spreads
Exile. 1.
He spreads his welcome where he goes,
Initial Love. 76.

Sprig

So sings in the wind a sprig of the pine;
Quat. Leasts. 2.

Spring

See Upspring; Wellspring.

He shall impose, to find a spring, trap
foxes, Adirondacs. 103.

'T is a tune of the Spring;
Ellen South. 5.

Only to youth will spring be spring.
Harp. 35.

The boy knew on the hills in spring,
Harp. 86.

Or teach thou, Spring! the grand recoil
Harp. 125.

From fall to spring, the russet acorn,
Holidays. 1.

Daughter of Heaven and Earth, coy
Spring, May-Day. 1.

The cagèd linnet in the Spring
May-Day. 83.

And bursts the hoops at hint of Spring:
May-Day. 91.

And o'er yon hazy crest is Eden's balmier
spring! May-Day. 103.

So Spring will not her time forerun,
May-Day. 126.

So Spring guards with surface cold
May-Day. 144.

Why chidest thou the tardy Spring?
May-Day. 164.

Wreaths for May! for happy Spring
May-Day. 263.

Spring is strong and virtuous,
May-Day. 271.

I saw the bud-crowned Spring go forth,
May-Day. 305.

The merry Spring threw wreaths on
them, May-Day. 314.

Beloved of children, bards and Spring,
May-Day. 396.

For thou, O Spring, canst renovate
May-Day. 441.

Under gentle types, my Spring
May-Day. 457.

His mighty psalm from fall to spring
Mountain. 19.

For me, in showers, in sweeping showers,
the Spring Musketaquid. 11.

And the untaught Spring is wise
Nature. I. 3.

I stay with the flowers of Spring:
Quat. Botanist. 2.

They feed the spring which they exhaust;
Saadi. 42.

For men mis-hear thy call in Spring,
Titmouse. 91.

but wake with bursting Spring,
*Violet. 11.

Spring still makes spring in the mind
World-Soul. 105.

Spring-flood

They thank the spring-flood for its fertile
slime, Musketaquid. 43.

Spring's

From Spring's faint flush to Autumn red.
Garden. 8.

Springs

In its mystic springs. Merlin. 8.

Springs from the life below.
Robbins Hymn. 20.

Spring-time

Friends of your spring-time,
Illusions. 8.

Spring-woods

I have come from the spring-woods,
Rhea. 5.

Sprinkled

See Toron-sprinkled.

Sprite

Alas! the Sprite that haunts us
World-Soul. 41.

Spruce

Barked the white spruce to weatherfend
the roof, Adirondacs. 35.

Linden and spruce. In strict society
Adirondacs. 39.

This thin spruce roof, this clayed log-
wall, Adirondacs. 318.

Pants up hither the spruce clerk
Monadnoc. 313.

Sprung

Sprung harmless up, refreshed by blows:
Worship. 2.

Spry

And not half so spry. Fable. 14.

Spurn

I spurn the Past, my mind disdains its
nod, To-Day. 13.

Spurneth

He spurneth the old. Sphinx. 88.

Spy

See Espy.

Spy behind the city clock Art. 14.

Disconcert the searching spy,
Astraea. 35.

The hidden-working Builder spy,
Monadnoc. 238.

To spy what danger on his pathway
creeps; Woodnotes. I. 91.

Squadrons

His couriers come by squadrons,
Song of Nature. 59.

Squalid

Is yonder squalid peasant all
Monadnoc. 75.

Squandering

Squandering your unquoted mirth,
Monadnoc. 186.

Squanders

And Nature squanders on the boy her
pomp, October. 3.

Square

Of the red deer, to aim at a square mist.
Adirondacs. 120.

Make his frame and forces square
Alphonso. 73.

Singing in the sun-baked square; Art. 8.

On the railway, in the square, Caritas. 2.

Squares

In palaces and market squares Harp. 17.

Squaw

Winds mindful still of sannup and of
squaw, Musketaquid. 28.

Squires

With squires, lords, kings, his craft compares, Fate. 8.

Squirrel

The mountain and the squirrel Fable. 1.

A very pretty squirrel track; Fable. 16.

Squirrel's

Was it a squirrel's pettish bark,
May-Day. 21.

Stab
Nor stab the love that orphans keep.
Frag. Life. VII. 4.

Stable
And imagest the stable good
Monadnoc. 387.

Stablish
See Establish.
And hands that stablish what these see:
Monadnoc. 109.
Phœbus stablish must.   Politics. 14.

Stablishing
Driving the foe and stablishing the
friend,—   Blight. 13.

Staff
Thou canst not wave thy staff in air,
Woodnotes. II. 168.

Stage
Pleasures to another stage
Frag. Poet. XI. 16.

Stagnant
To fire the stagnant earth with thought:
Solution. 4.

Staid
To greet staid ancient cavaliers
May-Day. 307.

Stain
Scatter the sloth, wash out the stain,
May-Day. 454.
The violets yon field which stain
Omar. 3.

Stained
See Unstained.

Stainless
Stainless soldier on the walls,
Voluntaries. 97.

Stains
No darkness stains its equal gleam,
Two Rivers. 19.

Stair
Ye shall climb on the heavenly stair,
Celestial Love. 9.

Stairs
At the first mounting of the giant stairs.
Adirondacs. 63.
Teach him on these as stairs to climb,
Art. 25.
In the chamber, on the stairs,
Frag. Life. VIII. 1.
Karnak and Pyramid and Giant's Stairs
Seashore. 15.

Stairway
By the stairway of surprise.'
Merlin. 38.

Stake
Round every windward stake, or tree, or
door.   Snow-Storm. 14.
Bound to the stake, no flames appalled,
Worship. 9.

Stalk
Loved the wood-rose, and left it on its
stalk?   Forbearance. 2.

Stalwart
Bow to the stalwart churls in overalls:
Adirondacs. 94.
And games to breathe his stalwart boys:
Monadnoc. 164.

Stanch
Stanch and strong the tendrils twine:
II Compensation. 16.

His gathered sticks to stanch the wall
Threnody. 84.

Stand
See Withstand.
Half for freedom strike and stand;—
Channing Ode. 96.
Of mother, father, sister, stand;
Daemonic Love. 6.
Stand upon this pasture hill,
Frag. Nat. XXVI. 7.
Fate grants each to stand aside;
Holidays. 18.
What care I, so they stand the same,—
Merops. 1.
Here amid clouds to stand?
Monadnoc. 209.
To stand the hurts of time, until
Monadnoc. 226.
Of minds that each can stand against the
world   Oh What. 2.
Saying, 'Stand in thy place;   Poet. 120.
Right out to sea his courses stand,
Quat. Poet. I. 3.
Not in their houses stand the stars,
Shah. Enweri. I. 1.
Stand not, pause not, in my going.
Song of Seyd. 20.

Stander
See Bystander.

Standeth
What in the Eternal standeth well,
Monadnoc. 87.

Stands
Who stands astonished at the meteor
light,   Adirondacs. 123.
Stands to each human soul its own,
Daemonic Love. 27.
On him who by the altar stands,
Robbins Hymn. 25.
And the secret stands revealed
Saadi. 173.
The painted sled stands where it stood;
Threnody. 82.
He stands in the meadows wide,—
Woodnotes. I. 9.

Star
See Day-star; Pole-star.
The fortunate star that rose on us sank
not;   Adirondacs. 337.
Over sun and star,   Celestial Love. 28.
They intertwine the farthest star:
Celestial Love. 108.
Electric star or pencil plays,
II Compensation. 8.
Minions of the Morning Star.
Daemonic Love. 102.
As moon from earth, or star from star.
Frag. Nat. VII. 2.
Strikes never moon or star.
Frag. Nat. XV. 4.
Face the eastern star until
Frag. Nat. XXVI. 8.
When every star is Bethlehem star?
Frag. Poet. XXVIII. 3.
Where the evening star so holy shines,
Good-Bye. 26.
Ah, brother of the brief but blazing star!
In Memoriam. 25.
With song and hue and star and state,
May-Day. 268.

Star—*Continued*

Each star, each god, each grace amain,
May-Day. 333.

When the star Canope shines in May,
Merlin's Song. 33.

An opaker star,   Monadnoc. 393.

For there's no rood has not a star above
it;   Musketaquid. 54.

And through man and woman and sea
and star   Poet. 69.

I see the pale lustres condense to a star:
Poet. 109.

Ah, happy if a sun or star   Poet. 165.

Out shone a star beneath the cloud,
Poet. 229.

In heaven no star, on earth no spark,—
Saadi. 132.

Tricked out in star and flower,
Song of Nature. 30.

As I behold yon evening star,
Thine Eyes. 3.

Was there no star that could be sent,
Threnody. 118.

Star by star his world resigning.
Threnody. 165.

Nail the wild star to its track
Threnody. 240.

The snowflake is her banner's star,
Voluntaries. 41.

In climates of the summer star.
Voluntaries. 50.

What oldest star the fame can save
Wealth. 22.

On him the light of star and moon
Woodnotes. II. 71.

This radiant pomp of sun and star,
Woodnotes. II. 208.

He is the axis of the star;
Woodnotes. II. 313.

Starbright

Brings book, or starbright scroll of
genius,   Day's Ration. 21.

The strong, star-bright companions
Dirge. 23.

Star-crowned

Star-crowned,   sole-sitting,   long   I
wrought   Solution. 3.

Star-dust

Of star-dust, and star-pilgrimages,
Woodnotes. II. 107.

Stare

And haughtily return us stare for stare.
Blight. 36.

Star-form

And why the star-form she repeats:
Woodnotes. I. 23.

Staring

With staring eye that seeth none,
Poet. 87.

Stark

Samson stark, at Dagon's knee,
Frag. Nat. XXXIV. 1.

All was stiff and stark;   May-Day. 36.

Scoff of yeoman strong and stark,
Monadnoc. 189.

The needful sinew stark as once,
Terminus. 27.

Built he heaven stark and cold;
Threnody. 273.

Starkly

Its onward force too starkly pent
Threnody. 247.

Starlike

Opens the eye to Virtue's starlike meed
Enchanter. 14.

Star-lit

In the star-lit minster aisled.
May-Day. 50.

Star-pilgrimages

Of star-dust, and star-pilgrimages,
Woodnotes. II. 107.

Starred

Where the starred, eternal worm
Celestial Love. 36.

Incensed and starred with lights and airs
and shapes,   October. 9.

Let the starred shade that nightly falls
Woodnotes. II. 225.

Starry

Skirts of angels, starry wings,
Art. 16.

Blends the starry fates with thine,
Freedom. 18.

Such tidings of the starry sphere
May-Day. 13.

Tired of their starry periods,
May-Day. 328.

Who heard the starry music
Ode to Beauty. 58.

Starry   space   and   lily-bell
Ode to Beauty. 78.

The morn is come: the starry crowds
Poet. 177.

And over the moon were the starry studs
Quat. Excelsior. 3.

But fell the starry influence short,
Song of Nature. 71.

Stars

Evening drew on; stars peeped through
maple-boughs,   Adirondacs. 46.

The spiritual stars rise nightly, shedding
down   Adirondacs. 222.

Loved by stars and purest winds,
Astraea. 32.

Our eyes Are armed, but we are strangers to the stars,   Blight. 29-30.

Stars rose; his faith was earlier up:
Character. 2.

The conscious stars accord above,
Concord Ode. 33.

Sails, astonished, amid stars.
Daemonic Love. 55.

Bread, kingdoms, stars, and sky that
holds them all.   Days. 6.

Stars flame and faded as they bade,
Dirge. 34.

O patient stars!   Frag. Nat. VIII. 5.

But the Stars of God remain.
Frag. Nat. XVI. 2.

I kept the sun and stars at bay,
Frag. Poet. II. 7.

Go, speed the stars of Thought
Frag. Poet. VI. 9.

Hide all the stars you boast;
From Hafiz. 3.

Stars abide—   Hamatreya. 31.

Outlive the newest stars.   House. 24.

See the stars through them,
Illusions. 14.

Know the stars yonder,   Illusions. 16.

The stars everlasting,   Illusions. 17.

Of the seven stars and the solar year,
Informing Spirit. 6.

And holds all stars in his embrace.
Initial Love. 117.

Go, speed the stars of Thought
I Intellect. 1.

And mark the rising of the early stars.
Letter. 15.

Forging double stars,   Merlin. 94.

Where stars their perfect courses keep,
Monadnoc. 101.

With its stars of northern fire,
Monadnoc. 217.

Sailing through stars with all their history.   Monadnoc. 278.

Shall not be forms of stars, but stars,
Monadnoc. 307.

'T is not in the high stars alone,
Music. 13.

And stars from the ecliptic road.
Poet. 30.

Stars rose, his faith was earlier up:
Poet. 135.

The great stars did not shine aloof,
Poet. 146.

In vain: the stars are glowing wheels,
Poet. 171.

Cast wishful glances at the stars
Poet. 191.

And yet, dear stars, I know ye shine
Poet. 233.

Suns and stars their courses keep,
Poet. 271.

Ere he was born, the stars of fate
Quat. Horoscope. 1.

And fetch her stars to deck her hair:
Rhea. 52.

The keen stars twinkle in our eyes,
Romany. 22.

You doubt we read the stars on high,
Romany. 25.

The stars may hide in the upper sky,
Romany. 27.

For Saadi's nightly stars did burn
Saadi. 84.

Not in their houses stand the stars,
Shah, Enweri. I. 1.

From thy worth and weight the stars gravitate,   Shah, Enweri. II. 1.

And light from meliorating stars
Song of Nature. 19.

And broken stars I drew,
Song of Nature. 26.

And kind acquaintance with the morning stars   Summons. 8.

The punctual stars will vigil keep,—
Titmouse. 18.

Hung idle stars and suns?   Wealth. 4.

Or the stars of eternity?
Woodnotes. II. 304.

Stars taunt us by a mystery
World-Soul. 47.

Stars weave eternal rings;
World-Soul. 62.

Stars'

The stars' own ether beams;   Poet. 100.

Start

See Upstart.

Time takes fresh start again,
Adirondacs. 328.

Can make the wild blood start
Merlin. 7.

Started

Each tramper started; but the feet
Threnody. 106.

Starve

Turn pale and starve.   Blight. 49.

Where forests starve: Monadnoc. 354.

State

State of hermit, state of lover;
Alphonso. 56.

There is no king nor sovereign state
Astraea. 3.

Have not hazarded their state;
Astraea. 34.

Which fired the little State to save
Boston. 94.

Shall constitute a state.
Boston Hymn. 32.

In church and state and school.
Boston Hymn. 44.

Each from your proper state,
Celestial Love. 13.

The state may follow how it can,
Channing Ode. 69.

To build an equal state,—
Concord Ode. 14.

Weapons to guard the State, or scourge
In Memoriam. 65.

With song and hue and star and state,
May-Day. 268.

And granted me the freedom of their state,   Musketaquid. 5.

Each spot where tulips prank their state
Omar. 1.

There, while hot heads perplexed with fears the state,   Phi. 9.

And give to hold an even state,
Poet. 167.

Cannot rear a State.   Politics. 10.

Then the perfect State is come,
Politics. 25.

And compromise thy peaceful state;
Saadi. 66.

And, though thy rede be church or state,
Visit. 25.

Building for their sons the State,
Voluntaries. 25.

State-house

And here in a pine state-house
Boston Hymn. 41.

When the state-house is the hearth,
Politics. 24.

Statelier

Statelier forms and fairer faces;
Rhea. 67.

Stately

O fair and stately maid, whose eyes
Eva. 1.

Stately lords in palaces,
Frag. Poet. I. 26.

Yet it is a stately tomb;
In Memoriam. 15.

Filing single in stately train.
May-Day. 308.

Stately marching in cap and coat
Threnody. 76.

Self-sown my stately garden grows;
Walden. 9.

States
> *See* United States.
> Behold the famous States
> > Channing Ode. 16.

Statesman
> Where the statesman ploughs
> > Politics. 21.

Statesman's
> Or statesman's rant.   Channing Ode. 6.

Statesmen's
> Past clerks' or statesmen's art or passion.
> > Monadnoc. 178.

Statue
> Let statue, picture, park and hall,
> > Art. 9.
> As the sculptor uncovers the statue
> > Boston Hymn. 19.

Stature
> By turns we praised the stature of our
> > guides,   Adirondacs. 80.
> Saadi, see! they rise in stature
> > Saadi. 171.

Statures
> Form of forms, and mould of statures,
> > Bacchus. 20.

Statute
> To take the statute from the mind
> > Concord Ode. 15.
> But make the statute of this land.
> > Rhea. 30.

Stay
> *See* Overstay.
> Up with your towns and stay!'
> > Boston. 52.
> To stay in the Syrian land;   Exile. 16.
> Upon my cheek to stay;
> > *Farewell. 24.
> He will spell in the sculpture, 'Stay.'
> > Garden. 64.
> Wished to stay, and is gone,
> > Hamatreya. 56.
> He cannot go, he cannot stay,   Poet. 84.
> Which none can stay, and none accel-
> > erate.'   Poet. 125.
> But will ye stay?   Poet. 259.
> I stay with the flowers of Spring:
> > Quat. Botanist. 2.
> Go thou, sweet Heaven, or at thy pleasure
> > stay!'   Sursum Corda. 9.
> This child should ills of ages stay,
> > Threnody. 135.
> Askest, 'How long thou shalt stay?'
> > Visit. 1.

Stayed
> Pitiless, will not be stayed;
> > Daemonic Love. 113.
> The plague is stayed.   Past. 4.
> And Ages went or stayed.   Peter. 24.
> Stayed on his subtile thought,
> > Voluntaries. 80.

Stays
> *See* Overstays.
> The lover rooted stays.   Friendship. 4.
> That Genius goes and Folly stays.
> > In Memoriam. 110.

Stead
> For God's vicegerency and stead?
> > Monadnoc. 77.

Steadfast
> Not yet a steadfast morn,   Poet. 102.

Steadfastly
> Be of good cheer, brave spirit; stead-
> > fastly   Good Cheer. 1.

Steads
> Steads not to work on the clean jump,
> > Alphonso. 61.
> On two days it steads not to run from
> > thy grave,   On Two Days. 1.

Steal
> Almost a smile to steal to cheer her sons,
> > Adirondacs. 342.
> Steal in by window, chink, or hole,
> > Past. 17.

Stealing
> Stealing with paddle to the feeding-
> > grounds   Adirondacs. 119.
> Stealing grace from all alive;   Give. 46.
> Stealing away the memory
> > Voluntaries. 77.

Steals
> He palters and steals;   Sphinx. 52.

Stealth
> Between two sleeps a short day's stealth,
> > Poet. 183.

Steam
> Galvanic wire, strong-shouldered steam.
> > Wealth. 41.
> Time-and-space-conquering steam,—
> > World-Soul. 14.

Steamer
> The steamer built.   Channing Ode. 65.

Steeds
> I saw fair boys bestriding steeds,
> > Harp. 111.
> They are his steeds, and not his feature;
> > Initial Love. 36.

Steel
> Or gleam which use can paint on steel,
> > Frag. Poet. I. 24.
> Charmed from fagot and from steel,
> > Frag. Poet. V. 30.
> As if the dust were glass and steel.
> > Poet. 6.

Steep
> The steep be graded,
> > Channing Ode. 59.
> To the snow-capped steep,
> > Frag. Nat. III. 37.
> He dives the hollow, climbs the steep.
> > May-Day. 72.
> Tumbling steep   Monadnoc. 328.
> The height of Fancy's far-eyed steep.
> > Poet. 170.
> And rankly on the castled steep,—
> > Voluntaries. 120.

Steeped
> Steeped in the light are beautiful.
> > Frag. Nat. XXVI. 18.
> Steeped in her quality,   Hermione. 23.
> Steeped in each forest cave?
> > Walden. 28.

Steeper
> No stouter fence, no steeper wall!
> > Boston. 62.

Steeple
> Rallying round a parish steeple
> > Monadnoc. 129.

Steeps
> On Adirondac steeps, I know
> > Frag. Nat. IV. 7.

Steer

Who steer the plough, but cannot steer
their feet   Hamatreya. 15.

Cooped in a ship he cannot steer,—
Monadnoc. 336.

Right to the heaven they steer and sing.
Poet. 26.

Steerer

Zigzag steerer, desert cheerer,
Humble-Bee. 7.

Steering

Steering north with raucous cry
May-Day. 24.

Steers

Steers his bark and trims his sail;
Quat. Poet. I. 2.

Stem

To climb a lofty stem, clean without
boughs   Adirondacs. 83.

To transmute crime to wisdom, so to
stem   Frag. Poet. XXII. 1.

Every tree and stem and chink
May-Day. 340.

The insanity of towns to stem
Monadnoc. 116.

Cut a bough from my parent stem,
Woodnotes. II. 51.

Stemmed

See Thick-stemmed.

Stems

The river, hill, stems, foliage are obscure,
Musketaquid. 83.

Step

Their step is forth, and, ere the day
Forerunners. 3.

Nor my unseasoned step disturbs
Frag. Nat. XVIII. 4.

Pilgrims wight with step forthright.
May-Day. 311.

Step by step, lifts bad to good,
May-Day. 464.

And thief-like step of liberal hours
Monadnoc. 64.

Step the meek fowls where erst they
ranged;   Threnody. 94.

To make no step until the event is
known,   Woodnotes. I. 88.

Stepped

Or where he stepped the soil did peal
Poet. 5.

Forward stepped the perfect Greek:
Solution. 14.

Stepping

Stepping daily onward north
May-Day. 306.

Steps

See Footsteps.

In many lands, with painful steps,
House. 11.

Then would I seek where God might
guide my steps,   Letter. 7.

The halting steps of aged Fate.
May-Day. 155.

And unimagined splendor waits his steps.
October. 5.

With sounding steps the poet came;
Poet. 2.

Thy steps to watch, thy place to know:
Threnody. 33.

What these with slowest steps attain.
Voluntaries. 54.

Sterile

When the old world is sterile
World-Soul. 97.

Sterility

Of genius the sterility;   Alphonso. 22.

Stern

As if on such stern forms and haunts
Frag. Nat. XXIX. 3.

And the stern Parcæ on his part.
Initial Love. 129.

To greet yon stern head-stone,
In Memoriam. 12.

The stern old war-gods shook their
heads,   Uriel. 27.

Stern benefit abides.
Waldeinsamkeit. 16.

It was her stern necessity: all things
Xenophanes. 5.

Sterner

A sterner errand to the silken troop
Summons. 1.

Sternly

And sternly calls to being souls
Quat. Fate. 3.

Steward

Ale, and a sup of wine. Our steward gave
Adirondacs. 178.

Stewards

Stewards of stipend and of rent;
Guy. 28.

Sticks

His gathered sticks to stanch the wall
Threnody. 84.

Stiff

All was stiff and stark;   May-Day. 36.

Stifling

With stifling beams on these retreats,
Titmouse. 72.

Still

Still are rulers, or Mildew?
Alphonso. 40.

The ring you gave is still the same;
Amulet. 2.

Torments me still the fear that love
Amulet. 11.

Which till obeys the mind.   Angelo. 5.

In the still abodes.   Celestial Love. 57.

Still to the proprietor;
Celestial Love. 78.

Of self in other still preferred,
Celestial Love. 118.

Would serve things still;—
Channing Ode. 42

Still keeps that golden day
Cosmos. 26.

In crowded and in still resorts,
Daemonic Love. 46.

Draws men to their likeness still.
Daemonic Love. 67.

And I am still the same;
Days Pass. 2.

Of thoughts and things at home, but still
adjourn   Day's Ration. 31.

Was woven still by the snow-white choir.
Each. 32.

For so I must interpret still   Eva. 4.

Sit still and Truth is near:
Frag. Life. XXXV. 2.

The Gordian noose was still untied.
Frag. Nat. VI. 6

Still—*Continued*
Than still to entertain his ear
                    Frag. Poet. V. 6.
A bolder foot is still rewarded.
                    Frag. Poet. XXXI. 2.
On waves and hedges still they burn.
                    Garden. 60.
Still thou playest;—short vacation
                    Holidays. 17.
And, being two, shall still be one.
                    Initial Love. 146.
Still enriches and transforms,
                    May-Day. 199.
Be still his arm and architect,
                    May-Day. 443.
Songs can the tempest still,   Merlin. 55.
And copious language still bestowed
                    Merops. 11.
Ere yet the summoning voice was still,
                    Monadnoc. 31.
Was   not   altogether   still,
                    Monadnoc. 196.
Where I gaze, and still shall gaze,
                    Monadnoc. 211.
Still is the haughty pile erect
                    Monadnoc. 373.
Holding us at vantage still,
                    Monadnoc. 376.
I hear a sky-born music still: Music. 2.
Winds mindful still of sannup and of
    squaw,   Musketaquid. 28.
Would mortify me, but in vain; for still
                    Musketaquid. 69.
The master-stroke is still her part.
                    Nature. II. 23.
Yet fly me still,   Ode to Beauty. 43.
In the woodwalks still and low
                    Poet. 254.
Are registered and answered still.
                    Prayer. 8.
Still floats upon the morning wind,
                    Problem. 59.
Still whispers to the willing mind.
                    Problem. 60.
her eye still seemed to see,
                    Quat. A. H. 3.
For still, where'er the trees grow biggest.
                    Quat. Artist. 3.
And the sharpest you still have survived,
                    Quat. Borrowing. 2.
For still the craft of genius is
                    Quat. Poet. 2. 3.
Unmeasured still my Shakespeare sits,
                    Quat. Shakespeare. 3.
To thee. He watches for thee still. His
    love   Rome. 24.
So shaped, so colored, swift or still,
                    Solution. 30.
And pour the deluge still;
                    Song of Nature. 12.
And still the man-child is not born,
                    Song of Nature. 43.
Accompany still;   Sphinx. 38.
Still plan and smile,   Terminus. 20.
Thine eyes still shined for me, though far
                    Thine Eyes. 1.
Still plotting how their hungry ear
                    Threnody. 50.
And garden,—they were bound and still.
                    Threnody. 109.

Through ruined systems still restored,
                    Threnody. 283.
Still for journeys she is dressed;
                    Una. 3.
Will thy clear blue eye, upward bent,
    still keep its chastened glow,
                    *Violet. 3.
Still tearless lift its slender form above
    the wintry snow?   *Violet. 4.
Still on the seeds of all he made
                    Waldeinsamkeit. 25.
In forests I am still at home
                    Walden. 47.
Still, through her motes and masses, draw
                    Wealth. 46.
It may blow north, it still is warm;
                    Woodnotes. I. 100.
Or south, it still is clear;
                    Woodnotes. I. 101.
Body with shadow still pursued.
                    Woodnotes. II. 163.
Still celebrate their funerals,
                    Woodnotes. II. 226.
Still, still the secret presses;
                    World-Soul. 57.
Spring still makes spring in the mind
                    World-Soul. 105.
Stillman
And Stillman, our guides' guide, and
    Commodore,   Adirondacs. 183.
Stillness
What majestic stillness broods
                    Frag. Nat. XXVI. 19.
Sting
Which past endurance sting the tender
    cit,   Adirondacs. 174.
Stings
Stings the strong with enterprise,
                    May-Day. 293.
In stings of remorse.   Sphinx. 92.
Stipend
Stewards of stipend and of rent;
                    Guy. 28.
Stirred
Throbs of a wild religion stirred;—
                    Daemonic Love. 8.
One deity stirred,—   Sphinx. 36.
And stirred the devils everywhere,
                    Uriel. 18.
Stock
None from its stock that vine can reave.
                    II Compensation. 18.
My stock of art,   Letter. 20.
In whom the stock of freedom roots;
                    Monadnoc. 93.
And drifting sand-heaps feed my stock,
                    Woodnotes. II. 11.
Stoic
When happy stoic Nature grieves,
                    Nun. 12.
Stole
It was from Jove the other stole his fire,
                    Adirondacs. 290.
Beauty through my senses stole;
                    Each. 50.
The air stole into the streets of towns,
                    May-Day. 342.
Stole over the celestial kind,   Uriel. 44.
Stolen
Like stolen fruit;   Channing Ode. 91.

Stone

See Head-stone; Hearth-stone.

Hid in gleaming piles of stone; Art. 4.

Which did not slumber like a stone,
Beauty. 3.

We set to-day a votive stone;
C. Hymn. 10.

Floating in air or pent in stone,
II Compensation. 26.

O, wondrous craft of plant and stone
Monadnoc. 66.

Where flowers each stone rosette and
metope brave; Monadnoc. 372.

But borrowed in atoms from iron and
stone, Nature. II. 21.

On prince or bride no diamond stone
On Prince. 1.

The conscious stone to beauty grew.
Problem. 24.

Are locked in sparkling stone.
Rubies. 8.

To mimic in slow structures, stone by
stone, Snow-Storm. 26.

I am seeker of the stone,
Song of Seyd. 9.

And crouched no more in stone;
Sphinx. 122.

Becomes a ruby stone; They. 2.

A spell is laid on sod and stone,
Unity. 7.

See thou bring not to field or stone
Waldeinsamkeit. 41.

Once slept the world an egg of stone,
Woodnotes. II. 266.

Stone-cleaving

Earth-baking heat, stone-cleaving cold.
Monadnoc. 57.

Stone-incarved

Dear memory's stone-incarved traits,
Daemonic Love. 14.

Stones

Let not unto the stones the Day
Monadnoc. 12.

These trees and stones are audible to me,
River. 22.

Sings in my ears, my hands are stones,
Titmouse. 13.

All spheres, all stones, his helpers be;
Woodnotes. II. 78.

O mortal! thy ears are stones;
Woodnotes. II. 126.

Stony

Hang roses on the stony fate.
Frag. Poet. X. 4.

The stony pathway to the wood.
May-Day. 358.

Or prayers the stony Parcæ soothe,
Nemesis. 10.

Stood

See Understood.

Here once the embattled farmers stood
C. Hymn. 3.

Around me stood the oaks and firs;
Each. 44.

And stood beneath the firmament,
Frag. Nat. XXVI. 13.

He stood before the tumbling main
Frag. Poet. I. 50.

Said Saadi, "When I stood before
Frag. Poet. III. 1.

On the summit as I stood,
Monadnoc. 193.

Not on its base Monadnoc surer stood,
Phi. 13.

Unseen by such as stood around.
Poet. 16.

She stood Monadnoc's head.
Sphinx. 128.

The painted sled stands where it stood;
Threnody. 82.

Stoop

Instant to my grave I stoop,
From Hafiz. 15.

See the plum redden, and the beurré
stoop. Quat. Gardener. 4.

Stoop not then to poor excuse;
Sursum Corda. 5.

Could stoop to heal that only child,
Threnody. 122.

Stooping

Stooping, his finger wrote in clay
Solution. 69.

Stoops

Daily stoops to harbor there.
Astraea. 48.

And nearer stoops the moon. Peter. 16.

Stopped

Time they stopped for shame. Gifts. 4.

The sled and traveller stopped, the courier's feet Snow-Storm. 6.

Stops

Stops his horse, and lists with delight,
Each. 7.

Store

The secret store Dull. 9.

He shall bring store of seeds and crumbs.
Titmouse. 82.

Stored

Then docks were built, and crops were
stored, Wealth. 42.

Stores

From the stores of eldest matter,
Frag. Life. XXIX. 1.

Storm

In flame, in storm, in clouds of air.
Beauty. 6.

A wintry storm more fitly fell.
Frag. Nat. XXIX. 4.

Frowned in my foe and growled in storm,
Frag. Poet. IV. 29.

Hither rolls the storm of heat;
May-Day. 192.

Like the lightning trough the storm,
Ode to Beauty. 69.

He, when the rising storm of party
roared, Phi. 7.

The storm is my best galley hand
Quat. Northman. 3.

In a tumultuous privacy of storm.
Snow-Storm. 9.

I trim myself to the storm of time,
Terminus. 34.

Storms

There for purifying storms; Astraea. 41.

Unhurt be a thousand storms,
May-Day. 321.

Storm-wind

His words like a storm-wind can bring
Saadi. 127.

The storm-wind wove, the torrent span,
Wealth. 38.

Storm-winds
The storm-winds urge the heavy weeks
along, Adirondacs. 227.

Stormy
Along the stormy coast, Boston. 46.
Scattered on the stormy air, Merlin. 56.

Story
Who all the day of life his summer story
tells; Enchanter. 2.

Stout
The men of yore were stout and poor,
Boston. 5.
It requireth courage stout. Give. 19.
So frolic, stout and self-possest?
Titmouse. 53.
For well the soul, if stout within,
Titmouse. 75.

Stouter
No stouter fence, no steeper wall!
Boston. 62.

Stoutness
Sparta's stoutness, Bethlehem's heart,
Monadnoc. 299.

Straight
Straight, into double band
Channing Ode. 94.
And straight begins again;
World-Soul. 92.

Straightest
And trim the straightest boughs;
Boston Hymn. 34.
Though thou kept the straightest road,
Rhea. 23.

Straightway
Him it would straightway blind or craze,
Guy. 22.
Straightway, a forgetting wind
Uriel. 43.

Strain
Graces of a subtler strain,
Daemonic Love. 57.
You must add the untaught strain
Destiny. 3.
Singing an immortal strain, Dull. 4.
Spirits of a higher strain
Frag. Life. XXII. 3.
Like the strain of all Frag. Nat. III. 27.
That the slave who caught the strain
Freedom. 3.
How strangely wise thy strain!
Harp. 42.
So sweet and mournful falls the strain.
Harp. 102.
Of Lord Christ's heart, and Shakspeare's
strain. Informing Spirit. 8.
In the heart of the music peals a strain
Merlin's Song. 8.
Resist in vain his motive strain,
Poet. 37.
Up and down their glances strain.
Threnody. 81.
A genius of so fine a strain,
Threnody. 141.
Low and mournful be the strain,
Voluntaries. 1.
To find what bird had piped the strain:—
Woodnotes. II. 249.

Strained
Oft he keeps his fine ear strained,
Initial Love. 66.

Strains
Strains every sense to larger scope,
May-Day. 153.

Which never strains its rocky beams;
Monadnoc. 273.
Fall like sweet strains, or pensive smiles;
Problem. 4.

Strait
Too strait and low our cottage doors,
May-Day. 220.
Too long shut in strait and few,
Mithridates. 20.

Straitly
Straitly charged him, 'Sit aloof;'
Saadi. 12.

Straits
Filled the straits and filled the wide,
Frag. Nat. III. 13.

Strand
And gems from the sea-washed strand,
Exile. 14.

Strange
In strange junctures, felt, with awe,
Guy. 11.
In strange lands unblest;
Hermione. 48.
And for strange coincidence.
Initial Love. 69.
To his own blood harsh and strange.
Insight. 6.
To see strange forests and new snow,
Monadnoc. 206.
Planting strange fruits and sunshine on
the shore, Seashore. 47.

Strangely
How strangely wise thy strain!
Harp. 42.
Time and tide are strangely changed,
Initial Love. 7.

Stranger
Thou intimate stranger,
Ode to Beauty. 15.

Stranger's
Our angel, in a stranger's form,
World-Soul. 27.

Strangers
Whether thy sons or strangers eat the
fruit: Adirondacs. 300.
Our eyes Are armed, but we are strangers to the stars, Blight. 29-30.
And strangers to the mystic beast and
bird, Blight. 31.
And strangers to the plant and to the
mine. Blight. 32.
And strangers, fond as they, their furrows plough. Hamatreya. 12.

Stratagem
With simpleness for stratagem.
Monadnoc. 117.

Stratum
Draw from each stratum its adapted use
Musketaquid. 39.

Straw
Is but a straw to anthracite;
May-Day. 139.

Stray
And pleased I stray
Frag. Nat. XXI. 2.
And there I cannot stray. Walden. 48.
And fear what foe in caves and swamps
can stray, Woodnotes. I. 87.

Strayed
As 'mid the virgin train she strayed,
Each. 30.

Streak
Its spot of purple, and its streak of brown,   Naples. 8.

Stream
Of the Ausable stream, intent to reach
                     Adirondacs. 3.

Père Raquette stream, to a small tortuous
pass   Adirondacs. 22.

From a log cabin stream Beethoven's
notes   Adirondacs. 313.

Down the dark stream   C. Hymn. 8.

On this green bank, by this soft stream,
                     C. Hymn. 9.

By lake and stream and gleaming hall
               Frag. Poet. I. 15.

Stream could not so perversely wind
                     Guy. 35.

Fall, stream, from Heaven to bless; return as well;   Inscription. 1.

And loiter willing by yon loitering
stream.   Musketaquid. 14.

Sun, moon, man, undulate and stream,
                     Poet. 173.

And wishful saw the Ocean stream:—
                     Poet. 192.

The stream, the trees,   River. 28.

And one by Avon stream,
              Song of Nature. 66.

The brook into the stream runs on;
               Threnody. 96.

The stream I love unbounded goes
              Two Rivers. 6.

I hear the spending of the stream
             Two Rivers. 10.

So forth and brighter fares my stream,—
             Two Rivers. 17.

As sunbeams stream through liberal space
             Woodnotes. II. 1.

Along Thought's causing stream,
             World-Soul. 70.

Streamers
Her stripes the boreal streamers are.
             Voluntaries. 42.

Streams
Or like the Atlantic streams, which run
             Bacchus. 29.

Up the far mountain walls the streams
increase   Frag. Nat. XXVI. 22.

With spouting streams and waves of
light   Frag. Nat. XXVI. 24.

With light that streams from gracious
eyes.   Frag. Poet. VII. 6.

Of the new-delivered streams,
             May-Day. 229.

My daily load of woods and streams,
             Monadnoc. 271.

Low, open meads, slender and sluggish
streams,   Musketaquid. 2.

The pit wherein the streams are rolled
             Quat. Alcuin. 3.

To leave my woods and streams and the
sweet sloth   Summons. 4.

Whose streams through Nature circling
go?   Threnody. 239.

Bound in by streams which give and take
             Waldeinsamkeit. 7.

That flows in streams, that breathes in
wind: Woodnotes. II. 233.

Street
On the city's paved street   Art. 5.

Each street leads downward to the sea,
             Boston. 57.

You shall not know me in the noisy
street,   Frag. Life. XV. 2.

The maple street   Frag. Nat. III. 21.

To crowded halls, to court and street;
             Good-Bye. 11.

In the street, if he turned round,
             Guy. 23.

Each street and spire and roof, incontinent.   Letter. 6.

Streets
The air stole into the streets of towns,
             May-Day. 342.

Oft, in streets or humblest places,
             Ode to Beauty. 64.

Trade and the streets ensnare us,
             World-Soul. 21.

Strength
Their rival strength and suppleness, their
skill   Adirondacs. 81.

By strength and terror skirted;
             Daemonic Love. 61.

From all the seas of strength Fate filled a
chalice,   Day's Ration. 2.

From strength to strength, and for night
brings   Frag. Life. XXXI. 2.

Of a true monarch's soul. Beauty and
strength,   Good Cheer. 8.

Adds to oak and oxen strength,
             May-Day. 201.

Wait his returning strength.
             Merlin. 62.

Her strength and soul has laughing
France   Quat. Leasts. 3.

This matchless strength. Where shall he
find, O waves!   Seashore. 32.

Of heart and soul, of strength and
pleasure,   Solution. 36.

In equal strength through space abide;
             Voluntaries. 116.

Hither I come for strength
             Waterfall. 5.

Unnerves his strength, invites his end.
             Woodnotes. II. 50.

Strengths
Which bind the strengths of Nature wild
             Wealth. 48.

Stretch
See Outstretch.

Friendly hands stretch forth to him,
             Frag. Poet. XI. 6.

Stretched
The prairie stretched away.
             Boston. 44.

And when I am stretched beneath the
pines,   Good-Bye. 25.

The Doctor stretched the hours,
             Walden. 34.

Strew
Flowers they strew,—I catch the scent;
             Forerunners. 11.

This must the leaves of ages strew
             Wealth. 15.

Strewing
Strewing my bed, and, in another age,
             Seashore. 36.

Strew'st
The wheat thou strew'st be souls.
             Frag. Poet. VI. 12.

Strew'st —*Continued*
The wheat thou strew'st be souls.
I Intellect. 4.

Stricken
See Sorrow-stricken.

Strict
Linden and spruce. In strict society
Adirondacs. 39.
And, in her strict resort Hermione. 71.

Stricter
And a stricter privacy; Initial Love. 144.

Stride
See Outstride.
The feet of millions stride. Boston. 40.

Strides
Unheeded Danger near him strides,
Daemonic Love. 87.

Strife
Traditioned fame of masters, eager strife
Adirondacs. 324.
Their doubts, and aid their strife.
Robbins Hymn. 12.
And ever in the strife of your own
thoughts Rome. 15.
Goethe, raised o'er joy and strife,
Solution. 65.
Of Death and Fortune, Growth and
Strife.' Woodnotes. II. 32.

Strike
Half for freedom strike and stand;—
Channing Ode. 96.
Thy foes to hunt, thy enviers to strike
down, Shah-Hafiz. 1.
For freedom he will strike and strive,
Voluntaries. 57.

Strikes
Strikes never moon or star.
Frag. Nat. XV. 4.
Strikes the loud pretender down.
Nature. I. 11.
Then the Spirit strikes the hour:
Threnody. 235.

String
If once again that silent string,
Harp. 105.
Shall string Monadnoc like a bead.
Monadnoc. 286.
My hand upon the silent string,
Poet. 95.
Two touch the string, Saadi. 19.

Strings
See Heart-strings.
Or like the thrill of Æolian strings
Frag. Poet. I. 41.
From the eager opening strings
Harp. 47.
Nor tinkle of piano strings, Merlin. 6.
And the countless leaves of the pine are
strings Woodnotes. II. 95.

Strip
Care not to strip the dead To J. W. 11.

Stripe
Henceforth I wear no stripe but thine;
Titmouse. 54.

Stripes
Her stripes the boreal steamers are.
Voluntaries. 42.

Stripling
Mad Destiny this tender stripling played;
Epitaph. 2.

How snatch the stripling from their
toils?— Frag. Life. X. 7.

Strive
Miss the aim whereto I strive.
Angelo. 9.
To speak the truth—for truth to strive.
Hymn. 8.
Usurp the seats for which all strive;
Merlin's Song. 17.
For freedom he will strike and strive,
Voluntaries. 57.

Strives
The moon-drawn tide-wave strives;
Promise. 2.

Striving
See Upward-striving.
And, striving to be man, the worm
May-Day. 81.
And, striving to be man, the worm
Nature. Mot. 5.

Stroke
See Master-stroke.
Thanked Nature for each stroke she
dealt; Poet. 209.
And give or take the stroke of war,
Saadi. 109.

Strokes
Three times ten thousand strokes, from
morn to eve. Adirondacs. 90.
Merlin's blows are strokes of fate,
Merlin. 16.
On his tense chords all strokes were felt,
Poet. 210.

Strolling
Said I, strolling through the pastures,
Berrying. 4.

Strong
See Headstrong.
Thence, in strong country carts,
Adirondacs. 2.
Homeward brought the oxen strong;
Apology. 18.
He saw strong Eros struggling through,
Beauty. 18.
And as behemoth strong.
Boston Hymn. 80.
The strong gods pine for my abode,
Brahma. 13.
Lands and goods go to the strong.
Celestial Love. 76.
Stanch and strong the tendrils twine:
II Compensation. 16.
Or strong, or rich, or generous;
Destiny. 2.
Broad his shoulders are and strong;
Destiny. 31.
The strong, star-bright companions
Dirge. 23.
Dearest Nature, strong and kind,
Experience. 18.
Sometimes their strong speed they slack-
en, Forerunners. 27.
Him strong Genius urged to roam,
Frag. Life. XX. 1.
And know the only strong?
Frag. Nat. III. 30.
Gropes for columns strong as he;
Frag. Nat. XXXIV. 2.
And by the sea-waves he was strong;
Frag. Poet. V. 18.

Strong crab with nobler blood did fill;
Guy. 42.
Ah! heedless how the weak are strong,
Hermione. 27.
Spring is strong and virtuous,
May-Day. 271.
Stings the strong with enterprise,
May-Day. 293.
It is mightier than the strong,
Merlin's Song. 3.
Adhere like this foundation strong,
Monadnoc. 115.
Strong as giant, slow as child.
Monadnoc. 132,
Sets the life-pulse strong but slow:
Monadnoc. 158.
And of the fibre, quick and strong,
Monadnoc. 169.
Scoff of yeoman strong and stark,
Monadnoc. 189.
'Monadnoc is a mountain strong,
Monadnoc. 256.
What these strong masters wrote at large
in miles, Musketaquid. 52.
Sounded like a tempest strong   Poet. 28.
Because they are not strong.
Quat. Orator. 4.
The opaline, the plentiful and strong,
Seashore. 18.
In slumber I am strong.
Song of Nature. 8.
Forth speed the strong pulses
Sphinx. 103.
Helps who for their own need are strong,
Titmouse. 87.
Musketaquit, a goblin strong,
Two Rivers. 13.
Strong Hades could not keep his own,
Uriel. 33.
The strong they slay, the swift outstride:
Voluntaries. 118.
Knew the strong task to it assigned,
Wealth. 10.
Which knits the world in music strong,
Woodnotes. II. 157.
Strong art and beautiful pretension,
Woodnotes. II. 207.

Stronger
Races by stronger races,
Channing Ode. 84.
Stronger Custom brought him home.
Frag. Life. XX. 2.
Stronger and bolder far than I,
Harp. 115.

Strongly
Well the Planter knew how strongly
Monadnoc Afar. 5.

Strong-shouldered
Galvanic wire, strong-shouldered steam.
Wealth. 41.

Strook
An inch of ground the lightning strook
Frag. Poet. XXXII. 3.

Strove
When Chaos and Order strove,
Cosmos. 2, 6.
Which, for the Genius that there strove,
Poet. 197.

Struck
Then struck a light and kindled the
camp-fire. Adirondacs. 36.

We struck our camp and left the happy
hills. Adirondacs. 336.
Structures
To mimic in slow structures, stone by
stone, Snow-Storm. 26.
Struggles
And all our struggles and our toils
Nemesis. 15.
Struggling
He saw strong Eros struggling through,
Beauty. 18.
Struggling through the drifted roads;
May-Day. 40.
Strung
Right good-will my sinews strung,
Forerunners. 6.
Which God in human hearts hath strung.
Hymn. 16.
On prayer and music strung;
Monadnoc. 234.
Studied
The old men studied magic in the flowers,
Blight. 23.
Studied thy motion, took thy form,
Lines. 16.
Studiously
Like Cupids studiously inclined;
Threnody. 65.
Studs
And over the moon were the starry studs
Quat. Excelsior. 3.
Study
My study for their politique,
Channing Ode. 8.
'T is his study and delight   Rhea. 47.
Books, Muses, Study, fireside, friends and
love, Summons. 13.
Stuff
Stuff their nine brains in one hat;
Alphonso. 72.
Of the same stuff, and so allayed,
Monadnoc. 167.
Stuff sharp thorns beneath the head
Saadi. 68.
Stuffs
The merchant hath stuffs of price,
Exile. 13.
Ponderous gold and stuffs to bear,
Merlin's Song. 26.
Stumbling
Or stumbling on through vast self-similar
woods Adirondacs. 105.
Stunted
The stunted trees look sick,   Blight. 50.
Style
Up to his style, and manners of the sky.
Threnody. 271.
Styled
And, for I'm styled Alphonse the Wise,
Alphonso. 47.
Style-discerning
Can thy style-discerning eye
Monadnoc. 237.
Styx
Of Styx and Erebus;   Bacchus. 9.
Subdividing
And, ever subdividing, separate
Frag. Nat. XVII. 3.
Subdued
Sinew that subdued the fields;
Woodnotes. II. 32.

Sublime
But ever the free race with front sublime,
Adirondacs. 293.
And matched his sufferance sublime
Character. 5.
Is weaving the sublime proportions
Good Cheer. 7.
Its peace sublime his aspect kept,
In Memoriam. 101.
Bathing, in thy day sublime.   Poet. 133.
And matched his sufferance sublime
Poet. 138.
His vision as sublime: Poet. 296.
Draws the heart a lore sublime."'
Saadi. 71.
Their meaning sublime.   Sphinx. 72.
To wrap the errors of a sage sublime.
To J. W. 9.
Or on the mountain-crest sublime,
Waldeinsamkeit. 9.

Subsiding
Of the old flood's subsiding slime,
Woodnotes. II. 109.

Subsisteth
What subsisteth, and what seems.
Uriel. 14.

Substance
Into substance, into Law.
Frag. Poet. VIII. 10.
Substance mixed of pure contraries;
Initial Love. 91.
And though the substance us elude,
Monadnoc. 390.
Know, each substance and relation,
Visit. 3.

Substances
Substances at base divided,
Celestial Love. 44.
All substances the cunning chemist Time
Day's Ration. 6.
But the substances survive.
Woodnotes. II. 261.

Substructs
And Nile substructs her granite base,—
Solution. 10.

Subtile
Stayed on his subtile thought,
Voluntaries. 80.

Subtle
And a prime end of the most subtle element
Adirondacs. 258.
Many and subtle are my lays,
Aeolian Harp. 20.
They know not well the subtle ways
Brahma. 3.
And infusing subtle heats,
Humble-Bee. 26.
A subtle chain of countless rings
May-Day. 79.
What time the subtle mind   Merlin. 44.
Subtle rhymes, with ruin rife,
Merlin. 123.
A subtle chain of countless rings
Nature. Mot. 1.

Subtler
Graces of a subtler strain,
Daemonic Love. 57.

Subtlety
To vex with odious subtlety   Saadi. 47.

Suburb
In the suburb, in the town.   Caritas. 1.

Succeed
Who shall succeed,   Hamatreya. 41.
No sire survive, no son succeed!
Monadnoc. 124.

Succeeds
In simple words succeeds,
Quat. Poet. 2. 2.

Success
A sycophant to smug success?
Chartist. 14.
That one thing is Success,—   Destiny. 46.
Born for success he seemed,
In Memoriam. 60.
When success exalts thy lot,
Prayer. 1.

Succession
Succession swift and spectral Wrong,
Experience. 8.

Succor
And ye shall succor men;
Boston Hymn. 49.
Thou dost succor and remede
Monadnoc. 405.

Succory
Grapevine and succory,
Frag. Nat. II. 3.
Succory to match the sky,
Frag. Nat. II. 8.
Succory to match the sky,
Humble-Bee. 45.

Such (Partial list.)
Of such delight and wonder as there
grew,—   Adirondacs. 250.
With sorrow such as mine,   Dirge. 46.
As if on such stern forms and haunts
Frag. Nat. XXIX. 3.
Such have I never seen.   Hamatreya. 36.
Such sweetness crowned me,
*Lines. 11.
Such tidings of the starry sphere
May-Day. 13.
Such resurrection of the happy past,
Naples. 22.
And thoughtest thou such guest
Threnody. 224.
And such I knew, a forest seer,
Woodnotes. I. 30.

Sucked
Like fiery honey sucked from roses.
Initial Love. 53.

Suckle
Suckle him with the she-wolf's teat,
Quat. Power. 2.

Sudden
With laughter sudden as the crack of
rifle;   Adirondacs. 128.
For who can tell what sudden privacies
Adirondacs. 191.
In which the sudden wind-god rings.
Frag. Poet. I. 42.
The heavy grouse's sudden whir,
Harp. 89.
With sudden passion languishing,
May-Day. 2.
Sudden, at unawares,   Merlin. 74.
Sudden gusts came full of meaning,
September. 9.
With sudden roar the aged pine-tree
falls,—   Woodnotes. I. 73.

Suddenly
Of loud Bog River, suddenly confront
Adirondacs. 233.
That suddenly caught the flame.
Cosmos. 12.
Suddenly it will uplift
Frag. Life. XXXV. 3.
Suddenly betook them all,
May-Day. 389.

Suffer
Off soundings, seamen do not suffer cold;
Adirondacs. 56.
Suffer no savor of the earth to scape.
Bacchus. 5.
I suffer them no more;
Boston Hymn. 6.
Nor suffer sense to win from wit
Fame. 21.
Though it hate thee, suffer long;
Poet. 291.

Sufferance
And matched his sufferance sublime
Character. 5.
And matched his sufferance sublime
Poet. 138.

Suffice
This wild plantation will suffice to chase.
Adirondacs. 319.
Why need I volumes, if one word suffice?
Day's Ration. 26.
He to his wants can well suffice:
Frag. Life. XVII. 5.
Suffice to hold the festival.
May-Day. 223.

Suffices
A little hut suffices like a town.
Seashore. 10.

Suger
Panax, black birch, sugar maple,
Frag. Nat. II. 15.
Sugar spends to fatten slaves,
Heroism. 2.

Suits
'This suits me for a pasture; that's my
park;   Hamatreya. 19.

Sultry
But soft! a sultry morning breaks;
May-Day. 58.
Surcharged and sultry with a power
Unity. 10.
Here sultry Summer overstays
Walden. 7.

Sum
Crowds in a day the sum of ages,
Frag. Poet. IX. 11.
Graced by each change of sum untold,
Monadnoc. 56.
Orbit and sum of Shakspeare's wit.
Solution. 40.
And the sum of the world   Sphinx. 47.
I've learned the sum of that sad history
Summons. 18.
Sum their long experience,   Visit. 19.

Summer
See Midsummer.
In winter, lumberers; in summer, guides;
Adirondacs. 88.
the summer short,   Blight. 50.
Hung out their summer pride,
Boston. 38.
Ere yet the red Summer
Ellen South. 18.

Who all the day of life his summer story
tells;   Enchanter. 2.
Soothing with thy summer horn
Frag. Nat. XXII. 3.
A gleam of sun, a summer rain,
Frag. Nat. XXVIII. 3.
Summer and winter, o'er the wave,
Frag. Poet. I. 47.
From her summer diadem.   Give. 42.
In the hall at summer eve   Harp. 45.
The summer bird   Hermione. 4.
Buries himself in summer waves,
Initial Love. 98.
The summer dells, by genius haunted,
May-Day. 43.
And Summer came to ripen maids
May-Day. 303.
'Many feet in summer seek,
Monadnoc. 199.
Nor the red rainbow of a summer eve,
Naples. 16.
Mourning summer laid in shrouds.
Nun. 22.
Yet wreathed and hid by summer blooms.
Nun. 28.
Not less are summer mornings dear
Promise. 7.
Am I not always here, thy summer home?
Seashore. 3.
And I like less when Summer beats
Titmouse. 71.
The mountain chase, the summer waves,
To J. W. 3.
Thy summer voice, Musketaquit,
Two Rivers. 1.
When summer light is fading, and autumn
breezes sigh;   *Vlioet. 10.
When the violets were in their shrouds,
and Summer in its pride,   *Violet. 15.
In climates of the summer star.
Voluntaries. 50.
Here sultry Summer overstays
Walden. 7.
I see the summer glow, World-Soul. 110.

Summer's
April's cowslip, summer's clover,
Ellen South. 30.
The surge of summer's beauty; dell and
crag,   Musketaquid. 22.
What without him is summer's pomp,
Song of Natutre. 55.
In summer's scorching glow.
Woodnotes. II. 12.

Summers
And many a thousand summers
Song of Nature. 17.

Summer-time
And pass the burning summer-time
Frag. Poet. V. 7.

Summit
On the summit as I stood,
Monadnoc. 193.
The summit of the whole.
Song of Nature. 44.

Summit-levels
And, on cheap summit-levels of the snow,
Musketaquid. 44.

Summits
In their summits are united;
Celestial Love. 45.
Hint summits of heroic grace;
Monadnoc. 111.

Summon
They summon thee, dearest,—
            Ellen South. 14.

Summoning
Ere yet the summoning voice was still,
            Monadnoc. 31.

Summons
Thy sumons called our sires,   Bell. 10.

Sumptuous
Our sumptuous indigence,
            Monadnoc. 377.

Sun
For one sun suply us twenty.
            Alphonso. 54.
Like the torrents of the sun   Bacchus. 27.
To sun the dark and solve the curse,
            Beauty. 19.
Of the round day, related to the sun
            Blight. 15.
Clouds shade the sun, which will not tan
our hay,   Blight. 51.
And make just laws below the sun,
            Boston Hymn. 47.
Over sun and star,   Celestial Love. 28.
The sun set, but set not his hope:
            Character. 1.
O Sun! I curse thy cruel ray:
            Chartist. 17.
Will take the sun out of the skies
            Concord Ode. 39.
The everlasting sun,   Day by Day. 2.
To make the sun forgotten.   Destiny. 28.
Fronted the sun with hope as bright,
            Dirge. 7.
With the sun and the sand and the wild
uproar.   Each. 28.
A tiny scene of sun and shower,
            Ellen. 4.
I wait the sun on them should shine.
            Frag. Life. XIV. 2.
And bleaching all souls like the sun.
            Frag. Life. XXVIII. 4.
To bring their first fruits to the sun.
            Frag. Nat. II. 20.
And walk on earth as the sun walks in
the sphere.   Frag. Nat. V. 12.
The sun athwart the cloud
            Frag. Nat. IX. 1.
And unstainèd as the sun.
            Frag. Nat. XXIII. 18.
A gleam of sun, a summer rain,
            Frag. Nat. XXVIII. 3.
I kept the sun and stars at bay,
            Frag. Poet. II. 7.
Sun and moon must fall amain
            Frag. Poet. V. 34.
Waits unblamed to-morrow's sun.
            Frag. Poet. XI. 19.
Sun and moon are in my way.
            Frag. Poet. XXV. 4.
If bright the sun, he tarries,
            Frag. Poet. XXXIII. 1.
They bleach and dry in the sun.
            Garden. 16.
And the world's sun seemed to rise
            Guy. 39.
Frost and sun and eldest night,
            Hermione. 62.
Which dances round the sun—
            House. 20.
Insect lover of the sun,
            Humble-Bee. 11.
Find me a slope where I can feel the
sun   Letter. 14.

And aim a telescope at the inviolate sun.
            Letter. 22.
To fruitful field and sun and moon.
            Limits. 10.
Nor cloy us with unshaded sun,
            May-Day. 128.
And sun this frozen side.   May-Day. 161.
To see the southing of the sun?
            May-Day. 176.
As that whereof the sun is made,
            Monadnoc. 168.
Old as the sun,   Monadnoc. 204.
The sun obeys them and the moon.
            Monadnoc. 248.
And the searching sun to see
            Mountain. 16.
Onward and nearer rides the sun of
May;   Musketaquid. 19.
The sun and sea,   Ode to Beauty. 39.
Live, robed with beauty, painted by the
sun;   Pan. 5.
For in those lonely grounds the sun
            Peter. 13.
He sowed the sun and moon for seeds.
            Poet. 32.
The sun set, but set not his hope:—
            Poet. 134.
Ah, happy if a sun or star   Poet. 165.
Sun, moon, man, undulate and stream,
            Poet. 173.
By love behold the sun at night.
            Poet. 288.
The sun goes down, and with him takes
            Romany. 1.
And held them to the sun;   Rubies. 2.
When shall that sun arise?   Rubies. 12.
For Saadi sat in the sun,   Saadi. 74.
Leaves, when the sun appears, astonished
Art   Snow-Storm. 25.
The sportive sun, the gibbous moon,
            Song of Nature. 3.
Will never my wheels which whirl the
sun   Song of Nature. 47.
The sun is its toy;   Sphinx. 44.
But thought will glow when the sun
grows cold,   Thought. 7.
Who gazed upon the sun and moon
            Threnody. 142.
I dine in the sun; when he sinks in the
sea,   Titmouse. 69.
Her morning sun shone bright and calmly
purely set;   *Violet. 14.
With the offspring of the Sun;
            Voluntaries. 46.
The all-seeing sun for ages hath not
shone;   Woodnotes. I. 65.
On him the sun looked more serene;
            Woodnotes. I. 113.
Primal chimes of sun and shade,
            Woodnotes. II. 160.
This radiant pomp of sun and star,
            Woodnotes. II. 208.
The sun himself shines heartily,
            World-Soul. 63.

Sun-baked
Singing in the sun-baked square;   Art. 8.

Sunbeam
And invite the sunbeam,
            Frag. Life. XXVII. 3.
"Erect as a sunbeam,   Sphinx. 17.
As if a sunbeam showed the place,
            Woodnotes. I. 44.
Or only a flashing sunbeam
            World-Soul. 29.

Sunshine—*Continued*
Chained the sunshine and the breeze,
Guy. 8.
Was frolic sunshine, dear to all men,
Holidays. 11.
Live in the sunshine, swim the sea,
Merlin's Song. 31.
Sunshine in his heart transferred
Saadi. 80.
Planting strange fruits and sunshine on
the shore, Seashore. 47.
Sunshine cannot bleach the snow,
Test. 11.
Life, sunshine and desire, Threnody. 2.

Sun-spark
But by the sun-spark on the sea,
Celestial Love. 103.

Sup
Ale, and a sup of wine. Our steward gave
Adirondacs. 178.

Superior
Superior to all its gaudy skirts.
Adirondacs. 220.
I am superior to my human weeds."
Frag. Life. XVIII. 4.
I see him with superior smile
In Memoriam. 73.

Supersolar
Sparks of the supersolar blaze.
Merlin. 15.
Lit by the supersolar blaze.
Threnody. 202.

Supped
'I have supped to-night with gods,
Poet. 142.

Supper
Or how thy supper is sodden;'
Destiny. 26.

Supplanters
Supplanters of the tribe, the farmers
dwell. Musketaquid. 31.

Supplants
And, by herself, supplants alone
Daemonic Love. 15.

Supple
To supple Office, low and high;
Good-Bye. 10.

Supplement
Shall supplement henceforth all trodden
ways, Adirondacs. 244.
Nature, the supplement of man,
Miracle. 19.

Supplemental
Supplemental asteroid,
II. Compensation. 12.

Suppleness
Their rival strength and suppleness, their
skill Adirondacs. 81.

Suppliants
We are its suppliants. By it, we
Poet. 283.

Supplied
Supplied me necessary food;
Woodnotes. I. 136.

Supplies
Furnished several supplies;
Ode to Beauty. 49.
But when it seeks enlarged supplies,
Woodnotes. II. 55.

Supply
For one sun supply us twenty.
Alphonso. 54.
Which well it can supply,
Waterfall. 6.

Supported
See Unsupported.

Suppose
But, in my simple ignorance, suppose
Rhodora. 15.

Surcharge
While the soul it doth surcharge,
Etienne. 18.

Surcharged
Surcharged and sultry with a power
Unity. 10.

Surcoat
He dons a surcoat which he doffs at
morn: Adirondacs. 77.

Sure
See Slowsure; Unsure.
Wise and sure the issues are.
Channing Ode. 77.
And be sure at last came Love,
Garden. 27.
Ran sure, Hamatreya. 38.
One musician is sure, Harp. 1.
For of this lore be thou sure,—
Rhea. 27.
This his slow but sure reclining,
Threnody. 164.
Sure some god his eye enchants:
Woodnotes. I. 11.
And be sure the all-loving Nature
World-Soul. 35.

Surely
Untold, unknown, and I could surely
spell Blight. 10.
Surely he carries a talisman Destiny. 29.
Who the road had surely kept;
Forerunners. 18.
But surely say them better.
Frag. Life. XII. 4.
Surely now will the curtain rise,
Woodnotes. II. 212.

Surer
Of swifter life, a surer hope,
May-Day. 152.
Not on its base Monadnoc surer stood,
Phi. 13.

Surf
Moist perhaps by ocean surf, Nun. 26.

Surface
Or whipping its rough surface for a
trout; Adirondacs. 111.
Fast to surface and outside, Circles. 3.
Surface and Dream, Experience. 7.
And the glassy surface in ripples brake
Frag. Poet. I. 37.
So Spring guards with surface cold
May-Day. 144.
Surface with surfaces did swim.
Poet. 216.

Surfaces
For I am weary of the surfaces,
Blight. 2.
Surface with surfaces did swim.
Poet. 216.

Surge
The surge of summer's beauty; dell and
crag, Musketaquid. 22.

Surging
The surging sea outweighs,
　　　　　　　　　Friendship. 2.
I sing it to the surging crowd,—
　　　　　　　　　Merlin's Song. 5.
O'erlooks the surging landscape's swell!
　　　　　　　　　Monadnoc. 11.
Surly
Where feeds the moose, and walks the
　surly bear,　　Woodnotes. I. 66.
Surmise
First vague shadow of surmise　Give. 36.
Surpass
Art might obey, but not surpass.
　　　　　　　　　Problem. 46.
Surprise
Use and Surprise,　　Experience. 6.
Their unspent beauty of surprise,
　　　　　　　　　Freedom. 14.
But when the surprise,　　Give. 35.
Surprise the exulting soul.　Hymn. 24.
Can your lurking thought surprise,
　　　　　　　　　Initial Love. 62.
By the stairway of surprise.'　Merlin. 38.
Casualty and Surprise　　Nature. I. 7.
And earth's fit tenant me surprise;—
　　　　　　　　　Woodnotes. II. 213.
Disconcerts with glad surprise.
　　　　　　　　　Worship. 18.
Surprises
Judge with what sweet surprises Nature
　spoke　　　　Adirondacs. 198.
Surveyors
Time and Thought were my surveyors,
　　　　　　　　　Song of Nature. 33.
Surveys
Which the brooding soul surveys,
　　　　　　　　　Uriel. 2.
Survive
No sire survive, no son succeed!
　　　　　　　　　Monadnoc. 124.
Which five hundred did survive?
　　　　　　　　　Test. 14.
But the substances survive.
　　　　　　　　　Woodnotes. II. 261.
Survived
Survived the Flight and swam the Flood,
　　　　　　　　　May-Day. 94.
And the sharpest you still have survived,
　　　　　　　　　Quat. Borrowing. 2.
Survives
The parent fruit survives;　Promise. 4.
Sustain
It was not ripe yet to sustain
　　　　　　　　　Threnody. 140.
Swain
The brother of the fisher, porter, swain,
　　　　　　　　　Frag. Life. XXX. 5.
Swainish
Swainish, coarse and nothing worth:
　　　　　　　　　Frag. Poet. XI. 14.
Swains
Swains by winter pinched and worn.
　　　　　　　　　Frag. Nat. XXII. 4.
To swains that live in happiness
　　　　　　　　　Nature. I. 18.
Swallow
That all the wine at once we swallow
　　　　　　　　　Good Hope. 3.
The sympathetic swallow swept the
　ground.　　　　Hermione. 7.

Swallows
'Higher, dear swallows! mind not what I
　say.　　　　　Hermione. 26.
Swam
Survived the Flight and swam the Flood,
　　　　　　　　　May-Day. 94.
Swamp
Loud hammered, and the heron rose in
　the swamp.　　Adirondacs. 148.
Sink, O mountain, in the swamp!
　　　　　　　　　Monadnoc. 121.
With cloverheads the swamp adorn,
　　　　　　　　　Monadnoc. 137.
Swamps
Bridge gulfs, drain swamps,
　　　　　　　　　Monadnoc. 150.
And fear what foe in caves and swamps
　can stray,　　Woodnotes. I. 87.
Swandown
Swandown clouds dappled the farms,
　　　　　　　　　September. 6.
Swan-like
A swan-like form invests the hidden
　thorn;　　　Snow-Storm. 19.
Swarmed
And round me swarmed in shadowy troop
　　　　　　　　　Peter. 27.
Swart
Nor haughty hope, nor swart chagrin,
　　　　　　　　　Past. 8.
Forging, through swart arms of Offence,
　　　　　　　　　Spiritual Laws. 11.
To Fin and Lap and swart Malay,
　　　　　　　　　Woodnotes. II. 154.
Swarthy
My swarthy tint is in the grain,
　　　　　　　　　Romany. 19.
Swathed
They swather their too much power.
　　　　　　　　　Song of Nature. 32.
Swear
He invented oaths to swear;
　　　　　　　　　Initial Love. 115.
Sweat
To coin his labor and sweat,
　　　　　　　　　Boston Hymn. 62.
Sweat and season are their arts,
　　　　　　　　　Monadnoc. 133.
At forge and furnace thousands sweat;
　　　　　　　　　Saadi. 107.
Swede
The Swede Emanuel leads the soul.
　　　　　　　　　Solution. 46.
Swedenborg
Luther, Fox, Behmen, Swedenborg, grew
　pale,　　　　Adakryn. 3.
Sweep
Whilst his files sweep round yon Alpine
　height;　　　　Each. 8.
Sweep ruins from the scarped mountain,
　　　　　　　　　May-Day. 449.
Sweeping
For me, in showers, in sweeping showers,
　the Spring　　Musketaquid. 11.
Sweeps
That sweeps my native shore.　Bell. 16.
Sweet
　See Bitter-sweet.
Judge with what sweet surprises Nature
　spoke　　　Adirondacs. 198.

Sweet—*Continued*

Comes the sweet sadness at the retrospect,   Adirondacs. 216.

I've come to live with you, sweet friends,
                 Aeolian Harp. 18.

Plant gardens lined with lilacs sweet;
                 Art. 6.

So sweet to Seyd as only grace
                 Beauty. 2.

Feeding on the Ethiops sweet,
                 Berrying. 7.

By sweet affinities to human flesh,
                 Blight. 12.

But the sweet affluence of love and song,
                 Blight. 42.

Flowed with naphtha fiery sweet;
                 Celestial Love. 16.

His action won such reverence sweet
                 Character. 9.

Will the sweet sky and ocean broad
                 Chartist. 15.

Sweet songs of liberty.
                 Concord Ode. 32.

Which drives me mad with sweet desire,
                 Destiny. 13.

Thy sweet dominion o'er my will,
                 Eva. 5.

Make the morning proud and sweet;
                 Forerunners. 10.

And, best with best in sweet consent,
                 Frag. Life. XXIX. 5.

Sweet fern, mint and vernal grass,
                 Frag. Nat. II. 14.

Sweet and scent for Dian's table,
                 Frag. Nat. II. 16.

Sweet willow, checkerberry red,
                 Frag. Nat. II. 23.

How sweet the west wind sounds in my
own trees!   Hamatreya. 6.

(Sweet is art, but sweeter truth,)
                 Harp. 44.

So sweet and mournful falls the strain.
                 Harp. 102.

And sung his sweet regrets
                 Hermione. 2.

Sweet to me thy drowsy tone
                 Humble-Bee. 33.

Sipping only what is sweet,
                 Humble-Bee. 55.

The sweet delight I found in fields and
farms,   I Bear. 6.

In the sweet odor of her memory.
                 Letter. 18.

Were tenanted by thy sweet ghost,
                 Lines. 4.

And the sweet air with thee was sweet.
                 Lines. 14.

Their sweet and lofty countenance
                 Manners. 5.

All the sweet secrets therein hid
                 May-Day. 45.

Drug the cup, thou butler sweet,
                 May-Day. 279.

Fans in all hearts expectance sweet,
                 May-Day. 296.

Hid in song's sweet influence.
                 Merlin. 42.

And sweet varieties of chance,
                 Monadnoc. 62.

Drain sweet maple juice in vats.
                 Monadnoc. 142.

Thine elegy, sweet singer, sainted wife.
                 Naples. 27.

Sweet tyrant of all!   Ode to Beauty. 12.

Sweet, extravagant desire,
                 Ode to Beauty. 77.

Sweet is death forevermore.   Past. 7.

To whom sweet angels ministered,
                 Poet. 202.

Fall like sweet strains, or pensive smiles:
                 Problem. 4.

Virtue alone is sweet society,   Rome. 8.

In the bower of dalliance sweet
                 Saadi. 55.

Creating a sweet climate by my breath,
                 Seashore. 23.

Flushed in the sky the sweet May-morn,
                 Solution. 7.

Well I love the meaning sweet,—
                 Song of Seyd. 23.

In difference sweet,   Sphinx. 26.

"Say on, sweet Sphinx! thy dirges
                 Sphinx. 67.

To leave my woods and streams and the
sweet sloth   Summons. 4.

Sweet twilight walks and midnight solitude   Summons. 7.

Go thou, sweet Heaven, or at thy pleasure
stay!'   Sursum Corda. 9.

And whither now, my truant wise and
sweet,   Threnody. 30.

Who heard the sweet request,
                 Threnody. 44.

With sunny face of sweet repose,
                 Threnody. 68.

Of the most beautiful and sweet
                 Threnody. 107.

Nature's sweet marvel undefiled,
                 Threnody. 123.

The riches of sweet Mary's Son,
                 Threnody. 222.

I see the inundation sweet,
                 Two Rivers. 9.

There will be nought to shelter thee when
their sweet leaves are gone.
                 *Violet. 8.

And the sweet heaven his deed secures
                 Voluntaries. 92.

Blows the sweet breath of song,
                 Waldeinsamkeit. 38.

Which breathes his sweet fame through
the northern bowers.
                 Woodnotes. I. 71.

Sweet influence from every element;
                 Woodnotes. I. 77.

Sweet the genesis of things,
                 Woodnotes. II. 105.

Sweetens

Sweetens its toil—   *Lines. 3.

The innocent mirth which sweetens daily
bread,   Summons. 10

Sweeter

(Sweet is art, but sweeter truth,)
                 Harp. 44.

Brother, sweeter is the Law   Poet. 281

But sweeter rivers pulsing flit
                 Two Rivers. 3.

Sweetest

Lurks the joy that is sweetest
                 Sphinx. 91

Sweetheart
Saying, Sweetheart! the old mystery remains,—   Flute. 3.
Sweetheart's
His sweetheart's idolatry   Rhea. 39.
Sweetly
Is sweetly solemnized. Then flows amain
                Musketaquid. 21.
Sweetness
Of gulfs of sweetness without bound
                Humble-Bee. 36.
Such sweetness crowned me, *Lines. 11.
With sweetness untold,   Sphinx. 86.
Sweets
The hero is not fed on sweets,
                Heroism. 7.
I should like to die in sweets,
                Mountain. 14.
Swell
Arrived in time to swell his grain;
                Guy. 34.
Joy-tides swell their mimic ocean.
                Initial Love. 49.
O'erlooks the surging landscape's swell!
                Monadnoc. 11.
Will swell and rise with wonted grace;
                Woodnotes. II. 54.
Swells
Swells a rain-drop to a tun;
                Frag. Poet. IX. 8.
Swells, and mellows, and matures,
                May-Day. 196.
Swells hitherward, and myriads of forms
                Pan. 4.
When the wind swells.
                Woodnotes. II. 92.
Aloft, abroad, the pæan swells;
                Woodnotes. II. 100.
Swept
Next morn, we swept with oars the Saranac,   Adirondacs. 7.
All day we swept the lake, searched every cove,   Adirondacs. 108.
And Time the ruined bridge has swept
                C. Hymn. 7.
Clean swept herefrom.   Hamatreya. 52.
The sympathetic swallow swept the ground.   Hermione. 7.
Where every wind that swept my tomb
                Mountain. 11.
Swerve
Beware from right to swerve.
                Boston Hymn. 52.
But the day of day may swerve.
                Poet. 274.
Swerved
For fear of human eyes swerved from his plan.   Entombed. 4.
Swerves
For Destiny never swerves
                World-Soul. 73.
Swerving
And without a swerving
                Celestial Love. 12.
Swift
Two of our mates returning with swift oars.   Adirondacs. 234.
Are ever rivals: but, though this be swift,   Adirondacs. 287.
Be swift their feet as antelopes,
                Boston Hymn. 79.

Succession swift and spectral Wrong,
                Experience. 8.
Swift cathedrals in the wild;
                May-Day. 48.
So shaped, so colored, swift or still,
                Solution. 30.
Silent rushes the swift Lord
                Threnody. 282.
Hatred's swift repulsions play.
                Visit. 30.
The strong they slay, the swift outstride:
                Voluntaries. 118.
Swifter
Of swifter life, a surer hope,
                May-Day. 152.
Swifter-fashioned
Swifter-fashioned than the fairies,
                Initial Love. 90.
Swiftlier
Turn swiftlier round, O tardy ball!
                May-Day. 160.
Swiftly
And they that swiftly come and go
                Daemonic Love. 41.
Sail swiftly through your amber vault,
                Poet. 163.
Sad-eyed Fakirs swiftly say   Saadi. 49.
Swim
To row, to swim, to shoot, to build a camp,   Adirondacs. 82.
Will rive the hills and swim the sea,
                II Compensation. 27.
Live in the sunshine, swim the sea,
                Merlin's Song. 31.
Surface with surfaces did swim.
                Poet. 216.
Can swim the flood and wade through snow,   Quat. Love. 2.
And I will swim the ancient sea
                Woodnotes. II. 45.
Swimmer
Swimmer through the waves of air;
                Humble-Bee. 14.
Swims
Glad when the solid mountain swims
                Frag. Poet. V. 28.
Swims the world in ecstasy,   Saadi. 134.
Swing
Swing me in the upas boughs,
                Mithridates. 18.
Swinging
The swinging spider's silver line,
                Ode to Beauty. 27.
Sword
Carries the eagles, and masters the sword.
                Destiny. 50.
Nor sword of angels could reveal
                Merlin. 76.
Swords
Swords cannot cut the giving hand
                Frag. Life. VII. 3.
Through with living swords,
                Frag. Poet. XIII. 2.
In the next age, are flaming swords.
                Solution. 58.
Sybarites
By Sybarites beguiled,   Merlin. 49.
Sycophant
A sycophant to smug success?
                Chartist. 14.

Syllable
Keen ears can catch a syllable,
Garden. 29.
Told every word and syllable
Miracle. 33.
In his every syllable Saadi. 129.

Syllables
These syllables that Nature spoke,
Harp. 95.
I understand their faery syllables,
River. 24.

Sylvan
As if associates of the sylvan gods.
Adirondacs. 156.
O, when I am safe in my sylvan home,
Good-Bye. 23.
Sylvan deities encamp, Saadi. 38.
Sped, when I passed his sylvan fort,
Titmouse. 35.

Symmetry
His own symmetry with law; Guy. 12.

Sympathetic
The sympathetic swallow swept the
ground. Hermione. 7.

Sympathize
Know me, as does my dog: we sympathize; Hamatreya. 9.

Sympathy
Of sympathy so large, that ours was
theirs, Adirondacs. 257.
Yield sympathy and signs of mirth;
Celestial Love. 110.
A sympathy divine. Eva. 6.
And somewhat of majestic sympathy,
River. 33.
They knew by secret sympathy
Woodnotes. I. 116.

Symphony
Was the symphony of spheres,
Frag. Poet. IV. 23.

Synod
Sometimes the airy synod bends,
Daemonic Love. 43.

Syrian
To stay in the Syrian land: Exile. 16.
Thou to the Syrian couldst belong?
Hermione. 30.
Of Syrian peace, immortal leisure,
Humble-Bee. 38.
Drugging herbs with Syrian spices,
May-Day. 250.
Where Syrian waters roll,
Waterfall. 18.

Syrup
Gushed with syrup to the brink.
May-Day. 341.

Systems
Through ruined systems still restored,
Threnody. 283.

Tabernacle
For who defends our leafy tabernacle
Adirondacs. 171.

Table
Sweet and scent for Dian's table,
Frag. Nat. II. 16.
And what is writ on Table Round
Harp. 25.
Wrote in thy mind's transparent table,
Threnody. 199.

Tables
His children fed at heavenly tables.
Art. 18.
At rich men's tables eaten bread and
pulse? Forbearance. 3.
Was writ on tables yet unbroken;
Problem. 56.

Tablet
With this tablet on their neck,
Astraea. 11.

Tablets
Upon the tablets blue, Bacchus. 66.
Save in tablets of the heart,
In Memoriam. 49.

Taciturnity
The taciturnity of time.
Character. 6.
The taciturnity of Time. Poet. 139.

Taháwus
Taháwus, Seaward, MacIntyre, Baldhead,
Adirondacs. 10.

Tail
In tail, Hamatreya. 39.

Take
See Overtake.
And wit to trap or take him in his lair.
Adirondacs. 86.
They give and take no pledge or oath,—
Celestial Love. 85.
To take the statute from the mind
Concord Ode. 15.
Will take the sun out of the skies
Concord Ode. 39.
And take the mortal leap undaunted,
Fame. 17.
Of her faults I take no note,
Frag. Life. XVI. 5.
All things through thee take nobler form,
Friendship. 13.
Leave the chaff, and take the wheat.
Humble-Bee. 57.
And take their youth again.
Merlins Song. 13.
Hither! take me, use me, fill me,
Mithridates. 31.
Take the bounty of thy birth,
Monadnoc. 25.
But their long hands it thence will take;
Monadnoc. 146.
I take him up my rugged sides,
Monadnoc. 315.
And if I take you, dames, to task,
Romany. 9.
And give or take the stroke of war,
Saadi. 109.
So take thy quest through nature,
Spinx. 117.
To take in sail:— Terminus. 2.
Would in thy hall take up his rest?
Threnody. 225.
Bound in by streams which give and take
Waldeinsamkeit. 7.
Take off thine eyes, thy heart forbear,
Woodnotes. II. 87.
And take their shape and sun-color
World-Soul. 71.

Taken
Must be taken in together, Fable. 7.
If I had not taken the child.
Threnody. 178.

Takes
Twirl the old wheels! Time takes fresh
start again,   Adirondacs. 328.
Peace now each for malice takes,
Caritas. 5.
A thing that takes no more root in the
world   Frag. Life. XXVI. 3.
When Fate by omens takes is part,
Initial Love. 76.
He takes a sovran privilege
Initial Love. 118.
The kind Earth takes her children's part,
May-Day. 66.
He takes no mark of night or day,
Poet. 83.
The sun goes down, and with him takes
Romany. 1.
Through smallest chambers takes it way,
Threnody. 218.
Takes hearts like thine in special charge,
Titmouse. 86.

Taking
See Overtaking.

Tale
See Tell-tale.
It was ever the self-same tale,
Daemonic Love. 19.
Its heavy tale divine.   Dirge. 48.

Talents
Talents differ; all is well and wisely put;
Fable. 17.
For the talents not thine own,
Saadi. 90.

Tales
Wins the believing child with wondrous
tales;   Enchanter. 5.
The tragic tales of crime and fate;
Frag. Nat. XXVI. 34.
Tales of many a famous mount,—
Monadnoc. 95.

Talisman
Surely he carries a talisman Destiny. 29.
Guy possessed the talisman   Guy. 5.
Is this colossal talisman
Monadnoc. 89.

Talismans
Their talismans are ploughs and carts;
Monadnoc. 134.

Talk
Shall hear far Chaos talk with me;
Bacchus. 39.
To hear, when, 'mid our talk and games,
May-Day. 56.
The gods talk in the breath of the woods,
Poet. 73.
They talk in the shaken pine, Poet. 74.
I talk with kings the while.]
Walden. 32.
Talk no more with feeble tongue;
Woodnotes. II. 137.

Talked
And with snake and seraph talked.
Daemonic Love. 22.
The winds took flesh, the mountains
talked,   Frag. Poet. I. 55.
We talked at large of worldly fate,
Hermione. 38.

Talker
Talker! the unreplying Fate?
Threnody. 250.

Talking
As if we men were talking in a vein
Adirondacs. 256.
Seyd overheard the young gods talking;
Uriel. 8.

Talks
To birds and trees who talks?
Woodnotes. I. 4.

Tall
Mountain tall and ocean deep
II Compensation. 3.
Among the legs of his guardians tall,
Experience. 15.
And modest copse and the forest tall,
Frag. Poet. I. 16.
In the hemlocks tall, untamable,
Garden. 31.
Tall and good my kind among;
Monadnoc. 257.
Thou seest, O watchman tall,
Monadnoc. 385.
The tall green trees, that shelter thee,
*Violet. 7.
And up the tall mast runs the wood-
pecker.   Woodnotes. I. 67.
The date fails not on the palm-tree tall;
Woodnotes. II. 245.

Tallies
No numbers have counted my tallies,
Song of Nature. 9.

Tamable
See Untamable.

Tame
Salt and basalt, wild and tame:
Mithridates. 11.

Tamed
See Untamed.
Not tamed and cleared cumber the
ground   Letter. 12.

Tampered
Night and Day were tampered with,
Unity. 8.

Tan
'T will not now avail to tan
Alphonso. 11.
Clouds shade the sun, which will not tan
our hay,   Blight. 51.

Tap
See Tap-roots.

Tapering
A tapering turret overtops the work.
Snow-Storm. 22.

Taper's
A belt of mirrors round a taper's flame;
Xenophanes. 16.

Tapers
Or tapers light the chaos dark?
Nemesis. 12.

Tap-roots
Or grew on vine whose tap-roots, reaching through   Bacchus. 3.

Tardily
Æons which tardily unfold   Nun. 41.

Tardy
Turn swiftlier round, O tardy ball!
May-Day. 160.
Why chidest thou the tardy Spring?
May-Day. 164.
To lead the tardy concert of the year.
Musketaquid. 18.

Tarn
Lone mountain tarn, or isle forgot,
Astraea. 46.

Tarnish
Which tarnish not, but purify
Rhea. 3.
Sheen will tarnish, honey cloy,
Waldeinsamkeit. 17.

Tarried
One tarried here, there hurried one;
Threnody. 156.

Tarries
If bright the sun, he tarries,
Frag. Poet. XXXIII. 1.
Tarries yet behind? Merops. 4.
Where tarries he the while?
Song of Nature. 38.

Tarry
"Thou didst not tarry while I prayed.
Frag. Poet. II. 2.
Here from youth to age I tarry,—
Poet. 128.
Shall flock to you and tarry by your side,
Rome. 6.

Tartary
Tented Tartary, columned Nile,—
Solution. 11.

Task
Freely as task at eve undone
Frag. Poet. XI. 18.
He shall no task decline; Merlin. 50.
To falter ere thou thy task fulfil,—
Merlin's Song. 27.
Go thou to thy learned task,
Quat. Botanist. 1.
And if I take you, dames, to task,
Romany. 9.
Knew the strong task to it assigned,
Wealth. 10.

Tasks
The oar, the guide's. Dare you accept the
tasks Adirondacs. 102.
Of scholars furloughed from their tasks
and let Adirondacs. 193.
Plied for thee thy household tasks.'
Saadi. 176.
And oft at home 'mid tasks I heed,
Walden. 41.

Taste
Taste the lordship of the earth.'
Monadnoc. 26.
For homes of virtue, sense and taste.
Monadnoc. 152.
Wilt not give the lips to taste
Ode to Beauty. 80.
In its fulness he should taste Poet. 45.

Tasted
He has not tasted wine impure,
Harp. 3.

Taught
See Untaught.
That human part may be described and
taught, Frag. Life. XVIII. 7.
Me too thy nobleness has taught
Friendship. 17.
Ye taught my lips a single speech,
Merops. 7.
I never taught it what it teaches me;
Self-Reliance. 9.
Taught by Plinlimmon's Druid power,
Solution. 34.

Taught me new lessons in the lore of life.
Summons. 17.
Said, "Who taught thee me to name?
Sphinx. 110.
Taught he not thee—the man of eld,
Threnody. 183.
I taught thy heart beyond the reach
Threnody. 197.
Taught thee each private sign to raise
Threnody. 201.
It seemed as if the sparrows taught him;
Woodnotes. I. 47.

Taunt
Or taunt us with our hope decayed?
May-Day. 427.
And airy tongues did taunt the town,
Walden. 23.
Stars taunt us by a mystery
World-Soul. 47.

Taunted
Taunted the lofty land
Channing Ode. 25.

Tautest
Yet holds he them with tautest rein,
Initial Love. 50.

Tavern
In tavern cheer and tavern joke,
Monadnoc. 120.
Rude poets of the tavern hearth,
Monadnoc. 185.

Tawny
Loved of bee,—the tawney hummer.
Ellen South. 20.
He found the tawny thrushes' broods;
Woodnotes. I. 56.

Tax
Tax not my sloth that I Apology. 5.
You shall pay us a tax on tea;
Boston. 66.

Taylor
Taylor, the Shakspeare of divines.
Problem. 68.

Tea
You shall pay us a tax on tea;
Boston. 66.
If *Indians* seized the tea,
Boston. 77.
Wild tea and wild pea,
Frag. Nat. II. 2.

Teach
And teach his nimbleness to earn his
wage, Adirondacs. 268.
Teach your pupils now with plenty,
Alphonso. 53.
Teach him on these as stairs to climb,
Art. 25.
Food which teach and reason can.
Bacchus. 35.
For you can teach the lightning speech,
Boston. 110.
Explored they teach us to explore.
Dull. 22.
O, be my friend, and teach me to be
thine! Forbearance. 8.
Teach me your mood,
Frag. Nat. VIII. 5.
Teach him gladly to postpone
Frag. Poet. XI. 15.
And best can teach its Delphian chord
Harp. 103.

Or teach thou, Spring! the grand recoil
Harp. 125.
And, generous, teach his awkward race
May-Day. 404.
Teach thy feet to feel the ground,
Monadnoc. 22.
These the masters who can teach.
Monadnoc. 174.
'Bard, when thee would Allah teach,
Saadi. 60.
What rainbows teach, and sunsets show?
Threnody. 261.

Teaches
I never taught it what it teaches me;
Self-Reliance. 9.

Teaching
Teaching barren moors to smile,
May-Day. 3.

Teal
Where the deer feeds at night, the teal by
day,   Adirondacs. 20.

Tear
No craven cry, no secret tear,—
In Memoriam. 99.
Though it tear thee unexpressed;
Rhea. 12.

Tearless
Still tearless lift its slender form above
the wintry snow?   *Violet. 4.

Tears
have wine for tears;   Fame. 16.
And my tears are dry.   *Lines. 28.
Some tears escaped, but his philosophy
Philosopher. 8.
Built of tears and sacred flames,
Threnody. 278.
Waters with tears of ancient sorrow
Threnody. 286.

Teat
Suckle him with the she-wolf's teat,
Quat. Power. 2.

Tedious
Traveller, to thee, perchance, a tedious
road,   Musketaquid. 32.

Tediousness
Not to be conned to tediousness
Threnody. 229.

Teem
Teem with unwonted thoughts:
Daemonic Love. 47.

Teeth
His teeth and bones to buy a name,
Fame. 10.
For teeth and hair with shopmen deal;
Romany. 18.

Telegraph
And the light-outspeeding telegraph
World-Soul. 15.

Telescope
And aim a telescope at the inviolate sun.
Letter. 22.

Tell
Tell the sun's time,   Adirondacs. 104.
For who can tell what sudden privacies
Adirondacs. 191.
But birds tell it in the bowers.
Apology. 16.
Tell men what they knew before;
Frag. Life. XIX. 1.
And tell what's there enjoyed,
Garden. 2.

Which thus the buried Past can tell,
Harp. 62.
And if I tell you all my thought,
Initial Love. 23.
And, truth to tell, amused by pain.
II Intellect. 2.
Tell me, maiden, dost thou use
Lines. 1.
That pierced my trance its drift to tell,
Miracle. 30.
By million changes skilled to tell
Monadnoc. 86.
Which who can tell what mason laid?
Monadnoc. 369.
Seeks how he may fitly tell   Poet. 89.
Tell them, dear, that if eyes were made
for seeing,   Rhodora. 11.
I cannot tell rude listeners
September. 13.
"Who'll tell me my secret,   Sphinx. 5.
Who shall tell what did befall,
Wealth. 1.
Who can tell him what he is?
Woodnotes. I. 27.
And tell its long-descended race.
Woodnotes. I. 45.
Hark! in thy ear I will tell the sign
Woodnotes. II. 192.
I will tell thee the mundane lore.
Woodnotes. II. 253.

Teller
See Foreteller.

Telleth
"Who telleth one of my meanings
Sphinx. 131.

Tells
Your letter tells, O changing child!
Amulet. 3.
Who all the day of life his summer story
tells;   Enchanter. 2.
And in their causes tells,—   Harp. 12.
But my minstrel knows and tells
Harp. 19.
Tells of countless sunny hours,
Humble-Bee. 34.
And tidings of the future tells.
Hymn. 4.
Bards, Roys, Scanderbegs and Tells;
Monadnoc. 97.
hear'st thou half it tells?
Woodnotes. II. 101.

Tell-tale
Half the tell-tale South-wind said,—
September. 14.

Temper
See Attemper.
Temper to face wolf, bear, or catamount,
Adirondacs. 85.

Temperament
Temperament without a tongue,
Experience. 9.
Combined a new temperament.
Frag. Life. XXIX. 6.

Temperance
But she has the temperance
May-Day. 130.

Tempering
Tempering the pitch of all   Harp. 9.
Through tempering nights and flashing
days,   Monadnoc. 212.

Tempest
Songs can the tempest still,   Merlin. 55.
Toil and tempest are the toys
                        Monadnoc. 163.
Sounded like a tempest strong   Poet. 28.
Or bow above the tempest bent;
                        Threnody. 277.
With tempest of the blinding flakes.
                        Titmouse. 74.
A tempest cannot blow;
                        Woodnotes. I. 99.
And anchored in the tempest ride.
                        Woodnotes. II. 257.

Tempests
Planted these, and tempests flowed it.
                        Garden. 20.
Dark with more clouds than tempests
are,   Threnody. 99.

Temple
The temple of a nation's vows.
                        Frag. Life. XXII. 2.
Knew every temple and kiosk
                        Frag. Poet. I. 7.

Temples
These temples grew as grows the grass;
                        Problem. 45.
Then temples rose, and towns, and marts,
                        Wealth. 34.

Tempted
Tempted by thy praise of wit,
                        Saadi. 88.

Ten
Ten men, ten guides,   Adirondacs. 6.
Ten scholars, wonted   Adirondacs. 50.
Three times ten thousand strokes, from
  morn to eve.   Adirondacs. 90.
Found ten years since the Californian
  gold?   Adirondacs. 280.
My counsel is, kill nine in ten,
                        Alphonso. 68.
O'er ten thousand, thousand acres,
                        Ellen South. 9.
Unless to learn it ten times ten.
                        Miracles. 8.
Come ten, or come a million,
                        Saadi. 32.
God, though he were ten times slain,
                        Voluntaries. 103.
Can find with glass in ten times ten.
                        Walk. 8.

Tenant
House and tenant go to ground,
                        Threnody. 288.
And earth's fit tenant me surprise;—
                        Woodnotes. II. 213.

Tenanted
Were tenanted by thy sweet ghost,
                        Lines. 4.

Tend
O, whither tend thy feet?
                        Threnody. 31.
Which the four seasons do not tend
                        Threnody. 112.

Tendency
Of tendency distribute souls.
                        Celestial Love. 82.
Of tendency through endless ages,
                        Woodnotes. II. 106.

Tender
Which past endurance sting the tender
  cit,   Adirondacs. 174.

And tender to the spirit-touch
                        Culture. 7.
A very tender history   Dirge. 55.
Mad Destiny this tender stripling played;
                        Epitaph. 2.
So guilt not traverses his tender will.
                        Frag. Life. II. 3.
Or match with words that tender sky?
                        Garden. 40.
Nor Collins' verse of tender pain,
                        Harp. 79.
Which for a spike of tender green
                        May-Day. 233.
With tender light and youthful cheer,
                        May-Day. 269.
And what his tender heart hath felt
                        Saadi. 123.
Low and tender in the cell
                        Voluntaries. 5.
Thy gait too slow, thy habits tender
                        Woodnotes. II. 187.

Tenderer
I await a tenderer touch,
                        Aeolian Harp. 6.

Tenderly
O tenderly the haughty day
                        Concord Ode. 1.

Tenderness
Power have they for tenderness;
                        Celestial Love. 90.
Shot million rays of thought and tender-
  ness.   Musketaquid. 10.

Tendrils
Whose ample leaves and tendrils curled
                        Bacchus. 15.
Stanch and strong the tendrils twine:
                        II Compensation. 16.
And the new-born tendrils twine,
                        May-Day. 88.

Tenements
The innumerable tenements of beauty,
                        Musketaquid. 61.
From humble tenements around
                        Robbins Hymn. 13.

Tenfold
The tenfold clouds that cover   Dull. 12.

Tense
With joy too tense for sober brain;
                        Frag. Poet. I. 51.
Thou grand affirmer of the present tense,
                        Monadnoc. 359.
On his tense chords all strokes were felt,
                        Poet. 210.

Tent
But I can see the elastic tent of day
                        Frag. Nat. V. 4.
A watchman in a dark gray tent,
                        Frag. Nat. XXVI. 14.
I know each nest and web-worm's tent,
                        Miracle. 3.
To compass of a tent.   Terminus. 11.
Or like a traveller's fleeing tent,
                        Threnody. 276.

Tented
Or tented armies on a plain.
                        May-Day. 256.
Tented Tartary, columned Nile,—
                        Solution. 11.

Ten-tongued
By the ten-tongued laurel speaking,
                        May-Day. 419.

Tents
And huts and tents; nor loved he less
                    Frag. Poet. I. 25.
through tents of gold,   October. 6.
Through these green tents, by eldest
Nature dressed,   Woodnotes. I. 80.

Term
And nothing thrives to reach its natural
    term;   Blight. 52.
Girds the world with bound and term;
                    Celestial Love. 37.
Since genius too has bound and term,
                    Harp. 74.
Plans immense his term prolong;
                    Initial Love. 139.
Is the term of convenance,   Visit. 24.
They reach no term, they never sleep,
                    Voluntaries. 115.

Terms
And live on even terms with Time;
                    Art. 26.
Through worlds and races and terms and
    times   Poet. 71.
Timely wise accept the terms,
                    Terminus. 17.

Terraces
Laid the terraces, one by one;
                    Garden. 14.
Was ever building like my terraces?
                    Seashore. 7.

Terrene
For Love draws might from terrene force
                    Waterfall. 7.

Terror
By strength and terror skirted;
                    Daemonic Love. 61.
When wrath and terror changed Jove's
    regal port,   Frag. Life. XXXIV. 1.
Terror and Hope and wild Remorse,
                    Miracle. 12.
Whilst love and terror laid the tiles.
                    Problem. 32.
Terror and beauty on their wing;
                    Saadi. 128.
With spasms of terror for balm of hope.
                    Solution. 24.
Walled with mortal terror round,
                    Voluntaries. 90.

Test
In sooth, red flannel is a saucy test
                    Adirondacs. 97.
Test of the poet is knowledge of love,
                    Quat. Casella. 1.

Testify
He is here to testify.   Day by Day. 13.

Tethered
Tethered by a liquid cord
                    Daemonic Love. 3.

Than (Partial list.)
No faster than his planted trees,
                    Alphonso. 78.
Than thine no deeper moat can be,
                    Boston. 61.
Not firmer based than they.
                    Frag. Life. XXXVI. 4.
Wiser far than human seer,
                    Humble-Bee. 52.
Plainer than the day,   Initial Love. 42
It is mightier than the strong,
                    Merlin's Song. 3.

Than wine or sleep or praise;
                    Rome. 13.
Older than all thy race.   Seashore. 17.
Better it is than gems or gold,
                    Thought. 5.
Than the meeting of the eyes? Visit. 12.
Than Walden's haunted wave,
                    Walden. 26.

Thank
I thank the joyful juice   Bacchus. 45.
They thank the spring-flood for its fertile
    slime,   Musketaquid. 43.
And thank thee for a better clew,
                    Titmouse. 100.

Thanked
Thanked Nature for each stroke she
    dealt;   Poet. 209.

Thankful
Six thankful weeks,—and let it be
                    Goethe. 1.
Shepherds are thankful and nations gay.
                    Merlin's Song. 34.

Thanks
Thanks if your genial care
                    Aeolian Harp. 2.
Wherefor thanks God his daily praise,
                    Frag. Poet. XI. 2.
Thanks the atoms that cohere.
                    Prudence. 6.
And thanks was his contrition;
                    Saadi. 75.
Thanks to the morning light,
                    World-Soul. 1.
Thanks to the foaming sea,
                    World-Soul. 2.
Thanks to each man of courage,
                    World-Soul. 5.

That (Partial list.)
That mortals miss the loyal heats,
                    Alphonso. 33.
That I, drinking this,   Bacchus. 38.
Hireling and him that hires;
                    Boston Hymn. 40.
The circles of that sea are laws
                    Celestial Love. 58.
And the wind that we perfume
                    Ellen South. 35.
Or say, the foresight that awaits
                    Fate. 15.
That each for each doth fast engage;
                    Hermione. 32.
Power that by obedience grows,
                    Insight. 1.
That the word the vessel brings
                    Letters. 5.
Who knows this or that?   Limits. 1.
What was that I heard   May-Day. 8.
That they may render back   Merlin. 12.
He looks on that, and he turns pale.
                    Monadnoc. 330.
To swains that live in happiness
                    Nature. I. 18.
From Eden's vats that run.   Rubies. 12.
Of that be none afraid.   September. 12.
There's not enough for this and that,
                    Terminus. 12.

Thatch
Thatch his flesh, and even his years
                    Alphonso. 75.
And thatch with towns the prairie broad
                    World-Soul. 67.

That's
From all that's fair, from all that's foul,
Music. 5.
That's writ upon our cell;
World-Soul. 46.

Thaw
As we thaw frozen flesh with snow,
May-Day. 125.
In the wide thaw and ooze of wrong,
Monadnoc. 114.
As snow-banks thaw in April's beam,
Poet. 35.
But fire to thaw that ruddy snow,
Rubies. 9.

Thawing
Thawing snow-drift into flowers.
Monadnoc. 65.

The (Partial list.)
The sallow knows the basket-maker's
thumb; Adirondacs. 101.
The midge, the blue-fly and the mosquito
Adirondacs. 166.
The other slow,—this the Prometheus,
Adirondacs. 288.
The lynx, the rattlesnake, the flood, the
fire; Adirondacs. 316.
Yet is understood the better;
Astraea. 22.
And the cloud-shadow on the lea,
Celestial Love. 104.
The universe, Daemonic Love. 73.
The master's requiem.' Dirge. 60.
The kingly bard Merlin. 9.
With the marches of the brave;
Merlin. 25.
Great is the art, Merlin. 27.
The rhyme of the poet Merlin. 77.
The Seraph's and the Cherub's food.
Saadi. 162.
The poultry-yard, the shed, the barn,—
Threnody. 89.

Theatre
Thine own theatre art thou. Poet. 252.

Thebes
In her hundred-gated Thebes every cham-
ber was a door, Frag. Nat. XII. 2.
Lo! here is Rome and Nineveh and
Thebes, Seashore. 14.
What boots it here of Thebes or Rome
Walden. 45.

Thee (Partial list.)
Thee to guide and to redeem.
Celestial Love. 62.
I found by thee, O rushing Contoocook!
Channing Ode. 21.
The shaft we raise to them and thee.
C. Hymn. 16.
From each to each, from thee to me,
Daemonic Love. 79.
'They loved thee from their birth;
Dirge. 50.
Would pay my debt to thee.
*Farewell. 22.
I gave my heart to thee. *Farewell. 40.
Go match thee with thy seeming peers;
Frag. Life. XXV. 2.
Draws angels nigh to dwell with thee,
Freedom. 19.
Of a joy apart from thee, Give. 38.
She shall find thee, and be found.
Hermione. 76.

And the sweet air with thee was sweet.
Lines. 14.
We in thee the shadow find.
Monadnoc. 391.
Traveller, to thee, perchance, a tedious
road, Musketaquid. 32.
Informed by thee, Ode to Beauty. 40.
To thee. He watches for thee still. His
love Rome. 24.
And lift thee to his holy mount,
Saadi. 61.
Seek nothing,—Fortune seeketh thee.
Saadi. 144.
To fetch thee birds of paradise:
Saadi. 148.
Admits thee to the perfect Mind.
Saadi. 164.
Plied for thee thy household tasks.'
Saadi. 176.
A music heard by thee alone
Threnody. 78.
To works as noble led thee on.
Threnody. 79.
Night came, and Nature had not thee;
Threnody. 102.
The eager fate which carried thee
Threnody. 160.
Taught he not thee—the man of eld,
Threnody. 183.
'I came to thee as to a friend;
Threnody. 209.
Dearest, to thee I did not send
Threnody. 210.
Heart's love will meet thee again.
Threnody. 269.
Thee of thy faith who hath bereft,
Woodnotes. II. 183.
To thee the horizon shall express
Woodnotes. II. 196.
Come, lay thee in my soothing shade,
Woodnotes. II. 219.
Enough for thee the primal mind
Woodnotes. II. 232.

Thefts
And thefts from satellites and rings
Song of Nature. 25.

Their (Partial list.)
Their rival strength and suppleness,
their skill Adirondacs. 81.
Their fragrance, and their chemistry ap-
ply Blight. 11.
Their noble meanings are their pawns.
Celestial Love. 88.
Their unspent beauty of surprise,
Freedom. 14.
Their pulses beat, Merlin. 46.
From their rifle or their snare;
Monadnoc. 144.
Their doubts, and aid their strife.
Robbins Hymn. 12.

Theirs (Partial list.)
Of sympathy so large, that ours was
theirs, Adirondacs. 257.
Earth-proud, proud of the earth which is
not theirs; Hamatreya. 14.
'They called me theirs, Hamatreya. 53.
How am I theirs, Hamatreya. 57.

Theist
See Atheist; Pantheist.
Let theist, atheist, pantheist, Saadi. 96.

Them (Partial list.)
Nay, we saluted them Auxiliaries,
    Adirondacs. 169.
Give them again to shine; Bacchus. 58.
Men their fortunes bring with them.
    Celestial Love. 74.
The key is gone with them; Dirge. 58.
The service done to me as done to them.
    Frag. Life. XXX. 7.
The merry Spring threw wreaths on
 them,   May-Day. 314.
You must be like them if you desire them,
    Rome. 11.
He wants them all, Saadi. 26.

Theme
When that bird sang, I gave the theme;
    Miracle. 27.
Theme no poet gladly sung,
    Prudence. 1.
I choose a novel theme, a bold abuse
    To-Day. 7.

Themselves
How they diffuse themselves into the
 air, Frag. Nat. XVII. 2.

Then (Partial list.)
A pause and council: then, where near the
 head Adirondacs. 29.
A union then of honest men,
    Boston. 35.
And then as now from far admired,
    Harp. 117.
Many hamlets sought I then,
    Monadnoc. 127.
Then, at last, I let him down
    Monadnoc. 344.

Thence (Partial list.)
Thence, in strong country carts,
    Adirondacs. 2.
To fetch one ingot thence Dull. 16.
They pluck Force thence, and give it to
 the wise. Seashore. 29.

Thenceforth
And the brains of men thenceforth,
    Daemonic Love. 45.

Thenceforward
I thenceforward and long after
    Forerunners. 35.

There (Partial list.)
There, growing slowly old at ease
    Alphonso. 77.
There the holy essence rolls,
    Celestial Love. 46.
None can reënter there,— Past. 14.
And finds his prison there.
    Woodnotes. II. 29.
But it carves the bow of beauty there,
    Woodnotes. II. 170.

Thereafter
And where thereafter in the world he
 went. River. 7.

Thereby
Five-leaved, three-leaved and two-leaved,
 grew thereby. Adirondacs. 41.
And the vine that grows thereby?
    Exile. 4.

Therefore
Therefore they shove us from them, yield
 to us Blight. 40.
Turn pale and starve. Therefore, to our
 sick eyes, Blight. 49.

Therefore comes an hour from Jove
    Daemonic Love. 116.
Therefore was the world so wide.
    Frag. Life. XXI. 2.
In love, he cannot therefore cease his
 trade; Philosopher. 3.

Therein
In its white block; yet it therein shall
 find Angelo. 3.
And Love led Gods therein to bide.
    Frag. Poet. XX. 2.
And seldom therein could I look,
    Goethe. 4.
Therein I hear the Parcæ reel
    Harp. 99.
All the sweet secrets therein hid
    May-Day. 45.
I too therein could challenge part
    Security. 11.
I hear continually his voice therein.
    Self-Reliance. 5.
No breath therein, no passage out,
    Poet. 190.

Thereon
And the poor spinners weave their webs
 thereon Frag. Nat. XXXIII. 2.
As with diamond dews thereon.
    May-Day. 413.

There's
For there's no sequestered grot,
    Astraea. 45.
There's a melody born of melody,
    Destiny. 5.
There's fruit upon my bararen soil
    Mondnoc. 295.
There's a berry blue and gold,—
    Monadnoc. 297.
For there's no rood has not a star above
 it; Musketaquid. 54.
There's not a sparrow or a wren,
    Threnody. 110.
There's not a blade of autumn grain,
    Threnody. 111.
Where his clear spirit leads him, there's
 his road Woodnotes. I. 94.

Therewith
In me therewith beatified? Poet. 278.
Builds therewith eternal towers;
    Spiritual Laws. 4.

Thermometer
Hang in the air a bright thermometer
    Letter. 21.

These (Partial list.)
All these are fading now; *Farewell. 14.
That seeth as God seeth. These are their
 gifts, Good Cheer. 12.
What hast thou to do with these
    In Memoriam. 26.
These the masters who can teach.
    Monadnoc. 174.
These the siroc could not melt, Test. 7.
Speak it firmly, these are gods,
    Voluntaries. 121.
But in these sunny solitudes
    Walden. 19.

Thessaly
The fields of Thessaly grew green,
    Peter. 19.

They (Partial list.)
Made them to boys again. Happier that
 they Adirondacs. 61.

They (Partial list.)—*Continued*
They are the doctors of the wilderness.
                        Adirondacs. 95.
And they serve men austerely,
                        Celestial Love. 121.
They treated Nature as they would.
                        Dirge. 32.
Perform the feat as well as they;
                        Frag. Life. X. 2.
They are ashamed.
                        Frag. Life. XXXIII. 6.
Not firmer based than they.
                        Frag. Life. XXXVI. 4.
For they drew no blood,   *Lines. 19.
What they conceal.   Merlin. 77.
In perfect time and measure they
                        Merlin. 126.
Youth, for a moment free as they,
                        Monadnoc. 21.
They feed the spring which they exhaust;
                        Saadi. 42.
They reach no term, they never sleep,
                        Voluntaries. 115.

They're
And feats achieve before they're named.
                        Nature. I. 21.

Thick
The old Sphinx bit her thick lip,—
                        Sphinx. 109.

Thicket
The matted thicket low and wide,
                        Wealth. 14.
They led me through the thicket damp,
                        Woodnotes. I. 125.

Thicket's
And guessed within the thicket's gloom,
                        Woodnotes. 1. 59.

Thickets
Me through trackless thickets led,
                        Woodnotes. I. 119.

Thick-stemmed
Through thick-stemmed woodlands rough
  and wide.   Woodnotes. I. 120.

Thief
No thief so politic,   Past. 15.

Thief-like
And thief-like step of liberal hours
                        Monadnoc. 64.

Thieves
And in the midst of spoils and slaves, we
  thieves   Blight. 46.
On thieves, on drudges and on dolls.
                        Woodnotes. II. 203.

Thieving
Thieving Ambition and paltering Gain!
                        Beauty. 24.

Thin
This thin spruce roof, this clayed log-
  wall,   Adirondacs. 318.
Daily to a more thin and outward rind,
                        Blight. 48.

Thine (Partial list.)
What pictures and what harmonies are
  thine!   Adirondacs. 212.
O, be my friend, and teach me to be
  thine!   Forbearance. 8.
If thou go in thine own likeness,
                        Frag. Life. XXVII. 7.
Blends the starry fates with thine,
                        Freedom. 18.

To seal the marriage of these minds with
  thine,   Good Cheer. 14.
Throb thine with Nature's throbbing
  breast,   Threnody. 207.
Henceforth I wear no stripe but thine;
                        Titmouse. 54.
"Am I not thine? Are not these thine?"
                        Woodnotes. II. 148.
'Alas! thine in the bankruptcy,
                        Woodnotes. II. 217.

Thing
Law for man, and law for thing;
                        Channing Ode. 54.
One thing is forever good;   Destiny. 45.
That one thing is Success,—
                        Destiny. 46.
Unto the thing so signified;   Fate. 14.
A thing that takes no more root in the
  world   Frag. Life. XXVI. 3.
Every thing is kin of mine.
                        Mithridates. 5.
Thou bloomest here a lonely thing
                        *Violet. 6.
And live with living nature, a pure re-
  joicing thing.   *Violet. 12.
But to each thought and thing allied,
                        Woodnotes. II. 175.

Things
Things deteriorate in kind;
                        Alphonso. 3.
Preferring things to names, for these
  were men,   Blight. 26.
Where unlike things are like;
                        Celestial Love. 38.
Would serve things still;—
                        Channing Ode. 42.
Things are of the snake.
                        Channing Ode. 43.
Things are in the saddle,
                        Channing Ode. 50.
Of thoughts and things at home, but still
  adjourn   Day's Ration. 31.
But the poor, unsightly, noisome things
                        Each. 26.
But all sorts of things and weather
                        Fable. 6.
We have not better things to say,
                        Frag. Life. XII. 3.
The portraiture of things to be.
                        Frag. Life. XXXV. 6.
All things shine in his smoky ray,
                        Frag. Nat. III. 15.
Many things the garden shows,
                        Frag. Nat. XXI. 1.
Nor offered words till they were things,
                        Frag. Poet. V. 27.
And carolled undeceiving things
                        Frag. Poet. V. 42.
Things writ in vaster character;
                        Frag. Poet. V. 46.
Chasing with words fast-flowing things;
  nor try   Frag. Poet. XXIX. 5.
All things through thee take nobler form,
                        Friendship. 13.
In his plenty things so rare?
                        Goethe. 8.
Interchangeable with things,   Guy. 3.
That all things from him began;
                        Guy. 6.
That panteth after things unseen,
                        Hymn. 3.

Two things thou shalt not long for, if
thou love a mind serene;—
      Ibn Jemin. 1.
Return to be things, Illusions. 30.
And where it cometh, all things are;
      Informing Spirit. 3.
And touches all things with his rose.
      Initial Love. 77.
All things wait for and divine him,—
      Initial Love. 78.
From the things which he compares,
      Insight. 4.
Adding wings through things to range,
      Insight. 5.
And a change has passed on things.
      May-Day. 34.
All things return, both sphere and mote,
      May-Day. 179.
Made all things in pairs. Merlin. 80.
Justice is the rhyme of things;
      Merlin. 114.
Things of the heavenly mind,—
      Merops. 2.
Smug-routine, and things allowed,
      Mithridates. 29.
Minorities, things under cloud!
      Mithridates. 30.
It sounds from all things old,
      Music. 3.
It sounds from all things young,
      Music. 4.
But in the darkest, meanest things
      Music. 11.
But in the mud and scum of things
      Music. 17.
She will be all things to all men.
      Nature. II. 4.
Queen of things! I dare not die
      Ode to Beauty. 94.
Things past and things to come.
      Peter. 28.
The things whereon he cast his eyes
      Poet. 9.
How all things sparkle, Poet. 105.
My heart at the heart of things
      Poet. 130.
O fire of fire! O best of things!
      Poet. 161.
Nor mount, nor dive; all good things
keep   Saadi. 145.
And out of spent and aged things
      Song of Nature. 27.
Heedless of inferior things;
      Song of Seyd. 32.
As love old things *for age,* and hate **the**
new.   To-Day. 12.
But now and then, truth-speaking things
      Uriel. 47.
Lover of all things alive.
      Woodnotes. I. 24.
Sweet the genesis of things,
      Woodnotes. II. 105.
Melts things that be to things that seem,
      Woodnotes. II. 114.
Of things with things, of times with
times,   Woodnotes. II. 159.
Hitherto all things fast abide,
      Woodnotes. II. 256.
It was her stern necessity: all things
      Xenophanes. 5.

Deceive us, seeming to be many things,
      Xenophanes. 8

Think
 See Bethink.
Think nature barely serves for one;
      Alphonso. 36.
Think me not unkind and rude
      Apology. 1.
Think ye I made this ball
      Boston Hymn. 9.
If the red slayer think he slays,
      Brahma. 1.
Or if the slain think he is slain,
      Brahma. 2.
And I think it no disgrace Fable. 10.
Nor think it long. Frag. Nat. XXI. 9.
For I had too much to think,
      Goethe. 5.
Yet I think on them in the silent night,
      I Bear. 9.
And think Nature in these towers
      Monadnoc. 98.
Think me not numbed or halt with age,
      Nun. 33.
I think no virtue goes with size;
      Titmouse. 60.
I think old Cæsar must have heard
      Titmouse. 95.
Thus or thus they are and think.
      Woodnotes. II. 288.

Thinks
Little thinks, in the field, yon red-cloaked
clown   Each. 1.
Blooms in beauty, thinks in wit,
      May-Day. 292.
The air is wise, the wind thinks well,
      Walden. 37.

Think'st
Think'st Beauty vanished from the coast
      Threnody. 181.

Thinly
Thinly dieted on dew, Mithridates. 21.

Third
One third part of the sky unrolled
      Concord Ode. 11.
The third adds heat's indulgent spark;
      Woodnotes. II. 291.

Thirst
False waters of thirst;
      Ode to Beauty. 14.
Or by thirst and appetite Saadi. 89.
Who drink it shall not thirst again;
      Two Rivers. 18.

Thirsting
Thirsting in that pure for a purer sky?
      Adirondacs. 210.

Thirsts
By man who thirsts to be deceived.
      Frag. Nat. XXXI. 6.

Thirsty
Will song dissuade the thirsty spear?
      Voluntaries. 18.

This (Partial list.)
This feat of wit, this triumph of mankind;
      Adirondacs. 255.
That I, drinking this, Bacchus. 38.
On this green bank, by this soft stream,
      C. Hymn. 9.
Saying, 'This be thy portion, child; this
chalice,   Day's Ration. 3.

This (Partial list.)—*Continued*
This poor tooting, creaking cricket,
Frag. Nat. I. 6.
This Hermione absorbed   Hermione. 12.
Who knows this or that?   Limits. 1.
Knowest thou this?   Monadnoc. 241.
The keys of this breast,—
Ode to Beauty. 2.
This is lordly man's down-lying,
Threnody. 163.

Tho'
Not to regret the changes, tho' they cost
River. 20.

Thorn
The wild rose and the barberry thorn
Boston. 37.
A swan-like form invests the hidden
thorn;   Snow-Storm. 19.
And the fresh rose on yonder thorn
Song of Nature. 83.

Thorns
Stuff sharp thorns beneath the head
Saadi. 68.

Thorough
An energy that searches thorough
May-Day. 459.
Thorough a thousand voices Sphinx. 129.
Thorough nature's operation,   Visit. 4.

Thoroughfares
As chapels in the city's thoroughfares,
Adirondacs. 195.

Thoroughly
I have thought it thoroughly over,—
Alphonso. 55.
And, so thoroughly is known
Celestial Love. 91.

Those (Partial list.)
Or those we erring own,
Celestial Love. 55.
Ah, not to me those dreams belong!
Frag. Poet. XXX. 1.
To those who go, and those who come;
Good-Bye. 13.

Thou (Partial list.)
Thou darling town of ours!
Boston. 119.
Out of that delicate lay could'st thou
Dirge. 47.
Right thou feelest, rush to do.'
Freedom. 24.
What art thou? His wicked eye
Limits. 11.
And comest thou   Monadnoc. 205.
If thou trowest   Monadnoc. 228.
Grow early old with grief that thou
Threnody. 130.
The deep Heart answered, 'Weepest
thou?   Threnody. 176.
But thou, my votary, weepest thou?
Threnody. 195.
When Duty whispers low, *Thou must,*
Voluntaries. 73.
The wood is wiser far than thou;
Woodnotes. II. 172.

Though (Partial list.)
'Welcome, though late, unknowing, yet
known to me.'   Adirondacs. 45.
Are ever rivals: but, though this be swift,
Adirondacs. 287.
What care though rival cities soar
Boston. 45.

But though aye one in heart,
*Farewell. 32.
Though with boom and spar
Frag. Nat. XV. 2.
A woman to thy wife, though she were a
crowned queen;   Ibn Jemin. 2.
And, though a pyramid, will bound.
Monadnoc. 255.
And though thy knees were never bent,
Prayer. 5.
Though thou kept the straightest road,
Rhea. 23.
For, though he scoop my water in his
palm,   Seashore. 45.
What though he pains and joys
Threnody. 40.
Though beloved, I miss her not;
Una. 10.
Though, feigning dwarfs, thy crouch and
creep,   Voluntaries. 117.
Grave, chaste, contended, though retired,
Woodnotes. II. 69.

Thought
See Forethought; Methought.
Nor doubt but visitings of graver thought
Adirondacs. 188.
I have thought it thoroughly over,—
Alphonso. 55.
Goes home loaded with a thought.
Apology. 12.
And his thought the penal worm.
Astraea. 30.
And good men thought thy sacred voice
Bell. 11.
He thought it happier to be dead,
Beauty. 25.
My honied thought   Channing Ode. 4.
I thought the sparrow's note from
heaven,   Each. 13.
To the dear object of his thought,
Frag. Life. XVII. 13.
Thought and its mansions fair.
Frag. Life. XXIV. 4.
The sun athwart the cloud thought it no
sin   Frag. Nat. IX. 1.
Go, speed the stars of Thought
Frag. Poet. V. 9.
For thought, and not praise;
Frag. Poet. VIII. 1.
Thought is the wages
Frag. Poet. VIII. 2.
Unless to Thought is added Will,
Frag. Poet. XVIII. 3.
The vice of Japhet by the thought of
Shem.   Frag. Poet. XXII. 2.
His instant thought a poet spoke,
Frag. Poet. XXXII. 1.
And omens above thought.   Garden. 56.
A spot that is sacred to thought and God.
Good-Bye. 22.
To music, and to music's thought,
Hermione. 74.
And, if I tell you all my thought,
Initial Love. 23.
Can your lurking thought surprise,
Initial Love. 62.
Nor thought of fame.   In Memoriam. 6.
Go, speed the stars of Thought
I Intellect. 1.
And to speak my thought if none forbids
May-Day. 326.

Newest knowledge, fiery thought,
    Miracle. 13.
I thought to find the patriots
    Monadnoc. 92.
Works thy form on human thought;
    Monadnoc Afar. 6.
Shot million rays of thought and tender-
    ness.   Musketaquid. 10.
The bosom thought which thou must
    speak;   Nemesis. 2.
Ah me! it was my childhood's thought,
    Nun. 7.
In latent fire is secret thought,
    Poet. 14.
By one thought to one same sphere;
    Poet. 268.
Of thought in their mysterious caves
    Poet. 276.
Unsure the ebb and flood of thought,
    Poet. 279.
Not from a vain or shallow thought
    Problem. 9.
Every thought is public,
    Quat. Hush. 1.
To clothe the fiery thought
    Quat. Poet. 2. 1.
I never thought to ask, I never knew:
    Rhodora. 14.
I looked again,—I thought them hearts
    Rubies. 5.
To fire the stagnant earth with thought:
    Solution. 4.
Then by better thought I lead
    Solution. 25.
Time and Thought were my surveyors,
    Song of Nature. 33.
But thought will glow when the sun
    grows cold,   Thought. 7.
And, pregnant with his grander thought,
    Threnody. 144.
Through love and thought, through pow-
    er and dream.   Two Rivers. 12.
In the homestead, homely thought,
    Una. 5.
At home a deeper thought may light
    Una. 13.
I am but a thought of hers,   Una. 19.
Haughty thought be far from me;
    Voluntaries. 2.
Stayed on his subtile thought,
    Voluntaries. 80.
[If Thought unlock her mysteries,
    Walden. 29.
So waved the pine-tree through my thought
    Woodnotes. II. 3.
But to each thought and thing allied,
    Woodnotes. II. 175.
He shoots his thought, by hidden nerves,
    World-Soul. 75.
Song, picture, form, space, thought and
    character   Xenophanes. 7.

Thoughtest
And thoughtest thou such guest
    Threnody. 224.
Thoughtful
And the balm of thoughtful words;
    Frag. Poet. X. 2.
Of thoughtful maids and manhood bold.
    Hymn. 12.

Thoughtless
Thoughtless of its anxious freight,
    Monadnoc. 333.
Discrowned and timid, thoughtless, worn,
    Poet. 181.
Thought's
Greet the glad miracle. Thought's new-
    found path   Adirondacs. 243.
For out of Thought's interior sphere
    Problem. 39.
Thought's holy light.   Thought. 4.
With Thought's perilous, whirling pool;
    Threnody. 233.
Along Thought's causing stream,
    World-Soul. 70.
Thoughts
There my thoughts the matter roll,
    Alphonso. 45.
Teem with unwonted thoughts:
    Daemonic Love. 47.
Of thoughts and things at home, but still
    adjourn   Day's Ration. 31.
By thoughts I lead   Frag. Poet. XII. 1.
And makes thy thoughts archangels be;
    Freedom. 20.
And the thoughts that in him woke,
    Harp. 96.
And with glad thoughts of faith and hope
    Hymn. 23.
Thoughts come also hand in hand;
    Merlin. 101.
Who, in large toughts, like fair pearl-
    seed,   Monadnoc. 285.
Itself with thoughts of thee adorning;
    Ode to Beauty. 87.
Shadows of the thoughts of day,
    Quat. Memory. 2.
He mixes music with her thoughts,
    Rhea. 53.
Here holy thoughts a light have shed
    Robbins Hymn. 5.
And ever in the strife of your own
    thoughts   Rome. 15.

Thousand
Three times ten thousand strokes, from
    morn to eve.   Adirondacs. 90.
On for a thousand years of genius more.'
    Adirondacs. 329.
Six thousand pounds a year.   Boston. 72.
The nearest matters for a thousand days?
    Day's Ration. 32.
O'er ten thousand, thousand acres,
    Ellen South. 9.
And proverb of a thousand years,
    Frag. Poet. IV. 24.
Through the cold slab a thousand gates,
    May-Day. 122.
Where a thousand pallid towns
    May-Day. 254.
Unhurt by a thousand storms,
    May-Day. 321.
Faithful through a thousand years,
    May-Day. 373.
The flowing fortunes of a thousand
    years;—   Merlin. 73.
And a thousand silences.   Merops. 8.
To a thousand humors shift it,
    Mithridates. 23.
Thousand minstrels woke within me,
    Monadnoc. 1.

Thousand—*Continued*
In many a thousand years?
Monadnoc. 218.
Has thousand faces in a thousand hours.
Musketaquid. 25.
In thousand far-transplanted grafts
Promise. 3.
A thousand men shall dig and eat;
Saadi. 106.
And many a thousand summers
Song of Nature. 17.
It through thousand natures ply;
Sphinx. 118.
Thorough a thousand voices
Sphinx. 129.
He who has a thousand friends has not a
friend to spare, Taleb. 1.

Thousands
Let the blood of her hundred thousands
Boston. 106.
The astonised Muse finds thousands at
her side. Channing Ode. 97.
At forge and furnace thousands sweat;
Saadi. 107.
And thousands sail the purple sea,
Saadi. 108
Ever on thousands shine, Webster. 2.

Thrall
I found me thy thrall,
Ode to Beauty. 10.
Is freed forever from his thrall.
Rhea. 75.

Thread
To thread by night the nearest way to
camp? Adirondacs. 106.
Feeling only the fiery thread
Voluntaries. 88.
Oft didst thou thread the woods in vain
Woodnotes. II. 248.

Threading
Threading dark ways, arriving late,
Worship. 12.

Threads
The threads of man at their humming
wheel, Harp. 100.
The threads of life and power and pain,
Harp. 101.
She threads dark Alpine forests
House. 9.
Draws the threads of fair and fit.
Wealth. 33.

Threatening
Threatening and young. Destiny. 33.

Three
Three conifers, white, Adirondacs. 40.
Three times ten thousand strokes,
Adirondacs. 90.
When of our little fleet three cruising
skiffs Adirondacs. 231.
The rocky nook with hilltops three
Boston. 1.
Miles off, three dangerous miles, is home;
Titmouse. 9.
In my garden three ways meet,
Walden. 1.
Three moons his great heart
Woodnotes. I. 84.

Three-leaved
Five-leaved, three-leaved and two-leaved,
grew thereby. Adirondacs. 41.

Threw
Which the Zodiac threw, May-Day. 108.
The merry Spring threw wreaths on
them, May-Day. 314.
Threw to each fact a tuneful name.
Poet. 8.

Thrice
And thrice outstretched my hand,
Song of Nature. 62.
Thrice the spot is blest; Walden. 2.

Thrice-piled
Are hid behind the thrice-piled clouds;
Poet. 178.

Thrift
fold the hands of thrift,
Frag. Life. XXXV. 1.
Thy thrift, the sleep of cares;
Waldeinsamkeit. 46.

Thrill
Urging astonished Chaos with a thrill
Adirondacs. 264.
And thrill our tuneful frames;
April. 2.
As erst it wont, would thrill and ring.
Harp. 106.
Or like the thrill of Æolian strings
Frag. Poet. I. 41.

Thrilled
See Over-thrilled.
Upward the ninth heaven thrilled and
moved Waterfall. 19.

Thrilling
Into those wise, thrilling palms.
Initial Love. 59.
The thrilling Delphic oracle;
Problem. 12.

Thrills
Whose throbs are love, whose thrills are
song. Monadnoc. 170.
It thrills to the antipodes, Waterfall. 11.
Electric thrills and ties of law,
Wealth. 47.

Thrive
Thrive in all weathers without fear,—
Walden. 15.

Thrives
And nothing thrives to reach its natural
term; Blight. 52.
Thrives here, unvalued, underfoot.
Monadnoc. 184

Thriving
'You are thriving well,' said he;
Boston. 64.

Thro'
See Through.
Thyself thro' Nature to diffuse?
Lines. 2.

Throat
When thrushes ope their throat, 't is he
that signs, Enchanter. 10.
Out of sound heart and merry throat,
Titmouse. 28.
My billets to his boiler's throat,
Woodnotes. II. 44.
Breathed from the everlasting throat.
Woodnotes. II. 123.

Throb
Throb in each manly vein; Boston. 107.
Should throb until he snapped his chain.
Freedom. 4.

This mound shall throb his face before,
Monadnoc. 288.

Throb thine with Nature's throbbing breast,
Nature. Mot. 11.

Throb thine with Nature's throbbing breast,
Threnody. 207.

And God said, "Throb!" and there was motion
Woodnotes. II. 268.

Throbbed

It throbbed up from the brook.
Hermione. 60.

The sod throbbed friendly to my feet,
Lines. 13.

Throbbing

A spasm throbbing through the pedestals
Adirondacs. 262.

The throbbing sea, the quaking earth,
Celestial Love. 109.

You must bring the throbbing heart.
Miracle. 10.

Throb thine with Nature's throbbing breast,
Nature. Mot. 11.

Nature's throbbing breast,
Threnody. 207.

Love wakes anew this throbbing heart,
World-Soul. 107.

Throbs

Throbs of a wild religion stirred;—
Daemonic Love. 8.

Whose throbs are love, whose thrills are song.
Monadnoc. 170.

Throbs with an overmastering energy
Pan. 7.

Throes

Throes that were, and worlds that are,
Woodnotes. II. 209.

Throne

Bad news from George on the English throne;
Boston. 63.

And Love ascends his throne,
Cosmos. 22.

The Genius from its cloudy throne.
Fate. 12.

And his heart the throne of Will.
Frag. Poet. XIV. 4.

With every king on every throne,
Initial Love. 125.

Hath granted his throne?
Ode to Beauty. 36.

And his heart the throne of will.
Power. 4.

Composed the network of his throne;
Woodnotes. I. 107.

Throned

Which, o'er passion throned sedate,
Astraea. 33.

Throng

All men would to my gardens throng,
Garden. 3.

Throngs

Ah! late I spoke to silent throngs,
I Compensation. 7.

Throttled

And throttled all his passion. Is't not like
Philosopher. 10.

Through (Partial list.)

Or grew on vine whose tap-roots, reaching through
Bacchus. 3.

He saw strong Eros struggling through,
Beauty. 18.

Beauty through my senses stole;
Each. 50.

Through the innumerable years.
Frag. Life. XXV. 4.

Every nook on Nature through:
Love and Thought. 6.

Till green lances peering through
May-Day. 123.

And through the priest the mind inspires.
Problem. 54.

All were winnowed through and through,
Test. 3.

And roamed the pastures through;
Thine Eyes. 6.

In equal strength through space abide;
Voluntaries. 116.

Throughout

Throughout the solid realm.
World-Soul. 76.

Thrown

Thrown to lions for their meat,
Worship. 7.

Throws

See, every patriot oak-leaf throws
May-Day. 113.

Thrush

See Hermit-thrush.

A quest of river-grapes, a mocking thrush,
Musketaquid. 73.

The thrush plies his wings;
Sphinx. 22.

Thrushes'

He found the tawny thrushes' broods;
Woodnotes. I. 56.

Thrushes

Ask votes of thrushes in the solitudes.
Channing Ode. 74.

When thrushes ope their throat, 't is he that sings,
Enchanter. 10.

Thrust

And trust the weak aside;
World-Soul. 94.

Thumb

The sallow knows the basket-maker's thumb;
Adirondacs. 101.

Thunder

Reply to the thunder of river and main.
May-Day. 240.

Artful thunder, which conveys
Merlin. 13.

Or coax the thunder from its mark?
Nemesis. 11.

Laughter rich as woodland thunder,
Threnody. 214.

Or west, no thunder fear.
Woodnotes. I. 103.

Thunderbolt

My thunderbolt has eyes to see
Boston Hymn. 87.

And the rash-leaping thunderbolt fell short.
Frag. Life. XXXIV. 2.

Thundercloud

To the thundercloud.
Frag. Nat. III. 38.

Thunder-clouds

Thunder-clouds are Jove's festoons,
Heroism. 4.

Thunder's

Disarmed the thunder's fires.
Bell. 12.

Thundertops

Yon thundertops,
Adirondacs. 260.

Thus (Partial list.)
Elect, to dreams thus beautiful?'
Berrying. 10.
A blessing through the ages thus
Boston. 116.
Thus to himself the poet spoke,
Poet. 141.
Thus or thus they are and think.
Woodnotes. II. 288.

Thwarted
I am bitter, vacant, thwarted,
Etienne. 7.
And his will is not thwarted;
World-Soul. 85.

Thwarts
to make our poles and thwarts,
Adirondacs. 34.

Thy (Partial list.)
Thy voice upon the deep Bell. 5.
And in thy valleys, Agiochook!
Channing Ode. 22.
Thy sight is growing blear;
Sphinx. 106.
Thy steps to watch, thy place to know:
Threnody. 33.

Thyself (Partial list.)
Though thou loved her as thyself,
Give. 43.
Thyself dost give forever more.
Hymn. 28.
Thyself thro' Nature to diffuse Lines. 2.
And being latent, feel thyself no less?
Musketaquid. 81.
Unmake me quite, or give thyself to me!
Ode to Beauty. 99.
See to thyself, O Universe! Rhea. 72.

Tidal
In changing moon and tidal wave
II Compensation. 5.
Wilt thou freeze love's tidal flow,
Threnody. 238.

Tide
See Joy-tide.
They heed not moon or solar tide,—
Garden. 23.
And made each tide and element
Guy. 27.
'T is the turning of the tide.
Holidays. 20.
Time and tide are strangely changed,
Initial Love. 7.
And troops of friends enjoyed the tide,—
In Memoriam. 71.
A momentary music. Being's tide
Pan. 3.
Knowing and doing. Ebbs the tide, they
lie Pan. 8.
Will heap in me their highest tide,
Poet. 277.
Must time and tide forever run?
Song of Nature. 45.
Time and tide their faults may find.
Test. 2.

Tides
Tides that should warm each neighboring
life Rubies. 7.
And give love's scarlet tides to flow,—
Rubies. 11.
And tides of life and increase lend;
Threnody. 113.

Wise harbinger of spheres and tides,
Woodnotes. I. 33.

Tide-wave
The moon-drawn tide-wave strives;
Promise. 2.

Tidings
No tidings *since* it came. Amulet. 4.
The joy-bells chime their tidings down,
Concord Ode. 7.
And tidings of the future tells.
Hymn. 4.
Such tidings of the starry sphere
May-Day. 13.
Some to their friends the tidings say;
Threnody. 154.

Tie
See Untie.
Burns up every other tie.
Daemonic Love. 115.
The tie of blood and home was rent:
Frag. Poet. I. 53.
And, least of all, the loyal tie
In Memoriam. 81.

Tied
See Untied.

Ties
Till Beauty came to snap all ties;
Daemonic Love. 11.
The frost-king ties my fumbling feet,
Titmouse. 12.
Electric thrills and ties of law,
Wealth. 47.

Tight
See Air-tight.

Tighter
Tighter wind the giant coils.
Nemesis. 16.

Tigris
I ask how far is the Tigris flood,
Exile. 3.
Is the Tigris to float me away.
Exile. 20.

Tile
Furnished with tile, the fierce artificer
Snow-Storm. 12.

Tiles
While love and terror laid the tiles.
Problem. 32.

Till (Partial list.)
Till your kind abound with juice?
Alphonso. 66.
Till Freedom cheered and joy-bells rung.
Boston. 99.
Till these echoes be choked with snows,
Boston. 104.
Round they roll till dark is light,
Channing Ode. 78.
Till the poor is wealthy grown,
Etienne. 19.
Till late he learned, through doubt and
fear, Fate. 9.
And drain his heart till he be dead.
Voluntaries. 58.
All is waste and worthless, till
Wealth. 30.
The sage, till he hit the secret,
World-Soul. 51.

Tilled
The glebe tilled, Channing Ode. 63.

Timely
In his rich nurseries, timely skill
Guy. 41.
Timely wise accept the terms,
Terminus. 17.

Time's
The evil time's sole patriot,
Channing Ode. 2.
Nor Time's snows hide the names he set.
Poet. 11.

Times
Three times ten thousand strokes,
Adirondacs. 90.
Shorter days and harder times.
Alphonso. 6.
Shame the times and live apart,—
Frag. Poet. IV. 6.
In weak, unhappy times, Merlin. 60.
I have trod this path a hundred times
Miracle. 1.
Over tribes and over times,
Monadnoc. 214.
To myriad kinds and times one sense
Monadnoc. 381.
Nine times folded in mystery:
Nature. Mot. 8.
Times wore he as his clothing-weeds,
Poet. 31.
Through worlds and races and terms and
times Poet. 71.
Adorned with them my country's primi-
tive times, River. 41.
Men read the welfare of the times to
come, Threnody. 169.
He who, in evil times, Voluntaries. 84.
God, though he were ten times slain,
Voluntaries. 103.
Through times that wear and forms that
fade, Waldeinsamkeit. 27.
Can find with glass in ten times ten.
Walk. 8.
Of things with things, of times with
times, Woodnotes. II. 159.

Timid
Discrowned and timid, thoughtless, worn,
Poet. 181.
Timid, self-pleasing, sensitive,
Poet. 213.
The timid it concerns to ask their way,
Woodnotes. I. 86.

Timorous
Its timorous ways, big trifles, and we
planned Adirondacs. 161.

Timour
I scorned the fame of Timour brave;
Frag. Poet. III. 3.
Timour, to Hassan, was a slave.
Frag. Poet. III. 4.

Tinge
Why tinge thy lustres jubilant
Frag. Nat. VIII. 3.

Tinged
And a blush tinged the upper sky,
Uriel. 55.

Tinkle
Nor tinkle of piano strings,
Merlin. 6.

Tint
The maple-tops their crimson tint,
May-Day. 60.

New tint the plumage of the birds,
May-Day. 447.
My swarthy tint is in the grain,
Romany. 19.

Tints
Refresh the faded tints, Bacchus. 62.
Illusions like the tints of pearl,
Frag. Nat. XXXII. 1.
Tints the human countenance
Humble-Bee. 24.
And the tints of heaven reply.
May-Day. 262.
Tints that spot the violet's petal,
Woodnotes. I. 21.

Tiny
A tiny scene of sun and shower,
Ellen. 4.
The Flowers—tiny sect of Shakers—
Ellen South. 11.
The wood-fly mocks with tiny voice
May-Day. 75.
When piped a tiny voice hard by,
Titmouse. 25.

Tipped
Were tipped with down, *Lines. 18.

Tips
See Finger-tips.

Tiptoe
And Reason on her tiptoe pained
Initial Love. 67.

Tire
I tire of shams, I rush to be: Nun. 37.
I tire of globes and races,
Song of Nature. 53.

Tired
See Untired.
God said, I am tired of kings,
Boston Hymn. 5.
Tired of their starry periods,
May-Day. 328.

'Tis
Let them hear well! 't is theirs as much
as ours. Adirondacs. 261.
'T is the privilege of Art Art. 19.
'T is very small,—no load at all.—
Boston. 67.
'T is nobleness to serve;
Boston Hymn. 50.
'T is fit the forest fall,
Channing Ode. 58.
'T is a sparkle passing
Daemonic Love. 78.
'T is a brave master; Give. 7.
Saying, "T is mine, my children's and my
name's. Hamatreya. 5.
'T is the turning of the tide.
Holidays. 20.
Publishes when 't is inclined.
Merlin. 69.
'T is not in the high stars alone,
Music. 13.
"T is man's perdition to be safe,
Quat. Sacrifice. 3.
'T is written on the iron leaf, Rhea. 34.
'T is his study and delight Rhea. 47.
'T is because a general hope
Threnody. 132.
'T is not within the force of fate
Threnody. 193.
Whose omen 't is, and sign.
Threnody. 259.

And 't is far in the deeps of history,
World-Soul. 19.

Titan
The Titan heeds his sky-affairs,
Monadnoc. 58.

Titan-born
Titan-born, to hardy natures
May-Day. 136.

Titans
And other Titans without muse or name.
Adirondacs. 11.

Titmouse
To the titmouse dimension.'
Titmouse. 64.

To (Partial list.)
See Flies-to; Fly-to; Whereto.
To men below, Celestial Love. 52.
Thee to guide and to redeem.
Celestial Love. 62.
And kind to kind. Celestial Love. 80.
To and fro perpetually;
Daemonic Love. 80.
To and fro the Genius flies,
Frag. Life. XVI. 1.
'In to the upper doors, Merlin. 35.
Hands to hands, and feet to feet,
Merlin. 88.
Short-lived wandering to and fro,
Merlin. 107.
Most like to bachelors, Merlin. 108.
And the gods from side to side.
Quat. Hush. 4.
Magic-built to last a season;
Threnody. 256.

Tobacco-leaf
Tobacco-leaf, or poppy, or rose;
Mithridates. 2.

To-day
And not to-day and not to-morrow
Aeolian Harp. 14.
To-day unbind the captive,
Boston Hymn. 65.
We set to-day a votive stone;
C. Hymn. 10.
To-day, when friends approach, and every
hour Day's Ration. 20.
We separate to-day, *Farewell. 35.
I leave untold to-day, *Farewell. 42.
She spared no speech to-day:
Frag. Nat. III. 9.
Of better men than live to-day;
Garden. 62.
Keep thee to-day, Give. 30.
To-day shall all her dowry bring,
May-Day. 264.
Thus far to-day your favors reach,
Merops. 5.
And what they say they made to-day,
Nature. II. 11.
Her planted eye to-day controls,
Quat. Fate. 1.
To-day slinks poorly off unmarked be-
tween: Quat. Heri. 2.
The open secret of to-day. Solution. 70.
The harvests sown to-day Walden. 14.
I, that to-day am a pine,
Woodnotes. II. 276.

Toe
See Tiptoe.

Together
Call the people together,
Boston Hymn. 37.
Must be taken in together, Fable. 7.
Together sad or gay, *Farewell. 33.
Ever, when twain together play,
Saadi. 15.

Toil
Only what to our griping toil is due;
Blight. 41.
Nor art, nor power, nor toil can find
Bohemian. 10.
And none but Toil shall have.
Boston Hymn. 28.
Of care and toil, Celestial Love. 64.
Toil could never compass it;
Destiny. 7.
Belonged to wind and world the toil
Guy. 49.
Possessed the land which rendered to
their toil Hamatreya. 2.
Day's toil and its guerdon, Illusions. 10.
In lands remote, in toil and pain,
In Memoriam. 75.
Sweetens its toil— *Lines. 3.
Toil and tempest are the toys
Monadnoc. 163.
Toil whistles as he drives his cart.
Saadi. 154.
His wistful toil to do his best
Voluntaries. 21.
For famine, toil and fray?
Voluntaries. 66.
The shop of toil, the hall of arts;
Wealth. 35.

Toilette
His brief toilette: at night, or in the rain,
Adirondacs. 76.

Toiling
I shunned the toiling Hassan's glance."
Frag. Poet. III. 12.

Toil's
Worship Toil's wisdom that abides.
Frag. Poet. III. 10.
Toil's hard hap with scorn accuse.
Monadnoc. 126.

Toils
How snatch the stripling from their
toils?— Frag. Life. X. 7.
And all our struggles and our toils
Nemesis. 15.

Token
Assured to find the token once again
Frag. Nat. IV. 9.
His vice some elder virtue's token,
Initial Love. 92.
It is a sound, it is a token
May-Day. 32.

Tokens
Tokens of benevolence.
Frag. Poet. VII. 12.

Told
See Untold.
our company all told. Adirondacs. 6.
A burst of joy, as if we told the fact
Adirondacs. 252.
To them their secret told; Boston. 14.
Those idle catches told the laws
Frag. Poet. V. 11.
Nor ran to speak till she him told;
Frag. Poet. V. 25.

Told—*Continued*

The fire winds told him what they knew,
Frag. Poet. V. 37.

Reporting what old minstrels told
Harp. 53.

And told his amulets: Hermione. 3.

And told the truant by his marks,—
Initial Love. 4.

His many signs cannot be told;
Initial Love. 130.

He told no pang, he knew no fear;
In Memoriam. 100.

That the bondage-days are told,
May-Day. 109.

Told every word and syllable
Miracle. 33.

The word by seers or sibyls told,
Problem. 57.

When sixty years are told;
World-Soul. 106.

Tolling

The setxon, tolling his bell at noon,
Each. 5.

Tomb

Gave an impartial tomb to all the kinds.
Adirondacs. 140.

Break not my dream, obtrusive tomb!
Harp. 124.

Yet it is a stately tomb;
In Memoriam. 15.

Slips behind a tomb.   Manners. 20.

Where every wind that swept my tomb
Mountain. 11.

And build to them a final tomb;
Woodnotes. II. 224.

Tombs

Forgotten amid splendid tombs,
Nun. 27.

To-morrow

And not to-day and not to-morrow
Aeolian Harp. 14.

And make to-morrow a new morn.
Art. 12.

To-morrow they will wear another face,
Experience. 20.

To-morrow, forever,   Give. 31.

As if to-morrow should redeem
May-Day. 297.

Or in what far to-morrow due;
May-Day. 417.

Ever from one who comes to-morrow
Merlin's Song. 20.

To-morrow, when the masks shall fall
Threnody. 189.

Apples of Eden ripe to-morrow.
Threnody. 287.

To-morrow's

Waits unblamed to-morrow's sun.
Frag. Poet. XI. 19.

Tone

Oft pealed for him a lofty tone
Beauty. 11.

And mute thy music's dearest tone,
Ellen. 10.

Or tone of silver instrument
Forerunners. 12.

Of one import, of varied tone;
Garden. 42.

From tone of joy to inward wail,
Harp. 8.

Speaks not of self that mystic tone,
Harp. 67.

Sweet to me thy drowsy tone
Humble-Bee. 33.

Chiming with the forest tone,
Merlin. 17.

To every tone beat answering tones,
Merlin. 83.

Nor in the redbreast's mellow tone,
Music. 15.

Tones

To every tone beat answering tones,
Merlin. 83.

One, with low tones that decide,
Uriel. 15.

Tones of penitence and pain,
Voluntaries. 3.

To the song of its waterfall tones,
Woodnotes. I. 2.

These echoes are laden with tones
Woodnotes. II. 127.

Tongue

See Adder's-tongue.

Spelling with guided tongue man's messages   Adirondacs. 269.

Nor speak with double tongue.
Concord Ode. 20.

Under his tongue;   Destiny. 30.

Temperament without a tongue,
Experience. 9.

Without tongue, yellow-cheeked, full of
winds that wail and sigh;   Flute. 2.

The tongue is prone to lose the way,
Frag. Life. XII. 1.

And love, for words thy tongue could say.
Frag. Poet. II. 8.

Harvests grew upon his tongue,
Frag. Poet. V. 31.

I framed his tongue to music,
Frag. Poet. XIV. 1.

Slighted Minerva's learnèd tongue,
Frag. Poet. XXXV. 1.

On its mystic tongue,   Harp. 51.

It is the tongue of mundane laws.
Harp. 72.

Already trembling on their tongue,
Hymn. 14.

Of keenest eye and truest tongue.
Merlin's Song. 15.

His tongue was framed to music,
Power. 1.

Like the volcano's tongue of flame,
Problem. 16.

Perforce must use his tongue;
Quat. Orator. 2.

His tongue can paint as bright, as keen;
Saadi. 122.

That wit and joy might find a tongue,
Solution. 15.

By wondrous tongue, and guided pen,
Threnody. 136.

Talk no more with feeble tongue;
Woodnotes. II. 137.

Tongued

See Ten-tongued.

Tongues

And why, when mirth unseals all
tongues,   I Compensation. 5.

Speaking by the tongues of flowers,
May-Day. 418.

The birds gave us our wily tongues,
                    Romany. 23.
And airy tongues did taunt the town,
                    Walden. 23.
Ocean tongues to islanders,
                    Woodnotes. II. 153.
To-night
'I have supped to-night with gods,
                    Poet. 142.
Too
Then turns to bound away,—is it too
late?   Adirondacs. 124.
The lightning has run masterless too
long;   Adirondacs. 266.
And these instructed by their wisest too,
                    Adirondacs. 294.
Men and gods are too extense;
                    Alphonso. 63.
Earth, crowded, cries, 'Too many men!'
                    Alphonso. 67.
Turned and departed silent. I, too late,
                    Days. 10.
He pays too high a price   Fame. 7.
Too soon those spires are lost,
                    *Farewell. 5.
Too fast we leave the bay,
                    *Farewell. 6.
Too soon by ocean tost   *Farewell. 7.
Too kind, too good to me;
                    *Farewell. 20.
With joy too tense for sober brain;
                    Frag. Poet. I. 51.
Gift too precious to be prayed,
                    Freedom. 8.
Me too thy nobleness has taught
                    Friendship. 17.
For I had too much to think,
                    Goethe. 5.
Too weak to win, too fond to shun
                    Manners. 17.
too slow the pearl: May-Day. 156.
Too strait and low our cottage doors,
                    May-Day. 220.
Too long shut in strait and few,
                    Mithridates. 20.
Or for my turn to fly too fast.   Nun. 32.
Whose shining sons, too great for fame,
                    Nun. 45.
Too credulous lover   Ode to Beauty. 3.
Too busied with the crowded hour to
fear to live or die.   Quat. Nature. 4.
Thy softest pleadings seem too bold,
                    Rhea. 21.
Why, Rome is lonely too;—   Rome. 1.
I too have arts and sorceries;
                    Seashore. 41.
I too therein could challenge part
                    Security. 11.
All too much to him they said,
                    September. 10.
Too much of donning and doffing,
                    Song of Nature. 49.
Too slow the rainbow fades,
                    Song of Nature. 50.
Too long the game is played;
                    Song of Nature. 54.
I am too much bereft.   Threnody. 170.
Its onward force too starkly pent
                    Threnody. 247.
I too have a hole in a hollow tree;
                    Titmouse. 70.

Late in the world,—too late perchance
for fame,   To-Day. 5.
Life is too short to waste   To J. W. 18.
And the treason, too long pent,
                    Uriel. 9.
Or by knowledge grown too bright
                    Uriel. 41.
Heart too soft and will too weak
                    Voluntaries. 15.
Thy cheek too white, thy form too slen-
der,   Woodnotes. II. 186.
Thy gait too slow, thy habits tender
                    Woodnotes. II. 187.
Took
    See Betook; Overtook.
Took Boston in its arms;   Boston. 4.
Took a few herbs and apples, and the
Day   Days. 9.
They took this valley for their toy,
                    Dirge. 29.
Him by the hand dear Nature took,
                    Experience. 17.
He took the flower of all their worth,
                    Frag. Life. XXIX. 4.
I took the friendly noble by the hand,
                    Frag. Life. XXX. 3.
The winds took flesh, the mountains
talked,   Frag. Poet. I. 55.
In as far as I took note,
                    Initial Love. 83.
Gave the law which others took,
                    In Memoriam. 45.
With shining gifts that took all eyes,
                    In Memoriam. 62.
Studied thy motion, took thy form,
                    Lines. 16.
The pious wind took it away,   Poet. 17.
He took the color of his vest
                    Quat. Forester. 1.
Took counsel from his guiding eyes
                    Threnody. 56.
Took the eye with him as he went;
                    Threnody. 71.
Took the largest part of me:
                    Threnody. 161.
Tools
Perversely borrowing from the shop the
tools   Adirondacs. 283.
Tooting
This poor tooting, creaking cricket,
                    Frag. Nat. I. 6.
Tooting, creaking,   Frag. Nat. I. 9.
Top
    See Hilltop; Overtop.
The fresh ground loves his top and ball,
                    May-Day. 69.
To the zenith's top can soar,—
                    Merlin. 64.
Whose giddy top the morning loved to
gild.   Woodnotes. I. 79.
Topmost
Giddy with day, to the topmost spire,
                    May-Day. 232.
Tops
    See City-tops; Maple-tops; Thunder-
tops.
Climb to their tops,   Frag. Nat. III. 19.
On windy hills, whose tops with morning
glow,   I Bear. 7.

Torch
When they with torch of genius pierce
Dull. 11.
At the same torch that lighted mine;
Eva. 3.

Torches
It seemed the world was all torches
Cosmos. 11.

Tore
Which tore from oaks their branches
broad,   Poet. 29.

Tormenting
Tormenting Pan to double the dose.
Alphonso. 26.

Torments
Torments me still the fear that love
Amulet. 11.
But what torments of grief you endured
Quat. Borrowing. 3.

Torn
And one by one has torn off quite
Rhea. 15.
And seeing rashly torn and moved
Threnody. 128.
And torn the ensigns from thy brow,
Woodnotes. II. 184.

Torrent
Cleanse the torrent at the fountain,
May-Day. 450.
I rest on the pitch of the torrent,
Song of Nature. 7.
The storm-wind wove, the torrent span,
Wealth. 38.

Torrents
Like the torrents of the sun
Bacchus. 27.

Torrid
From his Afric's torrid plains.
Voluntaries. 8.

Torrid-zone
Thou animated torrid-zone!
Humble-Bee. 6.

Tortuous
Père Raquette stream, to a small tortuous
pass   Adirondacs. 22.

Torture
Want and woe, which torture us,
Humble-Bee. 62.

Tossed
    See Tost.
Long I've been tossed like the driven
foam;   Good-Bye. 5.
The least breath my boughs which tossed
Woodnotes. II. 144.

Tosses
When the pine tosses its cones
Woodnotes. I. 1.
The sea tosses and foams to find
Woodnotes. II. 242.

Tossing
Tossing one sparkle to the eyes:
Peter. 38.

Tost
    See Tossed.
Too soon by ocean tost   *Farewell. 7.
Asks of the urchin to be tost.
May-Day. 64.

Total
The total air was fame;   Cosmos. 10.
He has a total world of wit;
Initial Love. 103.

The total freight of hope and joy
May-Day. 354.

Totter
They totter now and float amain.
Poet. 38.

Touch
    See Spirit-touch.
I await a tenderer touch,
Aeolian Harp. 6.
I touch this flower of silken leaf,
Dirge. 37.
Who leap from horse to horse, but never
touch the ground.
Frag. Poet. XIX. 2.
I was by thy touch redeemed;
Hermione. 36.
To touch with prophet's hand the chord
Hymn. 15.
O touch thy servant's lips with power,
Hymn. 26.
Two touch the string,   Saadi. 19.
And touch with soft persuasion,
Saadi. 126.
My touch thy antidote, my bay thy bath?
Seashore. 6.
Respond to the touch of man;
Waterfall. 10.

Touched
    See Untouched.
Touched with life by every beam.
Frag. Nat. XXVI. 29.
The dead log touched bursts into leaf,
May-Day. 208.
Are touched with genius. Yonder ragged
cliff   Musketaquid. 24.
Thou hast touched for my despair;
Ode to Beauty. 91.
There the red morning touched him with
its light.   Woodnotes. I. 83.

Touches
Touches a cheek with colors of romance,
Enchanter. 6.
But it touches his quick heart
Initial Love. 70.
And touches all things with his rose.
Initial Love. 77.

Touching
And with softness touching all,
Humble-Bee. 23.

Tower
    See Snow-tower.
The maple eight, beneath its shapely
tower.   Adirondacs. 43.
Tower of observance searching space;
Monadnoc. 83.
'What prizes the town and the tower?
Woodnotes. II. 30.

Towering
Seemed to me, the towering hill
Monadnoc. 195.

Towers
Shield all thy roofs and towers!
Boston. 117.
Along the mountain towers,—
Daemonic Love. 110.
And think how Nature in these towers
Monadnoc. 98.
Builds therewith eternal towers;
Spiritual Laws. 4.
Whose living towers the years conspired
to build,   Woodnotes. I. 78.

Town

We trode on air, contemned the distant
town, Adirondacs. 160.

Was it a college pique of town and
gown, Adirondacs. 277.

In the country and the town,
Astraea. 10.

The good town on the bay,
Boston. 42.

Penn's town, New York and Baltimore,
Boston. 47.

O happy town beside the sea,
Boston. 59.

Or over the town blue ocean flows.
Boston. 105.

Thou darling town of ours! Boston. 119.

In the suburb, in the town, Caritas. 1.

The last builds town and fleet,
Channing Ode. 55.

The cannon booms from town to town,
Concord Ode. 5.

Farewell the busy town, *Farewell. 10.

On the first wheels that quit this weary
town Letter. 3.

Once more into his dapper town,
Monadnoc. 345.

in a river town; Naples. 14.

Shines not as on the town, Peter. 14.

Men consort in camp and town,
Saadi. 7.

With war and trade, with camp and town;
Saadi. 105.

To court and mart, to gown and town.
Solution. 68.

The crowded town, thy feet may well
delay. To J. W. 4.

Seek him in his native town, Una. 23.

And airy tongues did taunt the town,
Walden. 23.

'What prizes the town and the tower?
Woodnotes. II. 30.

The fopperies of the town.
World-Soul. 60.

Town-incrusted

Farm-furrowed, town-incrusted sphere,
Monadnoc. 332.

Towns

Up with your towns and stay!'
Boston. 52.

Where a thousand pallid towns
May-Day. 254.

The air stole into the streets of towns,
May-Day. 342.

Purge alpine air by towns defiled,
May-Day. 451.

The insanity of towns to stem
Monadnoc. 116.

Our towns and races grow and fall,
Monadnoc. 386.

Then temples rose, and towns, and marts,
Wealth. 34.

And thatch with towns the prairie broad
World-Soul. 67.

Townsmen

The townsmen braved the English king,
Boston. 82.

Town-sprinkled

And all town-sprinkled lands that be,
Monadnoc. 277.

Toy

They took this valley for their toy,
Dirge. 29.

Toy with the bow, yet hit the white,
Frag. Poet. V. 2.

To be the children's toy. Holidays. 4.

Toy no longer—it has duties;
Holidays. 7.

Corrupted by the present toy
Initial Love. 112.

Toy with the bow, yet hit the white.
Merlin's Song. 38.

The sun is its toy; Sphinx. 44.

Toy's

Of the toy's purchase with the length
of life. Blight. 62.

Toys

Toil and tempest are the toys
Monadnoc. 163.

Abandon all those toys with speed to
obey Summons. 23.

Whereof it spoke were toys
Threnody. 41.

In an age of fops and toys,
Voluntaries. 59.

Shuts his sense on toys of time,
Voluntaries. 81.

Trace

Leaves on the wind melodious trace;
Forerunners. 13.

No trace of age, no fear to die.
Frag. Nat. VIII. 8.

Of Eden's bower some dream-like trace
May-Day. 93.

Night-dreams trace on Memory's wall
Quat. Memory. 1.

Track

Leave no track on the heavenly snow.
Daemonic Love. 42.

A very pretty squirrel track; Fable. 16.

No scout can track his way,
Frag. Poet. VI. 2.

On the soft path each track is seen,
May-Day. 61.

Secrets of the solar track, Merlin. 14.

Nail the wild star to its track
Threnody. 240.

Trackless

Me through trackless thickets led,
Woodnotes. I. 119.

Tract

Deep in a woodland tract, a sunny farm,
Letter. 8.

Tracts

Through tracts and provinces of sky,
May-Day. 25.

Trade

Of traders, led by corporate sons of trade,
Adirondacs. 282.

And where they went on trade intent
Boston. 7.

The world was made for honest trade,—
Boston. 11.

The world was made for honest trade,—
Boston. 53.

Trade and counting use Merlin. 115.

In love, he cannot therefore cease his
trade; Philosopher. 3.

With war and trade, with camp and
town; Saadi. 105.

Trade—*Continued*
In newer days of war and trade,
Solution. 59.
Let war and trade and creeds and song
Song of Nature. 77.
Trade and the streets ensnare us,
World-Soul. 21.
And what if Trade sow cities
World-Soul. 65.

Traders
Of traders, led by corporate sons of
trade, Adirondacs. 282.

Traditioned
Traditioned fame of masters, eager strife
Adirondacs. 324.

Tragedy
That the high gods love tragedy;
Saadi. 73.

Tragic
The tragic tales of crime and fate;
Frag. Nat. XXVI. 34.
The tragic and the gay, Harp. 24.
Nor lives the tragic bard to say
Nun. 47.

Trail
On trail of camel and caravan,
Frag. Poet. I. 6.

Trails
To hunt upon their shining trails.
Forerunners. 8.

Train
As 'mid the virgin train she strayed,
Each. 30.
A train of gay and clouded days
Frag. Life. I. 1.
And hither come the pensive train
Hymn. 9.
And the firm soul does the pale train defy
I Bear. 11.
Hunted by Sorrow's grisly train
In Memoriam. 74.
Filing single in stately train.
May-Day. 308.
Marching duly in her train,
May-Day. 335.
Came up the pensive train,
Robbins Hymn. 14.

Trained
Of books and arts and trained experiment, Adirondac. 307.

Training
And his training should not scant
Poet. 41.

Trains
I greet with joy the choral trains
May-Day. 392.
And trains us on to slight the new, as if
it were the old: Quat. Nature. 2.

Trait
And drew truly every trait.
Hermione. 39.

Traits
Dear memory's stone-incarved traits,
Daemonic Love. 14.
Whereon their traits are found.
Manners. 12.

Tramper
Each tramper started; but the feet
Threnody. 106.

Trance
That pierced my trance its drift to tell,
Miracle. 30.

In trance upborne past mortal goal
Solution. 45.
Can't trance him again, Sphinx. 78.

Trances
Trances the heart through chanting
choirs, Problem. 53.

Tranquil
Their tranquil mien bereaveth him
Manners. 15.

Transcend
Doth as far transcend Bohemian. 5.

Transferred
Sunshine in his heart transferred
Saadi. 80.

Transfix
Wilt thou transfix and make it none?
Threnody. 246.

Transforming
Transforming what it doth infold,
May-Day. 202.

Transforms
Still enriches and transforms,
May-Day. 199.

Transient
Since they are transient, and thou dost
abide. Unbar. 4.

Translucent
Translucent through the mortal covers,
Daemonic Love. 33.

Transmute
To transmute crime to wisdom, so to
stem Frag. Poet. XXII. 1.

Transmuted
Transmuted in these men to rule their
like), Musketaquid. 49.

Transmuting
Food which needs no transmuting,
Bacchus. 32.

Transparency
He hides in pure transparency;
Woodnotes. II. 310.

Transparent
Of joyful and transparent mien.
Daemonic Love. 77.
Transparent air, all-feeding earth,
Frag. Life. XXIX. 3.
Lighted each transparent word,
Saadi. 81.
Wrote in thy mind's transparent table,
Threnody. 199.

Transplanted
See Far-transplanted.

Trap
And wit to trap or take him in his lair.
Adirondacs. 86.
He shall impose, to find a spring, trap
foxes, Adirondacs. 103.

Travail
I travail in pain for him,
Song of Nature. 57.
My creatures travail and wait;
Song of Nature. 58.

Travel
Cannot travel in it two: Unity. 3.

Travelled
See Far-travelled.
And for travelled eyes what charms
Frag. Nat. XXVI. 3.
I travelled and found it at Rome;
Frag. Poet. IV. 32.

I travelled grateful by their side,
Woodnotes. I. 123.

Traveller
Caught from a late-arriving traveller,
Adirondacs. 236.
The joyful traveller gives, when on their
verge Adirondacs. 311.
Hearest thou, O traveller, Dirge. 43.
The traveller and the road seem one
Etienne. 21.
Seems, by the traveller espied,
Hermione. 43.
Shod like a traveller for haste;
Initial Love. 12.
Traveller, to thee, perchance, a tedious
road, Musketaquid. 32.
Admired, sage doubting whence the
traveller came,— River. 4.
The sled and traveller stopped, the cour-
ier's feet Snow-Storm. 6.
What recks such Traveller if the bowers
Woodnotes. II. 301.

Traveller's
Than doth the traveller's shadow on the
rock. Frag. Life. XXVI. 4.
Or like a traveller's fleeing tent,
Threnody. 276.

Travellers
I met many travellers Forerunners. 17.
Two well-assorted travellers use
Love and Thought. 1.
Makes travellers long for Indian skies,
May-Day. 294.
And who, and who are the travellers?
May-Day. 309.
Loveliest of travellers. Una. 20.

Travelling
From bold intrusion of the travelling
crowd,— Adirondacs. 172.
And travelling often in the cut he makes,
Blight. 20.

Travels
In the wood he travels glad,
Woodnotes. I. 13.

Traverses
So guilt not traverses his tender will.
Frag. Life. II. 3.

Trays
Give to barrows, trays and pans
Art. 1.

Treacherous
Through treacherous marbles.
Illusions. 15.
'T is even so, this treacherous kite,
Monadnoc. 331.

Treacherously
And treacherously bright to show
Chartist. 11.

Tread
Forbore the ant-hill, shunned to tread,
Frag. Poet. XXIV. 1.
I tread on the pride of Greece and
Rome; Good-Bye. 24.
To tread the forfeit Paradise,
May-Day. 96.
And tread uplifted land?
Monadnoc. 207.
I tread the book beneath my feet.
Song of Seyd. 24.
At the tread of the jubilant soul.
Waterfall. 20.

Treading
All too nimble for my treading.
Etienne. 4.

Treason
And the treason, too long pent,
Uriel. 9.

Treasure
Whispering hints of treasure hid
May-Day. 422.

Treasured
Crooning ditties treasured well
Voluntaries. 7.

Treasures
I fetched my sea-born treasures home;
Each. 25.
Disclosing treasures more than true,
May-Day. 416.
And to her son will treasures more
Walk. 5.

Treasury
Masks her treasury of heat
May-Day. 132.

Treated
They treated Nature as they would.
Dirge. 32.
And thus the high Muse treated me,
Frag. Poet. IV. 15.

Tree
See Apple-tree; Palm-tree; Pine-
tree; Poplar-tree.
Hark to that muffled roar! a tree in the
woods Adirondacs. 121.
Yea, plant the tree that bears best apples,
plant, Adirondacs. 298.
Singing aloft in the tree! Dirge. 42.
Runs round the pine and maple tree
Frag. Nat. XIX. 2.
From tree to tree Frag. Nat. XXI. 3.
Till the slow ripening, secular tree
Frag. Nat. XXI. 7.
Hills and islands, cloud and tree,
Hermione. 14.
Ere she can find a tree. House. 12.
Every tree and stem and chink
May-Day. 340.
Tree and lichen, ape, sea-lion,
Mithridates. 12.
Blue-coated,—flying before from tree to
tree, Musketaquid. 16.
Ascends as gladly in a single tree
Musketaquid. 56.
And over the tree was the moon,
Quat. Excelsior. 2.
And life pulsates in rock or tree.
Saadi. 138.
Round every windward stake, or tree, or
door. Snow-Storm. 14.
I too have a hole in a hollow tree;
Titmouse. 70.
One crash, the death-hymn of the perfect
tree, Woodnotes. I. 74.
Of the tree and of the cloud.
Woodnotes. I. 111.
One dry, and one the living tree.
Woodnotes. II. 21.
To fling his voice into the tree,
Woodnotes. II. 121.

Trees
See Plum-trees.
We cut young trees to make our poles
and thwarts, Adirondacs. 34.

Trees—*Continued*
The wood was sovran with centennial
trees,— Adirondacs. 37.
No faster than his planted trees,
Alphonso. 78.
The stunted trees look sick,
Blight. 50.
Go, cut down trees in the forest
Boston Hymn. 33.
Cut down trees in the forest
Boston Hymn. 35.
As the overhanging trees
Celestial Love. 71.
See yonder leafless trees against the sky,
Frag. Nat. XVII. 1.
The sleeps of trees or dreams of herbs.
Frag. Nat. XVIII. 5.
The trees were rich,
Frag. Nat. XXVII. 5.
In caves and hollow trees he crept
Frag. Poet. I. 43.
How sweet the west wind sounds in my
own trees! Hamatreya. 6.
In trees, with beasts, in mines and caves,
Initial Love. 99.
Haunting this bank's historic trees?
In Memoriam. 27.
Mount in the pipes of the trees,
May-Day. 231.
built of new-fallen trees,
Musketaquid. 30.
For still, where'er the trees grow big-
gest, Quat. Artist. 3.
These trees and stones are audible to me,
River. 22.
The stream, the trees, the grass, the
sighing wind, River. 28.
I feel as I were welcome to these trees
River. 36.
Trees in groves, Saadi. 1.
I see my trees repair their boughs;
Threnody. 10.
The tall green trees, that shelter thee,
*Violet. 7.
To feed the North from tropic trees;
Wealth. 37.
To birds and trees who talks?
Woodnotes. I. 4.

Trellised
When trellised grapes their flowers unmask, May-Day. 87.

Tremble
These idle flowers, that tremble in the
wind, River. 23.

Trembler
Trembler, do not whine and chide:
Sursum Corda. 3.

Trembles
It trembles to the cosmic breath,—
Harp. 69.

Trembling
Trembling balance duly keep.
II Compensation. 4.
Already trembling on their tongue,
Hymn. 14.

Tremulous
Tremulous, impressional, Culture. 4.
Who was not tremulous with love-lore.
Quat. Casella. 4.
The tremulous battery Earth
Waterfall. 9.

Trenchant
Trenchant time behoves to hurry
Woodnotes. II. 258.

Trespass
As angel blind to trespass done,
Frag. Life. XXVIII. 3.

Tribe
If our brief tribe miss thy face,
Ellen South. 23.
Supplanters of the tribe, the farmers
dwell. Musketaquid. 31.
Which bound the dusky tribe,
Voluntaries. 28.

Tribes
While classes or tribes, too weak to
master Frag. Life. XXXI. 3.
Tribes and ages overheard:
Frag. Poet. V. 10.
Lo! how all the tribes combine
May-Day. 111.
Over tribes and over times,
Monadnoc. 214.
Where pastoral tribes their flocks infold,
Poet. 64.
Bestrode the tribes that knelt within.
Problem. 50.
No tribes my house can fill,
Song of Nature. 10.

Tribute
But for tribute never a cent.'
Boston. 75.

Trick
Which at the best is trick,
Channing Ode. 9.
No Satan with a royal trick Past. 16.

Tricked
Tricked out in star and flower,
Song of Nature. 30.

Trickling
Fresh as the trickling rainbow of July;
Seashore. 20.

Tried
See Untried.
Our heroes tried their rifles at a mark,
Adirondacs. 125.
You have tried famine: no more try it;
Alphonso. 51.
His beauty once their beauty tried;
Threnody. 146.

Tries
Will you catch crabs? Truth tries pretension here. Adirondacs. 100.

Trifler
He is no churl nor trifler,
World-Soul. 81.

Trifles
Its timorous ways, big trifles and we
planned Adirondacs. 161.
Scorn trifles and embrace a better aim
Rome. 12.

Trill
To the lark's trill unfolds the rose,
Waterfall. 15.

Trillium
Blue-vetch and trillium, hawkweed, sassafras, Blight. 6.

Trim
And trim the straightest boughs;
Boston Hymn. 34.
I trim myself to the storm of time,
Terminus. 34.

Trimmed
> *See* New-trimmed.

Trims
> Steers his bark and trims his sail;
> > Quat. Poet. I. 2.
> As the bird trims her to the gale,
> > Terminus. 33.

Trines
> Glittering twins and trines.   Merlin. 95.

Triple
> Triple blossoms from one root;
> > Celestial Love. 43.
> And Dante searched the triple spheres,
> > Solution. 28.

Triste
> Useful only, triste and damp,
> > Chartist. 5.

Triumph
> This feat of wit, this triumph of man-
> kind;   Adirondacs. 255.
> And their coming triumph hide
> > Voluntaries. 113

Triumphant
> Of his triumphant piercing sight:
> > Woodnotes. II. 66.

Triumphing
> Much triumphing,—and these the fields
> > River. 13.

Trivial
> Thy trivial harp will never please
> > Merlin. 1.

Trod
> Who trod with me this lovely vale;
> > Dirge. 22.
> And vulgar feet have never trod
> > Good-Bye. 21.
> I have trod this path a hundred times
> > Miracle. 1.
> In spirit-worlds he trod alone,
> > Solution. 51.
> And the impatient years that trod on it
> > Summons. 16.

Trodden
> Shall supplement hencefort all trodden
> ways,   Adirondacs. 244.

Trode
> We trode on air, contemned the distant
> town,   Adirondacs. 160.
> He trode the unplanted forest floor,
> whereon   Woodnotes. I. 64.

Troop
> In sleep their jubilant troop is near,—
> > Forerunners. 29.
> None so backward in the troop,
> > Monadnoc. 251.
> A moment, by the railway troop,
> > Monadnoc. 396.
> And round me swarmed in shadowy troop
> > Peter. 27.
> And hemmed me in their glittering troop.
> > Poet. 148.
> A sterner errand to the silken troop
> > Summons. 1.
> The centre of the troop allied,
> > Threnody. 67.

Troops
> And troops of friends enjoyed the tide,—
> > In Memoriam. 71.

Trophies
> Equal trophies of thine art;
> > Ode to Beauty. 89.

> And trophies buried: To J. W. 15.

Tropic
> Beneath the tropic ray,   *Farewell. 51.
> Mix polar night with tropic glow,
> > May-Day. 127.
> With dews of tropic morning wet,
> > May-Day. 395.
> Moanings of the tropic sea;
> > Voluntaries. 4.
> To feed the North from tropic trees;
> > Wealth. 37.

Troubadour
> Comes that cheerful troubadour,
> > Monadnoc. 287.

Trousers
> and kersey trousers make
> > Adirondacs. 75.

Trout
> Or whipping its rough surface for a trout;
> > Adirondacs. 111.
> Venison and trout, potatoes, beans,
> wheat-bread;   Adirondacs. 179.

Trout's
> Dissected the slain deer, weighed the
> trout's brain,   Adirondacs. 134.

Trowest
> If thou trowest   Monadnoc. 228.

Trows
> Port or pilot trows not,—
> > Monadnoc. 338.

Truant
> And told the truant by his marks,—
> > Initial Love. 4.
> And whither now, my truant wise and
> sweet,   Threnody. 30.

Truculent
> Truculent with fraud and force,'
> > Berrying. 3.

True
> Tell the sun's time, determine the true
> north,   Adirondacs. 104.
> Give me of the true,—   Bacchus. 14.
> 'May be true what I had heard,—
> > Berrying. 1.
> The true astronomy,   Celestial Love. 67.
> He serves all who dares be true.
> > Celestial Love. 132.
> Farewell, my brothers true,
> > *Farewell. 28.
> Hard to out-do the brave, the true,
> > Frag. Life. X. 3.
> For Nature, true and like in every place,
> > Frag. Nat. IV. 1.
> And estimation true,   From Hafiz. 5.
> Of a true monarch's soul.   Beauty and
> strength,   Good Cheer. 8.
> Above her will, be true;
> > Hermione. 70.
> I must end my true report,
> > Initial Love. 81.
> Disclosing treasures more than true,
> > May-Day. 416.
> And, chiefest prize, found I true liberty
> > Musketaquid. 66.
> Believed the eloquent was aye the true;
> > Phi. 16.
> A cripple of God, half true, half formed,
> > Poet. 185.
> True Brahmin, in the morning meadows
> wet,   Quat. Gardener. 1.

True —*Continued*
Nathless we read your fortunes true;
Romany. 26.
Be great, be true, and all the Scipios,
Rome. 4.
Another heart as large and true.
Security. 6.
I embrace the true believers,
Song of Seyd. 29.
I loved ye with true love, so fare ye
well! Summons. 14.
Five lines lasted sound and true;
Test. 4.
Ah, yes! but by the true heart's blood
They. 3.
For this losing is true dying;
Threnody. 162.
A lover true, who knew by heart
Woodnotes. I. 34.

Truer
And a truer bosom-glow
Frag. Poet. XI. 10.

Truest
Of keenest eye and truest tongue.
Merlin's Song. 15.

Truliest
And they who truliest love her, heralds
are Frag. Nat. V. 9.

Truly
And drew truly every trait.
Hermione. 39.

Trump
Trump of their rescue, sound!
Boston Hymn. 68.

Trumpet-lowing
And trumpet-lowing of the herds.
May-Day. 185.

Trumpets
Announced by all the trumpets of the
sky, Snow-Storm. 1.

Trundle
Or trundle on the glowing rail, Una. 18.

Trunks
Decayed millennial trunks, like moonlight
flecks, Adirondacs. 48.

Trust
See Mistrust.
Unarmed, faced danger with a heart of
trust? Forbearance. 4.
In thee to frame, in me to trust,
Hermione. 29.
And in this fleeting lifetime trust
Robbins Hymn. 23.
The hour of heaven. Generously trust
Rome. 21.
To such as trust her faithfulness.
Woodnotes. I. 138.

Trusted
O trusted broken prophecy!
Threnody. 173.

Trustee
I was the trustee of the hand-cart man,
Frag. Life. XXX. 4.

Trusting
Trusting well the matchless power
Initial Love. 84.

Trusty
I know the trusty almanac
May-Day. 378.

Truth
Will you catch crabs? Truth tries pre-
tension here. Adirondacs. 100.
Others applauded him who spoke the
truth. Adirondacs. 187.
The Muse the truth uncolored speaking)
Daemonic Love. 64.
Know Heaven's truth from lies that
shine— Dull. 21.
Then I said, 'I covet truth;
Each. 37.
Yet can one ray of truth divine
Frag. Life. X. 8.
Not Sense but Reason is the Judge of
truth; Frag. Life. XVIII. 5.
Sit still and Truth is near:
Frag. Life. XXXV. 2.
The eloquence of truth, the wisdom got
Good Cheer. 10.
(Sweet is art, but sweeter truth,)
Harp. 44.
To speak the truth—for truth to strive.
Hymn. 8.
And, truth to tell, amused by pain.
II Intellect. 2.
Or keep truth undecayed. Merlin. 112.
Men wait their good and truth to borrow.
Merlin's Song. 21.
And promise, on thy Founder's truth,
Monadnoc. 407.
When for the truth he ought to die.'
Quat. Sacrifice. 4.
His cold eye truth and conduct scanned,
Quat. S. H. 2.
Are welcome to the man of truth.
Saadi. 40.
The flood of truth, the flood of good,
Saadi. 161.
The truth, and hurl wrong-doers down.
Worship. 14.

Truth's
For truth's and harmony's behoof;
Channing Ode. 68.
O truth's and nature's costly lie!
Threnody. 172.

Truths
Give me truths; Blight. 1.
Not with flatteries, but truths,
Rhea. 2.

Truth-speaking
But now and then, truth-speaking things
Uriel. 47.

Try
You have tried famine: no more try it;
Alphonso. 51.
In many forms we try Bohemian. 1.
Try the might the Muse affords
Frag. Poet. X. 1.
Chasing with words fast-flowing things;
nor try Frag. Poet. XXIX. 5.

Tubs
Youth is (whatever cynic tubs pretend)
To-Day. 17.

Tufted
O tufted entomologist!
Frag. Nat. XIX. 4.

Tugs
Tugs at the heart-strings, numbs the
sense, Titmouse. 15.

Tulip's
Bring back the tulip's pride.
May-Day. 163.

Tulips
In my plot no tulips blow,—
Garden. 5.
Of tulips, in the morning's rays.
May-Day. 207.
Woven of tulips and painted moth.
May-Day. 330.
Each spot where tulips prank their state
Omar. 1.

Tullius
It spoke in Tullius Cicero,
Frag. Poet. IV. 30.

Tumble
Or tumble all again in heap
Alphonso. 29.

Tumbling
He stood before the tumbling main
Frag. Poet. I. 50.
Tumbling steep   Monadnoc. 328.
Under the tumbling mountain's breast,
Wealth. 27.

Tumult
Come the tumult whence it will,
May-Day. 30.

Tumultuous
In a tumultuous privacy of storm.
Snow-Storm. 9.

Tun
Swells a rain-drop to a tun;
Frag. Poet. IX. 8.

Tune
See Untune.
'T is a tune worth thy knowing,
Ellen South. 3.
'T is a tune of the Spring;
Ellen South. 5.
Sings a tune that's worth the knowing.'
Ellen South. 36.
Sings aloud the tune whereto
Merlin. 45.
And the atoms march in tune;
Monadnoc. 246.
To some tune by fairies played;—
Threnody. 77.
For Nature beats in perfect tune,
Woodnotes. II. 164.

Tuned
Tuned to the lay the wood-god sings.
Woodnotes. II. 96.

Tuneful
And thrill our tuneful frames;
April. 2.
I tuneful voices overhear;
Forerunners. 30.
The self-same tuneful muse;
Merlin. 116.
Threw to each fact a tuneful name.
Poet. 8.

Tunes
And annual tunes commemorate
Mountain. 20.

Tunnelled
The mountain tunnelled,
Channing Ode. 60.

Tupper
Entering Big Tupper, bound for the
foaming Falls   Adirondacs. 232.
Wild Tupper Lake; witness the mute all-
hail   Adirondacs. 310.

Turbulent
Checked in these souls the turbulent hey-
day   Adirondacs. 189.
In the turbulent beauty   September. 1.

Turf
And passing, light my sunken turf
Nun. 25.

Turk
On pirate and Turk.   Channing Ode. 89.

Turmoil
That in the wild turmoil,   Illusions. 34.

Turn
Turn pale and starve.   Blight. 49.
I keep, and pass, and turn again.
Brahma. 4.
Find me, and turn thy back on heaven.
Brahma. 16.
They turn his heart from lovely maids,
Frag. Poet. XI.. 12.
Turn swiftlier round, O tardy ball!
May-Day. 160.
But they turn them in a fashion
Monadnoc. 177.
They turn the frost upon their chemic
heap,   Musketaquid. 41.
Or for my turn to fly too fast.
Nun. 32.
Which in turn thy glory warms!
Ode to Beauty. 24.
I turn the proud portfolio
Ode to Beauty. 52.
Turn the key and bolt the door,
Past. 6.
Up and eastward turn thy face;
Poet. 121.
To infinite time his eager turn,
Poet. 188.
Day and night their turn observe,
Poet. 273.
Ah! could we turn the leaf.
Quat. Climacteric. 4.
Falls, in turn, a new degree.   Rhea. 40.
Who can turn the golden rhyme.
Saadi. 114.
Turn on the accuser roundly; say,
Sursum Corda. 6.
I homeward turn; farewell, my pet!
Titmouse. 80.

Turned
Turned and departed silent. I, too late,
Days. 10.
And, how oft soe'er they've turned it,
I Eros. 5.
Each maple leaf turned up its silver side.
Frag. Nat. III. 14.
And turned the drowsy world to flame.
Frag. Poet. I. 14.
In the street, if he turned round,
Guy. 23.
I turned to Cheshire's haughty hill.
Monadnoc. 32.
Has turned my child's head?' "
Sphinx. 64.

Turner
Small need have I of Turner or Daguerre,
Frag. Nat. IV. 8.

Turning
'T is the turning of the tide.
Holidays. 20.

Turns
By turns we praised the stature of our
guides, Adirondacs. 80.
Then turns to bound away,—is it too
late? Adirondacs. 124.
And turns the woe of Night,
Bacchus. 10.
Turns the sod to violets,
Humble-Bee. 27.
He looks on that, and he turns pale.
Monadnoc. 330.

Turret
A tapering turret overtops the work.
Snow-Storm. 22.

Turrets
Airy turrets purple-piled,
May-Day. 350.

Turtle
The turtle brave in his golden spots;
May-Day. 238.

Tutors
Can rules or tutors educate Culture. 1.
Tutors, but a joyful eye,
Threnody. 211.

Twain
Yet melted would be twain.
Initial Love. 150.
Ever, when twain together play,
Saadi. 15.

'T was
'T was always thus, Adirondacs. 286.
'T was high time they came; Gifts. 2.
His eye the eye 't was seeking found.
Guy. 24.
Or haply 't was the cannonade
May-Day. 15.

Twelvemonth
A twelvemonth he could silence hold,
Frag. Poet. V. 24.

Twenty
Six rods, sixteen, twenty, or forty-five;
Adirondacs. 126.
For one sun supply us twenty.
Alphonso. 54.
The wind may alter twenty ways,
Woodnotes. I. 98.

'T were
So like the soul of me, what if 't were me?
Adirondacs. 214.

Twice
And twice each day the flowing sea
Boston. 3.
Self-planted twice, like the banian.
Miracle. 6.
Twice I have moulded an image,
Song of Nature. 61.

Twigs
Limbs into branches, branches into twigs,
Frag. Nat. XVII. 4.

Twilight
And in the twilight of the forest noon
Adirondacs. 32.
Thou saw'st but now the twilight sad
Frag. Nat. XXVI. 12.
And twilight nook, Hermione. 54.
To twilight parks of beech and pine,
Monadnoc. 6.
Sweet twilight walks and midnight soli-
tude Summons. 7.
My twilight realm he disenchants,
Woodnotes. II. 28.

Twilight's
Or, in the evening twilight's latest red,
Adirondacs. 115.

Twilights
As the two twilights of the day
Merlin. 128.
Than noontide twilights which snow
makes Titmouse. 73.

'T will
'T will not now avail to tan
Alphonso. 11.
Where way is none, 't will creep and wind
Quat. Love. 3.
'T will soon be dark; To J. W. 21.

Twin-born
The slight Linnæa hang its twin-born
heads, Woodnotes. I. 69.

Twine
  See Intertwine.
Stanch and strong the tendrils twine:
II Compensation. 16.
To spin my sand-heap into twine.
Frag. Poet. XXXIV. 2.
And the new-born tendrils twine,
May-Day. 88.

Twinkle
The keen stars twinkle in our eyes,
Romany. 22.
Leaves twinkle, flowers like persons be,
Saadi. 137.

Twinkling
And in every twinkling glade,
Hermione. 53.

Twins
From the twins is nothing hidden,
Love and Thought. 3.
Glittering twins and trines. Merlin. 95.
Twins the world that has been.
Poet. 113.

Twirl
Twirl the old wheels! Adirondacs. 328.

Twisted
Where twisted hills betray
Cosmos. 18.
Caught with love's cord of twisted beams,
Nun. 36.

Two
Two creeping miles Adirondacs. 24.
Between two rocky arms, we climb the
bank, Adirondacs. 31.
Two Doctors in the camp
Adirondacs. 133.
Two of our mates returning with swift
oars. Adirondacs. 234.
There are two laws discrete,
Channing Ode. 52.
Day! hast thou two faces,
Chartist. 1.
Making one place two places?
Chartist. 2.
Only two in the garden walked,
Daemonic Love. 21.
The Pleiads' sheaf but two.
From Hafiz. 8.
Two things thou shalt not long for, if
thou love a mind serene;—
Ibn Jemin. 1.
And, being two, shall still be one.
Initial Love. 146.
Two well-assorted travellers use
Love and Thought. 1.

Eldest rite, two married sides
                                        Merlin. 90.
As the two twilights of the day
                                        Merlin. 128.
On two days it steads not to run from
    thy grave,   On Two Days. 1.
Between two sleeps a short day's stealth,
                                        Poet. 183.
Two touch the string,   Saadi. 19.
And the world has only two.
                                        Security. 8.
Make thy option which of two;
                                        Terminus. 13.
But two cannot go abreast,   Unity. 2.
Cannot travel in it two: Unity. 3.

Twofold
    Reason's twofold, part human, part
        divine;   Frag. Life. XVIII. 6.

Two-leaved
    Five-leaved, three-leaved and two-leaved,
        grew thereby.   Adirondacs. 41.

Type
        See Archetype.
    And type of permanence!
                                        Monadnoc. 360.

Types
    Under gentle types, my Spring
                                        May-Day. 457.

Tyranny
    His hot tyranny   Daemonic Love. 114.

Tyrant
    Bereaved a tyrant of his will,
                                        Merlin. 53.
    Sweet tyrant of all!   Ode to Beauty. 12.

Tyrants
    Where tyrants great and tyrants small
                                        Boston Hymn. 11.
    Tyrants despite their guards or walls.
                                        In Memoriam. 66.
    The tyrants of his doom,   Manners. 18.

Una
    Una lights my clouded dreams;   Una. 2.
    Half-seen Una sits beside.   Una. 8.

Unaffied
    Not unrelated, unaffied,
                                        Woodnotes. II. 174.

Unalterable
    Nor mourn the unalterable Days
                                        In Memoriam. 109.

Unaltered
    Look, here he is, unaltered, save that now
                                        River. 8.

Unanimous
    And greet unanimous the joyful change.
                                        Adirondacs. 53.

Unanswered
    "Thou art the unanswered question;
                                        Sphinx. 113.

Unappointed
    The appointed, and the unappointed day;
                                        On Two Days. 2.

Unarmed
    Unarmed, faced danger with a heart of
        trust?   Forbearance. 4.

Unashamèd
    "The waves, unashamèd,   Sphinx. 25.

Unauthenticated
    Whose unauthenticated waves we named
                                        Adirondacs. 131.

Unawares
    At unawares 't is come and past.
                                        Forerunners. 32.
    Sudden, at unawares,   Merlin. 74.
    Floods with blessings unawares.
                                        Worship. 20.

Unbar
    Who the Future's gates unbar,—
                                        Daemonic Love. 101.
    Then I unbar the doors: my paths lead
        out   Seashore. 38.
    And clerks the Janus-gates unbar,
                                        Solution. 62.
    Unbar the door, since thou the Opener
        art,   Unbar. 1.

Unbeguiled
    Drew his free homage unbeguiled,
                                        In Memoriam. 68.

Unbelieving
    Aches thine unbelieving heart   Poet. 265.

Unbending
    Valor unbending,   Give. 21.

Unbind
    Unbind and give me to the air.
                                        Aeolian Harp. 3.
    To-day unbind the captive,
                                        Boston Hymn. 65.
    To bind or unbind, add what lacked,
                                        Past. 18.
    And know my higher gifts unbind
                                        Threnody. 230.

Unblamed
    Waits unblamed to-morrow's sun.
                                        Frag. Poet. XI. 19.

Unblest
    In strange lands unblest;   Hermione. 48.
    Of blest and unblest? Ode to Beauty. 4.

Unborn
    Kings unborn shall walk with me;
                                        Bacchus. 40.
    An embryo god unborn.   Poet. 104.
    And we despoil the unborn.
                                        World-Soul. 24.

Unbound
    So only are ye unbound;
                                        Boston Hymn. 66.
    But thou, poor child! unbound, unrhymed,
                                        Woodnotes. II. 178.

Unbounded
    The stream I love unbounded goes
                                        Two Rivers. 6.

Unbroken
    Under low mountains, whose unbroken
        ridge   Adirondacs. 27.
    Was writ on tables yet unbroken;
                                        Problem. 56.

Unbrowned
    And, in the forest, delicate clerks, un-
        browned,   Adirondacs. 57.

Unbuild
    Build and unbuild our echoing clay.
                                        Merlin. 127.

Unburies
    Whose pipe and arrow oft the plough un-
        buries,   Musketaquid. 29.

Uncalled
    For I am wont to sing uncalled,
                                        Solution. 19.
    Wilt thou, uncalled, interrogate,
                                        Threnody. 249.

Uncertain
A dull uncertain brain,   Dull. 1.
Uncertain of thine own   Farewell. 39.
The world uncertain comes and goes;
                              Friendship. 3.
Unchain
And I unchain the slave:
                              Boston Hymn. 54.
Unchanged
The wintry garden lies unchanged;
                              Threnody. 95.
Unclean
Aught unsavory or unclean
                              Humble-Bee. 40.
Uncolored
The Muse the truth uncolored speaking)
                              Daemonic Love. 64.
Unconscious
To catch the unconscious heart in the
  very act.   Philosopher. 6.
Uncontinented
In the uncontinented deep."
                              Monadnoc. 329.
Uncounted
Glide its hours uncounted,—
                              Sphinx. 43.
Uncouth
Then in the uncouth solitude unlock
                              Letter. 19.
Uncover
Lo! I uncover the land
                              Boston Hymn. 17.
Uncovers
As the sculptor uncovers the statue
                              Boston Hymn. 19.
Undaunted
And take the mortal leap undaunted,
                              Fame. 17.
Undaunted are their courages,
                              Initial Love. 33.
Undaunted and calm;   Sphinx. 20.
To the boy with his games undaunted
                              World-Soul. 7.
Undecayed
Or keep truth undecayed.   Merlin. 112.
Undeceiving
And carolled undeceiving things
                              Frag. Poet. V. 42.
Undefiled
Nature's sweet marvel undefiled,
                              Threnody. 123.
Under (Partial list.)
Under low mountains, whose unbroken
  ridge   Adirondacs. 27.
Under the cinders burned the fires of
  home;   Adirondacs. 333.
Under the Andes to the Cape,
                              Bacchus. 4.
Language falters under it,
                              Bohemian. 8.
And under, through the cable wove,
                              Concord Ode. 35.
Under his tongue;   Destiny. 30.
Under Alps and Andes cold;
                              Frag. Nat. I. 16.
Under this cover   *Lines. 7.
Under east winds crossed with sleet.
                              May-Day. 133.
Under morn's unlifted lid,
                              May-Day. 423.
Under gentle types, my Spring
                              May-Day. 457.

Minorities, things under cloud!
                              Mithridates. 30.
Under clouds, my lonely head,
                              Monadnoc. 203.
And, under vines, on rocky isle,
                              Solution. 12.
Deep love lieth under   Sphinx. 69.
And under pain, pleasure,— Sphinx. 99.
Under pleasure, pain lies. Sphinx. 100.
Under the snow, between the rocks,
                              Woodnotes. I. 40.
Underfoot
Thrives here, unvalued, underfoot.
                              Monadnoc. 184.
Down on earth there, underfoot,
                              Song of Seyd. 33.
Underground
Through snows above, mines under-
  ground,   Solution. 47.
Or hide underground her alchemy.
                              Woodnotes. II. 167.
Undermining
Fears not undermining days,
                              Spiritual Laws. 6.
Underneath
Save underneath the sea
                              Concord Ode. 30.
Chaste-glowing, underneath their lids,
                              Eva. 11.
The world's light underneath a measure.
                              Fame. 24.
Underneath, within, above,—
                              Initial Love. 43.
Quickening underneath the mould
                              May-Day. 273.
Deep underneath deep?   Sphinx. 16.
Under-song
Present and Past in under-song,—
                              Concord Ode. 18.
O, listen to the undersong,
                              Woodnotes. II. 146.
Underspread
See New England underspread,
                              Monadnoc. 280.
Understand
For sea and land don't understand,
                              Concord Ode. 21.
He palmistry can understand,
                              Initial Love. 54.
I understand their faery syllables,
                              River. 24.
Understands
The water understands
                              Frag. Nat. XXIV. 1.
Understands the universe;
                              Woodnotes. II. 143.
Understood
Yet is understood the better;
                              Astraea. 22.
Underwoods
Rover of the underwoods,
                              Humble-Bee. 29.
Underwoods were full of pleasance,
                              Peter. 33.
Undid
Let wine repair what this undid;
                              Bacchus. 59.
By Fancy, ghastly spells undid.
                              May-Day. 46.

Undo
That use to undo the limb and sense of
age; I Bear. 2.

Undone
The gay enchantment was undone,
Each. 35.

Freely as task at eve undone
Frag. Poet. XI. 18.

And thou, by science all undone,
May-Day. 174.

Undulate
Sun, moon, man, undulate and stream,
Poet. 173.

Undulating
Like undulating layer of air,
Daemonic Love. 24.

Uneasy
Has quenched the uneasy blush that
warmed my cheek; Summons. 2.

Unenviable
Yet envies none, none are unenviable.'
Musketaquid. 84.

Unequal
Both death and pity, my unequal skill
Angelo. 13.

Unerring
Unerring to the ocean sand.
Woodnotes. I. 132.

Unespied
So walks the woodman, unespied.
Quat. Forester. 4.

Unexhausted
In silver lakes that unexhausted gleam
Frag. Nat. IV. 10.

Glowed unexhausted kindliness,
Friendship. 7.

Unexpressed
Though it tear thee unexpressed;
Rhea. 12.

Unfading
Of the unfading gold of Heaven
Dull. 17.

So bloom the unfading petals five,
Solution. 71.

Unfallen
Mature the unfallen fruit. Terminus. 22.

Unfamed
Who walk in ways that are unfamed,
Nature. I. 20.

Unfathomable
In those unfathomable orbs
Initial Love. 25.

Unfit
He could not frame a word unfit,
In Memoriam. 53.

Unfold
Never did sculptor's dream unfold
Angelo. 1.

Æons which tardily unfold Nun. 41.

Unfolds
To the lark's trill unfolds the rose,
Waterfall. 15.

Unfurled
Their flag to April's breeze unfurled,
C. Hymn. 2.

Ungiven
Or an ungiven maid, Merlin. 109.

Ungrateful
I ungrateful, I alone.
Frag. Poet. VII. 8.

Unhappy
In weak, unhappy times, Merlin. 60.

Unharmed
Right onward drive unharmed;
Terminus. 38.

Unheeded
Unheeded Danger near him strides,
Daemonic Love. 87.

And his air-sown, unheeded words,
Solution. 57.

Unhurt
Unhurt by a thousand storms,
May-Day. 321.

He roves unhurt the burning ways
Voluntaries. 49.

Unimagined
And unimagined splendor waits his steps.
October. 5.

And the unimagined good of men
World-Soul. 103.

Union
A union then of honest men,
Boston. 35.

Or union never more again.
Boston. 36.

But feels and seals this union:
Celestial Love. 112.

Lured by 'Union' as the bribe.
Voluntaries. 30.

Unit
Unit and universe are round; Uriel. 22.
Hath its unit, bound and metre;
Visit. 5.

But the unit of the visit, Visit. 9.

Unitarians
Were unitarians of the united world,
Blight. 27.

Unite
Which round the floating isles unite:—
Frag. Nat. XXVI. 25.

United
Were unitarians of the united world,
Blight. 27.

In their summits are united;
Celestial Love. 45.

United States
United States! the ages plead,—
Concord Ode. 17.

Unites
Each obstruction, it unites
Daemonic Love. 83.

Uniteth
Whom he uniteth, God installs;
Frag. Life. XVII. 12.

Universal
And the Universal Friend
Bohemian. 4.

Spoke the universal dame; Sphinx. 130.
And universal Nature, through her vast
Xenophanes. 17.

Universe
And beam to the bounds of the universe.
Beauty. 20.

And pirates of the universe, shut out
Blight. 47.

The solid, solid universe Cupido. 1.
The universe, Daemonic Love. 73.
The riches of the universe Dull. 13.
Nor thee, on the second, the Universe
slay. On Two Days. 4.

Universe—*Continued*
'Merge me in the brute universe,
Poet. 193.
See to thyself, O Universe! Rhea. 72.
For there is no might in the universe
Rome. 18.
Unit and universe are round; Uriel. 22.
Understands the universe;
Woodnotes. II. 143.

Unkind
Think me not unkind and rude
Apology. 1.

Unking
And doth the man unking.
Channing Ode. 57.

Unknowing
'Welcome, though late, unknowing, yet
known to me.' Adirondacs. 45.
Unknowing war, unknowing crime,
Saadi. 100.
I'm all-knowing, yet unknowing;
Song of Seyd. 19.

Unknown
Untold, unknown, and I could surely spell
Blight. 10.
Unknown, albeit lying near,
Daemonic Love. 39.
Unknown to Cromwell as to me
Fate. 3.
Unknown to him as to his horse,
Fate. 5.
All beside was unknown waste,
Humble-Bee. 50.
By lonely lakes to men unknown.
May-Day. 29.
Of friends to friends unknown;
Rubies. 6.
But walked the earth unmarked, un-
known. Solution. 52.
Known fruit of the unknown;
Sphinx. 11.
He is hidden and unknown. Una. 24.

Unlaurelled
Of critic charters, an unlaurelled Muse.
To-Day. 8.

Unless
Unless he conquer and prevail?
Destiny. 15.
Not unless God made sharp thine ear
Dirge. 45.
Unless to Thought is added Will,
Frag. Poet. XVIII. 3.
Unless to learn it ten times ten.
Miracle. 8.

Unlifted
Under morn's unlifted lid,
May-Day. 423.

Unlighted
Chill and wet, unlighted, mean,
Chartist. 4.

Unlike
Where unlike things are like;
Celestial Love. 38.
Like and unlike, Experience. 4.

Unlock
Quickened so, will I unlock Bacchus. 43.
'You cannot unlock your heart,
Dirge. 57.
So didst thou quarry and unlock
Hermione. 45.

Then in the uncouth solitude unlock
Letter. 19.
If fate unlock his bosom's door,
Saadi. 120.
Unlock doors of new delight;
Solution. 21.
[If Thought unlock her mysteries,
Walden. 29.
Mountain chains he can unlock:
Worship. 6.

Unlocks
Unlocks new sense and loftier cheer.
Aeolian Harp. 17.

Unmake
Unmake me quite, or give thyself to me!
Ode to Beauty. 99.
Nor time unmake what poets know.
Test. 12.

Unmakes
And, being so, the sage unmakes the man.
Philosopher. 2.

Unmarked
To-day slinks poorly off unmarked between: Quat. Heri. 2.
But walked the earth unmarked, unknown. Solution. 52.

Unmarred
Perfect kinds by vice unmarred,
Frag. Nat. XXIII. 2.

Unmask
When trellised grapes their flowers unmask, May-Day. 87.

Unmeasured
Unmeasured still my Shakspeare sits,
Quat. Shakespeare. 3.

Unmeet
And all unmeet our carpet floors;
May-Day. 221.

Unnerves
Unnerves his strength, invites his end.
Woodnotes. II. 50.

Unpeoples
Who peoples, unpeoples,—
Channing Ode. 82.

Unplanted
Her broad van seeks unplanted lands;
Voluntaries. 37.
He trode the unplanted forest floor,
whereon Woodnotes. I. 64.

Unplighted
Unplighted yet to me, *Farewell. 38.

Unploughed
Unploughed, which finer spirits pile,
Monadnoc. 43.
In unploughed Maine he sought the lum-
berers' gang Woodnotes. I. 62.

Unquoted
Squandering your unquoted mirth,
Monadnoc. 186.

Unregarded
Fell unregarded to the ground,
Poet. 15.

Unrelated
Not unrelated, unaffied,
Woodnotes. II. 174.

Unreligiously
We devastate them unreligiously,
Blight. 38.

Unremembering
Her unremembering prow *Farewell. 16.

Unrepenting
As unrepenting Nature leaves
In Memoriam. 95.

Unreplying
Talker! the unreplying Fate?
Threnody. 250.

Unreturned
If thy love is unreturned;   Rhea. 10.

Unrhymed
But thou, poor child! unbound, unrhymed,   Woodnotes. II. 178.

Unripe
Beauty is unripe childhood's cheat;
Each. 38.

Unrolled
One third part of the sky unrolled
Concord Ode. 11.

Unruly
A hid unruly appetite   May-Day. 151.

Unsavory
Aught unsavory or unclean
Humble-Bee. 40.

Unsealed
Are unsealed, that he may hear.
Garden. 48.

Unseals
And why, when mirth unseals all tongues,
I Compensation. 5.

Unseasoned
Nor my unseasoned step disturbs
Frag. Nat. XVIII. 4.

Unseen
That panteth after things unseen,
Hymn. 3.
Unseen by such as stood around.
Poet. 16.
Out of an unseen quarry evermore
Snow-Storm. 11.

Unserviceable
And my unserviceable limbs forego.
I Bear. 5.

Unshaded
Nor cloy us with unshaded sun,
May-Day. 128.

Unsightly
But the poor, unsightly, noisome things
Each. 26.

Unspared
With God's unspared donation;
Day by Day. 4.

Unspent
Their unspent beauty of surprise,
Freedom. 14.
With wing unspent,   Give. 13.

Unspheres
And Genius unspheres all souls that abide.
Frag. Poet. XXI. 2.

Unstainèd
And unstainèd as the sun.
Frag. Nat. XXIII. 18.

Unsuited
Nor yet unsuited to that solitude:
Adirondacs. 251.

Unsupported
And your heart is unsupported.
Etienne. 8.

Unsure
Unsure the ebb and flood of thought,
Poet. 279.

Untamable
In the hemlocks tall, untamable,
Garden. 31.

Untamed
Shy, untamed, inscrutable,
Initial Love. 89.

Untaught
You must add the untaught strain
Destiny. 3.
And the untaught Spring is wise
Nature. I. 3.

Untied
The Gordian noose was still untied.
Frag. Nat. VI. 6.

Unties
And the dogs of Fate unties.
Daemonic Love. 118.

Until (Partial list.)
Until he write, where all eyes rest,
Astraea. 7.
Face the eastern star until
Frag. Nat. XXVI. 8.
Should throb until he snapped his chain.
Freedom. 4.
That he will not demand the debt until
the Judgment Day.   Ibn Jemin. 4.
To stand the hurts of time, until
Monadnoc. 226.
That until now has put his world in fee
Rome. 23.
To make no step until the event is
known,   Woodnotes. I. 88.

Untired
Their sinewy arms pull at the oar untired
Adirondacs. 89.

Unto (Partial list.)
Unto the same again.' Celestial Love. 26.
Unto men these moonmen lend,
Daemonic Love. 58.
Unto the thing so signified;   Fate. 14.
Defeated day by day, but unto victory
born.   Frag. Life. XXIII. 4.
Let not unto the stones the Day
Monadnoc. 12.
Yet unto me not morn's magnificence,
Naples. 15.
As a man unto his friend.   Peter. 36.
The word unto the prophet spoken
Problem. 55.
In birdlike heavings unto death,
Threnody. 101.
As if he came unto his own,
Threnody. 143.
Unto every race and age
Woodnotes. II. 281.
Unto each, and unto all,
Woodnotes. II. 283.

Untold
Draw untold juices from the common
earth,   Blight. 9.
Untold, unknown, and I could surely
spell   Blight. 10.
That untold early love   *Farewell. 41.
I leave untold to-day,   *Farewell. 42.
Meek Nature's secret still untold.
Frag. Nat. VI. 8.
Untold intent;   Give. 14.
Graced by each change of sum untold,
Monadnoc. 56.

Untold—*Continued*
Realm beyond realm,—extent untold;
Nun. 42.
With sweetness untold,   Sphinx. 86.
Untouched
Or ardent youth untouched by pain,
Hymn. 11.
Untried
Of untried power and sane delight:
Monadnoc. 105.
Untune
Nor grief untune his voice,   Harp. 6.
Unvalued
Thrives here, unvalued, underfoot.
Monadnoc. 184.
Unveiled
The heaven where unveiled Allah pours
Saadi. 160.
Unveils
Unveils thy form.   Hermione. 55.
Unwilling
Nor bid the unwilling senator
Channing Ode. 73.
Unwind
Nor seek to unwind the shroud
To J. W. 6.
Unwonted
Teem with unwonted thoughts:
Daemonic Love. 47.
Unworthy
An act unworthy to be done;
In Memoriam. 54.
Up (Partial list.
See Heaped-up.
rode up the forks   Adirondacs. 2.
On through the Upper Saranac, and up
Adirondacs. 21.
Up with the dawn, they fancied the light
air   Adirondacs. 59.
I saw men go up and down,
Astraea. 9.
Up the horizon walls,   Bacchus. 28.
Up with your towns and stay!'
Boston. 52.
Up to my ear the morning brings
Boston Hymn. 7.
Life up a people from the dust,
Boston Hymn. 67.
Up! and the dusky race
Boston Hymn. 77.
Are shadows flitting up and down
Celestial Love. 56.
When the purple flame shoots up,
Cosmos. 21.
And dress up Nature in your favor.
Destiny. 44.
I wandered up, I wandered down,
Dirge. 15.
To make up a year   Fable. 8.
A friend to lift the curtain up
Hymn. 21.
'Up!—If thou knew'st who calls
Monadnoc. 5.
Up! where the airy citadel
Monadnoc. 10.
I wandered up, I wandered down,
Peter.11.
Ridiculously up and down   Poet. 88.
Up from the burning core below,—
Problem. 17.
Loveth downward, and not up;
Rhea. 36.

Came up the pensive train,
Robbins Hymn. 14.
Up and down their glances strain.
Threnody. 81.
Would in thy hall take up his rest?
Threnody. 225.
Up to his style, and manners of the sky.
Threnody. 271.
Up! mind thine own aim, and
To J. W. 22.
Upas
Swing me in the upas boughs,
Mithridates. 18.
Upbore
And, on the instant, rosier clouds upbore
Adakryn. 4.
Upborne
In trance upborne past mortal goal
Solution. 45.
Upbraid
Who can, like thee, our rags upbraid,
May-Day. 426.
Upheaved
The upheaved land, and bury the folk,
Channing Ode. 30.
Upheld
See Self-upheld.
Uphold
The rocks uphold thy name engraved,
Lines. 12.
Upland
The heifer that lows in the upland farm,
Each. 3.
A patch of meadow upland Waterfall. 1.
Uplands
O, few to scale those uplands dare,
Waldeinsamkeit. 39.
To the uplands of New Hampshire,
World-Soul. 3.
Uplift
New flowerets bring, new prayers uplift
Celestial Love. 4.
And I uplift myself into its heaven,
Day's Ration. 16.
Suddenly   it   will   uplift
Frag. Life. XXXV. 3.
Uplifted
Uplifted shall condense her powers,
Monadnoc. 99.
And tread uplifted land?
Monadnoc. 207.
Uplifting
In music and uplifting hymns.
Frag. Poet. V. 29.
Upon
Upon the tablets blue,   Bacchus. 66.
Thy voice upon the deep   Bell. 5.
Ah! let me blameless gaze upon   Eva. 7.
Put youth, joy, health upon the shrine,
Fame. 27.
Upon my cheek to stay;   *Farewell. 24.
To hunt upon their shining trails.
Forerunners. 8.
The gods upon their spheres.
Frag. Life. IV. 4.
And boys run out upon their leafy ropes.
Frag. Nat. III. 20.
Stand upon this pasture hill,
Frag. Nat. XXVI. 7.
Harvests grew upon his tongue,
Frag. Poet. V. 31.

I mourn upon this battle-field,
In Memoriam. 1.
His elfin length upon the snows,
May-Day. 114.
Leaf answers leaf upon the bough;
Merlin. 86.
There's fruit upon my barren soil
Monadnoc. 295.
They turn the frost upon their chemic heap,
Musketaquid. 41.
And as each flower upon the fresh hill-side,
Naples. 5.
My hand upon the silent string,
Poet. 95.
Upon him noble eyes did rest,
Poet. 196.
As the best gem upon her zone,
Problem. 34.
To gaze upon the Pyramids;
Problem. 36.
Still floats upon the morning wind,
Problem. 59.
For, whom the Muses smile upon,
Saadi. 125.
Who gazed upon the sun and moon
Threnody. 142.
But if upon the seas I sail,   Una. 17.
The moss upon the forest bark
Woodnotes. I. 133.
That's writ upon our cell;
World-Soul. 46.

Upper
On through the Upper Saranac, and up
Adirondacs. 21.
Whilst upper life the slender rill
Art. 27.
Were kindled in the upper skies
Eva. 2.
Replunged again into that upper sphere
Frag. Life. XVI. 8.
'In to the upper doors,   Merlin. 35.
These wonders rose to upper air;
Problem. 40.
The stars may hide in the upper sky,
Romany. 27.
And a blush tinged the upper sky,
Uriel. 55.

Upraised
That haply man upraised might keep
Poet. 169.

Uprear
Alps and Causasus uprear,
Monadnoc. 275.

Uprears
The scale of power uprears,
Frag. Life. IV. 2.

Uproar
With the sun and the sand and the wild uproar.
Each. 28.
Hear the uproar of their joy;
May-Day. 227.

Uprose
Uprose the merry Sphinx,   Sphinx. 121.

Upspringeth
Upspringeth the palm;   Sphinx. 18.

Upstart
To upstart Wealth's averted eye;
Good-Bye. 9.

Upward
And upward pries and perforates
May-Day. 121.

Right upward on the road of fame
Poet. 1.
My boreal lights leap upward,
Song of Nature. 41.
Will thy clear blue eye, upward bent, still keep its chastened glow,   *Violet. 3.
Upward the ninth heaven thrilled and moved   Waterfall. 19.

Upward-striving
In countless upward-striving waves
Promise. 1.

Urbane
Bookworm, break this sloth urbane;
Monadnoc. 16.

Urchin
Asks of the urchin to be tost.
May-Day. 64.
The gazing urchin walks   October. 6.

Urge
The storm-winds urge the heavy weeks along,   Adirondacs. 227.
Nor me can Hope or Passion urge
Nun. 17.

Urged
Him strong Genius urged to roam,
Frag. Life. XX. 1.

Urgeth
Whom the dawn and the day-star urgeth,
Woodnotes. II. 38.

Urging
Urging astonished Chaos with a thrill
Adirondacs. 264.

Uri
Wales, Scotland, Uri, Hungary's dells:
Monadnoc. 96.

Uriel
This was the lapse of Uriel,   Uriel. 5.
As Uriel spoke with piercing eye,
Uriel. 25.
On the beauty of Uriel;   Uriel. 36.

Uriel's
Came Uriel's voice of cherub scorn,
Uriel. 54.

Urn
Fills his blue urn with fire;
Concord Ode. 2.
Cannot be carried in book or urn;
Garden. 54.
His lot of action at the urn.   Poet. 188.

Urns
Replenishing   material   urns
Day by Day. 3.

Us (Partial list.)
Where all the sacred mountains drew around us,   Adirondacs. 9.
For one sun supply us twenty.
Alphonso. 54.
The injured elements say, 'Not in us;'
Blight. 33.
And haughtily return us stare for stare.
Blight. 36.
Therefore they shove us from them, yield to us   Blight. 40.
'Like us be free and bold!'   Boston. 16.
You shall pay us a tax on tea;
Boston. 66.
God with the fathers, so with us,
Boston. 118.
That can give us a glimpse of the battle
Cosmos. 15.

Us (Partial list.)—*Continued*
Explored they teach us to explore.
                              Dull. 22.
Escort us to a little grave.
                              Frag. Life. I. 4.
Draw us to these meadow farms,
                              Frag. Nat. XXVI. 4.
So shall he speak to us the word
                              Hymn. 27.
Fold us music-drunken in.   Merlin. 129.
Holding us at vantage still,
                              Monadnoc. 376.
And though the substance us elude,
                              Monadnoc. 390.
Recallest us,   Monadnoc. 401.
But leave us the horizon walls.
                              Romany. 8.
Trade and the streets ensnare us,
                              World-Soul. 21.
Alas! the Sprite that haunts us
                              World-Soul. 41.
Deceive us, seeming to be many things,
                              Xenophanes. 8.

Usage
He by false usage pinned about
                              Poet. 189.

Use
And seeming-solid walls of use
                              Bacchus. 49.
By lying use bestowed,
                              Celestial Love. 65.
Use and Surprise,   Experience. 6.
To use my land to put his rainbows in.
                              Frag. Nat. IX. 2.
All my force saith, Come and use me:
                              Frag. Nat. XXVIII. 2.
Or gleam which use can paint on steel,
                              Frag. Poet. I. 24.
That use to undo the limb and sense of
  age;   I Bear. 2.
Tell me, maiden, dost thou use
                              Lines. 1.
Or seemed to use his privilege
                              Lines. 19.
Two well-assorted travellers use
                              Love and Thought. 1.
Trade and counting use   Merlin. 115.
The richest of all lords is Use,
                              Merlin's Song. 29.
I will use the world, and sift it,
                              Mithridates. 22.
Hither! take me, use me, fill me,
                              Mithridates. 31.
It is pure use;—   Monadnoc. 355.
Which, one by one, they know to draw
  and use.   Musketaquid. 35.
Draw from each stratum its adapted use
                              Musketaquid. 39.
Perforce must use his tongue;
                              Quat. Orator. 2.
And doubt and reverend use defied,
                              Uriel. 16.

Used
Well used, it decketh joy,
                              Frag. Nat. XXIV. 7.
Ill used, it will destroy,
                              Frag. Nat. XXIV. 9.
Belike the one they used in parting
                              May-Day. 385.

Useful
Useful only, triste and damp,
                              Chartist. 5.

Uses
Of all wit's uses the main one
                              Frag. Life. XI. 1.
Of all wit's uses, the main one
                              Merlin's Song. 39.

Useth
Like God it useth me.
                              Waldeinsamkeit. 4.

Ushers
He has ushers many a one;
                              Initial Love. 75.

Usurp
Usurp the seats for which all strive;
                              Merlin's Song. 17.

Utmost
The dim horizon's utmost bound;—
                              May-Day. 425.

Utter
To utter God's infinity,   Bohemian. 2.
Can adequately utter none   Harp. 97.
All of them utter sounds of 'monishment
                              River. 29.

Utterance
Past utterance, and past belief,
                              Threnody. 203.

Utterly
Follow it utterly,   Give. 9.

Vacant
I am bitter, vacant, thwarted,
                              Etienne. 7.
To vacant bosoms brought.
                              Voluntaries. 82.

Vacation
Still thou playest;—short vacation
                              Holidays. 17.

Væ
Vae solis! I found this, Frag. Poet. IV. 7.

Vagrant
Or vagrant booming of the air,
                              May-Day. 11.

Vague
First vague shadow of surmise
                              Give. 36.

Vain
How spread their lures for him in vain
                              Beauty. 23.
And pine in vain the sacred Seven;
                              Brahma. 14.
That you are fair or wise is vain,
                              Destiny. 1.
The brook sings on, but sings in vain
                              Frag. Poet. XXVI. 1.
Pluck it now! In vain,—thou canst not;
                              Holidays. 5.
Hushed myriads hark in vain,
                              Merlin's Song. 11.
Would mortify me, but in vain; for still
                              Musketaquid. 69.
Resist in vain his motive strain,
                              Poet. 37.
In vain: the stars are glowing wheels,
                              Poet. 171.
Not from a vain or shallow thought
                              Problem. 9.
Fraudulent Time in vain concealed.—
                              Saadi. 174.

I make your sculptured architecture vain,
Seashore. 11.
Vain beside mine. I drive my wedges
home, Seashore. 12.
Which his eyes seek in vain.
Sphinx. 80.
Nature, Fate, men, him seek in vain.
Threnody. 29.
Now Love and Pride, alas! in vain,
Threnody. 80.
East, west, for aid I looked in vain,
Titmouse. 7.
In vain produced, all rays return;
Uriel. 23.
To the van called not in vain.
Voluntaries. 96.
Not vain, sour, nor frivolous;
Woodnotes. II. 67.
Behold! were in vain and in vain;—
Woodnotes. II. 210.
Oft didst thou thread the woods in vain
Woodnotes. II. 248.

Vainly
Vainly valiant, you have missed
Etienne. 9.
Ah, vainly do these eyes recall
Threnody. 58.

Vale
Who trod with me this lovely vale;
Dirge. 22.

Vales
He hath broke his banks and flooded all
the vales River. 9.

Valiant
Vainly valiant, you have missed
Etienne. 9.
And, to be valiant, must come down
Titmouse. 63.
To the valiant chief who fights;
Voluntaries. 107.

Valley
See Sea-valley.
They took this valley for their toy,
Dirge. 29.
They added ridge to valley, brook to
pond, Hamatreya. 17.
With its old valley, Hamatreya. 46.
Visits the valley;—break away the
clouds,— Musketaquid. 12.
in valley clods, Voluntaries. 119.

Valleys
And in thy valleys, Agiochook!
Channing Ode. 22.
Or valleys by the sea, House. 10.
From mountains far and valleys near
Walden. 13.

Valor
Valor unbending, Give. 21.
This scrap of valor just for play
Titmouse. 45.

Valued
See Outvalued; Unvalued.

Vamp
Chemist to vamp old worlds with new,
May-Day. 445.

Vampyre-fanned
Vampyre-fanned, when I carouse.
Mithridates. 19.

Van
Her broad van seeks unplanted lands;
Voluntaries. 37.

To the van called not in vain.
Voluntaries. 96.

Vanilla
Wild rose, lily, dry vanilla,—
Frag. Nat. II. 18.

Vanish
Vanish, and end their murmuring,—
Monadnoc. 367.
Vanish beside these dedicated blocks,
Monadnoc. 368.

Vanished
The vanished gods to me appear;
Brahma. 7.
The vanished rose of evening's dream.
May-Day. 298.
Think'st Beauty vanished from the coast
Threnody. 181.

Vanishing
They are all vanishing, Illusions. 11.
The vanishing are seen, Poet. 111.

Vanity
I lay my vanity and guilt; Nun. 16.
But, critic, spare thy vanity, Saadi. 45.

Vantage
Holding us at vantage still,
Monadnoc. 376.

Vantage-ground
Failed to plant the vantage-ground;
Merlin's Song. 19.

Vapor
The vapor the hill. Sphinx. 40.

Varied
Of one import, of varied tone;
Garden. 42.

Varieties
And sweet varieties of chance,
Monadnoc. 62.

Variety
We cannot spare variety. Alphonso. 58.

Various
Long and various the report,—
I Eros. 2.

Vase
And dip it in thy porcelain vase;
Woodnotes. II. 52.

Vast
Or stumbling on through vast self-similar
woods Adirondacs. 105.
Vast the realm of Being is,
Day by Day. 9.
Sleeps the vast East in pleasèd peace,
Frag. Nat. XXVI. 21.
To the vast soul that o'er him planned;
Problem. 48.
Hurling defiance at vast death;
Titmouse. 44.
And to thine eye the vast skies fall,
Woodnotes. II. 200.
And the vast mass became vast ocean.
Woodnotes. II. 269.
And universal Nature, through her vast
Xenophanes. 17.

Vaster
Beckon the wanderer to his vaster home.
Adirondacs. 229.
loftier walls, and vaster floor.
Frag. Nat. XII. 3.
Things writ in vaster character;
Frag. Poet. V. 46.

Vats
Drain sweet maple juice in vats.
Monadnoc. 142.
From Eden's vats that run. Rubies. 4.

Vault
The low December vault in June be lifted high, Frag. Nat. XX. 1.
Sail swiftly through your amber vault,
Poet. 163.
This vault which glows immense with light Woodnotes. II. 299.
But arched o'er him an honoring vault.
Worship. 10.

Vaulted
And emulate, vaulted, Illusions. 19.

Vaulters
Like vaulters in a circus round
Frag. Poet. XIX. 1.

Vaunt
O'er all that mass and minster vaunt;
Titmouse. 90.

Vaunted
And in their vaunted works of Art
Nature. II. 22.

Vedas
Expound the Vedas of the violet,
Quat. Gardener. 2.

Vegetable
From plum-trees vegetable gold;
Guy. 44.

Veil
See Unveil.
Or baffle by a veil, or slight by scorn?
Adirondacs. 176.
Crowds each on other, veil on veil,
Frag. Nat. XXXI. 4.

Veiled
See Unveiled.

Veileth
Night veileth the morning, Sphinx. 39.

Veiling
Shamed the angels' veiling wings;
Uriel. 48.

Veils
And veils the farm-house at the garden's end. Snow-Storm. 5.

Vein
As if we men were talking in a vein
Adirondacs. 256.
Throb in each manly vein;
Boston. 107.
Beauty of a richer vein,
Daemonic Love. 56.
Vein an artery, though ye kill me!
Mithridates. 32.

Veins
Which fed the veins of earth and sky,
Alphonso. 32.
Of blood through veins of kindred poured. Daemonic Love. 4.
But left a legacy of ebbing veins,
Terminus. 29.
Aloft, in secret veins of air,
Waldeinsamkeit. 37.

Venerable
Each to all is venerable, Astraea. 5.
And life, shorn of its venerable length,
Blight. 53.
We love the venerable house
Robbins Hymn. 1.

Veni
Paean! Veni, vidi, vici. Titmouse. 104.

Venison
Venison and trout, potatoes, beans, wheat-bread; Adirondacs. 179.

Venture
And venture, and to Guy the oil.
Guy. 50.

Venus
Venus, when her son was lost,
Initial Love. 1.

Verb
He must to school and learn his verb and noun Adirondacs. 267.

Verdict
The verdict said, Past. 2.
Verdict which accumulates
Threnody. 262.

Verge
The joyful traveller gives, when on the verge Adirondacs. 311.

Veritable
Lurketh Nature veritable; Saadi. 130.

Vermilion
With a vermilion pencil mark the day
Adirondacs. 230.

Vernal
Sweet fern, mint and vernal grass,
Frag. Nat. II. 14.
Foreteller of the vernal ides,
Woodnotes. I. 32.

Verse
Coin the moonlight into verse
Frag. Poet. XXIX. 3.
Freedom's pæan in my verse,
Freedom. 2.
Canst thou copy in verse one chime
Garden. 37.
Wonderful verse of the gods,
Garden. 41.
Nor Collins' verse of tender pain,
Harp. 79
Not one of all can put in verse,
Harp. 83.
And verses that all verse outlive.
Solution. 72.

Versed
He is versed in occult science,
Initial Love. 64.

Verses
And verses that all verse outlive.
Solution. 72.
I hung my verses in the wind, Test. 1.

Vervain
Rue, cinquefoil, gill, vervain and agrimony, Blight. 5.

Very
'T is very small,— no load at all,—
Boston. 67.
A very tender history Dirge. 55.
'You are doubtless very big; Fable. 5.
A very pretty squirrel track; Fable. 16.
Into the very best sole-leather.
Frag. Poet. XXIII. 2.
To catch the unconscious heart in the very act. Philosopher. 6.
But he would come in the very hour
Woodnotes. I. 42.

Vessel
The winged vessel flies, *Farewell. 25.

That the word the vessel brings
Letters. 5.

Vest
Why should the vest on him allure,
Problem. 7.
He took the color of his vest
Quat. Forester. 1.
In rings and painted vest. Riches. 8.

Vestures
Nor thou detain her vesture's hem.
Give. 40.

Vetch
See Blue-vetch.

Vex
And vex the gods with question pert,
Alphonso. 38.
To vex with odious subtlety
Saadi. 47.

Vice
Virtue, to love, to hate them, vice;
Daemonic Love. 9.
Perfect kinds by vice unmarred,
Frag. Nat. XXIII. 2.
The vice of Japhet by the thought of
Shem. Frag. Poet XXII. 2.
His vice some elder virtue's token,
Initial Love. 92.
Vice nestles in your chambers,
World-Soul. 11.

Vicegerency
For God's vicegerency and stead?
Monadnoc. 77.

Viceroy
And his viceroy is none,—
World-Soul. 82.

Vici
Pæan! Veni, vidi, vici. Titmouse. 104.

Victim
He goes in pawn to his victim
Boston Hymn. 63.
Victim of perpetual slight: Destiny. 19.

Victim's
No fate, save by the victim's fault, is low,
Frag. Life. II. 1.

Victor
Crowns him victor glorified,
Voluntaries. 104.
Victor over death and pain.
Voluntaries. 105.

Victor's
For action's field, for victor's car,
In Memoriam. 29.

Victors
The victors divide; Channing Ode. 95.
Victors over daily wrongs:
Voluntaries. 110.
Awful victors, they misguide
Voluntaries. 111.

Victory
Defeated day by day, but unto victory
born. Frag. Life. XXIII. 4.
I read great years of victory,
Frag. Poet. III. 6.
To float my child to victory,
Woodnotes. II. 46.

Vidi
Pæan! Veni, vidi, vici. Titmouse. 104.

Viewless
Heat with viewless fingers moulds,
May-Day. 195.

Vigil
The punctual stars will vigil keep,—
Titmouse. 18.

Vigilant
Some mystic hint accosts the vigilant,
Adirondacs. 203.

Village
Farm-gear and village picket-fence,
Poet. 59.
Each village senior paused to scan
Threnody. 72.

Vine
See Grapevine.
Or grew on vine whose tap-roots, reach-
ing through Bacchus. 3.
Vine for vine be antidote, Bacchus. 53.
Man's the elm, and Wealth the vine;
II Compensation. 15.
None from its stock that vine can reave.
II Compensation. 18.
And the vine that grows thereby?
Exile. 4.
Infant Bacchus in the vine,— Garden. 35.
Feels the bloom on the living vine,
May-Day. 90.
Dominion o'er the palm and vine.
Woodnotes. II. 48.

Vine-leaf
Rose and vine-leaf deck buffoons;
Heroism. 3.

Vines
Caught among the blackberry vines,
Berrying. 6.
The vines replied, 'And didst thou deem
Berrying. 11.
Singing over shrubs and vines.
Humble-Bee. 10.
Or, hid in vines, peeping through many a
loop, Quat. Gardener. 3.
And, under vines, on rocky isle,
Solution. 12.

Vintage
Than all vintage of the earth.
Monadnoc. 294.

Vintage-day
'T was the vintage-day of field and wood,
May-Day. 338.

Violet
In Farsistan the violet spreads
Exile. 1.
Willow and violet, maiden and man.
May-Day. 288.
Expound the Vedas of the violet,
Quat. Gardener. 2.
Her passions the shy violet
Quat. Hafiz. 1.
Why lingerest thou, pale violet, to see
the dying year; *Violet. 1.
O Violet, like thee, how blest could I lie
down and die, *Violet. 9.
I had a sister once who seemed just like
a violet; *Violet. 13.

Violet's
I inhaled the violet's breath; Each. 43.
Tints that spot the violet's petal,
Woodnotes. I. 21.

Violets
And dew-bent violets, fresh and new,
Frag. Nat. XXVI. 36.

Violets—*Continued*
Cinquefoils or violets in the grass,
                    Frag. Poet. XXVIII. 5.
Turns the sod to violets,
                    Humble-Bee. 27.
But violets and bilberry bells,
                    Humble-Bee. 42.
Peep the blue violets out of the black
    loam,   Naples. 25.
The violets yon field which stain
                    Omar. 3.
When the violets were in their shrouds,
    and Summer in its pride,   *Violet. 15.

Virgin
Yet shine forever virgin minds,
                    Astraea. 31.
As 'mid the virgin train she strayed,
                    Each. 30.
It opened in its virgin bower,
                    Woodnotes. I. 43.

Virgins
Of shining virgins every May,
                    May-Day. 302.

Virtue
Virtue palters; Right is hence;
                    Channing Ode. 32.
Virtue, to love, to hate them, vice;
                    Daemonic Love. 9.
The virtue of his lucky hand.   Guy. 14.
Imbibing virtue by his hand
                    Initial Love. 55.
Every joy and virtue speed,
                    May-Day. 334.
For homes of virtue, sense and taste.
                    Monadnoc. 152.
In spite of Virtue and the Muse,
                    Nemesis. 13.
And yet, if virtue abrogate the law,
                    Phi. 3.
God for thy virtue lays a plot:
                    Prayer. 2.
And prayers of humble virtue made
                    Robbins Hymn. 7.
Virtue alone is sweet society,   Rome. 8.
And virtue reaching to its aims;
                    Threnody. 279.
Exists to draw thy virtue forth.
                    Titmouse. 59.
I think no virtue goes with size;
                    Titmouse. 60.
Shed their virtue through his eye.
                    Woodnotes. II. 74.

Virtue's
Opens the eye to Virtue's starlike meed
                    Enchanter. 14.
His vice some elder virtue's token,
                    Initial Love. 92.

Virtues
O birds, your perfect virtues bring,
                    May-Day. 397.
O all you virtues, methods, mights,
                    Mithridates. 26.
They prove the virtues of each bed of
    rock,   Musketaquid. 37.
And bragged his virtues to each other,—
                    Poet. 204.
With the Virtues meet,   Politics. 16.

Virtuous
And rare and virtuous roots, which in
    these woods   Blight. 8.

Spring is strong and virtuous,
                    May-Day. 271.
She loves a poor and virtuous race.
                    Voluntaries. 38.

Visibly
Visibly revolves;   Celestial Love. 35.

Vision
    See Prevision.
And a vision without bound:
                    Celestial Love. 20.
Into vision where all form
                    Celestial Love. 31.
To that within the vision of small eyes.
                    Phi. 18.
At the new vision gape and jeer.
                    Poet. 22.
His vision as sublime: Poet. 296.
"To vision profounder,   Sphinx. 81.

Vision's
In his vision's narrow walls
                    Day by Day. 12.

Visit
But the unit of the visit,   Visit. 9.

Visiting
And thy grave smiled on by the visiting
    moon.   Mountain. 6.

Visitings
Nor doubt but visitings of graver
    thought   Adirondacs. 188.

Visitor
No door-bell heralded a visitor,
                    Adirondacs. 65.

Visits
Visits the valley;—break away the
    clouds,—   Musketaquid. 12.

Vital
Of vital force the wasted rill,
                    Alphonso. 28.

Vixen
A vixen to his altered eye;   Rhea. 20.

Vocal
All their vocal muse affords;
                    Monadnoc. 176.

Void
A makeweight flying to the void,
                    II Compensation. 11.
And leave the cities void.   Garden. 4.
Broadsowing, bleak and void to bless,
                    Threnody. 284.
Wanting wisdom, void of right,
                    Voluntaries. 60.

Voice
He heard a voice none else could hear
                    Beauty. 13.
Thy voice upon the deep   Bell. 5.
And good men thought thy sacred voice
                    Bell. 11.
A better voice peals through my song.
                    Frag. Poet. XXX. 2.
Nor grief untune his voice,   Harp. 6.
And some attain his voice to hear,
                    Harp. 57.
Or Wordsworth, Pan's recording voice,—
                    Harp. 82.
Till a clear voice spoke,—   *Lines. 27.
Voice of a meteor lost in day?
                    May-Day. 12.
Voice of sport, or rush of wings,
                    May-Day. 31.
The wood-fly mocks with tiny voice
                    May-Day. 75.

The far halloo of human voice;
May-Day. 76.
With the voice of orators;   Merlin. 22.
Ere yet the summoning voice was still,
Monadnoc. 31.
There came a voice without reply,—
Quat. Sacrifice. 2.
Is not my voice thy music, morn and eve?   Seashore. 4.
I hear continually his voice therein.
Self-Reliance. 5.
Obey the voice at eve obeyed at prime:
Terminus. 36.
Whose voice, an equal messenger,
Threnody. 38.
That winsome voice again might hear;
Threnody. 51.
Voice of earth to earth returned,
Threnody. 264.
When piped a tiny voice hard by,
Titmouse. 25.
Thy summer voice, Musketaquit.
Two Rivers. 1.
Came Uriel's voice of cherub scorn,
Uriel. 54.
Warned by an inward voice,
Voluntaries. 85.
Soothed by the voice of waters,
Waterfall. 3.
To fling his voice into the tree,
Woodnotes. II. 121.
In a voice of solemn cheer,—
Woodnotes. II. 147.
The voice that speaketh clear.
World-Soul. 20.

Voiced
Not clearly voiced, but waking a new sense   Adirondacs. 204.

Voices
And round the globe your voices reach.
Boston. 111.
Which children's voices bless.
Concord Ode. 8.
I tuneful voices overhear;
Forerunners. 30.
Voices followed after,
Frag. Nat. III. 23.
Wandering voices in the air   Garden. 49.
The sights and voices ravishing
Harp. 85.
Thorough a thousand voices
Sphinx. 129.

Volcano's
Like the volcano's tongue of flame,
Problem. 16.

Volumes
Why need I volumes, if one word suffice?
Day's Ration. 26.

Volunteers
And like a lover volunteers,   Walk. 4.

Votary
But thou, my votary, weepest thou?
Threnody. 195.

Vote
Each honest man shall have his vote,
Boston. 33.

Votes
Ask votes of thrushes in the solitudes.
Channing Ode. 74.

Votive
We set to-day a votive stone;
C. Hymn. 10.

Vowed
Hermit vowed to books and gloom,—
Hermione. 34.

Vows
Alas! that neither bonds nor vows
Amulet. 9.
There need no vows to bind
Celestial Love. 83.
The temple of a nation's vows.
Frag. Life. XXII. 2.
In heaven are kept their grateful vows,
Robbins Hymn. 3.

Voyager
Voyager of light and noon;
Humble-Bee. 15.

Vulgar
And vulgar feet have never trod
Good-Bye. 21.

Vulnerable
See Invulnerable.

Vulture's
Dove beneath the vulture's beak;—
Voluntaries. 17.

Wade
Can swim the flood and wade through snow,   Quat. Love. 2.

Wading
Chilled wading in the snow-choked wood.
Titmouse. 4.

Waft
That waft the breath of grace divine
Voluntaries. 69.

Wafted
Which wafted Lafayette!   Boston. 89.

Wafting
Wafting the puny seeds of power,
Wealth. 7.

Wage
And teach his nimbleness to earn his wage,   Adirondacs. 268.
If curses be the wage of love,
Frag. Life. XXXIII. 1.

Wages
Thought is the wages
Frag. Poet. VIII. 2.

Wagon
And, Calmuck, in his wagon roam
Poet. 52.
The babe in willow wagon closed,
Threnody. 62.

Wagon-frame
Or mend his wicker wagon-frame,
Threnody. 49.

Wail
Without tongue, yellow-cheeked, full of winds that wail and sigh;   Flute. 2.
From tone of joy to inward wail,
Harp. 8.

Wailing
Was the wailing song he breathed,
Voluntaries. 11.
Without wailing, without fear;
Woodnotes. II. 80.

Wails
Rehearsed to men the damnèd wails
Solution. 49.

Waistcoat
Fronts the north-wind in waistcoat gray,
Titmouse. 46.

Wait
I wait the sun on them should shine.
Frag. Life. XIV. 2.
I will wait Heaven's perfect hour
Frag. Life. XXV. 3.
Wait a little, you shall see
Frag. Life. XXXV. 5.
Wait, I prithee, till I come
Humble-Bee. 17.
All things wait for and divine him,—
Initial Love. 78.
Wait his returning strength. Merlin. 62.
Men wait their good and truth to borrow.
Merlin's Song. 21.
Not yet I sing: but I must wait,
Poet. 94.
As mountains for the morning wait,
Poet. 122.
The Furies wait beyond.
Quat. Pericles. 4.
Wait then, sad friend, wait in majestic
peace Rome. 20.
My creatures travail and wait;
Song of Nature. 58.
To wait an æon to be born.
Threnody. 149.
And the shy hawk did wait for him;
Woodnotes. I. 57.

Waited
For which the world had waited, now
firm fact, Adirondacs. 238.

Waiting
Waiting till God create the earth,—
Frag. Nat. XXVI. 15.
Never balk the waiting ear.
Monadnoc. 192.

Waits
No courier waits, no letter came or went,
Adirondacs. 66.
Waits through dark ages for the morn,
Frag. Life. XXIII. 3.
Waits unblamed to-morrow's sun.
Frag. Poet. XI. 19.
Far distant yet his chorus waits.
Garden. 36.
And unimagined splendor waits his steps.
October. 5.

Wake
Were fairly reached at last. Wake, echo-
ing caves! Adirondacs. 259.
He loved to watch and wake
Frag. Poet. I. 35.
To every child they wake, Promise. 8.
When Winter reigned I'd close my eye,
but wake with bursting Spring,
*Violet. 11.

Waken
And, when it lists him, waken can
Freedom. 15.
Whether it waken joy or rage
Merlin's Song. 10.

Wakes
Mind wakes a new-born giant from her
sleep. Adirondacs. 327.
And wakes the wish in youngest blood
May-Day. 95.
Song wakes in my pinnacles
Woodnotes. II. 91.

Love wakes anew this throbbing heart,
World-Soul. 107.

Waking
Not clearly voiced, but waking a new
sense Adirondacs. 204.
Out of sleeping a waking, Sphinx. 13.
Out of waking a sleep; Sphinx. 14.

Walden
In Walden wood the chickadee
Frag. Nat. XIX. 1.
Then drink in Walden water.
Frag. Nat. XIX. 6.
Blue Walden rolls its cannonade,
May-Day. 106.

Walden's
Than Walden's haunted wave,
Walden. 26.

Wales
Wales, Scotland, Uri, Hungary's dells:
Monadnoc. 96.

Walk
That I walk alone in grove and glen;
Apology. 2.
Kings unborn shall walk with me;
Bacchus. 40.
And walk on earth as the sun walks in
the sphere. Frag. Nat. V. 12.
I could walk days, years, away
Frag. Nat. XXI. 6.
But if I would walk alone,
Frag. Poet. IV. 13.
My garden spade can heal. A woodland
walk, Musketaquid. 72.
Who walk in ways that are unfamed,
Nature. I. 20.
The souls that walk in pain.
Waldeinsamkeit. 24.
I walk in marble galleries, Walden. 31.
In one wood walk, than learned men
Walk. 7.

Walked
Only two in the garden walked,
Daemonic Love. 21.
With me who walked through space and
time Dirge. 4.
Walked about with puzzled look.
Experience. 16.
She walked in flowers around my field
Frag. Life. XIII. 1.
As if in him the welkin walked,
Frag. Poet. I. 54.
Each of these landlords walked amidst
his farm, Hamatreya. 4.
When late I walked, in earlier days,
May-Day. 35.
(That one would say, meadow and forest
walked, Musketaquid. 48.
As I walked among the hills Poet. 144.
But walked the earth unmarked, unknown.
Solution. 52.

Walker
But, like a walker in his sleep Poet. 86.

Walkest
However long thou walkest solitary,
Rome. 26.

Walking
Once, among the Pleiads walking,
Uriel. 7.

Walks
See Woodwalks.
The garden walks are passional April. 3.

And walk on earth as the sun walks in
the sphere.   Frag. Nat. V. 12.
Or walks in mask almighty Jove,
                    May-Day. 215.
The gazing urchin walks through tents of
gold,   October. 6.
So walks the woodman, unespied.
                  Quat. Forester. 4.
Sweet twilight walks and midnight soli-
tude   Summons. 7.
Who speeds to the woodland walks?
                  Woodnotes. I. 3.
Where feeds the moose, and walks the
surly bear,   Woodnotes. I. 66.
Whoso walks in solitude
                  Woodnotes. II. 57.

Wall
    See Log-wall.
No stouter fence, no steeper wall!
                    Boston. 62.
The Dæmon ever builds a wall,
                Daemonic Love. 93.
Silvers the horizon wall,
                  Humble-Bee. 22.
Hark in the wall to the rat: Limits. 2.
Every one to his hole in the wall,
                  May-Day. 390.
Night-dreams trace on Memory's wall
                  Quat. Memory. 1.
Seek not beyond thy cottage wall
                    Saadi. 165.
Fills up the farmer's lane from wall to
wall,   Snow-Storm. 20.
His gathered sticks to stanch the wall
                  Threnody. 84.

Walled
Walled with mortal terror round,
                  Voluntaries. 90.

Wall-flower
One scent to hyson and to wall-flower,
                  Xenophanes. 2.

Walls
    See Seawalls.
Within four walls is possible again,—
                Adirondacs. 322.
Up the horizon walls,   Bacchus. 28.
And seeming-solid walls of use
                    Bacchus. 49.
Through from the empyrean walls
                Celestial Love. 25.
Shrivel the rainbow-colored walls,
                Daemonic Love. 120.
In his vision's narrow walls
                  Day by Day. 12.
Nor heeds Condition's iron walls,—
                  Frag. Life. XVII. 9.
loftier walls, and vaster floor.
                  Frag. Nat. XII. 3.
Up the far mountain walls the streams
increase   Frag. Nat. XXVI. 22.
Tyrants despite their guards or walls.
                  In Memoriam. 66.
And wood-fire flickering on the walls,
                  May-Day. 55.
Over the owner's farthest walls!
                  Monadnoc. 9.
Girt in by mountain walls
                    Mountain. 8.
Walls Amphion piled   Politics. 13.
But leave us the horizon walls.
                    Romany. 8.

Stainless soldier on the walls,
                  Voluntaries. 97.
Yon sky between the walls,
                  World-Soul. 38.

Wand
He bears no bow, or quiver, or wand,
                  Initial Love. 17.

Wander
Many an angel wander by,   Nun. 24.
We wander far by east and west.
                    Una. 4.

Wandered
    See Far-wandered.
I wandered up, I wandered down,
                    Dirge. 15.
I wandered up, I wandered down,
                    Peter.11.
And wandered backward as in scorn,
                  Threnody. 148.

Wanderer
Beckon the wanderer to his vaster home.
                  Adirondacs. 229.

Wanderest
'Now, deceived, thou wanderest
                  Hermione. 47.

Wandering
As wind and wandering wave.
                  Boston Hymn. 56.
Wandering voices in the air   Garden. 49.
Short-lived wandering to and fro,
                    Merlin. 107.
Wandering yester morn the brake,
                    Miracle. 15.
O pilgrim, wandering not amiss!
                  Monadnoc. 242.
A facile, reckless, wandering will,
                    Poet. 207.
After long months of weary wandering,
                    River. 37.
In wandering by the sea;
                  Waldeinsamkeit. 2.

Waneth
Waneth fast and spendeth all.
                  Woodnotes. II. 25.

Want
Before ye want a drop of rain,
                    Alphonso. 49.
Glows the feud of Want and Have.
                  II Compensation. 6.
By want and pain God screeneth him
                  Frag. Poet. V. 7.
Woe and want thou canst outsleep;
                  Humble-Bee. 61.
Want and woe, which torture us,
                  Humble-Bee. 62.
The deepest lore of wealth or want:
                    Poet. 42.
Of Fate and Will, of Want and Right,
                  Woodnotes. II. 130.

Wanted
For this fortune wanted root
                  Daemonic Love. 126.

Wanting
Wanting the echo in my brain.
                  Frag. Poet. XXVI. 2.
Wanting wisdom, void of right,
                  Voluntaries. 60.

Wanton
Nor wanton skip with bacchic dance,
                  May-Day. 129.

Wantonness
And, in its highest noon and wantonness,
Blight. 56.
Wants
He to his wants can well suffice:
Frag. Life. XVII. 5.
He wants them all,　　　Saadi. 26.
What he knows nobody wants.
Woodnotes. I. 12.
War
A field of havoc and war,
Boston Hymn. 10.
The ravage of a year of war.
May-Day. 278.
Unknowing war, unknowing crime,
Saadi. 100.
With war and trade, with camp and
town;　　　Saadi. 105.
And give or take the stroke of war,
Saadi. 109.
Oft shall war end, and peace return,
Saadi. 111.
In newer days of war and trade,
Solution. 59.
When Science armed and guided war,
Solution. 61.
Let war and trade and creeds and song
Song of Nature. 77.
Warble
Whose silver warble wild
Threnody. 12.
Warbler
See Pine-warbler.
what ails the warbler?　Adirondacs. 206.
War-bolt
Through good and ill the war-bolt hurled,
Boston. 98.
Ward
For watch and ward and furtherance,
Daemonic Love. 28.
Warder
Rhyme the pipe, and Time the warder,
Monadnoc. 247.
Ware
Be thou ware where Saadi dwells;
Saadi. 34.
War-gods
The stern old war-gods shook their heads,
Uriel. 27.
Warily
Slow and warily to choose　House. 5.
He is not fooled, but warily knoweth
Rhea. 44.
Warking
Foully warking in his nest?　Riches. 2.
Warm
Ten scholars, wonted to lie warm and
soft　　　Adirondacs. 50.
Bid my bread feed and my fire warm me
Destiny. 43.
For a warm breast of maiden to his
breast,　　　Epitaph. 3.
Drugged with spice from climates warm,
Hermione. 52.
The saffron cloud that floated warm
Lines. 15.
Nestle warm the highland people,
Monadnoc. 130.
Tides that should warm each neighboring
life　　　Rubies. 7.

Lie on the warm rock-ledges, and there
learn　　　Seashore. 9.
It may blow north, it still is warm;
Woodnotes. I. 100.
Of poles and powers, cold, wet, and
warm:　　　Woodnotes. II. 111.
The warm rosebuds below.
World-Soul. 112.
Warmed
And by great sparks Promethean warmed,
Poet. 186.
Has quenched the uneasy blush that
warmed my cheek;　　Summons. 2.
Warming
See Heart-warming; World-warming.
Warms
Bird and brier inly warms,
May-Day. 198.
Which in turn thy glory warms!
Ode to Beauty. 24.
Yet the love the world that warms
Security. 3.
Warn
Him to beckon, him to warn;
Frag. Poet. V. 43.
Warned
No placard on these rocks warned to the
polls,　　　Adirondacs. 64.
Warned by an inward voice,
Voluntaries. 85.
Warning
Warning to the blind and deaf,
Rhea. 33.
Annexed a warning, poets say,
Saadi. 13.
Warrant
He may, by warrant of his age,
Alphonso. 79.
Is there warrant that the waves
Poet. 275.
Wars
Is the ancestor of wars
Daemonic Love. 130.
By lapses or by wars,　House. 22.
With the cannonade of wars;
Merlin. 24.
Wary
Soften the fall with wary foot;
Terminus. 18.
And wary Nature knows her own
Walk. 2.
Was (Partial list.)
Let not him mourn who best entitled was,
Adirondacs. 296.
And ever was. Pay him.
Boston Hymn. 72.
Who made this world the feast it was,
Dirge. 26.
Since the world was, he has gnawed;
Limits. 3.
The lord is the peasant that was,
Woodnotes. II. 18.
Wash
Waters that wash my garden-side
Garden. 21.
The ground-pines wash their rusty green,
May-Day. 59.
Scatter the sloth, wash out the stain,
May-Day. 454.
And the seas wash the low-hung sky;
Poet. 66.

Put off thy years, wash in the breeze;
Woodnotes. II. 135.

Washed
See Sea-washed.
The mountain waters washed him clean
Frag. Poet. V. 17.
And washed with waterfalls
Mountain. 9.
Whence brought his sunny bubbles ere
he washed River. 5.

Washing
Washing out harms and griefs from memory,
Seashore. 24.

Waste
In the waste one nook is his;
Day by Day. 10.
And all the costly liquor runs to waste;
Day's Ration. 23.
It may be in wood or waste,—
Forerunners. 31.
All beside was unknown waste,
Humble-Bee. 50.
He came late along the waste,
Initial Love. 11.
And fit the bleak and howling waste
Monadnoc. 151.
So call not waste that barren cone
Monadnoc. 352.
Ill day which made this beauty waste,
Threnody. 150.
Life is too short to waste To J. W. 18.
All is waste and worthless, till
Wealth. 30.
As the sheep go feeding in the waste,
Woodnotes. II. 297.

Wasted
Of vital force the wasted rill,
Alphonso. 28.
This charm is wasted on the earth and
sky, Rhodora. 10.

Wastes
Must to the wastes of Nature go,—
Threnody. 131.

Watch
And water it with wine, nor watch askance
Adirondacs. 299.
For watch and ward and furtherance,
Daemonic Love. 28.
He loved to watch and wake
Frag. Poet. I. 35.
I watch your course, Poet. 156.
Thy steps to watch, thy place to know:
Threnody. 33.
To watch the convoy on the road;
Threnody. 61.
Not so the wise; no coward watch he
keeps Woodnotes. I. 90.

Watched
I, in my pleached garden, watched the
pomp, Days. 7.
The lover watched his graceful maid,
Each. 29.
As in the Andes watched by fleets at
sea, Frag. Nat. IV. 4.
I watched the singer with delight,—
Miracle. 22.

Watcher
No watcher in the firmament,
Trenody. 119.

Watches
And as through dreams in watches of the
night, Adirondacs. 201.
To thee. He watches for thee still. His
love Rome. 24.
Behold, he watches at the door!
Saadi. 157.

Watchful
Nor fear those watchful sentinels,
Eva. 9.

Watching
Watching when the loud dogs
Adirondacs. 110.
To the watching Pilgrims came,
Boston Hymn. 2.
Watching the white pear-bloom,
Frag. Nat. XXI. 4.
Watching the daylight fade,
Hermione. 59.
Couched like a cat sat watching close behind
Philosopher. 9.

Watchman
A watchman in a dark gray tent,
Frag. Nat. XXVI. 14.
Thou seest, O watchman tall,
Monadnoc. 385.

Water
To Follansbee Water and the Lake of
Loons. Adirondacs. 25.
Insatiate skill in water or in air
Adirondacs. 137.
As water poured through hollows of the
hills Adirondacs. 149.
And water it with wine, nor watch askance
Adirondacs. 299.
Each dimple in the water, April. 9.
Water and bread, Bacchus. 31.
Whether your jewel be of pure water,
Destiny. 35.
Man drinks the water, drinks the light.
Frag. Life. XXIII. 9.
The deep-eyed flame, obedient water,
Frag. Life. XXIX. 2.
Then drink in Walden water.
Frag. Nat. XIX. 6.
The water understands
Frag. Nat. XXIV. 1.
I cannot spare water or wine,
Mithridates. 1.
She drugs her water and her wheat
Nature. II. 15.
Made the black water with their beauty
gay; Rhodora. 6.
For, though he scoop my water in his
palm, Seashore. 45.
Or the speeding change of water,
Uriel. 52.
Beside the forest water sate;
Woodnotes. I. 105.

Watercourse
And when I sat by the watercourse,
Hermione. 58.

Watercourses
The watercourses were my guide;
Woodnotes. I. 122.

Waterfall
To the song of its waterfall tones,
Woodnotes. I. 2.

Waterfalls
To winds and waterfalls
Hermione. 72.

Waterfalls—*Continued*
And washed with waterfalls
                    Mountain. 9.
One sound to pine-groves and to water-
falls,   Xenophanes. 3.
Waterflag
You waterflag, yon sighing osier,
                    Poet. 221.
Water-haunting
Methought like water-haunting birds
                    Poet. 19.
Water-line
Water-line patterns of all art?
                    May-Day. 213.
Water's
I found the water's bed.
                    Woodnotes. I. 121.
Waters
The waters wild below,
                    Concord Ode. 34.
The mountain waters washed him clean
                    Frag. Poet. V. 17.
Waters that wash my garden-side
                    Garden. 21.
So that the common waters fell Guy. 29.
I fancy these pure waters and the flags
                    Hamatreya. 8.
And waters free as winds shall flow.
                    May-Day. 110.
False waters of thirst;
                    Ode to Beauty. 14.
And murmuring waters counselled me.
                    Rhea. 8.
Waters with tears of ancient sorrow
                    Threnody. 286.
Soothed by the voice of waters,
                    Waterfall. 3.
Where Syrian waters roll,
                    Waterfall. 18.
The falling waters led me,
                    Woodnotes. I. 129.
The foodful waters fed me,
                    Woodnotes. I. 130.
Watery
Down in yon watery nook,
                    Waldeinsamkeit. 33.
Wave
    See Tide-wave.
With the beryl beam of the broken wave;
                    Beauty. 8.
As wind and wandering wave.
                    Boston Hymn. 56.
In changing moon and tidal wave
                    II Compensation. 5.
The bubble of the latest wave
                    Each. 20.
Summer and winter, o'er the wave,
                    Frag. Poet. I. 47.
Asked no physician but the wave,
                    Frag. Poet. V. 20.
As the wave breaks to foam on shelves,
                    Initial Love. 147.
Then runs into a wave again,
                    Initial Love. 148.
Wave which severs whom it bears
                    Insight. 3.
A World-wide wave with foaming edge
                    May-Day. 245.
But not the less the eternal wave rolls on
                    Pan. 10.

I catch thy meaning, wizard wave;
                    Peter. 39.
For every wave is wealth to Dædalus,
                    Seashore. 30.
Illusion dwells forever with the wave.
                    Seashore. 42.
But what is land, or what is wave,
                    Song of Seyd. 13.
She flowed into a foaming wave:
                    Sphinx. 127.
And every wave is charmed.'
                    Terminus. 40.
Than Walden's haunted wave,
                    Walden. 26.
Ere wheat can wave its golden pride.
                    Wealth. 17.
Choosing light, wave, rock and bird,
                    Woodnotes. II. 59.
Thou canst not wave thy staff in air,
                    Woodnotes. II. 168.
The wood and wave each other know
                    Woodnotes. II. 173.
Like wave or flame,
                    Woodnotes. II. 274.
Waved
Waved the scoop-net, and nothing came
amiss;   Adirondacs. 138.
The wood-boughs with thy manners
waved,   Lines. 11.
So waved the pine-tree through my thought
                    Woodnotes. II. 3.
Wave's
On the wave's circulation,   Illusions. 23.
Waves
    See Sea-waves.
Whose unauthenticated waves we named
                    Adirondacs. 131.
The waves that rocked them on the deep
                    Boston. 13.
The honest waves refused to slaves
                    Boston. 17.
All day the waves assailed the rock,
                    Frag. Nat. XXV. 1.
With spouting streams and waves of light
                    Frag. Nat. XXVI. 24.
On waves and hedges still they burn.
                    Garden. 60.
Swimmer through the waves of air;
                    Humble-Bee. 14.
Flow, flow the waves hated,
                    Illusions. 1.
The waves of mutation;   Illusions. 3.
Buries himself in summer waves,
                    Initial Love. 98.
What joy in rosy waves outpoured
                    May-Day. 190.
But O, these waves and leaves,—
                    Nun. 11.
Is there warrant that the waves
                    Poet. 275.
In countless upward-striving waves
                    Promise. 1.
With his redundant waves.   River. 10.
The forest waves, the morning breaks,
                    Saadi. 135.
This matchless strength. Where shall he
find, O waves!   Seashore. 32.
"The waves, unashamèd;   Sphinx. 25.
The mountain chase, the summer waves,
                    To J. W. 3.

Waving
One held a printed journal waving high
Adirondacs. 235.
Let me chase thy waving lines;
Humble-Bee. 8.

Wax
Lixe wax, their fashioning skill betrays,
Monadnoc. 148.

Way
See Halfway; Highway; Midway;
Pathway; Straightway.
To thread by night the nearest way to
camp? Adirondacs. 106.
His way home to the mark.
Boston Hymn. 88.
Our brig hastes on her way,
*Farewell. 15.
And find a loftier way:
Frag. Life. X. 4.
The tongue is prone to lose the way,
Frag. Life. XII. 1.
The flowing conditions of life, give way.
Frag. Life. XXXI. 4.
Did as she pleased and went her way.
Frag. Nat. XXXV. 2.
No scout can track his way,
Frag. Poet. VI. 2.
Sun and moon are in my way.
Frag. Poet. XXV. 4.
The siroc found it on its way. Guy. 37.
Out of the forest way Hermione. 56.
Which lit my onward way with bright
presage, I Bear. 4.
And what they call their city way
Natutre. II. 9.
Is not their way, but hers,
Nature. II. 10.
In lowly homes have lost their way.
Ode to Beauty. 67.
Like meteors which chose their way
Poet. 55.
Huntsmen find the easiest way.
Quat. Artist. 4.
Where way is none, 't will creep and wind
Quat. Love. 3.
To find the narrow way.
Robbins Hymn. 24.
With aged eyes, short way before,—
Threnody. 180.
Through smallest chambers takes its way,
Threnody. 218.
Softly,—but this way fate was pointing,
Titmouse. 23.
Show me the forward way, since thou art
guide, Unbar. 2.
The timid it concerns to ask their way,
Woodnotes. I. 86.
The river knows the way to the sea;
Woodnotes. II. 239.
Its way up to the cloud and wind;
Woodnotes. II. 243.
He has his way, and deals his gifts,—
World-Soul. 79.

Wayfarer
Every wayfarer he meets Astraea. 25.

Ways
See Pathways.
Though late returning to her pristine
ways. Adirondacs. 55.
Its timorous ways, big trifles, and we
planned Adirondacs. 161.

So through all creatures in their form
and ways Adirondacs. 202.
Mark is capricious ways to draw the eye.
Adirondacs. 207.
Shall supplement henceforth all trodden
ways, Adirondacs. 244.
Their dauntless ways did all men praise,
Boston. 9.
They know not well the subtle ways
Brahma. 3.
Thy heart saith, 'Brother, go thy ways!
Destiny. 21.
Peace that hallows rudest ways.
Forerunners. 38.
Knee-deep snows choked all the ways,
May-Day. 37.
Who walk in ways that are unfamed,
Nature. I. 20.
Wormwood,—saying, "Go thy ways;
Saadi. 63.
He roves unhurt the burning ways
Voluntaries. 49.
In my garden three ways meet,
Walden. 1.
The wind may alter twenty ways,
Woodnotes. I. 98.
Threading dark ways, arriving late.
Worship. 12.

We (Partial list.)
And we the low-prized laymen.
Adirondacs. 96.
We flee away from cities, but we bring
Adirondacs. 302.
We praise the guide, we praise the forest
life: Adirondacs. 305.
We are budding, we are blowing;
Ellen South. 34.

Weak
Might harry the weak and poor?
Boston Hymn. 12.
While classes or tribes, too weak to mas-
ter Frag. Life. XXXI. 3.
Ah! heedless how the weak are strong,
Hermione. 27.
Battling for the weak and poor.
In Memoriam. 43.
Too weak to win, too fond to shun
Manners. 17.
In weak, unhappy times, Merlin. 60.
Though I am weak, yet God, when
prayed, Nun. 5.
As if to shame my weak behavior;
Titmouse. 47.
Heart too soft and will too weak
Voluntaries. 15.
And shock thy weak ear with a note
Woodnotes. II. 122.
Our bodies are weak and worn;
World-Soul. 22.
And thrust the weak aside;
World-Soul. 94.

Weakness
See Love-without-weakness.

Wealth
To feed this wealth of lakes and rivulets,
Adirondacs. 150.
Can drain its wealth of hope and sorrow;
Aeolian Harp. 15.
Man's the elm, and Wealth the vine;
II Compensation. 15.

Wealth—*Continued*
The wealth of forms, May-Day. 189.
The deepest lore of wealth or want:
Poet. 42.
For every wave is wealth to Dædalus,
Seashore. 30.
Wealth to the cunning artist who can
work Seashore. 31.
Wealth's
To upstart Wealth's averted eye;
Good-Bye. 9.
Wealthy
Till the poor is wealthy grown,
Etienne. 19.
The wealthy and the wise,
*Farewell. 11.
Weapon
To drug their crops or weapon their arts
withal. Musketaquid. 40.
Weapons
He did their weapons decompose.
Guy. 18.
Weapons to guard the State, or scourge
In Memoriam. 65.
Wear
To-morrow they will wear another face,
Experience. 20.
If thou wear no mask or lie,
Frag. Life. XXVII. 10.
There is no mask but he will wear;
Initial Love. 114.
To me seem not to wear Park. 2.
Wear out indoors your sickly days,
Romany. 7.
Henceforth I wear no stripe but thine;
Titmouse. 54.
Through times that wear and forms that
fade, Waldeinsamkeit. 27.
Wears
But Cupid wears another face,
Daemonic Love. 89.
Boy no more, he wears all coats,
Initial Love. 15.
Earth proudly wears the Parthenon,
Problem. 33.
I heed how wears the day; Walden. 42.
Weary
For I am weary of the surfaces,
Blight. 2.
Long through thy weary crowds I roam;
Good-Bye. 3.
On the first wheels that quit this weary
town Letter. 3.
Never heard thy weary name; Nun. 46.
I am neither faint nor weary, Poet. 126.
After long months of weary wandering,
River. 37.
I weary of my robe of snow,
Song of Nature. 51.
Weather
But all sorts of things and weather
Fable. 6.
Weatherfend
Barked the white spruce to weatherfend
the roof, Adirondacs. 35.
Weatherglass
Weatherglass and chemic phial,
Monadnoc. 53.
Weatherproof
Weave your chamber weatherproof;
Frag. Nat. XXIII. 12.

Here weave your chamber weather-proof,
May-Day. 401.
Weathers
Thrive in all weathers without fear,—
Walden. 15.
Weave
Weave roses for your mate.
Celestial Love. 14.
Web to weave, and corn to grind;
Channing Ode. 49.
Weave your chamber weatherproof;
Frag. Nat. XXIII. 12.
And the poor spinners weave their webs
thereon Frag. Nat. XXXIII. 2.
Fate and Beauty skilled to weave.
Harp. 46.
Here weave your chamber weather-proof,
May-Day. 401.
He shall not seek to weave, Merlin. 59.
Weave wood to canisters and mats;
Monadnoc. 141.
a crown to weave Phi. 1.
Come weave with mine a nobler rhyme.
Woodnotes. II. 139.
Stars weave eternal rings;
World-Soul. 62.
Weaves
Her nest beside the snow-drift weaves,
May-Day. 171.
Weaving
Weaving webs innumerable,
Frag. Nat. XXXI. 2.
Is weaving the sublime proportions
Good Cheer. 7.
Web
See Cobweb.
Web to weave, and corn to grind;
Channing Ode. 49.
With the web that's just begun;
Frag. Poet. IX. 5.
Play not in Nature's lawful web,
Garden. 22.
If He should make my web a blot
Nun. 8.
The poor man crawls in web of rags
Riches. 9.
Thy fortune's web to the beneficent hand
Rome. 22.
Webs
Weaving webs innumerable,
Frag. Nat. XXXI. 2.
And the poor spinners weave their webs
thereon Frag. Nat. XXXIII. 2.
Webster
Why did all manly gifts in Webster fail?
Webster, 1854. 1.
Webster's
Let Webster's lofty face Webster. 1.
Web-worm's
I know each nest and web-worm's tent,
Miracle. 3.
Wedged
Where yon wedged line the Nestor leads,
May-Day. 23.
Wedge-like
Wedge-like cleave the air the birds,
Saadi. 4.
Wedges
Put in, drive home the sightless wedges
Frag. Nat. XXX. 1.

Vain beside mine. I drive my wedges
home,   Seashore. 12.

Wee

At this pinch, wee San Salvador!
                          Titmouse. 51.

Weed

See Hawkweed; Milkweed.
Was a weed of self and schism;
                    Daemonic Love. 128.
And weed and rock-moss is preferred.
                          Threnody. 115.

Weeds

See Clothing-weeds.
Beauty for his sinful weeds,
                          Caritas. 6.
In coarsest weeds or in the best;
                          Destiny. 39.
I wiped away the weeds and foam,
                          Each. 24.
I am superior to my human weeds."
                    Frag. Life. XVIII. 4.
I knew their forms in fancy weeds,
                          Harp. 112.
Leave his weeds and heed his eyes,—
                    Initial Love. 19.
Now in sordid weeds they sleep,
                    Monadnoc. 171.
To mask a king in weeds.
                    Quat. Poet. 2. 4.
Flowering grass and scented weeds;
                    Threnody. 275.

Weeks

The storm-winds urge the heavy weeks
along,   Adirondacs. 227.
Six thankful weeks,—and let it be
                          Goethe. 1.

Weep

Maidens laugh and weep; Composure
                          Poet. 223.

Weepest

The deep Heart answered, 'Weepest
thou?   Threnody. 176.
But thou, my votary, weepest thou?
                          Threnody. 195.

Weighed

Dissected the slain deer, weighed the
trout's brain,   Adirondacs. 134.

Weight

See Makeweight.
From thy worth and weight the stars
gravitate,   Shah Enweri. II. 1.

Weird

With men and women weird.
                    Frag. Nat. X. 4.

Welcome

'Welcome!' the wood-god murmured
through the leaves,—
                    Adirondacs. 44.
'Welcome, though late, unknowing, yet
known to me.'   Adirondacs. 45.
Welcome back, you little nations,
                    Frag. Nat. XXIII. 7.
There was no frost but welcome came,
                          Guy. 47.
He spreads his welcome where he goes,
                    Initial Love. 76.
I feel as I were welcome to these trees
                          River. 36.
And opens you a welcome in them all.
                          Rome. 10.

Are welcome to the man of truth.
                          Saadi. 40.
Most welcome they who need him most,
                          Saadi. 41.

Welfare

Men read the welfare of the times to
come,   Threnody. 169.

Welkin

As if in him the welkin walked,
                    Frag. Poet. I. 54.
Bend happy to the welkin blue.
                          May-Day. 124.

Well

Let them hear well! 't is theirs as much
as ours.   Adirondacs. 261.
'Well done!' he cries;   Adirondacs. 315.
I alas! not well alive,   Angelo. 8.
And that which roses say so well.
                          Bacchus. 25.
He flung in pebbles well to hear
                          Beauty. 9.
'You are thriving well,' said he;
                          Boston. 64.
They know not well the subtle ways
                          Brahma. 3.
We greet you well, you Saxon men,
                          Boston. 51.
To please each other well;
                    Celestial Love. 7.
They can well communicate
                    Celestial Love. 95.
Well may Jove and Juno scorn.
                          Destiny. 11.
Yet well I know the royal mine,
                          Dull. 19.
Well that we loved, woe had we not,
                          Ellen. 8.
all is well and wisely put;   Fable. 17.
And loved so well a high behavior,
                          Forbearance. 5.
Perform the feat as well as they;
                    Frag. Life. X. 2.
Is to live well with who has none.
                    Frag. Life. XI. 2.
He to his wants can well suffice:
                    Frag. Life. XVII. 5.
edge well pleased beheld
                    Frag. Life. XXX. 6.
Well he knows his own affair,
                    Frag. Nat. I. 12.
The frost to spare, what scents so well.
                    Frag. Nat. II. 31.
Civilization well;   Frag. Nat. XXIV. 2.
Well used, it decketh joy,
                    Frag. Nat. XXIV. 7.
Yet mark me well, that idle word
                    Frag. Poet. IV. 21.
Well might then the poet scorn
                    Frag. Poet. V. 44.
As costly wine into his well.   Guy. 30.
The land is well,—lies fairly to the
south.   Hamatreya. 22.
With grace, with genius, well attired,
                          Harp. 116.
Trusting well the matchless power
                    Initial Love. 84.
It was well done.   In Memoriam. 10.
return as well;   Inscription. 1.
Well for those who have no fear,
                          Letters. 3.

Well—*Continued*

Looking seaward, well assured
                    Letters. 4.
Well accept her rule austere;
                    May-Day. 135.
To babes, and to old eyes as well.
                    May-Day. 348.
Knowing well to celebrate
                    May-Day. 267.
Ah! well I mind the calendar,
                    May-Day. 372.
Is to live well with who has none.
                    Merlin's Song. 40.
Well known, but loving not a name,
                    Monadnoc. 29.
What in the Eternal standeth well,
                    Monadnoc. 87.
And well the youngest can command
                    Monadnoc. 135.
Well embodied, well ensouled,
                    Monadnoc. 156.
They bide their time, and well can prove,
                    Monadnoc. 165.
And the learned lecture, well;
                    Monadnoc. 180.
But well I know, no mountain can,
                    Monadnoc. 258.
Well I hear the approaching feet
                    Monadnoc. 267.
Mute orator! well skilled to plead,
                    Monadnoc. 403.
Well the Planter knew how strongly
                    Monadnoc Afar. 5.
And like wise God she judges well.
                    Nature. I. 15.
And do well because they please,
                    Nature. I. 19.
And recount the numbers well;
                    Ode to Beauty. 59.
And well he loved to quit his home
                    Poet. 51.
I greet my office well,   Poet. 115.
High was her heart, and yet was well in-
clined,   Quat. A. H. 1.
Her manners made of bounty well re-
fined;   Quat. A. H. 2.
Well and wisely said the Greek,
                    Quat. Pericles. 1.
And well could honoring Persia learn
                    Saadi. 82.
My gardens ripened well,
                    Song of Nature. 18.
They laid their courses well,
                    Song of Nature. 34.
Well I love the meaning sweet,—
                    Song of Seyd. 23.
I loved ye with true love, so fare ye well!
                    Summons. 14.
The port, well worth the cruise, is near,
                    Terminus. 39.
Morn well might break and April bloom,
                    Threnody. 16.
For his lips could well pronounce
                    Threnody. 52.
His daily haunts I well discern,—
                    Threnody. 88.
Well, in this broad bed lie and sleep,—
                    Titmouse. 17.
For well the soul, if stout within,
                    Titmouse. 75.

The crowded town, thy feet may well de-
lay.   To J. W. 4.
Crooning ditties treasured well
                    Voluntaries. 7.
Long she loved the Northman well;
                    Voluntaries. 43.
O, well for the fortunate soul
                    Voluntaries. 75.
The air is wise, the wind thinks well,
                    Walden. 37.
Which well it can supply,
                    Waterfall. 6.
And well the primal pioneer   Wealth. 9.

Well-appointed

Below May's well-appointed arch,
                    May-Day. 332.

Well-assorted

Two well-assorted travellers use
                    Love and Thought. 1.

Well-born

Shall the well-born soul accept.
                    Celestial Love. 70.

Well-built

Well-built abode of many a race;
                    Monadnoc. 82.

Well-hung

In well-hung chambers daintily bestowed,
                    Adirondacs. 51.

Well-known

That rustles down the well-known forest
road—   River. 26.

Wellspring

From this wellspring in my head,
                    Monadnoc. 292.

Weltering

Shot through the weltering pit of the
salt sea.   Adirondacs. 270.
To weltering Chaos and to sleep.
                    Alphonso. 30.

Went

no letter came or went,   Adirondacs. 66.
Ask you, how went the hours?
                    Adirondacs. 107.
pictures came and went.
                    Adirondacs. 159.
No wisdom from our berries went?"
                    Berrying. 12.
And where they went on trade intent
                    Boston. 7.
As they went or they returned,
                    Forerunners. 25.
Did as she pleased and went her way.
                    Frag. Nat. XXXV. 2.
Northward he went to the snowy hills,
                    Frag. Poet. I. 9.
Were'er he went, the magic guide
                    Frag. Poet. I. 17.
Whither went the lovely hoyden?
                    Holidays. 13.
And Ages went or stayed.   Peter. 24.
Again by night the poet went
                    Poet. 225.
And where thereafter in the world he
went.   River. 7.
Took the eye with him as he went;
                    Threnody. 71.
Some went and came about the dead;
                    Threnody. 152.
Some went to write, some went to pray;
                    Threnody. 155.

Low lies the plant to whose creation
went   Woodnotes. I. 76.

Were (Partial list.)
The men of yore were stout and poor,
                                Boston. 15.
Sad, in sooth, it were to ours,
                                Ellen South. 22.
That were a man's and lover's part,
                                Etienne. 23.
That were Freedom's whitest chart.
                                Etienne. 24.
Were it not better done,   Fame. 13.
With their own harvest honored were.
                                Guy. 46.
If need were, their line from Jove;
                                Monadnoc. 166.
And pause were palsy to the world.—
                                Poet. 176.
I would he were nobler   Sphinx. 95.
When the violets were in their shrouds,
    and Summer in its pride,   *Violet. 15.

Wert
Though thou wert the loveliest
                                Rhea. 17.
Why thou wert there, O rival of the rose!
                                Rhodora. 13.

West
Or landward to the west.'   Boston. 58.
He shall cut pathways east and west
                                Boston Hymn. 15.
Which I hid of old time in the West,
                                Boston Hymn. 18.
Come, East and West and North,
                                Boston Hymn. 81.
They marched from east to west:
                                Experience. 13.
East, West, from Beer to Dan,
                                Fame. 3.
How sweet the west wind sounds in my
    own trees!   Hamatreya. 6.
And all is clear from east to west.
                                Nature. Mot. 12.
Will never my winds go sleep in the
    west?   Song of Nature. 46.
And all is clear from east to west.
                                Threnody. 208.
East, west, for aid I looked in vain,
                                Titmouse. 7.
East, west, north, south, are his domain.
                                Titmouse. 8.
We wander far by east and west.
                                Una. 4.
Space is ample, east and west,   Unity. 1.
Or west, no thunder fear.
                                Woodnotes. I. 103.

Western
    See Northwestern.
And where the western hills declined
                                Boston. 43.
Over yon western bridges I would ride
                                Letter. 4.

Wet
Chill and wet, unlighted, mean,
                                Chartist. 4.
With dews of tropic morning wet,
                                May-Day. 395.
True Brahmin, in the morning meadows
    wet,   Quat. Gardener. 1.
Heat, cold, wet, dry, and peace, and pain.
                                Song of Nature. 76.

Of poles and powers, cold, wet, and
    warm: Woodnotes. II. 111.
Wets
It wets my foot, but prettily
                                Frag. Nat. XXIV. 3.
We've
And we've the landscape overrun,
                                Etienne. 6.
Wharf
    See City Wharf.
What (Partial list.)
    See Somewhat.
What pictures and what harmonies are
    thine!   Adirondacs. 212.
What boots it? What the soldier's mail,
                                Destiny. 14.
What parts, what gems, what colors
    shine,—   Frag. Poet. XVIII. 5.
Not what I made, but what I loved,
                                Threnody. 129.
Saying, *What is excellent,*
                                Threnody. 266.
What subsisteth, and what seems.
                                Uriel. 14.
What his fault, or what his crime?
                                Voluntaries. 13.
What smiths, and in what furnace, rolled
                                Wealth. 18.
And what if Trade sow cities
                                World-Soul. 65.
Whate'er
Nor let us hide, whate'er our pleasure,
                                Fame. 23.
Whatever
And whatever glows or seems
                                Frag. Poet. VIII. 9.
Youth is (whatever cynic tubs pretend)
                                To-Day. 17.
What's
What's most theirs is not their own,
                                Nature. II. 20.
Whatsoever
Whatsoever hap befalls Day by Day. 11.
Wheat
The wheat thou strew'st be souls.
                                Frag. Poet. VI. 12.
Leave the chaff, and take the wheat.
                                Humble-Bee. 57.
The wheat thou strew'st be souls.
                                I Intellect. 4.
She drugs her water and her wheat
                                Nature. II. 15.
Furrow for the wheat,—   Politics. 22.
Ere wheat can wave its golden pride.
                                Wealth. 17.
Wheat-blade
The wheat-blade whispers of the sheaf.
                                May-Day. 209.
Wheat-bread
Venison and trout, potatoes, beans,
    wheat-bread;   Adirondacs. 179.
Wheat-sown
Frontier of the wheat-sown plains,
                                Quat. Alcuin. 2.
Wheel
In a region where the wheel
                                Celestial Love. 33.
Ring of axe or hum of wheel
                                Frag. Poet. I. 23.
The threads of man at their humming
    wheel,   Harp. 100.

Wheel—Continued
Grasp the felloes of her wheel,
     May-Day. 158.
Revolves the fatal wheel! Poet. 117.
Could chain the wheel of Fortune's car,
     Poet. 166.

Wheeling
And saw the wheeling sea-birds skim,
     Frag. Poet. I. 46.

Wheels
Twirl the old wheels! Adirondacs. 328.
On the first wheels that quit this weary
town   Letter. 3.
In vain: the stars are glowing wheels,
     Poet. 171.
On Nature's wheels there is no rust;
     Poet. 297.
Will never my wheels which whirl the
sun   Song of Nature. 47.
Yet whirl the glowing wheels once more,
    Song of Nature. 73.

When (Partial list.)
When linked hemispheres attest his deed.
     Adirondacs. 248.
When the pilgrimage is done,
     Etienne. 5.
When all their blooms the meadows
flaunt   Frag. Nat. VIII. 1.
When boughs buffet boughs in the wood;
     Merlin. 18.
As, when the all-worshipped moon at-
tracts the eye, Musketaquid. 82.
When the scanty shores are full
     Threnody. 232.

Whence (Partial list.)
To be the quarry whence to build
     Frag. Life. XXIV. 3.
Ebbing later whence it flowed,
     Garden. 15.
Whence a smokeless incense breathes.
     May-Day. 6.
Come the tumult whence it will,
     May-Day. 30.
Whence brought his sunny bubbles ere he
washed   River. 5.
Whence the fair flock of Nature sprang.
     Woodnotes. II. 125.
Whence camest thou, misplaced, mis-
timed,   Woodnotes. II. 179.

Where (Partial list.)
See Everywhere.
Where good and ill, Celestial Love. 39.
Where the wisest Muses falter,
     Etienne. 14.
Where forests starve: Monadnoc. 354.
And cities rise where cities burn,
     Saadi. 112.
Where a captive sits in chains,
     Voluntaries. 6.

Whereby
Whereby to model newer races,
     Rhea. 66.

Where'er
Where'er he went, the magic guide
     Frag. Poet. I. 17.
Let me go where'er I will, Music. 1.
The gallant child where'er he came
     Poet. 7.
For still, where'er the trees grow biggest,
     Quat. Artist. 3.

Wherefor
Wherefor thanks God his daily praise,
     Frag. Poet. XI. 2.

Wherefore
Wherefore? to what good end?
     Channing Ode. 40.

Wherein
Wherein every siren sung,
     Daemonic Love. 124.
Wherein was dropped the mortal spoil.
     Harp. 127.
October woods wherein October. 1.
The pit wherein the streams are rolled
     Quat. Alcuin. 3.

Whereinto
The world whereinto he was born,
     Threnody. 18.
Whereinto he loved to look.
     Threnody. 93.

Whereof
Whereof old chronicles relate
     Frag. Nat. XXVI. 33.
Of the gods, whereof she is one,—
     May-Day. 131.
As that whereof the sun is made,
     Monadnoc. 168.
And the sands whereof I'm made
     Ode to Beauty. 50.
Whereof it spoke were toys
     Threnody. 41.

Whereon
Whereon the purple iris dwells in beauty
     Adirondacs. 219.
Whereon their traits are found.
     Manners. 12.
Whereon ye sail, Monadnoc. 327.
The things whereon he cast his eyes
     Poet. 9.
Yet every scroll whereon he wrote
     Poet. 13.
He trode the unplanted forest floor,
whereon   Woodnotes. I. 64.

Wheresoever
And, wheresoever their clear eye-beams
fell,   Blight. 28.

Whereto
Miss the aim whereto I strive.
     Angelo. 9.
Sings aloud the tune whereto
     Merlin. 45.

Wherewith
The light wherewith all planets shone,
     Frag. Poet. IV. 25.

Whether (Partial list.)
Whether thy sons or strangers eat the
fruit: Adirondacs. 300.
Immensely curious whether you
     Alphonso. 39.
And whether I am angry or content,
     Day's Ration. 9.
Whether your jewel be of pure water,
     Destiny. 35.
But whether it dazzle me with light.
     Destiny. 37.
Nor whether your name is base or brave:
     Destiny. 40.
But whether you charm me,
     Destiny. 42.
Whether it waken joy or rage
     Merlin's Song. 10.

And whether formed for good or ill,
                                    Prayer. 7.
Whether doomed to long gyration
                                    Uriel. 39.
'Whether is better, the gift or the donor?
                                    Woodnotes. II. 5.
Whether she work in land or sea,
                                    Woodnotes. II. 166.

Which (Partial list.)
Which publish and which hide the cause.
                                    Celestial Love. 59.
Counsel which the ages kept
                                    Celestial Love. 69.
Which only angels hear;
                                    Merlin's Song. 9.
Life is life which generates,
                                    Threnody. 244.
To the aim which him allures,
                                    Voluntaries. 91.

While
   See Erewhile
The while, one leaden pot of alcohol
                                    Adirondacs. 139.
While the soul it doth surcharge,
                                    Etienne. 18.
With fire that draws while it repels.
                                    Eva. 12.
I murmur never while   *Farewell. 52.
These had crossed them while they slept.
                                    Forerunners. 20.
While oaks of pride   Frag. Nat. III. 18.
"Thou didst not tarry while I prayed.
                                    Frag. Poet. II. 2.
While Time shot by.   *Lines. 12.
While the solid curse and jeer
                                    Monadnoc. 191.
The day goes drudging through the
   while,   Nun. 2.
A little while attend;   Poet. 93.
And I the lady all the while.
                                    Romany. 12.
While thou sittest at thy door
                                    Saadi. 167.
Where tarries he the while?
                                    Song of Nature. 38.
While they slumbered and slept:—
                                    Sphinx. 8.
A little while   Terminus. 19.
A while to share his cordial game,
                                    Threnody. 48.
I laugh at those who, while they gape
   and gaze,   To-Day. 15.
I talk with kings the while.]
                                    Walden. 32.
A little while each russet gem
                                    Woodnotes. II. 53.

Whilst
If, whilst within thy heart abide
                                    Angelo. 12.
Whilst upper life the slender rill
                                    Art. 27.
Whilst his files sweep round yon Alpine
   height;   Each. 8.
Whilst the country's flinty face,
                                    Monadnoc. 147.
Whilst love and terror laid the tiles.
                                    Problem. 32.
He shall be happy whilst he wooes,
                                    Woodnotes. II. 83.

Whine
And whine, and flatter, and regret,
                                    Initial Love. 30.
Trembler, do not whine and chide:
                                    Sursum Corda. 3.
Whined
The Dervish whined to Said,
                                    Frag. Poet. II. 1.
Whipping
Or whipping its rough surface for a
   trout;   Adirondacs. 111.
Whips
For haircloth and for bloody whips,
                                    Saadi. 76.
Whip-scirpus
Orchis and gentian, fern and long whip-
   scirpus,   Adirondacs. 142.
Whipt
When the wing of the south-wind whipt
   the lake   Frag. Poet. I. 36.
Whir
The heavy grouse's sudden whir,
                                    Harp. 89.
Whirl
And grasping give the orbs another
   whirl.   May-Day. 159.
Will never my wheels which whirl the
   sun   Song of Nature. 47.
Yet whirl the glowing wheels once more,
                                    Song of Nature. 73.
Whirling
To the cadence of the whirling world
                                    House. 19.
Lost in whirling spheres I rove,
                                    Song of Seyd. 7.
With Thought's perilous, whirling pool;
                                    Threnody. 233.
Whirlwind
The whirlwind in ripples wrote
                                    Garden. 54.
Whirlwinds
Fleeter far than whirlwinds go,
                                    Visit. 16.
Whisper
My lips in whisper move   *Farewell. 43.
Serve that low whisper thou hast served;
   for know,   Good Cheer. 2.
Thy gossips spread each whisper,
                                    Quat. Hush. 3.
Me false to mine dare whisper none,—
                                    Romany. 15.
Whispered
Whispered, 'Darling, never mind!
                                    Experience. 19.
Whispered the Muse in Saadi's cot:
                                    Saadi. 86.
Whispering
And what the whispering grasses
   smother.   Garden. 32.
Whispering hints of treasure hid
                                    May-Day. 422.
In every whispering leaf I hear
                                    Peter. 31.
Whispers
The wheat-blade whispers of the sheaf.
                                    May-Day. 209.
Still whispers to the willing mind.
                                    Problem. 60.
When Duty whispers low, Thou must,
                                    Voluntaries. 73.

Whispers—*Continued*
It whispers of the glorious gods,
World-Soul. 43.
Whistle
The whistle of returning birds,
May-Day. 184.
Whistled
But Nature whistled with all her winds,
Frag. Nat. XXXV. 1.
Whistles
Toil whistles as he drives his cart.
Saadi. 154.
Whistlings
The air is full of whistlings bland;
May-Day. 7.
White
See Snow-white.
Through scented banks of lilies white and
gold, Adirondacs. 19.
Barked the white spruce to weatherferd
the roof, Adirondacs. 35.
Three conifers, white, pitch and Norway
pine, Adirondacs. 40.
In its white block; yet it therein shall
find Angelo. 3.
Black by white faces,—
Channing Ode. 85.
The wings of Time are black and white,
II Compensation. 1.
He flingeth white Cupido. 6.
A rose diamond or a white,
Destiny. 36.
She paints with white and red the moors
Frag. Nat. XIII. 1.
Watching the white pear-bloom,
Frag. Nat. XXI. 4.
Toy with the bow, yet hit the white,
Frag. Poet. V. 2.
Toy with the bow, yet hit the white.
Merlin's Song. 38.
White hollow shells upon the desert
shore, Pan. 9.
Grow red with joy and white with fear;
Saadi. 30.
Smite the white breasts which thee fed,
Saadi. 67.
Curves his white bastions with projected
roof Snow-Storm. 13.
And the meaning was more white
Test. 9.
Thy cheek too white, thy form too
slender,
Woodnotes. II. 186.
Whited
The whited desert knew me not,
May-Day. 41.
Seems nowhere to alight: the whited air
Snow-Storm. 3.
Whitest
That were Freedom's whitest chart.
Etienne. 24.
Whither
Whither gaunt Labor Adirondacs. 196.
Whither went the lovely hoyden
Holidays. 13.
Whither the angry farmers came,
In Memoriam. 4.
And whither now, my truant wise and
sweet, Threnody. 30.
O, whither tend thy feet? Threnody. 31.

Who (Partial list.)
Who is the owner? The slave is owner,
Boston Hymn. 71.
Who saw the hid beginnings
Cosmos. 1.
To those who go, and those who come;
Good-Bye. 13.
Who drinks of Cupid's nectar cup
Rhea. 35.
Denounce who will, who will deny,
Saadi. 94.
'Who has drugged my boy's cup?
Sphinx. 61.
Whoever
Whoever fights, whoever falls,
Voluntaries. 99.
Whole
And solve and oft resolve the whole.
Alphonso. 46.
I yielded myself to the perfect whole.
Each. 51.
Sphered and concentric with the whole.
Frag. Poet. I. 57.
Is made whole again. May-Day. 337.
And the whole flight, with folded wing,
Monadnoc. 366.
And for the whole. The gentle deities
Musketaquid. 59.
Better, the linked purpose of the whole,
Musketaquid. 65.
Was mingled from the generous whole;
Ode to Beauty. 47.
The summit of the whole.
Song of Nature. 44.
Nor see the genius of the whole
Threnody. 251.
God hid the whole world in thy heart.
Woodnotes. II. 235.
And crowded whole, an infinite paroquet,
Xenophanes. 18.
Wholes
Primordial wholes, Sphinx. 30.
Who'll
"Who'll tell me my secret, Sphinx. 5.
Wholly
And Nature has miscarried wholly
Woodnotes. II. 57.
Whom (Partial list.)
Or Shakspeare, whom no mind can
measure, Harp. 78.
Wave which severs whom it bears
Insight. 3.
Whom the Infinite One
Ode to Beauty. 35.
And I to whom your light has spoken,
Poet. 237.
For, whom the Muses smile upon,
Saadi. 125.
The hyacinthine boy, for whom
Threnody. 15.
Whom they will destroy,
Voluntaries. 112.
Whose (Partial list.)
Whose unauthenticated waves we named
Adirondacs. 131.
Whose roads lead everywhere to all;
Boston. 60.
Whose eyes pierce Daemonic Love. 72.
Whose balsam never grew. Dirge. 40.
'Happy,' I said, 'whose home is here!
Monadnoc. 68.

Whose throbs are love, whose thrills are song. Monadnoc. 170.
Whose soul sees the perfect, Sphinx. 79.
Whose eyes within his eyes beheld Threnody. 184.

Whoso
Whoso walks in solitude Woodnotes. II. 57.

Why (Partial list.)
My apprehension? Why seek Italy, Day's Ration. 29.
I knew not why *Lines. 10.
Knew my quarrel, how and why, Miracle. 31
Rhodora! if the sages ask thee why Rhodora. 9.
Why thou wert there, O rival of the rose! Rhodora. 13.
Alone in Rome. Why, Rome is lonely too;— Rome. 1.
And the gods shook, they knew not why. Uriel. 56.
Why did all manly gifts in Webster fail? Webster, 1854. 1.
Why Nature loves the number five, Woodnotes. I. 22.

Wicked
What art thou? His wicked eye Limits. 11.

Wicker
Or mend his wicker wagon-frame, Threnody. 49.

Wide
See World-wide.
They laughed to know the world so wide; Boston. 49.
Pouring as wide a flood Dirge. 18.
He scatters wide and wild its lustres here. Frag. Life. XVI. 9.
Therefore was the world so wide. Frag. Life. XXI. 2.
Filled the straits and filled the wide, Frag. Nat. III. 13.
For Genius made his cabin wide, Frag. Poet. XX. 1.
Now scattered wide thro' earth, and each alone, Good Cheer. 4.
Rich rents and wide alliance shares; Monadnoc. 59.
In the wide thaw and ooze of wrong, Monadnoc. 114.
And wide around, the marriage of the plants Musketaquid. 20.
Of his fate is never wide. Nemesis. 8.
Which, from Eden wide astray, Ode to Beauty. 66.
Every nook is wide; Quat. Hush. 2.
Far and wide she cannot find him; Threnody. 22.
I rake no coffined clay, nor publish wide To-Day. 1.
If from home chance draw me wide, Una. 7.
The matted thicket low and wide, Wealth. 14.
He stands in the meadows wide,— Woodnotes. I. 9.
The wide lake, edged with sand and grass, Woodnotes. I. 108.

Through thick-stemmed woodlands rough and wide. Woodnotes. I. 120.
Or see the wide shore from thy skiff, Woodnotes. II. 195.
Their arms fly open wide. World-Soul. 96.

Wider
We made our distance wider, boat from boat, Adirondacs. 14.
Belike has wider hospitality Frag. Nat. V. 5.

Wield
Wield the first axe Adirondacs. 33.

Wife
A gentle wife, but fairy none. Each. 36.
Disappeared in blessed wife; Holidays. 14.
A woman to thy wife, though she were a crowned queen; Ibn Jemin. 2.
Thine elegy, sweet singer, sainted wife. Naples. 27.

Wight
Pilgrims wight with step forthright. May-Day. 311.

Wild
Wild Tupper Lake; Adirondacs. 310.
This wild plantation will suffice to chase. Adirondacs. 319.
The wild rose and the barberry thorn Boston. 37.
But it runs wild, Channing Ode. 56.
The waters wild below, Concord Ode. 34.
Throbs of a wild religion stirred;— Daemonic Love. 8.
With the sun and the sand and the wild uproar. Each. 28.
He scatters wide and wild its lustres here. Frag. Life. XVI. 9.
Life would be too wild an ode. Frag. Nat. I. 18.
Wild tea and wild pea, Frag. Nat. II. 2.
Wild rose, lily, dry vanilla,— Frag. Nat. II. 18.
Him wood-gods fed with honey wild Frag. Poet. I. 33.
In numbers wild as dreams, Harp. 30.
The wild dissipation, Illusions. 25.
That in the wild turmoil, Illusions. 34.
He affects the wood and wild, Initial Love. 96.
Swift cathedrals in the wild; May-Day. 48.
In May beholds the blooming wild, May-Day. 99.
Can make the wild blood start Merlin. 7.
Drink the wild air's salubrity: Merlin's Song. 32.
Terror and Hope and wild Remorse, Miracle. 12.
Salt and basalt, wild and tame: Mithridates. 11.
The wild air bloweth in our lungs, Romany. 21.
Speeding, the myriad-handed, his wild work Snow-Storm. 15.
Whose silver warble wild Threnody. 12.

Wild—*Continued*

Worthier cause for passion wild
> Threnody. 177.

Nail the wild star to its track
> Threnody. 240.

Or ever the wild Time coined itself
> Uriel. 3.

Wild planters, plant away!   Walden. 16.

Which bind the strengths of Nature wild
> Wealth. 48.

Boughs on which the wild bees settle,
> Woodnotes. I. 20.

Wilderness

They are the doctors of the wilderness,
> Adirondacs. 95.

Of craggy Indian wilderness he hears
> Adirondacs. 312.

Earth's a howling wilderness,
> Berrying. 2.

Thy echoes in the wilderness,
> May-Day. 438.

I am a willow of the wilderness,
> Musketaquid. 70.

Plants with worlds the wilderness;
> Threnody. 285.

An exile from the wilderness,—
> Woodnotes. II. 189.

Wildernesses

In Indian wildernesses found;
> Humble-Bee. 37.

Wild-eyed

The wild-eyed boy, who in the woods
> Woodnotes. II. 33.

Wild-piled

And through the wild-piled snow-drift
> World-Soul. 111.

Wild-rose

A wild-rose, or rock-loving columbine,
> Musketaquid. 74.

Wiles

By mystic wiles   Cupido. 9.

Thy genius, wiles and blandishment?
> May-Day. 432.

Wilful

He is wilful, mutable,   Initial Love. 88.

Will (Partial list.) (Verb.)
> *See* 'Twill.

Come the tumult whence it will,
> May-Day. 30.

Fall on thee, as fall they will.
> Monadnoc. 223.

'Let him heed who can and will;
> Monadnoc. 224.

Let me go where'er I will,   Music. 1.

Denounce who will, who will deny,
> Saadi. 94.

Evil will bless, and ice will burn.'
> Uriel. 24.

Whom they will **destroy**,
> Voluntaries. 112.

Go where he will, the wise man is at
home,   Woodnotes. I. 92.

Will (Noun.)
> *See* Good-will.

My will fulfilled shall be,
> Boston Hymn. 85.

Their fierce and limitary will
> Daemonic Love. 66.

Which his ruthless will defies,
> Daemonic Love. 117,

To each they offer gifts after his will,
> Days. 5.

Thy sweet dominion o'er my will,
> Eva. 5

So guilt not traverses his tender will.
> Frag. Life. II. 3.

Or I might at will forbear;
> Frag. Poet. IV. 20.

And his heart the throne of Will.
> Frag. Poet. XIV. 4.

Unless to Thought is added Will,
> Frag. Poet. XVIII. 3.

Above her will, be true;   Hermione. 70.

To Heaven's high will his will is bent.
> In Memoriam. 89.

Fire fainting will,   May-Day. 440.

Bereaved a tyrant of his will,
> Merlin. 53.

When the God's will sallies free,
> Merlin. 71.

Through which at will our Indian rivulet
> Musketaquid. 27.

By its own meek and incorruptible will?
> Oh What. 3.

Fill thy will, O faultless heart!
> Poet. 127.

A facile, reckless, wandering will,
> Poet. 207.

Beams with a will compassionate
> Poet. 243.

And his heart the throne of will.
> Power. 4.

The bias of the will betray.
> Quat. Memory. 4.

Moulding Nature at his will,
> Solution. 29.

The pure shall see by their own will,
> Threnody. 191.

That works its will on age and hour.
> Unity. 11.

Heart too soft and will too weak
> Voluntaries. 15.

Arrives the wise selecting will,
> Wealth. 31

So long he roved at will the boundless
shade.   Woodnotes. I. 85.

Of Fate and Will, of Want and Right,
> Woodnotes. II. 130.

A single will, a million deeds.
> Woodnotes. II. 265.

And his will is not thwarted;
> World-Soul. 85.

Willard

Bulkeley,   Hunt,   Willard,   Hosmer,
Meriam, Flint,   Hamatreya. 1.

Willing
> *See* Unwilling.

Hereafter,—willing they, and more adroit.
> Adirondacs. 164.

And willing grow old
> Frag. Poet. VIII. 5.

And loiter willing by yon loitering
stream.   Musketaquid. 14.

Still whispers to the willing mind.
> Problem. 60.

To lead him willing to be led,
> Voluntaries. 56.

Willow

Sweet willow, checkerberry red,
> Frag. Nat. II. 23.

Wind—*Continued*
That flows in streams, that breathes in
wind: Woodnotes. II. 233.
The rain comes when the wind calls;
              Woodnotes. II. 238.
Its way up to the cloud and wind;
              Woodnotes. II. 243.

Wind-blown
Or on wind-blown sea-marge bleak,
              Solution. 13.
The winds and wind-blown seed,
              Walden. 10.

Wind-borne
To northern lakes fly wind-borne ducks,
              Saadi. 5.

Wind-god
In which the sudden wind-god rings.
              Frag. Poet. I. 42.

Wind-harp
Is the wind-harp which thou seest
              Harp. 39.
Save to his ear the wind-harp lone.
              Harp. 98.

Wind-harp's
Who but loved the wind-harp's note?
              Harp. 49.

Winding
Winding through grassy shallows in and
out,   Adirondacs. 23.
The winding Concord gleamed below,
              Dirge. 17.

Winding-sheets
A hill's leaves for winding-sheets,
              Mountain. 15.

Window
A window rose, and, to say sooth,
              Harp. 109.
Steal in by window, chink, or hole,
              Past. 17.
From the window I look out
              Threnody. 74.

Window-pane
In at the window-pane;   World-Soul. 30.

Wind's
Come see the north wind's masonry.
              Snow-Storm. 10.
Built in an age, the mad wind's night-
work,   Snow-Storm. 27.

Winds
See Head-winds; South-winds.
The April winds are magical   April. 1.
Loved by stars and purest winds,
              Astraea. 32.
Winds of remembering   Bacchus. 47.
Said the winds that sung the lads to sleep,
              Boston. 15.
Without tongue, yellow-cheeked, full of
winds that wail and sigh;   Flute. 2.
But Nature whistled with all her winds,
              Frag. Nat. XXXV. 1.
The winds took flesh, the mountains
talked,   Frag. Poet. I. 55.
The free winds told him what they knew,
              Frag. Poet. V. 37.
To winds and waterfalls   Hermione. 72.
And waters free as winds shall flow.
              May-Day. 110.
Under east winds crossed with sleet.
              May-Day. 133.
Bitter winds and fasts austere
              Monadnoc. 159.

Winds mindful still of sannup and of
squaw,   Musketaquid. 28.
Oh, south winds have long memories,
              September. 11.
Will never my winds go sleep in the
west?   Song of Nature. 46.
Must borrow his winds who there would
come.   Titmouse. 10.
The winds shall sing their dead-march
old,   Titmouse. 20.
And where he winds is the day of day.
              Two Rivers. 16.
The winds and wind-blown seed,
              Walden. 10.

Windward
Round every windward stake, or tree, or
door.   Snow-Storm. 14.

Windy
In his windy cave.   Harp. 10.
On windy hills, whose tops with morning
glow,   I Bear. 7.

Wine
Ale, and a sup of wine. Our steward gave
              Adirondacs. 178.
And water it with wine, not watch ask-
ance   Adirondacs. 299.
Nor wine nor brains perpetual pump.
              Alphonso. 62.
Bring me wine, but wine which never
grew   Bacchus. 1.
We buy diluted wine;   Bacchus. 13.
Wine of wine,   Bacchus. 18.
Wine that is shed   Bacchus. 26.
Wine which is already man,
              Bacchus. 34.
Wine which Music is,—   Bacchus. 36.
Music and wine are one,—
              Bacchus. 37.
Pour, Bacchus! the remembering wine;
              Bacchus. 51.
Let wine repair what this undid;
              Bacchus. 59.
With lotus wine obliterates
              Daemonic Love. 13.
His nectar smacks of wine.
              Daemonic Love. 92.
All he distils into sidereal wine
              Day's Ration. 11.
Laugh life away; have wine for tears;
              Fame. 16.
Because of the sons of wine;
              Frag. Life. X. 6.
Friends to me are frozen wine;
              Frag. Life. XIV. 1.
Not his the feaster's wine,
              Frag. Poet. VI. 5.
The wine-cup shakes, the wine is spilled.
              Frag. Poet. XVI. 2.
That all the wine at once we swallow
              Good Hope. 3.
As costly wine into his well.   Guy. 30.
He has not tasted wine impure,
              Harp. 3.
Ruby wine is drunk by knaves,
              Heroism. 1.
The old wine darkling in the cask
              May-Day. 89.
When magic wine for bards is brewed;
              May-Day. 339.
Poets praise that hidden wine
              May-Day. 406.

I cannot spare water or wine,
                    Mithridates. 1.
Costlier far than wine or oil.
                    Monadnoc. 296.
The ruby of the drop of wine,
                    Ode to Beauty. 28.
Shed in each drop of wine.
                    Quat. Leasts. 4.
Than wine or sleep or praise;
                    Rome. 13.
I said, they are drops of frozen wine
                    Rubies. 3.
Nor the wine-cup from the wine.
                    Song of Seyd. 4.
Hear what wine and roses say;
                    To J. W. 2.
His myrrh, and wine, and rings,
                    To J. W. 13.
Pouring of his power the wine
                    Woodnotes. II. 279.

Wine-cup
The wine-cup shakes, the wine is spilled.
                    Frag. Poet. XVI. 2.
Nor the wine-cup from the wine.
                    Song of Seyd. 4.

Wine-fed
Than the wine-fed feasters know.
                    Frag. Poet. XI. 11.

Wing
    See Redwing.
And fend you with his wing.
                    Boston Hymn. 16.
To the robin on the wing,
                    Ellen South. 7.
Solar insect on the wing
                    Frag. Nat. XXII. 1.
When the wing of the south-wind whipt
    the lake   Frag. Poet. I. 36.
With wing unspent,   Give. 13.
Every moth with painted wing,
                    Lines. 9.
When his fellows on the wing
                    May-Day. 85.
And the whole flight, with folded wing,
                    Monadnoc. 366.
New-bathed, new-trimmed, on healthy
    wing,   Poet. 25.
Terror and beauty on their wing;
                    Saadi. 128.
When the redbird spread his sable wing,
                    Thine Eyes. 9.
Flew near, with soft wing grazed my
    hand,   Titmouse. 38.
As 't would accost some frivolous wing,
                    Titmouse. 92.

Winged
Hast not thy share? On winged feet,
                    II Compenation. 23.
The winged vessel flies,   *Farewell. 25.
Emerge the wingèd words in haste.
                    Poet. 24.
Freedom all winged expands,
                    Voluntaries. 35.

Wings
Skirts of angels, starry wings,   Art. 16.
When me they fly, I am the wings;
                    Brahma. 10.
The wings of Time are black and white,
                    II Compensation. 1.
And he that paints the oriole's fiery
    wings.   Enchanter. 11.

He felt the flame, the fanning wings,
                    Frag. Poet. V. 26.
The birds brought auguries on their
    wings,   Frag. Poet. V. 41.
Adding wings through things to range,
                    Insight. 5.
Voice of sport, or rush of wings,
                    May-Day. 31.
Perfect-paired as eagle's wings,
                    Merlin. 113.
Rushing ages moult their wings,
                    Poet. 132.
O birds of ether without wings!
                    Poet. 159.
I hear the rustle of wings,   Poet. 260.
But when he flees on riches' wings,
                    Riches. 11.
Her wings are furled: Sphinx. 2.
The thrush plies his wings;   Sphinx. 22.
Shamed the angels' veiling wings;
                    Uriel. 48.
Which Music's wings infold,
                    Voluntaries. 76.
Wings of what wind the lichen bore,
                    Wealth. 6.

Winning
Hark to the winning sound!
                    Ellen South. 13.

Winnow
They set the wind to winnow pulse and
    grain,   Musketaquid. 42.

Winnowed
All were winnowed through and through,
                    Test. 3.

Wins
Wins the believing child with wondrous
    tales;   Enchanter. 5.

Winsome
That winsome voice again might hear;
                    Threnody. 51.

Winter
In winter, lumberers; in summer, guides;
                    Adirondacs. 88.
Swains by winter pinched and worn.
                    Frag. Nat. XXII. 4.
Summer and winter, o'er the wave,
                    Frag. Poet. I. 47.
In the dreaded winter time,
                    Monadnoc. 201.
Into the winter night's extinguished
    mood?   Musketaquid. 79.
And, in winter, Chic-a-dee-dee!
                    Titmouse. 94.
When Winter reigned I'd close my eye,
                    *Violet. 11.
Over the winter glaciers
                    World-Soul. 109.

Wintered
Wintered with the hawk and fox,
                    Quat. Power. 3.

Wintergreen
Mouse-ear, cowslip, wintergreen,
                    Frag. Nat. II. 29.

Winter's
Or winter's frozen shade?
                    Song of Nature. 56.

Winters
Winters know   Nature. I. 1.

Wintry
A wintry storm more fitly fell.
                    Frag. Nat. XXIX. 4.

Wintry—*Continued*
Ere yet arrives the wintry day
                    Monadnoc. 23.
The wintry garden lies unchanged;
                    Threnody. 95.
Still tearless lift its slender form above
    the wintry snow?   *Violet. 4.
Wipe
Whither gaunt Labor slips to wipe his
    brow   Adirondacs. 196.
Wiped
I wiped away the weeds and foam,
                    Each. 24.
Wire
Galvanic wire, strong-shouldered steam.
                    Wealth. 41.
Wire-cable
Of the wire-cable laid beneath the sea,
                    Adirondacs. 239.
Wires
The wires shall murmur through the
    main   Concord Ode. 31.
Wiry
Henceforth I prize thy wiry chant
                    Titmouse. 89.
Wisdom
No wisdom from our berries went?'
                    Berrying. 12.
That wisdom might in youth be gotten,
                    Fame. 5.
When wisdom not with me resides,
                    Frag. Poet. III. 9.
Worship Toil's wisdom that abides.
                    Frag. Poet. III. 10.
Mask thy wisdom with delight,
                    Frag. Poet. V. 1.
To transmute crime to wisdom, so to
    stem   Frag. Poet. XXII. 1.
The eloquence of truth, the wisdom got
                    Good Cheer. 10.
His wisdom will not fail,   Harp. 2.
But word and wisdom is a snare;
                    Initial Love. 111.
Of his wisdom, of his fraud   Limits. 4.
Mask thy wisdom with delight,
                    Merlin's Song. 37.
Wisdom of the gods is he,—   Saadi. 35.
And brought Olympian wisdom down
                    Solution. 67.
To make this wisdom earthly wise.
                    Threnody. 57.
Wanting wisdom, void of right,
                    Voluntaries. 60.
Oblivion here thy wisdom is,
                    Waldeinsamkeit. 45.
Wisdom-fruiting
Rainbow-flowering, wisdom-fruiting,
                    Bacchus. 33.
Wise
    See All-wise; Cross-wise.
Wise and polite,—and if I drew
                    Adirondacs. Motto. 1.
And, for I'm styled Alphonse the Wise,
                    Alphonso. 47.
Wise and sure the issues are.
                    Channing Ode. 77.
For He that worketh high and wise,
                    Concord Ode. 37.
That you are fair or wise is vain,
                    Destiny. 1.
Be wise without a beard?   Fame. 2.

Who sells his sinews to be wise,
                    Fame. 9.
The wealthy and the wise, *Farewell. 11.
To Grandeur with his wise grimace;
                    Good-Bye. 8.
He had so sped his wise affairs
                    Guy. 31.
To drudge all day for Guy the wise.
                    Guy. 40.
How strangely wise thy strain!
                    Harp. 42.
Wise Milton's odes of pensive pleasure,
                    Harp. 77.
And with this hint be wise,—
                    Hermione. 66.
Into those wise, thrilling palms.
                    Initial Love. 59.
O how wise are his discourses!
                    Initial Love. 104.
The wise and simple have one glance
                    In Memoriam. 11.
Refreshed the wise, reformed the clowns,
                    May-Day. 343.
Of Merlin wise I learned a song,—
                    Merlin's Song. 1.
Like wise preceptor, lure his eye
                    Monadnoc. 102.
And the untaught Spring is wise
                    Nature. I. 3.
And like wise God she judges well.
                    Nature. I. 15.
Your gold makes you seem wise;
                    Park. 10.
He bridged the gulf from the alway good
    and wise   Phi. 17.
Boded Merlin wise,   Politics. 5.
I know what say the fathers wise,—
                    Problem. 63.
And thus the wise Immortal doeth,—
                    Rhea. 46.
But wiser than I was, and wise enough
                    River. 19.
The Catos, the wise patriots of Rome,
                    Rome. 5.
Wise Saadi dwells alone.   Saadi. 22.
Wise Ali's sunbright sayings pass
                    Saadi. 151.
They pluck Force thence, and give it to
    the wise.   Seashore. 29.
And this wise Seer within me never errs.
                    Self-Reliance. 8.
Timely wise accept the terms,
                    Terminus. 17.
And whither now, my truant wise and
    sweet,   Threnody. 30.
So gentle, wise and grave,
                    Threnody. 45.
To make this wisdom earthly wise.
                    Threnody. 57.
The encounter of the wise,—   Visit. 10.
The air is wise, the wind thinks well,
                    Walden. 37.
Arrives the wise selecting will,
                    Wealth. 31.
Wise harbinger of spheres and tides,
                    Woodnotes. I. 33.
To please and win this pilgrim wise.
                    Woodnotes. I. 53.
Not so the wise; no coward watch he
    keeps   Woodnotes. I. 90.

Go where he will, the wise man is at
home,   Woodnotes. I. 92.
O wise man! hear'st thou half it tells?
                         Woodnotes. II. 101.
O wise man! hear'st thou the least part?
                         Woodnotes. II. 102.
And the wise soul expels disease.
                         Woodnotes. II. 191.

Wisely
Talents differ; all is well and wisely put;
                         Fable. 17.
Well and wisely said the Greek,
                         Quat. Pericles. 1.

Wiser
Wiser far than human seer,
                         Humble-Bee. 52.
I am not wiser for my age,
                         Quat. Climacteric. 1.
But wiser than I was, and wise enough
                         River. 19.
The wood is wiser far than thou;
                         Woodnotes. II. 172.

Wisest
And these instructed by their wisest too,
                         Adirondacs. 294.
And the wits of all her wisest,
                         Boston. 108.
Where the wisest Muses falter,
                         Etienne. 14.

Wish
And his wish is intimacy,
                         Initial Love. 142.
Is the word they wish to hear.
                         Letters. 6.
And wakes the wish in youngest blood
                         May-Day. 95.
Wish not to fill the isles with eyes
                         Saadi. 147.

Wished
Once I wished I might rehearse
                         Freedom. 1.
Wished to stay, and is gone,
                         Hamatreya. 56.
What Saadi wished to say;   Saadi. 83.

Wishes
Forgot my morning wishes, hastily
                         Days. 8.

Wishful
Cast wishful glances at the stars
                         Poet. 191.
And wishful saw the Ocean stream:—
                         Poet. 192.
Seldom seen by wishful eyes,
                         Woodnotes. I. 51.

Wisp
Wisp and meteor nightly falling,
                         Frag. Nat. XVI. 1.

Wistful
His wistful toil to do his best
                         Voluntaries. 21.

Wit
    See Outwit.
And wit to trap or take him in his lair.
                         Adirondacs. 86.
This feat of wit, this triumph of man-
kind;   Adirondacs. 255.
Since fortune snatched from wit the
lion's part?   Adirondacs. 276.
The great Idea baffles wit,
                         Bohemian. 7.

It came never out of wit;
                         Destiny. 9.
Or wit be ripe before 't was rotten?
                         Fame. 6.
Nor suffer sense to win from wit
                         Fame. 21.
He has a total world of wit;
                         Initial Love. 103.
Of eloquent lips, of joyful wit:
                         In Memoriam. 52.
Of wit, of words, of rest.
                         Manners. 16.
Blooms in beauty, thinks in wit,
                         May-Day. 292.
Or compass that, by meddling wit,
                         Merlin. 67.
Adamant is soft to wit: Monadnoc. 261.
Nor wit, nor eloquence,—no, nor even the
song   Naples. 19.
Tempted by thy praise of wit,
                         Saadi. 88.
That wit and joy might find a tongue,
                         Solution. 15.
Orbit and sum of Shakspeare's wit.
                         Solution. 40.
And, out of slime and chaos, Wit
                         Wealth. 32.
And leave thy peacock wit behind;
                         Woodnotes. II. 231.

Witchery
For the witchery of my own.
                         Cosmos. 24.

With (Partial list.)
    See Therewith; Wherewith.
That keeps intelligence with you,—
                         Amulet. 6.
God with the fathers, so with us,
                         Boston. 118.
With rifle and with knife!
                         Channing Ode. 18.
With the flower with which it came.
                         Days Pass. 4.
With forecast or with fear?
                         Frag. Nat. VIII. 4.
Now I live with all;   Hermione. 41.
As with hammer or with mace;
                         Merlin. 11.
Lovesick with rhyme;   Merlin. 97.

Withal
To drug their crops or weapon their arts
withal.   Musketaquid. 40.

Withdrew
Withdrew, that hour, into his cloud;
                         Uriel. 38.

Withering
A sad self-knowledge, withering, fell
                         Uriel. 35.

Withheld
The nectar and ambrosia, are withheld;
                         Blight. 45.

Withhold
Yet cannot all withhold.   Garden. 52.
Cannot withhold his conquering aid.
                         Nun. 6.

Within (Partial list.)
As one within whose memory it burned
                         Adirondacs. 278.
Within four walls is possible again,—
                         Adirondacs. 322.
The orb within the mind,
                         Day by Day. 6.

Within (Partial list.)—*Continued*

Of Merlin locked the harp within,—
                    Harp. 54.
Within earshot of thy hum,—
                    Humble-Bee. 18.
Underneath, within, above,—
                    Initial Love. 43.
No pain was within,   *Lines. 13.
Beneath the calm, within the light,
                    May-Day. 150.
Thousand minstrels woke within me,
                    Monadnoc. 1.
Spirit that lurks each form within
                    Nature. Mot. 13.
The morning mist within your grounds
                    Park. 11.
To that within the vision of small eyes.
                    Phi. 18.
Philosophers are lined with eyes within,
                    Philosopher. 1.
Bestrode the tribes that knelt within.
                    Problem. 50.
Hide thy grief within thy breast,
                    Rhea. 11.
Within the air's cerulean round,—
                    Threnody. 14.
Whose eyes within his eyes beheld
                    Threnody. 184.
'T is not within the force of fate
                    Threnody. 193.
For well the soul, if stout within,
                    Titmouse. 75.
And guessed within the thicket's gloom,
                    Woodnotes. I. 59.
Clean shall he be, without, within,
                    Woodnotes. II. 63.
And, far within those cadent pauses,
                    Woodnotes. II. 118.
Within, without the idle earth,
                    World-Soul. 61.

Without

And other Titans without muse or name.
                    Adirondacs. 11.
To climb a lofty stem, clean without
boughs   Adirondacs. 83.
And, without Jove,   Adirondacs. 291.
A mastiff that will bite without a bark.
                    Arrow. 2.
And love without a name.
                    Celestial Love. 5.
And without a swerving
                    Celestial Love. 12.
And a vision without bound:
                    Celestial Love. 20.
Go, without check or intervals,
                    Celestial Love. 24.
They can parley without meeting;
                    Celestial Love. 93.
Without a false humility;
                    Celestial Love. 123.
Nor skies without a frown
                    Concord Ode. 22.
And dark, without love, is the day;
                    Exile. 18.
Temperament without a tongue,
                    Experience. 9.
Omnipresent without name;—
                    Experience. 11.
Be wise without a beard?   Fame. 2.
How desert without you   *Farewell. 30.

Without tongue, yellow-cheeked, full of
winds that wail and sigh;   Flute. 2.
Hast thou named all the birds without a
gun?   Forbearance. 1.
Nor kind occasion without eyes;
                    Frag. Life. XVII. 7.
Without remission, without rest,
                    Frag. Life. XXVII. 2.
Without remoter hope or fear
                    Frag. Poet. V. 5.
Without fail,   Hamatreya. 42.
All without is martyrdom.
                    Humble-Bee. 19.
Of gulfs of sweetness without bound
                    Humble-Bee. 36.
Not without relation   Limits. 9.
Like a world without sin,   *Lines. 15.
Or a day without night.   *Lines. 16.
Without the baffled North-wind calls.
                    May-Day. 57.
Without halting, without rest,
                    May-Day. 465.
And send conviction without phrase,
                    Monadnoc. 404.
Merry and manifold without bar,
                    Nature. II. 7.
O birds of ether witout wings!
                    Poet. 159.
O heavenly ships without a sail!
                    Poet. 160.
There came a voice without reply,—
                    Quat. Sacrifice. 2.
Without cleanness, without rest.
                    Riches. 4.
And say it frankly without guile,
                    Romany. 10.
But without glass we fathom you.
                    Romany. 28.
What without him is summer's pomp,
                    Song of Nature. 55.
Without cloud, in its eyes;   Sphinx. 46.
Far beholding, without cloud,
                    Voluntaries. 53.
Thrive in all weathers without fear,—
                    Walden. 15.
Melancholy without bad.
                    Woodnotes. I. 15.
Without better fortune had,
                    Woodnotes. I. 14.
Clean shall he be, without, within,
                    Woodnotes. II. 63.
Without wailing, without fear;
                    Woodnotes. II. 80.
Without a pilot it runs and falls,
                    Woodnotes. II. 240.
Within, without the idle earth,
                    World-Soul. 61.

Withstand

That no mixture could withstand
                    Guy. 13.

Witness

O no, not we! Witness the shout that
shook   Adirondacs. 309.
Wild Tupper Lake; witness the mute all-
hail   Adirondacs. 310.
To him authentic witness bare;
                    Frag. Poet. V. 40.
Nay, God is witness, gave the names.
                    Miracle. 36.

Witnesses
Worthy the enormous cloud of witnesses,
Adirondacs. 247.

Wit's
Of all wit's uses the main one
Frag. Life. XI. 1.
Of all wit's uses, the main one
Merlin's Song. 39.

Wits
Sometimes their wits at sally and retort,
Adirondacs. 127.
And the wits of all her wisest,
Boston. 108.
Rear purer wits, inventive eyes,—
Monadnoc. 107.
I see all human wits
Quat. Shakespeare. 1.
"Dull Sphinx, Jove keep thy five wits;
Sphinx. 105.

Witted
See Quick-witted.

Wittily
It chills my life, but wittily,
Frag. Nat. XXIV. 4.

Wizard
The wizard South blew down the glen,
Frag. Nat. III. 12.
I catch thy meaning, wizard wave;
Peter. 39.

Woe
And turns the woe of Night,
Bacchus. 10.
In dens of passion, and pits of woe,
Beauty. 17.
Well that we loved, woe had we not,
Ellen. 8.
Woe is me for my hope's downfall!
Monadnoc. 74.
Woe and want thou canst outsleep;
Humble-Bee. 61.
Want and woe, which torture us,
Humble-Bee. 62.
The canticles of love and woe:
Problem. 18.
For out of woe and out of crime
Saadi. 70.

Woe-begone
Cities of mortals woe-begone
Waldeinsamkeit. 13.

Woes
And sore bested with woes. Riches. 10.

Woe-worn
Of woe-worn mortals darkling go,
Walden. 18.

Woke
And the thoughts that in him woke,
Harp. 96.
His purpose woke, his features slept;
In Memoriam. 102.
Thousand minstrels woke within me,
Monadnoc. 1.
And woke the fear lest angels part.
Poet. 256.

Wold
And murmurs in the wold Garden. 50.
And, echoed in some frosty wold,
Titmouse. 97.

Wolf
Temper to face wolf, bear, or catamount,
Adirondacs. 85.

And near the wolf and panther slept.
Frag. Poet. I. 44.
Of wolf and otter, bear and deer;
Monadnoc. 81.
For wolf and fox, bring lowing herds,
Monadnoc. 139.

Wolf's
See She-wolf's.

Wolves
Hear wolves barking at the moon;
Saadi. 54.
Wolves shed their fangs, and dragons scales;
Solution. 6.

Woman
A woman to thy wife, though she were a crowned queen; Ibn Jemin. 2.
Nor in the song of woman heard,
Music. 10.
Of any woman that is now alive,—
Naples. 20.
And through man and woman and sea and star Poet. 69.

Woman-born
All woman-born do know, that hoped-for days, Summons. 19.

Woman's
Will a woman's fan the ocean smooth?
Nemesis. 9.
Or woman's pleading eyes;
World-Soul. 28.

Womb
When from the womb the babe was loosed, Quat. Horoscope. 3.

Women
With men and women weird.
Frag. Nat. X. 4.
Princely women hard to please,
Frag. Poet. I. 27.
Graceful women, chosen men,
Manners. 3.
Make women of men;
Ode to Beauty. 18.

Won
Had won the brightest laurel of all time.
Adirondacs. 285.
His action won such reverence sweet
Character. 9.
The prizes in all lists he won;
In Memoriam. 79.

Wonder
Of such delight and wonder as there grew,— Adirondacs. 250.
And oh, the wonder of the power,
Miracle. 17.
The same blue wonder that my infant eye
River. 3.
Lovely locks, a form of wonder,
Threnody. 213.

Wonderer
Wonderer at all he meets,
Woodnotes. I. 25.
Wonderer chiefly at himself,
Woodnotes. I. 26.

Wonderful
Wonderful verse of the gods,
Garden. 41.

Wonders
These wonders rose to upper air;
Problem. 40.
Hold all the hidden wonders
World-Soul. 39.

Wondrous

Wins the believing child with wondrous
tales; Enchanter. 5.

O, wondrous craft of plant and stone
Monadnoc. 66.

And he, the wondrous child,
Threnody. 11.

By wondrous tongue, and guided pen,
Threnody. 136.

Wont

As erst it wont, would thrill and ring.
Harp. 106.

And through my rock-like, solitary wont
Musketaquid. 9.

For I am wont to sing uncalled,
Solution. 19.

Wonted

See Unwonted.

Ten scholars, wonted to lie warm and
soft Adirondacs. 50.

Their wonted convenance, cheerly hid the
loss Adirondacs. 181.

Beguile me with the wonted spell.
May-Day. 352.

Will swell and rise with wonted grace;
Woodnotes. II. 54.

Wood

See Dog-wood.

The wood was sovran with centennial
trees,— Adirondacs. 37.

I go to the god of the wood
Apology. 3.

Only the herbs and simples of the wood,
Blight. 4.

Bold as the engineer who fells the wood,
Blight. 19.

Gracing the rich man's wood and lake,
Chartist. 9.

Came with me to the wood. Dirge. 20.

It may be in wood or waste,—
Forerunners. 31.

Come search the wood for flowers,—
Frag. Nat. II. 1.

In the houseless wood,
Frag. Nat. III. 22.

In Walden wood the chickadee
Frag. Nat. XIX. 1.

Hay, corn, roots, hemp, flax, apples, wool
and wood. Hamatreya. 3.

Shaggy with wood, Hamatreya. 45.

He is come through fragrant wood,
Hermione. 51.

He affects the wood and wild,
Initial Love. 96.

'T was the vintage-day of field and wood,
May-Day. 338.

The stony pathway to the wood.
May-Day. 358.

When boughs buffet boughs in the wood;
Merlin. 18.

Weave wood to canisters and mats;
Monadnoc. 141.

Yet said yon ancient wood, Park. 14.

And every rood in the hemlock wood
Peter. 7.

The kennel by the corded wood;
Threnody. 83.

Chilled wading in the snow-choked wood.
Titmouse. 4.

In one wood walk, than learned men
Walk. 7.

In the wood he travels glad,
Woodnotes. I. 13.

The purple berries in the wood
Woodnotes. I. 135.

And inhabiteth the wood,
Woodnotes. II. 58.

The wood is wiser far than thou;
Woodnotes. II. 172.

The wood and wave each other know
Woodnotes. II. 173.

Wood-bell's

Of the wood-bell's peal and cry,
Garden. 38.

Wood-bird

That wood-bird sang my last night's
dream, Miracle. 28.

Woodbird's

Know'st thou what wove yon woodbird's
nest Problem. 25.

Wood-boughs

The wood-boughs with thy manners
waved, Lines. 11.

Woodchucks

The fox-hole which the woodchucks rent,
Miracle. 4.

Woodcock's

He heard the woodcock's evening hymn;
Woodnotes. I. 55.

Wooden

Low on their wooden bench.
Boston. 85.

And build me a wooden house.
Boston Hymn. 36.

Servant to a wooden cradle,
Holidays. 15.

I will not go under a wooden root:
Poet. 143.

Wood-fire

And wood-fire flickering on the walls,
May-Day. 55.

Wood-fly

The wood-fly mocks with tiny voice
May-Day. 75.

Wood-god

'Welcome!' the wood-god murmured
through the leaves,— Adirondacs. 44.

Tuned to the lay the wood-god sings.
Woodnotes. II. 96.

Wood-gods

Him wood-gods fed with honey wild
Frag. Poet. I. 33.

The partial wood-gods overpaid my love,
Musketaquid. 4.

For thus the wood-gods murmured in my
ear: Musketaquid. 76.

Wood-kinds

For, as the wood-kinds lurk and hide,
Quat. Forester. 3.

Woodland

Deep in a woodland tract, a sunny farm,
Letter. 8.

Sharp accents of my woodland bird;
Miracle. 24.

My garden spade can heal. A woodland
walk, Musketaquid. 72.

To leave the rudeness of my woodland
life, Summons. 6.

Laughter rich as woodland thunder,
Threnody. 214.

Who speeds to the woodland walks?
Woodnotes. I. 3.

Woodlands
They made the woodlands glad or mad.
Dirge. 36.
Like the bird from the woodlands to the cage;—
Each. 34.
Through thick-stemmed woodlands rough and wide.
Woodnotes. I. 120.

Woodman
So walks the woodman, unespied.
Quat. Forester. 4.

Woodpecker
The raven croaked, owls hooted, the woodpecker
Adirondacs. 147.
And up the tall mast runs the woodpecker.
Woodnotes. I. 67.

Wood-rose
Loved the wood-rose, and left it on its stalk?
Forbearance. 2.

Woods
See Pine-woods; Spring-woods; Underwoods.
Or stumbling on through vast self-similar woods
Adirondacs. 105.
Hark to that muffled roar! a tree in the woods
Adirondacs. 121.
And rare and virtuous roots, which in these woods
Blight. 8.
The wrinkled shopman to my sounding woods,
Channing Ode. 72.
And peaceful woods beside my cottage door.
Frag. Nat. IV. 11.
If I could put my woods in song
Garden. 1
Even from a brook, and where old woods
Letter. 11.
Firm-braced I sought my ancient woods,
May-Day. 39.
Up and away! where haughty woods
May-Day. 224.
To read the sense the woods impart
Miracle. 9.
My daily load of woods and streams,
Monadnoc. 271.
Slide with the sledge to inaccessible woods
Musketaquid. 45.
October woods wherein
October. 1.
The gods talk in the breath of the woods,
Poet. 73.
I found the fresh Rhodora in the woods,
Rhodora. 2.
Hides hills and woods, the river, and the heaven,
Snow-Storm. 4.
To leave my woods and streams and the sweet sloth
Summons. 4.
In these woods, thy small Labrador,
Titmouse. 50.
In the great woods, on prairie floors.
Titmouse. 68.
The woods at heart are glad.
Waldeinsamkeit. 20.
He saw the partridge drum in the woods;
Woodnotes. I. 54.
The wild-eyed boy, who in the woods
Woodnotes. II. 33.
Oft didst thou thread the woods in vain
Woodnotes. II. 248.

Woodwalks
In the woodwalks still and low
Poet. 254.

Wooes
Hunt knowledge as the lover wooes a maid,
Rome. 14.
He shall be happy whilst he wooes,
Woodnotes. II. 83.

Wool
The mottled clouds, like scraps of wool,
Frag. Nat. XXVI. 17.
Hay, corn, roots, hemp, flax, apples, wool and wood.
Hamatreya. 3.

Word
Answers not in word or letter,
Astraea. 21.
(Your Highness knows our homely word)
Boston. 73.
The word of the Lord by night
Boston Hymn. 1.
Why need I volumes, if one word suffice?
Day's Ration. 26.
Pronounced the word that mortals hate to hear—
Frag. Life. XVIII. 2.
Yet mark me well, that idle word
Frag. Poet. IV. 21.
Heedless that each cunning word
Frag. Poet. V. 9.
No word or feat
Frag. Poet. IX. 10.
One word more thy heart behoved,
Give. 28.
And Time, who keeps God's word, brings on the day
Good Cheer. 13.
They seek a friend to speak the word
Hymn. 13.
So shall he speak to us the word
Hymn. 27.
But word and wisdom is a snare;
Initial Love. 111.
He could not frame a word unfit,
In Memoriam. 53.
Every ship brings a word;
Letters. 2
That the word the vessel brings
Letters. 5.
Is the word they wish to hear.
Letters. 6.
One word, no more, to say.
Merops. 12.
Told every word and syllable
Miracle. 33.
Self-centred; when he launched the genuine word
Phi. 19.
Some random word they say
Poet. 78.
The word unto the prophet spoken
Problem. 55.
The word by seers or sibyls told,
Problem. 57.
Lighted each transparent word,
Saadi. 81.
The rash word boded ill to all;
Uriel. 30.

Words
Sentences him in his words;
Astraea. 28.
He spoke, and words more soft than rain
Character. 7.
Words of the air
Frag. Nat. III. 33.
And love, for words thy tongue could say.
Frag. Poet. II. 8.
Nor offered words till they were things,
Frag. Poet. V. 27.
And the balm of thoughtful words;
Frag. Poet. X. 2.
With adamantine words.
Frag. Poet. XIII. 4.

Words —*Continued*

Chasing with words fast-flowing things;
  nor try Frag. Poet. XXIX. 5.
Or match with words that tender sky
  Garden. 40.
Ever the words of the gods resound;
  Garden. 45.
Words of pain and cries of fear,
  Harp. 58.
Of wit, of words, of rest. Manners. 16.
Fourscore or a hundred words
  Monadnoc. 175.
Divers or dippers were his words,
  Poet. 20.
Emerge the wingèd words in haste.
  Poet. 24.
His words are music in my ear,
  Problem. 69.
In simple words succeeds,
  Quat. Poet. 2. 2.
His words like a storm-wind can bring
  Saadi. 127.
Saadi, so far thy words shall reach:
  Saadi. 139.
And his air-sown, unheeded words,
  Solution. 57.
Words that were persuasions.
  Threnody. 53.

Wordsworth

Or Wordsworth, Pan's recording voice,—
  Harp. 82.

Wore

With the high port he wore erewhile,
  In Memoriam. 77.
All wore thy badges and thy favors
  Lines. 7.
Times wore he as his clothing-weeds,
  Poet. 31.

Work

  See Network; Night-work.
Steads not to work on the clean jump,
  Alponso. 61.
And the cheerful round of work.
  Celestial Love. 106.
Every one to his chosen work;—
  Channing Ode. 75.
Time hath his work to do and we have
  ours. Frag. Life. XXXVII. 2.
There doth digest, and work, and spin,
  Initial Love. 46.
Work of his hand In Memoriam. 92.
They harness beast, bird, insect, to their
  work; Musketaquid. 36.
Wealth to the cunning artist who can
  work Seashore. 31.
Speeding, the myriad-handed, his wild
  work Snow-Storm. 15.
A tapering turret overtops the work.
  Snow-Storm. 22.
At my work I ramble not; Una. 6.
Whether she work in land or sea,
  Woodnotes. II. 166.

Worked

Worked on the Maker's own receipt,
  Guy. 26.

Worketh

For He that worketh high and wise,
  Concord Ode. 37.

Working

  See Hidden-working.

Which puts me in a working mood.
  Frag. Poet. XVIII. 2.

Works

He works, plots, fights, in rude affairs,
  Fate. 7.
Illusion works impenetrable,
  Frag. Nat. XXXI. 1.
All between that works or grows,
  Mithridates. 4.
Works thy form on human thought;
  Monadnoc Afar. 6.
And in their vaunted works of Art
  Nature. II. 22.
Works in close conspiracy;
  Ode to Beauty. 83.
Love works at the centre, Sphinx. 101.
Sole and self-commanded works,
  Spiritual Laws. 5.
To works as noble led thee on.
  Threnody. 79.
That works its will on age and hour.
  Unity. 11.

World

And presently the sky is changed; O
  world! Adirondacs. 211.
For which the world had waited, now
  firm fact, Adirondacs. 238.
The secret of the world imparts;
  Aeolian Harp. 13.
Blood of the world, Bacchus. 19.
And planted world, and full executor
  Blight. 16.
Were unitarians of the united world,
  Blight. 27.
Of man and earth, of world beloved and
  lover, Blight. 44.
The world was made for honest trade,—
  Boston. 11.
They laughed to know the world so wide;
  Boston. 49.
The world was made for honest trade,—
  Boston. 53.
But right is might through all the world;
  Boston. 96.
Girds the world with bound and term;
  Celestial Love. 37.
And fired the shot heard round the
  world. C. Hymn. 4.
It seemed the world was all torches
  Cosmos. 11.
Which melts the world into a sea.
  Destiny. 6.
Who made this world the feast it was,
  Dirge. 26.
The sense of the world is short,—
  I Eros. 1.
Therefore was the world so wide.
  Frag. Life. XXI. 2.
A thing that takes no more root in the
  world Frag. Life. XXVI. 3.
The world above, the world below.
  Frag. Nat. XXVI. 10.
See the world below
  Frag. Nat. XXVI. 26.
The moon was making amber of the
  world, Frag. Nat. XXVII. 3.
Groped for axle of the world.
  Frag. Nat. XXXIV. 4.
And turned the drowsy world to flame.
  Frag. Poet. I. 14.

The civil world will much forgive
Frag. Poet. IV. 1.
The world uncertain comes and goes;
Friendship. 3.
For, in the world of love
From Hafiz. 4.
Good-bye, proud world! I'm going home:
Good-Bye. I. 14.
But now, proud world! I'm going home.
Good-Bye. 6.
The salt of all the elements, world of
the world.   Good Cheer. 16.
Belonged to wind and world the toil
Guy. 49.
To the cadence of the whirling world
House. 19.
Is law and the world,—   Illusions. 32.
He has a total world of wit;
Initial Love. 103.
Since the world was, he has gnawed;
Limits. 3.
Like a world without sin,   *Lines. 15.
The world rolls round,—
May-Day. 177.
The world hath overmuch of pain,—
May-Day. 369.
I will use the world, and sift it,
Mithridates. 22.
'For the world was built in order,
Monadnoc. 245.
The rounded world is fair to see,
Nature. Mot. 7.
Of minds that each can stand against the
world   Oh What. 2.
A Brother of the world, his song
Poet. 27.
And the world that shall be   Poet. 112.
Twins the world that has been.
Poet. 113.
And pause were palsy to the world.—
Poet. 176.
The heedless world hath never lost.
Problem. 62.
And where thereafter in the world he
went.   River. 7.
That until now has put his world in fee
Rome. 23.
'Let the great world bustle on
Saadi. 104.
Swims the world in ecstasy,
Saadi. 134.
Yet the love the world that warms
Security. 3.
And the world has only two.
Security. 8.
And when his hours are numbered, and
the world   Snow-Storm. 23.
I formed the world anew;
Song of Nature. 28.
The sunburnt world a man shall breed
Song of Nature. 79.
She broods on the world.   Sphinx. 4.
And the sum of the world
Sphinx. 47.
The world whereinto he was born,
Threnody. 18.
The world and not the infant failed.
Threnody. 139.
Star by star his world resigning.
Threnody. 165.

The world dishonored thou hast left.
Threnody. 171.
Late in the world,—too late perchance
for fame,   To-Day. 5.
Which knits the world in music strong,
Woodnotes. II. 157.
God hid the whole world in thy heart.
Woodnotes. II. 235.
Once slept the world an egg of stone,
Woodnotes. II. 266.
The world is the ring of his spells,
Woodnotes. II. 285.
From world to world the godhead
changes;   Woodnotes. II. 296.
The world would blush in flame;
World-Soul. 50.
When the old world is sterile
World-Soul. 97.
The fairer world complete.
World-Soul. 100.

Worldly
We talked at large of worldly fate,
Hermione. 38.

World-old
The seat of the world-old Forces
Cosmos. 19.

World's
And the world's flowing fates in his own
mould recast.   Culture. 11.
The world's light underneath a measure.
Fame. 24.
And the world's sun seemed to rise
Guy. 39.
And let the world's affairs go by,
Threnody. 47.
Who layeth the world's incessant plan,
Woodnotes. II. 271.

Worlds
See Spirit-worlds.
Chemist to vamp old worlds with new,
May-Day. 445.
Through worlds and races and terms and
times   Poet. 71.
New worlds to find in pinnace frail.
Quat. Poet. I. 4.
When worlds of lovers hem thee in?
Threnody. 188.
Plants with worlds the wilderness;
Threnody. 285.
Of fruitful worlds the grain,
Waldeinsamkeit. 22.
Of rounded worlds, of space and time,
Woodnotes. II. 108.
Throes that were, and worlds that are,
Woodnotes. II. 209.

World-soul
The World-soul knows his own affair,
Monadnoc. 153.

World-warming
And worship that world-warming spark
Etienne. 15.

World-wide
Restores the world-wide mart;
Boston. 101.
A world-wide wave with foaming edge
May-Day. 245.

Worm
See Blindworm; Bookworm; Ground-
worm; Web-worm.
And his thought the penal worm.
Astraea. 30.

Worm—*Continued*

An angel as a worm. Bohemian. 6.

Where the starred, eternal worm
Celestial Love. 36.

There's no god dare wrong a worm;
II Compensation. 20.

And, striving to be man, the worm
May-Day. 81.

And, striving to be man, the worm
Nature. Mot. 5.

Worms

Of gem, and air, of plants, and worms.
Woodnotes. II. 275.

Wormwood

Wormwood,—saying, "Go thy ways;
Saadi. 63.

Wormy

And thou,—go burn thy wormy pages,—
Woodnotes. II. 246.

Worn

See Woe-worn.

Where now on heated pavements worn
Boston. 39.

Swains by winter pinched and worn.
Frag. Nat. XXII. 4.

He should have the helmet worn,
In Memoriam. 39.

Discrowned and timid, thoughtless, worn,
Poet. 181.

No ray is dimmed, no atom worn,
Song of Nature. 81.

Our bodies are weak and worn;
World-Soul. 22.

Worse

If he than his groom be better or worse.
Fate. 6.

Thou art better, and not worse.'—
Rhea. 73.

Alike to him the better, the worse,—
Woodnotes. II. 305.

Worship

In loyal worship, scorning praise,
Beauty. 22.

Worship him ever. Ellen South. 12.

And worship that world-warming spark
Etienne. 15.

You must worship fasting,
Frag. Nat. III. 31.

Worship Toil's wisdom that abides.
Frag. Poet. III. 10.

Worshiped

See All-worshiped.

Worst

And charm the anguish of the worst.
Aeolian Harp. 23.

Salve my worst wounds.
Musketaquid. 75.

Worth

'T is a tune worth thy knowing,
Ellen South. 3.

Sings a tune that's worth the knowing.'
Ellen South. 36.

He took the flower of all their worth,
Frag. Life. XXIX. 4.

All of worth and beauty set
Frag. Nat. XXIII. 3.

Swainish, coarse and nothing worth:
Frag. Poet. XI. 14.

A sun-path in thy worth.
Friendship. 16.

Know the worth of Oman's pearls?
Friendship. Trans. 2.

Is worth one barley-corn at most,
From Hafiz. 7.

Of the rich inherent worth,
In Memoriam. 50.

Fountain-drop of spicier worth
Monadnoc. 293.

When the Church is social worth,
Politics. 23.

From thy worth and weight the stars
gravitate, Shah. Enweri. II. 1.

The port, well worth the cruise, is near,
Terminus. 39.

Which all her harvests were not worth?
Threnody. 125.

There lives no man of Nature's worth
Woodnotes. II. 198.

Worthier

Worthier cause for passion wild
Threnody. 177.

Worthless

All is waste and worthless, till
Wealth. 30.

Worthy

See Unworthy.

Worthy the enormous cloud of witnesses,
Adirondacs. 247.

Chaucer had no such worthy crew,
Adirondacs. Motto. 3.

Worthy her design, House. 8.

Wot

Older am I than thy numbers wot,
Woodnotes. II. 254.

Would (Partial list.)

The frost might glitter, it would blight no
crop. Adirondacs. 68.

They treated Nature as they would.
Dirge. 32.

It would please me to die,
Mountain. 10.

Would I that cowlèd churchman be.
Problem. 6.

I would not the good bishop be.
Problem. 72.

I would he were nobler Sphinx. 95.

Wouldst (Partial list.)

Yet,—wouldst thou the mountain find
Freedom. 11.

And wouldst be my companion
Monadnoc. 210.

Wound

Its soft leaves wound me with a grief
Dirge. 39.

Wounds

Healed as fast the wounds it made.
Guy. 20.

Salve my worst wounds.
Musketaquid. 75.

Wove

And under, through the cable wove,
Concord Ode. 35.

Into chorus wove. Merlin. 99.

Know'st thou what wove yon woodbird's
nest Problem. 25.

The storm-wind wove, the torrent span,
Wealth. 38.

Woven

Was woven still by the snow-white choir.
Each. 32.

Woven of tulips and painted moth.
May-Day. 330.

Wrangle
Define and wrangle how they list,
Saadi. 97.

Wrap
Please God, I'll wrap me in mine inno-
cence, I Bear. 13.
To wrap the errors of a sage sublime.
To J. W. 9.

Wrath
Also (from the song the wrath
Daemonic Love. 62.
When wrath and terror
Frag. Life. XXXIV. 1.
As Southern wrath to Northern right
May-Day. 138.
All my wrath and all my shames,
Miracle. 35.

Wreath
See Flower-wreath.
Instead of flowers, crowned with a
wreath of hills. Adirondacs. 13.
The ground-pine curled its pretty wreath,
Each. 41.
My wreath shall nothing miss.
Song of Nature. 16.
I see the wreath, I hear the songs
Voluntaries. 108.

Wreathed
Yet wreathed and hid by summer blooms.
Nun. 28.

Wreathes
Oft as morning wreathes my scarf,
Monadnoc. 311.

Wreaths
See Cowslip-wreaths.
Drooping oft in wreaths of dread,
Heroism. 5.
Wreaths for May! for happy Spring
May-Day. 263.
The merry Spring threw wreaths on
them, May-Day. 314.
On coop or kennel he hangs Parian
wreaths; Snow-Storm. 18.

Wrecked
The gale that wrecked you on the sand,
Quat. Northman. 1.

Wrecks
With their centennial wrecks. Letter. 13.
He will from wrecks and sediment
World-Soul. 99.

Wren
Small bat and wren Channing Ode. 27.
A brown wren was the Daniel
Miracle. 29.
There's not a sparrow or a wren,
Threnody. 110.

Wrestled
Who wrestled here on a day.
Cosmos. 20.

Wretch
Call in the wretch and slave:
Boston Hymn. 26.

Wretched
In the wretched little beast Limits. 6.

Wrinkled
The wrinkled shopman to my sounding
woods, Channing Ode. 72.

Writ
For God hath writ all dooms magnificent,
Frag. Life. II. 2.
Things writ in vaster character;
Frag. Poet. V. 46.
And what is writ on Table Round
Harp. 25.
And round their circles is writ,
Initial Love. 41.
For it is on zodiacs writ,
Monadnoc. 260.
Was writ on tables yet unbroken;
Problem. 56.
That's writ upon our cell;
World-Soul. 46.

Write
Until he write, where all eyes rest,
Astraea. 7.
And write my old adventures with the
pen Bacchus. 64.
Be just at home; then write your scroll
Concord Ode. 25.
Write in a book the morning's prime,
Garden. 39.
And write, and reason, and compute,
Initial Love. 28.
More sense than sages write.
Peter. 32.
Some went to write, some went to pray;
Threnody. 155.
And I will write our annals new,
Titmouse. 99.

Writes
Writes a letter in my book. Apology. 8.

Written
'T is written on the iron leaf, Rhea. 34.

Wrong
By right or wrong, Celestial Love. 75.
There's no god dare wrong a worm;
II Compensation. 20.
Succession swift and spectral Wrong,
Experience. 8.
The partial wrong, Merlin. 120.
In the wide thaw and ooze of wrong,
Monadnoc. 114.
Put the Spirit in the wrong; Poet. 292.

Wrong-doers
The truth, and hurl wrong-doers down.
Worship. 14.

Wronged
But thine to thee, who never wronged
In Memoriam. 33.

Wrongs
Reputed wrongs and braggart rights,
Mithridates. 28.
Victors over daily wrongs:
Voluntaries. 110.

Wrote
Each the herald is who wrote
Astraea. 1.
Pay every debt as if God wrote the bill.
Frag. Life. XXXII. 2.
The whirlwind in ripples wrote
Garden. 54.
What these strong masters wrote at large
in miles, Musketaquid. 52.
Yet every scroll whereon he wrote
Poet. 13.
Stooping, his finger wrote in clay
Solution. 69.

Wrote —*Continued*
I wrote the past in characters
                    Song of Nature. 21.
Wrote in thy mind's transparent table,
                    Threnody. 199.
He wrote on Nature's grandest brow, For
Sale.   Webster, 1854. 2.
Wrought
When he has wrought his best;
                    Boston Hymn. 20.
Or Duty to grand purpose wrought.
                    Miracle. 14.
By eldest science wrought and shown!
                    Monadnoc. 67.
Wrought in a sad sincerity;
                    Problem. 21.
Star-crowned, sole-sitting, long I wrought
                    Solution. 3.

Yard
    See Poultry-yard.
Yawns
Atom from atom yawns as far
                    Frag. Nat. VII. 1.
Yawns the pit of the Dragon,
                    Sphinx. 75.
Ye (Partial list.)
Look to yourselves, ye polished gentle-
men!   Adirondacs. 91.
Think ye I made this ball
                    Boston Hymn. 9.
And ye shall succor men;
                    Boston Hymn. 49.
So only are ye unbound;
                    Boston Hymn. 66.
Fond children, ye desire
                    Celestial Love. 6.
'Ye drew one mother's milk,   Dirge. 53.
One chamber held ye all;   Dirge. 54.
Ye taught my lips a single speech,
                    Merops. 7.
Whereon ye sail,   Monadnoc. 327.
Yea
Yea, plant the tree   Adirondacs. 298.
Yean
All to yean and all to bury:
                    Woodnotes. II. 259.
Yeaned
Then Asia yeaned her shepherd race,
                    Solution. 9.
Yeaning
Is yeaning at the birth. World-Soul. 104
Year
Fit to grace the solar year.
                    Alphonso. 82.
Six thousand pounds a year.
                    Boston. 72.
Friends year by year more inly known.
                  Daemonic Love. 16.
Every year plays it over
                    Ellen South. 6.
To make up a year   Fable. 8.
To deck the morning of the year,
                    Frag. Nat. VIII. 2.
And, after many a year,   Friendship. 6.
And all the hours of the year   Guy. 45.
Year by year the rose-lipped maiden,
                    Holidays. 9.
Of the seven stars and the solar year,
                    Informing Spirit. 6

The spousals of the new-born year.
                    May-Day. 270.
The ravage of a year of war.
                    May-Day. 278.
Last year from yon oak or larch;
                    May-Day. 386.
Mould the year to fair increase,
                    Merlin. 57.
To lead the tardy concert of the year.
                    Musketaquid. 18.
O'er meadows bottomless. So, year by
year,   Musketaquid. 46.
Why lingerest thou, pale violet, to see
the dying year;   *Violet. 1.
Patient through Heaven's enormous year
                    Wealth. 11.
A minstrel of the natural year,
                    Woodnotes. I. 31.
He shall meet the speeding year,
                    Woodnotes. II. 79.
The specious panorama of a year
                    Xenophanes. 14.
Year's
The year's fresh bloom,
                    In Memoriam. 18.
and in the year's rich beauty
                    *Violet. 16.
Years
Or at the foresight of obscurer years?
                  Adirondacs. 217.
Found ten years since the Californian
gold?   Adirondacs. 280.
On for a thousand years of genius more.'
                  Adirondacs. 329.
Thatch his flesh, and even his years
                  Alphonso. 75.
For eternal years in debt.
                  Boston Hymn. 64.
And Ellen, when the graybeard years
                  Ellen. 1.
To dine and sleep through forty years;
                  Fame. 14.
My few and evil years!   *Farewell. 31.
Through the innumerable years.
                  Frag. Life. XXV. 4.
I could walk days, years, away
                  Frag. Nat. XXI. 6.
I read great years of victory,
                  Frag. Poet. III. 6.
And proverb of a thousand years,
                  Frag. Poet. IV. 24.
Five years elapse from flood to ebb.
                  Garden. 24.
In sidereal years.   Harp. 28.
Faithful through a thousand years,
                  May-Day. 373.
The flowing fortunes of a thousand
years;—   Merlin. 73.
In many a thousand years?
                  Monadnoc. 218.
And the impatient years that trod on it
                  Summons. 16.
Through years, through men, through
Nature fleet,   Two Rivers. 11.
Single moment years confessed.
                  Visit. 22.
Whose living towers the years conspired
to build,   Woodnotes. I. 78.
Put off thy years, wash in the breeze;
                  Woodnotes. II. 135.

When sixty years are told;
World-Soul. 106.

Yellow
On the desert's yellow floor,   Saadi. 168.
She spired into a yellow flame;
Sphinx. 125.

Yellow-breeched
Yellow-breeched philosopher!
Humble-Bee. 53.

Yellow-checked
Without tongue, yellow-cheeked, full of
winds that wail and sigh;   Flute. 2.

Yeoman
Scoff of yeoman strong and stark,
Monadnoc. 189.

Yeoman's
The order regnant in the yeoman's brain.
Musketaquid. 51.

Yes
Yes, sometimes to the sorrow-stricken
Frag. Life. XXVI. 1.
Ah, yes! but by the true heart's blood
They. 3.

Yester
Wandering yester morn the brake,
Miracle. 15.

Yesterday
Forth paced it yesterday;   Hermione. 57.
The yesterday doth never smile,   Nun. 1.
Yesterday was a bundle of grass.
Woodnotes. II. 277.

Yestermorn
I marked them yestermorn,
May-Day. 381.

Yet (Partial list.)
Or, later yet, beneath a lighted jack,
Adirondacs. 117.
Nor yet unsuited to that solitude:
Adirondacs. 251.
And yet I marked, even in the manly joy
Adirondacs. 271.
And that the Joy,—yet, howsoever hid,
Adirondacs. 289.
Yet is understood the better;
Astraea. 22.
Yet shine forever virgin minds,
Astraea. 31.
O day remembered yet!   Boston. 87.
Their reach shall yet be more profound,
Celestial Love. 19.
Yet do not I implore Channing Ode. 71.
Unplighted yet to me,   *Farewell. 38.
Yet I could never see their face.
Forerunners. 14.
Never yet could once arrive,
Forerunners. 24.
Yet Nature will not be in full possessed,
Frag. Nat. V. 8.
But never yet the man was found
Frag. Nat. VI. 1.
The trees were rich, yet ominous with
gloom.   Frag. Nat. XXVII. 5.
Yet,—wouldst thou the mountain find
Freedom. 11.
Far distant yet his chorus waits.
Garden. 36.
Yet, hear me, yet,   Give. 27.
Yet I think on them in the silent night,
I Bear. 9.
The impossibe shall yet be done,
Initial Love. 145.

Toy with the bow, yet hit the white.
Merlin's Song. 38.
Tarries yet behind?   Merops. 4.
Ere yet arrives the wintry day
Monadnoc. 23.
Ere yet the summoning voice was still,
Monadnoc. 31.
Coarse and boisterous, yet mild,
Monadnoc. 131.
Yet, will you learn our ancient speech,
Monadnoc. 173.
Yet envies none, none are unenviable.'
Musketaquid. 84.
Yet unto me not morn's magnificence,
Naples. 15.
Yet spake yon purple mountain,
Park. 13.
Yet said yon ancient wood,   Park. 14.
And yet, if virtue abrogate the law,
Phi. 3.
Not yet, not yet,   Poet. 91.
Yet not for all his faith can see
Problem. 5.
Was writ on tables yet unbroken;
Problem. 56.
And yet, for all his faith could see,
Problem. 71.
Yet thou errest far and broad. Rhea. 24.
And yet it seemeth not to me
Saadi. 72.
And yet his runes he rightly read,
Saadi. 78.
Yet before the listener's eye   Saadi. 133.
Yet the love the world that warms
Security. 3.
Which yet beholds not me.
Thine Eyes. 4.
Yet fairest dames and bearded men,
Threnody. 43.
It was not ripe yet to sustain
Threnody. 140.
Yet on the nimble air benign
Voluntaries. 67.
Yet happier he whose inward sight,
Voluntaries. 79.
Then will yet my mother yield
Woodnotes. I. 143.
Yet there in the parlor sits
World-Soul. 25.

Yield
A second crop thine acres yield,
Apology. 19.
Therefore they shove us from them, yield
to us   Blight. 40.
Yield sympathy and signs of mirth;
Celestial Love. 110.
What mystic fruit his acres yield
Dirge. 11.
Who, having more absorbed, more largely
yield,   Frag. Nat. V. 11.
What mystic fruit his acres yield
Peter. 3.
Redeemers that can yield thee all:
Saadi. 166.
When thou didst yield thy innocent
breath   Threnody. 100.
But all her shows did Nature yield,
Woodnotes. I. 52.
Then will yet my mother yield
Woodnotes. I. 143.

Yielded
I yielded myself to the perfect whole.
Each. 51.
Yields
Boon Nature yields each day a brag
which we now first behold,
Quat. Nature. 1.
Only what the pine-tree yields;
Woodnotes. II. 31.
Nor yields to men the helm;
World-Soul. 74.
Yoke
The yoke of conscience masterful,
Park. 3.
The yoke of men's opinions. I will be
Self-Reliance. 2.
Yoke-fellow
I am thy spirit, yoke-fellow;
Sphinx. 111.
Yon
Like yon slow-sailing cloudy promontory
Adirondacs. 218.
Bend nearer, faint day-moon! Yon
thundertops, Adirondacs. 260.
Yon pale, scrawny fisher fools,
Alphonso. 15.
Hearken to yon pine-warbler Dirge. 41.
Little thinks, in the field, yon red-cloaked
clown Each. 1.
Whilst his files sweep round yon Alpine
height; Each. 8.
In yon green palmy isle, *Farewell. 50.
O hide yon sun-filled zone,
From Hafiz. 2.
The violets yon field which stain
From Omar. 3.
Bosomed in yon green hills alone,—
Good-Bye. 16.
Its root has pierced yon shady mound;
Holidays. 6.
To greet yon stern head-stone,
In Memoriam. 12.
Over yon western bridges I would ride
Letter. 4.
Where yon wedged line the Nestor leads,
May-Day. 23.
And o'er yon hazy crest is Eden's balmier
spring.' May-Day. 103.
Or if yon realms in sunset glow
May-Day. 361.
Yon broidered zodiac girds.
May-Day. 377.
Last year from yon oak or larch;
May-Day. 386.
And loiter willing by yon loitering
stream. Musketaquid. 14.
Yet spake yon purple mountain,
Park. 13.
Yet said yon ancient wood, Park. 14.
Yon waterflag, yon sighing osier,
Poet. 221.
Know'st thou what wove yon woodbird's
nest Problem. 25.
'T would bring the blushes of yon maples
September. 15.
As I behold yon evening star,
Thine Eyes. 3.
Down in yon watery nook,
Waldeinsamkeit. 33.
Yon ridge of purple landscape,
World-Soul. 37.

Yon sky between the walls,
World-Soul. 38.
Yonder
See yonder leafless trees against the sky,
Frag. Nat. XVII. 1.
Know the stars yonder, Illusions. 16.
Passing yonder oak, I heard
Miracle. 23.
Is yonder squalid peasant all
Monadnoc. 75.
Are touched with genius. Yonder ragged
cliff Musketaquid. 24.
I pass with yonder comet free,—
Nun. 38.
And the fresh rose on yonder thorn
Song of Nature. 83.
Yonder masterful cuckoo Unity. 4.
Yore
The men of yore were stout and poor,
Boston. 5.
Never was poet, of late or of yore,
Quat. Casella. 3.
York
See New York.
You (Partial list.)
Ask you, how went the hours?
Adirondacs. 107.
Their several portraits, you would own
Adirondacs. Motto. 2.
Masters, I'm in pain with you;
Alphonso. 41.
Masters, I'll be plain with you;
Alphonso. 42.
That keeps intelligence with you,—
Amulet. 6.
Red when you love, and rosier red,
Amulet. 7.
We greet you well, you Saxon men,
Boston. 51.
'For you,' they said, 'no barriers be,
Boston. 55.
For you no sluggard rest; Boston. 56.
And fend you with his wing.
Boston Hymn. 16.
'You cannot unlock your heart,
Dirge. 57.
I serve you not, if you I follow,
Etienne. 1.
Neither can you crack a nut.'
Fable. 19.
Would you know what joy is hid
Frag. Nat. XXVI. 1.
As you spin a cherry.
Mithridates. 24.
But without glass we fathom you.
Romany. 28.
Young
We cut young trees Adirondacs. 34.
But these young scholars, who invade our
hills, Blight. 18.
The young men and the sires,
Boston Hymn. 38.
Threatening and young. Destiny. 33.
Keen my sense, my heart was young,
Forerunners. 5.
Though Adam, born when oaks were
young, Frag. Nat. VI. 3.
Flits across her bosom young,
Give. 37.
Playfellow of young and old,
Holidays. 10.

Of rich and poor, of young and old,
Hymn. 10.
Old man and young maid,   Illusions. 9.
Meaning always to be young.
Initial Love. 141.
On his young promise Beauty smiled,
In Memoriam. 67.
And danced as merrily as young men.
May-Day. 323.
It sounds from all things young,
Music. 4.
Which always find us young
Ode to Beauty. 62.
Beaming from a young man's eyes.
On Prince. 4.
His awful Jove young Phidias brought;
Problem. 10.
Fair to old and foul to young;
Prudence. 2.
And finds young pines and budding
birches;   Threnody. 25.
Seyd overheard the young gods talking;
Uriel. 8.
The young deities discussed   Uriel. 11.
Where from a hundred lakes young rivers
sprang;   Woodnotes. I. 63.
Chanted when the sphere was young.
Woodnotes. II. 99.
The ever old, the ever young;
Woodnotes. II. 117.

Younger
The younger Golden Lips or mines,
Problem. 67.

Youngest
And wakes the wish in youngest blood
May-Day. 95.
And well the youngest can command
Monadnoc. 135.

Young-eyed
Of this young-eyed emperor
Initial Love. 85.

Your (Partial list.)
Your picture smiles as first it smiled;
Amulet. 1.
We pay your governors here
Boston. 70.
Choose him to be your king;
Boston Hymn. 14.
I break your bonds and masterships,
Boston Hymn. 53.
Did in your childhood fall.   Dirge. 56.
And bend my fancy to your leading,
Etienne. 3.
Your eyelids to the sphere:
Frag. Life. XXXV. 4.
Your colors for our eyes' delight:
Frag. Nat. XXIII. 10.
Squandering your unquoted mirth,
Monadnoc. 186.

Yours (Partial list.)
The manhood that should yours resist,—
Etienne. 10.
'Mine and yours;   Hamatreya. 28.
With aim like yours   Poet. 155.

Yourselves (Partial list.)
Look to yourselves, ye polished gentlemen!   Adirondacs. 91.

Youth
I leave it behind with the games of
youth:'—   Each. 39.

That wisdom might in youth be gotten,
Fame. 5.
Go then, sad youth, and shine; Fame. 25.
Put youth, joy, health upon the shrine,
Fame. 27.
Only to youth will spring be spring.
Harp. 35.
Gay for youth, gay for youth,
Harp. 43.
I looked forth on the fields of youth:
Harp. 110.
Mates of my youth,—yet not my mates,
Harp. 114.
Of ardent youth untouched by pain,
Hymn. 11.
I bear in youth the sad infirmities
I Bear. 1.
His from youth the leader's look
In Memoriam. 44.
The youth sees omens where he goes,
May-Day. 73.
From youth to maid, from boy to man,
May-Day. 347.
Like thee the youth or maid:
May-Day. 435.
And take their youth again.
Merlin's Song. 13.
Youth, for a moment free as they,
Monadnoc. 21.
Long morrow to this mortal youth.
Monadnoc. 408.
Here from youth to age I tarry,—
Poet. 128.
And by her radiant youth delighted,
Rhea. 43.
And simple maids and noble youth
Saadi. 39.
Of human youth had left the hill
Threnody. 108.
Youth is (whatever cynic tubs pretend)
To-Day. 17.
The youth replies, I can.
Voluntaries. 74.
Immortal youth returns.
Waldeinsamkeit. 28.

Youthful
To fascinate each youthful heart,
Daemonic Love. 31.
What prayers and dreams of youthful
genius feign,   Frag. Nat. V. 2.
When, foremost of the youthful band,
In Memoriam. 78.
With tender light and youthful cheer,
May-Day. 269.
And quit proud homes and youthful
dames   Voluntaries. 65

Youth's
See youth's glad mates in earliest
bloom,—   Harp. 123.

Youths
Of keen competing youths, joined or
alone   Adirondacs. 325.
High destined youths and holy maids
Frag. Poet. VII. 3.

Zeal
What boots thy zeal, Channing Ode. 36.
When Nature falters, fain would zeal
May-Day. 157.

Zeal —*Continued*
Inexorable to thy zeal:
                Sursum Corda. 2.
The good, the bad with equal zeal,
                Poet. 211.
Zealous
    See Overzealous.
Zenith's
To the zenith's top can soar,—
                Merlin. 64.
Zephyr
Goes light the nimble zephyr;
                Ellen South. 10.
The zephyr in his garden rolled
                Guy. 43.
Zigzag
Zigzag steerer, desert cheerer,
                Humble-Bee. 7.
Zion
Zion or Meru, measure with man.
                Monadnoc. 259.
Zodiac
We seemed the dwellers of the zodiac,
                Adirondacs. 157.
Which the Zodiac threw, May-Day. 108.
Yon broidered zodiac girds.
                May-Day. 377.
On the half-climbed zodiac?
                Threnody. 241.

Zodiac's
Secure as in the zodiac's belt;
                Daemonic Love. 122.
Zodiacs
For it is on zodiacs writ, Monadnoc. 260.
Zone
    See Torrid-zone.
Match God's equator with a zone of art,
                Adirondacs. 245.
From nodding pole and belting zone.
                Beauty. 12.
And all the zone is green again.
                Frag. Nat. XXVIII. 4.
O hide yon sun-filled zone,
                From Hafiz. 2.
Above the floral zone, Monadnoc. 353.
As the best gem upon her zone,
                Problem. 34.
The zone that girds the incarnate mind.
                Threnody. 231.
Clinging to a colder zone
                Voluntaries. 39.
Zones
Climbing the northern zones,
                May-Day. 253.
From all zones and altitudes;—
                Mithridates. 9.
Of all the zones and countless days.
                Song of Nature. 80.